World Literature
and Its Times

VOLUME 4

British and Irish
Literature and Its
Times: The Victorian Era
to the Present
(1837–)

World Literature and Its Times

Profiles of Notable Literary Works and the
Historical Events That Influenced Them

Joyce Moss

GALE GROUP

Detroit
New York
San Francisco
London
Boston
Woodbridge, CT

World Literature and Its Times

Profiles of Notable Literary
Works and the Historical
Events That Influenced Them

VOLUME 4

**British and Irish Literature
and Its Times**

JOYCE MOSS

STAFF

Michael L. LaBlanc, *Production Editor*

Maria Franklin, *Permissions Manager*
Shalice Shah-Caldwell, *Permissions Associate*

Mary Beth Trimper, *Manager, Composition and Electronic Prepress*
Evi Seoud, *Assistant Manager, Composition Purchasing and Electronic Prepress*

Kenn Zorn, *Product Design Manager*
Pamela A. E. Galbreath, *Senior Art Director*
Michael Logusz, *Graphic Artist*

Barbara J. Yarrow, *Graphic Services Supervisor*
Randy Bassett, *Image Database Supervisor*
Robert Duncan, *Imaging Specialist*
Pamela A. Reed, *Imaging Coordinator*
Dean Dauphinais, *Senior Image Editor*
Robyn V. Young, *Senior Image Editor*
Kelly A. Quin, *Image Editor*

Joyce Nakamura, *Literature Content Capture Managing Editor*
Sara Constantakis, *Editor*
Motoko F. Huthwaite, *Associate Editor*
Arlene Johnson, *Associate Editor*
Michelle Poole, *Associate Editor*
Mary Ruby, *Technical Training Specialist*

∞™The paper used in this publication meets the minimum requirements of American National Standard for Information Sciences—Permanence Paper for Printed Library Materials, ANSI Z39.48-1984.

ISBN 0-7876-3729-7

Printed in the United States of America
10 9 8 7 6 5 4 3 2 1

Library of Congress Control Number: 2001089390

Contents

General Preface

The world at the turn of the twenty-first century is a shrinking sphere. Innovative modes of transmission make communication from one continent to another almost instantaneous, encouraging the development of an increasingly global society, heightening the urgency of the need for mutual understanding. At the foundation of *World Literature and Its Times* is the belief that within a people's literature are keys to their perspectives, their emotions, and the formative events that have brought them to the present point.

As manifested in their literary works, societies experience phenomena that are in some respects universal and in other respects tied to time and place. T. S. Eliot's poem *The Waste Land,* for example, is set in post-World War I London, when Europe was rife with disenchantment. Coincidentally, Juan Rulfo's novel *Pedro Páramo,* set in Latin America over a spread of decades that includes the post-World War I era, features a protagonist whose last name means "bleak plain" or "waste land." The two literary works, though written oceans apart, conjure a remarkably similar atmosphere. Likewise Aphra Behn's novel *Oroonoko,* set largely in the British colony of Surinam in the early 1660s, and Miguel Barnet's *Biography of a Runaway Slave,* beginning in 1860 in the Spanish colony of Cuba, both feature defiant slaves. The plots in this case take place two centuries apart, suggesting that time, as well as place, is of little consequence. A close look at the two slaves, however—and the two waste lands referred to above—exposes illuminating differences, indeed related to the times and places in which the respective works are set.

World Literature and Its Times regards both fiction and nonfiction as rich mediums for understanding the differences, as well as the similarities, among people and societies. In its view, full understanding of a literary work demands attention to events and attitudes of the period in which a work takes place and of the one in which it is written. The series therefore examines a wide range of novels, short stories, biographies, speeches, poems, and plays by contextualizing a work in these two periods. Each volume covers some 50 literary works that span a mix of centuries and genres. The literary work itself takes center stage, with its contents determining which issues—social, political, psychological, economic, or cultural—are covered in a given entry. Every entry discusses the relevant issues apart from the literary work, making connections to it when merited, and allowing for comparisons between the literary and the historical realities. Close attention is given as well to the literary work itself, in the interest of extracting historical understandings from it.

Of course, the function of literature is not necessarily to represent history accurately. Nevertheless, the images and ideas promoted by a powerful literary work—be it Miguel de Cervantes's *Don Quixote* (Spain), Nadine Gordimer's *Burgher's Daughter* (South Africa), or Rudyard Kipling's *Kim* (Britain)—leave impressions that are commonly taken to be historical. In taking literature as fact, one risks acquiring a mistaken notion of history. Kipling's *Kim,* for example, ascribes a number of negative traits to Easterners, conveying a common perception in his day of their being inferior to Westerners. To adjust for such portrayals, this series ties such perceptions to the era and distinguishes between historical facts and literary impressions.

On the other hand, literary works can broaden our understanding of history. They are able to convey more than the cut-and-dried record, by portraying events in a way that captures the fears and challenges of a period or that draws attention to groups of people who are generally left out of standard histories. This is well illustrated with writings that concern the position of women in different societies, such as Flora Nwapa's novel *Efuru* (Nigeria), Charlotte Brontë's *Jane Eyre* (Britain), or Edna O'Brien's *Country Girls* (Ireland). As demonstrated by these works, literature engages in a vigorous dialog with other forms of communication. It often defies stereotypes by featuring characters or ideas that are contrary to preconceptions. In fact, many of the literary works covered in this series feature characters and ideas that attack or upset deeply engrained stereotypes of their day, from Friar Bartolomé de Las Casas's *A Short Account of the Destruction of the Indies* (mid-1500s Latin America) to Thomas Hardy's *Jude the Obscure* (late-1800s Britain), to Mongo Beti's *Mission to Kala* (mid-1900s Cameroon Republic).

Even nonfiction must be anchored in its place and times to derive its full value. Octavio Paz's essay *The Labyrinth of Solitude* explains the character of contemporary Mexicans as a product of historical experience; the entry on the essay amplifies this experience. A second entry, on Albert Memmi's *Pillar of Salt*, uses the less direct genre of biography to describe the life of a Tunisian Jew during the Nazi occupation of North Africa. A third entry relates Charles Darwin's *On the Origin of Species* to scientific and religious developments in Britain at the time, and to challenges to its empire abroad.

The task of reconstructing the historical context of a literary work can be problematic. An author may present events out of chronological order, as Carlos Fuentes does in *The Death of Artemio Cruz* (Mexico), or may create works that feature legendary heroes who defy attempts to fit them neatly into a specific time slot (such as the warrior Beowulf of Denmark, glorified in England's epic poetry; or the emperor Sunjata of Mali

in the Western Sudan). In the first case, *World Literature and Its Times* unscrambles the plot, providing a linear rendering of events and associated historical information. In the second, the series profiles customs particular to the culture in which the epic is set and written, arming the reader with details that inform the hero's adventures. The approach sheds light on the relationship between fact and fiction, both of which are shown to provide insight into a people and their epics. As always, this approach is taken with a warm appreciation for the beauty of a literary work independent of historical facts, but also in the belief that ultimate regard is shown for that work by placing it in the context of pertinent events.

Beyond this underlying belief, the series is founded on the notion that a command of world literature bolsters knowledge of the writings produced by one's own society. Long before the present century, fiction and nonfiction writers from different locations influenced one another through trends and strategies in their literatures. In our postcolonial age, such cross-fertilization has quickened. Latin American literature, having been influenced by French and Spanish trends among others, itself influences Chinese writers of today. Likewise, Africa's literary tradition has affected and been affected by France's, and the same relationship holds true for the writings of India and Great Britain. The degree of such literary intermixture promises only to multiply given our increasingly global society. In the process, world literature and its landmark texts gain even greater significance, attaining the potential to promote understanding not only of others, but also of ourselves.

The Selection of Literary Works

The works chosen for *World Literature and Its Times 4: British and Irish Literature and Its Times* have been carefully selected by professors in the field at the universities detailed in the Acknowledgements. Keeping the literature-history connection in mind, the team made its selections based on a combination of factors: how frequently a literary work is studied, how closely it is tied to pivotal events in the past or present, how strong and enduring its appeal has been to readers in and out of the society that produced it, and how reflective it is of new developments in literature of the region. Attention has been paid to literary works set from the Victorian era to the present that have met with critical and/or popular acclaim. Those works by an author of this time span that are set in an earlier period have been placed in *World Literature and Its Times 3: British and Irish Literature and Its Times* (an example is George Eliot's *Middlemarch*). In both volumes, there has been a careful effort to include works from different reaches of Britain and Ireland, to represent female as well as male authors, and to cover a mix of genres, from poetry, to the novel, to drama, and the essay. There are, of course, many more integral works by pivotal writers than could be included. Again, the selection has been based on the above-delineated range of concerns.

Format and Arrangement of Entries

The volumes in *World Literature and Its Times* are arranged geographically. *World Literature and Its Times 3* and *World Literature and Its Times 4* are devoted to British and Irish literature and its times. The volumes are divided chronologically according to when the literary works are set. Covered in the *World Literature and Its Times 3* are works set from the Celtic migrations into the region to the early nineteenth century Reform Bill. *World Literature and Its Times 4* features works set from the Victorian era to the present.

Within a volume, entries are arranged alphabetically by title of the literary work. Each entry is organized as follows:

1. **Introduction**—identifying information in three parts:

   The literary work—specifies the genre, the place and time period in which the work is set, when it was written and/or first published, and, if applicable, when it was first translated.

   Synopsis—summarizes the storyline or contents of the work.

   Introductory paragraph—introduces the literary work in relation to the author's life.

2. **Events in History at the Time the Literary Work Takes Place**—describes social and political events that relate to the plot or contents of the literary work. The section may discuss background information as well as relevant events during the period in which the work is set. The subsections in this section vary, depending on the particular literary work. In general, the section takes a deductive approach, starting with events in history and telescoping inward to events in the literary work.

3. **The Literary Work in Focus**—summarizes in detail the plot or contents of the work, describes how it illuminates history, and identifies sources used by the author and the literary context in which the work was generated. After the summary of the work comes a subsection focusing on an aspect of the literature that illuminates our understanding of events or attitudes of the period. This second subsection takes an inductive approach, starting with the literary work and broadening outward to events in history. It is followed by a third subsection, which specifies sources that inspired elements of the work and discusses its literary context, or relation to other works.

4. **Events in History at the Time the Literary Work Was Written**—describes social, political, and/or literary events in the author's lifetime that relate to the plot or contents of a work. Also discussed in this section are the reviews or reception accorded the literary work.

5. **For More Information**—provides a list of all sources that have been cited in the entry as well as sources for further reading about the different issues or personalities featured in the entry.

If the literary work is set and written in the same time period, sections 2 and 4 of the entry on that work ("Events in History at the Time the Literary Work Takes Place" and "Events in History at the Time the Literary Work Was Written") are combined into the single section "Events in History at the Time of the Literary Work."

Additional Features

Whenever possible, primary source material is provided through quotations in the text and material in sidebars. There are also sidebars with historical details that amplify issues raised in the text, and with anecdotes that provide a fuller understanding of the temporal context. Timelines appear in various entries to summarize intricate periods of history. Finally, historically relevant illustrations enrich and further clarify information in the entries.

Comments and Suggestions

Your comments on this series and suggestions for future editions are welcome. Please write: Editors, *World Literature and Its Times,* The Gale Group, Inc., 27500 Drake Road, Farmington Hills, Michigan 48331-3535.

Acknowledgments

World Literature and Its Times 4: British and Irish Literature and Its Times is a collaborative effort that evolved through several stages, each of which was monitored by a team of experts in British and Irish Literature. A special thank you goes to John McLeod of University of Leeds, School of English, in the United Kingdom and to Robert Aguirre of Wayne State University, Department of English, in the United States for their careful guidance at every stage of the development process.

For their incisive participation in selecting the literary works to cover in this volume, the editors extend deep appreciation to the following professors:

Robert Aguirre, Wayne State University, Department of English

Julia Brown, Boston University, Department of English

Sandra Donaldson, University of North Dakota, Department of English

Carol Jago, Santa Monica Public High School, English Department

James Kincaid, University of Southern California, Department of English

John McLeod, University of Leeds, School of English

Indira Viswanathan Peterson, Mount Holyoke College, Chair, Asian Studies Department

The following professors carefully reviewed the entries to insure accuracy and completeness of information. Sincere gratitude is extended to these professors:

Robert Aguirre, Wayne State University, Department of English

Roger Beck, Eastern Illinois University, Department of History

James Berg, Minnesota State Colleges and Universities, Center for Teaching and Learning

Julia Brown, Boston University, Department of English

Sandra Donaldson, University of North Dakota, Department of English

Howard Eiland, Massachusetts Institute of Technology, Department of English

Barri Gold, Muhlenberg College, Department of English

William Hughes, Bath Spa University, Department of English

Farhad Idris, Frostburg State University, Department of English

James Kincaid, University of Southern California, Department of English

Jack Kolb, University of California at Los Angeles, Department of English

David Lloyd, Scripps College, Department of English

John McLeod, University of Leeds, Department of English

Acknowledgments

Martin McQuillan, University of Leeds, Department of Cultural Studies

Barbara Moss, Clark Atlanta University, Department of History

Josna Rege, Dartmouth College, Department of English

Ross Roy, University of South Carolina, Emeritus, Department of English; Editor, Studies in Scottish Literature

Patricia Smith, Hofstra University, Department of English

Asha Varadharajan, Queen's University, Department of English

Louise Yelin, State University of New York, Purchase College, Department of Literature

Steven Young, Pomona College, Department of English

For their painstaking research and composition, the editors thank the writers whose names appear at the close of the entries that they contributed. A complete listing follows:

Kimberly Ball, M.A. candidate, University of California at Berkeley

Anne Brannen, Associate Professor, Duquesne University

Matthew Brosamer, Lecturer, Mount St. Mary's College

Isaac Cates, Lecturer, Yale University

James Caufield, Ph.D. candidate, University of California at Los Angeles

Francesca Coppa, Assistant Professor, Muhlenberg College

Laura Franey, Assistant Professor, Millsaps College

Barri Gold, Assistant Professor, Muhlenberg College

Martin Griffin, Ph.D. candidate, University of California at Los Angeles

Elisabeth Rose Gruner, Associate Professor, University of Richmond

Ingrid Gunby, Ph.D. candidate, University of Leeds

Tracy Hargreaves, Lecturer, University of Leeds

Albert Labriola, Professor, Duquesne University

Susan Lonac, Instructor, Whatcom Community College

Pamela S. Loy, Ph.D., University of California at Santa Barbara; professional writer

Mary McGlynn, Assistant Professor, Baruch College, City University of New York

John McLeod, Lecturer, University of Leeds

Michelle Mimlitsch, Lecturer, University of California at Los Angeles

Danielle Price, Ph.D., University of California at Los Angeles

Diane Renée, B.A., University of California at Los Angeles; professional writer

Kathryn Stelmach, Ph.D candidate, University of California at Los Angeles

Erin Templeton, Ph.D. candidate, University of California at Los Angeles

Lawrence Warner, Executive Director, Australian Academy of the Humanities, Australian National University

Colin Wells, M.A., Oxford University; professional writer

Alan Williamson, Professor, University of California at Davis

Deep appreciation is extended to Michael L. LaBlanc of the Gale Group for his careful editing of the entries and to Joyce Nakamura of the Gale Group for her responsive and conscientious compilation of illustrations. Anne Leach indexed the volume with great sensitivity to readers and subject matter. Lastly, the final expression of gratitude goes to Monica Riordan for her deft copy editing, and to Lisa Blai for her proficient proofreading, word processing, and organizational management.

Introduction

"Th' whole worl's in a terrible state o' chassis!" says a character in *Juno and the Paycock*, drunkenly slurring the word "chaos" in a line that aptly evaluates recent history. In this one exclamation, Sean O'Casey's play captures the condition of grappling with uncertainty that surfaces in the literature of Britain (England, North Ireland, Scotland, and Wales) and Ireland from the Victorian era to the present. Early in the Victorian era, the uncertainty found its way into essay as well as poetry. Works of natural history, such as Charles Darwin's *On the Origin of Species* (1859), challenged certain common interpretations of the Bible, while poems like Alfred Tennyson's *In Memoriam* (1850) struggled mightily with new findings in geology, such as the geological record of mass extinctions in the earth's distant past. In the face of these developments, society's longstanding confidence in a controlling, benign divinity foundered. A rush of questions spewed forth more publicly than ever before: Was there a God? An afterlife? Was a person's soul immortal and distinct from a beast's? Was the human race intended for an awesome destiny, or doomed to vanish without a trace, like countless species before it? Tennyson makes his agonizing way through the minefield of such questions, emerging with his faith qualified but in tact. Similarly, another poet of the era, Robert Browning, wrote "Prospice," verse that suggests faith in the afterlife.

Influenced by the French Revolution and by Romantic innovations in poetry, Victorian novelists meanwhile made the everyday lives of common people a major concern. In response to the growth of women readers and writers, domestic realism became the dominant fictional mode. The focus riveted attention to an unparalleled degree on previously disenfranchised groups—women and youth. The Victorians both touted and assailed a dominant ideal of womanhood—the passive, morally superior, self-sacrificing, sexually disinclined angel of home and hearth, a fountainhead of nurturing sustenance. The image, while propagated throughout the century, was at the same time attacked for its falsity by, for example, the unconventional heroine of Charlotte Brontë's *Jane Eyre* (1847). By century's end, the image had been discredited, not only in novels, but also in drama, where the outspoken woman (see *The Importance of Being Earnest*) became fashionable to some degree. Still the ideal persisted, far from quashed by the counter-images, as shown in 1904 by its appearance in the drama *Peter Pan*, which would be adapted the next decade into the novel *Peter and Wendy*.

Featured even more conspicuously than the ideal woman in *Peter Pan* is the other disenfranchised group, children. Their heyday as fictional stars began early in the Victorian era, perhaps most notably in novels by Charles Dickens, whose *Great Expectations* (1860-61) follows the fortunes of an orphan, a familiar protagonist in Victorian fiction, often featured in "social-problem" novels, which had come into vogue by the middle of the century. Written by and for the middle class, these novels played an educational role, enlightening the uninformed about the plight of Britain's outcasts and newly industrialized working class. The orphan would often be depicted as beleaguered and forlorn, a neglected waif in a largely hostile environment. Yet optimism found its way into the social problem novel. The novelists, like the poets, showed an abiding belief in the possibility of worldly goodness. There were exceptions, of course, the novels of Thomas Hardy being perhaps the strongest. A philosophical streak of pessimism undergirds Hardy's plots, as does an iconoclastic bent, manifested in his then much reviled *Jude the Obscure* (1894-95), which addresses social barriers to education, female sexual inhibitions, and the religious as well as irreligious in late-nineteenth-century England.

Hardy's pessimism prefigures later developments in fiction and drama, but perhaps even more transitional, in style as well as content, is Joseph Conrad's *Lord Jim*. Conrad's novel concerns itself with empire, from the British point-of-view or, more accurately, points-of-view, since the novel conveys a rather elusive reality through the medium of more than one consciousness, or storyteller. In its preoccupation with empire, Conrad's novel follows on the heels of nineteenth-century colonial adventure stories (e.g., H. Rider Haggard's *King Solomon's Mines* or Rudyard Kipling's *Kim*) and anticipates twentieth-century postcolonial fictions, from V. S. Naipaul's *A House for Mr. Biswas* (1961) to Hanif Kureishi's *The Buddha of Suburbia* (1990). The problem of empire resurfaces over time, cast in different lights by various literary works. In much the same fashion, Jackie Kay's *The Adoption Papers* (1991) features the young outcast again, but now in the guise of a late-twentieth-century biracial girl in Scotland. The subject remains the same; the variables and outlooks change for these and other issues that recur in the various works:

- **Racism**—*Cambridge, Ulysses, Sour Sweet*
- **Evolution and degeneration**—*The French Lieutenant's Woman, Dracula, Arcadia*
- **Love and marriage**—*Sonnets from the Portuguese, The Country Girls, Under Milk Wood*
- **Catholicism**—*Brideshead Revisited, The Prime of Miss Jean Brodie, The Power and the Glory*
- **Fascism and socialism**—*Goodbye to Berlin,* "The Lion and the Unicorn," *The Remains of the Day*
- **War and betrayal**—*Juno and the Paycock,* "Anthem for Doomed Youth" and Other Poems, *The Heat of the Day*
- **Imperialism and the decline of empire**—*The Grass Is Singing, Midnight's Children, Troubles*

- **Crime and hypocrisy**—*Great Expectations, The Adventures of Sherlock Holmes, Dr. Jekyll and Mr. Hyde, Lord of the Flies*
- **Social climbing and social classes**—*Jude the Obscure, Howards End, Pygmalion, Disaffection*
- **Women's rights**—*Jane Eyre, Nights at the Circus, The Sea, The Sea*
- **Homosexuality**—*The Importance of Being Earnest, Women in Love, What the Butler Saw*
- **Psychology**—*Dr. Jekyll and Mr. Hyde, The Waste Land, Mrs. Dalloway*

The breadth of literary works for a given issue begins to convey the depth of the British and Irish experience. In the sampling above, racism moves from Africans in the early 1800s British West Indies (*Cambridge*) to the Irish in early 1900s Ireland (*Ulysses*) to Chinese immigrants in late 1900s Britain (*Sour Sweet*). Of course, a particular work addresses concerns beyond the one identified above. *Ulysses* could as easily be slotted into love and marriage, Catholicism, or psychology as into racism in Ireland.

Ireland is in fact a case apart, a country united to Britain (in 1800) shortly before the Victorian era, violently divided from it by war (1919-21) shortly after. These changes affected the stream of Irish literature, which reaches back to the ancient Celts (see **The Táin** in *WLAIT 3: British and Irish Literature and Its Times*). England exerted a powerful influence on Ireland, one that the Irish struggled consciously to shed in the early 1900s by mounting their own literary revival, which drew on native folklore, language, and popular culture. The result was a period of multifaceted Irish literature made evident by the disparate voices, not only within the revival (see William Yeats's "September 1913" and "Easter, 1916" and John Millington Synge's *Playboy of the Western World*) but also in contrast to or apart from it. James Joyce, whose *Ulysses* reflects a cosmopolitan approach, antithetical to the nationalistic one taken by participants in the revival, nevertheless emerges as vitally integral to the epoch.

During Joyce's time, in the throes of the profound disillusionment that followed World War I, the struggle to make sense out of existence intensified. There were new tools now, perhaps most notably the phenomenon of the unconscious, as revealed by Sigmund Freud, whose work first became known in Britain and Ireland around 1912. Writers experimented with the new psychology, redefining reality not as objective experience to be relayed by an omniscient narrator but rather as a subjective experience, filtered through the perspective of the narrator.

This redefinition led to fictional innovations such as stream of consciousness narration. In time, the experimentation grew into a movement, modernism, which would dominate the first half of the twentieth century without altogether displacing the traditional realistic style. Wilfred Owen's poetry of the 1920s, for example, stubbornly insisted on exposing World War I's horrors for what they were, while realistic novels of the 1930s and early '40s concerned themselves with fascism, socialism, and a resurgence of horrors engendered by World War II. In contrast to the note of optimism in Victorian literature, much of the modernist literature was laced with disillusionment, perhaps most conspicuously T. S. Eliot's poem *The Waste Land.*

Pessimism found its way as well into postmodern literature, a type that emerged after World War II and tended to manipulate conventions of the novel, featuring a narrator, for example, who stepped out of the storytelling mode to chat with the reader, as John Fowles's narrator does in *The French Lieutenant's Woman.* Drama too showed pessimism, Samuel Beckett's *Waiting for Godot,* which concerns the absurdity of the human condition, being a noteworthy example. The pessimism, however, was far from unrelieved. Rather it was infused with comedy, hardly a new element in British and Irish literature. Life without comedy would be impossible, observed Sean O'Casey, who had earlier invoked it in *Juno and the Paycock* to relieve tragic aspects of a family's life during the Irish Civil War. In similar fashion, Beckett used comedy to undercut a pervading sense of despair in his post-World War II drama.

Twenty years later Joe Orton would use comedy to hilarious effect in *What the Butler Saw,* not to relieve tragedy but to highlight sexual confusions of his day.

Here the grappling with uncertainty concerned not the meaning of existence, but one's sexual identity, a topic addressed more forthrightly in literature of the 1960s than ever before. The growing frankness bespoke a progress of sorts. In Oscar Wilde's 1890s, writers referred to homosexuality clandestinely, if at all; by D. H. Lawrence's 1910s the subject was no longer taboo—Lawrence, though he ultimately decided against it, even toyed with openly admitting one of his male character's physical desire for other men in *Women in Love.* By Joe Orton's late 1960s homosexuality has begun to become a viable option in society and is a directly broachable subject in comedy.

Likewise, postcolonial fiction showed a heightened frankness that bespoke progress. In decline before World War II, the British Empire was succeeded after it by a commonwealth of nations including dominions, such as Canada, and the newly independent nations of Africa, the Caribbean, and South Asia. The transition prompted a postwar immigration boom into Britain that enhanced its cultural mix, encouraging the growth of vigorous communities of East Indians, Africans, and Chinese, among others. There followed a not-always-peaceful grappling with uncertainty, over how the newcomers would fit into larger society—economically, politically, socially, and artistically.

In literature, new voices have broadened the amalgam of English, Scottish, Welsh, and Irish writings. V. S. Naipaul's *A House for Mr. Biswas* concerns the diversity of colonial society in Trinidad, as well as the title character's passion for a house. The novel slips easily into the established line next to E. M. Forster's *Howards End,* a work in the literary canon that concerns middle-class diversity and passion for a home in early-twentieth-century England. Postcolonial writings added dimension to the established collection of literary portrayals too. Salman Rushdie's *Midnight's Children,* published 80 years after Rudyard Kipling's *Kim,* adds perspective to its image of colonial India, even serves as something of a corrective to views propagated by such celebrated British novels.

Midnight's Children features a character living in a time of historical crisis. In fact, much of twentieth-century British and Irish literature conveys this sense of crisis, and not necessarily by depicting grand events. James Joyce's *Ulysses* conveys it through a commonplace day in the life of two Dubliners; J. G. Farrell's *Troubles* through the story of an Englishman's trip to an Irish hotel; Seamus Heaney's "Station Island" through a pilgrimage on which he wrestles with the very question of his responsibility to the explosive events around him; and Tom Stoppard's *Arcadia* by juxtaposing a household of late twentieth-century and early-nineteenth-century inhabitants.

Thus, British and Irish literature of the past two centuries is replete with the aura of historical crisis in *Juno and the Paycock,* which proclaims the world to be in a terrible state of "chassis." If this sense of chaos bears witness to upheavals of the two centuries, it also plays a vital role in their literary creativity. The chaos, in other words, is double edged. Today it can be tied to the diversity of voices that generate literary works, and, as earlier, it points not just to a troubled world but also to the end of old certainties and the possibility of change.

Chronology of Relevant Events

British and Irish Literature and Its Times

SOCIAL AND POLITICAL REFORM

In contrast to many of its European neighbors, Britain managed, with the help of social and political reform, to maintain a stable government in the nineteenth century. Members of the burgeoning middle and working classes strove to make their voices heard through demonstrations, petitions, and the formation of new political movements. While much of the population lived in straitened circumstances, the government adopted some important measures that began to address popular demands: a series of Reform Acts (1832, 1867, 1884) extended the voting franchise to the majority of adult males, a secret ballot was introduced, and Factory Acts established more reasonable hours and conditions for workers. Some of the most sweeping reforms were introduced by the early-twentieth-century Liberal Party, alternative to the Conservative Party in government. By the end of World War II, the Labour Party had become the alternative to the Conservatives. Winning the postwar election, Labour oversaw a government whose welfare reforms turned Britain into a partly capitalist, partly socialist society. A few decades later the Conservatives under Margaret Thatcher reversed the process, beginning to dismantle the welfare reforms.

Historical Events		Related Literary Works in *WLAIT 4*
1830-37	Reign of William IV	
1830s-40s	Number of convicts transported from Britain to Australia is estimated at 58,000; practice of transportation begins to taper off in succeeding decades	*Great Expectations* by Charles Dickens
1832	Passage of parliamentary Reform Bill extends voting franchise to smaller property holders and householders occupying property valued at £10 or more	
1833	Abolition of slavery throughout British territory at home and abroad; Factory Act sets minimum working age at nine	

Historical Events		Related Literary Works in *WLAIT 4*
1833-38	Bill abolishing slavery substitutes apprenticeship for bondage for seven years; substitution is abolished August 1, 1838	
1834	New Poor Law provides relief only to those who agree to abide by regimen of the workhouse	*Jane Eyre* by Charlotte Brontë
1837-1901	Reign of Queen Victoria, who ascends to throne of England at age 17	
1838	The Chartists, a large organization of workingmen, draw up a "People's Charter" advocating extension of the franchise, secret ballot, and other legislative reforms	
1839	Government begins to provide money for public schools	
1840	Queen Victoria marries Prince Albert of Saxe-Coburg-Gotha, becomes model wife, exhorting devotion to duty and domesticity; penny post (inexpensive mail service) is established	
1840s	The "Hungry '40s"—Britain suffers a severe economic depression, resulting in widespread unemployment; Chartists' riots erupt after Parliament rejects People's Charter	
1842	London police establish detective department	
1846	Prime Minister Robert Peel resolves to end traditional protectionism of British goods, advocates policy of Free Trade; Parliament repeals the Corn Laws of 1815	
1848	Revolutions erupt in France, Austria, Germany, and Italy; in England, Chartists stage demonstration after third presentation of People's Charter to Parliament; cholera epidemic highlights need for public-health measures	
1850s-70s	Britain recovers from depression, begins to experience economic prosperity as technology and industry advance	
1857	Transportation of convicts is abolished	
1861	Prince Albert dies of typhoid; the widowed Queen Victoria enters prolonged period of mourning	
1867	Representation of People Act (Second Reform Bill) extends voting franchise to almost all men over 21	
1868-80s	Prime Ministers Benjamin Disraeli and William Gladstone institute protection of children from abuse, higher sanitation and safety standards in housing, and other social reforms	
1870	W. E. Forster's Education Act makes elementary education available to all children in England and Wales	
1870s-1910s	Agricultural depression leads to a fall in the price of land	
1872	Police strike; secret ballot becomes compulsory; Education (Scotland) Act makes school compulsory in Scotland for children from ages five to 13	
1874	Factory Act establishes a maximum work week of 56 hours	
1878	Four police inspectors are found guilty of corruption; Detective Department of London police is reorganized as Criminal Investigation Division	
1880	Elementary education becomes compulsory for all children from age seven to 10	
1880s-90s	Gradual decline of Victorian values; increasing migration of people to the city—80 percent of the population recorded as living in towns; socialist organizations attract British intellectuals, including George Bernard Shaw and William Morris	

Historical Events		Related Literary Works in *WLAIT 4*
1884	Formation of the Fabian Society, an organization designed to promote socialism gradually	
1887	"Bloody Sunday"—Socialist League march in Trafalgar Square is disrupted by police brutality, hundreds of demonstrators are injured	
1888	The serial killer Jack the Ripper murders five London prostitutes but is never apprehended; county councils are established	
1889	London dock strike succeeds; spread of trade unionism; employment of children under 10 is prohibited	
1891	London police move to New Scotland Yard; elementary education becomes free in government schools	*The Adventures of Sherlock Holmes* by Arthur Conan Doyle
1897	First Workmen's Compensation Act is passed	
1899	School attendance is made compulsory until the age of 12	
1900	Labour Party is founded	
1901-10	Death of Queen Victoria; accession and reign of Edward VII	
1905-11	Liberal government institutes important social reforms, including old-age pensions, and health and unemployment insurance	
1910-36	Reign of George V	
1924	First Labour government is elected in Britain	
1926	A miners' dispute over wages and hours sparks a nine-day general strike	*Brideshead Revisited* by Evelyn Waugh
1930s	Worldwide economic depression, following the crash of Wall Street in the United States	
1931	Fall of Labour government in Britain	
1936	Death of George V; Edward VIII abdicates throne of England to marry American divorcee Wallis Simpson; Jarrow Crusade— 200 Englishmen stage hunger march to garner public sympathy and aid for the community after a major shipyard is closed, costing 8,000 workers their jobs	
1936-52	Reign of George VI	
1940	Winston Churchill is elected prime minister, forms a coalition government as Britain enters World War II	
1944	Education Act reorganizes secondary school system, makes school attendance compulsory until the age of 15	
1946-51	Labour Government is elected, nationalizes key industries and services, including the Bank of England, railroads, mines, steel, gas and electricity; National Health Service is instituted to give free medical treatment to all British citizens	
1951-64	Conservative Party reassumes power	
1952	Accession of Elizabeth II	
1964-79	Labour Party regains power in government	
1969	Abolishment of capital punishment	
1970	Age of majority is lowered from 21 to 18	
1970s	Conservative Party gains control of Parliament; decade is marked by inflation and industrial upheaval; rise of Scottish nationalist movement	

Historical Events	Related Literary Works in *WLAIT 4*
1979-97	Margaret Thatcher becomes prime minister; Conservative Party begins 18 years in government	
1980s-90	Thatcher's government targets economic problems, privatizes national industries and dismantles parts of the welfare state, reduces spending in education	*Disaffection* by James Kelman; *Adoption Papers* by Jackie Kay
1984	National coal miners' strike	
1989	Thatcher's government introduces poll tax	
1990-97	Thatcher resigns; John Major serves as prime minister	
1997	Labour government is returned to power; Anthony Blair becomes prime minister	
1999	Devolution in Scotland and Wales—power is partly transferred from British Parliament at Westminster to newly convened Scottish Parliament and Welsh Assembly	

WOMEN'S RIGHTS AND ROLES

For most of the nineteenth century, many women labored under the ideal that they be a self-sacrificing wife and mother, or "angel in the house." As the nineteenth century progressed, a woman's rights movement took hold and gained momentum. Generations of female mavericks petitioned for better working conditions, more control over their earnings, more freedom within their marriages, more power to leave unhappy marriages, and the right to vote. During the 1840s, the first petitions for women's suffrage were submitted to the British Parliament. Their failure did not deter the suffragists, who became increasingly militant as the twentieth century dawned. Women would at last gain the vote after the First World War, meanwhile taking large strides in social life and the work world. Nineteenth-century parliamentary acts gave women increasing and finally complete control over their own property. Also women were admitted to professions formerly closed to them—such as medicine—and allowed to study at newly established women's colleges at Oxford and Cambridge University. Reforms of the twentieth century further narrowed the gap between the social, political, and economic rights of women and those of men. The Matrimonial Causes Act of 1923 made the grounds for divorce the same for women and men. Armed with the vote, women continued to make political strides in the twentieth century too, finding their way into some of the highest offices in Britain before the century's end.

Historical Events	Related Literary Works in *WLAIT 4*
1830s-40s	Economic problems and dearth of available men contribute to surplus of single women; middle- and lower-class working women experience financial hardships; movements for women's suffrage gain momentum and petitions are submitted to Parliament	*Jane Eyre* by Charlotte Brontë
1837-1901	Reign of Queen Victoria	
1839	Child Custody Act makes it possible for a mother to gain custody of her children under seven years of age	
1842	Ashely's Mines Act excludes women and children from having to work in the mines	
1845	After a yearlong courtship, England's most renowned female poet, Elizabeth Barrett, elopes to Italy with poet Robert Browning	*Sonnets from the Portuguese* by Elizabeth Barrett Browning; "My Last Duchess and Other Poems" by Robert Browning

Historical Events	Related Literary Works in *WLAIT 4*
1848 Queen's College in London is established for women who intend to teach; Factory Act limits women's and children's working hours in textile mills to 10 a day	
1852 Women's Suffrage Petition is presented to the House of Lords but rejected; judge rules that a man may not force his wife to live with him	
1854-56 Florence Nightingale acquires lasting renown as a nurse in the Crimean War, introduces hygienic standards into military hospitals; publication of Coventry Patmore's "Angel in the House," one of best-selling poems in Victorian England	
1857 Matrimonial Causes Act allows divorce through law courts instead of private act of Parliament; husband must prove wife's adultery; wife must prove husband's adultery, plus incest, bigamy, cruelty, or desertion	
1860 Nightingale Training School for Nurses is established	
1864 Contagious Diseases Act forces prostitutes to undergo periodic examinations for venereal diseases; in response, movement to stamp out prostitution develops	*Nights at the Circus* by Angela Carter
1865 Barbara Bodichon forms Women's Suffrage Committee	
1867 First debate in Parliament on women's suffrage; John Stuart Mill tries but fails to amend reform bill to grant women the vote	*The French Lieutenant's Woman* by John Fowles
1869 National Society for Women's Suffrage is founded; Girton College—the first for women—is founded at Cambridge University	
1870 Married Woman's Property Act gives women full rights over money earned after marriage and willed to them by others	*Howards End* by E. M. Forster; *The Adventures of Sherlock Holmes* by Sir Arthur Conan Doyle
1870s-1900s Additional women's colleges are founded at Oxford and Cambridge; a growing number of middle- and upper-class women explore options beyond marriage and motherhood; an influx of wealthy American girls enter British high society, making advantageous marriages into the English aristocracy	
1871 Women receive right to vote in municipal elections but are denied the franchise at the national level	
1876 Women receive right to become licensed physicians	
1880-1902 Women are granted the vote in the Isle of Man, New Zealand, and Australia but not in England	
1882 Second Married Woman's Property Act gives women ownership over all property acquired by their own efforts; female students at Cambridge take examinations for the first time	
1886 Contagious Diseases Act is repealed	
1888 Women are granted the right to vote in elections for county councils, also established that year	
1893 Third Married Woman's Property Act gives women control of all their own property	
1894-1900s The phrase "New Woman" is coined by Sarah Grand, denotes the woman who seeks the same freedoms of thought, speech, and dress that men have possessed for generations	*The Importance of Being Earnest* by Oscar Wilde
1897 First large national suffrage movement forms under Millicent Fawcett	

Historical Events	Related Literary Works in *WLAIT 4*
1903-13 Emmeline Pankhurst founds a militant women's suffrage movement; countless suffragists are arrested and jailed for the cause, which acquires its first martyr after Emily Davidson throws herself in front of the king's horse on Derby day	
1914-18 As men fight in World War I, an increasing number of middle- and working-class women find jobs outside the home	
1918 Voting Act gives women over 30 and men over 21 the franchise	
1920 Women undergraduates gain right to hold degrees from Oxford University	
1921 Females make up 30 percent of the workforce in Britain	
1923 Matrimonial Causes Act makes the grounds for divorce the same for men and women	
1928 Passage of Equal Franchise act: the voting age for women is reduced to 21 to match the voting age for men	
1939-45 Number of women working outside the home increases during World War II; some even serve in the armed forces	
1959 Women's colleges at Oxford finally recognized as full colleges of the university	
1960s-70s Loosening of social and sexual mores contributes to increased emancipation of women in Britain; stigma against unwed mothers and illegitimate offspring fades	*The Sea, the Sea* by Iris Murdoch
1967 Abortion Act makes abortion legal for social as well as medical reasons	*The French Lieutenant's Woman* by John Fowles
1970 Equal Pay Act calls for men and women in equivalent lines of work to receive the same monetary compensation	
1971 Divorce Act allowing for no-fault divorces and for divorce on the grounds of mutual or individual unhappiness takes effect	
1975 Sex Discrimination Act allows men and women to bring their employers before a tribunal for sexual discrimination	
1976 Domestic Violence Act allows women to seek the arrest of husbands and boyfriends who beat them	
1979 Margaret Thatcher becomes Britain's first woman prime minister	
1983 Mary Donaldson becomes the first female lord mayor of London	
1996 Women account for over 44 percent of the workforce in Britain	

THE BRITISH EMPIRE: FROM EXPANSION TO DISSOLUTION

The Victorian Age is often called the Age of Empire. During the queen's long reign, Britain expanded its territorial and colonial holdings throughout the world, creating an empire on which the sun literally never set. Other nations competed strenuously against Britain for colonial acquisitions—especially France, Germany, Belgium, and the Netherlands. During the latter half of the nineteenth century, these countries and more strove to carve out "spheres of influence" in Africa and Asia, meanwhile exploiting the indigenous peoples and their resources. The British Empire reached its height at the turn of the twentieth century and endured well into that century, but after World War II, decolonization, a process that would take several decades, began. One consequence was a vast influx of immigrants to Britain from its former colonies. From the late 1940s to the 1960s, East Indians, West Indians, Pakistanis, Africans, and Asians poured into Britain, radically changing the ethnic balance in the population. Racial friction followed as society adjusted to the new multicultural mix.

	Historical Events	Related Literary Works in *WLAIT 4*
c. 1800	Slave population in the British West Indies numbers 500,000	*Cambridge* by Caryl Phillips
1834-1917	Approximately 144,000 East Indians move to Trinidad as indentured servants to work in colonial sugar industry	*A House for Mr. Biswas* by V. S. Naipaul
1837-1901	Reign of Queen Victoria—British empire expands, acquiring holdings throughout the world	*Peter Pan: Peter and Wendy* by J. M. Barrie
1839-42	Opium War—Britain annexes city of Hong Kong in China; Britain loses First Anglo-Afghan War to a claimant supported by Russia	*Sour Sweet* by Timothy Mo
1840s	British establish colony in Ceylon (present-day Sri Lanka); Canada is granted measure of self-government	
1840s-50s	British settlers arrive and settle in Natal, on eastern coast of South Africa	
1849	East India Company annexes the Punjab, in the northwest region of India	
1850s-1900s	Australia and New Zealand are granted measure of self-government; Britain, France and the Netherlands compete for colonial possessions in Africa and Asia	*Lord Jim* by Joseph Conrad
1853	British explorer David Livingston begins three-year expedition through uncharted Central Africa	
1854-56	Crimean War—Britain goes to war against Turkey, partly to protect trade routes to Asia	
1856-60	Second Opium War—Britain gains control of Kowloon on the mainland of China	
1857	Rebellion in the Bengal Army sparks Indian Mutiny, a revolt against British rule that claims thousands of lives	*Kim* by Rudyard Kipling; *The Moonstone* by Wilkie Collins
1858	Government of India Act transfers administrative power in India from East India Company to the British Crown; publication of R. M. Ballantyne's influential boys' adventure classic *The Coral Island*	
1860s-70s	British explorers and missionaries arrive in Uganda; Britain annexes additional territories in South Africa	
1861	British establish Lagos colony in Nigeria, marking beginning of British colonial rule in West Africa	
1867	Diamonds are found in South Africa near confluence of Vaal and Harte rivers	
1868	Britain annexes Lesotho (Basutoland) in South Africa	
1869	Suez Canal opens	
1870s	Diamond rush ensues after gems are discovered in South Africa; Britain annexes territory surrounding new diamond mine of Kimberley	*King Solomon's Mines* by H. Rider Haggard
1874	Gold Coast (future Ghana) becomes British colony	
1875	Britain gains shares in Suez Canal, safeguarding route to India	

	Historical Events	Related Literary Works in *WLAIT 4*
1877	Queen Victoria is proclaimed Empress of India; Britain annexes the Transvaal in South Africa	*Kim* by Rudyard Kipling
1878-80	Britain loses Second Anglo-Afghan War, again to a claimant supported by Russia	
1879	In South Africa, Zulu War begins with slaughter of British troops at Insandlwana, ends with capture of Zulu leader Cetshwayo	
1880s-90s	Cecil Rhodes colonizes territory in southern Africa; British gain control over Northern Somalia and Kenya (British East Africa)	
1882-1914	British forces occupy Egypt, which becomes a "Veiled Protectorate"	
1884-85	Mahdi uprising in the Sudan leads to the 10-month long siege of Khartoum; British Governor General Charles Gordon is killed	
1885-98	Period of Sudanese independence	
1890s	Ndebele and Shona peoples of southern Africa rebel against encroachment of British colonists but are defeated by colonists' strategy and sophisticated weaponry; colony of Southern Rhodesia is established; British expand territorial holdings in southwestern Nigeria	*The Grass Is Singing* by Doris Lessing
1894	Uganda becomes British protectorate	
1895	British East Africa becomes a British protectorate	
1898-1956	Egypt and Britain jointly rule the Sudan	
1899-1902	South African War (Anglo-Boer War)—Britain fights settlers of Dutch descent over territorial holdings in South Africa; British victory marks final stage in colonial conquest of South Africa	
1914	Egypt is formally named a British protectorate	
1920	British East Africa is officially named a colony	
1921	Irish independence begins as southern Ireland achieves free-state status (see timeline below—Ireland: Act of Union to Late-Twentieth-Century "Troubles")	
1922	Britain grants Egypt formal but nominal independence	
1931	Statute of Westminister brings British Commonwealth of Nations into existence as collection of states within British Empire	
1936	British and Egyptian governments sign agreement restricting British military occupation to the Canal Zone	
1946	British colonial rule over Trinidad, a British possession since 1737, begins to wane; universal suffrage is granted in Trinidad *A House for Mr. Biswas* by V. S. Naipaul	
1947	British Empire begins process of dissolution; India is granted independence and the subcontinent is divided into India (Hindu) and Pakistan (Muslim)	*Midnight's Children* by Salman Rushdie; *A House for Mr. Biswas* by V. S. Naipaul
1948	British Nationality Act ascribes British citizenship to people of the United Kingdom, its colonies, and newly independent Commonwealth countries; *SS Empire Windrush* carries 492 Jamaicans to Britain; large-scale twentieth-century immigration of blacks to Britain begins	
1950s-60s	Relatively few nonwhite children in need of families are adopted in Britain	*Adoption Papers* by Jackie Kay
1951	Egypt asserts sovereignty, abrogates treaties that made it a virtual colony of Britain	

	Historical Events	Related Literary Works in *WLAIT 4*
1956	Egypt seizes control of Suez Canal; Britain, France, and Israel attack but back down after United Nations calls for end to hostilities; Britain withdraws forces from the Canal Zone; the Sudan gains independence	
1957	Britain grants independence to Ghana	
1958-68	Vast quantities of formerly colonial peoples immigrate to Britain, changing ethnic makeup of nation; race riots in Nottingham and London in 1958	*The Buddha of Suburbia* by Hanif Kureishi;
1960	Britain grants independence to Nigeria and territory of Somalia	
1961	South Africa secedes from British commonwealth and becomes an independent nation	
1962	British Commonwealth Immigrants' Act abolishes automatic right of British citizenship for Commonwealth citizens; Trinidad and Uganda are granted full independence from Britain	*Sour Sweet* by Timothy Mo
1963	Kenya and Northern Rhodesia (Zambia) are granted independence from Britain	
1965	Race Relations Act bans discrimination in public places, makes the promotion of ethnic-based hatred an offense, and institutes a Race Relations board to handle complaints; Rhodesia declares independence from British control	*Adoption Papers* by Jackie Kay
1966-68	Botswana, Lesotho, and Swaziland in southern Africa become independent	
1968	Race Relations Act bans discrimination in housing and employment in Britain; Member of Parliament Enoch Powell proclaims opposition to African and Asian immigration, delivers "rivers of blood" speech assailing Race Relations Act	
1970s	Formed in 1967, National Front Party gains prominence by capitalizing on fears inspired by increasing number of immigrants	
1976	Race Relations Commission is set up to further equal opportunity and harmonious relations between races	
1977	Support for National Front Party peaks; anti-Nazi League forms to alert voters to fascist tendencies in National Front Party	
1980-85	Urban riots erupt, instigated in part by racially motivated arrests of blacks by police	
1984	Britain and China, in anticipation of 1997 expiration of Britain's lease on Hong Kong, agree that Hong Kong's British-established legal, education and financial systems will remain in effect until 2047	
1991	Ethnic groups in Britain first enumerated in census—African and Asian immigrants comprise 5 percent of the population	

RELIGION AND SCIENCE

Early in the nineteenth century, the faith of Britain's practicing Christians was tested by various new findings. Scientific and archaeological discoveries challenged interpretations of biblical scripture, touching off a debate between religion and science that would last for decades. A growing number of Victorians suffered crises of faith, questioning lifelong beliefs, even as their society expanded to encompass a variety of religious creeds. Startling new theories about the nature of the world and the evolution of humanity were introduced, while scientific research yielded vital information about life-threatening diseases and the possibility of cures. Scien-

Historical Events	Related Literary Works in *WLAIT 4*

tific developments would continue to transform life on both the theoretical and practical levels for the next two centuries. Late in the nineteenth century, anthropologists and naturalists journeyed to parts of the empire for scientific investigation, and psychology became a major new area of scientific study. The ideas of Sigmund Freud spread through Britain early in the twentieth century, followed by the development and spread of computers that quickened computation and other intellectual tasks.

	Historical Events	Related Literary Works in *WLAIT 4*
1830s-90s	Evangelical movement of the Anglican Church, combined with such factors as political uprisings in Europe and the subsequent reevaluation of political and social perspectives, fosters a climate of moral and intellectual earnestness	*The Importance of Being Earnest* by Oscar Wilde
1830-33	Publication of Sir Charles Lyell's *Principles of Geology,* which influences scientific and religious thought in ensuing decades	*In Memoriam* by Alfred Tennyson; *On the Origin of Species* by Charles Darwin; *The Time Machine* by H. G. Wells
1833-45	The "Oxford" Movement—Anglican clergymen, led by John Henry Newman, react against liberalizing tendencies within Church of England and call for the revival of certain Roman Catholic rituals and doctrines	*Jude the Obscure* by Thomas Hardy
1840s-90s	Modern phonetics begins to develop, with the experiments of Sir Isaac Pitman, Alexander Melville, and Henry Sweet	*Pygmalion* by George Bernard Shaw
1844	Robert Chambers's *Vestiges of the Natural History of Creation* is published, advancing argument that changes are the result of natural forces at work, not acts of God	*In Memoriam* by Alfred Tennyson
1848	Cholera epidemic throughout Britain reveals need for public health reforms	
1850	Publication of the elegy *In Memoriam* sums up many of the contemporary attitudes on faith, science, and doubt; Roman Catholic hierarchy regains measure of prominence in England	*In Memoriam* by Alfred Tennyson
1851	About 60 percent of able-bodied Britons attend church services	
1853	Queen Victoria uses chloroform during the birth of her eighth child, leading to its subsequent use as an anesthetic	
1858	Lionel Nathan Rothschild becomes the first Jewish member of Parliament; Medical Act establishes a register of qualified physicians	
1859	Charles Darwin's *On the Origin of Species* is published, positing evolution of species through natural selection	*On the Origin of Species* by Charles Darwin; *The French Lieutenant's Woman* by John Fowles
1861	Prince Albert, consort of Queen Victoria, dies of typhoid fever	
1869	Charitable Organization Society formed to connect religious and private charities	
1870s	Scientific debate takes place regarding the "split personality" and its possible link to evolutionary theory; Jewish refugees from Eastern European pogroms immigrate to Britain, settling in Liverpool, Manchester, and London's East End	*The Strange Case of Dr. Jekyll and Mr. Hyde* by Robert Louis Stevenson
1872	Publication of Darwin's *Descent of Man*	
1875	Theosophical Society, an influential group interested in occultism, is founded by Russian immigrant Madame Blavatsky	*Dracula* by Bram Stoker
1878	The Salvation Army is organized by Catherine and William Booth as a mission to the poor	

	Historical Events	Related Literary Works in *WLAIT 4*
1880s	Psychology, the study of human behavior and consciousness, becomes increasingly popular among European intellectuals	*The Strange Case of Dr. Jekyll and Mr. Hyde* by Robert Louis Stevenson
1890	Jews achieve full civil rights in Britain	
1902	Decline in church attendance to 20 percent of the population is observed	
1912	Sigmund Freud's theories of psychology spread through Britain	*Mrs. Dalloway* by Virginia Woolf; *Ulysses* by James Joyce
1928	British bacteriologist Alexander Fleming discovers penicillin	
1940s	British and American scientists develop early models of electronic and digital computers	*Arcadia* by Tom Stoppard
1942	Council of Christians and Jews is founded to combat religious intolerance	
1943	British scientists Max Newman, Donald Michie, and Alan Turing build Colossus I, the first electronic computer, used for breaking enemy communications codes during World War II	
1950s-60s	Freudian psychology continues to dominate medical and scientific views on sexuality and homosexuality; Britain experiences influx of minority races and faiths	*What the Butler Saw* by Joe Orton; *The Buddha of Suburbia* by Hanif Kureishi
1953	British scientist Francis Crick and his American colleague James Watson discover the structure of DNA	
1967	Sexual Offences Acts partially decriminalizes homosexuality	*What the Butler Saw* by Joe Orton
1970	Census reports that 230,000 Hindus are living in Britain	
1980s	AIDS epidemic spreads throughout world, sparking health-awareness programs and a "safe-sex" movement	*Adoption Papers* by Jackie Kay; *Arcadia* by Tom Stoppard

INDUSTRY, TECHNOLOGY, AND LEISURE

The Victorian Age saw Britain transform itself from an agricultural kingdom into a major industrial power. The very face of the terrain changed as thousands of miles of railroad track were laid, shortening journeys that had once taken days by foot or horse into a few hours' duration. In 1851 a Great Exhibition was held to celebrate Britain's numerous industrial and technological achievements. The industrial boom continued in the latter half of the nineteenth century as use of electrical power became increasingly widespread. While the nineteenth century produced a number of ambitious, hardworking inventors and entrepreneurs who effected these achievements, it also gave rise to generations of Victorians who played as hard as they worked. During the 1880s and 1890s, people of all classes found new venues and activities to supply entertainment. Included were music halls, circuses, and leisure sports, such as lawn tennis and bicycling. In the twentieth century, the options multiplied with the introduction of film, television, and rock music in the region.

1825-55	First railroad boom in Britain—8,000 miles of track are laid over the next three decades	
1830s-60s	Iron steamships begin to replace wooden sailing ships; propellers replace paddle wheels on sides of steamships, shortening Atlantic Ocean crossings	
1834	The Hansom Safety Cab, a two-wheeled horse-drawn vehicle, is patented and becomes a popular means of transportation	
1840s-50s	Construction of Houses of Parliament and the clock tower Big Ben, two London landmarks	

Historical Events		Related Literary Works in *WLAIT 4*
1842	Railway from Manchester to London opens	
1843	First telegraph line is in operation	
1851	Great Exhibition celebrating progress and industry is held at the Crystal Palace	
1852	Canterbury Hall opens, initiating music hall form of entertainment	
1854-63	Construction of London Underground (future subway system) begins, opening for regular passenger service nine years later	
1856	Henry Bessemer develops process that will inexpensively allow iron to be turned into steel	
1866	Transatlantic telegraph cable is in service	
1870s-80s	Electric lighting is installed in large buildings such as the Royal Albert Hall, the British Museum Library, and Victoria Station; public electric generating plants are built to supply power for developments such as trams and streetlights	
1871	The *Oceanic*, the first luxury liner, is built by the White Star Line for passenger service to Australia	
1875-1900s	Municipalities pave city streets, build reservoirs, provide adequate water supplies, and establish sanitary drainage	
1878	Electrical lights are installed on some streets in London	
1879	First dining car is installed on the railway	
1880	Stores begin to stock canned fruits and meats	
1881	The Savoy Theatre, the first to be lit with electricity, opens	
1883	First electric tram is in operation	
1884	Football League is formed to control professional soccer matches	
1886	Safety bicycles become available for sale	
1887	Queen Victoria's Golden Jubilee marks her fiftieth anniversary as monarch	
1888	Barnum and Bailey's circus comes to England for the first time	*Nights at the Circus* by Angela Carter
1890s	First moving-picture shows appear; aesthetic and decadent movements acquire a following in London society	*The Importance of Being Earnest* by Oscar Wilde
1895	Playwright Oscar Wilde is convicted of homosexuality and sentenced to two years' imprisonment	
1897	Queen Victoria's Diamond Jubilee celebrates her 60 years on the throne	
1899	First motor bus begins service	
1900s	A focus of many novels becomes the experience of Europeans in Asia, Africa, and South America	*The Grass Is Singing* by Doris Lessing; *The Power and the Glory* by Graham Greene
early 1900s	Britain ranks highest in world as producer of coal	*Women in Love* by D. H. Lawrence; *Under Milk Wood* by Dylan Thomas
1900-45	First acting schools open in London; members of the middle and upper class who enter the acting profession enjoy celebrity status and privileges	*The Sea, the Sea* by Iris Murdoch
1907	Henry Royce and C. S. Rolls build Silver Ghost, the first Rolls-Royce	
1910s	The motor car becomes increasingly popular among the wealthy and socially ambitious	*Howards End* by E. M. Forster

Historical Events		Related Literary Works in *WLAIT 4*
1912	The *Titanic* sinks on its maiden voyage from Southampton to New York	
1920s	The "stream of consciousness" technique becomes a noted feature of the modern novel	*Mrs. Dalloway* by Virginia Woolf; *Ulysses* by James Joyce
1913-23	Decline of the music hall and rise of variety theater	
1922	Formation of the British Broadcasting Corporation	
1926	Scottish inventor John Logie Baird gives first practical demonstration of television	
1930s-50s	Film and television compete with the theater as a source of public entertainment	
1950s-60s	Decline of variety theater; numerous literary innovations in drama take place, resulting in the composition of verse plays, "kitchen-sink" realist plays, and absurdist plays	*Waiting for Godot* by Samuel Beckett
1960s	The London-based Arts Council delegates much of its grant-giving responsibility to regional arts councils, resulting in growing confidence among artists outside London and a renaissance of regional literature	
1963	The Beatles, a rock group from Liverpool, top the British music charts for the first time, going on to attain worldwide fame	
1968	Censorship of the theater by the Lord Chamberlain's office ends	
1969	Oil is discovered in the North Sea	
1969-96	Decline in number of manufacturing jobs from 9.1 to 4 million; rise in number of jobs in service industries and public administration from 7.2 to 12 million	
1960s-70s	Rock music becomes associated with liberal approaches towards sex, drugs, and politics	
1970s	Punk rock music attracts following; groups adopt Caribbean rhythms of reggae music	*The Buddha of Suburbia* by Hanif Kureishi
1987-91	Channel Tunnel between England and France is constructed	*Arcadia* by Tom Stoppard

FROM WORLD WAR I TO THE PERSIAN GULF WAR

Britain's relations with Germany, a country whose customs and culture it had once admired, grew increasingly volatile in the late nineteenth century as German leaders became more aggressive and militaristic. By the outbreak of World War I, many British believed war was inevitable. The ensuing conflict between the Allies (Britain, France, at first Russia, and later the United States) and Central Powers (Germany, Austria-Hungary, Turkey, and Bulgaria), cost Britain dearly. Ill-prepared for modern warfare, an estimated 780,000 British soldiers perished. By the end of the war, Britain, as well as France, had lost almost an entire generation of young men, a circumstance that likely influenced the harsh reparative terms levied against Germany in the Treaty of Versailles. Crippled economically and emotionally after the war, Germany turned to fascism for solutions. The rise of totalitarian governments in Europe—Hitler's Nazi Germany and Mussolini's fascist Italy—in the 1920s and 1930s led to another world war, this time between the Allies (Britain, France, the Soviet Union, and the United States) and Axis (mainly Germany, Italy, and Japan) powers. The Allies won again, but at great cost; the British lost about half as many soldiers as in World War I, and more than 43,000 civilians in 1940-41 during the

Historical Events	Related Literary Works in *WLAIT 4*
blitz. Exhausted by war, Britain afterward lost dominance as a world power, but managed nonetheless to maintain an active presence on the global political scene.	

	Historical Events	Related Literary Works in *WLAIT 4*
1890s-1910s	Tensions develop between Britain and the increasingly militaristic Germany; many believe that conflict, even war, is inevitable	
1914-18	World War I—Britain goes to war against Germany after the assassination of Archduke Ferdinand in Sarajevo; horrific new forms of war technology are introduced, including trench warfare, tanks, and poison gas	"Anthem for Doomed Youth" and Other Poems by Wilfred Owen; *Women in Love* by D. H. Lawrence
1918	Allied terms of the Treaty of Versailles exact harsh penalties from the defeated nations, especially Germany, which is blamed for starting the war	
1920s	Disillusionment in the years following the First World War results in the development of a cynical, aesthetic "Lost Generation," whose members reject the values of their predecessors; after demobilization, many ex-officers who fought in World War I find themselves in menial jobs or unemployed	*The Waste Land* by T. S. Eliot; *Mrs. Dalloway* by Virginia Woolf; *Brideshead Revisited* by Evelyn Waugh
1930s	Fascist governments are established in Italy and Germany, awakening some fascist sympathies in British society; communist and socialist movements also take root in Europe and other parts of the world, swaying some of the British to their cause	*The Remains of the Day* by Kazuo Ishiguro; *The Prime of Miss Jean Brodie* by Muriel Spark; *Goodbye to Berlin* by Christopher Isherwood; *The Power and the Glory* by Graham Greene.
1932	Sir Oswald Moseley founds the British Union of Fascists	*The Remains of the Day* by Kazuo Ishiguro
1936-39	Spanish Civil War—about 2,500 British citizens fight as volunteers in Spain, most of them against Franco and on the side of the Republicans; British prime ministers Stanley Baldwin and Neville Chamberlain implement policy of appeasement as Germany invades other European countries	*The Prime of Miss Jean Brodie* by Muriel Spark
1937-39	British government under leadership of Neville Chamberlain practices policy of appeasement towards Adolf Hitler, Chancellor of Germany	
1938	British Prime Minister Chamberlain appeases Hitler at Munich, requires Czechoslovakia to surrender the Sudetenland to Hitler to maintain peace	
1939	September 1—Britain declares war on Germany after German invasion of Poland; London's children undergo mass evacuation to safer locations in the country	*Lord of the Flies* by William Golding
1939-45	World War II—Britain fights Germany and Japan	*The Heat of the Day* by Elizabeth Bowen; "The Lion and the Unicorn" by George Orwell
1940	Battle of Britain in skies over southern England begins, pits the British Royal Air Force against the German Luftwaffe; British are forced to retreat to Dunkirk, a port city in France, Allied armies are evacuated from Dunkirk mainly by Royal and Merchant Navy ships	
1940-41	September 1940 to May 1941—London and other major industrial cities in Britain undergo aerial bombardment by the Germans (the "blitz")	*The Heat of the Day* by Elizabeth Bowen
1941	British Navy sinks the German battleship Bismarck; British secret service officially begins resistance against Nazis in France	*Waiting for Godot* by Samuel Beckett
1945	United States, backed by Allied forces, drops atomic bombs over on Hiroshima and Nagasaki, Japan, effectively ending the war	*Lord of the Flies* by William Golding

	Historical Events	Related Literary Works in *WLAIT 4*
1945-90	The United States and the Soviet Union fight the Cold War for world leadership; Britain allies itself to the United States	
1945-92	Britain engages in series of small wars and military actions in Korea, Kenya, Malaysia, Palestine, the Falkland Islands, the Persian Gulf, and other areas of the world	
1947	Exhausted financially and emotionally by war, Britain reduces its land, air, and sea defenses to about 690,000 personnel	
1949	Britain joins the North Atlantic Treaty Organization (NATO), a defense alliance to safeguard western Europe from domination by the Soviet Union	
1950-53	Britain enters the Korean War, sending troops and ships to aid South Korea	
1952	The British develop and tests their own atomic bomb	
1968-71	Britain begins process of withdrawing forces from Malaysia, Singapore, and the Persian Gulf	
1973	Great Britain joins the European Economic Community (EEC)	
1982	Britain defeats Argentina in war over the Falkland Islands	
1991	Britain participates in the Persian Gulf War against Iraq	

IRELAND: ACT OF UNION TO LATE-TWENTIETH-CENTURY "TROUBLES"

Ireland, united to Britain at the start of the nineteenth century and divided from it in the first half of the twentieth, continued to develop its own separate traditions in politics, social life, science, and art. For much of the nineteenth century, Britain and Ireland clashed over Home Rule, the drive to return limited domestic powers to Ireland. Irish nationalists and politicians rallied to the cause, but by the end of World War I, Home Rule had largely been rendered moot by the more radical demand for the formation of a separate Irish republic. Fighting the British for independence, the Irish Republican Army emerged with a truce that resulted in 26 counties becoming the Irish Free State within the British Commonwealth. Meanwhile, six Protestant-majority counties, known collectively as Ulster, remained part of the United Kingdom of Great Britain and Northern Ireland. Over the years grievances mounted among Catholics in Northern Ireland, leading to a civil rights movement in the 1960s. Years of mass rioting and terrorist strife followed, the goal of the terrorists being to achieve a united Ireland free of Britain. In fact, since 1937 the Irish Republic had officially laid claim to Northern Ireland in its constitution. This claim would be removed at the close of 1999, when the Irish Republic, Britain, and Northern Ireland joined together to effect a peaceful solution.

1800	Act of Union forms the United Kingdom of Great Britain and Ireland, abolishes Irish Parliament	
1823-43	Daniel O'Connell wins fight for granting of partial civil rights to Catholics, but fails to obtain Home Rule for Ireland	
1831	Free elementary education begins	
1832	Small party of 39 Irish Members of Parliament in Britain pledge to secure repeal of the Act of Union	
1834-50s	Most of Ireland's railway is laid	

Historical Events	Related Literary Works in *WLAIT 4*
1846-51 Irish population decreases because of potato crop failures, famine, disease, and large-scale emigration	
1848-67 The Fenians, a secret revolutionary group, instigates unsuccessful risings in Ireland	
1852-53 Industrial exhibitions are held in Cork and Dublin, though Ireland remains highly rural	
1861 Abortion is outlawed in Ireland under the Offences against the Person Act	
1869-70 British Prime Minister William Gladstone disestablishes Protestant Church of Ireland and introduces land reforms	
1870 Irish Land Act gives tenants compensation for eviction	
1871 The Alhambra, first structure designed as a music hall in Ireland, opens in Belfast	*Waiting for Godot* by Samuel Beckett
1877-91 Member of Parliament Charles Parnell advocates Irish Home Rule, but his involvement with the married Kitty O'Shea destroys his popularity	
1885 John O'Leary, Irish nationalist, returns to Dublin after years of exile and imprisonment, draws many Irish to the nationalist cause	
1886 Gladstone introduces First Home Rule Bill in House of Commons, but it is defeated; anti-Catholic rioting takes place in Belfast	
c. 1890-1914 Irish literary revival features poets, prose writers, and playwrights who draw on Irish folklore and popular culture for material	*Ulysses* by James Joyce; *Playboy of the Western World* by John Millington Synge
1892 Education becomes compulsory for children between ages six and 14; colleges in Belfast, Galway, and Cork open all courses to women	
1893 Second Home Rule Bill is defeated in the House of Lords; Douglas Hyde founds Gaelic League to encourage Irish cultural revival	
1900s Poverty in Ireland exacerbated by migration of young people from rural areas to cities and emigration of Irish to the United States	*Playboy of the Western World* by John Millington Synge
1903 Land Act gives tenant farmers government loans to buy farms	
1904 Arthur Griffiths establishes the Sinn Féin (Ourselves Alone) Party	
1912-14 Third Home Rule Bill is introduced into Parliament and passed, despite opposition in Ulster (Northern Ireland); home rule is suspended when World War I breaks out	
1913 Sir Hugh Lane offers his collection of Impressionist paintings to city of Dublin but rescinds his offer after plans for proposed art gallery in Dublin are criticized by nationalist press	"September 1913" and "Easter 1916" by William Butler Yeats
1914 John Joly, one of several distinguished Irish scientists of the era, pioneers use of radioactivity to treat cancer	
1914-18 206,000 men from Ireland serve in World War I to support British war effort, about 30,000 die	
1916 Forces of Irish Republican Army seize Dublin Post Office on Easter Monday and proclaim a republic; the rebellion is suppressed and the leaders are executed	"September 1913" and "Easter 1916" by William Butler Yeats
1918-19 Fighting erupts between Irish Republican Army (IRA) and British forces over conscripting Irishmen into the British Army	

Historical Events		Related Literary Works in *WLAIT 4*
1919-21	IRA fights British forces for independence; war ends in Anglo-Irish Treaty	
1921	Ireland is partitioned; Anglo-Irish Treaty establishes Irish Free State within the British Commonwealth and accepts Northern Ireland's separate status; Sinn Féin leaders split over treaty's terms	*Troubles* by J. G. Farrell
1922-23	Civil war breaks out between pro-treaty faction, which controls the government, and anti-treaty faction, led by Eamon de Valera	*Juno and the Paycock* by Sean O'Casey
1926	De Valera founds Fianna Fáil (Warriors of Destiny) Party	
1932	Fianna Fáil and de Valera come to power; oath of allegiance to British crown is abolished; economic war with Britain develops; both nations raise tariff barriers against each other's goods	
1937	New constitution declares Ireland a sovereign state; southern Ireland is renamed Éire; Douglas Hyde becomes president; constitution lays claim to all of Ireland	
1938	Compromises reached on tariffs lead to settlement of economic war between Britain and Ireland; Britain relinquishes naval bases in southern Ireland	
1939-45	Southern Ireland is officially neutral during World War II but tacitly assists British; more than 43,000 from southern Ireland join British forces; 38,000 from Northern Ireland join British forces	
1940s-50s	Population of Dublin increases to 500,000 as rural dwellers migrate to the cities	*The Country Girls* by Edna O'Brien
1947	Education Act provides for universal free secondary education	
1948	General Election; Fianna Fáil is defeated	
1949	Republic of Ireland is formally declared, removing southern Ireland from the British Commonwealth; Northern Ireland remains part of the United Kingdom	
1950s	Half of all Irish homes still have no piped water, making housework burdensome; decline in maternal and infant mortality rates	*The Country Girls* by Edna O'Brien
1956-62	IRA wages unsuccessful border campaign in the north	
1955	Ireland joins the United Nations	
1959	Sean Lemass is named prime minister of Republic of Ireland; begins campaign to attract foreign investors and industrialize the nation; Eamon De Valera is elected President	
1961	Irish television service begins	
1965	Talks between Lemass and Terence O'Neill, prime minister of Northern Ireland	
1967	Formation of Northern Ireland Civil Rights Association; British Abortion Act of 1967 is not enacted in Northern Ireland; abortion continues to be illegal in southern Ireland	
1968	First civil rights march held; though banned, Derry civil rights march is held but broken up by police brutality	
1968-69	Tensions between Protestants and Catholics in Northern Ireland almost lead to civil war; British troops are sent in to keep peace, at request of Ulster government; Sinn Féin splits over best way to reclaim Ulster— more radical faction forms the Provisional IRA (Provos) and commit themselves to destroying British influence in Ireland	"Station Island" by Seamus Heaney

Historical Events	Related Literary Works in *WLAIT 4*
1969 O'Neill resigns; Chichester Clark becomes prime minister of the Republic	
1970 Charles Haughey and Neil Blaney are dismissed from Ulster government, arrested for conspiracy to import arms; Haughey is later acquitted in Dublin Arms Trial	
1970-95 More than 3,000 people are killed in sectarian violence in Northern Ireland; IRA is joined by similar groups (e.g., Irish Nationalist Liberation Army) and opposed by Protestant terrorist organizations (e.g., Ulster Defence Association)	
1971 First British soldier is killed by IRA in Belfast; series of attacks and bombings in Northern Ireland lead to British police interning without trial anyone suspected of terrorist activity	
1972 "Bloody Sunday"—13 are killed when police fire on Catholic demonstrators in Northern Ireland; Stormont (Irish parliament) is suspended; British government introduces direct rule from London; Irish Republic joins the European Economic Community	"Station Island" by Seamus Heaney
1973 Sunningdale agreement between Northern Ireland and Britain provides for a new type of executive in Northern Ireland in which power is to be shared between representatives of both Catholic and Protestant communities in a joint government; an assembly is established	
1974 Ulster Workers' Strike cripples Sunningdale agreement; direct rule by Britain is reimposed; Loyalists bomb Dublin and Monaghan, killing 30 people	
1981-82 Ten Republicans die in hunger strikes in Maze Prison in Northern Ireland; Bobby Sands, a dying hunger-striker, is elected to British Parliament	
1985 Anglo-Irish agreement is negotiated calling for Irish Republic to consult regularly with Britain on major policy in Northern Ireland	
1993 Downing Street Declaration: British government accepts Irish people's right to self-determination	
1994 IRA declares cease-fire	
1995 Unconditional ban on divorce in Republic of Ireland is repealed by referendum	
1996 Cease-fire breaks down when Conservative British government bars Sinn Féin from all-party talks in Northern Ireland	
1997 IRA cease-fire resumes; talks in Belfast between British Labour government, Irish Republic government, and political parties of Northern Ireland begin	
1998 Initial peace plan is approved by all parties	
1999-2000 Irish Republic removes claim to all Ireland from its constitution; devolution—power is partly transferred from British government at Westminster to assembly and executive in Northern Ireland	

Contents by Title

Contents by Title

Contents by Author

Contents by Author

Photo Credits

~

Kay, Jacqueline Margaret, photograph. © Jerry Bauer. Reproduced by permission. —Davis, Angela (speaking into microphone), photograph. AP/Wide World Photos, Inc. Reproduced by permission. —Doyle, Arthur Conan, photograph of a painting. UPI/Bettmann. Reproduced by permission.—Book illustration from *The Adventures of Sherlock Holmes.* —Owen, Wilfred, photograph. Corbis. Reproduced by permission. —American World War I soldier, photograph. © Hulton-Deutsch Collection/Corbis. Reproduced by permission. —Stoppard, Tom, photograph. AP/Wide World Photos. Reproduced by permission. —From a theatre production of *Arcadia* by Tom Stoppard, Directed by Eric Forsythe at University Theatres Mainstage production, The University of Iowa, November, 1997, photograph. University of Iowa. Reproduced by permission. —Waugh, Evelyn (sitting at desk, checked jacket), photograph. The Library of Congress. —Andrew, Anthony, Diana Quick, and Jeremy Irons in front of the set for the 1981 television adaptation of *Brideshead Revisited*, photograph. Virgin Vision. Reproduced by permission. —Kureishi, Hanif, photograph. © Jerry Bauer. Reproduced by permission. —Idol, Billy (wearing large cross pendant on chest), photograph by Ken Settle. Reproduced by permission. —Phillips, Caryl, photograph. © Jerry Bauer. Reproduced by permision. —West Indies Negro slave, photograph. Corbis Corporation. Reproduced by permission. —O'Brien, Edna, photograph. © Jerry Bauer. Reproduced by per-

mission. —Kelman, James, photograph by Alan Wylie. Reproduced by permission. —Council housing at Blackhill, Glasgow, Scotland, photograph. —Stevenson, Robert Louis (sitting at desk, pen in right hand), engraving. The Library of Congress. —March, Frederic (as Mr. Hyde, swinging a poker), in the 1932 movie *Dr. Jekyll and Mr. Hyde,* photograph. Del Valle Gallery. Reproduced by permission. —Stoker, Bram, photograph. AP/Wide World Photos. Reproduced by permission. —Lugosi, Bela, in the film *Dracula,* 1930, photograph. AP/Wide World Photos, Inc. Reproduced by permission. —Fowles, John (head tilted right, black glasses), photograph. Camera Press Ltd./Archive Photos, Inc. Reproduced by permission. —Ammonite, photograph by Derek Hall. Frank Lane Picture Agency/Corbis. Reproduced by permission. —Isherwood, Christopher, photograph. Archive Photos, Inc. Reproduced by permission. —Nazi students and SA members unloading materials for the public book burning on the Opernplatz, in Berlin, Germany, May 10, 1933, photograph by Abraham Pisarek. USHMM Photo Archives.

Lessing, Doris, photograph. © Jerry Bauer. Reproduced by permission. —Harvesting maize in Rhodesia, photograph. © Hulton-Deutsch Collection/Corbis. Reproduced by permission. —Dickens, Charles, photograph. Viking Press. —Wager, Anthony, as Magwich, grabbing Pip, in the film *Great Expectations,* 1946, photograph. Springer/Corbis-Bettmann. Reproduced by permission. —Bowen, Elizabeth (in checked skirt, white scarf at collar), 1973, photograph. AP/Wide World Photos, Inc. Reproduced by permission. —Two German Dornier 217 aircraft on bombing raid, photograph. © Hulton-Deutsch Collection/Corbis. Reproduced by permission. —Naipaul, V. S., photograph. AP/Wide World Photos. Reproduced by permission. —Forster, E. M., photograph. AP/Wide World Photos, Inc. Reproduced by permission. —Forster, E. M., photograph. Hulton Getty Picture Library/Archive Photos. Reproduced by permission. —Wilde, Oscar (seated, hand on chin), photograph. The Library of Congress. —Illustration of "The Closing Scene at the Old Bailey: Trial of Oscar Wilde," which appeared in *The Illustrated Police News.* —Tennyson, Lord Alfred, photograph. Archive Photos. Reproduced by permission. —Trinity College Gate, from *Tennyson,* written by Peter Levi. —Brontë, Charlotte (hair parted in center, wearing lace cap), painting. Archive Photos. Reproduced by permission. —Fontaine, Joan, Orson Welles (his arms around her), in the film *Jane Eyre,* 1944, photograph. Archive Photos, Inc. Reproduced by permission. —Hardy, Thomas (wearing dark suit, checked tie), photograph. Archive Photos, Inc. Reproduced by permission. —Stonemasons at work, carving architectural decorations, photograph. © Hulton-Deutsch Collection/Corbis. Reproduced by permission. —O'Casey, Sean, photograph. AP/Wide World Photos. Reproduced by permission. —Snipers kneeling on sidewalk behind mailbox, photograph. © Hulton-Deutsch Collection/Corbis. Reproduced by permission. —Kipling, Rudyard, photograph. Source unknown. —Kim and the Letter Writer, terracotta plaque, photograph by John Lockwood Kipling. The Granger Collection, New York. Reproduced by permission. —Haggard, H. Rider, photograph. The Library of Congress. —Kimberly Diamond Mines, photograph. © Bettmann/Corbis. Reproduced by permission. —Orwell, George (wearing a wool blazer, v-neck sweater), photograph. AP/Wide World Photos. Reproduced by permission. —Members of the General Post Office Home Guard, photograph. © Hulton-Deutsch Collection/Corbis. Reproduced by permission.

Conrad, Joseph, 1904, photograph. Archive Photos, Inc. Reproduced by permission. —Golding, William (pen in right hand, wearing cable knit sweater) 1983, photograph. AP/Wide World Photos. Reproduced by permission. —Edwards, Hugh, Tom Chap (wearing dirty, tattered clothing), in the film *Lord of the Flies,* 1963, photograph. Archive Photos. Reproduced by permis-

sion. —Rushdie, Salman (in white shirt, belack vest), photograph. Archive Photos, Inc. Reproduced by permission. —Hundreds of Muslim refugees, photograph. AP/Wide World Photos. Reproduced by permission. —Collins, (William) Wilkie (gazing down), photograph. The Library of Congress. —Interior of the Metropolitan Police Criminal Museum at Scotland Yard, photograph of engraving. © Corbis. Reproduced by permission. —Woolf, Virginia (left hand cupping face, wearing fur), photograph. AP/Wide World Photos. Reproduced by permission. —Suffragettes, carrying banners, photograph. © Hulton-Deutcsh Collection/CORBIS. Reproduced by permission. —Browning, Robert (white hair, goatee and mustache), photograph. —Azulejo tile portrait of King Afonso II of Portugal, photograph by Tony Arruza. Corbis. Reproduced by permission. —Carter, Angela, photograph. © Jerry Bauer. Reproduced by permission. —Ringling Brothers and Barnum & Bailey circus poster, photograph. © Bettmann/Corbis. Reproduced by permission. —Darwin, Charles, line drawing. Photo Researchers, Inc. Reproduced by permission. —Illustration of the H.M.S. *Beagle,* photograph. © Bettmann/Corbis. Reproduced by permission. —Barrie, Sir James M. (standing, hands in pocket, watch chain), photograph. The Library of Congress. —Martin, Mary, as Peter Pan, flying across the stage. © Bettmann/Corbis. Reproduced by permission. —Synge, John Millington (arms folded), drawing. Irish Tourist Board. —Woman holding broom over her head in a scene from *Playboy of the Western World*, photograph by John Springer. Corbis. Reproduced by permission. —Greene, Graham, photograph. AP/Wide World Photo. Reproduced by permission. —Mexican Federal troops, photograph. © Bettmann/Corbis. Reproduced by permission. —Spark, Muriel, photograph. AP/Wide World Photos. Reproduced by permission. —Cityscape of Edinburgh, Scotland, photograph. © Sean Sexton Collection/Corbis. Reproduced by permission. —Shaw, George Bernard, photograph. The Library of Congress. —From a production still of *Pygmalion.* Mander & Joe Mitchenson Theatre Collection. Reproduced by permission.

Ishiguro, Kazu, photograph. AP/Wide World Photos. Reproduced by permission. —Vaughn, Peter, and Sir Anthony Hopkins in a production still from *The Remains of the Day.* The Kobal Collection / Derrick Santini / Columbia / Merchant Ivory. Reproduced by permission. —Murdoch, Iris, photograph by Sophie Bassouls/ SYGMA. Reproduced by permission. —London feminists marching, photograph. © Bettmann/Corbis. Reproduced by permission. —Yeats, William Butler, photograph. Library of Congress.

Frame of a burned car, photograph. © Hulton-Deutsch Collection/Corbis. Reproduced by permission. —Browning, Elizabeth Barrett (seated, in dark dress with lace collar), print. Archive Photos, Inc. Reproduced by permission. —Browning, Robert, illustration. Archive Photos, Inc. Reproduced by permission. — Mo, Timothy, photograph. © Jerry Bauer. Reproduced by permission. —Heaney, Seamus (wearing a dark tweed sports coat, floral pattern tie), photograph. © Jerry Bauer. Reproduced by permission. —A masked IRA gunman, photograph by Michael McQueen. Camera Press Ltd./Michael McQueen/Archive Photos. Reproduced by permission. —Wells, H.G., photograph. The Library of Congress. —First Kodak camera (1888). Reproduced by permission of Eastman Kodak Company. —Farrell, J. G., 1973, photograph. Topham/The Image Works. Reproduced by permission. —Bomb damaged buildings on Sackville Street, Dublin, photograph. © Hulton Deutsch Collection/Corbis. Reproduced by permission. —Joyce, James, photograph. AP/Wide World Photos. Reproduced by permission. —Corrected proof for 1922 edition of *Ulysses,* from *Joyce Images,* written by Bob Cato. —

Thomas, Dylan (wearing checked jacket, dotted tie), 1953, photograph. AP/Wide World Photos. Reproduced by permission. —Beckett, Samuel, photograph. Archive Photos, Inc. Reproduced by permission. —From a production still from *Waiting for Godot.* Mander & Joe Mitchenson Theatre Collection. Reproduced by permission. —Eliot, T(homas). S(tearns)., photograph. International Portrait Gallery. Reproduced by permission. —Corrected proof for *The Waste Land* from *T. S. Eliot's The Waste Land: A Facsimile and Transcript of the Original.* edited by Valerie Eliot. —Orton, Joe (standing in front of a tree), London, England, 1967, photograph. AP/Wide World Photos. Reproduced by permission. —From a theatre production of Joe Orton's *What the Butler Saw* with Richard Wilson and Debra Gillet at the National Theatre, London, March, 1995, Gillet is standing in her underwear while Wilson holds a gun to her, photograph by Robbie Jack. Robbie Jack/Corbis. Reproduced by permission. —Lawrence, D.H., photograph. © Hulton-Deutsch Collection/Corbis. Reproduced by permission. —D. H. Lawrence (left), on his wedding day, standing with (l-r) Katherine Mansfield, Frieda von Richthofen (his wife), and John Middleton Murry, from *Lawrence and His Women: The Intimate Life of D. H. Lawrence,* written by Elaine Feinstein.

The Adoption Papers

by

Jackie Kay

Jackie Kay was born in Edinburgh, Scotland, in 1961. A black child adopted by white working-class socialist parents, she was brought up in Glasgow. The experience of transracial adoption has informed Kay's work from "The Adoption Papers" to her recent prize-winning novel, *Trumpet* (1998). In addition to poetry and fiction, Kay has also written for television and for theater. *Chiaroscuro*, presented in 1986, was the result of a fruitful collaboration between the Theatre of Black Women, which commissioned her to write the piece (and who eventually performed it), and the Gay Sweatshop theater. *The Adoption Papers*, Kay's first published collection of poetry, won an Eric Gregory Award (1991), together with the Saltire and Forward prizes (1991) and for her second collection of poems, *Other Lovers*, she garnered a Somerset Maugham Award (1993). More success followed, this time in fiction, with Kay's winning *The Guardian* Fiction Prize for her 1998 novel *Trumpet*, loosely based on the life of the American transgendered jazz musician, Billy Tipton. Jackie Kay has also written biography (*Bessie Smith*, 1997) and poetry for children (*The Frog Who Dreamed She Was an Opera Singer*, 1998). *The Adoption Papers* contains poetry about, rather than for, children, treating some of the very different issues that concerned Kay during the 1990s, from her personal experience of transracial adoption to her poetic accounts of Margaret Thatcher's socially divided Britain.

THE LITERARY WORK

A narrative poem set in Glasgow from 1961 to 1990 and a collection of 17 poems set in various parts of Britain in the 1980s; published in 1991.

SYNOPSIS

"The Adoption Papers," a narrative poem for three voices, tells the story of an adoption from the points of view of the birth mother, the adoptive mother, and the adopted child. "Severe Gale 8," a collection of 17 poems, chronicles private experiences relating to the sociopolitical landscape and to the emergence of AIDS-related deaths in Britain during the Thatcher era.

Events in History at the Time of the Poems

The Adoption Acts. The Adoption of Children Act was passed in 1926 in England and Wales, and in Scotland four years later in 1930. Up until these dates, birth parents had been able to reclaim their children when they reached wage-earning status. A further Adoption Act was passed in 1950, "which outlawed so-called 'third-party' adoptions in which children could be placed for adoption without the intervention of a local authority or recognised adoption agency" (Gaber, p. 13). The number of adoptions rose

Jackie Kay

dramatically over the 30-year period following the passing of the Adoption Act in Scotland. The total of 339 adoption petitions in the sheriff courts of Scotland in 1930 climbed to over 2,000 in the late 1960s, then dropped during the late 1970s to about 1,600 (McNeill, Preface, p. vii).

Historically, during the late 1950s, it was difficult to place children from ethnic minority backgrounds in suitable permanent family homes precisely because of their color. In "The Adoption Papers," it is only when the adoptive mother comments that she doesn't mind what color the baby might be that the waiting is over "just like that" ("The Adoption Papers," p. 14). Until she has said that color is irrelevant to her, the agency had told her that they had no babies, presumably on the assumption that a white woman wouldn't want to adopt a racially mixed child (in the poem, the daughter's birth mother was white, her birth father black). *Adoption and the Coloured Child*, published less than ten years after the 1961 start date of "The Adoption Papers," asserts that "few adoptions involving coloured children appear to come under the 'third-party' heading [i.e., occur outside authorized adoption agencies or local authorities], and that other placements of such children remain at rather less than 3 per-

cent of all adoptions. Indeed, only a minority of agencies will accept the responsibility of finding suitable adopters for a non-white child" (Kareh, p. 30). This point is underlined by a research project for the National Council of Civil Liberties undertaken in 1960, which discovered only five agencies that were willing to place "colored" children: in London, Bristol, Edinburgh, the Church of England Children's Society, and Dr Barnardo's (Gaber, p. 15).

By 1962, there was concern about the high number of children from ethnic minorities who were still in local authority care and an Action Committee was formed, which resulted in the founding of the British Adoption Project in 1965, specifically to address the need to locate a permanent home for children in care.

Postwar immigration. Large-scale twentieth-century immigration of blacks to Britain began in 1948 when the *SS Empire Windrush* docked at Tilbury with 492 Jamaicans on board. The immigration resulted from a number of factors. One popular perception has been that the immigrants on the *SS Empire Windrush* were the fruit of a recruitment drive: 1948 witnessed the end of British postwar austerity and, with it, the need for an increased work force. Other reasons have been suggested as well: "If they [the immigrants] were moved by anything it was their own drive to escape the boundaries of colonialism, allied to a unique combination of historical circumstances, the most important of which was to do with the logistics of travel" (Phillips, p. 46). In 1948, the government adopted the British Nationality Act, which ascribed British citizenship to the United Kingdom, its colonies, and newly independent Commonwealth countries such as India, which had gained independence from Britain the previous year, in 1947. According to Mike and Trevor Phillips, "The juxtaposition of the Nationality Act and the arrival of the *Windrush* was a pure coincidence, but the two events seem to fit together because the Act itself enshrines what became a classic uncertainty about how to define the nature and the boundaries of British citizenship" (Phillips, p. 74). This "classic uncertainty" was profoundly problematic: if the postwar breakup of the British Empire led to crises of what now constituted British identity, some of those crises were undeniably racist: "The debate on the Nationality Act was actually the beginning of a trauma about citizenship, race and nationality which swiftly became associated with the arrival of Caribbean immigrants" (Phillips, p. 75). The numbers escalated rapidly. From 1948 to 1961, Britain would receive 66,000 West Indians along with 48,000 Indian and Pakistani immigrants (Porter in Phillips, p. 159).

In 1962 the first Immigration Act to curb black immigration became law. Growing racial prejudice in Britain also led to the Race Relations Act in 1965, which prohibited racial discrimination in public places, outlawed the promotion of racial hatred, and formed a Race Relations Board to hear complaints. The Act's mandate did not extend to racial discrimination in private places. In contrast, the Sexual Offences Act, passed two years later, legalized private homosexual acts (under specified conditions) but kept them subject to prosecution if indulged in public.

The passage of the Race Relations Act points to mounting racial discrimination by 1965. Although "Commonwealth immigrants were in fact British citizens . . . nevertheless racial discrimination was ubiquitous and continuous" (Sinfield, p. 126). For example, Baroness Valerie Amos, who came to Britain from Guyana in 1963, recalled the imperialist and erroneous geography lessons that her sister received at school: "I mean, they were talking about Africa rather than South America, and they started to show the kinds of houses that they thought people like us lived in, and it was all wrong" (Amos in Phillips, pp. 205-206). Evidence of racist abuse is alluded to in Part Two of "The Adoption Papers" when the daughter is at school. This takes the form of physical violence that is perpetrated by her peers. But she is also subject to a different form of abuse by her teacher, who attributes racist stereotypes to her. The daughter's experience of domestic and public spaces is a shared one, evident in Baroness Amos's recollections:

> I think they [her parents] spent a lot of time guarding us from the overt kind of racism which I don't really remember as being a real part of my childhood. I think that my parents had a lot to do with that, and quite a lot to do with the fact that I was so much into social justice issues from a very early age.
>
> (Amos in Phillips, p. 206)

In part, Valerie Amos's recollections agree with those of Jackie Kay herself, who recalled not only being subjected to physical and verbal racist abuse when growing up in Glasgow, but also being nurtured in an environment that introduced her to such positive black role models as the activists Angela Davis and Martin Luther King, as well as to blues, jazz, and politics. This environment has clearly been influential for the subjects of her poetry.

Assimilation and difference. Two distinct phases emerge in adoption and fostering practices. The pre-1970s era saw these practices being based on the concept of the fully racially integrated society, "as symbolised by the multicultural family" (Gaber, p. 15):

> This philosophy was based on the notion that skin colour was irrelevant and that everyone was the same underneath—the melting pot theory of the decade of peace, love and flower power. It was at a time when the persistence of white racism and the need for ethnic minority groups to sustain themselves through their own cultures was not fully recognised. Such philosophies were prevalent in social services departments and adoption agencies throughout the country. Transracial placements were seen as positive steps towards a more integrated society.
>
> (Gaber, p. 15)

Notions of assimilation were to be replaced, during the 1970s, with 'the politics of black self-identity, and, for some, separatism' (Gaber, p. 19). This change is reflected in the rites of growing up experienced by the daughter in "Adoption Papers." The cultural figures that the child turns to when she is growing up are all black (and American): the celebrated singer, actress, and advocate of humanitarian issues Pearl Bailey (1918-90), the blues singer Bessie Smith (1894-1937), and the political activist Angela Davis (1944-).

Notably, the daughter's heroines are all black women. In his survey of the history of sexuality post-1800, Jeffrey Weeks notes "[t]he emergence of a powerful black feminist presence in the women's movement" during the 1970s and 80s (Weeks, p. 299). For Weeks, this presence has repercussions in terms of the dynamics and construction of the family unit, and these repercussions are interesting because of the ways in which the family unit was being utilized by the Conservative Government of the 1980s:

> The debates over the family and the whole question of reproductive rights were transformed by the black presence. It became less easy to criticise 'the family' as if it were an unproblematic unity when black people in their own communities were struggling to protect family integrity against immigration legislation and racist attacks.
>
> (Weeks, p. 299)

For the Conservatives, the family was seen as the necessary foundation of a good and moral society. Sex education in schools during the 1980s emphasized the importance of a stable married life and responsible parenting skills. Anxieties that family life was under attack by alternative or nontraditional familial models (for example single parent or same sex families) were in fact unfounded. Although divorce statistics were on the increase, so too were marriage and remarriage:

> Nearly 400,000 marriages took place in 1986, lower than the peak figure of 480,000 in 1972, but up on the low figures of the early part of the decade. And there was evidence of the continued growth of stable non-marital relations. Some 21 per cent of live births were illegitimate, but half of these were registered by both parents.
>
> (Weeks, p. 296)

However, in the 1987 Local Government Act, the Conservatives added a contentious provision, Clause 28, which outlawed the "promotion" in schools of homosexual lifestyles and sexuality. While liberal agendas since the 1960s had promoted a greater degree of toleration towards homosexuality, the 1980s witnessed the attempted reining in of this perceived permissiveness. Schools were now prohibited from "promoting the acceptability . . . of homosexuality as a 'pretended' family relationship" (Weeks, p. 295). And yet, during the 1970s and 1980s, alternative forms of sexual identities were increasingly visible, evidenced by gay and lesbian sexualities, same-sex parented families, transvestite practices and so on. Clause 28 had prohibited the "promotion" (or toleration) of same-sex lives, and in the process had inadvertently helped mobilize and unite gay communities.

While race and immigration had been high on the political agenda during the 1960s, by the 1980s, sexual issues had been added to it. One critical issue emerged not as a result of the Thatcher administration, although it would help fuel the moral agendas of the new right conservatives. The critical issue was AIDS—acquired immune deficiency syndrome and HIV—human immuno-deficiency virus. The AIDS crisis in Britain came to be associated predominantly with promiscuous gay sexual practices. Weeks estimates that by 1988, there had been "some 1500 cases of people with AIDS, over half of whom had died, with the numbers doubling every ten months. At least 10,000 people were known to be infected with the HIV virus which caused AIDS, with the likelihood that many thousands more were similarly at risk (Weeks, p. 300).

The Thatcher years and "Severe Gale 8." While the voices in "The Adoption Papers" look to Europe and America as locations of profound significance, the subpoems in the poem "Severe Gale 8" are concerned with matters much closer to home: Britain during the Thatcher years. All five poems are concerned with events in the 1980s. Margaret Thatcher was Britain's first woman Prime Minister, elected in the General Election of May 1979. Her premiership was marked, for those on the left, by profound social unease and unrest. By August 1980, unemployment had surpassed 2 million for the first time since 1935. Anxieties ran high, but developments gave way to new hope by the 1990s. In view of the looming threat of nuclear war, for example, the Labour Party voted for unilateral nuclear disarmament in September 1980. In South Africa, the government began to dismantle apartheid in the mid-1980s, and the activist Nelson Mandela was released after 27 years in prison. (In "The Third Hurricane," last in the sequence of "Severe Gale 8," the poet envisages children bringing a turtle dove, emblem of peace, to the newly released Mandela, who is un-named in the poem.) Urban violence was rife and was given dramatic expression in a series of race riots across the country. Unemployment remained high. Against the odds, Thatcher was re-elected to a second term in office in June 1983 following a wave of patriotic fervor that had swept Britain following the Falkland Crisis of 1982. But by July of 1983, £500 million had been cut from government spending, £140 million of which was from the health service. By December 1983, records showed that Britain had, that year, experienced the lowest level of economic growth since the Second World War" (Peacock, p. x). A miner's strike began in 1984 after the National Coal Board laid off 20,000 miners, leading to violent disputes between police and striking miners. In September 1985, there were more urban riots in Handsworth, in Birmingham, and in Brixton, South London. The following months, violent riots broke out on the Broadwater Farm Housing Estate in London. But these were not the same kinds of riots as those that had occurred in Nottingham and Notting Hill in the late 1950s, of white against black. The 1980s riots register a change in attitude in multi-cultural Thatcherite Britain, forcing a recognition that "black people and their interests were no longer marginal" (Phillips, p. 368). Riots in the early 1980s were due to any number of socially motivated problems, but they were also clearly happening in response to racially motivated arrests of black men by the police. What finally sparked the 1981 Brixton riot, for example, was the stop and search of a black taxicab driver. The police claimed that he was hiding drugs in his socks; in fact, this was where he kept his cab fares. They then decided to search his car, in spite of the fact that a crowd of young and angry black men were surrounding the vehicle. One of these men blocked a policeman's path; he was arrested and bundled into a van. Bricks were then thrown in protest at the van, more police arrived, and the riots escalated from there.

In June 1987, Thatcher won a third election victory, and in July she announced what many would see as the beginning of her downfall, the Poll Tax. This tax was to replace the old property-based rates tax, but it sparked public outrage because it taxed people, rather than property, and levied the same basic charge, irrespective of the different kinds of property people occupied. The introduction of the Poll Tax in Scotland in April 1989 produced widespread revolt; further violent riots ensued in London's Trafalgar Square in March 1990, prior to the introduction of the tax in England in April of that year. Kay's poem "Death to Poll Tax" weaves private experience in and out of the violent public responses to the poll tax. The poem's voice addresses a friend or lover whose mother's death is imminent. As the poet/persona tries to get out of the subway s/he discovers that most of the exits are closed, and in the first stanza, s/he begins to imagine some sort of violent disturbance. In the second stanza, it's not clear where the reality and the fantasy of violence begin and end, but the images nonetheless convey the anger of the people and the violent tactics of the police:

> The third thing is a man screaming
> DEATH TO POLL TAX - a policeman
>   punching him every time
> he gets to Poll. Death to Poll THUD Tax.
>   (*The Adoption Papers*, p. 60)

In November 1990, after internal dissent within the Conservative party, Thatcher resigned.

The Poem in Focus

Contents summary. "The Adoption Papers" is a poem in three parts. Part One: 1961-1962 (subdivided into five chapters) traces the period of birth and adoption from the perspectives of the

birth mother, adoptive mother, and daughter: the three voices are distinguished by different typefaces (Palatino for the daughter, Gill for the adoptive mother, Bodoni for the birth mother). The voices of the birth and adoptive mothers follow each other, the birth mother speaks of the ease with which she conceived the child, the adoptive mother of her longing to be pregnant and to endure the discomforts and pain of pregnancy.

The poem first establishes that the child is mixed race (a white Scottish mother, a black Nigerian father) and illegitimate and thus doubly stigmatized in terms of the moral climate of the early 1960s.

"SCIENTIFIC" RACISM

So-called "scientific" racism was . . . discredited by many biologists in 1951, but the belief that black people belong to a different and inferior race, and that 'interbreeding' would harm the white race, lingered on in popular consciousness, and many whites continued to show strong disapproval for white-black marriages. According to a Gallup poll in 1958, 71 percent of respondents disapproved of mixed marriages, while only 13 percent approved. A Gallup poll conducted in the United States that same year found that over 90 percent disapproved. Patterson's field study in Brixton (South London), carried out in 1955-58, showed that local attitudes to mixed relationships varied from the mildly disapproving to outright distaste: "Disgusting. I don't know how a decent woman could let a blackie touch her" (Patterson in Tizard and Phoenix, p. 23). The study claims that few "respectable" local white girls would be seen out with a West Indian. The late 1960s saw the beginning of more liberal white attitudes. The proportion of people disapproving of marriages between whites and nonwhites fell to 57 percent in a 1968 Gallup poll, and to 42 per cent in 1973. (The comparable U.S. proportions were 76 percent and 65 percent [Spickard in Tizard and Phoenix, p. 23].)

Next the poem traces the beginning of the daughter's attempts to locate her birth mother, interspersing the daughter's voice with the birth mother's thoughts after the birth. Then comes the adoptive mother's voice, narrating the processes of visiting different adoption agencies and then making her house "look ordinary" for the social worker who comes to assess her suitability for adoption ("The Adoption Papers," p.

15). (This involves hiding her books by Karl Marx, Friedrich Engels and Vladimir Lenin, the communist newspaper *The Daily Worker*, her "dove of peace" and her poster of the singer, actor, and political and human rights activist Paul Robeson.) The section then describes the adoptive mother's excitement about going to see the new baby, interspersing this with the voice of the birth mother, who stages an imaginary and symbolic funeral for her baby, digging a hole in the garden and burying the clothes that she'd bought for the infant. Shifting its focus, the poem moves to the anxiety of the adoptive mother that the birth mother will come back to claim her daughter, interweaving this with the adoptive daughter's continued search for her birth mother.

Part Two: 1967-1971 re-introduces the voice of the daughter, not as the adult voice tracing her birth mother, as she was in the first section, but as the child either protesting or working out how she came into being:

> Ma mammy bot me oot a shop [my mammy
>   bought me from a shop]
> Ma mammy says I was a luvly baby
> Ma mammy picked me (I wiz [was] the best)
> your mammy had to take you (she'd no
>   choice)
> ("The Adoption Papers," p. 21)

In this section the adoptive mother reveals to her daughter that she is adopted. The daughter's difference is not only marked out by her adopted status and her blackness in contrast to her parents' whiteness, but also by her cultural preferences. She and her best friend reject the white American popular cultural influences embraced by their peers (singers Donny Osmond, David Cassidy, TV cops Starsky and Hutch), preferring to mime, instead, to the songs of blues singers Pearl Bailey and Bessie Smith. Next the section moves to the racist abuse that the daughter suffers at school, both from her peers and her teachers. The adoptive mother wants to disavow the issue of her daughter's skin color, believing that "colour matters to the nutters [colloquial reference to a mad or eccentric person]" ("The Adoption Papers," p. 24). But color also matters to the daughter.

Although the daughter is able to stand up for herself against the bullying and racist abuse of her peers, it's the supposedly educated voice of her teacher she can't understand, "like that time she said Darkies are like coal" ("The Adoption Papers," p. 25). Interspersed with this recollec-

tion is that of her birth mother's own recollection of the hostile stares that she and Olubayo, the birth father (and the only protagonist in the poem to be given a name) attracted as they walked down the street. The daughter searches for a role model to support a sense of her fragmented identity, lighting on white American movie stars (Bette Davis, Katharine Hepburn, and the British-born though American-based Elizabeth Taylor) as possible models for imitation, since they have greater visibility in popular cultural media. In the end, though, it's not Bette Davis that she settles for as a role model, but the African American black rights activist Angela Davis. Again, the issue of cultural visibility and paucity of role models is underlined. The daughter realizes that she has only seen one black woman on TV, playing a nurse. As Kay herself has said in interview:

> Most black children brought up in a white environment will experience some form of psychological distress. It's hard to get a strong sense of being black and proud when there is nothing to reinforce this notion.
> (Kay, Interview, p. 38)

Part Three of the poem incorporates the years 1980-1990, continuing to intersperse the three voices. The birth mother shows awareness of herself as the subject of gossip; the daughter imagines her painful birth (she was pulled out by forceps) and the faithful visits made by her adoptive mother. The cultural and environmental considerations that constituted the second part of the poem now give way to the daughter's desire to know her birth mother and to know her genetic inheritances.

The poem ends with the daughter's imagining what it would be like to meet her birth mother; envisioned is an understated reunion that takes place on a walk along the seashore and in a room with "no sentiment" ("Adoption Papers, p. 32). Although the adoptive mother acknowledges that she, too, would want to have met her birth mother, she still believes that there's no one closer than the two of them: "Closer than blood./ Thicker than water. Me and my daughter" ("The Adoption Papers," p. 34).

Five subpoems make up "Severe Gale 8," the opening poem of the collection's second section: "NHS," "£££," "Cardboard," "The Pound," "The Third Hurricane." The third subpoem in the sequence, "Cardboard," makes this clear: "It had come to this when Poll Tax / arrived that winter of the second hurricane" (*The Adoption Papers*, p. 37). The 1980s was the decade of power for the former British Prime Minister, Margaret Thatcher, and the poems stage some of the despair due to the effects of Thatcher's period of office, such as the decline of the National Health Service ("NHS"), the introduction of the poll tax ("Death to Poll Tax"), increases in pollution and traffic congestion, and the rise of the so-called "cardboard city"—a reference to visible increases in homelessness ("Cardboard").

Other poems in the second half of the collection can be read alongside "The Adoption Papers" in terms of common themes of maternal loss and longing. "The Underground Baby Case" chronicles the theft of a small child on a crowded underground [subway] train by a woman whose own child has recently died. "Summer Storm, Caplona" recalls a memory of an unmarried woman with a small child taking shelter from a storm in Caplona; the two invite the pity of the old couple who offer them refuge. The image of running through the rain and getting soaked is also used in "Pounding Rain," a poem that focuses on a renewed friendship between two old schoolfriends who embark on a lesbian relationship when they're much older. "Mummy and Donor and Deirdre" deals with lesbian parents from the perspective of a child as well as the parents, and the ways in which childhood innocence and acceptance are corrupted by adults who uphold one particular parental model as the only possible alternative. Other lesbian-associated poems in the section are "In the Seventh Year" and "Photo in the Locket." "Close Shave" explores the consciousness of a working-class man who is married but is also involved in a gay relationship with his barber that must be kept secret. "Dressing Up" is about a working-class male-to-female cross-dresser and his relationship with his parents: his mother is highly critical of her son's cross-dressing practice. Meanwhile, the poem itself is critical of the parent's own violent and abusive relationship, which suggests the absurdity of the situation: violence within heterosexual relationships is tolerated whereas the cross-dressing son is open to censure. While all of these poems speak to the emerging visibility of different social and sexual identities, other poems in the collection address issues that are specific to the decade in which they were written. "Dance of the Cherry Blossom," "He Told Us He Wanted a Black Coffin," and "Lighthouse Wall" all concern AIDS-related illness and death. "My Grandmother's Houses" explores the notion of the grandmother in the poem as a figure at the intersection of postwar private and public memo-

Angela Davis, a positive role model for the daughter in *The Adoption Papers*.

ries and histories and "Death to Poll Tax" again engages with the location of private memory at a historically specific moment.

Against the grain. "The Adoption Papers" concerns the impact of learned responses from familial environments and the movement of a child out into the mid-to-late-twentieth-century public world of politics and history. In "The Adoption Papers" only one of the protagonists in the poem (Olubayo, the birth father) is mentioned by name, but the poem refers explicitly to several real historical figures, mainly in the first two parts of the poem, which cover the periods 1961-2 and 1967-71. These include the clandestine communists Ethel and Julius Rosenberg and show business personalities Pearl Bailey, Bessie Smith, Bette Davis, Katharine Hepburn, Elizabeth Taylor, Donny Osmond, David Cassidy, and the fictional Starsky and Hutch. By naming these figures the poem evokes issues of profound political concern (communism, the desire for world peace) beginning in the late 1950s; also the poem shows the daughter rejecting some of the depoliticized role models available to her (white American and Anglo-American) in favor of more radical black figures who straddle political and cultural fields of representation. More generally, the references make apparent a global political culture. This emerges not just in relation to immigration and transracial adoption in postwar Britain, but also in the adoptive parents' concerns for world peace (evident in their support for the Campaign for Nuclear Disarmament, or CND) and for civil rights (evident in their support of Paul Robeson). They also stress the importance

---

PAUL ROBESON (1898-1976)

Robeson, the son of a former slave, was a prominent black and civil rights activist. His was a distinguished career, both celebrated and reviled in turn. He was only the third African American to enter Rutgers in 1915. He began his career as a professional footballer, earned a law degree from Columbia University in New York (he resigned when a white secretary refused to take dictation from him), and debuted as a professional actor in 1922. Robeson was politically active. He spoke out against Nazism, and in 1934, the film director Sergei Eisenstein invited Robeson to the Soviet Union, a place he admired for the apparent equality with which people were treated. Also Robeson visited Spain during the Civil War and sang for the Republican forces, who were fighting against Franco's Fascists. But by 1943 (the same year he was awarded the Abraham Lincoln Medal), the FBI accused Robeson of being a leading communist. After denouncing the Korean War and refusing to deny that he was a Communist, his US passport was revoked in 1950. Nikita Kruschev's revelation of Stalin's crimes against humanity in 1956 led to a two-month emotional collapse for Robeson. Following the return of his passport in 1958, he traveled regularly between London and Moscow: he and his wife Essie did not return to the States until 1963. The FBI renounced any further need for investigations into Paul Robeson in 1974. He died at the age of 77 in 1976. Although his passport had been re-issued by the time the adoptive mother hides the poster urging its restitution, the very fact that she has the poster remains an important sign of her support for civil rights in general, and Robeson's in particular.

---

of not forgetting the fate of Ethel and Julius Rosenberg, who, with very little evidence against them, had been executed by the electric chair on June 19, 1953, for allegedly selling state secrets to the Russians. The political concerns of the parents are passed down to the daughter, seen to support the then current plight of the jailed Angela Davis.

When the adoptive mother is in the process of being surveyed by social workers, she is aware that certain cultural items are acceptable while others are not. Consequently, her bust of the Scottish poet Robert Burns (1759-96), her complete works of Percy Bysshe Shelley (1792-1822) and her more "low-brow" detective stories are left exposed to view (the assumption here is probably that the social worker would perceive Shelley as a high cultural poet and not as a revolutionary figure). As the voices in the poem engage with a series of human rights activists and high profile African American entertainers, the daughter begins to forge a deliberate historical, political and cultural agenda that she can claim as her own. She chooses and rejects certain cultural figures as being important to the formation of her own sense of self in the world. This sense of self is obviously informed by the fact of her personal (transracial) adoption and her relationship with her adoptive mother and imagined relationship with her birth mother. At the same time, the poem suggests that she is also formed by more public factors of her twentieth-century global environment. In the daughter's case, the influence of Paul Robeson, Angela Davis, Pearl Bailey and Bessie Smith are lasting, whereas the products of white Anglo-American mainstream popular culture are rendered negligible and transient. And it's in "The Adoption Papers" particularly that Kay's poetry reaches out to a history of Black oppression, civil rights and Black culture, making this history important also to Black British identity.

Literary context. Valerie Mason John's interview with Kay points to a vacuum her verse begins to fill: "Kay is concerned about the lack of recognition of black women writers in Britain and points out that although the U.S. appears to foster black women's talent, with the success of writers like Alice Walker and Toni Morrison, one cannot be complacent" (Mason John in Kay, p. 38) Bruce Woodcock identifies two significant moments in Britain's postcolonial publishing history of black women's poetry: the publication, in 1977, of a special edition of *Savacou*, (a magazine run by the Caribbean poet Edward Kamu Brathwaite) that was called "Caribbean Women." And in 1980, the publisher Heinemann produced an anthology called *Jamaica Woman*, featuring 15 Caribbean women poets. Into this emerging context, Woodcock notes Kay as one of "a number of women poets not included in these collections, but who can be found in other recent anthologies not devoted to Caribbean writing or in individual volumes" (Woodcock, p. 58). The best British examples of Caribbean women poets, according to Woodcock, are Jackie Kay and Maud Sulter, (although he mistakenly assumes that Kay is of Caribbean rather than part-African descent). Kay's work has appeared in *A Dangerous Knowing* (1983), a collection of poetry by black British women poets Barbara Burford, Gabriela Pearse and Grace Nichols. At that point in the 1980s, Kay's work had only appeared in anthologies. In common with Grace Nichols (b. 1950 Guyana), Kay's early work points to a need to recognize and assert the specificity of black women's experiences. But even in the 1980s, while "The Adoption Papers" was being written, the circumstances of Kay's upbringing were contributing to a distinctive poetic voice: motherhood in relation to adoption, Black-Scottish (particularly Glaswegian) identity, and lesbian relationships. Woodcock points out Kay's poem "Happy Ending" (not in *The Adoption Papers*) as significant for "wryly rejecting the enforced tragedies of past writings on lesbianism" (Woodcock, p. 69). While Kay's voice has been located in the context of the growing volumes of Black British and Caribbean women's writing (including, for example, Paula Burnett's edition of *The Penguin Book of Caribbean Verse*, published in 1986) her poetic voice has remained distinctly and recognizably hers in its global and insistently local (Glasgow and London) geographies.

Reception. Sections of "The Adoption Papers" were published and performed on BBC Radio 3 before publication on October 10, 1991, in the collection to which the poem gives its name. Kay was showered with prizes: the Eric Gregory Prize, the Saltire and the Forward Prizes for poetry.

Asked whether she felt that reviewers tended to pigeonhole her work, Kay responded affirmatively:

> Yes, I think reviewers do review your work depending on who you are. That's annoying for me, particularly because I have a whole set of labels which reviewers could put after my name—like Scottish, woman, black, lesbian, socialist, adopted. . . . It is very irritating for me. In my children's poetry books, for example, I write lots of poems about lots of different topics, but reviewers still find a reason to name me as: 'Jackie Kay who is black and adopted and was brought up in Scotland.' And that won't necessarily have anything to do with the poems.
>
> (Goodman, p. 255)

One reviewer, at least, did respond to her poems rather than to Kay herself as a series of labels: Robert Potts reviewed *The Adoption Papers* in the *Times Literary Supplement* shortly after its publication. He found the collection to be "an inspiring volume" (Potts, p. 30) for its "remarkable technique and knack for quick, telling characterisation" in the series of poems that make up "Severe Gale 8" (Potts, p. 30). But he also sin-

---

ANGELA DAVIS (1944-)

Angela Davis was dismissed from her post as Assistant Professor in Philosophy at the University of California at Los Angeles for her involvement with the Communist Party, to which she belonged from 1968-91. Through her involvement with prisoners' rights, Davis met George Jackson, one of the Soledad brothers (jailed in Soledad Prison), who had been falsely charged with killing a prison guard in January 1970. She established friendships with the Jackson family, and especially with George's brother Jonathon, who became one of her bodyguards. In August 1970, in order to draw attention to prison conditions and abuses perpetrated against the Soledad Brothers, Jonathan carried guns into a courtroom in the Marin County Civic Center, in northern California, and took the judge, district attorney, and members of the jury hostage. In the ensuing standoff, Jonathon Jackson was killed. Davis, who was out of California at the time, was named as accomplice because the guns were registered in her name. She escaped underground, and, as the daughter in "The Adoption Papers" notes, the American Federal Bureau of Investigation (FBI) put her on its most wanted list. Taken prisoner in October 1970, Davis remained in jail for the rest of that year. She was released on bail during the preparation for her trial, which in June 1972 ended in a not-guilty verdict. Acquitted by an all-white jury, Davis became a symbol of the fight against racial oppression in America.

---

gled out for praise "The Adoption Papers": "the juxtaposition of dialects and perspectives, married to a sureness of phrase and metaphor, raise questions of blood and identity (both cultural and biological) skilfully and almost tacitly" (Potts, p. 30).

—Tracy Hargreaves

For More Information

Foner, Philip S. *Paul Robeson Speaks: Writings, Speeches, Interviews, 1918-74.* London: Quartet, 1978.

Gaber, Ivor, and Jane Aldridge, eds. *In the Best Interests of the Child: Culture, Identity and Transracial Adoption.* London: Free Association, 1994.

Goodman, Lizbeth. *Feminist Stages: Interviews with Women in Contemporary British Theatre.* Amsterdam: Harwood Academic, 1996.

James, Joy. *The Angela Y. Davis Reader.* Oxford: Blackwell, 1998.

Kay, Jackie. *The Adoption Papers.* Newcastle: Bloodaxe, 1991.

———. Interview by Valerie Mason John. *The Guardian,* 10 October 1991, 38.

McNeill, Peter G. B. *Adoption of Children in Scotland.* Edinburgh: W. G. Green & Son, 1982.

Peacock, Keith D. *Thatcher's Theatre: British Theatre and Drama in the Eighties.* London: Greenwood, 1999.

Phillips, Mike, and Trevor Phillips. *Windrush: The Irresistible Rise of Multi-Racial Britain.* London: Harper Collins, 1998.

Potts, Robert. Review of *The Adoption Papers. The Times Literary Supplement,* 22 May 1992, 30.

Sinfield, Alan. *Literature, Politics and Culture in Postwar Britain.* Oxford: Blackwell, 1989.

Tizard, Barbara, and Ann Phoenix. *Black, White or Mixed Race? Race and Racism in the Lives of Young People of Mixed Parentage.* London: Routledge, 1993.

Weeks, Jeffrey. *Sex, Politics and Society: The Regulation of Sexuality Since 1800.* London: Longman, 1989.

Woodcock, Bruce. "'Long Memoried Women': Caribbean Women Poets." In *Black Women's Writing.* Ed. Gina Wisker. Basingstoke: Macmillan, 1993.

The Adventures of Sherlock Holmes

by
Sir Arthur Conan Doyle

⁓

Arthur Conan Doyle (1859-1930) was born in Edinburgh, Scotland, where his father had moved from London after taking a job as a civil servant. In 1882, after studying medicine at Edinburgh University, he established a medical practice near the southern English city of Portsmouth. He had begun writing short stories to supplement his income while still a student, and he continued to do so while starting out as a doctor. Doyle's first published novel, *A Study in Scarlet*, which appeared in the popular magazine *Beeton's Christmas Annual* in 1887, introduced the characters of Sherlock Holmes and Dr. Watson. The story enjoyed only modest success in Britain, however, and Doyle continued work on what he considered more important projects, such as the historical novels *Micah Clark* (1889) and *The White Company* (1890). A second Sherlock Holmes novel, *The Sign of Four*, appeared in 1890, but not until the 12 short stories later collected as *The Adventures of Sherlock Holmes* did the fictional detective and his creator achieve sudden fame. Published in the new monthly magazine *The Strand*, the stories caused a literary sensation and contributed significantly to the magazine's great success. Doyle himself went on to become one of the most successful writers of his age, ultimately producing over 30 books and 150 short stories, in addition to plays, poems, essays and pamphlets. While Holmes would ultimately feature in four novels and 56 short stories, it was the 12 *Adventures of Sherlock Holmes* stories that made him into one of the most popular and recognizable fictional characters of all time. Aside

> ## THE LITERARY WORK
>
> A collection of 12 short stories set in England in the 1880s and early 1890s; published individually in London's *The Strand Magazine* in 1891-92, and in book form in London in 1892.
>
> ## SYNOPSIS
>
> Using his unusual powers of deduction, detective Sherlock Holmes solves mysteries involving murder, blackmail, theft, and other crimes and misdeeds.

from catapulting him to fame, the stories reflect the anxieties of Doyle's age as well as its optimistic faith in human reason.

Events in History at the Time of the Stories

Empire and anxiety in late Victorian Britain. The mid-Victorian period (c. 1851-1875) saw dramatic growth in almost every area of British life, from developments in science, technology and industry, to the consolidation of a worldwide British Empire. Although expansion continued in some areas during the late Victorian period (c. 1875-1901), it slowed or halted in others, particularly in agriculture and industry after the mid-1870s, when Britain suffered a major economic slump. London kept its place as the

Arthur Conan Doyle

world's banking and financial capital, and Britain remained the world's leading power, but by the beginning of the 1890s a number of factors had combined to create an atmosphere of growing doubt and anxiety.

Britain scored vast new territorial acquisitions for the empire in Africa and Asia, but they were periodically offset in the public mind by severe and demoralizing defeats for the British imperial army. By the 1880s much of Africa (including South Africa and Egypt) had come under British colonial control, but British army expeditions had been either decimated or virtually wiped out at Isandhlwana (1879) in the Zulu War, at Majuba Mountain (1881) in the Anglo-Transvaal War, and at El Teb (1884) and Khartoum (1885) in the Sudanese War. In Asia the worst defeat came at the battle of Maiwand (1880) in Afghanistan, where the British sought to create a buffer zone that would protect British-ruled India (often called the jewel in the imperial crown) from Russian encroachment. The fictional Dr. Watson, Holmes's friend and chronicler, is portrayed as having served in the imperial army and been badly wounded at Maiwand; his wound is mentioned several times in *The Adventures of Sherlock Holmes*. When the two initially meet in *A Study in Scarlet*, Holmes's famous first line to Watson illustrates both his deductive powers and his knowledge of Victorian imperialism: "You

have been in Afghanistan, I perceive" (Doyle, *A Study in Scarlet and The Sign of Four*, p. 13).

The rise of other Western powers by the 1880s and 1890s, especially Germany and the United States, threatened Britain's imperial and economic supremacy, also fueling British anxiety. The German Empire arose after Germany unified under Prussian leadership and won a decisive victory over France in the Franco-Prussian War (1870-71). Germany's new colonies (in Africa and the Pacific Islands) supplied raw materials that promoted economic expansion, while her rapidly growing navy threatened the global naval superiority upon which British security traditionally rested. In one of *The Adventures of Sherlock Holmes*, "The Engineer's Thumb," Germans are portrayed as sinister counterfeiters who kidnap and mutilate an English engineer. Germans would become more frequent villains in later Holmes stories, and as war between Britain and Germany grew imminent, Holmes would battle German spies.

The United States was also emerging as an economic and possibly an imperial rival to Britain. Inexpensive U.S. wheat flooded the British market, for example, contributing to the woes of British farmers from the 1870s. Anglo-U.S. cultural ties, however, made this rivalry a more ambivalent one than that with Germany. Reflecting that ambivalence, Holmes's American adversary Irene Adler in "A Scandal in Bohemia," the first of *The Adventures of Sherlock Holmes*, is a ruthless opponent but an attractive one. America produces shadowy threats in many of Holmes's cases. In *The Adventures of Sherlock Holmes*, for example, "The Five Orange Pips" features an American organization, the Ku Klux Klan, waging a secret terror campaign against a British family. Doyle, who himself had traveled in the American South, may have heard stories about the Ku Klux Klan and about how they threatened victims.

Like America, Australia was seen as a land of violence and opportunity. The British had gained this island-continent for their empire in the late eighteenth century. Until the 1830s they used it primarily as a penal colony, and the white population there consisted mostly of convicts sent over from Britain. Different British settlers began arriving in the 1830s, but it was the discovery of gold in the 1850s that brought prospectors and others flocking to Australia, creating a rough-and-ready frontier society similar to the American West. In the 1860s, thieves known as bushrangers held up and robbed a number of gold shipments; examples are the Eugowra Rocks Robbery (1862) and the Mudgee Mail Robbery (1863). Doyle based one of *The Adventures of Sherlock Holmes*, "The Boscombe Valley Mystery," on these two incidents, which (like other such robberies) were well publicized in Britain.

Threats to social order. For the late Victorians, however, violence and the threat of violence was not restricted to foreign lands such as Germany, the United States, or Australia. It also originated closer to home. Victorian society was highly regimented, and (ideally, at least) each member of society was expected to know his or her place within the social order. Fundamentally different patterns of behavior were expected from men and women and from members of the three main social classes (upper-class aristocrats, middle-class professionals and other well-paid workers, and lower-class manual laborers). By the late Victorian period, however, these once rigid social distinctions were being successfully challenged.

For example, women were traditionally expected to defer to men of their class, and their ideal role was perceived to be that of a wife and mother. In charge of running the household, they ideally had little interaction with the outside world, which was seen as the province of men. People regarded women as naturally passive creatures who were ruled by their emotions, men as the energetic doers in society, practical and rational. Women were not allowed to vote, and their property and money were generally controlled by male relatives, usually their fathers or husbands.

By the middle of the century, the women's suffrage movement had begun pressing for greater social freedom and political power for women. Acts of Parliament gave increasingly broad voting rights to women in 1869, 1870, 1880, and 1894, though the vote would not be extended to all women until 1918. The Married Women's Property Act of 1870 gave married women control of their own earnings, while a similar act in 1882 gave them control of all other property, including inherited wealth. Unmarried women already had legal control of their own money, but social convention often dictated that real control be turned over to the father, as head of the family; similarly, social pressure often allowed husbands to exercise such control, even after 1882. Three of the 12 *Adventures of Sherlock Holmes* tales—that is, fully one quarter of the stories—hinge upon a father or stepfather wishing to prevent a young woman's marriage in order to retain control of her independent income,

which he exercises by virtue of his position as head of the family.

Other economic and social changes help comprise the stories' more general background. At the beginning of Queen Victoria's reign in 1831, the small upper class and the rapidly expanding middle class held virtually all political power. Stringent property qualifications prevented working-class men from voting. While the Reform Act of 1867 extended the vote to most male urban workers, and a similar act of 1884 did the same for male agricultural laborers, other issues—such as pay, hours, and working conditions—continued to cause strife between workers and employers. Also unemployment, which had escalated in the economic slump, remained high after the mid-1870s. The result was a series of unsettling protests and strikes in London in the late 1880s and early 1890s, supported by a growing socialist movement:

MASCULINE ANXIETIES

Critics have linked Holmes's resonance with male readers to concerns about masculinity and manliness that arose in the turbulent 1880s and 1890s. Many of the stories deal with the question of what constitutes appropriate male behavior, leading one critic to claim that "the subject of the *Adventures* tales *is* masculinity" (Kestner, p. 81; emphasis original).

- **February 1886:** Riots by the unemployed poor in London's Trafalgar Square last several days and spread to other areas; panic spreads throughout the city.
- **November 1887:** Further unrest is centered in Trafalgar Square; authorities respond with the infamous and violent police crackdown of Bloody Sunday on November 13, 1887.
- **1889:** In the "Great London Dock Strike," dock workers shut down the London waterfront.
- **1890:** Police strike for higher wages and pensions (police had made similar demands in an 1872 strike).

Among other effects, such events undermined public confidence in the police as a force for order in society. Historians have suggested that the public associated such social agitation with crime, which in the 1880s loomed larger as a perceived threat to order than it had in earlier times. Faith in the police was furthermore shaken by the murder spree of the serial killer known to history as Jack the Ripper, who cut the throats of at least seven London prostitutes between August and November 1888. This still-unidentified killer terrified London residents and held the British public in thrall, sending taunting notes to the police, who seemed powerless. Public outcry over the failure to catch Jack the Ripper forced London's police commissioner to resign. In the Sherlock Holmes stories, Holmes's deductive prowess stands in stark contrast to the inefficiency of the police, who are represented primarily by the character of the slow and often bumbling Inspector Lestrade.

SCOTLAND YARD

ᴄᴡ

Founded in 1829, at first the London Metropolitan Police (called Scotland Yard after their location) were poorly trained and paid. There was a police strike in 1872; then scandal rocked the organization's Detective Department when three out of its four chief inspectors were found guilty of corruption in 1878. In a reshuffle later that year, the Detective Department was reorganized as the Criminal Investigation Division (C.I.D.), and in 1891, the year that Doyle wrote the first Sherlock Holmes story, the London police moved to a site called New Scotland Yard, where they would remain until 1967.

The Short Stories in Focus

Plot summaries. The Sherlock Holmes that readers met in the short stories that appeared in *The Strand Magazine* differed in small but telling ways from the often antisocial hero of the earlier novels. In the very last sentence of *The Sign of Four*, for example, Holmes is pictured as reaching for his cocaine bottle, about to partake of the addiction that relieves him from the boredom of daily existence. In contrast with these early novels, Holmes's cocaine habit is mentioned only once in *The Adventures of Sherlock Holmes*, at the beginning of the first story, "A Scandal in Bohemia." And while Holmes is still clearly eccentric, the former characterization of him as an often brusque detective has changed. Holmes now smiles or laughs frequently and possesses an "easy courtesy" that makes his clients comfortable (Doyle, *The Adventures of Sherlock Holmes*, p. 32). Furthermore, while Holmes solved outlandish murders in the two early novels, his cases now tend to pose mysteries arising from more commonplace or whimsical situations (such as an attempt to return a lost hat and an abandoned Christmas goose to their owner in "The Blue Carbuncle"). In many of them, no actual crime is committed, though one may be threatened. Finally, in most of the stories Holmes and Watson no longer share rooms at 221B Baker Street in London; Watson has moved out and married, and, as Holmes predicted at the end of *The Sign of Four*, he and Holmes have drifted apart. Yet Watson's wife remains firmly in the background, and the reader only meets her briefly in two of the 12 adventures in *The Adventures of Sherlock Holmes,* many of which begin with Watson dropping by 221B Baker Street to say hello to his friend.

A Scandal in Bohemia. The first story opens as Watson finds himself passing by 221B Baker Street and is seized by a sudden urge to see how Holmes "is employing his extraordinary powers" (*Sherlock Holmes*, p. 6). Holmes has been engaged by the king of Bohemia, who is about to marry. He has employed Holmes because the king's former mistress, an American opera singer named Irene Adler, possesses compromising letters that he wrote her along with a photograph of them together, which she threatens to use to cause a scandal and wreck the marriage. Disguising himself as an unemployed groom, Holmes manages to insinuate himself into Adler's presence, and is even asked to be the official witness as she marries a man named Godfrey Norton. Using another disguise (this time as a clergyman), Holmes then infiltrates Adler's house and discovers where she has hidden the documents.

The next morning Holmes and Watson accompany the king to Adler's house, where Holmes expects to recover these documents. However, Holmes is startled to be told that Adler and Norton have left the country. She has, however, addressed a note to "My Dear Mr. Sherlock Holmes," which relates how she had become suspicious of the clergyman and followed him to the detective's famous address (*Sherlock Holmes*, p. 27). Now, happily married to "a better man" than the king (who, she says, "has cruelly wronged" her), she tells Holmes she no longer loves the king and will not bother him further (*Sherlock Holmes,* p. 28). She leaves behind the documents, along with the memory of "how the best plans of Sherlock Holmes were beaten by a woman's wit" (*Sherlock Holmes*, p. 29).

A Case of Identity. A young woman named Mary Sutherland engages Holmes to locate her fiancé, a Mr. Hosmer Angel, who disappeared without a trace on their wedding day, minutes before the wedding was to take place. By comparing typewritten notes from Angel and Miss Sutherland's stepfather, Mr. Windibank, Holmes proves that Windibank created the fictitious character of Hosmer Angel in order to retain control of his stepdaughter's independent income, which the stepfather had access to while Miss Sutherland lived at home. Wearing a disguise, he had wooed his stepdaughter until she had fallen in love with him as Hosmer Angel. Then, just before his disappearance, in the character of Angel he had mysteriously asked her to wait for him whatever happened, claiming that if they were parted he would one day return. By abandoning her in that way, he counted on her love for Hosmer Angel to keep the hope of his return alive in her heart and thus to prevent her from ever marrying.

The Red-Headed League. Holmes is hired by Jabez Wilson, a redhead whose strange tale attracts Holmes's interest. Wilson, who owns a small pawn shop, was hired by an organization calling itself the "League of Red-Headed Men." The league purported to have been endowed by a redheaded American financier, who wished to support other redheads by paying them well to perform undemanding jobs. Accordingly, the league offered Wilson a good salary to come to its London office and copy the *Encyclopedia Britannica* by hand. Wilson left the pawnshop in the hands of his assistant, whom he had recently hired but who seemed responsible and capable. After performing the strange job for several weeks, he turned up one morning to find the office locked and a note saying that the league had been dissolved. The man who had hired him was nowhere to be found. Wilson had come straight to Sherlock Holmes that very morning in hopes of tracing the league and perhaps resuming his lucrative and undemanding job.

Holmes laughs at the tale, then tells Wilson that the case is "a most remarkable one" and that "graver issues may hang from it than might at first sight appear" (*Sherlock Holmes,* p. 60). Suspecting that the league was simply a ruse to remove Wilson from his pawnshop, Holmes establishes that the recently hired assistant is in fact the leader of a gang of bank robbers, who planned to tunnel from the pawnshop into the vaults of a bank across the street. The disbanding of the fictional league, he deduces, means that they are ready to strike. That night, when they attempt the robbery, Holmes, Watson, and

the police are waiting in the vaults and the thieves are arrested.

The Boscombe Valley Mystery and *The Five Orange Pips.* These two stories are the only *Adventures* tales in which Holmes is called upon to solve a murder, and both murders turn out to be motivated by revenge. In "The Boscombe Valley Mystery" Holmes and Watson travel to Boscombe Valley to investigate the murder of Charles McCarthy, for which McCarthy's son James has been arrested. Holmes determines that the murderer is in fact an old associate of McCarthy's, John Turner, who lives nearby. The two had known each other in Australia, where Turner had participated in the robbery of a gold convoy in which McCarthy had driven one of the wagons. Later, living off the proceeds in England under an assumed name, Turner had run into McCarthy on

THE MANY FACES OF SHERLOCK HOLMES

A master of disguise, Sherlock Holmes is most recognizable peering through a magnifying glass, wearing his deerstalker hat and checked Inverness cape, clutching a curved calabash pipe in his teeth as he exclaims "Elementary, my dear Watson." In fact, of these famous Holmes trademarks only the magnifying glass appears in Doyle's original stories. The deerstalker hat, cape, and pipe were added by illustrators, and while Holmes does say "elementary" and refer to his friend as "my dear Watson," he never does both at the same time.

the street, and McCarthy had blackmailed him for years. Securing the innocent son's release, Holmes agrees to let Turner go at the end of the story, saying that it is not up to him to judge the killer of a blackmailer.

The Five Orange Pips. In this tale, Holmes is engaged by John Openshaw, whose uncle and then father had both died, years apart, under similar mysterious circumstances: each had received in the mail an envelope containing five dried orange seeds ("pips" in British usage) shortly before his death and the letters K.K.K. written on a single piece of paper. The uncle, in his former years the owner of a plantation in the southern United States, had incurred the enmity of the Ku Klux Klan before returning to England. Holmes ultimately fails to protect his client from the long arm of the U.S. terror organization, and Openshaw is murdered.

An illustration from the original 1892 edition of *The Adventures of Sherlock Holmes.*

The Man with the Twisted Lip. Holmes untangles the disappearance of Neville St. Clair, a London businessman. Though St. Clair's body was never found, a deformed beggar named Hugh Boone had been apprehended with the businessman's bloodstained clothes and arrested for murder. After examining the evidence, Holmes deduces that Boone and St. Clair are in fact the same man; St. Clair has been pursuing a career as a beggar in London, finding it more profitable than a respectable business career, to which he had only pretended to commit himself. He used theatrical make-up to give himself a deformed lip in his disguise as a beggar. Since no crime was committed, St. Clair beseeches Holmes and the police to keep his waywardness secret; they agree and St. Clair promises that Hugh Boone will never reappear. The implication is that St. Clair will resume his respectable Victorian life.

The Adventure of the Blue Carbuncle. One Christmas morning, a man brings Holmes a hat and a Christmas goose that he has found on the street, hoping that Holmes can locate their rightful owner. The case takes a more serious turn when the finder, preparing to cook the unclaimed goose, discovers that it contains a famous gemstone (the "blue carbuncle") stolen in a recent hotel robbery. Tracing the goose's trail from wholesaler to retailer to customer, Holmes tracks

down the thief, who had hidden the gem in the goose to elude detection.

The Adventure of the Speckled Band. A young woman named Helen Stoner comes to Holmes two years after her sister became engaged and then died in unexplained circumstances. The two young women lived in the country with their stepfather, a violent man named Roylott who served in the army in India and has a collection of exotic animals from there. Miss Stoner says she heard her sister scream in the middle of the night, then heard a low-pitched whistle. Her sister ran from her bedroom, gasping, "It was the band! The speckled band!" before she collapsed and died (*Sherlock Holmes*, p. 178). Miss Stoner, who now lives alone with Roylott, has just become engaged. Owing to work that Roylott ordered done on the house, she has moved into her sister's old bedroom. The night before she heard the same low-pitched whistle, and so fears that the same fate awaits her as befell her sister.

Holmes and Watson travel to the house, where they foil Roylott's attempt to murder Miss Stoner as he had her sister: by sending a poisonous Indian snake (the source of the whistle) into her room through a ventilator shaft and down a rope pull that hangs above the bed. Holmes, who has deduced the method by observing the room, drives the snake—which resembles a speckled band—back into Roylott's room, where it kills him. The attempts on both sisters' lives had been prompted when each of them had become engaged, threatening the debt-ridden Roylott's control of their inheritances from their mother.

The Adventure of the Engineer's Thumb. Dr. Watson is awoken early one morning by Mr. Victor Hatherley, an engineer who needs emergency treatment for an amputated thumb. When Hatherley tells Holmes how he lost his thumb, Holmes deduces that Hatherley has been unwittingly working for counterfeiters and, together with the police, goes to round up the gang. However, the criminals, who are headed by a "sinister German," have escaped (*Sherlock Holmes*, p. 219).

The Adventure of the Noble Bachelor. Holmes is engaged by Lord Robert St. Simon, a British aristocrat who has recently married a young and wealthy American heiress, Miss Hatty Doran. Unhappily, Miss Doran disappeared shortly after the wedding and has not been seen since. Holmes's investigation establishes that Miss Doran was in fact already married to an American who had been presumed dead but who suddenly appeared at her wedding to St. Simon. Holmes locates the couple and persuades the woman to explain her situation to an unforgiving St. Simon.

The Adventure of the Beryl Coronet. Holmes is asked to recover the fabled Beryl Coronet, a rare and historical piece of jewelry that has been stolen from the home of banker Alexander Holder. The police have arrested Holder's son, but using footprints and other evidence Holmes establishes that Holder's niece was manipulated by her crooked lover into acting as his accomplice in the theft.

The Adventure of the Copper Beeches. Holmes is engaged by Miss Violet Hunter, a resourceful and observant young woman who wonders whether she should accept a strange job offer. She has been offered unusually high pay to act as a governess at an estate called the Copper Beeches on the bizarre conditions that she cut her hair short, wear a blue dress, and, when asked, sit prominently in front of a large window in the house with her face turned away from the window.

Holmes and Watson journey to the country house when its owners, the Rucastles, are away. Holmes establishes that Rucastle, a widower who had remarried, had a daughter named Alice from his first marriage, to whom his deceased wife had left a substantial amount of money. While Alice was single, Rucastle could use her money, but then she became engaged to a local man named Fowler. If Alice married, Rucastle knew, her husband would expect to take over the money. Imprisoning his daughter in a locked room in the house, Rucastle had hired Miss Hunter to impersonate her, hoping to give the persistent Fowler the impression that Alice was no longer interested in him (so that he would stop courting her). Her father's scheme is foiled, and Alice is freed. She marries Fowler, and Miss Hunter goes on to become the successful head of a private school.

Science, rationalism, and order. To many late Victorian middle-class men, the best hope for maintaining social order lay in the proper application of reason to society's problems. Shaped by decades of scientific and technological progress, the middle-class male Victorian prized reason above all else as the key to improving the human condition. He furthermore viewed reason as a particularly male quality.

At the beginning of the first story, "A Scandal in Bohemia," Watson describes Holmes as "the most perfect reasoning and observing machine that the world has ever seen" (*Sherlock Holmes*, p. 5). Holmes's defining characteristic, his machinelike use of reason, idealizes him by exag-

gerating the Victorian male ideal of rationality. Yet while Holmes's reasoning abilities set him apart from society, those abilities also let him function as society's protector in a way that the more conventional police cannot. They even justify his sometimes unconventional behavior, as when he lets John Turner, the murderer of a blackmailer, go free in "The Boscombe Valley Mystery." Holmes's superior intellect thus not only distinguishes him from other men—such as the middle-class male readership that made the stories a commercial success—but it also allows him to be both judge and jury in removing hidden threats to the Victorian social order. Critics have noted that these threats are posed not only by the criminal element in the stories, but also by a number of their male authority figures (such as aristocrats and fathers), whose greed has driven them to irrational or antisocial behavior.

For the late Victorians, a leading embodiment of reason was biologist Charles Darwin, whose work ***On the Origin of Species*** (1859; also in *WLAIT 4: British and Irish Literature and Its Times*) was the most important scientific publication of the nineteenth century. In it Darwin established the fact of biological evolution and proposed a theory, called natural selection, to explain how evolution occurs. To Darwin's many followers, reason had evolved in humans alone and (in the language of the times) it alone separated "men" from "beasts." Though controversial, Darwinism ultimately permeated late Victorian culture, offering a reassuring vision of human society in which evolution was taken as the equivalent of progress and was believed to have reached a pinnacle in human reason.

As a doctor and a man of science, Doyle stood squarely within this rationalist milieu. So do both of his leading characters: like Doyle, Watson is a doctor, and Doyle based many of Holmes's mannerisms and techniques on those of his own former teacher, Dr. Joseph Bell, a professor of medicine at Edinburgh University (to whom he dedicated *The Adventures of Sherlock Holmes*). Holmes mentions Darwin several times in stories other than those in *The Adventures of Sherlock Holmes*; in "The Five Orange Pips" he compares his deductive methods to a biologist's, specifically to those of Darwin's famous predecessor, French naturalist Georges Cuvier (1769-1832):

> The ideal reasoner . . . would, when he has been shown a single fact in all its bearings, deduce from it not only all the chain of events which led up to it, but also all the results which would follow from it. As Cuvier could correctly

describe a whole animal by the contemplation of a single bone, so the observer who has thoroughly understood one link in a series of incidents, should be able accurately to state all the other ones, both before and after.

(*Sherlock Holmes*, p. 114)

Finally it is the pursuit of solutions through reason that matters most in these stories. Not always does Holmes solve a mystery or best an opponent (see *Scandal in Bohemia* and *Five Orange Pips*) but usually he does—through the use of reason.

Sources and literary context. While basing Holmes's incisive rationality partly on that of his real-life teacher Dr. Joseph Bell, Doyle also had literary models for his detective. American author Edgar Allen Poe (1809-49) is credited with inventing the detective story, and his French hero, C. Auguste Dupin, clearly inspired Doyle's portrayal of Holmes. Like Dupin, for example, Holmes frequently surprises and impresses bystanders with his prodigious feats of deduction. Poe's Dupin appeared in three short stories published in the 1840s, best known of which is the first, "The Murders in the Rue Morgue" (1841). The leisurely Dupin solved mysteries by reason alone—often from his armchair. A French writer, Émile Gaboriau (c. 1832-1873), enjoyed Poe's stories so much that he created his own more active detective in the 1860s: Monsieur Lecoq, who as a policeman took a leading role in tracking down clues and criminals. Alternating between idleness at home and energy on the crime scene, Holmes combines both approaches.

A changing literary market also shaped the stories. Print media such as newspapers and magazines expanded rapidly in the 1880s and 1890s, developing new technologies, adopting fresh formats, and above all reaching new and larger audiences. In 1891 pioneer publisher George Newnes founded a monthly magazine called *The Strand*, after the London thoroughfare near its offices. While *The Strand* included brief sections for women and even children, its primary audience was men. Sold in city shops, bookstalls, and train stations, it was directed at middle-class urban workers such as clerks and businessmen—especially the new and growing class of businessmen who commuted by train between cities like London and their suburbs. Previous nineteenth-century magazines (for example Charles Dickens's popular weekly *Household Words*) had generally been aimed at a family audience. In such journals fiction had taken the form of long novels, serialized in short installments that were de-

signed to be read aloud to the family. This meant that one had to follow the entire series in order to fully enjoy a single issue of the journal. By contrast, *The Strand*—with its on-the-move male audience in mind—would specialize in short, action-packed stories that could be completely enjoyed on their own.

Note was made, however, of the fact that readers enjoyed developing familiarity with the characters in serials. Capitalizing on this pleasure, *The Strand* also pioneered the idea of a serial character who would return in story after story. Writing later, Doyle himself took credit for this new literary formula:

It had struck me that a single character running through a series, if it only engaged the attention of the reader, would bind that reader to that particular magazine. . . . Clearly the ideal compromise was a character that carried through, and yet installments that were complete in themselves. . . . I believe I was the first to realize this and *"The Strand Magazine"* the first to put it into practice.

(Doyle, *Memories and Adventures*, p. 90)

Reception. With the publication of the 12 stories starting in July 1891, this marriage of character familiarity with self-contained installments of a series made Sherlock Holmes the most spectacularly successful serial character of all. The stories were collected and published by Newnes in 1892 in book form as *The Adventures of Sherlock Holmes*, and the collection garnered a positive critical response:

There is hardly any waste of time about subtle character-drawing, but incident succeeds incident with the most businesslike rapidity, and the unexpected always occurs with appropriate regularity. Of the dozen stories of which the book is made up, there is not one which does not contain a thorough-paced mystery . . . the reader is worked up to such a pitch of nervous excitement that he is ready for almost anything.

(*The Athenaeum* in Hall, pp. 215-216)

The Strand commissioned a second series of 12 stories in 1893, with Doyle—now worried that the famous detective would monopolize his literary output and reputation—killing Holmes off in the last one. However, public outcry over Holmes's death was tremendous, and Doyle received many letters calling him a murderer. *The Strand* received more than 20,000 cancellations from subscribers upon Holmes's death. People wore black armbands as a sign of public mourning; papers the world over reported Holmes's demise as newsworthy. Indeed, Holmes felt so real to readers that Doyle constantly received letters asking Holmes to look into real-life mysteries.

Sherlock Holmes fan clubs still exist, and a number of books and articles have been written purporting to supply biographical details about Holmes and Watson. Bowing to popular pressure, Doyle produced another Holmes novel, *The Hound of the Baskervilles*, which was serialized in *The Strand* beginning in 1901. Further stories and another novel, *The Valley of Fear* (1914) followed, with the last appearance of Sherlock Holmes taking place in 1927, a few years before Doyle's death.

—Colin Wells

For More Information

Booth, Martin. *The Doctor, the Detective, and Arthur Conan Doyle: A Biography of Arthur Conan Doyle*. London: Hodder and Stoughton, 1997.

Doyle, Arthur Conan. *The Adventures of Sherlock Holmes*. Oxford: Oxford University Press, 1993.

———. *Memories and Adventures*. Boston: Little Brown, 1924.

———. *A Study in Scarlet and The Sign of Four*. New York: Berkley, 1963.

Hall, Sharon K., ed. *Twentieth-Century Literary Criticism*. Detroit: Gale Research, 1982.

Harrison, J. F. C. *Late Victorian Britain 1875-1901*. London: Routledge, 1991.

Jarrett, Derek. *The Sleep of Reason: Fantasy and Reality from the Victorian Age to the First World War*. London: Weidenfeld and Nicolson, 1988.

Jaffe, Jaqueline A. *Arthur Conan Doyle*. Boston: Twayne, 1987.

Keating, H. R. F. *Sherlock Holmes: The Man and His World*. New York: Scribner, 1979.

Kestner, Joseph A. *Sherlock's Men: Masculinity, Conan Doyle, and Cultural History*. Brookfield, Vt.: Ashgate, 1997.

Mitchell, Sally. *Daily Life in Victorian England*. Westport, Conn.: Greenwood, 1996.

Orel, Harold. *Critical Essays on Sir Arthur Conan Doyle*. New York: Macmillan, 1992.

"Anthem for Doomed Youth" and Other Poems

by
Wilfred Owen

Wilfred Edward Salter, born on March 18, 1893, in the village of Oswestry in Shropshire, England, was the eldest son of a minor railway official. Educated at the Birkenhead Institute and at Shrewsbury Technical College, Owen matriculated in 1911 but without the honors necessary to enter a university. Like his mother, to whom he was quite close, Owen was religious and even considered pursuing a career in the church. In 1911-12, he worked as an unpaid lay assistant to a vicar in the poor country parish of Dunsden, where he taught Bible classes, led prayer meetings, and attended missionary gatherings. Owen meanwhile began to compose poetry. After suffering a serious illness in 1913, Owen left to teach English in Bordeaux, France, and was there when World War I broke out. Owen eventually enlisted in the army, which led to his fighting as an officer at the western front in 1917. Hospitalized for some months with "shell shock," Owen met the war poet, Siegfried Sassoon, whose realistic verse deeply influenced Owen's own work. Continuing to write poetry, Owen returned to the army in November 1917, serving with distinction—he received the Military Cross. He was killed in action a week before the war ended. Sassoon oversaw the posthumous first publication of Owen's poems, which garnered critical praise for their mastery of rhyme and their unflinchingly realistic depiction of the horrors of modern war.

THE LITERARY WORK

War poetry written and set in France during World War I, 1914-18; first published in 1920.

SYNOPSIS

Owen's poetry portrays the grim horrors of trench warfare and the futile waste of youthful manhood.

Events in History at the Time of the Poetry

Owen's wartime experiences. Originally, Owen did not intend to enlist in the British army, but following a visit to a hospital for the wounded, he decided, in September 1915, to return to England and join up. After 14 months of training with the Artists' Rifles in various parts of England, Owen was commissioned a second lieutenant in the Manchester Regiment on June 4, 1916, and posted to the western front later that same year.

The winter of 1916-17 was a particularly difficult time in the war—the Battle of the Somme, an Allied offensive campaign launched the previous summer, was proving unsuccessful. By November 1916, torrential autumn rains had turned the battlefield into a sea of mud, preventing Allied armies from advancing more than five miles

Wilfred Owen

and helping the Germans retain their seemingly impregnable positions in the trenches. Owen's first task once he was sent to the front lines was to hold positions in No Man's Land—the unoccupied territory between the Allied and German armies—in the Beaumont Hamel region in France; later, he was sent behind the lines for a transport course. Owen had a number of close calls in that period, falling into a cellar and suffering a concussion in March 1917, then getting blown into the air by a shell while participating in a successful attack on the village of Fayet in April. This action lasted 12 days, and Owen was forced to spend several of those days sheltering in a hole near the dismembered remains of a fellow officer.

Although Owen escaped physical injury, soon after the action he was judged "unfit to command troops" and diagnosed as suffering from neurasthenia—"shell shock," or what today is called posttraumatic stress disorder. Many soldiers, including Owen's contemporary and fellow war poet Robert Graves, suffered from "shell shock," which involved symptoms such as sporadic fits of uncontrollable weeping, twitching, voiding of the bowels, nightmares, and periodic depression. Owen was sent to Craiglockhart Hospital in Edinburgh, Scotland, a facility famous for its treatment of shell shock victims. While at Craiglockhart, Owen met Siegfried Sassoon, an older poet who not only helped Owen

with poetry but also influenced him to adopt a more critical view of England's role in the war. Both Owen and Sassoon contributed to the *Hydra,* a literary magazine produced by the patients at Craiglockhart. Owen even took over the editorship of the magazine for the issue of August 4, 1917.

Discharged from Craiglockhart in November 1917, Owen was posted to Scarborough to take charge of the domestic affairs of a large hotel that was being used as a barracks, then later to Ripon. Much of Owen's war poetry was composed during that time. By August 1918, Owen was judged fit for active duty, and he returned to the front lines in France. Although he suspected he might not return alive from the war, he accepted his probable fate calmly and led his troops with an increased confidence and authority. In early October 1918, shortly before he was awarded the Military Cross, England's equivalent of the Purple Heart, for capturing a German machine-gun emplacement and turning it upon the enemy, Owen wrote to his mother, "I came out in order to help these boys—directly by leading them as well as an officer can; indirectly, by watching their sufferings that I may speak of them as well as a pleader can. I have done the first" (Owen, *War Poems and Others,* p. 107). On November 4, 1918, just one week before the armistice, Owen was killed while leading his men across the Sambre Canal near Ors, France. He was 25 years old at the time. The bells in his home town in Shropshire were ringing on November 11, 1918, in celebration of the armistice when the doorbell buzzed at his parents' home, bringing them the telegram with news of their son's death.

Trench warfare. Among the innovations of war on the western front was the system of trench warfare. There were normally three lines of trenches. The front-line trench was anywhere from 50 yards or so to a mile from its enemy counterpart, the area between them being known as No Man's Land. Several hundred yards behind the front-line trench was the support trench, and several hundred yards behind that was the reserve line.

There were actually three kinds of trenches: firing trenches (the front-line trenches); communication trenches, running roughly perpendicular to the lines and connecting the three lines; and "saps," shallower ditches thrust out into No Man's Land and used as observation posts, listening posts, grenade-throwing posts, and machine gun positions. Saps were usually manned at night.

British troops normally rotated trench duty. After a week of so-called "rest" behind the lines, a unit would move up—at night—to relieve a unit in the front-line trench. After three days to a week or more in that position, that unit moved back for a similar length of time to the support trench, and finally back to the reserve trench. Then it was time for another week of rest. In the three lines of trenches the main business of the soldier was to exercise self-control while being shelled. Casualties were heavy, as soldier's diaries and letters attest. T. S. Eliot, in a letter he sent to *The Nation* magazine on July 23, 1917, quoted the following anonymous soldier's account:

> Perhaps you are tempted to give them a picture of a leprous earth scattered with the swollen and blackening corpses of hundreds of young men. The appalling stench of rotting carrion mingled with the sickening smell of exploded lyddite and ammonal. Mud like porridge, trenches like shallow and sloping cracks in the porridge— porridge that stinks in the sun. Swarms of flies and bluebottles clustering on pits of offal. Wounded men lying in the shell holes among the decaying corpses: helpless under the scorching sun and bitter nights, under repeated shelling. Men with bowels dropping out, lungs shot away, with blinded, smashed faces, or limbs blown into space. Men screaming and gibbering. Wounded men hanging in agony on the barbed wire, until a friendly spout of liquid fire shrivels them up like a fly in a candle. But these are only words, and probably convey only a fraction of their meaning to their hearers. They shudder, and it is forgotten.
>
> (Eliot in Hibberd, p. 100-01)

Along with trench warfare came new weaponry during World War I. The war saw the introduction of tanks, planes, and submarines. Also new was poison gas—an element that figures in Owen's poetry. Germany was the first nation to use tear gas, on October 27, 1914. In the battle of Ypres during April 1915, many of the 60,000 were killed by chlorine gas attacks, because England had not yet come up with the box respirator, forerunner of the modern gas mask.

Propaganda and the outbreak of war. Since the late nineteenth century, Britain had uneasily watched Germany's rise as a military and industrial power. By the time World War I broke out in 1914, many had come to believe that conflict with Germany was inevitable, a belief encouraged by vast amounts of pro-war propaganda circulated by the government, the press, private patriotic organizations, and even popular British authors. Historian Cate Haste argues that the

purpose of pro-war propaganda entails "building up the image of national and allied leaders as the embodiment of courage, heroism, and resolution, while the enemy leaders become the embodiment of evil and the scapegoats for the war"; also "propaganda builds an image of war itself" as "glorious and heroic, and exciting enough to arouse the desire to take part," leaving out grue-

---

"WASTAGE" IN WORLD WAR I

World War I had its share of famous battles, although as the scholar Paul Fussell has said, "To call these things *battles* is to imply an understandable continuity with earlier British history and to imply that the war makes sense in a traditional way," when in fact such terms are used "in the interest of neatness and the assumption of something like a rational causality" (Fussell, p. 9). The German attempt to break through at Verdun in 1916 (February-July) involved 2 million men, and caused 1 million casualties. It failed. The British offensive on the Somme in June 1916, designed to force the Germans to end the Verdun offensive, cost Britain 420,000 dead— 60,000 on the first day of the attack. It is not surprising that in the memory of the British and French, who fought most of the war on the western front, World War I remained the "Great War," more terrible and traumatic than World War II. A list of some of the major actions follows:

- **Ypres** (Belgium) April 22, 1915: 60,000 killed.
- **Loos** (France) September 15-26, 1915: 60,000 killed.
- **Somme** (France) British attack, on July 1, 1916: 60,000 out of a total force of 110,000 killed or wounded on the first day of battle; 20,000 dead in No Man's Land.
- **Ypres** (Belgium) Third battle of Ypres on April 9, 1917: 160,000 killed or wounded.
- **Passchendaele** (Belgium) July 31-November 15, 1917: 370,000 dead or wounded; many men frozen to death or literally drowned in mud.
- **Somme** (France) Germans attack, on March 21-27, 1918: 300,000 British killed.

The British used the euphemistic term "wastage" for casualties. Battlefield cemeteries in France and Belgium are famous for their vast expanses of orderly white crosses, and while these white crosses give visitors the illusion that each soldier has his own grave, in fact most of these fields constitute mass graves where men and parts of men were buried in bulk and not in neat rows.

A soldier in the heat of battle in World War I.

some or shocking details that would discourage support (Haste, p. 3).

In the early years of World War I, the British government did not need to establish a *formal* propaganda machine at the home front. After Germany invaded Belgium, which France and Britain were pledged to protect, most British firmly felt that their country would be fighting in a just cause and supported the ensuing war. On behalf of the British government, Henry Herbert Asquith, the prime minister, issued a statement defining the nature of the conflict: "We are fighting to vindicate the principle that small nationalities are not to be crushed in defiance of international good faith by the arbitrary will of a strong and over-mastering power . . . not for the maintenance of its own selfish interests, but . . . for principles the maintenance of which is vital to the civilized world" (Asquith in Haste, pp. 22-24).

Asquith's sentiments were reiterated and expanded upon in other media as well. Patriotic organizations, such as the Central Committee for National Patriotic Organizations, were quickly formed and circulated pro-war pamphlets. The popular press published inflammatory cartoons and sketches. One cartoon in *Punch* depicted Germany as a towering bully armed with a cudgel advancing upon a child ("Little Belgium") carrying only a stick, and in September 1914, 53 of Britain's authors signed a public statement in *The Times* supporting the war (Haste, p. 23). Signatories included the novelists H. G. Wells, Rudyard Kipling, and Arthur Conan Doyle.

Other writers published stories, poems, and songs that further fueled nationalistic and patriotic impulses. In November 1914, Jessie Pope, a poetess and the author of several pre-war children's books, exhorted the young men of England to take up arms in "The Call":

> Who's for the trench—
> Are you, my laddie?
> Who'll follow the French—
> Will you, my laddie?
> Who's fretting to begin,
> Who's going to win?
> And who wants to save his skin—
> Do you, my laddie?
> (Pope in Stallworthy, p. 227)

Such poems as Pope's appealed blatantly to idealistic young men's hunger for glory, as well as making veiled insinuations of cowardice towards those opposed to the war or reluctant to enlist. It was just this sort of saber-rattling verse that Owen and his fellow war poets found so appalling after they had actually experienced combat on the western front, especially in the later years of the war.

The British public, however, remained largely ignorant of the true conditions under which their troops were fighting: newspaper correspondents were not allowed to visit the front and, as a form of "negative propaganda," military leaders and the government itself restricted access to all information, thus promoting a false image of the war and Britain's success in it. As late as 1917, despite increased criticism of the war in some circles, the poet Sir Henry Newbolt published *Book of the Happy Warrior*, which told the story of chivalry in the medieval era and was intended to inspire boys in wartime England to noble deeds. E. B. Osborn edited a collection of war poems, *The Muse in Arms*, in which parallels between sport and the current war were continually established. In "Rugby Football—written on receiving the football-match list from Ilkley Grammar School," the speaker asks, "Can you hear the call? Can you hear the call / That drowns the roar of Krupp / But hark, can you hear it? Over all— / 'Now, School! Now, School! Play up'" (Osborn in Girouard, p. 286).

The Poetry in Focus

Contents summary. Owen's war poems—23 of which were printed in the first edition of his poetry—depict the grim facts of trench warfare, stressing in particular the human cost of war: the ravages of gas attacks on their victims, the horrors of seeing the frail bodies of beautiful young men crushed and broken by industrially mass-produced armaments, and the desolation in witnessing an entire generation laid waste. The romanticized view of war, presented in the works of many of Owen's contemporaries, continually gives way to an unsparingly realistic perspective of a soldier at the front, which at the same time manifests compassion. Owen himself wrote in a draft preface meant to precede his poems when they were published:

> This book is not about heroes. English Poetry is not yet fit to speak of them.
> Nor is it about deeds, or lands, nor anything about glory, honour, might, majesty, dominion, or power, except War.
> Above all I am not concerned with Poetry.
> My subject is War, and the pity of War.
> The Poetry is in the pity.
> (*War Poems and Others*, p. 137)

"Anthem for Doomed Youth"

What passing-bells for these who die as
    cattle?

—Only the monstrous anger of the guns.
Only the stuttering rifles' rapid rattle
Can patter out their hasty orisons.
No mockeries now for them; no prayers nor
    bells;
Nor any voice of mourning, save the choirs,—
The shrill demented choirs of wailing shells'
And bugles calling for them from sad shires.

What candles may be held to speed them all?
Not in the hands of boys but in their eyes
Shall shine the holy glimmers of goodbyes.
The pallor of girls' brows shall be their pall;
Their flowers the tenderness of patient minds,
And each slow dusk a drawing-down of
    blinds.

In the sonnet "Anthem for Doomed Youth," the speaker asks what rites are most appropriate for the ill-fated soldiers of this modern war. The conventional symbols of mourning—the "passing bells," the "hasty orisons," the flowers, and candles—are revealed as hollow "mockeries" to those who perish before "the monstrous anger of the guns" to the sounds of "wailing shells." Rather, the speaker calls for quieter, more thoughtful observances and memorials to dead soldiers: "the holy glimmers of goodbyes" in the eyes of young boys, the "pallor of girls' brows," the "tenderness of patient minds, / And each slow dusk a drawing-down of blinds." The empty ceremonies that usually attend the dead are replaced by something simpler yet more heartfelt, which the speaker feels is more appropriate to doomed youth "who die as cattle."

"Dulce et Decorum Est"

Bent double, like old beggars under sacks,
Knock-kneed, coughing like hags, we cursed
    through sludge,
Till on the haunting flares we turned our
    backs,
And towards our distant rest began to trudge.
Men marched asleep. Many had lost their
    boots,
But limped on, blood-shod. All went lame, all
    blind;
Drunk with fatigue; deaf even to the hoots
Of tired, outstripped Five-nines [5.9 caliber
    shells] that dropped behind.

Gas! GAS! Quick, boys! —An ecstasy of
    fumbling
Fitting the clumsy helmets just in time,
But someone still was yelling out and
    stumbling
And flound'ring like a man in fire or lime . . .
Dim through the misty panes and thick green
    light,

As under a green sea, I saw him drowning.
In all my dreams before my helpless sight
He plunges at me, guttering, choking,
    drowning.

If in some smothering dreams, you too could
    pace
Behind the wagon that we flung him in,
And watch the white eyes writing in his face,
His hanging face, like a devil's sick of sin,
If you could hear, at every jolt, the blood
Come gargling from the froth-corrupted lungs
Bitter as the cud
Of vile, incurable sores on innocent tongues,—
My friend, you would not tell with such high
    zest
To children ardent for some desperate glory,
The old Lie: Dulce et decorum est
Pro patria mori.

A far angrier note is sounded in "Dulce Et Decorum Est," which depicts, by turns, the unglamorous march of sick, weary soldiers, some bootless and "blood-shod," towards their "distant rest," the sudden horror of a gas attack, followed by the lingering nightmare—continually relived in dreams by the speaker—of seeing one comrade, who failed to don his mask in time, "guttering, choking, drowning" in the poison gas, then hearing "the blood / Come gargling from the froth-corrupted lungs" of the dying victim as he is borne off in a wagon. In the final lines, the speaker addresses a particular reader—identified by Owen scholars as Jessie Pope—and declares that, had she experienced "in some smothering dreams" the horror of what he himself had seen, "you would not tell with such high zest / To children ardent for some desperate glory, / The old line: Dulce et decorum est / Pro patria mori." The Latin tag, from Horace, meant, as Owen explained to his mother, "*It is sweet and meet* to die for one's country. Sweet! and *decorous*!" (Owen in Stallworthy, p. 228).

"Futility"

Move him into the sun—
Gently its touch awoke him once,
At home, whispering of fields unsown.
Always it awoke him, even in France,
Until this morning and this snow.
If anything might rouse him now
The kind old sun will know.

Think how it wakes the seeds—
Woke, once, the clays of a cold star.
Are limbs so dear-achieved, are sides
Full-nerved, still warm, too hard to stir?
Was it for this the clay grew tall?

—O what made fatuous sunbeams toil
To break earth's sleep at all?

"Futility" is written in a tone distinctive from the elegiac somberness of "Anthem for Doomed Youth" and the furious indignation of "Dulce et Decorum Est." The first stanza reveals that a man—presumably a soldier—has died, though the cause of death is unclear. The speaker exhorts that the man's body be moved "into the sun" whose touch has always awakened him before: "If anything might rouse him now / The kind old sun will know." But as the man remains lifeless, the speaker is moved to contemplate nature's power to awaken life in seeds and "the clays of a cold star," contrasted with nature's inability to revive *mortal* "clay," as represented by the dead soldier: "Are limbs, so dear achieved, are sides / Full nerved, still warm, too hard to stir? / Was it for this the clay grew tall?" "Futility" concludes on a note both pensive and poignant as the speaker wonders, "O what made fatuous sunbeams toil / To break earth's sleep at all?"

Poets at the front. Although Owen's war poetry has attained fame for its brutal honesty about fighting in the trenches, it must be noted that initially he was as susceptible as any other idealistic young man of his generation to the lure of honor and glory that the Great War seemed to promise those who enlisted. In August 1914, shortly after war had been declared, young Englishmen were joining up by the thousands. At the time, Owen was working on a poem tentatively titled "The Ballad of Peace and War," which contained the lines: "O meet it is and passing sweet / To live in peace with others, / But sweeter still and far more meet / To die in war for brothers" (Owen in Stallworthy, p. 104). Upon deciding to enlist himself in 1915, Owen wrote to a friend, "I don't imagine that the German War will be affected by my joining in, but I know my own future Peace will be. . . . Having now some increase of physical strength I feel proportionately useful and proportionately lacking in sense if I don't use it in the best way—The Only Way" (*War Poems and Others*, p. 59).

Owen's enthusiasm survived training and even his arrival in France. On first hearing the Drum & Fife Band after enlisting, he admitted that it roused the fighting spirit in him: "The sound, together with the gallant bearing of the twenty fifers, has finally dazzled me with Military Glory" (*War Poems and Others*, p. 59). He even described his first hearing of the guns while in France as "a sound not without a certain sublimity" (Owen in Stallworthy, p. 153). And in the early months of 1917, as Britain struggled through the unsuccessful aftermath of the Somme offensive, Owen wrote to his mother, "There is a fine heroic feeling about being in France, and I am in perfect spirits. A tinge of excitement is about me, but excitement is always necessary to my happiness" (*War Poems and Others,* p. 60). As the war continued and Owen's own combat experience increased, that "fine heroic feeling" was succeeded by dismay at the cold and filth soldiers were forced to endure in camps and trenches, pity for his dead and wounded comrades, and anger over the carnage caused by war. In February 1917, Owen wrote again to his mother:

> I suppose I can endure cold, and fatigue, and the face-to-face death, as well as another; but extra for me there is the universal pervasion of *Ugliness.* Hideous landscapes, vile noises, foul language and nothing but foul, even from one's own mouth (for all are devil ridden), everything unnatural, broken, blasted; the distortion of the dead, whose unburiable bodies sit outside the dug-outs all day, all night, the most execrable sights on earth. In poetry we call them the most glorious. But to sit with them all day, all night . . . and a week later to come back and find them still sitting there, in motionless groups, THAT is what saps the "soldierly spirit."
>
> (*War Poems and Others,* p. 64)

Many of the "war poets"—including Edward Thomas (1878-1917), Isaac Rosenberg (1890-1917), Ivor Gurney (1890-1937), and Siegfried Sassoon (1886-1967)—had wartime experiences similar to Owen's. However idealistically or romantically they had viewed or written about the war when they first enlisted, they soon awakened to its dangers, horrors, and squalor after they were sent to the front. While "Georgian" poets in Britain—so named because they were writing during the reign of King George V—continued to compose meditative, even nostalgic poems on such subjects as the English countryside or stirring patriotic verses praising the gallantry of young Englishmen fighting for king and country, the war poets integrated their visceral reactions to the war—shock, disgust, disillusionment, black humor—into *their* writing. Brutally honest subject matters and innovative poetic techniques were two of the hallmarks of the war poets' works. In "Dead Man's Dump," for example, Rosenberg eschews rhymes and traditional verse forms in favor of stark, terse sentences:

> The air is loud with death,
> The dark air spurts with fire,
> The explosions ceaseless are.
> Timelessly, now, some minutes past,
> These dead strode time with vigorous life,
> Till the shrapnel called "An end!"
> (Rosenberg in Abrams, p. 1841)

Sassoon, by contrast, often retained rhymes and traditional forms, letting his scathingly critical tone and startling images communicate his increasingly anti-war sentiments, as in his sonnet "Glory of Women":

> You can't believe that British troops "retire"
> When hell's last horror breaks them, and they run,
> Trampling the terrible corpses—blind with blood.
> O German mother dreaming by the fire,
> While you are knitting socks to send your son
> His face is trodden deeper in the mud.
> (Sassoon in Abrams, p. 1843)

While the need to express and perhaps exorcise their traumatic experiences at the front was arguably the war poets' primary motive for writing, in the case of Sassoon and Owen, the need to educate the largely ignorant British public about the horrors of modern warfare was equally compelling. As Owen somberly wrote in the draft preface to the book of poems he was never to see printed in his lifetime: "[T]hese elegies are to this generation in no sense consolatory. They may be to the next. All a poet can do today is warn. That is why the true Poets must be truthful" (*War Poems and Others,* p. 137).

Sources and literary context. Owen's war poetry was primarily drawn from his experiences and observations as an officer serving in World War I. In some poems, Owen also reacted to the writing of his contemporaries and their expressed views on the war. John Stallworthy, Owen's biographer, contends that "Anthem for Doomed Youth" may have been Owen's response to an anonymous prefatory note in *Poems of Today* (1916), a collection of verse that Owen possessed, which announced,

> Most of the writers [in this book] are living and the rest are still vivid among us, while one of the youngest, almost as these words are written, has gone singing to lay down his life for his country's cause . . . there is no arbitrary isolation of one theme from another; they mingle and interpenetrate throughout, to the music of Pan's flute, and of Love's viol, and the bugle-call of Endeavour, and the passing-bell of Death.
> (Anonymous in Stallworthy, p. 216)

OTHER VOICES: OWEN'S CONTEMPORARIES

~

Two contrasting viewpoints on war can be found in the poems of Rupert Brooke (1887-1915) and Siegfried Sassoon (1886-1967). "Went to war with Rupert Brooke," went a popular saying of the time, "and came home with Siegfried Sassoon" (Abrams, p. 1849). Brooke, who composed a series of "war sonnets" in 1914, died of dysentery and blood poisoning before ever seeing combat—on a troop ship bound for Gallipoli. His famous sonnet "The Soldier" expresses the romanticism and idealism shared by many of his contemporaries early in the war. By contrast, Siegfried Sassoon experienced the horrors of trench warfare firsthand, and his biting, pungent verses reflect that reality.

Siegfried Sassoon's "They"

The Bishop tells us: "When the boys come back
They will not be the same; for they'll have fought
In a just cause: they lead the last attack
On Anti-Christ; their comrades' blood has bought
New right to breed an honourable race,
They have challenged Death and dared him face to face."

"We're none of us the same!" the boys reply.
"For George lost both his legs; and Bill's stone blind;
Poor Jim's shot through the lungs and like to die;
And Bert's gone syphilitic: you'll not find
A chap who's served that hasn't found *some* change."
And the Bishop said: "The ways of God are strange!"

(Sassoon in Abrams, p. 1842)

As a second lieutenant in the army, "Mad Jack" Sassoon fought courageously at Mametz Wood and in the Somme Offensive of July 1916, receiving the Military Cross. After being wounded in the chest by a sniper's bullet, Sassoon was invalided back to England in April 1917. While recovering, he sent this declaration to his commanding officer: "I am making this statement as an act of wilful defiance of military authority, because I believe that the war is being deliberately prolonged by those who have the power to end it. . . . I have seen and endured the sufferings of the troops, and I can no longer be a party to prolong these sufferings for ends which I believe to be evil and unjust" (Sassoon in Stallworthy, p. 206). The military authorities responded to Sassoon's manifesto by announcing that he was suffering shell shock and sending him to Craiglockhart Hospital in Edinburgh for treatment.

The trenchant opening line of Owen's sonnet—"What passing-bells for these who die as cattle?"—certainly lends some credence to Stallworthy's argument. Similarly, the poem "Dulce et Decorum Est" was directed at a contemporary's pro-war writings, in this case, Jessie Pope's patriotic children's books and poems. Early drafts of "Dulce et Decorum Est" carried bracketed dedications "To Jessie Pope etc" and "To a certain Poetess."

As a child, Owen began experimenting with verse, and his war poems are distinguished particularly by the use of pararhymes, rhymes in which two words are identical in consonant sounds not only after but also before different stressed vowel sounds. In "Futility," for example, Owen uses pararhymes like "star/stir," "seeds/sides," and "tall/toil." Pararhymes had been used to some small effect by modern French poets but were also a feature of some ancient Welsh poems, a fact of which Owen, himself partly Welsh, was likely aware.

Owen's most obvious poetical influences seem to have been John Keats and Percy Bysshe Shelley (see **"Eve of St. Agnes,"** and **"England in 1819" and Other Poems,** in *WLAIT 3: British and Irish Literature and Its Times*). There is evidence that in his late teens, Owen read widely in the work of the loose grouping of contemporary poets who came to be called Georgians, named for King George V, who ascended the British throne in 1910. By the end of 1917 he had read recent books by such contributors to the well-known anthology *Georgian Poetry* as Harold Munro, John Masefield, Robert Nichols, John Drinkwater, Rupert Brooke, Walter de la Mare, and Sassoon.

Of those named, Sassoon was to have the most profound effect upon Owen's poetry, encouraging the younger man to adopt a leaner, more colloquial style and censuring "the over-luscious writing of [Owen's] immature pieces" (Sassoon in Poupard, p. 199). Sassoon noted and rejoiced in his friend's rapid poetic development and the growing confidence that soon helped Owen find his own voice. In later years, he insisted,

> The truth of the matter was that I arrived just when he needed my stimulation and advice. It was my privilege to be in close contact with him while he was attaining a clear view of what he wanted to say and deploying his technical resources to a matured utterance. . . . I count it among my most satisfactory performances that I was able to be of service to his genius.
>
> (Sassoon in Poupard, p. 199)

Reception. Only five of Owen's poems were published in his lifetime. Sassoon edited the first collection, which appeared in 1920. The reaction to the first collection was, for the most part, favorable, although some readers took issue with Owen's stance on the war and his attacks on those who had supported it. Sir Henry Newbolt, who had written numerous patriotic poems in the late nineteenth century, admitted in a letter that Owen's poems were "terribly good, but of course limited, almost all on one note," complaining, "Owen and the rest of the broken men rail at the Old Men who sent the young to die . . . what Englishman of fifty wouldn't far rather stop the shot himself than see the boys do it for him?" (Newbolt in Poupard, p. 199). Several years later, W. B. Yeats would exclude Owen's work from his 1936 edition of the *Oxford Book of Modern Verse*, dismissing it in a letter as "all blood and dirt and sucked sugar-stick" (Yeats in Hall, p. 262).

Overall, however, most commentators admired Owen's poems. The reviewer for the *Times Literary Supplement* wrote, "[Owen] is pitiless with his readers, but for the sake of utter truth and faithfulness where pity belongs. And the tenderness behind his relentlessness gives the hard brutal words a strange, improbable beauty" (Anonymous in Poupard, p. 198). The critic John Middleton Murry declared,

> Here in thirty-three brief pages is the evidence that Wilfred Owen was the greatest poet of the war. . . . In these poems there is no more rebellion, but only pity and regret, and the peace of acquiescence. It is not a comfortable peace, this joyless yet serene resignation; but it is a victory of the human spirit. We receive from it that exalted pleasure, that sense of being lifted above the sphere of anger and despair which the poetic imagination alone can give.
>
> (Murry in Hall, p. 359)

—James Caufield and Pamela S. Loy

For More Information

Abrams, M. H. *The Norton Anthology of English Literature,* Vol. 2. 6th ed. New York: Norton, 1993.

Bell, John, ed. *Wilfred Owen: Selected Letters.* Oxford: Oxford University Press, 1998.

Buitenhuis, Peter. *The Great War of Words: British, American, and Canadian Propaganda and Fiction, 1914-1933.* Vancouver: University of British Columbia Press, 1987.

Fussell, Paul. *The Great War and Modern Memory.* London: Oxford University Press, 1975.

Girouard, Mark. *The Return to Camelot: Chivalry and the English Gentleman.* New Haven: Yale University Press, 1981.

Hall, Sharon K., ed. *Twentieth-Century Literary Criticism.* Vol. 5. Detroit: Gale Group, 1981.

Haste, Cate. *Keep the Home Fires Burning: Propaganda in the First World War.* London: Penguin, 1977.

Hibberd, Dominic. *The First World War.* London: Macmillan, 1990.

Owen, Wilfred. *War Poems and Others.* London: Chatto & Windus, 1973.

Poupard, Dennis, ed. *Twentieth-Century Literary Criticism.* Vol. 27. Detroit: Gale Group, 1988.

Stallworthy, Jon. *Wilfred Owen.* London: Oxford University Press, 1970.

Arcadia

by

Tom Stoppard

S ir Tom Stoppard, often thought of as the quintessential contemporary English play-wright and gentleman, was actually born Tomas Straussler in Zlin, Czechoslovakia, on July 3, 1937. Stoppard took the name of his stepfa-ther, Kenneth Stoppard, a British officer who married his mother after his natural father was killed during the Second World War. In the 1960s Stoppard began to write plays that treat a breathtaking variety of topics, from nuclear physics to metaphysics. Stoppard's early play, *Rosencrantz and Guildenstern Are Dead*, which retells the story of *Hamlet* from the point of view of its most minor characters, was a huge success when it premiered in 1966. Stoppard's subse-quent plays include *The Real Inspector Hound* (1968), *Jumpers* (1972), *Travesties* (1974), *The Real Thing* (1982), *Hapgood* (1988), and *The In-vention of Love* (1997). While known primarily as a playwright, Stoppard has also written both fic-tion (*Lord Malquist and Mr. Moon*, 1966) and screenplays, including those for *Brazil* (1986), *Empire of the Sun* (1987), and *Rosencrantz and Guildenstern Are Dead* (1991). Most recently, Stoppard won the Best Screenplay Oscar for the 1998 film *Shakespeare In Love*. Like this film, Stoppard's *Arcadia* moves back in time, explor-ing history to tell us more about our own era.

Events in History at the Time the Play Takes Place

Chronological note. *Arcadia* takes place in the same room during two different time periods:

THE LITERARY WORK

A play set in Derbyshire, England, from 1809-1812 and in "the present"; first published and performed in 1993.

SYNOPSIS

Three modern-day scholars—a literature don, a historian, and a mathematician—convene at Sidley Park to try to piece together the past history of the Park and its inhabitants.

1809-1812, and "the present" day. The plot has characters from the contemporary era trying to learn about the historical characters, and the two time periods are set before the viewer for com-parison and contrast.

The Napoleonic Wars (1792-1815). The Napoleonic Wars were a series of conflicts be-tween the French and most of the other Euro-pean powers. The French troops intended at first to defend and spread the republican ideals of the French Revolution (1789), but the war soon turned into French conquest for its own sake. By 1809, when the earlier part of *Arcadia* is mainly set, the French Empire under Napoleon con-trolled nearly all of Europe, including Belgium, Luxembourg, Spain, Prussia, and most of Italy. This left Britain essentially alone to oppose France.

Napoleon was eventually brought down by his own vast ambitions. In 1813 a new coalition of

Tom Stoppard

European powers finally managed to raise an army greater than Napoleon's, and they began to liberate nations one by one. In 1814, this coalition invaded France, reaching Paris in March. Napoleon abdicated and was exiled in Elba for a year. However, he escaped and returned to France in 1815 to raise his final army. England, Russia, Prussia, and Austria swiftly and effectively opposed him, bringing Napoleon to defeat at Waterloo in June of 1815. The Napoleonic Wars are an important, if unseen, backdrop to *Arcadia*. For Lady Croom, the war is merely an inconvenience to travelers: "The whole of Europe is in a Napoleonic fit, all the best ruins will be closed, the roads entirely occupied with the movement of armies, the lodgings turned to billets and the fashion for godless republicanism not yet arrived at its natural reversion" (Stoppard, *Arcadia*, p. 41).

Lord Byron and Romanticism. While Lord Byron, also known as George Gordon (1788-1824), never actually appears in *Arcadia*, he is nevertheless a major presence in the play. One of the key plot points concerns whether Lord Byron ever visited Sidley Park, and what he may or may not have done during his stay there.

Lord Byron is an actual literary and historical figure, a poet and satirist whose very name has become synonymous with Romantic masculinity;

we speak even today of a "Byronic" hero. Stoppard's fictional protagonist Septimus Hodge is a friend of Byron's from both Harrow (middle/high school) and Trinity College (Cambridge University), and in *Arcadia*, Septimus and Byron move in the same literary and social circles.

Both Byron's life and work exemplify important qualities of the Romantic Movement, which emphasizes individuality, high emotions, irrationality, spontaneity, sensuality, and imagination. Romanticism was a rebellion against classical and neoclassical values, which included reason, moderation, the intellect, tradition, and observance of aesthetic and moral rules. Romantic writers like Byron, Percy Bysshe Shelley, his wife Mary Shelley, Samuel Taylor Coleridge, William Wordsworth, and others lived lives full of passion and imagination—they traveled widely, wrote intensely, and had various love affairs (see **"England in 1819" and Other Poems** by Percy Bysshe Shelley, **Frankenstein** by Mary Shelley, and **Lyrical Ballads** by Wordsworth and Coleridge in *WLAIT 3: British and Irish Literature and Its Times*).

Byron's fictional behavior in Stoppard's *Arcadia* certainly reflects aspects of the poet's real life. One of the play's modern characters, the literature professor Bernard Nightingale, tries to figure out why Lord Byron left England so suddenly in the year 1809. The solution he comes up with is wrong, but the mystery is historically a real one—Byron did in fact suddenly and mysteriously leave England, and to this day no one knows why. In the play, Byron has affairs with all the play's adult female characters; in real life, Byron was very promiscuous and had affairs with women across Europe, most notoriously with his own married half-sister Augusta, Mary Shelley's niece Claire, and Lady Caroline Lamb.

Byron is today admired not only for his literary works (e.g. the epic poems *Childe Harold's Pilgrimage* (1812-18) and **Don Juan** (1819-24) (in *WLAIT 3: British and Irish Literature and Its Times*) but for his zestful and passionate life. When he wasn't writing, traveling, or attending to his various mistresses, Byron was challenging himself to swim across the Dardanelles (a strait connecting the Aegean Sea and the Sea of Marmara), or leading a brigade of Greek revolutionaries in their war against the Turks. In *Arcadia*, Septimus Hodge, like his friend Byron, is also a wit, a literary critic, and a seducer of women who gets challenged to a duel.

Sir Isaac Newton and classical physics. In *Arcadia*, Septimus Hodge teaches Lady Thomasina the scientific and mathematical principles that were current in the early nineteenth century. These principles were drawn almost entirely from the work of Sir Isaac Newton (1643-1727). Newton's work figures into *Arcadia* in several important ways, but perhaps the most important concepts can all be explained in terms of Newton's three laws of motion: 1) unless a force operates upon them, objects in motion stay in motion and objects at rest stay at rest; 2) the change of motion in an object is proportional to the force exerted upon that object; 3) for every action, there is an equal and opposite reaction. All three laws deal with Newton's discovery of force, which is actually now measured in units called newtons. Force is in fact the basis for Newton's famed law of gravity as well. Newton discovered that any particle of matter in the universe attracts any other with a force varying directly as the product of the masses and inversely as the square of the distance between them. The moon and the earth, for example, attract each other in proportion to their masses, which keeps the one orbiting around the other. Newton called the force that keeps the moon circling around the earth *gravitas*, a Latin word that literally means "heaviness" or "weight."

In *Arcadia*, these Newtonian ideas inspire a lot of confidence in the universe. If objects that are in motion remain in motion, for instance, then we don't need to worry that the planets will one day suddenly stop dead in their orbits. All motion is predictable. The planets will keep moving in their elliptical paths the way each and every atom in the universe moves—according to Newton's laws—and they will all presumably keep moving that way forever and ever. This idea does cause the characters some philosophical problems. For instance, Septimus poses the question, "If everything from the furthest planet to the smallest atom of our brain acts according to Newton's law of motion, what becomes of free will?" (*Arcadia*, p. 5). In other words, if all the motion in the universe is governed by physical law, do human beings have any real choice about their actions?

Newton's deterministic laws of motion turned out not to be the only laws governing the universe. Early nineteenth-century scientists like the Anglo-American Benjamin Thompson (1753-1814), and the Frenchman Sadi Carnot (1796-1832) made discoveries that laid the groundwork for what would come to be called the science of thermodynamics, or the study of heat. Thompson argued that heat was a form of motion and

not a substance: when its molecules move quickly, a thing is hot; when they move slowly, a thing is cold. Thus heat and motion are *essentially the same science*. Carnot's work showed that there is no way for a perfectly efficient engine to exist because working engines give off heat, which escapes and cannot be used productively as an energy source. Therefore no engine produces enough power to run itself—the energy output of a machine is always less than the energy input. This may seem obvious, but the fact that heat escapes, that things move from hotter to colder and not the other way around, contradicted an important consequence of Newton's laws, which suggest that physical events are reversible, that they can run backwards as well as forwards. Where Newton's laws of motion suggested a universe that would keep moving forever, the science of thermodynamics suggested that energy escapes a system over time, and thus the universe is slowly growing colder and slowing down.

The science of thermodynamics therefore was the first major challenge to the Newtonian Universe. While historically, the laws of thermodynamics were not formulated until later in the nineteenth and twentieth centuries, *Arcadia*'s Lady Thomasina turns out to be a scientific genius. Sidley Park happens to be in possession of an early steam engine, and Thomasina, though brought up with Newtonian ideas, figures out that "Mr. Noakes's engine cannot give the power to drive Mr. Noakes's engine" (*Arcadia*, p. 87). With this stroke of brilliance, Thomasina contradicts Newton, anticipates thermodynamics, and profoundly shocks her tutor Septimus, who realizes that "the Improved Newtonian Universe must cease and grow cold. Dear me." (*Arcadia*, p. 93).

Landscape gardening. In the modern part of the play, gardening historian Hannah Jarvis notes that:

> The history of the garden says it all, beautifully. There's an engraving of Sidley Park in 1730 that makes you want to weep. Paradise in the age of reason. By 1760 everything had gone—the topiary, pools and terraces, fountains, an avenue of limes—the whole sublime geometry was ploughed under by Capability Brown. The grass went from the doorstep to the horizon and the best box hedge in Derbyshire was dug up for the ha-ha so that the fools could pretend they were living in God's countryside.
>
> (*Arcadia*, p. 27)

In other words, Sidley Park has experienced all three of the main styles that characterize eighteenth- and nineteenth-century landscape gardening: the neoclassical, the natural, and the picturesque. Until 1760, Sidley Park's garden and grounds had been designed in the *neoclassical* style, which technically speaking isn't landscape gardening at all, but really a form of architecture. The neoclassical style emphasized geometric precision, so that for instance the garden at Hampton Court Palace was characterized by avenues radiating out from a central point like the spokes from the hub of a wheel.

Landscape gardening properly refers to the movement in eighteenth-century English gardening in which gardens were modeled on landscape paintings. As such, it was a rebellion against the formal, classical garden. Landscape gardeners were inspired by "nature," or rather famous paintings of nature. In trying to make the landscape seem more *natural*, landscape gardeners did away with the fences (or in the case of Sidley Park, hedges) that divided the formal gardens from the larger parkland that comprised an aristocratic estate. Gardeners instead substituted a *ha-ha*, a sunken ditch that was invisible from the house but kept a large estate's grazing animals—like cows and sheep—out of the garden proper without destroying the illusion of one single, sweeping vista. The famous gardener Lancelot "Capability" Brown (1715-83) created a number of "natural" landscapes consisting mainly of grass, irregularly shaped lakes, and clumps of trees.

However, Capability Brown's view of nature came to be itself challenged by a style known as the *picturesque*. The argument of the picturesque style is that "real" nature is messy and disorganized, characterized by chaos—rotting trees, overgrown ruins, waterfalls, swamps, jutting cliffs and the like. Of course, all of these elements—the trees, the ruins, the cliffs—would be carefully constructed in the new garden by an expert designer. In *Arcadia*, the fictional nineteenth-century landscape gardener Richard Noakes has plans for Sidley Park that include such features as "gloomy forest and a towering crag," "ruins where there was never a house," "water dashing against rocks where there was neither a spring nor a stone," "a fallen obelisk overgrown with briars," and—lest we forget—a hermitage (*Arcadia*, p. 12).

The rise of the waltz. It might be difficult to imagine now, but the waltz used to be considered an unsophisticated and even a scandalous dance. Coming from the German word *waltzen*, which means tramping, the waltz was born in

the eighteenth century as a German peasant dance. Other nations became interested in the waltz in the years after the French Revolution, which stimulated an interest in folklore and other cultures. However, England didn't begin to accept the waltz until about 1810, during the time when *Arcadia* is set. While the waltz quickly became a social phenomenon, it was still considered risqué. Unlike the minuet, the highly precise and formal dance that had previously dominated upper-class society, the waltz forced couples into a close embrace and sent them whirling around the room at dizzying speeds. (The speeds then were, in fact, much faster than today's waltzes.) Doctors claimed that waltzing would cause injury. Moralists claimed that the waltz was indecent and would corrupt European youth. But the flying, gliding freedom of the waltz was perfectly in tune with the Romantic spirit of the era. Lord Byron wrote a poem about waltzing in 1812, "The Waltz; An Apostrophic Hymn," in which he described "Hands promiscuously applied/Round the slight waist, or down the glowing side" (Byron, *The Poetical Works*, p. 277). In 1812 in *Arcadia*, Lady Thomasina begs Septimus to teach her how to waltz, promising that "If mama comes I will tell her we only met to kiss, not to waltz" (*Arcadia*, p. 92). Apparently Thomasina would rather be discovered having an affair with her tutor than dancing the scandalous waltz!

The Play in Focus

Plot summary. *Arcadia*'s seven scenes (scenes 1-4 constitute Act 1; 5-7 constitute Act 2) all take place in one garden-front room of the Sidley Park estate during two different times, the early nineteenth century and "the present." The last scene takes place simultaneously in the two time periods, although the characters are separated by time and do not interact with each other. The set for both times is the same: the room is furnished sparsely with a large wooden table and chairs and an architect's stand. Over the course of the play, the table accumulates items from both periods.

ACT 1, Scene 1 (1809). Thirteen-year-old Lady Thomasina Coverly is studying with her tutor, Septimus Hodge; motionless on the table is Septimus's pet tortoise, Plautus. Thomasina asks Septimus an unexpected question about sex. She has overheard that Mrs. Chater, their houseguest, was discovered in "carnal embrace" in the gazebo and wants to know what carnal embrace means. Septimus realizes that he himself has been

Thomasina interrupted at her studies, from a 1997 stage production of *Arcadia* at the University of Iowa.

caught. He has been having an affair with Mrs. Chater. A servant brings him a letter from Ezra Chater, Mrs. Chater's husband, challenging Septimus to a duel. Septimus puts the letter into the book he is reading and planning to review, an epic poem by Mr. Chater called "The Couch of Eros." Shortly thereafter Mr. Chater himself storms into the room, wanting vengeance. Septimus placates Chater by persuading him that his wife was only trying to get him a good review.

Lady Croom, Thomasina's mother, sweeps in, upset about the gazebo. Chater and Septimus immediately assume she is condemning the love affair, when, in fact, she is merely complaining that the gazebo is about to be demolished by the landscape gardener Mr. Noakes, who is redoing the Sidley Park grounds in the picturesque style. Noakes shows the group his drawing book of the proposed new landscape. It contains, among other features, a decorative hermitage. Lady Thomasina, in a fit of whimsy, draws a picture of a hermit into Mr. Noakes's book.

Scene 2 (the present). Writer Hannah Jarvis is temporarily living at Sidley Park because she is researching a book about its gardens. In particular, Hannah is interested in the hermit who lived there—whose only known likeness appears in the surviving copy of Mr. Noakes 1809 gar-

den book. Rumor has it that the hermit lived in the garden for years, scribbling endless pages about how the world was coming to an end. Hannah considers the hermit a perfect symbol of "the Romantic sham," which she conceives of as "the decline from thinking to feeling" (*Arcadia*, p. 27).

A literature don named Bernard Nightingale arrives but lies about his identity; he doesn't want Hannah to know who he is because he wrote a terrible review of her last book. Bernard tells Hannah that he is doing research on the minor poet Ezra Chater. But Bernard's real identity is soon exposed; he is actually a famous scholar of Romanticism and Lord Byron. Bernard has found "The Couch of Eros" in Lord Byron's library, and that copy contains a challenge from Ezra Chater to a duel. (This copy of "The Couch of Eros," as we already know, actually used to belong to Septimus, and the challenge was made to Septimus also.) But Bernard is convinced that Byron dueled with Chater and killed him, which solves the famous mystery as to why Lord Byron fled England in 1809. Hannah thinks Bernard's theory is wrong, but admits that her research has revealed that Sidley Park's tutor, Septimus Hodge, was a classmate of Byron's.

Scene 3 (1809). Back in the past, during her morning lessons, Thomasina tells Septimus that she thinks her mother is in love with Lord Byron, who is in fact currently a guest at Sidley Park. She also tells Septimus that at breakfast that morning, Lord Byron revealed that Septimus actually wrote a terrible review of Ezra Chater's last book. Septimus tries to change the subject by criticizing Thomasina's math homework: Lady Thomasina is trying to develop mathematical equations that describe not just simple curves and lines but natural shapes like leaves and flowers.

Lady Croom's brother Captain Brice and Mr. Chater storm in. Chater is even angrier than before about Septimus's affair with his wife, since he no longer believes that Septimus will give his poem a good review. Chater again challenges Septimus to a duel, and Septimus objects that he is not the only one having an affair with Mrs. Chater—Captain Brice is too—whereupon Captain Brice also challenges Septimus to a duel. Septimus wearily accepts them both, saying that he will fight Chater the next morning at 5:00 A.M., and that he "can fit [Captain Brice] in at five minutes after five" (*Arcadia*, p. 42).

Scene 4 (the present). Jumping forward to the present again, the play shows Hannah reading Thomasina's math books to Valentine Coverly, the heir of Sidley Park and himself a mathematician: "I, Thomasina Coverly, have found a truly wonderful method whereby all the forms of nature must give up their numerical secrets and draw themselves through number alone" (*Arcadia*, p. 43). Valentine says that Thomasina must have been lying. What Thomasina claims to have discovered—fractal geometry and iterated equations—has only been known for the last 20 years.

Hannah informs Bernard that Captain Brice married Mrs. Chater in 1810—so presumably Mrs. Chater was a widow by 1810. Bernard is thrilled. He thinks this supports his theory that Byron killed Chater. Hannah points out that Bernard has no proof—in fact, Bernard can't even prove that Byron was ever at Sidley Park. Valentine pipes up that Lord Byron certainly was at Sidley Park—in the game books, there is a record of Byron shooting a hare. Bernard is thrilled at this news.

Hannah asks Valentine why Thomasina couldn't have done iterated equations in 1809, since they're not that complicated, mathematically speaking. Valentine, exasperated, explains that there was not enough time or enough paper back then—what we can do today in seconds with a calculator or computer would have taken Thomasina years and years, and reams of paper. Valentine concludes that anyone who did end-less, boring calculations on paper would a) have to have a really good reason for doing it and b) would have to be essentially insane.

ACT 2, Scene 5 (the present). Bernard is reading his research paper to Hannah, Valentine, Valentine's sister, Chloe Coverly, and Valentine's mute "genius" brother, Gus Coverly. Bernard is rehearsing for a press conference he will be giving in London. He plans to announce that Lord Byron killed Ezra Chater and fled England to escape murder charges. Hannah points out that Bernard fails to mention all the evidence that does not fit his theory.

Before he leaves for London, Bernard shows Hannah an excerpt from a book which describes the Sidley Park hermit and his pet tortoise Plautus. Hannah then reads Valentine a letter she has found, which claims that the hermit was driven insane by: "Frenchified mathematick that brought him to the melancholy certitude of a world without light or life . . . as a wooden stove that must consume itself until ash and stove are as one, and heat is gone from the universe" (*Arcadia*, p. 65). This surprises Valentine; the letter seems to be describing the Second Law of Thermodynamics. But thermodynamics—like iterated equations—hadn't been discovered yet. Hannah notes that the Sidley Park hermit was born in 1787—the same year as Thomasina's tutor Septimus Hodge.

Scene 6 (1809). Back in the past again, it is early in the morning and we hear the sound of a shot. But it isn't the duel; it is just Septimus shooting a rabbit. Septimus has been waiting for the duel, but the butler informs him that during the previous night Mrs. Chater was discovered having an affair with Lord Byron, and Lady Croom threw all of them—the Chaters, Byron, and Captain Brice—out of the house! Byron is on his way to Europe and has taken Septimus's copy of "The Couch of Eros" with him; the Chaters and Captain Brice are going on an expedition to the West Indies.

Scene 7 (1812 and the present, simultaneously). The modern characters are preparing for a fancy dress ball to be held at Sidley Park in nineteenth-century costume. Bernard's sensational theory has made all the newspapers, giving rise to headlines such as "Bonking Byron Shot Poet" (*Arcadia*, p, 74). Valentine confesses to Hannah that he's working on Thomasina's equations. He's done what she couldn't do—put her equations into a computer—and he plans to publish the results. But Valentine still doesn't believe that Thomasina realized what she had accomplished.

He claims that if Thomasina had really discovered iterated equations she'd have been famous. But Hannah tells Valentine that Thomasina didn't have time to be famous—she died in a fire the night before her seventeenth birthday. If anyone knew about and understood Thomasina's discovery, says Hannah, it would be her tutor, Septimus Hodge.

At this point a young man rushes into the room—he looks like Valentine's brother Gus, but he is really Lord Augustus, Thomasina's brother (who is played by the same actor.) Sixteen-year-old Thomasina chases her brother in, and for the first time modern and historical characters occupy the same stage at the same time. Septimus arrives, separates the fighting siblings, and sits them down to take their drawing lesson. Thomasina asks Septimus if he liked her latest mathematical equation—it is, we understand now, an iterated equation—and explains that she didn't have enough paper to finish working on it. Septimus studies Thomasina's math book.

Elsewhere on the stage, among the present-day characters, Hannah is studying the same math book. Valentine explains to her that iterated equations are the mathematics of nature. If the laws of thermodynamics mean that the world is going to end, then iterated equations may show how this world started and how the next world may begin.

The early nineteenth-century Septimus puts down Thomasina's equations and picks up his own book to read. He then shows the book to Thomasina; it is a French essay about heat. Thomasina reads the essay, and suddenly we hear the rhythmic pounding of a steam engine in the distance. Mr. Noakes is using a new engine to dig up the garden.

Lady Croom enters carrying a pot of dahlias, which have come from the West Indies. She tells us that Mr. Chater died in Martinique of a monkey bite, and that Captain Brice has married Mrs. Chater.

Thomasina finishes reading the French essay and announces that, just as she thought, Newton's theories are incomplete. Just as Newton's geometry does not describe nature, Newton's theories of motion don't account for the way heat works. Thomasina sits down and tries to draw a picture of what she means.

Lady Croom complains to Mr. Noakes that if he is going to build a hermitage in her garden, he ought to supply her with a hermit to live in it.

Thomasina leaps up and gives her drawing to Septimus, explaining that it shows how you can never get the same power out of a heat engine that you put into it. In fact, usable energy is always decreasing—this is the Second Law of Thermodynamics.

Lady Croom is understandably puzzled by Thomasina's statements, and suggests that perhaps Thomasina has had enough education—it may be time for her to get married. Thomasina meanwhile has been continuing to draw. This time she has sketched a portrait of Septimus and his tortoise, Plautus. Lord Augustus takes possession of the picture, and all leave the room.

ENGLISH COLONIALISM IN THE CARIBBEAN

In *Arcadia*, several characters go off on a Caribbean expedition. In fact, the English were the dominant colonial power in the West Indies during the nineteenth century. By the early part of the century, they controlled Dominica, Saint Lucia, Saint Vincent, Tobago, Grenada, Trinidad, Barbados, Jamaica, Nevis, Antigua, and Montserrat among other places. They did not control Martinique, the French colony from which Lady Croom receives an exotic plant, the dwarf dahlia, in the play. British interests in the West Indies focused on the trade of slaves, sugar, and manufactured goods. Often the Englishman went there only temporarily, setting up plantations, then leaving them to function—and profit—in his absence while he himself returned home.

The present-day Bernard arrives and Hannah tells him the bad news: Ezra Chater wasn't killed by Byron; he died of a monkey bite in Martinique. She has found this information in Lady Croom's gardening diary, where Lady Croom explained how she came by her exotic dahlias. Hannah plans to correct Bernard publicly in the *Times* the next day. The modern characters put on period costumes for that night's ball and leave the room to pose for a picture.

The light changes; night falls.

Septimus enters the dark room carrying an oil lamp and Thomasina's mathematical papers. A few minutes later Thomasina sneaks in wearing her nightgown. She has come to beg Septimus to teach her to waltz. Someone is playing piano in the next room, but not a waltz. While they wait for the right music, they discuss Thomasina's scientific theories.

Hannah and Valentine enter the room in period dress. Valentine is excited because he's realized what Thomasina's first drawing means. It's a diagram of heat exchange, and now Valentine believes that Thomasina really was a genius who discovered the Second Law of Thermodynamics ahead of her time.

Septimus is at that very moment learning about the Second Law directly from Thomasina. He is also realizing to his horror what the Second Law means—that the universe is doomed to go cold and die. Septimus doesn't know what to do in the face of this devastating knowledge, but Thomasina remains cheerful: if you are facing the end of the world, she tells him, all you can do is dance. Septimus takes Thomasina into his arms and begins to teach her the waltz. He stops, kisses her intensely, and then they continue waltzing.

SAFE AND SAFER SEX

The upper-class characters in the early-nineteenth-century part of *Arcadia* seem to enjoy relatively carefree sexual affairs in contrast to the late-twentieth-century characters. Although AIDS (acquired immune deficiency syndrome) was identified as early as 1981, the disease didn't really reach widespread public consciousness until the mid to late 1980s. A fatal disease that still has no cure, AIDS effectively ended an era of careless or carefree sex and ushered in an era of safe sex. *Arcadia*'s modern characters live—and even joke about—this new, grimmer world. As Valentine notes, "My mother's lent [Bernard] her bicycle. Lending one's bicycle is a form of safe sex, possibly the safest there is" (*Arcadia*, p. 51).

Bernard rushes back into the room. Chloe's mother has discovered that Chloe and Bernard have been having an affair. Bernard grabs his jacket and heads for the door, wishing Hannah good luck with her book. Hannah says that she can guess who the Sidley Park hermit was, but she can't prove it.

Septimus stops the waltz lesson and tells Thomasina she should go to bed, reminding her to be careful with her candle. Thomasina asks Septimus to come to bed with her, but Septimus refuses. Thomasina then refuses to leave Septimus. They will dance again, once more, in celebration of her seventeenth birthday tomorrow.

The mute Gus Coverly comes into the room with a present for Hannah. He has found Thomasina's second picture, the drawing of Septimus and Plautus. This is the final piece of evidence that Hannah needs to prove that Septimus Hodge became the Sidley Park hermit. Hannah now knows that Septimus and the hermit were the same age, that Septimus/the hermit had a pet tortoise named Plautus, that Septimus/the hermit spent the rest of his life working on Thomasina's equations in the hermitage, that Septimus/the hermit knew about both iterated equations and thermodynamics, and that Septimus/the hermit had a reason to devote himself obsessively to this task. He was probably driven to madness by his grief at the sudden death of his beautiful and brilliant student. Gus then bows to ask Hannah to dance, and the play ends with the two couples—Septimus and Thomasina, Gus and Hannah—whirling around and around and around.

From Waterloo to Waterloo—things fall apart. Tom Stoppard's play *Arcadia* takes place in two different time periods: the early nineteenth century and the late twentieth century. One of the important ideas of the play concerns the discovery of the Second Law of Thermodynamics, which says that the amount of usable energy in the universe is decreasing. In other words, things decay; systems become more disorderly and less effective over time.

Stoppard illustrates this point by implicitly comparing the two time periods of his play. Metaphorically speaking, we can see things decaying even in the relatively short time span of two hundred years. For instance, the earlier part of the play is set from 1809-12, during the time when, as Lady Croom notes, "Europe is in a Napoleonic fit" (*Arcadia*, p. 41). Napoleon had extended the French empire throughout Europe (see entry above), conquering practically every major European power except for Great Britain. As the English audience for *Arcadia* already knows, the British Empire, led by the Duke of Wellington, would eventually bring Napoleon down at the famous Battle of Waterloo, which took place in 1815 and represented the beginning of a century of British world domination.

The only hint of the triumph of Waterloo present in *Arcadia*'s modern era is the implied reference to London's Waterloo Train Station, where the Eurorail train from Paris terminates. Literature professor Bernard Nightingale tells us that he found Lord Byron's books when the house they were in was "sold to make way for the Channel Tunnel Rail-link" (*Arcadia*, p, 30). Consider that England and France have historically been enemies (as they were during the

Napoleonic wars). Consider that England has always felt protected from Europe, because it is an island separated from the mainland by the English Channel. Then think about what it means for the English that the Channel Tunnel has been built, allowing trains to move easily between England and the continent. The Channel Tunnel has taken away England's island defenses, and has linked it, rather controversially, to France in particular and to Europe more generally. Arguably, England is no longer strong enough to exist entirely separately from Europe; the Channel Tunnel thus can be seen as a symbol of England's global decline.

An English audience would understand how profoundly England has changed between the Battle of Waterloo (1815) and the digging of the tunnel to Waterloo Station (1987-1991), and might well think that the changes have not been for the better. *Arcadia*'s modern era suffers in comparison to the earlier time in other ways as well. For instance, the nineteenth-century character Septimus Hodge is a brilliant wit, scientist, literary critic, and lover. He reads physics in French, translates Shakespeare into Latin, reviews poetry, teaches drawing, dances the waltz. He is, in short, a man of many and various talents. In the modern era, the characters of Bernard Nightingale, Hannah Jarvis, and Valentine Coverly are all *specialists*. They have a particular area of expertise and cannot move fluidly between different areas of knowledge the way Septimus can. They don't even dance well! Even in terms of sex, the nineteenth-century characters triumph. They have numerous affairs and intrigues, while their modern counterparts are all essentially celibate, save for the Bernard-Chloe affair which is painted as essentially sordid and unsatisfactory. In short, Stoppard seems to be saying that the world has grown worse since the early nineteenth century—we know less, love less, have less grace, charm and adventure, and have generally lost status and power—and that this is perfectly in accord with what science would tell us to expect.

However, there are certainly grounds in *Arcadia* for a contrary argument. From a late-twentieth-century perspective, the early-nineteenth-century world Stoppard describes is problematic in terms of class, race, and gender. The characters we see are primarily wealthy aristocrats, and so their lives are certainly not indicative of how things were for the average English person at the time. Some of Stoppard's characters travel to the West Indies, but Stoppard doesn't mention that England was the dominant colonial power there,

or that the colonies were dependent on slave labor. Stoppard does a little better when it comes to women: he recognizes that, even though she's a genius, Lady Thomasina's formal education would shortly have come to an end; as her mother notes, it's about time for Thomasina to get married. Unlike Septimus, Thomasina would not have been able to study at Cambridge. Modern woman Hannah Jarvis, on the other hand, has been able to pursue her studies and remain unmarried yet respectable.

Overall, *Arcadia* asks us to compare nineteenth- and twentieth-century scholars, lovers, dancers, and England. In each case, the play seems to find the former century superior to the latter. However, it is up to the reader to weigh all the evidence and decide if the nineteenth-century grass was actually greener.

THE CHANNEL TUNNEL RAIL LINK

Also called the "Eurotunnel" or the "Chunnel," the Channel Tunnel runs for 31 miles underneath the English Channel and connects Folkstone, England to Calais, France. The idea of constructing a tunnel to Europe was revived in 1986 and caused a controversy which lasted for years. England has always had a diffident relationship to Europe in general and to France in particular. As an island, England has often been protected from events on the continent. However, with the advent of the Chunnel, that island status has been significantly compromised. Dug between 1987 and 1991, the Channel Tunnel officially opened in May, 1994, a year after *Arcadia* premiered in England.

Sources and literary context. As noted, Tom Stoppard's *Arcadia* makes reference to a number of real people and events. Obviously Lord Byron was a real poet; less obviously, he did have an affair with Lady Caroline Lamb, the subject of Hannah Jarvis's previous book. More obscurely, the play's Newcomen Steam Engine was named for the actual English engineer, Thomas Newcomen (1663-1729), who improved heat engines early in the eighteenth century.

The scientific ideas that *Arcadia* refers to—Newton's laws of motion, thermodynamics, iterated equations, fractal geometry, Fermat's last theorem, and so on—are also real. As Stoppard explained to the journalist David Nathan, "I got tremendously interested in a book called *Chaos* by James Gleick which is about this new kind of mathematics. . . . I thought, here is a marvelous metaphor. But, as ever, there wasn't really a play until it had connected with stray thoughts about other things" (Nathan, p. 13). Some of Stoppard's stray thoughts were literary. Most of the poems and books *Arcadia* refers to are also real: Byron's "Childe Harold's Pilgrimage" and his *English Bards and Scotch Reviewers*, Horace Walpole's *The Castle of Otranto*, and Ann Radcliffe's **The Mysteries of Udolpho** (in *WLAIT 3: British and Irish Literature and Its Times*). Stoppard's only real invention was Ezra Chater and his apparently terrible poem, "The Couch of Eros," and even he reflects reality in that his verse typifies poor literature of the era.

Other characters in *Arcadia* seem to be based on real people. For example, Lady Croom's fictional gardener Richard Noakes evokes the real gardener Humphry Repton (1752-1818). Repton was the first to advertise himself specifically as a landscape gardener and, like the fictional Mr. Noakes, was famous for making picture books that provided "before" and "after" views of the gardens on which he worked. Similarly, in 1812 Septimus Hodge shows Thomasina a prize-winning French essay from the Scientific Academy in Paris. While Stoppard never names the scientist, the Baron Jean-Baptiste Joseph Fourier (1768-1830) won the prize of the French Academy of Sciences in 1811 for his mathematical description of heat in solids. Septimus tells Thomasina that she is the French scientist's prophet, and in fact Fourier did go on to make some of the same discoveries that Thomasina makes in *Arcadia*.

Events in History at the Time the Play Was Written

The quest for knowledge in the age of technology. If Stoppard's historical and modern characters have one thing in common, it's that they are all curious about the world and how it works. They deeply desire to learn and to make discoveries, both literary and scientific. Hannah wants to learn about the Sidley Park hermit; Bernard wants to learn about Byron; Thomasina and Valentine, in different eras, want to learn about the relationship between mathematics and nature. In fact, Hannah Jarvis claims that "It's wanting to know that makes us matter. Otherwise we're going out the way we came in" (*Arcadia*, p. 75).

Valentine Coverly, the present heir of Sidley Park, is a scientist, and one of his roles is to explain a number of recent scientific discoveries that are central to the plot of the play. In particular, Valentine explains to Hannah (and to us, the audience) iterated equations, fractal geometry, and the importance of computers in mathematics.

As Valentine eloquently explains, an iterated algorithm "is an algorithm that's been . . . iterated" (*Arcadia*, p, 43). Eventually he does manage to come up with a more precise definition. Take a simple algebraic equation like $2x + 1 = y$. If, say, $x = 1$, then $y = 3$ ([2 x 1] + 1 = 3). If $x = 2$ then $y = 5$, and so on. In an iterated equation, you feed your answer back into the question, making your value for y into your next value for x. So, to iterate the sample equation above ($2x + 1 = y$): if $x = 1$, then $y = 3$, if $x = 3$ then $y = 7$, if $x = 7$, then $y = 15$, and so on. Thomasina actually discovered iterated equations back in her time, but nobody recognized the fact because she died so young. Thomasina calls her iterated equation a "rabbit equation" because "It eats its own progeny"—in other words, the solution of the equation is "fed" back into it, just as rabbits sometimes eat their own offspring (*Arcadia*, p. 77).

It turns out that, as Thomasina suspected, many natural phenomena can be described by using iterated equations, where the answer feeds back into the question. For instance, population biologists—who, like the play's Valentine Coverly, try to find equations that explain the rise and fall of animal populations—use iterated equations. Last year's ending population y is the starting point for this year, or is this year's x. The iterated equation into which each year's x is fed to determine y is designed to describe and predict how the population will rise and fall depending on external factors, like famine or an abundant food supply.

Year	Starting Population (x)	Δ	Ending Population (y)
1995	10,000	Δ	15,000
1996	15,000	Δ	13,000
1997	13,000	Δ	12,000
1998	12,000	Δ	19,000
1999	19,000	Δ	21,000

In the example above, the ending population for 1995 (15,000) is the starting population for 1996 (15,000) and Δ stands for the transformation, or the equation, that turns each of the starting numbers into the ending numbers. The equation in the above examples always stays the same. What

Valentine is trying to do with his game books (which provide a whole bunch of starting and ending numbers representing the varying population of birds on the estate) is to discover the iterated equation that describes the population change.

But iterated equations are not just for population biologists. They are also the basis for something called fractal geometry. In 1809 Thomasina decides to iterate her equations because she is trying to draw pictures of leaves and flowers on a graph. She doesn't want her x and y graphs to be just boring old lines and arcs. It turns out that iterated equations, when plotted extensively on a graph with millions of numbers—plotted more extensively than Thomasina could ever do with pen and paper—can make pictures that look a lot like leaves, snowflakes, and mountains! As Thomasina says, she has discovered "a truly wonderful method whereby all the forms of nature must give up their numerical secrets and draw themselves through number alone" (*Arcadia*, p. 43).

But these graphs take millions of numbers to turn into recognizable pictures, and one of the key points of *Arcadia* is that Thomasina wasn't able to push enough different numbers through an equation with just a paper and pencil. Presumably even Septimus Hodge, alone in his hermitage, wasn't able to put enough different points onto the graph to make an equation draw itself like a leaf or a snowflake. Computers, however, make such tasks comparatively easy. They can do thousands of calculations in mere seconds.

Computers are a twentieth-century invention. John V. Atanasoff built the first electronic digital computer in 1939, and the first stored-program computers were introduced in the late 1940s. The desktop personal computer is an invention of the 1970s and 1980s, and the laptop computer that Valentine uses to do his grouse research in *Arcadia* was top of the line at the time. It enables him to calculate infinitely more quickly than anyone in the past would have dreamed possible. In the remaining 22 years of his life, Septimus, the hermit, could not perform the number of calculations that Valentine can do with a personal computer in a month. *Arcadia* shows another use for Valentine's computer. He employs it to compare some anonymous essays to actual samples of Lord Byron's writing, hoping to determine whether or not Byron actually wrote the essays. While some scholars of literature have used computers to authenticate anonymous prose, many (like Bernard) are skeptical

about a computer's ability to make sophisticated literary judgments. Literature professors want to make discoveries, too, but appear to prefer the human touch.

Reception. *Arcadia* was almost instantly a critical and public success, winning both the Olivier and the Evening Standard awards for Best Play of 1993, and moving from the Royal National Theatre to the West End for a long and profitable run. The expression "*almost* instantly" is used because the reviews of the play immediately after its premiere were more mixed. The daily reviewers may at first be divided roughly into two groups: those who "got" the play, and those who did not. *Arcadia*'s references to various complicated, intellectual subjects obviously make it something of a challenge. Some reviewers, like Michael Coveney, confessed themselves, "enthralled . . . but frankly perplexed" (Coveney, p. 57). Coveney went so far as to title his article "Head-Scratching in Stoppard's *Arcadia*."

There were still differences of opinion among those critics who did get the play's difficult concepts. Some found the play clever but emotionally dry: "It is elegant, complicated, densely argued, serenely inconclusive and cold as ice," writes John Peter in *The Sunday Times* (Peter, sec. 9, p. 12). Others found *Arcadia* to be a romantic and spiritual experience: "[T]ears prick the eyes. . . . [The] production achieves an emotional resonance that goes too deep for words," confessed Charles Spencer in the *Daily Telegraph* (Spencer, p. 18). This division—between thinking and feeling—is actually a theme of *Arcadia* itself. In fact, the deepest divide over Tom Stoppard's work as a whole concerns whether he is capable of touching an audience's heart as well as its brain.

In any case, critical consensus was quickly reached: *Arcadia* is currently thought to be Stoppard's finest play. Charles Spencer spoke for many when he wrote, "I have never left a new play more convinced that I'd just witnessed a masterpiece" (Spencer, p. 18).

—Francesca Coppa

For More Information

Alwes, Derek B. "'Oh, Phooey to Death!': Boethian Consolation in Tom Stoppard's *Arcadia*." *Papers on Language & Literature* 36, no. 4 (fall 2000): 392-405.

Bloom, Harold, ed. *Tom Stoppard*. Modern Critical Views. New York: Chelsea House, 2000.

Byron, (George Gordon). "The Waltz; An Apostrophic Hymn." In *The Poetical Works of Lord Byron*. London: Oxford University Press, 1996.

Coveney, Michael. "Head-scratching in Stoppard's *Arcadia*." *The Guardian*, 18 April 1993, 57.

Gleick, James. *Chaos: Making a New Science*. London: Penguin, 1988.

Gussow, Mel. *Conversations With Stoppard*. London: Nick Hern, 1995.

Jenkins, Anthony. *The Theatre of Tom Stoppard*. Cambridge: Cambridge University Press, 1989.

Lahr, John. "Blowing Hot and Cold: Chaos Meets History in a Brilliant New Play." *New Yorker,* 17 April 1995, 112.

Nathan, David. "What's Tom Stoppard's New Stage Play All About?" *Sunday Telegraph*, 28 March 1993, 13.

Peter, John. "What Time Is It?" *The Sunday Times*, 18 April 1993, sec. 9, p. 12.

Spencer, Charles. "Stoppard's Thrilling Workout." *The Daily Telegraph*, 26 May 1994, 18.

Stoppard, Tom. *Arcadia*. London: Faber and Faber, 1993.

Brideshead Revisited

by
Evelyn Waugh

Arthur Evelyn St. John Waugh was born in London on October 28, 1903. His father, Arthur Waugh, was the director of the Chapman and Hall publishing company. Educated first at Lancing College and then at Oxford, Evelyn Waugh studied art and tried his hand at both teaching and journalism before settling down to write full-time. Waugh's body of works is usually divided by scholars into three distinct categories. Those works written before 1939 are mainly witty and savage satires of Britain in the interwar years. They include *Decline and Fall* (1928), *Vile Bodies* (1930), *Black Mischief* (1932), and *A Handful of Dust* (1934). During and after the Second World War, Waugh, like many other authors of his generation, started writing novels that were more reflective, more spiritual, and greater in scope. *Brideshead Revisited* (1945), the first of these, was described by Waugh as "an attempt to trace the workings of the divine purpose in a pagan world" (*Brideshead* in Gardiner, p. 536). Other works of this period include *Helena* (1950), about the mother of Catherine the Great, the wartime trilogy: *Men at Arms* (1952), *Officers and Gentlemen* (1955), and *Unconditional Surrender* (1961). Waugh also wrote nonfiction, including a number of travel books, biographies, and the first part of an autobiography, *A Little Learning*. To a great extent, all of Waugh's work is autobiographical, based on people that he knew, experiences that he had, and places that he visited. However Waugh's tone and purpose in each of the different categories can vary considerably. *Brideshead Revisited*, written while

> ## THE LITERARY WORK
>
> A novel set in the English countryside during World War II, with reflections back to 1923; published in 1945.
>
> ## SYNOPSIS
>
> While supervising training exercises in the countryside, an army Captain traces his own development by recollecting his interactions with the Flyte family.

Waugh himself was on leave from the army in 1944, shows his growing nostalgia for the now-lost world he once so bitingly satirized.

Events in History at the Time the Novel Takes Place

World War I (1914-18). The earliest events in *Brideshead Revisited* take place in 1923, five years after the end of the First World War, yet the war hangs over the novel and its characters. Touted as the war to end all wars, the conflict pitted the Central Powers (primarily Germany, Austria-Hungary, and Turkey) against the Allies (France, Great Britain, Russia, Italy, Japan and, from 1917, the United States). Both sides fought with new, modern weaponry—machine guns, mustard gas, barbed wire, airplanes. These are the basic, easily understood facts; more difficult to grasp is the effect of the war on the world's psyche, and for

Evelyn Waugh

our purposes, the British psyche. The death-count of this war far surpassed any in previous wars: over 8,500,000 soldiers died of wounds or disease. Forecasters predicted that the war would be over in six months: it lasted four years. Comprised of eager volunteers, the original British Army was all but wiped out by November of 1914, a mere three months into the war. New volunteers were sought, and when these had died in the trenches, conscription began. An entire generation of British men were killed—fathers, sons, brothers, husbands, lovers, friends. The few who survived returned home suffering from a condition the world had never known before—shell shock, which covered a broad range of psychological and nervous disorders. Soldiers broke down mentally from the constant bombardment of bullets, grenades, shells and bombs. The human, social, and geographic destruction of the war was unprecedented and unexpected, and thus the world was totally unprepared for it. As the poet Edmund Blunden wrote later: "Neither race had won, nor could win, the War. The War had won, and would go on winning" (Blunden in Fussell, p. 13).

The interwar years: Oxford, the Lost Generation, and the rise of aestheticism. The generation of men who came of age in the years after World War I carried a burden that they inherited from their fathers and older brothers.

On the one hand, they felt as if they'd missed their chance for wartime patriotism and bravery; on the other hand, they were highly critical of these same values: they had survived to see the devastation that such values had wreaked on the world. The result was in many ways a cynical and disillusioned generation, often labeled the "Lost Generation." Theirs was a disillusionment that took many different forms. At Oxford University in the 1920s, the disillusion was expressed by a resurgence of the cult of aestheticism, a late-nineteenth-century movement that argued that art exists for its own sake, and that it doesn't serve any political, didactic or moral purpose. In its nineteenth-century form, aestheticism was a reaction against the perceived ugliness of the new industrial age. But in the years after the First World War, aestheticism was a reaction against the Victorian values (including manly seriousness, duty, and responsibility) that were seen as having produced the war. In contrast, aesthetes prized effeminacy, triviality, drunkenness, and the appreciation of beauty and art for its own sake. The aesthetic persona was designed as a rebuke to the manly, athletic types who had previously dominated Oxford life and who represented parental values. To be an aesthete was therefore to be anti-establishment.

According to Paul Fussell, the "war" that young aesthetes were fighting against the establishment was a kind of substitution for the actual war that they had missed. These young men couldn't fight the Great War, but they could fight a war of their own: "The sensitive and the intelligent conceived of their relations with the rest of the university as a form of fighting. The lines were drawn: on one side, aesthetes, wits, subversives, and winners; on the other, dons, hearties, 'stooges,' and 'losers'" (Fussell, p. 110).

Throughout the first book of *Brideshead Revisited*, which is called "*Et In Arcadia Ego,*" we see these battle lines drawn. At Oxford, Charles Ryder, Sebastian Flyte, Anthony Blanche, and their aesthetic friends define themselves against various dons, bullies, athletes, and dutiful "Victorian" types such as Charles's cousin Jasper. Jasper scolds Charles by noting that he has fallen "straight, hook, line and sinker, into the very worst set in the University"—a group of aesthetes (Waugh, *Brideshead Revisited*, p. 41).

Anglo-Catholicism and the Oxford Movement. The Oxford Movement sought a renewal of Roman Catholic thought and practice within the Church of England. It started in the early part of the nineteenth century (1830s and 1840s), at a time when old laws requiring that corporate or government personnel be members of the Church of England were repealed. Up until that point, the Church of England drew a lot of its moral authority from its privileged position in relation to the government. Now that the connection between church and state was weakening, many Anglicans wanted to compensate by showing that the Church of England, or Anglican Church, had the same authority as the Roman Catholic Church: the Anglican Church taught Christian Truth and its bishops were part of the Apostolic Succession (in other words, that they could trace their offices back in an unbroken line to the Apostles.)

Some important leaders of the Oxford Movement were John Henry Newman (1801-90), John Keble (1792-1866), and Edward Pusey (1800-82). Newman was the author of 24 of the *90 Tracts for the Times*, a series of documents that asserted the authority of the catholic church to be absolute ("catholic" in this context meaning "faithful to the teaching of the early and undivided church"). These Anglican clergymen believed the Church of England to be a "catholic" church in these terms.

The Oxford Movement gradually spread its influence throughout the Church of England. Some of the results were increased use of ceremony and ritual in church worship, the establishment of Anglican monastic communities for men and women, and better-educated clergy who were more concerned with the care of their church members. However, not everyone approved of this trend. Some Anglicans strongly resisted the attempt to bring Roman Catholic doctrines, prayer, and ritual back into the Church of England. They also disliked the increased role and influence of women in church affairs, feeling that such actions were improper for Victorian "ladies." This dislike even extended to women participating in the sacrament of confession: presumably well-bred ladies either had no sins or should not be compelled to voice their sins aloud. Moreover, these Anglicans felt that the elaborate rituals of Catholicism were not quite "manly," and dismissed many of the young men attracted to ritualism as unmanly, unnatural, and un-English. In the other camp, many so-called Anglo-Catholics, or Anglicans in the Oxford Movement, came to feel that there was not *enough* Roman Catholic influence in the Church of England and decided to convert to Roman Catholicism itself. John Henry Newman himself converted to Catholicism in 1845 and eventually became a cardinal.

The fight between "manly" Anglo-Christianity and "unmanly, un-English" ritualized Anglo-Catholicism continued to rage throughout the nineteenth century and well into the twentieth. Most of the characters of *Brideshead Revisited* participate in this argument in one way or another. For example, the character Sebastian is urged by his mother to participate in the Newman Club while at Oxford, and Charles's cousin warns Charles to "beware of the [Oxford] Anglo-Catholics" since "they're all sodomites with unpleasant accents" (*Brideshead*, p. 26). In other words, Anglo-Catholics were perceived by the mainstream not only as unmanly foreigners, but also as not properly "English."

"ET IN ARCADIA EGO"

"Et In Arcadia Ego," the title of the first book of *Brideshead Revisited*, is often translated in two different ways. Ironically, the wrong translation—"And I have dwelt in Arcadia, too," or "Here I am, in Arcadia"—is generally the more popular. The emphasis here is on Arcadia being a rural paradise in which one lives a contented, simple existence. This translation has a sense of optimism—I, too, lived in that wonderful place. However, the correct translation is a lot bleaker: "Even in Arcadia, I, Death, hold sway." Death is the "I" who is speaking—Death is all around us, even in Arcadia.

The General Strike of 1926. In a general strike, laborers in a number of different industries stop working in a collaborative attempt to achieve economic or political goals. A general strike is therefore a form of collective bargaining. In 1926, the Trades Union Congress orchestrated one of the largest of all general strikes in support of Great Britain's coal miners. Some 3 million out of the nation's 5 million union members went on strike on May 4, 1926. Prime Minister Stanley Baldwin declared a state of emergency and organized volunteers to provide essential services to the population. Like many people, Baldwin felt that the general strike was a precursor to a political revolution, which meant it had to be stopped at any cost. He therefore refused to negotiate with the unions until the strike was called off. On May 12, 1926, when the workers realized that they were unable to stop important services from running, they ended the strike.

Chapter Eight of *Brideshead Revisited* begins, "I returned to London in the spring of 1926 for the General Strike" (*Brideshead*, p. 200). The character Charles Ryder comes home from Paris to be a government volunteer; he, like many others, is convinced that the strike "foretold revolution and civil war" (*Brideshead*, p. 201). It is important to remember that the communist Russian Revolution had happened less than a decade earlier, so that it seems almost logical to expect "Revolution—the red flag on the post office, the overturned tram, the drunken N.C.O.'s, the gaol open and gangs of released criminals prowling the streets" (*Brideshead*, p. 201). As noted above, young men of this era felt that they had missed the chance to be in the First World War—a fact that helps explain why some of them were so eager to participate in the conflict prompted by the General Strike.

In the end, the class war that people feared never did transpire; the strike lasted only eight days. The novel's Charles Ryder joins a unit whose job is to deliver milk, and the most "action" he sees is a small street fight at an intersection.

Spanish Civil War (1936-39). In Spain in 1936, the Nationalists, led by General Francisco Franco, revolted against the Republican government. The fear, on Franco's side, was that the Republican government would usher in revolutionary programs and upset the status quo. Support for the Nationalists came from Fascist Italy and Nazi Germany; the Republicans received support from the Soviet Union, France, and Mexico. Technically, Britain remained neutral in the Spanish Civil War, refusing to sell arms to either side, but many individual British citizens volunteered for service in the conflict, and generally they fought on the Republican side.

In hindsight, it is easy to see that the Spanish Civil War prefigured the Second World War: Italy and Germany on the one side, France and the Soviet Union on the other. The foes, in fact, tried out in Spain many of the military tactics that they would use in World War II. Franco and the Nationalists triumphed in 1939, after three long bloody years of conflict.

The Spanish Civil War hovers in the background of the later chapters of *Brideshead Revisited*, with several of the characters participating in one way or another. Cordelia Flyte, Sebastian's youngest sister, goes to Spain as part of the ambulance corps and stays to help refugees once

the fighting ends. Lord Marchmain, Sebastian's father, is living in Italy for most of the novel but returns home to England when the political situation in Italy becomes dangerous for British citizens. In the novel, as in reality, the Spanish Civil War shows the international situation rapidly declining into brutal conflict, and prefigures the more devastating changes for Europe that would be brought about by World War II.

The Novel in Focus

Plot summary. *Brideshead Revisited* begins with a short prologue. Captain Charles Ryder is moving from one army training camp to another in middle England in 1944; he is enmeshed in the routines, drudgeries, and drab hierarchies of army life. When he arrives at the new camp, he asks, "What's this place called?" and the unspoken answer—Brideshead—triggers the memories that constitute the rest of the novel (*Brideshead*, p. 15).

The novel is divided into two parts. Book One, "Et In Arcadia Ego," focuses on Ryder's homoerotic friendship with Sebastian Flyte, whom he meets at Oxford and with whom he experiences London, Venice, and the Flyte family's manor home of Brideshead. Book Two, "A Twitch upon the Thread," is focused on Ryder's affair with Sebastian's sister Julia ten years later, and how that affair brings him back into the sphere of the Flyte family and from there to a spiritual awakening.

Book One: "Et In Arcadia Ego." Charles's introduction to Lord Sebastian Flyte at Oxford University in 1923 is both unusual and prophetic: the drunken Sebastian leans through Charles's window and vomits. To apologize, Sebastian sends flowers to Charles and a friendship is born. Sebastian introduces Charles to his circle of friends, including the aesthete Anthony Blanche, who talks nonstop of gossip, literature, and love affairs, and stutters for dramatic effect. Sebastian also takes Charles to visit Brideshead Castle, but chooses a day when his family is not there. Charles is disturbed when Sebastian refers to Brideshead not as his home, but as "where my family live" (*Brideshead*, p. 35).

Over the summer vacation Charles goes home to his father, a cold man with a dry wit. A telegram from Sebastian—"Gravely injured. Come at once."—allows Charles to escape to Brideshead (*Brideshead*, p. 74). Sebastian is in a wheelchair, having cracked a tiny bone in his foot. At Brideshead, Charles briefly meets Sebastian's sister Julia, who is just leaving, and then

Anthony Andrews (left) as Sebastian Flyte, Diana Quick as Julia, and Jeremy Irons as Charles Ryder in front of Castle Howard in Yorkshire, England, the setting for the 1981 television adaptation of *Brideshead Revisited.*

spends some weeks alone with Sebastian, painting and drinking large quantities of wine. Sebastian and his family are Catholics, which is relatively rare in England, so Charles begins to question Sebastian about his religious faith. Sebastian believes in Catholic doctrine but finds it hard to observe. He also describes variations in how the various members of his family—a brother, two sisters, and his parents—practice the faith:

> [W]e're a mixed family, religiously. Brideshead and Cordelia are both fervent Catholics; he's miserable, she's bird-happy; Julia and I are half-heathen; I am happy, I rather think Julia isn't; Mummy is popularly believed to be a saint and Papa is excommunicated—and I wouldn't know which of them was happy."
> (*Brideshead*, p. 89)

In fact, Sebastian's parents, Lord and Lady Marchmain, are separated, (though not divorced, as Catholics don't believe in divorce). Lord Marchmain lives in Venice with his mistress Cara, and Lady Marchmain resides in England. By the end of this visit, Charles has met Sebastian's brother Brideshead and his sister Cordelia, and is surprised to find that they really are fervent Catholics who talk about religion all the time.

Sebastian suggests that Charles come with him to visit his father in Venice. Charles is nervous, but finds Lord Marchmain and his mistress Cara to be like any other socially respectable couple. However, Cara tells Charles that despite the calm appearances, Lord Marchmain hates his wife and Sebastian hates his mother; furthermore, she believes that Lady Marchmain represents something inside themselves that they are hating. Lastly, Cara warns Charles that Sebastian is drinking too much, and that if he does not take care, he will become a drunkard.

In the fall, Sebastian and Charles return to Oxford, only to find that a lot of their aesthetic friends have left school. Charles meets Lady Marchmain when she comes to Oxford to consult a history professor, Mr. Samgrass, who is helping her write a book about her brothers, soldiers who died in World War I. Soon after this, Sebastian, Charles, and a casual friend called Boy Mulcaster are arrested for public drunkenness (and in Sebastian's case, the more serious crime of drinking and driving) after attending a party given by Julia and her new, boorish boyfriend, Rex Mottram. They are all eventually let off with fines, but after this, Sebastian begins to feel haunted by Mr. Samgrass, who has been charged by Lady Marchmain to keep an eye on him. This leads to a very bad cycle for Sebastian, who rebels and drinks more the more he is watched.

The cycle worsens; Sebastian drinks ever-increasing amounts. Lady Marchmain tries to stop him by tightening her control over him, but this

ALCOHOLISM AND HOMOSEXUALITY WITHIN LIMITS

During a trip to Venice, Lord Marchmain's mistress Cara gives Charles two warnings about his friend Sebastian: first, that "Sebastian is in love with his own childhood," and second, that "Sebastian drinks too much" (*Brideshead*, p. 103). All the novel's characters drink much more alcohol than most people today would think healthy, although people today often regard teenage drinking as commonplace, if regrettable. There is a popular attitude that teenagers will grow out of their desire to get drunk. However, there is no longer the sense that homosexuality is a youthful indulgence and that adolescents will grow out of it. In the novel, Cara believes that romantic friendship between young men is a temporary phase to be eventually outgrown. A period of homosexuality is acceptable in a young man's life, but, as with his drinking, Sebastian overdoes it, refusing to grow out of what the novel sees as an adolescent sexuality. There were other parallels drawn between alcoholism and sexuality at the time of the novel too. Society variously labeled both as sins, crimes, and diseases, despite the labels being contradictory. Moreover, the new field of psychology tried to "cure" alcoholism and homosexuality with similar techniques. ("Aversion therapy," which used poisons or electric shocks to dissuade patients from their habit, was developed to treat alcoholism and later used to treat homosexuality—the "cure" was ineffective in both cases.) Finally, people looked to religion to help the homosexual as well as the alcoholic. Alcoholics Anonymous (AA) was in fact founded in 1935 by Robert Holbrook Smith and William Griffith Wilson, who were strongly influenced by the Oxford Movement.

only makes Sebastian a more deceptive alcoholic. When she asks Charles for advice, her appeal makes Sebastian think that Charles has gone over to his mother's "side," and the friendship between the two men weakens. Finally, Sebastian is caught drinking at Oxford shortly after a visit from his mother. Again, Lady Marchmain seeks

Charles's advice; again, Charles tries to warn her that the more she watches her son, the worse he will get. Disregarding the warning, Lady Marchmain pulls Sebastian out of Oxford and sends him abroad with the hated Mr. Samgrass. Charles finds Oxford depressing without Sebastian and drops out to attend art school in Paris.

Back at Brideshead for Christmas, Charles learns that the situation has deteriorated from bad to worse. Sebastian escaped Mr. Samgrass and went off traveling and drinking with Anthony Blanche instead. Now at home again, Sebastian has been given no money and no alcohol. Charles is both sympathetic and horrified. Clearly, Sebastian has been drinking too much, but Charles believes that Sebastian's family bears the blame for turning him into a drunk due to their suspicion and mistrust. In Charles's opinion, treating Sebastian like an alcoholic only encourages him to be deceptive; if the family were not so insistent and controlling, Sebastian might not be so defensive and determined to drink. Charles has made up his mind to treat his friend like a normal person, so when Sebastian asks him for money, Charles gives it to him. This comes to Lady Marchmain's attention and upsets her greatly. Charles leaves Brideshead at her request, thinking that he is leaving the house and its inhabitants behind for good.

Charles learns what happened after he left by talking to others. Over dinner in Paris, Rex Mottram tells Charles that Sebastian ran away while Rex was trying to take him to see a doctor in Switzerland. Rex also gives Charles news about the rest of the family: most importantly, Rex wants to marry Julia, and Lady Marchmain has fallen seriously ill. Charles later reads in the paper that Rex and Julia were married quietly, which is unusual for aristocrats of their wealth and stature. Filling in the details, Charles then gives the reader the full story. Rex was planning to convert to Catholicism in order to marry Julia, but it turned out that he had already been married and divorced in his native Canada. Since divorced people can't be married in the Catholic Church, the Marchmain family canceled the wedding. However, Julia rebelled against this, and decided to marry Rex anyway. The scandal associated with marriage to a divorced man keeps most society people away from the wedding. This is a great disappointment to Rex, who wanted to marry Julia precisely because of her lofty social connections. Thus, Julia and Rex's marriage is troubled from the start.

Charles returns to London in 1926 to serve as a government volunteer during the General Strike and meets up with Anthony Blanche and Boy Mulcaster. From them, Charles hears more news: Sebastian has settled in Tangier with a disabled German solider. Finding Charles, Julia asks him to bring Sebastian home; Lady Marchmain wants to see her son before she dies. Charles obligingly flies to North Africa and finds Sebastian in the hospital; drink and sickness have taken their toll. In the end, Lady Marchmain dies without ever seeing Sebastian again, but Charles stays with Sebastian until he is well enough to go home, after which Sebastian chooses to return to his German soldier. Sebastian explains to Charles that he'd rather look after someone else than be looked after himself. Nevertheless, Charles continues to look after Sebastian, arranging for him to get an allowance from his family. Book One ends with Charles having dinner with Cordelia, who explains that even though it seems like Lord Marchmain, Sebastian, and Julia have all left the Catholic Church, "God won't let them go for long, you know" (*Brideshead*, p. 220). But things look bleak for the family's Catholic faith; after Lady Marchmain's death, the Roman Catholic chapel at Brideshead Castle is closed down.

Book Two: "A Twitch upon the Thread." Book Two picks up the story ten years later. Charles, we learn, has married Boy Mulcaster's sister Celia, has had two children, and has become a respected artist. We also learn that the marriage is not going well. Charles and his wife are aboard an ocean liner, crossing back from America to England; Julia also happens to be on board. A storm hits the ship, making most of the passengers sick, but Julia and Charles are both good sailors and spend a lot of time together. They catch up on each other's lives and begin having an affair: Charles tells Julia that he loved her brother Sebastian, who was "the forerunner," presumably to his relationship with her (*Brideshead*, p. 257).

Back in England, Charles and Julia continue their affair while both are still married—Charles's wife Celia is totally involved in her world of art and fashion; Julia's husband Rex, now a politician, is busy worrying about the Spanish Civil War, the rise of Hitler, and the possibility of war with Germany. The affair continues for more than two years, during which time Charles and Julia move in together at Brideshead. Then Lord Brideshead, Sebastian's older brother, arrives with plans to marry. This causes two problems

for Charles and Julia: first, Bridey wants to live at Brideshead Castle, and second, his pious bride will not share living space with a couple who are living in sin. This upsets Julia greatly—she is hurt by her brother's holier-than-thou attitude, and bothered by her own conscience. Julia and Charles finally decide to divorce their spouses and get married.

Next Cordelia comes back to Brideshead; she has been helping war victims in Spain. Cordelia reports that she has seen Sebastian; he is now at a monastery in Tunis. He had wanted to become a monk, but, too sick to do so, he has become an under-porter at the monastery instead. Cordelia thinks that Sebastian will stay there, sometimes drunk, sometimes not, until he dies.

Sebastian is not the only one who is sick; his father, Lord Marchmain, is now fatally ill, and decides that because of the political situation in Italy he will come home to Brideshead to die. Lord Brideshead and Cordelia are eager for their father to be reunited to God and the Catholic Church before his death. Julia feels ambivalent about this idea, and Charles is downright hostile to it, believing that they are essentially blackmailing a dying man. As Lord Marchmain's health deteriorates, the family argues about whether or not to get a priest to give him the sacrament of last rites. They try, but Lord Marchmain sends the priest away. Lord Marchmain's health continues to fail, but there are moments when he rallies and tells stories about the family history. Finally, he slips into a near-coma. This time Julia calls the priest, who gives the unconscious Marchmain the last rites. To their relief, Lord Marchmain makes the sign of the cross, thus accepting the sacrament. He dies that night, and Julia and Charles end their relationship.

The short epilogue returns us to Brideshead in 1944. In the prologue, there were hints that Charles had converted to Catholicism after his break-up with Julia. Now we see Captain Ryder stop into the re-opened chapel to pray. He returns to camp "looking unusually cheerful," having renewed his faith by remembering the past (*Brideshead*, p. 351).

Revaluing the past. Most of the critics of *Brideshead Revisited* find the novel elitist in its nostalgia. Narrator Charles Ryder seems to long for the "good old days" of the 1920s—for the aristocratic privileges, class snobbery, and luxurious wealth of that era, which he finds vastly superior and more civilized than the drab, egalitarian Britain of 1944. Waugh seemed to like dwelling in that earlier world as well, for the two parts of his novel are not equally proportioned. Nearly twice as much narrative time is spent in the 1920s than in the 1930s and 1940s.

But to think that the novel is only looking back to the 1920s is to miss an important part of the story. *Brideshead Revisited* is primarily a novel of religious conversion. All the lost sheep—Sebastian, Julia, Lord Marchmain, and then, finally, Charles Ryder himself—are eventually converted or reconverted back to the Catholic faith. To convert to Catholicism, from the point of view of the novel, is to connect oneself back to the "one true church," and to the earliest Christians, the Apostles. To become a Catholic is to reconnect oneself both to God and to an ancient, deep-rooted history.

Castle Brideshead itself embodies this connection to God and history. "Why is this house called a 'Castle'?" Charles asks Sebastian early in the novel:

> "It used to be one until they moved it."
> "What can you mean?"
> "Just that. We had a castle a mile away, down by the village. Then in Inigo Jones's time we took a fancy to the valley and pulled the castle down, carted the stones up here and built a new house."
>
> (*Brideshead*, p. 79)

So Brideshead itself is an older house than it appears: it was rebuilt from the stones of an ancient castle by the famous architect Inigo Jones (1573-1652), who designed not only Charles I's famous Banqueting House and the Queen's House at Greenwich, but supervised the restoration of the old St. Paul's Cathedral. At the end of the novel, the dying Lord Marchmain fills in another part of Brideshead's history:

> You can see where the old house stood near the village church; they call the field 'Castle Hill'. . . . They dug to the foundations to carry the stone for the new house. . . . Those were our roots in the waste hollows of Castle Hill, in the briar and nettle; among the tombs in the old church and the chantrey where no clerk sings.
>
> (*Brideshead*, p. 332)

The "old house" is connected to the "old church"—and so is the Marchmain family itself, through the old family tombs located there. House, family, and church were once all rooted in the same spot. "We were knights, then," Lord Marchmain explains, "barons since Agincourt; the larger honours came with the Georges" (*Brideshead*, p. 332). The Marchmain family history dates from before Agincourt, the famous battle that Henry V fought and won against the

French on St. Crispian's Day (see *Henry V* in *WLAIT 3: British and Irish Literature and Its Times*). The Battle of Agincourt was quite literally a miraculous victory; won against incredible odds, it was thought to symbolize God's approval of Henry V and the British cause. So Lord Marchmain is not only establishing his family's heritage as noblemen, or even as Englishmen, but as specifically God-sanctioned Catholic Christians. In Henry V's time, Britain was a Catholic country—it would be a later king, Henry VIII, who would bring Protestantism to England.

Thus, for Charles Ryder to "revisit" Brideshead is not, as it seems at first glance, only for him to remember his visits there in the 1920s. Rather, Captain Charles Ryder—a soldier in another perilous British battle: the Second World War—revisits a house that has come to represent British history, British victory, and British Catholic faith in times of crisis. Captain Ryder finds strength in the small red flame he sees burning in the Brideshead chapel. The flame represents the presence of the Eucharist, and in the closing paragraphs of the novel, Charles notes that it "burns again for other soldiers, far from home, farther, in heart, than Acre or Jerusalem. . . . [T]here I found it this morning, burning anew among the old stones" (*Brideshead*, p. 351). Charles Ryder, a modern soldier, draws strength from the ancient flame that the soldiers in the religious Crusades carried with them to Acre and Jerusalem. No wonder Charles returns to his camp looking "unusually cheerful"; he's drawn courage from an ancient historical and religious past. Charles may feel lost in this modern war and this modern world, but the red flame of faith now burns inside of him the way it burns among the old stones of Brideshead, connecting both of them invisibly to the past.

Sources and literary context. Like his protagonist Charles Ryder in *Brideshead Revisited*, Evelyn Waugh was a soldier in the British Army during World War II. Waugh had seen active service earlier in the war, but by 1942 he had been relegated to noncombatant status and was stationed at various training posts in Britain itself, which gave him some time to think about writing a new novel. The event that triggered *Brideshead* happened in 1943, when Waugh went to visit a dying friend, Hubert Duggan, and persuaded his reluctant family to call in a priest. Like Lord Marchmain, Duggan crossed himself after receiving the sacrament. Waugh referred to the moment in his diary: "we spent the day watching for a spark of gratitude and saw the spark" (Waugh, *Diaries*, p. 553).

The protagonist-author (Ryder-Waugh) and dying father-dying friend (Marchmain-Duggan) connections are not the only autobiographical ones; in fact, *Brideshead Revisited* is based on so many autobiographical elements that Waugh had to insist in an Author's Note to *Brideshead Revisited*: "I am not I; thou are not he or she; they are not they" (Waugh, p. v). Robert Murray Davis identifies sources of incidents and characters in the novel:

> Waugh drew the arrest for public drunkenness . . . from an episode involving him and his aristocratic co-defendant Matthew Ponsonby in 1925. Anthony Blanche is based upon a blend of the characters and tastes of Brian Howard and Harold Acton. Lord Marchmain's family and exile abroad . . . have obvious origins in Lord Beauchamp and the Lygon family. Minor characters like Mr. Samgrass and Rex Mottram have been linked with Sir Maurice Bowra, a popular Oxford don with whom Waugh maintained a mutually derisive friendship for most of his life, and Brendan Bracken, Winston Churchill's wartime minister of information.
>
> (Davis, p. 6)

Although Waugh certainly drew upon his own circle of friends at Oxford and elsewhere for inspiration, his novel transcends the particular circumstances of his own life. *Brideshead Revisited* is one of a number of religious-themed novels that appeared in Britain in the late 1940s. The experience of war made many British writers turn their minds and pens to religious themes: for example, W. H. Auden and T. S. Eliot wrote poetry infused with Christian themes and imagery, and Graham Greene wrote such Catholic-themed novels as **The Power and the Glory** (1940; also in *WLAIT 4: British and Irish Literature and Its Times*) and *The End of the Affair* (1951).

Events in History at the Time the Novel Was Written

The Second World War (1939-45). World War II pitted the Allies (England, France, the Soviet Union, and other nations—including, eventually, the United States) against the Axis Powers (Germany, Italy, and Japan). From the British perspective, World War II was fought in three distinct phases.

The first phase was characterized by a number of German victories. Nazi Germany overran the Allied nations of Denmark, Norway, Belgium, Luxembourg, and finally, France. By June of 1940, Germany had conquered much of Europe, leaving Great Britain to fight the second phase—the "heroic" phase—alone. During this second phase, Britain mobilized against near-constant German bombing raids. In the last six months of 1940, 23,000 British civilians were killed. This bombardment is known as "The Battle of Britain." The third phase of the war, known as the "Grand Alliance" began in late 1941. Prompting this third phase were two events: first, the successful Soviet defense of Moscow, and second, the bombing of Pearl Harbor by the Japanese, which brought the United States into the war. The British had gained two very powerful allies: the Russians were fighting hard in the east, and the Americans were fighting hard in the west. Bit by bit, the Allies took back Europe, and the war finally ended in 1945.

The Second World War is generally considered to represent a time of unparalleled national unity for Britain. Historically, Britain was a country divided by class differences; the lines between the aristocracy, middle classes, and working classes had been very firmly drawn. But during the war, all of these socioeconomic classes worked together to defeat their common enemies. Everybody contributed: men and women alike, upper class and working class alike. Everybody made sacrifices: food, fuel, fabric and other resources were rationed to support the war effort. People who would never have met under ordinary conditions worked shoulder to shoulder during the war. As a result, British politicians began taking steps to ensure that everyone who had worked so hard to end the war would share equally in the benefits of peace. If the nation's inhabitants could work together in wartime, couldn't they also work together in peacetime?

The novel's Prologue and Epilogue show Charles Ryder living on the cusp of this newly egalitarian world and feeling somewhat lost in it. The language of his fellow soldiers indicates that they are from a number of different classes, mostly lower than his own. As noted, many people saw this class-intermingling as positive, but Charles seems only to notice that lots of soldiers have thrown cigarette butts and other garbage into the dry well of Brideshead Castle's beautiful fountain. Charles draws strength from his religious faith as he faces a new world brought about by the war.

"Young England" and the development of the welfare state. One of the ways that the British government planned to reward its citizens for their wartime efforts was with the development of the welfare state. Beginning in 1944, a number of acts were passed to improve housing, education, health insurance, and other benefits. The final years of the war thus brought about a radical reorganization of British society. In this context of national unity and optimism about the future, *Brideshead Revisited* sounds a sour note. Waugh does not appear to share the opinion that Britain is moving towards a new, more egalitarian future. Instead, his narrator, Captain Charles Ryder, looks with disdain upon the working-class members of his military unit and mourns the passing of his aristocratic world.

The new world is represented by Charles's military subordinate, Mr. Hooper, who is described as "a sallow youth with hair combed back, without parting, from his forehead, and a flat, Midland accent" (*Brideshead*, p. 7). In the class-conscious world of the novel, the Midland accent alone is enough to mark Hooper as a member of the working classes; he is precisely the sort of man whom Charles Ryder would never have had to speak to, let alone work with, in the years before the Second World War. However, Hooper is precisely the sort of young soldier that the welfare state intended to reward, and he comes to symbolize to Charles all the social changes that are in the air:

> In the weeks that we were together Hooper became a symbol to me of Young England, so that whenever I read some public utterance proclaiming what Youth demanded in the Future and what the world owed to Youth, I would test these general statements by substituting 'Hooper' and seeing if they still seemed as plausible. Thus in the dark hour before reveille I sometimes pondered: "Hooper Rallies," "Hooper Hostels," "International Hooper Co-operation" and "the Religion of Hooper."
>
> (*Brideshead*, p. 9)

Charles sees what he calls "the age of Hooper" on the horizon and finds it desolate and dreary, unlike the lush aristocratic world he remembers fondly throughout the novel. (Waugh's own dislike of the welfare state led him to consider emigrating to Ireland in 1947.) This nostalgic attitude was seen as unbearably snobbish, which greatly affected the reception accorded *Brideshead Revisited* when it was published in 1945.

Reception. In a "Warning" on the dust jacket of the 1945 edition, Evelyn Waugh declares what the novel aims to achieve:

> [It is] an attempt to trace the workings of the Divine purpose in a pagan world, in the lives of an English Catholic family, half-paganized themselves, in the world of 1923-1939. The story will be uncongenial alike to those who look back on that pagan world with unalloyed affection, and to those who see it as transitory, insignificant, and, already, hopefully passed. Whom, then, can I hope to please?
>
> (Waugh in Gardiner, p. 536)

Waugh's fears about the reception of his work were to some degree justified. While the book was generally well received in the United States, becoming a Book-of-the-Month Club selection, *Brideshead Revisited* faced a rockier reception in Britain. The book faced three serious obstacles there. First, it sounded a sour note about Britain's future just at the historical moment when Britain was celebrating its wartime victory and experiencing great optimism about its social future. Secondly, *Brideshead* is a novel about conversions to Catholicism, and Britain was—and is—a primarily Protestant country. Finally, and perhaps most importantly, many of the intellectuals whose job it was to review the book were Waugh's own friends and contemporaries at Oxford—people whom he had modeled his characters after, or satirized, in the novel. Waugh tried to address this in the aforementioned Author's Note by insisting that "I am not I; thou are not he or she; they are not they," but nonetheless trying to guess who was based on whom became a popular intellectual game.

Perhaps the most vocal critic of the novel was the American writer Edmund Wilson. Wilson, previously a great fan of Waugh's work, liked the first book of *Brideshead*. However, he thought that Book Two was "disastrous," full of "romantic fantasy," "dispiriting clichés," and "shameless and rampant" snobbery; it contained "no genuine religious experience," but was only "a Catholic tract," mere propaganda (Wilson, pp. 71-74). Wilson's charges of elitism and Catholic propaganda stuck to the novel, and dominated criticism for many years. Kingsley Amis summed up these two strands in a review entitled: "How I Lived In a Very Big House and Found God."

On the other hand, Paul Baumann expounds on an enduringly positive reaction to *Brideshead Revisited*, despite its flaws:

> Grappling with my addiction [to *Brideshead Revisited*], I found some comfort in learning that [novelist and critic] Anthony Burgess was similarly afflicted. Though he selected *Brideshead* as one of the best novels of the last fifty years, he readily acknowledged its glaring

flaws. "A sham and a snobbish sham," was the judgment of many critics, Burgess conceded. Waugh's romance with the doomed Flyte family was egregiously sentimental, the celebration of the landed aristocracy risible, the sex scenes ludicrous, the theology medieval by way of the Catholic Truth Guild. And a death-bed reconciliation to boot!

Yet Burgess confessed to having read *Brideshead* at least a dozen times. A dozen! As he noted, the novel somehow triumphs over its showy snobbery and idiosyncratic piety. "This is one of those disturbing novels in which the faults do not matter," Burgess professed. "It is a novel altogether readable and magical."

(Baumann, p. 6)

—Francesca Coppa

For More Information

Amis, Kingsley. "How I Lived in a Very Big House and Found God," *Times Literary Supplement,* 20 November 1981, 1352.

Baumann, Paul. "Flytes of Fancy," *Commonweal* 123, no. 2 (26 January 1996): 6.

Davis, Robert M. *Brideshead Revisited: The Past Redeemed.* Boston: Twayne, 1990.

Fussell, Paul. *The Great War and Modern Memory.* Oxford: Oxford University Press, 1975.

Gardiner, Harold C. "Follow-up on Waugh," *America* 74 (16 February 1946): 536.

Waugh, Evelyn. *A Little Learning: An Autobiography: The Early Years.* Boston: Little, Brown, 1964.

———. *Brideshead Revisited: The Sacred and Profane Memories of Charles Ryder.* Boston: Little, Brown, 1945.

———. *The Diaries of Evelyn Waugh.* Ed. Michael Davie. Boston: Little, Brown, n.d.

Wilson, Edmund. Review of *Brideshead Revisited,* by Evelyn Waugh. In *Evelyn Waugh: The Critical Heritage.* Ed. Martin Stannard. London: Routledge and Kegan Paul, 1984.

———. "Splendors and Miseries of Evelyn Waugh," *New Yorker,* 5 January 1946, 71-74.

Wirth, Annette. *The Loss of Traditional Values and Continuance of Faith in Evelyn Waugh's Novels: A Handful of Dust, Brideshead Revisited and Sword of Honour.* New York: Peter Lang, 1990.

The Buddha
of Suburbia

Hanif Kureishi

Hanif Kureishi was born in Bromley, a South London suburb, in December 1954. His mother was British; his father, an immigrant from India with family in Pakistan, was a civil servant whose true obsession was writing novels. The younger Kureishi read philosophy at King's College of the University of London, where he embarked on a career as a playwright. His play *Outskirts* won the George Devine Award in 1981, and in 1982 he became writer-in-residence at the prestigious Royal Court Theatre. In the mid-1980s he turned to screenwriting, debuting with *My Beautiful Laundrette* (1984), which garnered an Oscar nomination for Best Screenplay. Other films followed: *Sammy and Rosie Get Laid* (1987); *London Kills Me* (1991), which he directed; and *My Son the Fanatic* (1997), based on one of his short stories. *The Buddha of Suburbia* was Kureishi's first novel. He would subsequently write three more novels, *The Black Album* (1995), *Intimacy* (1998), and *Gabriel's Gift* (2001), and publish two short-story collections, *Love in a Blue Time* (1997) and *Midnight All Day* (1999). Throughout his career, Kureishi has also written essays. His novel *The Buddha of Suburbia* explores the new London being forged in the 1970s.

Events in History at the Time of the Novel

Immigration and racism. *The Buddha of Suburbia* takes place in the 1970s, but its events are in many ways determined by changes in England's

demography dating to the years after World War II. The ravages of that war called for massive efforts at rebuilding, but depleted the supply of potential workers. To meet the shortfall, Great Britain called upon citizens in its colonies and former colonies; by the mid-1950s, around 10,000 immigrants per year were arriving from India and Pakistan. India had just recently (in 1947) achieved independence from British rule and divided into two nations, India and Pakistan, now both members of the Commonwealth—those nations formerly under British rule. British recruitment combined with administrative changes in the dispersal of passports (the process was now localized in India and Pakistan rather than being centralized in London) helped stimulate a massive influx of new citizens. Roughly one million immigrants entered England in the decade from 1958 to 1968. As a result, Great Britain became a country increasingly ethnically

Hanif Kureishi

their economic footing in Britain by opening ethnic corner shops, grocers, restaurants, and laundrettes (the latter of which are celebrated in Kureishi's first film, *My Beautiful Laundrette*); others, like Haroon, the father of *The Buddha of Suburbia*'s protagonist, worked in better-paying jobs such as the Civil Service. In either case, people maintained ties with their heritages through Asian newspapers, which proliferated in Britain in the 1960s. The Urdu-language weekly *Mashriq* was followed by eight other weeklies in various Indian languages, as well as the English-language *India Weekly*.

The changing mix of British society frightened a portion of the native British population, who held racist views of Asian and African immigrants. In fact, the British government had to take official measures against racism. A 1965 Race Relations Act banned discrimination in public places, made the promotion of ethnic-based hatred an offense, and instituted a Race Relations board to handle complaints. A 1968 act banned ethnic discrimination in housing and employment, and a 1976 act called for a Race Relations Commission to further equality of opportunity and harmonious relations. Though these measures tried to address a current of disharmony, they did little to stem the mounting racism. Economic distress in the 1970s meanwhile fanned the fires of discontent. Inflation was rife, and attempts to reign it in were accompanied by rising numbers of unemployed workers. Unemployment soared from 3 percent in 1971, around the time the novel opens, to 5 percent in 1979, when it ends and Margaret Thatcher assumes power. It would climb still higher to 12.3 percent in 1983, after Thatcher mounted a no-holds-barred attack on inflation (Williamson, p. 202). Partially in reaction to this hardship, white extremists vented frustrations on Asians and Africans. Blaming them for joblessness, the extremists resorted to "Paki-bashing" and acts of violence. The Asians responded variously. For many, the 1970s became a decade of alienation in which Asian immigrants and their descendants felt they "had to look to their own defences and find strength in their own communities"; others, especially the young, saw a need for "more racial mixing and tolerance" (Williamson, p. 222).

Included in mainstream society were those who agreed with this last attitude. Racism was by no means a uniform response among white Britons. An anti-racist current manifested itself in such movements as Rock against Racism, a musical reaction to singer Eric Clapton's en-

mixed. Yet, as Kureishi remarked in 1990, it did "not yet have a vision of itself as a mixed place. The feeling is that blacks and Asians were invited to Britain to work, but maybe they'll somehow go back again. Britain still hasn't re-cast itself as a multi-racial, multi-cultural society" (Kureishi in Collins, p. 20). This was true particularly in the 1940s and '50s, when white Britons harbored appalling racist stereotypes of their new neighbors' former lifestyles. A 1948 survey suggested that many whites thought of those in the former British colonies as people who practiced cannibalism, lived in mud huts, ate strange foods, had "primitive" sexual urges, and were illiterate and uneducated. White Britons, moreover, were often not sensitive to the differences between various ethnic groups and tended to treat immigrants as if they were all alike.

The truth was that lifestyles and beliefs among the immigrants, as among white Britons, varied greatly. The immigrants hailed from various countries, spoke an assortment of languages, and practiced different religions. Nor were their experiences in their new home uniform. Some adopted the customs of their new environs, seeking to assimilate; others built communities based on customs from their homelands. Many found

THE NATIONAL FRONT AND ENOCH POWELL'S "RIVERS OF BLOOD" SPEECH

The Labour and Conservative parties were not the only ones on the British political scene of the 1970s. A notable feature of the decade was the emergence of the National Front, whose platform was almost solely anti-immigration, which prompted people to associate the party with fascist or neo-Nazi groups. The thuggery of some of its younger adherents, and their police-protected march through Lewisham, a South London suburb, on August 13, 1977, are featured in *The Buddha of Suburbia*. The National Front capitalized on sentiments that attained a veneer of respectability from such politicians as Member of Parliament (MP) Enoch Powell, who, Kureishi asserts, "helped to create racism in Britain and was directly responsible not only for the atmosphere of fear and hatred, but through his influence, for individual acts of violence against Pakistanis" (Kureishi, "Rainbow Sign," pp. 74-75). Powell articulated his racist policy in his famous "rivers of blood" speech (the phrase is from Virgil's epic poem *The Aeneid*), delivered in Birmingham on April 21, 1968. Here are the closing lines, in which Powell lambastes the Race Relations Bill of 1968 for "showing that the immigrant communities can organise . . . to overawe and dominate the rest with the legal weapons which the ignorant and ill-informed have provided":

> As I look ahead, I am filled with foreboding. Like the Roman, I seem to see, 'the River Tiber foaming with much blood.' That tragic and intractable phenomenon which we watch with horror on the other side of the Atlantic but which there is interwoven with the history and existence of the States itself, is coming upon us here by our own volition and our own neglect. Indeed, it has all but come. In numerical terms, it will be of American proportions long before the end of the century. Only resolute and urgent action will avert it even now.
>
> (Powell in Cosgrave, p. 250)

Some white Britons took such "officially" expressed sentiments to be endorsements of their own racism, which manifested itself in acts of violence against nonwhites. "Powell's awful prophecy was fulfilled: the hate he worked to create and the party of which he was a member, brought about his prediction," mourns Kureishi. "The River Tiber has indeed overflowed with much blood—Pakistani blood" (Kureishi, "Rainbow Sign," p. 94).

dorsement in a 1976 concert of the racist immigration policies that were being promoted by Enoch Powell. There was also the Anti-Nazi League (1977), which sought to alert voters to the fascist tendencies of the increasingly popular National Front Party. Indians and Pakistanis themselves fought back politically, forming, for example, the Anti-Racist Committee of Asians in East London in 1976, which took to the streets, demonstrating against police harassment and ethnic attacks. Key to all this activism were Asian British women, represented aptly in *The Buddha of Suburbia* by the militant Jamila. Late in the decade they helped form the Organization of Women of Asian and African Descent (1978-83),

which would foster "an increasingly positive sense of self and blackness" and led to the formation of other, similar groups. Meanwhile, demonstrations and counter-demonstrations became an indelible part of the landscape in 1970s London, as dramatized in Kureishi's novel. It is during this turbulent era that its protagonist Karim comes of age.

British politics of the 1970s. *The Buddha of Suburbia* opens around the time that the Conservative Party regained control of Parliament via Edward Heath's election as Prime Minister in June 1970, and ends on May 3, 1979, the day Margaret Thatcher assumed the conservative mantle and reset the nation's course. This was a tumultuous decade, marked by inflation and industrial upheaval. The Heath years witnessed the Arab oil embargo of 1973 and a miners' strike in the winter of 1973-74, which together exerted enormous pressure on his government. Heath called an election in 1974, but lost to Labour's Harold Wilson, who was succeeded by James Callaghan in 1976. But neither Labour leader could reign in inflation; so great union unrest ensued, culmi-

---

THE BROMLEY CONTINGENT: BOWIE AND THE BUDDHA

In the essay "The Boy in the Bedroom" (1994), Kureishi speaks about his circle of friends in high school, called "The Bromley Contingent" by Johnny Rotten, leader of the punk group Sex Pistols. The more adventurous members of The Bromley Contingent formed spin-off pop music groups—Siouxie and the Banshees, and Generation X. Nor were these the only pop heroes to emerge from Kureishi's Bromley school. Billy Idol, then known as Bill Broad, was one of his grade-school mates ("although I haven't seen him since I was 16," Kureishi remarked in 1990 [Kureishi in Collins, p. 20]). In fact, Idol is a major model for Charlie Hero in *The Buddha of Suburbia*. Even Kureishi's art teacher had cachet in the pop music world; he was Peter Frampton's father. Certainly the most notable figure to emerge from Bromley was David Bowie. "Bowie, then called David Jones, had attended our school several years before," relates the narrator of *The Buddha of Suburbia*. "Boys were often to be found on their knees before this icon, praying to be made into pop stars and for release from a lifetime as a motor-mechanic, or a clerk in an insurance firm, or an architect" (*Buddha*, p. 68). As a result of Kureishi's 1993 interview with Bowie, the pop star composed an original soundtrack for the British Broadcasting Corporation's television version of *The Buddha of Suburbia*.

---

nating in the "winter of discontent" of 1978-79. As the novel's narrator puts it, "the bitter, fractured country was in turmoil: there were strikes, marches, wage-claims" (Kureishi, *The Buddha of Suburbia*, p. 259). When the Liberal and Nationalist parties broke away from their alliance with Labour in March 1979, Callaghan's hold on Parliament collapsed, and he was dismissed by a vote of no-confidence.

Pop music and theater galvanize a generation. Both the novel's Karim and Kureishi himself are self-conscious products of the remarkable flourishing of the arts in Britain in the 1960s and 1970s. Kureishi relates that when he started to write in the early 1970s, he worried that "this tiny skill" was "elegantly useless," but he was aware "of the potency and influence of another language that spoke to millions—pop music (Kureishi, *Plays*, p. xii). At stake was the political empowerment of a generation and a nation.

In the essay "Eight Arms to Hold You" (1986), Kureishi says that the Beatles not only entertained British youth, but also "came to represent opportunity and possibility. They were careers officers, a myth for us to live by, a light for us to follow" (Kureishi, "Eight Arms," p. 110). In fact, the music's importance to Kureishi, and to many of his generation, is more powerful than as a guiding light. Kureishi's second novel, *The Black Album*, characterizes pop music (its title refers to a bootlegged album that originated with the musician Prince) as a means of liberation that defends the individual against the fascist mindset of religious fundamentalism. In the early 1970s, rock music was indelibly associated with developments deemed "'progressive' or 'experimental'"—whether they were the "drum solos or effeminate synthesizers" of the music or liberal approaches towards sex, drugs, and politics (*Buddha*, p. 130). By the late 1970s such attitudes would themselves have become mainstream (and seemed narcissistic) enough to be cast aside by the punk movement and its anarchic tendencies, most explosively in the Sex Pistols' album *Anarchy in the U.K.* and in the 1977 single "God Save the Queen."

British theater, too, had a major impact upon postwar British society (and a more tangible one upon Kureishi than pop music). The production of John Osborne's *Look Back in Anger* in London's West End in 1956 signaled the arrival of the British stage as a powerful cultural force. The play, which features Jimmy Porter of working-class heritage and his turbulent marriage to the upper-middle-class Alison, became renowned for Jimmy's condemnations of the social status quo. Subsequent plays, such as Edward Bond's *Saved* (1965), Harold Pinter's *The Homecoming* (1965), and Tom Stoppard's *Travesties* (1974) proved unsettling, even shocking to theatergoers.

In the 1970s, Kureishi writes, fringe theater seemed the best venue for exploring the changed Britain, "which involved violence, the contamination of racism and years of crisis. The questions that a multi-cultural society had to ask had hardly been put" (Kureishi, *Plays*, p. xvi). In large part because it explored such issues, fringe theater also served as fertile soil for supposedly radical political ideals—ones that, Kureishi seems to believe, adherents tended not to put into action in the world outside art. Thus, in his novel's portrayal of a fringe production (ironically of the non-radical *Jungle Book*), we find a Trotskyite hoping that society becomes as miserable as possible so that a communist revolution will transpire in Britain.

The Novel in Focus

Plot summary. *The Buddha of Suburbia* is divided into "In the Suburbs" (South London) and "In the City" (the metropolis itself), both parts narrated by Karim Amir. At the opening of the novel, in the early 1970s, Karim is a 17-year-old living in the suburbs of South London. His mother, Margaret, is a British woman neglected by her family; his father, Haroon, is a civil servant who immigrated to Britain from India in 1950. Karim also has a brother, Allie, who is preoccupied with fashion. The novel's title refers to the events of chapter one, in which Karim accompanies his father to the home of another white British woman, Mrs. Eva Kay, where Haroon dispenses "Eastern" wisdom to groups of suburbanites. Here Karim learns that his dad and Eva are having an affair and has an exciting sexual encounter of his own with Eva's charismatic son, Charlie, who is a burgeoning rock star.

Other vivid characters soon enter the picture. Anwar is Haroon's business-minded friend from their childhood days together in Bombay; his wife, Jeeta, runs their grocer's shop. Anwar mocks his friend's new role as "Buddha," or dispenser of Eastern wisdom. At a second suburban gathering, Margaret's sister Jean shows up with her husband Ted in order to monitor and report on Haroon's activities to Margaret, who knows that her husband is "impersonating a Buddha" and carrying on with another woman (*Buddha*, p. 44). The gathering is eventful for Karim. He meets Helen, who becomes his girlfriend for a time, and whose father ("Hairy Back") heaps racial epithets upon him. Helen is as smitten with Charlie, the burgeoning rock star, as Karim himself.

Karim's concern over his father's infidelity is soon superseded by the appearance of Jamila, daughter of Anwar and Jeeta. Radical political activist and sometime lover of Karim, she has just learned that Anwar has arranged for her to marry

Punk-rock singer Billy Idol, a model for Charlie Hero in *The Buddha of Suburbia*.

a 30-year-old Indian man (who will, he hopes, be helpful around the shop as well). Her father has undertaken a hunger strike to force her to submit to his wishes. Jamila decides to capitulate. So into the picture comes Changez, nicknamed "Bubble," whose laziness and one good hand render moot Anwar's hopes that he himself will benefit from this union. Changez, eager to discover London, becomes good friends with Karim, although it seems that he will never become intimate with his new wife. Karim makes matters worse by having sexual relations with Jamila after the marriage.

Meanwhile, Haroon and Eva have moved in together at Eva's, and Margaret has left the house to live with Ted and Jean. Eva, having enlisted Ted (who had quit his plumbing job at Haroon's urging) to renovate her house, decides to move her new family to London, in search of both a more sophisticated lifestyle and her son Charlie, "who was only rarely around now," because he clearly believed that "our suburbs were a leaving place" (*Buddha*, p. 117).

Part Two, "In the City," begins at Eva's dingy new flat in West Kensington, located around the corner from a club at which Karim and Charlie witness the explosion of punk music. Charlie runs off with the band and is next seen as "Charlie Hero," its leader. Meanwhile, Karim's own road to fame begins when Eva's friend Jeremy Shadwell casts him as Mowgli in a play that is adapting Rudyard's Kipling's *The Jungle Book* to the stage. Karim especially enjoys getting to know Terry, a Trotskyite, who becomes dismayed when the famous director Matthew Pyke chooses Karim over him for a new production.

Pyke instructs Karim to choose someone from his own background, "someone black" as a model for his role, whereupon Karim muses, "I didn't know anyone black, though I'd been at school with a Nigerian" (*Buddha*, p. 170). Pyke's romanticized prejudices about race are revealed when he specifies that Karim should choose someone from his own family. Anwar on his hunger strike, thinks Karim. But when Tracey, the troupe's one black actress, accuses Karim of portraying black people as "irrational, ridiculous, as being hysterical," he switches models to Changez, despite his Indian friend's refusal to grant permission (*Buddha*, p. 180). Karim begins an affair with Eleanor, a fiery redhead; but especially after a bizarre gathering that involves group sex together with Pyke and his wife, Karim becomes suspicious of the power games lying behind the supposedly progressive mindset of this group of artists.

After attending mosque one day, Anwar decries Changez as a "useless cripple," and attempts to bash him with a walking stick (*Buddha*, p. 209). Changez returns the blow; having visited sex shops, he whacks his father-in-law smartly over the head with a newly-purchased dildo. Alas, the blow is fatal. This situation prompts Jamila to move to a commune, and, at Karim's urging, she allows Changez to accompany her.

Back on stage, Karim winds up basing his character "Tariq," on the "Dildo Killer," though he gives Changez his word of honor that this is not the case. In the wake of an attack on Changez by National Front thugs, Karim agrees to join Jamila in protesting a neo-Nazi party march scheduled for the following Saturday. When Karim tries to enlist Eleanor, her response is strange: suspicious, he skips the protest, instead gathering evidence that she is sleeping with Pyke. Their own affair, Karim informs Eleanor, is over.

After the play's opening night, Terry, the Trotskyite actor, enjoins Karim to ask Pyke and Eleanor for money for "the Party"; Changez, obliviously delighted by the performance, tells Karim that Jamila and he are expecting a baby

(not his own, though); Jamila berates Karim for failing to march against the National Front; and Margaret wonders why her British son is playing an Indian character.

> "Wasn't I good, eh, Mum?"
> "You weren't in a loin-cloth as usual," she said. "At least they let you wear your own clothes. But you're not an Indian. You've never been to India. . ."
> " . . . Aren't I part Indian?"
> "What about me?" Mum said. "Who gave birth to you? You're an Englishman, I'm glad to say."
> "I don't care," I said. "I'm an actor. It's a job."
> "Don't say that," she said. "Be what you are."
> "Oh yeah."
>
> (*Buddha*, p. 232)

Karim and the troupe later accept Pyke's invitation to perform the show in New York. Once there, Karim seeks out Charlie, who has moved to America, birthplace of blues and rock' n' roll: they can be "two English boys in America, the land where music came from, with Mick Jagger, John Lennon and Johnny Rotten living round the corner" (*Buddha*, p. 249). Since his play runs for just a month, Karim spends a lot of time with Charlie, but this does little to mitigate Karim's depression and self-hatred. Two events make him return to England: Charlie's physical brutality towards a journalist who chases him in a street for a story, and the pop star's night of sado-masochism with a prostitute as Karim looks on.

Upon returning to London, Karim lands a lucrative job in a television soap opera. He also finds London a changed city, politically and aesthetically. "I walked around Central London and saw that the town was being ripped apart; the rotten was being replaced by the new, and the new was ugly. The gift of creating beauty had been lost somewhere. The ugliness was in the people, too. Londoners seemed to hate each other" (*Buddha*, p. 258).

Eva, the home-refurbisher, is interviewed about her work by reporters who are keen to learn about Charlie Hero; Haroon has decided to quit his job; and Margaret has a new boyfriend. Karim goes to Jamila's commune, where he meets the new baby and witnesses Changez's unwavering, yet unrequited, love for Jamila, who has taken a lesbian lover. The novel ends on the day Thatcher is elected the new Prime Minister. Karim invites his father, Haroon, and Eva, his brother, Allie, Allie's new girlfriend, and his friends Changez and Jamila to the most expensive restaurant he knows in Soho (Jamila is too busy with politics and the baby to join them).

"GOING SOMEWHERE": H. G. WELLS AND SUBURBIA

Karim twice reminds his readers that H. G. Wells was from Bromley, his own home. "I got off my bicycle and stood there in Bromley High Street, next to a plaque that said 'H. G. Wells was born here,'" he tells us just before the encounter with his father in the phone booth (*Buddha*, p. 64). Later, in describing his new environs in West Kensington: "Unlike the suburbs, where no one of note—except H. G. Wells—had lived, here you couldn't get away from VIPs" (*Buddha*, p. 126). Wells is perhaps most famous today for such science fiction works as **The Time Machine** (also in *WLAIT 4: British and Irish Literature and Its Times*), but he was also a noted social commentator. Some of his comments, from *The New Machiavelli*, serve as an apt backdrop to Karim's own reaction to suburban life:

> The outskirts of Bromstead were a maze of exploitation roads that led nowhere, that ended in tarred fences studded with nails (I don't remember barbed wire in those days; I think the Zeitgeist did not produce that until later), and in trespass boards that used vehement language. Broken glass, tin cans, and ashes and paper abounded. Cheap glass, cheap tin, abundant fuel, and a free untaxed Press had rushed upon a world quite unprepared to dispose of these blessings when the fulness of enjoyment was past.
>
> (Wells, pp. 44-45)

The phrase "roads that led nowhere" resonates powerfully in Kureishi's novel, whose Karim describes himself as "from the South London suburbs and going somewhere" (*Buddha*, p. 3). Karim goes on to say that he is "restless and easily bored. Perhaps it is the odd mixture of continents and blood, of here and there, of belonging and not, that makes me restless and bored. Or perhaps it was being brought up in the suburbs that did it" (*Buddha*, p. 3). The novel bears out the sense that it not an either/or situation: suburbia is the English landscape's embodiment of the sense of "belonging and not" that is an indelible aspect of Karim's life, of the experience of immigrants and their descendants, and even of England itself. In his essay "The Rainbow Sign" Kureishi extends this sense of separation inherent in the English suburban condition beyond geography to include time itself: "A boy in a bedroom in a suburb, who had the King's Road constantly on his mind and who changed the picture on his wall from week to week, was unhappy, and separated from the 1960s as by a thick glass wall against which he could only press his face" (Kureishi, "Rainbow Sign," p. 86). The threat of being held captive by this suburban glass wall hovers over Karim and Charlie in the novel: "You're not going anywhere—not as a band and not as a person," Karim taunts his friend in very Wellsian language in the novel (*Buddha*, p. 121). But soon after, the tables are turned: when Karim questions Charlie's enthusiasm for punk rockers, Charlie "turned on me with one of his nastiest looks. 'You're not going anywhere, Karim. You're not doing anything with your life because as usual you're facing in the wrong direction and going the wrong way'" (*Buddha*, p. 132). *The Buddha of Suburbia* is fundamentally about finding the roads that lead out of the Bromley of H. G. Wells, David Bowie, and Kureishi: of breaking through the glass wall, facing in the right direction, and carving out new paths to follow.

Their table becomes the center of attention, and Haroon announces that he and Eva will be getting married. Karim closes by observing that he "felt happy and miserable at the same time. I thought of what a mess everything had been, but that it wouldn't always be that way" (*Buddha*, p. 284).

Racial violence, class, and assimilation. A disturbing current of racial violence runs through the otherwise very comical plot of *The Buddha of Surburbia*. While the violence itself is a fact of life in Karim's England, a number of approaches to the problem are represented among his family and friends. Karim himself is at the opposite spectrum from Jamila on this issue:

> Compared to Jammie I was, as a militant, a real shaker and trembler. If people spat at me I practically thanked them for not making me chew the moss between the paving stones. But Jamila had a PhD in physical retribution. Once a greaser rode past us on an old bicycle and said, as if asking the time, "Eat shit, Pakis." Jammie sprinted through the traffic before throwing the bastard off his bike and tugging out some of his hair, like someone weeding an overgrown garden.
>
> (*Buddha*, p. 53)

Karim's mother Margaret, on the other hand, seeks to distance her husband from popular stereotypes associated with the immigration wave of the late 1940s that inspired overt prejudices. Haroon's family, she claims, was

> higher [in social class] than the Churchills. . . . This ensured there would be no confusion between Dad and the swarms of Indian peasants who came to Britain in the 1950s and 1960s, and of whom it was said they were not familiar with cutlery and certainly not with toilets, since they squatted on the seats and shat from on high.
>
> (*Buddha*, p. 24)

Changez, the only recent immigrant in the novel, takes to the extreme assumptions about the value of assimilation into the upper-class world of white "Englishmen." To be accepted, he asserts, the Indians and Pakistanis he sees walking to their menial jobs have to take up English ways.

> [They need to] forget their filthy villages! They must decide to be either here or there. Look how much here I am! And why doesn't that bugger over there look the Englishman in the eye! No wonder the Englishman will hit him!
>
> (*Buddha*, p. 210)

In his 1986 essay "The Rainbow Sign," Kureishi explores the premise behind Changez's belief: that if the British could see among the Pakistanis "the rich, the educated, the sophisticated, they wouldn't be so hostile." His Pakistani companions "couldn't understand when I explained that British racists weren't discriminating in their racial discrimination: they loathed all Pakistanis and kicked whoever was nearest" (Kureishi, "Rainbow Sign," p. 93). *The Buddha of Suburbia* dramatizes this point only a few pages after Changez's outburst, when he is attacked by a gang of National Front thugs "who called him a Paki, not realizing he was Indian" (*Buddha*, p. 224).

Another variation on this attitude is articulated by Allie, lover of high fashion. Allie disdains the "self-pity" of "people who go on all the time about being black, and how persecuted they were at school, and how someone spat at them once" (*Buddha*, p. 267). Unlike the Indians who were kicked out of Uganda, Allie says to Karim, "no one put people like you and me in camps, and no one will. We can't be lumped in with them, thank God" (*Buddha*, p. 268). Allie combines the attitude of his mother (differentiating between his own social background and those of less fortunate immigrants) with the scorn for others of his own race shared by Changez, except that Allie's antipathy is targeted against idealists and artists rather than the lower classes. Like Margaret and Changez, he takes refuge in the fantasies that his difference from the truly oppressed exempts him from racism: "we can't," he says, as noted above, "be lumped in with them."

Finally, there is the approach of the two genuine immigrants, Haroon and Anwar. "Maybe there were similarities between what was happening to Dad, with his discovery of Eastern philosophy, and Anwar's last stand. Perhaps it was the immigrant condition living itself out through them," observes the narrator. By taking on the roles of "Buddha of Suburbia" and hunger-striker, respectively, Haroon and Anwar are fulfilling many of the stereotypes that Britons held of the East: hence the pain the 19-year-old black actress Tracey feels upon seeing Karim portray Anwar on stage. "Now, as they aged and seemed settled here, Anwar and Dad appeared to be returning internally to India, or at least to be resisting the English here" (*Buddha*, p. 64). Their attitude reflects a phenomenon that Kureishi describes in "The Rainbow Sign": the belief among British-born Indians and Pakistanis that "they are in exile, awaiting return to a better place, where they belong, where they are welcome" (Kureishi,

"Rainbow Sign," p. 100). This view, he continues, contains much "illusion and falsity," for it denies "the extent to which [they] have been formed by England and the depth of attachment [they] feel to the place, despite everything" (Kureishi, "Rainbow Sign," p. 100). On the other hand, neither Anwar nor Karim's father "expressed any desire actually to see their origins again. 'India's a rotten place,' Anwar grumbled" (*Buddha*, p. 64).

The final word of *The Buddha of Suburbia* on this topic, then, must be the first: "I am an Englishman born and bred" (*Buddha*, p. 3). It is not a question of immigrants or their children becoming like Englishmen, or distancing themselves from the peasants, or seeking to return to a homeland, whether internally or literally. The point is that the very meaning of "Englishman" has fundamentally changed, both with regard to Karim's world and the world of English literature: "Being British is a new thing now. It involves people with names like Kureishi or [Kazuo] Ishiguro or [Salman] Rushdie, where it didn't before. And we're all British too" (Kureishi in Kaleta, p. 7; for Ishiguro and Rushdie, respectively, see **Remains of the Day** and **Midnight's Children,** also in *WLAIT 4: British and Irish Literature and Its Times*). *The Buddha of Suburbia* is a comic and often poignant celebration of that fact, as well as a lament that so many do not yet acknowledge it.

Sources and literary context. *The Buddha of Suburbia*'s first incarnation was as a short story by that name, published in *Harper's* in 1987. Kureishi recollects that he conceived of the idea for the novel "on the balcony of a hotel room in Madras, my father's birthplace. . . . Ever since [the short story] had appeared in print the characters and situation remained with me"; he knew he had material for a whole book but needed to find a way to organise it" (Kureishi, "Something Given"). The material sprang in large part from the author's own experiences coming of age in the 1970s: as noted, Billy Idol became Charlie Hero; Kureishi's father became Haroon; Kureishi's apprenticeship in the Royal Court Theatre gave rise to the Matthew Pyke plot. But Kureishi warns against putting too much stock in autobiographical elements; actually whether a writer's work is autobiographical, seems an odd, "redundant" question to him—from where else could the work come? As to Karim's being based on Kureishi, the author notes, "There's one difference, one main difference, between me and that guy in *The Buddha*, which is that when I was

young, from the age of fourteen, I fully knew that I wanted to be a writer. And so I had a great sense of purpose and direction in my life all through those years" (Kureishi in Kaleta, p. 74).

The Buddha of Suburbia extends the strong contemporary tradition of immigrant voices, represented by such writers as Anita Desai and Salman Rushdie (see **Midnight's Children,** also in *WLAIT 4: British and Irish Literature and Its Times*). Rushdie celebrated the prominence of these immigrant voices in his essay "The Empire Writes Back With a Vengeance" published in *The Times* (3 July 1982, p. 8). According to A. Robert Lee, this tradition "has somewhat too often had the effect of laying down a pre-emptive configuration, that of post-independence, first-generation immigration, with a kind of internal colonialism to follow" (Lee, p. 72). Much of the impact of *The Buddha of Suburbia,* by contrast, lies in its status as one of the harbingers of a group of writings in which "indigenous lives 'of colour' [are] pursued and articulated wholly, or almost wholly, as from inside the very grain of British society" (Lee, p. 71). Lee places Kureishi together with David Dabydeen and Mike Phillips, whose fiction "speaks out of, and to, the absolute centre of 'England'. That is, whatever their author's literal place of birth, they proceed from, and inscribe, a quite ineradicable and historic multicultural Englishness or Britishness" (Lee, p. 75). Nor are such voices limited to the medium of literature: "One consequence, on the page and in theatre and music has been the rise of new, hybrid styles" in music (e.g., "a pop tradition embracing east-west Beatles lyrics and groups from The Two Tones to Steven Kapur's Apache Indian") and in theatre (Jatinder Verma's "Indian" version of Molière's Tartuffe).

Events in History at the Time the Novel Was Written

Thatcherism and its opponents in the 1980s. With the fall of Prime Minister James Callaghan in 1979, *The Buddha of Suburbia*'s Terry says, "The chickens are coming home to die. It's either us or the rise of the Right" (*Buddha*, p. 258). It was the latter, by far, for upon her victory a few weeks after Terry's remark, Prime Minister Margaret Thatcher invoked her policies of economic rationalism—wholesale attention to fiscal responsibility, whatever the costs to the society supposedly being served by the government. Thatcher undertook to dismantle Britain's socialist structures by selling its share of public utilities to private companies, and undermined what she saw as the labor unions' stranglehold on the economy, most dramatically by crushing the miners' strike of 1984-85. The narrator of Kureishi's 1998 autobiographical novel *Intimacy* reflects upon the ways in which Thatcherism unhinged his generation:

> We were dismissive and contemptuous of Thatcherism, but so captivated by our own ideological obsessions that we couldn't see its appeal. Which isn't to say we didn't fight it. There was the miners' strike, and the battles at Wapping [1986 industrial strife after the dismissal of 5,500 workers by the media conglomerate News Corporation in the wake of its relocation from Fleet Street to Wapping, near London's Docklands]. We were left enervated and confused. Soon we didn't know what we believed. Some remained on the left; others retreated into sexual politics; some became Thatcherites. We were the kind of people who held the Labour party back. Still, I never understood the elevation of greed as a political credo.
>
> (Kureishi, *Intimacy,* pp. 53-54)

Fathomable or not, Thatcher would stay in power until 1990, the year *The Buddha of Suburbia* was published.

The combination of the economic turmoil of Thatcher's early years and her own attitude towards racial minorities ensured the racial tensions of the 1970s would not dissipate under her tenure: indeed, Thatcherism in large part rendered the National Front moot. In January 1978, the future Prime Minister said on television that the white community's fears about being "swamped" by non-whites were legitimate. Two years into her ministership, severe economic strains upon the working classes led to a rash of about 20 disturbances in British towns and cities, notably in Brixton, a multiracial community near London with a high population of unemployed young blacks. In April 1981, 279 policemen and large numbers of civilians were injured in serious disturbances there, and 28 buildings were damaged or destroyed by fire (Young, p. 233). Many white Britons, including members of Thatcher's administration, saw evidence in such violence not of the dramatic economic hardships the nation's non-whites were being forced to endure, but rather of the supposition that there were, in the words of one unemployed white moulder in 1982, "too many Indians"; Those riots at Brixton," he added, "I'd send all them darkies back home" (Williamson, p. 237).

Given the prevalence of such attitudes, it is hardly surprising that the non-white residents of council-housing estates continued to experience racial abuse. As in the 1970s, Asian homes and businesses were petrol-bombed, and verbal abuse was hurled at their owners and inhabitants. There were Asians who reacted by rising above the racism.

Yet children of the first wave of postwar immigrants continued to assimilate into mainstream British culture. Some intermarried, with as many as 20 percent of British-born Indian and African Asian men wedding white women by the early 1990s. The novel's Haroon, an immigrant himself, marries two white women, the first in the 1950s, the second in the 1970s. Such developments in the novel reflect aspects of real-world society in mid-to-late twentieth-century Britain. Though the era was one of economic and social hardships for Pakistani and Indian inhabitants, they nevertheless managed to become an integral part of contemporary British society, which has been irreversibly changed as a consequence. But they continue to face uncertainties—a fact that surely contributes to the unresolved conclusion to Karim's story.

1989: The end of the Cold War. Between the first draft of *The Buddha of Suburbia* in December 1987 and its publication in April 1990, two events indelibly changed global society, and the role of literature in the world. The first was the collapse of the communist-democratic polarity, the competition for world leadership that ended with the fall of the Berlin Wall in November 1989. This fall had a domino effect, leading to the collapse of Soviet-style communism in eastern Europe, and indeed of the Soviet Union itself. Here, *The Buddha of Suburbia*'s Terry could not have been further off the mark with regard to his hopes for the rise of the Communist Party in Britain. In retrospect, the Soviet collapse, while widely heralded as a triumph of freedom, confused many of Kureishi's generation, just as Thatcherism had. In a passage of his novel *Intimacy* the narrator remarks, "We were the last generation to defend communism" (Kureishi, *Intimacy,* p. 53).

1989: The *Fatwa* against Rushdie. The other event of 1989, to which Kureishi felt much more immediately connected, occurred on February 14. Iran's leader Ayatollah Ruhollah Khomeini declared a *fatwa* (death sentence) upon Indian-born British novelist Salman Rushdie because of the supposed anti-Muslim blasphemies in his novel *The Satanic Verses.* Rushdie was forced into hiding, emerging only in 1998. This event "was devastating for him, for all of us," remarked Kureishi in 1990, whose family had long known Rushdie's. In 1986, Kureishi's own film *My Beautiful Laundrette* had been picketed by the Pakistan Action Committee in New York City because of its frank treatment of sexuality and characterization of immigrant culture. "People think you're supposed to show them exclusively as strong, truthful and beautiful," observed Kureishi. "Looking back on it [the picketing], I can see in it the seeds of the Rushdie situation" (Kureishi in Collins p. 20). *The Buddha of Suburbia* dramatizes precisely such a reaction. According to the young black actress Tracey, Karim's depiction of Anwar shows black people as being "irrational, ridiculous, as being hysterical. And as being fanatical" (*Buddha*, p. 180). In retrospect, Tracey's use of the term "fanatical" strikes an especially ironic chord, since the Rushdie affair would show that a fanatical approach towards or reaction to creative representation can be deadly.

Reception. *The Buddha of Suburbia* garnered mostly positive reviews in the press, winning the Whitbread Prize for best novel of 1990. Not all the reviews were favorable, however. In the *Times Literary Supplement,* Neil Berry described the plot as "chaotic"; in the past, complained Berry, Kureishi has written "with elliptical brilliance about being at once English and Asian, and about the bankruptcy of Britain's traditional self-images. Such challenging topics bob tantalizingly into view in *The Buddha of Suburbia*—and as quickly vanish" (Berry, p. 339). But others praised the novel as sharp satire on racial relations, and within a decade many recognized it as an attempt to redefine Britishness. "This reform(ulation)," explains Anuradha Dingwaney Needham, "insists that riven as Britishness is with mixtures which are a product, in large part, 'of migration and miscegenation,'. . . a 'singular sense of Britishness' ought to be unacceptable"

(Needham, p. 114). *The Buddha of Suburbia* advances this reformulation by featuring a protagonist in the process of shaping his identity, one that acknowledges his diverse heritage. More generally, it aims for minorities in Britain to be seen as not deviant from the norm but rather an integral part of it.

—Lawrence Warner

For More Information

Berry, Neil. Review of *The Buddha of Suburbia. Times Literary Supplement,* 30 March 1990, 330.

Collins, Glenn. "Screen Writer Turns to the Novel To Tell of Race and Class in London." *The New York Times*, 24 May 1990, 17, 20.

Cosgrave, Patrick. *The Lives of Enoch Powell.* London: Bodley Head, 1989.

Kaleta, Kenneth C. *Hanif Kureishi: Postcolonial Storyteller.* Austin: University of Texas Press, 1998.

Kureishi, Hanif. *The Buddha of Suburbia.* London: Faber and Faber, 1990.

———. *Hanif Kureishi Plays One.* London: Faber and Faber, 1999.

——— "Something Given: Reflections on Writing." Available on the internet at: [http://www.hanifkureishi.com]. Accessed October 14, 2000.

———. *Intimacy.* New York: Scribner, 1999.

———. "The Rainbow Sign" and "Eight Arms to Hold You." In *My Beautiful Laundrette and Other Writings.* London: Faber and Faber, 1996.

Lee, A. Robert, ed. *Other Britain, Other British: Contemporary Multicultural Fiction.* East Haven, Conn.: Pluto Press, 1995.

Needham, Anuradha Dingwaney. *Using the Master's Tools: Resistance and the Literature of the African and South-Asian Diasporas.* New York: St. Martin's, 2000.

Young, Hugo. *One of Us: a Biography of Margaret Thatcher.* London: Macmillan, 1989.

Williamson, Bill. *The Temper of the Times; British Society since World War II.* Oxford: Basil Blackwell, 1990.

Wells, H. G. *The New Machiavelli.* London: William Clowes, 1911.

Cambridge

by

Caryl Phillips

Born in 1958 on the West Indian island of St. Kitts, Caryl Phillips was raised in Britain, where his family immigrated soon after his birth. While studying English literature at Oxford University, Phillips took a five-week bus trip through the United States. During the journey, he read works by African American authors such as Richard Wright, Ralph Ellison, and James Baldwin, which he found deeply inspiring for his own writing. After graduating from Oxford in 1979, Phillips began writing plays for stage, radio, and television. His works enjoyed immediate success, and on the proceeds Phillips was able to travel back to the West Indies for the first time. A subsequent tour of Europe in the mid-1980s resulted in a book of essays, *The European Tribe* (1987), criticizing European ethnocentricity. As a black man traveling in America and Europe, as during his youth in Britain, Phillips frequently encountered racism, which has been a central issue in his writing. From the plays with which he began his career to the novels, essays, documentary filmscripts, articles, interviews, and one screenplay that have followed, Phillips's work combines moral and psychological insight with a keen interest in the black experience. His novels—including *A State of Independence* (1986), *Higher Ground* (1989), *Cambridge* (1991), *Crossing the River* (1994), and *The Nature of Blood* (1997)—focus on the centuries-old interaction between Europe, Africa, and the Caribbean. Of the novels, *Cambridge* has reached the widest audience and is generally regarded as effectively reflecting the historical com-

> ## THE LITERARY WORK
>
> A novel set in the British West Indies in the early nineteenth century; first published in London in 1991.
>
> ## SYNOPSIS
>
> Emily Cartwright, a young Englishwoman, journeys to her father's sugar plantation in the West Indies, where she becomes involved in a deadly contest of wills between the plantation's manager, Mr. Brown, and a slave, Cambridge.

plexities and moral ambiguities of this triangular relationship.

Events in History at the Time the Novel Takes Place

Slavery in the British West Indies. Like the Spanish before them, by the middle of the seventeenth century both the British and the French had established a number of plantation colonies in the West Indies. Following the Spanish model, the colonies employed slave labor imported from West Africa to raise cash crops that were shipped back to the mother country. While early crop experiments included tobacco and cotton (both grown more successfully on plantations in the southern United States), the West Indian plan-

Caryl Phillips

tations soon came to rely almost exclusively on sugarcane.

The first successful British colony in the West Indies was founded in the 1620s on the small island of St. Kitts, Caryl Phillips's birthplace and the model for the unnamed island in the novel. By the early nineteenth century, when the novel is set, British plantations had been flourishing for nearly 200 years throughout the West Indies—from the Bahamas in the north (near Florida), to Barbados in the south (off the Venezuela coast), and from Jamaica in the west to the Leeward Islands (including St. Kitts, one of the most prosperous islands) in the east.

Historians estimate that altogether some 8-15 million Africans were transported to the Spanish, British, French, Portuguese, and other European plantations in the New World between the mid-seventeenth and mid-nineteenth centuries. On top of that total, an estimated 2 to 3 million Africans died in chains during the harrowing "Middle Passage," the brutal trip across the Atlantic Ocean. In the novel Cambridge survives this trip twice, returning to Africa after achieving freedom a first time, where he is again kidnapped and resold into slavery once more.

Conditions for slaves were particularly harsh in the Caribbean. Diseases—dysentery, diarrhea, smallpox, and others—flourished in the tropics, where medical care on the isolated estates was

minimal. In the novel Emily Cartwright meets Mr. McDonald, who cares for a few whites and "many hundreds of blacks" on several plantations; McDonald charges more for doctoring the whites, which he says "demands closer attention," and complains about the "bizarre imaginary diseases" he says the blacks use as a pretext for not working (Phillips, *Cambridge*, p. 34). Such sentiments both reflect contemporary white attitudes to slaves' health and point to a subtle means invoked by slaves to resist slave labor.

Typically slaves worked in gangs according to strength and age. The gangs assembled at daybreak to begin work, then stopped at 9:00 A.M. for about a half-hour breakfast, after which they resumed work until 11:00 A.M. Next they left the fields for anywhere from an-hour-and-a-half to three hours, after which they resumed labor there until about 30 minutes before sunset, when they stopped to pick grass. Their workday thus amounted to at least 10 hours, at harvest-time longer, to keep the mill that ground the sugarcane operating all night. During the ten hours, they labored under the watchful gaze of slave drivers, as reported by an observer at a plantation on St. Kitts: "Every ten Negroes have a driver who walks behind them holding a short whip and a long one. . . . They are naked, male and female, down to the girdle, and you constantly observe where the application [of the whip] has been made" (Schaw in Goveia, p. 131).

According to another observer on Antigua,

> The negroes are turned out at sunrise and employed in gangs from twenty to sixty, or upwards under the inspection of white overseers. . . ; subordinate to these overseers are drivers . . . who are mostly black or mulatto fellows . . . and these men are furnished with whips, which they are obliged, on pain of severe punishment to have with them, and are authorised to flog wherever they see the least relaxation from labor.
>
> (Luffman in Goveia, p. 131)

The physical requirements of work in the sugarcane fields meant that men were in higher demand than women. Combined with poor nutrition, the other hardships suffered by Caribbean slaves raised their mortality rate and lowered their fertility rate, so that the slave population had to be replenished constantly with new shipments from West Africa. Modern estimates suggest that the "depletion rate" (that is, the rate at which death outstripped natural reproduction) among West Indian slave populations averaged

A West Indies slave rolls a barrel of sugar syrup aboard a ship. While planters first experimented with tobacco and cotton in the West Indies, plantations there came to rely almost exclusively on sugarcane and on the labor of black slaves.

between 20 percent and 30 percent before 1800 (Ward, p. 121).

Between c. 1650 and c. 1800, for example, British slave ships brought an estimated 1.5 million slaves to the British West Indies, but at the end of that time the slave population there stood at only about 500,000. In the American South, by contrast, where conditions were better and where women and children were in higher demand for lighter duties (such as domestic service), reproduction outpaced mortality beginning in the mid-eighteenth century, so that fewer slaves needed to be imported. Only in the early nineteenth century did the West Indian slave population's reproductive rate begin to approach its death rate.

The British antislavery movement. Significant opposition to slavery did not arise in Britain until near the end of the eighteenth century, when the abolitionist leaders William Wilberforce and Thomas Clarkson, together with their supporters, founded the Anti-Slavery Society in 1787. Opposing the abolitionists was the powerful lobby known as the West Indian Interest, a coalition of planters, merchants, and proslavery politicians. With Wilberforce leading the way in the British Parliament, after decades of political struggle the abolition movement achieved two major victories: first, in 1807 Parliament abolished the British slave trade; second, in 1834 Parliament abolished slavery itself on British territory, emancipating British slaves in the West Indies and elsewhere.

Cambridge takes place at an unspecified time between these two events, a period in which Wilberforce and others continued to press for emancipation. Wilberforce's 1823 pamphlet "An Appeal to the Religion, Justice, and Humanity of the Inhabitants of the British Empire, in Behalf of the Negro Slaves in the West Indies" outlines the abuses of slavery and raises many issues touched on in the novel:

- Wilberforce argues that the slaves remain "under-fed and over-worked," lacking "due medical care and medical comforts," and still suffering "a progressive decrease by mortality" (Wilberforce, pp. 7, 8). The white doctor in the novel, by contrast, claims that "lazy" slaves feign illness in order to "lie at ease in the sick-house" (*Cambridge*, p. 34).
- Wilberforce objects to "the driving system" employed on the plantations, in which a black "driver," a slave elevated by the white manager to a position of authority, uses a whip—"a dreadful instrument of punishment"—to force a gang of his fellow slaves to work harder (Wilberforce, pp. 12-

13). The novel's main conflict, between the slave Cambridge and the manager Mr. Brown, arises when Cambridge refuses Brown's request that he act as Head Driver.

- Wilberforce calls "absenteeship"—that is, the ownership of the plantations by Englishmen who never live in or even visit the West Indies—"perhaps one of the most injurious" aspects of the British system, because it allows the other abuses to continue unchecked (Wilberforce, p. 27). In the novel Emily's father is an absentee owner, and she decries the practice, writing home repeatedly in hopes of persuading him to visit his estate.

- The proslavery forces repeatedly claim, writes Wilberforce, "that these poor degraded beings, the Negro slaves, are as well or even better off than our British peasantry; a proposition so monstrous that nothing can possibly exhibit in a stronger light the extreme force of the prejudices which must exist in the minds of its asserters" (Wilberforce, pp. 33-34). In the novel Emily makes precisely this claim as her exposure to slavery's degradation hardens her own prejudices: "If I were to be asked if I should enter life anew as an English labourer or a West Indian slave I should have no hesitation in opting for the latter" (*Cambridge*, p. 42).

Worst of all, according to Wilberforce, is the complete lack of "religious and moral instruction among the slaves" (Wilberforce, p. 19). Wilberforce was an Evangelical Christian whose antislavery views were rooted in his passionate religious convictions. In the novel Cambridge's own story underscores the strong historical link in Britain between Evangelical Christianity, which underwent a major revival in the early nineteenth century, and the antislavery movement. Cambridge himself becomes an Evangelical Christian after being brought to England, receives "a Christian education" before being freed, and returns to Africa as a Christian missionary, hoping to convert those "in my unChristian native land" (*Cambridge*, pp. 144, 154).

British society, colonial society, and slave society. After victory over the French emperor Napoleon at the battle of Waterloo in 1815, Britain's national pride ran high and its mastery of the seas was unchallenged. Naval dominance boosted the British economy, opening new markets for British goods throughout the world—especially textiles, which the Industrial Revolution now allowed British weavers to make more cheaply in Britain than elsewhere. Having begun in British textile manufacturing in the mid-to-late eighteenth century, the Industrial Revolution would soon spread throughout the British economy, making Britain the first nation to change from an agricultural economy to a manufacturing one. These developments ultimately brought greater freedom and new political power to a broader part of the population, as Britain took the first steps towards social reform and universal suffrage. Historians see the Reform Bill of 1832, which doubled the number of men eligible to vote in British elections, as an early sign of this new democratic spirit.

As the limited focus of the Reform Bill suggests, however, not all Britons were immediately included in the political and social reforms. While the Reform Bill expanded voting rights, it extended the vote only from upper-class men to some middle-class men, about 1 million voters in all: working-class men and all women remained disenfranchised. These groups were socially repressed as well as politically marginalized, and in the novel both Emily Cartwright and Cambridge object to the deference that, as a woman and a freed black slave respectively, they are constantly expected to show in British society. Society generally demanded that women defer to their fathers and later their husbands, and that middle- and upper-class women limit their activities to the household. In the novel, Emily's father has arranged for her to marry an older, wealthy man whom she has never met, an arrangement she bitterly complains about but with which she plans to comply. This was the dawning though, of advocacy on behalf of women's rights; they were increasingly being considered in public debate, and Emily's hopes for a writing career accurately reflect a climate that, a few decades later, would result in the onset of the Women's Suffrage movement in Britain. By contrast, the racism that Cambridge encounters in Britain (for example, he and his white wife are ostracized by the townspeople after settling in a small English village) would remain more firmly entrenched despite legal and political reforms. In an interview Caryl Phillips has commented on the irony of a situation in which racial prejudices are held by Emily, a woman of her times who herself objects to the prospect of "a life sacrificed to the prejudices which despise my sex" (*Cambridge*, p. 113).

White society in the plantation colonies was isolated and often reactionary; it generally lagged behind the social changes that occurred at home. Cultural institutions were sparse and the white population largely transient, especially after profits declined in the 1820s. With the end of the

British slave trade, the cost of slaves from other sources than British ships had nearly tripled. Combined with depressed sugar prices, higher costs drove a number of plantations into poverty. The rise of absenteeism—between the 1760s and the 1820s the proportion of plantations owned by absent landlords rose from about one-third to about two-thirds—meant that many were run by managers who were young, single men. White female company was rare, so that the planter, regarding female slaves as property to do with as he pleased, often engaged in sexual liaisons with slave women, as the manager Mr. Brown does in *Cambridge*. "Faced with conditions such as these," writes one historian, "it was not remarkable if planters sank into torpor, and spent too many evenings drinking alone"—a picture reflected by the uncouth Mr. Brown (Ward, p. 266).

The slaves themselves most often lived in small villages on or near the plantation, as described in the novel by Emily and Cambridge. It was the owner's responsibility to care for and feed the slaves, whose living conditions varied somewhat according to the owner's or manager's character. Minimum standards were specified by law, but slaves on owner-operated plantations were generally better cared for than those on absentee-owned estates. Particularly after the end of the British slave trade, slaves were encouraged to cultivate their own food and to live in family units, practices that were seen as "producing healthy, fertile, and contented slaves" (Craton in Beckles, p. 235). Slave marriages were generally informal arrangements, unsanctified by the church, as Cambridge's is to his second wife, the slave woman Christiania, in the novel. The Anglican Church, which until 1827 was the only church in which formal weddings could occur under law, made no attempt to convert slaves to Christianity. In the novel Cambridge, echoing Wilberforce's complaint quoted above, is contemptuous of an Anglican priest who has no interest in the slaves' religious beliefs.

Both among themselves and by whites, slaves were divided into two classes, Africans (those born in Africa) and Creoles (those born under slavery in the New World). By the time of the novel Africans were numerically few, and Creole slave culture, more closely modeled on European cultural patterns, predominated. Yet many African cultural traits persisted, and within the slave society Africans tended to be chosen over Creoles for positions of leadership or authority, as Cambridge is in the novel. Of surviving African folkways, the most important were in the related areas of medicine and religion. The two areas blended together in the practice of obeah, the Caribbean slaves' African-based folk religion. In the novel Cambridge's second wife Christiania is an "obeah woman," a healer and occult practitioner whose powers cause other slaves to fear her (*Cambridge*, p. 74).

The Novel in Focus

Plot summary. The main body of the novel is narrated in two first-person accounts: the first and longer of the two is cast as the journal of the young Englishwoman Emily Cartwright; the second is a shorter statement made by Cambridge. A third section of just a few pages takes the form of a lurid, journalistic account, perhaps from a newspaper, of the conflict between the manager Mr. Brown and the "insane" slave Cambridge (*Cambridge*, p. 171). These three nineteenth-century voices are framed by a Prologue and an Epilogue, both presented in modern, contemporary language.

OBEAH

In West African folklore the obeah is a huge animal that, under a shaman's control, sneaks into villages and kidnaps young girls. In West Indian slave culture, the term was extended to designate the slaves' shamanic folk religion as a whole. Obeah practitioners functioned as healers and priests, though the white slaveowner associated them with superstition, witchcraft, and poison. Indeed, obeah constituted one of the slaves' scant retaliatory recourses; obeah practitioners were known to curse whites, and even poison them (in *Cambridge* the obeah woman Christiania utters spells against Emily Cartwright). Obeah also served as a rallying point for more direct slave resistance, as when obeah men led the 1760 Tacky Rebellion in Jamaica.

Emily's journal opens as she and her maid Isabella embark on their voyage to the West Indies, where Emily's father has sent her to report on the state of his sugar plantation. On her return her father has arranged for her to marry a wealthy man some 30 years her senior, whom she has never met. Emily's discomfort during the sea voyage is compounded by grief and loneliness when Isabella dies only a few days after they set sail from England.

Arriving on the island, Emily finds that Mr. Wilson, her father's plantation manager, has mysteriously disappeared and has been replaced by a subordinate, Mr. Brown, whose coarse manners shock her. However, before she can make any inquiries she falls ill with fever. After a severe month-long illness, she takes as her new maid the estate's housekeeper, a slave named Stella, who has tenderly nursed Emily back to health. She also meets Mr. McDonald, the local physician. Her health recovered, Emily questions Mr. McDonald and Stella closely about the circumstances in which the plantation's slaves live and work. With Stella as her guide, she begins to explore the plantation. While walking through the grounds she is appalled to encounter Mr. Brown ruthlessly whipping "a black Hercules of

MULTIPLE NARRATORS, BORROWED LANGUAGES

"A central concern in Phillips's later novels has to do with loss of speech, and distortions of self through borrowed languages. *Cambridge* (1991) . . . seeks[s] to re-fashion and re-enter varieties of voices and written language, and to show characters who struggle to communicate through them, or whose vision is obscured through the language they attempt to use."

(Lee, p. 26)

a brute," an older man who despite the whipping "steadfastly refused to flinch away" (*Cambridge*, pp. 41-42). She learns later that the aged slave's name is Cambridge.

On her first evening at the Great House (the common term for a plantation's main residence), Emily had been irked by the inappropriate presence at the dining table of a strangely bold black woman, to whom Stella, though nominally in charge of the household, seemed to defer. While ill Emily had dined alone in her room. Now rejoining Mr. Brown at dinner, she is again offended by the unaccountable presence at the table of "the same insolent negro woman," whose name is Christiania (*Cambridge*, p. 58). Emily's attempts to make the slave woman leave escalate into a shouting match when Christiania refuses, claiming that Mr. Brown (who is absent when the altercation takes place) has allowed her at the

table. After Emily flees from this disconcerting and humiliating situation, Stella tells her that Christiania is an obeah woman, an occult practitioner whose powers make the other slaves fear and respect her. Emily also suspects that Brown has been enjoying a sexual relationship with Christiania, which explains her presence at the table. Emily orders Brown to keep the woman away, and Christiania no longer appears at the table.

Subsequently Emily finds a new closeness developing between herself and the increasingly attentive Brown, as he walks the estate with her and explains the process of growing the sugarcane and extracting the sugar from it. He also defends his brutal punishment of the slaves as the only way to keep them from rebelling, a concern that he says was underestimated by the lax Mr. Wilson, whom he also accuses of stealing from the estate.

At the same time, to her growing alarm, Emily repeatedly discovers Christiania muttering imprecations and scratching symbols in the dirt at night under Emily's window. Only Cambridge seems to have any influence over the woman, and he is appointed to stand watch at Emily's bedroom at night. Emily is surprised to find him—a supposedly uneducated heathen slave—reading the Bible as he does so. When she quizzes him about it, his self-assured response seems to lack suitable deference, offending her.

Emily's relationship with Mr. Brown, whom she begins calling "Arnold" in her narrative, becomes more intimate. One day they return from a picnic to find Cambridge charged with stealing meat from the kitchen, "an opportunity," Emily says, "for the testing of Arnold's theories on negro punishment" (*Cambridge*, p. 111). Brown goes to confront Cambridge with the accusation and returns enraged, claiming that the slave has attacked him. Several weeks later, as Brown considers Cambridge's punishment, Christiania disappears, creating a second topic for gossip among both whites and blacks on the plantation. Adding to the increasing tension, Mr. Wilson suddenly reappears and appeals to Emily, claiming that he stole nothing from the estate, and that "his only crime" in running the plantation was to pursue "the maximum profit compatible with humane decency" in his treatment of the slaves (*Cambridge*, p. 125).

Unsure of how to handle the matter, Emily collapses emotionally and physically, fearing that Mr. Brown will abandon her if she takes Wilson's side (we later learn that their relationship has progressed to one of sexual intimacy and that she is in fact carrying Brown's child). A final journal entry on Christmas Day relates starkly that Brown has been killed, ambushed by Cambridge while returning from church, and that Cambridge himself has been hanged for the murder. As Mr. McDonald attends her bedside, Emily records that Wilson has resumed his old position as manager. Ashamed for reasons she does not specify, she fears her father's arrival will result in "a major scandal" (*Cambridge*, p. 128).

Cambridge's statement, at just over 30 pages about one-quarter the length of Emily's narrative, purports to be recorded as he awaits execution. Aside from his "true Guinea name, Olumide," Cambridge remembers little of his early life on the Guinea coast of West Africa, just a vague impression of loving parents before his abduction, at about age 15, by African slave traders who sold him to the English (*Cambridge*, p. 134). Turned over to the mysterious "men of no color," he and his fellow captives wonder if they are going to be eaten (*Cambridge*, p. 135). Cambridge survives the harsh Middle Passage, arriving in the Carolinas, from where, having been sold to a London sea captain, he immediately sails for England. During this journey a kindly English clerk teaches him a little English, introduces him to Christianity, and persuades him to answer to his new name as a slave, Thomas.

For most of the next decade he lives in London, serving his master, a retired slave ship captain (the narrative fixes this time as shortly after the abolition of the slave trade in 1807). At the same time, with his master's approval, he studies English and the Bible under an Evangelical Christian, Miss Spencer. Taking the name David Henderson, he eventually marries a fellow servant in the household, a Christian Englishwoman named Anna. Freed after his master's death, at Miss Spencer's suggestion Cambridge travels the country with his white wife. As David Henderson, he lectures on Christian salvation and the evils of slavery. After Anna dies, Miss Spencer suggests that Cambridge extend his Christian mission to his native Africa, but en route to Africa Cambridge is robbed and enslaved by the ship's corrupt captain. He again finds himself in chains, enduring the psychological and physical traumas of the Middle Passage—which are made all the worse by his continuing grief for Anna, and his deep indignation at his treatment as a free English Christian. This time he arrives in the West Indies, where he is purchased by Mr. Wilson, who gives him the name Cambridge.

As the years pass Cambridge at first holds out hope of achieving freedom and returning to his former life in England. Forming a bond with a strange and unpopular slave girl whose sufferings have left her mentally ill, he eventually takes her as his wife, giving her the name Christiania. When Brown replaces Wilson as the plantation's manager, Cambridge's dignified demeanor provokes Brown's bullying, and Cambridge relates how Brown eventually takes out his anger at Cambridge by repeatedly forcing himself on the increasingly deranged Christiania. This escalat-

---

SLAVE REBELLIONS IN THE BRITISH CARIBBEAN

How real was the threat raised in the novel by the plantation manager Mr. Brown, of slaves fomenting a rebellion around the time of the novel? Slaves of the region launched a successful revolution in French-controlled Saint-Domingue (now Haiti) in 1791, so the fear was well-founded. British-controlled areas in the region would not experience a similarly successful revolution. In St. Kitts and the other Leeward Islands, white society prevented slaves from associating with one another and from challenging it, which kept the slaves divided, weak, and unable to mount a large-scale rebellion. They, however, did plan insurrections, including one on St. Kitts in 1778, whose perpetrators intended "to murder the Inhabitants, to deliver the Island to the French, or any Persons who would make them Free" (Goveia, p. 95). Elsewhere, in Barbados, Demerara, and Jamaica, rebellions broke out in 1816, 1829, and 1831, respectively. "The Barbados rebellion seems to have been part of a new pattern of rebellions . . . aimed at forcing local governing assemblies to implement reforms which were suspected by slaves of having been ordered by Great Britain" (Beckles and Shepherd, p. 383).

---

ing conflict sets the stage for their violent confrontation after Cambridge is accused of theft (he presents his act as borrowing). In the ensuing struggle, Brown is killed. Cambridge now awaits his execution for Brown's death.

Part III relates these events in sensational journalistic style from the perspective of the white West Indian slaveowner. Brown's sexual predation of Christiania is called "an innocent amour," like that carried out by "many other white men on this island," while Cambridge's marriage with her is labeled the "fanciful notions of a Christian life of moral and domestic responsibility which he, in common with his fellow slaves, was congenitally unsuited to" (*Cambridge*, pp. 171-72). The account ends with Cambridge's trial, hanging, and gibbeting (the display of an executed criminal's body). In the Epilogue we learn that Emily, having lost Brown's child in childbirth, lives in disgrace and poverty off the plantation. Cared for by the loyal Stella and supported by the charity of the slaves who live nearby, she hopes only for a quick death.

Levels of racism. In its opening pages the novel makes explicit reference to the changing political atmosphere that permitted the abolitionists to prevail over the planters' coalition. Emily Cartwright's father owns a large plantation that he has never visited, and may be presumed to belong to the West Indian Interest, the political lobby opposing the abolitionists. As she sets out on her voyage to survey the estate on her father's behalf, Emily has the following hope:

> Perhaps my adventuring will encourage Father to accept the increasingly common, though abstract, English belief in the iniquity of slavery. It is increasingly . . . argued with much vigour, that the lordship over one's own person is a blessing far beyond mere food and shelter.
>
> (*Cambridge*, pp. 7-8)

Yet her exposure to slavery's degradation soon modifies the liberal outlook with which she began her journey. Within days of arriving, she concludes that the antislavery movement has in fact been misguided in assuming that the slaves would value freedom: "It would appear that Mr Wilberforce and his like have been volleying well wide of the mark, for the greatest fear of the black is not having a master who they know they can turn to in times of strife" (*Cambridge*, p. 37). Soon after that, she writes to her father suggesting that on her return she undertake a lecture tour and a writing career in support of slavery.

Actually Emily reveals a tendency to racial prejudice before her shift from opposing slavery to supporting it. As soon as she lands on the island, she shows a willingness to accept the white racism that prevails there: "Generally speaking, the lighter the shade of black, the nearer to salvation and acceptability was the negro. A milkier hue signified some form of white blood, and it should be clear to even the most egalitarian observer that the more white blood flowing in a person's veins, the less barbarous will be his social tendencies" (*Cambridge*, p. 25). Later Emily endorses similar views that she hears expressed

by the "intelligent and humane" Mr. McDonald (*Cambridge*, p. 33). She calls him "a man of impartial mind" because he argues against those who believe that Africans are inhuman, though he at the same time maintains their "self-evident inferiority" and inherent suitability for labor under the superior and more civilized white Europeans (*Cambridge*, p. 35).

Two levels of racism are thus at work: the prevalent strong form, which holds that blacks are subhuman (a common belief was that, like animals, they did not possess souls); and the more "intelligent and humane" racism that accepts blacks' humanity but still maintains their inferiority to whites. This last is the racism held by McDonald and Emily, who look down on the other form as unenlightened. Yet there were a few white voices in the early nineteenth century that rejected racism in whatever form it took. Often they were the voices of Nonconformist (Non-Anglican) Christians, such as the Quakers in both England and America, who in the late eighteenth century began condemning slavery and proclaiming the equality of blacks in the eyes of God. In his 1823 pamphlet Wilberforce too explicitly attacks racism, which he refers to as a "contemptuous aversion to the Negro race" found "in the minds of Europeans in general" (Wilberforce, p. 9).

Sources and literary context. Phillips has explained that the inspiration for *Cambridge* came to him in the British Library in London, where he discovered the *Journal of a Lady of Quality*, an account by a Scottish woman named Janet Schaw of her trip from Edinburgh to the Caribbean in the early nineteenth century. She went, in fact, to Phillips's native St. Kitts, and Phillips realized that his brother had once lived next door to the ruins of the Great House at which Schaw recorded attending a large formal dinner. In recreating the experiences of both Emily and Cambridge, Phillips relied heavily on similar historical documents, often incorporating substantial portions of text word for word. Emily's narrative draws on the published accounts such as Matthew Gregory ("Monk") Lewis's *Journal of a West Indian Proprietor* (pub. 1834) and Lady Nugent's *Journal of her Residence in Jamaica from 1801 to 1805*, among several others, while Cambridge's statement is closely modeled on the popular autobiography of the African-born abolitionist and former slave Olaudah Equiano (1750-97). Critic Evelyn O'Callaghan has suggested that by incorporating such verbal echoes and structural parallels, the novel attempts "to interrogate and, possibly, rewrite the European record of the West Indies" (O'Callaghan, p. 34).

Events in History at the Time the Novel Was Written

Immigration and racism in Britain. After World War II, leaders in the West Indies and elsewhere in the British Empire increasingly demanded the right of self-government. In the Leeward Islands, the subsequent process of decolonization resulted in the creation of the independent West Indies Federation in 1958. However, economic problems caused massive emigration, mostly to Britain. In 1962 the federation was replaced by the West Indies Associated States, in which the individual states (Antigua, Dominica, Grenada, St. Kitts-Nevis and Anguilla, St. Lucia, and St. Vincent) retained internal self-government, but voluntarily gave Britain authority over foreign affairs, defense, and fiscal policy. The associated states each achieved full independence in the 1970s and early 1980s, except for Anguilla, which opted to remain under British control.

Meanwhile, the British government had promoted immigration under the 1948 British Nationality Act, which permitted citizens of Commonwealth nations to settle in Britain as a way of ameliorating a shortage of labor in the expanding postwar economy. By the late 1950s, however, racial hostility from the white British population had become front-page news. In the summer of 1958, for example, violent riots erupted between crowds of mutually antagonistic whites and blacks in London's Notting Hill area. Such events made immigration a burning political issue. Meanwhile, newcomers continued to arrive, so that by 1962 over 300,000 black West Indians had immigrated to Britain, Caryl Phillips's family among them. In that year the 1962 Commonwealth Immigrants' Act removed the automatic right of Commonwealth citizens to settle in Britain, a reversal that many observers have seen as aimed at excluding blacks from immigrating to Britain.

Race relations continued to be a divisive problem in Britain into the 1990s, aggravated by events that had transpired since but dating back to the developments at mid century. As one historian noted in 1988, "the decade between 1948 and 1958 was formative in the development of Britain's modern race relations, and the seeds of many of today's conflicts and challenges were sown then" (Pilkington in Panayi, p. 172).

Reception. Critics almost uniformly applauded *Cambridge*, singling out Phillips's sensitive recreation of the nineteenth-century voices—one female and upper-class, one enslaved and Evangelical Christian—which tell the bulk of the story. While praising the book as "a virtuoso exercise in narrative voice," Rita Ciresi sounded a dissonant note, finding that the story "loses some of its emotional grip" when the focus shifts to

---

PARALLELS BETWEEN *CAMBRIDGE* AND HISTORICAL ACCOUNTS

Cambridge's story closely parallels that of Olaudah Equiano, whose autobiography, published posthumously in 1798, was a bestseller in Britain in the early nineteenth century. Like *Cambridge* (whose original name, Olumide, recalls Equiano's first name), Equiano was born in Africa, captured as a boy, enslaved under various names, converted to Christianity, and freed. Also like Cambridge, Equiano married an Englishwoman and traveled in England lecturing against slavery. Throughout the novel, Phillips paraphrases or quotes *verbatim* from Equiano's writings and other historical sources, as when Cambridge is re-enslaved while returning to Africa:

- CAMBRIDGE: My former passage rose in dreadful review and showed only misery, stripes and chains. In one moment of weakness I called upon God's thunderous avenging power to direct the sudden state of death to myself, rather than permit me to become a slave and be passed from the hand of one man to another. . . .
- EQUIANO: My former slavery now rose in dreadful review to my mind, and displayed nothing but misery, stripes, and chains; and, in the first paroxysm of my grief, I called upon God's thunder and his avenging power to direct the stroke of death to me rather than permit me to become a slave, and be sold from lord to lord.

(Adapted from O'Callaghan, pp. 34-47)

Cambridge himself (Ciresi, p. 127). Yet Maya Jaggi found *Cambridge* "a masterfully sustained, exquisitely crafted novel" that achieves "a profound marriage of stylistic virtuosity and artistic purpose," writing in the *Times Literary Supplement* that it "offers a startling anatomy of the age of slavery and of the prejudices that were necessary to sustain it" (Jaggi, p. 10). Another critic found that "Events and ideas matter in this fictional world, but not as much as the humanity, with all its depths and nuances, of the characters," going on to assert that with *Cambridge*, Caryl Phillips "takes a firm step towards joining the company of the literary giants of our time" (Garrett, p. 1).

—Colin Wells

For More Information

Beckles, Hilary, and Verene Shepherd, eds. *Caribbean Slave Society and Economy.* London: James Currey, 1991.

Ciresi, Rita. Review of *Cambridge,* by Caryl Phillips. *Library Journal* 117 (1 February 1992): 127.

Garrett, George. Review of *Cambridge,* by Caryl Phillips. *New York Times Book Review,* 16 February 1992, 1.

Goveia, Elsa V. *Slave Society in the British Leeward Islands at the End of the Eighteenth Century.* Westport, Conn.: Greenwood Press, 1965.

Harrison, Brian. *Peaceable Kingdom: Stability and Change in Modern Britain.* Oxford: Oxford University Press, 1982.

Jaggi, Maya. Review of *Cambridge,* by Caryl Phillips. *Times Literary Supplement,* 15 March 1991, 10.

Lee, A. Robert. *Other Britain, Other British: Contemporary Multicultural Fiction.* London: Pluto, 1995.

O'Callaghan, Evelyn. "Historical Fiction and Fictional History: Caryl Phillips' *Cambridge.*" *Journal of Commonwealth Literature* 39, no. 2 (1993): 34-47.

Panayi, Panikos. *Racial Violence in Britain in the Nineteenth and Twentieth Centuries.* London: Leicester University Press, 1996.

Phillips, Caryl. *Cambridge.* London: Bloomsbury, 1991.

Solow, Barbara L., and Stanley L. Engerman, eds. *British Capitalism and Caribbean Slavery: The Legacy of Eric Williams.* Cambridge: Cambridge University Press, 1987.

Ward, J. R. *British West Indian Slavery, 1750-1834: The Process of Amelioration.* Oxford: Oxford University Press, 1988.

Wilberforce, William. "An Appeal to the Religion, Justice, and Humanity of the Inhabitants of the British Empire, in Behalf of the Negro Slaves in the West Indies." In *Slavery in the West Indies.* New York: Negro Universities Press, 1969.

The Country Girls

by
Edna O'Brien

Edna O'Brien was born in 1932 in County Clare, a region between the Shannon and the Atlantic coast of Ireland. She had a rural Catholic upbringing, and moved to Dublin in 1948, where she graduated from Pharmacy College. In 1954 she married and, a couple of years later, moved with her husband to London. Encouraged by a publisher for whom she was working, she began writing the fictional account of growing up in rural Ireland that ultimately became *The Country Girls*. When the novel first appeared, it was banned in Ireland under the Censorship of Publications Act—a fate shared by many works of Irish and foreign origin during this period. By the time the Censorship Act was reformed and largely dismantled in 1967, a younger generation had become the audience for Edna O'Brien's early novels, all of which now became available. O'Brien wrote two sequels. *The Country Girls* was quickly followed by *The Lonely Girl* (also published as *Girl with the Green Eyes*) in 1962 and *Girls in their Married Bliss* in 1964, forming a trilogy of novels with Kate and Baba as the central characters. *The Country Girls* and its two sequels established Edna O'Brien as a distinctive and courageous voice in modern Irish literature.

Events in History at the Time the Novel Takes Place

The Age of De Valera. In the Ireland of the late 1940s, when Kate and Baba are about 14 years old in *The Country Girls*, a dour feeling of isola-

> ## THE LITERARY WORK
>
> A novel set in the West of Ireland and Dublin in the late 1940s and early 1950s, first published in Britain and Ireland in 1960.
>
> ## SYNOPSIS
>
> Two teenage girls, Kate and Baba, survive the terrors of their convent boarding school and move to the big city, learning about life, men, and each other along the way.

tion could be clearly sensed by both native inhabitants and visitors. Ireland had maintained a posture of neutrality throughout World War II and then was politically marginalized by the changes and opportunities of the postwar world in Europe and beyond. The United States, facing the complex challenges of the Cold War, the competition with the Soviet Union for world leadership, was less than interested in Ireland's local and rather dismal problems. Although for all practical purposes, Irish neutrality had operated to the benefit of the Allies, its continuation of diplomatic relations with Nazi Germany, including the expression of condolences to the German ambassador in Dublin upon the death of Adolph Hitler on April 30, 1945, had led to a ban against Ireland on membership in the new United Nations organization, which would not be removed until 1955.

The Country Girls

Edna O'Brien

In economics, the depression of the 1930s had left a deep mark on Ireland, deeper than on many other places; its standard of living was low, particularly when compared with Britain. The bleak prospects facing the population made emigration an easy choice.

Finally, the cultural vitality of the nation had been distorted and disabled by the application of rigorous and undiscriminating Catholic moral standards to movies, literature and all forms of public media. Movies were cut or banned for reasons that seem extremely peculiar now. Not only pornographic material, but mainstream novels and short stories, whether by Irish or foreign writers, could be presented to the Publications Censorship Board and banned from Irish shores on the most absurd grounds. In the case of the novel *The Land of Spices* by Kate O'Brien, for instance, just one sentence referring to homosexuality was enough to justify banning (Brown, p. 151). Theaters had to be careful in their choice of plays. Paintings with a hint of nudity, even those with clearly religious subjects, were refused for exhibition in public buildings. The shadow of Church disapproval hung over public debates on reforms in social policy, health, sports, and education. What made things worse was that the low level of economic activity, the constant stream of young people "voting with their feet,"

that is, emigrating across the Irish Sea to Britain, and the sense of isolation from the outside world were often answered, not by an admission that something was seriously wrong, but by a kind of smug paternalism, assuring the population that Ireland was in fact an oasis of wholesomeness and Catholic piety in a world of secular materialism and corruption. The roots of this phenomenon can be found in the previous decade.

From independence to conservative isolationism. In 1937, to the satisfaction of Prime Minister Eamon De Valera, the proposed new Constitution of Ireland was passed by the electorate in a referendum, and with this document a long period of conflict in Irish history was laid to rest. Ireland had emerged from a long period of war and turmoil, but rather than entering on a journey into the future with all the optimism and robustness a newly liberated nation might be expected to show, the people embarked on an era of social conservatism, inflexible and narrow Catholic values, and cultural isolation. For most of the previous 70 years, a national struggle against the imperial authority of Great Britain had been carried on in one form or another, sometimes through peaceful, parliamentary methods such as those of Charles Parnell and the Irish Party between the 1880s and 1914, sometimes in the shape of armed rebellion, like the one that took place in Dublin during Easter Week 1916. A new militant nationalist movement formed in 1917 called Sinn Féin (pronounced "shin fane," it means, in rough translation, "ourselves"). Ireland finally fought the War of Independence (1919-1921). Afterwards, representatives of the British government and the "underground" Irish government, which was led by Sinn Féin, hammered out the Treaty of 1922, which granted a high level of autonomy to an Irish Free State but at the same time established Partition—that is, the separation of the six largely Protestant counties in northeast Ireland to be retained under British rule. This arrangement provoked a split in Sinn Féin and armed conflict within its military wing the IRA (Irish Republican Army). The first group (led by Michael Collins) believed that Ireland needed peace and that the limited independence gained under the Treaty from the British government offered the best chance for successful self-rule; the second group (led by De Valera) felt that the Treaty with its partition of the country was a gross and unacceptable betrayal of the ideals of national independence. Ultimately the armed conflict escalated into the Irish Civil War, which lasted 10 months from

1922 to 1923, leaving a bitter and rancorous wound across Ireland, one that would take at least two generations to heal. In 1925 De Valera founded the Fianna Fáil party to represent the defeated side in the Civil War, and in 1927 he led the party into the Dáil, the national parliament. Fianna Fáil went on to win the 1932 general election, and De Valera became Prime Minister.

The later 1920s meanwhile saw some very positive developments outside government: the establishment of the national broadcasting station Radio Eireann brought the modern world to remote villages and farms and, most importantly, the River Shannon Hydro-electric Scheme provided power to rural towns and communities in the midlands and West. With these new developments came the potential and pressing need for innovation in Irish education and other fields. Unfortunately, however, the range of political and social debate in Ireland was becoming increasingly marked by a combination of conservative anti-intellectualism and authoritarian Catholic teaching.

The victory of this concept of Irish national identity over a more diverse and multicultural version was relatively recent. Before 1922, both the size of the Protestant population in Ireland (about 25 percent of the total) and the historical contribution by Protestant leaders to the struggle for national independence meant that Irish nationalism had to promote a more open, complex and secular ideal than an exclusionary focus on majority Catholic rule. The long agony of World War I, the chaos of the War of Independence and the Civil War, and the creation of Northern Ireland had brought traditional Protestant Ireland to a very weakened state, however. Yes, the new mini-state of Northern Ireland had a Protestant majority, but a Presbyterian one that differed distinctly from the Anglicans in the South. These southern Protestants were in a tight spot: seeing little to attract them in Northern Ireland, they were meanwhile a minority with little chance of making their presence felt in the new Irish Free State. Moreover, thousands of Protestant families emigrated from Ireland to Britain, Australia, and South Africa, decreasing their substantial 25 percent of the population. In the end, the Irish Protestant minority sported a largely negative or equivocal attitude toward the Irish Free State that was affected by their decreasing numbers and declining political strength. During the 1920s, Protestants discovered they were becoming foreigners in their own land, partly due to their own failure to embrace the project of Irish national independence with enthusiasm, and partly due to the growing opinion that those who identified themselves as Protestant and Anglo-Irish, with some kind of residual loyalty to Britain, could no longer be considered part of the nation. The nation was now Catholic, Gaelic, and nationalist, characteristics that would define the shape of Irish society in the future. The arrival into power of De Valera and the Fianna Fáil party was to be the final nail in the coffin of Anglo-Irish Protestant hegemony. Its demise would be cemented by the 1937 Constitution.

The Constitution was De Valera's way of putting on record what had never really been in doubt: that the Irish Free State was a Catholic nation and public policy would adapt itself to this fact whether anyone liked it or not—and most everyone did like it. Certain provisions of the document were also Fianna Fáil's peace offering to the Catholic Church hierarchy, whose members had been either neutral or hostile toward militant nationalism. Article 44, which would be removed by referendum in 1972, stated that the Catholic Church had a "special position" in Irish society. Article 41 gave constitutional force to the notion that a married woman's place is in the home, not on the job market. The social engineering of the De Valera Constitution would be felt deeply in Irish society over the following decades. Despite his history as a revolutionary nationalist and the secular vision of Irish republicanism, De Valera's message was clear: there would be no social revolution in Ireland, no cultural experimentation, no open engagement with the modern world, but rather the maintenance of a conservative, inflexible Catholic philosophy, an obsessive idealization on a Gaelic past allied to mandatory teaching of the Irish language in schools in ways that ignored the economic reasons for its decline, and a consciously inward-looking isolation from the struggles and issues of the wider world. This is the Ireland in which the novel's Kate and Baba are growing up.

Leaving the rural past. Despite the advances made since independence, Ireland in 1950 was not a place of prosperity or optimism. At the same time, it was not simply a failed political experiment collapsing into violence and despair. What you saw depended on one's perspective. From one angle of observation, Ireland was one of the most successful examples of postcolonial development: it was a functioning democracy; it was administered by a noncorrupt civil service;

its military and police forces obeyed the civil authority without question; it educated its children better than some countries, though less well than others; it was a society governed by the rule of law. From another angle, however, Ireland evinced the confusion afflicting a society emerging from long years of colonial domination. An aspect of this confusion was a conflict between rural and urban values, experiences, and ideas of social change.

THE RURAL VISION

The poet Patrick Kavanagh (1904-67), author of *The Great Hunger*, was born in the northern county of Monaghan and grew up in a world of small, subsistence farming. A largely self-educated man who had no formal education after the age of 14, he went to Dublin in the early 1930s and began to attract considerable attention for his laconic, conversational poems. His poetry was anti-heroic; not political or nationalist, it focused on everyday experience and its unexpected depths. In 1942 Kavanagh took a different path and brought out *The Great Hunger*, a long poem dealing with the tragedy of the rural small farmer and a society in a cycle of emptiness and decline. Always suspicious of urban intellectuals and their tendency to romanticize country life as part of a nationalist cultural formula, Kavanagh's poem took bleak irony to new heights. Realistic and implacably honest, *The Great Hunger* (the name echoes the Irish Famine of the nineteenth century) follows the life of Patrick Maguire from when he is an awkward young man embarrassed by girls and worried by thoughts of sin, through the increasing loneliness and sexual frustration of his adult years, to the hopelessness of his old age. Unmarried, childless, Maguire cut a haunting figure at the door of his house. The verse envisions him as "a ragged sculpture" molded by the wind that "Screams the apocalypse of clay / In every corner of this land," evoking one of the most memorable poetic images to emerge from Irish writing in this period (Kavanagh, p. 23).

Although the flight from the countryside had been going on for some time, Ireland remained a remarkably rural society. It was hardly though, despite this steadfastness, a confident society. Its steadfastness reflected a deep-seated fear of change and adversity rather than self-confidence in rural values and culture.

Irish rural life was like a raft afloat in the calm after a great storm. The Famine had betrayed so many that the survivor, conscious of the frailty of his craft and of the likelihood of future buffetings, calculated its precise seaworthiness and supported a social order that allowed no significant role in the countryside for those sons and daughters who could neither inherit the land nor make an appropriate marriage. For them emigration was the only possible route to a life without the frustrations and indignities of their position as helpers about the farm they neither owned nor, accidents apart, would ever own.

(Brown, pp. 19-20)

A casualty of this social order was the eldest son, who, designated to inherit the family farm, remained single into his forties and fifties because he had no property of his own as yet; with a father who seemed likely to live a long and healthy life, the son had no place to bring a wife of his own or to raise a family. Patrick Kavanagh's social-realist epic poem "The Great Hunger" (1942) is the definitive piece of writing that takes as its theme the grim tragedy of penury, loneliness, and sexual frustration that was lurking behind the myths of rural family values and the rugged farming life. The hard reality was that the daughters and the younger sons (Irish families were generally large at this time) would move to the bigger towns, to Dublin or Cork, or across the sea to Britain. Emigration to the United States was an option for those who were more adventurous or had family connections across the Atlantic Ocean. Even young women and men who at first only moved away to go to college, rather than for economic or personal reasons, were unlikely to return except for visits. The continual seepage of young people meant that the chances of marriage in the localities they were leaving were becoming slimmer and slimmer, which encouraged more emigration. As one commentator has put it: "Rural Ireland was filled with broken families, whose fate seemed quite at variance with . . . a society which constructed itself on the sacredness of family life" (Kiberd, p. 477).

From country to city. For many, the journey to Cork or Dublin, or further on to Manchester or London, was a journey out of a depressing and restrictive environment—the farm, the village, the remote small town—to lively, exciting urban centers full of people to meet and socialize with at a large selection of locales. As Kate says in *The Country Girls* when she and Baba arrive in Dublin for the first time: "I knew now that this was the place I wanted to be. Forevermore I would be restless for crowds and lights and noise. I had gone from the sad noises, the lonely rain pelting on the galvanized roof of the chicken house" (O'Brien, *The Country Girls*, p. 132). For Kate and hundreds of thousands like her in real life, the city offered not only the bustle and the vitality that they had not known before, but also something almost as important: anonymity. Life in a rural small town could become unbearable precisely because it was almost impossible to maintain anything like a private life, particularly if you were a woman. In the days when, if you had a phone, all calls went via the village postmistress who acted as the exchange, holding a confidential conversation was difficult. Your borrowing record at the local library, the number of visits to the doctor, anything could become an item of local gossip. Despite the welcome anonymity of city life, the confrontation with the urban milieu could also be an unpleasant one. The standard of working-class housing in Dublin was appalling and had been for many decades, despite some limited success with suburban-style developments built by the city as public housing projects. Often young people who came from poor family circumstances in the country were confronted with a disturbingly different and uglier kind of poverty than they had ever known at home. It was one thing to stare admiringly at the solid, upper-middle-class houses in the leafy neighborhoods of Ballsbridge and Drumcondra in Dublin, quite another to see the decaying, crumbling tenements that housed much of the Dublin poor, along with the violence and squalor that haunted their areas.

No matter how fresh and exciting Dublin appeared to the Kates and Babas stepping off the train at one of its main railway terminals, it was still a comparatively non-urban center. The rural structures of Irish society were often surprisingly alive even among streets, stores, and office buildings of the city, as well as in its residential neighborhoods and suburban outskirts. Social conservatism and a prurient curiosity were as well established as in any small town, and municipal politics was orientated around a "client" system of personal favors and backdoor negotiations rather than issues or policies. In dealings with public agencies, personal contact was considered more important than filling out the forms correctly. As in the countryside, the Church exerted a strong influence in Dublin: if anything, the level of religious observance was higher there than in many rural areas. The expansion of the population of the greater Dublin area had been met with a well-planned strategic response on the part of the Catholic Church, whose aggressive church-building and parish-creating program from the late 1940s on resulted in the mass concentrations of people in new suburbs and satellite towns being as close to the Church and its traditional institutions as villagers were. Moreover, labor organizations played only a marginal role in the spectrum of national politics in the mid-twentieth century, which meant that the dominating ideology in both major parties, despite their bitter differences over issues of national destiny, was that of the small storekeeper or the farmer. As for the professional classes, far from being open to talent from all social backgrounds they were small and tended to act as a self-perpetuating elite. Rather than a society on the move, urban Ireland appeared to be as static and as culturally conservative as the countryside from which it drew its burgeoning population.

Dublin at mid-century, then, offered a confusing mixture of the urban experience and the rural sensibility. From a positive standpoint, it was a city with the friendly informality and relaxed atmosphere of a small town; from a negative standpoint, it had all the problems of urban decay with few of the advantages of a developed urban culture. The population was a mixture too, a diverse mixture with subpopulations that expressed certain prejudices. Although living in Dublin and raising families in the growing city, many migrants from rural areas continued to look condescendingly at their urban home and its city-born inhabitants, continuing to hold a sentimental, somewhat unrealistic notion of the qualities of the rural environment they had been so eager to leave. Recruitment policies and unspoken preferences had led to the demographic make-up of the police force and the civil service being distinctly rural in mid-twentieth-century Dublin, creating feelings of distance and alienation between these institutions and native Dubliners. The "hayseed cop" confronting the "sharp-witted slum kid" is a standard motif in Dublin folklore. In sum, despite its population of 500,000 and growing, the Dublin of the early 1950s, to which the novel's Kate and Baba migrate, was more like the home village than they would probably have cared to admit.

The Novel in Focus

Plot summary. In a small village in Clare, in the more southerly part of the West of Ireland, two girls are growing up. Caithleen Brady, called

Kate, and Bridget Brennan, known as Baba, are friends, but their friendship is distinctly unequal. Baba is confident, cheeky, and clearly the dominant member of the partnership. As the daughter of the local veterinarian, she belongs to a higher social niche in the community than Kate, whose father is an unsuccessful farmer. Kate, who is the first-person narrator of the story, continually portrays herself as less smart, less interesting, and less assured than Baba. Unlike Baba, Kate is indecisive, timid, and likely to defer to Baba's authority on every occasion. Kate's mother is the long-suffering wife of a blustering failure given to bouts of uncontrolled drinking. When the girls are 14 years old, at the beginning of *The Country Girls,* Mrs. Brady drowns in a boating accident. Unable to bear living with her domineering father, Kate spends that summer with the Brennan family; in the fall, Kate leaves for boarding school on a scholarship grant. Baba's parents, worried about her bad grades and general lack of progress, have decided to send her to the same school. Before leaving, Kate makes a trip into Limerick, the nearest big town, to buy her school uniform. In Limerick she bumps into "Mr. Gentleman," an older man, half-French, who lives with his wife near Kate's village. His real name, Monsieur du Maurier, is regarded as exotic and unpronounceable by the local people, who have provided him with a substitute identity, as shown by his nickname. Mr. Gentleman invites Kate to lunch, and she accepts, flattered by his attentions and attracted by the air of culture and wistful charm that he radiates. He drives her back home from Limerick, and they hold hands in the car.

Kate's and Baba's boarding school is a grim and joyless convent. The food is almost inedible, in the dorms the girls have to undress for bed under their bathrobes, and the atmosphere is one of authoritarian piety. The two girls are at the Catholic boarding school for three years until a wild and obscene prank, organized by Baba, leads to their hoped-for expulsion. Baba writes a pornographic message (involving a priest's private parts and a nun) on a sheet of paper and cajoles Kate into signing her name to it along with Baba's. An elderly nun finds the paper. She begins reading it aloud under the impression that it is a prayer, and faints from horror when she realizes what she is reciting. The trick works, and the girls are expelled from the school with the reputation of being evil, despicable creatures. They return home, where Kate is physically attacked by her enraged father in Baba's house.

Baba convinces her parents to let her move to Dublin to take secretarial classes. Kate decides to go with her and obtains the promise of a job in a store. It is now around the year 1950. Arriving in Dublin one fine spring evening, the young women rent a room together in a north city lodging house run by an Austrian woman, Joanna, whose English (spoken with a German accent) becomes a kind of comic soundtrack as the story progresses. Exhilarated by the freedom of being away from home and school, and by the bustle and energy of the city in contrast to the lonely silences of their rural background, Kate and Baba blossom.

Their personality differences begin to shift the balance of their relationship, with Kate tending more to resist Baba's browbeating and indomitable cynicism, at least some of the time. Kate's love for books and reading, always a source of irritation to Baba, becomes an issue when on one occasion Baba begs her furiously, if they are out together on a date, not to keep asking men if they have read James Joyce's *Dubliners* as it tends to put them off. Kate does not have Baba's single-minded energy and commitment when it comes to looking for male company, and so often ends up accompanying Baba to meet people whom Kate does not like and who tend not to like her. After one particularly disastrous evening with two older men, Kate returns home to discover to her joy that Mr. Gentleman has driven up to Dublin to visit her. They spend the night talking in his car and watching the sunrise over Dublin Bay. Mr. Gentleman stays in the city for several weeks and his and Kate's relationship develops. He becomes the first man to whom she reveals herself naked, although they do not sleep together. Before returning to the West, he invites her to come with him on a trip to Vienna. Kate, who has never traveled outside Ireland, is overwhelmed and delighted. Meanwhile, Baba, who suspects she has tuberculosis, finds it necessary to go into a sanatorium, and Kate is left on her own. On the evening Mr. Gentleman is supposed to take her to the airport, Kate places herself at the agreed-upon meeting place. Expecting to wait a few minutes, she stands for hours as the night life of the city surges around her. Mr. Gentleman never shows up. When she returns to the lodging house, Johanna gives her a telegram from him, in which he explains that both his wife and Kate's father have found out about their affair, and he had to call the whole thing off. Kate is left with the bleak remains of her romantic illusions.

The price of a good dinner. In one of the final chapters of *The Country Girls*, Baba and Kate go out on a date with two prosperous businessmen whom Baba has met previously. Harry and Reginald are middle-aged, self-assured and, in Harry's case, exploiting the opportunities offered by the absence of his wife. Baba's date, Reginald, is reasonably civil and courteous, but Kate develops her usual antipathy to Harry, her partner for the evening. He is egoistic and pompous, not to mention older than Kate would like; Kate feels uneasy in principle about Baba's interest in older men. As she says to Baba earlier in the evening: "But we want young men. Romance. Love and things" (*Country Girls*, p. 145). Baba is convinced that there is no future there: "Young men have no bloody money. At least the gawks we meet . . . a cup of damp tea in a damp hostel. Then out in the woods after tea and a damp hand fumbling under your skirt. No, sir" (*Country Girls*, p. 145). The present evening becomes fraught with sexual tension and mismatched expectations. At one point, the four are returning from an expensive meal in an exclusive hotel for which the men have paid:

> We drove back just after ten o'clock, and there was a stream of cars coming from the opposite direction.
> "Sit close to me, will you?" Harry said in an exasperated way. As if I ought to know the price of a good dinner.
>
> (*Country Girls*, p. 152).

Harry drives them to his house, where Reginald and Baba disappear for a time, leaving Kate and Harry alone. Harry makes sexual advances to Kate who repels him forcibly. His response to Kate's protests is "Why in God's name did you come, then?" Eventually, he drives the two women back home, Reginald having drifted off to sleep. It's not quite clear whether or not Baba and Reginald have actually slept together or not. Baba claims that Reginald is not married, but Kate does not quite believe it.

Kate's visceral dislike of the date at the house and the evasiveness of Baba regarding the nature of her relationship with Reginald reflect the pressures and double standards that young single women had to negotiate in the particular atmosphere of that period in modern Irish history. The deeply Catholic stamp on the society's moral guidelines meant that an intense hypocrisy was often the norm when socializing with the opposite sex. Reginald and Harry are obviously respectable men in the usual sense of the term—upright citizens and prosperous members of the community. They use their money to attract women as men with their resources might do anywhere else. The difference is that the reigning social ideology in Ireland at the time denied that any such thing happened. Even if a married

THE IRISH AND TUBERCULOSIS

At the conclusion of *The Country Girls*, Baba has to go away to a sanatorium for suspected tuberculosis (TB). The threat of TB was one of the major unsolved health and social problems haunting Ireland at mid-century. The TB statistics were dismaying—a fatality rate of well over one in 1,000 Irish in 1950, including many young people.

Family members who contracted TB were often kept isolated at home. There were extremely limited in-patient medical facilities available, even in Dublin, leaving parents with one sick child torn between wanting to care for him or her and to keep the infection away from the rest of the family. In 1948 De Valera's government was defeated at the polls for the first time in 16 years. The new government was an unstable coalition in which a small, left-orientated party held the reins of power. With these changes came a desire for reform. A young doctor named Noel Browne ran for election, won a seat, and was appointed Minister of Health and Social Welfare. Browne had seen three members of his family die of tuberculosis and was passionately convinced that the problem needed to be tackled immediately and aggressively. Facing a conservative government bureaucracy and a suspicious Irish Medical Association, Browne managed nonetheless to put through an ambitious, targeted health services plan that involved radical increases in the number of sanatoriums available throughout the country, use of the new BCG vaccination, and the drug streptomycin. Trying something that no government official had ever attempted, he tapped into the assets of the Irish Hospitals Sweepstakes (a kind of national lottery), using them to raise further independent funding for his project. Although the coalition government lasted less than two years, collapsing after a controversy over universal health care, Browne's contribution to defeating the threat of TB in Ireland has become part of the nation's political folklore. From a death toll of 3,103 in 1948, deaths from tuberculosis fell to 432 in 1961 (Coogan, p. 648). Browne would be elected to parliament many times over the next 35 years but never again occupy a government office. His combination of organizational energy and moral passion, however, left an indelible mark on Irish society.

man took advantage of his wife's brief absence to go out on the town, trawl the bars, and find a woman, the national pretense was that such things only went on abroad, say in London or Paris, never in Dublin. Pregnancy resulting from such a liaison was a horrific prospect: a woman had little recourse when faced with a social structure that protected the established family and the husband against all accusations. To be an unmarried mother was simply impossible. Contraception was generally unavailable. Termination meant an expensive back street abortion, probably in England. Even having a child out of wedlock and giving it up for adoption, an option administered entirely by the Catholic Church, meant a humiliating procedure involving several months in a convent, where one lived in an atmosphere of moral censure and authoritarian discipline.

Despite all this, Kate is not so much under the pressure of Catholic moral teaching as disgusted, in an instinctive way, by the limited and degrading nature of what constitutes relations between the sexes in the Dublin scene. It was assumed that the man would pay for dinner and entertainment and, depending upon personality and expectation, some kind of sexual activity was seen as the legitimate compensation for that expenditure. She senses that this is wrong, that this cannot be all there is, but is confused by Baba who operates confidently on precisely that principle. Balancing the different demands of a guilt-inducing Catholic upbringing against normal desires for a social life as well as for love and intimacy was a subtle juggling act for women in Ireland, and Kate is not unusual in feeling each one of these elements tugging at her at different times, or even the same time. As Declan Kiberd points out, Kate and Baba are "believable, fallible, flesh-and-blood women, neither paragons nor caricatures" (Kiberd, p. 566). Edna O'Brien's achievement was, in many ways, to open up the unspoken dimensions of Irish women's lives with both a sense of their everyday frustrations and an ear for the satirical and anarchic backchat that young women engage in when alone with each other and away from the public eye.

Literary context. The first person narration and the theme of *The Country Girls* would suggest some autobiographical influence from the writer's own history. The apparently casual and informal style in which Kate tells her story, however, giving the impression of a close connection between author and narrator, is also doing some-

thing unusual, even risky. It was not only the presence of sexual plot elements that caused the book to be banned, or what was perceived as the anti-Catholic polemic of *The Country Girls*; it was also the comic grotesquerie and "vulgar" detail that got O'Brien into trouble.

> The brassiere I bought was cheap. Baba said that once brassieres were washed they lost their elasticity, so we might as well buy cheap ones and wear them until they got dirty. We threw the dirty ones in the dustbin, but later we found that Joanna [the landlady] brought them back in and washed them.
> "Christ, she'll resell them to us," Baba said, and bet me sixpence.
>
> (*Country Girls*, p. 141)

O'Brien's willingness to casually mention what young ladies just did not talk about in public—underwear is a good example—gives her novel a ribald energy that it would not have had if it had been more "serious" in its approach. Whereas other novels employed a demure vagueness about the nitty-gritty of everyday life, hers favored a brazen frankness. *The Country Girls* is clearly a comic novel in some respects, but not in others. The characters in Kate's village, such as Baba's unstable mother leave little room for humor. What results from this mix of tone is an unashamedly realistic, female coming-of-age story that challenges the large number of male-centered narratives, by Irish writers, in this vein (for example, James Joyce's *Portrait of the Artist as a Young Man*, D. H. Lawrence's *Sons and Lovers*, and Brian Moore's *The Emperor of Ice Cream*). The specific references to Joyce's *Dubliners* in Edna O'Brien's novel point to a conscious attempt to appropriate some of the narrative elements and the psychological intensity of the *Dubliners* stories and use them for different purposes. As one critic has put it, O'Brien's commitment to a realistic rather than a fantastic or whimsical style leads her to imitate the "tart, desperate comedy" of *Dubliners* (Gillespie, p. 111).

The Country Girls and its sequel, *The Lonely Girl*, could be regarded also as Kate's account of how she came to understand the progress of her life. Several years after her first novels appeared, Edna O'Brien published a short quasi-autobiography, accompanied by photos of Irish life and landscapes, called *Mother Ireland*. The text consisted of a number of lyrical prose chapters, one of which was entitled "The Books We Read." Here, she describes her childhood reading fantasies bumping up against the cold fabric of rural existence. After drifting off into a reverie stimulated by the tear-jerking melodrama of *East Lynne*, an immensely popular nineteenth century romantic novel, O'Brien describes waking up to her surroundings:

> Nothing could be further from reality. The topped egg had gone cold in its cup. There was scum on the cocoa, a voice was saying, "Have you done your exercise" or "Get that table cleaned." Outside it was growing dark. The cows were already milked, there was half a candle left which you were enjoined to spare.
>
> (O'Brien, *Mother Ireland*, p. 81)

Kate in *The Country Girls* seems to embody something of this willingness—which Baba never suffers from—to let the dream take over, to retreat from life into fiction. Her readiness to accept Mr. Gentleman's offer when he invites her on the trip to the Continent is rooted in her tendency to want more than she sees, to search beyond the everyday routine of work in the grocery store and nights spent at the dance-hall. This dimension of *The Country Girls* is continually undermined, however, by the situation comedy of life in the lodging house with Joanna and her husband Gustav. As Michael Gillespie has suggested, "a both/and incorporating impulse rather than an either/or exclusivity stands as the feature distinguishing O'Brien's humor from that of most Irish male writers" (Gillespie, p. 109).

Events in History at the Time the Novel Was Written

From silence to talk show. On a dark January evening in 1962, roughly a year after *The Country Girls* was released, the small number of Irish households that possessed television sets stared at their screens. A flickering Saint Bridget's Cross, the Celtic logo designed for RTE, the national broadcasting service, appeared. The bells of the Angelus, the prayer at 6 A.M. and 6 P.M., in Catholic churches sounded out. The announcer came on, and the Irish television age was born. The first transmission was a Mass to celebrate the event. The arrival of the national television service combined elements that symbolized its role and personality in the years to come. It would make its gestures toward the Catholic ethos of the nation, but it would change Irish society radically. As the number of households with television sets in both rural and urban areas climbed higher and higher, regional news broadcasts and documentary films brought a searching light into the dim corners of Irish life, and a late-night talk show, called *The Late Late Show*, began to open

up public debate among Irish people in ways that would have been simply inconceivable only a few short years earlier. Hosted by Gay Byrne, *The Late Late Show* tackled women's liberation, censorship of movies and books, education, health and sexuality, and so on. The invited guests argued passionately about things that had, for generations, existed under a cloak of peasant silence.

This new cultural atmosphere went hand-in-hand with the economic renewal of the country. In 1958 Eamon De Valera left office after decades in power (1932-58). Grim stagnation gave way to innovative thinking. The new Prime Minister, Sean Lemass, working with the budgetary policy expert and senior advisor T. K. Whitaker, turned around two generations of economic conservatism and protectionism. Lemass opened up the country to foreign investment and industrial expansion, and the results were extraordinary. Ireland quickly became one of the most profitable industrial locations in Europe. This altered the character of the Irish economy and had the effect of slowing down but not stopping, emigration, and also spurred the rise of a modern consumer society in Ireland. Even though many had reservations about the effects on religious faith and others questioned the sustainability of this economic boom—which was not all upward—nobody could deny that a new energy, a new optimism, and a feeling that it was indeed possible to improve life were defining elements of this period.

A number of what had seemed unshakeable cornerstones of Irish society began to vibrate and crumble. One of them was the tendency of the broad majority of Irish women to maintain a decorous silence in public life, unless they were addressing safe issues where no suspicion of "unfeminine" behavior could arise. But, despite the memorable contributions made by women like Lady Augusta Gregory, Constance Markievicz, and Hannah Sheey-Skeffington during the struggle for national independence, women's voices were not particularly welcome in Irish public life. Female candidates were rarely nominated to stand for election to local councils or the national parliament, except in rare cases where they were the widows of recently deceased public representatives. In the more revolutionary 1920s there had been attempts to increase the number of women in the Dáil political party, but these had foundered upon women voters' disinclination to vote for their own sex. Female government employees had to retire upon getting married, with the convenient result that the senior ranks of the civil service were entirely male. These inequitable conditions began now to change.

Reception. The more dramatic tale of how Edna O'Brien's *The Country Girls* was received revolves around its banning by the Censorship of Publications Board for indecency. Beyond this, the novel received some very positive reviews, mostly in Britain and the United States. In the *New Statesman* V. S. Naipaul praised *The Country Girls* as "A first novel of great charm by a natural writer," going on to describe it as "so completely, so truly realized in the writer's mind that everything that comes out has a quality of life which no artifice could achieve." Patricia Mac-Manus in the *New York Herald Tribune* commented that it "combines a guileless wit and crisp directness with a certain innocent earthiness."

In Ireland, neither the quality of the writing nor the "innocent earthiness" of the story impressed those who saw Edna O'Brien as just the latest in a long line of disrespectful writers purveying filth. The Censorship of Publications Board banned *The Country Girls* from sale or distribution in the Republic of Ireland on June 21, 1960. Two points are useful to bear in mind in relation to censorship of books in Ireland: one is that the censorship laws were supported by the majority of the population; they were not the arbitrary action of some political elite opposed by the rest of the nation. Secondly, Ireland did not operate like a police state, so the ability to bring a banned book into the country from abroad depended entirely on whether the customs officials at the airport or the harbor were going to search your luggage and, if they did, if they were interested in what you were reading. If the banned books were not found or confiscated at the port of entry, they could sit openly on your bookshelf at home and circulate among your friends. This meant that many educated people who were interested in modern Irish writing could read O'Brien's works and others that had been banned.

In 1967 the censorship law would be radically reformed, providing for the automatic lapsing of banning orders 12 years after they had been issued and an efficient appeals system for authors and publishers who felt that their books had been unjustly censored. In effect, this meant that censorship of publications in Ireland, as far as fiction was concerned, would practically cease to exist. Importation of journals and magazines was still strictly controlled, however. A couple years earlier, in 1965, an Irish glossy magazine had arranged a semiprivate deal with the government minister to whom the Censorship Board reported to publish *The Country Girls* in serial form; this seems to have been the only time that such an application was made to republish, rather than import for sale, a work under a banning order. Over the following few years after the new legislation was passed, *The Country Girls* and Edna O'Brien's other early novels—as well as those of censored colleagues—gradually appeared on bookstore and library shelves, securing their place in modern Irish writing.

—Martin Griffin

For More Information

Adams, Michael. *Censorship: The Irish Experience.* University, Ala.: University of Alabama Press, 1968.

Brown, Terence. *Ireland: A Social and Cultural History, 1922 to the Present.* Ithaca: Cornell University Press, 1985.

Coogan, Tim Pat. *De Valera: Long Fellow, Long Shadow.* London: Arrow Books/Random House, 1993.

Gillespie, Michael Patrick. "(S)he Was Too Scrupulous Always: Edna O'Brien and the Comic Tradition." In *The Comic Tradition in Irish Women Writers.* Gainesville: University Press of Florida, 1996.

Hargreaves, Tamsin. "Women's Consciousness and Identity in Four Irish Women Novelists." In *Cultural Contexts and Literary Idioms in Contemporary Irish Literature.* Totowa, N.J.: Barnes & Noble, 1988.

Kavanagh, Patrick. *The Great Hunger.* London: MacGibbon and Kee, 1966.

Kiberd, Declan. *Inventing Ireland: The Literature of the Modern Nation.* London: Vintage/Random House, 1996.

Lee, J. J. *Ireland 1912-1985: Politics and Society.* Cambridge: Cambridge University Press, 1989.

MacManus, Patricia. Review of *The Country Girls,* by Edna O'Brien. *New York Herald Tribune,* 10 April 1960, 8.

Naipaul, V. S. Review of *The Country Girls,* by Edna O'Brien. *New Statesman* 60 (16 July 1960):97.

O'Brien, Edna. *The Country Girls.* In *The Country Girls Trilogy.* New York: Plume/Penguin, 1987.

———. *Mother Ireland.* Photographs by Fergus Bourke. New York: Harcourt Brace Jovanovich, 1976.

A Disaffection

by

James Kelman

With his use of Scots vernacular and ample profanity, James Kelman has altered the landscape of the contemporary British literary scene. Kelman was born in 1946 near shipyards in the Glasgow neighborhood of Govan. At the age of eight he moved with his family to Drumchapel—an infamous housing estate on the edge of town, remote from shops and public transportation. The youngest of the five sons of struggling working-class parents, Kelman left school at age 15, dismissing its structure and lessons as irrelevant. For the next seven years, he read insatiably, educating himself while performing various menial jobs, from asbestos factory worker to bus driver before settling down to write. Convinced that working-class characters seldom occupied any role other than servant, criminal, or comic relief, he set out to express the voices of the underprivileged, making the crucial decision early in his career to use the language of those characters, in all its slang, vulgarity, and nonstandard constructions. Kelman's first short stories conformed to this model, which was so unheard-of that the typesetter refused to finish working on them. With the help of small presses, however, Kelman's fiction was published and did find a loyal audience. His early work in short stories, in such volumes as *An Old Pub Near The Angel* (1973), *Not While the Giro and other stories* (1983), and *Greyhound for Breakfast* (1985), laid the groundwork for the novels he wrote in the 1980s, including *The Busconductor Hines* (1984) and *A Chancer* (1985). Kelman's *A Disaffection* became a finalist for

THE LITERARY WORK

A novel set in the working-class neighborhoods of unemployment-torn Glasgow in the 1980s; published in 1989.

SYNOPSIS

Secondary-school teacher Patrick Doyle agonizes over his social and political alienation, seeking solace in drinking, constructing a musical instrument, starting an affair with a married colleague, and reaching out to his loving but distant family.

Britain's prestigious Booker Prize in 1989 and his *How Late it Was, How Late* won this same award in 1995. Despite this public acclaim, he has continued to live in the neighborhood he writes about, agitating for other oppressed groups in Britain and criticizing both the literary and the political establishment for their elitism. His plays, essays, and fiction draw on Glasgow speech to convey the loneliness of individuals and challenges of being male in modern society, the frustration with bureaucracy, and a yearning for beauty. *A Disaffection* traces about a week in the life of an instructor who is highly conscious of his social distance from his less-educated parents, meanwhile raising questions about the role teachers play in maintaining or challenging the status quo and about the relationship of the personal to the political.

James Kelman

Events in History at the Time the Novel Takes Place

Thatcherism and economics. As a writer interested in social change, Kelman's works deal with the present. In the 1980s, when he began to publish, the United Kingdom was experiencing a period of economic hardship rooted in the economic policies of the previous 30 years. After the shortages and hardships of World War II, the British government had nationalized such major industries as coal and the railroads and supplemented its already well-established social insurance system with socialized medical care. While prosperity marked the postwar years, the British pound was weakened by a trade imbalance, in which imports far exceeded exports. Wages were frozen and the pound was devalued in an effort to maintain good times while balancing trade, and this resulted in rapid inflation accompanied by high taxes. By the late 1970s, it became clear that Britain was in serious trouble, its former status as a world leader jeopardized. Unemployment rose ever higher as Britain's standard of living declined in the years leading up to Margaret Thatcher's election as prime minister in 1979. As if these economic woes were not enough, the

"troubles" between Protestant Unionists and the Irish Republican Army kept erupting into violence, racial tensions continued to rise, and a Scottish Nationalist movement was in the making. Thatcher took measures to contain these problems, often making very controversial choices. Many of Thatcher's policies, designed to restore the economy to its former strength, also reflected Thatcher's own beliefs that such social services as medical care and housing assistance caused people to depend too much on government aid, rather than on their own hard work.

In its departure from cradle-to-grave care, Thatcher's regime diverged from the bipartisan consensus that had marked the previous 30 years. Reversing the postwar policies of nationalization, her government privatized major industries; it dismantled parts of the welfare state, faced down union leaders and labor strikes, and sought tax cuts for the wealthy. As Britain's economy sputtered back into motion, many working-class citizens felt that their needs had been overlooked and that Thatcher's rhetoric unfairly characterized their hardships as their own fault. In her economics and accompanying discussion, Thatcher resembled her good friend, American President Ronald Reagan, who was a proponent of trickle-down economics and welfare cutbacks at the same time. Thatcher advocated, for instance, a poll tax based on the premise that all citizens should pay equally for the social services they received. Unemployment remained high, especially in traditional industries such as mining and manufacturing, fields in which Patrick Doyle's family works in *A Disaffection*. By 1987, with the third election of Thatcher and her Conservative (often called Tory) government to power, the split in Britain was clear: the Conservatives had no hold in the industrial North, including Scotland, while the progressive Labour party had little support in the economically recovering South. It is in this time of angry division that Kelman writes, as a citizen of the part of Great Britain not prospering under Thatcher's policies.

Scottish identity in Great Britain. At the same time, and especially significant for a Scottish novel, there was a rise in Scotland of a nationalist movement. Scotland had united with England to form Great Britain in 1707, and since that time the two nations had shared political leaders and economic, religious, and legal systems. There was a feeling in mid-twentieth century Scotland that the British government did not speak to Scottish interests, and a series of candidates for office proposed a devolution of power as one of their aims. These nationalist tendencies reached an apex in the 1970s, at which time the discovery of oil in the North Sea offered the promise of Scottish prosperity. Still, despite a majority in a 1977 referendum about independence, the Scottish Nationalist Party did not manage to garner enough of a popular vote to begin the move to self-governance. Class solidarity came into conflict with national solidarity, and many of the Scottish supported Britain's Labour party instead. The failure of the Scottish nationalists in the 1970s to capitalize on their natural allies against the Tories, the strong Labour party, revealed a movement out of touch with the very working class it claimed as its base. For Kelman and others like him, Scots nationalism would merely replace one government unreceptive to workers with another.

Yet Kelman's novel seems to reserve special dislike for the British government, placing condemnations of its imperialist tendencies in the mouth of the character Patrick Doyle. Indeed, Kelman's own distance from the British mainstream can be seen in his literary influences. The German writer Johann Wolfgang von Goethe, the French writer Honoré de Balzac, and the Russian writer Feodor Dostoyevsky all receive mention in *A Disaffection*, though stylistically and thematically, Austrian-born Franz Kafka and Irish-born Samuel Beckett are the most prominent literary forefathers. Worth noticing here is the absence of British influences, which, according to Kelman, is not so much a nationalist or isolationist statement as a matter of necessity. From his readings, it seemed to Kelman that no one in British literature had ever written from anything like his own experience before. "So because of this dearth of home-grown literary models I had to look elsewhere. As I say, there was nothing at all in English literature, but in English Language literature—well, I came upon a few American writers," as well as writers in Russian, German, and French (Kelman, *Some Recent Attacks*, p. 83).

Glasgow. In this rejection of a British canon, Kelman resembles other Scottish writers of his time, in particular a group called the Glasgow School. Such figures as Alasdair Gray, Liz Lochhead, Tom Leonard, and Janice Galloway are seen as major figures in the contemporary Glasgow scene. Known for their working-class perspective, use of urban landscapes, reliance on local dialect, and resistance to a dominant British perspective, many of the writers focus on the plight of the individual isolated within society. While their formal techniques may vary, these writers share a commitment to using Scots language as the standard voice in their texts, and a tendency to focus their stories on the everyday existences of urban, working-class characters. Their storylines have led many critics, reviewers, and readers to expect gritty realist texts in coarse local dialect, in a manner much like the "kailyard" texts pub-

GLASGOW AND LANGUAGE

In his essay collection *Some Recent Attacks* (1994), Kelman discusses how British literature's historical depiction of class distinctions have made such differentiations seem natural, inevitable, and aesthetic. He notes that historically the working-class character, whose language is so quaintly garbled, has been equipped with an equally inaccessible inner life:

What gobbleydygook! Beautiful! Their language a cross between semaphore and Morse code; apostrophes here and apostrophes there; a strange hotchpotch of bad phonetics and horrendous spelling—unlike the nice stalwart upperclass English here (occasionally Scottish but with no linguistic variation) whose words on the page were always absolutely and splendidly proper and pure and pristinely accurate, whether in dialogue or without, and what grammar! Colons and semicolons! Straight out of their mouths! An incredible mastery of language . . . the narrative belonged to them and them alone. They owned it. The place where thought and spiritual life exists. Nobody outwith the parameters of their sociocultural setting had a spiritual life. We all stumbled along in a series of behaviouristic activity, automatons, cardboard-cut-outs, folk who could be scrutinised, whose existence could be verified in a social or anthropological context. In other words, in the society that is English literature, 80 to 85 percent of the population simply did not exist as human beings.

(Kelman, *Some Recent Attacks*, p. 82)

lished about village life in Scotland a century before. Drawing its name from the Scots word for "a small kitchen garden," the kailyard movement relied on a natural-seeming, unsophisticated style to tell sentimental stories of humble folk. While Kelman and other writers in the Glasgow school similarly write about everyday events and common people, they actually write in reaction to such stereotypes as the kailyard tales created, often challenging the conventions of realism

(such as linear plot and a controlling narrative perspective) that marked earlier texts, instead aiming for a nuanced reproduction of working-class voices that carry the narrative authority to tell their own stories. With an ear for the ca-dences of Glasgow speech and a vernacular at once poetic and profane, Kelman leads the drive to give equal time to voices outside conventional expectations.

Glasgow is unique in Britain and in Scotland. First recognized as a town in the twelfth century, the city came into its own in the 1800s, when it dominated in shipbuilding and other heavy man-ufacturing industries. Because of its community of skilled laborers, it has historically boasted a strong worker's movement and progressive pol-itics. Unemployment has lingered in Glasgow, es-pecially in the poverty-stricken estates, longer than elsewhere in Scotland, in large part because of the permanent decline in shipbuilding and the gradual shift to a service and tourist economy. Moreover, it has always supported the arts, with a thriving opera and vigorous local literary scene. Industry, however, has meant pollution, and Glasgow is notorious for its slums, from the in-ner-city Gorbals to the more recently built es-tates such as Castlemilk on the outskirts of town. Kelman's fiction, set in dingy public buildings, fetid bus shelters, and grimy pubs, portrays a city as alienated as the characters themselves.

The educational system and red-brick uni-versities. Universal elementary education in Great Britain was made free and compulsory dur-ing the reformist Victorian era, but the goals of that education varied with the intentions the state had for various students. A university edu-cation was reserved for a tiny fraction of the very elite; most students received more vocational training. This fact hindered the population hardly at all, since the majority of jobs did not require a college degree (a concept that is itself only about 150 years old). Yet higher education in Britain has a long history; it dates to the twelfth and thirteenth centuries, with the found-ing of the oldest colleges within Oxford and Cambridge universities. It was not until the nine-teenth century, though, that higher education spread to the general population. Late in the cen-tury, many industrial towns built universities to serve their local inhabitants. Known as red brick universities to distinguish their buildings from the older stone colleges of "Oxbridge" (Oxford and Cambridge), these universities made educa-tion available to a wider pool of people. A fur-ther move to broaden university access came in 1963, with the release of the Robbins Report, which recommended that "courses of higher ed-ucation should be available for all those who are qualified by ability and attainment to pursue them and who wish to do so" (Robbins in Bligh,

HOUSING ESTATES

At the end of the Second World War, Glasgow contained some of the most decrepit and overcrowded slums in Eu-rope. Its inner-city neighborhoods were disease-ridden and un-comfortable. Families of five or even ten crowded into one or two rooms in tenements that had been built years before. Be-cause the private sector was not building enough homes, the government stepped in, funding what became known as "Council Housing" or "housing estates." At the same time, the government engaged in slum clearing, knocking down inner-city buildings. While the new housing was a significant im-provement over the tenement slums, much of it was poorly de-signed. Moreover, rebuilding was often poorly coordinated with demolition, resulting in the devastation of local commu-nities long before reconstruction took place. A further problem with the new estates came in their locations. While some were built in the inner city neighborhoods that had been cleared, others were erected on the outskirts of Glasgow, based on the assumption that car ownership would soon become universal. A strong system of public transportation was never put into place, leaving many residents stranded in poor neighborhoods that were unable to sustain local markets and shops. A cycle ensued in which estates with little public transportation and few shops were evacuated by all except the poorest tenants, which in turn led to businesses closing and further cuts in trans-portation.

> Leaving his brother Gavin's house, Pat had passed a bus stop before the end of the road but no point waiting there accord-ing to Gavin. People died of exposure waiting there. It was one of those bus stops you find in outer-city housing schemes all over Glasgow, only there for the benefit of the fucking canine population and a few desperate drunks because no buses ever went there.
>
> (Kelman, *A Disaffection*, p. 327)

The picture Pat paints characterizes the worst problems of the postwar exurban estates. Scenes throughout *A Disaffection* ex-plore the ways such remote and inaccessible housing increased both unemployment and a feeling of alienation among Glas-gow's working class.

Blackhill council housing in Glasgow, Scotland. Characters in *A Disaffection* live in council housing much like the housing in Blackhill, shown here.

p. 24). The report noted the rise in demand for education after the Second World War and the need for teachers to educate the growing populace. For the next decade, funds and access were increased; however, Margaret Thatcher's 1972 White Paper "A Framework for Expansion" called for the reduction of the number of trainees in teacher education. Further cuts throughout the 1970s and 1980s were made in response to Britain's continuing economic downturn.

While *A Disaffection*'s main character Patrick Doyle, a teacher, appears to have attended University of Glasgow, an institution with a longer history than the red bricks, his presence there stems from the inclusive admissions fostered by more open access to education through the red brick schools. The students Pat Doyle teaches are not expected to go on to college any more than he himself had been. Rather, their formal education will presumably end when they complete secondary education. For Pat, the near-inevitability of their futures outside the educational, social, and economic elite obscures the value of the material he teaches. His disenchantment with the teaching process can be attributed to the tension between economic trimming under Thatcher and an expanding student body at the secondary school level.

The Novel in Focus

Plot summary. *A Disaffection* opens with the information that "Patrick Doyle was a teacher. Gradually he had become sickened by it" (Kelman, *A Disaffection*, p. 1). This sick feeling pervades the story, which traces about a week of Pat's life. Curiously, there is very little plot development throughout the novel. This is not to say that things do not happen, just that the events resemble those of real life, with their randomness, occasional banality, and unresolved issues, especially at the novel's end. Most of the narrative is in the form of third-person interior monologue; that is, we read Pat's thoughts while they are occurring but as told to us by someone else, without use of the pronoun "I." Reading the novel feels like reading Pat's mind, a sense amplified both by the various formal, philosophical, slang, and vulgar linguistic registers that Pat uses, and by Kelman's willingness to let certain thoughts trail off as unfinished sentences and others to enter and exit Pat's mind unpredictably.

In the first scene, Pat retreats behind a building to urinate while out for drinks after work with his fellow teachers. While behind the building, he discovers a pair of cardboard pipes that he determines he can blow into like musical instruments. These pipes occupy a significant portion of Pat's thoughts throughout the story, representing the sort of purity that he feels he has lost as a teacher. Dispirited, Pat comes to feel that he cannot change the world, that he is but a cog in a machine he wants to resist. Teaching, in Pat's mind, influences children without actually offering them tools or hope for a better life. Instead, most teachers he knows are asked to help prepare children to accept the socioeconomic status into which they are born. In trying to combat the establishment he knows himself to be a part of, Pat encourages his students in subversive thoughts: "now then, I want you all to repeat after me: the present government in suppressing the poor, is suppressing our parents. . . . Our parents, who are poor, are suffering from acute poverty of the mind" (*A Disaffection*, p. 24). Working class Glasgow in the 1980s is about as unfortunate a lot as Pat can imagine, and he feels compromised by the institutional expectations of the school and guilty that he cannot give more to the "weans," or children, that he teaches.

To add to Pat's angst, he is lonely. A bachelor living on his own, he has trouble relating to other people, speaking awkwardly and often appearing to lash out at others. His experience with women is limited, and he is desperate for female companionship; mainly, he seeks the company of Alison Houston, a colleague who happens to be married, although in his typical indecisive self-dialogue, he considers bars, clubs, and prostitutes as alternatives. "What about a prostitute? A prostitute was sensible. Surely a prostitute was sensible? If it came right down to that did he really feel as low as all that and the notion that female company, that [unfinished sentence]" (*A Disaffection*, p. 79). Somewhat estranged from his parents and brother—his father is a machinist at a factory and his brother a chronically unemployed construction worker—Pat has no one he feels he can relate to, no one in whom he can confide. The pipes he brings home offer him a chance to take definitive action in a life that seems stagnated, so the day after he finds them, he paints them and begins to imagine the environment in which he would perform with them.

Meanwhile, the situation at Pat's school is deteriorating. Increasingly irritated by the conversations in the staff room, Pat announces his intention to quit his job. He is jealous of the attention Alison receives from other men and fed up with his role in perpetuating the status quo. Already frustrated, Pat plans to meet Alison for a drink after work, only to feel thwarted when

another teacher accompanies them. As Pat struggles with his emotions, often more inside his own head than participating in conversation, he also grapples with the question of how much to drink, especially as he is driving. Choosing to call it an early evening, he starts out for home, intending to play his pipes once his head is clear. In a moment of massive emotional need, he leaves his flat in a rush, desperate to make some human contact. Once in his car, he considers going to clubs, but recalls that his students frequent such places. He contemplates trying to contact Alison, reflects on former girlfriends, and thinks of a friend in England he hasn't seen in a few years. As he passes a bar he used to frequent, he contemplates entering, but "he probably wont know anybody to talk to. And even if he does . . . he is not able to talk. If he could talk he wouldn't be here" (*A Disaffection*, p. 63). As he continues to drive further and further out of Glasgow, it seems as though Pat may finally make some sort of definitive change in his life. But after a while, he turns the car around and heads home, unable or unwilling to radically change his life. The pipes offer some comfort to him, but his thoughts dart around suicide. The remainder of the weekend traces Pat's lonely wanderings—to a football match, to his parents (where he takes a bath to avoid awkward conversation), to a strained meeting with Alison in which he cannot muster the nerve to express his feelings. The emptiness in his life is crushing, seeping into the repetitive rhythm of the narrative.

Upon his return to school Monday morning, Pat is informed by his headmaster that a transfer to another school that Pat applied for has come through. As he cannot recall putting in for such a transfer, Pat is disconcerted and reacts with suspicion. The sense of a controlling state bureaucracy looms as Pat warns his students of conspiracies around them all. He leaves campus alone at the lunch hour and gets drunk, later falling down some stairs, continuing to rant to his students, and getting sick in his classroom. Later that day, he arranges to meet with Alison that night and finally makes clear to her his interest in her. She holds his hand sympathetically but says she does not want a relationship and asks him to stop calling her at home. The next day Pat sneaks away from school early and goes to his brother's house, where a drinking session is in progress. Gavin and his unemployed friends welcome Pat, although Gavin is wary. He feels resentful of his brother's dissatisfaction with his job and affluent lifestyle when he himself cannot find work at all. As Pat notes, "The levels of irony were become slippery" (*A Disaffection*, p. 255). The brothers' joking has an edge to it throughout the afternoon, and by the time Gavin's wife, Nicola, returns home, there is tension in the air. Pat agrees to stay for dinner, and to pass the time, creates for his young niece and nephew a fantastic version of the story of his discovery of the pipes, one of the few moments in the text in which Pat seems to achieve warm human contact. He also finds intimacy in a conversation with his careworn sister-in-law before leaving the house on foot, unable to drive due to the alcohol he has consumed. When no buses arrive, Pat begins to walk home, eventually running through the rain into his future, a seemingly bleak one: "It was dark and it was wet but not cold; if it had not been so dark you would have seen the sky. Ah fuck off, fuck off" (*A Disaffection*, p. 337).

Social mobility and guilt. Part of Pat's abundant discomfort with his life comes from the guilt he feels at not being happy when he believes it is such a privilege to attend college, become a teacher, and collect such a large salary. Pat's family, his brother Gavin included, sacrificed to make it possible for him to attend university. As he notes, he now earns twice as much as Gavin, and that is when Gavin can find the construction work that is his trade. Pat feels guilt and disconnection as a consequence of his upward mobility. While his family wanted him to have a "uni" education, they have little contact with the college-educated and don't quite know how to communicate with Pat; his own feelings, while sometimes phrased in the language he has acquired at college, reveal a similar discomfort in his acquired milieu. Pat is acutely aware of the disjunction between the language he grew up with and the one he now speaks; his egalitarian politics are confronted by assumptions about the superiority of educated speech that seem imbedded within language itself. During the strained weekend visit to his parents, as Pat contemplates his guilt in avoiding them, the narrative moves towards their grammar: "He should have gone straight home after the match. He just shouldni have come here? How come he came? He shouldni have fucking came" (*A Disaffection*, p. 114). From the proscriptively proper past conditional, the language shifts to a slang, "shouldni," before shifting into an incorrect construction, "have came," perhaps brought on by the slang, or perhaps by sitting at the dinner table of parents who would say "have came" and whom

Pat senses would feel awkward in the presence of their son's educated speech.

This issue of speech permeates the novel. Kelman avoids the use of quotation marks, which creates an effect of interpenetration of narrative and character voices. While many novels have a controlling narrator who translates for readers or tells them how to interpret events, Kelman offers readers of *A Disaffection* only a narrator who uses Pat's phrases but does not clarify for his audience. As the quotation above has made evident, profanity is inevitable. Kelman's own mother objects to the language he uses, but he feels that it would be a disservice to his readers and his subjects to pretend that the everyday language of Glasgow were not suffused with swearing. "In fiction whole groups in society have been suppressed by virtue of the way they speak and the language they use. If the language is taboo, the people are taboo. A culture can't exist without the language of the culture" (Kelman in Jack, p. 26). For Kelman, then, the plot of *A Disaffection* may be secondary to the language used to relate it. The characters he focuses on—particularly Pat and Gavin—give voice to the "taboo" people of this world. As literary historian Cairns Craig has pointed out, "Kelman's novels take place not in the traditional sites of the working-class struggle for power (the trades union, the educational system as liberator), nor in the traditional sites of working-class escape from work and exploitation (sport, domestic solidarity), but along the margins of that traditional working-class life . . . because that life has been decimated" by the destruction of traditional Glasgow industries (Craig, p. 101). Pat does not feel ennobled and set free by his advanced degrees, nor does Gavin find solidarity at work since he never does work. Moreover, home provides no safe haven. Rather it is a place of tension for Gavin and loneliness for Pat. Nor is the traditional escapism offered by sport an outlet: at the one football match that Pat attends, distracted by his woeful reflections, he misses seeing the only goal.

All the conventions of working-class fiction are resisted by *A Disaffection*, which then offers its readers new perspectives on characters they would perhaps never meet otherwise. Actually Pat plays in his mind with the conventions of the "poor boy makes good" novel, recalling "far-off days at the sun-drenched uni" (*A Disaffection*, p. 171). But now, we learn, he is "sickened" by his life. Pat's guilt arises from his sense of having betrayed his family and his background for a set of values that offers no comfort or direction to him.

Literary context. Kelman's distinctive writing style appeared on the British literary scene at an interesting time in history, and despite his forswearing of British influences, his work marks an important evolution in a century of powerful texts. Early twentieth-century British modernism, a diverse movement that focused on subjective experience and textual experimentation, featured writers that were by and large connected to a central, London-based literary scene or were living and writing abroad. Though Irish, James Joyce is often considered a preeminent example of British modernism (see *Ulysses,* also in *WLAIT 4: British and Irish Literature and Its Times*). Kelman's writing draws on Joyce's in its intense interiority, its attention to the varieties of voice, and its willingness to discuss banal, everyday, and even vulgar events. His awareness of the frustrations and dehumanizations inflicted

---

STAYING HOME

～

Kelman's commitment to his hometown of Glasgow and its residents was made evident in 1989, when *A Disaffection* was shortlisted for the prestigious and lucrative Booker Prize. Citing a writing course he would not cancel, Kelman declined to attend the awards ceremony in London. His decision announced his distance from both literary and political establishments.

---

by bureaucracy is often compared to the work of another modernist, Franz Kafka of Prague—then part of Austria-Hungary. Literary historians frequently designate World War II as the unofficial end to modernism and the beginning of postmodernism, that is, writing that commonly takes modernist innovations to extremes while undercutting such concepts as unity of time, self, or place. Writing in self-imposed exile as Joyce did, the Irishman Samuel Beckett represents the strain of postmodernism on which Kelman seems to draw. Beckett employed a type of black comedy (see *Waiting for Godot,* also in *WLAIT 4: British and Irish Literature and Its Times*). Like Beckett's characters, Pat Doyle is prone to bleak yet funny insights, alienated in the extreme, and hopeful for some undefinable relief to rescue him from the horrors of everyday existence. Unlike either of his Irish influences, however, Kel-

man has remained at home, writing in solidarity with the people in his neighborhood, where he has continued to live despite his financial success. Indeed, Kelman's choice to remain in Scotland distinguished him from generations of expatriates and exiles who believed that they needed to move to metropolitan centers like Paris and London to achieve their goals. This rootedness, especially in combination with Kelman's decision to write in local language, has had measurable effects on other Scottish writers. Describing how it felt to read Kelman's work for the first time, author Duncan McLean claims to have been most affected by "the voice. For the first time I was reading a book about the world I lived in. I didn't know literature could do that" (Downer, p. 44).

This is not to say that Kelman was the first working-class writer, or even the first to use local language. In the 1950s, when the literary establishment appeared to some to grow more and more disconnected from realist fiction's depictions of daily life in recognizable settings, a group of working-class writers known as the Angry Young Men began publishing fiction, drama, and poetry about working-class people and using some working-class language. Like the "Kitchen Sink" films often based on their works, these authors focused on gritty, realistic scenes of factory life, pub life, and class tensions. While Kelman has moved away from what swiftly became the clichés of their style, his fiction recalls theirs in its attention to underrepresented characters and settings and in its vernacular vocabulary and syntax, a technique that he has innovatively extended to the narrative voice as well. John Osborne's 1956 play *Look Back in Anger,* with its striving working-class boy uncomfortable with his social mobility and with women, offers a good example of a Pat Doyle-like character three decades earlier. Kelman's novel draws on the strengths of much of the fiction that preceded it but distinguishes itself in its particular willingness to portray the downside to social "advancement" and use a local vernacular suffused with both philosophy and profanity. In contrast to *Look Back in Anger,* whose protagonist hates the people and longs for what they have, Kelman's protagonist is skeptical about the entire project of social mobility, given its implications of losers and winners and hierarchies of tastes and values.

Kelman's own decision to write came upon him swiftly, during his years of menial labor. But he knew no other writers, until 1972, when he enrolled in a University of Glasgow evening class conducted by the poet Philip Hobsbaum. "Immediately Philip talked to me as a writer and a colleague in this straight Oxbridge accent of his, and that was quite powerful, to be treated like that" (Kelman in Jack, p. 26). It was through Hobsbaum that Kelman met other writers from similar backgrounds and established a social and work atmosphere that has been productive for the already mentioned Glasgow School. In turn, these authors have mentored others from backgrounds that do not traditionally foster a writer's life. This Glasgow School has challenged the mainstream British literary culture, arguing for the inclusion of working class and Glaswegian perspectives in the canon, or for the destruction of exclusionary concepts like a canon altogether. A beneficiary himself of a supportive community of writers, Kelman has gone on to foster the careers of other writers, perhaps most notably Janice Galloway. At the same time, his tireless efforts to articulate a Glasgow voice have made it possible for such writers as Duncan McLean and Irvine Welsh to reach audiences, and he may be credited to some degree for recent interest in Scottish film, particularly such urban-based movies as *Trainspotting* and *Small Faces*.

Reviews. While most critics acknowledged Kelman's command of his language and his deft use of literary and philosophical allusions in *A Disaffection*, not all appreciated the intense trip into one man's troubled mind. Martin Kirby, writing for *The New York Times*, felt that there was "not very much dramatic excitement," adding that he saw the Scottish schoolteacher as familiar, over-explored terrain and suggesting Kelman write about a Scottish criminal instead (Kirby, p. 14). (Ironically, while it is exactly this sort of pigeonholing that Kelman has sought to avoid in his varied career, his next novel, *How Late it Was, How Late,* did focus on an ex-convict.) There was also a tendency to overlook or underestimate the literary craftsmanship of the work, as reflected in a comment by Howard Jacobson, who on the night in 1989 that *A Disaffection* failed to win the Booker Prize, told his television audience that all Kelman's work amounted to was Billy Connolly (a well-known Scottish comedian) with philosophical pretensions.

However, other reviewers found *A Disaffection* haunting and beautiful, acknowledging the importance of Kelman's project, a view affirmed by critics in the decade since its publication. Writing for *The Times* in London, John Walsh hailed the novel's experiments "with prose that meanders and loses its way, a technique as effective as it is daring, for it conveys the circular, circuitous ruminations of the protagonist" (Walsh, p. F1). Jill Neville, for *The Independent*, cited the significance of the "combination of knowing patois and intellectual range" (Neville, p. 29). It is this unification of hauntingly complicated concepts and free-flowing vernacular that emerges as perhaps *A Disaffection*'s greatest strength.

—Mary McGlynn

For More Information

Bligh, Donald. *Understanding Higher Education.* Oxford: Intellect, 1999.

Craig, Cairns. "Resisting Arrest: James Kelman." *The Scottish Novel Since the Seventies: New Visions, Old Dreams.* Ed. Gavin Wallace and Randall Stevenson. Edinburgh: Edinburgh University Press, 1993.

Downer, Lesley. "Beats of Edinburgh." *The New York Times Magazine.* 31 March, 1996, 42-45.

Jack, Ian. "Uncensored voice of a native son; James Kelman writes in the ripe vernacular rhythms of Glasgow." *The Independent* (London) 28 April 1991, 26.

Kelman, James. *A Disaffection.* London: Farrar, Strauss, & Giroux, 1989.

———. *Some Recent Attacks: Essays Cultural and Political.* Stirling, Scotland: AK Press, 1992.

Kirby, Martin. "A Prufrock In Glasgow." *The New York Times.* 18 June 1989, Late Edition—Final, sec. 7, p. 14, col. 1.

Leventhal, F. M., ed. *Twentieth Century Britain: An Encyclopedia.* New York: Garland, 1995.

Neville, Jill. "O Pat. Lessons from Glasgow: 'A Disaffection'—James Kelman." *The Independent*, 18 February 1989, 29.

Walsh, John. Review of *A Disaffection,* by James Kelman. *The Times* (London), 24 September 1989, no. 8615, Features, 1.

Dr. Jekyll and Mr. Hyde

by

Robert Louis Stevenson

Robert Louis Stevenson (1850-94), the son of a Scottish engineer, was born and grew up in Edinburgh, Scotland. Expected to follow his father into engineering, as an undergraduate at Edinburgh University, he rebelled against his parents' wishes, declaring his intention to become a writer instead. Soon after graduating, he also openly rejected his parents' strict Calvinist religious outlook, igniting a long disagreement between the sternly devout father and the bohemian, agnostic son that would last until the father's death in 1887. Stevenson suffered from tuberculosis from childhood on, and spent much of his life traveling in search of a healthy climate. At the Swiss health resort of Davos in 1882 he completed *Treasure Island,* which was published the following year and immediately acclaimed as a classic. Another classic adventure, *Kidnapped,* was published in 1886, the same year as *Dr. Jekyll and Mr. Hyde,* while Stevenson was living in the southern English resort of Bournemouth. With these three novels Stevenson established himself as one of the most popular British writers of his day; in addition to several other novels, he composed essays, poems, and nonfiction before dying of tuberculosis in 1894. In *Dr. Jekyll and Mr. Hyde* Stevenson created a gripping Gothic horror story, a timeless allegory of human psychology, and a reflection of behavior particular to his era but not unknown in ours. The focus is on the rigid ideal of social respectability in Stevenson's era that stood in stark contrast with less acceptable inner impulses and appetites.

THE LITERARY WORK

A novella set in London in the mid-1880s; first published in London in 1886.

SYNOPSIS

A respectable Victorian scientist, Dr. Henry Jekyll, creates a drug that releases a dark part of his personality by physically transforming him into the depraved and bestial Edward Hyde.

Events in History at the Time of the Novella

Uncertainty, respectability, and repression. The late Victorian period (c. 1875-1901) was a time in which British society increasingly questioned the comfortable assumptions of an earlier age. After several decades of stability and prosperity, starting in the 1870s a series of social and economic crises led to an atmosphere of growing disquiet. To many Britons it seemed that even hallowed traditional institutions in British life were being cast into doubt. Most significantly, perhaps, religious skepticism became the order of the day, as many in the late Victorian era questioned the unhesitating faith that had distinguished their forebears.

One such literary figure was Robert Louis Stevenson's mentor Sir Leslie Stephen, a leading man of letters who from 1871 to 1882 edited the influential *Cornhill Magazine,* in which many of

Robert Louis Stevenson

Stevenson's early stories and poems were published. Declaring his agnosticism in terms that were echoed by other late Victorian writers, Stephen stated: "I now believe in nothing, to put it shortly; but I do not the less believe in morality . . . I mean to live and die like a gentleman if possible" (Stephen in Newsome, pp. 194-5).

As Sir Leslie Stephen's declaration suggests, skeptics of the late Victorian era may have abandoned their faith, but that did not mean they gave up the moral values that had earlier been associated with religious belief. Indeed, like Sir Leslie Stephen, late Victorian agnostics often took great pains to stress their adherence to traditional morality. In particular, many followed their older contemporary, the influential critic and historian Thomas Carlyle (1795-1881), in exalting the moral value of hard work, which had long been proclaimed by authorities in the various British Protestant churches as a path to spiritual salvation. Hard work and piety had earlier gone hand in hand as essential elements of "respectability," which was the catchword of social acceptance for the middle and lower classes throughout the Victorian period (1837-1901). By espousing a stringent work ethic, late Victorian agnostics could remain socially respectable even though they questioned or openly rejected traditional religious beliefs. In the novella, Henry Jekyll introduces himself to the reader by establishing his credentials as a respectable Victorian: he is, he says, "by nature inclined to industry, [and] fond of the respect of the wise and good among my fellow-men" (Stevenson, *Dr. Jekyll and Mr. Hyde,* p. 60).

While agnostics could gain respectability by compensating with hard work, it was nevertheless even more respectable—and easier—to cloak oneself in the outward trappings of religion. Many in whom the inner faith had flickered out did precisely that. For instance, Sir Leslie Stephen's brother, Sir James Stephen, confessed in a private letter that he did not accept the truth of the New Testament or of Christ's having performed miracles. "As to Christian morals," he continued, "I cannot regard them as either final or complete" (Stephen in Harrison, p. 123). Yet in public he continued to behave like a good Christian, taking his family to church and leading them in regular prayer. If open skepticism first flourished among intellectuals of the late Victorian era, public devotion—such as being regularly seen in church—remained a pillar of British society. In the novella Henry Jekyll (though a bachelor) maintains a similar veneer of conventional public piety. He never shows any signs of real Christian faith; in fact, his only interest in religion comes when, for a brief period, he stops transforming himself into Hyde and tries to live a blameless life: "whilst he had always been known for charities, he was now no less distinguished for religion" (*Dr. Jekyll and Mr. Hyde,* p. 32). This vague description (which probably means that Jekyll did nothing more than go to church regularly for a short time) makes Jekyll a man whose behavior was not uncommon in terms of late Victorian era religious practices.

Of course, respectability encouraged conformity in other areas than just religion. Throughout the Victorian era, both men and women were expected to comply with rules governing behavior: for middle-class professional men, rules of gentlemanly conduct included propriety, discretion, and above all self-control, sexual or otherwise. "A man who cannot learn self-control is a cad. . . . A loose man is a foul man. . . . He is a beast," preached the late Victorian philosopher Fredric Harrison in a lecture to his son that resembled Stevenson's description of Jekyll's bestial alter ego, Edward Hyde (Harrison in Newsome, p. 194).

Victorian science and medicine. Part of gentlemanly self-control was the dominance of reason over the emotions, and the leading model of Victorian rationalism was the new professional scientist. The era gave rise to unprecedented scientific progress, much of which encouraged the prevailing intellectual climate of religious skepticism. From biology came the single most influential idea of the later nineteenth century, Charles Darwin's theory of evolution, which was proposed in his revolutionary book **On the Origin of Species** (1859; also in *WLAIT 4: British and Irish Literature and Its Times*). In this controversial work, Darwin made the most compelling argument yet that organisms evolve, that is, they change form over generations, and he proffered a theory called natural selection to explain how the process works. Some religious authorities, by contrast, maintained that God created the various forms of life directly and that all species existed unchanged since He had created them. The situation was more complicated than a clear-cut conflict between religion and science, though. There were, for example, religious thinkers who accepted evolution, arguing that it was evidence of God's magnificence. Certainly the debate caused a great stir.

Throughout the 1860s, a series of highly publicized disputes followed Darwin's publication, often pitting religious leaders against scientific experts. The most famous debate took place in 1860 between Bishop Samuel Wilberforce and biologist Thomas Henry Huxley, and focused public attention on the question of whether humans and apes had evolved from a common ancestor.

This idea rapidly became the central point of contention in the evolutionary controversy, and by the 1870s some scientists were using it to explain a mysterious phenomenon they had noticed earlier in the century, the "split personality." They had noticed that people who suffered from this rare syndrome lived perfectly normal lives but occasionally experienced episodes in which they seemed to take on separate, usually antisocial personalities, complete with different voices, mannerisms, and even names. Such cases had been reported as early as 1816, but in the 1870s a German scientist named Dr. Franz Hoffman, who studied several of them, developed a theory based on current evolutionary thinking. Hoffman suggested that split personality (now called multiple personality disorder) represented a temporary reversion to an earlier stage in evolution, or in the common parlance of the time, a "throwback" (Milner, p. 418).

At the time many biologists thought of evolution in terms of either "progress" towards "higher" forms of life or "degeneration" towards "lower" ones, and Hoffman's theory fit well with such concepts. Biologists today prefer to describe evolutionary processes as a matter of adaptation to local environments, but in stressing humanity's animal nature and origins, Darwin himself had thought in terms of "high" and "low": "with all his . . . exalted powers," Darwin wrote in his 1871 book *Descent of Man,* "Man still bears in his bodily frame the indelible stamp of his lowly origin" (Darwin in Milner, p. 127). In keeping with all this theory, many Victorians, in their strictly controlled social environment, came to see any antisocial or overtly sexual behavior as closer to a "lower," more animal-like stage in human evolution. Thus, when Dr. Jekyll becomes Mr. Hyde in the novella, he manifests "lower-order" features: while Jekyll is tall and handsome, Hyde is "pale and dwarfish," an "ape-like" and "brutish" creature whose hands are dark, knobby, and hairy (*Dr. Jekyll and Mr. Hyde,* pp. 15, 23, 70).

By the 1880s human behavior and consciousness had become a major new area of scientific study, as scientists such as Austrian physician Sigmund Freud (1856-1939) and others laid the foundations of modern psychology. In 1885 the young Freud was in Paris to see French neurologist Jean Martin Charcot give a public demonstration of hypnotism, which was being successfully used to treat some forms of mental illness. Charcot's demonstration inspired another French scientist, Pierre Janet, to suggest that consciousness comprised a number of separate strands that could operate independently of each other. In succeeding years Freud would use the ideas of Charcot, Janet, and others in formulating his theory of the conscious and the unconscious, as well as his theory of the id, the ego, and the superego. Dual and multiple personality disorders would continue to be studied, and eventually Freudian psychologists would characterize the illnesses as a dissociation and projection of the superego, the mental entity that imposes social and moral norms on an individual's behavior.

The field of psychology would continue to develop in the last decade of the nineteenth century, with the theory and interpretation of dreams playing an increasingly important role in revealing how the mind works. The notion that dreams could be scientifically significant was new in the 1890s. While in the early 1800s poets, artists, and philosophers in Europe and the United States had embraced the idea that dreams are an integral part of life and a highly creative process, by mid-century a shift in thinking had reduced the perception of dreams to "a meaningless by-product of automatic and uncoordinated brain activity occurring during sleep" (Ellenberger, p. 304). Despite this skepticism about the importance of dreams, three pioneers—Karl Albert Scherner, Alfred Maury, and Marie-Jean-Léon Hervey de Saint-Denis—conducted groundbreaking research that became foundational to subsequent work in dream theory from 1880 to 1900 and, still later, to the dream theories of Freud (*The Interpretation of Dreams,* 1900) and Swiss psychiatrist Carl Gustav Jung (1875-1961). Their investigation into the nature of dreams explored the origin and significance of dream images as well as other phenomena.

MULTIPLE PERSONALITY DISORDER

Stevenson's novella would prove remarkably accurate in its insights into multiple personality disorder and human consciousness. Most genuine cases of multiple personality start with dual personalities, alternating between a "good" personality that behaves properly, and a "bad" personality that behaves without regard for social or moral guidelines. As Stevenson has Dr. Jekyll suggest in the novella, other personalities may later appear. Jekyll speaks of his

> partial discovery . . . that man is not truly one but truly two. I say two, because the state of my knowledge does not pass beyond that point. Others will follow, others will outstrip me on the same lines; and I hazard a guess that man will ultimately be known for a mere polity of multifarious, incongruous and independent denizens.
>
> (*Dr. Jekyll and Mr. Hyde,* p. 61)

A collection of "independent denizens" is, in fact, precisely how many psychologists view human consciousness today.

Dreams fascinated Robert Louis Stevenson in an era on the cusp of the new regard for them as scientifically significant. Over the years, he had learned to consciously direct certain aspects of his dream life. In his book, *Across the Plains* (1892), Stevenson explains that he received many of the ideas for his novels from the "Little People" or "Brownies"—that part of his psyche that does "one-half my work for me whilst I am fast asleep." (Stevenson, pp. 247-248). The behavior of the character in the dream that Stevenson says inspired the Jekyll/Hyde transformation in his novella could be said to anticipate what Jung would later describe as the "shadow"—the sum of those personal characteristics that individuals wish to hide from others and from themselves. According to this theory, the more an individual tries to conceal these undesirable traits, the more the shadow "may become active and evil-doing" (Ellenberger, p. 707).

While most of the progress in psychology lay in the future when Stevenson wrote the novella, the five years immediately preceding the book saw some of the most dramatic advances in medicine that have ever taken place within a comparable time period. After decades of work, the French physician and bacteriologist Louis Pasteur (1822-95) conclusively demonstrated the new germ theory of medicine, with a series of experiments in which he isolated the viruses or bacteria responsible for causing several diseases. Building on the work of German biologist Robert Koch (1843-1910) and others, Pasteur also showed that a weaker form of a disease-causing germ could be used to inoculate or immunize a person against the disease. Between 1881 and 1885, working independently, Pasteur and Koch isolated the agents of a number of diseases and created inoculations for them: anthrax, tuberculosis, diphtheria, cholera, and—most spectacularly—rabies. In July 1885, amid great publicity, Pasteur succeeded in inoculating a young boy who had been bitten by a rabid dog; the feat fixed him in the public mind as a medical miracle worker, for until then, the always fatal disease was greatly feared. By the time Stevenson wrote *Dr. Jekyll and Mr. Hyde* later that same year, probably no medical achievement seemed outside the capability of a solitary, ingenious, hardworking doctor and his chief weapon, a flask of serum.

The Novella in Focus

Plot summary. Though the novella totals less than 100 pages in most editions, its narrative structure is unusual and complex. The first eight of its ten chapters are told in the third person, primarily from the perspective of Dr. Jekyll's lawyer, Gabriel Utterson. The last two chapters are told in the first person, purporting to be factual statements, first by Dr. Jekyll's friend, Dr. Lanyon, and finally by Henry Jekyll himself. It is a structure that keeps the reader in suspense regarding several key points in the story until the end of the book and Dr. Jekyll's own account of the events.

Mr. Utterson, a cold, unemotional, "yet somehow lovable" middle-aged lawyer who lives in London, goes for regular Sunday walks with his distant relative, Richard Enfield (*Dr. Jekyll and Mr. Hyde,* p. 3). On one of these walks, Enfield points out the door of a building on a quiet London side street, saying that the door is connected in his mind "with a very odd story" (*Dr. Jekyll and Mr. Hyde,* p. 5). Enfield had been coming home at about three o'clock one morning, and along the deserted streets he had suddenly seen two figures hurrying, "a little man stumping along eastwards at a good walk," and a little girl running towards the same corner (*Dr. Jekyll and Mr. Hyde,* p. 5). They were coming at right angles to each other, so that one could not see the other. They collided at the corner—and the man simply knocked over the little girl as if she hadn't been there at all. He then continued on his way, leaving the girl screaming on the ground. Enfield chased the man and brought him back to the scene of the accident, where neighbors had gathered, awakened by the girl's screams.

Something about the little man antagonized everyone in the crowd, including a doctor, who arrived shortly, and for whom the little girl had apparently been sent in the first place. The little girl was not hurt, but Enfield and the others threatened the man with publicity and ruin until he agreed to pay the girl's family a sum of £100. The man then led them to the same door that Enfield and Utterson were now looking at, and taking out a key he disappeared inside, shortly afterward emerging with a check for £100, signed by a well-known gentleman of very good reputation, someone whose name Enfield had often seen in the newspapers. The little man, who calls himself Hyde, has an unsettling quality that is vague and undefinable, says Enfield: "I never saw a man I so disliked, and yet I scarce know why. He must be deformed somewhere; he gives a strong feeling of deformity, although I couldn't specify the point" (*Dr. Jekyll and Mr. Hyde,* p. 8).

Hyde, guesses Utterson, has disappeared into the house of Dr. Henry Jekyll, a friend and client of Utterson's. Utterson guesses this on the strength of his having already drawn up a will for Jekyll naming one Edward Hyde as sole beneficiary. The will is an unusual document, bequeathing Jekyll's large fortune to Hyde not only if Jekyll dies, but also if he disappears for more than three months. Wondering why the respectable Jekyll has left his large fortune to someone so disreputable under such strange terms,

Frederic March in his Academy Award-winning performance in the 1932 film version of *Dr. Jekyll and Mr. Hyde.*

Utterson approaches their mutual friend Dr. Hastie Lanyon. Lanyon, however, has had a falling out with Jekyll. He says that he has seen "devilish little of the man" (*Dr. Jekyll and Mr. Hyde,* p. 12). Nor has he heard of Mr. Hyde, whom Utterson decides to track down: "If he be Mr. Hyde," Utterson tells himself, "I shall be Mr. Seek" (*Dr. Jekyll and Mr. Hyde,* p. 13). Mounting a watch on Jekyll's back door, one night he spots Mr. Hyde and accosts him. They exchange a few words, and Utterson gets a good look at Hyde's face before Hyde runs nimbly into the house. Going around to the front, Utterson learns from Poole, Jekyll's servant, that Jekyll has given Hyde the key. Hyde never comes in the front, however, but always enters through the back, where Dr. Jekyll has his laboratory.

Some time later, all of London is startled by the murder of a respected old gentleman named Sir Danvers Carew, who is brutally bludgeoned to death on a street corner late at night. An eyewitness identifies Hyde as the murderer. However, when Utterson accompanies the police to Hyde's shabby Soho address, Hyde is not there. Utterson goes to Jekyll's house and demands to know if Jekyll is concealing Hyde, but Jekyll denies it, swearing he will have nothing further to do with the murderer. He tells Utterson that

Hyde is gone and will never be heard from again. The two resume their friendship, seeing each other frequently, but two months later when Utterson pays a social call on Jekyll he is suddenly turned away at the door. After several more unsuccessful attempts to see Jekyll, the concerned Utterson approaches Dr. Lanyon. He is shocked to see that Lanyon is clearly a very sick man, and Lanyon confirms that he does not have long to live. He and Jekyll have had another quarrel, Lanyon says, and he wants nothing to do with the man. After Utterson writes to Jekyll the next day, Jekyll writes back, confessing that he has done something terrible, something he must keep to himself, and begging Utterson "to respect my silence" (*Dr. Jekyll and Mr. Hyde,* p. 34). Two weeks later, Lanyon is dead, leaving Utterson a sealed envelope, with instructions to open the envelope in the event of Jekyll's death or disappearance.

As time goes by, Utterson stops making efforts to see the increasingly reclusive Jekyll. But eventually Utterson receives a visit from Poole, Jekyll's servant, who urgently beseeches the lawyer to come quickly to Jekyll's house. Poole fears that Jekyll has been murdered and that the murderer has locked himself in Jekyll's laboratory. At Jekyll's house he tells Utterson that whoever—or whatever—is locked inside the laboratory "has been crying night and day for some sort of medicine" (*Dr. Jekyll and Mr. Hyde,* p. 42). Jekyll's habit has been to leave instructions outside the door for drugs and other supplies needed for his experiments, and Poole would then go make the purchases. Lately, though, Jekyll has repeatedly rejected the purchased drugs as impure. Also inside the laboratory, Poole has caught sight of a grotesque creature he swears is the long-vanished Edward Hyde. Poole and Utterson go to the laboratory, where Utterson hears Hyde's voice inside. By the time they manage to break down the door to the laboratory, Hyde has taken poison and is dead. They see no sign of Jekyll, but Utterson finds a letter in Jekyll's handwriting and a package: the letter instructs Utterson first to read Lanyon's narrative (the letter Lanyon left with Utterson) and then to read Jekyll's firsthand account in the package.

Dr. Lanyon's narrative begins by relating how one day Lanyon received a note from his friend Henry Jekyll asking him for a favor: Lanyon should retrieve the contents of a certain drawer from Jekyll's laboratory and bring them back to Lanyon's house. There a messenger from Jekyll will meet him at midnight. Lanyon does so—the drawer contains, among other items, some packets of a white powder and a phial of red liquid—and the messenger duly arrives. He is a small and oddly dressed man, with "something abnormal and misbegotten" in his appearance (*Dr. Jekyll and Mr. Hyde,* p. 56). Lanyon watches as the man mixes together some of the powder with a small amount of the red liquid and drinks the mixture down. Before Lanyon's eyes, the small man staggers, his features seem "to melt and alter"—and suddenly before Lanyon stands Henry Jekyll (*Dr. Jekyll and Mr. Hyde,* p. 59). Lanyon is so deeply shocked by what he has seen that he feels his days are numbered. He closes his account by stating that Jekyll has revealed to him that the "creature" who arrived at his house that night was Edward Hyde, "hunted in every corner of the land as the murderer of Carew" (*Dr. Jekyll and Mr. Hyde,* p. 59).

The novella's final chapter is entitled "Henry Jekyll's Full Statement of the Case" and purports to be Jekyll's own account of his experiment and its results, written out in the laboratory before his final transformation into Edward Hyde. Tormented by his own dual propensity for good and evil, Jekyll hopes to discover a drug that will separate the two parts of his personality:

> If each, I told myself, could but be housed in separate identities, life would be relieved of all that was unbearable; the unjust might go his way, delivered from the aspirations and remorse of his more upright twin; and the just could walk steadfastly and securely on his own path, doing the good things in which he found his pleasure, and no longer exposed to disgrace and penitence by the hands of this extraneous evil.
>
> (*Dr. Jekyll and Mr. Hyde,* p. 61)

After many experiments, Jekyll develops a mixture that transforms his physical body to reflect only "the lower elements of my soul," just as his original body reflected his soul as a whole (*Dr. Jekyll and Mr. Hyde,* p. 62). After the first transformation, he enjoys the new and sweet sensation of being purely evil, noticing that his new body is smaller and much younger than Jekyll's 50 years. This, he realizes, is because his evil side was less developed, since he had lived a life that was "nine-tenths a life of effort, virtue, and control" (*Dr. Jekyll and Mr. Hyde,* p. 64).

As he starts to use the mixture regularly, he takes rooms in Soho under the name Edward Hyde and makes sure that his servants know that Hyde is to have full access to Jekyll's house. He relishes the "vicarious depravity" in which he now freely engages; as Henry Jekyll, he feels no remorse for wicked deeds he has performed as Edward Hyde (*Dr. Jekyll and Mr. Hyde*, p. 66). About two months before Hyde murders Sir Danvers Carew, however, Jekyll begins at times to turn into Hyde without taking the drug, but still requires the drug in order to turn back into Dr. Jekyll. Hyde is also becoming larger, and he needs more and more of the drug in order to resume his Jekyll identity. Hyde, Jekyll realizes, is taking over. For two months, like a drunkard, says the novella, he abstains from becoming Hyde, but then he can stand it no more and takes the drug. That night he murders Sir Danvers, and when he learns that the murder was witnessed he knows that he must never become Hyde again. For two more months, as the police hunt Hyde, he lives a blameless life, struggling to make up for the evil deeds he has done as Hyde.

Then he starts longing to do those deeds again, and one day as he sits on a park bench remembering his evil experiences, he turns into Hyde once more. This time he cannot return home for fear of the police, so he turns to Lanyon to fetch the drug from his cabinet. Safely home afterwards, he finds the change coming over him every few hours, and discovers as well that it takes larger and larger quantities of the drug to change him back. He begins to run low and sends Poole to purchase new ingredients, but the new mixture is ineffective. He realizes that there must have been an impurity in the original ingredients, and that the impurity must have been necessary for the transformation. Finally, his supply of the old drug runs out, and he knows that the next change will be his last—for without the drug, he can never change back to Jekyll. He is doomed to be Hyde forever. Hyde too, cornered in the laboratory, is doomed either to be hung as a murderer, or, if he has the courage, to take his own life. As Henry Jekyll lays down his pen to wait for the transformation he knows is coming, he himself does not know which it will be.

A study in hypocrisy. In its depiction of a conventionally respectable but ultimately hypocritical man who deliberately brings alive his own evil side, *Dr. Jekyll and Mr. Hyde* dramatizes the question of what it meant "to live and die like a gentleman." The strict Victorian code of gentlemanly behavior offered little forgiveness to transgressors, so that those who fell short of it were generally forced into pretense. In Stevenson's novella, Jekyll's primary fault is identified as precisely such hypocrisy. Even before discovering the drug that transforms him into Edward Hyde,

Jekyll has experienced a "profound duplicity of life," in which his "imperious desire" for reputation and respectability coexists with "an impatient gaiety of disposition" that has led him to commit "irregularities" as a young man (*Dr. Jekyll and Mr. Hyde*, p. 60).

The cumulative pressure of his past "irregularities" and the fond memory of his recent ones as Edward Hyde eventually replace the drug as the agent of the transformation, as when Jekyll sits on a park bench and is overtaken by memories of his illicit pleasures:

> I sat in the sun on a bench; the animal within me licking the chops of memory. . . . After all, I reflected, I was like my neighbors; and then I smiled, comparing myself with other men, comparing my active goodwill with the lazy cruelty of their neglect. And at the very moment of that vainglorious thought a qualm came over me, a horrid nausea and the most deadly shuddering.
>
> (*Dr. Jekyll and Mr. Hyde*, p. 73)

This "shuddering" marks the change into Hyde, which comes as Jekyll first indulges his memory and then reflects that he is no different (perhaps better—hence "vainglorious") than others. In the next sentence, the reader discovers that one of the sensations he feels as Hyde is a loosening of social responsibility, "a solution of the bonds of obligation" (*Dr. Jekyll and Mr. Hyde*, p. 73). This recalls that Jekyll undertook the experiment in the first place largely in order to escape social accountability in the form of "disgrace."

The novella universalizes Jekyll's predicament by putting him on a par with everyone else in Victorian society and by stressing that Hyde revels in freedom from social obligation as much as in evil deeds. *Dr. Jekyll and Mr. Hyde* furthermore underscores this universality by repeatedly letting the reader know that other gentlemen such as Utterson and Enfield have their own dark secrets. Enfield, for example, is a man about town who first sees Hyde when he himself is out on the streets at three in the morning (a distinctly unrespectable hour to be abroad). Finally, critics have noted the deliberately vague way in which the novella describes both Hyde and his activities. Aside from knocking down the little girl and murdering Sir Danvers Carew, the only explicit evil we know Hyde has committed is striking a woman on the face. Anything else he may have done is left to the imagination. By leaving what we suppose to be the bulk of Hyde's evil deeds unspecified, the novella invites readers to supply their own personal "irregularities" when imagining them, and thus to ponder their own hypocrisy.

Sources and literary context. Like another classic of Gothic horror, Mary Shelley's **Frankenstein** (1818; in *WLAIT 3: British and Irish Literature and Its Times*), the immediate inspiration for *Dr. Jekyll*

STEVENSON'S DREAM LIFE

In a chapter on dreams in his book *Across the Plains,* Stevenson writes that his childhood was plagued by disturbing nightmares, which later evolved into dream adventures. Soon he began to dream in sequence and lived what he called a sort of double life, dipping in and out of a dreamland whose characters suggested concepts and plot twists he never could have consciously imagined—guided by a muse he called his "Brownies." He had tried for a long time to create a story for *Dr. Jekyll and Mr. Hyde,* struggling to find the right vehicle for "that strong sense of man's double being which must at times come in upon and overwhelm the mind of every thinking creature" (Stevenson, *Across the Plains,* p. 249).

> I went about racking my brains for a plot of any sort; and on the second night I dreamed the scene at the window, and a scene afterwards split in two, in which Hyde, pursued for some crime, took the powder and underwent the change in the presence of his pursuers. All the rest was made awake, and consciously, although I think I can trace in much of it the manner of my Brownies. The meaning of the tale is therefore mine, and had long pre-existed in my garden of Adonis, and tried one body after another in vain; indeed, I do most of the morality, worse luck! and my Brownies have not a rudiment of what we call a conscience. . . . Mine, too, is the setting, mine the characters. All that was given me was the matter of three scenes, and the central idea of a voluntary change becoming involuntary.
>
> (Stevenson, *Across the Plains,* pp. 249-251)

Addressing critics, Stevenson goes on to suggest that he is not to blame for the sections of the novella that have been censured, but rather the "Brownies" who made decisions about the story while he slept.

---

and *Mr. Hyde* came to its author in a dream, after which he wrote a first draft of the novella in three days. Though the dream inspired characters in his story, the "profound duplicity of life" that Henry Jekyll/Edward Hyde personifies was an idea that Stevenson had already explored both in his own life and in earlier literary efforts. For a period in his youth, Stevenson and his friends frequented the bars and brothels of urban Edinburgh, behavior that the young man found difficult to reconcile with his parents' moralistic Calvinism, and which thus left him deeply conflicted. It may have been this inner conflict that led to his fascination with the story of Deacon William Brodie (1741-88), a real life "Jekyll-and-Hyde" who led a blameless life as an Edinburgh religious official by day but caroused in the city's taverns and brothels and led a band of robbers by night. Convicted and hung before a huge crowd, Brodie was an almost legendary figure in local Edinburgh lore; as a teenager Stevenson had written a play about him, rewriting it for theatrical production (1880) as *Deacon Brodie or The Double Life.* A number of Stevenson's other works (for example, *Macaire,* 1885; "Thrawn Janet," 1886; "Markheim," 1887; *The Master of Ballantrae,* 1889) deal in various ways with the theme of a double life too.

Stevenson had also read a number of works by other authors that explored the same idea. The German author of fantastic tales E. T. A. Hoffman wrote a story called "The Devil's Elixir" (1816) in which a sinner exploits his resemblance to someone else in order to gratify his lust with impunity. Thomas Jefferson Hogg's novel *The Private Memoirs and Confessions of a Justified Sinner* (1824) features a protagonist with a shape-shifting double and has structural similarities to Stevenson's novella. In Edgar Allen Poe's short story "William Wilson" (1839), the wicked William Wilson is repeatedly thwarted by the supernatural appearance of an identical William Wilson whose good deeds undo his own evil ones. Finally, French author Théophile Gautier's story "Le Chevalier Double" ("The Double Knight"; 1840) pits a good knight born under a double star against his evil twin; when the good knight strikes a blow against his enemy, he suffers the pain of the blow himself.

Reception. While his *Treasure Island* (1883) had proved a popular classic, *Dr. Jekyll and Mr. Hyde* created a literary sensation that made Stevenson one of the best-known writers in Britain. The book sold a sensational 40,000 copies in England in the first six months following publication. Soon after its release in January 1886, an anonymous reviewer wrote in the London *Times:* "Nothing Mr. Stevenson has written yet has so strongly impressed us with the versatility of his very original genius" and suggested that the tale "should be read as a finished study in the art of fantastic literature" (Hammond, p. 115). The influential literary critic Andrew Lang warned in the *Saturday Review* that the effect of the work should not obscure its literary subtlety: "while one is thrilled and possessed by the horror of the central fancy, one may fail, at first reading, to recognise the delicate and restrained skill of the treatment of accessories, details, and character" (Lang in Hammond, p. 115).

—Colin Wells

For More Information

Calder, Jenni. *Stevenson and Victorian Scotland.* Edinburgh: Edinburgh University Press, 1981.

Ellenberger, Henri F. *The Discovery of the Unconscious.* New York: Basic Books, 1970.

Geduld, Harry M. ed. *The Definitive Dr. Jekyll and Mr. Hyde Companion.* New York: Garland, 1983.

Hammond, J. R. *A Robert Louis Stevenson Companion.* London: Macmillan, 1984.

Harrison, J. F. C. *Late Victorian Britain: 1875-1901.* London: Routledge, 1991.

Jarrett, Derek. *The Sleep of Reason: Fantasy and Reality from the Victorian Age to the First World War.* London: Weidenfeld and Nicolson, 1988.

Milner, Richard. *The Encyclopedia of Evolution: Humanity's Search for its Origins.* New York: Holt, 1990.

Newsome, David. *The Victorian World Picture: Perceptions and Introspections in an Age of Change.* London: John Murray, 1997.

Stevenson, Robert Louis. *Across the Plains: With Other Memories and Essays.* New York: Scribner, 1892.

———. *Dr. Jekyll and Mr. Hyde and Other Stories.* New York: Knopf, 1992.

Veeder, William, and Gordon Hirsch, eds. *Dr. Jekyll and Mr. Hyde After One Hundred Years.* Chicago: University of Chicago Press, 1988.

Wolf, Leonard, ed. *The Essential Dr. Jekyll and Mr. Hyde.* London: Plume, 1995.

Dracula

by

Bram Stoker

Anglo-Irish author Bram Stoker (1847-1912) was born in Dublin, Ireland, where he spent a decade as a civil servant before moving to London in 1878. The move was prompted by Stoker's becoming the business manager of the era's best known actor, Henry Irving (1838-1905), who had just taken over London's Lyceum Theater. For the next 27 years, until Irving's death, Stoker helped run the theater, managing and promoting Irving's career, writing letters in his name, and accompanying the actor on tours to various parts of the world (including the United States, which Stoker avidly admired). Stoker began a supplementary career as a novelist when he published *The Snake's Pass* in 1890; his later novels include *The Mystery of the Sea* (1902), *The Jewel of Seven Stars* (1903), *The Lady of the Shroud* (1909), and *The Lair of the White Worm* (1911). Like *Dracula*, these works combine elements of Gothic horror and often grotesque fantasy. None, however, has enjoyed *Dracula*'s lasting success. Written in a period of national anxiety in Britain, the novel reflects a society that fears its own vitality may somehow be draining away.

Events in History at the Time of the Novel

Certainty and doubt in late Victorian Britain. The late Victorian period (c. 1875-1901) was an age of contrasting certainties and doubts for the British. On one hand, national confidence was high as Britain's worldwide empire expanded rapidly in the last quarter of the nineteenth century. By 1897, when the nation marked Queen Victoria's sixtieth year of rule with an exuberant public celebration called the Diamond Jubilee, Britain held sway over about a fourth of the world's population and landmass. Of that territory, 2.5 million square miles—an area the size of the entire Roman Empire at its peak—had come under British rule in the previous twelve years alone, from 1884 to 1896. From Ireland to India, from the Americas to Asia and Africa, Britain seemed destined to rule.

Yet even as British world power reached its apogee, some believed they saw signs of vulnerability, portents of a feared and inevitable decline. Subject peoples in Ireland, India, Africa, and elsewhere had resisted British rule, at times violently. In addition, other Western nations, particularly Germany and the United States,

Bram Stoker

seemed to possess energy and ambition that threatened to undo Britain's global leadership should the British grow soft or degenerate. Such apprehensions, while pushed into the background in the grandly imperial 1890s, nonetheless reflected nagging concerns about Britain's future.

Much more overtly worrisome to most cultural observers at the time was a deep religious crisis that was seen as undermining society's very foundations. Fueled by the impersonal harshness of an industrial revolution that resulted in urban poverty, and by scientific developments such as Charles Darwin's **On the Origin of Species** (1859; also in *WLAIT 4: British and Irish Literature and Its Times*), religious skepticism flourished on an unprecedented scale in the later decades of the nineteenth century. Though this crisis of faith had its best known expression in Alfred, Lord Tennyson's Poem **In Memoriam** (1850; also in *WLAIT 4: British and Irish Literature and Its Times*), a number of novelists addressed the issue too toward the end of the century. One of them, a then-popular but now forgotten writer named Hall Caine (1853-1931), sold 50,000 copies of his novel *The Christian* in the first month of publication. Published (like *Dracula*) in 1897, the book tells the story of a clergyman, torn between his faith and his love for a woman, who revolts against organized religion and devotes himself to

aiding the poor in crowded cities. Caine was a good friend of Stoker's, and *Dracula* is dedicated to him (under the nickname "Hommy-Beg"). While it does not invoke Caine's type of realism, *Dracula* does portray its protagonist as planning to prey on London's "teeming millions" (Stoker, *Dracula*, p. 51).

By the end of the nineteenth century, science and industrialization had combined to produce a newly secular outlook in contrast to the long-standing religious one. This new outlook was "conducive to demystification," not an altogether welcome development (Harrison, p. 130). Many Victorians felt the loss of mystery keenly, and the void it left created an often ambivalent reaction to the new secularism. Stoker's novel reflects this ambivalence clearly. For example, the band of friends that opposes Dracula includes two scientists and enthusiastically relies on rational, modern scientific methods to demystify the alien threat represented by the vampire Count. In the end, however, they are forced to fall back on religious symbols as well, such as the crucifix and the Host (communion wafer). One of them, Jonathan Harker, a British lawyer imprisoned in Dracula's castle in the novel's early pages, acknowledges fearfully in his "up-to-date" shorthand diary that "the old centuries . . . have powers of their own that mere 'modernity' cannot kill" (*Dracula*, p. 36).

Modern technology and "the New Woman." Along with shorthand (which had actually been around for some two centuries but was coming into wider business and personal use), the modern weapons in the vampire hunters' arsenal include such high-tech communications and information processing tools as the telegraph, the phonograph, and the typewriter. (The telephone had been invented and would come into commercial use just a few years after the novel is set.) Dr. Seward, one of the vampire hunters in the novel, keeps his journal on an early phonograph that records his voice on wax cylinders. The typewriter had been invented in the 1860s by American Christopher Sholes, who contracted with the arms manufacturer Remington and Sons to mass produce the machines in the 1870s. Remington opened a British dealership in 1886, and by the 1890s typewriters had come into widespread use in British businesses. In *Dracula*, Mina Murray (who marries Jonathan Harker midway through the novel) plays a key role in the hunt for Dracula by efficiently collecting and transcribing relevant but scattered documents on her typewriter, including various telegrams, her husband's shorthand diary, and Dr. Seward's phonograph journal.

As Mina's central part in the story suggests, the advent of the typewriter and other technologies created a revolutionary new role for women in British society. Suddenly, women were offered avenues of employment far different from any available to them before. One Englishman, returning to England in 1904 after a 30-year absence, was shocked to find women pursuing jobs that had either been reserved for men or had not even existed when he left:

> So far as I remember in days gone by the only lines of employment open to girls or women were: teaching, assisting in a shop, dress-making, or bar-keeping. In these days there is hardly an occupation . . . into which a girl may not aspire to enter. Type-writing provides a living for many thousands, perhaps hundreds of thousands. There are women newspaper reporters almost as numerous as men. Accountants and book-keepers crowd the trains morning and evening . . . while many branches of postal, telegraph and telephone work are entirely managed by women.
>
> (Harrison, p.168)

The typewriter led the way in this revolution in the 1890s, as girls and young women skilled in shorthand and typing found work as secretaries in otherwise all-male offices. Wages, however, were too low for such employees to live independently, and they were expected to leave when they married. If they did not leave by their mid-twenties, they were generally replaced by younger, newly trained girls or women. Those women who did work nevertheless had a significant impact on late Victorian society; their jobs gave them a degree of financial independence, which contributed greatly to the formation of an assertive female identity.

Limited independence was more than women had enjoyed before, and in 1894 feminist novelist Sarah Grand coined the phrase "the New Woman" to describe the phenomenon. The New Woman was neither a prostitute nor a confirmed homebody; in fact, she did not consider the home her exclusive sphere. While Grand introduced the phrase "the New Woman," the writer Ouida (pen name for Marie Louise de la Ramée) popularized it. She replied to Grand that this variety of female was a bore, and controversy ensued. Novelists meanwhile helped define the image. Middle-class and educated, as portrayed in popular novels by Grant Allen, Thomas Hardy, George Gissing, and others, the typical New Woman sought greater sexual freedom, smoked cigarettes, and drank in public. She also supported the growing women's suffrage movement, which aimed to secure the vote for British women (a goal that would not be achieved until 1918 for women over the age of 30, until 1929 for women 21 and older, and until 1969 for those 18 and older). As Sally Ledger notes, the New Woman was an invented persona too, a characterization in reaction to this growing movement.

> The New Woman of the fin de siècle had a multiple identity. She was, variously, a feminist activist, a social reformer, a popular novelist, a suffragette playwright, a woman poet; she was also often a fictional construct, a discursive response to the activities of the late nineteenth-century women's movement.
>
> (Ledger, p. 1)

In *Dracula,* Mina, an assistant schoolmistress at a girls' school, rejects the New Woman's radical values but seems to appreciate her abilities, having acquired typing and other secretarial skills in order to assist her husband's career as a lawyer. Mina's ambivalence regarding the New Woman reflects a genuine widespread cultural anxiety of the day. Many feared that new opportunities would lead women to neglect their civic responsibility to become mothers. The New Woman was perceived as an internal threat to national strength and security—a threat every bit as grave as the threat of colonial resistance. There was also a fear that if other nations did a better job of reproducing than Britain, they would grow stronger and the two threats would combine to dislodge the preeminence of the British. In view of this fear, what happens to Mina in the novel is doubly reassuring. She bears a British baby and is also prevented from helping to reproduce threatening outsiders, in this case, vampires.

Occultism and psychology. The late Victorians' questioning of previous scientific, religious, and social certainties may help explain a surge of interest in the occult as the century drew to a close. Certainly many of the same people doing the questioning were drawn to the occult, which perhaps served to restore a sense of mystery to lives increasingly illuminated by the glaring spotlight of Victorian rationalism. Séances, clairvoyance, mesmerism (hypnosis), astrology, palmistry, crystal-gazing, faith healing, alchemy, witchcraft, astral projection—these and other mysterious practices and entertainments flourished, both in public spaces such as theaters and in private homes. Clubs and societies pursued occult ideas with avid curiosity, their members often sport-

THE "CRIMINAL TYPE"

Oₙe discipline that blended science and the occult was phrenology, which held that character traits and mental qualities can be discerned by the shape of the head or the dimensions of the brow. The discipline, now thoroughly discredited, played a part in late Victorian criminology. Society boasted "scientific" criminologists, men who based their study of criminals on dissection and anatomy, as well as on observation of the head. In *Dracula*, Mina Harker names one such criminologist, Cesare Lombroso (1835-1909), when she describes Count Dracula as "a criminal type," and elsewhere the novel echoes very closely Lombroso's description of the typical criminal when it describes Count Dracula (*Dracula*, p. 342):

Stoker Describes Dracula

- "[Count Dracula's] face was . . . aquiline, with high bridge of the thin nose and peculiarly arched nostrils."
- "His eyebrows were very massive, almost meeting over the nose."
- "His ears were pale and at the tops extremely pointed. . . ."

Lombroso Describes the Criminal Type

- "[The criminal's] nose . . . is often aquiline, like the beak of a bird of prey."
- "The eyebrows are bushy and tend to meet across the nose."
- "A relic of the pointed ear. . . ."

(Adapted from Wolf, p. 300)

ing an attitude of scientific detachment. Many believed that occult phenomena could be scientifically explained.

For example, the Society for Psychical Research attempted to inquire scientifically into curiosities such as thought reading and haunted houses. The society also hosted a talk that Stoker may have attended on the groundbreaking work of Sigmund Freud, the Viennese doctor who was laying the foundations of modern psychology. Stoker incorporates contemporary ideas about mental illness into Dracula, citing Jean Martin Charcot, a French neurologist who worked with Freud in Paris in 1885 and who demonstrated the usefulness of hypnosis in treating mental illness. In the novel Dr. Seward runs a "lunatic asylum" (institution for the mentally ill) in which one of the patients, Renfield, is depicted as being psychically linked with Count Dracula, though Renfield is never properly bitten. Like Dracula's female victims, Renfield is controlled through his psychic link with the vampire, who possesses supernaturally hypnotic powers of mind control.

The most influential of the many occult groups was the Theosophical Society, founded in 1875 by the eccentric Russian immigrant Helena Petrova Blavatsky (1831-91), who is also credited with popularizing the term "occultism." Madame Blavatsky (as she was known) promoted both mysticism and science as paths toward enlightenment, and the Theosophical Society attracted a wide range of Victorian nonconformists, including feminists, socialists, and vegetarians. Though not a "Theosophist" himself, Stoker belonged to a social set that included Theosophical Society members. One was Constance Wilde, wife of the celebrated writer and wit Oscar Wilde, a friend, fellow-Dubliner, and one-time rival of Stoker's. (Before marrying Constance, Wilde had unsuccessfully wooed Florence Balcombe, who became Stoker's wife in 1878.)

Oscar Wilde's own occult novel, *The Picture of Dorian Gray*, published in 1890, features a sexually ambiguous central character who (like Dracula) acquires eternal youth from the powers of darkness.

The Novel in Focus

Plot summary. The story is told through the journal entries, letters, newspaper articles, notes, and telegrams that Mina Harker assembles and transcribes during the course of the developing

campaign against the vampire. The longest continuous narrative is the first, from the journal of Jonathan Harker. The young British lawyer has traveled to the Balkans at the request of his firm's client, a certain Count Dracula, who wishes to purchase a house in London. Jonathan writes the first entry as he arrives in Transylvania (today the center and northwest of Romania), the region of the Balkans where the Count lives in his castle. As he awaits a coach that will take him closer to Castle Dracula, he is perturbed when an innkeeper's wife implores him not to go and then gives him a crucifix, which she says will protect him. The coach is met later by another, smaller coach, driven by a tall man who hides his features but who has eyes that seem to gleam red in the lamplight. Dogs howl as the coach passes farms along the way, and, as it approaches the castle, wolves join in, forming a chorus of howling animals.

At the castle Jonathan is welcomed by Dracula, "a tall old man, clean-shaven save for a long white moustache, and clad in black from head to foot, without a single speck of colour about him anywhere" (*Dracula,* p. 15). At first, Dracula's friendly welcome allays Jonathan's growing sense of foreboding, but after a few days his nervousness returns. Several strange incidents add to his fears: the Count does not seem to cast a reflection in mirrors, for example, and reacts violently to the sight of blood when Jonathan cuts himself. Then from a window one night he sees the Count crawling headfirst, like a lizard, down the outside of the castle wall. Furthermore, Dracula only seems to be around at night; Jonathan never sees him during the day, when the castle doors are all locked. Gradually Jonathan realizes that he is a prisoner in the castle.

Against his host's orders Jonathan explores the castle. In one of the rooms he experiences what seems to be a nightmare: he is menaced by three voluptuous women who excite in him a "deadly fear" yet also "a wicked burning desire" to be kissed with their red lips (*Dracula,* p. 37). One of the women is about to touch her sharp teeth to his neck when Dracula suddenly appears. His eyes glowing red with rage, the Count pushes them away with a furious warning: "This man belongs to me!" (*Dracula,* p. 39). The women seem to vanish, and Jonathan awakens in his room. Yet he feels certain the experience was real and dreads that the women still wish to suck his blood. He also sees and hears evidence that Dracula and the women are preying on young children. Another time, while exploring in the base-

Bela Lugosi in the 1931 classic film version of *Dracula.*

ment, he discovers 50 large wooden crates of earth, in one of which rests the Count himself, seemingly dead. In growing panic Jonathan decides to flee the castle, and his last entry is written as he plans to climb down the steep outer stone wall. Better, he resolves, to die in the attempt than to suffer whatever fate the Count and the ghoulish women have in store for him.

The next documents in the narrative are letters between Mina Murray and her upper-class friend Lucy Westenra, a beautiful and stylish young woman. Mina looks forward to her fiancé Jonathan Harker's return, and Lucy has recently received three proposals of marriage: one from the aristocratic Arthur Holmwood, Lord Godalming, and two others from his friends Dr. Jack Seward and Quincey Morris from Texas in the United States. She agrees to wed Arthur Holmwood, and the rejected suitors gallantly pledge their friendship and best wishes. Mina and Lucy have planned to meet in Whitby, a small coastal resort town in the northern English county of Yorkshire. By the time they do so, Mina has grown anxious about Jonathan, from whom she has not heard in over a month. Meanwhile, entries from Dr. Seward's journal reveal that (despite sadness at Lucy's rejection) he has grown interested in what he calls a "zoophagous" (life-eating) patient in his lunatic asylum (*Dracula,* p.

70). The man, whose name is Renfield, catches flies in his cell, first eating them, but then feeding them to spiders and eating the spiders; he soon progresses to feeding the spiders to sparrows and eating the birds himself. Renfield has asked for a kitten.

Entries from Mina's journal reflect her growing concern about Jonathan, who still has not been heard from; Mina also mentions that Lucy has begun walking in her sleep. A newspaper cutting relates that a violent and sudden storm at sea off Whitby has resulted in the shipwreck of the Russian sailing vessel *Demeter*, driven aground in Whitby harbor. Oddly, the cargo ves-

BLOODTHIRSTY TYRANTS, VAMPIRE LEGENDS

The clearest historical model for Count Dracula was a notoriously bloodthirsty Balkan nobleman called Vlad Tepes or Vlad the Impaler, after his preferred method of executing his enemies. The ruler of the Balkan principality of Wallachia from 1456 to 1462, he was also known as Vlad Dracula. Dracula means "Devil" or "Dragon" in Wallachian; Stoker makes clear in the novel that Dracula's powers originate with the Devil, and hints that he may be the Devil himself. Another Central European historical figure, the sixteenth-century Hungarian countess Elizabeth Bathory, was infamous for killing young girls and bathing in their blood in order to rejuvenate herself. While vampires have been a staple of folklore in many cultures since ancient times, such behavior may have helped give rise to an epidemic of vampire sightings in the early eighteenth century in Central Europe.

sel was empty except for a huge dog that leaped off as the vessel came to rest, and the dead captain, who had lashed himself to the wheel. The captain's log tells how the crew disappeared at night one by one during the voyage until only the captain was left; terrified, the man lashed himself to the wheel, and was found with a crucifix and rosary beads around his bound wrists. The vessel's cargo includes 50 large boxes of earth, which are sent on to their destination.

As Mina records, Lucy's sleepwalking worsens. Mina follows her friend one night to the ruins of a local abbey, where she seems to see a figure with gleaming red eyes bending over Lucy. When Mina approaches, the figure is gone, and Lucy is unconscious. She has two small pinpricks

in her throat. Two nights later, Mina finds Lucy sitting up in bed, asleep, pointing to her bedroom window, around which Mina sees a large bat flying. Lucy grows languid and exhausted during the daytime, and she starts talking in her sleep. Instead of healing, the two wounds in her throat get larger. A document records the shipping of 50 crates to Carfax, the ruined manor house next to Dr. Seward's asylum in London that Jonathan's firm arranged for Dracula to purchase.

Mina finally receives word of Jonathan, who has been ill in a hospital in the Hungarian city of Budapest for some six weeks. She journeys to Budapest, where she and the now recovering Jonathan are married. Dr. Seward makes entries in his phonograph journal that chart the strange behavior of Renfield, who babbles excitedly about awaiting the commands of his approaching master. Holmwood, worried about Lucy, asks Dr. Seward to examine her. Seward can find nothing wrong, but writes to his old teacher, the renowned Dutch scientist Professor Abraham Van Helsing. Arriving from Amsterdam, Van Helsing transfuses blood from Holmwood to Lucy, then repeats the operation with blood from himself, Seward, and Quincey Morris at intervals of several days, as Lucy somehow keeps losing blood and growing paler and weaker. Despite Van Helsing's efforts, Lucy dies; she is entombed in her family's crypt in Hampstead, close to London.

Mina and Jonathan, who have returned to England, are in London where Jonathan, aghast, sees the Count on the street one day. Dracula has somehow grown younger, with black hair instead of gray. Meanwhile, newspaper cuttings report that several young children, missing after playing on Hampstead Heath, have returned with tales of a "bloofer lady" (beautiful lady) who lures them away (*Dracula*, p. 177). The children also came home with unexplained wounds on their throats. Mina, having read Jonathan's journal, prepares herself for the struggle she senses coming against "that fearful Count" by typing up her husband's record of his days as Dracula's prisoner (*Dracula*, p. 179). The Dutch scientist Van Helsing contacts her to ask for Lucy's diary, which Mina has also typed out; she gives him both documents. Van Helsing alarms Seward with talk of hypnotism and thought-reading, insisting that Seward keep an open mind while declaring that it was Lucy who attacked the children on Hampstead Heath. That night they go to the crypt, entering the cold dark chamber to find that Lucy's coffin is empty. The next day, however, they find her again in the coffin.

Van Helsing tells the disbelieving Seward that Lucy has become a vampire, one of the "Un-Dead," and that they must kill her by driving a stake through her heart and cutting off her head (*Dracula,* p. 201). They must do the same, he says, to Dracula, "the great Un-Dead," who has made Lucy into a vampire by sucking her blood (*Dracula,* p. 203). After the vampire Lucy attacks them on a subsequent visit, Holmwood, Morris, and Seward believe Van Helsing. The night following the attack they return with him to the crypt, where Lucy's fiancé, Holmwood, hammers a stake through her heart and Van Helsing and Seward cut off her head. Van Helsing says that only after this can her soul rest in peace.

Mina comes to Dr. Seward's asylum, where she transcribes the doctor's phonograph journal and gives him typescripts of her and Jonathan's diaries to read. Seward realizes that Renfield's odd behavior, alternately violent and peaceful, has been "a sort of index to the coming and going of the Count" (*Dracula,* p. 225). Van Helsing's occult research has taught him that Dracula's powers are at their lowest by day, when the vampire must rest, and he can only do so on his native soil. They must find the boxes of earth and "sterilize" them by placing pieces of the Host (sanctified communion wafer) in them (*Dracula,* p. 242). Once they have done so, the vampire will be unable to rest. They can then find and attack him during his weakest hours, between noon and sunset.

While the men begin tracking the boxes, some of which Dracula has removed to other houses he has purchased, Dracula goes on the offensive against his hunters. Taking the form of mist, he enters Mina's bedroom at night and begins to suck her blood as he sucked Lucy's. Soon afterward, Renfield is found beaten in his cell; his back broken, he dies after revealing that Dracula, his assailant, has targeted Mina. Van Helsing and the others hurry to Mina's room, where they find Jonathan in a trance-like stupor as Dracula, having drunk Mina's blood, forces her to drink his own in turn. This, the vampire has told her, will place her mind under his command from any distance. Some hours later, as the men locate and sterilize the last of the boxes except for one, Dracula attacks them, but they drive him back with a crucifix, and he flees.

Mina suggests that Van Helsing hypnotize her. As she hopes, under hypnosis her mind-link with the vampire provides a vital clue to his whereabouts. She hears water lapping and sails creaking: Van Helsing assumes that Dracula has fled England in the remaining box and is returning to Transylvania. But the struggle is not over, for Van Helsing says they must pursue him—both for Mina's sake, since she will remain under the vampire's influence, and also "for the sake of humanity," since he is immortal and will continue to make new vampires unless stopped (*Dracula,* p. 319). They travel to the Black Sea port of Varna, where they await Dracula's arrival. Overcoming a number of obstacles, they finally intercept the band of gypsies that is transporting Dracula's box from the ship to the castle. Just as the sun is about to set, the men fight their way through the gypsies to the box, where the mortally injured Quincy Morris plunges his bowie knife through Dracula's heart as Jonathan Harker simultaneously cuts Dracula's throat. The vampire's body immediately crumbles into dust.

Evolution and degeneration. Throughout *Dracula* Stoker portrays the Texan Quincey Morris as a man of action who outshines his British fellow vampire hunters in resourcefulness, initiative, and strength. At one point in the novel, Renfield flatters Morris by predicting that America will become a world power: he foresees a day when "the Pole and the Tropics may hold allegiance to the Stars and Stripes" (*Dracula,* p. 244). Dr. Seward, the Victorian man of science, puts this potential in terms of breeding: "If America can go on breeding men like that, she will be a power in the world indeed" (*Dracula,* p. 173). In other words, imperial success results from breeding. And breeding, the Victorians had realized, is closely linked to the process of evolution.

The publication of Charles Darwin's *On the Origin of Species* in 1859 had made evolution the most influential idea of the later nineteenth century. Whereas Darwin had limited himself to the area of biology, by the 1870s British thinkers such as Herbert Spencer had applied Darwin's ideas, popularly summed up in the phrase "survival of the fittest," to the social realm. In contrast to Darwin's explanation of biological success, however, this "social Darwinism" was invoked not merely to explain but also to justify social or political success. Politically powerful nations and individuals, the argument went, were inherently superior to less powerful ones, and therefore justified in expanding their power. The imperial Victorians viewed evolution as a ladder of progress, a ladder at the top of which they themselves stood. From the top of a ladder, however, one can easily go down. Progress thus also entails an implicit threat, the danger of its opposite, degeneration, which was (like evolution) a widely discussed idea at the time of the novel.

This often unconscious recognition lay behind the vague fears of the imperial 1890s. Like other nineteenth-century Europeans, the Victorians viewed blood and bloodlines as closely linked to the idea of racial vitality, and saw both as subject to degeneration. Degeneration could come through moral laxness or indulgence, vices they believed had caused the earlier downfall of the Roman Empire, with which the Victorians were fond of comparing their own. Or degeneration

---

HOMOEROTIC UNDERTONES

In a sensational trial in 1895, two years before *Dracula* was published, Stoker's friend Oscar Wilde was sentenced to prison for his part in a homosexual love affair. In general, Victorian society viewed homosexuality as an evil perversion. Stoker, who as a young man had idolized the homosexual American poet Walt Whitman, adopted an attitude of similar hero-worship toward his employer, the actor Henry Irving. Discerning homoerotic undertones in *Dracula,* modern critics have speculated about Stoker's own sexual orientation. Stoker depicts the seductive and commanding Dracula as physically resembling Irving, and he attempted in vain to interest the actor in playing the vampire in a stage version. Some critics have therefore argued that Stoker's novel cloaks an attraction toward Irving that the author felt unable to show openly. Regardless of the truth, the dangers of such impulses in Victorian society were clearly demonstrated by the fate of Oscar Wilde, who emerged from prison a broken man in May 1897, the very month of *Dracula*'s publication.

---

could come simply with age. In *Dracula*, these imperial fears are symbolized by the foreign vampire's draining of British blood in the very process through which he breeds vampires. Recounting medieval battles in his homeland, Dracula describes himself as belonging to "a conquering race" but one whose "blood" is old and needs to be revived (*Dracula*, p. 29). Drinking blood from his British victims physically rejuvenates him as it enervates them. The vampire thus demonstrates that a degenerate, parasitical fate potentially awaits those whose conquests lie in the past—as many feared was the case with Britain and her empire by the 1890s.

Sources and literary context. Aside from Central European vampire legends and the historical figures of Vlad the Impaler and Elizabeth Bathory, Stoker also drew on an already existing body of vampire tales in English. Like Mary Shelley's *Frankenstein* (1818; in *WLAIT 3: British and Irish Literature and Its Times*), they originated in the Romantic movement, which was dominated by such poets as Percy Bysshe Shelley (Mary's husband) and Lord Byron. Some of these Dracula predecessors include:

- Lord Byron's "The Giaour" (1813), an occult narrative poem that mentions a vampire emerging from its tomb to suck the blood of humans.
- Dr. John Polidori's *The Vampyre* (1819), featuring a seductive and aristocratic vampire modeled on Lord Byron himself. Polidori was Byron's physician, and he was present when Byron and the Shelleys held a horror story contest one stormy night in June 1816. Polidori based *The Vampyre* on an idea Byron himself had that night; Mary Shelley's contribution would become *Frankenstein*.
- James Malcolm Rymer's *Varney the Vampire* (1847), a long (nearly 900 pages) and turgidly written potboiler that introduces features Stoker would borrow for *Dracula*: Central European origins; long, fanglike canine teeth; a black cloak; the abilities to climb down sheer castle walls and put female victims in a trancelike state; arriving in Britain in a shipwrecked vessel.
- Sheridan Le Fanu's *Carmilla* (1872), in which a sensuous female vampire preys on female victims.

Reception. Published on May 26, 1897, *Dracula* received mixed reviews and enjoyed only moderate sales during Stoker's lifetime. Seeing the novel as a straightforward Gothic adventure story in which good triumphs over evil, Victorian readers and reviewers alike ignored the sexual elements that have proven so alluring for modern literary critics.

In addition to the novel's sexual aspects, critics have found the figure of Count Dracula himself a strikingly rich source of symbolism, most of which plays off taboos or alienation of one kind or another. As one critic writes in the introduction to a recent edition, Dracula has been seen as standing for "perversion, menstruation, venereal disease, female sexuality, male homosexuality, feudal aristocracy, monopoly capitalism, the proletariat, the Jew, the primal father, the Antichrist, and the typewriter" (Ellmann in *Dracula*, p. xxviii). Along with being perennially fashionable among literary critics, Dracula has proven immensely popular on both stage and screen, where (beginning with Bela Lugosi's classic 1931 film portrayal) he has found his widest exposure in popular culture.

—Colin Wells

For More Information

Belford, Barbara. *Bram Stoker: A Biography of the Man Who Wrote Dracula.* New York: Knopf, 1996.

Glover, David. *Vampires, Mummies, and Liberals: Bram Stoker and the Politics of Popular Fiction.* Durham, N.C.: Duke University Press, 1996.

Harrison, J. F. C. *Late Victorian Britain 1875-1901.* London: Routledge, 1991.

Hughes, William, and Andrew Smith, eds. *Bram Stoker: History, Psychoanalysis and the Gothic.* London: Macmillan, 1998.

Jarret, Derek. *The Sleep of Reason: Fantasy and Reality from the Victorian Age to the First World War.* London: Weidenfield and Nicolson, 1988.

Jenner, Michael. *Victorian Britain.* London: Weidenfield and Nicolson, 1999.

Leatherdale, Clive. *The Origins of Dracula.* London: William Kimber, 1987.

Ledger, Sally. *The New Woman: Fiction and Feminism at the Fin de Siècle.* New York: St. Martin's, 1997.

Mitchell, Sally. *Daily Life in Victorian England.* Westport, Conn.: Greenwood, 1996.

Rosenbach Museum. *Bram Stoker's Dracula: A Centennial Exhibition at the Rosenbach Museum and Library.* Philadelphia: Rosenbach Museum, 1997.

Stoker, Bram. *Dracula.* Ed. Maud Ellmann. Oxford World's Classics Series. Oxford: Oxford University Press, 1996.

Wolf, Leonard. *The Annotated Dracula.* New York: Clarkson N. Potter, 1975.

The French Lieutenant's Woman

by

John Fowles

❧

John Robert Fowles was born March 31, 1926, at Leigh Upon Sea, Essex. He served two years in the military before attending Oxford University, where he studied French language and literature. After graduating in 1950, Fowles went on to teach English in France, Greece, and Britain. In 1954 he married Elizabeth Whitton, whom he had met in Greece, becoming at the same time stepfather to her daughter from a prior marriage. Fowles's first published novel, *The Collector* (1963) sold well and was generally, if not universally, well reviewed (Aubrey, pp. 91-92). Its success enabled Fowles to leave teaching and write full time. His second, *The Magus* (published in 1965, although actually written much earlier) fared less well, often being dismissed as pretentious (Aubrey, p. 100). Therefore, the success of his third novel, *The French Lieutenant's Woman*, which catapulted him to fame as an important and popular writer, came as a surprise. Fowles continued to publish consistently thereafter, releasing several novels, as well as collections of short stories, essays on philosophy and natural history, poems, and translations of French literature. He wrote *The French Lieutenant's Woman* shortly after moving to Lyme Regis, where he and his wife lived in an old farmhouse on the edge of the Undercliff that served as a model for The Dairy in the novel. Although no longer living at Underhill Farm, Fowles still resides in Lyme Regis, where he acted as curate for the town's local history museum in the 1980s.

THE LITERARY WORK

A novel, set primarily in Lyme Regis, England, but also in Exeter and London, England, and in the United States in 1867; written 100 years later in 1967; published in 1969.

SYNOPSIS

A Victorian gentleman, staying in Lyme Regis with his pretty and conventional fiancée, becomes intrigued with "the French Lieutenant's Woman," an enigmatic figure with a scandalous past. The relationship that develops between them forces him to choose between the safety and security of conventionality and the freedom of following his own heart.

Events in History at the Time the Novel Takes Place

Evolutionary thinking and the crisis of faith. The pursuit of science was crucial to Victorian intellectual culture and industrial development, but posed difficult challenges to Christian descriptions of the world, its origins, and humanity's place within it. In particular, developments in geology and biology led many to question the Biblical account of the world's creation and, along with it, traditional Christianity. Sir Charles Lyell (1797-1875) published his *Principles of Ge-*

John Fowles

ology (3 volumes) between 1830 and 1833, which demonstrated that the earth was millions of years old rather than thousands, and that the world itself had changed over long periods of time as the result of processes like erosion. Biologist Charles Darwin (1809-82), working in part from Lyell's research on fossils, published the theory of natural selection in his watershed book, **On the Origin of Species** (also in *WLAIT 4: British and Irish Literature and Its Times*) in 1859. Its impact was enormous, both within scientific circles and in the popular culture. Indeed, evolutionary thinking became a hallmark of the era.

Many Victorian thinkers were concerned with the notion of "progress"—where their society had been, where it was going, and how it might get there. Evolutionary thinking provided a model within which to conceptualize progress, and was soon applied beyond the sciences, to social and economic theory as well. Herbert Spencer (1820-1903) devoted himself to producing "a theory in which evolution could provide a total explanation for all phenomena," introducing the phrase "survival of the fittest" (usually, and incorrectly, attributed to Darwin) in his writings about social evolution (Hoppen, p. 475). For Spencer, the same natural laws applied to biology and society; thus class inequalities (among many other social characteristics)

could be understood (and, for some, justified) as the manifestation of different individuals' "fitness" for life in modern society.

At the same time, scientific evidence that the world was ancient and its inhabitants evolved over time rather than being created all at once undermined the credibility of the Genesis story in the Bible, leading many to question Christian history and Christian faith along with it. Moreover, other branches of scholarship contributed to this doubt: at mid-century, German Biblical scholars began publishing work in "higher criticism" that challenged previous assumptions about the authorship and sources of Biblical texts. Taken together, these intellectual developments created for many a kind of crisis of faith; with evidence mounting that the Bible could not be taken as literal truth, many struggled to reconcile religion with knowledge. Certainly, Fowles's Charles Smithson is just such a man. This is not to say, however, that religious doubt swept through the entire populace. On the contrary, "never was Britain more religious than in the Victorian age" (Hoppen, p. 425). In the 1830s, for example, the Oxford Movement, led by John Newman (1801-90; after 1879, Cardinal John Newman) thrived as an influential religious revival. Actually, the agonizing over religious doubt that appears in so much Victorian writing and culture indicates the continuing strength of religious thought; had faith and the Church been less powerful elements in society, they would have been much easier for intellectuals troubled by counterevidence to leave behind.

Social transformation and the Second Great Reform Bill. Along with industrialization in the nineteenth century came urbanization, accompanied by important demographic shifts in the British population. Manufacturing provided a new economy in which riches could be amassed, creating a new class of well-off (occasionally fabulously rich) families who owed their financial status to industry rather than landownership. The aristocracy had traditionally been the wealthiest—and concomitantly most powerful—group in society because of its landholdings, but political power and influence shifted to the wealthy industrial class (the upper middle class) as the Victorian era progressed. The furor over the Corn Laws is indicative of this change. The Corn Law tariffs prohibited the importation of foreign grain unless domestic grain prices went above a very high set price. These tariffs protected landlords by keeping food prices high, which, in turn, opponents argued, limited trade and made manufactured goods more costly. The repeal of the Corn Laws in 1846 indicated a policy shift in favor of the new wealthy.

At the same time, industrialization drew workers to the city and trade (in the broadest sense) created many new white-collar jobs both in the offices of the companies doing business and in aspects of the infrastructure necessary to support urban living, such as retail shops. As a result, in addition to shifting from agricultural labor to factory work, many in the working class were able to leave manual labor behind altogether and move into the lower rungs of the middle class by acquiring jobs as clerks, secretaries, or shopkeepers. Indeed, this subgroup of the middle class increased more rapidly than most others. In *The French Lieutenant's Woman*, Sam's dreams of his own haberdashery shop represent his desire to make the leap from working to middle class, and although he is unable to achieve them, his eventual success in Mr. Freeman's department store demonstrates how working-class members could indeed rise economically and socially in this period.

Social mobility—whether up or down the class scale—is rarely easy, however, and can be accompanied by social unrest. Significant aspects of English political policy during the 1800s were structured with the intention of quelling potential rebellion in the lower classes. Britain's conservative leadership, anxious about the possibility of revolution, passed a series of gradual reforms across several decades designed to appease radical demands for greater political equality without actually implementing radical change. Most important among these were the two great franchise reform bills of 1832 (the year usually identified as the beginning of the Victorian period) and 1867 (the year in which *The French Lieutenant's Woman* takes place). Although carefully structured to minimize their impact on the actual balance of power between the wealthy and the poor, these reforms enfranchised hundreds of thousands of men. The 1867 bill granted the vote to every male property owner living in a borough constituency, and to male lodgers paying at least £10 per year in rent. It also included redistricting provisions that took one parliamentary seat away from any borough with less than 10,000 inhabitants, freeing 45 seats for redistribution. Ten went to towns that had never had a Member of Parliament (MP), four were given as second seats to Liverpool, Manchester, Birmingham and Leeds, one was assigned to the University of London, and 25 were given to coun-

ties whose population had grown since 1832. These provisions reduced the impact of new working-class votes by giving more parliamentary seats to the landholding counties than to industrialized urban areas. Even after the 1867 bill, only around a third of British men over 21 had the right to vote in national elections.

Class consciousness was in fact just beginning to develop in this period. Karl Marx (1818-83) and Friedrich Engels (1820-95) composed the *Communist Manifesto* in the 1840s; it would be published in an English translation in 1888. In the epigrams to the chapters of *The French Lieutenant's Woman*, Fowles often quotes Marx. These quotations reflect his era's hindsight on the shifting class structures of Britain (and indeed all of Europe), for although these ideas appeared and gained influence as the nineteenth century progressed, they were by no means the dominant theory of social interaction and progress at the time. Indeed, during the mid-nineteenth century, "many began to believe that the heat was being taken out of social antagonisms; that, occasional strikes notwithstanding, physical force and revolution were giving way to gradualism under the impress of prosperity" (Hoppen, p. 240). This mid-Victorian faith in gradualism, although contradictory to radical theories under development by European thinkers such as Marx and Engels, nevertheless set Britain on a course of reform that complemented its shifting economic and class structures and established precedents for future emancipations.

Gender inequality and the sexual double standard. Among those left out by the Great Reform Bills were Britain's women, although in the debates over the 1867 bill John Stuart Mill was able to convince 73 MPs to vote in favor of extending suffrage to women. The novel cites this moment as "the beginning of feminine emancipation in England" (Fowles, *The French Lieutenant's Woman*, p. 115). But Mill's radicalism was a minority position—196 MPs voted against the measure; and women would not achieve even partial suffrage in national elections until after the First World War. Instead, the dominant mode of thought about women in the nineteenth century consisted of a not-always compatible set of ideas regarding women's nature and role in society. On one hand, women were considered by many to be morally superior to men; they were idealized as "The Angel in the House" (the title of a popular mid-century poem by Coventry Patmore) who would counteract the influence of the wicked world on their husbands and children with their inherent gentleness and virtue. On the other hand, society regarded women as weaker than and intellectually inferior to men; females were considered incapable of managing the demands of professions or business. In other words, women ought to be dependent upon and subordinate to men, despite the pedestal of virtue upon which they were placed.

The idea (and idealization) of the angel in the house developed largely as a result of shifting work patterns in the middle and working classes. Whereas in previous centuries husbands and wives had often worked together to sustain a family through small-scale farming and cottage industry, the shift toward work in factories or businesses took earning a living out of the home. This initiated the now-familiar dichotomy between a (usually male) wage earner who goes out to work each day and a (usually female) family caregiver who stays in the home with responsibility for the children and domestic chores. The arrangement indicates a certain level of socioeconomic status and respectability (since the husband is clearly earning enough on his own to support the entire family) that quickly became romanticized as the ideal family structure—something good and proper, rather than simply practical. Of course, for many working-class families this ideal was completely out of reach; in families battling poverty, women often sought work as well, although employers systematically discriminated against them in wages and other respects. Women, then, suffered unequal treatment in both public and private life, living under an ideology that prized their virtue but insisted upon an environment thoroughly dominated by men.

Another aspect of the inequality of women in the nineteenth century was a sexual double standard under which chastity before marriage and fidelity thereafter were demanded of women whereas a certain discreet indulgence and variety of sexual experience were expected of men. The scope of female prostitution at the time provides evidence of this dichotomy, as thousands of "fallen" women provided outlets for men's sexuality. It is impossible to know today how many prostitutes really worked in Victorian England, in part because contemporary estimates varied widely, ranging from 25,000 to 368,000 for England and Wales, but clearly the numbers were high (Hoppen, p. 322). Fowles's novel captures the contradictions between the Victorians' stated values and actual behavior in its description of the nineteenth century: "An age where woman was sacred; and where you could buy a thirteen-year-old girl for a few pounds—a few shillings, if you only wanted her for an hour or two" (Fowles, *French Lieutenant's Woman*, p. 266). The novel likewise reminds us of the double standard among respectable people, explaining early in the story that Charles has dallied with many women abroad whereas Ernestina forbids herself even thoughts about sex.

The Novel in Focus

Plot summary. *The French Lieutenant's Woman* opens with its three primary characters all out walking on the Cobb, a stone breakwater that forms the manmade harbor of Lyme Regis. Charles Smithson and his fiancée, Tina Freeman, banter affectionately about Charles's acceptance of "the Darwinian position" and fondness for fossils until Charles notices that standing at the end of the Cobb is a mysterious figure, whom Tina identifies as "poor Tragedy"—"The French Lieutenant's . . . Woman" (*Woman,* pp. 7, 9). Tina's hesitation, indicated by the ellipsis in the text, alludes to the "gross name" the fishermen call her—"The French Lieutenant's Whore"—although that name will not be voiced until much later in the novel (*Woman,* p. 9). Intrigued by the woman, Charles demands that Tina tell him her story. The woman waits, Tina explains, for a French lover who abandoned her—but in fact Tina knows little for certain, admitting "it is all gossip" (*Woman,* p. 9). Nonetheless, the woman's presence discomfits Tina, who asks Charles to turn away with her. Charles insists on approaching her, however, and is profoundly startled by the look she gives him when he speaks to her. From this moment it is clear that a romantic triangle has formed. Walking away, Charles comments to Tina that the trouble with provincial towns is that "there is no mystery. No romance," two elements the French Lieutenant's Woman is about to bring into Charles's life with striking consequences (*Woman,* p. 10).

The following chapters familiarize us with the histories of several major players in Fowles's drama: Charles, the minor aristocrat, who is likely to inherit his uncle's baronetcy although he has not inherited his attitudes and interests; Mrs. Poulteney, the hypocritical, unkind, and self-righteous widow with whom Sarah Woodruff, the French Lieutenant's Woman, currently resides; Ernestina, the intelligent and sexually self-repressed young woman whose manners, like her face, are exactly right for the Victorian age; Sarah Woodruff herself, albeit

Ammonite fossils at Lyme Regis, England, of the type Charles gives to Ernestina in *The French Lieutenant's Woman.*

through versions of her story told by others; Sarah, it appears, rashly left her post as a governess to elope with a French Lieutenant she had nursed after he was injured in a shipwreck.

Although the people who claim to know the story all believe that Sarah Woodruff lodged with a female cousin when she followed the French Lieutenant to Weymouth (a port nearer to France), and that she refused the Lieutenant when it became clear that he planned to seduce rather than marry her, her conduct remains "highly to be reprobated" in the eyes of rigidly moralistic respectable Victorian society (*Woman,* p. 34). Mrs. Poulteney, we learn, has taken Sarah in as a kind of personal secretary in a charitable gesture, intended both to earn Mrs. Poulteney a surer place in heaven and to spite a rival of hers known in the community for her generosity and kindness.

As the plot progresses, Charles sets out fossil hunting. In the course of his walk, he stumbles upon Sarah, asleep on a hidden ledge at the edge of a seaside meadow. She seems to him "childlike," "immensely tender and yet sexual" in the "abandonment of deep sleep" (*Woman,* p. 70). Charles is "tranced by this unexpected encounter," and overcome by a conviction that she has been "unfairly outcast" (*Woman,* p. 71). In

the awkward moment after she awakes they share another powerful, disconcerting look before Charles "[comes] to his sense of what was proper," apologizes, and walks away (*Woman,* p. 71). Significantly, Charles does not tell Ernestina he has met Sarah at all—an omission he justifies on the grounds of Ernestina's apparent wish to hear nothing about the woman, but that suggests the secrecy of a man having an affair.

The narrative then looks backward, to explain that Sarah's wish for secrecy is due to Mrs. Poulteney's having forbidden her to walk in that area, Ware Commons, because of its association in the minds of the townspeople with midsummer dancing and sexual impropriety. On that day, in fact, Sarah had contemplated suicide, but the narrator declares he cannot explain her thoughts or feelings precisely, nor answer the perplexing question, "Who is Sarah?" (*Woman,* pp. 95-96). At this point in *The French Lieutenant's Woman,* the narrator—speaking in the voice of the author, John Fowles—makes a startling intrusion into the plot, inserting an entire chapter (13) that discusses his philosophy and methods of writing, and asserts that his characters, although fictional, choose their own paths through the novel. Although the narrative voice has interrupted the plot several times already to provide background information like the details of Charles's proposal to Tina or Sarah's positive influence on Mrs. Poulteney's household, this intrusion is by far the most self-conscious yet, and sets the stage for further insertions of the authorial presence as the novel continues. At the same time, Chapter 13 explicitly states the creed of freedom that Fowles

---

THE WICKEDNESS OF THE FRENCH

~

Sarah's actions seem all the more sinful to the righteous of Lyme Regis because the man she followed was French. The stigma reflects a long history of animosity between France and England, during which the two countries fought many wars. It also reflects a stereotype. As Mrs. Poulteney makes clear in the novel, many Britons believed the French to be generally wicked and wanton in their ways and beliefs. France, the novel also suggests, has gained ill repute simply because it is foreign, and therefore associated with the excesses of travelers. While abroad, people could indulge in, for example, the services of prostitutes without anxiety about social repercussions that would accompany such indiscretions closer to home. Finally the French were overwhelmingly Catholic, which seemed sinful in itself to many English Protestants. During the nineteenth century, France's recent political history provoked further anxiety in Britain. Although many British intellectuals had been enthusiastic about the French Revolution when it began in 1789, the chaos and violence that followed led a large number to adopt the view of English philosopher Edmund Burke, whose *Reflections on the Revolution in France* (1790) argued that revolution would only lead to anarchy and tyranny, and that gradual reform was the superior way to improve society. Anxiety about the possibility of violent revolution underscored British politics throughout the nineteenth century and contributed to the series of reforms (notably the franchise) that are one hallmark of the Victorian period. Thus, in addition to associating the French with immorality and excess, Britons were also likely at this time to associate them with the threat of dangerous social and political disorder.

---

sets forth in the larger plot of *The French Lieutenant's Woman*, declaring, "There is only one good definition of God: the freedom that allows other freedoms to exist" (*Woman*, p. 97).

In the following chapters, Charles meets Sarah a series of times, at first unintentionally, but with a growing interest in her. At a visit to Mrs. Poul-

teney, Charles is again impressed by her apparent intelligence and strangely self-confident reserve. On another hunt for fossils, he is struck by her appearance, and his perception of her shifts toward a heightened appreciation of her sensuality. They have their first real conversation, in which Charles expresses kindness and sympathy and Sarah reveals that although she knows the French Lieutenant will never return, she feels tied to Lyme Regis despite the town's condemnation of her.

By now it is becoming apparent even to Charles himself that he has grown to be somewhat obsessed with Sarah, "or at any rate with the enigma that she presented," so it is not surprising when he sets out again walking in the direction of the place they have met twice before (*Woman*, p. 128). Charles plans to avoid Sarah, but she appears and approaches him, bearing as a gift two of the fossilized starfish that he especially seeks. Sarah speaks of her isolation and suffering, and pleads with a disconcerted Charles to meet her again so that she may tell him her story. Charles reluctantly agrees, recognizing that "he was about to engage in the forbidden, or rather the forbidden was about to engage in him" (*Woman*, p. 146).

When they next meet, Sarah confesses that she is "a doubly dishonored woman. By circumstances and by choice" because in fact she did not stay with a female cousin in Weymouth and, when the Lieutenant made his intentions clear, "I gave myself to him" (*Woman*, p. 174). She explains that she has "married shame" because it is the only way she could find to "break out of what I was" and achieve a kind of personal freedom (*Woman*, p. 175). Her explanations confuse Charles, but her tears touch him, and he appears more drawn to her than ever. It becomes clear now that they are in love, but they agree that they must never meet alone again.

Fowles's plot speeds up at this point, with delicate character development giving way to a rapid sequence of events. A disturbing surprise is in store for Charles: he has been called to his uncle's estate, to be informed that his uncle plans to marry—an event that will most likely disinherit Charles when the union produces children. Upon his return, he learns that Sarah has been dismissed by Mrs. Poulteney (having intentionally allowed another household servant to see her leaving Ware Commons). At first Charles fears for Sarah's safety, but two notes from her relieve his anxiety. Although disturbed by her carelessness, he decides to try to help her.

Charles gives Sarah some money and advises her to leave Lyme Regis immediately because there is talk of committing her to an asylum. Painfully, they part, and, following Charles's advice, Sarah goes to Exeter.

Charles, on the other hand, travels to London, where he discusses his changed prospects with Ernestina's father. Much to Charles's dismay, Mr. Freeman suggests that Charles join him in the family business. This proposal horrifies Charles, who thinks of himself as a gentleman of the sort who has nothing to do with trade or industry. In his distress, Charles embarks on an evening of drinking and debauchery that concludes in the room of a prostitute. Already nauseous from excessive drinking, Charles becomes violently ill when she tells him her name is Sarah. Back at his London residence, Charles receives a letter from Sarah, containing nothing but her Exeter address.

The next chapter of the novel presents one possible conclusion to the story. Charles and Ernestina settle down to marriage and, eventually, seven children; Charles never hears from Sarah again. But, the narrator then tells us, this "thoroughly traditional ending" is actually only what Charles has imagined on the train (*Woman*, p. 339). He in fact stops in Exeter to visit Sarah. Within a few passionate moments, Charles and Sarah have abruptly consummated their affair in her small bedroom, but when Charles suggests that he break off his engagement, Sarah protests. She insists that she could not ask him to give up his position in the world for her sake, and declares herself unworthy to be his wife. He disagrees, until he realizes that she has lied to him: she never had sex with the French Lieutenant. Charles cannot fathom the reason for her deceit, but, refusing to explain, Sarah sends him away.

After a night of soul-searching, Charles has an epiphany: it is essential to be free, to follow one's own heart regardless of the expectations of the world around one. He comes to understand Sarah's deceit and actions as "stratagems" to help him see that if he so chooses, he is free to reject the dictates of convention, duty, and restrictive moral codes just as she has. With this knowledge, Charles determines to break off his engagement and remain with Sarah (*Woman*, p. 368). He declares his resolve in a letter, which he asks his manservant, Sam Farrow to deliver, and heads off to Lyme Regis to speak with Ernestina, confident that Sarah will await him upon his return.

Throughout the novel, Sam Farrow has been the protagonist of an important subplot: a romance between himself and a maid working for Ernestina's Aunt Tranter. Sam dreams of opening his own haberdashery shop, and hopes that Charles will give him enough money to do so. His hopes—and his machinations in his own best interest—grow more urgent when he and Mary get engaged. In the manner of personal servants who know a great deal about their employers' goings-on, Sam observes the relationship developing between Charles and Sarah. He at first views the information as potentially valuable, but after Charles is effectively disinherited, it becomes crucial to Sam's plans that Charles marry the wealthy Tina. When Sam realizes that Charles intends to choose Sarah instead, he develops an alternative strategy based on offering the information he has about the affair to Ernestina's family. Sam, therefore, keeps Charles's letter of intentions instead of delivering it to Sarah.

After breaking his engagement with Ernestina, Charles travels to London, to explain everything to her father, Mr. Freeman. Here, Fowles writes himself into the narrative, as a traveler in Charles's train compartment, and explains that he doesn't know quite what to do with Charles and will, therefore, offer two endings to the novel rather than just one.

In London, Charles is browbeaten by two developments: Sarah has disappeared, and Mr. Freeman forces him to sign a legal document admitting his guilt in breaking the contract of his engagement and forfeiting his right to be considered a gentleman. Although he hires detectives to find her, and places inquiries in the *Times*, Charles cannot locate Sarah, and eventually decides to go abroad. He travels widely for over a year before receiving word that Sarah has been found in London. When Sarah is found, Charles is in the United States, a nation that restores in him "a kind of faith in freedom"; he thinks Sarah would have been at home there (*Woman*, p. 434). Indeed, Charles finds Sarah looking very much like an American woman when he returns to London and goes to her new residence, the home of painter Dante Gabriel Rossetti (*Woman*, p. 443). She has joined Rossetti as a kind of assistant, and tells Charles that she has found happiness in this life. After a difficult conversation, she introduces Charles to the daughter she bore after their intercourse and the first ending closes with a passionate family embrace.

Here Fowles again appears in the novel, this time as a dandy in the street below, and turns back the hands of his watch. In the second conclusion, there is no child and Sarah refuses Charles when he urges her to marry him, choosing, finally, freedom and independence over love.

Anachronisms in *The French Lieutenant's Woman.* Although Fowles writes with the tone of a conventional Victorian omniscient narrator in *The French Lieutenant's Woman*, several aspects of the novel make it unmistakably of its own time. Among these is the persistent anachronistic commentary that calls our attention to the similarities and differences between the 1860s and the 1960s. These anachronisms—in this case definable as comments or ideas belonging to a time in the future of the novel's setting—allow Fowles to shape our perception of the Victorian era by comparing and/or contrasting it to a more familiar twentieth-century, environment, while also suggesting that many contemporary trends have parallels or, indeed, origins, in the Victorian era.

Fowles introduces this approach in the novel's third paragraph. Having described the Cobb at Lyme Regis in enthusiastic terms, his narrator comments: "I exaggerate? Perhaps, but I can be put to the test, for the Cobb has changed very little since the year of which I write; though the town of Lyme has, and the test is not fair if you look back towards land" (*Woman*, p. 4). Asserting both continuity and change, the narrator overtly asks his reader to "look" as he bids, at the Cobb of 1867 rather than the Lyme Regis of 1967. From this point forward the novel is peppered with narratorial comments that point out the differences between Victorian times and our own. These comments might be socio-historical, as when describing Charles's skin as "suitably pale," the narrator reminds us that "this was a time when a suntan was not at all a desirable social-sexual status symbol, but the reverse: an indication of low rank" (*Woman*, p. 41). At other times, the comments are philosophical, as when the narrator explains to us that "In spite of Hegel, the Victorians were not a dialectically minded age; they did not think naturally in opposites, of positives and negatives as aspects of the same whole" (*Woman*, p. 248). At still other times, the comments are psychological:

Such a sudden shift of sexual key is impossible today. A man and a woman are no sooner in any but the most casual contact than they consider the possibility of a physical relationship. We consider such frankness about the real drives of human behavior

healthy, but in Charles's time private minds did not admit the desires banned by the public mind.

(*Woman*, p. 176)

Another anachronistic device Fowles adopts to remind us that the novel takes place in a historical period removed from our own is the inclusion of footnotes explaining certain terms or historical situations. These pull us out of the illusion of reality created by fictional narratives, reminding us that we are reading a text, and indeed, one that may require historical education for comprehension. In effect, although the setting of the *story* is 1867, the setting of the *text* is clearly and explicitly 1967.

Even more striking is Fowles's appearance in the narrative on two separate occasions as himself—the author—first attempting to determine what he should do with his characters and then later, having decided, interrupting the flow of textual time by setting his watch back 15 minutes, a gesture that facilitates the shift from one possible ending for the novel to another. Obviously, John Fowles could not have been present in historical 1867, but he can insert himself into the fictional 1867 of his imagination in anachronistic moves that allow him to comment directly on his own choices as the author. Notably, he identifies the precise period of time that separates himself from his characters—and the problems that creates for him as an author—in one of these episodes: "I have pretended to slip back into 1867; but of course that year is in reality a century past. It is futile to show optimism or pessimism, or anything else about it, because we know what has happened since" (*Woman*, p. 406).

These anachronisms also enable Fowles to remind his readers that many of the liberal tendencies of the 1960s, perhaps most notably the liberation of women, have beginnings in the earlier century. Sarah, with her personal and sexual independence, is clearly a precursor to modern women, and Fowles uses another anachronistic narratorial comment about Ernestina's conventionality to locate the origins of political emancipation for women in 1867 as well:

Ah, you say, but women were chained to their role at that time. But remember the date of this evening: April 6th, 1867. At Westminster only one week before John Stuart Mill had seized an opportunity in one of the early debates on the Reform Bill to argue that now was the time to give women equal rights at the ballot box. His brave attempt . . . was greeted with smiles from the average man, guffaws from *Punch* . . . and disapproving frowns from a sad majority of educated women. . . . Nonetheless, March 30th, 1867 is the date from which we can date the beginning of feminine emancipation in England.

(*Woman,* p. 115)

Here the narrator challenges his contemporary audience's notions about women and feminism in Victorian Britain, encouraging readers to connect women's liberation not just with the social movements of their own time, but with the nineteenth century as well.

The Rossettis and 16 Cheyne Walk. The painter and poet Dante Gabriel Rossetti, with whom Sarah lives and works at the close of *The French Lieutenant's Woman,* was a founding member of the Pre-Raphaelite Brotherhood, a group of young artists who admired the style of the early Italian masters of the fourteenth and fifteenth centuries, and sought to create paintings that emulated the virtues they saw therein. In a short manifesto, they detailed ideals, including the expression of "genuine ideas," an attentive study and reproduction of nature, and sympathy with "what is direct and serious and heartfelt in previous art," along with the rejection of "what is conventional and self-parading and learned by rote" (Ash, p. 383). Initially they kept their society a secret, exhibiting paintings signed only with the enigmatic initials "P.R.B." When the secret came out, there was a brief scandal in the London art world because all of the artists involved were young and considered audacious for their rejection of contemporary artistic standards. However, although the actual Brotherhood only lasted for about five years from its inception in 1848, their work gained respect and influence as the esteemed art critic John Ruskin touted their creations in publications and lectures.

Throughout his career, Rosetti often painted medieval themes, frequently featuring the characters of Dante (the Italian poet for whom he was named) and Beatrice, the woman who leads Dante through Hell, Purgatory and Paradise in his masterpiece, *The Divine Comedy.* In addition to echoing Beatrice as a guide or tutor leading a man toward redemption, Fowles's Sarah Woodruff also appears to look much like the women that populate Rossetti's paintings.

In the late 1860s (the point at which Charles finds Sarah at Rossetti's house at 16 Cheyne Walk) Rossetti was sharing a home with the writers Algernon Charles Swinburne and George Meredith, as well as his mistress and model,

Fanny Cornforth, who "moved in with the euphemistic title of 'housekeeper'" (Ash, p. 388). When Charles knocks, she is undoubtedly the woman answering the door whom he finds so difficult to place on the hierarchical scale of servants and masters (*Woman,* p. 441). Christina Rossetti, the younger sister of Dante Gabriel, who Charles mistakenly believes for a moment to be Sarah's lover, was a respected poet in her own right (*Woman,* p. 455). She is known both for religious writing and for poems like "Goblin Market" (1862) that subtly challenge Victorian stan-

---

LITERARY ALLUSIONS IN *THE FRENCH LIEUTENANT'S WOMAN*

Many literary works allude with more or less subtlety to earlier texts or stories as part of the development of their own narratives. *The French Lieutenant's Woman,* however, does so explicitly and self-consciously. Ernestina points out to Charles, for example, that as they walk along the Cobb they pass "the very steps that [novelist] Jane Austen made Louisa Musgrove fall down in *Persuasion* [1817]," and when the narrator introduces Sam Farrow he reminds his audience of Sam's literary predecessor, "the immortal Sam Weller"—the Cockney servant in Charles Dickens's *The Pickwick Papers,* published serially in 1836 and 1837 (*Woman,* p. 8, 41). Similarly, the narrative voice (sounding very much like Fowles at this point, although he is not speaking as a character) expounds on the fact that his work comes "under the shadow" of Thomas Hardy, who "was the first to try to break the Victorian middle-class seal over the supposed Pandora's box of sex" in his novels set in Dorset, the county of England that contains Lyme Regis (*Woman,* pp. 8, 271; see *Jude the Obscure,* also in *WLAIT 4: British and Irish Literature and Its Times*).

---

dards and expectations regarding women and their roles. These are the poems Charles remembers as marked by "passionate obscurity" and "rather absurdly muddled over the frontiers of human and divine love" (*Woman,* p. 456). Swinburne's poetry was politically radical, and his personal life—marked by alcoholism, self-publicized homosexuality, masochism, and bestiality—flouted conventional Victorian morality. A novelist, Meredith is perhaps most respected for *The Egoist* (1879), a critique of male chauvinism. By placing Sarah in this household,

Fowles aligns her with these multiple rejections of Victorian values, both political and social. Here, she can declare, "I belong," whereas in the respectable homes of Lyme Regis she has no comfortable place (*Woman*, p. 451).

Sources and literary context. In a well-known essay, "Notes on an Unfinished Novel" Fowles ties the origin of *The French Lieutenant's Woman* to a haunting visual image that interrupted the work he had underway, absorbing his attention. This image is the one that opens the novel, both within the text and in the author's mind: "A woman stands at the end of a deserted quay and stares out to sea" (Fowles, *Notes on an Unfinished Novel*, p. 161). Later he adds, "The woman had no face, no particular degree of sexuality. But she was Victorian; and since I always saw her in the same static long shot, with her back turned, she represented a reproach on the Victorian Age" (Fowles, *Notes,* p. 162). In its inscrutability, this image also prefigures the enigmatic nature of Sarah, who even at the close of the novel insists to Charles, "I am not to be understood even by myself" (*Woman*, p. 452).

This resistance to interpretation is also a hallmark of the literary mode with which *The French Lieutenant's Woman* is generally associated: postmodernism. "Postmodernism" is a decidedly slippery term, carrying different meanings in fields ranging across the arts and social sciences. Describing certain tendencies in the arts and culture of Western society after World War II, "postmodernism" is associated with (among other things) a suspicion of intellectual reason and its assumption that there is clear or universal "truth" to be determined by rational study, a rejection of high modernism's distinction between "high" and "low" culture, and (in a famous formulation from Jean-Francis Lyotard's 1979 book, *The Postmodern Condition*) a profound doubt about any narratives that propose to explain grand scale historical processes or the meaning of life. These "metanarratives" might include religions, political theories like Marxism, or even scientific formulations about the origins of the universe or life on earth.

In literature, certain forms or stylistic devices are also consistently associated with postmodernism, including a playful irony, parody, fragmentation, intertextuality (a more substantial borrowing of elements from other books than we see in allusion), and explicit self-consciousness within the text about its nature as a text (exemplified in *The French Lieutenant's Woman* by Fowles's descriptions of how he is going about

writing the novel). Because "postmodernism" is associated with so many different ideas, postmodern texts may display only some postmodern qualities. *The French Lieutenant's Woman* clearly demonstrates several postmodern tendencies—self-consciousness, multiple and contradictory endings, a challenge to linear notions of time and narrative, and profound resistance to the idea that Sarah (or the novel) can be rationally interpreted. Nevertheless, it also accepts some metanarratives (e.g., evolutionary thinking, suggested in the novel by Charles's decline and Sam's success) and argues for a philosophy of freedom that one might regard as being at odds with the cynical irony in much postmodern thought. The approach reflects Fowles's own interests in philosophy and natural history, while the mixture of genres testifies to the reality that classifications like "postmodern" are usually applied after the fact rather than as manifestos by which authors set out to write.

Events in History at the Time the Novel Was Written

The permissive society. The 1960s saw dramatic changes in the mood of British society and culture as the growing influence of youth culture created "swinging London" and a society that perceived itself to be "throwing off the Victorian shackles and the legacy of post-war austerity and Puritanism" (Morgan, p. 255). Young men with long hair and young women wearing short skirts both enjoyed and symbolized a wave of personal freedom and experimentation that included forays into drug use and freewheeling sexual activity. These youth, described by themselves and others as rebellious, rejected older notions of morality, respectability, and, in many cases, class division.

Despite deep-seated macroeconomic problems that led to the devaluation of the pound in 1967 and serious damage to Britain's economy, throughout much of the '60s full employment combined with a booming property and consumer market meant that many in the middle and working classes had the means to participate in the burgeoning "consumer culture" (Morgan, p. 256). The new permissiveness (as it was identified at the time) was closely associated with consumerism, in both booming retail sales and in a thriving mass-market culture, perhaps best exemplified by the stunning success (and record sales) of the Beatles musical ensemble, which appeared in 1963. In this framework, permissiveness was often associated with materialism and hedonism, much to the chagrin of those Britons who longed for a more conventional and unified society.

At the same time, Britain's legislators were advancing a series of reform bills that echoed the permissive society's emphasis on liberalization and individual freedoms. Capital punishment was abolished in 1965, and both abortion and private homosexual acts between consenting adults were legalized in 1967. After years of pressure from middle-class women, divorce laws were also reformed in 1969. Of course, part of the impetus for these legal reforms came from civil rights movements like those calling for women's or gay liberation—movements that reflected a new determination on the part of many individuals to assert their personal and civil rights. This liberalization of both law and culture reflects a societal interest in personal freedom that parallels the philosophy of freedom Fowles champions in *The French Lieutenant's Woman*; Sarah, with her back turned on restrictive Victorian conventionality, can be read in some ways as an icon of Fowles's own time.

The Cold War and the threat of nuclear annihilation. The Cold War, the competition for world leadership between the United States and the Soviet Union and their respective allies, was one of the dominant issues on the international stage throughout the 1960s. Nuclear buildup and the principles of deterrence implicated not only the nations directly involved, but all others as well because of the threat that nuclear war might destroy not only the participants but the entire world. Britain, allied to the United States through the North Atlantic Treaty Organization (NATO), had little actual influence on the course of the Cold War, despite attempts by Prime Minister Harold Wilson (1916-95) to act as a mediator between the United States and the Soviet Union in 1967. Nevertheless, events outside Britain's control routinely reminded her citizens of the nuclear threat. The Cuban Missile Crisis of 1962 brought the world to the brink of nuclear disaster, while the involvement of United States' troops in the war in Vietnam (beginning in 1965) provided ongoing evidence that Cold War ideological differences could lead to actual military conflict. The Six-Day War between Israel and Egypt in 1967 (which created a shock in the British economy when it temporarily closed the Suez canal, a major route for British shipping) also raised the specter of nuclear war because the involvement of the Arab and Israeli combatants with the su-

perpowers led to the possibility of escalations that could pit the United States and the Soviet Union against each other in a direct conflict.

Fowles has identified the nuclear threat as an important historical context for *The French Lieutenant's Woman*. In "Notes on an Unfinished Novel," Fowles explains that he believes "the great nightmare of the respectable Victorian mind" was the new understanding of human insignificance and "hideously mechanistic explanation of human reality" offered by the science of men like Lyell and Darwin; "Just as we 'live with the bomb,'" said Fowles, "the Victorians lived with the theory of evolution" (Fowles, "Notes," p. 166). In both cases, Fowles suggests, scientific progress creates a terrifying situation in which our knowledge or achievement forces us to reassess our understanding of human nature, our past, and the potential future of our species.

Reception. Although Fowles expected otherwise, *The French Lieutenant's Woman* was both a critical and a popular success. Reviews were enthusiastic. Like many reviews, the *Times Literary Supplement*'s assessment praised Fowles's handling of the interaction between the nineteenth and twentieth centuries, observing that he "has found a way, in this tour de force, to emulate the great Victorians, to supplement them without patronage" (*Times Literary Supplement,* p. 629). The reviewer for *Punch* declared Fowles "the most stunningly original novelist since William Golding" and the novel's handling of transitions back and forth from the Victorian past to the contemporary present "breathtaking" (Price, p. 35). In a front-page article for *The New York Times Book Review*, Ian Watt wrote that "our final impression is of pleasure and even, on occasion, awe, at so harmonious a mingling of the old and the new in matter and manner" (Watt, p. 74). *New Statesman* reviewer James Price declared the novel "a splendid, lucid, profoundly satisfying work of art" (Price, p. 850). Fowles won the 1970 W. H. Smith Literary Award for the novel. In less than a decade after its 1969 publication, it sold over 3 million copies (Aubrey, p. 108) and a major film adaptation was in development, with a script written by noted English playwright Harold Pinter.

—Michelle N. Mimlitsch

For More Information

Adams, Robert M. *The Land and Literature of England*. New York: Norton, 1983.

Ash, Russell. *Victorian Masters and Their Art.* London: Pavilion, 1999.

Aubrey, James R. *John Fowles: A Reference Companion.* Westport, Conn.: Greenwood Press, 1991.

Dennis, Barbara, and David Skilton, eds. *Reform and Intellectual Debate in Victorian England.* World and Word Series. London: Croom Helm, 1987.

Fowles, John. *The French Lieutenant's Woman.* Boston: Back Bay Books/Little, Brown, 1998.

———. "Notes on an Unfinished Novel." *Afterwords: Novelists on Their Novels.* Ed. Thomas McCormack. New York: Harper & Row, 1969.

Hoppen, K. Theodore. *The Mid-Victorian Generation, 1846-1886.* Oxford: Oxford University Press, 1998.

Morgan, Kenneth O. *The People's Peace: British History 1945-1989.* Oxford: Oxford University Press, 1990.

Price, James. "Self-Dependence." *New Statesman* 77 (1969): 850.

Price, R. G. G. "Four New Novels" *Punch* 257 (1969): 35.

Review of *The French Lieutenant's Woman*, by John Fowles. *Times Literary Supplement*, 12 June 1969, 629.

Watt, Ian. Review of *The French Lieutenant's Woman*, by John Fowles. *The New York Times Book Review*, 9 November 1969, 1, 74.

Waugh, Patricia. *Postmodernism: A Reader.* London: Edward Arnold, 1992.

Goodbye to Berlin

by
Christopher Isherwood

Christopher Isherwood (1904-86) was born in High Lane, Cheshire, England. In 1929 he went to Berlin, where, like his novel's narrator, he remained for four years. This period saw the curtain come down on Germany's first parliamentary democracy, the Weimar Republic, when the constitution and the political culture proved unable to withstand the continual attacks from both the Nazi Party with its uniformed cohorts on the right of the political spectrum and the communists on the left. Isherwood experienced Berlin during a period of political tension and violence that was, at the same time, a period of cultural experimentation and artistic energy. He published two novels based on his experiences, *The Last of Mr. Norris* (1935) and *Goodbye to Berlin* (1939). Adapted to the stage in the postwar years, the latter became the 1951 Broadway play *I Am a Camera*. The Broadway play, in turn, became the basis for the extremely successful stage musical and the 1972 movie *Cabaret*, starring Liza Minelli as club singer Sally Bowles. Isherwood moved to the United States in 1939, and later took up residence in Santa Monica, California. During the 1970s he became a kind of elder statesman for the growing Gay Rights movement in America and Britain, in particular because of his autobiography *Christopher and his Kind* (1977), in which the homosexual subtext of his *Goodbye to Berlin* moved more into the foreground of the story. More generally, Isherwood's Berlin stories portray the legendary artistic, cultural, and sexual tolerance that

THE LITERARY WORK

A semi-autobiographical novel, set in Berlin at the end of the Weimar Republic and the beginning of the Nazi era; first published in 1939.

SYNOPSIS

Christopher, a young Englishman, lives in Berlin in the early 1930s and earns a small income from teaching English in private homes. Over a three-year period he becomes deeply involved with a number of memorable Berlin characters and observes the disintegration of the German political system that leads to Hitler's rise to power.

reigned in the city during the years leading up to the Third Reich.

Events in History at the Time the Novel Takes Place

The world turned upside down. When Christopher Isherwood, the narrator of Isherwood's novel, arrives, the city of Berlin is one in which no political or social certainty seems to have been left undamaged by the events of the previous ten years. (Hereafter "Christopher" will refer to the narrator of *Goodbye to Berlin*, and "Isherwood" to the author himself.) The humiliation of Germany's defeat in World War I (1914-18), the ab-

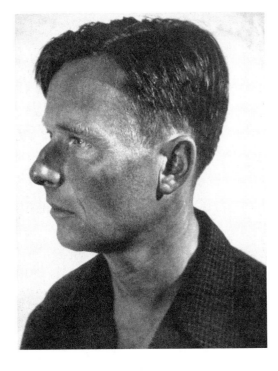

Christopher Isherwood

dication of Kaiser Wilhelm II, the establishment of parliamentary democracy, the economic trauma of the currency inflation of 1923—all these dramatic events seem to be appropriately summed up by Christopher's landlady, Fräulein Schroeder, when she observes in a resigned tone, "Twenty years ago, if anyone had told me to scrub my own floors, I'd have slapped his face for him. But you get used to it. You can get used to anything" (Isherwood, *Goodbye to Berlin*, p. 3). Fräulein (the "miss" emphasizing her unmarried status) Schroeder is reduced to taking in paying boarders and sleeping on a couch in her living room. Her way of dealing with her considerably diminished status in life is to regard her boarders as her guests. She is concerned for Christopher's welfare, and regards him as a gentleman in the tradition of all her previous male tenants. With her little snobberies and obsessive housecleaning, Fräulein Schroeder is a memorable character in *Goodbye to Berlin*, but even more notably she is an image of the countless Berliners who had grown up in a world of stable hierarchies and respectable social status, and now feel that the world has gone terribly wrong.

Pre-World War I Berlin had certainly been powerfully and repeatedly shaken. Before a child born in Berlin during the early years of the century saw his or her seventeenth birthday, the world would have changed beyond belief. By

1918 three of the most notable empires in the world, the Austro-Hungarian empire ruled by the Hapsburg monarchy, the Ottoman Empire in the Eastern Mediterranean and Levant, and Tsarist Russia—all of them with roots in the Middle Ages—had collapsed beyond repair. In Russia, a communist government had taken power and was speedily transforming the most basic social structures of the country. In the last weeks of World War One, the German Empire saw the spirit of revolution stirring in the air there too: in October 1918 sailors from the naval base at the port city of Kiel mutinied and marched on Berlin; a few days later, on November 9, 1918, the reigning monarch, Kaiser Wilhelm II, abdicated and left the country, and a constitutional democracy was proclaimed by the SPD, the Social Democratic Party, the largest political party in Germany. The proclamation, however, rested on an undeniably shaky foundation. The winter of 1918-19 saw a situation of political chaos in Berlin, with a number of radical parties and armed militias made up of ex-servicemen all demanding that Germany move faster in the direction of a Soviet-style communist revolution.

Armed groups of ex-army and ex-navy men could be found also on the other side of the political divide. Ultimately the left-wing and communist movements were violently put down by the liberal SPD administration using the right-wing (and anti-Semitic) *Freikorps*, semi-official paramilitary units under loose army command; the repression aggravated anger and resentment in the young republic. Dispensing with niceties, the *Freikorps* restored "order" in Berlin by killing between 1,200 and 1,500 of their opponents on the streets and barricades while, in a surreal way, the life of the big city went on around the violence (Large, pp. 165-66). The intensity of German political feelings sometimes found violent expression in the fate of government personnel too: in 1922 the foreign minister, Walter Rathenau, who happened to be a Jew, was shot down in a Berlin street by right-wing fanatics who resented his commitment to pay the war reparations demanded by the victors of World War I.

Berlin's economy had suffered serious setbacks as a result of the First World War. From 1920 on Berliners experienced the personal and social chaos that erupted as the Reichsmark, the German currency, underwent hyperinflation. Cash and savings spiraled downward in value, becoming next to useless. At the worst point in 1923 the price of a meal in a restaurant could treble between the customer ordering it and the waitress bringing it to the table, and people literally needed a large sack to bring home their wages. At the end of November of that year, one U.S. dollar was worth 4,210,500,000,000 marks (Large, p. 174). Although a measure of monetary and economic stability would be reestablished by 1924, this economic trauma caused not only misery and poverty but also humiliation, paranoia and political fantasy: passionately convinced that someone had to be responsible for these national disasters, many people turned for guidance to the extreme right.

The fledgling National Socialist German Workers' Party (NSDAP)—soon to be known by its German abbreviation, the Nazis—began to gain popularity founded on a mixture of national glorification and anti-Semitic propaganda. The propaganda claimed, among other things, that German Jews had profited by doing business on the black market during the War. Despite the services of many young Germans of Jewish faith in the armed forces between 1914 and 1918, it was claimed that Jews had been living comfortably at home while "real" Germans were being killed on the Front.

The menacing activism on the political right was mirrored by the revolutionary ambitions of the KPD, the German Communist Party. Many Berliners from working-class backgrounds—along with many intellectuals—were attracted to the radical and uncompromising demands for socialist revolution represented by the KPD. The belief that a new era of humanity had dawned in Soviet Russia was held deeply by many people, in Germany and elsewhere, and even those who had no love for the philosophy of the communists had an uneasy feeling that history was on their side. The communists represented everything that right-wing supporters hated most passionately. Yet the communists had as little respect for the Weimar Republic (the original constitutional assembly had been held in January 1919 in the city of Weimar, and the name had stuck) and its democratic constitutional order as their opponents the Nazis did. Indeed, the phrase used by the KPD about the Nazi Party was "After them, us!" This belief that even a Nazi victory, gained by elections or otherwise, could bring about a catastrophe ultimately benefitting the communists caused some strange political alliances. For example, both the KPD and the NSDAP joined forces in an anti-government bus and subway strike in 1932, and a common thread in each party's political rhetoric was contempt for the moderate Social Democrats, whose commit-

ment to the Weimar Constitution had been a crucial force in enabling the German democratic experiment to survive, even for a few years. By 1930, however, the strain was beginning to show. The worldwide depression that began in 1929, moving out from the U.S. economy to impact the rest of the world, had started to whittle away at the political legitimacy of the SPD, who were seen as badly managing unemployment and economic collapse. In fact, not only was the Weimar Republic threatened from outside by the hostile political forces that worked for its destruction, but it was also being dismantled from within. By and large, the civil service, the armed forces, the judiciary, the industrial leaders, and the schoolteachers and university professors were authoritarian and antidemocratic. They may not have wanted a Nazi takeover with all its consequences, but they showed no loyalty to the new democratic institutions and indeed worked consistently to malign and disrupt the Weimar experiment. Anti-Semitic attitudes proliferated in schools and universities, and the police and judiciary ignored Nazi street violence while condemning left-wing activities. Meanwhile, the armed forces followed their own secret agenda of building up their strength in defiance of the limits on German military forces imposed by the 1918 Treaty of Versailles. The big industrial corporations like Krupp and I. G. Farben funded the Nazi Party (NSDAP), seeing it primarily as a nationalist and anti-communist movement, despite its socialist-sounding name.

The average Berliner had to do what he or she could to survive the violence and chaos of the postwar years, to keep body and soul together during the Inflation, and to avoid being drawn into the brutal street battles that flared at regular intervals between the different political camps. Many managed to do so successfully. Still, the system, the social and political environment that surrounded the individual, was in violent flux. Nothing was certain, except that political change would be equally violent. The future had become like a vortex into which everyone was being pulled. Towards the end of Isherwood's novel, the following scene appears in which a Nazi is explaining drunkenly to his girlfriend in a café that it is not only important to win political power—they will achieve that anyhow—but that blood must flow too. The Nazi's girlfriend reassures him, "But, *of course*, it's going to flow, darling" (*Goodbye to Berlin*, p. 199). In real life, patrons in such a café might soon align themselves with a Nazi, or alternatively with a communist. To a great extent, chance figured into whether an individual would end up identifying with one political party or another. Otto's brother in the novel is working-class and pro-Nazi; he would be equally believable had he been working-class and communist at the time.

The scapegoats. The irony of anti-Semitism in Germany in the early pre-Hitler twentieth century is that it asserted itself when the social and legal status of German Jews appeared to have finally been put on an equal footing with that of Protestants and Catholics. Forming the vast majority of the German population, these two groups predominated in different regions of the country, the Catholics in the South and West, and the Protestants in the North and East. From the early nineteenth century onwards, age-old anti-Jewish laws and restrictions were dismantled and discarded in several European countries, including Germany, and Jewish communities responded by emerging from the ghetto and taking their place in the broader society. German Jews made names for themselves in intellectual and artistic life (for example, the painter Max Liebermann) and in industry (Emil Rathenau built up AEG, Germany's largest electric corporation). Such distinction seemed to promise a bright future in an enlightened Germany, which had shed much of its legacy of medieval prejudice (Gay, pp. 169-87).

This progress was, however, not the whole story. Large segments of the population had at least a passive suspicion of Jews and continued to regard them as not "real" Germans (the resentful diatribes of the novel's Fräulein Mayr, one of Christopher's fellow tenants, in which she complains bitterly that all the department stores are owned by Jews, offer a fictional example of this attitude). Such attitudes appear to have been even more deeply embedded in Austrian than in German social life (Adler, pp. 110-11), which may help explain the heavy presence of Austrians in the upper ranks of the Nazi Party—including Hitler himself, of course. In Germany, the larger, more industrially advanced of the two countries, the significant undercurrent of anti-Semitism was often kept to private exchanges rather than raised openly. In the early years of the twentieth century there was even evidence of public rejection of traditional Jew-baiting and race hatred. Cases involving anti-Semitic libel and perjury led to prosecutions, and most individuals who considered themselves political progressives (Social Democrats, liberal intellectuals, and the like) thought that anti-Semitism would

gradually die out as a result of better general education and the growth of a more socially advanced, less superstitious society (Adler, p. 106).

Some German Jews distrusted the apparent conduciveness of German society to their assimilation, however, and the denial of Jewish identity that seemed to be the price for this. Often this distrust went hand-in-hand with a Zionist perspective, that is, with the desire for a Jewish homeland rather than full integration into the European nations. Sometimes it stemmed from the uncomfortable suspicion that, down deep, most Germans hated Jews and always would, and that the contribution of Jews to Germany's cultural and intellectual life triggered hostility rather than respectful recognition. In realistically sizing up future prospects for German Jews, some Jewish leaders took into account this basic attitude. "We Jews administer the intellectual property of a people which denies us the right and the ability to do so," asserted the Jewish writer Moritz Goldstein in a famous and controversial article in 1912 (Goldstein in Arendt, p. 30).

The years during and just after World War I would see both the most integration into German society for Jews *and* the opening of a new abyss of prejudice and hatred. This paradox emanates from two contradictory historical realities: first, 100,000 young German Jews fought for the Fatherland during the First World War, a very respectable number in proportion to a total count of Jews in the German Reich of around 555,000 (Adler, p. 114); second, there was a widespread belief after Germany's humiliating surrender and the punitive Treaty of Versailles that Jewish economic interests had sold out the nation and brought about defeat from within. Indeed, the first intimations of this could be sensed in 1916, when an anti-Semitic member of Parliament asked the War Department to survey how many Jews were in the armed forces, with the unspoken suggestion that most were not fighting for their country but rather staying at home to run their businesses. The War Department conducted the survey but refused to release the results to the public, probably to avoid giving the impression that a large number of Jews *were* indeed serving at the front (Gay, p. 221).

The contradictory realities are reflected in Bernhard Landauer's comments to Christopher in the chapter "The Landauers": "My elder brother had been killed, right at the beginning of the War. . . . Later, certain business rivals of my father began to make propaganda against him . . . it was rumored that we were spies" (*Good-*

In *Goodbye to Berlin,* Christopher sees the Nazis raid a liberal publisher and haul off his stock. In real life, Nazi-organized book burnings, often supported by students, as shown here, were common after Hitler assumed power in 1933.

bye to Berlin, p. 169). The true story, the contribution of Jewish soldiers, sailors, and airmen to the German nation, was being continually drowned out, as it were, by the blaring of the alternative, paranoid narrative, the so-called Jewish "stab in the back" directed against the Fatherland. In an atmosphere of "cold, irrational hatred," the combination of distorted figures regarding military service, old anti-Jewish prejudices to do with business acumen, and an ethnic nationalism that divided Germans into "real" Germans and others came together to make a potent brew (Gay, p. 244). The idea took root that German Jews had profited from black-marketeering and exploiting the economic problems of the country while thousands of other Germans died daily on the battlefield—and in vain, for Germany was defeated in the end.

As portrayed by Isherwood on the model of the fictional Landauer family, Jews in Berlin at the end of the Weimar era were caught between feelings of mounting nervousness on the one hand and of denial on the other. Convinced that the victory of extreme politics in the shape of the Nazi Party could not be prevented, the majority of the Jewish community at the same time regarded Germany as their homeland and re-

mained unwilling to abandon their professions, businesses, and property. In the early 1930s there were very few German Jews who realized that, in a very short time, going into exile would become the only alternative to a gradually tightening noose of regulation, humiliation, and finally mass murder.

In *Goodbye to Berlin*, the final few pages of "The Landauers" hint at the darkening horizon for Jews in Germany as the Nazis move to implement their extreme racial policies. Christopher overhears a conversation between two businessmen in a restaurant: "'Concentration camps,' said the fat man, lighting a cigar. 'They get them in there, make them sign things. . . . Then their hearts fail'" (*Goodbye to Berlin*, p. 185). The years 1930 to 1933 were, in many ways, the last years of Central European Jewish life and culture as they had been known for generations. The growing brutality and state repression directed at Jews in Germany—reflected in similar events across Central and Eastern Europe—would culminate in Hitler's "Final Solution," the plan to exterminate all Jews in Nazi-occupied Europe. This blueprint for mass murder was put together at a meeting in the wealthy Berlin suburb of Wannsee. In *Goodbye to Berlin* it is in a luxurious villa in this same green tree-lined neighborhood that Bernhard Landauer and Christopher have a tortured conversation about Jews, Germans, and the English, and later it is where Christopher attends a beach party to which Bernhard has invited him. Observing the crowd of guests, the many friends and relatives of the Landauers, Christopher is struck by the disturbing gap between the apparently cheerful atmosphere at the villa and the rapidly disintegrating society outside the gates. "This evening is the dress-rehearsal of a disaster. It is like the last night of an epoch" (*Goodbye to Berlin*, p. 177).

The Novel in Focus

Plot summary. There is a basic chronological narrative underpinning *Goodbye to Berlin*, but rather than proceeding sequentially from 1930 to 1933, from the narrator's arrival to his final departure, the novel is structured around Christopher's various interactions with three particular individuals or groups of individuals, Sally Bowles, the Nowak family, and the Landauer family. These three partly self-contained chapters are balanced, at the beginning and again at the end of the novel, by two "Berlin Diary" pieces in which Christopher recounts, in a loose, fragmentary style, various incidents he has seen or participated in, and meditates on his personal feelings about Berlin. A middle chapter, "On Ruegen Island," is the story of what happens to Christopher when he is on vacation off the Baltic coast during the summer of 1931.

The opening section, "A Berlin Diary (Autumn 1930)," begins with an interior monologue in which the narrator is staring out at the city from his bedroom window, caught suddenly by the feeling that, as he says, "I am in a foreign city, alone, far from home" (*Goodbye to Berlin*, p. 1). As the focus of the narrative moves out of the mind of the narrator and takes in the surrounding reality, we meet Christopher's landlady, the snobbish but good-hearted Fräulein Schroeder, and several of her other tenants, including the loud and politically pro-Nazi Fräulein Mayr and the attractive young Fräulein Kost, who appears to earn her living as a prostitute. Fräulein Schroeder cannot pronounce Christopher's last name, and continually addresses him as "Herr Issyvoo" throughout the novel, which becomes a kind of character marker for her.

Christopher moves on to describe some of the peculiarities of Berlin nightlife: in a dance bar that he visits there are no customers as yet; the musicians, gigolos, and bartenders are lounging around chatting to each other. When a small group arrives in the bar, everything swings into action. Some of the staff pretend to be customers drinking at the bar, while the band strikes up a tune and a young couple—who also work there—move onto the dance floor as if they were regular customers too. Berlin entertainment spots, the incident reveals, have a kind of "standby mode," a passive state in which they wait for custom until real paying guests arrive, whereupon they immediately switch into active gear. Customers must believe that everything—the music, the fun—will still go on without them when they leave, without realizing that it is all a front to entice them in to spend money. We also meet one of Christopher's pupils to whom he is giving English lessons, Hippi Bernstein. He visits her in her family's mansion in the prosperous Grünewald area, described by Christopher as a "millionaire's slum," as the expensive houses are built on tiny, constricted plots due to the exorbitant cost of land in that part of the city (*Goodbye to Berlin*, p. 14).

Introduced in the second chapter of *Goodbye to Berlin* is the famous, or infamous, Sally Bowles. Sally Bowles enters the novel as the very embodiment of the good-time girl, painting her fingernails a luminous green, singing in a bar and trying to rope the next wealthy male patsy into supporting her as the Weimar Republic descends into a vortex of anarchy and street violence all around. Sally is English, as is Christopher himself, which leads to a certain tension between the two figures, stemming from Christopher's somewhat prim reaction to Sally's vulgarities. Like Fräulein Schroeder's "Herr Issyvoo," Sally's atrocious German becomes a comic signal for her presence, as, later in the novel, the Germanized English of the character Natalia Landauer will become her most identifiable trait.

Sally and Christopher initiate a friendship in late fall of 1930, and she moves into a vacant room at Fräulein Schroeder's house. Soon after, Christopher and Sally meet a rich American, Clive, who spends money like water and appears to have no problem buying friendship and company with his generosity. After Clive disappoints Sally's fond hopes of serving as her permanent sugar daddy when he suddenly leaves Berlin without telling her or Christopher, she discovers that she is pregnant by an earlier lover, the musician Klaus, a situation that ends with her having an illegal abortion. Klaus, who had accompanied Sally's singing on the piano, has abandoned her for an opportunity to compose film scores in Europe. In the late summer of 1931, Sally and Christopher have a falling out. He's had enough of her grabby, self-centered behavior; they make up a few days later, but shortly after that Sally leaves Berlin for Rome. She sends Christopher two postcards from Italy, and that, he says, is the last he ever hears from Sally Bowles. (She makes a cameo appearance, however, in Isherwood's next novel, *Prater Violet* [1945].)

Christopher spends the early summer of 1931 at Ruegen Island, a popular North German vacation resort on the Baltic coast. Portrayed here is the difficult, clearly sexually charged relationship between Otto Nowak, a young working-class Berliner, and Peter Wilkinson, a sensitive and highly-strung Englishman, and their individual relationships with Christopher. Peter, Otto, and Christopher stay in the same boarding house. Whereas Peter appears to be completely obsessed with—and dominated by—Otto, Otto is interested not only in Peter but also in women, and strikes up a relationship with a teacher accompanying a group of inner-city children. Peter, a tortured soul who believes in psychoanalysis, is in many ways an unhappier and more self-absorbed version of Christopher himself. For his part, Christopher plays something of neutral diplomat, moving back and forth between the warring parties of Peter and Otto. Otto teases Peter unmercifully. Peter, who cannot abide this teasing, ultimately leaves for Britain, frustrated and troubled—"I feel I've got to keep traveling until I'm clear of this bloody country," he comments—and Otto returns to Berlin (*Goodbye to Berlin*, p. 99). Suddenly lonely, Christopher misses Peter and Otto's daily round of arguments.

Back in Berlin himself in the winter of 1931-32, Christopher leaves Fräulein Schroeder and moves in with Otto's family, who occupy a cramped apartment in a run-down, working-class neighborhood. The cheerful and emotional Nowaks offer a complete contrast to the prim and proper Fräulein Schroeder. Otto, his younger sister, Grete, and their mother regularly shout at each other in fury, then make up with hugs and endearments. The father, Herr Nowak, is a war veteran with a taste for grotesque horror stories. The mother suffers from a lung disease of some kind, not helped by the damp, unaired apartment and the Berlin winter. Shortly before Christmas, her doctor decides that Frau Nowak should be confined to a sanatorium for treatment. Her leaving seems to drain all the life out of the

family. Christopher gets a well-paid job around the same time, and moves out to a more attractive part of the city. Some time afterwards, Otto asks Christopher to come with him to visit his mother in the sanatorium out in the country. They travel out together, and during the visit it becomes clear that Frau Nowak's condition has worsened. It seems unlikely that she will ever leave the sanatorium alive: "her body seemed to break in half like a hinged doll. Clasping her hands over her breast, she uttered short yelping coughs like a desperate injured animal" (*Goodbye to Berlin*, p. 138).

From the bleak lives of the Berlin working poor, the novel moves in its next-to-last chapter to the prosperous and civilized lifestyle of an upper-middle-class Jewish family in Berlin, the Landauers. Christopher's interactions with the Landauers take place over 1930 to 1933 (encompassing the periods he spends with the Nowak family and Sally Bowles). He gives English lessons to the daughter of the family, Natalia Landauer. Natalia's virtuous behavior—as well as her education and interest in literature—sets her up as a polar opposite of Sally Bowles. On one occasion, Christopher makes the mistake of introducing the two women to each other. Predictably, it is a disaster: Sally gossips in atrocious German about sex, drugs, and the Berlin nightlife while Natalia sits horrified, staring at Sally's painted green fingernails.

Through Natalia, Christopher meets her cousin Bernhard. He is the manager of the Landauer's big department store in Berlin, but in private seems to be more of a tortured intellectual, not unlike Peter Wilkinson, the Englishman on Ruegen Island. Bernhard lives alone in an apartment surrounded by works of art that he has collected during his earlier travels, and his general demeanor is one of a courteous but emotionally distant personality, with a hint of sexual ambivalence. He takes an interest in Christopher and invites him out to his villa on the lake in Wannsee. There, on one particular evening, they have a long discussion during which Bernhard tries to explain to Christopher something about his family's history. His brother had been killed in World War I, but, on account of their Jewishness, the family was still regarded as "un-German" and hostile to the nation; after his brother's death, his mother withdrew from reality. Bernhard is at the same time both envious of Christopher's Englishness and resentful of the secure identity he seems to possess. Despite his economic security and his respectable place in the world of business, Bernhard seems to be suffering on a psychic level. He echoes the uncertainty of German Jews who have had to make weighty and sudden decisions: Germany or exile; trust the future to get better or make a run for it. It is as if Bernhard is transfixed at the moment of reaction, caught between "fight or flight," as it were, and thus cannot react at all. At the end of "The Landauers" it is May 1933 and Christopher, having left Berlin for the last time, overhears a conversation in a café in Prague between two businessmen who reveal that Bernhard Landauer is dead of a mysterious "heart attack" that the two men don't quite seem to accept as the true story of what has happened.

The final chapter of *Goodbye to Berlin*, "A Berlin Diary (Winter 1932-3)," mirrors the opening chapter. Fragmentary and highly subjective, it discloses Christopher's ideas and fantasies about Berlin, providing intense descriptions of his social and physical environment: people, places, incidents. The year is now 1933, just before Christopher leaves Berlin. The Nazis have finally taken over the government after indecisive elections and months of political jockeying. Street violence with fatalities and continual demonstrations are the norm, and Christopher's meetings with his students and others are full of fearful, coded conversations, as if everyone is hypnotized by the political crisis, not knowing what they should do or say. On his final morning in Berlin, Christopher goes for a stroll, noticing that everything on this sunny day is so oddly normal and familiar despite the fact that Hitler is now securely in power. The last sentence of the novel emphasizes the sense of distance that Christopher suddenly begins to feel toward his years in Berlin, toward all the people whose lives have crossed his and everything that he has experienced: "Even now I can't altogether believe that any of this has really happened" (*Goodbye to Berlin*, p. 207). He will write the novel to make it real again.

The personal and the political. One of the substantial threads woven into *Goodbye to Berlin* is the issue of Christopher's sexuality. Although there is no specific plot element or scene in the novel that clearly establishes it (until a comic incident with an American in the final chapter, during which Christopher makes what could be an admission of his same-sex orientation), and although his relationships with both Sally Bowles and Natalia Landauer have a flirtatious tone at times, Christopher seems to be homosexual. It is for the most part implicit rather than explicit throughout *Good-*

bye to Berlin, even in the "On Ruegen Island" chapter with Otto and Peter. One example of this oblique approach is a passage in which Christopher has been invited to stay to dinner with the Landauers. Natalia's father is expounding on the topic of art and morality, mentioning the suspicions of incest that have surrounded the British poet Lord Byron and going on to ask Christopher directly about his opinions on the popular dramatist and wit Oscar Wilde, who in a well-known court case in the 1890s was found guilty of sodomy and imprisoned (see *The Importance of Being Earnest,* also in *WLAIT 4: British and Irish Literature and Its Times*):

> "Your dramatist Oscar Wilde . . . this is another case. I put this case to you, Mr. Isherwood. I should like very much to hear your opinion. Was your English Law justified in punishing Oscar Wilde, or was it not justified? Please tell me what you think?"
>
> Herr Landauer regarded me delightedly, a forkful of meat poised halfway up to his mouth. In the background, I was aware of Bernhard, discreetly smiling.
>
> "Well . . ." I began, feeling my ears burning red. This time, however, Frau Landauer unexpectedly saved me, by making a remark to Natalia in German, about the vegetables.
>
> (*Goodbye to Berlin*, p. 151)

In the above exchange, it is not altogether clear just what Christopher has been saved from, but it is obvious that to be brought into connection with Wilde's homosexuality, even by an innocent question, causes him embarrassment. Bernhard's "discrete smile" suggests that he shares something with Christopher (and Wilde) and knows exactly why Christopher was uncomfortable.

The question of sexuality is bound up with one important aspect of the novel that is never dealt with openly: why Christopher has come to live in Berlin in the first place. His only comment is an obviously fraudulent response to one of his pupils, Hippi Bernstein: "The political and economic situation," I improvised authoritatively, in my schoolmaster voice, "is more interesting in Germany than in any other European country" (*Goodbye to Berlin*, p. 15). This unconvincing cliché is justifiably ignored by Hippi Bernstein, who has correctly ascertained that Christopher does not have many friends in Berlin at all, and that life might be a little dull for him. Christopher does not, however, find Berlin particularly dull. In fact, the occasional sense of loneliness, of being far from home, seems to be the attraction of the city, as shown in the "Berlin Diary" chapters. Christopher meets characters such as Sally Bowles, whom he would be very unlikely to meet back home in England. And he enjoys the exile's compensation prize of at times being, as he says, a passive observer, like a camera. As a narrator, Christopher prefers to focus on the characters around him, which tends to make him a somewhat flat character himself, but he does participate in the action and in the lives of other characters.

Christopher also enjoys—and this would seem to be one of his primary motives for coming to Berlin—the tolerance and the decadence. That is, he enjoys the tolerance of the fringe, the quasi-private social and sexual milieus that were a staple of the Berlin of the Weimar Republic, and the much-vaunted "decadence" of the city—the bars that rarely closed, the morbid hedonism, the delicious sense of dancing too close to the edge of the political abyss. As the British artist Francis Bacon, living in Berlin around the same time as Isherwood, once commented: "There was something extraordinarily open about the whole place. . . . You had this feeling that sexually you could get absolutely anything you wanted. I'd never seen anything like it . . . it excited me enormously" (Bacon in Large, p. 222). The reputation of Berlin had spread abroad and a part of that reputation was that the "anything goes" rule applied in Berlin despite its daytime atmosphere of grim Prussian "Ordnung." As Isherwood himself later admitted when looking back on the experience in *Christopher and His Kind*, Berlin's liberal atmosphere appealed to him in no small part because of its sexual possibilities. In short, "To Christopher, Berlin meant boys" (Isherwood, *Christopher and His Kind*, p. 2).

Many of the unspoken, or partly spoken, implications of *Goodbye to Berlin* were dealt with openly many years later. In Berlin, one could join the free cosmopolitan nation of the sexually different, as Isherwood comments in his autobiography in plain language (Isherwood, *Christopher*, p. 12). *Goodbye to Berlin* is clearly, as much as anything else, a tale of individual sexual liberation. As David Large explains, Isherwood came to Berlin to get away from family and country, and these two oppressive entities could be lifted with the help of a (male) lover who was working-class and foreign. The working-class aspect undermined the snobberies of Isherwood's upper-middle-class background; the foreign dimension was a gesture of rejection aimed at an insular, self-righteous Britain of the 1920s that

looked down on Germans as nothing more than defeated enemies (Large, p. 230).

Sources and literary context. As *Goodbye to Berlin* is substantially an autobiographical novel, later admitted to be such by Isherwood, some of the real individuals behind the characters in the novel appear in his actual autobiography. The novel's Bernhard Landauer was inspired by the real-life Wilfrid Israel, who, Isherwood explains, helped run a department store founded by his family, one of the largest of such stores in Berlin

PAGAN GERMANS, EMBARRASSED BRITS

Not only the fictional Christopher and the real Isherwood, but thousands of tourists from Europe and America descended upon Berlin in the 1920s and early 1930s because of the city's reputation for sexual tolerance, availability, and openness. These phenomena were obvious, but a foreigner might often miss the connection between them and specific German traditions of physical exercise and the value of the body. Nineteenth-century health reformers encouraged civic-sponsored programs of gymnastics and sport in schools and communities so that even working-class German children growing up in industrial cities were more physically robust than their counterparts in other countries. Connected to this focus on physical health was a lack of embarrassment about nudity, a kind of de-sexualized nudity that involved open pleasure in physical health and attractiveness. In the novel, Christopher's feelings about Otto Nowak seem to be less an expression of sexual desire than an admiration of a pagan vitality and energy connected to such attitudes to physical health and the body: "Otto himself, squatting there on the bed, was so animally alive, his naked brown body so sleek with health" (*Goodbye to Berlin*, p. 114). By contrast, Christopher, the Englishman, seems more self-conscious about his body and his sexuality.

(Isherwood, *Christopher,* p. 65). In *Christopher and His Kind,* we also meet the original of the character Otto Nowak. Isherwood does not reveal his real name, but does fill in the background to the narrative in *Goodbye to Berlin,* particularly the cover-up of the homosexual motives for the move to the Nowak family. Isherwood and Otto are lovers, and they think it will be fun to live together in the family apartment. Aware of the relationship, Frau Nowak appears to accept it with good grace.

Moving up in society through a series of better apartments, the real Isherwood ends up renting a room from Fräulein Thurau, the model for the memorable Fräulein Schroeder. In this period of his life, he meets Jean Ross, the figure on whom he based Sally Bowles. Isherwood and Ross became close friends, but never had any kind of sexual feelings for each other. There was no ambiguity in this regard, while there is in the relationship depicted in *Goodbye to Berlin*. Isherwood admired Ross's pluck and her spirited way of dealing with adversity. Isherwood gave the story of Sally Bowles and Christopher a more poignant and complete ending in the novel than was the case in real life: "Unlike the novel's protagonist and Sally, Isherwood and Jean did not part forever when she left Berlin. Circumstances separated them for long intervals, but they continued to meet, as affectionate friends, throughout the rest of Jean's life. She died in 1973" (Isherwood, *Christopher*, p. 64).

One aspect of British literary history is particularly important for the context of *Goodbye to Berlin*: the English left-wing writers of the 1930s. Mostly poets rather than novelists, the writers W. H. Auden, Louis MacNeice, Stephen Spender, and Cecil Day-Lewis are often set alongside that of Isherwood. All of the same generation, a few years too young to have fought in World War I, these men were fascinated by the culture and science of modernity (Freud, Marx, Einstein, and Picasso, they thought, had radically and irreversibly redefined the human psyche, politics, science and art) and were also drawn to socialist—sometimes communist—politics by the experience of the Great Depression and the threat of fascism. They knew each other and sometimes collaborated in their writing. In the cases of Isherwood, Auden, and Spender, their homosexual (or, in Spender's case, bisexual) orientation added a sharper edge to their feelings of alienation from the polite, respectable British society that they were born into. The works of all three, without making an explicit issue of their sexual interests, tended to covertly interweave the personal and the political; often there was a suggestion that a communist society, for example, would bring about an end to sexual exclusion and rigid bourgeois morality. Christopher's brief account of the Communist Party café that he visits in the last "A Berlin Diary" chapter, however, suggests that he was less than convinced that the Berlin Communist milieu held the key to a better, more liberated future in which the whole range of human sexuality could be freely expressed.

Events in History at the Time the Novel Was Written

The inevitability of war. Although the increasing aggressiveness of Nazi German foreign policy and the successful establishment of fascist regimes in countries like Spain and Italy could hardly be ignored, even in 1939 very few people in Europe—and even fewer in the United States—wanted to face the fact that armed hostilities of some kind seemed unavoidable. When *Goodbye to Berlin* finally appeared in Britain at the end of the thirties, Berlin had become a very different place from the open city that Christopher had experienced ten years earlier. It was now the capital of the Third Reich, an authoritarian and militaristic political system that flew the curious symbol of the swastika. The famous tolerance and decadence had disappeared, although the Nazis made an exception for the 1936 Summer Olympic Games, permitting a brief and temporary expansion of prostitution and allowing a few homosexual bars to reopen (Large, p. 295). Never a Nazi stronghold in the manner of Munich, even the city of Berlin responded to the seemingly irresistible force of Hitler's New Germany that had been expanding continuously over the last five years: independent Austria had been incorporated into the German Reich, the city of Danzig had been taken from the Poles, and the Sudetenland region of Czechoslovakia had been practically handed to Nazi Germany on a plate after Britain and France had made it clear at Munich in September 1938 that they would not support Czech resistance to the German ultimatum in any way.

The Landauers would have long since had their property confiscated and their possibilities of study or employment closed down or at least greatly restricted, as did the German Jewish family on whom they were based, the Israels. Others would have escaped from Germany to France, America, Palestine, or a dozen different destinations.

In 1938 the *Reichskrystallnacht* (a melodramatic term using an image of shattered glass), in which Jewish businesses and property were attacked and destroyed all over Germany in a concerted effort to terrorize the community, convinced everyone that the Nazis' anti-Semitism was not just a rhetorical flourish to satisfy the Party faithful, but a central plank in Hitler's scheme for a future German nation with all "foreign" elements removed. Despite the obvious threat, however, Berlin still had a Jewish community numbering 70,000 people, most of whom would ultimately be deported to concentration and extermination camps. Self-imposed exile was still possible, but it presented formidable obstacles. Already some countries had closed their borders to Jewish refugees, and the British administrators in Palestine were disinclined to encourage a Jewish immigration that they feared would anger the Arab population and destabilize British rule. Indeed, Nazi ideologists such as Joseph Goebbels saw the unwillingness to accept Jewish refugees as proof that they were not wanted anywhere—that the Nazis' own attitude was echoed and confirmed by the lack of sympathy for Jews elsewhere in the world.

Such events served to strengthen the single-minded focus of German diplomatic and military planning. Apart from the Axis powers (Nazi Germany, Italy, and later Japan), nobody was really well prepared for war, even in 1939. America was still largely isolationist, and the countries of Western Europe recognized that they would have trouble resisting a decisive German invasion. Fear of air raids was widespread; governments feared that large-scale panic among the population would be the result of bombing raids by enemy aircraft. France, a country that still ruled a worldwide empire from the Caribbean to Southeast Asia, was transfixed by the anxiety that Germany would invade and overrun the country for the third time in 75 years—which indeed would happen in a few months' time. Britain took war-related measures such as partial evacuation of children from the inner cities, but even these were half-hearted.

Goodbye to Berlin is a memorial to a time of immense energy and openness, as well as violence and chaos, that existed in one peculiar city between two world wars. The survival of the image of Berlin during the Weimar Republic testifies to the power of that experience. People such as Isherwood discovered freedoms in Berlin that were unknown at home. By the time Christopher Isherwood published *Goodbye to Berlin*, however, aggressive expansion, mystical nationalism, and anti-Semitism had long since taken over the levers of power in the German capital.

Reception. *Goodbye to Berlin* existed as a series of "short stories" before it coalesced into its final form as a novel. Isherwood had published "The Nowaks," and "The Landauers" for example, in an avant-garde literary magazine called *New Writing*. He submitted the piece entitled "Sally Bowles," an earlier version of the chapter of the same name in *Goodbye to Berlin*, to the editor of

New Writing John Lehman, who liked it but thought that it was too long for the magazine. Lehman arranged for the story to appear as a small book on its own. *Sally Bowles* found such an enthusiastic response from readers when it came out in 1937 that Isherwood knew it would be an important part of his planned novel (Isherwood, *Christopher*, p. 245).

When *Goodbye to Berlin* was finally published as a single novel in 1939 it attracted significant attention, and a number of well-known names in literature and criticism were among the reviewers on both sides of the Atlantic, including the New York literary scholar Alfred Kazin, the German émigré intellectual Klaus Mann, and the

---

THE END OF JEWISH BERLIN

Already in the spring of 1933 a sequence of tightening restrictions on Jews (as well as on those identified as anti-social persons or political subversives) began to remove any rights connected with citizenship or previous military service. Education, personal qualities, public service—all became irrelevant: "When the Nazis took power in 1933, eleven of the forty German winners of a Nobel prize in the sciences had been Jews. But they, too, were no longer regarded as anything but members of an 'inferior race'" (Gay, p. 256). In 1941 the Nazis started deporting Berlin's Jews east to labor and death camps. Some 5,000 managed to hide out or disguise their identity for the duration of the war while another 14,000 led "an open if precarious existence" as spouses of non-Jews; thousands more, however, were brutally killed in the Nazi gas chambers and camps, which overall claimed the lives of 170,000 German Jews (Gay, p. 281).

---

critic Edmund Wilson. Wilson, for example, was generous in his evaluation of Isherwood's novel in the *New Republic* (May 17, 1939) and commented on the ability the author showed to write the kind of transparent prose that allowed the perceptions of the narrator and the reader to merge: "you seem to look right through Isherwood and see what he sees" (Wilson, p. 51). In Britain, a review of *Goodbye to Berlin* in *The Spectator* magazine (March 3, 1939) by Irish novelist Kate O'Brien focused in, as Wilson did, on the objective atmosphere of Isherwood's writing. Using a phrase that would be echoed a few years later, she asserted that the striking quality of the novel was the sense that it possessed "the laconic and unemotional selectiveness of the camera" (O'Brien, p. 364). The title chosen for the 1951 play that was adapted from *Goodbye to Berlin* would be *I Am a Camera*.

—Martin Griffin

For More Information

Adler, H. G. *The Jews in Germany: From the Enlightenment to National Socialism.* Notre Dame, Ind.: University of Notre Dame Press, 1969.

Arendt, Hannah. Introduction to *Illuminations: Essays and Reflections,* by Walter Benjamin. Trans. Harry Zohn. New York: Schocken, 1969.

Berg, James J., and Chris Freeman. *The Isherwood Century: Essays on the Life and work of Christopher Isherwood.* Madison: University of Wisconsin Press, 2000.

Gay, Ruth. *The Jews of Germany: A Historical Portrait.* New Haven: Yale University Press, 1992.

Isherwood, Christopher. *Christopher and his Kind, 1929-1939.* New York: Farrar, Straus and Giroux, 1976.

———. *The Berlin Stories.* Containing *Goodbye to Berlin* and *The Last of Mr. Norris.* New York: New Directions, 1963.

Large, David Clay. *Berlin.* New York: Basic Books, 2000.

O'Brien, Kate. Review of *Goodbye to Berlin,* by Christopher Isherwood. *The Spectator* 162 (3 March 1939): 364.

Page, Norman. *Auden and Isherwood: The Berlin Years.* London: Macmillan, 1998.

Wilson, Edmund. Review of *Goodbye to Berlin,* by Christopher Isherwood. *New Republic* 99 (17 May 1939): 51.

The Grass
Is Singing

by

Doris Lessing

THE LITERARY WORK

A novel set in early 1900s rural Southern Rhodesia; published in 1950.

SYNOPSIS

Feeling displaced on the veld in Southern Rhodesia, a white woman breaks the color bar by becoming too intimate with her African servant and pays for the indiscretion with her life.

Born October 22, 1919, in Kermanshah, Persia (present-day Iran), Doris Lessing moved to a farm in Southern Rhodesia with her family in 1925. Her father was an unsuccessful maize farmer who, like thousands of his British contemporaries, ventured into southern Africa in search of freedom and prosperity but found instead isolation and despair. Lessing left the countryside for the capital of Salisbury in 1937 (present-day Harare, Zimbabwe). In Salisbury, she found a job as a typist and joined the Communist Party, which led to her becoming an active member of the movement for African rights. After two unsuccessful marriages and three children, Lessing left Africa for London in 1949 to concentrate on professional writing. Her fiction has been acclaimed for its humanist portraits as well as provocative subject matter. It was with the publication of her first novel, *The Grass Is Singing*, that Lessing established herself as one of the most formidable novelists to emerge since World War II—a writer unafraid to tackle taboo subjects of the day and to challenge the status quo. She continued to focus on African issues in her widely acclaimed five-volume *Children of Violence* series, featuring the autobiographical heroine, Martha Quest (1952-69), as well as in short stories and memoirs, including her nonfiction *African Laughter*. With *The Grass Is Singing* Lessing initiated a lifelong investigation into the Afro-European experience and broke with convention to bring controversial, thought-provoking subject matter into the public eye.

Events in History at the Time of the Novel

Southern Rhodesia and imperialism in Africa. At the turn of the twentieth century, the leading colonial nations—Portugal, Great Britain, France, Belgium, and Spain—were scrambling for African land and resources to fuel the Industrial Revolution in Western Europe. Rich in minerals, such as gold, platinum, asbestos, and coal, Africa was a veritable treasure chest for imperialists who, for the most part, seemed to have no moral qualms about exploiting human and natural resources for their own personal gain.

Cecil Rhodes, diamond magnate and founder of the British South Africa Company—more commonly known as the Chartered Company—was a leading British imperialist who, by age 36, owned the world's largest company (De Beers

Doris Lessing

Consolidated Mines) and controlled nearly all of Southern Africa. Like many of his contemporaries, Rhodes considered Africa the "dark" continent—backward and in need of enlightenment. At the same time, he recognized that it held a wealth of fertile land and minerals with which he could build and expand his empire.

In 1890 Rhodes sent an expedition up from South Africa into Mashonaland and Matabeleland to add to his agricultural and mineral interests. White encroachment finally led to outright rebellion by the local Ndebele (in 1893 and 1896) and Shona peoples (in 1896-97) against the colonists. The concerted strategy of the colonists, and to some degree their machine guns and artillery, helped them emerge victorious, after which they went on to create Southern Rhodesia. In 1894 the colonists set up reserves, or specially designated areas, for the Ndebele, and in 1898 for the Shona, relegating them to "locations" on the desolate outskirts. White settlers received the choicest parcels; to each white settler the Chartered Company granted 3,000 acres on which to farm maize, wheat, and tobacco for export via the Company. Rhodes also established a white-only government, giving no representation or rights to the native peoples—precedents that would have devastating long-term effects on African-European relations in the region. Comparing the groups and evincing white attitudes,

in 1912 Belgian lawyer Henri Rolin spoke of the blacks "two castes below the whites . . . one has only to see [the Africans] in their sordid villages . . . to appreciate the immense difference which divides the victors from the vanquished" (Rolin in Blake, p. 158).

Monetary slavery. Lured by promises of land ownership and prosperity, disenchanted and adventure-seeking British subjects, like those in *The Grass Is Singing* and Lessing's own family, came by the tens of thousands to Southern Rhodesia from 1907 through World War II, initiating the most dramatic economic transformation ever witnessed to that point in southern Africa. Whites were initially granted 21 million acres of prime land, which they could purchase for the low sum of five shillings per acre (government loans were readily available). In contrast, the indigenous African peoples—though they outnumbered colonists 30 to 1—were apportioned just 24 million acres of barren land. Through 1914, African farmers produced as many or more cash crops as settlers but new laws, as well as taxes, and the colonists' monopoly of the finest lands, eliminated their ability to compete. In 1930-31 the Land Apportionment Act granted 43 million more acres to colonists, along with seven million to Africans, and made it illegal for indigenous peoples to purchase land in European areas. The Land Apportionment Act disabled African farmers from competing economically with European farmers and merchants and legalized segregation across the board. In sum, developments forced the Africans to become wage earners rather than independent farmers.

Though the colonists had every economic advantage, they still needed cheap labor in order to become profitable. Farming and mining for export required an abundance of menial workers and there were simply not enough colonists willing or able to meet the demand. In the interest of creating a workforce, first a hut and then a poll tax of £1 were imposed on all African men. At the time, the Shona-speaking majority had no hard currency system—they traded in commodities or bartered. The tax law forced them to work for colonists in order to earn British pounds so that they could meet their new financial obligations. Since slavery had been abolished in the British Empire in 1834, technically the colonists could not enslave locals. However, they managed to do so indirectly, by forcing every African man to pay taxes and by limiting freedom of movement so that nonpayers would not escape. The colonist government restricted movement between districts by requiring visiting passes and registration certificates of all African men, to be carried at all times and produced upon demand. Separated from their families, African men were transported into "locations," the urban equivalent of a reserve, where they either rented or built their own dwellings. The idea was to live here on a temporary basis, long enough to earn their tax money after which they could return to their family dwellings in the rural reserves.

Lodged in these shoddy locations, on the outskirts of white enterprises, African men provided farm labor and domestic service for the Europeans; if they attempted to flee, they would be hunted down and punished as tax evaders. The effect on indigenous life was dramatic. Back on the homestead, by the 1930s, women were forced to take on tasks formerly performed by the men—threshing, for example, in addition to the planting, hoeing, weeding, and harvesting. An investigating committee sized up the impact: "This uncontrolled and growing emigration [of black men to white farms] brings misery and poverty to hundreds and thousands of families and the waste of life, happiness, health and wealth [is] colossal" (Hallett, p. 525).

Re-education Victorian-style. Along with the forced labor came a climate of racism and cultural misunderstanding. Out of a combination of ignorance, arrogance, greed, and fear, most European colonists from the outset discriminated against the locals, known by the British as "Kaffir" (a denigrating term equivalent to the disparaging American term "nigger"). The British viewed what they perceived to be the Africans' lack of "progress" and non-British ways as abhorrent, dismissing the indigenous people as idle and lazy, interested only in drinking and making love. Under the guise of "Christian duty," some of the colonists set out to re-educate the local peoples and teach them British values of thrift, individualism, self-help, and hard work. The colonists banned alcohol sales to locals in 1903 and restricted production of "Kaffir beer," which was vital to many tribal rituals. According to the leading colonial politician Godfrey Huggins (1883-1971), the Europeans were acting as a "leaven of civilization," and "the black man would inevitably revert to a barbarism worse than before" if left to his own devices (Huggins in Hallett, p. 533). Like Huggins, most British colonists believed they had a "dual mandate" to "re-educate" the African peoples, whom they considered backward, and to extract resources to fuel industrialization and further Western progress (which they believed was promoting the progress of the world).

But the re-education aimed to go only so far. While the colonists wanted a diligent, tax-paying, and subordinate African community, they in no way wanted it to mix with their own. Yes, the colonists felt more secure as their population increased, but many of them continued to feel threatened by the African majority, who by 1930 numbered over 1 million while whites numbered 50,000 (Blake, p. 161). For the Europeans, segregation was the key to maintaining control and,

---

PSEUDO-SCIENTIFIC SUPREMACY

By the time British colonists founded Southern Rhodesia, Charles Darwin's theories of evolution were well known (see *On the Origin of Species,* also in *WLAIT 4: British and Irish Literature and Its Times*). Having produced the railroad, telegraph, and machine gun, Europeans felt immense pride in their contributions to what is known as the late-nineteenth-century Age of Progress. Many Europeans considered these inventions evidence that they were indeed more highly evolved than other races. Cecil Rhodes himself is said to have subscribed to this theory, adding further that the British sat atop the European hierarchy because their Empire controlled the world (Thomas, p. 109). White-owned newspapers such as *The Cape Times* wrote that South Africa's indigenous peoples were "among the lowest" and the *Cape Argus* added, "the lower people are in the scale of humanity, the more will they be taught by working, obeying and submitting" (Thomas, pp. 108, 109). From the point of view of their countrymen, then, the colonists had a pseudo-scientific basis that condoned their treatment of Africans, a basis that deemed this treatment not only correct but in accordance with the natural order of things.

---

just as the land grants and commercial incentives had been introduced to attract white settlers, segregation laws, such as the Land Apportionment Act, which outlawed the purchase of land in "European areas" by indigenous peoples, were passed to placate and reassure them.

The economics of the Africans and the colonists became inextricably mixed. While the Africans lived mostly on subsistence agriculture, they came to depend greatly on an infusion of money from relatives in towns and the Europeans likewise depended on African labor. But socially they were strictly segregated, as observed by Henri Rolin in 1913.

> The white man will not take his meals at the same table as the black; he will not meet him on the footpath of the streets; he travels by rail in separate wagons. . . . The farmer sees him as a pilferer and cattle-thief. . . . Those who know the natives add besides that the antipathy of black for white is not less, and that is easily to be understood in view of the brusqueness, the complete lack of consideration with which the European often treats the native.
>
> (Rolin in Blake, pp. 157-58)

This was the state of affairs even from the start. Early in the twentieth-century colonists imposed

---

LYNCH MOBS IN AFRICA

Southern Rhodesian whites were unlike some other frontier communities in that they showed no affinity for invoking lynch law; in fact just two lynchings were publicly recorded. Instead the Southern Rhodesians passed stern, discriminatory laws against the local Africans and administered them with white-male-only personnel. The intent was not to end lynchings but rather to establish a semblance of law and order. Relying on export trade, the colonists actually feared that lynchings would damage their international reputation and the economy. One local leader stopped a lynching, then rewarded the mob with free drinks. On the other hand, the discriminatory laws were frequently invoked. There were numerous cases of black men charged and convicted on the thinnest of evidence for rape and attempted rape of white women.

---

strict laws to keep African men from European women, addressing the main fear of European males. In 1903 the Immorality Suppression Ordinance passed, making it illegal for an African man and a white woman to have sexual relations (there was, by contrast, no edict making it illegal for white men to have sex with black women). The Rhodesia Women's League lobbied, unsuccessfully, for equal punishment for white men under this Ordinance. White women risked jail time for being with a black man; white men were not punished for being with a black woman. Also in 1903 a law passed extending the death penalty not only to any African man who raped a white woman, but to any African man who attempted to rape a white woman (it was assumed that no

white woman would willingly agree to have sexual relations with a black man, therefore all sexual advances were considered attempted rape). Some whites argued that these laws were passed to end lynchings, but the juries were made up only of voting males (white men), so that in effect the laws inaugurated what can be described as legal lynching.

The color bar. The color bar, or legal and customary separation between Africans and whites, pervaded Rhodesian society. In addition to segregation in housing, the workplace, and public facilities, there was a social convention—insisted on particularly by lower-class whites—that Africans would keep to their subordinate station and not coexist or communicate with Europeans on an equal level. Africans were to lower their eyes when addressing Europeans and, as Mary Turner says in the *Grass Is Singing*, were not to speak in English, for then they would be acting above their station, or being "cheeky" (Lessing, *The Grass Is Singing*, p. 180). A famous missionary and Yao folk hero, John Chilembwe, observed that a local African "was often times beaten by a white man if he did not take his hat off his head some thousand yards away, even a mile away of a white man" and that Europeans took strong exception to "natives who got above their station" (Chilembwe in Hallett, p. 527).

Moreover, the blacks were not the only ones expected to abide by prescribed behavior and "stay in their place." Whites, taught the colonists, ought to act "above" their subordinates and not get too familiar with Africans. They were to keep their affairs private, live in a "more civilized" manner, and—especially in the case of white women—not show emotion or dress in front of African domestic servants. In *The Grass Is Singing*, this is the line that Mary Turner crosses, and her white neighbors cannot tolerate the transgression. As Victoria Middleton observes, the novel depicts the "white woman as a cherished luxury or valuable prize" (Middleton in Kaplan, p. 138). Mary sins against society by lowering herself and allowing her servant Moses close proximity to her. She thus outrages her fellow colonists and condemns herself. The Turners' successful neighbor in the novel, Charlie Slatter, articulates the prevailing European attitude, the so-called "first law of South Africa" that said: "Thou shalt not let your fellow whites sink lower than a certain point; because if you do, the nigger will see he is as good as you are" (*Grass*, p. 210).

Lower than low. Of course, not all whites expressed such blatant racism in public. There were even whites who did not subscribe to such views—including some missionaries, officials of the Department of Native Affairs, and philanthropists. However, the lower down the socioeconomic scale were the colonists, the more outward contempt they seemed to show for Africans:

> The Petite Commercant (small businessman) will not hesitate to tell you that the black is a 'stupid animal'. . . . Educated men are naturally more prudent 'more discreet' in their language.
> (Rolin in Blake, p. 158)

When officials in Salisbury, the capital of Southern Rhodesia, attempted to implement a policy of assimilation in 1910, arguing that better educated, English-speaking Africans would make for a more prosperous Rhodesia, the white laboring classes strongly objected. Increasingly hardpressed to keep up their standard of living—even with all the low-cost labor and market monopoly—they felt more than threatened by any leveling of the playing field and made sure the Legislative Council, which they controlled, passed no such measures.

Isolation and decimation. European colonists came to Southern Rhodesia with dreams of wealth and freedom. What greeted most instead was a harsh landscape, overtaxed resources, and severe isolation. Droughts caused already difficult harvests to dwindle, and price-drops in maize from 25 shillings per bag to 9, which lasted until the end of World War II, further decimated earnings. Large farms that concentrated on major cash crops, such as tobacco, were those that succeeded, but small farms, such as those run by Dick Turner in Lessing's novel and by Lessing's own father in real life, barely eked out a living from year to year. As political scientist Colin Leys notes, "The first Europeans came to seek fortunes from gold; the second influx came to live by farming the land. Both resources were seriously overvalued, and not even a virtual monopoly of them both was sufficient in itself to provide the European population with the standard of living it had expected" (Leys in McEwan, p. 333). Pre-World War II farm output never exceeded £4 million. After the war, it increased more than tenfold, but by this time many small farmers, such as Lessing's father and the fictional Dick Turner, were already bankrupt.

In the novel and in other writings, Lessing depicts Southern Rhodesia as a wasteland, not only because of the infertile crops but because of the extreme isolation that colonists often experienced. Living on about 3,000-acre farms at least five miles from their nearest neighbor and refusing to establish equal relations with locals, European farmers found themselves utterly alone. Lessing describes her own experience, noting that, though, the whole family felt isolated, most affected was her mother, the farmer's wife:

> My father went to Southern Rhodesia on an impulse, to farm . . . he took a very large tract of land to grow maize. Thus I was brought up in a district that was very sparsely populated indeed, by Scottish people who had left

---

MISSIONARY MIXED BAG

British missionaries traveling to Africa were inspired by anti-slavery crusaders who wanted to establish agriculture and commerce and spread Christianity to make amends for British involvement in the slave trade. Patronizing as it may seem now, the missionaries felt they were saving the "savages" of the "dark continent" and bringing them into the light. It was "the Bible and the plough," felt the missionaries, that would regenerate Africa (Thomas, p. 106). So they founded missionary schools, took in orphaned Africans and taught them to speak English. By 1928, 86,000 of 1 million Africans had converted to Christianity. The ability of the converts to speak the language of their conquerors gave them a tremendous advantage for future advancement and change—an unhappy consequence in the eyes of most working-class whites. These working-class whites preferred for Africans employed in their homes as domestic servants or field workers to address them in "Kaffir" (actually a mixture of several African languages), enough of which the whites learned to state basic orders. Language books, such as Mary Turner's "Kitchen Kaffir" in the novel, were common among whites, who preferred to know what the Africans were saying but did not want them to understand the talk in English of whites. In *The Grass Is Singing*, Moses is a "mission boy." This, notes Mary, "explained a lot: that irritatingly well-articulated 'madame' instead of the usual 'missus,' which was somehow in better keeping with his station in life" (*Grass*, pp. 180-81). Like many real-life contemporaries, Mary does not approve of higher education for blacks. Close by in Nyasaland (between Northern and Southern Rhodesia) Scottish missionaries established primary schools and by the 1930s raised the African literacy rate to the highest on the continent. This hardly mattered, however, to the whites of Southern Rhodesia, who did not allow Africans to attend secondary school until after World War II.

Maize has long been a major crop in Zimbabwe (formerly known as Southern Rhodesia), although the novel's Dick Turner is unsuccessful raising it there.

Scotland or England because it was too small for them. I spent most of my childhood alone in a landscape with very few human things to do in it.

[I]t was my mother who suffered. . . . Poor woman, for the twenty years we were on the farm, she waited for when life would begin for her and for her children.
(Lessing, *A Small Personal Voice*, pp. 45-46, 91)

Both the novel's Mary Turner and Lessing's mother exemplify the lonely existence of the colonial farmer's wife. Even more than the men's, colonial women's lives wasted away on the veld, cut off from community, the modern world, and any professional outlet.

The Novel in Focus

Plot summary. Beginning at the scene of her death, *The Grass Is Singing* retraces the tragic life of Mary Turner, a white woman in Southern Rhodesia. Her parents had emigrated to Africa to achieve success through farming, but like so many other hopeful Europeans met with little success and even less happiness. Determined to make a different life for herself, Mary leaves the veld for the city and becomes a professional secretary. She lives in a boarding house with other

single women and, managing to support herself, feels quite content to go on like this forever. Though she still dresses like a schoolgirl, Mary is getting older, and one day she overhears some of her roommates mocking her. They call her an old maid and make fun of her dress, intimating that she should stop acting like a child and get married.

It is at this point that Mary meets Dick Turner, a young British emigrant who moves to Southern Rhodesia to farm. He buys thousands of acres out on the veld and comes to the city to find a wife to share it with. For Mary, returning to the veld is a nightmare, but the social pressure to conform and get married persuades her to accept Dick's proposal, and off they go.

In contrast to her contentment as a professional woman in the city, Mary becomes distraught and increasingly withdrawn on the farm. She has no income, no social connection with her neighbors, no real intimacy with her husband, and no other family to sustain her. Moreover, her relations with the Africans who worked on the farm are abominable. Both fearful and fiercely racist, Mary cannot bear to be in the company of locals and speaks even more disparagingly of them than her other white neighbors. She repeatedly fires her domestic workers and quickly earns a reputation for being very difficult to serve. Since there is not an abundance of available domestic workers, this creates problems with fewer and fewer workers coming around to replace those Mary fires or drives away.

Farm labor in general grows increasingly difficult to acquire. Though Dick has a reputation as a fair employer, Mary's antics cost him dearly, and, unable to get enough workers to harvest and plant, he is also extremely unlucky when it comes to weather and crop selection. While his neighbor, Charlie Slatter, makes a fortune in tobacco, Dick barely survives year-to-year with his diverse fields of maize, wheat, and vegetables. His farm is always the most devastated by drought and storm, and price-drops seem to affect only his harvests. He continually comes up with schemes, like gold divining and bee keeping, to remedy his dismal situation and finally achieve wealth and success, but they all fail, leaving him broke and broken.

With each passing year of struggle and failure, Mary's mental state worsens, as does Dick's physical health. When Moses, a very competent, mission-educated man, comes looking for work as a domestic servant, Dick hires him instantly and sternly warns Mary against firing him. They desperately need help now, and Dick fears that if Moses leaves, no others will ever come to take his place.

As Mary slips deeper and deeper into depression, Moses becomes her only lifeline and human contact. Dick works morning to night on the farm while Mary, unable to even do the most menial task, sleeps all day and talks to herself. Moses becomes her caretaker, forcing Mary to eat and get fresh air. He makes her bed, combs her hair, and even begins to dress her, breaking with social convention, exhibiting practically criminal behavior for Southern Rhodesia. Such intimacy with a black man was taboo for a white woman. Once Mary had personally whipped Moses for speaking to her in what she considered an insolent manner. Now she cries in front of him and relegates all authority and control to him. "What had happened was that the formal pattern of black-and-white, mistress-and-servant, had been broken by the personal relation" (*Grass*, pp. 166-67). In her first substantive contact with an African man Mary finds herself shedding her racist beliefs and becomes enthralled by this taboo figure. She daydreams about him, admires his muscular physique, imagines him watching her from the shadows, listens intently for his breathing on the other side of the wall where he sleeps at night. Mary becomes obsessed with Moses, but her attraction is mixed with both guilt and racist contempt and adds to her increasing state of dementia.

The way Mary acts does not escape the attention of her neighbors. They are outraged by her behavior and seek to get her off the farm and away from Moses. Charlie Slatter finally persuades Dick to sell out to him so that Dick can take Mary to the Cape Colony (in South Africa), where she could get mental help and get away from Moses, who is embarrassing all the whites of the area by acting as their equal with Mary.

When Mary realizes she is being forced to leave the farm and Moses, she panics. By this point she is gravely ill, wholly dependent on Moses, and beyond rational thought. In her mind, her only recourse is to fire him and rescind his authority over her. Mary is convinced this action will prompt Moses to kill her. However rational or irrational this thought is, in real life the ultimate colonial fear was that Africans would retaliate against whites by murdering them.

The night before she is to leave, Mary sits outside her dilapidated house in the dark and waits for Moses to come. She'd rejected him harshly and knew he would now come to take revenge.

> Then, as she heard the thunder growl and shake in the trees, the sky lit up, and she saw a man's shape move out from the dark and come towards her, gliding silently up the steps. . . . Two yards away Moses stopped. . . . [A]t the sight of him, her emotions unexpectedly shifted, to create in her an extraordinary feeling of guilt; but towards him, to whom she had been disloyal.
>
> (*Grass*, p. 243)

Mary's inner torment was quelled finally when Moses stabbed her in the throat. "'And then the bush avenged itself:' that was her last thought" (*Grass*, p. 243). Moses left Mary bleeding to death on the porch and waited for the authorities to come and arrest him.

Trapped by taboos. In the novel, Lessing uses the intimate relationship of Mary and Moses to illustrate the human tragedy of racism in the Southern Africa of her youth. Trapped by taboos, Mary and Moses cannot connect. Culturally they do not understand and trust one another. Physically they cannot be together under penalty of death for Moses and jail for Mary (under the Immorality Suppression Ordinance of 1903 white women could receive two years hard labor for being with black men). Socially they cannot be seen as equals because that would be breaking what Charlie Slatter terms "the first law of South Africa," which states that whites must always act superior to blacks in all aspects or the black man will realize he is just as capable. In each of these cases, the inability of whites and blacks to form meaningful relationships results in some form of death: spiritual, physical, and social.

At the time, sex was considered the "touchstone," or ultimate test of race relations and because many European colonists believed that Darwinism proved they were a superior race, they viewed mating with Africans as "an act of much deeper degradation than a casual affair" (Blake, p. 158). Even affairs between white men and black women earned disdain. While the affairs themselves were tolerated, white society shunned racially mixed children, and European men generally did not acknowledge their "coloured" offspring. The ultimate sin was a white woman's having any measure of intimacy with a black man:

> The deepest degradation of all was any relationship between a white woman and a black man. For this there could be no excuse whatever and it was taken for granted that it could only occur as a result of *force majeure* by the black man, or criminal immorality on the part of the white woman.
>
> (Blake, p. 158)

By pairing Moses and Mary, Lessing shows that this attitude, as well as racist segregation in general, caused misery and death. Moses is the only person who can possibly "save" Mary yet by her befriending and confiding in him, she condemns them both.

> The connection between Mary and Moses breaks the great taboo of the color bar between the black and white races, with disastrous results, and yet in a way that both emphasizes the decadence and sterility of the life in which Mary is trapped, and hints that her only hope of renewal is through the forbidden bond which is being created with Moses.
>
> (Vinson, p. 64)

Lessing visually depicts the destruction caused by racism—particularly to Moses and Mary—with the barren landscape of the veld. It is a dying wasteland just as the souls of its inhabitants are stripped of humanity. Taking the title of the novel from T. S. Eliot's *The Waste Land* (also in *WLAIT 4: British and Irish Literature and Its Times*), Lessing makes it clear that racism has robbed Southern Africa of its value and fertility ("In this decayed hole among the moun-

tains / In the faint moonlight, the grass is singing"—*Grass*, preface). After Mary sends Moses away, she sees nothing but doom and despair on the horizon:

> A lean, sun-flattened landscape stretched out before her, dun-colored, brown and olive-green, and the smoke-haze was everywhere, lingering in the trees and obscuring the hills. The sky shut down over her, with thick yellowish walls of smoke growing up to meet it. The world was small, shut in a room of heat and haze and light.
>
> (*Grass*, p. 228)

Tormented by the society in which she lives and the belief system she has been taught, Mary protests that she is not a "criminally immoral" woman for befriending Moses. She has been brought up within the system and for the majority of her life adheres to the color bar. But when she gets to know Moses as simply a person and not a black person, her beliefs begin to change. Mary's new boarder, Tony Marston, discovers her relationship with Moses and observes that she "behaves simply as if . . . other people's standards don't count" (*Grass*, p. 221). Indeed, Mary retreats into her own world to escape the harsh reality of the society she lives in, creating a refuge in which she and Moses can relate as equals. But when Tony enters this world she is forced to revert back to the "official rules" and send Moses away. "It was all right till you came!" Mary screams at Tony and collapses in a "storm of tears," illustrating her outrage at a society that will not allow her to befriend the one person who can save her from her lonely existence.

Lessing leaves the union of Moses and Mary deliberately ambiguous to show that any intimate relationship between a black man and a white woman—no matter how innocent—was strictly forbidden. As was customary colonial society, represented in the novel by Tony and Charlie Slatter, succeeds in destroying it because in fact in the southern Africa of Lessing's youth, any equitable relationship between a black man and white woman could only end in death. Like the inhospitable climate that withered crops, the novel shows that the color bar induced its own physical and spiritual draught, producing a devastatingly inhospitable climate that brought to whites as well as blacks misery and death.

Sources and literary context. Based on her formative years in Southern Rhodesia from 1925 to 1948, *The Grass Is Singing* draws on Lessing's personal experiences. She uses the story she heard as a girl of a European woman dressing in front of her African servant—gossip that spread from porch to porch like wildfire across the veld—as the basis for the illicit relationship between Moses and Mary. But she alters the viewpoint of the real-life story from one of condemnation to one that evokes the human tragedy produced by the color bar. Lessing bases many of Mary's early choices—for example, leaving the farm to work as a typist in the city—on her own life. She portrays the coldness she witnessed between her own parents in the frigidity between Mary and Dick. The isolation experienced by Mary is akin to that of her mother, who longed for England and her former social life, and the bad luck and lack of success experienced by Dick echo the fate of her father, who tried many of the same schemes as Dick to no avail. Though clearly full of personal detail, Lessing is quick to point out that the general story and behavior "could have been about white people anywhere south of the Zambezi, white people who were not up to what is expected of them in a society where there is very heavy competition from the black people coming up" (Lessing, *A Small Personal Voice,* p. 46).

In the tradition of realist, humanist writers of the Victorian Age such as Charles Dickens, Lessing believed she was producing "art which springs from a strongly-held, though not necessarily intellectually defined, view of life that absorbs symbolism" (Lessing, *Small,* p. 4). She wrote *The Grass Is Singing* to carry on what she termed propagandist literature in the tradition of Dickens's *Oliver Twist* (Lessing, *Small,* pp. 3-4). Writing in the tumultuous yet hopeful post-World War II era, Lessing's novel aimed to both enlighten European society and inspire positive change, objectives that testify to a fundamental faith in mid-twentieth century humanity.

Events in History at the Time the Novel Was Written

African awakening-a turning point in history. Lessing witnessed the harsh experience of her parents and was fortunate enough to come of age in a more hospitable era when she could choose a different path. Opting off the farm as soon as she could, she ventured into Salisbury in about 1937 when great changes were taking place in Africa and the world. Two years later World War II broke out, initiating a boom in the local economy that continued in the postwar era. Meanwhile, Rhodesia's African majority began demonstrating their discontent through strikes in the cities. In 1948 a general strike in Bulawayo

erupted in riots that paralyzed the country's second largest city. Resistance leaders Joshua Nkomo and Benjamin Burumbo called for higher wages, desegregation, access to secondary education, and government representation. Though the African National Congress of Southern Rhodesia had been founded in 1934, it did not establish itself as a powerful force of change until 1945, by which time African members had achieved the necessary educational and nationalistic skills to organize effectively.

An ANC-backed railway strike in Salisbury in 1945 succeeded in gaining higher wages for the laborers as well as official union recognition, which prompted many to proclaim, "The railway strike has proved that Africans have been born" (Hallett, p. 532). The strike's success led to the establishment of African Representative Councils in 1946, the general strike of 1948, and the prelude to 15 years of mounting political excitement in every part of British Central Africa—literally the dawning of "a new era" (Hallett, p. 530). Brought on by increased industrialization of the country, a switch from rural to urban occupation, and a huge population surge, Africans were determined to rid themselves of their colonial chains and were gaining the power in monetary and physical numbers to do so.

Communism and African rights. Leading the fight on behalf of African rights was the Communist Party in Southern Rhodesia. It was the only public institution in which whites and blacks worked together on an equal footing and the first to champion the end of both segregation and monetary servitude. "The Communist Party had an enormous effect on politics because it ignored the colour bar" and fought for labor organization and workers rights across the board (Lessing, *A Small Personal Voice,* p. 74). Because Russia was a British ally during World War II, the Party was tolerated at the time, but after the war, it came under suspicion until it went underground, so to speak, and become a clandestine organization. Lessing joined the Party when it was considered "seditious, dangerous, and above all kaffir-loving" (Lessing, *Under My Skin,* p. 199). The suspicion under which it fell did not deter Party members from holding secret meetings under the auspices of the Left Bank Book Club and circulating pamphlets calling for education and better pay and working conditions for Africans. By this time even mainstream whites recognized the growing power of the Africans and the necessity of addressing some of their needs. As Prime Minister Godfrey Martin Huggins noted in 1948, "We are witnessing the emergence of a proletariat and in this country it happens to be black" (Huggins in Blake, p. 240).

For Lessing, the Left Bank Book Club and one of its principals, Gladys Maasdorp (to whom *The Grass Is Singing* is dedicated), gave credibility to her instinctive belief that the color bar was wrong. Though she had been raised by parents who very much believed in the system as it was, Lessing had always rebelled against it. "We were quarrelling about the Colour Bar, the Native Question," she writes. "The trouble is, I had no ammunition in the way of facts or figures, nothing but a vague but very strong feeling there was something terribly wrong with the System" (Lessing, *Under My Skin*, p. 179). The Communist Party provided those facts and figures—evidence of the physical, emotional, and economic suffering of both blacks and whites under the color bar—which Lessing then used in her writing. In other words, the movement for African rights and the Communist Party validated Lessing's ideas and enabled her to publicly denounce segregation and discrimination in *The Grass Is Singing*.

Though her views on the Communist Party changed markedly over time, Lessing was originally inspired by its message of equality and its efforts to improve living and working conditions. As with Lessing, the postwar social movements had a transfiguring effect. They altered the course of colonial rule and the rights of Africans, rousing the continent and, with it, Lessing herself, who would go on to further this postwar awakening through her writing.

Reviews. Though criticized for flat depictions of the African characters—particularly Moses—Lessing was otherwise widely praised for her first novel. *Spectator* reviewer Marghanita Laski called *The Grass Is Singing* "the best first novel for a long time. Mrs. Lessing has written in a prose of exceptional strength and maturity" (Laski in James and Brown, p. 552). London's *Times Literary Supplement* hailed the novel as "a powerful and bitter book," and South African author J. M. Coetzee praised the novel too, deeming it "an astonishingly accomplished debut" (*Times* in James and Brown, p. 552; Coetzee in Peacock, p. 278). Across the Atlantic Ocean, America's R.

Anthony Appiah found the novel "intensely humane in its attentiveness to the minutest details of the mental life of this central character" and distinguished Lessing as "the finest new novelist since the war" (Appiah in Peacock, p. 278). The novel, said Anthony White in the *New Statesman* "is full of those terrifying touches of truth, seldom mentioned but instantly recognised" (White in James and Brown, p. 552). Written and revised from 1948 until its publication in 1950, *The Grass Is Singing* was among the first works to tackle the taboo subject of sexual relations between the races in southern Africa and spawned a distinguished career for Lessing, who would continue to tackle timely and controversial topics in her future novels, short stories, essays, poems, and plays.

—Diane Renée

For More Information

Blake, John S. *A History of Rhodesia.* New York: Knopf, 1978.

Hallett, Robin. *Africa Since 1875.* Ann Arbor: University of Michigan Press, 1974.

James, Mertice M., and Dorothy Brown. *The Book Review Digest: March 1950-February 1951.* Vol. 46. New York: H.W. Wilson, 1951.

Kaplan, Carey, and Ellen Cronan Rose, eds. *Doris Lessing: The Alchemy of Survival.* Ohio: Ohio University Press, 1988.

Lessing, Doris. *The Grass Is Singing.* New York: Crowell, 1950.

———. *A Small Personal Voice.* New York: Knopf, 1974.

———. *Under My Skin.* New York: Harper Collins, 1995.

McEwan, P. J. M., ed. *Twentieth-Century Africa.* London: Oxford University Press, 1968.

Peacock, Scot, ed. *Contemporary Authors, New Revision Series.* Vol. 76. Detroit: Gale, 1999.

Singleton, Mary Ann. *The City and the Veld.* Lewisburg: Bucknell University Press, 1977.

Thomas, Anthony. *Rhodes.* New York: St. Martin's, 1996.

Vinson, James, ed. *Novelists and Prose Writers.* New York: St. Martin's, 1979.

Wesseling, H. L. *Divide and Rule.* London: Praeger, 1996.

Great Expectations

Charles Dickens

reat Expectations was the penultimate novel completed by the most popular novelist of Victorian England, Charles Dickens. Born in Kent, England, in 1812 to a family of modest means but great pretensions, Dickens's early life was marked by both humiliation and ambition. Dickens never forgot the period of financial crisis during his childhood, when following his father's bankruptcy, he was taken out of school and forced to work in a shoe-polish warehouse. While the episode was relatively brief, it marked Dickens's later life in many ways: in the development of his own ambitions, in his sympathy for the poor and especially children, and in his outrage at social injustice and bureaucratic heartlessness. *Great Expectations*, written when Dickens was at the height of his popularity and success, demonstrates all these concerns. His thirteenth novel, it was not overtly autobiographical, as his earlier *David Copperfield* (1850) had been, but in writing it Dickens employed a first-person narrative that elicits mixed sympathy and judgement for the protagonist Pip, an orphan raised by an abusive elder sister and her saintly husband, a blacksmith. Pip's story invokes an assortment of real-life issues of Victorian England, ranging from its relationship to its colonies, to its imperfect educational system, to its overarching concern with social mobility and status.

Events in History at the Time the Novel Takes Place

Economic anxiety and social mobility. Dickens set the substance of *Great Expectations* at

THE LITERARY WORK

A novel set in England in the first half of the nineteenth century; published in 1860-61.

SYNOPSIS

The orphan Pip, a blacksmith's apprentice, harbors aspirations to gentility that are inspired by his love for the disdainful Estella and that are mysteriously supported by an anonymous benefactor.

roughly the time of his own childhood; the action of the novel begins in 1812, the year Dickens was born, when Pip is seven. This was a time of great economic anxiety in England; the American Revolution, Napoleonic wars, and the War of 1812 had caused a drain on the national economy, and industrial developments were putting agricultural as well as other manual laborers out of work. The development of the threshing machine in farming (patented 1788; in widespread use by 1830) and mechanized looms in cloth-making (patented 1786; in widespread use 1815-1840) were two significant changes in labor practice; both inventions increased production, which led to greater economic security for their owners and managers, but also reduced the need for unskilled laborers, which created unemployment at the lower ends of the economic scale. Manual labor, always a marker of lower social status, was giving way to industrialized forms of doing business, and the new industrial elite was

Charles Dickens

reshaping the English class system. Alongside the old class system, which was based on land and status, a new economy arose, based on industry, information, and capitalist investment. While these changes generated anxiety, especially among the landed aristocracy, they at the same time augmented opportunity and excited hopes among the lower orders. If hard work could earn money, perhaps it could also earn higher social standing.

Education, always a marker of class standing, was beginning to be a means to social mobility as well. In an era before compulsory or standardized education (attendance at elementary school would not be made mandatory until 1880), a "gentleman's" education in classics, mathematics, and literature conveyed a social standing that more technical or skill-based education did not. At the beginning of the nineteenth century, there was no national educational system in England. Wealthy children were usually educated at home, and middle-class children attended private schools. The options for poor and working-class children were limited to unregulated, unprofessional schools like "dame schools," often run by poorly trained women who supervised children in cottage industries (such as plaiting straw or lacemaking) while they performed a perfunctory instruction in reading. In the novel Biddy improves on her dame-school

education and uses it as a means of self-support and social improvement.

Poor or laboring-class children, and even some middle-class youths, might also serve an apprenticeship as their education into a trade. In the apprentice system, a child or youth was legally "bound" for seven years to a master who would, in return for a premium paid at the beginning of the contract and free labor throughout its term, teach him the trade. After seven years an apprentice could become a "journeyman," free to hire himself out for daily wages. Blacksmithing, shoemaking, and millinery—as well as law and surgery—were taught through the apprenticeship system, which varied widely in efficacy and professionalism.

As the century progressed, a variety of educational organizations were formed to provide free or inexpensive education for the poorer classes; both religious and secular educations were provided through these philanthropic organizations. Basic literacy and arithmetic skills could and did increase one's economic viability in the new economy, as they opened up white-collar professions such as clerk, accountant, or trader.

But economic improvement did not always translate into social mobility. England at the beginning of the nineteenth century was still a very hierarchical, socially stratified society. Social status depended on blood and birth, land and leisure. While money could not buy blood or birth, or lineage, (except through a socially advantageous marriage), fresh sources of wealth such as factory-owning and overseas trade meant that land and leisure could now occasionally be purchased by a new social strata, the middle-class professional. A gentleman's status was derived primarily from his leisure: a gentleman lived off investments (or land) and hired servants. While most of the newly rich were not themselves considered "gentlemen," having derived their wealth through hard work, their children might possibly aspire to that status, with an education to polish off the rough edges and servants to maintain their households. Pip's education with Mr. Pocket is concerned with giving him the appearance of gentility, while his legacy provides him leisure. Ironically, in *Great Expectations*, when Pip is given both the financial means and the education to become a gentleman, a role he has aspired to only for Estella's sake, he is given them by an escaped convict who also turns out to be her father. Social status, the novel suggests, is both ephemeral and implicated in the very crimes it condemns.

Crime and punishment. *Great Expectations* begins and ends with the pursuit and apprehension of an escaped convict, and crime and punishment figure largely in the plot of the novel. The criminal justice system was changing in England at the turn of the nineteenth century; in 1800, there were over 200 crimes for which capital punishment could be imposed, while by 1841 only eight remained (Philips, p. 156). Dickens had treated the failures of the criminal justice system directly in his early novel *Oliver Twist* (1838), in which his young thieves are threatened with the death penalty for stealing silk handkerchiefs. His outrage at the injustice of the death penalty for relatively minor crimes against property was widely shared, and contributed to the changing climate of criminal justice in the early part of the nineteenth century.

"Transportation," or forced resettlement in one of England's colonies (first America and, after American independence, Australia) offered an alternative to capital punishment, which was felt to be far more humane, and indeed some former prisoners prospered in the colonies. Convicts working under government supervision were allowed some hours a day to work for themselves; others, however, labored under "private assignment" to non-government employers, who might maintain them in virtual slavery. Their terms and conditions varied widely, as did the entire administration of criminal justice before the various reforms of the nineteenth century.

By 1830 about 58,000 convicts had come to Australia; this marked the high point of transportation, after which the practice began a gradual decline because anti-slavery feeling came to influence the convict system as well. Private assignment of transported criminals was abolished in 1840, the sentence of transportation was abolished in 1858, and the practice of transportation in lieu of execution gradually decreased after that time. Like Magwitch in the novel, most transported criminals were career criminals and thieves, though some were political prisoners as well. Transported criminals were barred, under penalty of their original death sentences, from ever returning to England, even after their terms of labor (usually between seven and fourteen years) had expired.

The crimes in *Great Expectations* include both the "white collar" crimes of forgery and fraud, and more violent attacks on persons and property. Of course the class system infected the criminal justice system; the lower-class Magwitch is condemned far more harshly for his part in the

forgery and swindling scheme than his more genteel partner Compeyson. Access to legal representation could make the difference between life and death for the accused prisoner, and in the absence of a public defense system, many accused criminals were unable to defend themselves. Prisoners did not speak in their own defense, nor did they speak directly to the lawyers who would represent them in court. Legal cases were prepared by an attorney or solicitor, such as the novel's Mr. Wemmick, who would then usually turn over the actual arguing of the case to a "barrister," a lawyer licensed to appear in court, such as Mr. Jaggers. The system set up barriers between the lower-class accused and the upper-class legal community that often resulted in the former's being only seen, not heard.

Criminal justice in the early nineteenth century was as swift as it was severe. In London, criminals awaited trial only briefly (although in some rural areas criminal trials were held only once a year), and sentencing and punishment followed rapidly upon conviction. Prisons were for the most part mere holding cells, often operated by private individuals for profit. The concept of the prison as a locus of either reform or punishment was still relatively new in the nineteenth century; convicted criminals were either executed or served hard labor, either on the "Hulks"—prison ships that also provided lodging for prisoners awaiting transportation—or in Australia.

England and its colonies. England had been a colonial power for over two centuries by the era depicted in *Great Expectations*; the nineteenth century was, however, a time of great expansion and re-evaluation of England's colonial presence. England began to settle Australia in 1788 as a penal colony. Having lost the American colonies in the Revolution, England maintained its presence in Canada and Australia, and began expanding its political and economic presence in Asia and Africa as well. By the end of the Napoleonic Wars in 1815, England had expanded its holdings in the Indian subcontinent to include Afghanistan and Burma, and had acquired Holland's former colonial holdings in South Africa as well. Both commerce and conviction underlay England's imperial development; what novelist Rudyard Kipling would later call "the white man's burden" to spread Christianity and, more generally, "Englishness" throughout Asia and Africa co-existed, more or less comfortably, with capitalist expansion of trade throughout the world. Among the colonial reaches of the empire, India and Africa, in particular, provided a combination of missionary and capitalist opportunities for the younger sons of the gentry and for the hard-working sons of modest families, who could become rich and respected through trade or government service. In *Great Expectations,* empire is the source of wealth, even redemption, for convict and respectable citizen alike.

The Novel in Focus

Plot summary. The action of the novel takes place between 1812 and 1829, and is narrated by its main character, Pip (Philip Pirrip) from the vantage point of adulthood, sometime in the late 1850s or early 1860s. His story begins on Christmas Eve, when Pip is in his seventh year; an orphan being raised by his sister, known always as Mrs. Joe, and her husband Joe, a blacksmith, Pip is visiting his parents' and brothers' gravesites when he is accosted by a convict. The convict threatens to kill him if he does not bring food the next day; this Pip does, stealing the food out of his sister's pantry. On his way to deliver the food, he encounters another, younger, escaped convict, but eludes him to deliver the food. On Christmas Day, during a family party, soldiers arrive at the blacksmith's house—not to arrest Pip for pilfering the food, as he at first believes, but to enlist the blacksmith's help in mending some handcuffs. Pip and Joe join the soldiers in their search for the escaped convicts. Both are apprehended, and Pip sees "his" convict take responsibility for the stolen food before being taken away in chains.

Months pass. Pip endures his sister's abuses and the difficulties of life in the forge, as well as a growing sense of guilt at his still unacknowledged theft. An eccentric wealthy woman living in the town, Miss Havisham, requests Pip's presence at her manor house (Satis House). There, Pip meets a proud and beautiful girl, Estella, who is Miss Havisham's ward. Miss Havisham lives with her in almost complete isolation and decay, surrounded by the appurtenances of a wedding that never occurred. Miss Havisham asks to have Pip visit often, and amuse her by playing cards with Estella. During one of these visits, Pip meets relatives of Miss Havisham's who resent him for his assumed closeness to her; among them is a boy of his own age who challenges him to fight. Pip does so reluctantly; he beats the boy, and for the first time Estella seems pleased with him. After eight or ten months, Miss Havisham ends the

arrangement when she pays the requisite premium to have Pip apprenticed to Joe. The visits with Estella cease, but Pip continues to call upon Miss Havisham once a year, on his birthday.

During this early time, Pip attends a local school, run by an incompetent old woman and her great niece, Biddy. Pip confesses to Biddy that he wants to become a "gentleman" to impress Estella, though he laments openly not having chosen a more attainable object, like herself. Biddy teaches Pip as much as she can, and lets him know that she is bothered by the attentions of the blacksmith's journeyman, a worker named Orlick. Orlick resents the fact that Pip's relationship with Joe makes him "superior," and after Pip is apprenticed, his resentment only increases. One evening, while both Pip and Joe are out of the house, Mrs. Joe is attacked and left for dead; Pip suspects Orlick, but cannot prove his suspicions. In the aftermath of the attack, Biddy moves to the forge to help care for Mrs. Joe.

Pip feels ashamed of Joe and the forge because of his attachment to the heartless and snobbish Estella. Thus, he is delighted when, after he has served four years of his apprenticeship, Miss Havisham's lawyer, Mr. Jaggers, announces that Pip has come into "great expectations," and that he is to be released from his apprenticeship and educated in London to be a gentleman. The only two conditions attached to his new status are that he will not attempt to identify his benefactor and that he will retain the name Pip. While Pip assumes that Miss Havisham is his benefactor, Mr. Jaggers will not confirm his suspicions.

Pip moves to London, where he lodges with a distant relative of Miss Havisham's, Herbert Pocket (the young boy who had challenged him to fight at Satis House) and is educated by Herbert's father, Matthew. Herbert tells him Miss Havisham's story: the daughter of a brewer, she was engaged to be married when her fiancé jilted her on the morning of the wedding. The fiancé, now revealed as a forger and swindler, was in league with a half-brother of Miss Havisham's. Her heart broken, Miss Havisham laid waste to her house and stopped all the clocks at the moment she learned of her failed engagement (twenty minutes past nine). Estella, he learns, was adopted by Miss Havisham when a child, and has been brought up to wreak Miss Havisham's revenge on the male sex.

Befriended by Jaggers's clerk, Mr. Wemmick, Pip also learns more about Mr. Jaggers's criminal practice. Wemmick is a businesslike man who maintains a tiny "castle," complete with

In a scene from the 1946 film version of *Great Expectations,* Anthony Wager, as Magwich, grabs Pip when he encounters him in the graveyard.

drawbridge, turrets, and cannon, in Walworth, a suburb of London, where Pip visits him and meets his father, known as the "Aged Parent." At Walworth, Wemmick becomes a friend and confidant to Pip, but he adopts an air of businesslike unapproachability in the office, maintaining a strict separation of private and public life. Another curious character enters the picture, Mr. Jaggers's housekeeper, a former client whom Mr. Jaggers claims to have "tamed" (Dickens, *Great Expectations,* p. 195). The housekeeper, it is said, had murdered a younger woman whom she perceived as a rival; Jaggers has engineered her acquittal and with it her continuing service to him.

Estella moves to Richmond, another suburb of London, and Pip sees her frequently. Suspecting that Miss Havisham intends Estella for him, he does not speak to her of his attachment, but suffers when she seems to flirt with other men.

Pip and Herbert fall greatly into debt, not being educated for any profession, yet having great expectations of themselves. Mrs. Joe dies, and Pip makes a rare return to the forge to attend her funeral. Since coming into his "expectations" he has distanced himself from Joe and the forge even further than when he was visiting Miss Havisham. When Pip turns 21, he is given an annual income but does not learn any further details about his benefactor. He resolves, however, to use part of his income to endow a position for Herbert at a shipping and trading company, Clarriker's, without Herbert's knowledge, and Herbert begins to succeed in the business, learning all about England's trade with its Asian colonies.

Estella becomes engaged to a former student of Matthew Pocket's, a well-to-do man named Bentley Drummle (nicknamed the "Spider" by Mr. Jaggers for his sneaky, brutal appearance). Drummle is brutal and cruel, and Pip remonstrates with Estella about her choice, but she claims that, since she has been brought up without a heart, she cannot bestow it on anyone. Even Miss Havisham is shocked at her cruelty, but Estella reminds her that she is Miss Havisham's creation and cannot be expected to act otherwise.

Pip is 23 when he learns the true identity of his benefactor: it is not Miss Havisham, but the convict he had fed on the marshes that long-ago Christmas Eve, a man named Abel Magwich. Magwich had been transported to Australia for his crimes (as yet unnamed) and in returning to England, he risks the death penalty. He has prospered as a sheep-farmer in Australia, and devoted all his income (via Jaggers, who had been his attorney) to Pip's education and transformation into a "gentleman." Ashamed of his benefactor, Pip endeavors to hide him, and soon learns that the other convict, a man named Compeyson, is aware of Magwitch's return. Through Herbert Pocket, Pip also discovers that Compeyson is the man who jilted Miss Havisham. Details in Magwitch's story convince Pip that Estella is his

VICTORIAN PHILANTHROPY

The Victorian period was a great age of philanthropy. The rise of evangelical Christianity in the late eighteenth and early nineteenth centuries awakened the consciences of many, and indeed it is impossible to contemplate Victorian society without being aware of the great social injustices which divided it. While in earlier times private charity or church-based charity had been common, the large-scale social change of the Victorian period rendered such solutions impotent, and many philanthropic organizations sprang up to fill the void. Organizations such as the Royal Society for the Prevention of Cruelty to Animals (founded 1824), the National Society for the Prevention of Cruelty to Children (founded 1884), the National Society for Promoting the Education of the Poor in the Principles of the Church of England (1811), the British and Foreign Schools Society (1808), and many others, were motivated to a great extent by the energetic women who found in philanthropy a socially acceptable outlet for their skills and talents. Dickens was ambivalent about such efforts. In *Bleak House* he satirizes the philanthropic women who tirelessly raise money for evangelizing Africa but ignore their own children, in characters like Mrs. Jellyby. Yet he was himself involved in a small-scale effort, spearheaded by his friend Angela Burdett-Couts, to train former prostitutes in useful skills and help them to emigrate. Dickens seems to have preferred such private generosity as Magwitch's and Pip's, which was based on personal connection rather than self-aggrandizement or a desire for structural reform.

daughter and that Jaggers's "tamed" housekeeper is her mother. Jaggers is the surprising link between all these disparate characters; his legal profession connects him across class boundaries to virtually everyone in the novel.

After learning the truth about his benefactor, Pip returns to Satis House to confront Miss Havisham. She admits that she has used him and his

expectations to confound her own relatives (by letting them believe he, not they, might inherit her substantial wealth) but has otherwise had nothing to do with his legacy. Pip forgives Miss Havisham and as he is leaving, a fire breaks out and he saves her from the conflagration, at some cost to himself. Injured, he returns to London. Miss Havisham survives the fire but dies soon thereafter.

Pip resolves to leave England with Magwitch, whom he has learned to love and respect. He sequesters him in a boarding house near the Thames River and plans to depart with him on a freighter to Europe as soon as Wemmick suggests that it is safe. Just before the planned departure, Pip receives a mysterious message inviting him to a limekiln near the old forge; he complies, and is met by Joe's former journeyman Orlick who, now mysteriously in league with Compeyson, has resolved to kill Pip. Mystified by Orlick's malevolence, Pip learns that the journeyman's resentment motivated the attack on Mrs. Joe as well as this final attack. Saved by Herbert Pocket, who has followed him, Pip returns to London and tries to carry out the escape plan, but Orlick has warned Compeyson, and their boat is met before Magwitch can escape. Magwitch and Compeyson struggle, and Compeyson is drowned. Magwitch is condemned to death, his wealth a forfeit to the crown. But before he can be executed, Magwitch dies of injuries sustained in the struggle with Compeyson. As he lies dying, Pip reveals to Magwitch that he knows and loves Magwitch's daughter.

Pip falls ill, and is nursed back to health by Joe, who also pays his debts. When he is fully recovered, Pip returns to the forge, intending to discard his expectations and propose to Biddy. However, she and Joe have just been married, and Pip wisely says nothing of his plan. Chastened, he joins Herbert Pocket at Clarriker's and rises from clerkship to partnership; he lives in Cairo in charge of the Eastern Branch of the business.

Eleven years pass. Pip returns to England, where he sees that Joe and Biddy have a child named for him. Visiting Satis House for a final time, he meets Estella there. Bentley Drummle, who mistreated her, has died in a fall from a horse. Estella and Pip are reconciled in the ashes of Satis House, and as the novel ends they leave the house together, hand in hand.

Gender and violence. *Great Expectations* depicts male-female relationships as violent and destructive in all but a few rare cases. Mrs. Joe beats both her husband and Pip; Joe is himself a victim and witness of domestic violence. As he informs Pip, Joe's father, also a blacksmith, "were given to drink, and when he were overtook with drink, he hammered away at my mother, most onmerciful. It were a'most the only hammering he did, indeed, 'xcepting at myself" (*Great Expectations*, p. 61). Miss Havisham inflicts her own violence on herself at the failure of her intended marriage, and Estella is, we learn after the fact, "used with great cruelty" by her husband, Bentley Drummle (*Great Expectations*, p. 437). Although Wemmick and Herbert Pocket both marry, presumably happily, in the course of the novel, as do Biddy and Joe, their peaceful relationships are anomalous in this novel. Orlick evidently beats and leaves Mrs. Joe for dead, and Estella's mother has killed a woman out of sexual jealousy. Pip himself seems to understand his relationship with Estella in violent terms; he claims, for example, that he has "suffered every kind and degree of torture that Estella could cause [him]" (*Great Expectations*, p. 280).

The novel's emphasis on the violence seemingly inherent in sexual relations comes at a time when issues of gender were hotly debated. Although England was ruled by a queen, women in general had few if any legal rights at the beginning of Victoria's reign; throughout the century, what came to be called "The Woman Question" grew ever more urgent, as women (and some men) pressed for female emancipation in marriage, in property rights, in child custody, and in social and professional relations. In 1839 the Infant Custody Act was passed, allowing women to petition for custody of their infant children in the rare case of divorce or separation; this was the first instance in English legal history of legislation specifically concerning women's rights. The act was followed by decades of debate about, and the eventual passage of, the Matrimonial Causes Act (1857) and the Married Woman's Property Acts (1870, 1882), the first of which legislated more liberal divorce laws and the second of which allowed women to retain some control of their property in marriage. A corollary to the Matrimonial Causes Act was a right gained by magistrates in 1878 to grant separation to wives if their husbands were convicted of aggravated assault. Although women would not be granted the vote in England until 1928, the foundation of a woman's movement was laid in the nineteenth century even in politics: John Stuart Mill introduced the first bill for woman suffrage in 1867, during his brief career as a member of Parliament.

The debates about custody, married women's property, and divorce made public the private operations of the Victorian home. They revealed the ugly and often violent realities of gendered power relations that lay behind the public ideology of domesticity. Put baldly, they demonstrated that domestic bliss was frequently an illusion based on the often-violent suppression of one human being's rights, most often the wife.

THE TWO ENDINGS OF *GREAT EXPECTATIONS*

Great Expectations was completed in June 1861, with the final episode scheduled for publication in August. During that year, Dickens had been in constant contact with the novelist Edward Bulwer-Lytton, whose novel *A Strange Story* was scheduled to follow the serial publication of *Great Expectations* in the magazine *All the Year Round*. The two novelists had read and critiqued each other's work throughout the year, and when Bulwer-Lytton read the conclusion to *Great Expectations* in proof, he advised Dickens to change it. Dickens had originally written a briefer, more somber conclusion in which Pip and Estella—who had remarried after Bentley Drummle's death—meet only briefly on the street and are parted forever. Bulwer-Lytton objected to the sadness of this ending, and Dickens's revised version, with the meeting between Estella and Pip at Satis House, was published in its place. Dickens continued to edit the final words of the novel; in manuscript and in proof, he wrote, "I saw the shadow of no parting from her but one." However, at the proof stage he dropped the last two words, and the sentence appeared in *All the Year Round* as "I saw the shadow of no parting from her." Finally, in the 1862 one-volume edition, the line appears as, "I saw no shadow of another parting from her" (*Great Expectations*, pp. 440-41). This is the version quoted above, as it is the standard printed version. While the differences between these latter versions may seem minor—especially compared to the major difference wrought between the proof and published versions—they indicate Dickens's continued wrestling with the question of Pip and Estella's future even after the novel was published.

Dickens's depictions of gendered violence likewise operate to reveal the failures of domesticity and its disconnection from romantic love. His violent women, often brutally tamed by even more violent men, are aberrations, women who have seized power and often masculine identity and are then punished for it. Mrs. Joe is the most striking example of a woman who is masculinized by her dominance in the household, and who is tamed by Orlick, an even more brutal force than herself.

Conversely, both Wemmick and Herbert Pocket find brides for themselves who support their desire for a quiet domesticity; like Biddy, Wemmick's Miss Skiffins and Herbert's Clara are quiet, efficient, and long-suffering women who willingly enter a secluded domesticity based on mutual concern, companionship, and care, rather than property or status. Pip's fruitless attachment to Estella, and his inability to recognize until too late the love and care that someone like Biddy could offer him, are symptomatic of the failure of his romantic ideals, which had—as so many nineteenth-century novels do—linked love and status, here with disastrous results. It is significant in this regard that Pip's ultimate union with Estella is accomplished only after she has been ill-treated by her first husband, Bentley Drummle; like Mrs. Joe, perhaps, she is brutally "tamed" into domesticity.

Sources and literary context. Dickens was the most popular novelist in England at the time he was writing *Great Expectations*. The realistic novel had become the dominant literary form by then, due in large part to Dickens's and other writers' development of it in the earlier part of the century. The novel's most direct antecedent, though, is not another novel but the Renaissance sonnet cycle by Sir Philip Sidney, *Astrophil and Stella*. In that cycle, the helpless lover (Astrophil, or "star-lover," a stand-in for the author), pines for his beloved, Stella (or "star"). The cycle is written in the traditional Petrarchan mode, in which the beloved becomes the metaphoric light by which the lover steers, but is also the source of all his frustration and anxiety. By taking the names (Philip/Pip; Stella/Estella) and the basic relationship from the sonnet cycle and turning them into a realistic novel, Dickens explores the destructiveness as well as the power of romantic love.

Estella is the one character in the novel for whom biographers and critics have consistently sought a real-life counterpart. Dickens's personal life at the time he was writing *Great Expectations* was itself public knowledge, even public scandal: he had separated from his wife, Catherine (née Hogarth) in 1858, and was living with her sister Georgina and nine of his children while Catherine stayed in London with their eldest son Charley. In a strikingly open admission of the failure of his domestic ideal, Dickens published a statement in his magazine *Household Words* soon after the split, recognizing the separation but claiming that all parties involved were guiltless. Georgina's position in the household was officially that of housekeeper and substitute mother, and Dickens was widely believed to be involved at the time with an actress, Ellen Ternan, who retired in 1859. Dickens's financial responsibilities in 1860, then, were legion: he sup-

DICKENS AS PUBLISHER

Dickens's first novel, *The Pickwick Papers*, which began appearing in 1836, marked the beginning of a revolution in publishing. Dickens had first come to public attention with *Sketches by Boz* earlier that same year; these were a series of illustrations accompanied by Dickens's text, originally meant simply to illuminate the image, but used by Dickens to develop longer and more complex characters and incidents. Dickens turned the sketch, a popular eighteenth-century form, into something larger, a novel, in his *Pickwick Papers*, with the text now dominating in the illustrations. Both the *Sketches* and *Pickwick Papers* were published in monthly "numbers," paperbound booklets containing a single episode. Often working only hours ahead of a printer's deadline, Dickens continued to publish his subsequent novels serially. Readers eagerly anticipated the next installment of their favorite novel, passing the current issue from reader to reader while they awaited further development of their hero's life.

Already popular beyond imagination, Dickens took control of the publishing process for his novels in the 1850s. As editor of the magazines *Household Words* and later *All the Year Round*, Dickens serialized his own and other authors' novels. *Great Expectations* was originally designed for monthly publication, but Dickens decided to issue it in weekly parts in *All the Year Round* when sales for another novel by Charles Lever proved disappointing. Sales of the magazine increased dramatically when Dickens's novel replaced Lever's, thus suggesting—along with the number of other venues in which the novel appeared—its immediate popularity. The novel appeared in *Harper's Weekly* in the United States while it was running in *All the Year Round* in England; Harper's subsequently published it in a two-volume book form, while Dickens's English publishers, Chapman & Hall, issued it in a three-volume version for libraries, and at least four other editions appeared in England and the United States in the next three years.

ported his wife and one child in one home, himself, his sister-in-law, and nine children in another, his mother, her daughter-in-law, and five children in yet a third, and Ellen Ternan and, at times, her mother and two sisters in a fourth. If Ternan was not the cold and contemptuous Estella, she may have served that function in Dickens's imagination, as she was certainly a financial and emotional drain on him (Carlisle, "Introduction," p. 15).

Another potential model for Estella is Maria Beadnell, Dickens's first serious love, whom he courted in the early 1830s. Seductive, witty, and both older and better educated than he was, Maria seems never to have taken Dickens's suit seriously, and she wounded him desperately by calling him a "boy" at his coming-of-age party; Estella is similarly contemptuous of Pip (Kaplan, p. 53). Whether Estella's original is Maria Beadnell, Ellen Ternan, or Sir Philip Sidney's "Stella," however, she remains the motivating force of the novel and entirely Dickens's own creation as well.

Finally, *Great Expectations* is a realistic novel. Realism, the dominant literary form of the middle nineteenth century, is a set of literary conventions that equate the "real" with material life in society; works that take for their subject the daily lives of relatively ordinary people, in a believable setting, are thus classed as "realistic." While events in the novel may strain credulity at times, Dickens's emphasis on the economic and social struggles of a single character, and the relationships he makes and breaks during those struggles, mark it as realistic in a solidly Victorian sense. Dickens emphasizes the conditions of Pip's life and Pip's own concerns with social status and hierarchy throughout the novel. Realism took many forms in the Victorian period, from the broad social satire of William Makepeace Thackeray (see **Vanity Fair**, in *WLAIT 3: British and Irish Literature and Its Times*) to the working-class fictions of Elizabeth Gaskell (in, for example, *Mary Barton*). Dickens's *Great Expectations* shares significant elements with works at both ends of the spectrum.

Events in History at the Time the Novel Was Written

England and India. In the beginning of the nineteenth century, England's presence in India was controlled by a single private enterprise, the British East India company. In 1857, however, the Sepoy Rebellion (also known as the Indian Mutiny) demonstrated to the English at home that all was not well in their distant colony. The thrust of the rebellion by Indian soldiers (known as sepoys) who served the East India Company lasted from May to December 1857, and marked the beginning of widespread Indian resistance to British rule. The British reaction was to transfer control of India from the East India Company directly to the English government. Victory for the British was hard-won, with traces of armed resistance erupting until the spring of 1859. Mean-

DICKENS AND COMEDY

A brief summary cannot convey the tone or quality of the comic writing for which Dickens was so justly famous. *Great Expectations*, to some reviewers' minds, marked Dickens's welcome return to his earlier, comic style, after the publication of "darker" masterpieces such as *Dombey and Son* and *Bleak House*. While the emphasis on crime and punishment, violence and degradation may not seem funny to contemporary readers, Dickens's genius lay in his ability to move freely between tragedy, melodrama, and comedy, sometimes even in one scene. In *Great Expectations* much of the comedy derives from the persistent social climbing of a variety of characters, from Mrs. Joe's "Uncle Pumblechook" to the church clerk, Mr. Wopsle, to Miss Havisham's obsequious and fawning relatives. Mr. Wopsle's abandonment of the church for the stage is the occasion of a famously comic scene in which Herbert and Pip attend an extremely unskilled production of *Hamlet*, which features a ghost who has a cough and a Hamlet who is badly overplayed by the foolish Wopsle. Pip himself does not escape the satirist's eye; his desperate attempts at gentility are often foiled by his own excesses, as when he hires a servant (whom he refers to as the "Avenger") and then has nothing for him to do.

while, the popular press in England published accounts of the rebellion that captured the English imagination, which led to India and things Indian becoming extremely popular. From perceptions of it as a rather distant colony, India became central to England's conception of itself; popular imperialism took hold and was consolidated when England's Queen Victoria crowned herself Empress of India in 1877. In *Great Expectations* the fictional firm Clarriker profits from the India trade, and the shift in the novel from Australia as a place of punishment to India as a source of wealth parallels the larger shift in England's imperial ambitions during the period.

Criminal justice. Although there were over 200 capital offenses on the books in the beginning of the nineteenth century, by the time Dickens was writing *Great Expectations* the death penalty was rarely invoked. Also by 1860, the hulks had been demolished and the sentence of transportation had been abolished. The middle nineteenth century saw the increasing professionalization of criminal justice, with the development of a professional police force, sentencing reforms, and the introduction of parole. Our sympathy for the convict Magwitch is thus consonant with the tenor of the times; an increasing emphasis on repentance and reform had replaced the earlier, more punitive system of criminal justice.

Reception. Early reviews of *Great Expectations* were somewhat mixed. While the critic in *Saturday Review* found it "new, original, powerful, and very entertaining," the novelist Margaret Oliphant, writing in *Blackwood's Edinburgh Magazine*, claimed that it "occupie[d] itself with incidents all but impossible, and in themselves strange, dangerous, and exciting . . . " (Oliphant in Rosenberg, pp. 617, 625). Writers such as George Gissing, G. B. Shaw, and George Orwell all praised *Great Expectations* for its realistic depiction of childhood, its use of the first-person narrator, and—as Shaw said—its "consistent truthful[ness]" (Shaw in Rosenberg, pp. 627, 633, 641). Edward Whipple, reviewing the novel in *Atlantic Monthly* in 1861, particularly praised Dickens's achievement in the character of Magwitch, and voiced the opinion which still stands today:

> The character [of Magwitch] is not only powerful in itself, but it furnishes pregnant and original hints to all philosophical investigators into the phenomenon of crime. In this wonderful creation Dickens follows the maxim of the great master of characterization and seeks "the soul of goodness in things evil." . . .

Altogether we take great joy in recording our opinion that *Great Expectations* is a masterpiece.
> (Whipple in Tredell, p. 23)

—Elisabeth Rose Gruner

For More Information

Carlisle, Janice. "Introduction." *Great Expectations*. Boston: Bedford, 1996.

Cody, David. "British Empire." *The Victorian Web*. 1988. http://landow.stg.brown.edu/victorian/history/empire/Empire.html (12 Oct. 2000).

Dickens, Charles. *Great Expectations*. Ed. Janice Carlisle. Boston: Bedford, 1996.

Everett, Glenn. "Political and Economic History of Great Britain." *The Victorian Web*. 1987. http://landow.stg.brown.edu/victorian/history/empire/Empire.html (12 Oct. 2000).

Gilmour, Robin. *The Idea of the Gentleman in the Victorian Novel*. London: Allen & Unwin, 1981.

Kaplan, Fred. *Dickens: A Biography*. New York: William Morrow, 1988.

Mitchell, Sally, ed. *Victorian Britain: An Encyclopedia*. New York: Garland, 1998.

Patten, Robert L. *Charles Dickens and his Publishers*. Oxford: Oxford University Press, 1978.

Philips, David. "'A New Engine of Power and Authority': The Institutionalization of Law-Enforcement in England 1780-1830." *Crime and the Law: The Social History of Crime in Western Europe since 1500*. Ed. V. A. C. Gatrell, et al. London: Europa, 1980.

Pool, Daniel. *What Jane Austen Ate and Charles Dickens Knew: From Fox-Hunting to Whist—the Facts of Daily Life in 19th-Century England*. New York: Simon & Schuster, 1993.

Rosenberg, Edgar, ed. *Great Expectations: A Norton Critical Edition*, by Charles Dickens. New York: Norton, 1999.

Tredell, Nicholas, ed. *Charles Dickens: Great Expectations*. New York: Columbia University Press, 1998.

Walder, Dennis. "Reading *Great Expectations*." *Approaching Literature: The Realist Novel*. Ed. Dennis Walder. London: Routledge in association with The Open University, 1995.

The Heat of the Day

by

Elizabeth Bowen

Elizabeth Bowen was born in 1899 into an Anglo-Irish family, the Bowens of Bowen's Court in County Cork in Dublin, Ireland. The relative security of her early years was shattered in 1906 by her father's nervous breakdown, after which her mother took Elizabeth to live in England. More upheaval followed when Elizabeth was 13 and her mother died of cancer. Elizabeth Bowen's first collection of short stories, *Encounters*, was published in 1923, and was followed soon after by her marriage to Alan Cameron. The couple settled in Oxford in 1925, and it was there that Bowen established important and lifelong friendships with other writers and intellectuals. The next 13 years were extremely productive, resulting in the publication of three further collections of stories and six novels, including *The Last September* (1929), *The House in Paris* (1935), and *The Death of the Heart* (1938). The outbreak of war in 1939 found Bowen living in London, where she and her husband remained throughout the war, except for occasional visits to Bowen's Court, which Bowen had inherited on her father's death in 1930. Bowen wrote two memoirs, *Seven Winters* and *Bowen's Court* (both 1942) and she continued to write short stories (which would be collected in *The Demon Lover and Other Stories* in 1945), but found that the stress and disruption of wartime prevented her from working successfully on longer fiction. Thus, although she began *The Heat of the Day* in 1944, Bowen finished it only after the war was over. When the novel finally appeared in 1949, it was instantly acclaimed for its

THE LITERARY WORK

A novel set in London during the middle of the Second World War; published in 1949.

SYNOPSIS

Stella Rodney's faith in her lover is called into question when she is told that he is a Nazi spy, in a novel that explores a woman's perspective on the psychological impact of war.

accurate portrayal of the atmosphere of wartime London, and of the intense, dislocated lives of those who remained there throughout the war.

Events in History at the Time of the Novel

The blitz. The main action in *The Heat of the Day* takes place between the beginning of September and the middle of November 1942, with a coda covering the period up to June 1944. However, the affair between Stella Rodney and Robert Kelway started earlier, in September 1940, at the beginning of the *blitzkrieg* ("lightning war"), or blitz, the air raids on British cities by the German Luftwaffe (air force) from September 1940 to May 1941.

Although war had been declared in September 1939, the British public saw little evidence of it until mid-1940 when, having overrun Holland, Belgium, Luxembourg, and France, Ger-

Elizabeth Bowen

many turned its attention to preparations for an invasion of Britain.

The Luftwaffe first attacked British coastal shipping and southern ports, and then its fighter defenses, which led to spectacular dogfights over the skies of southern England in what came to be known as the Battle of Britain. Then, from the end of August on, came the blitz: night bombing raids on London and other British cities. Germany's primary objective was to facilitate an invasion by crippling British war production, but as time went on and it became obvious that Germany would not gain the air superiority necessary to launch an invasion of Britain, the objective increasingly became to cause as much damage and terror as possible, in the hope that British morale would collapse.

The blitz transformed the phrase "the home front" from a metaphor into a reality. The destruction wrought by the bombing was enormous: by the time the blitz ended in mid-1941, more than 43,000 civilians had been killed and around 139,000 had been injured, and over 2 million houses had been damaged or destroyed, 60 percent of them in London (Calder, *The People's War*, p. 223). Never before had the civilian population of Britain been so closely involved in a war. As historian Angus Calder explains, this was:

the battle of an unarmed civilian population against incendiaries and high explosives; the battle of firemen, wardens, policemen, nurses and rescue workers against an enemy they could not hurt. The front line troops were doctors, parsons, telephonists, and people who in peacetime life had been clerks, builders, labourers and housewives.
(Calder, *The People's War*, p. 156)

The blitz was exhilarating as well as traumatic and exhausting. As Bowen explains in Chapter Five of *The Heat of the Day*, the sense of nightly danger gave the early days of the blitz a strange glamour: "one bought the poetic sense of it with the sense of death" (Bowen, *The Heat of the Day*, p. 90). Furthermore, by fostering a new sense of shared suffering and effort, and at the same time exposing shocking differences between the standards of living of the well-off and those of the poor, the blitz also gave rise to aspirations for a better, more democratic future.

The people who are holding the Front Line are fighting and suffering for a new democracy, . . . to which they themselves are giving the meaning . . . and its superscription is that simple remark of the docker "We are all in it together." Because, if it is not a "we-are-all-in-it-together" democracy, there is going to be hell to pay.
(Richie Calder in Hewison, p. 46)

"The lightless middle of the tunnel." Despite the damage done, the bombing raids of the blitz did not significantly disrupt British industry, nor crush people's resolve to fight, and in May 1941, having postponed indefinitely his plans to invade Britain, Hitler turned his attention to the invasion of Russia. The blitz itself was over, although British cities continued to be bombed intermittently throughout the rest of the war, and there was a renewal of intensive bombing in January-March 1944, known as the "little blitz." This little blitz reached its peak with five major raids on London between the 18th and the 24th of February. After the heroism of what Prime Minister Winston Churchill referred to as Britain's "finest hour"—its holding out against Germany during the Battle of Britain and the blitz—the months that followed were distinctly dispiriting. From the middle of February 1941 until October 1942, "the British public was not to hear of one victory on land . . . which seemed at all meaningful" (Calder, *The People's War*, p. 242). Instead there were endless "reverses, losses, deadlocks" and a "deadening acclimatization" to the routines of war (*The Heat of the Day*, p. 92). Paramount among these routines were the material discomforts of rationing and of blackouts that "transformed a capital city into a network of inscrutable canyons" and the psychological stress of dealing with the "stupefying" magnitude of the conflict (Bowen, *The Demon Lover*, pp. 219-23). In the novel, it is during this "lightless middle of the tunnel," when it was by no means clear that the Allies would eventually win, that Stella's faith in her lover, and her allegiance to her country, are tested by Harrison's allegation that her lover is a spy. (*The Heat of the Day*, p. 93)

El Alamein to D-Day. The first good news for the British public came on November 4, 1942, when British commander Bernard Montgomery's Eighth Army defeated General Erwin Rommel's forces at Al-Alamein in Egypt. Five days later, on November 9, forces of the Allied powers (Britain, France, and Russia) landed in French northwest Africa to do battle with forces of the Axis powers (Germany, Italy, and Japan), and the good news mounted. By early May 1943, the Allied forces had completely defeated the Axis forces on the southern side of the Mediterranean. The summer of 1943 saw the Allied landings in Italy, and the defeat of German forces on the Russian front, and from then on, Hitler's only hope of victory was to delay his own defeat so long that the Allies would fall apart (Parker, p. 177). However, the Allies finally opened a "Second Front" in western Europe in the summer of 1944, landing over 2 million troops in northwestern France in the three months that followed D-Day, June 6, 1944, the day the allies invaded German-occupied Europe. Also, the Russians began an offensive in the East, after which Germany's defeat was inevitable.

Ireland's neutrality during World War II. The Irish Free State had won its independence from Britain in 1922, and, although it remained a formal member of the British Commonwealth until 1949, in practical terms it had been fully independent since 1937. The new state, Eire, remained neutral during the Second World War, and although on balance its neutrality favored Britain, there was mutual mistrust between the two countries: Britain suspected Eire of harboring Axis agents and of secretly helping to re-supply its U-boats, while "when the Germans accidentally bombed a Dublin suburb, most of those on the ground thought the British had raided them" (Dear and Foot, p. 324). On an individual basis, however, many citizens of Eire committed themselves to the Allied cause: around 50,000 volunteered for the British

armed forces, and many more were employed in civilian war work in Britain (Calder, *The Myth of the Blitz*, pp. 65-66).

For the Anglo-Irish, descendants of the English Protestant ruling class that had established itself in Ireland from the early seventeenth century onwards, wartime allegiances were particularly complicated. In *The Heat of the Day*, the Anglo-Irish Cousin Francis fiercely defends Eire's right to independence and to determine its own position in the war, but hopes that it will enter the war on the Allied side, and, when this does not happen, Francis travels to England to offer his services.

DUNKIRK

As France was falling to the German "blitzkreig," or lightning war, in May 1940, plans were made to evacuate British soldiers fighting in France from the northern French port of Dunkirk. The Dunkirk evacuation is famous as much for the method of the rescue as for the number of soldiers saved: between 850 and 950 ships and small craft were involved, and for the last five days of the evacuation, these included civilian vessels with volunteer crews. Over eight days, under heavy attack from the Luftwaffe, these vessels succeeded in evacuating around 338,000 Allied troops, including 110,000 French soldiers (Dear and Foot, pp. 312-13; Keegan, p. 81). This success was, initially at least, a boost to civilian morale, but as Prime Minister Winston Churchill said at the time, "wars are not won by evacuations": Dunkirk was a "colossal military disaster" (Churchill in Calder, *The People's War*, p. 110). Many of the evacuated soldiers themselves shared this view, feeling humiliated and resentful of those—their own commanders—whom they considered responsible. In *The Heat of the Day*, Robert Kelway attributes his decision to betray his country to the disgust he felt during his experience at Dunkirk.

Women's roles in wartime. With the conscription of men into the armed forces, and the need for increased production to meet demand for war supplies, the war prompted women to work outside the home in unprecedented numbers. Two million British women took on paid work, or moved from domestic service into different jobs between 1939 and 1942 (Parker, p. 141). Some joined the armed forces in noncombat roles, while others worked as air raid wardens or am-

Two German aircraft over London in autumn 1940. Nazi aircraft launched night-time bombing raids
on London to cause destruction and deflate British morale.

bulance drivers, in factories or on farms as so-
called "land girls." By 1943 it had become almost
impossible for a woman younger than 40 to avoid
war-related work unless she had heavy family duties, or was caring for a war worker whom she
lodged: 90 percent of single women between 18
and 40 years old, and 80 percent of married
women, were in the forces or in industry (Calder,
The People's War, pp. 331-32).

War work offered some women more freedom
and a wider range of experiences than they had
ever known. Others, however, particularly many
working-class women, were trapped in monoto-
nous factory work, and found themselves burdened with two jobs—toiling at laborious employment outside the house, and raising the

children and managing the housework within. In
the novel, Stella Rodney's perception of the war
as a social opportunity, and her employment in
"secret, exacting, not unimportant work" for a
(fictional) government organization "better called
Y.X.D." are much more typical of the experience
of middle- and upper-class women than of the
majority (*The Heat of the Day*, p. 26). Perhaps
more representative are the experiences of two
of the novel's other characters, Louie Lewis and
her friend Connie. Louie is married to a soldier
and so is exempt from compulsory war work but,
like many who found they could not survive on
the allowance they received as servicemen's
wives, has to work in a factory. Connie, single
and in her early thirties, and therefore classed as

a "mobile woman," eligible to be sent wherever in the country labor was required, worked in a tobacco kiosk before the war, and volunteered to become an air raid warden in September 1939. Although she finds she dislikes the work, it is better than the alternative of being allocated, with little say in the matter, to factory work or to a women's branch of the services: "a Mobile Woman," she thinks, "dared not look sideways these days—you might find yourself in Wolverhampton . . . or at the bottom of a mine, or in the A.T.S. [Auxiliary Territorial Service] with some bitch blowing a bugle at you till you got up in the morning" (*The Heat of the Day*, p. 148). Connie's fear of finding herself at the bottom of a mine is perhaps excessive, as even with the labor shortage no women went down the coal mines. But Wolverhampton, one of the industrial cities in the Midlands where many women were sent to work, and the A.T.S., a women's service that supported the army by taking over many noncombat tasks and freeing men for frontline duty, would have been strong possibilities.

The Novel in Focus

Plot summary. *The Heat of the Day* opens in Regent's Park in central London on the evening of the first Sunday of September 1942. Louie Lewis, who has spent the day wandering in the park looking for company, meets the as-yet-unnamed Harrison at an outdoor concert, and, intrigued by his seemingly "cryptic behaviour," tries to strike up a conversation. He rebuffs her, saying he has a date (*The Heat of the Day*, p. 9). Meanwhile, Stella Rodney waits apprehensively in her nearby flat: despite her having already firmly rejected Harrison's advances, he has asked to see her again, and some "undefined threat" has been implied (*The Heat of the Day*, pp. 22-23).

When Harrison arrives, he tells Stella that her lover, Robert Kelway, who works at the War Office, is passing information to the enemy. Harrison, who has been watching Robert for an unnamed counterespionage organization, claims that he can prevent him from being arrested if Stella will agree to end her relationship with Robert and take up with him. Incensed and incredulous, Stella rejects the proposal, but Harrison gives her a month to consider it. Later that evening, Stella's son Roderick arrives for two days' leave from the army. Having borrowed Robert's robe, he finds a piece of paper in the pocket, and Stella's reaction reveals to the reader that the seeds of suspicion about Robert have taken root.

Chapter Four goes back four months to the funeral of Francis Morris, a cousin of Stella's former husband Victor. At the funeral, Stella is snubbed by most of the family, who believe her to be a *femme fatale* and responsible for the breakdown of her marriage. She discovers, however, that in the absence of any child of his own, Cousin Francis has left his estate in Ireland, Mount Morris, to her son, Roderick. She also meets Harrison for the first time; initially she takes him to be an inmate of Wistaria Lodge, the home for uncertified mental patients in which Francis's wife Nettie has been living. She is forced

---

BOWEN'S WAR "ACTIVITIES"

Elizabeth Bowen worked as an air raid warden during the war, but she also volunteered her services to the Ministry of Information, thinking she might be able to help in relation to Ireland. Her activities in this regard, which had the added benefit of allowing her to come and go between London and Bowen's Court, involved attempting to understand Irish attitudes to the war, and in particular whether Eire could be persuaded to allow Britain to use ports in the south and west of the country. In her report to the Ministry, she stressed that Britain must not attempt to use force to gain access to the ports. She also, "castigated . . . the Anglo-Irish for presenting themselves as England's stronghold in Ireland. If they merged their interests with the Irish people, she said, they could make Ireland a very much more solid and possible country with which to deal" (Glendinning, p. 162). Bowen's work for the Ministry led to her essay "Eire" (1941), an attempt to explain to the British the situation in wartime Eire, and its reasons for choosing neutrality in the war.

---

to abandon this notion after Harrison tells her that he was a friend of Cousin Francis's, had visited Francis at Mount Morris, and had met with him in London shortly before his death. Still, she is uncertain about what sort of man Harrison is and what his profession might be.

Chapter Five looks even further back, to describe the beginning of Stella and Robert's relationship in the "heady autumn of the first London air raids" (*The Heat of the Day*, p. 90). Having chosen to remain in London because she found that "the climate of danger" suited her, Stella felt "on furlough from her own life," and, if anything, this distance from her everyday outer world increased when she fell in love with Robert: they lived in their own private sphere, "afloat on [a] tideless, hypnotic, futureless day-to-day" (*The Heat of the Day*, p. 100). Harrison's visit has disturbed this world, however, and a few days later, Stella tentatively raises with Robert the question of what she should feel if somebody told her something "preposterous" about him (*The Heat of the Day*, p. 102). He responds flippantly.

In early October, Robert takes Stella to meet his mother and his sister Ernestine at their house,

---

MI5 AND MI6

During the war, responsibility for intelligence relating to national security was divided between MI5 (the Security Service), MI6 (the Secret Intelligence Service), and the Special Branch of the (London) Metropolitan Police. MI5 had the role of "evaluating and advising on all intelligence relating to subversion (other than that relating to known Irish and anarchist groups and to the maintenance of public order, which remained in the province of the Special Branch) and to espionage" within the United Kingdom and, with the co-operation of local authorities, the countries of the empire. MI6 gathered foreign intelligence in relation to national security. MI5 was responsible for detecting and intercepting German spies in Britain; it would therefore have been MI5 that was watching the novel's Robert Kelway if he was suspected of passing information to the Germans. In the latter years of the war, MI6 had a number of notable successes; in particular, agents' reports, along with photographic reconnaissance, allowed the Allies to neutralize radar defenses around the German heartland, and to disrupt the development and deployment of German V-weapons—flying bombs and bombardment rockets that could be fired at British cities from across the channel—thus saving many Allied lives.

Holme Dene, on the outskirts of a Home Counties dormitory town. The visit is not a success: to Stella, the place seems like "a bewitched wood," and the widowed Mrs. Kelway the malign presence at its heart (*The Heat of the Day*, p. 110). As they leave, Stella notices that Robert is limping from his Dunkirk wound, something she has previously observed that he does only when he feels like a wounded man.

The sinister atmosphere of the Holme Dene edifice seems to follow Stella back to London,

where, when she returns to her flat, she finds Harrison waiting for her. He says that he knows she has been thinking things over, adding that her visit to Holme Dene was a "look at the first place where rot could start" (*The Heat of the Day*, p. 131). They quarrel, Stella telling him that she cannot bear the way he has "distorted love" by "making a spy of [her]," and eventually he leaves, promising to return (*The Heat of the Day*, pp. 138-42).

Meanwhile, Louie, intrigued by her encounter with Harrison in the park, hopes to run into him again. Chapter Eight describes Louie's loneliness without her soldier husband and her parents, who have been killed by a bomb, and her attempt to find recognition and understanding in a series of one-night stands. From Connie, an acerbic ARP (Air Raid Precautions) warden who moves into her building and befriends her, Louie acquires an addiction to newspapers. But whereas Connie's attitude to the news is suspicious, Louie reads the papers in order to feel included in the "one big family" of the nation at war (*The Heat of the Day*, p. 152).

At the end of October, Stella goes to Mount Morris to attend to some business on Roderick's behalf. While she is there, she finds that Harrison's account of having visited Cousin Francis is true. She also has a vision of the generations of women of Mount Morris going "not quite mad" from the isolation of a purely private life in which they "knew no choices, made no decisions" and "suspected what they refused to prove"(*The Heat of the Day*, p. 174). These revelations prompt an obscure change in her: walking in the woods near the house, she seems to draw strength and hope that "something might intervene to save her" from the place itself. At this moment she hears that "Montgomery's through" in Egypt (*The Heat of the Day*, pp. 177-78). She returns to London and confronts Robert with Harrison's allegations. He denies them, and later that evening proposes to her but, although she accepts his denial, she cannot agree to marry him.

While Stella is in Ireland, Roderick arranges to visit Nettie, Cousin Francis's widow, to set his mind at rest over the fact that he has inherited what he thinks of as her house. From Nettie he learns that it was his father Victor, and not Stella, who ended his parents' marriage: he left Stella so that he could live with the nurse who had cared for him after he was wounded in World War I. When Roderick rings his mother to ask her why she never told him this, Harrison is at her flat, and she and he discuss the issue: Stella explains that she did not challenge the story that she had been the one to leave Victor because she would "rather sound a monster than look a fool" (*The Heat of the Day*, p. 224).

Harrison takes Stella to dinner and says he knows she has alerted Robert that others suspect Robert of being a spy. Convinced by Harrison's account of the changes in Robert's behavior since the night she returned from Ireland—changes that would be consistent with guilt—Stella is on the brink of agreeing to save Robert by becoming Harrison's mistress when Louie, who has mistakenly come to the same bar looking for Connie, interrupts them. A furious Harrison turns viciously on Louie, and as she is about to leave, Stella indicates to Harrison that "a friend is out of danger," meaning that she agrees to his proposal (*The Heat of the Day*, p. 240). But Harrison unexpectedly sends both women home.

While Stella, Harrison, and Louie are in the bar, Robert is at Holme Dene. He has been called there by Ernestine and Mrs. Kelway to discuss the offer they have received for the house, which has been for sale for many years. Their farcical and inconclusive exchange is terminated by a mysterious telephone call, which no one answers. The following night, Robert goes to Stella's flat and confesses that he has indeed been passing information to the enemy: the ringing telephone, he says, suddenly brought home to him the possibility that he might be arrested and never see her again. The lovers spend a final night together, during which Robert explains that he chose to side with the enemy because England seems to him to be "muddled, mediocre, damned," while Nazism represents a better, more definite, future (*The Heat of the Day*, p. 268). In the early morning, believing the other exits from the flat to be watched, Robert leaves through a skylight onto the roof. He slips, or jumps, to his death.

The last two chapters form a coda to the novel. The morning of Robert's death brings news of the Allied landings in North Africa. A week later, on the day when, for the first time in three years, church bells across the country were rung to celebrate the Allies' victories in the desert, Stella visits Roderick to talk to him about his father and to explain what happened to Robert. She finds, however, that she cannot explain it because she knows "less than her little part" of the story (*The Heat of the Day*, p. 296).

Because she wants to understand what happened, Stella longs to see Harrison, but he has disappeared. He eventually reappears in the middle of the "Little Blitz" of February 1944, but their meeting is far from conclusive: Harrison cannot tell her what happened because the night before Robert's death he was switched to another case and since then, he has been out of England. He seems to hope that they might now be able to begin an affair, but Stella insists that it is impossible, because the link between them—Robert—is gone. She plans, she says, to get married to a cousin of a cousin.

That same week finds Roderick at Mount Morris, taking possession of his inheritance and becoming aware for the first time of the claims on him of both the past and the future. In London, too, a future is taking shape: Louie announces to Connie that she is going to have a baby. The child is not her husband's, and Connie takes charge of helping Louie through the pregnancy. Just at the point that Connie sits down to write a letter to Tom, trying to explain Louie's unfaithfulness, a telegram is delivered saying that he has been killed. Louie's child, Thomas Victor, is finally born in June 1944, shortly after the D-Day landings. The novel closes in September 1944 with Louie's return, with her son, to Seale-on-Sea where she grew up.

"You have been my country": the individual in wartime. While Stella still believes in Robert's innocence and in the integrity of their love, she thinks of Harrison as "an enemy," and compares him to the Gestapo (*The Heat of the Day*, pp. 23,33). Once she is convinced of Robert's guilt, however, she faces a choice between loyalty to her lover—which would require her to give him up for Harrison—and loyalty to her country, which would mean Robert's arrest. By the time she chooses to try to save Robert, the chain of events that will lead to his death has already begun.

The choice between lover and country is particularly difficult for Stella because she feels profoundly disconnected from the things that would give personal meaning to loyalty to her country. Her dislocation is brought home to her at Holme Dene, where she becomes acutely aware that, as a divorced, 40-year-old working woman who has lost touch with her family and her social class, she is a "hybrid" who has "come loose from her moorings," and whose past has "dissolved behind her" (*The Heat of the Day*, pp. 114-15). The disruptions of war have only accentuated this feeling; indeed, for all three of the novel's main characters, as Harrison puts it, the war "hasn't started anything that wasn't there already" (*The Heat of the Day*, p. 33).

Robert's account of the reasons for his betrayal of his country, as almost every critic who has written about the book has noted, is singularly unsatisfying. He offers only fragments of an explanation; Stella's description of it as just "wildness and images" seems justified (*The Heat of the Day*, p. 282). As far as his reasons can be re-

BRITISH FASCISTS AND NAZI SPIES

Robert Kelway is not unusual in his dissatisfaction with English society: such feelings were common in the years between the wars. He *is* unusual in that his dissatisfaction turns him into a fascist rather than a communist, as would have been more likely in Britain at the time, and even more unusual in that this does not happen until 1940, after Dunkirk. In the 1930s, on the other hand, fascist sympathizers were far from unknown in Britain; at its peak in 1934, Sir Oswald Mosley's British Union of Fascists had perhaps 30,000 members (Calder, *The People's War*, p. 133). But support for fascism had declined by the beginning of World War II, and never recovered, while popular sympathy for communism seems to have risen during the war (Calder, *The Myth of the Blitz*, p. 77). Despite this decline, fascists were seen as a threat to British security. In May 1940, when paranoia over the possibility of a German invasion of Britain was at its height, Mosley's party was banned, and he and 1,600 other fascists, along with others thought to pose a threat to national security, were imprisoned without trial.

Fears of a Nazi "Fifth Column" waiting to destabilize Britain from within turned out to be unjustified. In reality, Germany was singularly unsuccessful in establishing agents in Britain. By the end of 1940, all of the 21 agents dispatched so far had been captured and either imprisoned or "turned" to become double agents, sending misinformation to their German controllers. The German strategy to infiltrate Britain, which continued into 1943, failed miserably. Later in the war the double agents gave very useful information to the Allies, helping them deceive Germany about the location of the D-Day landings.

constructed from these fragments, it seems that he grew up in a malevolent, inquisitorial atmosphere at Holme Dene, with imitation antique architecture and passages that resemble "swastika-arms" (*The Heat of the Day*, p. 258). The experience has bred in him an instinct to conceal what he is up to, and a loathing for his "unwhole," rootless "race"—by which he means the

men of his generation, growing up in a world dominated by Mrs. Kelways, and born too late to believe in the ideals of patriotism and honor for which a slightly earlier generation had died in World War I (*The Heat of the Day*, pp. 272, 276; see Rawlinson, p. 102). Robert believes that the humiliating retreat from Dunkirk showed that England was doomed by its own emptiness and weakness to be defeated by Germany.

His turning to the other side, he tells Stella, gave him "a new heredity" and a new confidence that came not only from being able to get away with acting secretly, but from the sense that the fascists stand for a more noble future—one that has cut the unmanly "cackle" out of life, one based on totalitarian power rather than freedom (*The Heat of the Day*, pp. 273, 282).

Stella rejects Robert's justification of his treachery, seeing it as a betrayal of *their* country, the London in which they have loved each other, and of the other people who inhabited it with them (*The Heat of the Day*, pp. 274-75). She concludes, however, that she cannot judge him; he is a product of his time.

Although Robert dies believing that his ideas are worth living for, the revelation of his betrayal has awoken in Stella a realization: in her belief that their love had nothing to do with the times in which they were living, she had been under an illusion. As the anonymous narrator observes, "they were not alone, nor had they been from the start. . . . Their time sat in the third place at their table. They were the creatures of history" (*The Heat of the Day*, p. 194). But the dilemmas of allegiance in *The Heat of the Day* are not resolved in favor of an uncomplicated affirmation of patriotism and commitment to the Allied war effort. Indeed, it has been argued that "the precise project of the book is to entertain the thought that vulgarity dwells with the democratic victors of 1945, and civilization with fascism" (Sinfield, p. 17). Literary historian Mark Rawlinson contends, however, that Bowen is not endorsing fascism, let alone suggesting that the war should not be fought, but expressing fear about the cost of the war, even in the event of an Allied victory.

The war affected almost every aspect of people's lives, from what they ate and wore to where they worked. Furthermore, the government expected all citizens to support the war effort, whatever their personal beliefs. These aspects of wartime life prompted fears, even among those who were committed to the Allied cause, "that the survival of private life"—which the Allies believed they were fighting to preserve from totalitarianism—"demanded its surrender" to the needs of the wartime state (Rawlinson, p. 33). Many writers on the right and on the left worried that the legacy of the war would be a devaluation of the individual in the face of an increasingly powerful state. These fears grew as the war dragged on, and they lasted into the immediate postwar years, when Bowen was writing *The Heat of the Day* (Hewison, pp. 106-202).

Despite her active involvement in war work, Bowen seems to have had doubts about the kind of society that was emerging from the war, and particularly about the incoming Labour Government's vision of an increased role for the state. Writing to a friend in the summer of 1945, she stated that although she had adored Churchill's England for its "stylishness," she "[couldn't] stick [put up with] all these little middle-class Labour wets with their Old London School of Economics ties and their women. Scratch any of those cuties and you find the governess. Or so I have always found" (Bowen in Glendinning, p. 166). Certainly, Bowen felt very strongly the war's threat to private life, and the need to assert the importance of the individual. In her postscript to her collection of wartime stories, *The Demon Lover*, she suggests that all wartime writing is "resistance writing," in which "personal life . . . put up its own resistance to the annihilation that was threatening it—war" (*The Demon Lover*, p. 220). This resistance, as Bowen saw it, meant clinging to "every object or image or place or love or fragment of memory with which [individual] destiny seemed to be identified, and by which the destiny seemed to be assured" (*The Demon Lover*, p. 220). But, as Stella discovers in *The Heat of the Day*, an attachment to a personal world inevitably brings one back to face the "hammerlike chops" of the war (*The Demon Lover*, p. 219). Remembering the "crystal ruined London morning when she had woken to [Robert's] face," she realizes that he has betrayed both their love *and* the "country"—the time and place—of which it was a part (*The Heat of the Day*, p. 274). Having thought that, through their love, she had "turned away from everything to one face," she instead finds herself "face to face with everything" (*The Heat of the Day*, p. 195). Stella's awareness of her unavoidable involvement in the war is experienced as a loss rather than a gain: when we last see her in February 1944 she has learned how to be a survivor, but seems to care little about whether she lives or dies.

Some critics have argued that Stella's difficulty in choosing between allegiance to Robert and to her country is compounded by her sense that, as a woman, she is marginal to the largely masculine enterprise of war. For these critics, despite Stella's work for "Y.X.D.," in the espionage plot she is the object of both Robert's and Harrison's desires: both men assume that she has no opinion of her own about the larger political questions at stake; and the choice that Harrison offers her—to take up with him or let Robert be arrested, is far from real decisionmaking. In this reading *The Heat of the Day* is an exploration not only of the status of the individual, but also of women in wartime.

Sources and literary context. *The Heat of the Day* was a product of Bowen's own experiences in wartime London and Ireland. The sense it conveys of the strange combination of excitement and fear during the blitz, and the exhaustion that succeeded it, were Bowen's own. The relationship between Stella and Robert, too, is generally thought to be modeled on Bowen's own affair with the Canadian diplomat Charles Ritchie, seven years her junior, whom she met in 1941, and to whom she dedicated *The Heat of the Day*. Specific details of their affair found their way into the novel: the description of the roses in Regents Park in Chapter One, for example, seems to come from a visit Bowen and Ritchie paid to the Park in September 1941 (Glendinning, pp. 148-49). More importantly, Bowen seems to have drawn on the intensity of her relationship with Ritchie, and their shared sense of being "outsider-insiders" in England, in depicting Stella and Robert's affair and the issues of allegiance it raises. The Anglo-Irish Bowen, and the Anglo-Canadian Ritchie, writes Glendinning, were able to "pass" in England, but felt "in a subtle sense secretly different, like spies" (Glendinning, pp. 138-39). *The Heat of the Day* has affinities with other British wartime fiction. Its descriptions of the blitz, for example, echo those of Henry Green's *Caught* and Graham Greene's *The Ministry of Fear* (both 1943), the latter of which, as Hermione Lee points out, is another "novel about treachery and concealment between lovers" (Lee, p. 169). *The Heat of the Day*'s portrayal of the malaise of middle-class England in the deadly atmosphere of Holme Dene also has much in common with other writings of the 1930s and 1940s, as does its anxiety about the shape of the postwar world, which found its best-known expression in Evelyn Waugh's **Brideshead Revisited** (1945; also in *WLAIT 4: British and Irish Literature and Its Times*).

Reception. *The Heat of the Day* was an instant success when it appeared in February 1949, selling 45,000 copies almost immediately. But critics had reservations about the novel. The reviewer for *The New York Times* complained that "its principal characters are . . . never believable human beings," and wished for "the sure hand of an expert in psychological thrillers such as Graham Greene" (Prescott, p. 21). This view was echoed by the anonymous reviewer for the *Times Literary Supplement*, who found the scene in which Robert explains his actions "the least satisfactory in the book," and lamented that "if only we fully understood him, what a magnificent book this would be" ("Climate of Treason," p. 152). Bowen's friend and fellow-novelist Rosamond Lehmann disagreed with these complaints about Robert's plausibility, arguing that Robert "had to be discovered through Stella"; Lehmann was, however, concerned by the lack of explanation in their final scene. She was bothered by the absence of any real justification for Robert's not having "been a Communist and therefore pro-Russian, pro-Ally, rather than pro-'enemy'" (Lehmann in Glendinning, p. 151).

Subsequent critics have tended to argue, however, that Bowen was not interested in writing a conventional spy novel or thriller, but in exploring what she called the psychological war-climate. Lee, for example, acknowledges that considered "as a spy-fiction against the work of Conrad or Kipling, Buchan or Greene, Fleming or le Carré, [*The Heat of the Day*] is obviously risible," containing as it does "no scenes of recruitment, no government department meetings, no stories of infiltration, no details of espionage or counter-spying, no information about Intelligence, nothing about the operations of M.I.5 or S.I.S"; she argues, however, that the novel is actually "a woman's view of the male world of 'Intelligence,' rendering in personal terms 'a war of dry cerebration inside windowless walls'" (Lee, p. 175).

—Ingrid Gunby

For More Information

Bowen, Elizabeth. *The Demon Lover*. London: Jonathan Cape, 1952.

———. *The Heat of the Day*. London: Vintage, 1998.

Calder, Angus. *The People's War: Britain 1939-1945*. London: Jonathan Cape, 1969.

"The Climate of Treason." Review of *The Heat of the Day*, by Elizabeth Bowen, *The Times Literary Supplement*, 5 March 1949, 152.

Dear, I. C. B., and M. R. D. Foot, eds. *The Oxford Companion to the Second World War*. Oxford: Oxford University Press, 1995.

Glendinning, Victoria. *Elizabeth Bowen: Portrait of a Writer*. London: Weidenfeld and Nicolson, 1977.

Hewison, Robert. *Under Siege: Literary Life in London 1939-45*. London: Methuen, 1988.

Lassner, Phyllis. *Elizabeth Bowen*. Basingstoke: Macmillan, 1990.

Lee, Hermione. *Elizabeth Bowen: An Estimation*. London: Vision; and Totowa, N.J.: Barnes and Noble, 1981.

Parker, R. A. C. *The Second World War: A Short History*. Rev. ed. Oxford: Oxford University Press, 1997.

Prescott, Orville. "Books of the Times." Review of *The Heat of the Day*, by Elizabeth Bowen. *The New York Times*, 21 February 1949, 21.

Rawlinson, Mark. *British Writing of the Second World War*. Oxford: Clarendon Press, 2000.

Sinfield, Alan. *Literature Politics and Culture in Post-war Britain*. 2d ed. London and Atlantic Highlands, N.J.: Athlone Press, 1997.

A House for
Mr. Biswas

by

V. S. Naipaul

The descendent of East Indian indentured servants, Vidiadhar Surajprasad Naipaul was born August 17, 1932, in Chaguanas, Trinidad. His father, Seepersad Naipaul (1906-53), was a journalist and an aspiring writer whose literary ambitions spread to his sons Vidiadhar and Shiva. A bright student, Vidiadhar Naipaul gained admission to Queen's Royal College—one of just four secondary schools on the island—and in 1948 won a coveted government-sponsored scholarship to study abroad. He entered University College at Oxford in England as a literature student in 1950, graduated in 1953, and began working for the British Broadcasting Corporation, hosting the program *Caribbean Voices*. He also wrote for the *New Statesman* literary journal and published his first novel, *The Mystic Masseur*, in 1957. Two novels followed, earning him a reputation as a formidable new novelist, but it was with the publication of *A House for Mr. Biswas* in 1961 that Naipaul's work achieved masterpiece status. Not part of the colonial ruling establishment, nor of the native culture, the protagonist is an East Indian in Trinidad, an ethnic outsider searching for a sense of self and place. Through this protagonist, the novel focuses on a displaced people reinventing themselves in a foreign and often inhospitable land.

Events in History at the Time of The Novel

From indentured servant to twentieth-century minority. Trinidad's cultural and ethnic melange

> ## THE LITERARY WORK
> A tragicomic novel set in Trinidad at the turn of the century through the 1950s; published in 1961.
>
> ## SYNOPSIS
> An East Indian searches for meaning, identity, and a sense of place in colonial Trinidad.

stems from its 500-year history of conquest and foreign occupation. Originally the home of Amerindian peoples, the island was sighted in 1498 by Admiral Christopher Columbus, who claimed it for Spain. With the Spanish came thousands of European settlers and African slaves to develop the colony, driving out native peoples and dramatically transforming the landscape. By the 1790s the immigrant population, mainly French Catholics settlers and African slaves, had wholly displaced the indigenous peoples, outnumbering them by a factor of 16 to 1.

By this time sugar had become "king," and plantations dominated the island and economy. Lured by the lucrative trade, the British seized control of the West Indian colony in 1797. A wave of British settlers followed the Spanish and French, while African slaves continued to comprise the bulk of the workforce. In 1834, slaves in the British Empire were emancipated, and indentured servants from another of Britain's colonies, India, were brought to Trinidad as re-

V. S. Naipaul

placements. From 1838 to 1917 some 144,000 East Indians moved to Trinidad under a policy of unrestricted immigration to support the sugar industry. Typically indentured for five years, East Indians received land grants at the expiration of their contracts or after ten years of residence—often in place of return passage to India—in the interest of keeping a low-wage workforce on the island. Approximately one-third of the servants returned to India, while the majority stayed and established shops, opened businesses, and farmed sugar on their newly acquired land.

Because of its colonial heritage and legacy of slavery and indentured servitude, twentieth-century Trinidad lacked a unified national cultural identity. White Europeans dominated the government and upper classes, yet people of African or East Indian descent comprised 80 percent of the population. Racism and discrimination were rampant in society, with the inhabitants strictly divided along economic and color lines.

> Whites in the Caribbean did not fully accept the changing reality of the new post-slavery conditions . . . [and] as long as sugar remained "king," all social goals were subordinated to boosting production. Little positive incentive was given to develop the arts, to inculcate a

sense of national identity that was faithful to the plurality of the peoples.

> (Knight, p. 188)

What emerged in place of a national identity were two strong "minority" communities who shared only their rejection of European culture and who openly clashed with each other. While white elites remained at the top of society, East Indians and the descendants of African slaves were forced to compete for the same meager allotments of land and opportunities. Put in this competitive position, they showed a general distrust for each other and segregated themselves socially. The two communities adapted differently: while the descendants of African slaves, whose ancestors had come from diverse regions, created their own new culture in Trinidad, East Indians held firmly to old Asian traditions, showing a steadfast refusal to assimilate or change cultural patterns that impressed many of the African descendants as arrogance. Tensions festered and at times flared. The sight of East Indians cheering India's cricket team over that of the West Indies was enough to nearly start a "war" (Saft, p. 77).

The sense of displacement and lack of a national community in Trinidad are key concerns in *A House for Mr. Biswas*, as they were for Naipaul personally. Both Mr. Biswas and Naipaul seek identity—a "home"—a sense of place and self that did not readily exist for East Indians in Trinidad at the time. In the novel Mr. Biswas marvels that Pastor, an African who makes his living filling out forms for illiterates outside the county courthouse, has discovered and assumed his role in society. "Even Pastor, for all his grumbling, had found his place," Mr. Biswas notes. Upon this revelation, Mr. Biswas "perceived that the starts of apprehension he felt at the sight of every person in the street did not come from fear at all; only from regret, envy, despair" (Naipaul, *A House for Mr. Biswas*, p. 318). As an East Indian colonial in a British colony, Mr. Biswas is physically in one place and culturally in another, and so struggles to find his identity.

Exile off Main Street. As a consequence of immigrating as servants, East Indians were "at the bottom of the social scale" in Trinidad (Rodman, p. 19). Their dark skin, comparable to that of the African slave, only intensified their lowly status. According to Trinidad's first black prime minister, Eric Williams (1956-81), West Indians' "concern with colour and lightness of skin was almost an obsession" during the first part of the twentieth century (Williams in Rodman, p. 20).

The legacy of slavery and servitude had long-term effects on living conditions and social interaction in Trinidad. Division existed not only between Europeans and their Asian and African counterparts, but also within Trinidad's Asian and African communities, of which no segment was more removed or outcast than the East Indians. Physically they were separated because they lived in rural Trinidad. East Indians made up just 4 percent of the population of Trinidad's chief town, the Port of Spain, before 1917, although they comprised approximately 40 percent of the total population. Socially they were barred because of their distinct cultural and low-status farm labor.

The living and working conditions of East Indians in Trinidad further isolated them. The 25-cent wage of indenture was tantamount to slavery (a full 43 cents below the recommended minimum wage in 1919). Poverty was widespread, with nearly 20 percent of the population filing for poor relief in 1911 and their numbers surging annually. Through the 1940s, malnutrition soared—80 percent of the rural, mostly East Indian population in 1920 was infested with hookworms. Meanwhile, wages, instead of rising with inflation, dropped annually through 1935.

Compounding the poverty, housing was scarce. Just 48,000 houses existed on the island in 1911, which together with an additional 45,000 barrack rooms (former slave quarters) had to provide shelter for the bulk of Trinidad's 300,000 inhabitants. As evidenced in the novel, dozens of East Indians lived in a single dwelling or squatted in ramshackle squatter's cabins erected illegally on others' property, as Mr. Biswas's mother and many aunts and uncles do in the novel. Ideally the East Indian household sheltered one nuclear family or one extended family (traditionally a mother, father, unmarried children, and married sons with their wives and children), with the family sharing "a common kitchen" and "family purse" (Klass, p. 44). But the complications of life in Trinidad, including the dearth of dwelling places, often interfered with realizing the ideal. The acute housing problem among East Indians helps explain why home ownership is an all-consuming passion for Mr. Biswas in the novel (as does Biswas's search for individual identity).

East Indian social life in Trinidad. East Indians at first voluntarily segregated themselves from other communities, in large part because of cultural tradition. They practiced Hindu or Muslim religions, which were not officially recognized by the colonial government, and married within their own religious group. As evidenced in the novel, interaction between cultural groups in Trinidad was very limited. Occasionally Mr. Biswas sneaks off to Chinese restaurants, but this is a clear act of defiance against his wife's family. In fact, friendships, business relationships, and formal marriages between Trinidad's various cultural groups were rare in Trinidad until the 1940s, when social and political change began to occur. In the novel, Mr. Biswas's uncle marries a Chinese woman, whom the family never formally recognizes. They acknowledge only Hindu marriages, ironically, since the British government only acknowledged Christian marriages at the time. Similarly children borne by Chinese or African women to East Indian men were not officially recognized by East Indian families; such "illegitimate" children could not inherit property and were otherwise ostracized.

While East Indians in Trinidad maintained Hindu (85 percent) and Muslim traditions by keeping the patriarchal family structure and to some extent the caste system alive, both traditions weakened over time. Most Hindus practiced daily *puja,* or worshipful offerings to gods; ate in accordance with religious teachings; and observed customary religious holidays and rites (though, like the Tulsis in the novel, many eventually adopted the celebration of Christmas). Women usually filled traditional roles as wife, mother, and homemaker, laboring also in agriculture or at home-based businesses, while men worked outside the home. The education of boys took priority over that of girls—a policy reinforced by the local school system in which just three in 200 girls advanced to secondary school (Williams, p. 22). As in India, women dressed modestly in *saris* or *salwar kameez*; men sported Eastern or Western attire. Dowries were required for Hindu girls to marry, and their marriages were arranged, ideally to someone above their family's station. In the novel, Mr. Biswas is paired with Shama, one of the Tulsi family daughters, because he is a Brahmin—the highest caste. Though he has no real occupation or property, his caste brings honor to the Tulsi family. Their daughter is "marrying up."

Unequal education. The educational system proved to be another dividing factor in Trinidad. Until World War II, the government had no universal system of primary education and spent little on the education it did provide. The majority of schools were private and secular, operated by Christian religious institutions that did not cater to Hindus or Muslims. The consequences of the government abdicating responsibility for public education were serious: racial and economic differences were accentuated. Poor, non-Christians were discriminated against, performance standards for teachers were nonexistent,

---

"DOWN BY LAW"

With no right to vote, little education, and no political representation until 1946, East Indians felt persecuted by the law and distrusted the official legal system in Trinidad, so they implemented their own system of justice: the law of the cutlass. "The Indian agricultural worker in Trinidad was a man with the cutlass [blade that cuts sugar cane], oppressed by the law which, instead of being his protector, was his principal enemy" (Williams, p. 20). In the novel, East Indians invoke the "law of the cutlass" to settle disputes among themselves, and maintain control over their households. The successful way to resolve conflicts in the Tulsi home is via physical force, not through the legal system. When considering the possibility of local law enforcement's getting involved in a dispute, Mr. Biswas has a "fleeting vision of black policemen, courthouses, gallows, graves, coffins" (*Biswas,* p. 135). Resorting to official law is clearly a frightening option. In fact, the police force was dominated by foreigners—90 percent from Barbados or other islands. Routinely the Tulsi women give their children "a dose of licks" as a sort of "ritual" to make them "big men"; and when Mr. Biswas is exasperated with his children he has "visions in which he cutlassed, poisoned, strangled, burned, Anand and Savi" (*Biswas,* pp. 197, 154, 273). The one time that Mr. Biswas decides to resolve a problem by hiring a lawyer, he is sued for slander and loses his case. British law, as demonstrated by this incident, favored the upper classes, not the commoner or the ethnic outsider.

---

and there was no uniformity of curriculum. As a result, just one in ten East Indian boys attended primary school, one in 14 East Indian girls. In contrast, the island average at the time was one in two boys, three in five girls.

An even worse situation existed at the secondary-school level. There were just four secondary schools in Trinidad, all very expensive and strictly urban. The only bridge for poor kids to secondary school was via government-sponsored exhibitions, whose winners received free tuition plus textbooks. A second exhibition or academic contest enabled winners to attend college abroad—usually Cambridge or Oxford in England—but the number of awards granted for each contest was extremely small. While just 800 students of about 47,000 advanced to secondary school in 1911, only four attended with exhibition scholarships, and only three advanced from secondary school to college abroad as exhibition winners. Of the lucky few, Mr. Biswas's son, Anand, and Naipaul himself won the secondary and college scholarships, as did Trinidad's first black prime minister, Eric Williams. For East Indians and Africans, the exhibitions were often the only opportunity for educational and socioeconomic advancement, and so were of paramount importance to families wishing to better themselves.

Ironically, though higher education enabled poor children to advance, it also became a social barrier separating students from family and friends, and dividing the generations. The main purpose of education in Trinidad was the Anglicization of the colony, and the secondary curriculum, according to Eric Williams, was indistinguishable from that of an English public school. Textbooks were written by J. O. Cutteridge, an aristocratic, non-Trinidadian British official who emphasized the classics and mathematics. There was no teaching of Creole, African, or East Indian culture and history, and the literary and scientific styles were "affected, pompous, high-flown and ponderous"—a far cry from colloquial speech or daily experience in the cane fields or Port of Spain (Williams, p. 23). Non-European students exposed to this type of education became far more "British" than their families, yet remained clearly *not* British in the eyes of mainstream society. Like Mr. Biswas, an avid reader, and his educated children, the students themselves often felt alienated from, even repelled by, their inherited traditions and questioned their cultural identity. Naipaul's characterization of the ethnic outsider seems to stem from his own experience as a product of this educational system, from his "rootlessness" as a colonial divided from his cultural heritage yet unable to share in that of Trinidad's imperial ruler (Chapman, p. 303).

"Picong"—a tradition of satire. In Trinidad, a unique tradition of political satire became a major force in society. By the mid-twentieth century there were no less than four daily newspapers and an abundance of weeklies for a population of one million, with each featuring humorous political attacks on local government, bureaucracy, and traditions. Called "picong," this unique form of "sniping satire," which originated in Calypso music, conveyed the popular "Trinidadian" attitude of refusing to take anyone or anything too seriously (Saft, p. 81). Most Trinidadians viewed the established order as unrepresentative and corrupt. Yet an inherent *joie de vivre* generally provided "a studied philosophy of life which rests upon a highly developed sense of humor" (Saft, p. 82). In the weeklies no topic was sacrosanct and "a major part of the attraction" was "their punching holes in public figures" (Saft, p. 82). The humor "level[ed] all hierarchies" and, as in the novel, poked fun at tradition and the status quo (Saft, p. 82).

Naipaul's novel is a masterpiece of "picong." A newspaper columnist, Mr. Biswas specializes in biting satire. He, like Naipaul's father, exposes the folly of society and finds his muse in his editor Mr. Burnett (for Naipaul's father, it was Mr. MacGowan), who openly encourages his outlandish stories. With nothing above reproach, Mr. Biswas constantly satirizes his own life and experiences, recording events in his mind: "Amazing scenes were witnessed in St. Vincent Street yesterday when Mohun Biswas, 31, unemployed, of no fixed address, assaulted a receptionist at the offices of TRINIDAD SENTINEL. People ducked behind desks as Biswas, father of four, walked into the building with guns blazing, shot the editor and four reporters dead, and then set fire to the building" (*Biswas*, p. 319). Of course, Mr. Biswas does none of these things—they are random thoughts passing through his mind that illustrate his sensational, black sense of humor. The general focus of the newspaper he writes for conveys the same black humor, an attribute appreciated in Trinidad: "The peasant was then reported as saying that he read the *Sentinel* every day, since no other paper presented the news so fully, so amusingly, and with such balance" (*Biswas*, p. 328). In deference to Trinidad's penchant for "picong," the *Sentinel* editor includes "amusingly" in his description, a quality outside newspapers often do not equate with fine reporting.

Big changes on a small island. A mix of variables characterized Trinidadian society. "Class, colour, caste and race combined to create an immensely complex pattern of human relationships" and made it extremely difficult for change to occur (Bridget Brereton in Rogozinski, p. 317). The

elite Protestant British and Roman Catholic French-Creole classes agreed on nothing but money. As mentioned earlier, blacks and East Indians clashed. Oil and farm workers were pitted against middle-class white-collar workers. And even within the East Indian community, Hindus and Muslims divided along religious lines. Reinforced by the social and educational systems, the divisions helped isolate power in the hands of a privileged few. In 1934, however, when the

MILK AND PRUNES—BRAIN FOOD

Because it was a life-making or life-breaking event, the government-sponsored educational exhibitions were a family priority in Trinidad. Families poured their energy and resources into the education of a select child as preparation for the scholastic exams. He or she would be tutored at the family's expense and would receive certain privileges. In the novel, milk from the dairies and prunes are the special diet East Indian families prescribed for educational brilliance. Both foods were not only precious commodities but were seen as possessing special intellectual qualities. As a rule, milk would not be purchased from European-operated diaries but acquired from family cows or bought from "a man six lots away who, oblivious of the aspirations of the district, kept cows and delivered milk in rum bottles stopped with brown paper"; prunes were believed to be "especially nourishing to people who exercised their brains" (*Biswas*, pp. 336-37). Mr. Biswas at first scoffs at Mrs. Tulsi for indulging Owad [her son] in these excesses. But soon Mr. Biswas not only sees the wisdom of her choice but hopes his own son will some day be worthy of the treatment. "He was watching and learning, with an eye on his own household and especially on Anand. Soon, he hoped, Anand would qualify to eat prunes and drink milk from the Dairies" (*Biswas*, p. 337).

Wages Advisory Board recommended that peoples' needs were less, wages fell below those paid in 1920, at which point the repressed classes finally banded together for change. East Indians in particular became more public in their demands for improved wages and working conditions, staging a hunger strike. They also staged demonstrations, with East Indian sugar workers marching from San Fernando to Port of Spain, inspiring workers in other industries to follow suit.

About this time East Indian advocate Krishna Deonarine, came to the fore of local politics. The grandson of indentured servants, he changed his name to Adrian Cola Reinzi to pass as a more-privileged Spaniard. Reinzi organized the Oilfield Workers Trade Union and the All Trinidad Sugar Estates and Factory Workers Trade Union in 1937, inaugurating a major turning point in race relations on the island, as "oil and sugar, African and Indian . . . joined hands" (Saft, p. 45). By 1941, 12 unions had been established in Trinidad, with workers finally putting aside cultural differences to form coalitions and agitate for change.

A second important impetus for change occurred three years later with the arrival of American service personnel. In September 1940 the British leased its military bases in Trinidad to the United States. Inadvertently the presence of Americans helped erode color and class distinctions because, in contrast to the British, the Americans provided high-paying jobs to Trinidadians, regardless of their cultural heritage. Also, whereas the British had maintained a very separate and formal public relationship with the general population, Americans "labored bareback, got drunk and brawled, and white respectability crumbled" (Saft, p. 46). In other words, they worked and lived with the public, frequented Port of Spain nightclubs, and dated locals. Meanwhile, the standard of living rose, aided by World War II oil exports (which rose by 1/3), increased urbanization, and American dollars. With more financial resources, people gained status, servility decreased, and society radically changed. By the war's end, a nationalist movement had evolved that would produce a new, self-governing Trinidad.

Postwar Trinidad. The close of World War II signaled the end of British colonial rule in Trinidad (though it would not gain full independence until 1962). Universal suffrage was granted in 1945 and "rowdy" elections took place the following year (Saft, p. 48). Because of the island's lack of party affiliation outside the British Crown Colony, elections were wide open, with 141 candidates vying for 18 seats in parliament. Politicians appealed to the citizenry along race and class lines. East Indians candidates sought the Hindu and Muslim vote. Among them was Ajodha Singh, a popular candidate because of his reputation as a colorful campaigner and "mystic masseur," who massages a person's aura or karma (Saft, p. 48). Naipaul's father, Seepersad, a local journalist, covered the political developments when Naipaul was just a boy. Drawing on these memories, and on his father's stories, Naipaul satirized the events surrounding Trinidad's first elections in his novels *The Mystic Masseur* and *The Suffrage of Elvira*. He also incorporated some of the characters into his masterpiece, *A House for Mr. Biswas*, including a fictionalized version of Ajodha Singh.

The postwar years in Trinidad brought a nationalist surge and increased prosperity, with the economy benefitting greatly from higher oil prices through the 1950s. Testament to the independent spirit sweeping the island, Eric Williams was elected prime minister in 1956. A respected intellectual and skilled politician, Williams was instrumental in Trinidad's achieving total independence from Great Britain in 1962, after a brief membership in the West Indies Federation (1958-62). Williams helped unify Trinidadians, instilling a strong sense of community and national pride where neither had existed before. He called for "nationalism and democracy" and "a mobilisation of all the forces in the community, cutting across race and religion, class and colour" (Williams in Rogozinski, p. 318).

With wages up 10 to 20 times what they had been before World War II, prosperity continued to grow and to help erase class and color lines. As Mr. Biswas does in the novel, East Indians migrated to the cities where educational and white-collar job opportunities increased. Literacy rates rose to 90 percent. Children of all races mixed at school, as did their parents in the workplace. Caste and culture barriers eroded in the desegregated urban environment, and the standard of living rose across the board. "Since the Second World War, the sense of self and the sentiment of nationalism intensified throughout the Caribbean," and "Hindu and Muslim East Indians formed coalitions with black Trinidadians" (Knight, pp. 302, 303). For the first time, East Indians—through education—became part of the recognized middle class as barriers of all forms began to erode and a new national society formed.

The Novel in Focus

Plot summary. Tracing the life of Mohun Biswas, a humble East Indian born and raised in Trinidad, *A House for Mr. Biswas* begins at the end, in the house Mr. Biswas spends his life pursuing. It then flashes back to the onset of Mohun Biswas's troubles. Because of chronic illness, he is fired by the *Trinidad Sentinel*, his employer since he moved to Port of Spain. Mohun has a considerable mortgage, his children, on whom he may have depended, are abroad at school, and he is dying of stress and a bad heart. Yet he is content at the thought of going to his final resting place from his own home, "his own portion of the earth. That he should be responsible for this seemed to him, in these last months, stupendous," and it was (*Biswas*, p. 8).

Born to indentured servants in "a crumbling mud hut in the swamplands," Mohun Biswas seems doomed from the outset (*Biswas*, p. 15). He has six fingers and comes out feet first—bad omens in his community—and shortly thereafter is inadvertently the cause of his father's death. To increase his fortune in life, he is named Mohun, which means "the beloved," but for years the trick does not seem to fool the gods and bad luck hovers overhead like a rain cloud. His mother sells the family shack just before oil is discovered on the property. The sale leaves her destitute, his brothers with a life of hard labor in the cane fields, and Mohun without vocation or direction. He tries in vain to become a *pundit*, or holy man, because of his birth into the Brahmin caste, but questions Hindu teachings and has neither the horoscope nor, quite literally, the hands for it. He works in rum shops and at odd jobs, but succeeds at nothing. In fact, Mohun's only marketable skill is sign painting—a craft from which he can at best eke out a minor living. But he has dreams—and books. Mohun is a voracious reader, devouring all the books he can acquire. They enable his escape into the outside world and fuel his desire to make his own place in it. For many years Mohun remains directionless, working as a sign painter for various businesses around town. One day a job brings him into contact with a 16-year-old East Indian girl named Shama. He thinks little of marriage and his mother has all but given up on the prospect when Shama's family abruptly intervenes. The Tulsis are one of the most influential Hindu families in Trinidad. They own sugar plantations, stores, and cinemas, and wield considerable power in the community. When Mrs. Tulsi realizes Mohun's attraction to Shama, as well as his Brahmin caste status, she quickly arranges his marriage to her daughter. Before Mohun fully realizes what is happening, he is part of the Tulsi household and living in their home in Arwacas: Hanuman House, named for the monkey god.

Life for Mohun in Hanuman House becomes quite literally like life in a monkey house. All of Shama's siblings and their families live there together—some 30 or more—with Mrs. Tulsi and her son Seth reigning supreme. Mohun bristles at everything having to do with the living situation, feels he has nothing in common with the Tulsis, and continually causes disruptions and quarrels. Though he clearly does not fit into the family structure or show aptitude for working on their plantations like the other sons-in-law, the Tulsis find places for him to serve the family business and interests. He is sent to other properties—first to operate a small general store, then to supervise fieldworkers on their plantation. During these years his own family continues to

ALLEGORICAL NAMES

A House for Mr. Biswas invokes allegorical names, drawing on East Indian history and Hindu legend. The protagonist's name, Mohun, meaning "beloved," was the title most often associated with Mohandas Gandhi (though he did not approve of it). In this way, Naipaul is illustrating his sympathy for this flawed character and indicating that his experience as a confused, fallible non-hero or "Everyman" is honorable. Appropriately Naipaul dedicates the Tulsi residence to Hanuman, monkey god and savior in the Hindu epic *Ramayana*, an intricate tale of good and evil about the creation of Hindustan (India). In doing so, he employs the double-entendre of Hanuman House as monkey house and of Hanuman's unifying role in the epic. In the epic, Hanuman rescues Sita (the hero Rama's beloved) by building a bridge across the water to another land, and in the novel the Tulsi home serves as the bridge from India to Trinidad.

grow with the birth of three daughters and a son, but he remains disconnected from them as well as from his in-laws. Shama's loyalty lies with the Tulsis, and Mohun feels a stranger around his own children.

With the dream of building a home always firmly in the back of his mind—ever more so since living in Hanuman House—Mohun makes two attempts to realize his goal: the first while working at the plantation at Green Vale and the second when the Tulsis move to the country in Shorthills. But ill fortune still dogs him. Both homes are destroyed by natural disaster, leaving Mohun more dispirited, yet more determined, than ever. He "yearned after the outside world;

A House for Mr. Biswas

he read novels that took him there" and, with the destruction of his houses, felt he had nothing to lose by finally going to explore it for himself (*Biswas*, p. 207).

Following the lead of a friend who has gone to Port of Spain to work in the world's first psychiatric hospital, Mohun moves to the city and lands a job as a reporter for the *Trinidad Sentinel*. He teams up with a bold, bawdy Hindu editor who capitalizes on Mohun's keen powers of observation and black sense of humor. Mohun begins writing sensational columns, such as the roving Scarlet Pimpernel, about a reporter who seeks out the common man and, if recognized, pays him or her a reward.

With memories coming from he knew not where, he wrote:

SCARLET PIMPERNEL SPENDS NIGHT IN A TREE

Anguish of Six-Hour Vigil
Oink! Oink!

The report then described a sleepless night, encounters with snakes and bats, two cars that passed in the night, heedless of the Scarlet Pimpernel's cries, the rescue early in the morning by peasants who recognized the Scarlet Pimpernel and claimed their prize.

(*Biswas*, p. 329)

Most of his subject matter is made up; Mohun converts his disillusionment with his life into fuel for his creativity: His stories are largely fictional and thoroughly outrageous, as when he pens "I am Trinidad's Most Evil Man." Suddenly Mohun is respected by society—even by his family! His audacity and bold humor is rewarded, and his fortune begins to change.

Though the newspaper is eventually bought out and his writing assignments become more mundane, Mohun is content with his career and begins to focus on his family. All the Tulsis move to Port of Spain and for the first time he bonds with his children—especially his son, Anand, to whom he transfers his ambitions. They share a passion and gift for reading and composition, and Mohun invests his time and energy preparing Anand for the secondary school exhibition. Anand eventually wins a scholarship and, that accomplished, Mohun turns his sights one final time to owning a home.

The price is too high, the structure unsound, the seller unscrupulous, but Mohun purchases a house on Sikkim Street and at long last moves his family into a home of his own. Everything he dreamed of comes true. His relationships with his wife and children radically transform: "Since

they had moved to the house Shama had learned a new loyalty, to him and to their children . . . and to Mr. Biswas this was a triumph almost as big as the acquiring of his own house" (*Biswas*, p. 8). He is awestruck at the wonder of being in his own house each time he enters,

to walk in through his own front gate, to bar entry to whoever he wished, to close his doors and windows every night, to hear no one's noise except those of his family, to wander freely from room to room and about his yard, instead of being condemned, the moment he got home to the crowded room in one or the other of Mrs. Tulsis houses, crowded with Shama's sisters, their husbands, their children.

(*Biswas*, p. 8)

He is thrilled to find his place in the world and, though short-lived, his happiness and life are at last complete. He dies in his own home, and his daughter Savi returns to pay the mortgage and care for the family while her brother is away at college.

Hanuman House as a microcosm of East Indian society. In colonial Trinidad, where the population outnumbered that of single dwellings sixfold and the majority lived in cramped quarters, slept on floors, and often cooked and bathed outdoors, the home could be seen as a microcosm of life in the immigrant community. Hanuman House, where the Tulsi family resides, is a perfect example of the living conditions of East Indians in Trinidad: crowded, undemocratic, chaotic, and part of, yet far removed from, mainstream society.

Relationships within Hanuman House are complex. As in the local political and social structure, one must forge alliances to survive. Mr. Biswas realizes this the moment he moves in: "It was a strain living in a house full of people and talking to one person alone, and after some weeks Mr. Biswas decided to look around for alliances. Relationships at Hanuman House were complex and as yet he understood only a few, but he had noted that two friendly sisters made two friendly husbands, and two friendly husbands made two friendly sisters" (*Biswas*, p. 105). Biswas seeks to ally with like-minded family members to change some of the "house rules" but cannot even secure the allegiance of his own wife. Within the house, sheltered by her family, Shama's first loyalty is to the Tulsis and she does not alter her sentiments until much later when Biswas breaks free from the Tulsis and buys his own home.

Seated firmly atop the hierarchy like the British colonials who ruled Trinidad, Seth and

Mrs. Tulsi run the family enterprise—Seth the business, Mrs. Tulsi the household. Despite his bold assertions to Shama that he is "not at his beck and call, like everyone else in this house," Mr. Biswas must answer to Seth and follow his directives (*Biswas,* p. 107). Mrs. Tulsi, hearing that he is making fun of Seth's spoiled children and refusing to work for the family, reminds Biswas of his obligations. Like an indentured servant, he is indebted because they have taken him in, "penniless, a stranger" and given him their daughter, a home, food and shelter (*Biswas,* p. 109). Mr. Biswas declares that his motto is "paddle your own canoe" yet, as an East Indian without a trade he literally cannot (*Biswas,* p. 107). He acquiesces to the family because he has no choice. Like most East Indians in his situation, he must become part of the system and not forget his place in it: at the bottom.

In time—even in Hanuman House—the system evolves, though not necessarily harmoniously. Like the rest of the community, Hanuman House is comprised of old and new generations, with those seeking to modernize and those clinging to old world tradition inhabiting the same small space. Brothers-in-law Hari and Govind represent the old-world East Indian culture, with Hari practising *puja* for the family and performing Hindu rites, and Govind committing the *Ramayana* to memory and singing its verses at every opportunity. At the opposite extreme are Mr. Biswas and the brother-in-law he nicknames W. C. Tuttle. They are avid readers who both feel "that by marrying into the Tulsis they had fallen among the barbarians" (*Biswas,* p. 459). While Hari and Biswas maintain a quiet disdain for each other, Tuttle and Govind opt for duelling gramophones: Govind "*Ramayana*-grunting" and Tuttle blaring modern "music of celebration" at full volume simultaneously from adjacent rooms (*Biswas,* p. 461).

In this setting, East meets West head on and, as in general society, the mixture is disjunctive; it does not blend smoothly. Yet the blending continues nonetheless. Seth marries a Protestant woman, the children study in Christian schools (the older boys attend British universities) and the Hindu family starts celebrating the Christian holiday Christmas. They eat traditional curries and *roti* but sample store-bought ice cream and Coca-Cola as well. The children learn English and forget Hindi, which becomes a "secret" language spoken only among the elders, and little by little the household becomes increasingly con-

fused, as society in general desegregates and modernizes.

In less than 50 years the Tulsis build a strong foundation in Trinidad, acquiring real estate, cinemas, and businesses throughout the island, but still never feel at home.

> Despite the solidity of their establishment the Tulsis had never considered themselves settled in the town of Arwacas or even Trinidad. It was no more than a stage in a journey that began when Pundit Tulsi left India . . . and ever since they had talked, though less often . . . of moving on, to India.
>
> (*Biswas,* p. 390)

But the Tulsis, now the third and fourth generations who know only Trinidad, would never return east. Like others of their community they become part of the island, even as they remain outsiders, maintaining East Indian identities and adapting to change, however reluctantly. The result is a permanently displaced people—colonial immigrants who do not wholly belong to the land and are slowly losing ties to their cultural roots.

Hanuman House mirrors mid-twentieth-century East Indian life in Trinidad: the social stratification, the complex politics and economics of the upper and lower classes, the growing generation gap, and the East-West culture clashes. Along with these realities, it illustrates the isolation of the colonial immigrant searching for a sense of self and belonging in a foreign and often hostile environment. In the context of this house, Mr. Biswas struggles in pursuit of his own identity, or a place of his own. "As a boy he had moved from one house of strangers to another; and since his marriage he felt he had lived nowhere but in the houses of the Tulsis" (*Biswas,* p. 8). His experience and pursuit parallels that of the East Indian immigrant community as a whole—indentured servants, moving to an unfamiliar land, living with strangers, obligated to those who provide food and shelter. Hanuman House symbolizes the community within a community—East Indians in the West Indies, double-edged in that it has been both protective and repressive. For most of the Tulsi sisters, Hanuman House is a place of refuge where the brutal and unfamiliar outside world evaporates, but for Biswas it is a prison from which he must free himself in order to take his place in society and forge his own identity.

Sources and literary context. Naipaul based *A House for Mr. Biswas* on his own experiences in Trinidad, patterning the characters of Mr. Biswas and his son, Anand, on his father and himself.

In his most recent book, *Between Father and Son: Family Letters* (2000), Naipaul reveals that the relationship between himself and his father was strikingly similar to that of the characters. Like his own father, Mr. Biswas dreams of literary success, transfers those dreams to his son, and

---

ENGLISH INFLUENCES

When Naipaul arrived in Britain as a young student, the nation was rebuilding after the ravages of World War II. Colonies in Britain's once vast empire gained independence, and British ties shifted from the areas of Caribbean, Africa, and Southeast Asia to the areas of Europe and the United States. In spite of Britain's demise as a colonial power, national pride remained strong at the time, especially in its ancient aristocratic institutions. At Cambridge and Oxford Universities, though more students of the lower classes were being admitted, many in the privileged class still believed that they alone deserved their place in Britain's finer institutions. The Dean of Balliol College, Oxford, is described as having often spoken derogatorily of the lower-class students—of whom Naipaul would have been considered one. "The snobbery," said one former student, "was absolute—as if they felt now was the last chance to re-establish things as things ought to be and as life had been before the war" (J. MacNaughton in Williamson, p. 100). There were some who publicly decried the leveling of society in the postcolonial era, arguing that "a recognisable and secure upper class . . . represents far less danger than would-be elites in an egalitarian' society, whose privileges would be hidden and therefore uncontrolled" (Worthestone in Williamson, p. 101). Class distinctions remained prevalent in British society, and nostalgia for the old colonial past was "coupled with a suspicion of strangers and some resentment of the newcomers who were increasingly arriving" (Williamson, p. 105). It is in the context of this climate of conditional acceptance, on top of his own background as an immigrant outsider, that Naipaul creates such a convincing portrayal of the East Indian colonial experience in Trinidad.

---

dies financially burdened but gratified that he is leaving a better future for his children. Naipaul, like Anand, was "torn between self-absorption and familial concern, writing home out of duty, need and affection" (Kakutani). Showing his deep affection and a growing realization of the relevance of his father's experience as a univer-

sal struggle for identity, Naipaul records and embellishes upon the life and memories of the man he knew.

The novel draws on what Naipaul describes as ostracized peoples, estranged from societies to which they ostensibly belong, seeking ways to genuinely belong. He deliberately broadened out from his family experience to that of the West Indian community in Trinidad, as he describes in his book *Reading and Writing*: "One day . . . I began to see what my material might be: the city street from whose mixed life we had held aloof, and the country life before that, with the ways and manners of a remembered India" (Naipaul in Schmitt, p. 132). He specifically portrayed the reality of descendants of indentured servants, of which he was one, and in so doing, conveyed larger truths about the general colonial predicament in Trinidad.

Reviews. Most critics agree that *A House for Mr. Biswas* is Naipaul's literary masterpiece, but not all responses to the novel have been positive. Naipaul has been criticized for depicting Third World peoples as culturally inferior to Westerners, and his works have received a less-than-favorable initial reception in India and the West Indies. But at least one reviewer identified with the portrayal in *A House for Mr. Biswas*, saying that "for the first time, he is able to feel his own history not merely as a squalid farce, but as an adventure in sensibility" (Schmitt, p. 151). Another reviewer praised the metaphors embedded in the novel: "The book is powerfully symbolic, but it is never crudely or obtrusively so"; Biswas "represents all things because he is fully presented as a person whose every quirk and idiosyncrasy we know" (Rohlehr in Schmitt, p. 153). Others agreed, calling Biswas "an archetypal figure"—the "Third World Everyman," the wanderer-stranger searching for his role in the universe (Schmitt, pp. 153, 133). Still others celebrated the novel's engaging humor, and the comic dimension of its epic hero. "If," said Paul Theroux writing in the *New York Times Book Review*, "the silting up of the Thames coincided with a freak monsoon" causing him to be marooned in South London, the one book he would want with him would be *A House for Mr. Biswas* (Theroux in Chapman, p. 303).

—Diane Renée

For More Information

Chapman, Jeff, and Pamela S. Dear, eds. *Contemporary Authors, New Revision Series*, Vol. 51. Detroit: Gale, 1996.

Kakutani, Michiko. "Naipaul's Letters Reveal True Nature of Mr. Biswas and Son." *Seattle Post Intelligencer.* 16 Feb. 2000. http://www.seattlepi.nwsource.com/books/boox166.shtml (20 Jan. 2001).

Klass, Morton. *East Indians in Trinidad.* Prospect Heights, Ill.: Waveland Press, 1961.

Knight, Franklin W. *The Caribbean: The Genesis of a Fragmented Nationalism.* New York: Oxford University Press, 1990.

Naipaul, V. S. *A House for Mr. Biswas.* New York: Penguin, 1961.

———. *Between a Father and a Son.* New York: Alfred A. Knopf, 2000.

Rodman, Hyman. *Lower-Class Families.* New York: Oxford University Press, 1971.

Rogozinski, Jan. *A Brief History of the Caribbean.* New York: Facts on File, 1999.

Saft, Elizabeth, ed. *Trinidad & Tobago.* Boston: APA, 1993.

Schmitt, Deborah A., ed. *Contemporary Literary Criticism,* Vol. 105. Detroit: Gale Group, 1998.

Williams, Eric. *Inward Hunger: The Education of a Prime Minister.* Chicago: University of Chicago Press, 1969.

Williamson, Bill. *The Temper of the Times.* Oxford: Basil Blackwell, 1990.

Wolpert, Stanley. *A New History of India.* New York: Oxford University Press, 1997.

Howards End

by

E. M. Forster

B orn in London in 1879, Edward Morgan Forster was the only son of the architect Edward Morgan Llewellyn Forster and Alice Clara Whichelo. The future novelist was only one year old when his father died of tuberculosis; in 1882, the infant Forster and his mother moved to Rooksnest, a country house in Hertfordshire, where he was brought up by his mother and paternal aunts. Forster attended Tonbridge School as a day pupil, later matriculating at King's College, Cambridge University. From 1900 to 1901, he traveled with his mother extensively throughout Europe, including Italy, Sicily, and Austria. In 1902 he took a position as an instructor with the Working Men's College in London, while pursuing publication as an author. His first short story "Albergo Empedocle" was printed the following year in the literary journal *Temple Bar*. Forster also contributed essays and short stories to the newly founded *Independent Review*. His first novel, *Where Angels Fear to Tread*, was published in 1905, and was followed in quick succession by *The Longest Journey* (1907) and *A Room with a View* (1908). *Howards End*, his fourth novel and first major success, was published in 1910. During World War I, Forster spent three years as a civilian war worker in Egypt. Two visits to India, in 1912 and 1921, led to his highly lauded novel *A Passage to India* (1924). During World War II, Forster won respect for his lack of sympathy with all forms of totalitarianism, and in 1946 he received an honorary fellowship that enabled him to live in Cambridge. Forster died in Coventry, England,

---

THE LITERARY WORK

A novel, set in England, during the early 1900s; published in 1910.

SYNOPSIS

A country house plays a pivotal role in the intertwined lives of two middle-class families and a struggling clerk.

---

in 1970. Among his other achievements, *Howard's End* had established him as a master of domestic realism in his time.

Events in History at the Time of the Novel

The Edwardian Age—an overview. Queen Victoria's 64-year reign ended with her death in 1901; her eldest son, the Prince of Wales, succeeded her as Edward VII. Although the new king of England was close to 60 years old when he took the throne and was to rule only until 1910, during his brief reign he nonetheless left his own mark on the age. After the horrors of World War I (1914-18), the English looked back on the Edwardian Age as a golden time of ease, luxury, lavish display, and perpetual sunshine. While this nostalgic view may have been true for the wealthy, titled, and socially ambitious who found their way into the king's social circle, matters were quite different for political activists, lower-

E. M. Forster

class workers, and the struggling poor. Literary scholar Alistair M. Duckworth describes the Edwardian period as "a time of social and political strife," marked by bitter conflicts between Irish nationalists and Ulster unionists, between organized labor and management, between militant suffragists and men equally determined to deny women the voting franchise (Duckworth, p. 3).

The international picture of the time was likewise troubled. Edward VII had assumed the throne in the midst of an international conflict. The Anglo-Boer or South African War (1899-1902), also called the Second War of Liberation, divided Britons at home and exposed British soldiers to the horrors of trench warfare for the first time. Even more ominously, Britain's relations with Germany were becoming increasingly tense and volatile. The British War Office and Admiralty, both of which regarded Germany's expansionist policies with alarm, committed Britain to a costly armaments race in anticipation of German threats. Britain's fears would be realized with the outbreak of the Great War in 1914.

For better and for worse, the Edwardian Age was also a period of industrial development and rapid urban growth. At the turn of the century, most of Britain's wealth as a nation was derived from trade and industry rather than from agriculture, although large landowners and aristocrats continued to dominate British government and society. The British themselves had become an urban people: according to the census of 1901, over 25 million people lived in towns, 4.5 million of them in London alone. Ten years later, 41 percent of the population of England and Wales were recorded as living in such industrial areas as London, South-East Lancashire, Merseyside, the West Midlands, and West Yorkshire (Cecil, p. 43). As more displaced rural workers drifted into the cities in search of employment and housing, the already wretched quality of the overpacked slums and tenements deteriorated still further. Cities were simply not prepared to accommodate the influx of migrant workers; during the 1900s, there was a 15 percent decline in the construction of new housing, despite the acute need for it. Although the Housing and Town Planning Act of 1909 enabled local authorities to demolish slum property and rebuild, overcrowding continued to be a problem well into the 1910s.

Meanwhile, the metropolis, especially London, was undergoing a rapid expansion, a trend that had begun in the previous century and only accelerated during the dozen or so years leading up to the First World War. A novelist of the time, Frank Swinnerton, speculated as to whether London's urban sprawl would eventually extend throughout the southern counties and obliterate rural England entirely. Swinnerton even anticipated that the tall houses in the heart of London would have to be demolished and their place taken by "enormous blocks of flats and dwellings 'built with some beauty'" (Pearsall, p. 57).

Technology also kept pace with the times, as the motorcar—initially a luxury only the rich could afford—became a more familiar sight on British roads, and the flying machine—the prototype of the modern airplane—presented exciting new possibilities in transportation. Although *Howards End* is a novel of character rather than of historical incident, Forster nonetheless imbues his novel with the issues of the Edwardian period, from the impact of motorcars cherished by the materialistic Wilcoxes, to the relentless urban expansion of London that eventually claims the Schlegels' family home, to the financial struggles of Leonard Bast, who ultimately finds himself unemployed and adrift in a society marked by conspicuous and extravagant display.

The Edwardian middle class. Like that of the nineteenth century, the British social structure of the early twentieth century was hierarchical. Most Edwardians tended to think of their society as divided into three classes—an aristocratic upper class; a middle class made up of lawyers, physicians, and merchants; and a lower class consisting of laborers and poor workmen. During the Edwardian period, however, the middle class underwent a significant expansion in several ways.

> There was a noticeable proliferation of the "lower middle class": that army of clerks and office workers who were neither factory laborers nor factory owners but who merged into the working class beneath and the prosperous middle class above. There was a pronounced growth of the professions: those lawyers, doctors, teachers, and civil servants whose numbers, qualifications, and incomes were all expanding rapidly at this time. And there was a new plutocracy of super-rich bankers, financiers, and businessmen that emerged (or bought its way) into the traditional aristocracy.
>
> (Cannadine, pp. 120-121)

As the era progressed, more and more people began to fall under the umbrella title of "middle class," despite vast differences in income, occupation, and way of life.

Such diversity often created its own problems within class strata. According to author J. B. Priestley, who grew up during the Edwardian Age, most contemporary tensions originated among this increasingly populous and diverse middle class. Lacking the confidence of their Victorian predecessors, Priestly argues, middle-class Edwardians were quick to denounce startling or unconventional new ideas—artistic, religious, political—that posed a potential challenge to their safely ordered world:

> The members of the upper middle class felt that property and position were being threatened. In the lower middle class respectability itself, often newly won, had to be guarded. There was a feeling that religion, the family, decency, social and political stability, the country itself, were all in danger . . . during these years the English middle classes were at war with themselves. This odd conflict did much to give the Edwardian Age its peculiar character.
>
> (Priestley, p. 87)

Forster demonstrates his own awareness of middle-class tensions and diversity in *Howards End*. Indeed, his major characters all embody different subcategories of the middle class: the super-rich Wilcoxes amass their wealth through Mr. Wilcox's business acumen, the idealistic Schlegels lead a cultured existence made possible by sound investments and an independent income, while at the lower end of the spectrum,

Leonard Bast toils as a clerk, barely managing to hang on to his hard-won middle-class status. Mutual tolerance between these characters proves difficult, and, in some cases, impossible to achieve. Disillusioned early by the Wilcoxes, Helen Schlegel detests them for their dedication to

THE MOTORING AGE

First introduced in Britain in the 1890s, the motorcar quickly became the ultimate status symbol for wealthy Edwardians. Most models came from France or Germany, such as the petrol-driven, 4 hp (horsepower) Panhard & Lavassor car that the Honorable Evelyn Ellis purchased in 1895. A devotee of this new vehicle, Ellis backed the motoring industry in Britain with about 20,000 pounds of his own money. Ellis, along with J. A. Koosen—who owned another variety, the Lutzmann—and Sir David Salomons, became one of the country's earliest and best-known motorists. Exhibitions, motor shows, and the press further exposed motorcars to the public. In November 1895, *Autocar* magazine was founded, in anticipation of an interested readership. A year later, the speed limit on British roads was increased from 4 mph to 12 mph, to the delight of new motorists and the dismay of law enforcement officers. The motoring craze escalated in the early years of the twentieth century: in 1904, there were apparently 24,201 cars registered in the United Kingdom, one-third of them in London alone (Pearsall, p. 134). Two years later, that number had almost doubled; again, it was only the rich who could afford to purchase and maintain this new toy at first. "The Edwardian car," writes one historian, "was expensive to buy, complicated and costly to run. . . . No gentleman could be expected to mess around in the crude smoking interior of a motor-car, and the new domestic was introduced, the motor servant" (Pearsall, pp. 130-131). His services were frequently invoked, for the Edwardian car tended to be unreliable—tires were continually getting punctured, the engine frequently overheated, and pistons were easily ruined. As the decade progressed and technology advanced, however, sturdier, faster motorcars were built, and motoring enthusiasts eagerly traded in their old cars for bright new models, such as Rolls-Royce's Silver Ghost.

the outer life of "telegrams and anger" at the expense of human feelings (Forster, *Howards End*, p. 28); meanwhile, the Wilcox children regard the Schlegels with deep suspicion, especially after Margaret becomes engaged to their father; and the wretched Leonard Bast is ultimately destroyed through his interactions with both families.

Women, property, and inheritance. From Norman times—the late eleventh century—the English Crown encouraged landholders to leave their property to one heir, usually the eldest son, in order to keep the land intact so it could economically support a military force that could come to the aid of the king. This practice, which became known as primogeniture, remained the norm among English landowners for the next 800 years. By the nineteenth century, the Crown had since found other means of protection and support, but landed families still considered primogeniture a means of preserving their name and ancestral greatness, an attitude that persisted until the early twentieth century and was upheld by the legal courts: "So powerful was the hold of the idea [of primogeniture] that, until 1925, by law the land of someone dying without a will went to the eldest son, and middle-class efforts to change the law and have the land divided among all the children were consistently defeated by the old families" (Pool, p. 90).

As a general rule, girls did not inherit the great estates because the line could die out if they remained single, while if they wed, the property would pass to a male outside the family. Having to leave the premises when the new heir took up residence was often a traumatic experience for a woman who had long been attached to the family home (see *Sense and Sensibility* in *WLAIT 3: British and Irish Literature and Its Times*). However, among the middle and lower classes, women could conceivably inherit the family property, as Ruth Wilcox—formerly Howard—does, in the absence of any surviving male heirs. In Forster's novel, the Howards are presented as belonging to the yeomanry—gentlemen farmers and small landholders—who were a dying breed in the late nineteenth century. Owing to the economic pressures of the Victorian Age (foreign competition, rising agricultural costs, etc.), many yeomen lost their land, descending to the level of rural laborers or becoming tenant farmers to the owners of the large country estates. The Howards' fate is poignantly implied by the very name of their farm, Howards End. As Miss Avery, the old housekeeper, tells Margaret, the second Mrs. Wilcox, "Things went on [at Howards' End] until there were no men [left]" (*Howards End*, p. 287).

With the death of Ruth Wilcox, ownership of Howards End passes to her widower, Henry,

again an accepted and established custom of the Victorian and Edwardian eras. Traditionally, a woman's property legally became her husband's upon marriage. In the latter half of the nineteenth century, however, the law gradually increased wives' powers over their possessions. The passage of the Married Women's Property Acts of 1870, 1882, and 1893, in turn, granted wives full rights over

- Their own earnings after marriage and over money they were willed by others
- Property they acquired by their own efforts
- All their own property so that husbands had no rights over anything legally owned by their wives

The Acts also gave women the rights to sue and be sued over property and to enter into property contracts. In the novel, the dying Mrs. Ruth Wilcox seeks to distribute her own property as she pleases, by choosing Margaret Schlegel as the next owner of her beloved Howards End. The unconventional nature of her bequest—a brief note, scribbled in pencil, informing her husband of her wishes—leads her surviving family to disregard her desires and destroy the note.

Sexuality. Ironically, despite the dawn of a new age and the accession of a new monarch, Edwardian attitudes towards sexuality remained largely unchanged from those of the Victorian Age, a circumstance that author Duncan Crow terms "hardly surprising, because the change of a century or the death of a statute does not necessarily invoke a whole new personality in the psyche of a nation" (Crow, p. 171). The same sexual double standard that had prevailed in the nineteenth century was firmly in place during the early twentieth century. Proper young ladies of the middle and upper classes were still expected to have no sexual experience or contact before marriage—during courtship, "a hand around the waist, a kiss, and a fervent pressing of the hand was probably the accepted limit in most cases" (Pool, p. 187). Moreover, the prevailing view, as put forth by Dr. William Acton in the mid-1860s, held that "the majority of women are not very much troubled by sexual feelings of any kind" (Acton in Pool, p. 186). A Scottish gynecologist attempted to refute that claim in the 1890s, reporting that, out of the 190 women who responded to his questions (his original sample consisted of 504 women), 152 admitted that they did have sexual desires, while 134 even admitted that they had orgasms (Pool, 187). Nonetheless, many Victorian and Edwardian men re-

Forster on horseback with his mother in front of his childhood home, Rooksnest, near Stevenage, Hertfordshire; basis for the fictional *Howards End*.

mained convinced that only "harlots" enjoyed the sex act, while "pure women" dreaded it. Certainly, ignorance of sexual matters did not contribute to a proper young woman's enjoyment of intercourse: most brides went to their wedding nights ill-prepared and frightened.

Abstinence and chastity were not, however, demanded of upper and middle-class men, many of whom engaged in dalliance with domestic servants and lower-class prostitutes. Discretion was expected, however—illicit sexual adventures had to be concealed at all costs: "This was, indeed, the crux of Edwardian morality. To those who could avoid being found out almost everything was permitted. If your vice or indiscretion was exposed, ostracism of some kind was sure to follow" (Cecil, p. 162). The outrageousness of this double standard is illustrated in Forster's novel: the unmarried, pregnant Helen Schlegel is shunned by her brother-in-law, Henry Wilcox, who has himself been unfaithful to his first wife. As Helen's enraged sister, Margaret—Henry's second wife—points out, "You have had a mistress—I forgave you! My sister has a lover—you drive her from the house. Do you see the connection? Stupid, hypocritical, cruel—oh, contemptible!—a man who insults his wife when she's alive and cants with her memory when she's dead" (*Howards End*, p. 322).

The Novel in Focus

Plot summary. The novel begins with a series of letters written by Helen Schlegel to her older sister, Margaret. While vacationing in Germany the previous spring, the earnest, idealistic Schlegel sisters had made the acquaintance of the prosperous Wilcox family, who later invited the Schlegels to visit them at their country house, Howards End, in Hertfordshire, England. Margaret declines the invitation because she must nurse her ailing brother, Tibby, but Helen accepts. While staying at Howards End, Helen becomes enchanted with the Wilcoxes—the forceful patriarch, Henry; his quiet, self-contained wife, Ruth; and their grown children, Charles, Evie, and Paul. Helen and Paul, the younger son, fall in love, but Helen's ardor cools when she sees how willing Paul is to back off because he fears his family's disapproval. Unfortunately, Helen has already written to Margaret about her feelings for Paul, news that sends the sisters' interfering Aunt Juley down to Hertsfordshire to discuss the matter with Helen herself. An awkward situation subsequently arises, which is partially smoothed over by Mrs. Wilcox. An embarrassed Helen returns to London, having lost her illusions about the Wilcoxes, and the acquaintance between the families cools.

Some months later, the Schlegels also meet Leonard Bast, whose umbrella Helen absent-mindedly filches at a concert both are attending. When Leonard calls to retrieve his umbrella at the Schlegels' house, the sisters take a keen interest in the young man, especially after they learn that he has intellectual aspirations and wishes to improve himself. Bast, for his part, comes to idealize the cultured Schlegels and despairs of being able to rise above his poverty or disentangle himself from his relationship with Jacky, a vulgar, older woman he has promised to marry. An intellectual from Germany, Herr Schlegel had married an Englishwoman and landed a position as a teacher at a local university, which helps explain his children's cultured upbringing. Meanwhile, the Wilcoxes have come to London for Charles Wilcox's wedding and, co-incidentally, rented a flat just opposite the Schlegel home. Although Helen no longer loves Paul, she decides to visit cousins in Germany to avoid an awkward meeting. Mrs. Wilcox, however, informs Margaret that Paul has gone to Nigeria so the former lovers will not encounter each other. What Paul does in Nigeria, which by then had been colonized by the British, remains obscure.

Despite their different interests and personalities, Mrs. Wilcox and Margaret become friends. Mrs. Wilcox is especially sympathetic when she hears the Schlegels will eventually have to leave their London home when their lease expires; she invites Margaret to visit her beloved Howards End. Before they can carry out their plans, Mrs. Wilcox falls ill and dies. During her final days, however, Mrs. Wilcox scribbles a note to her husband in which she expresses her wish that Margaret have Howards End. Astonished and rather offended by Mrs. Wilcox's bequest to a stranger, the Wilcoxes decide to discard the note without telling Margaret of its existence.

Two years pass, during which the Schlegels become slightly better acquainted with Leonard Bast, now married to Jacky and still doggedly pursuing the acquisition of culture. The sisters sense something genuine in Leonard's spirit, despite his intellectual posturing, and determine to find some way to help him. One evening in London, the sisters unexpectedly encounter Mr. Wilcox again and the subject of Leonard Bast comes up. Mr. Wilcox passes along the information that the Porphyrion Fire Insurance Company, at which Bast is employed as a clerk, is unstable and that Bast should find another position elsewhere. The sisters pass along Mr. Wilcox's advice to Leonard, who resents their interference but adopts their suggestion nonetheless.

Meanwhile, Mr. Wilcox begins to take an interest in Margaret, actively seeking her company. When he learns she and her siblings will soon have to leave their home and have not found a suitable replacement, he offers them the lease of his own London house, which he has decided to give up when his daughter Evie marries. Margaret goes with Mr. Wilcox to inspect the house; while they are there, Mr. Wilcox makes a proposal of marriage that Margaret, after some reflection, accepts. A horrified Helen tries to dissuade her sister, but Margaret remains determined to marry Mr. Wilcox, even though she recognizes his emotional and spiritual limitations. He is embarrassed by passionate feelings and overly concerned with appearances.

While visiting Mr. Wilcox's married son, Charles, and his wife Dolly in the country, Margaret gets her first sight of Howards End, deserted by a tenant who has now gone abroad. While exploring the neglected house, Margaret briefly encounters Miss Avery, the old housekeeper, who informs her that she has the late Ruth Wilcox's "way of walking" (*Howards End,* p. 211). Although startled by this meeting, Margaret soon dismisses it from her mind as preparations for Evie Wilcox's wedding—to be held at another family property, Oniton Grange near Salisbury—begin.

On the day of the wedding, however, an outraged Helen, with Leonard and Jacky Bast in tow, barges in on the reception. Helen, who kept in touch with Leonard through correspondence, angrily reveals to Margaret that Leonard has lost everything, including his new position at Dempster's bank, through the bad business advice of the Schlegels and Mr. Wilcox. Leonard had left his former place of employment based on advice from Wilcox that the company would founder, but it did not, and Dempster's bank had fired him. Helen demands that Mr. Wilcox make financial restitution to Leonard. Annoyed by her sister's outburst, Margaret nonetheless agrees to intercede for the young man, but after she persuades Mr. Wilcox to meet the Basts, a tipsy Jacky reveals that she was Mr. Wilcox's mistress ten years before. Mortified, Mr. Wilcox offers to release Margaret from their engagement, but she forgives him, reasoning that it was his late wife, not herself, who had suffered from his indiscretion. Margaret decides that, under the circumstances, Mr. Wilcox should not be expected to help the Basts and writes a note to Helen, who is staying with Leonard and Jacky at a local hotel, informing her of this decision. Helen and Leonard are sitting together in the hotel coffee room when the bad news arrives that evening.

The next morning, Margaret learns to her dismay that Helen and the Basts have left the hotel separately, leaving no clue as to their whereabouts. Meanwhile, a distraught Helen visits her brother Tibby, now at Oxford, informs him of what happened at Oniton Grange, and asks him to send a large sum of money—made over from her personal fortune—to the Basts, as she is about to go abroad. Tibby obeys, but the money is quickly returned, and on following up the situation at Helen's request, Tibby learns that the Basts have been evicted from their home and disappeared.

Soon after Evie's wedding, Margaret and Mr. Wilcox marry quietly and have a honeymoon in Innsbruck, Austria. Margaret hopes for a meeting with her sister, but Helen remains elusive. Returning to England, the newlyweds search for a permanent country home since Mr. Wilcox has decided to let Oniton Grange. Not long after their return, Margaret learns from her husband's daughter-in-law Dolly Wilcox that the Schlegels' furniture, which has been stored at the deserted Howards End since the demolishment of the Schlegels' home, has been mistakenly unpacked and set up in the house. Traveling down to Hertfordshire to straighten out the situation, Margaret again encounters the housekeeper Miss Avery, who tells her more about the house and the Howards, while calmly refusing to believe Margaret's claim that she will not be living at Howards End. After her visit, Margaret resolves to have all the furniture repacked and sent to a warehouse, but her plans are upset when her Aunt Juley falls seriously ill.

After a long period of nursing, Aunt Juley recovers but Margaret and Tibby are disturbed by Helen's continued absence from England, which has now lasted eight months. Margaret's anxiety increases when Helen does return to England but still avoids a direct meeting. In desperation, Margaret colludes with Mr. Wilcox to force a meeting by luring Helen down to Howards End to pick up some of her books. When Margaret surprises Helen at the house, she sees that her sister is pregnant.

Shocked by Helen's situation, Mr. Wilcox and his son, Charles, demand to know the identity of the baby's father, but Margaret shields her sister from their prying. Alone, Helen confesses to Margaret that her child is the result of a night spent with Leonard Bast. She also tells Margaret that she is going abroad for the birth but asks if she can spend one night at Howards End with her sister. Margaret passes along Helen's request to Mr. Wilcox, who refuses to allow a "fallen woman" to stay in his late wife's house. Furious, Margaret berates her husband for his hypocrisy and his inability to see the similarity between his transgression and Helen's. She then leaves him, returning to Helen at Howards End.

The following day, two more people converge on Howards End: Leonard Bast, who, guilt-ridden over his night with Helen, wishes to confess his sin to Margaret and Charles Wilcox, who is determined to evict the sisters from the house. Owing to an inadvertent slip on the part of Tibby, whom Charles visited the previous day, the younger Wilcox has deduced the identity of Helen's lover. Seeing Leonard at Howards End, Charles seizes an old German sword belonging to the Schlegels and beats Leonard with the flat of it. Reeling from the blows, Leonard pulls the bookcase down on top of himself. Once extricated, he is discovered to be dead. Although doctors declare that Leonard's death was due to heart disease, Charles is convicted of manslaughter and sentenced to three years in prison. Broken by his son's disgrace, Mr. Wilcox turns to his estranged wife for comfort. Despite having planned to leave England with Helen, Margaret moves her brokenhearted husband and sister into Howards End.

Fourteen months later, Margaret, Mr. Wilcox, Helen and her baby are still living at Howards End and have managed to become a family. Mr. Wilcox assembles his children at the house to inform them of the terms of his new will: all his money will be divided among his offspring, but Howards End will go to Margaret, and after her death, to her nephew, Helen's son. The Wilcox children accept the terms and take their leave. The novel ends with Margaret's chance discovery that Ruth Wilcox had always intended her to have Howards End and with the triumphant cutting of hay in the Hertfordshire meadow.

Home, sweet home. Howards End itself is as much a character in Forster's novel as the Wilcoxes and Schlegels. Indeed, much of the story's action focuses on the process of finding a suitable home—throughout the novel, houses are purchased, furnished, abandoned, demolished, and, in the case of Howards End, rediscovered and brought to life again.

The unique nature of Howards End—originally a Hertfordshire farmhouse—is established in Helen's first letter to Margaret, in which she describes the house as "old, and little, and altogether delightful—red brick" and not at all the kind of dwelling they would expect the Wilcoxes to own (*Howards End*, p. 3). Further details of

---

"ONLY CONNECT . . ."

Forster's famous epigraph—the literary motto—that serves as a prelude to *Howards End* has elicited considerable critical commentary. Literary scholar Claude J. Summers argues that "the idea of connection fuels the novel's attempts to fuse into wholeness individuals divided within themselves and a society equally fragmented and to reconcile the various dualities of existence: the inner life and the outer life, the past and the present, the body and the soul, the masculine and the feminine, the city and the country, the visible and the invisible, the prose and the passion, life and death" (Summers, pp. 106-107). Similarly, Alistair M. Duckworth contends that the epigraph "expresses a wish—for the emergence of a just, harmonious, and whole society—and it acknowledges that the Edwardian world was disconnected at the social, political, economic, cultural, and sexual levels" (Duckworth, p. 8). The character in the novel who most embodies this philosophy and hope for connection is Margaret Schlegel, whose unexpected love for Henry Wilcox leads her to attempt to bridge the chasm between their disparate worlds and values: "Only connect! That was the whole of her sermon. Only connect the prose and the passion, and both will be exalted, and human love will be seen at its height. Live in fragments no longer. Only connect, and the beast and the monk, robbed of the isolation that is life to either, will die" (*Howards End*, p. 195). Firmly believing that personal relations are the basis of meaningful human existence, Margaret is stunned and appalled to learn that her new husband cannot connect, that he refuses to see any parallel between his infidelity to the first Mrs. Wilcox and Helen's pregnancy by a married lover. Henry's inability to "connect" causes Margaret to leave him, and only a greater tragedy—the sudden death of Leonard Bast and Charles Wilcox's imprisonment as his killer—can reunite them.

the house's history—its wide meadow and great wych-elm tree—are provided by Ruth Wilcox who inherited Howards End after the deaths of all the male heirs. As her friendship with Ruth develops, Margaret Schlegel discovers "that Mrs.

Wilcox, though a loving wife and mother, had only one passion in life—her house—and that the moment was solemn when she invited a friend to share this passion with her" (*Howards End*, p. 89).

Indeed, it is Mrs. Wilcox's devotion to Howards End that allows her to sympathize so completely with the Schlegels when she hears that their London house is to be torn down to make room for a block of flats: "To be parted from your house, your father's house—it oughtn't to be allowed. It is worse than dying. . . . Oh, poor girls! Can what they call civilization be right, if people mayn't die in the room where they were born?" (*Howards End*, p. 86). Love for Howards End also prompts the dying Wilcox matriarch to leave the house to Margaret rather than to her own uncomprehending family: "To them Howards End was a house; they could not know that to her it had been a spirit, for which she sought a spiritual heir" (*Howards End*, p. 103). Unaware of her late friend's bequest for most of the novel, Margaret is nonetheless recognized as Mrs. Wilcox's "spiritual heir" by old Miss Avery, former housekeeper of Howards End, who unpacks the Schlegels' old furniture in full expectation of their future residence there: "You think you won't come back to live here, Mrs. Wilcox, but you will" (*Howards End*, p. 284).

Ruth Wilcox's passion for her country home—a passion that her successor, Margaret, comes to share—hearkens back to the Victorian period, in which a home was considered a haven and a refuge from the cares and pressures of the outside world. The passion for the English countryside, however, has taken on a new intensity; it acquired a heightened keenness during the Edwardian Age. The well-to-do often tried to maintain a place in the country as well as in the town; the construction of the railroads throughout the nineteenth century had made it possible for city-dwellers to visit their country homes for the weekend and be back in town by Monday. Certainly the stay was reward enough for the trouble of the journey there: "In terms of the picturesque the countryside was at its best during the period, and townees sought succour and inspiration amidst flora and fauna" (Pearsall, p. 118).

For farmers, yeomen, and poor rural laborers, country life was rather less idyllic. Agriculture had been steadily losing ground as an industry since the 1880s and 1890s; the monetary value of land had fallen dramatically. A 700-acre Wiltshire farm, worth 27,000 pounds in 1812, sold for only 7,000 pounds in 1892 (Pearsall, p. 121). After 1871, farms also suffered from a diminished supply of laborers, many of whom, as noted, flocked to industrial cities to work in mills and factories. Finally, the countryside itself was under attack, as the growing suburbs of large towns encroached upon hill and meadowland. At the end of Forster's novel, Helen points out "a red rust" in the distance and wistfully observes "London's creeping" towards Howards End, a circumstance that even the optimistic Margaret cannot deny (*Howards End*, p. 355). Significantly, the knowledge of what is coming only makes the Schlegels—like their real-life contemporaries—value what they have even more: "The Edwardian period was one in which many people looked on the English countryside with new eyes; some knew it would never be so beautiful again" (Cecil, p. 131).

Sources and literary context. As early as 1908 Forster had begun thinking about the novel that would eventually become *Howards End*. He had already considered the idea of a plot involving two cultured, idealistic sisters, one of whom would wed a businessman and face a troubled marriage. Forster numbered among his acquaintances several intellectual women who provided partial inspiration for these characters, including the three sisters of Cambridge instructor Goldsworthy Lowes Dickinson, and the Stephen sisters, Vanessa and Virginia (who later became the novelist Virginia Woolf; see **Mrs. Dalloway,** also in *WLAIT 4: British and Irish Literature and Its Times*). Forster also drew on his own experiences in Germany as a tutor to Countess Von Arnheim's children in 1905, who provided the German origins of the Schlegels. Arguably, the most autobiographical of Forster's sources for the novel was the country house, Rooksnest, in Hertfordshire, where Forster lived for much of his boyhood and which served as the model for Howards End.

Forster's novel is often considered an example of the English realistic tradition in its attempt to convey the details of Edwardian life as the author experienced them. Forster himself was an admirer of such realistic novelists as George Eliot and William Makepeace Thackeray (see **Middlemarch** and **Vanity Fair** in *WLAIT 3: British and Irish Literature of Its Times*). Yet *Howards End* may also be read as a comic satire on the values and foibles of the middle class, which is represented in all its diverse aspects by the materialistic Wilcoxes, the idealistic Schlegels, and the struggling Leonard Bast. Looking at the novel from

yet another vantage point, literary scholar Frederick P. McDowell calls *Howards End* "the quintessential Bloomsbury novel"; the reference here is to a group of Edwardian writers and thinkers, many of whom were Forster's acquaintances. They used to meet for intellectual discussions at 46 Gordon Street in the neighborhood of Bloomsbury, laying "stress upon the overriding importance of personal relationships" and placing "high valuation" on art and culture (McDowell, p. 65). Moreover, Forster's heroine, Margaret Schlegel, could be considered the "quintessential Bloomsbury intellectual," owing to her habit of "skeptically and rationally testing social and philosophical values and balancing the polarities of the objectively real and the visionary" (McDowell, p. 65).

Reviews. *Howards End* was favorably received from the outset of its publication. Most critics expressed admiration for Forster's attention to detail and ability to convey believable emotional states. A. N. Monkhouse, writing for the *Manchester Guardian* called *Howards End* "a novel of high quality written with what appears to be a feminine brilliance of perception. . . . It is always a humane presentment of real men and women even when their doings surprise us into some kind of protest" (Monkhouse in Gardner, pp. 123-124). A reviewer for *The Times Literary Supplement* similarly declared, "Mr. E. M. Forster . . . has written a book in which his highly original talent has found full and ripe expression," adding, "where quick-fingered lightness and deftness are demanded, there Mr. Forster never fails; and he has caught in this book a sensitive reflection of life on which he is very heartily to be congratulated" (Gardner, pp. 125-126).

Critics were also taken with Forster's characters. A reviewer for *The Standard* singled out the Schlegel sisters, Mr. and Mrs. Wilcox, and Leonard Bast as "wonderfully rendered" and contended that "[w]ith this book [Forster] seems to us to have arrived, and if he never writes another line, his niche should be secure" (Gardner, p. 129). There were, however, some quibbles regarding Forster's plot, especially the sexual encounter between Helen and Leonard, which a reviewer for *The Daily Telegraph* complained "strikes a false note" because "[w]e do not feel that it is inevitable, but that it is the author's will, and that he is doing violence to his characters in bringing it about" (Gardner, p. 131). Similarly, a reviewer for the *Daily Graphic* observed that "the ending is brought about, or at any rate is accompanied, by incidents which, in any other juxtaposition, we should call sensational; and which in their sober surroundings have a disturbing crudity" (Gardner, p. 146).

Nonetheless, the general consensus on *Howards End* echoed the review of the critic for *The Daily Mail*, who declared that "the faults of this book are as nothing compared to its merits. The way in which the characters . . . are made to live before us is of the essence of all great fiction. . . . *Howards End* is packed full of good things. It stands out head and shoulders above the great mass of fiction now claiming a hearing. The autumn season has brought us some good novels, but this is, so far, the best of them" (Gardner, pp. 144-145).

—Pamela S. Loy

For More Information

Cannadine, David. *The Rise and Fall of Class in Britain*. New York: Columbia University Press, 1999.

Cecil, Robert. *Life in Edwardian England*. London: B. T. Batsford, 1969.

Crow, Duncan. *The Edwardian Woman*. New York: St. Martin's, 1978.

Duckworth, Alistair M. *Howards End: E. M. Forster's House of Fiction*. New York: Twayne, 1992.

Forster, E. M. *Howards End*. New York: Vintage, 1989.

Gardner, Philip, ed. *E. M. Forster: The Critical Heritage*. London: Routledge & Kegan Paul, 1973.

McDowell, Frederick P. W. *E. M. Forster*. Boston: Twayne, 1982.

Pearsall, Ronald. *Edwardian Life and Leisure*. Newton Abbot: David & Charles, 1973.

Pool, Daniel. *What Jane Austen Ate and Charles Dickens Knew: From Fox-Hunting to Whist—the Facts of Daily Life in 19th-Century England*. New York: Touchstone, 1993.

Priestley, J. B. *The Edwardians*. New York: Harper & Row, 1970.

Summers, Claude J. *E. M. Forster*. New York: Frederick Ungar, 1983.

Widdowson, Peter. *E. M. Forster's Howards End: Fiction as History*. London: Sussex University Press, 1977.

The Importance of Being Earnest

by
Oscar Wilde

~

Born in Dublin in 1854, Oscar Wilde was the son of the distinguished surgeon Sir William Wilde and of Jane Francesca Elgee, a feminist and ardent proponent of Irish nationalism. After studying classics at Trinity College, Dublin, Wilde won a scholarship to Oxford University, where he earned a reputation as a brilliant scholar. After his graduation in 1878, Wilde took up residence in London, where he soon established himself as a writer and leader of a new aesthetic movement that championed "art for art's sake" and promoted the works of contemporary French poets and critics. Witty, outspoken, and flamboyant, Wilde enjoyed great success as a spokesman for aestheticism in both England and America; he also attracted considerable notoriety—in 1881, Sir William Schwenk Gilbert and Sir Arthur Sullivan poked fun at Wilde and aestheticism in their comic opera, *Patience*. That same year, Wilde's novel *The Picture of Dorian Gray*, in which a handsome young man's moral corruption is reflected in the increasing ugliness of his portrait, caused a sensation among the English reading public. Outside the novel, Wilde was a successful poet and essayist too, but he achieved his greatest triumphs as a writer of social comedies for the stage—*Lady Windermere's Fan* (1892), *A Woman of No Importance* (1893), *An Ideal Husband* (1895). Best-known is his masterpiece *The Importance of Being Earnest* (1895). Although the play purports to deal with trivialities (Wilde actually subtitled the play "A trivial comedy for serious people"), it deftly satirizes institutions and characteristics

---

THE LITERARY WORK

A play set in London and Hertfordshire, during the 1890s; first performed in 1895; published in 1899.

SYNOPSIS

Comic mishaps ensue when two gentlemen court two ladies who have a fondness for the name Ernest.

---

of the era—from social class, marriage, and morality, to hypocrisy, social conformity, and the desire for respectability.

Events in History at the Time of the Play

The importance of earnestness. Above all, Wilde's play satirizes "earnestness," a peculiarly Victorian quality usually associated with sober behavior and a serious turn of mind. The concept of "earnestness" had its origins in several nineteenth-century phenomena: the outbreak of revolutions in Europe; the subsequent reevaluation of political and social attitudes; the growing reaction of the rising middle class to the selfish hedonism of the aristocracy; and the Evangelical Movement of the Anglican Church, which had advocated worthy causes (such as the abolition of slavery), had favored the observance of a strict code of morality, and had rigorously censured worldliness in others. "Earnestness" also carried multiple meanings:

The Importance of Being Earnest

Oscar Wilde

To be in earnest meant *intellectually* is to have or to seek to have genuine beliefs about the most fundamental questions in life, and on no account merely to repeat customary and conventional notions insincerely. . . . To be in earnest *morally* is to recognize that human existence is . . . a spiritual pilgrimage from here to eternity in which [one] is called upon to struggle with all his power against the forces of evil, in his own soul and in society. . . . The prophets of earnestness were attacking a casual, easygoing, superficial, or frivolous attitude, whether in intellectual or moral life; and demanding that men should think and men should live with a high and serious purpose.

(Houghton, pp. 220-22)

In *The Importance of Being Earnest*, the comedic conflict between "earnestness" and frivolity manifests itself in a number of ways: from the pun in the title, to the squabbles between serious Jack Worthing and the more lighthearted Algernon Moncrieff, to the irresistible fascination the name "Ernest" holds for the play's two heroines. Jack's intended, Gwendolen Fairfax, ardently declares that "[Ernest] is a divine name. It has music of its own. It produces vibrations" (Wilde, *The Importance of Being Earnest*, p. 13). Similarly, Cecily Cardew confesses to a smitten Algernon that "it has always been a girlish dream of mine to love someone whose name was Ernest. There is something in that name that seems to inspire absolute

confidence. I pity any poor married woman whose husband is not called Ernest" (*Importance of Being Earnest*, p. 41). Even Algernon demonstrates his awareness of the Victorian passion for "earnestness" when he reacts to Jack's revelation of his true name: "You answer to the name of Ernest. You look like an Ernest. You are the most earnest-looking person I ever saw in my life. It is perfectly absurd your saying that your name isn't Ernest" (*Importance of Being Earnest*, p. 6).

Ironically, the term "earnestness" had yet another, more exotic, meaning:

> Homosexual members of [Wilde's] audience probably grasped the pun's other significance in the subculture of the nineties, for Uranian "love in earnest" was the love of the same sex. The term *Uranian* was derived from the name of the Greek God Uranus ("Heaven"), whose genitals were severed by his son, Chronus, and cast into the sea, the bubbling foam around them generating the birth of Aphrodite. The focus in the myth is on the male's creative capacity without the female. In fin-de-siècle London, a Uranian . . . was a male homosexual.
> (Beckson, *London in the 1890s*, p. 186)

As a practicing homosexual, Wilde would almost certainly have been aware of the additional implications of the term "earnestness." He may even have taken a secret pleasure in perpetrating this esoteric pun on a largely unsuspecting Victorian audience, which would have perceived nothing untoward in the plot of *The Importance of Being Earnest*, ending as it does with two heterosexual marriages.

Courtship, marriage, and social class. Throughout the nineteenth century, courtship and marriage were conducted according to certain rules, especially among the upper classes. For the wealthy and well-established, courtship revolved around the "London Season," a three-month-whirligig of social occasions, ranging from parties and balls to sporting events and artistic exhibitions. The Season began after Easter, coinciding with the opening of Parliament, and ended around late July, after Parliament declared a recess, at which point the aristocrats retired to their country estates.

The Season's main objective was far more serious than the calendar of events suggests, the goal being suitable marriage matches. For 17- or 18-year-old young women, this meant matches to men of equal or superior wealth and status. The population of debutantes grew more mixed in the latter half of the century; the season "in Oscar Wilde's London" took on an extra dimension, providing "the social link between the old landed gentry and the new industrial wealth" (Von Eckhardt, Gilman, and Chamberlin, p. 116). Featured, along with aristocrats' daughters, were the daughters of successful businessmen and bankers, who showed an eagerness to marry into "good families" and a willingness to spend thousands of pounds to do so. Wealthy young American women entered the mix too, finding the often impoverished English lord receptive; apparently their money was not too "new" for these lords, the way it was for upper-class families in New York. England's aristocrats were encumbered at the time not only by their everyday expenses but also by the imposition on their estates of heavy taxes or "duties," to be paid during their lives and even after their deaths. In the play, Lady Bracknell demonstrates her awareness of this circumstance when she declares, "What between the duties expected of one during one's lifetime; and the duties exacted from one after one's death, land has ceased to be either a profit or a pleasure. It gives one position, and prevents one from keeping it up" (*Importance of Being Earnest*, p. 16).

In many respects, steps in courtship and marriage were the same as earlier in the century. Men and women still chose prospective partners with care. The man especially looked upon marriage as a career move since the woman's property became his after the wedding, although the Married Women's Property Acts of 1870 and 1882, respectively, gave the wife some control over bequests and over property that she managed to acquire on her own. After a man proposed and a woman accepted, he was expected to inform her parents of his intentions and acquaint them with his financial circumstances. Her parents, in turn, acquainted him with the amount of their daughter's fortune. Then lawyers for the bride and groom negotiated a marriage settlement, resolving such concerns as the wife's spending or "pin" money, the "portions" that would go to any children of the marriage, and the "jointure"—in the form of money or property—that would be bequeathed to the wife should her husband predecease her. In *The Importance of Being Earnest,* Wilde satirizes the mercenary and businesslike aspects of Victorian courtship in his depiction of a grueling interview between Lady Bracknell and Jack after Jack has proposed to her daughter, Gwendolen. Producing a pencil and notebook, Lady Bracknell interrogates the suitor on every particular from his income—between 7,000 and 8,000 pounds a year—to the address of his London townhouse:

> LADY BRACKNELL: What number in Belgrave Square?
> JACK: 149.
> LADY BRACKNELL: (*shaking her head*) The unfashionable side. I thought there was something. However, that could easily be altered.
> JACK. Do you mean the fashion, or the side?
> LADY BRACKNELL: (*sternly*) Both, if necessary, I presume.
> (*Importance of Being Earnest*, p. 17)

A fly in the ointment—marriage and the "New Woman." In Wilde's time, the rituals of courtship and marriage were complicated by a social phenomenon: the rise of the "New Woman." The term was mostly applied to a vanguard of middle- to upper-class women of the 1880s and 1890s who increasingly forsook the traditional female role of self-effacing wife and mother and sought lives beyond the domestic sphere. In her most extreme form, the New Woman sought to claim the same freedoms of thought, speech, and dress that men had possessed for generations. Many in the mainstream regarded her with alarm and disdain—in the popular press, she was derided, ridiculed, and exhorted to return to hearth and home. "There is a New Woman" quipped *Punch* magazine on May 26, 1894, "and what do you think? / She lives upon nothing but Foolscap and Ink! / But though Foolscap and Ink are the whole of her diet, / This nagging New Woman can never be quiet!" (*Punch* in Marks, p. 11). From the vantage point of the mainstream press, she was a wild woman, a social insurgent, a manly woman. She threatened to take the initiative, reverse gender roles, and confuse society altogether. Certainly she confounded the etiquette of courtship.

From a *Punch* Cartoon, September 26, 1896

"Two Sides to a Question"

"Oh, Flora, let us be man and wife. You at least understand me—the only woman who ever did!"

"Oh yes, I understand *you* well enough, Sir Algernon. But how about your ever being able to understand *me*?"

(*Punch* in Marks, p. 35)

Marriage-minded masculine contemporaries wondered how to court this more assertive female. How dominant was she going to be? They worried about being "emasculated by feminine aggressiveness" (Marks, p. 38). In *The Importance of Being Earnest,* Wilde examines the more comic aspects of this potential situation. Gwendolen and Cecily are not representative of the New Woman—both grew up in sheltered upper-class households with the expectation of marrying. Nonetheless, they are more aggressive and forthright than their suitors. Gwendolen criticizes Jack for taking so long to propose and notes his lack of polish when he at last makes her an offer of marriage. Cecily meanwhile informs an astonished Algernon, masquerading as Jack's brother Ernest, that in her imagination she has carried out an entire romance—complete with courtship, engagement, and separation—with his alter ego.

Aesthetes, decadents, and dandies. During the latter half of the nineteenth century, many artists and intellectuals were caught up in the aesthetic movement that had spread throughout Europe. The movement had its roots in a German theory proposed by philosopher Immanuel Kant that a pure aesthetic experience resulted from disinterested contemplation of an object, without reference to reality or consideration of the object's utility or morality. French intellectuals further developed the doctrine, declaring that works of art were self-sufficient and had no purpose beyond existing and being beautiful. French aestheticism adopted as its slogan *L'art pour l'art* or "art for art's sake," a rallying cry taken up by converts to the movement, who included Charles Baudelaire and, later, Oscar Wilde.

Some aesthetes, notably Baudelaire, also became involved in another movement, called the decadence, which admired the artistic qualities of ancient, even decaying, cultures such as those of the late Roman Empire and Byzantine Greece. The Decadent writer usually adopted a highly artificial style and bizarre subject matter, seeking to shock, enthrall, or even to appall the audience. In its most extreme forms, Decadence "emerged as the dark side of Romanticism in its flaunting of forbidden experiences, and it insisted on the superiority of artifice to nature" (Beckson, *London in the 1890s*, p. 33).

The Decadent movement, in its turn, helped to revive and redefine the concept of the "dandy," a term that, at the beginning of the nineteenth century, was usually applied to foppish men of fashion largely concerned with fine clothes and polished manners. In his essay "Le Dandy" (1863), however, Baudelaire argued that the dandy's taste for satorial elegance was only "a symbol of the aristocratic superiority of his mind" (Baudelaire in Beckson, *London in the 1890s,*

p. 35). The new dandyism of the late Victorian Age shared several characteristics with Decadence, including "worship of the town, and the artificial; grace, elegance, the art of the pose; sophistication and the mask. The wit of epigram and paradox was called upon to confound the bourgeois" (Baudelaire in Beckson, *London in the 1890s,* p. 35).

In *The Importance of Being Earnest,* the characters reflect the aesthetic, decadent, and dandified attitudes of Wilde himself, albeit in exaggerated form. Artifice, not nature, rules the play's drawing-room milieu. Jack exhibits the dandy's preference for London when he remarks to Algernon: "When one is in the town one amuses oneself. When one is in the country one amuses other people. It is excessively boring" (*Importance of Being Earnest,* p. 2). The young women in the play also express their preference for the artificial and beautiful over the natural and genuine. When Cecily praises the "wonderful beauty" of Algernon's explanation for his deceit, Gwendolen concurs, declaring, "In matters of grave importance, style, not sincerity is the vital thing" (*Importance of Being Earnest,* p. 55).

The play itself, on the other hand, goes beyond art for art's sake, its dialogue constituting satiric social commentary on earnestness, courtship, and other aspects of late Victorian life. Farce was a popular genre in Wilde's era and *The Importance of Being Earnest* invokes many ingredients of the average Victorian farce—the vacation resort, the imaginary identity, competing claims to the same name, and the figure of the foundling or homeless child (see **Great Expectations** and **Jane Eyre,** also in *WLAIT 4: British and Irish Literature and Its Times*). There was an iconoclastic bent to other farce too; the forward female was a common type of character, for instance. But in other farce of Wilde's time, the iconoclasm remains beneath the surface; after getting laughs, characters apologize for their transgressions "as a violation of the good order and just standards of society" (Powell, p. 120). In contrast, Wilde's dialogue shows open irreverence for those standards, and without apology or retraction.

> JACK: If you don't take care, your friend Bunbury will get you into a serious scrape some day.
> ALGERNON: I love scrapes. They are the only things that are never serious.
> JACK: Oh, that's nonsense, Algy. You never talk anything but nonsense.
> ALGERNON: Nobody ever does.
> (*Importance of Being Earnest,* pp. 23-24)

The Play in Focus

Plot summary. The play opens with Algernon Moncrieff, a young dandy, preparing to entertain his formidable aunt, Lady Bracknell, and her daughter, Gwendolen Fairfax, for afternoon tea. As his butler, Lane, sees to the refreshments, Algernon receives a visit from his friend, Ernest Worthing, newly returned to London after a short stay in the country. Ernest is delighted to hear that Gwendolen, whom he hopes to wed, will be coming to tea. Algernon, however, demands that his friend explain the meaning of the inscription on a cigarette case he left behind at Algernon's: "From little Cecily, with her fondest love to her dear Uncle Jack." After several futile attempts at prevarication, Ernest finally admits that he has a young ward, Cecily Cardew; that his real name is "Jack"; and that he has invented "Ernest"—a profligate younger brother—to serve as a scapegoat for his own adventures in town. Amused by these disclosures, Algernon reveals that to escape boring social obligations in London, such as his aunt's dinner parties, he resorts to a similar ruse—he has invented an imaginary invalid friend, "Bunbury," who frequently requires Algernon's companionship and assistance in the country.

Lady Bracknell and Gwendolen arrive for tea; Jack contrives to be alone with Gwendolen so he can propose marriage. Gwendolen delightedly accepts, telling Jack that it has long been her fondest dream to wed a man named Ernest. Dismayed by Gwendolen's aversion to his real name, Jack inwardly resolves to be christened "Ernest" as soon as possible. Meanwhile, he and Gwendolen break the news of their engagement to a displeased Lady Bracknell, who subjects Jack to an interrogation regarding his finances and family history. Although Jack can reassure Lady Bracknell that he is wealthy enough to support a wife, he is ultimately forced to admit he knows nothing of his family history: as an infant, he was found in a leather handbag in the cloakroom of the Victoria Railway Station by one Mr. Thomas Cardew. Cardew named him and raised him. Shocked, Lady Bracknell refuses to consider a marriage between her daughter and a foundling. Despite her opposition, Jack and Gwendolen vow eternal devotion and resolve to remain in contact. Unknown to Jack, Algernon secretly writes his friend's country address on his shirt cuff and plans a "Bunburying" expedition to Hertfordshire to meet the mysterious Cecily.

Living in quiet seclusion with Miss Prism, her governess, Cecily is thrilled to receive a visit from her uncle Jack's so-called younger brother "Ernest"—in reality, a disguised Algernon—about whom she has woven several romantic fantasies. Algernon, for his part, falls instantly in love with Cecily and begins to court her; he also learns that, like Gwendolen, Cecily is enamored of the name "Ernest." The lovers' idyll is interrupted by the arrival of Jack who, on his own, has decided to "kill off" his troublesome younger brother and is displeased to see Algernon impersonating "Ernest" and wooing Cecily. The two friends quarrel vehemently, especially after they learn that each has approached Dr. Chasuble, the local clergyman, about being rechristened "Ernest" to please his respective sweetheart.

Meanwhile, Gwendolen arrives at Jack's country house and makes Cecily's acquaintance; for a time, both ladies mistakenly believe they are rivals for the same man, leading to an exchange of insults over the tea table. The appearances of Jack and Algernon clear up this confusion but the ladies accuse their suitors of wooing them under false pretenses and retire to the house in high dudgeon. Alone, Jack and Algernon argue over who has the superior claim to the name of "Ernest"—and who gets to eat the last muffin on the tea table.

Gwendolen and Cecily decide to forgive their suitors but remain firm in their resolve only to wed men named Ernest. Jack and Algernon quickly reassure the ladies that they plan to be christened that very afternoon. The couples' reconciliations, however, are interrupted by the arrival of Lady Bracknell, who has come in search of her missing daughter. Discovering Gwendolen with Jack, Lady Bracknell again forbids their engagement. She is doubly astonished to hear that Algernon has affianced himself to Cecily and subjects the girl to the same cross-examination she earlier suffered Jack to undergo. On learning that Cecily has a fortune of 130,000 pounds, Lady Bracknell quickly withdraws her objections to the match. Jack, however, informs Lady Bracknell that Cecily cannot wed without his consent until she is 35 years old and coldly voices his own opposition to the marriage, citing Algernon's lack of moral character. But Jack offers to give his consent to Algernon and Cecily's marriage if Lady Bracknell will consent to his and Gwendolen's. Lady Bracknell indignantly refuses his terms.

Matters seem at an impasse until Lady Bracknell recognizes Miss Prism as a former nurse who had worked in Lord Bracknell's household. Many years ago, Miss Prism had taken one of the children—a male infant—out in his pram one day, only to disappear with him completely. Lady Bracknell demands to know what became of the baby. A shamefaced Miss Prism admits that she had gotten the baby mixed up with a manuscript for a three-volume novel she had written. The manuscript was left in the pram, and the baby was placed in a leather handbag that she deposited in a cloakroom at the Victoria Railway Station. Stunned, Jack produces that handbag, which Miss Prism verifies as her own. Believing Miss Prism to be his long-lost mother, Jack attempts to embrace her, but Lady Bracknell sets the record straight, informing Jack that he is the son of her sister, Mrs. Moncrieff, making him Al-

---

WILDEAN WIT

~

One trademark of Wilde's wit is his use of the epigram, a short, polished, often paradoxical verbal statement intended to surprise and amuse its audience. *The Importance of Being Earnest* contains many memorable examples of Wildean epigrams:

Divorces are made in Heaven.
The truth is rarely pure and never simple. Modern life would be very tedious if it were either, and modern literature a complete impossibility.
[I]n married life three is company and two is none.
All women become like their mothers. That is their tragedy. No man does. That's his.

(*Importance of Being Earnest*, pp. 3, 7, 9, 20)

---

gernon's older brother. Jack embraces Algernon as his brother, then quickly searches through army lists for the name of his true father, for whom he himself was named. Finally locating the correct list, Jack discovers to his astonishment that his Christian name really is "Ernest John." The last obstacles to his happiness are removed and the two couples (plus Miss Prism and Dr. Chasuble) joyously unite, while Jack assures the still-censorious Lady Bracknell that he has at last realized "the vital Importance of Being Earnest" (*Importance of Being Earnest,* p. 17).

Double lives. Much of the comedy of Wilde's play hinges upon the elaborate double lives led by the two dandy-heroes, Algernon and Jack. Both have created an imaginary person who serves as a "blind" for their activities, but while Algernon's invalid friend, Bunbury, merely functions as his excuse to avoid boring social responsibilities, Jack's scapegrace brother "Ernest" is actually a facet of Jack himself, a facet that he wishes to conceal from his young ward, Cecily. Exhibiting the typically Victorian concern for propriety and respectability, Jack explains to Algernon:

When one is placed in the position of guardian, one has to adopt a very high moral tone on all subjects. It's one's duty to do so. And as a high moral tone can hardly be said to conduce very much to either one's health or one's happiness, in order to get up to town I have always pretended to have a younger brother of the name of Ernest, who lives in the Albany, and gets into the most dreadful scrapes.

(*Importance of Being Earnest*, p. 7)

The whole concept of leading a double life was by no means unheard of among Victorians. Indeed, Victorian life seemed to incline naturally towards duality, with public and private spheres making up the separate halves of existence. For men, life in the public sphere involved duty, service, and pursuit of a profession. The private sphere, usually presided over by women, provided men with a domestic haven, a retreat from public duties, in the form of a peaceful home and, ideally, a loving marriage. The separation between public and private life could take on sinister implications, however—especially for men, who possessed more freedom and autonomy than their wives. It was entirely possible for an otherwise respectable middle-class husband to lead a life of promiscuity and depravity, of which his wife might be kept completely unaware. Indeed, during the 1880s, an anonymous Victorian gentleman published *My Secret Life*, an 11-volume series of memoirs chronicling his many sexual encounters with servants, prostitutes, courtesans, and women of his own class. The author marries twice, once unhappily—which he cites as a partial justification for his promiscuity—and once happily, yet he continues with his secret life despite having found domestic bliss:

For fifteen months, I have been contented with one woman. I love her devotedly. I would die to make her happy. Yet such is my sensuous temperament, such my love of women, that much as I strive against it, I find it impossible to keep faithful to her, to keep to her alone . . . . My life is almost unbearable from unsatisfied lust. It is constantly on me, depresses me, and I must yield.

(Marcus, p. 96).

In 1886 Robert Louis Stevenson also explored the hazards of a double life, though in a more fantastic form. In his novel **Dr. Jekyll and Mr. Hyde**, (also in *WLAIT 4: British and Irish Literature and Its Times*), the upright physician Henry Jekyll divides himself in two by becoming the sensualist Edward Hyde, who pursues diabolical pleasures that Jekyll denies himself. Both identities perish, however, when a guilt-ridden Jekyll commits suicide.

While Jekyll's carnal excesses remained confined to the pages of Stevenson's novel, there were, as revealed in *My Secret Life,* Victorians in real life who had illicit sexual and other experiences while wearing an outward mantle of respectability. Wilde's play alludes to this deception when Cecily tells Algernon, "If you are not [wicked], then you have certainly been deceiving us all in a very inexcusable manner. I hope you have not been leading a double life, pretending to be wicked and being really good all the time. That would be hypocrisy" (*Importance of Being Earnest,* p. 29).

For some, including Wilde himself, homosexuality represented perhaps the most extreme example of a double life, as noted by literary scholar Elaine Showalter:

> By the 1880s . . . the Victorian homosexual world had evolved into a secret but active subculture, with its own language, styles, practices, and meeting places. For most middle-class inhabitants of this world, homosexuality represented a double life, in which a respectable daytime world often involving marriage and family, existed alongside a night world of homoeroticism.
>
> (Showalter, p. 106).

The consequences of being caught in homosexual acts were severe. From the time of Henry VIII, the crime of "buggery," or sodomy, had carried the death penalty, although history does not record anyone ever being executed for the crime. The law was not officially changed until 1861, with the passage of the Offenses against the Person Act of 1861, which imposed prison sentences ranging from 10 years to life on those caught committing anal intercourse or sexually exploiting people under the legal age of 21. In 1885, the Criminal Law Amendment Act, which had been passed to protect women and girls by suppressing brothels, was revised to include an amendment making "any act of gross indecency" between males an offense punishable by a year—later two years—in prison, with or without hard labor. The law considered males who were inti-

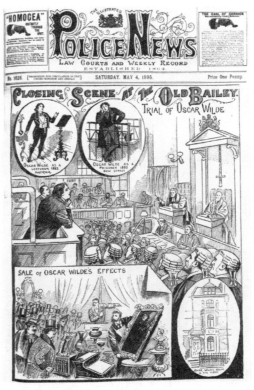

From *The Illustrated Police News* of May 4, 1895, depicting Wilde's fall from the height of fashionable grace to the depth of public contempt.

mate with each other criminals, whether the two males were in a committed relationship or not. In 1889, several male aristocrats narrowly escaped prosecution when the police discovered a male prostitution ring in London's West End. Sir Arthur Somerset, a frequent customer at the brothel and superintendent of the Prince of Wales's stables, was permitted to escape to the Continent, where he would remain until his death in 1926. To protect the royal family from publicity, other clients were likewise saved from exposure; the British press provided virtually no coverage of the scandal.

Wilde himself was less fortunate. A decade after its passage, the conditions of the Criminal Law Amendment Act imposed a sentence of two years' imprisonment with hard labor on the playwright: his own double life was over. Wilde's prison sentence began in 1895, after the debut that same year of *The Importance of Being Earnest.* In the play, Jack becomes indignant and offended when Algernon, drawing a parallel between their similar ruses, refers to Jack as "one of the most advanced Bunburyists I know" and offers to explain to Jack how the pretense can be maintained after marriage (*Importance of Being Earnest,* p. 5).

"I am not a Bunburyist at all," Jack retorts. "If Gwendolen accepts me, I am going to kill my brother. . . . And I strongly advise you to do the same with Mr. . . . with your invalid friend who has the absurd name" (*Importance of Being Earnest.* p. 8). Jack's reluctance even to utter the name Bunbury may be significant if, as one re-

---

FALL FROM GRACE

~

Wilde's triumph with *The Importance of Being Earnest* was short-lived. In the spring of 1895, Wilde was accused of homosexuality—then considered a serious criminal offense—by the Marquis of Queensberry, the irascible father of Lord Alfred Douglas, with whom Wilde had established a relationship several years earlier. At Lord Alfred's urging, Wilde sued the marquis for libel. Although Wilde's friends advised him to withdraw the suit, the playwright pursued the case, only to find the tables turned on him when Queensberry produced male prostitutes who testified as to Wilde's sexual preferences. Wilde was subsequently arrested, convicted of sodomy, and sentenced to two years of hard labor in prison. He served most of his imprisonment at Reading Gaol. During his incarceration, Wilde wrote *De Profundis*, a confessional letter addressed to Lord Alfred Douglas, in which he dissected the self-destructive impulses that had led to his fall from grace. After being released from jail in 1897, his reputation in tatters, his health seriously undermined, Wilde emigrated to France, where he lived for the rest of his life, mainly on the financial support of his friends. Estranged from his wife, Constance, who had visited him in prison and sent him money from her own dowry, Wilde was denied access to their two sons. The notoriety and grief of Wilde's conviction probably contributed to Constance's early death in 1898. Wilde himself was prompted by the hardships and indignities he suffered in jail to compose *The Ballad of Reading Gaol* (1898) and to advocate prison reform in Britain. He died of cerebral meningitis in 1900 in Paris, where he was buried.

---

cent critic argues, the play was using the name as a "private joke" because it was a term that Wilde used for a homosexual pickup (Beckson, *London in the 1890s*, p. 187). There is, however, no evidence that the term was used in this way *before* Wilde's play opened, though "bunburying" did acquire homosexual implications soon *after*

the play's performance and Wilde's trial for homosexuality.

Sources and literary context. While *The Importance of Being Earnest* is justly celebrated for its originality, Wilde did in fact draw on his own life and history for some particulars, especially names and personalities he had known. Wilde's biographer Richard Ellmann speculates that the original for Lady Bracknell may have been Wilde's maternal aunt, Emily Thomazine Warren, who was several years older than Wilde's mother, married to an officer in the British army, and disapproving of her sister's Irish nationalist activities. Other acquaintances lent only their names—for example, Henry St. Bunbury, a classmate of Wilde's at Trinity, whose surname became the term used to describe Algernon's elaborate ruse in the play. As a student, Wilde stayed with the Cardews at their country house, promising to name the heroine of his next play Cecily Cardew after one of the family. Similarly, names of real places, such as Worthing and Bracknell, became surnames for characters.

While the preposterous workings-out of the plot were Wilde's own invention, the playwright had recourse to the tried-and-true devices of Victorian stage melodrama and, as noted, farce: secret engagements, tyrannical parents, hidden family scandals, missing heirs, and foundling babies.

Wilde may have owed a debt to a particular play if he saw *The Foundling*, a three-act farce by W. Lestocq and E. M. Robson, performed at Terry's Theatre in the autumn of 1894. Dick Pennell, the hero of the play, is a foundling who, after various misadventures, discovers that his mother was a woman of rank, lawfully married, and his father pursued a career in India, discoveries likewise made by Jack Worthing, himself a foundling, in *The Importance of Being Earnest*. But if Wilde drew some inspiration from this farce, his sources were multiple; he drew also upon his own classical scholarship: his use of the device of the misplaced baby was taken from the works of Menander, a dramatist of ancient Greece. Moreover, *The Foundling* was a conventional farce, emphasizing fast-paced action, more than the quick-witted turn of a phrase. The ordinary farce stressed the physical over the verbal; Wilde's comedy, on the other hand, featured clever epigrams and elegant phrases. It used language to subvert ordinary farce, creating a "new sensation" and heightening the comic effect of such fare (Powell, p. 119). "Such playing with language . . . was for Wilde one of the . . . secrets of his art, of absurdly reversing the tendencies of language in *The Foundling* specifically, in Victorian farce generally" to produce a play that became a "stage classic while almost all other farces of the day vanished" (Powell, p. 120).

The wit, wordplay, and worldliness of *The Importance of Being Earnest* is not, however, unprecedented; it recalls some of the more lighthearted comedies of the seventeenth and eighteenth centuries, such as William Congreve's *Way of the World* and Oliver Goldsmith's **She Stoops to Conquer** (in *WLAIT 3: British and Irish Literature and Its Times*). Like these predecessors, *The Importance of Being Earnest* shuns sentimentality: its potentially maudlin moments are invariably interrupted by squabbles between the characters and by frequent pauses for food and drink.

Reviews. *The Importance of Being Earnest* first opened on February 14, 1895, to great critical and popular acclaim. In a distinct minority, fellow playwright and Irishman George Bernard Shaw was unenthusiastic. Shaw wrote of his displeasure in *The Saturday Review*: "I cannot say that I greatly cared for *The Importance of Being Earnest*. It amused me, of course; but unless comedy touches me as well as amuses me, it leaves me with a sense of having wasted my evening" (Shaw in Beckson, *Wilde: The Critical Heritage*, p. 195).

Other critics, however, were dazzled by Wilde's display of wit and absurdity, even those who found fault with his earlier plays. H. G. Wells, who had not liked Wilde's previous play *An Ideal Husband*, offered the author warm congratulations in the *Pall Mall Gazette* for his "delightful revival of theatrical satire" (Wells in Beckson, *Wilde: The Critical Heritage,* p. 188). Similarly, William Archer, writing for the *World*, called *The Importance of Being Earnest* "an absolutely wilful expression of an irrepressibly witty personality" (Archer in Beckson, *Wilde: The Critical Heritage,* p. 190) A. B. Walkley, reviewer for the *Speaker*, hailed Wilde as "an artist in sheer nonsense" and said of his new play that "better nonsense, I think our stage has not seen" (Walkley in Beckson, *Wilde: The Critical Heritage*, p. 196). Finally, Hamilton Fyfe, the London correspondent for the *New York Times*, cabled America with the news that the opening night audience responded to *The Importance of Being Earnest* with "unrestrained, incessant laughter from all parts of the theatre" (Fyfe in Beckson, *Wilde: The Critical Heritage*, p. 189). The knowledge that Wilde had created a masterpiece was not lost on the actors either. Allan Aynesworth, who originated the role of Algernon Moncrieff, later recalled, "In my fifty-three years of acting, I never remember a greater triumph than the first night of *The Importance of Being Earnest*. The audience rose in their seats and cheered and cheered" (Aynesworth in Beckson, "Oscar Wilde," p. 214).

—Pamela S. Loy

For More Information

Beckson, Karl. *London in the 1890s: A Cultural History*. New York: Norton, 1992.

————, ed. *Oscar Wilde: The Critical Heritage*. London: Routledge & Kegan Paul, 1970.

Ellmann, Richard. *Oscar Wilde*. New York: Vintage, 1987.

Houghton, Walter E. *The Victorian Frame of Mind, 1830-1870*. New Haven: Yale University Press, 1957.

Marcus, Steven. *The Other Victorians: A Study of Sexuality and Pornography in Mid-Nineteenth Century England*. New York: Basic, 1964.

Marks, Patricia. *Bicycles, Bangs, and Bloomers: The New Woman in the Popular Press*. Lexington: University of Kentucky Press, 1990.

Pool, Daniel. *What Jane Austen Ate and Charles Dickens Knew: From Fox-Hunting to Whist—the Facts of Daily Life in 19th-Century England*. New York: Touchstone, 1993.

Powell, Kerry. *Wilde and the Theatre of the 1890s*. Cambridge: Cambridge University Press, 1990.

Sammells, Neil. *Wilde Style: The Plays and Prose of Oscar Wilde*. Harlow: Pearson Education, 2000.

Showalter, Elaine. *Sexual Anarchy: Gender and Culture at the Fin de Siècle*. New York: Viking Penguin, 1990.

Von Eckhardt, Wolf, Sander L. Gilman, and J. Edward Chamberlin. *Oscar Wilde's London: A Scrapbook of Vices and Virtues 1880-1900*. New York: Anchor Press, 1987.

Wilde, Oscar. *The Importance of Being Earnest*. Essex: Longman, 1983.

In Memoriam

by
Alfred Tennyson

THE LITERARY WORK

An elegiac poem set in nineteenth-century England, spanning the years 1833 to 1850; published anonymously in 1850.

SYNOPSIS

While mourning the death of a close friend, the poet struggles to resolve his questions on such issues as personal immortality, religious faith, and new science.

Born in Somersby, Lincolnshire, in 1809, Alfred Tennyson was the fourth of 12 children, the son of a country parson and a vicar's daughter. Except for a brief unhappy stint at Louth Grammar School in York, Tennyson was educated at home by his father until he left for Trinity College at Cambridge University in 1827. That same year, Tennyson—who showed signs of poetic promise from an early age—and his brother Charles published *Poems by Two Brothers*, a feat that attracted the attention of a group of gifted Cambridge undergraduates. These students, called "The Apostles," befriended Tennyson, encouraging him to devote his life to poetry and building his confidence by involving him in their intellectual and political discussions. Arthur Henry Hallam, one of the leaders of The Apostles, became an especially close friend and later was even engaged to Tennyson's younger sister, Emily. Financial pressures led to Tennyson's ultimately leaving Cambridge without a degree, but he returned home to study and write poetry, publishing two volumes in 1830 and 1832. In 1833, however, the Tennysons were shocked to learn that Arthur Henry Hallam had unexpectedly fallen ill and died while traveling in Europe. In 1850, after 17 years of composition and revision, Tennyson published *In Memoriam*, his elegy for Hallam, which comes to grips with some pressing issues of Tennyson's day, particularly with religious faith in view of the powerful and troubling questions raised by new scientific discoveries and theories.

Events in History at the Time of the Poem

The death of Arthur Henry Hallam. Like all elegies, *In Memoriam* is, first and foremost, a poem of lamentation for the dead, in this case Tennyson's close friend, Arthur Henry Hallam. The Hallam-Tennyson friendship began in 1829 while both young men were attending Cambridge University and competing for the Chancellor's Gold Medal for English Verse, a prize that Tennyson won. Two years younger than Tennyson, Hallam was the eldest surviving son of Henry Hallam, a noted historian. The ambitious elder Hallam encouraged his son's education and intellectual development; as a child, Arthur became proficient in both French and Latin. At Cambridge, he took a passionate interest in politics and metaphysics, as well as poetry, and gained a reputation as an outstanding debater. A

Alfred Tennyson

brilliant future awaited him, predicted his family and a wide circle of friends, which included Tennyson and William Ewart Gladstone, the future prime minister.

Hallam was popular among his friends at Cambridge. One contemporary, Henry Alford, described Hallam as "full of blessings, full of happiness, drawing active enjoyment from every thing, wondering, loving, and being loved" (Alford in Martin, p. 74). Tributes to him in his lifetime mentioned his kindness to others, especially his tenderness towards distressed or afflicted friends. Apparently Hallam was prone to hiding this capacity for tenderness behind a mask of flippancy. Another friend, James Spedding, wrote to his younger brother Edward, who did not care for Hallam: "I do not agree with you as to A. H. H.'s flippancy. It seems to me to be all very graceful & courteous—and the medium nicely hit" (Spedding in Martin, p. 75). One of Tennyson's biographers, Robert Bernard Martin, sums up Hallam's character:

> The truth is that Hallam was neither perfect nor despicable, but that the separate aspects of his character were often kept discrete, rather than being mingled as in most men. He was at his best with those who elicited his sympathy, for to them he could show his own weaknesses without fear.
>
> (Martin, p. 75)

The Hallam-Tennyson friendship ripened after Tennyson was elected to the Cambridge Conversazione Society—informally known as "The Apostles"—in October 1829. Although Tennyson's shyness and dread of public speaking eventually led to his resigning from The Apostles, he remained on friendly terms with them, especially Hallam, who had been a member since the previous spring. As the intimacy between the two young men grew, they visited each other's respective homes and traveled through France, Spain, and the Pyrenees during their summer holidays in 1830.

Although Tennyson's Cambridge career ended after the death of his father in 1831, he and Hallam remained in close correspondence, especially since Hallam had fallen in love with Tennyson's sister, Emily. Hallam's father disapproved of the attachment and forbade his son to visit the Tennysons' home at Somersby or even to write Emily until he was of age. The Tennysons had little money, and their father had been emotionally disturbed, given to violent outbursts and excessive drinking. Arthur Hallam weathered his father's ban, and soon after he attained his majority the couple became engaged. Meanwhile, Hallam faithfully supported Tennyson's writing, encouraging him to publish his most recent work. Tennyson acceded to his friend's urging, and *Poems* was published in early 1833.

By this time, Hallam had completed his education at Cambridge—after winning both the college English essay prize and the declamation prize—and was studying for a career in law. He had begun to experience severe headaches, however, and that spring he caught influenza, taking more than a month to recover. In the summer of 1833, Hallam accompanied his father on an extended trip to Europe, visiting, among other countries, Austria and Hungary. While staying in Vienna, Hallam fell ill with what he believed to be an ague, but a few days later he seemed to have made a partial recovery. After taking a short walk with his father, he lay down to rest on the sofa in their hotel. When the elder Hallam returned from a further stroll, he found his son apparently sleeping. Only after some time had passed did he realize that Arthur had not moved. A surgeon confirmed that the 22-year-old Hallam had died in his sleep; a post-mortem examination revealed a brain hemorrhage as the cause of death.

Hallam's family and friends were devastated by his sudden demise. Emily Tennyson collapsed and spent most of the following year as a bedridden invalid. Meanwhile, Tennyson and Hallam's other friends drew closer together in their shared loss and reverence for Hallam's memory, which took on an even greater luster as a result of his early death. It was a luster developed and nurtured in the epistles they sent to one another: "The letters of the circle at the time are full of affectionate condolences to each other, sympathy for the Tennysons and reassurances of Hallam's greatness, as if their own being were dependent upon his having been a man of transcendent promise. The Hallam mythology had begun" (Martin, p. 183). Tennyson's *In Memoriam*, labored over for 17 years before publication, set the seal on that myth, transforming Hallam from a young man of considerable talent to one who possessed a "[s]eraphic intellect and force / To seize and throw the doubts of man" (Tennyson, *In Memoriam*, 109.5-6). In death, Hallam became, to Tennyson and his contemporaries, a symbol of the best human nature can offer.

Religious doubt. During the early decades of the nineteenth century, practicing Christians in England tended to regard the Bible as a sacred, infallible text, whose meaning was to be taken literally. As the century progressed, however, linguistic criticism, which originated among German intellectuals, and new geological discoveries challenged the accuracy of the Scriptures, shaking the faith of many Victorians.

Sectarian conflicts, some of which originated in the early 1800s, also weakened religious certainties. Among other movements, Materialism, the doctrine that esteems physical or worldly well-being and material progress above all, gained currency. Materialist thinker Jeremy Bentham (1772–1832) established a philosophy known as Utilitarianism which favored the abolishment of all social institutions that were not determined to be "useful," that is, to be a contribution to the greatest happiness for the greatest number of individuals. Benthamite Utilitarians generally agreed that religion failed to meet that criteria and was no more than an outmoded superstition. At the other end of the spectrum, philosophical conservatives, including Samuel Taylor Coleridge and Thomas Carlyle, argued that people needed faith as surely as they needed material sustenance, while religious conservatives, like John Henry Newman, argued for the establishment of a powerful, traditional religious institution to deflect the narrow tenets of Benthamitism.

Ongoing religious debates and the emergence of scientific theories regarding the nature of man and his world contributed to many Victorians' suffering crises of faith. Was there a God? Was there an afterlife, with the possibility of heaven and hell to follow? Was the human soul indeed immortal, or was it no better than that of a beast? Was the human race intended for a greater destiny, or was it doomed to vanish without a trace like countless species before it? These questions troubled many Victorian thinkers and writers, including Tennyson. The pathos of *In Memoriam* is derived not only from the poet's loss of his beloved friend but also from his doubts and fears regarding the worth of any human soul—Hallam's, his, anyone's—in the universal scheme of things. In the poem, Nature discourages the speaker; he is disheartened by what he considers her utter indifference to humanity—"She cries: 'A thousand types are gone: / I care for nothing, all shall go'" (*In Memoriam*, 56.3-4). Fearful, the speaker wonders about "Man, her last work, who seemed so fair" (*In Memoriam*, 56.9). "Who lov'd, who suffer'd countless ills, / Who battled for the True, the Just"; is he destined to "Be blown about the desert dust, / Or seal'd within the iron hills?" (*In Memoriam*, 56.17-20).

Tennyson later realizes that even these agonized questions can lead to a renewal, rather than a decline, of faith, in a stanza that may refer as much to his own spiritual journey as to Hallam's: "Perplext in faith, but pure in deeds, / At length he beat his music out. / There lives more faith in honest doubt, / Believe me, than in half the creeds" (*In Memoriam*, 96.9-12).

Geology and evolution. *In Memoriam* was published in 1850, nine years before Charles Darwin's **On the Origin of Species** (also in *WLAIT 4: British and Irish Literature and Its Times*), which would make the most compelling argument yet that organisms evolve over generations, using Darwin's theory of natural selection to explain how this occurred. Other works, however, preceded Darwin's, and these earlier works, by scientists such as Sir Charles Lyell and J. F. W. Herschel, left their mark on Tennyson and on many of his contemporaries. Indeed, Lyell's *Principles of Geology* (1830–33), which would prove revolutionary, had an impact not only on the geological theories of the time but on religious thought as well.

Basing his arguments on studies conducted by his predecessors and his own observations over a period of several years, Lyell proposed that the present state of the earth was the result of natural forces—wind and water erosion, rock faulting, sedimentation—operating over time, rather than the result of catastrophic occurrences, as had been argued by French naturalist Georges Cuvier. Lyell also contended that geology revealed continual physical changes, which, in turn, seemed to indicate the extinction of many different species throughout the earth's history. These extinct species died out, Lyell maintained, because they were unable to cope with new conditions in their ever-changing environment.

While Lyell was not the first scientist to arrive at these conclusions (James Hutton and Georges-Louis de Buffon advanced similar arguments in the preceding century), his works achieved unprecedented popular success and enjoyed a wide readership. Tennyson was deeply immersed in *Principles of Geology* in 1837, and its tenets regarding extinction influenced the sections of *In Memoriam* dealing with the speaker's sudden crisis of faith. In particular, Tennyson, along with many others, felt troubled by the conclusion Lyell reached from his study of fossils that people, like all other parts of the globe, "are subject to change. It is not only the individual that perishes, but the whole species" (Lyell in Wilson, p. 160). Such teachings inspired Tennyson's images of nature's indifference to humanity in his poem, and of the crisis of faith this engenders in man: "Who trusted God was love indeed / And love Creation's final law— / Though Nature, red in tooth and claw / With ravine, shrieked against his creed" (*In Memoriam*, 56.13-16).

If Lyell's arguments regarding extinction represented one pessimistic extreme of scientific thought, Herschel's *Preliminary Discourse on the Study of Natural Philosophy* (1830) and Robert Chambers's *Vestiges of the Natural History of Creation* (1844) provided a partial corrective, although the latter advanced its own disturbing hypotheses. Herschel vigorously refuted the idea that the study of science cast doubt on the belief in the immortality of the soul; rather, he argued, the study of science left the mind "open and free to every impression of a higher nature which it is capable of reaching . . . encouraging rather than suppressing, every thing that can offer a prospect of a hope beyond the present obscure and unsatisfactory state" (Herschel in Tennyson, p. 130).

Chambers's work, however, was somewhat less reassuring, especially to those who sought to reconcile scientific discoveries with religious faith. While asserting the existence of "a primitive almighty will, of which these [physical] laws are merely the mandates," *Vestiges of the Natural History of Creation* nonetheless argued that natural laws, not acts of God, were responsible for the process of organic creation (Chambers in Tennyson, p. 130). Chambers's work, furthermore, upset the widespread belief that humans were superior to animals, maintaining that humanity was part of the animal kingdom and subject to the same process of organic development that affected every living species on the planet. Moreover, the fate of the individual was a matter of complete indifference to the forces of nature; it was up to the individual, said Chambers, "to take his chance amidst the melee of the various laws affecting him" (Chambers in Tennyson, p. 131).

Chambers's revelations, like those of Lyell, proved highly disturbing to many Victorians. Historian Walter E. Houghton explains the reason behind their disconcertion:

> Nature had been thought of [by the Victorians] as the manifestation of a good and beneficent God . . . the nurse and guide of life. But once Lyell's *Principles of Geology* had appeared (1830–1833), followed by Chambers' *Vestiges of Creation* (1844) and Darwin's *Origin of Species* (1859), nature became a battleground in which individuals and species fought for their lives and every acre of land was the scene of untold violence and suffering.
>
> (Houghton, p. 68)

But while Chambers's work refuted the idea of a loving and concerned Providence, it offered some counter-reassurances to the effect that nature's very ruthlessness might be part of a larger, perfect plan. The extinction of one species, Chambers argued, could lead to the development of another, superior species that would take its place and fulfill the aspirations of its predecessors: "Is our race but the initial of the grand crowning type? Are there yet to be species superior to us in organization, purer in feeling, more powerful in device and act, and who shall take a rule over us! . . . There may then be occasion for a nobler type of humanity, which shall complete the zoological circle on this planet, and realize some of the dreams of the purest spirits of the present race" (Chambers in Tennyson, p. 132).

Chambers's speculations on the evolution of man into a superior being were instrumental in resolving the speaker's crisis of faith in *In Memoriam*. Initially cast into despair by the evidence of extinction and death, the poet is later able to conceive of man as a "herald of a higher race," to be purified, like iron in a furnace, and re-shaped into a being who will "[m]ove upward, working out the beast, / And let the ape and tiger die" (*In Memoriam*, 118.14, 27-28).

The Poem in Focus

Plot summary. *In Memoriam* ("In memory of") possesses an unusual structure of individual lyric units that can stand on their own but are also integrated into the body of the entire poem. The narrative of Tennyson's elegy is likewise unusual: it does not follow a purely linear progression from the poet's despair over the death of his friend to his acceptance of the loss and renewal of hope. While some sections of *In Memoriam* occur in a specific temporal context—like the three Christmases following the death of Arthur Henry Hallam (sections 28, 78, 104)—other sections reflect only the trend of Tennyson's thought processes as he contemplates such issues as faith, doubt, and immortality. Paradoxically, *In Memoriam* seems to encompass two time periods: the three years following Hallam's death and the 17 years Tennyson spent composing, revising, and organizing his elegy.

Numerous critics have suggested different ways in which to read and interpret *In Memoriam*. Tennyson himself suggested that the main body of the poem fell into nine natural groups that marked the stages of his grief and thought:

- Sections 1 to 8 describe the first onset of grief;
- Sections 9 to 19 recount the return of Hallam's remains to England;
- Sections 20 to 27 recall the four years of the Hallam-Tennyson friendship;
- Sections 28 to 49 balance thoughts of personal immortality against overwhelming personal loss;
- Sections 50 to 59 give full rein to the speaker's philosophical doubts and terrors;
- In Sections 59 to 71, the speaker expresses his dependence on Hallam's spirit;
- Sections 72 to 98 reiterate that dependence, yet introduce a fragile element of hope or optimism;
- Sections 99 to 103 depict a spiritual reunion of sorts between the severed friends, which represents the turning point of the entire poem;
- Finally, sections 104 to 131 affirm the speaker's faith in a loving God and his belief that his lost friend lives again in that God

In Memoriam begins with a prologue that addresses the "Strong Son of God" and affirms the speaker's belief that faith is superior to knowledge and more enduring: "Our little systems have their day; / They have their day and cease to be: / They are but broken lights of thee, / And thou, O Lord, art more than they" (*In Memoriam*, Prologue.17-20). Acknowledging God's love and wisdom, Tennyson asks Him to forgive his "wild and wandering cries" for the lost Hallam and "in thy wisdom make me wise" (*In Memoriam*, Prologue.41, 44).

In the opening segments of the poem, the speaker muses upon the nature of sorrow and how it comes unexpectedly upon those who love the departed—his parents, friends, and sweetheart—just as they anticipate his return to them. In sections 9 through 20, his reflections take on a more personal significance with the revelation that Arthur Hallam's remains are being borne back to England for burial: "Calm on the seas, and silver sleep, / And waves that sway themselves in rest, / And dead calm in that noble breast / Which heaves but with the heaving deep" (*In Memoriam*, 11.17-20). Even after Hallam's body is placed "in English earth" and the initial pangs of grief begin to fade, the speaker remains devastated by his loss (*In Memoriam*, 18.2). The pealing of the bells on the first Christmas after Hallam's death "bring [him] sorrow touch'd with joy" and make him wonder "With such compelling cause to grieve / As daily vexes household peace / And chains regret to his decease / How dare we keep our Christmas-eve" (*In Memoriam*, 28.19, 29.1-4).

After that first sad Christmas, the speaker finds himself contemplating the nature of personal immortality and wondering whether the individual soul somehow survives or is absorbed back into some universal Godhead. His readings on natural history—particularly, the phenomena of evolution and extinction—further color his thoughts, which take a pessimistic turn: "Are God and Nature then at strife, / That Nature lends such evil dreams? / So careful of the type she seems, / So careless of the single life" (*In Memoriam*, 55.5-8). His most pressing questions, however, remain unresolved at this juncture; what persists is his love for Hallam's spirit and his need to praise him.

The second Christmas brings calm and a lessening of sorrow to the speaker, who acknowledges regretfully that this is but the inevitable progression of grief: "Her deep relations are the same, / But with long use her tears are dry" (*In Memoriam*, 78.19-20). Calmer, but still melancholy, he ponders the life his dead friend might

The gate to Trinity College, Cambridge. It was at Trinity College that Tennyson first met Arthur Henry Hallam, whose death inspired *In Memoriam*.

have had and the marriage between their families that would have drawn them closer together. Yet he realizes that he has come to terms with his loss and is still able to feel Arthur's continuing influence on him even in death: "Whatever way my days decline, / I felt and feel, tho' left alone, / His being working in mine own, / The footsteps of his life in mine" (*In Memoriam*, 85.41-44). Moreover, he can even extend friendship to other men, although the level of intimacy will never quite match what he shared with Hallam.

Revisiting "the reverend walls" of Trinity College, where he and Hallam first met, the speaker recalls their happy times together—their past conversations, walks, picnics—at Cambridge and at his family home. Knowing that he will never again behold Hallam in the flesh, the speaker nonetheless wonders whether his friend's spirit may be hovering near. Back at the country parish of Somersby, he experiences an epiphany when he rereads Hallam's letters to him: "So word by word, and line by line, / The dead man touch'd me from the past, / And all at once it seem'd at last / The living soul was flash'd on mine" (*In Memoriam*, 95.33-36). The speaker realizes anew the power of the connection, a connection that persists even in death. He feels Arthur's presence; his living soul manifests itself in the letters. On the eve of the family's departure from their home at Somersby, the poet experiences a dream—"a vision of the dead, / Which left my after-morn content" (*In Memoriam*, 103.3-4). In this vision, he and Hallam, accompanied by the Muses, are reunited aboard a ship bound for the next world.

The third Christmas section sees the family ensconced in their new home, which is not haunted by memories of the dead. Turning his thoughts wholly to the future, the speaker exhorts the tolling Yule bells to "ring out the old, ring in the new . . . / Ring out the want, the care, the sin, / The faithless coldness of the times; / Ring out, ring out my mournful rhymes, / But ring the fuller minstrel in" (*In Memoriam*, 106.5, 17-20).

In the sections that follow, the speaker pays tribute to his lost friend's many virtues, accepts his own fate of remaining on earth for the time being, and resumes once more his meditation on faith and science. This time, however, he concludes that modern scientific discoveries do not presage the end of the human race, but rather, hold out hope for its further evolution, seeing modern man as "[t]he herald of a higher race" (*In Memoriam*, 118.14). Ultimately, he rejects scientific materialism and reaffirms his faith, believing that the human and divine elements of his beloved friend are to be found again in the God who created him: "My love involves the love before; / My love is vaster passion now; / Tho' mix'd with God and Nature thou, / I seem to love thee more and more" (*In Memoriam*, 130.9-12). The main body of the poem ends with the speaker's exhortation that humanity place its faith in God and accept "[t]he truths that never can be proved / Until we close with all we loved, / And all we flow from, soul in soul" (*In Memoriam*, 131.10-12).

The epilogue to *In Memoriam* leaps ahead to the 1842 nuptials of the speaker's friend (Edmund Lushington), to his youngest sister (Cecilia Tennyson), a wedding that symbolically replaces the wedding that never took place between Hallam and the speaker's other sister (Emily Tennyson). Reflecting on the passage of time since Hallam's death, the speaker reveals that "Regret is dead but love is more / Than in the summers that are flown, / For I myself with these have grown / To something greater than before" (*In Memoriam*, Epilogue.17-20). Rejoicing in the union of his friend and sister, he watches them depart after the ceremony and imagines how, on their wedding night, "[a] soul shall draw from out the vast, / And strike his being into bounds, / And, moved thro' life of lower phase, / Result in man" (*In Memoriam*, Epilogue.123-126). That unborn child he envisions will become a living

link between the present generation and the higher human race which the process of evolution seems to presage, as well as part of that "one far-off divine event, / To which the whole creation moves" (*In Memoriam*, Epilogue: 143-144).

Male friendship. One aspect of *In Memoriam* that has often surprised readers is the intensity of the Hallam-Tennyson friendship as revealed in the poem. Tennyson continually addresses his lost friend in language that seems, to some modern audiences, more suited to a lost beloved: "My Arthur, whom I shall not see / Till all my widow'd race be run; / Dear as the mother to the son, / More than my brothers are to me" (*In Memoriam*, 9.17-20). Repeated references are made throughout *In Memoriam* to the poet shedding "tears of the widower" as he mourns "the comrade of [his] choice," reinforcing the im-

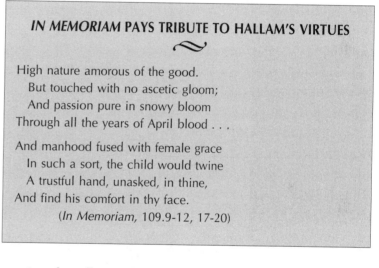

IN MEMORIAM PAYS TRIBUTE TO HALLAM'S VIRTUES

High nature amorous of the good.
   But touched with no ascetic gloom;
   And passion pure in snowy bloom
Through all the years of April blood . . .

And manhood fused with female grace
   In such a sort, the child would twine
   A trustful hand, unasked, in thine,
And find his comfort in thy face.
      (*In Memoriam*, 109.9-12, 17-20)

pression of an affection that appears to be more than platonic (*In Memoriam*, 13.1, 9). Even in Tennyson's own time, one reviewer complained of the note of "amatory tenderness" in *In Memoriam*, and, after quoting two especially tender stanzas, remarked, "Very sweet and plaintive these verses are; but who would not give them a feminine application?" (Hunt, p. 104).

Some twentieth-century critics, such as Lionel Trilling and Harold Bloom, have gone even further in their speculations, suggesting that *In Memoriam* is a poem of repressed passion from one man to another. Other critics and scholars, however, firmly refute these claims. Tennyson biographer Robert Bernard Martin writes:

> It has been the tendency in post-Freudian times to look at such [friendships] in an increasingly unsubtle fashion and to fashion categorical

labels that are inexact at best. . . . Sexual feelings may be the most common stimulus to love, but even in relationships that are deeply sexual there are many other factors that have little to do with sex. Sympathy, companionship, likeness of interests, and even habitual proximity often form a great part of love. . . . It was surely these feelings that were at the heart of Tennyson's friendship with Hallam.

(Martin, p. 94)

HALLAM'S BRIDE-TO-BE

Ironically, Alfred Tennyson's intense emotional reaction to his friend's death overshadowed and obscured that of his own sister, Hallam's betrothed. Devastated by Hallam's 1833 death, Emily Tennyson, always in uncertain health, suffered a complete breakdown and was ill in bed for over a year afterwards. In 1834, Emily met the other Hallams for the very first time and was taken into the family. During Emily's visit, the Hallams gave a dinner party in honor of her twenty-third birthday. Among the guests was a Mr. Jesse, who attended another party at the Hallams' a month later. In 1841, Emily became engaged to Richard Jesse—in all probability the same man—who was a lieutenant in the navy. Hallam's family was shocked by this development—afterwards, they claimed always to have detested Richard Jesse. Tennyson too was startled, although he accepted the couple's 1842 marriage. But he never cared much for Richard, who was a compulsive talker, and frequently made excuses to be absent from home when Emily and her husband came to visit. Old Mr. Hallam also accepted the situation and generously continued to pay Emily an annuity of 300 pounds even after her marriage. Others were less understanding; the poet, Elizabeth Barrett, on hearing the news, declared that Emily was "a disgrace to womanhood! . . . to marry at all—bad!—to keep the annuity, having married—worse!" (Barrett in Martin, p. 258). In the end, the Jesses' marriage appears to have been neither better nor worse than most marriages; Emily had two children and named the eldest son Arthur Henry Hallam Jesse, but she appears to have made her peace with the past. Many years later, she and her husband attended a séance, at which she was told by the medium that she would spend her afterlife with Arthur Hallam. Emily indignantly declared to Richard, "I consider that an extremely unfair arrangement and shall have nothing to do with it. We have been through bad times together in this world and I consider it only decent to share our good times, presuming we have them, in the next"

(Jesse in Martin, p. 259).

Moreover, Martin continues, "[t]he pairing of friends such as Hallam and Tennyson was both common in the Apostles and perfectly open. . . . As Maurice and Sterling had been each other's closest friends at an earlier date, so Kemble and Donne, Robert Monteith and Francis Garden, G. S. Venables and Henry Lushington, all found a special friendship within the larger group, one to give a centre to their affections" (Martin, p. 95).

The closeness between Hallam and Tennyson and their fellow Apostles was not unprecedented, but rather, part of a larger phenomenon. Historian Mark Girouard writes, "Romantic friendships had always been an inevitable feature of the male life at public schools and universities. They tended to be more in fashion, however, at some periods than others. In the 1820s and 1830s they were very much the vogue at Cambridge; they were called 'arm-in-arms'" (Girouard, p. 216). However, Girouard, adds, "Such romantic friendships need not necessarily, or even usually, lead to sexual relationships" (Girouard, p. 217). Indeed, Hallam himself made it abundantly clear to another member of his circle—Richard Monckton Milnes, who *was* apparently homosexual—that he desired no special intimacy in their relationship and that his own sexual preferences lay in another direction. In a letter dated July 1831, Hallam wrote to Milnes: "I am not aware . . . that, in the lofty sense which you are accustomed to attach to the name of Friendship, we ever were or ever could be friends. . . . That exalted sentiment I do not ridicule—God forbid—nor consider it as merely ideal: I have experienced it, and it thrills within me now—but not—pardon me, my dear Milnes, for speaking frankly—not for *you*" (Hallam in Martin, p. 96). Significantly, the timing of Hallam's letter coincides with his attachment to Emily Tennyson, to whom he was engaged at the time of his death in 1833.

Sources and literary context. The main source of inspiration for *In Memoriam* was, of course, the early death of Tennyson's closest friend and future brother-in-law, Arthur Henry Hallam. Tennyson drew upon other people and incidents from his life as well, most notably in the epilogue to *In Memoriam*, which, as mentioned, celebrates the wedding of his sister Cecilia to his friend Edmund Lushington. However, Tennyson remained wary of placing too close or narrow an autobiographical framework about his work, asserting that

[*In Memoriam*] is a poem, *not* an actual biography. It is founded on our friendship, on the engagement of Arthur Hallam to my sister, on his sudden death at Vienna, just before the time fixed for their marriage, and on his burial at Clevedon Church. The poem concludes with the marriage of my youngest sister Cecilia. It was meant to be a kind of *Divina Commedia*, ending with happiness. . . . 'I' is not always the author speaking of himself, but the voice of the human race speaking thro' him.

(Tennyson in Palmer, p. 93)

Moreover, *In Memoriam* is a meditative as well as a semibiographical or elegiac poem: Tennyson's musings on works of natural history—including the previously mentioned *Principles of Geology* by Sir Charles Lyell and *Vestiges of the Natural History of Creation* by Robert Chambers—comprise the basis of other sections.

In Memoriam is most often categorized as an elegy, a poem of lamentation for the dead. Comparisons invariably arise with two great English elegies, John Milton's *Lycidas* and Percy Bysshe Shelley's *Adonais*, with which Tennyson was almost certainly familiar. However, unlike Milton and Shelley, Tennyson does not make extensive use of the conventions associated with the pastoral elegy, such as depicting the speaker and the deceased as shepherds, invoking the muse, showing a procession of mourners, and strewing flowers upon the hearse of the deceased. Rather, Tennyson's expression of sorrow for Hallam remains firmly rooted in the contemporary world, and it is to the Christian God that he directs his thoughts, prayers, and questions, not to the classical deities of Greek or Roman mythology.

Reviews. Tennyson had planned to have *In Memoriam* published anonymously. But word leaked out even before publication, and on the day of its release the *Publishers' Circular* described *In Memoriam* as the work of Tennyson. The poet was apparently not upset by the revelation of his identity as the author, yet he never permitted an edition to be published with his name on the title page during his lifetime. Perhaps he felt the subject was too personal for such public display, or he wanted to maintain some portion of his original intent to publish the poem anonymously.

All questions of anonymity aside, *In Memoriam* was, for the most part, warmly and enthusiastically received. One of the few unfavorable critiques appeared in *The Times*, where an anonymous reviewer admitted to finding "the enormous exaggeration of the grief" for Hallam rather off-putting, complaining, "Instead of a memorial we have a myth. Hence the subject suffers loss even from its magnitude. The hero is beyond our sympathy" (Hunt, p. 103). The *Times* reviewer was also unsettled by the note of "amatory tenderness" expressed towards Hallam, which, he felt, would be more appropriate if directed towards a female subject; the reviewer recommended that *In Memoriam* be shortened considerably in subsequent editions (Hunt, p. 104).

The general consensus among contemporary critics, however, was that Tennyson had composed a great and beautiful poem that would endure. J. Westland Marston, writing for the *Athenaeum*, praised the poem's honesty and straightforwardness in expressing grief:

[The verses] come upon us with all the truthfulness of a diary:—but it is a diary of a love so profound, that though using the largest symbols of imagination, they appear to us as the homeliest language. The beauty and melody of illustration are so absorbed in the pervading feeling, that we become fully conscious of the former attributes only by a recurrence to the poems.

(Marston in Hunt, pp. 63-64)

The noted critic G. H. Lewes, writing for *The Leader*, was similarly enthusiastic. Although Lewes considered *In Memoriam* not quite on a par with such elegies as Milton's *Lycidas* and Shelley's *Adonais*, he nonetheless found much to commend in Tennyson's work: "But how beautiful, how simple, and how touching are the poems when you read them uncritically, giving full sway to the feelings which that music rouses in you! . . . We shall be surprised if [*In Memoriam*] does not become the solace and delight of every house where poetry is loved. A true and hopeful spirit breathes from its pages" (Lewes in Hunt, p. 68). Finally, Franklin Lushington, critic for *Tait's Edinburgh Magazine*, called *In Memoriam* "one of the most touching and exquisite monuments ever raised to a departed friend—the pure and unaffected expression of the truest and most perfect love; and as such, it ought to be, and . . . will be, a memorial more lasting than bronze" (Lushington in Hunt, p. 72).

—Pamela S. Loy

For More Information

Girouard, Mark. *The Return to Camelot: Chivalry and the English Gentleman.* New Haven: Yale University Press, 1981.

Houghton, Walter E. *The Victorian Frame of Mind, 1830-1870.* New Haven: Yale University Press, 1957.

Hunt, John Dixon, ed. *Tennyson: In Memoriam*. London: Macmillan, 1970.

Levi, Peter. *Tennyson*. New York: Charles Scribner's Sons, 1993.

Martin, Robert Bernard. *Tennyson: The Unquiet Heart*. New York: Oxford University Press, 1980.

Mattes, Eleanor Bustin. *In Memoriam: The Way of a Soul*. New York: Exposition Press, 1951.

Palmer, D. J. *Writers and Their Backgrounds: Tennyson*. London: G. Bell & Sons, 1973.

Peltason, Timothy. *Reading "In Memoriam."* Princeton: Princeton University Press, 1985.

Steane, J. B. *Tennyson*. New York: Arco, 1969.

Tennyson, Alfred. *In Memoriam*. ed. Robert H. Ross. New York: W. W. Norton, 1973.

Wilson, A. N. *God's Funeral: A Biography of Faith and Doubt in Western Civilization*. New York: Ballantine, 1999.

Jane Eyre

by

Charlotte Brontë

THE LITERARY WORK

A novel set in rural England during the early nineteenth century; published in 1847.

SYNOPSIS

An orphan draws upon her own strength of character, the kindness of a few allies, and supernatural aid as she matures from schoolgirl to governess to independent adult and married woman.

Born in Yorkshire on April 21, 1816, Charlotte Brontë was the third child of clergyman Patrick Brontë, rector of Hayworth, and Maria Branwell Brontë. Living a sequestered life with her four sisters and one brother, Charlotte read voraciously and rambled on the moors. Her mother died of stomach cancer when she was five, after which the four eldest girls suffered from protracted hunger, illness, and cold at the harsh Clergy Daughters' School at the Cowan Bridge in Lancashire, model for the Lowood School of *Jane Eyre*. In fact, Charlotte's two older sisters, Maria and Elizabeth, died at the school before Charlotte and her younger sister Emily were withdrawn and brought home in 1825. Together, the four remaining Brontë children (Charlotte, Emily, Anne, and Branwell) created vividly detailed imaginary worlds in story form, recording them in miniature volumes written in minute script. The three sisters, when adults, drew on these early literary efforts and published a book of poems together under the pen names Currer, Ellis, and Acton Bell, neutral appellations that could have belonged to men at a time when female authors were "liable to be looked on with prejudice" (Brontë in Gordon, pp. 139-40). Undeterred by the fact that their book of poems sold only two copies and determined to support themselves as writers, the young women began work on novels thereafter. Charlotte's first mature effort, *The Professor*, was rejected by numerous publishers, but the firm Smith, Elder & Co. urged her to try a three-volume novel with more action and excitement. The result was the immediately successful *Jane Eyre,* a novel that treats the social realities of mid-nineteenth-century Britain in a context of gothic mystery.

Events in History at the Time of the Novel

England's orphans and orphanhood. Scholars and critics often comment on the literary usefulness of orphanhood in the world of the novel. The orphans of fiction, they observe, have a wider field of experiences open to them than would a child raised in a family: there are no protective parents to prevent interesting adventures or misadventures from befalling an orphan as the action of a novel proceeds. This is certainly true for Jane Eyre, who is thrown into several crises from which a parent might have rescued her.

As convenient a device for fiction as orphanhood might have been, there was a social and

Charlotte Brontë

historical basis for the large number of orphan-heroes in nineteenth-century British novels. Orphanhood occurred with substantial frequency in nineteenth-century Britain, particularly among the poor: "In mid-century working-class areas it appears that 8 percent of the children lost both parents by the time they were fifteen and almost a third had lost at least one" (Pool, p. 235).

Once a child was orphaned, he or she had to rely principally on the sometimes grudging willingness of relatives to assume guardianship. In *Jane Eyre*, the heroine's cold-hearted aunt, Mrs. Reed, takes Jane in only because it was Mr. Reed's dying wish that she do so. If no one consented to take in a child as a ward, that child was thrown on the mercy of the parish for aid. Orphanages run by charities were few and far between, and many were reserved just for very young children. Frequently, then, circumstances compelled orphans to seek aid from the same sources as impoverished adults: neighbors, the parish, and—in the most desperate cases—the poorhouse.

In the 1790s, many rural parishes had adopted poor-relief policies, dubbed "outdoor relief," which supplemented the incomes of needy parishioners while still allowing them to live outside of poorhouses. The aid, however, was woefully inadequate, and with it for most recipients came the stigma of social shame. Moreover, the comparatively generous outdoor relief policies

lasted only a short while. In 1834 the New Poor Law curtailed such policies in favor of sending able-bodied adults and children to live in one of a swelling number of increasingly prison-like workhouses where they earned their food by hard manual labor like stonebreaking or grinding corn (Altick, p. 123). Another common task was tearing apart fibers of old ropes until the fingers bled and were scarred with cuts. By 1836 more than 42,000 children under the age of 16 lived in such houses. The regimen varied, but in 1836 inmates typically rose at 5:00 A.M. in summer, 6:00 A.M. in winter, then labored 10 or 9 hours, respectively. Three of the hours were spent in school, at lessons taught by ordinary, often illiterate workhouse officers. Scant diets resulted in malnourished children, who, if disobedient, risked reduction of even this minimal diet, as well as beatings for boys, and confinement in darkened rooms for both genders. The conditions were dismal enough to strike terror in adults and children alike for more than a century. From 1834 until after World War II, when workhouse premises passed into the control of the National Health Service—the threat of living in such an institution inspired dread in the poor. In Brontë's novel, Jane herself is threatened with a fate of this kind. After a bout of bad behavior, the servant Bessie warns her, "You ought to be aware, Miss, that you are under obligations to Mrs. Reed: she keeps you: if she were to turn you off, you would have to go to the poor-house" (Brontë, *Jane Eyre*, 10).

The life of the governess. Like the orphan, the governess was a familiar figure in Victorian fiction and society. Ostensibly the governess's job was to teach the children of affluent families; in practice, however, her responsibilities often extended to more general childcare that supplemented the care provided by the children's nursemaid, and to miscellaneous chores at the whim of her employers. Care and instruction of boys under the age of seven generally fell to the governess, after which the boys were either sent away to school or transferred to the care of a male tutor. Girls often remained under the care of the governess, gaining tutelage in "accomplishments" deemed appropriate for a lady, until they were 17 or 18, the proper age to "come out" into society. Over the years the roster of subjects that a governess was expected to teach grew lengthier and more elaborate, expanding to include a variety of arts and languages and embracing such arcane skills as spinning glass or molding artificial flowers from paper and wax. Hence Jane's observation on her own preparedness to serve as governess: she is qualified, she says, "to teach the usual branches of a good English education, together with French, Drawing, and Music," then remarks in an aside, "in those days, reader, this now narrow catalogue of accomplishments would have been held tolerably comprehensive" (*Jane Eyre*, p. 76).

Despite their refined attainments and often superior education, governesses held an ambiguous rank within the household, supposedly above the servants but clearly not in the same social stratum as the family. Thus, Jane must be deferential to her employer Rochester and his upper-class visitors, such as the Ingram party; however, the housekeeper, Mrs. Fairfax, distinguishes Jane (and herself) from Leah and John, referring to the latter two as "only servants" (*Jane Eyre*, p. 84). Related to the governess's unclear social standing was her vulnerability to the sexual advances of an employer, for which governesses themselves were sometimes blamed. Governesses were refined young women not immediately distinguishable from marriageable women of the upper-class, yet many Victorians looked askance at the governess, considering her a temptation to her employer and therefore a threat to middle-class values. In fact, a governess risked sexual predation by an employer since she was economically dependent on him and lacked social power or connections that might protect her.

Never handsomely compensated for their work, governesses began suffering severe economic hardship in the 1830s and 1840s, a period in which widespread bank failures brought trouble for workers in most occupations. Adding to the national economic difficulties was another problem: swelling numbers of so-called "redundant women," single women compelled to support themselves because of their lack of inheritance and the period's dearth of marriageable men. Historians speculate that one source of this problem may have been the large-scale emigration of single Englishmen to the Americas and Commonwealth colonies during the period. In any case, demographics and economics forced increasing numbers of women into the workforce. Since governessing was one of very few socially acceptable occupations open to females at the time, the majority of middle-class working women chose this profession. Their options were, in fact, limited, by a sad irony of the era:

> At the same time that the economic pressure to work increased, the range of activities considered socially acceptable for middle-class

women decreased; whereas in the 1790s, middle-class women had worked as jailors, plumbers, butchers, farmers, seedsmen, tailors, and saddlers, by the 1840s and 1850s, dressmaking, millinery, and teaching far outstripped all other occupational activities.
> (Poovey, pp. 126-27)

So fierce was the competition for a position that job openings grew scarce and salaries dropped. By 1841 there was an abundant supply of governesses; in fact, so abundant did they become and so dismal their circumstances that the Christian Socialists founded a charity for them, the Governesses' Benevolent Institution.

Center of social controversy. As the charity suggests, people of the period exhibited growing concern about the lives of governesses and about the effect of their increasing numbers upon the social order in general. By the 1830s, the governess and her "plight" had become a popular subject for English novels; by the 1840s, essayists and other public moralists had begun declaring their concern for the welfare of the well-educated, middle-class young woman thrust into a frequently ascetic, lonely, and thankless way of life. While female servants of lower stations vastly outnumbered governesses and lived under far more deplorable conditions, the governess's life was what seized the imaginations of the era's social commentators, themselves largely middle-class men and women. Writers for periodicals like the *English Woman's Journal* and the *Saturday Review* offered up a wide spectrum of criticisms, from worries about the morality of a woman hired to educate their daughters (work perceived by conservative commentators as "naturally" belonging to mothers), to concerns about the physical and emotional well-being of the governesses themselves (Poovey, pp. 128-34).

The so-called "governess novels" of the period—such as *Jane Eyre* and Anne Brontë's *Tenant of Wildfell Hall*—became vehicles used by writers to expound on the psychological difficulties of the governess's life. They furthermore became vehicles for the portrayal of upper- and middle-class domestic life: the "neither-an-outsider-nor-insider status of the post [of the governess] . . . made it a marvelous, relatively detached standpoint from which the novelist could describe at close quarters the workings of a household" (Pool, p. 225). It is this standpoint that enriches the descriptions of life at Thornfield Hall in *Jane Eyre*. Through the governess, a novelist might even level criticism at mid-nineteenth-century limitations placed on women.

The life of the governess, constrained and limited as it was for anyone of active intellect and lively feeling, becomes intolerable to Jane in her fictional world, as it was to Brontë herself when she worked as a governess in 1839. The constraints lead Jane to speak her mind in a passage of the novel that would become well-known to the period's agitators for women's rights:

> Women feel just as men feel; they need exercise for their faculties and a field for their efforts as much as their brothers do; they suffer from too rigid a restraint, too absolute a stagnation, precisely as men would suffer; and it is narrow-minded in their more privileged fellow-creatures to say that they ought to confine themselves to making puddings and knitting stockings, to playing on the piano and embroidering bags. It is thoughtless to condemn them, or laugh at them, if they seek to do more or learn more than custom has pronounced necessary for their sex.
>
> (*Jane Eyre*, p. 96)

Empire and evangelism. Though the action of *Jane Eyre* takes place entirely within England, the events in the novel are by no means sealed off from the wider world. There is an "offstage" global presence—recounted in the contents of letters from abroad, in Rochester's narration of his misadventures in continental Europe and in Jamaica, and in the discussions of whether Jane will accompany the missionary St. John Rivers to India. The combined weight of these "offstage" influences shapes the plot unmistakably, creating a sense of danger that periodically intrudes upon the safer world of domestic England.

During the early years of the nineteenth century, England was still benefiting from strong imperial control of the West Indies. The English conquered Jamaica (the island on which Rochester made his fortune) in 1655, and starting in the 1700s, Englishmen ran lucrative sugar plantations there with labor provided predominantly by African slaves. Not explicitly mentioned in the novel, but surely present in the minds of both author and readers, was this specter of slavery, the primary mechanism by which British plantation owners were able to make spectacular profits.

> Sugar enriched many planters as well as their European creditors and suppliers—and sugar made slavery necessary. The labor of black slaves was the basis for life on the sugar islands from the 17th century. . . . By the 1750s, almost nine out of ten men and women were slaves on all the islands where sugar was grown. (Rogozinski, p. 125).

The slave trade was still legal in the West Indies in the early nineteenth century, despite the ongoing efforts of secular and evangelical humanitarians who pressed for its abolition. It was 1833 before abolitionists finally succeeded in outlawing slavery in British colonies, but long before then the force of increased public concern about the treatment of "uncivilized" peoples had rendered the practice shameful in the eyes of the English at home.

Of course, slavery and other forms of exploitation in the colonies were originally made possible in part by the English people's long-standing belief in their own cultural superiority to the African and indigenous peoples living in their colonies, and this belief complicates the growing British humanitarian concern on their behalf. In India, this English ethnocentrism led some early missionaries there to portray the indigenous population in negative and condescending terms. Missionary Charles Grant, for example, concluded his 1792 tract on English missionary efforts in these words: "Upon the whole, then, we cannot avoid recognizing in the people of Hindostan a race of men lamentably degenerate and base, retaining but a feeble sense of moral obligation . . . and sunk in misery by their vices" (Grant in Moorhouse, p. 67).

Despite Brontë's conscious efforts at egalitarian thinking in other contexts, this widely held fear of different cultures manifests itself in *Jane Eyre*'s portrayal of both India and the West Indies as suspicious, even threatening places. Some of this anxiety was warranted. The resident English were indeed frequently in danger in these colonies because of the prevalence of tropical diseases, crime, and (specifically in the Caribbean) periodic slave rebellions, hundreds of which marked the West Indian slave era. As a result, the sense of threat was pervasive among the white settlers, particularly in the West Indies, and with good reason: they were vastly outnumbered by the population they exploited. By 1775 "fewer than 19,000 whites ruled over 193,000 slaves" (Rogozinski, pp. 117, 155).

At the root of much of Brontë's negative portrayal of the West Indies and India was not just latent ethnocentrism, however; the ethnocentrism was tinged with genuine disapproval of exploitative English practices in these reaches of the empire. Brontë was well aware of the problem of slavery and in private letters spoke reverently of the work of abolitionists. Moreover, she may easily have shared the widespread English disgust with Caribbean sugar planters as part of the

Joan Fontaine as Jane and Orson Welles as Mr. Rochester in the 1944 film version of *Jane Eyre*.

larger "ill-mannered and ostentatious gang" who were earning wealth overseas in pursuits of questionable morality (Moorhouse, p. 41). It follows that in *Jane Eyre*, the Mason family's involvement in the West Indies serves as an implicit indica-

tor of their social and moral degradation; their "madness" is a logical corollary of their environment, which was imagined to be both inherently uncivilized and corrupted from without by the British. This view undergirds Rochester's characterization of the West Indies as "hell," a "bloody . . . bottomless pit" from which his only rescue is a "sweet" wind "fresh from Europe" (*Jane Eyre*, p. 271).

A similar set of assumptions about alien cultures (together with religious and commercial motives) informed nineteenth-century British attitudes toward India. The English were well established in India by the time of *Jane Eyre*, having arrived there as merchants with the East India Trading Company in the early seventeenth century. At first, English involvement in India was strictly commercial; in fact, the British government forbade missionary activity there until Lord Wellesley began supporting maverick Anglican clergymen who defied the government's ban. Soon thereafter, concern on the behalf of indigenous Indians, coupled with a widespread conviction that the Christian faith was superior to other belief systems, led to the development of a vast network of Christian missionary settlements in India. This project was energetically supported at home in England by prominent public figures such as the avid abolitionist William Wilberforce, who maintained that converting India to Christianity was "the greatest of all causes, for I really place it before Abolition" (Wilberforce in Moorhouse, p. 69). Evangelical Christians (of whom St. John Rivers is a representative in *Jane Eyre*) were particularly vigorous in their efforts to convert the "heathen." Evangelicals at home and abroad "sought to impose their standards of right living (of whose absolute authority, residing in divine inspiration, they had no doubt) upon society as a whole" (Altick, p. 181).

Evangelical aims were not universally supported by the English at home or in India. Some thinkers, such as philologist Horace H. Wilson and Asiatic Society member Colonel Stewart, criticized Evangelical infringements upon Hindu sacred traditions, which they regarded as every bit as fine and noble as Christian traditions (Moorhouse, p. 70). However, the collective ambition of the Evangelicals nevertheless led to colonized cultures' being altered substantially by the introduction of Christian spirituality and ideology.

The Novel in Focus

Plot summary. *Jane Eyre* opens with the narrator, the adult Jane, recounting her childhood persecution at the hands of her adoptive family, the Reeds. In the midst of cruel insults, exclusion from family festivities, and even violence, Jane finds solace in reading imaginative fiction and looking at pictures of far-off landscapes in Thomas Bewick's *History of British Birds*. Though she reaps some small comfort from the occasional attentions of the servant Bessie, eventually the chronic ill treatment proves too much for Jane to withstand. After an explosion of long-suppressed anguish and rage, Jane is locked into the "red room," locus of her uncle Reed's death, where she believes she sees a supernatural presence and faints in terror.

When Jane regains consciousness, she finds that she is being treated by a kindly local apothecary, who intercedes with Mrs. Reed on her behalf and recommends that Jane be sent away to school. Mrs. Reed, glad at the prospect of being rid of Jane, complies with the apothecary's recommendations and sends her to Lowood, a charity school. There, though she is relieved to be away from the Reeds, Jane discovers new trials. The school is run by the stinting, hypocritical Mr. Brocklehurst, who administers unjust punishments to the girls and allows them to suffer conditions of severe cold, hunger, and illness. While at Lowood, Jane gains some comfort and learns a measure of self-control from her devout friend Helen Burns and her gentle, generous teacher Miss Temple. Soon, however, Helen contracts typhus and dies, along with many of the other girls. When news of the abominable conditions at the school finally reaches the wider public, some improvements are made, and Jane eventually goes on to become a teacher there herself.

A few years pass uneventfully before Jane decides she needs more stimulus and a wider field of action than Lowood can provide. She advertises for a position as a governess and is soon employed at Thornfield, the large, old country manor of the wealthy Mr. Rochester. Jane's pupil, Adèle, is Rochester's "ward," a girl whose exact relationship to Rochester is at first unclear. Adèle soon grows attached to Jane, as does Jane's other frequent companion, the genial housekeeper Mrs. Fairfax. Rochester himself proves to be mysterious and unpredictable, by turns seeming interested in Jane and then ignoring her, playing elaborate tricks on her, and offering overtures of intimacy but then taunting her with the presence of a sham fiancée. Also mysterious are the doings of the inscrutable servant, Grace Poole, whose role in the household is withheld from Jane. As Jane and Rochester's relationship blooms into romance, Jane becomes increasingly alarmed by unexplainable events within the household, events seemingly connected with Grace Poole. Eerie laughter from the third floor, a near-fatal fire stealthily set in Rochester's bedroom, a bloody attack on Rochester's business associate Mason, and a late-night visit to Jane's room from a ghoulish stranger lead up to the final revelation of the house's central secret. As Jane and Rochester are about to be married, Mason interrupts the ceremony and declares that Rochester already has a wife. The wife is in fact Mason's sister Bertha, a violent madwoman whom Rochester has kept locked in a third-floor room with Grace Poole as her attendant.

After this revelation, Rochester attempts to explain his actions and reveals a personal history of pain, disappointment, and subsequent debauchery. He narrates how he was duped into marrying Bertha by her family, English plantation owners in Jamaica. He goes on to describe how, in despair upon discovering her madness, he housed her at Thornfield and left for Europe, where he plunged into a series of affairs in search of solace. At this point we learn that Adèle is the daughter of one of Rochester's mistresses, though probably fathered by one of her other lovers. Rochester begs Jane to have mercy and stay with him, but Jane, heartbroken but resolute, determines that she must leave Rochester.

Before dawn, Jane sets out on foot with no destination in mind, carrying only a few small belongings and 20 shillings in her purse. In her haste and distress, she gives all her money to a coachman and then forgets her belongings on the coach at the end of the trip. Absolutely destitute, she wanders alone on the moors and sleeps in the open air until she is reduced to begging charity from strangers. In her last extremity of hunger and fatigue, she falls on the doorstep of Marsh End, the home of the local clergyman, St. John Rivers, and his sisters, Diana and Mary. Though Jane uses an assumed name and will not divulge her history to them, they take her in, nurse her back to full health, and finally find her work as a village schoolmistress. Before long, St. John discovers Jane's identity and history and learns that they are, in fact, cousins. Moreover, their uncle has named Jane as his sole heir to a sum of 20,000 pounds, a fortune that Jane generously shares with her newfound relatives. As Jane, Diana, and Mary grow ever closer, the impassive St. John observes Jane closely and eventually draws her into his preparations for his life as a missionary in India.

One day, St. John surprises Jane with a loveless and perfunctory offer of marriage; he has identified in her all the qualities necessary for a missionary's wife. Even though she does not love St. John, Jane is tempted to pursue the rigorous life he offers her, believing that the vocation is worthy and that she could do the work well. Just as she nearly gives in to St. John's forceful efforts at persuasion, she is startled to hear the unearthly voice of Rochester, seeming to call to her over a great distance. She immediately leaves to seek him. Upon returning to Thornfield, she discovers that the house was long ago burnt to the ground by Bertha Mason, who threw herself to her death from the flaming battlements as Rochester tried to save her. Rochester himself was blinded and maimed in the fire and soon afterwards moved his household to Ferndean, an abandoned ancestral home in a dank, overgrown forest. There Jane finds him and marries him. They send his ward Adèle to school and begin a happy life together. Rochester eventually recovers his sight partially, and together he and Jane have a child.

Jane Eyre and "the Woman Question." Jane, as narrator and heroine, expounds throughout the novel on the needs and abilities of women and the injustice of a culture that circumscribes their lives so tightly. For example, at Lowood, she "gasp[s]" and "pray[s] for liberty," but settles for "a new servitude" because it is all she can imagine getting (*Jane Eyre*, p. 74). Later, at Thornfield, she decries men who would require women to be tame and domestic, calling them "narrow-minded" and "thoughtless," and asserts her right to a fuller existence (*Jane Eyre,* p. 96). Finally, at Ferndean, she requires of Rochester a partnership of equals that will allow her to be "a free human being with an independent will" (*Jane Eyre,* p. 223). In doing so, Jane presages the massive social changes yet to come in the mid- to late-Victorian period, at which time "the Woman Question" would become a prominent feature of public debate and political agitation.

As of the early nineteenth century, British women had few avenues for social or economic independence open to them, and the restrictions against which Jane struggles would have been widespread among women in real life. The call for a meaningful education for girls and women issued by Mary Wollstonecraft's *A Vindication of the Rights of Woman* (in *WLAIT 3: British and Irish Literature and Its Times*) in 1798 went largely unheeded for the first half of the nineteenth century. Because of the period's insistence that women be refined, decorative, and non-threatening, girls from affluent families were not so much educated as trained in elegant uselessness, learning only "the polite accomplishments which were calculated to help her first to win a husband and then, after that primary goal was reached, to infuse her household with an air of the softer graces so as to maintain its separation from the gritty world of affairs" (Altick, p. 54). Higher education was not available at all to women until the founding of Queen's College in 1848, and even if a woman were to complete a university education, she could not hold an official degree until 1880. For most of the century, once an affluent young woman had completed her secondary education, such as it was, the nineteenth-century social doctrine of "separate spheres" for men and women guaranteed that the professional world would be closed to her.

While affluent girls were trained in ornamental idleness, lower-middle and working-class girls, if educated at all, were trained in propriety and deference to their social superiors. "Charity schools" for "respectable" girls in reduced circumstances, such as the Lowood School in *Jane Eyre*, churned out modest, well-mannered graduates who would become governesses or schoolmistresses. Rural working-class girls, such as those educated in Jane's village schoolhouse in the latter half of the novel, might receive some part of a basic elementary education (grammar, geography, and arithmetic) and then return to work as farmhands, mine laborers, or various kinds of servants. In England in 1851, "over 10 percent of the female population were working as maids, washerwomen, and charwomen" (Altick, p. 52). Urban working-class girls, with or without an education of any kind, generally labored at exhausting, menial, and often dangerous factory jobs in trades such as textile production, nailmaking, and match-making.

If opportunities were limited for single women, the lives of married women did not offer many more options. Women in all social classes were denied legal identities separate from their husbands:

> Once married, a wife could not sue or make a contract on her own nor make a will without her husband's consent. If he wished to confine her against her will, as Mr. Rochester does his wife at Thornfield Hall, until 1891 he was well within his rights in doing so. He could "correct" her if he wished, too, a right which was supposed to mean only verbal chastisement but in practice often meant physical punishment.
> (Pool, p. 185)

Just as married women had limited legal protection bodily, they also had highly restricted legal rights to their children and property. In case of divorce, custody of the children automatically reverted to the husband; the situation improved somewhat with the passage of the Infants' Custody Act of 1839, which allowed a mother to petition for custody of children under the age of seven. Finally, prior to the Married Women's Property Act of 1882, any property that a woman owned automatically became her husband's upon marriage. G. M. Trevelyan wryly notes the irony in this last feature of early nineteenth-century law: "The law was in curious contrast to the words of the marriage service, when the man was made to say 'with all my worldly goods I thee endow.' It was really the other way around" (Trevelyan, p. 24).

Given the monotony of women's paid work and the risks and indignities that accompanied marriage, it is hardly surprising that the most Jane can wish for herself as she leaves Lowood is "a new servitude" (*Jane Eyre*, p. 74). It becomes that much more remarkable, then, that by the novel's close she has built for herself a life of sustained intellectual discourse (with Diana and Mary, as well as with Rochester), uncompromised personal integrity, and deeply felt equality with her husband, of whom she says, "I am my husband's life as fully as he is mine" (*Jane Eyre*, p. 396). The impassioned speech Jane makes to Rochester midway through the novel especially takes on a new resonance in view of the period's entrenched belief in the inferiority of women:

> Do you think, because I am poor, obscure, plain, and little, I am soulless and heartless? You think wrong!—I have as much soul as you,—and full as much heart! . . . I am not talking to you now through the medium of custom, conventionalities, nor even of mortal flesh—it is my spirit that addresses your spirit; just as if both had passed through the grave, and we stood at God's feet, equal,—as we are!
> (*Jane Eyre*, p. 222)

Brontë's literary advocacy of private, emotional, and psychological freedoms for women helped set the stage for the later public advances made by women's rights advocates like Barbara Bodichon and Harriet Taylor in England, as well as Elizabeth Cady Stanton and Susan B. Anthony in the United States. Though the women's rights movement had barely begun at the time *Jane Eyre* was published, Brontë was not alone in expressing her passionate desire for an expanded field of action and experience for women. In the 1840s, literary contemporaries of Brontë, such as writer-activist Harriet Martineau, expressed social criticisms similar to Brontë's. Martineau in particular was a strong influence on Brontë; her novel *Deerbrook* impressed Brontë with its critique of social injustices, and her pioneering work as an abolitionist and advocate of educational and professional opportunities for women elicited Brontë's admiration. However, it would not be until subsequent decades that literary and political feminism became a widely recognized public force in England.

Sources and literary context. The literary influences on *Jane Eyre* were multiple and disparate. As children, the Brontës read surprisingly sophisticated materials that varied widely, ranging from the poetry of Byron, to the novels of Sir Walter Scott, to periodicals like *Blackwood's Magazine*. From these sources and their own fertile imaginations sprang their juvenilia: stories of the kingdoms of Gondal (written mostly by Emily and Anne) and Angria (by Charlotte and Branwell). These stories revealed the strong influence of Gothic and Romantic literary traditions on the young authors' minds, traditions that would continue to inform Charlotte's later work in less obvious ways.

The works of many novelists had their effect on Brontë's mature fiction. Brontë was conscious early in her career of the influence of Samuel Richardson's novels on her work (see **Pamela**, in *WLAIT 3: British and Irish Literature and Its Times*). More exactly, Brontë worked to correct what she saw as Richardsonian defects in her own writing (Gordon, p. 124). She aspired to the moral trenchancy of William Makepeace Thackeray and Harriet Martineau, and later in her career she was befriended by another novelist with a sharply developed social conscience, Elizabeth Gaskell, a writer whom Brontë admired and who would eventually become her first and most famous biographer. Brontë's famous contemporary Charles Dickens would likewise both influence and be influenced by her work. Lyndall Gordon has suggested that Brontë's reading of Dickens's serialized *Nicholas Nickleby* may well have been what first inspired her to draw on her own environment and experiences to create her form of realistic fiction (Gordon, p. 85). Indeed, she drew on her personal experiences to write *Jane Eyre*: her own memories of life as a clergyman's daughter, a schoolgirl, a governess, a student abroad, and a teacher furnished much of the raw material for the novel.

In addition to the many autobiographical sources, there were a host of specific literary influences on the novel. John Bunyan's **Pilgrim's Progress** (in *WLAIT 3: British and Irish Literature*

and Its Times) forms a structural basis for Jane's movement through life, and allusions to that work pepper the novel. At key stages in her progress, Jane evokes Bunyan's protagonist, for example whispering to herself at Gateshead "the words of Bunyan's Christian: 'What shall I do?—What shall I do?'" (Gilbert and Gubar, *Madwoman in the Attic*, p. 343). Likewise, elements from fairy tales (Jane as "Cinderella," Rochester as "Bluebeard"), folk tales (England's Yorkshire stories), Greek and Roman myths, lore of the Freemason society (Rochester's and Jane's association with fire and air imagery, respectively) and the Bible all contribute to the novel. In terms of subgenre, *Jane Eyre* bears the marks of several popular categories: the governess novel, as noted above; the post-Gothic romance; and most notably the *bildungsroman*, or novel of growth and development.

Reception. Since its earliest reviews, the literary conversation surrounding *Jane Eyre* has been impassioned. Brontë's publishers began receiving enthusiastic letters from readers soon after the novel's publication. One notable response came from no less a personage than William Makepeace Thackeray, author of the social satire **Vanity Fair** (in *WLAIT 3: British and Irish Literature and Its Times*) and an intellectual figure whom Charlotte admired greatly. In a letter dated 23 October 1847, Thackeray had this to say to W. S. Williams of Smith, Elder, & Company:

> I wish you had not sent me *Jane Eyre*. It interested me so much that I have lost (or won if you like) a whole day in reading it. . . . Who the author can be I can't guess—if a woman she knows her language better than most ladies do, or has had a 'classical' education. It is a fine book though—the man & woman capital—the style very generous and upright so to speak.
>
> (Dunn, p. 430)

Also favorably impressed with the novel was G. H. Lewes, best known now as novelist George Eliot's lifelong lover but himself also a writer of note. In December of 1847 he reviewed *Jane Eyre* for *Fraser's Magazine*:

> This, indeed, is a book after our own heart; and, if its merits have not forced it into notice by the time this paper comes before our readers, let us, in all earnestness, bid them lose not a day in sending for it. The writer is evidently a woman, and, unless we are deceived, new in the world of literature. But, man or woman, young or old, be that as it may, no such book has gladdened our eyes for a long while. Almost all that we require in a novelist she has:

perception of character, and power of delineating it; picturesqueness; passion; and knowledge of life.

(Dunn in Brontë, p. 436)

Both Thackeray and Lewes had their criticisms about the novel, but even these are couched in very generous terms. Thackeray considered the character of St. John Rivers "a failure . . . but a good failure," and Lewes chided Brontë gently for indulging in "too much melodrama and improbability" (Dunn in Brontë, pp. 430, 436). Overall, however, their remarks were energetically laudatory, as were those of many other reviewers.

After such a glowing response, Brontë was dismayed when several sharply condemnatory reviews began to appear, reviews that, to her, seemed to misunderstand the spirit of the novel. One critic for *The Christian Remembrancer* accused the book of unfeminine "coarseness" and anti-Christian leanings (Dunn in Brontë, p. 439); to his charges, an irked Brontë replied, "His shafts of sarcasm are nicely polished, keenly pointed; he should not have wasted them in shooting at a mark he cannot see" (Dunn in Brontë, p. 440). Later, Brontë was badly shaken by the untimely criticisms of Elizabeth Rigby, whose lacerating review unfortunately appeared immediately after Branwell Brontë's death and as Emily Brontë lay dying. Rigby damned the novel for "sheer rudeness and vulgarity," calling the character of Rochester "coarse" and "brutal" and reserving particularly excoriating remarks for the character of Jane:

> We hear nothing but self-eulogiums on the perfect tact and wondrous penetration with which she is gifted, and yet almost every word she utters offends us, not only with the absence of these qualities, but with the positive contrasts of them, in either her pedantry, stupidity, or gross vulgarity. . . . Jane Eyre is throughout the personification of an unregenerate and undisciplined spirit . . . She has inherited in fullest measure the worst sin of our fallen nature—the sin of pride.

(Rigby in Brontë pp. 441-42)

Though this review and others like it wounded Brontë, she defended her work in firm replies published in the various periodicals and in the introductions to subsequent novels. Brontë, moreover, was not the only one to speak up in *Jane Eyre*'s defense. In 1849 Brontë met her longtime heroine Harriet Martineau, who declared to Brontë that she thought *Jane Eyre* was "a first-rate book," then went on to defend it from Rigby's criticism: "[T]o the coarse-minded alone *Jane Eyre* is coarse" (Gordon, p. 208). Readers in later eras would further vindicate Brontë's fiction, finding, as novelist Virginia Woolf described it, "a beauty, a power, a swiftness" unlike that of any other writing in its time (Woolf in Brontë, p. 456).

—Susan Lonac

For More Information

Altick, Richard. *Victorian People and Ideas*. New York: Norton, 1973.

Brontë, Charlotte. *Jane Eyre: a Norton Critical Edition*. Ed. Richard Dunn. New York: Norton, 1987.

Gilbert, Sandra M., and Susan Gubar. *The Madwoman in the Attic: The Woman Writer and the Nineteenth-Century Literary Imagination*. New Haven: Yale University Press, 1979.

———. *The Norton Anthology of Literature by Women*. New York: Norton, 1985.

Gordon, Lyndall. *Charlotte Brontë: A Passionate Life*. New York: Norton, 1994.

Moorhouse, Geoffrey. *India Britannica: A Vivid Introduction to the History of British India*. Chicago: Academy Chicago Publishers, 2000.

Morgan, Kenneth O., ed. *The Oxford Illustrated History of Britain*. Oxford: Oxford University Press, 1997.

Pool, Daniel. *What Jane Austen Ate and Charles Dickens Knew: From Fox Hunting to Whist—the Facts of Daily Life in 19th-Century England*. New York: Touchstone, 1993.

Poovey, Mary. *Uneven Developments: The Ideological Work of Gender in Mid-Victorian England*. Chicago: University of Chicago Press, 1988.

Rogozinski, Jan. *A Brief History of the Caribbean*. New York: Facts on File, 1999.

Trevelyan, G. M. *Illustrated English Social History*. Vol. 4. London: Longmans, Green, 1957.

Jude the Obscure

by

Thomas Hardy

Thomas Hardy was born June 2, 1840, in the village of Upper Bockhampton, in Dorset. He was the eldest of four children of Thomas Hardy, a builder and master mason, and Jemima Hand. Both parents were from long-established Dorset families. The younger Thomas attended school from 1848-1856, entering the work world at age 16 as an apprentice to an architect and church restorer in Dorchester. In 1862 Hardy moved to London, where he worked for an architectural firm and became immersed in a program of self-education. He regularly attended church, both mainstream Anglican services and nonconformist evangelical services, and even considered entering the university, with an eye toward a career in the church. Religious doubts put an end to this scheme, and Hardy resumed his former employment in Dorchester in 1867. He meanwhile pursued his writing, both poetry and fiction, publishing his first novel, *Desperate Remedies,* in 1871. Hardy married Emma Lavinia Gifford in 1874, and the couple lived in London and Dorset before settling in 1885 at Max Gate—in a house that Hardy designed—on the outskirts of Dorchester. He was living here when *Jude the Obscure,* his fourteenth novel, appeared in book form in 1895. For the remaining 33 years of his life Hardy published only verse. He died on January 11, 1928. His ashes were placed in Westminster Abbey, and his heart was buried, as he had requested, in the church at Stinsford, near his birthplace. Hardy claimed that his turn from fiction to poetry was due at least partly to the

---

THE LITERARY WORK

A novel set in southwest England from about 1855-85; published in serial form in *Harper's Magazine* in 1894-95, in book form in 1895.

SYNOPSIS

Jude Fawley, an orphan from a remote rural village in Dorsetshire, experiences professional and personal frustrations that lead to the extinction of his dreams.

---

negative reviews received by *Jude the Obscure*, a novel that powerfully criticized some aspects of society in the late Victorian era.

Events in History at the Time of the Novel

Class barriers to university admission. A central aspect of *Jude the Obscure* is Jude's boyhood dream of attending the great university at Christminster in Hardy's fictional world of Wessex. (Christminster is based on Oxford University, and Wessex on Hardy's native county of Dorset.) In fact, a working-class boy like Jude would have no formal training to realize his dream. Free elementary education for all children in England was not mandated until the Education Act of 1870 or made compulsory until 1880. When Jude was a child, in the late 1850s, day schools of various sorts provided the only access to ed-

Thomas Hardy

ucation for children of the lower classes. These day schools came in an assortment of types— charity schools, independent schools run by religious dissenters from outside the Church of England, and a few ancient grammar schools dating from the sixteenth century and supported by the Church of England. Locally administered, they were elementary schools and varied enormously in quality and curriculum. Attempts were made in the early nineteenth century to provide a national system of free elementary schools, but religious antagonisms between the Anglican church and the many nonconformist sects made organization impossible. In the novel, Jude does not attend the day school in Marygreen but works during the day and receives occasional instruction in the evenings from the local schoolmaster, an arrangement frequently found in the mid-nineteenth century among lower-class boys whose labor was of more immediate importance to the survival of their families than was their education. The upper classes, on the other hand, received the training necessary for attendance at Christminster (Oxford). For centuries Oxford functioned primarily as a preserve of the wealthy upper classes, whose children prepared for service in the Anglican clergy or for posts in the upper levels of government administration at home or in the colonies.

Aside from lack of training, Jude's working-class status excludes him from attending an elite university like Oxford. Hardy's novel accurately reflects the historical situation of higher education in mid-nineteenth-century England. Not only were Oxford and Cambridge universities too costly for middle- and lower-class students, they also remained virtually closed to dissenters and Roman Catholics until reform of the Test Acts in 1871, which had required taking communion according to the rites of the mainstream Church of England. Reform removed the religious obstacle, but class barriers remained to attendance at Oxford and Cambridge. Other universities, however, would have been realistic possibilities for Jude. By the time Hardy wrote the novel, London University (known today as University College London) was providing education for middle- and lower-class men, as were universities in Durham, Manchester, Birmingham, Liverpool, Leeds, and other provincial centers. University education for women also developed in the latter decades of the nineteenth century.

In pursuit of his dream, Jude begins a rigorous course of self-instruction, teaching himself Greek and Latin and reading deeply in classical and religious literature as well as popular works of science. While working-class men of Jude's seriousness and industry might have been rare, they were not so uncommon as to render Jude's character improbable, for this was the age of the literature of self-improvement. The Society for the Diffusion of Useful Knowledge was founded in 1826, aiming to impart useful information to all classes of the community. The Society produced many works designed to show that factual knowledge about nature and history was of practical advantage, and their works sold widely among the middle and lower classes. While Jude's studies are primarily theological, he represents the type of working-class individual for whom self-instruction was the only educational option available in the 1850s and 1860s. In the novel, Jude also belongs to the Artizans Mutual Improvement Society until the society learns of his unconventional relations with Sue Bridehead and ostracizes him. Innumerable working-class associations of this kind were common at the time, helping to spread popular scientific and technical knowledge as well as socialist ideology. Organizations such as the Salvation Army, association football leagues, and craft unions were also devoted to the entertainment and improvement of working-class life.

Religion and agnosticism. In *Jude the Obscure*, the central characters discuss many social and religious topics, all of which were of great relevance when the novel was written. Jude develops a thorough knowledge of the Bible and religious literature, and his awareness of current theological controversies is representative of contemporary attitudes toward religion.

Among the theological disputes of the day was the Oxford Movement, also known as the Tractarian Movement, which began in 1833 with sermons and tracts published by John Keble, Edward Pusey, John Henry Newman, and other eminent Anglican clergymen at Oxford. The Tractarians sought to renew the Church of England by reviving certain Roman Catholic doctrines and rituals abandoned since the reformation. They were reacting against liberalizing tendencies within the Church of England, tendencies that originated primarily in a faction known as the Broad Church, whose principles envisaged the church as a partner of the state, a relationship to which theological doctrine was strictly subordinate. Politically these liberalizing tendencies culminated in the Reform Bill of 1832, a measure that extended the franchise slightly to the newly populated industrial centers, disfranchising 56 boroughs, including ones with very small populations, and giving representation to 42 cities and towns that had previously lacked it. The measure transferred political power from the landowning aristocrats to the middle class, and the Tractarians saw it and other such measures as steps on the way to national apostasy. They wished to restore the Anglican Church to a position of spiritual preeminence in the nation and to resist the general trend toward secularization in British society. The Oxford Movement, at least at Oxford itself, effectively ended in 1845 when Newman and some of his followers converted to Roman Catholicism. With their conversion, the extremely conservative Tractarian Movement lost its most powerful supporters, and for the rest of the century a political and theological liberalism assumed the dominant position in the university. The successors of the Tractarians, however, continued to influence the contemporary religious mood outside Oxford. These second-generation Tractarians fostered personal piety and a respect for the church's spiritual function in society, in opposition to the secular tendencies of liberalism, and their influence is evident in *Jude the Obscure*. When Jude gives up his study of religion and burns his library of theological and ethical works, into the incinerator go the writings of "Jeremy Taylor, Butler, Doddridge, Paley, Pusey, and Newman." (Hardy, *Jude the Obscure*, p. 234). The latter three—William Paley, Edward Pusey, and John Henry Newman—were leaders of the Oxford Movement, while Joseph Butler and Philip Doddridge were eighteenth-century Anglican divines, and Taylor was a seventeenth-century bishop famous for his sermons. This group gives a fair cross-section of Jude's beliefs: one nonconformist, Doddridge, and five High Churchmen, members of the traditional faction that favored hierarchy and ceremony.

COMTE, MILL, AND FREE THOUGHT

Auguste Comte was a nineteenth-century French philosopher who founded the school of philosophy known as Positivism, which taught that science was the only legitimate form of knowledge and positive facts the only valid goal. Comte placed religion above sociology as the highest science, but it was a religion shorn of metaphysical trappings, with humanity itself as the object of worship. He also coined the term "sociology" and in fact is called the father of the field of sociology. In his efforts as a social reformer, Comte envisaged a society in which individuals and nations could live in harmony and comfort.

John Stuart Mill was the most influential British philosopher in the nineteenth century. He wrote important works on logic and economics, and in his ethical and political works he pointed out a sentiment of social solidarity and unity that was similar to Comte's religion of humanity. Among Mill's most influential essays were *On Liberty* (1859) and *On the Subjection of Women* (1869).

In other words, Jude is conventionally orthodox in his religious opinions.

Sue Bridehead, on the other hand, quotes liberal philosophers such as John Stuart Mill and August Comte in the novel, which marks her as a religious skeptic and freethinker. Along with the ideas of Mill and Comte, Sue is also influenced by another movement of the day, the Higher Criticism, which began in Germany in the early nineteenth century and went on to gain many adherents in mid-century England. The Higher Criticism movement brought the study of history and philology to bear on the Bible in order to establish its textual accuracy and secure its legitimacy as the basis of Protestantism. But in many ways these efforts to apply scientific standards to Bible criticism had the opposite effect, casting doubt on the historical basis of many Old and New Testament events, on the veracity of miracles, and on the historical existence of Jesus. In *Essays and Reviews* (1860), a group of notable Oxford scholars—nicknamed the "Seven Against Scripture"—articulated many of these doubts. (Members of the group include Benjamin Jowett, Mark Pattison, and Baden Powell.) Other scientific endeavors contributed to the spread of religious agnosticism among intellectuals in England as well, in such fields as geology, archaeology, astronomy, and physics. Integral to scientific progress of the day was Charles Darwin's **On the Origin of Species** (1859; also in *WLAIT 4: British and Irish Literature and Its Times*), itself an important element in the decline of church authority and the growth of secularism. Lastly, the fields of anthropology and comparative religion, which developed with the arrival of information from the furthest reaches of England's colonial empire, helped construct a larger picture of human beliefs, and this picture encouraged the increasingly secular climate in the "mother country."

Woman's emancipation. When *Jude the Obscure* was written, women in England could neither vote nor attend any of the older universities, nor sit on a borough or county council, nor enter any of the leading professions except medicine or teaching. Feminism in England is traceable in a variety of forms back to the eighteenth century and earlier (see **A Vindication of the Rights of Woman**, in *WLAIT 3: British and Irish Literature and Its Times*). In the 1880s and 1890s, feminism advanced onto new fronts as women began to demand equality of education, jobs, and personal habits in terms particular to the era. Feminist leaders were espousing new ideas about women—their nature, sexuality, and interests—and Hardy was well aware of these new ideas. The mid-to-late-nineteenth-century women's movement, for example, demanded greater employment opportunities for working-class women and an end to legislation that specifically excluded women from certain kinds of high-skilled jobs. At the same time, related questions of industrial legislation and trade union membership drew many women into socialist organizations and the labor movement toward the end of the century.

In *Jude the Obscure*, the character of Sue Bridehead is often identified with a feminist position. The critic Robert Gittings has argued, though, that Sue is representative of the emancipated women of the 1860s rather than the 1890s. For Gittings, Sue's interest in the works of John Stuart Mill and Auguste Comte was common among certain women of the 1860s—known as the "Girl of the Period"; it was more typical of her than of the so-called "New Woman" of the 1890s, who sought greater sexual freedom, drank and smoked in public, and supported the woman's suffrage movement (Gittings, p. 93). "The genuine New Woman of the 1890s was likely to have political affiliations with socialism, to play some part in opening the professions to women, and probably to have received some sort of university training," and Sue has none of these characteristics (Gittings, p. 94). For Gittings, Hardy was clearly modeling Sue, when she was anti-religious, rationalist, and positivist, on a woman of the 1860s.

Sexual liberation was another important element of Victorian feminism, along with the political and economic elements. The Married Women's Property Acts of 1882 and 1893 gave a wife the same right to her property as an unmarried woman, which was considered a triumph, since prior to these acts a woman's property became her husband's upon marriage. However, many feminists continued to decry the economic and sexual oppression of prostitutes and the exposure of married women to venereal diseases because of the infidelities of their husbands. One strain of discourse about women rejected marriage, motherhood, and sexuality, and this strain also emerges in the opinions of Sue Bridehead.

The "marriage problem." *Jude the Obscure* focuses on marriage as a social and religious institution, particularly the unhappy marriage. Divorce law in England was reformed by the Matrimonial Causes Act of 1857, which made more generally attainable for the first time what had long been nearly impossible to all but the wealthiest British subjects. The act established a Court for Divorce and Matrimonial Causes, but the provisions for unhappy wives differed from those for unhappy husbands. The husband had the right to a divorce simply on the grounds of his wife's adultery, but a wife had to have proof that her husband committed not only adultery but also desertion, cruelty, rape, incest, or sodomy. Another act in 1878 allowed magistrates' courts to recognize separation between spouses in the case of violence or desertion. Still, divorce remained relatively rare; as late as 1913 there would be only 577 in England and Wales combined (Cannon, p. 298).

The question of marriage and divorce came to the forefront of public attention in 1890 with the case of the Irish political leader Charles Stewart Parnell. In December 1889, Captain William O'Shea filed a petition for divorce from his wife, Katherine, on the grounds of her adultery with Parnell. The case caused a storm of controversy and immense public discussion on the whole issue of love, marriage, and divorce. It was in this climate of opinion that serial publication of *Jude the Obscure* began in *Harper's New Monthly Magazine* in December 1894. Other specifically literary events also contributed to the topicality of the marriage question. Among these were current interest in the plays of Norwegian dramatist Heinrik Ibsen, first staged in England in the early 1890s, and interest in the novels of Grant Allen and the essays of Edward Carpenter. Ibsen's powerful indictments of the evasions and lies of middle-class marriage occur in such works as *The Doll's House* (1879), *Ghosts* (1881), *Rosmersholm* (1886), and *Hedda Gabler* (1890), all of which Hardy had read and some of which he saw performed in 1893. Allen's novel *The Woman Who Did* (1895) follows the fortunes of an unconventional woman who rejects marriage as oppressive, lives and bears a child with her lover, and endures social condemnation and suffering after his death. Published the same month as *Jude the Obscure*, Allen's novel is sensational and, in the opinion of feminists of the 1890s, even reactionary, yet less discerning reviewers classed both novels as attacks on the conventional pieties surrounding the sacrament of marriage. Finally, in essays such as "Love's Coming of Age" (1896), Edward Carpenter discussed forthrightly the relationship between the sexes.

Modernization and industrialization. By the mid-nineteenth century, industrialization in England had turned the nation into the first predominantly urban society in human history. Rapid and unregulated growth of manufacturing towns disrupted the settled patterns of rural folkways, many of which had persisted largely unchanged for centuries. The countryside and the character of its people changed as it adapted to the new conditions. Among the changes was loss of population, as a number of forces coalesced to drive thousands off the land and into the new factory towns. Railroad expansion as well as new technologies and capitalistic methods meanwhile drastically altered farming, with ongoing shifts in rural society growing sharper between the years of Hardy's birth and the end of the century. English agriculture during the third quarter of the nineteenth century had been prosperous, but after 1875 a series of disastrous harvests coincided with an influx of cheap grain from the United States to cause heavy losses for English farmers. Two "great depressions," in 1875–84 and 1891–99, made it appear that the independent grain industry could not survive as it was then organized. On top of their other problems, in the light of the depopulation, the farmers had to cope with an acute labor shortage, which forced them to raise the wages of those workers who stayed on the land. In fact, by the end of the century the exodus from country to town had depleted the rural population enough for some critics to warn that English rural society was on the verge of collapse.

Commentators differed markedly in their proposals for reform: liberal economists advocated free trade and scientific farming as the solution, radicals called for a Socialist revolution, and others suggested land-reform measures that would make small-scale ownership the basis of England's agriculture. Beginning in the 1860s, union organizing among rural laborers led to higher wages and improved conditions. Joseph Arch's National Union spread quickly in the early 1870s among the southern counties of England, including Hardy's Dorsetshire, relieving extreme cases of oppression, hunger, and misery among the rural laborers. Meanwhile, many reformers called for more education for the rural poor, while others demanded the complete abolition of education for the lower classes, claiming it was making the rural laborers discontented with their place in the social hierarchy. Hardy came to maturity during this period of ferment in rural England, and his novels chronicle the upheaval that changing social forces caused in individual lives. The critic Raymond Williams describes Hardy's original contribution to the literature of the rural working class:

> It is not only that Hardy sees the realities of laboring work. . . . It is also that he sees the harshness of economic processes, in inheritance, capital, rent and trade, within the community of the natural processes and persistently cutting across them. The social process created in this interaction is one of class and separation, as well as of chronic insecurity, as this capitalist farming and trading takes its course. The profound disturbances that Hardy records cannot then be seen in the sentimental terms of a pastoral: the contrast between country and town. The exposed and separated individuals, whom Hardy puts at the center of his fiction, are only the most developed cases of a general exposure and separation.
>
> (Williams, p. 115)

The Novel in Focus

Plot summary. *Jude the Obscure* is set in Hardy's fictional region of Wessex. The hero, Jude Fawley, was orphaned in early childhood and raised by his widowed aunt Drusilla Fawley in the remote rural village of Marygreen in Dorsetshire. After receiving encouragement from his schoolmaster, Richard Phillotson—whose parting words to Jude direct him to "be kind to animals and birds, and read all you can"—Jude aspires to attend the university at Christminster and become a clergyman (*Jude*, p. 34). Industrious, he shows remarkable scholarly aptitude, but lacks

---

BEHIND THE ARCHITECTURAL TIMES

With the growth in the economy and population of England came an increase in the demand for buildings, which helps explain why the figure of the architect first emerges at this time as a discrete and recognizable professional. Hardy distinguished himself as an architect, winning two awards in 1863—a silver medal from The Institute of British Architects and first prize from the Architectural Association for design of a country mansion. Hardy's attitudes toward architectural styles was formed during the height of England's Gothic Revival, a movement traceable to the 1830s but at the peak of its popularity in the 1850s and waning by the late 1860s. This shift in taste is reflected in *Jude the Obscure*; the provincial Jude, whose own training as a stonemason was in the Gothic style, arrives in Christminster when Gothic has fallen out of favor and the Classical style is dominant, another example of societal circumstances under which Jude vainly labors.

---

formal education. Jude is a self-taught man; he reads theology and classical literature as possible during the day, when he drives his aunt's bakery cart, and studies late into the night. At age 20, before he attains his goal of applying for admission to the university, Jude enters a disastrous marriage with the vital but vulgar Arabella Donn, who feigns pregnancy in order to trap Jude. In despair over his miserable situation, Jude walks to the middle of a frozen lake, hoping to fall through the ice and die. When this fails, he gets drunk. After cohabiting with her husband for three years, Arabella abandons Jude and immigrates to Australia. Jude then revives his interest in the university, moves to Christminster, and

finds work as a stonemason while continuing his studies, still hoping for admission.

In Christminster, the 23-year-old Jude meets his cousin, Sue Bridehead, a 27-year-old woman with unconventional attitudes and religious opinions who works in a shop making ecclesiastical ornaments. Though strongly attracted to each other, Sue and Jude both believe members of their family are constitutionally unsuited to marriage. They nevertheless fall in love. Jude introduces Sue to his former schoolmaster, Phillotson, who now teaches in a village school near Christminster. Phillotson offers Sue a job as an instructor at his school, suggests she enroll in a teacher-training school, and eventually proposes marriage. In spite of the age difference—Phillotson is about 40—Sue agrees to marry him after she finishes teacher training, though Jude is the one whom she loves. Sick at heart at seeing Phillotson woo Sue, and having failed to gain admission to the university, Jude returns to his ailing old aunt at Marygreen and decides to spend the next few years preparing to enter the ministry.

When Sue later learns of Jude's first marriage (to Arabella), she quits her training and abruptly marries Phillotson in what seems to be a fit of impulsive masochism. Jude agrees to give her away at the wedding. Sexual relations with Phillotson disgust and repulse Sue, whereupon she flees to Jude. Their own love remains unconsummated until Arabella returns and Sue grows desperate to retain Jude for herself.

Jude and Sue have two children together and also raise his child with Arabella, Little Father Time. The fact that Jude and Sue never married mortifies their respectable neighbors, so the two begin moving from place to place to find work and avoid scandal, which grows progressively more difficult. In the novel's most horrific scene, Little Father Time, who seems to embody a Schopenhauer type of pessimism, hangs his two younger siblings and himself, leaving a note that reads, "Done because we are too menny" (*Jude*, p. 405). The shock and grief of this slaughter convince Sue that she has offended the Christian God by deserting Phillotson, taking up with Jude, and espousing free thought. Jude tries to reason with Sue:

> "You have been fearless, both as a thinker and as a feeler, and you deserve more admiration than I gave. I was too full of narrow dogmas at that time to see it."
> "Don't say that, Jude! I wish my every fearless word and thought could be rooted out of my

Stonemasons at work. The main character, Jude Fawley, labors as a stonemason while nurturing dreams of attending the university at Christminster.

history. Self-renunciation—that's everything! I cannot humiliate myself too much. I should like to prick myself all over with pins and bleed out the badness that's in me!"

(*Jude*, pp. 353-54)

Sue insists on seeing the death of the children as a just retribution for her sins, and she gradually slips into an irrational process of self-punishment that finally leads her to return to Phillotson and submit to the repugnant sexual relations with him. Jude tries to reason with Sue but is unable to penetrate her by-now-extreme Christian dogmatism. In his sorrow, he imbibes alcohol, and his health gradually deteriorates. Through an unusual series of events Jude is reunited with the ever-calculating Arabella, who nurses him through his final illness with callous contempt, leaving him to die alone in his room with the bitter words from the biblical book of Job on his lips: "Wherefore is light given to him that is in misery, and life unto the bitter in soul?" (*Jude*, p. 408).

Sue Bridehead and the vicissitudes of Victorian sex. Critics have continued to scrutinize the problematic nature of Sue's sexuality since *Jude the Obscure* was published, and for this reason she often seems the novel's most interesting character. After a few weeks of marriage to Phillot-

son, Sue tells Jude of the sexual "repugnance" she feels toward her husband, with whom conjugal relations raise "a physical objection—a fastidiousness or whatever it may be called" (*Jude*, pp. 227, 230). She cryptically explains that what tortures her so "is the necessity of being responsive to this man whenever he wishes, good as he is morally!—the dreadful contract to feel in a particular way, in a matter whose essence is its voluntariness" (*Jude*, p. 230). Sue informs Phillotson of her feelings, saying she wishes to leave him and live with Jude, a scandalous proposal in Victorian England. To support her argument for such an unconventional arrangement, Sue quotes John Stuart Mill's essay *On Liberty*. Any man or woman, says Mill, "who lets the world, or his portion of it, choose his plan of life for him, has no need of any other faculty than ape-like imitation" (*Jude*, p. 239). Phillotson agrees to the separation, though he pays a high price: he experiences a loss of respectability in the eyes of the community that costs him his career. Once Sue and Jude begin cohabiting, their relations also remain sexless for many months, and they make love only seldom after first being physically intimate. "My nature is not so passionate as yours!" Sue tells Jude, to which he replies, "I think you are incapable of real love" (*Jude*, p. 255).

The source of Sue's sexual inhibitions remains obscure, although the speculation of critics has ranged from frigidity to homosexuality. Hardy's friend and reviewer Edmund Gosse, for instance, supposes that Sue's shrinking from sex and marriage was motivated by lesbianism. But Hardy re-

PESSIMISM AND SCHOPENHAUER

Hardy once wrote to a friend: "My pages show harmony of view with Darwin, Huxley, Spencer, Comte, Hume, Mill, and others." Among these others was Arthur Schopenhauer (1788-1860), the German idealist philosopher who is sometimes called the father of pessimism. Schopenhauer maintained that an honest assessment of human existence in its totality reveals that suffering far outweighs pleasure and that, objectively considered, never to have been born at all is vastly preferable to existence under any conditions. The central postulate of Schopenhauer's metaphysical system was his conception of the *will,* a blind and irrational striving that pervades nature and is ceaseless and insatiable. Compassion was the cardinal virtue in Schopenhauer's ethics, since an awareness of the universality of human suffering leads the individual to sympathize and commiserate with all fellow sufferers. Schopenhauer's philosophy is akin to Buddhist thought, a relation he himself was aware of, as both deem it possible to escape from enslavement to the will by transcending the ego, which is the way, the two philosophies teach, to ultimate salvation. For Hardy, Schopenhauer's thought fit well with current notions of a universal struggle for survival as the basis of organic life and of human life as occurring within a context of vast, impersonal cosmic forces, where the desires and aspirations of individual human beings are meaningless or very nearly so. When Jude explains Little Father Time's actions, he echoes Schopenhauer: "The doctor says there are such boys springing up amongst us—boys of a sort unknown in the last generation—the outcome of new views of life. They seem to see all its terrors before they are old enough to have staying power to resist them. He says it is the beginning of the coming universal wish not to live."

(*Jude,* p. 346)

sponded that Sue's "abnormalism consists in disproportion: not in inversion, her sexual instinct being healthy so far as it goes, but unusually weak and fastidious" (Hardy in Kramer, p. 173). Repeatedly in the novel, she evinces a tepid de-

sire. Jude often refers to Sue as if she had no body: she is "the ethereal, fine-nerved, sensitive girl, quite unfitted by temperament and instinct to fulfill the conditions of the matrimonial relation with Phillotson, possibly with any man" (*Jude,* p. 235). By relating Sue's psychological situation to the social institution of marriage, the novel renders her attitude even more complex. Sue repeatedly expresses a sense of "dread lest an iron contract" of marriage should extinguish the tenderness she and Jude share (*Jude,* p. 273):

> Jude, do you think that when you *must* have me with you by law, we shall be so happy as we are now? The men and women of our family are very generous when everything depends upon their good-will, but they always kick against compulsion. Don't you dread the attitude that insensibly arises out of legal obligation? Don't you think it is destructive to a passion whose essence is its gratuitousness?
>
> (*Jude,* p. 286)

Whatever causes her sexual inhibitions, Sue's staunch efforts to intellectualize, rationalize, and politicize an issue that she dare not confront in all its sensuousness and intimacy provides the novel with an excellent platform upon which to air related questions about the social and psychological conditioning of women and their sexual exploitation in marriage. Sue articulates many of the standard feminist views current in the 1890s. Furthermore, her attitude echoes an image propagated in Victorian society by Dr. William Acton, a venereal-disease specialist. According to Dr. Acton, the Victorian female was passionless: "I should say that the majority of women (happily for society) are not very much troubled with sexual feeling of any kind" (Acton in Hellerstein, p. 177). Particularly when a woman is with child, said Acton, she loathes familiarity. "In some exceptional cases, indeed, feeling has been sacrificed to duty, and the wife has endured, with all the self-martyrdom of womanhood, what was almost worse than death" (Acton in Hellerstein, Hume, and Offen, p. 178). In view of such teachings, Sue Bridehead hardly seems like an anomaly for her time.

Sources and literary context. Like Jude, Hardy himself was largely self-taught, and his reading and its influences on his craft were very broad. He had a profound knowledge of the Bible and the Anglican Church's *Book of Common Prayer* and was thoroughly familiar with the works of Shakespeare. The English romantic poets were another important influence on Hardy, particularly Sir Walter Scott, William Wordsworth,

Percy Bysshe Shelley, Robert Browning, and Algernon Charles Swinburne. As indicated above, Hardy read widely in science and philosophy, Darwin and Thomas Huxley especially influencing his attitude toward life. Among English novelists, George Eliot is probably Hardy's most direct forebear. Jude's speech to the Christminster townspeople in part 6, for example, is modeled on a speech to workingmen given by one of Eliot's characters in "Address to Working Men, by Felix Holt" (1867). Though Hardy claimed that *Jude* contained less autobiographical material than any of his other novels, critics have found abundant evidence that Hardy in fact put a great deal of his own circumstances and experiences into *Jude*.

Reception. Hardy's novel was greeted with righteous indignation by the defenders of moral propriety in literature. Reviews with headlines such as "Jude the Obscene" and "Hardy the Degenerate" were among the more vituperative reactions, an experience Hardy later said had the effect of "completely curing me of further interest in novel-writing" (Hardy in Page, p. 6). As indicated above, *Jude the Obscure* was seen by some reviewers as an attack on the sanctity of marriage as a religious sacrament. Margaret Oliphant, a prolific author of popular romances and novels, reviewed *Jude* in *Blackwood's Magazine* in January 1896 and found some parts of the novel "of the most unutterable foulness" and the whole "an assault on the stronghold of marriage, which is now beleaguered on every side" (Oliphant, pp. 139, 141). Oliphant was especially indignant that a writer of Hardy's stature, whose works sold very widely, would descend to such depths of corruption. "There may," she said, "be books more disgusting, more impious . . . more foul in detail, in those dark corners where the amateurs of filth find garbage to their taste; but not, we repeat, from any Master's hand" (Oliphant, p. 138). Other guardians of public morality reacted similarly. The Bishop of Wakefield burned his copy of *Jude the Obscure*, prompting Hardy to remark in the "Postscript" to the 1912 edition that the bishop must have done so "in his despair at not being able to burn me" (Hardy in Page, p. 6).

Not all reviewers, however, were blind to the novel's merits; before Hardy's death it was recognized as a masterpiece, a status it continues to hold today. In fact, William Dean Howells lauded the novel in an early review in *Harper's Weekly* (December 7, 1895), saying that *Jude the Obscure* "has not only the solemn and lofty effect of a tragedy . . . but it has unity very uncommon in

the novel, and especially the English novel . . . . This tragedy of fate suggests the classic singleness of means as well as the classic singleness of motive" (Howells in Page, pp. 378-79).

—James Caufield

HARDY'S FICTIONAL WESSEX

The setting for many of Hardy's most successful novels is the region he called Wessex, and the localities in Hardy's Wessex often correspond to real places in England. Some of these correspondences are listed below.

Hardy's Fictional Name	Real-Life Parallel
Aldbrickham	Reading
Alfredston	Wantage
Casterbridge	Dorchester
Christminster	Oxford
Exonbury	Exeter
Kennetbridge	Newbury, on river Kennet
Marygreen	Fawley
Melchester	Salisbury
Mellstock	Stinsford
Mid-Wessex	Wiltshire
Nether Wessex	Somerset
North Wessex	Berkshire
South Wessex	Dorset
Stoke-Barehills	Basingstoke
Wintonchester	Winchester

Hardy also renamed many of Oxford's most famous colleges, though scholars differ over some of the designations, as the question marks here indicate.

Cardinal College	Christ Church
Crozier College	Oriel?
Oldgate College	New College
Rubric College	Brasenose?
Sarcophagus College	All Souls?
Tudor College	Merton

For More Information

Cannon, John, ed. *The Oxford Companion to British History*. Oxford: Oxford University Press, 1997.

Draper, Jo. *Thomas Hardy's England*. London: Cape, 1984.

Gittings, Robert. *Young Thomas Hardy*. London: Heinemann, 1975.

Hardy, Thomas. *Jude the Obscure*. 1895. Reprint, London: Macmillan, 1974.

Hellerstein, Erna Olafson, Leslie Parker Hume, and Karen M. Offen. *Victorian Women: A Documentary Account of Women's Lives in Nineteenth-Century England, France and the United States*. Stanford, Calif.: Stanford University Press, 1981.

Jedrzejewski, Jan. *Thomas Hardy and the Church*. New York: St. Martin's, 1996.

Kramer, Dale, ed. *The Cambridge Companion to Thomas Hardy*. Cambridge: Cambridge University Press, 1999.

Oliphant, Margaret. "The Anti-Marriage League." *Blackwood's Edinburgh Magazine* 159 (January 1896): 135-49.

Page, Norman, ed. *Thomas Hardy Jude the Obscure*. Norton Critical Edition. 2nd ed. New York: Norton, 1999.

Rothblatt, Sheldon. *Tradition and Change in English Liberal Education: An Essay in History and Culture*. London: Faber, 1976.

Williams, Raymond. *The English Novel: From Dickens to Lawrence*. London: Chatto & Windus, 1973.

Juno and
the Paycock

by
Sean O'Casey

S ean O'Casey was born John Casey in 1880 in Dublin and baptized in the Church of Ireland. After the death of his father, in 1886, the family sank into the poverty of the Dublin tenements. Throughout the beginning of the twentieth century, O'Casey was politically active, becoming a nationalist, joining the Irish Republican Brotherhood (forerunner of the Irish Republican Army), and also a socialist, joining a union in 1911 and participating in a major Dublin strike of 1913. *The Shadow of a Gunman* was accepted for production by the Abbey Theatre in 1923. In the following year, the Abbey produced *Juno and the Paycock*. Though the play established his reputation in Ireland, O'Casey would ultimately find that in order to draft the plays he was interested in writing, and see them produced, he would have to leave Ireland. His next major play, *The Plough and the Stars*, set in the 1916 Rebellion, caused riots in Dublin, and the following play, *The Silver Tassie*, written in 1928 and set in World War I, was rejected by the Abbey as too experimental. By that time, O'Casey was living in England. He would be buried there in 1964. An immediate hit when performed in 1924, *Juno and the Paycock* remains one of O'Casey's most popular plays; the world it gives us is "unpredictable, fickle, but surviving" (Maxwell, p. 567).

Events in History at the Time of the Play

Poverty in Dublin. At the beginning of the twentieth century, the state of life in the Dublin ten-

THE LITERARY WORK

A play, set in 1922 in Dublin, Ireland, during the Civil War; first performed in 1924, at the Abbey Theatre in Dublin.

SYNOPSIS

In this tragicomedy, the Boyle family, living in the Dublin slums, is shattered by poverty, alcoholism, illegitimate pregnancy, and the Irish Civil War.

ements—filthy, disease-ridden, overcrowded— was appalling. From the time of the Potato Famine, in the 1840s, which devastated the rural social structure of the country, people had been leaving the rural areas, many for other countries entirely, but many others for Dublin, where they found, increasingly, little room and little work. In 1880, the year Sean O'Casey was born, the death rate in Dublin was 44.8 per 1000, the worst in Europe—worse even than Calcutta, India, where the death rate was 37.0, or Alexandria, Egypt, where the death rate was 40.0 (Krause, p. 4). By the 1920s, at the time *Juno and the Paycock* is set, the situation had improved only slightly (Hughes, p. 64). F. S. L. Lyons provides some of the details:

About thirty per cent (87,000) of the people of Dublin lived in the slums which were for the most part the worn-out shells of Georgian mansions. Over 2,000 *families* lived in single

Sean O'Casey

room tenements which were without heat or light or water (save for a tap in a passage or backyard) or adequate sanitation. Inevitably, the death-rate was the highest in the country, while infant mortality was the worst, not just in Ireland, but in the British Isles. Disease of every kind, especially tuberculosis, was rife and malnutrition was endemic; it was hardly surprising that the poor, when they had a few pence, often spent them seeking oblivion through drink.

(Lyons, pp. 277-78)

O'Casey was not born in the Dublin slums, but he grew up in them and knew them well. The Boyle family in *Juno and the Paycock*, living a hand-to-mouth existence, subsisting more on dreams than wages, is taken from his direct experience and the lives he saw his neighbors lead.

O'Casey's portrayal of Dublin tenement life seems to have been not merely entertaining and evocative, but accurate as well. Former residents of the slums who knew his plays often refer to them when speaking of tenement life. Patrick O'Leary, for instance, says, "I've *absolutely no doubt* that Sean O'Casey didn't invent a single thing. All he did was keep his ears open" (Kearns, p. 143). All the key elements of *Juno and the Paycock* are taken directly from tenement life, at its most infamous and most stereotypical.

Captain Boyle and Joxer, for instance, illustrate one of the most conspicuous social problems of the tenements: excessive drinking. As historian Kevin C. Kearns relates, "most men drank heartily and many over-indulged, leading to deprivation at home and abuse of wife and children" (Kearns, p. 52). Mary Boyle, at the end of the play, is also not an unusual figure. She is unmarried and pregnant, in desperate trouble, and her menfolk want to throw her out of the house, a common reaction among family members to the problem of illegitimate pregnancy. At the end of the play, she is indeed going away, but, happily, with her mother, the strong, enduring Juno. Juno herself represents yet another well-known figure of Dublin tenement life, the mother who holds the impoverished family together. Una Shaw, who lived in the Dublin tenements near the time in which *Juno* is set, says, "the women were the mainstay, they were *everything*. They were mother, father, counselor, doctor . . . everything" (Kearns, p. 49).

Socialism in Dublin. The situation of the Dublin poor made the city a natural place for socialist organizing. O'Casey became a socialist early in the century. He joined the Irish Transport and General Workers' Union in 1911, serving as the Secretary of the Women and Children's Relief Fund in 1913 during the Dublin Lockout. He also joined the Irish Citizen's Army, the force created by the union to protect the striking workers during the Lockout. Anxious about worker militancy, a group of employers led by the head of the Dublin United Tramways company (William Martin Murphy) had closed ranks, pressuring employees to withdraw from the union or be fired. In response, the firebrand union leader James Larkin called a strike against the Dublin United Tramways Company, after which union members were locked out of the offices of the Tramway Company as well as other enterprises—newspapers, dockyards, and building suppliers. Within a month, some 25,000 men were off work (Lyons, p. 282). In the end, management proved stronger than the unions; the strike failed after about six months, but the strikers' protective force, the Irish Citizens' Army (ICA), stayed vital, due in large part to Sean O'-Casey, who at the time was secretary of the ICA. Irish socialism, a movement whose intent was to establish a workers' republic, disappeared during World War I, but it resurfaced thereafter in the form of the Irish Labour Party.

In *Juno and the Paycock*, Mary Boyle, a factory worker, is on strike, and though the play is set a decade after the Dublin Lockout, the issues remain the same: the tenement dwellers in the play live a hand-to-mouth existence, working—when they can get work at all—under horrible conditions for tiny wages; their unions have not been strong enough to change the situation; and every day Mary spends on strike means one day less of wages coming into her impoverished home. In the Boyle family, Johnny, the son, can't work; Joxer, the father, won't. The family is dependent on Mary's wages and what money Juno can bring in. While Mary is on strike, the financial position of the family is especially unstable. Though O'Casey remained committed to socialist ideals, he was disappointed that the theories tended to turn into empty talk rather than into meaningful action, as illustrated in *Juno* by both Mary Boyle and Jerry, her first suitor.

The Irish Civil War. The background of the Irish Civil War is the Irish Revolution. In 1916, on April 24, Easter Monday, combined nationalist forces (including the Irish Volunteers, the associated Irish Republican Brotherhood, and the Irish Citizens' Army, which by this time O'Casey had left) occupied government buildings in Dublin and in other towns throughout Ireland. Since this occupation took place while Britain was fighting World War I in Europe, the British executed the leaders as traitors in time of war. The structure of the nationalist forces was temporarily shattered, but by April 1917, it had reorganized as the Irish Republican Army. Its war against Britain continued until July 1921, when a treaty was signed, which ended the conflict with a compromise: 26 counties (today's Ireland) would become autonomous; 6 counties (today's Northern Ireland) would remain part of Britain. While the Republican forces that had fought against Britain were not happy with the treaty, the majority of them nevertheless saw it as the lesser of two evils, the greater evil being continued war; Dr. Patrick McCartan, for example, who would remain neutral in the Civil War that followed the signing of the Treaty, nevertheless resigned himself to it.

> I see no glimmer of hope. We are presented with a *fait accompli* and asked to endorse it. I, as a Republican, will not endorse it, but I will not vote for chaos.
>
> (McCartan in Neeson, p. 62)

Chaos did follow. There were outbreaks of violence in the North, and the army split. By March 1922 the Civil War had started, with the groups that splintered off from the government forces portraying themselves as "the lawful army of a sovereign republic proclaimed at Easter 1916, which [the government that signed the treaty] had betrayed" (Hughes, p. 56). In *Juno and the Paycock*, the pro-treaty forces, or Free State forces, are called "Staters"; the anti-treaty forces, or Republicans, are called "Diehards."

The Civil War necessarily involved the shattering of old alliances, with former comrades turning on each other, as shown in *Juno and the*

CALL FOR CIVIL WAR, 28 JUNE 1922

Fellow citizens of the Irish Republic: The fateful hour has come. At the dictation of our hereditary enemy our rightful cause is being treacherously assailed by recreant Irishmen. The crash of arms and the boom of artillery reverberate in this supreme test of the Nation's destiny. Gallant soldiers of the Irish Republic stand vigorously firm in its defence and worthily uphold their noblest traditions. The sacred sprits of the Illustrious Dead are with us in this great struggle. "Death before Dishonour," being an unchanging principle of our national faith as it was of theirs, still inspires us to emulate their glorious effort. We, therefore, appeal to all citizens who have withstood unflinchingly the oppression of the enemy during the past six years, to rally to the support of the republic and recognize that the resistance now being offered is but the continuation of the struggle that was suspended with the British. We especially appeal to our former comrades of the Irish Republic to return to that allegiance and thus guard the Nation's honour from the infamous stigma that her sons aided her foes in retaining a hateful domination over her. Confident of victory and of maintaining Ireland's Independence this appeal is issued by the Army Executive on behalf of the Irish Republican Army.

(*Poblacht na hEireann War News*, 29 June 1922, in Hughes, p. 119)

Paycock by Johnny Boyle's betrayal of his old friend and comrade Robbie Tancred. Johnny's early faithfulness to the Republican cause has cost him an arm, and, in the 1916 Rebellion, he was shot in the hip as well. At the start of the Civil War, he stayed with the Republican forces, but he has since left and has betrayed a former comrade to the Free State troops. Before the start of the play this comrade has been murdered, which leads directly to Johnny's own death at the close of the play. The war formally

Snipers in Dublin in 1922 during the Irish Civil War.

ended in May 1923, when the anti-treaty forces agreed to dump arms—significantly, not a full surrender (Hughes, p. 57). By 1924, when O'-Casey wrote *Juno and the Paycock*, conditions were peaceful, the Republican forces temporarily quieted, and the Irish focused on rebuilding and stabilizing the new country. The bitterness left by the Civil War remained, however, and would surface again.

The Play in Focus

Plot summary. *Juno and the Paycock* opens with Mary Boyle, the 22-year-old daughter of the family, reading the paper in the Boyle's tenement living-room to her brother, Johnny. (The play is staged entirely in the living-room; there is one other room to the tenement dwelling, but it is offstage.) When Mary shares details from the newspaper about the death of a neighbor's son—a former comrade of her brother Johnny—Johnny leaves in distress. By this time, Mary's mother, Juno Boyle (the "Juno" of the title), has arrived. Mary, a factory worker, is on strike, and her father, "Captain" Boyle (the "paycock," or "peacock," of the title), is out of work and likely to remain so. Meanwhile, Johnny, due to wounds he received in the Easter Uprising, is unable to work.

Mary's suitor, Jerry Devine, a socialist, arrives with news of a possible job for the Captain, but on hearing her suitor arriving, Mary leaves. In a humorous scene, the Captain and his best buddy, Joxer (whom Juno considers a particularly bad influence on Captain Boyle) arriving, and Juno hides herself. The Captain and Joxer are interrupted in their quest for food ("Ah, a cup o' tay's a darlin' thing, a daarlin' thing—the cup that cheers") when Juno reveals herself (*Juno*, p. 209). At this point, Joxer and the Captain lie about trying to find work; Joxer subsequently leaves. Juno and the Captain bitterly discuss the Captain's inability to find work while he is getting drunk in the pub. In comes Jerry Devine to inform the Captain of the job prospect. Mary appears, and it becomes clear that she is seeing another man. All leave, except for the Captain, who begins to eat the breakfast he proudly refused to consume earlier, when he was annoyed at Juno for berating him about his shiftlessness. Joxer returns, whereupon he and the Captain eat and discuss, with great boastfulness and inaccuracy, Irish politics and religion. When Juno reenters, the men hide the dishes, and Joxer sneaks out the window. Mary returns with Charlie Bentham, an Englishman, who has a copy of the last will and testament of Captain Boyle's cousin. The cousin has left all his goods "to be divided between my two first and second cousins" (*Juno*, p. 223); half of the property will amount to between £1500 and £2000, a fortune, so financially, at least, things seem to be looking up for the Boyles at the end of Act One.

Act Two opens in the same living room. Although it is only two days after the action of the first act, there are more items, especially garish ones, around the room. Captain Boyle is sleeping on the sofa but pretends, when Joxer enters, to be working on papers. They discuss the Boyle finances, which appear to now include a vast and complex fortune. Juno and Mary arrive with a gramophone. It becomes clear that all the new furniture and knickknacks have been purchased on credit, on the strength of the cousin's will. Johnny enters; he is moody and wan, and we learn that he has not been sleeping. When Charlie Bentham walks in, the Captain tries to impress him with misunderstood bits of economic news. Mary enters, and she and Juno pour out tea. It becomes obvious that Mary and Bentham are romantically interested in each other. Bentham discusses his philosophy; he's a Theosophist, he says, a term that means nothing to his listeners, even though he helpfully explains that he believes in an "all-pervading Spirit—the Life-Breath" (*Juno*, p. 228). There is a discussion about religion; when ghosts are mentioned, Johnny turns pale and leaves. He screams from the room offstage and reenters, having seen the ghost of Robbie Tancred, the dead comrade mentioned at the beginning of the play. There follows an amusing party. Mrs. Madigan, one of the neighbors, comes in, and the company drinks whiskey. There are Irish songs, one sung by Mary and her mother and one attempted by Joxer, though he cannot finish it, since he forgets the words. Mrs. Tancred—the mother of the dead comrade—comes downstairs with other neighbors. Entering the Boyle rooms, she keens for her son, and the mourners leave. The company discusses the tragedy. Juno explains that Robbie and Johnny had been good friends in the Republican force, but Johnny denies that they were ever close. Next Juno enumerates the many dead and wounded sons and husbands of neighbors and friends. The Captain recites a maudlin poem, then plays a record on the gramophone. Needle Nugent, the tailor, objects. Robbie Tancred's funeral is passing outside the window, and playing a record at this time, says Nugent, is in poor taste. All the company but Johnnie goes to the window to watch the funeral, then almost everyone exits to the street. Johnny has been left alone

in the room; interrupting his solitude, a young man enters and informs Johnny that he must go to a Battalion Staff meeting in two nights to answer questions about the death of Robbie Tancred. Johnny refuses, saying he has done his share in getting wounded: "I've lost me arm, an' me hip's desthroyed so that I'll never be able to walk right agen! Good God, haven't I done enough for Ireland?" (*Juno*, p. 238).

Act Three is set two months later. Mary is sitting, dejected. In fact, Juno is about to take Mary to the doctor because is so wan and depressed. As Juno readies herself, she asks Mary when she last heard from Bentham. A month earlier, we learn. They leave, while the Captain remains offstage in the next room. Joxer and Nugent, the tailor, enter and discuss the Boyles' finances. The family has been buying a great deal on credit, but has paid nothing off. Nugent asks the Captain, still offstage, for some of the money owed on his new clothes. The Captain not only refuses to pay, but he asks for more credit. Unwilling to give him any, Nugent leaves with the Captain's new suit. Joxer steals a bottle of stout. When the Captain comes into the living room, Joxer pretends not to know anything about the previous exchange with the tailor and blames the disappearance of the stout on Nugent. The neighbor Mrs. Madigan comes in, asking for some money that the Boyles owe her. Refused payment, she takes the gramophone and leaves. Joxer departs too, after which Johnny and a solemn-looking Juno return, separately. Mary is pregnant, and Bentham, the father, has disappeared. The Captain and Johnny both take this as a personal affront and demand that Mary be thrown out of the house. At this point, the Captain admits that he is not going to receive any money from his deceased relative. The will said "first and second cousins," but it did not specify the two people meant. Now cousins are coming out of the woodwork. There will be no money once everything is divided up, yet the Captain has been buying more and more on credit, even though he knows the family cannot pay the bills. He leaves to get drunk, and some furniture removal men arrive to confiscate their wares. Mary comes home, and Jerry Devine enters, telling her that he will take her back, though he retracts the offer when he discovers that she is pregnant. Afterwards Johnny berates Mary, and she runs out. The play winds down to a near finish. First, the votive candle for the Virgin expires and Johnny panics, with just cause, since two members of the IRA come to drag him away for betraying his comrade Robbie Tancred to the Free State forces. Then the curtain falls. It rises again on a mostly empty living room, the furniture having been confiscated. Mary and Juno are there, awaiting news of Johnny. Word finally arrives that he has been found dead. Juno prays for an end to hatred in the country, and she and Mary leave to identify the body and start a new life with Juno's sister. Afterward Captain and Joxer wander in drunk, wondering what happened to the furniture. The play ends with their maudlin ramblings about the state of Ireland and the world in a scene both hilarious and appalling: "Irelan' sober . . . is Irelan'. . . free," Boyle manages to say, observing, ". . . th' whole worl's . . . in a terr . . . ible state o' chassis" (*Juno*, p. 254).

Betrayal. The foundation of the action in *Juno and the Paycock* is betrayal: Johnny's betrayal of

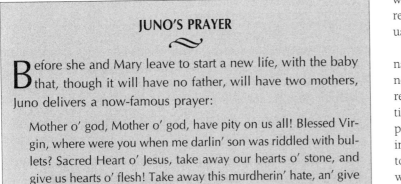

JUNO'S PRAYER

Before she and Mary leave to start a new life, with the baby that, though it will have no father, will have two mothers, Juno delivers a now-famous prayer:

Mother o' god, Mother o' god, have pity on us all! Blessed Virgin, where were you when me darlin' son was riddled with bullets? Sacred Heart o' Jesus, take away our hearts o' stone, and give us hearts o' flesh! Take away this murdherin' hate, an' give us Thine own eternal love!

(*Juno*, p. 253)

his comrade Robbie Tancred; the Captain's betrayal of his family, financially and emotionally; Bentham's betrayal of the pregnant Mary. All these betrayals intertwine and magnify each other, but the betrayals of the Civil War are the background of the play that the author referred to as a play about Johnny Boyle (Fallon, p. 19). At the time when the play was written, Ireland was trying to recover from the damage done by the Revolution (1917–21) and the Civil War (1922–24). Though there had of course been much physical damage done in the wars, the longest lasting damage was the legacy of bitterness left by the Civil War. A civil war in itself necessitates violence turned against fellow citizens, and in the case of the Irish Civil War, violence was turned against former comrades, as the military forces that had fought for Ireland in the

Revolution split into those willing to accept the 1921 Treaty with Britain and those unwilling to accept it. In the Revolution, horrific crimes had been committed against the people, by both Irish forces and British forces, but the Black-and-Tans (British mercenaries brought in during 1920 to reinforce the police force) were much more feared than the Irish forces of the IRA. Also, the war had been fought against a distinct enemy, Britain. But the Civil War involved Irishmen fighting Irishmen. The horrific crimes committed against soldiers and civilians were entirely the doings of the Irish themselves. The Free State imprisoned men who had fought to create it; the Republicans killed men alongside whom they had fought a year before. This occurred at the highest levels of the government, as well as at grass-root levels. Kevin O'Higgins, for instance, Minister of Home Affairs for the new government, had Rory O'Connor, the best man at his wedding, executed in one of the Free State reprisals (Lyons, p. 487). It was a humiliating situation, with very little moral high ground.

When O'Casey wrote *Juno and the Paycock*, the nation as a whole was pulling itself together. The new government had to be stabilized, buildings reconstructed, lives refocused. But at the same time that the Irish focused on the rebuilding process, the horror of the Civil War was still fresh in their minds. Johnny's fate—being dragged off to be shot, for betraying a former IRA comrade—was one that the audience and actors had known well, either from firsthand experience or from stories circulating throughout Dublin.

O'Casey's disgust at these betrayals is especially clear in that the reason Johnny has betrayed Robbie Tancred is never clear in the play. Tancred had been his neighbor, a boyhood friend, and a comrade-in-arms in the IRA after the treaty was signed. By the time of the play, not long after the civil war begins (the play is set in 1922, the same year the war started), Johnny has left the IRA—a source of satisfaction to his mother, who does not like his involvement in the violent politics of the day. But we never learn why he has left. And we never learn why, in the process of leaving the IRA, he betrayed Tancred. In any case, he did; and so two young men are dead at the end of the play. It is vital to the drama that Johnny's betrayal of Tancred seems to make no sense. The violence is senseless. The betrayal seems senseless. Johnny shatters himself—long before the IRA shows up at the door he is clearly in grave emotional trouble. He becomes a powerful symbol of the horror of civil war.

Sources and literary context. For the poverty-stricken family in *Juno and the Paycock*, O'Casey drew on the poverty-stricken Dublin he grew up in; his source for the pattern of betrayal in the play, and especially the betrayal of a former comrade, was the civil war the country had just endured. W. B. Yeats urged O'Casey to write about what he knew, and in the end his finest plays for the Abbey Theatre were grounded in realism.

After Yeats suggested to him that he write about the life of the Dublin slums, O'Casey wrote *The Shadow of a Gunman*, which was accepted without revision (other than that the title had been changed). The next year, *Juno and the Paycock* appeared and was a great success. O'Casey and the Abbey Theatre both benefited from their connection. There would be riots in 1926 when his play *The Plough and the Stars* was produced, and in 1928 his association with the Abbey Theatre would be severed, when his experimental play *The Silver Tassie* was rejected by Yeats. However, O'Casey made his reputation at the Abbey Theatre and wrote his best known plays for its company; and the staging of his plays there gave the theater its first wildly popular, sellout performances.

The subject matter of *Juno and the Paycock* was somewhat unusual for the Abbey, however. True, the realism of *Juno* was in large part common to the Abbey plays of the early twentieth century. While many Abbey plays dealt with themes connected to either the mythological underpinnings of cultural nationalism (Yeats's *On Baile's Strand*, for instance, or Synge's *Deirdre of the Sorrows*), others concerned the Irish political situation. One example is Yeats's early play, *Cathleen ni Houlihan* (performed in 1902); others were Lady Gregory's *Rising of the Moon* (in 1907) and O'Casey's first produced play, *The Shadow of a Gunman* (in 1923). And, though there was considerable pressure on the Abbey Theatre to produce plays that portrayed the Irish in a positive way, the company had produced plays with questionable characters—the riots which had broken out in 1907 at the opening of Synge's **Playboy of the Western World** (also in *WLAIT 4: British and Irish Literature and Its Times*) were a reaction to its "supposed defamation of the peasantry's moral and linguistic purity" (Maxwell, p. 563). But only *Juno and the Paycock* dealt with the Irish Civil War, so soon on its heels. For a brief time, its negative view of both Irish politics and Irish morality was not only tolerable but welcomed. To be sure, other writers addressed the Civil War at the time. Yeats, for instance, wrote "Meditations in Time of Civil War," first published in *The Dial*, in January of 1923; but *The Dial* was a literary magazine published in America. Also, Frank O'Connor would deal with the Civil War in some of the short stories contained in his collection, *Guests of the Nation*, published in 1931. But *Juno and the Paycock* is unique in that it addressed the Civil

---

O'CASEY DESCRIBES A CIVIL WAR BETRAYAL

Many of O'Casey's friends remembered his retelling of the stories he heard of the atrocities of the civil war. They affected him strongly, especially the stories of comrades killing other comrades. Later, in his autobiographies, he mentions those terrible years and, in *Inishfallen, Fare Thee Well*, retells one of the stories. In this excerpt, Lanehin, an IRA member, has bombed a house where Free State troops are quartered and has been captured by Colonel Clonervy, who had been "Sergeant of his company when they had both fought the Tans":

> He advanced with his two men towards Lanehin; advanced without a word, till they were so close, Lanehin fancied he felt their breaths tickling his cheeks. They stood as they had sat— in a closer semicircle, staring curiously at him. He stared back at them for a little; dropped his gaze; lifted his head again, knowing not what to do, for his mind overflowed with prayer. . . .
> —I surrendher, he said plaintively at last; what are you going to do with me? I surrendher.
> —A wise thing to do, said one of the civilian-clad men.
> —After all, went on the frightened man, there wasn't a lot of damage done. . . .
> —I'm an old comrade of yours, Mick, the young man pleaded . . . .
> —Jesus! whimpered the half-dead lad, yous wouldn't shoot an old comrade, Mick!
> The Colonel's arm holding the gun shot forward suddenly, the muzzle of the gun, tilted slightly upwards, splitting the lad's lips and crashing through his chattering teeth.
> —Be Jasus! We would, he said, and then he pulled the trigger.
> (O'Casey, *Inishfallen*, pp. 142-44)

War so immediately after the war ended, and in so public a fashion.

Reception. As has been mentioned, *Juno and the Paycock* was an immediate success. Its original run of a week was extended for another week, the first time such a thing had happened in the history of the Abbey Theatre. The company knew by the dress rehearsal how good it was; after hearing Juno's prayer, spoken after the death of her son Johnny, for the Lord to "take away this murdherin' hate, an' give us Thine own eternal love," Lady Gregory told Yeats, "this is one of the evenings at the Abbey that makes me glad to have been born" (Cowasjee, pp. 51-52). The reviewer for the *Freeman's Journal* (4 March 1924) would write:

AN ACTOR DISCUSSES THE PLAY

Gabriel Fallon, the Abbey Theatre actor who played Bentham in the first production, describes the rehearsals for the play, and its production, in his book concerning his friendship with Sean O'Casey. According to Fallon, the first read-through was hardly promising; the company thought they had a failure on their hands:

We could make nothing of the reading of *Juno and the Paycock* as it was called. It seemed to be a strange baffling mixture of comedy and tragedy; and none of us could say, with any certainty, whether or not it would stand up on the stage . . . . All were agreed that the title of the play was not a good one and that the dialogue written for the part of Jerry Devine, which was to be played by the manly forthright actor P. J. Carolan, was possibly the most stilted ever written in the history of the Abbey Theatre. There was a general feeling that the play lacked form, that it was much too "bitty," that the mixture of tragedy and comedy "would not go" and that the author of *The Gunman* might well have overshot his mark.

(Fallon, p. 19)

No one who saw the *Shadow of a Gunman* will ever forget its strong ironic bite. Here we have that same irony, centrifugal and indiscriminating as to character, but with a finer point. If the point is finer, however, the thrust is deeper. In the last act, touching the vitals, it becomes unbearable.

(*Freeman's Journal* in Cowasjee, p. 43)

Its brilliant combination of horrible tragedy and hilarious comedy precisely caught the mood of the Dublin citizens. As O'Casey's friend Joseph Holloway put it, the play was "backgrounded by the terrible times we have just passed through, but his characters are so true to life and humorous that all swallow the bitter pill of

fact that underlies both pieces" (Harrington, p. 494). But there would be a limited time when O'Casey could be presented without trouble in Ireland, since the mood would shift quickly. Some hint of the future trouble that O'Casey would run into with *The Plough and the Stars* surfaced when the Abbey Theatre took the show to Cork, where it had to be performed in a bowdlerized version, with every reference to religion expunged and every mention of sex cleaned up.

Even the beautiful and poignant prayer spoken by Mrs. Tancred and Juno Boyle, one of the most important speeches in the play, was cut out; and to avoid the undesirable fact that an Irish girl had been seduced, albeit by an Englishman, some dialog was added to indicate that Bentham had married Mary Boyle before he deserted her.

(Krause, p. 39)

The main problem in Cork had to do with the sexuality in the play, not the politics. The next year, the play opened in London, where it was again successful; in London, neither the sexuality nor O'Casey's bitter view of Irish politics was a problem. Reviewing the first London production for the *Sunday Times* (November 16, 1925), James Agate applauded the play's finish:

There are some tremendous moments in this piece, and the ironic close—in which the drunken porter returns to his lodging unconscious of his son's death, daughter's flight to river or streets, and wife's desertion—is the work of a master.

(Agate, p. 77)

The next year, 1926, the play won the Hawthornden prize in London, for the finest work of the previous year by a new writer. In 1930, Alfred Hitchcock would direct a movie version, which would in short order be burned in the streets of Limerick by Irish nationalists; but by then, O'Casey had moved to England.

But at the dress rehearsal, the play hit its mark for Fallon and the others in the theater:

I sat there stunned. So, indeed, so far as I could see, did Robinson, Yeats and Lady Gregory. Then Yeats ventured an opinion. He said that the play, particularly in its final scene, reminded him of a Dostoievsky novel. Lady Gregory turned to him and said: "You know, Willie, you never read a novel by Dostoievsky." And she promised to amend this deficiency by sending him a copy of *The Idiot*. I turned to O'Casey and I found I could only say to him: "Magnificent,

Sean, magnificent." Then we all quietly went home.

(Fallon, p. 22)

—Anne Brannen

For More Information

Agate, James. "Juno and the Paycock." In *Sean O'-Casey: Modern Judgements*. Ed. Ronald Ayling. Nashville: Aurora, 1969.

Ayling, Ronald. "Sean O'Casey and the Abbey Theatre." In *Sean O'Casey: Centenary Essays*. Ed. David Krause and Robert G. Lowery. Irish Literary Studies 7. Buckinghamshire: Colin Smythe, 1980.

Cowasjee, Saros. *Sean O'Casey: The Man behind the Plays*. Edinburgh and London: Oliver & Boyd, 1963.

Fallon, Gabriel. *Sean O'Casey: The Man I Knew*. Boston: Little, Brown, 1965.

Harrington, John P., ed. *Modern Irish Drama: A Norton Critical Edition*. New York & London: W. W. Norton, 1991.

Hughes, Michael. *Ireland Divided: The Roots of the Modern Irish Problem*. New York: St. Martin's, 1994.

Kearns, Kevin C. *Dublin Tenement Life: An Oral History*. 1994. Reprint, Penguin, 2000.

Krause, David. *Sean O'Casey: The Man and His Work*. New York: Macmillan, 1975.

Lyons, F. S. L. *Ireland since the Famine*. Glasgow: Weidenfeld & Nicolson, 1971.

Maxwell, D. E. S. "Irish Drama 1899–1929: The Abbey Theatre." In *The Field Day Anthology of Irish Writing*. Vol. 2. Derry: Field Day, 1991.

Neeson, Eoin. *The Civil War in Ireland, 1922–23*. Cork: The Mercier Press, 1966.

O'Casey, Sean. *Inishfallen, Fare Thee Well*. New York: Macmillan, 1949.

———. *Juno and the Paycock*. In *Modern Irish Drama*. Ed. John P. Harrington. New York: W. W. Norton, 1991.

Kim

by
Rudyard Kipling

Joseph Rudyard Kipling (1865–1936) was born in Bombay, India, where his father, John Lockwood Kipling, was a professor of Indian art and architecture. After being educated in England, Kipling returned to India in 1882, where he worked for the next seven years as a reporter. During this time his short stories about life in British-ruled India (published in 1888 as *Plain Tales from the Hills*) won him a literary reputation there, and when Kipling came back to Britain in 1889 he was rapidly accepted on the London literary scene as something of a young genius. By the following year he had published a novel, *The Light That Failed* (1890), along with further collections of short stories and several books of poetry that focused on the British colonial experience in India. Forever linking Kipling's name with the British Empire, his poems (e.g., "Gunga Din," 1882) and stories (e.g., "The Man Who Would Be King," 1888) are highly original in their often sympathetic portrayals of both Indians and the common British soldiers serving in India. During the 1890s, Kipling's series of children's stories featuring Mowgli, a boy raised by wolves, was published as the two *Jungle Books* (1894 and 1895). Along with the *Just So Stories* (1902), also for children, they remain among his most widely read works today. Begun in the early 1890s, *Kim* was completed in 1900. At once a young reader's adventure story and a serious adult novel, it not only describes the meeting of cultures under British rule in India, but also dramatizes India's strategic importance within the larger British Empire.

THE LITERARY WORK

A novel set in India in the late 1880s; first published in London in 1901.

SYNOPSIS

Kim, a young white orphan who has been raised as an Indian street urchin, becomes both a spy for the British Secret Service and the disciple of a Tibetan lama (holy man).

Events in History at the Time of the Novel

The British in India. Britain's presence in India began in the seventeenth century, when the English East India Company established a handful of coastal trading forts (called "factories") at sites from Surat in the west (1619) to Calcutta in the east (1690). Only in the middle of the eighteenth century, however, with the breakup of India's Mughal Empire into warring states, did British influence begin to extend inland from the coast. In 1757 East India Company forces under Robert Clive won a major victory north of Calcutta at Plassey; they defeated the Bengali ruler Siraj-ud-Daula, who had temporarily captured the factory in Calcutta. Another military victory followed in 1764, over the deteriorating Mughal armies further inland at Buxar. The British victories at Plassey and Buxar—after which the Company controlled the rich province of Bengal directly—

Rudyard Kipling

marked a turning point for British power in India, in that the company's military strength began to transform Britain's economic influence into political control. Over the next half century, the Company extended its dominance into southern India by defeating Tipu Sultan of Mysore in 1799, and into central India by defeating the Maratha Confederacy in 1818. Finally, in 1849 the Company annexed the region of northwestern India known as the Punjab. Ruling either directly or through client kings, the British East India Company now controlled all of India from its headquarters in Bengal.

In 1857, however, the situation changed dramatically when a violent revolt broke out in northern India against the Raj, as British rule had come to be known (from "rajah," the Sanskrit word for "king"). The unrest originated among Indian soldiers, called "sepoys," who served under British officers in the British Indian Army. Reflecting India's religious makeup, many of the soldiers were either Hindus or Muslims, and the army had offended both by ordering them to handle cartridges greased with cows' fat (unclean to Hindus) and pork fat (unclean to Muslims). The soldiers' insurrection triggered widespread unrest among the civilian population of north-

ern and central India, where decades of British political domination, economic exploitation, and cultural Westernization had created deep resentment among many Indians. Both the revolt and the British suppression of it in the following year were violent and bloody, with each side committing brutal atrocities against soldiers and against civilian men, women, and children.

In the novel, which is set approximately three decades after the unrest, Kim meets an old Indian soldier who participated in the conflict on the side of the British. For remaining loyal to the "sahibs," as Indians referred to the whites (the word was originally Arabic and means "master"), the old soldier was given good land in his village and is "still a person of consequence" often visited by British officials who pass near the village (Kipling, *Kim*, p. 94). As scholar and critic Edward Said points out in his introduction to a recent edition of the novel, Kipling's novel offers only one side of the story, through the old soldier, for his loyalty hardly represents general Indian opinion. Indeed, the old soldier would have been viewed as a traitor by at least a substantial proportion of the Indian population.

Significant changes in British policy followed the unrest of 1857–58. The British East India Company was shut down, and the colonial administration and army, formerly under the Company's private control, were turned over to the British government, which appointed a governor general to command both. Massive public works programs begun under the Company were continued and new ones undertaken: irrigation systems, telegraphs, roads, railroads, and British-run schools and universities created a modern infrastructure that in large part survives today. Railroads and the famous highway called the Grand Trunk Road, which was built under the Company's rule, figure prominently in the novel. Founding a number of universities in major cities, the government deliberately fostered Western education for Indians in the interest of breaking down India's traditional caste system and encouraging greater participation by Indians in colonial administration. As a result, by the time of the novel a middle class of Indian civil servants and other professionals had begun to emerge. In the novel this newly Westernized segment of Indian society is represented by the character Hurree Chunder Mookerjee, known as the Babu, a Westernized Hindu Bengali with an M.A. degree from the first such institution, British-run Calcutta University, which was founded in 1857.

INDIA'S RELIGIOUS VARIETY

~

- Followers of India's oldest major religion, Hindus today make up about 85 percent of India's population. Hindus worship a complex array of gods and goddesses and have traditionally been segregated into castes, social classes originally defined by occupation. Much of the resentment against British rule was inspired by British attempts to reform or abolish the caste system, which the British viewed as backward. Hindus are represented in the novel by such characters as the old soldier and the widow of Saharunpore (who befriends Kim and the lama).

- Islam arrived in India from the north with the Mughal conquerors of the sixteenth century and remained strongest in India's north, especially in the Punjab and Bengal (the two regions that split from India after independence from Britain in 1947 to form Muslim-dominated Pakistan). In general the British tended to favor Muslims, whom they viewed as warlike and aristocratic, over Hindus. Muslim characters in the novel include the colorful Afghan horse trader and spy Mahbub Ali, who drafts Kim into the British Secret Service.

- While Buddhism originated in India around the sixth century B.C.E. (when its founder, the Buddha or Enlightened One, is thought to have lived) and shares many of its precepts with Hinduism, it failed to displace Hinduism in India. Instead it spread eastward and became predominant in many parts of East and Southeast Asia. Buddhism is represented in the novel by the wise Tibetan lama (or holy man) who befriends Kim, and who some critics have suggested is the novel's true hero.

- Christianity arrived in India with European explorers in the fifteenth century, and Christian missionaries comprised an important element of British colonialism. The novel features two Christian priests, one Anglican and one Catholic, whose worldly behavior contrasts sharply with the lama's simple spirituality.

- Other religions mentioned in the novel include Sikhism and Jainism. Although both derived from a blend of Hindu with Muslim or Buddhist beliefs, they are separate faiths.

The Great Game. Since 1876 Queen Victoria had been styled "Empress of India" in addition to her other royal titles; thereafter she appointed a Viceroy of India (her personal representative) who replaced the governor general as commander of the colonial administration and the Indian Army. The Queen's imperial title reflected India's preeminent role among the vast territories Britain now controlled. In 1897, when it held an extended and extravagant public celebration of Queen Victoria's Diamond Jubilee (she had come to the throne in 1837), Britain ruled vast chunks of Asia, Africa, the Americas, and the islands of the Pacific—about a quarter of the world's land mass and population. Because of its lucrative trade opportunities and strategic value as a gateway to the rest of Asia, India was considered "the jewel in the crown" of this worldwide empire.

Protecting this "jewel" had worried the British as far back as the Napoleonic Wars that England and her allies fought, and finally won, against France from 1803 to 1815. At that time it was feared that Napoleon might invade Egypt, another British-controlled territory, and defeat British forces there, thus opening the way for a move against British India. This threat came to nothing, but after the defeat of Napoleon's France, a further menace to India was perceived in the expansionist Russia of Czar Alexander I and his successors, who in fact began a campaign of conquest and diplomacy that brought Russian armies steadily closer to the Indian border. By the middle of the century, agents and officers of each government were at work trying to advance their nation's cause by winning over the khans and emirs of Central Asia, north of India, where the contest was being played out. It was one such officer, a British captain named Arthur Conolly, who first called this struggle the "Great Game"— several years before a fatal miscalculation on his part led to his execution by a hostile emir in the Central Asian town of Bokhara in 1842.

That same year a British military expedition was driven out of Afghanistan in southern Central Asia, a defeat that concluded the First Anglo-Afghan War (1839–42). A Second Anglo-Afghan War followed from 1878 to 1880, in which the British were again frustrated in their attempts to control the remote, mountainous, and landlocked region. In both wars Russia and Britain supported rival claimants to power in Afghanistan, which the British hoped to establish as a buffer zone to protect India from Russian encroachment.

THE "TE-RAIN" AND THE GRAND TRUNK ROAD

In the first half of the novel Kim and the lama travel together across northern India, from the Punjabi city of Lahore (now in Pakistan) to Lucknow and Benares near Bengal, a journey of about 1,000 miles. They travel by train and by foot on the Grand Trunk Road. A 1,500-mile-long highway, the road is India's major thoroughfare. It was constructed by the East India Company to facilitate military and commercial transportation (parts had been built by sixteenth-century rulers for the same purposes). Spanning northern India, the Grand Trunk Road runs northwest from Calcutta through Benares, Delhi, and Lahore to the Punjab-Afghan border.

While Arthur Conolly originated the phrase the "Great Game," it came into common use only decades later with the publication and success of *Kim.* Kipling uses it repeatedly in the novel, for it is as a player in the Great Game that Kim is trained and deployed by the novel's spymasters. These include the Afghan horse trader Mahbub Ali and the Babu, both loyal to the British, and both of whom ultimately work for the enigmatic Colonel Creighton. Creighton, a British officer, poses as an ethnological researcher, his academic inquiries into Indian folkways serving as a perfect cover for his true job as head of the British Secret Service in India. In the real world, the British did engage in espionage and counteres-

pionage throughout the century, but there was no single "Secret Service" as such in India: the actual British spy system in India and Central Asia was less centralized than that depicted in the novel.

By the 1880s three separate organizations were working to further British strategic interests in India. In 1879 the Indian Army had established an Intelligence Department under Major General Sir Charles MacGregor, which at first consisted of only five officers plus native clerks. MacGregor himself put together a confidential 1883 handbook, *The Defense of India,* providing a detailed analysis of India's vulnerability to Russian attack from the north. In addition, the colonial government's Political Department employed its officers in intelligence gathering along the mountainous frontiers, where they did their best to monitor Russian troop movements. Finally, topographical intelligence was the province of a government organization called the Survey of India, whose Colonel T. G. Montgomerie, journalist and author Peter Hopkirk suggests, was the model for the novel's Colonel Creighton.

In the 1860s the Viceroy of India had forbidden British officers to travel north of India's borders because of the high probability that they would be captured and executed (as Arthur Conolly and others had been). Therefore, Montgomerie, then a young captain working for the Survey of India, came up with the idea of sending specially trained native inhabitants, who would be better able to escape detection, north of the border to conduct undercover surveying of the vital mountain passes and other strategic points. Known as "pundits" (a Hindi word meaning "learned man"), Montgomerie's operatives obtained a wealth of valuable information this way from the 1860s into the 1880s. Hopkirk concludes that Kipling, with a reporter's deep knowledge of British India, modeled the novel's Mahbub Ali and the Babu on Montgomerie's pundits, right down to similar code names (Mahbub Ali and the Babu are designated C25 and R23, respectively).

In one particularly effective technique, Montgomerie had the pundits disguise themselves as Buddhist pilgrims and carry specially modified versions of pilgrims' gear. For example, Montgomerie trained them to measure the distances they covered by taking uniform steps, counting the steps, then noting every hundredth step by moving a bead on a rosary, the string of 108 beads that devout Buddhists carried. By removing eight beads, Montgomerie made it easy to calculate that one rosary's worth of walking equaled 10,000 steps. The "pilgrim" recorded each day's distance on a paper cylinder concealed in the Buddhist prayer wheel that he spun as he walked. In the novel Kim is trained to collect topographical intelligence in precisely this way.

The Novel in Focus

Plot summary. The novel opens in the Punjabi city of Lahore, as 13-year-old Kim plays with other boys outside the Lahore Museum, known to Indians (and to Kim) as the Wonder House. Kim is the orphaned son of a British nursemaid and an Irish sergeant in the Indian Army. His real name is Kimball O'Hara, but Indians who know him call him Little Friend of all the World. Kim's father, who left the army and "fell to drink and loafing," lived with an opium-smoking "half-caste woman" (a woman of mixed European and Asian descent) before his death several years earlier, and she now looks after the boy (*Kim*, p. 49). But Kim has grown up largely on his own, acquiring an intimate knowledge of the streets of Lahore, playing with young Indian boys and evading the charitable workers, missionaries, and other representatives of the British establishment who might seek to curtail his cherished freedom. His only connection to the past is the leather pouch that hangs around his neck, into which the woman has sewn the few official papers that constitute Kim's inheritance from his father.

Suddenly Kim and some other boys are approached by "such a man as Kim, who thought he knew all castes, had never seen," a tall strangely dressed man with wrinkled yellow skin and a holy man's rosary (*Kim*, p. 52). The stranger, a Buddhist lama, or holy man, says he is from Tibet and asks about the museum. He has come to India on a pilgrimage to the Buddhist holy places there, and to Lahore because he has heard about the sacred objects in its museum. Kim, his curiosity aroused, escorts the lama to the museum's curator, a kindly white-bearded Englishman who possesses a wide knowledge of Buddhism and other Eastern religions. Listening at the door while the two men talk in the curator's office, Kim overhears the lama tell the curator that the real reason for his pilgrimage is to seek the legendary River of Healing, which formed at the place where an arrow shot by the Buddha fell to the ground. As the lama leaves the museum to continue the search for the mythical river—which, he says, "washes

"Kim and the Letter Writer," a terra cotta plaque by Rudyard Kipling's father, John Lockwood Kipling, for the first edition of *Kim*.

away all taint and speckle of sin"—he tells Kim that his quest has been jeopardized by the death from fever of his *chela*, or disciple (*Kim*, p. 58). The *chela* was a boy who traveled with the lama and begged for him, and since his *chela*'s death, the lama has been lonely and hungry. Always eager for fresh sights and sounds, Kim decides that he will be the lama's new *chela*. In making this decision, Kim also conceives a quest of his own, based on some dimly remembered words of his father, who had once said that Kim's destiny would lie with a group of men whose god was a red bull in a green field (the emblems on his father's regimental flag).

The lama and Kim set out for Benares, a city of many temples, in which the lama will consult another holy man. But before beginning the journey, the lama and Kim spend the night with Kim's friend Mahbub Ali. Mahbub Ali is a large man with a red beard, an Afghan horse trader who divides his time between Lahore and his homeland, "that mysterious land beyond the [mountain] Passes of the North," (*Kim*, p. 66). He often employs Kim to watch certain men and report on their movements, although Kim does not yet know Mahbub Ali's status as a spy for the

British. Mahbub Ali has just returned with valuable intelligence: five kings north of India's borders have allied with Russia. He needs to communicate this information to the British garrison in Umballa, a city that is on the way to Benares. Since he is being watched by agents of the five kings, he asks the boy to deliver a small package to a bungalow there. He tells Kim that the matter concerns a horse, and that Kim is to find a certain British officer at the bungalow, give him the package, and say that "the pedigree of the white stallion is fully established" (*Kim*, p. 68). Kim agrees "with a giggle, his eyes aflame" (*Kim*, p. 68). Not for a moment does he believe the story about the horse, instead imagining his mission to involve romantic intrigue of some sort.

After journeying by train with the lama from Lahore to Umballa, Kim finds the bungalow and delivers both the package and the message. He then conceals himself near the bungalow and eavesdrops on Colonel Creighton, the British officer to whom he has delivered the message. As Creighton discusses the situation with another officer—whom Kim discovers to be the British Commander-in-Chief of the Indian Army—Kim learns that his message has triggered the movement north of some 8,000 British troops to punish the five kings. For Kim, this is much more exciting than romantic intrigue. "It is big news," he tells himself excitedly (*Kim*, p. 86). The next day, when Kim and the lama continue their journey, they spend the night in a village where they meet a Hindu priest and an old soldier who served with the British in the Great Mutiny of 1857.

The following morning, the old soldier accompanies them to the Grand Trunk Road, the highway that will take them to Benares. Along the way they befriend the widow of a wealthy *rajah* (princeling) from Sarunhapore in the Himalayan foothills. The widow is on a religious pilgrimage and, charmed by Kim's lively wit and the lama's modesty and wisdom, she invites them to travel with her. That evening Kim sees several British soldiers marching with flags that depict a red bull on a green field—the sign that he remembers his father describing, and that he believes will be associated with his destiny. A long column of British troops marches into sight behind the flags and begins pitching tents nearby. Later that evening Kim sneaks away from the widow's camp and creeps into the soldiers' encampment, but he is apprehended by the regiment's Anglican chaplain, Reverend Bennett. Believing the boy to be a thief, Bennett summons his Roman Catholic colleague, Father Victor, and

the two search Kim and find the papers that the "half-caste" woman had sewn into the leather pouch Kim carries around his neck. The two priests are amazed to discover that the boy they take for a little Indian beggar speaks English, even if haltingly, and is in reality the son of a former sergeant in their own regiment.

Meeting with Kim and the two priests, the lama is heartbroken to learn that Kim has deceived him, and that his *chela* is in fact "a Sahib and the son of a Sahib" who can no longer accompany the lama on his quest for the River of Healing (*Kim*, p. 139). He blames himself, however, explaining that his attachment to Kim goes against the precepts of Buddhism, which hold that all passions (including affection) are obstacles to spiritual enlightenment. When it appears that Kim will have to go to a military orphanage and become a soldier, and that the only alternative is an expensive British school in Lucknow, the lama suggests that he himself pay Kim's tuition fees at the school. The priests doubt that the lama can do so, however. The lama departs and Kim—desperate to escape from the sahibs and rejoin the lama on the road—sends a letter to Mahbub Ali pleading for the horse trader to come to his rescue. Responding quickly, Mahbub Ali arrives a few days later and takes Kim to meet with Colonel Creighton. Identifying Kim as the boy who delivered the earlier message, Mahbub Ali explains the situation, stressing (in the language of horse trading) that Kim is a "colt" who "has no equal" (*Kim*, p. 156). Fluent in many of India's various languages, resourceful, adept at disguise, Kim is perfect for the Great Game and should not be wasted as a soldier, the Afghan tells Creighton. Creighton agrees, and when the lama in fact sends the tuition money (presumably from his monastery's treasury, though the novel does not say so), Creighton escorts Kim by train to Lucknow. Creighton tells Kim that at the school he will learn surveying skills, hinting that Kim will eventually be called on to assist him in the Survey of India, perhaps in disguise.

Creighton and Mahbub Ali carefully monitor Kim's progress at the school, which is called St. Xavier's. Although Kim likes the school and learns how to behave like a young sahib, when he hears that he is expected to spend the long summer holiday at an army barrack-school in a remote hill station, he rebels. Darkening his skin with dye, he disguises himself as a low-caste Hindu boy and goes "back to the Road again," promising Mahbub Ali by letter that he would be back at school for the start of term and asking Mahbub Ali to defend him to Creighton (*Kim*, p. 177).

Later in the holiday, however, Kim meets up with Mahbub Ali and, on Creighton's instructions, travels to Simla in the Himalayan foothills, summer capital of the colonial government. There, in some of the novel's most colorful scenes, Kim is trained in the arts of espionage by an eccentric and mysterious Briton named Lurgan, with whom he lives until it is time to return to school in Lucknow. There, too, he meets Lurgan's friend Hurree Chunder Mookerjee, a British-educated Bengali known as the Babu, a master of disguise who also works for Creighton and who further instructs Kim in spy techniques. Kim returns to Lurgan's house in Simla for subsequent Christmas and summer holidays and eventually tries out his skills in the field. He helps Mahbub Ali thwart a Briton who is illegally smuggling arms north of the border and accompanies the horse trader to the remote city of Bikanir, which Kim maps using the secret surveying techniques he has learned.

After the operation in Bikanir, Mahbub Ali finally persuades Creighton to take the boy out of school and bring him into the Great Game before his abilities are blunted. No longer the dirty 13-year-old ragamuffin who arrived at St. Xavier's, Kim is now a tall, confident, and handsome young sahib of 16. He has kept in touch with the lama, who visited Kim regularly at school while continuing his quest for the River of Healing. Now Creighton gives Kim six months to travel with the lama before beginning his work in the Great Game, but before the six months are up, Kim stumbles into the novel's last two Great Game adventures.

First, during a train journey, Kim rescues another agent who is being stalked by assassins. Then, in his last adventure, Kim and the lama go north to Sarunhapore, where they stay with their friend, the widow whom they had met on the road years earlier. There they happen upon the Babu, also a guest of the widow, but now in disguise as a doctor. He tells Kim that two men, one French and one Russian, have crossed through the mountain passes from the north pretending to be on a hunting expedition while actually surveying the valleys and passes that are close to the Indian border. After journeying into the mountains to help the Babu stop this hostile intelligence operation, Kim, the lama, and the Babu return to Sarunhapore. It is here, as the novel closes, that the lama finally finds enlightenment, locating his River of Healing in a

modest irrigation ditch. In accordance with Buddhist doctrine, he now believes he is ready to leave the cycle of birth, death, and reincarnation that is the human lot. Instead, however, he decides to stay in the world and help others reach enlightenment as well—specifically, to help his beloved disciple, Kim.

"Little Friend of all the World": *Kim* and imperialism. When first meeting Mahbub Ali, the reader learns that he is a spy for Britain and that "five confederated Kings, who had no business to confederate, had been informed by a kindly Northern Power [i.e. Russia] that there was a leakage of news from their territories into British India" (*Kim*, p. 69). Mahbub Ali—whose spying is the source of the leakage—thwarts the kings' surveillance by having Kim deliver to the British the news of their alliance with Russia, after which Kim overhears Creighton conferring with the British Commander-in-Chief about how they should respond. They plan to send troops north to attack the five kings, but when Creighton asks, "Then it means war?" the Commander-in-Chief replies, "No. Punishment" (*Kim*, p. 85).

These two passages reflect the essentially paternal quality of Britain's attitude toward India, the British Empire, and indeed much of the world as a whole in the late Victorian era. It was an attitude that rested on one simple, pervasive, and largely unquestioned assumption: that the British had an absolute right to rule other peoples. From such a premise comes the conclusion that the five kings—whose kingdoms lie outside of "British India"—have "no business" forming their own foreign policies, despite their positions as the heads of sovereign states. The British often used the threat of military force to impose treaty obligations on Central Asian rulers (for example, at the end of the Second Anglo-Afghan War in 1880). Similarly, the distinction made by the Commander-in-Chief in his subtle correction of Creighton—not war, but punishment—implies that, as he sees it, the five kings owe obedience to Britain: punishment is for disobedient children, while war is for equal opponents.

In his introduction to the novel, Edward Said points out that the novel provides no hint of Indian dissatisfaction with British rule, dissatisfaction that certainly existed and that found a voice in such organizations as the Indian National Congress, which was founded in 1885 and became the focal point of India's growing independence movement. In the world of *Kim*, however, British imperial rule is a benevolent gift that no one would ever wish to refuse. As one historian of the empire notes, it was at the time of the novel's composition in the 1890s that Kipling, "more than anyone, gave voice to the national emotions" of imperial Britain (Morris, p. 348). Like Kim, many Britons thought of their small island nation as a Little Friend of all the World.

Sources and literary context. Colonel Creighton and his espionage network are not the only part of the novel inspired by real life. In its rich and detailed descriptions of Indian sights and sounds, *Kim* explores Kipling's memories of his own boyhood in India. According to Peter Hopkirk, whose research is presented

---

QUESTIONS OF RACE, CULTURE, AND EMPIRE

In modern studies of *Kim* and Kipling, controversy has arisen over the question of whether—and if so, how—Kipling's writings are racist. Certainly the novel abounds with broad generalizations regarding "Oriental" disorganization, ineptitude, or duplicity. In describing the chaos of Lahore's train station at night, for example, Kipling writes that "all hours of the twenty-four are alike to Orientals, and their passenger traffic is regulated accordingly" (*Kim*, p. 74). Similarly, we are told that "Kim could lie like an Oriental" (*Kim*, p. 71). Some critics have argued that such stereotypes reveal racial prejudice on Kipling's part. Others, arguing that the novel's nonwhite characters often compare favorably to the whites, suggest that cultural stereotyping does not necessarily stem from racially based prejudgments. It has furthermore been suggested that the "brilliance of *Kim* lies in its ability to represent cultural multifariousness" while at the same time illustrating the power of a "monolith," the colonial system (Suleri, p. 119).

---

in his recent book *Quest for Kim*, many (though not all) of the novel's other characters and settings are based on actual people and places Kipling knew. Most significantly perhaps, the white-bearded curator of the Wonder House is widely recognized to be an accurate and affectionate portrait of Kipling's father, John Lockwood Kipling, who held that same position at the real Lahore Museum when Kipling himself was a boy. Both of Kipling's parents helped him as he wrote the novel, offering critical advice and suggestions; his father, an accomplished artist, produced illustrations for the novel's first American edition.

Kipling also knew a colorful Afghan horse trader named Mahbub Ali, whose father had sided with the British during the First Anglo-Afghan War (1829–32). While the real Mahbub Ali kept his friend "Kuppeleen Sahib" up to date about events in Afghanistan when Kipling was a reporter, he does not seem to have spied for the British (Hopkirk, *Quest,* p. 60). Other characters such as the lama may also originally have had real-life models, though it seems certain that Kipling added his own creative touches to their fictional counterparts.

Kim is a highly original work and does not stand squarely within any single literary tradition, but it has been compared with Mark Twain's *Adventures of Huckleberry Finn* (1884), which also describes a young boy's coming of age within the context of a colorful journey. The wise yet often naïve lama, critics have suggested, has much in common with Huck's companion Jim, the escaped slave with whom Huck journeys on the Mississippi.

Reception. *Kim* was serialized in *McClure's Magazine* in the United States from December 1900 to October 1901 and in *Cassell's Magazine* in Britain from January to November 1901. It appeared in book form in Britain and America in 1901. Early reviews were muted, considering Kipling's status as a leading British author, partly because public attention at the time was preoccupied with the South African War (1899–1902). This bitter and often brutal colonial struggle pitted the British against the Afrikaners (white descendents of Dutch colonials in South Africa, formerly called Boers). Kipling himself traveled to Africa to report on the South African War for British newspapers. The conflict had sharply reduced popular enthusiasm for imperial ventures, and Kipling's name was firmly linked with such ventures in the public mind. Popular enthusiasm also flagged with the death of Queen Victoria in January 1901; along with the war, her death seemed to mark the passing of the imperial era.

Yet critics soon recognized *Kim* as an artistic masterpiece and the best of Kipling's novels. Edward Shanks, for example, praised it as celebrating "the infinite and joyous variety of India for him who has the eyes to see it and the heart to rejoice in it" (Shanks in Page, p. 152). Even more laudatory were the words of novelist Kingsley Amis, who called *Kim* "not only the finest story about India" but "one of the greatest novels in the language" (Amis, p. 83).

—Colin Wells

For More Information

Amis, Kingsley. *Rudyard Kipling and His World.* New York: Scribner's, 1975.

Bloom, Harold. *Rudyard Kipling.* New York: Chelsea House, 1987.

Carrington, Charles. *Rudyard Kipling: His Life and Work.* Harmondsworth: Penguin, 1970.

Green, Roger Lancelyn, ed. *Kipling: The Critical Heritage.* London: Routledge, 1971.

Hopkirk, Peter. *The Great Game.* New York: Kodansha, 1994.

————. *Quest for Kim.* London: John Murray, 1996.

Kipling, Rudyard. *Kim.* London: Penguin, 1987.

Morris, James. *Pax Britannica: The Climax of an Empire.* Harmondsworth: Penguin, 1979.

Page, Norman. *A Kipling Companion.* London: Macmillan, 1984.

Rutherford, Andrew. *Kipling's Mind and Art.* London: Oliver & Boyd, 1964.

Suleri, Sara. *The Rhetoric of English India.* Chicago: University of Chicago Press, 1992.

King Solomon's Mines

by

H. Rider Haggard

The prolific late Victorian author Henry Rider Haggard (1856–1925) mesmerized the British public with his stirring, romantic tales of adventure. He wrote 68 books altogether, many of which are set in Africa. Along with his friend Rudyard Kipling, who also set his stories in far-off corners of the British Empire, Haggard both defended and glorified Britain's imperial aspirations. *King Solomon's Mines,* the book that brought him overnight celebrity in 1885, is based on the author's personal experience in British South Africa. Haggard went to South Africa in 1875 as a 19-year-old assistant to the lieutenant-governor of the British colony of Natal. Holding posts of increasing responsibility, he traveled widely in Africa over the next six years, returning to Britain in 1881. His experiences gave him material not only for *King Solomon's Mines,* but also for his later books, which include *She* (1887), *Allan Quatermain* (1887), *Maiwa's Revenge* (1888), *Nada the Lily* (1892), and *Queen Sheba's Ring* (1910). A number of them feature Allan Quatermain, the big-game hunter who narrates *King Solomon's Mines* and who became Haggard's most popular character.

Events in History at the Time of the Novel

Zulus, Boers, and British in South Africa. By the second half of the nineteenth century, a number of conflicting populations were struggling for land and power in South Africa. Bantu-speaking

THE LITERARY WORK

A novel set in southern Africa; first published in London in 1885.

SYNOPSIS

Three Englishmen seek a fabulous lost diamond mine in the remote interior of southern Africa.

Africans, of whom the Zulus would later become the most powerful, had entered from the north, perhaps before 300 C.E., driving the indigenous Khoikhoi and San peoples into less fertile regions of desert and scrub. Europeans arrived more than a millennium later—first the Portuguese, who founded trading settlements such as Delagoa Bay in Natal on the eastern coast in the early 1500s, and then in greater numbers the Dutch, who founded the first permanent white settlement at Cape Town in 1652. During the golden age of Dutch commercial expansion in the seventeenth century, Cape Town served as a stopover for Dutch East India Company ships that sailed between Europe and Asia. Cape Town and the fertile land around it were settled by Dutch merchants and farmers. Their descendants called themselves *Afrikaners* (the Dutch word for "African"; their language, derived from Dutch, is Afrikaans, and they are known also as *Boers* from the Dutch word for "farmer"). The city and its adjacent territory remained in Dutch hands

H. Rider Haggard

fective use a new shorter spear, the *assegai,* used for stabbing in hand-to-hand combat. But there were some unhappy troops under him. Shaka had a disaffected lieutenant named Mzilikazi, who led a group of the Zulus' allies north into the Transvaal, then further into today's southwestern Zimbabwe. Called the Ndebele, the group was Haggard's model for the Kukuana in *King Solomon's Mines,* the people deep in the interior who welcome the English explorers.

Thus, by about 1870 the situation stood as follows:

- Britain exercised colonial rule over the highly developed Cape Colony (population about 30,000) and over Natal, with its seaport city of Durban (where Quatermain and the other Englishmen arrive by ship in *King Solomon's Mines.*) In addition, the British controlled much territory indirectly, through client states such as Griqualand, southeast of the Transvaal.
- *Voortrekker* farming settlements had been contested and often curbed both by the British and by African peoples such as the Zulus. Nevertheless, the Afrikaners had established two independent states in the interior: the South African Republic, in the Transvaal (1852), and the Orange Free State, south of the Transvaal (1854).
- Having absorbed many neighboring peoples, the Zulu nation controlled the territory between Natal and the Transvaal. Persistent border disputes occurred between the Zulus and the Afrikaner descendants of European settlers. Other indigenous peoples who resisted the Europeans included the Xhosa (on the Cape frontier), the Swazi (north of Natal) and the Pedi (in the northern Transvaal).
- The Ndebele (also called Matabele) occupied a wide strip of land in today's southwestern Zimbabwe, along the border with Botswana.

Diamonds, British annexation, and the Zulu War. The region's unsettled situation was exacerbated by the discovery, in 1870, of rich diamond deposits in territory already contested by various groups: the two Afrikaner states, a breakaway Griqua (mixed race) state, and chiefs of the neighboring southern Tswana peoples. A diamond rush ensued, and by the end of the following year nearly 50,000 fortune seekers had arrived, creating the sprawling boom town of Kimberley. British adjudication awarded Kimberley to the Griqua, who then requested British protection. Britain formally annexed the area as Griqualand West in 1871, incorporating it into the Cape Colony nine years later.

until 1795, when the area was captured by the British, who made Cape Town the capital of what became the new British-ruled Cape Colony. For a brief few years (1803–06), the Dutch regained control, after which Britain remained the reigning colonizer until 1910.

As large numbers of British immigrants began arriving in the early nineteenth century, both groups of white Europeans (the Afrikaners and the British) competed for land against each other and against black African peoples. Displaced Afrikaners moved northeastward from the Cape Colony into the interior, at first in scattered groups, but after 1835 in a mass migration of large, organized groups called the "Great Trek." By 1840 about 6,000 Afrikaner men, women, and children had migrated from the Cape Colony. Crossing the Vaal River, many of these so-called *Voortrekkers* ("pioneers") occupied the area known as the Transvaal ("across the Vaal"). Others moved into Natal on South Africa's eastern coast, where thousands of British settlers also arrived beginning in the 1840s and 1850s. Meanwhile, under their kings Shaka (1816–28), and Dingane (1828–40), the Zulus conquered much of the interior between Natal and the Transvaal, using new tactics and combat techniques to create a powerful military force. Shaka (also spelled Chaka) is said to have organized and trained his troops in innovative ways and to have put to ef-

The annexation of Griqualand West marked a shift in British policy; the British were taking a new, aggressively imperial stance. This change in attitude sprang not only from events in South Africa (such as the discovery of diamonds and, in 1886, of gold), but also from a growing sense among the British of their own place at the head of a worldwide empire. For the most part, the British Empire before the 1870s had grown haphazardly and without conscious design; from the 1870s to the early 1900s it would grow as the result of self-conscious and deliberate purpose.

The 19-year-old Haggard arrived in South Africa in 1875, at a critical period in this transition. In his first year, as assistant to the lieutenant-governor of Natal, Sir Henry Bulwer, Haggard accompanied Bulwer on visits to a number of Zulu *kraals,* or villages. The following year, he went with Sir Theophilus Shepstone, the influential secretary for native affairs, on a fact-finding mission into the Transvaal. Shepstone, having just returned from meetings in London with the British colonial secretary Lord Carnarvon, had instructions to see if conditions favored British annexation of the unstable Afrikaner state there. Under threat from the formidable Zulu king Cetewayo (whose accession Shepstone had helped secure in 1872), the Afrikaners agreed to annexation. On May 24, 1877—Queen Victoria's birthday—Haggard himself hoisted the British flag in the Transvaal capital of Pretoria.

With the Transvaal in British hands, the Zulus became a British problem, not an Afrikaner one. In December 1878 the British high commissioner for Southern Africa, Sir Bartle Frere, issued an ultimatum to Cetewayo, ordering him to disband his troops and accept British government. As anticipated, Cetewayo ignored the ultimatum, which then gave Frere a pretext to invade Zululand. Early the following year, under the inexperienced Lord Chelmsford, a British expeditionary force of some 1,700 men was almost completely wiped out by the Zulus at Isandhlwana. Although the Zulus were defeated later that year, and Zululand was eventually incorporated into Natal, the battle of Isandhlwana remained a strong memory for the British in South Africa. Shepstone, Haggard, and other experienced colonists had opposed Frere's making an ultimatum to the Zulus. Haggard's fictional narrator, Allan Quatermain, served as "one of Lord Chelmsford's guides in that unlucky Zulu War," though he had the good fortune to be away from the camp when the Zulus attacked (Haggard, *King Solomon's Mines,* p. 46). Like his narrator, Haggard had friends who died at Isandhlwana, and he viewed the expedition as a tragic error. After the British victory in the Zulu War, Haggard's respect for the Zulus—the "Romans of Africa," he called them—remained undiminished (Haggard in Pocock, p. 21).

Afrikaner rebellion. Following a visit to England (where he got married in 1880), Haggard returned to Africa. Buying a home in eastern Natal near the Transvaal border, he switched from a career in colonial government to one as an ostrich farmer. His decision to leave colonial government was partly influenced by the extreme

---

NDEBELE CIVIL WARS

Haggard himself identified the Ndebele as his model for the novel's Kukuana, though he portrays his fictional people as having settled Kukuanaland long before the Ndebele's trek north to Zimbabwe in the mid-1800s. Like the Zulu, from whom they split, the Ndebele suffered from frequent civil wars between leaders. Mzilikazi's son Lobengula displaced his rival in one such war, perhaps providing a model for the novel's war between Twala, the usurper, and Ignosi, the Kukuana's rightful king. The character Quatermain in Haggard's novel refers to Lobengula as "a great scoundrel" (*King Solomon's Mines,* p. 50). In real life, Lobengula was responsible for the deaths of two of Haggard's African servants, Khiva and Ventvögel. Haggard had sent them to accompany some English friends on a friendly expedition to the Ndebele, but the whole party was wiped out by Lobengula's soldiers. Haggard paid tribute to the two by reproducing them as the faithful servants Khiva and Ventvögel who die in *King Solomon's Mines.*

---

unpopularity of the British administration in the Transvaal. Shepstone had handled the annexation with tact and deftness, but his superiors had removed him from office after the debacle against the Zulus at Isandhlwana. British policy afterward ignored the demands of the Afrikaners, who, once the British defeated the Zulus, no longer needed British protection against them in any case. By the time Haggard returned to the area, the Afrikaners had broken out in open revolt against the British. The tough, heavily armed farmers defeated the British in a series of battles, most notably at Majuba Hill in 1881, and shortly after that Britain restored self-rule to the Transvaal. Haggard viewed this so-called Retrocession ("giving back") as a betrayal of the British colonials by the government in London. Ironically, at his house in Natal, Haggard—who had personally raised the British flag in Pretoria—also personally hosted the five weeks of negotiations that returned the Transvaal to the Afrikaners.

Abandoning the dangers of South Africa, Haggard and his family went back to England, where he turned his hand first to a legal career and then to writing. *Cetywayo and His White Neighbors* (1882), his first book, provides a history of the Zulu War and a defense of Shepstone's policies. The book, which has been highly praised by modern historians, argues that British rule was necessary in the Transvaal to protect the black Africans from abuse at the hands of the Afrikaners. It also predicts that political strife will continue to trouble South Africa, a prediction that

HAGGARD'S VIEW OF THE AFRIKANERS

In contrast to his respect for the Zulus, Haggard had contempt for the Afrikaners. Like many British colonials in South Africa, he saw the Afrikaners as a backward people who were racist and brutal in their treatment of blacks. Modern historians generally agree with this assessment. Haggard was chastised by his superiors for portraying the Afrikaners unfavorably in a magazine article at a time of sensitive negotiations over the fate of the Transvaal, which (along with his hostility) may partly explain why *King Solomon's Mines* has few references to them.

would be fulfilled when the British and the Afrikaners clashed again in the long and bitter South African or Anglo-Boer War of 1899–1902. That war, which Britain won only with difficulty, would mark the final stage in Britain's colonial conquest of South Africa.

The Novel in Focus

Plot summary. The story begins as Allan Quatermain, the 55-year-old trader and big-game hunter who narrates the novel, returns home to Durban from Cape Town by ship after an unsuccessful elephant hunt. On board the ship he meets two Englishmen traveling together from Britain to Natal, Sir Henry Curtis and Captain John Good. He strikes up a shipboard acquaintance with the two friends, who are opposites in physical appearance. Sir Henry, a large muscu-

lar man with blond hair, looks like a Viking, while Captain Good, an officer in the British navy, is short, heavy-set, and dark-haired. They have come to Africa in hopes of tracing Sir Henry's missing brother. He disappeared five years earlier while searching for King Solomon's mines, the legendary lost diamond mines that supposedly belonged to the ancient Hebrew monarch.

Quatermain once met the missing brother, it turns out, who at the time was traveling under the name Neville as he searched for the lost mines. Quatermain himself had heard of the mines from another elephant hunter 20 years earlier. But since this was well before the discovery of diamonds at Kimberley, there was no proof of diamonds in the region, so he discounted the story at the time. Then, years later in Manicaland (today's eastern Zimbabwe), Quatermain met a Portuguese prospector named José Silvestre, who emerged from the western desert and, dying of fever, gave Quatermain a map, which had been drawn in blood, to the mines. The map had been drawn 300 years earlier by an ancestor of Silvestre, one of the first Portuguese in Natal. With the map, which directed seekers to cross the desert to the land of the Kukuanas and pass between two mountains called Sheba's Breasts, came instructions. The instructions warned readers to beware "the treachery of Gagool the witchfinder" (*King Solomon's Mines*, p. 28). Quatermain did not take the map seriously, but he relayed directions to the mines to Neville's black servant, Jim, to pass along to Neville. Quatermain had never seen or heard of Neville again.

After telling them this story and showing them the map, Quatermain agrees to help Sir Henry and Captain Good find the mines, in hopes of also locating Neville. Staying at Quatermain's home in Durban, the three prepare supplies for the long expedition north into the interior, including weapons and ammunition. They also hire five black servants, among them a Khoikhoin tracker named Ventvögel, a Zulu named Khiva, and a man named Umbopa who describes himself as "of the Zulu people yet not of them" (*King Solomon's Mines*, p. 48). Umbopa says that he wants the job because he wishes to return to his people in the north, who were "left behind when the Zulus came down here 'a thousand years ago'" (*King Solomon's Mines*, p. 48). Quatermain remembers Umbopa from the British camp at Isandhlwana, where Umbopa had commanded a unit of "native auxiliaries," black African troops fighting under British command (*King Solomon's*

Mines, p. 47). Umbopa, in fact, had warned him that the camp was in danger. Quatermain had ignored the warning at the time but remembered it later, after the Zulu attack. Umbopa is a large and "magnificent-looking man," every bit as impressive as Sir Henry, who likes him and decides to take him as his personal servant (*King Solomon's Mines,* p. 49).

It takes the group nearly four months to make the more than 1,000-mile journey from Durban north to Sitanda's Kraal, the remote village in Manicaland where Quatermain had met Silvestre years earlier. Quatermain skips over most of the trip, though he does pause to relate the events surrounding an elephant hunt that the group engages in on the way. At the end of the hunt, Captain Good—who insists on wearing formal clothes or "civilized dress" in the bush—slips in his smooth-soled boots and falls while fleeing a charging elephant (*King Solomon's Mines,* p. 62). Khiva, his young Zulu servant, bravely stops and hurls his *assegai,* or long-bladed spear, at the enraged animal, which seizes him and tears him in two. After burying Khiva, the group moves on.

Finally the men reach Sitanda's Kraal, on the edge of the western desert. There they hear of a white man and his black servant named Jim who went into the desert a few years ago and never returned. Making arrangements to leave their elephant rifles and other heavy gear with an old man in the village, they venture into the desert, resting by day and traveling by night. Their only hope of survival is to find a single water hole that is marked on the map halfway across the desert, for without replenishing their water supply they cannot complete the journey. The experienced Ventvögel saves them by finding water. Now their problem is food, for they have eaten the last of their provisions. They reach the mountains and begin climbing, and as it gets colder they suffer all the more for not having nourishment. They find the little cave that marks the entrance to the mines and sleep in it, losing Ventvögel who dies during the night.

The next morning they find another body besides Ventvögel's inside the cave. It is Silvestre's ancestor, the man who drew the old map that led them there and whose remains have been preserved by the cold. That day they shoot some antelope, eating the meat raw since there is no wood for a fire. Taking some of the meat with them, they press on, using a mysterious 50-foot wide highway marked on the map as Solomon's Great Road. The road, artfully carved out of the solid stone, appears abruptly at the bottom of the

mountain and runs through the plain that lies ahead. As they camp that evening, they encounter a group of men who identify themselves as Kukuanas and who speak a language very similar to Zulu. The Kukuanas are about to kill them when Captain Good terrifies them by pulling his false teeth down and letting them snap back (a habit of his in times of stress). Quatermain further shocks them by shooting an antelope with his rifle. Convinced that the whites must be gods, the Kukuanas escort them back to their king, whose name is Twala.

Their Kukuana escort is led by Infadoos, King Twala's half-brother, and by Scragga, his son. Infadoos tells Quatermain that Twala seized power years ago in a civil war, overthrowing the rightful king, Twala's older twin brother Imotu. Imotu was killed, but his wife escaped with their infant son, Ignosi. The two disappeared in the desert and were never seen again. If he had survived, however, Ignosi would be the rightful king of the Kukuana. As Infadoos answers his questions, Quatermain notices Umbopa, Sir Henry's servant, listening attentively.

They travel for three days through Kukuanaland before arriving at Loo, the large town where the king makes his residence. They meet Twala and the "wizened monkey-like figure" named Gagool, a terrifying old woman who acts as the king's prophetess (*King Solomon's Mines,* p. 147). In a trancelike state, Gagool foresees rivers of blood, and she seems to recognize Umbopa before collapsing in a fit and being carried away. The travelers are told that in the evening they will witness "the great witch-hunt," in which the leading Kukuanas assemble and Gagool singles out those she identifies as witches, who are killed on the spot (*King Solomon's Mines,* p. 151). In reality, Infadoos tells them, she points out those who have property the king covets or who have in some other way incurred his wrath. Twala is a harsh tyrant. "The land," says Infadoos, cries out with his "cruelties" (*King Solomon's Mines,* p. 151). Twala has been tolerated by the people only because the son, Scragga, is even more cruel than the father.

Before the witch-hunt begins, Umbopa reveals that he is Ignosi, the rightful king, and that he plans to overthrow Twala. Infadoos swears loyalty to him and says that he will speak with the Kukuana chiefs, who will in turn speak with their soldiers. After they witness the horrible spectacle of the witch hunt—and are themselves nearly singled out by Gagool—they are met in their hut by a number of Kukuana chiefs. Believing them

An aerial photo of the Kimberly diamond mine taken in 1875, the same year that Haggard arrived in British South Africa.

still to be gods, the chiefs ask for a sign to show that Umbopa is in fact Ignosi, the rightful king. After they leave, Captain Good reads in his almanac that a solar eclipse will happen the next day. Returning later, the chiefs agree that if the white "gods" can block out the sun, the chiefs will accept Umbopa as Ignosi. The eclipse occurs, and under cover of darkness Ignosi and the whites escape to prepare for battle against Twala, taking a young Kukuana girl named Foulata, whom they have rescued from death at the hands of Twala's son Scragga.

Sir Henry, Captain Good, and Quatermain fight bravely on the side of the victorious Ignosi, and after the battle Sir Henry kills Twala in single combat. Calling Gagool "the evil genius of the land," Ignosi states his intention to execute her, but he has also promised to take the whites to the diamond mines, and Quatermain points out that Gagool can show the way (*King Solomon's Mines*, p. 245). Captain Good develops a fever from his wounds, and is nursed back to health by Foulata, the young Kukuana girl. After he heals, they all set out for the mines, taking the muttering and cursing Gagool with them. She hints that she is the same Gagool the old Portuguese warned them about (beware "the treachery of Gagool, the witch-finder"), and that she may be hundreds of years old.

The travelers approach the three towering mountains that surround the mines, and as they get closer, they find a pit that Quatermain recognizes, having seen similar mining pits at Kimberley. On the other side of the pit they come upon three huge statues of stone, one female and two male figures, which the Kukuana call the "Silent Ones" (*King Solomon's Mines*, p. 258). Past the Silent Ones lies the cave called the "Place of Death," where all the kings of the Kukuana are entombed and where Gagool says they will find "the store of bright stones" (*King Solomon's Mines*, pp. 259, 260). Led by Gagool, they enter the cave, where they find numerous stalagmites created by water dripping from the ceiling over the centuries. They go through a passage to an inner cavern, where one stalagmite has been sculpted into a huge skeleton that presides over a massive table. Around the table are nearly 30 stalagmites that contain the bodies of the Kukuana kings, slowly encased by the minerals in the dripping water. Even Twala is there, a thin mineral film already covering his body.

Gagool triggers a secret mechanism, and a stone wall at the back of the cavern slowly rises, creating an opening into the treasure chamber. Inside they find crates of gold and huge stone chests filled with diamonds. Suddenly, the men hear Foulata cry out from the passage, where Gagool has returned and triggered the secret mechanism again to lower the massive stone wall. She stabs Foulata, who grapples with Gagool, delaying her, so that just as Gagool wriggles free and scrabbles under the wall it closes on her with "a long sickening crunch" (*King Solomon's Mines*, p. 280). Gagool is dead. Foulata dies too, declaring her love for Good, and shortly afterward their only oil lamp slowly goes out. They realize that although Gagool is dead, she has left them entombed in the treasure chamber.

Sparingly using the eight matches they have left, the men desperately begin to search for a way out. They find a stairway, and before exploring it Quatermain fills his pockets with diamonds. At the bottom, Captain Good notices a draft of air, which they walk against, encountering numerous intersecting tunnels and an underground stream and retracing their steps several times. Finally they see a patch of light, which turns out to be a small hole in the ground. Gratefully, they climb out and rejoin Infadoos, who has been waiting at the pit. After two days spent recovering their strength, they are unable to find the small hole through which they escaped, nor can they discover the secret mechanism with which Gagool opened the stone door to the treasure chamber. Returning to the town Loo, they bid a sad farewell to Ignosi, who says he will allow no other white men to come into Kukuanaland.

The travelers start across the desert, making their way toward an oasis to which the Kukuanas have directed them—where they find none other than Sir Henry's brother and his servant Jim. The two had been marooned at the oasis after Sir Henry's brother broke his leg badly. Together they manage to transport the brother back across the desert to Sitanda's Kraal and thence to Durban, where the Englishmen catch a ship back to Britain. They apportion the diamonds that Quatermain pocketed, which are enough to make them all rich men. As he finishes writing his account of the adventure, Quatermain receives an invitation to join his friends at Sir Henry's home in Yorkshire, where Quatermain's son Harry (who attends Oxford University) will be spending his Christmas vacation. Quatermain ends his story with plans to sail to England.

Race, greed, and imperialism. In his classic study of imperialism, the British historian J. A. Hobson has written that although "the year 1870 has been taken as . . . the beginning of a conscious policy of Imperialism . . . the movement did not attain its full impetus until the middle of the eighties" (Hobson, p. 19). As the remarkable career of the South African diamond magnate and imperialist statesman Cecil Rhodes illustrates, events in South Africa were central to this gathering momentum, and diamonds were central to events in South Africa. When Haggard wrote *King Solomon's Mines* in 1885, Rhodes was still in the process of consolidating his control of the Kimberley mines, which would form the cornerstone of his economic and political power. Haggard showed remarkable insight in putting diamonds at the center of *King Solomon's Mines,* a deceptively simple adventure story published at the exact historical moment (according to Hobson) of imperialism's full impetus.

CECIL RHODES AND THE KIMBERLEY DIAMONDS

The quintessential imperialist Cecil Rhodes (1853–1902), was 17 years old when he landed in Durban, South Africa in 1870. He had planned a career in law, then fallen ill; to recuperate, he took a voyage to see his brother Herbert, a recent immigrant to South Africa. Rhodes proceeded, with his brother, to seek his fortune in the Kimberley diamond fields in the 1870s. First buying a number of small mines, he formed the De Beers Mining Company, which acquired other mines until Rhodes controlled 90 percent of the world's diamond production. He parlayed his economic success into a political career, becoming Prime Minister of the Cape Colony from 1890 to 1896 and engineering British commercial and political expansion into two vast areas that were named for him: Southern Rhodesia, now Zimbabwe; and Northern Rhodesia, now Zambia. "Expansion is everything," Rhodes declared, continuing, "I would annex the planets if I could" (Rhodes in Arendt, p. 4).

Haggard is often cited as an imperialist writer, and *King Solomon's Mines* as an unabashedly imperialist work. Yet in its portrayal of European motives in Africa, the novel's sense of romance and adventure is balanced by its often stark acknowledgment of greed and racism. For example, as the African king Ignosi (a complex and sympathetically drawn character) bids goodbye to his white friends, he delivers a perceptive anti-imperialist speech that explicitly links white expansion in Africa to greed for diamonds:

> If a white man comes to my gates I will send him back; if a hundred come, I will push them

back; if an army comes, I will make war on them with all my strength, and they shall not prevail against me. None shall ever come for the shining stones; no, not an army. . . .

(*King Solomon's Mines*, p. 306)

Elsewhere both Ignosi and Gagool deride the whites' hunger for the shining diamond stones, which seems ridiculous to them. Perhaps Sir Henry captures Haggard's ambivalence when he responds indignantly to Ignosi that "wealth is good, and if it comes our way we will take it; but a gentleman does not sell himself for wealth" (*King Solomon's Mines*, p. 155). Yet a gentleman, it seems, has trouble taking wealth even when it is there for the picking; it is Quatermain, the

---

AFRICA'S MYTHIC INTERIOR

Throughout the nineteenth century, a series of highly publicized British expeditions ventured into the African interior, helping to feed an appetite for romance and adventure in the British public. The most sensational of these expeditions was that of the British-American journalist Henry Morton Stanley, who located the missing explorer and missionary David Livingstone in 1871. To European audiences, one intriguing element in their lore about Africa was a speculative connection between Africa and ancient white races. In 1871 the German geologist Karl Mauch suggested that the giant stone ruins at Great Zimbabwe had been built by the ancient Phoenicians; for centuries Portuguese traders speculated that the rock mines near Great Zimbabwe had been built by King Solomon. Modern historians have discounted these theories, attributing such remains to indigenous African peoples.

---

practical trader, not the gentlemanly Sir Henry, who will soon fill his pockets when diamonds come their way in the treasure chamber. Race, too, is subject to similar ambivalence. When pondering what makes a gentleman, Quatermain refuses to use the derogatory word "nigger," explaining that he has known blacks who were gentlemen and whites who were not. Yet Quatermain chides Ignosi (very much a "gentleman" in behavior even when he is still Umbopa the servant) for speaking too familiarly to the whites. He also decides that Foulata's death, while tragic, was a blessing in disguise, because "no amount of beauty or refinement could have made an entanglement between Captain Good and herself a

desirable occurrence; for, as she herself put it, 'Can the sun mate with the darkness, or the white with the black?'" (*King Solomon's Mines*, p. 300). Quatermain thus exemplifies a common attitude among British South Africans: horror at the allegedly open and brutal racism of the Afrikaners, paternal affection and respect for some black Africans, yet revulsion at the idea of mixing too closely with them.

Sources and literary context. In addition to well-known and exotic lore about the African interior, Haggard's own experiences in Africa provided many of the novel's details and background. The characters of the two servants Khiva and Ventvögel, he records elsewhere, were as true to life as he could make them. For the cave he calls the "Place of the Dead," Haggard drew on a visit to a real stalagmite cave at Wonderfontein, where he saw rows of glistening pillars formed by dripping, mineral-laden water. A friend's description of a Zulu ceremony served as a model for the novel's witch-hunt. As Haggard recalled the tale, there stood "some five thousand armed warriors in a circle," with "witch-doctors" dancing around them: "Everyone was livid with fear, and with reason, for now and again one of these creatures would come crooning up to one of them and touch him, whereupon he was promptly put out of this world by a regiment of the king's guard" (Haggard in Higgins, p. 19).

Haggard's childhood in England also offered inspiration. One of his schoolteachers told a strange tale about a friend who had come upon an ancient burial site in Peru, where the corpses were seated around a table. Haggard combined this image with the caves at Wonderfontein in his rendering of the "Place of the Dead." Also, as a boy he had known a farmer named Quatermain, whose name he appropriated for the novel's hero. Scholars have suggested (though Haggard himself denied it) that Quatermain's character was based on the well-known explorer and hunter Frederick Selous, whose popular book *A Hunter's Wanderings in Africa* (1881) Haggard had probably read. Around this time a number of "boys' adventure" novels about Africa captured the public's imagination, such as the prolific G. A. Henty's *By Sheer Pluck: A Tale of the Ashanti War* (1884), and these too may have influenced Haggard's writing of the novel. Finally, Haggard owed at least some inspiration to Robert Louis Stevenson, author of *Treasure Island* (1883) and **Dr. Jekyll and Mr. Hyde** (1886; also in *WLAIT 4: British and Irish Literature and Its Times*). It was after discussing *Treasure Island* with his brother that Haggard boasted he could match it. His brother bet him he could not, and *King Solomon's Mines*—written, Haggard later said, in some six weeks—was the result.

Reception. Haggard won the bet, for like *Treasure Island, King Solomon's Mines*—Haggard's first deliberate attempt at children's fiction—was an immediate success. Published by Cassell (Stevenson's publisher) in September 1885, *King Solomon's Mines* sold an impressive 31,000 copies in its first year. "KING SOLOMON'S MINES— THE MOST AMAZING STORY EVER WRITTEN," Haggard's publishers proclaimed on advertising posters in London, and most reviews were nearly as enthusiastic. *The Athenaeum* declared the novel "one of the best books for boys— old or young—that we remember to have read" (*King Solomon's Mines,* vii). A reviewer for *The Spectator* compared it favorably to similar works by Jules Verne and Herman Melville, and Stevenson himself thought it showed "flashes of a fine weird imagination and a fine poetic use and command of the savage way of talking: things which both thrilled me" (Stevenson in Cohen, p. 95).

Ultimately, the novel's influence was profound if unmeasurable, for (as historians point out) an entire generation of British children— along with many adults—took their impression of Africa directly from *King Solomon's Mines.* Like other budding empire-builders, the young Winston Churchill read it as a schoolboy, sending Haggard an avid fan letter: "I hope you will write a great many more books," the future leader announced (Churchill in Cohen, p. 96). As a later observer wrote in 1926, by creating a powerfully romantic vision of Europeans in Africa, Haggard's novels (of which *King Solomon's Mines* remained the most popular) "helped to accomplish the dreams and aims of [Cecil] Rhodes," encouraging young males to support and later advance the cause of British empire-building (Hutchinson in Katz, p. 1).

—Colin Wells

For More Information

Arendt, Hannah. *Imperialism.* New York: Harcourt Brace Jovanovich, 1968.

Cohen, Morton N. *Rider Haggard: His Life and Works.* New York: Walker, 1960.

Ellis, Peter Berresford. *H. Rider Haggard: A Voice from the Infinite.* London: Routledge & Kegan Paul, 1978.

Etherington, Norman. *Rider Haggard.* Boston: Twayne, 1984.

Haggard, H. Rider. *King Solomon's Mines.* 1885. Reprint, World's Classics Series. Oxford: Oxford University Press, 1989.

Harrison, J. F. C. *Late Victorian Britain 1875-1901.* London: Routledge, 1991.

Higgins, D. F. *Rider Haggard: A Biography.* New York: Stein & Day, 1981.

Hobson, J. A. *Imperialism, A Study.* Ann Arbor: University of Michigan Press, 1965.

Katz, Wendy R. *Rider Haggard and the Fiction of Empire: A Critical Study of British Imperial Fiction.* Cambridge: Cambridge University Press, 1987.

Pocock, Tom. *Rider Haggard and the Lost Empire.* London: Weidenfeld & Nicolson, 1993.

"The Lion and the Unicorn"

by

George Orwell

THE LITERARY WORK

An essay on the necessity of a socialist revolution in wartime Britain, written between August and October 1940; published in February 1941.

SYNOPSIS

Analyzing the situation in Britain in 1940–41, Orwell argues that the war has demonstrated the failure of private capitalism and that if Britain is to win the war, it must embrace socialism.

George Orwell was born Eric Arthur Blair on June 25, 1903, at Motihari in Bengal to a father who served as a middle-ranking official in the Opium Department of the Government of India. In 1904 Blair's mother took him and his older sister Marjorie "home" to England, their father joining them on his retirement in 1911. Blair had a comfortable middle-class upbringing and, upon finishing his schooling at Eton, joined the Imperial Indian Police, which posted him to Burma. After five years' service, however, he resigned, partly, as he later put it, "because the climate had ruined my health"—a reference perhaps to the tuberculosis that was to kill him at the age of 46 in 1950; "partly," he continued, "because I already had vague ideas of writing books, but mainly because I could not go on any longer serving an imperialism which I had come to regard as very largely a racket" (Orwell, *Complete Works* 12, p. 147). On his return to Europe, Blair chose to spend a year and a half living in poverty in London and Paris, trying to share the life of the destitute and oppressed and doggedly teaching himself to write. In 1933, using the name George Orwell, he published his first book, *Down and Out in Paris and London*, and a new book followed every year for the rest of the 1930s. During this decade, his politics developed into a unique variety of revolutionary socialism; his socialism "engaged in a continual dialogue with the anti-Stalinist revolutionary left," or those opposed to mainstream Russian communism, but always tried "to relate [their] ideas to what he understood to be the realities of

British society and culture" (Newsinger, p. 21). This political journey was one that Orwell would chronicle in *The Road to Wigan Pier* (1937) and *Homage to Catalonia* (1938). With the outbreak of war in September 1939, his politics took what seemed to be an even more surprising turn. In the late 1930s Orwell had opposed the coming war in Europe, believing it to be a clash between rival capitalist imperial powers that would lead to Britain's becoming a totalitarian state; now he argued not only that it was necessary for the British to fight Hitler, but that this struggle must be accompanied by a socialist revolution in Britain. By 1940, he believed that German victories in Europe, and the threat that Britain itself would be invaded, had exposed the inadequacies of Britain's economic and political system and brought its people to the brink of revolutionary change. It was this mood of "revolutionary pa-

George Orwell

triotism" that produced "The Lion and the Unicorn" (Crick, *George Orwell*, p. 257).

Events in History at the Time of the Essay

Britain in the 1930s. The 1930s in Britain are often seen as a time of "economic disaster, social deprivation and political discontent" (Stevenson and Cook, p. 4). This image is certainly not without foundation. Throughout the 1920s and 1930s there were never less than one million people out of work—a tenth of the working population that had unemployment insurance. In the depths of the international economic crisis that followed the Wall Street Crash of October 1929, unemployment soared to three million, exacerbating existing social problems of chronic poverty, ill-health, and poor housing. These mounting social problems were brought to the public's attention as never before by pioneering social researchers and by the protests of the unemployed themselves.

As Orwell (in *The Road to Wigan Pier*) and many others observed, however, the effects of the "Great Slump" were not felt evenly across the nation. They were much worse in regions of Wales, Scotland, and the north of England that were economically dependent on the old industries: coal, textiles, iron and steel, and shipbuilding. In some

of these areas, up to three-quarters of the insured population found itself out of work. London, parts of the Midlands, and the southeast of England, on the other hand, were virtually booming. For those who did have jobs, standards of living improved during the 1930s. The cost of living was falling, as was family size, and as a result many people could, for the first time, afford to own their own houses, operate a car, and buy consumer goods such as electrical appliances. Thus, argue Stevenson and Cook, we must add to "the pictures of the dole queues and hunger marches . . . those of another Britain, of new industries, prosperous suburbs and a rising standard of living" (Stevenson and Cook, p. 4).

The left in Britain during the 1930s. Left-wing organizations might have been expected to thrive in Britain's economic crisis of the 1930s. But neither the extreme left nor the extreme right were able to capitalize on the situation and build mass movements for radical change.

The two most important moderate left-wing organizations were the Labour Party and the Trades Union Congress (TUC). Although there were internal divisions within these organizations, they were on the whole committed to working within the existing parliamentary system to bring about the advent of socialism and, in the interim, to improving the pay and conditions of working people under capitalism. More radical were the British Communist Party (CP) and the National Unemployed Workers' Movement (NUWM), which was affiliated to, but somewhat independent of, the CP.

In the late 1920s, under directions from Moscow to foment a revolution through a "class-against-class" policy, the British CP severed all connections with more moderate left-wing organizations and dissolved groups that contained communist and non-communist members. After Hitler came to power in Germany in 1933, Moscow changed its policy, and the CP and the NUWM sought to build a "united front" against fascism by re-establishing links with the Labour Party and the Trades Union Congress. These organizations, however, were not only committed to a moderate line but also deeply suspicious of the CP, and they rejected all such overtures.

Left-wing views became somewhat fashionable in Britain from the mid-1930s on, stimulated in particular by the rise of fascism abroad, by Sir Oswald Mosley's British Union of Fascists at home, and by the Spanish Civil War. It was not, however, the working class that the CP attracted. Many of those who joined the Communist Party or became "fellow travelers" (sympathizers) were from the middle classes and the intelligentsia. It is estimated that of the several million who were unemployed or threatened with unemployment in the 1930s, only 3,140 joined the CP. Those among the working classes who were politically active tended to retain their traditional allegiances to the Labour Party and the TUC; in fact, many of them were suspicious of communism as a "foreign" political creed (Stevenson and Cook, pp. 136-44, 290).

The mood in Britain in 1940–41. The situation in Britain in mid-to-late 1940 was unprecedented. Dunkirk had revealed that "Britain had barely the means to defend itself, let alone to attack" (Addison, p. 111). Critics in Britain laid the blame—somewhat unfairly, in view of the fact that many on the left had advocated pacifism during the 1930s—at the door of the Conservatives. In power since 1931, it was argued, the Conservatives had failed to re-arm, hoping instead to appease Hitler. Amid strong feelings of "patriotism, rage against the Nazis, and the fear of invasion," there arose a widespread feeling that the country had been misgoverned, along with calls for change (Addison, p. 104). As the blitz—the night bombing raids on Britain's cities during 1940—progressed, the popular appetite for change was fueled by resentment of the more well-to-do, cushioned by their wealth from the worst hardships of the war. Ultimately, public discontent was partially addressed by social and economic reforms that began during the war and that developed, after the Labour party's election victory in 1945, into the postwar welfare state. But in the summer and autumn of 1940 many on the left, including Orwell, were anticipating a revolution. On June 20, 1940, Orwell wrote in his diary: "if only we can hold out [against Germany] for a few months, in a year's time we shall see red militia billeted in the Ritz" (Orwell, *Complete Works* 12, p. 188).

The Essay in Focus

Contents summary. The first section of "The Lion and the Unicorn," "England Your England," begins with the assertion that one cannot understand the modern world without acknowledging the power of patriotism and, moreover, that the peoples of different nations are divided by "real differences of outlook" (Orwell, "The Lion and the Unicorn" in *Complete Works* 12, p. 392). Orwell then turns to the task of identifying the distinctive characteristics of English life

and civilization, because, he writes, "it is . . . of the deepest importance to try and determine what England *is*, before guessing what part England *can play* in the huge events that are happening" ("Lion and the Unicorn," p. 393).

The list of English characteristics that Orwell identifies include a lack of artistic ability; "a horror of abstract thought"; a devotion to private life; a "hatred of war and militarism"; a respect for constitutionalism and legality; and a deep xenophobia, particularly among the working class ("Lion and the Unicorn," pp. 393-99). Orwell is not overly idealistic about English civilization. Its antimilitarism, for instance, "ignores

---

HUNGER MARCHES

The National Unemployed Workers Movement (NUWM) was active in organizing "hunger marches," and related demonstrations, throughout the 1920s and 1930s. However, the march that has come to stand for the protests of the unemployed in popular memory was organized not by the NUWM but by Ellen Wilkinson, the local Labour member of the parliament, and by the Mayor and Council of Jarrow, a shipbuilding community in northeast England. The Jarrow march, or "Crusade," of 1936 was atypical in that it was avowedly "nonpolitical," refusing affiliation with the NUWM: its aim was not to change the government's policies as a whole, but simply to get help for Jarrow, which, with the closure of Palmer's Shipyard, had lost almost 8,000 jobs. The dignified and disciplined conduct of the 200 men chosen to represent the community on the march to London gained them much public sympathy, although the march "achieved few tangible results" (Stevenson and Cook, p. 188).

---

the existence of the British Empire," won and maintained by naval force, and it is "the most class-ridden country under the sun"; but, nonetheless, most English people feel themselves to be one nation and tend to "act together in moments of extreme crisis" ("Lion and the Unicorn," pp. 396, 400). England, Orwell famously concludes, is like "a rather stuffy Victorian family . . . with the wrong members in control" ("Lion and the Unicorn," p. 401).

Orwell then turns his attention to what he sees as the failure of leadership on the part of the English ruling class during the last three-quarters of a century, and particularly since 1920.

THE SPANISH CIVIL WAR

For many, the Spanish Civil War of 1936–39 embodied the great ideological conflicts of the age: between democracy and fascism, and between Christianity and communism. In July 1936 the Spanish military, supported by the old ruling class and the Catholic Church, rebelled against the Popular Front Government of the Spanish Republic. The rebellion was prompted by fears that the Popular Front, which had the support of the enlightened middle class and most of the working class, would bring in a revolutionary program aimed at ending economic underdevelopment and exploitation as well as social and religious conservatism. At first, the attempt to overthrow the government seemed likely to fail: it was met by a popular uprising that went on, in many Republican areas, to develop into the beginnings of a socialist revolution. But German and Italian aid, along with internal divisions on the Republican side, enabled Franco's Nationalists—essentially a fascist movement—to ultimately seize control of the country.

The Republicans received assistance from the Soviet Union, but Britain's policy was not to intervene. At odds with this policy, around 2,500 British citizens fought as volunteers in Spain, most of them for the Republicans in the International Brigades, which were organized by national Communist Parties from around the world. Many more became involved in political and humanitarian campaigns in support of the Republic. The idealism of these volunteers, however, often gave way to disillusionment when they realized that the war was much more complex, and less heroic, than they had imagined.

Orwell himself volunteered to fight in the Spanish Civil War, in the *Partido Obrero de Unificación Marxista* (POUM), or United Marxist Workers' Party militia, an independent socialist group, which, along with the anarchists, was dedicated to completing the economic and social revolution that had taken place behind the Republican lines. The Communists, however, were pursuing a different agenda. Under orders from Moscow, which was keen to secure an alliance with Britain and France against Hitler and therefore did not wish to see socialism established in Spain, the Communists were determined to reverse the socialist revolution. To this end, the Communist secret police hunted down and arrested or executed so-called "traitors" and dissidents and misrepresented revolutionary groups such as the POUM as pro-Fascist. Orwell could not forgive the Communists for this betrayal. In fact, it was this experience that led him to see communism as a totalitarian system equivalent to fascism, and totally incompatible with democratic socialism (Crick, *George Orwell*, pp. 207-36; Newsinger, pp. 42-54).

Although England's rulers have been neither treacherous nor corrupt, their inability to "grasp what century they are living in," and their "infallible instinct for doing the wrong thing," prevented them from seeing the danger posed by fascism until it was too late ("Lion and the Unicorn," p. 404). The English left-wing intelligentsia also played a part in allowing the war to happen; their contempt for English institutions and for any form of English patriotism throughout the crucial years of the 1930s damaged English morale and encouraged the fascist nations to believe that England was "decadent" and that she would not fight ("Lion and the Unicorn," p. 406).

In the last section of "England Your England," Orwell notes some of the changes that have taken place in England since the end of the First World War. Technological progress has led to improved living standards for the working and middle classes and to a less differentiated culture, especially in the south of England, "in the light-industry areas and along the arterial roads" ("Lion and the Unicorn," p. 408). The war, he predicts, will complete the process of eliminating class privileges. But "England will still be England, an everlasting animal stretching into the future and the past, and, like all living things, having the power to change out of recognition and yet remain the same" ("Lion and the Unicorn," p. 409).

In Part 2, "Shopkeepers at War," Orwell argues that Hitler's conquest of capitalist Europe has proved that "private capitalism"—that is, an economic system in which land, factories, mines and transport are owned privately and operated solely for profit "*does not work*" ("Lion and the Unicorn," p. 409). Compared to the planned economies of fascist or socialist states, capitalism is hopelessly inefficient at directing resources to achieving the nation's objectives because its main aim is maximizing private profit. But if Dunkirk and the blitz have opened English eyes to the merits of a planned economy, the wrong members of the English family are still in control. As a result the British war effort is halfhearted: the ruling class are at least as afraid of Bolshevism and of losing their economic and social privilege as they are of Hitler. The suffering of wartime, moreover, is far from equally shared, and here Orwell sees danger, for without "equality of sacrifice," ordinary people may sooner or later begin to feel that they would be no worse off under Hitler and lose the will to fight ("Lion and the Unicorn," p. 415).

In Part 3, "The English Revolution," Orwell reiterates his belief that traditional English social structures are beginning to break down and that England is already moving towards socialism. He insists, however, that further progress toward this end must be made if the war is to be won:

> The war and the revolution are inseparable. We cannot establish anything that a Western nation would regard as Socialism without defeating Hitler; on the other hand we cannot defeat Hitler while we remain economically and socially in the nineteenth century.
>
> ("Lion and the Unicorn," p. 418)

Such changes would not be made by Churchill's government, or any similar one: they must come from a genuinely popular socialist movement. Such a thing, Orwell acknowledges, has never existed in England before, a fact he blames on the inadequacies of the socialist organizations: the Labour Party has always been primarily interested in improving wages and working conditions for British workers, not in overthrowing capitalism; and the more extreme left-wing parties, including the Communist Party, merely

alienated the middle classes—whom Orwell sees as vital to the success of a socialist revolution. By threatening the very survival of England, however, the war has made socialism a "realizable policy"; if the alternative is being conquered by Hitler, not only the working classes but "the great mass of middling people" on incomes between £6 a week and £2000 a year will choose socialism ("Lion and the Unicorn," pp. 421-22). And even though there will be resistance from the upper and upper-middle classes, it is likely that—patriotism and a sense of national unity being stronger in England than class hatred,

ORWELL'S ATTITUDE TO WORLD WAR II

Orwell's view of events in Spain profoundly shaped his attitude to the coming war with Germany in the late 1930s. The Communists' advocacy of a "popular" or "united front" against fascism, he argued, was a way of getting the working class to unite with the bourgeoisie in a war that would actually protect the interests of British imperialism. "Communism," he wrote in "Spilling the Spanish Beans," "is now a counter-revolutionary force; . . . Communists everywhere are in alliance with bourgeois reformism and using the whole of their powerful machinery to crush or discredit any party that shows signs of revolutionary tendencies" (*Collected Works 11*, p. 42). When war broke out in September 1939, however, Orwell was in the process of changing his mind and coming out in favor of the war effort. Britain was now facing both the major totalitarian powers, because on August 23, 1939, Germany and Russia had signed a Non-Aggression Pact—confirming Orwell's view that there was little difference between the two. Moreover, as he described in "My Country Right or Left" in the autumn of 1940, Orwell had discovered "that I was patriotic at heart" and that he could not do other than support the war effort. But this patriotism, he insisted, did not compromise his revolutionary politics. One could be "loyal both to [then Prime Minister] Chamberlain's England and to the England of tomorrow" (Orwell, *Complete Works* 12, p. 271). Indeed, the one required the other, for only if Hitler were resisted could a socialist revolution take place in Britain, and only if such a revolution occurred could Britain be saved. He went on to develop this argument at much greater length in "The Lion and the Unicorn." But it also underlay his involvement in the Local Defense Volunteers or Home Guard, which he saw as a revolutionary militia in waiting.

England's Home Guard performing a bayonet drill in London in 1941. Orwell, who joined the Home Guard in 1940, regarded it as a revolutionary militia in waiting.

especially in a time of war—the will of the majority will prevail.

Orwell then goes on to outline a six-point program that "aims quite frankly at turning this war into a revolutionary war and England into a Socialist democracy" ("Lion and the Unicorn," p. 422). The first three points are intended to eliminate gross structural inequalities within English society: they are the transfer of ownership of all major industry, land, and infrastructure to the State, as representative of the people; the limitation of incomes, so that the highest "tax-free" (Orwell presumably means "after-tax") income would be ten times the lowest at most; and reforming the education system to ensure that all children receive an education appropriate to their ability, regardless of their parents' wealth. Points four and five concern England's relationship with the Empire. Orwell insists that England cannot truly call itself a socialist democracy unless it ceases to exploit the peoples of its Empire. He therefore argues that Britain must offer India, and many other of her "possessions," partnership on equal terms, meaning that Dominion status must be granted immediately, along with the right to secede completely once the war is over; and that an Imperial General Council representing all the peoples of the Empire must be formed. The sixth point

extends this responsibility to oppressed peoples still further, calling for England to declare a formal alliance with other nations, such as China and Abyssinia, that have been overrun by Fascist powers (i.e. Japan and Italy respectively).

Orwell declares himself to be extremely optimistic that within a year, if England is not conquered, a specifically *English* Socialist movement will have developed and, by sheer strength of numbers, will have become the government. Its policies, he argues, will be distinctly English, retaining many of the essential aspects of England that he has already outlined. It will be neither "doctrinaire" nor "logical," "[leaving] anachronisms and loose ends everywhere," including, perhaps, the monarchy and the lion and the unicorn, the emblem of the old state, on soldiers' cap-buttons ("Lion and the Unicorn," p. 427). It will keep its tradition of compromise and of respect for a law that is above the State, and it will be tolerant of dissent, as well as of religion—although it will nonetheless shoot traitors (after a "solemn" trial) and "crush any open revolt promptly and cruelly" ("Lion and the Unicorn," p. 427). It will furthermore fight the war wholeheartedly, and with all its forces mobilized, not being afraid of stirring up revolution in other states.

"The Lion and the Unicorn" concludes by reiterating the necessity of England's fighting, and winning, the war. Although the left-wing intelligentsia is in the habit of arguing that democracy is just as bad as totalitarianism, the two are as different as the rent-collector and the Nazi S.S. man, and it is frivolous to suggest otherwise. Hitler's totalitarianism has as its aim the establishment, over Europe, Africa, the Middle East, and parts of Russia, of a racially stratified empire, whereas British, or English, democracy, although far from perfect, contains within itself the seeds of socialism.

English democracy cannot simply be preserved in this war, Orwell concludes: it must be extended to become *socialist* democracy. He concedes that it is possible that England might follow this advice and still lose the war. But even such a defeat would be better than compromising with Hitler, for, if the English revolution had already taken place, "bringing the real England to the surface," she could never be *utterly* defeated ("Lion and the Unicorn," p. 432).

The idea of "England" in "The Lion and the Unicorn." It is noticeable that, in "The Lion and the Unicorn," Orwell refers almost exclusively to "England" rather than to "Britain," which would include Scotland and Wales, let alone "the United Kingdom," which would include Northern Ireland as well. Yet it seems that he intends his call to revolution to apply to the whole of Britain. He himself notes that "Welsh and Scottish readers are likely to have been offended because I have used the word 'England' oftener than 'Britain,' as though the whole population dwelt in London and the Home Counties and neither north nor west possessed a culture of its own" ("Lion and the Unicorn," p. 398). But for Orwell the question of national differences within Britain—which he here conflates with regional differences within *England*—are almost nonexistent compared to the difference between a Briton and anyone else, and are, in any case, less important than the difference between rich and poor.

Orwell is far from unique in conflating "England" and "Britain" in this way. Because England has always been the dominant nation within Britain, England has been taken—especially by the English—to stand for the whole in a way that Scotland and Wales have not. Only in the last two decades or so have politicians and the public become more conscious of the need to distinguish between "Britain" and "England," in large part because of the growing debate over the devolution of powers to the constituent nations of the Union. In Orwell's time, it was easy to write as though England *was* Britain, without thinking too hard about whether one's comments about the national character really applied to Scotland and Wales as well. When we examine how Orwell characterizes his England, we find that his specific references do tend to be English.

IMPERIALISM AND ANTI-IMPERIALISM

By 1910 there were two distinct sides to the British Empire: the white settler colonies of Australia, New Zealand, Canada, and South Africa had all become self-governing Dominions, but the remaining, nonwhite, parts of the Empire were still ruled by Britain in an authoritarian fashion. Nationalist feelings in these countries were steadily growing, and the British government was coming under increasing pressure to grant them a greater degree of self-government. Pressure was also being applied from within Britain itself, where anti-imperialists were questioning both the motives for European expansion and the way the Empire was administered.

In India, which was by far Britain's most important single colony, Britain made a series of reforms between 1909 and 1935 that gave Indians a greater role in the governance of their nation. Britain even announced that its intention was that India should eventually be granted Dominion status—on Britain's timetable. But Indian nationalist organizations continued to press for independence; the most significant of these was the Indian National Congress, which combined constitutional politics with M. K. Gandhi's strategy of *satyagraha*, or peaceful resistance.

When Britain declared war on Germany in September 1939, the Empire, with the exception of Ireland, declared war too. By and large, there was considerable enthusiasm for the war effort throughout the Empire, and its nations made significant contributions of both manpower and supplies: around 5,580,000 citizens of the Empire and Commonwealth served in the war, compared with 6,500,000 Britons (Jeffery in Brown and Louis, pp. 307-8). But anti-imperial sentiment did not disappear; indeed, in India, it hardened. Britain's failure to commit itself to Indian independence led to the campaign of 1942 to drive the British out of India. The campaign was swiftly suppressed by the British, and the Congress itself was banned for the duration of the war. In August 1947, however, India and Pakistan became independent from Britain, although both remained within the Commonwealth.

Here, for example, he summons up the following typical "fragments . . . of the English scene":

the clatter of clogs in the Lancashire mill towns, the to-and-fro of the lorries on the Great North Road, the queues outside the Labour Exchanges, the rattle of pin-tables in the Soho pubs, the old maids biking to Holy Communion through the mists of the autumn mornings.

("Lion and the Unicorn," p. 392)

The essay, then, can best be understood as referring not to Britain, but specifically to England—or, perhaps, to an *idea* of England. In fact, "The Lion and the Unicorn" is part of a long tradition of writing about England and Englishness. Debates about the nature of Englishness have gone on for centuries, but they were particularly intense in the years from 1900 to 1950. During this period, concepts of national identity were important in articulating war aims and in attempts to sustain the public's morale during both world wars. Between the two world wars, during the 1920s and 1930s, there were economic crises and social changes that called into question the inclusiveness of older images of England.

To judge both what "The Lion and the Unicorn" shares with much other writing of the period about England and how it differs from it, one might compare it with a famous speech by the Conservative politician Stanley Baldwin, three times the Prime Minister of Britain during the 1920s and 1930s. Baldwin's speech, which was delivered to the Royal Society of St. George on May 6, 1924, begins by outlining the essential elements of the English character, elements that overlap with those highlighted by Orwell. Both men emphasize the anti-intellectualism of the English, their predilection for action without forethought, their distrust of foreigners, their sense of national unity, and their determined individuality. But Baldwin laments social and economic change and warns that the real England, which for him is the countryside, is in danger of being lost as its fields are converted into towns. Orwell's imagined England, on the other hand, while certainly not excluding the country, consistently includes the England of "the factories and the newspaper offices, . . . the aeroplanes and the submarines" ("Lion and the Unicorn," p. 415). And, at least as important, Orwell looks not back into the past, but into the future, for the real England.

Baldwin's primary concern as a politician, argues one historian, was "the preservation of parliament and the British character from extremism" of the left or of the right (Addison, p. 27).

Orwell's was to reconcile English patriotism and socialist revolution. In his 1980 biography of Orwell, Bernard Crick avowed that "The Lion and the Unicorn" was "the only book that has ever been written about the possibility of revolution in terms of English national character" (Crick, *George Orwell*, p. 257); it is probably still the only one. Given this aim, Orwell was understandably concerned to argue that England after a revolution would still be England—that, indeed, revolution would make England more fully itself, setting free the "native genius of the English people" ("Lion and the Unicorn," p. 415). The continuity that Orwell envisages between the old England and the new is embodied in the essay's title. The lion and the unicorn, the emblem of the old state, would not be replaced the way national symbols had been in Russia or Germany, but would remain on soldiers' cap-buttons. England's revolution would be as "peculiar" as England itself. But it would be a revolution nonetheless ("Lion and the Unicorn," p. 427).

Sources and literary context. "The Lion and the Unicorn" was the first of "a series of short books on war aims for a better future" planned during the summer of 1940 by Orwell, Fredric Warburg, and Tosco Fyvel (Newsinger, p. 71). The Searchlight series was a reflection of the revolutionary hopes of 1940–41, and "The Lion and the Unicorn" needs to be understood, writes Newsinger, as "a work of propaganda, not of analysis," intended to "help inspire, mobilise and direct" the masses of people who, Orwell believed, were ready to support a socialist transformation of British society (Newsinger, pp. 75-76).

As well as recognizing the relation of "The Lion and the Unicorn" to traditions of writing about Englishness, we need to understand Orwell in the context of socialist writing and thought. For, despite his idiosyncrasies, Orwell was "a pretty typical English left-wing socialist in the tradition of Morris, Blatchford, Carpenter, Cole, Tawney, Laski, Bevan and Foot"; this socialism is "egalitarian, libertarian, environmental, individualist in practice if not in theory, highly principled but somehow untheoretical, or if tinged with Marxism, then only in its broadest and most libertarian forms" (Crick, "Orwell and English Socialism", p. 4).

Furthermore, as noted, in the early part of the war, other left-wing thinkers shared Orwell's belief that a revolution was imminent, which gave rise to a tide of books, pamphlets, and essays calling for—or prophesying—change. It has been suggested that one such work in particular may have influenced Orwell: *The Malady and the Vision* (1940) by Tosco Fyvel, co-editor of the Searchlight series. In this book, Fyvel argues that the real England has been kept down by a class of the "idle rich" fostered by the Empire, but that "with the first crash of bombs over British troops in Norway, the whole cracked edifice of Chamberlainism and outdated British Imperialism was blown up," and "the real England," whose "enduring spirit" is the spirit of freedom, could once again show itself (Fyvel in Newsinger, p. 71).

Orwell's style in "The Lion and the Unicorn" is intimately connected to his political purpose. Orwell wanted, as he said in "Why I Write" (1946), "to make political writing into an art" (Orwell, *Complete Works* 18, p. 319). His "famous clear, plain, simple, colloquial and forceful style" was modeled on those of political writers such as Jonathan Swift and Daniel Defoe (see **Gulliver's Travels** and **Moll Flanders,** in *WLAIT 3: British and Irish Literature and Its Times*). Like them, he wanted to reach a popular audience—specifically, the self-educated working and lower-middle classes for whom Dickens and H. G. Wells had written (Crick, "Orwell and English Socialism," p. 3). But his style was also an expression of his belief that "plain language speaks the truth whereas polysyllabic neologisms are either obfuscations or lies" (Crick, "Orwell and English Socialism", p. 16).

Reception. "The Lion and the Unicorn" sold well when it appeared in February 1941. Five thousand copies were initially printed, and good sales meant that this run was soon increased to 7,500. In March, a further 5,000 were ordered, but only 1,000 had been delivered when the Mayflower Press was hit in a German bombing raid on Plymouth (Orwell, *Complete Works 12*, p. 391). Reviewers praised Orwell's polemical skill, even if they did not agree with his politics. V. S. Pritchett, for example, writing in *The New Statesman and Nation*, placed Orwell with Cobbett, Defoe, and G. B. Shaw among the finest English pamphleteers:

> His virtue is that he says things which need to be said; his vice that some of those things needed saying with a great deal more consideration. But, damn thoughtfulness! Pamphleteers have to hit the bull's eye every time, or, failing that, somebody else's eye.
>
> (Pritchett in Crick, *George Orwell*, p. 280)

As time went on, and hopes of an English revolution faded, Orwell's predictions came to seem mistaken. In March 1942, reviewing "The Lion and the Unicorn" for the American journal *Partisan Review*, Dwight Macdonald pointed out that there were still "no signs of the English socialist movement Orwell so confidently predicted. Despite an almost unbroken string of humiliating defeats, . . . the reins of power are still firmly in the hands of Churchill," the anti-revolutionary (Macdonald, p. 193). Toward the end of 1942, Orwell himself concluded that revolutionary change was unlikely in Britain, and in 1949, preparing for his own death, he drew up instructions stipulating that "The Lion and the Unicorn," along with the related essay "The English People," and two of his novels, *A Clergyman's Daughter* and *Keep the Aspidistra Flying*, should not be reprinted. Nonetheless, in an obituary for Orwell after his death on January 21, 1950, Arthur Koestler insisted on the essay's importance in the literature of the war: "Among all the pamphlets, tracts and exhortations that the war produced, hardly anything bears re-reading today, except, perhaps, E. M. Forster's *What I Believe*, a few passages from Churchill's speeches, and, above all, Orwell's 'The Lion and the Unicorn'" (Koestler in Crick, *George Orwell*, p. 273).

Since Orwell's death, his legacy has been strongly contested. In the 1950s and early 1960s, his criticism of communism caused many on the left to repudiate him, although this began to change in the late 1960s with the rise of the new left outside of traditional affiliations to either the Labour Party or the Communists. Meanwhile, his critique of totalitarianism, most famously in *Animal Farm* (1945) and *Nineteen Eighty-Four* (1949), led some on the political right to ignore his lifelong commitment to socialism and to claim him as, in Newsinger's words, "an emotional conservative who had given terrible warning of the totalitarian logic inherent in the socialist cause" (Newsinger, p. 155).

Like Orwell's more famous works, "The Lion and the Unicorn" has been caught up in this struggle over his memory. In April 1993, in a clear allusion to "England Your England," British Prime Minister John Major evoked a vision of an unchanging nation of "long shadows falling across the country [cricket] ground, . . . warm beer, . . . invincible green suburbs, dog lovers and pools fillers . . . and old maids bicycling to Holy Communion through the morning mist" (in Porter, p. 2). This echo of "The Lion and the Unicorn" in a speech by a Conservative Prime Minister might well have surprised Orwell himself. But it indicates his essay's complex relationship to traditions of thinking about England and his singular achievement in turning such traditions to revolutionary ends.

—Ingrid Gunby

For More Information

Addison, Paul. *The Road to 1945: British Politics and the Second World War*. Rev. ed. London: Pimlico, 1994.

Brown, Judith M., and Wm. Roger Louis, eds. *The Oxford History of the British Empire, Vol. 4, The Twentieth Century*. Oxford: Oxford University Press, 1999.

Crick, Bernard. *George Orwell: A Life*. London: Secker & Warburg, 1980.

———. "Orwell and English Socialism." In *George Orwell: A Reassessment*. Ed. Peter Buitenhuis and Ira B. Nadel. Basingstoke: Macmillan, 1988.

Giles, Judy, and Tim Middleton, Eds. *Writing Englishness 1900-1950: An Introductory Sourcebook on National Identity*. London: Routledge, 1995.

Macdonald, Dwight. "The Lion and the Unicorn." In *George Orwell: The Critical Heritage*. Ed. Jeffrey Meyers. London: Routledge, and Boston: Kegan Paul, 1975.

Newsinger, John. *Orwell's Politics*. Basingstoke: Macmillan, and New York: St. Martin's Press, 1999.

Orwell, George. *The Complete Works of George Orwell, Vol. 9: Facing Unpleasant Facts, Volume 12: A Patriot after All*, and *Vol. 18: Smothered under Journalism*. Ed. Peter Davison. London: Secker & Warburg, 1998.

Porter, Henry. "England, Our England." *Guardian*, 28 July 1993, sec. 2, pp. 2-3.

Stevenson, John, and Chris Cook. *The Slump: Society and Politics during the Depression*. London: Jonathan Cape, 1977.

Thomas, Hugh. *The Spanish Civil War*. 3rd ed. Harmondsworth: Hamish Hamilton, 1977.

Lord Jim:
A Tale

by
Joseph Conrad

〜

Joseph Conrad was born in Russian-occupied Poland in 1857 to an aristocratic family involved in anti-Russian activities. For two decades (c. 1878 to 1895), he traveled to many parts of the world while working on various merchant vessels that plied trade routes between Europe, Africa and Asia. Conrad spoke and wrote three languages fluently—Polish, French, and English—but he published mainly in English and became a British citizen. His illustrious writing career began in 1895 with the publication of *Almayer's Folly*, a novel that takes place in what is now the Indonesian archipelago and set the tone for much of his later work about the colonial world. First published in book form in 1900, *Lord Jim*, his fourth major work, established him as one of the foremost English-language writers of the time. The novel shares its setting with *Almayer's Folly*, but goes far beyond that work in respect to experimental style and psychological depth. Although Conrad would go on to write several novels that take place in Europe, he remains best known for his colonial fiction, especially *Heart of Darkness* (1899), *Lord Jim* (1899–1900) and *Nostromo* (1904).

Events in History at the Time of the Novel

European imperialism and trade in south and southeast Asia. *Lord Jim* begins with an evocation of various port cities in the "east." The first narrator directly cites Bombay, Calcutta, Rangoon, Penang, and Batavia as just a few of the

> ### THE LITERARY WORK
>
> A novel set in southeast Asia, including the archipelagos of the south Asian seas, in the late nineteenth century; serialized 1899–1900 and published in book form in 1900.
>
> ### SYNOPSIS
>
> A young English sailor named Jim becomes the unofficial leader of a rural community of Malays. His leadership is an attempt to atone for an earlier act of cowardice he had performed while employed on a steamship carrying Muslim pilgrims to Mecca from south Asia.

places where the title character worked for short periods of time as a clerk. The reader is thus whisked immediately into a world of colonial relationships, for Britain, the Netherlands, and France all had come to possess both formal and informal control over most of south Asia and southeast Asia by the late nineteenth century. The coastal cities of Bombay and Calcutta in India proper, Rangoon in Lower Burma, and Penang, an island off peninsular Malaysia, all served—along with Singapore—as key nodes in a trading network that enabled the far-flung British empire in the eastern world to move goods and people in an attempt to solidify Britain's economic and political predominance in the region. These cities, which also functioned

Joseph Conrad

symbolically as the dividing line between the greater world outside and the interior regions of ruled territories, became cosmopolitan centers, attracting members of various indigenous groups from inland areas as well as different types and classes of Europeans. The ships themselves reflected that cosmopolitan nature, as is evident in the composition of the crew and passengers on board the *Patna* (the steamship that is the main setting of much of the first half of Conrad's novel). The *Patna* is "owned by a Chinaman, chartered by an Arab, and commanded by a . . . New South Wales German," besides boasting English crewmen and two Malay steersmen (Conrad, *Lord Jim*, p. 13).

The British Empire had a formidable rival in the form of a Dutch colonial system that had grown steadily in the archipelagos of southeast Asia from the first appearance of Dutch ships in the Java Sea in 1596. The city of Batavia (now called Jakarta), on the island of Java, became the center of Dutch colonial power, and Dutch rule—both direct and indirect—came by the end of the nineteenth century to involve a region stretching from Sumatra in the west to Irian Jaya in the east. Though only a "minor state" in Europe at that time, the Netherlands nonetheless possessed stakes in the region that the British were not likely to contest, unless those claims interfered too greatly with Britain's commercial

preeminence in the area. In contrast to Britain's governance in the Indian subcontinent, which became more formalized after the great Mutiny or Rebellion of 1857, the Dutch relied mostly "on contracts and treaties with indigenous states and were more concerned with questions of commerce than questions of government" (Tarling, p. 13). In this way, the Dutch exercised a measure of control over various aspects of life in the colonies.

Besides frequently enjoying a level of formal control over law, education, and religion, both the Dutch and British oversaw trade networks. Sometimes they effectively squashed local commerce through the introduction of large-scale organizations and monopolies. This was the case, for instance, with the British North Borneo Company, which administered a region on the island of Borneo. But oftentimes the colonial powers also allowed private companies to participate in trade, a fact reflected in the presence of "Stein's Trading Company" in *Lord Jim*. This trading company is owned, as its title indicates, by Stein, a "wealthy and respected [German-born] merchant" (*Lord Jim*, p. 122).

Europeans in south and southeast Asia. Somewhat surprisingly, given the fact that Europe enjoyed such hegemony in south and southeast Asia, the number of Europeans who lived there in actuality was never very large, even in India. Since the time of Magellan's round-the-world voyage in the sixteenth century, small numbers of Europeans had been coming to the East—both voluntarily and involuntarily. A few had missionary intentions; both Catholic and Protestant groups sent out missionaries with the aims of gaining converts, educating people in Western modes of thought, and spreading the Gospel. Others had governing intentions: various officials were needed to administer the colonies and oversee the other Europeans who had made the East home. New civil servants were often brought from Europe, especially in the early years of colonialism, because few indigenous people were given the opportunity and training necessary for government service.

Some Europeans came in small groups in order to found communities centered around a particular crop that Europeans thought might prove profitable in the region. A good example of this sort of entrepreneurial activity was the formation of a colony of British people in Ceylon (now Sri Lanka) in the 1840s. The government thought that coffee could become a profitable item of trade, and several families with mercantile ties decided to try their luck with the crop. The experiment ultimately failed, as did many such schemes. In fact, the majority of the families went back to England, which points to another important characteristic of European populations in south and southeast Asia: they were highly transitory. People came and went, often very rapidly. These unsettled conditions proved to be a perfect breeding ground for the kind of European adventurer whose shadow hangs over the last few chapters of *Lord Jim*.

Far from the social and class regulations of Europe, people had a certain amount of freedom to reinvent themselves. This reinvention could take a positive direction—as in the case of Jim—or a negative direction as in the case of Gentleman Brown. Brown, whose presence in Patusan ultimately leads to Jim's final dishonor, is described by one of the narrators as a "ruffian" whose "lawless life" and terrorizing tendencies became the stuff of stories both in the colonies and back home (*Lord Jim*, p. 209). Implicit in this description is a leniency against crime in many areas of southeast Asia, which meant that criminal acts by Europeans often went unpunished. This state of affairs attracted to the region shady Europeans, more interested in preying on people and making a quick—and often illegal—fortune than engaging in what was considered legitimate commerce.

Also involved in at least temporary migrations from Europe to both colonized and independent areas of south and southeast Asia were scientists of various stripes. People who today would be identified as cultural or social anthropologists traveled there to find out about "primitive" religion, society, and politics. After about 1875, those who would come to be known as physical anthropologists went there in search of people to measure in order to determine the physiological differences between "races." But the most common type of European scientist to visit the region was the naturalist. Interested in both flora and fauna, naturalists usually collected specimens of animals and plants and studied the characteristics of the life they found around them. Naturalists intended ostensibly to increase human knowledge about the natural world, but sometimes the information could also be used to aid in imperial rule. Stein, the aforementioned merchant in *Lord Jim*, who ultimately launches Jim on his final career as a virtual ruler, combines an interest in natural history with his commercial activities. Marlow, the narrator of the second half of the novel, hints that Stein's hunting of animal specimens to send back to Europe is part of a general attempt to control and dominate the area in which he lives: "Stein never failed to *annex* on his own account every butterfly or beetle he could lay his hands on" (Conrad, *Lord Jim*, p. 124, emphasis added). Stein's life essentially combines many elements that figured prominently in the lives of various Europeans who immigrated. Born in Bavaria, he was forced to flee Europe after participating in the political upheavals of 1848, and he decided to travel in the Dutch possessions in the South China Sea upon the invitation of a famous Dutch naturalist. After the naturalist's return to Europe, Stein stayed on with a Scotch trader in the Celebes and after inheriting that trader's wealth upon his death, developed his own company.

Village life and ethnic groups in the Malay Archipelago. Most of mainland southeast Asia as well as the Malay peninsula and the islands that now form the nation-state of Indonesia were characterized by a complex mix of peoples in the late nineteenth century. These areas grew increasingly diverse as the British and Dutch colonial regimes developed trade and encouraged—or forced—migrations between the constituent parts of their respective empires. Added to the various indigenous Malay peoples of the area were groups of Chinese and Indian immigrants, many of whom took advantage of British protection to become successful merchants, traders, and occasionally farmers. These Chinese and Indian groups frequently experienced cool treatment by European officials because of racism as well as outright resentment from indigenous Malays because of the relative economic prosperity they enjoyed.

Despite being united through language and some cultural and social practices, the Malay peoples were nevertheless divided into various ethnic or tribal groupings. Most commentators in the Victorian period split the Malays into Forest Dyaks and Sea Dyaks because cultural practices depended on whether a group lived in the interior of an island or near the coast. Within each of those large groupings, however, were many different subgroupings, such as the Kayan, Iban, Buginese (or Bugis, as Conrad refers to them), and Makasarese. Malay was the lingua franca of the archipelago that later became the nation-states of Indonesia and Malaysia; it was used for trade and communication between various peoples. Malay life often was centered around water; small communities of people lived either in coastal regions or along rivers leading into the interior. The people subsisted mainly on fish and rice. Small villages under the leadership of one (often charismatic) man functioned as the main unit of social and political organization.

As an anthropologist observed of the Malay during a trip made less than a decade after Conrad published *Lord Jim*: "Even though single-family houses may be placed in scattered hillside clearings, the occupants consider themselves members of some community and subject to its chief or headman. This leader has considerable power and prestige, for he is judge, he officiates at weddings, and he conducts most of the dealings with outsiders" (Cole, p. 115). These are precisely the types of powers which Jim comes to enjoy after he has become a respected part of Malay society in the second half of the novel.

In terms of religion, the original beliefs of most Malay peoples—as with most Indonesians generally before the introduction of Hinduism, Buddhism, Islam, and Christianity—included a notion of a plurality of different types of beings, including human beings, animals, and numerous spirits or deities. Malays saw the world as a mix of positive and negative forces and practiced rituals organized around the human life-cycle and the worship of personalized natural objects such as mountain peaks or celestial bodies. Many groups, however, including the Bugis, had converted to Islam prior to the coming of the Europeans. *Lord Jim* features Muslim Malays led by a rajah; Malays practicing traditional, pre-Muslim religion in a simple fishing village; and a community of Muslim Bugis from the Celebes.

Eurasians, products of relationships between Europeans and Malays or other Asians, made up a small but culturally and politically significant proportion of the population in most large ports and sometimes in rural regions as well. Though they enjoyed certain advantages because of their European inheritance, Eurasians, or "half-castes" as they were often called during the Victorian era and earlier, often suffered by being caught in a sort of no-man's land between the privileged Europeans, colonized peoples like the Malays, and more well-to-do migrants like the Chinese and Indians. In Conrad's novel, the woman whom Jim calls "Jewel" and who becomes his companion (if not wife—Conrad does not clarify their relationship) has a Malay mother and a European father (*Lord Jim*, p. 155). Mistreated by her stepfather, another European (Portuguese), and unable to fit into the indigenous society that her mother had effectively rejected by living with two different European men consecutively, Jewel has no comfortable niche in Patusan and finds happiness only with another European interloper—Jim.

Victorian racial thought and faith in progress. The second half of the nineteenth century was a time of hardening racial distinctions in Europe, attributable in large part to increased contact between Europeans and so-called "primitive" peoples, to scientific investigation of human bodies, and to the new theories of human evolution such as Charles Darwin's **On the Origin of Species** (also in *WLAIT 4: British and Irish Literature and Its Times*). An earlier humanitarian position that considered individuals of any race capable of advancement gave way to more rigid hierarchies that declared it impossible for particular "races" to attain the intellectual and technological level of Europe. This is not to say that racism did not exist prior to the Victorian period; it only means that racial categories became solidified as supposedly scientific realities at that time.

As anthropology developed as an academic discipline out of the earlier study of ethnology, and as Darwin's ideas about evolution became popularized, human beings came to be seen as objects to be studied. Victorian investigators reached the conclusion that "laws of nature" determined which race would survive and which would fall by the wayside. They came to see "primitive peoples," including those who lived in the southeast Asian archipelagoes, as lacking the right tools not only to move up the ladder of racial hierarchy but even to perpetuate themselves. The so-called primitive peoples, thought the Victorians, were a vestige of some earlier stage of mankind.

The Novel in Focus

Plot summary. The plot of *Lord Jim* is relatively simple, but it might appear complex to many readers because the narrative does not unfold in a straightforward manner. The novel opens with a third-person narrator describing an Englishman named Jim who works as a water-clerk in various ports in the south Asian seas. Jim is said to be "an inch, perhaps two, under six feet, powerfully built" and "spotlessly neat, appareled in immaculate white from shoes to hat" (*Lord Jim*, p. 7). His work is defined as "racing under sail, steam, or oars against other water-clerks for any ship about to anchor, greeting her captain cheerily, forcing upon him a card . . . and on his first visit on shore piloting him firmly but without ostentation to a vast, cavern-like shop" where the visitor can buy things necessary for the next voyage (*Lord Jim*, p. 7). Though an excellent clerk, Jim is said to have the mysterious habit of quitting a job abruptly and moving to another port, usually farther east, where he gets another clerking position.

After this introduction to Jim's character, the novel takes the reader back to the years of Jim's upbringing and the reasons for his current rootlessness. We learn that Jim is one of five sons of an English clergyman and that he entered the merchant marine with dreams of grand adventure and courageous action: in his imagination "he confronted savages on tropical shores, quelled mutinies on the high seas, and in a small boat upon the ocean kept up the hearts of despairing men—always an example of devotion to duty, and as unflinching as a hero in a book" (*Lord Jim*, p. 9). Eventually he became a chief mate and found his life mostly satisfactory but felt disappointed at the lack of adventure. He finally did find excitement—albeit excitement of the wrong kind—when he was involved in a scandal over a pilgrim ship, a steamer called the *Patna*. The steamer, which was carrying over eight hundred Muslim pilgrims to Mecca, struck a hidden obstacle, whereupon the captain arranged to have the white crew abandon the ship before it sank. Jim debated internally about whether or not to join the crew in this cowardly act that ran counter to honorable behavior on the high seas. Ultimately he chose to leave the ship, but this choice came to have serious ramifications because the ship did not sink after all. The pilgrims were rescued by a French ship, and the crew of the *Patna* was brought before a court of inquiry in an "Eastern port" to answer for its dishonorable behavior. During the time of the inquiry, Jim met an old sailor named Marlow, a fact that we learn after the narrative point of view shifts to a first-person story by Marlow upon the conclusion of the inquiry.

Marlow first chronicles what he knows about the fates of the other crew members of the *Patna*, what he has heard of the suicide of one of the judges at the inquiry, and what he heard about the *Patna* from an officer of the French ship that rescued the pilgrims. After recounting these events, he narrates the steps he took to get Jim settled in good employment once Jim decided not to return to England (because he was embarrassed by the incident and anxious not to bring shame on his family).

After watching Jim leave one good job after another whenever he hears the *Patna* incident discussed, Marlow sends him to see a friend of his named Stein. A trader, collector, and entomologist, Stein offers Jim a chance to go to Patusan, "a remote district of a native-ruled state" within the Indonesian archipelago (*Lord Jim*, p. 133). Despite the possibility of danger in this place where few white European men even visited, Jim accepts this challenge because he desires to prove himself trustworthy. He wants to make reparations, somehow or other, for his failure to do the right thing on board the ship so many years before. The rest of the novel describes his experiences in Patusan, resulting in a decided shift of tone from the mysteriousness of the first half of the novel to a more straightforward detailing of events.

VICTORIAN ORIENTALISM

The phrase "the East" appears over and over again in the pages of Conrad's novel, and in the first few pages as Jim tries to bury more deeply his memory of a shameful act he moves to ports "generally farther East" (*Lord Jim*, p. 8). Rather than having a simple geographical meaning—"an area in particular geographical relation to Europe"—the phrase had a wide range of connotations for Victorian Britons that indicated some sense of the West as politically, spiritually, and economically superior over the East. "The East," a term that in the Victorian era referred to an expansive area from Egypt and Palestine through India and southeast Asia to Japan, was associated with irrationality, mysteriousness, secrecy, and sensuality. Europeans perceived the East as directly opposed to Western rationality, clarity, honesty, and intellectualism and therefore in need of European rule or at least close supervision, as propounded in Edward Said's now-classic study *Orientalism*: "There are Westerners, and there are Orientals. The former dominate; the latter must be dominated, which usually means having their land occupied, their internal affairs rigidly controlled, their blood and treasure put at the disposal of one and another Western power" (Said, p. 36). Significantly, too, Westerners frequently imagined the Orient and the Occident in sexualized terms: the East, feminine and the West, masculine. Conrad employs this distinction in subtle ways in *Lord Jim*. As Jim approaches a village where he will eventually become the *de facto* ruler, the narrator says that Jim's "opportunity [sits] veiled by his side like an Eastern bride waiting to be uncovered by the hand of the master" (*Lord Jim*, p. 147). In accord with Victorian conceptions, then, Jim's virility as a Westerner is contrasted to the supposed passivity of the land and people of Patusan.

There are three men in Patusan who have power: the Rajah Tunku Allang; Doramin, who has immigrated there with a group of people from another island; and Sherif Ali, who leads another group of Muslims trying to take control of the area. Ultimately Jim sides with Doramin and helps him defeat Sherif Ali and cow the Rajah Allang into virtual submission to Jim's will. Jim's sojourn in Patusan does not, however, start off promisingly. Upon his arrival in a canoe that has brought him up a river from the sea, he is made a sort of hostage in the home of the local rajah, Tunku Allang. After three days, he escapes and goes to see Doramin, the leader of 60 Bugis families who immigrated to Patusan from the island Celebes. Jim moves into the household of the only other European in the region—Cornelius, a Malacca man of Portuguese descent. Living in that household also is Cornelius's stepdaughter, whom Jim calls "Jewel." Jewel's mother was a Dutch-Malay woman and her father a white man, a "high official" whose career ended under a cloud (*Lord Jim*, p. 165). Cornelius lords over his stepdaughter and treats Jim badly because he is suspicious about Jim's intentions and wary about his increasing influence in the region. Jim hates him for this ill-treatment and eventually manages to escape from the household after discovering a plot to kill him. He escapes with Jewel's help and then settles in a house with Jewel as his companion and with a devoted Malay servant named Tamb' Itam. According to Marlow, Jim and Jewel have an ideal relationship: Jewel dotes on Jim while maintaining her own sense of self-worth, and Jim treats her very kindly.

Jim helps the Bugis defeat the warriors of Sherif Ali, a half-Arab, half-Malay who attempted to gain control over trade in the region. By virtue of his leadership abilities and his courageous fighting, Jim becomes the virtual ruler of Patusan society—in fact local "legend . . . gift[s] him with supernatural powers" (*Lord Jim*, p. 159). The rajah acquiesces in Jim's newfound role as preeminent figure and does not challenge his authority.

Despite the fact that Jim has now become the trusted leader of the people, he still does not feel that he has fully vindicated himself for his cowardly act of deserting the pilgrim ship headed to Mecca. He tells his friend Marlow, "If you ask [the people] who is brave—who is true—who is just—who is it they would trust with their lives?—they would say, Tuan [Lord] Jim. And yet they can never know the real, real truth . . ." (*Lord Jim*, p. 181). He cannot rid his mind of the *Patna* episode, and ultimately he does fail the people of Patusan in a similar fashion.

The situation begins to unravel when a piratical adventurer named Brown, known ironically around the colonial world as "Gentleman Brown," appears in the waters off the coastal outlet of the river on which Patusan is situated. According to Marlow, Brown comes to Patusan while running from the law. Spanish authorities had arrested him for gun-running and were in the process of taking him to the Philippines for trial when he stole one of their ships. With a motley crew of "a couple of simple, blond Scandinavians, a mulatto of sorts, one bland Chinaman who cooked . . . and the rest of the nondescript spawn of the South Seas," Brown headed for Madagascar (*Lord Jim*, p. 211). In need of supplies, he stops at Patusan to see what he and his men can steal. They are attacked by Doramin's men, and their boat winds up stuck in the narrow creek that leads into Patusan. They manage to defend themselves against the Malays for a time, then the situation stagnates. A council is called among the various indigenous factions in Patusan, and the representative of the rajah decides to make overtures to Brown. Encouraged by this turn of events, Brown begins to dream of "stealing the whole country" (*Lord Jim*, p. 217). In the meantime, Cornelius begins to think that here might be an opportunity to rid the region of his main enemy, Jim.

Doramin calls on Jim for help in dealing with this new threat to the stability of Patusan. Though the Malays urge the immediate annihilation of these motley intruders, Jim decides to approach Brown personally and discuss the possibility of letting him and his crew return to the sea peacefully. When they meet, Brown appeals to him on the basis of their shared European heritage, whereupon Jim promises Brown safe passage back to the sea. The move proves disastrous for Doramin and his people because of Cornelius's interference and Brown's lack of faithfulness. Cornelius boards Brown's ship and shows him another creek that will lead back to the sea. On his way down this new creek, Brown's boat sneaks up on a contingent of men sent out in boats to watch Brown's movements away from Patusan. Doramin's son, Dain Waris, who had earlier become a close friend of Jim's, dies in the attack. Jim feels responsible for his death; once again he has let down those who placed their faith in him. Ignoring Jewel's pleas that he defend himself against the attack against him that will probably come from Doramin's people after this horrendous event, Jim decides to give himself up to Doramin and accept whatever judgment is passed against him. He proceeds to Doramin's house, walks up to the grieving father, and meets his tragic end: "Doramin, struggling to keep his feet, made with his two supporters a swaying, tottering group; his little eyes stared with an expression of mad pain, of rage, with a ferocious glitter, which the bystanders noticed, and then, while Jim stood stiffened and with bared head in the light of torches, looking him straight in the face, he clung heavily with his left arm round the neck of a bowed youth, and lifting deliberately his right, shot his son's friend through the chest" (*Lord Jim*, p. 246).

Imperialism as the "white man's burden." In *Lord Jim*, Marlow conceives of Jim's leadership as a type of sacrifice for people who do not necessarily appreciate what Jim is giving of himself. Marlow argues that though Jim may think of himself as ruler, it is actually the Malay people who rule him. He can never be completely free now of the obligations he owes them and the duties he must perform for them. "Jim the leader was a captive in every sense. The land, the people, the friendship, the love, were like the jealous guardians of his body. Every day added a link to the fetters of that strange freedom" (*Lord Jim*, p. 157). As Marlow sees it, Jim has placed himself in the role of self-sacrificing colonialist, reflecting a genuine perception of Conrad's time.

In 1899, the year Conrad's *Lord Jim* was first serialized in *Blackwood's Magazine*, another British writer, Rudyard Kipling, articulated a view of Western imperialism that saw colonizers not as arrogant, greedy invaders but rather as self-sacrificing heroes. They were humanitarians, declared this view, intent on giving up their own freedom and happiness for the sake of those whom they governed. Kipling dubbed imperialism "the white man's burden" in a poem of the same title. Kipling wrote the poem on the occasion of America's debate about whether or not it should rule imperially over the Philippines after having taken those islands from Spain during the Spanish-American War. Appealing to the United States of America, Kipling invited its leaders to join the Western nations that had all sacrificed of themselves to "civilize" other peoples and pacify other lands. The following excerpt encapsulates the altruistic view of imperialism:

> Take up the White Man's burden—
>   Send forth the best ye breed—
> Go bind your sons to exile
>   To serve your captives' need;

> To wait in heavy harness
>   On fluttered folk and wild—
> Your new-caught, sullen peoples,
>   Half devil and half child.

> Take up the White Man's burden—
>   In patience to abide,
> To veil the threat of terror
>   And check the show of pride;
> By open speech and simple,
>   An hundred times made plain,
> To seek another's profit,
>   And work another's gain.
>
> (Kipling, p. 602)

Sources and literary context. The five years that Joseph Conrad spent as a sailor in the south Asian seas—1883 to 1888—served as the inspiration for seven of his major literary works, including his first novel, *Almayer's Folly*, and the novel that one critic claimed put him "in the front ranks of living novelists": *Lord Jim* (Sherry, *Conrad: The Critical Heritage*, p. 120). On board various merchant marine vessels, Conrad visited not only the largest ports, such as Singapore and Bangkok, but also smaller trading posts on islands like Borneo and the Celebes. When transforming those events and experiences into the stuff of fiction, Conrad turned to travelers' books and other documents about the area that now makes up Malaysia and Indonesia; in one letter he refers to consulting "dull, wise books" for the kinds of sociological and historical facts that allowed him to create minutely detailed worlds for his characters (Conrad in Sherry, *Conrad's Eastern World*, p. 139). The two most influential among those books was naturalist Alfred Wallace's *The Malay Archipelago* (1869) and Major Fred McNair's *Perak and the Malays* (1878). Several of Conrad's Malay characters, including Rajah Tunku Allang, Doramin, and Tamb' Itam, take their names from real Malays discussed by McNair. The name of Jim's village, Patusan, probably comes from a pirate stronghold discussed in Henry Keppel's *Expedition to Borneo*, published in 1846.

The first half of the novel, which deals with Jim's experiences on board the *Patna*, are based on a similar real-life incident that took place in 1880. A steamship called the *Jeddah* left Singapore on July 17, 1880, carrying nearly 1,000 Muslim pilgrims and a few European officers. A few weeks later, the captain, his wife, the chief engineer and the second engineer and 16 "natives" were rescued from a lifeboat; they reported that the ship had sunk and all the people had perished. This turned out to be untrue, however, when the ship was discovered still afloat and the ship was towed into Aden, a port on the Red Sea.

Many Europeans were shocked to hear of this dereliction of duty. Subsequently a Court of Inquiry was held at Aden, and the captain had his "certificate of competency . . . suspended for a period of three years" (Sherry, "Pilgrim-Ship Episode," p. 338). The court also expressed its disapproval of actions taken by the first engineer, Augustine Williams, whom at least one critic has viewed as a possible original for Jim.

James Brooke, rajah of Sarawak, has been proposed as a source for Jim's experiences as a trusted ruler in the second half of the novel. Born in India in 1803, Brooke participated in the Anglo-Burmese war of the 1820s and then traveled to the archipelago in search of adventure on a schooner that he had purchased in the 1830s. He offered his services to the Sultan of Brunei, an area in northeast Borneo, who was currently fighting against peoples in the nearby territory of Sarawak. The victorious sultan thanked Brooke for his aid by naming him rajah of Sarawak in

---

FROM LONDON'S *DAILY CHRONICLE* ON THE *JEDDAH* INCIDENT

~

"It is to be feared that pilgrim ships are officered by unprincipled and cowardly men who disgrace the traditions of seamanship." (Sherry, "Pilgrim-Ship Episode," p. 322)

1841 and making the position inheritable by his descendants in 1846. Thus, an anomalous situation occurred whereby a private British citizen was also the independent ruler of a foreign land. Though the British public lionized and admired Brooke for his adventuring spirit, the British government expressed some dissatisfaction about this arrangement. They did not interfere much in this personal raj, however, and the Brooke family continued to rule the region until the last of these "white rajahs" ceded Sarawak to Great Britain in 1946.

Lord Jim shares some elements with the adventure novels and maritime fiction that enjoyed immense popularity in the late Victorian period, especially among young male audiences (see **King Solomon's Mines** and **Kim,** for example, also in *WLAIT 4: British and Irish Literature and Its Times*). It took place in a world seen by most Europeans as incredibly "exotic," and it included a romance with a "native" girl and a confronta-

tion with what amounted to an English pirate. Yet it also differed from adventure novels very significantly in terms of its focus on psychological development rather than plot, its concentration on a fundamentally ambiguous character who cannot easily be classified as wholly good or bad, and its unusual narrative style. Stylistically the novel shifts around in time, sometimes without being clear about which period is being described; without much warning, it switches from an omniscient third-person narrator to a first-person narrator, Marlow; and it pursues tangents—especially when Marlow narrates.

Reception. Despite the complexity of its language and structure, *Lord Jim* was generally well received by critics and public alike in 1900, a fact reflected in a statement Conrad himself made in a letter written soon after publication: "I am the spoiled child of the critics" (Conrad in Sherry, *Conrad: The Critical Heritage*, p. 16). Many reviewers, even those who expressed some reservations, referred to Conrad as a genius and saw this work as perhaps the best of those writings he had published thus far. Journal reviews stressed Conrad's "originality" and deemed the novel "remarkable" both for its ability to tease out subtle psychological elements of its title character and its capturing of the "odd parti-coloured life" of Southeast Asia (Sherry, *Conrad: The Critical Heritage*, pp. 111, 118, 115).

While the content of *Lord Jim* was almost universally praised, its form attracted criticism. One reviewer declared *Lord Jim* "tedious, over-elaborated, and more than a little difficult to read"; others complained about the narrative's tendency to drift into stories that did not appear immediately relevant to the protagonist's tale (Sherry, *Conrad: The Critical Heritage*, p. 123). Several reviewers emphasized the ways in which Conrad's prose differed from his contemporaries': "In striking antithesis to many writers of to-day he gives us too many episodes, too many side issues"; another critic saw his writing as unique but predicted Conrad's work would endure: "If he keeps on writing the same sort, he may arrive at the unique distinction of having few readers in his own generation, and a fair chance of several in the next" (Sherry, *Conrad: The Critical Heritage*, pp. 114, 128). In the end, this prophecy would prove both right and wrong. Not only did Conrad's works fare well in his own generation but they found multitudes of enthusiastic readers in subsequent generations.

—Laura Franey

For More Information

Cole, Faye-Cooper. *The Peoples of Malaysia.* New York: D. Van Nostrand, 1945.

Conrad, Joseph. *Lord Jim.* Ed. Thomas C. Moser. New York: Norton, 1996.

Eliade, Mircea, ed. "Southeast Asian Religions: Insular Cultures." In *The Encyclopedia of Religion.* New York: Macmillan, 1987.

Indonesia: A Country Study. Ed. William H. Frederick and Robert L. Worden. Washington, D.C.: Library of Congress, 1993.

Keppel, Henry. The *Expedition to Borneo of H. M. S. Dido for the Suppression of Piracy.* London: Chapman & Hall, 1846.

Kipling, Rudyard. "The White Man's Burden." In *The Portable Kipling.* Ed. Irving Howe. Harmondsworth, England: Penguin, 1982.

Lorimer, Douglas A. "Race, Science and Culture: Historical Continuities and Discontinuities, 1850–1914." In *The Victorians and Race.* Ed. Shearer West. Aldershot, England: Scholar Press, 1996.

Said, Edward W. *Orientalism.* New York: Random House, 1979.

Sherry, Norman, ed. *Conrad: The Critical Heritage.* London: Routledge & Kegan Paul, 1973.

———. *Conrad's Eastern World.* Cambridge: Cambridge University Press, 1966.

———. "The Pilgrim-Ship Episode." In *Lord Jim,* by Joseph Conrad. New York: Norton, 1996.

Stape, J. H., ed. *The Cambridge Companion to Joseph Conrad.* Cambridge: Cambridge University Press, 1996.

Stocking, George, Jr. *Victorian Anthropology.* New York: Free Press, 1987.

Tarling, Nicholas, ed. *Cambridge History of Southeast Asia,* Vol. 2. Cambridge: Cambridge University Press, 1992.

Lord of the Flies

by
William Golding

William Golding was born at St. Columb Minor, Cornwall, on September 19, 1911. His father, Alec Golding, the Senior Assistant Master at the Marlboro Grammar School, specialized in science and wrote textbooks (on chemistry, botany, zoology, physics, and geography). Golding himself attended the Marlboro School, then studied in science at Brasenose College, Oxford. After graduation, Golding became a settlement-house worker while composing plays and acting. In 1939, having wed Ann Brookfield, he began teaching English and philosophy at Bishop Wordsworth's School in Salisbury. His career there was short term; by the following year, he had enlisted in the Royal Navy. Golding served in the navy for five years during World War II. His first published novel, *Lord of the Flies*, manifests his disillusionment with human nature—a result, in large part, of his experience in World War II. Continuing to focus on violence and evil, Golding went on to write *The Inheritors* (1955; about prehistoric inhabitants), *Pincher Martin* (1956; about a drowned sailor), and eight more novels (from *Free Fall*, 1959, to *The Paper Men*, 1984), establishing "a rhythm of contrasted sea-stories and land-stories all of which are concerned with extremity and isolation" (Sanders, p. 596). His *Lord of the Flies* is now recognized as a modern classic, a chilling fable of total war and the darkness lurking in all human hearts, including those of children.

> ## THE LITERARY WORK
>
> A novel set on an uninhabited tropical island somewhere in the South Pacific during the post-World War II years; first published in 1954.
>
> ## SYNOPSIS
>
> Marooned on a desert island after a plane crash, a group of British schoolboys tries to establish a cooperative society but ultimately descends into violence and savagery.

Events in History at the Time of the Novel

Hitler, social prohibitions, and the nature of evil. Although *Lord of the Flies* is set in the 1950s, memories of World War II—and the atrocities of the totalitarian National Socialist (Nazi) regime in Germany, in particular—provide a dark undercurrent to the story. Golding himself had been profoundly affected by his experiences in the British Navy during the war. In a conversation with a friend, Golding explained,

> I was gradually coming up against people and I was understanding a bit more what people were like, and, also, gradually, learning that the things I hadn't really believed, that I had in fact taken as propaganda, were, in fact, *done* . . .

William Golding

going [into occupied territory in France] twice—meeting a man one time and the next time not meeting him, and being told that he was probably being tortured to death at that moment. This kind of thing one gradually began to *see*, and at the end, I *fully* believed in [the fact of] Nazism; one couldn't do anything else.
(Golding in Biles, p. 34)

The prewar rise of Nazism—and Nazi dictator Adolf Hitler—has been attributed, among other factors, to the economic depression and political turmoil experienced by Germany after World War I. Ordered by the Treaty of Versailles to make substantial financial reparations to the victor nations, Germany suffered multiple financial woes. A disastrously inflated national currency, large-scale unemployment, and a worldwide economic depression (following the Wall Street crisis in the United States in 1929) exacerbated its postwar economic stress. Meanwhile, the Weimar Republic, established in 1919 after the abdication of the Kaiser, was proving unstable. Together the economic and political disarray, combined with the Germans' desire to recover their lost "honor" and "greatness" as a nation, allowed Hitler's growing Nazi party to step in and assume power in 1933. The new regime aroused nationalist fervor, promised—and delivered—economic stability, emphasized the importance of the community over the individual, and predicted a glorious national and racial destiny for Germany, especially after the elimination of "traitors and Jews" (Kedward, p. 67). Welcoming the authoritarian control provided by Hitler and his followers, most Germans became fervent believers in Nazism, even adopting Hitler's view that Jews were a hindrance to Germany's greatness. Ultimately, the Nazis' dedication to the machine of the state overrode all else: the state was all, the individual—especially the Jewish or foreign individual—was nothing. Enemies of the state were to be eliminated at all costs and could expect neither mercy nor humane treatment from the state itself.

With the Nazi regime as the most blatant example, World War II provided numerous incidences of man's inhumanity to man. Throughout Germany and other parts of Eastern Europe, Hitler and the Nazis set up firing squads and concentration camps where an estimated 5,721,800 victims (mostly Jews) were killed in gas chambers or through forced hard labor, or were gunned down in cold blood and left for dead in pits such as Babi Yar in the Ukraine. Forced to dig the pits, undress, then stand at the edge of the new graves, they became targets for the gunfire of the Nazi militia and even of the local population. In several camps, Jews were also made the "guinea pigs" for Nazi "medical experiments," exposed, for example, to extremes of high pressure and freezing temperatures at the Dachau concentration camp in Germany. Other nations were equally savage in their treatment of "the enemy." In Japanese prison camps, enemy civilians and POWs were starved, beaten, and subjected to experimental surgery, without anesthesia, by Japanese physicians. Those who survived the medical procedures were usually killed afterwards. The Americans meanwhile interned Japanese residents, and the British did likewise to Italian, Austrian, and German (including Austrian and German Jewish) refugees within their borders.

The British internment of aliens began after Denmark, Norway, and Holland fell to the Nazis and when Germany threatened to invade Britain. The major fear of the British issued from their perception that Holland fell because of so-called "Fifth Columnists," the Dutch populace favoring a German takeover and working subversively to promote it. Most internees were kept on the Isle of Man, but as many as 7,000 were transported to Canada and Australia. Overcrowding, rationed food, restrictions on communication, and routines of camp life created intense psychological anxiety that led to depression and even suicide among internees. Over time life in the camps improved, with the help of educational, artistic, and literary activities and entertainment, such as cabarets and concerts. Still, prejudice and hostility were manifested toward aliens, who were always treated with suspicion.

After the war, the revelation of atrocities committed by the Nazis and others led many, including Golding, to reflect on the nature of good and evil. Summing up his own experiences, Golding concluded,

> I had seen enough in the last five years to know that these people [the "nice people"] are capable of [atrocities] too; that really this was an extension of the human condition; that what the Nazis were doing, they were doing because certain capacities in them, certain deficiencies . . . had been freed, and they were just people like us, in different circumstances.
>
> (Golding in Biles, p. 34)

However, Golding also argued, "There must be an explanation of why there is a Nazi system in one place and not in another, because even if [people] were held back only by certain social sanctions or social prohibitions, the social prohibitions were there" (Golding in Biles, p. 36).

The Blitz and the Great Evacuation. Hitler's plan to invade Britain, called Operation Sea Lion, involved the use of amphibious warfare. British naval strength made it imperative for Germany to gain dominance in the air. To achieve this, Germany amassed 1,300 bombers and dive bombers, as well as 1,200 fighter aircraft. Deployed from Norway to northern France, the German air force, or Luftwaffe, attacked Britain from all directions, except from the sea at the west. The attackers encountered British antiaircraft guns and the Royal Air Force (RAF), whose 600 fighters, chiefly Spitfires and Hurricanes, intercepted the Germans in the air. As the Battle of Britain unfolded, the attack at sea saw the German naval force strike along the coast of the English Channel, then move inland.

Without a strategic plan, the German air force struck diverse targets, not simply military but also civilian, such as populated urban areas and historical and cultural monuments in Britain. In the end, the RAF prevailed, the British scoring a military and psychological victory. While the British lost approximately 900 fighter aircraft, the Germans lost almost 1,700 bombers and fighters. The British meanwhile staged an air raid on Berlin. In retaliation, Hitler ordered the bombing of populous cities in England, including London, Manchester, and Coventry. Britain's most intense period of aerial bombardment by the Germans—which became known as the "Blitz"—began in September 1940 and ended in May 1941.

Even before the Blitz, many city families were planning to send their most vulnerable members—the children—to safety. In 1939, the British government formulated a plan to sponsor the evacuation from London of children and their mothers, expectant mothers, and certain classes of the population, such as the blind, to more isolated locations in the country. Workers and those willing to contribute to the war effort were encouraged to stay behind; others remained in London at their own risk or left at their own expense. In late summer of 1939, even before war had been officially declared between Britain and Germany, many London families were receiving letters containing instructions for evacuation procedures, like the following from the West Ham Council:

> In the event of an Emergency, arrangements have been made to evacuate school children from the London area to safe places in the country. It is hoped that your child/children will participate in this scheme. On receipt of further instructions, he/she/they should report to Star Road School bringing with him/her/them hat, raincoat, haversack containing nightclothes, towel, soap, tooth brush and toothpaste, and he/she/they should wear a card round his/her/their neck(s) giving his/her/their full name(s), age(s), School, home address and names of next of kin.
>
> (West Ham Council in Mosley, pp. 5-7)

On September 1, 1939, shortly after Britain received news of Germany's invasion of Poland, the British government issued orders to transport London's children to safety, and the Great Evacuation began. For the next 24 hours, people everywhere in London came to watch as long processions of children trekked to a railway or bus station. Around the neck of each child was a small square cardboard box that held a gas mask, and pinned to their lapels were name tags. "Brothers and sisters clung to each other's hands like grim death, and refused to be parted" (Mosley, p. 14). An estimated 1 million children and 200,000 mothers left London in the Great Evacuation. Evacuees who had relatives in the country took refuge with them, while others were housed by rural families who had consented to serve as a safe haven. Some of the wealthier Londoners sent their children overseas, to the United

States and Canada, where they would remain throughout the war.

Lord of the Flies centers on British schoolboys who are being evacuated to a safe haven after a deadly nuclear war breaks out but end up marooned on a deserted tropical island. It is one of the novel's many ironies that Britain's attempt to spare such boys from the horrors of war backfires, ultimately embroiling them in a violent, primitive, and equally deadly struggle for survival on the island.

Nuclear technology and total war. In the European theater, the concept of total war involved the devastation not only of military installations and personnel but also of civilians and urban

---

NO TO NUCLEAR WEAPONS

Less than a decade after the dropping of the atomic bomb on Japan, the specter of nuclear war was revived during another armed conflict. Britain found itself embroiled in grim warfare in Korea for 37 months (July 1950-August 1953) preceding the publication of *Lord of the Flies*. The United Kingdom suffered 1,078 killed in action, 2,674 wounded, and 1,060 missing or taken prisoner during the conflict (Hickey, p. 366). United States President Harry Truman promised British Prime Minister Clement Atlee that no nuclear weapons would be fired on Korea or Red China, but the devastation was staggering nonetheless. Two million civilians are estimated to have perished in North Korea, which translates into 20 percent of the region's population at that time. Clearly man's inhumanity to man had not been quashed by the excesses of World War II.

---

areas. Because twentieth-century nations relied on their country's industrial capability for military equipment and materials, civilians, though non-combatants, were perceived as vital to the war effort. Consequently, they and the factories in which they labored became targets for air raids, as in the aforementioned Battle of Britain. This concept of total war enlarged considerably with the invention of the atomic bomb. First developed in the United States under the Manhattan Project, atomic weaponry resulted in a potential for mass destruction on a scale previously unimagined. On August 6, 1945, the United States detonated an atomic bomb over Hiroshima, Japan, destroying an area of 4 square miles at the center of the city, where close to

350,000 residents dwelled. The number of dead and injured amounted to almost 140,000. On August 9, 1945, the United States dropped another atomic bomb over Nagasaki, Japan, killing nearly 65,000 people. Since that time, the specter of nuclear conflict has virtually terrorized humankind.

The United States' decision to bomb Hiroshima and Nagasaki has been the focus of heated debate ever since. Initially, there was little outcry against the bombings—indeed, many Allied nations agreed with U.S. President Harry Truman's argument that dropping the bomb forestalled an invasion of Japan and prevented a costly land war, bringing World War II to a speedier end than would otherwise be the case. Within a few years, however, Truman's decision fell under scrutiny; in July 1946, a panel he had appointed to study the Pacific War submitted a report, *The United States Strategic Bombing Survey*, expressing the opinion that Japan would probably have surrendered before the end of 1945, even if the atomic bomb had never been dropped. Seconding this view, Henry Stimson, the U.S. Secretary of War in Truman's administration, wondered in his memoirs—published in 1948—if a change in negotiating tactics would have brought about peace without the bombings. The 1950s and '60s saw the emergence of new opponents to the bombings and to atomic warfare in general. Critics, said Robert J. Maddox, "have accused President Harry S Truman and his advisers of everything from failing to explore alternatives to engaging in a monstrous conspiracy to slaughter all those people for no more compelling reason than to employ 'atomic warfare' against the Soviet Union" (Maddox, p. 1). P. M. S. Blackett, a British scientist, even charged that the bombings of Hiroshima and Nagasaki represented the first chapter of the Cold War, that is, the competition between the United States and the Soviet Union for world leadership, rather than the last chapter of World War II. In 1950, Admiral William D. Leahy, Truman's personal chief of staff, denounced the bombings in his own memoirs as "barbarous," maintaining that they provided "no material assistance in our war against Japan" and declaring, "I was not taught to make war in that fashion and wars cannot be won by destroying women and children" (Leahy in Maddox, p. 120).

In *Lord of the Flies*, sophisticated and primitive warfare exist alongside each other. Not only have the British schoolboys been evacuated because of a nuclear war, but also aerial battles take place over the tropical island on which the boys find themselves stranded. As they revert to savagery, hunting each other with knives and spears, their elders employ the technological advancements of civilization to elevate the destructive impulses of human nature to the most catastrophic levels. The boys are ultimately rescued from the island by a naval officer whose ship is armed with a submachine gun and whose gaze is trained on the horizon, in search of the enemy he must hunt and destroy.

The Novel in Focus

Plot summary. The novel begins as two boys—fair-haired, even-tempered Ralph and fat, bespectacled, asthmatic Piggy—meet on the beach of an apparently deserted tropical island. Both were passengers on an aircraft transporting British 6-to-12-year-old schoolboys to a safe destination while England wages a nuclear war. The aircraft crashed, claiming the life of the pilot. Ralph and Piggy, who were traveling in the passenger compartment, which had landed safely on the island, somberly wonder if they are the sole survivors. Drawn by Ralph's blowing upon a conch shell, more children emerge from the jungle and quickly assemble. Last to join the group are a black-clad boys' choir, led by bossy, red-haired Jack Merridew.

Discovering that they are without adult supervision, the boys try to establish rules for life on the island while they wait to be rescued. Jack is discomfited when Ralph is elected leader by the other boys but is appeased when he and the rest of the choir are appointed to be hunters, responsible for obtaining food for the whole group. Ralph, meanwhile, decrees that shelters be erected on the beach and that a signal fire be built on top of a nearby mountain to attract rescuers. The first attempt to build the fire—using Piggy's glasses as a lens to focus the sunlight on their kindling—ignites a blaze that scorches a large portion of the forest, but eventually the boys succeed in lighting a proper signal fire, which Jack and the other hunters promise to keep ablaze during the day. At this point, one small boy, who claimed to have seen "a beastie"—a snakelike thing that moves by night—gets lost in the confusion (Golding, *Lord of the Flies*, p. 31).

In the days that follow, tensions begin to develop between Ralph and Jack. Ralph complains that after having agreed to build huts, many of the boys work briefly on that project, then scat-

ter to swim, eat fruit, or play. Only Ralph and Simon—an introverted boy prone to fits—are building the huts. Meanwhile, Jack becomes increasingly intent on his role of hunter, painting his face with colored clay as he stalks wild pigs in the hope of slaying one for food. Finally, he and the other hunters succeed in killing a pig; unfortunately, they are so involved in the hunt that they neglect to tend the signal fire, which dies out just as the other boys sight a vessel on the horizon. A furious Ralph berates Jack for costing them their chance to be rescued, and a fight ensues during which one of Piggy's lenses is shattered. Peace is restored after Jack apologizes for neglecting the fire, and all the boys roast and eat the pig.

The truce between Ralph and Jack proves temporary, however, and other fears—chiefly surrounding the mysterious "beastie" described by the lost boy—start to erode the tenuous bonds that hold the group together. At one assembly Jack challenges Ralph's leadership and summons the rest of the hunters to follow him instead. Jack and his band depart, leaving Ralph, Piggy, and Simon to fret about the group's dissolving and to lament the absence of adults on the island.

That night the body of a dead parachutist—killed in a nearby air battle—is carried by the wind to a mountainside on the island. Periodically, a breeze elevates the head and chest of the corpse, so that it appears upright and gazing when held in place by the tangled lines of the parachute. Meanwhile, the older boys have formed a search party to locate the "beastie," or beast. One night, Ralph, Jack, and another boy, Roger, scale the mountain where the beast was supposedly sighted. Close to the summit, they view the decomposing corpse of the parachutist; the gruesome sight causes the boys to flee down the mountain in terror of "the beast."

In the resulting panic, Jack again stirs up trouble at an assembly, challenging Ralph's status as chief. He accuses Ralph of cowardice in the presence of the so-called beast and of simply barking out orders and expecting others to obey. The other boys remain silent and fail to support Jack's claim to be the new leader, after which Jack angrily leaves the group to form his own tribe. Later, the rest of the hunters and several other boys slip off to join him. Jack and his followers paint their faces, then track and kill a sow, disemboweling her and mounting her head on a stick to appease the beast on the island. Both the pig's head and offal attract hordes of flies.

Hugh Edwards as Piggy and Tom Chapin as Jack in the 1963 film version of *Lord of the Flies*.

To cook the sow, Jack's boys need fire, so they steal it from Ralph's band, which by now has dwindled to himself, Piggy, Simon, and two other boys. Jack informs Ralph and his followers about the killing of the sow and invites them to the feast. Simon, who has wandered off into the forest by himself, meanwhile encounters the pig's head and undergoes a visionary experience that causes him to lose consciousness. After regaining his senses, Simon resumes his wanderings, encounters the corpse of the parachutist, and recognizes it for what it is. Freeing the body from its moorings, Simon goes to inform the other boys of his discovery.

Ralph and his followers arrive at the feast, over which a painted, garlanded Jack is presiding. After the meal, Jack invites the remaining boys to join his tribe, then commands his followers to enact the dance of the hunt. Storm clouds appear overhead. The boys, frenzied by their dance and chanting, see Simon emerge from the forest, mistake him for the beast, and attack him, ignoring his cries for help. When the storm breaks, the boys finally scatter, seeking shelter. A great wind dislodges the corpse of the parachutist from the mountain and sweeps it out to sea. Simon's lifeless body is also carried off by the tide.

Shaken by Simon's death and their own participation in it, Ralph, Piggy, and their last two followers try to concentrate on the signal fire—now located on the beach. That night, Jack and his followers raid Ralph's camp, while the boys are asleep, stealing Piggy's glasses, the vital tool for starting fires. The next morning, Ralph's band plans to reason with the hunters, and request the return of Piggy's glasses. Approaching Jack's group, the party of four are astonished to find his mountain camp guarded by armed followers who deny them admission. Jack, returning from a hunt with two other boys, tells Ralph that he is not welcome and orders him to keep to his part of the island. Ralph demands the return of Piggy's glasses; but Jack refuses, and the boys engage in hand-to-hand combat with spears. Meanwhile, at Jack's command, his hunters capture Sam and Eric, the other two boys in Ralph's band. As Ralph and Jack continue to fight, Piggy tries to muster the group's attention with the conch shell used to call everyone to assembly. But atop the mountain, Roger, one of Jack's followers, dislodges a boulder that careens downhill, shatters the conch shell, and strikes Piggy, who falls 40 feet to his death in the sea below. Jack hurls his spear at Ralph, wounding him and forcing him to flee alone into the forest.

After hiding and examining his wounds, Ralph secretly returns to Jack's camp, where he encounters Sam and Eric, who warn him that Jack's tribe plans to hunt him next. Concealing himself in a thicket, Ralph hopes to avoid discovery but is ultimately spotted by a hunter. Fleeing through the forest, he learns that the hunters have started a fire to smoke him out, so he heads for the open beach with Jack and the others in hot pursuit. Suddenly, Ralph finds himself face to face with a naval officer, whose vessel was attracted to the island by the smoke. The other boys, though painted and savage in appearance, emerge from the forest behind him and come to a halt when they see their rescuer. The officer questions Ralph about the situation and expresses disappointment that "a pack of British boys" failed "to put up a better show" (*Lord of the Flies*, p. 186). Overwhelmed by his experiences on the island, Ralph begins to shake and sob over "the end of innocence, the darkness of man's heart" and the deaths of Simon and Piggy (*Lord of the Flies*, pp. 186-87). The other boys are soon crying along with him. Uncomfortable with such a naked display of emotion, the officer turns away to study "the trim cruiser in the distance" (*Lord of the Flies*, p. 187).

THE TITLE IN BIBLICAL CONTEXT

The title of the novel refers to Beelzebub, who was the patron god of the Philistines in ancient Palestine. In Judeo-Christian mythology, Beelzebub—the Greek translation of the Hebrew *Baal-Zevuv*—is the prince of demons or devils, whose idol, called Baal, included the image of an animal, at times propped up on a pole. Such idols became objects of worship in ancient Phoenicia, Syria, and Palestine. Periodically the Israelites would capture or destroy the idols. At times, moreover, the idols wound up in Gehenna, a refuse dump outside Jerusalem where they attracted hordes of flies. Hence, Beelzebub was also called "Lord of the Flies."

War, society, and civilization. The emphasis on destruction in *Lord of the Flies* derives from Golding's own experience in the war. As a lieutenant in the Royal Navy, he commanded a rocket ship that engaged enemy battleships, submarines, and airplanes. He even participated in D-Day operations. Interviewed in 1963 by Douglas A. Davis for an article in *New Republic* (4 May 1963), Golding himself explained how the war affected him, saying that when he was younger, he had some unrealistic views about human nature, but the war changed him (Golding in Dick, p. 4).

A decade earlier, in his reply to a publicity questionnaire from the American publishers of *Lord of the Flies*, Golding revealed how his conception had shifted:

The theme is an attempt to trace the defects of society back to the defects of human nature. The moral is that the shape of a society must depend on the ethical nature of the individual and not on any political system however apparently logical or respectable. The whole book is symbolic in nature except the rescue in the end where adult life appears, dignified and capable, but in reality enmeshed in the same evil as the symbolic life of the children on the island. The officer, having interrupted a manhunt, prepares to take the children off the island in a cruiser which will presently be hunting its enemy in the same implacable way. And who will rescue the adult and his cruiser?

(Golding in Epstein, p. 189)

CLASS CONSCIOUSNESS ON THE ISLAND

Initially, the stranded boys in *Lord of the Flies* cling closely to the strictures of the worldly society from which they hail, including class-related strictures. Ralph proudly reveals that he is the son of a naval officer, a fact that gives him a certain standing in the eyes of the other children. Likewise, Jack clings to his own status in the outside world as chorister and "head boy" at his school. By contrast, the orphaned Piggy demonstrates by his ungrammatical speech—"There ain't nothing we can do"—that he is of a lower social class than Ralph or Jack, which sets him apart from the group as much as his overweight, myopia, and asthma do (*Lord of the Flies*, p. 40). Once the society the boys attempt to create on the island begins to collapse, however, class designations cease to matter: most of the boys become indistinguishable in their savagery. The naval officer who rescues them cannot tell the commander's son from the choir boy; he sees only "little boys, their bodies streaked with colored clay, [and] sharp sticks in their hands" who have, to his disapproval, been conducting themselves like "small savages" (*Lord of the Flies*, pp. 185-86).

In the novel, the boys' actions increasingly reflect their consciousness of war and their own capacity for violence. Even before the struggle for the island begins, the children play at war—Ralph pretends to be "a fighter-plane, with wings swept back, and machine-gun[s] Piggy," while some of the other boys scale the cliffs, cheering when they manage to dislodge a boulder and send it crashing "like a bomb" to the forest below (*Lord of the Flies*, pp. 9, 24). Most ominous of all is the first appearance of the boys' choir;

led by Jack Merridew, they enter "marching approximately in two parallel lines and dressed in strangely eccentric clothing . . . each boy wore a square black cap with a silver badge on it. Their bodies, from throat to ankle, were hidden by black cloaks which bore a long silver cross on the left breast and each neck was finished off with a hambone frill" (*Lord of the Flies*, p. 16). The description of the almost military organization and demeanor of the choir brings to mind the black-shirted followers of Italian dictator Benito Mussolini or Hitler's own goose-stepping Nazis, who wore black uniforms and iron crosses during World War II.

Freed from adult strictures, Jack and his followers quickly become a force for darkness and violence, like the Nazis but on a far more primitive level. At home, Jack "was a part of society; on the island he is all of it," much as a dictator would be (Golding in Biles, p. 46). Also, the chants that Jack and his followers reiterate as they stalk pigs on the island, encircle, and kill them with spears—"Kill the pig! Cut his throat! Kill the pig! Bash him in!"—seem to echo the hysteria that typified Nazi rallies (*Lord of the Flies*, p. 106). Perhaps Jack and his hunters are primitive counterparts of fervent Nazis whose own chants led to aggression, first against their neighboring countries and then against the Allies in World War II.

It would not be entirely accurate to describe Golding's novel as a parable about Nazism. It can, however, be argued that the breakdown of certain social prohibitions on the island causes the collapse of "government" that the British schoolboys attempt to establish there, creating an environment in which violence, savagery, and inhumanity can flourish, as they did in Nazi Germany. Like the post-World War I Germans, the boys in Golding's novel find themselves in a state of disarray after a disaster—the crash of their aircraft leaves them stranded on a deserted island. At first, they are jubilant at being without adult restriction and confident in their ability to create a viable communal society on the island, declaring, "We're English and the English are best at everything" (*Lord of the Flies*, p. 38). But in the end, the English, like the Americans (with their internment camps), the Japanese (with their prisoner-of-war camps), and the Nazis (with their death camps), succumb to what Golding perceives as a pervasive human depravity.

The view is not an entirely bleak one, however. Golding conceives of the depravity as pervasive, but not as absolute:

It is the ordered society which keeps us in . . . this viable shape, this social shape, and which enables us to show our bright side. . . . Take away these sanctions, and we fall into the dark side. But you must remember this, that the sanctions, the shape of society, are also the product of the human being. Here is where it gets so damned difficult.

(Golding in Biles, p. 44)

Sources and literary context. *Lord of the Flies* is Golding's reaction to, and critique of, a work of children's literature in England, Robert Michael Ballantyne's *The Coral Island* (1857), written during the heyday of Victorian society. In this classic novel, three boys—Ralph Rover, Jack Martin, and Peterkin Gay—are shipwrecked on a Pacific island. In accordance with the traditions and values of Victorian society, the boys interact cooperatively and happily on the island. They are resourceful; their killing of a sow, which, unlike *Lord of the Flies*, does not ensue in a bloodthirsty frenzy, will provide the hide from which they craft shoes for future use. They encounter cannibals, who eventually are converted to Christianity, and a resounding affirmation of God echoes in the novel.

Golding perceived Ballantyne as an idealist, whose fanciful children's story lacks realism. Throughout Golding's novel, there are periodic reminders of Ballantyne's work when characters refer to the "coral island" on which they are stranded. Golding's schoolboys initially compare their marooned situation to an adventure story, citing such books as *Treasure Island, Swallows and Amazons*, and *Coral Island* (*Lord of the Flies*, p. 30). At the end of the novel, the uncomprehending naval officer makes a similar reference when the exhausted, traumatized Ralph tries to explain what has been happening to them: "I know. Jolly good show. Like the Coral Island" (*Lord of the Flies*, p. 186). As an antidote and counterargument to Ballantyne's idealism, Golding revives the narrative of the shipwreck and boys stranded on a Pacific island. Ballantyne's Ralph and Jack become the identically named characters in Golding's novel, and Peterkin, as Golding revealed in an interview with literary scholar Frank Kermode, is transformed into Simon—"Peterkin . . . is Simon, by the way. Simon called Peter, you see [as in the Bible]. It was worked out very carefully in every possible way, this novel" (Golding, p. 201).

In a larger sense, Golding's *Lord of the Flies* reflects a longstanding trend in "island literature."

Whereas Ballantyne's *Coral Island* dramatizes how children cope with the challenge of being stranded, other works such as Daniel Defoe's *Robinson Crusoe* (1719) and Johann Rudolf Wyss's *Swiss Family Robinson* (1827) feature adults, as well, on an island. Often the aim of such literature has been to present a society from its inception and chart whether the community that evolves becomes a utopia or dystopia, the former a model of harmony and cooperation, the latter of dysfunction, disharmony, and competitive disintegration.

Reviews. At its publication in 1954, *Lord of the Flies* elicited mixed reviews. In the *New Statesman*, Walter Allen questioned the plausibility of the degeneration of the schoolboys into barbarism: "These children's crosses, it seems to me, were altogether too unnaturally heavy for it to be possible to draw conclusions from Mr. Golding's novel" (Allen in Nelson, p. 3). Louis J. Halle in the *Saturday Review* also expressed reservations about *Lord of the Flies*, arguing that Golding "cannot quite find his meaning in his material. The heroes come to a bad end, having contributed nothing to such salvation as the society achieves. There is a great deal of commotion and the last page is nothing more than a playwright's contrivance for bringing down the curtain. One is left asking: What was the point?" (Halle in Nelson, p. 5).

Other critics were more favorably impressed. In *The Manchester Guardian*, Douglas Hewitt found the book "completely convincing and often very frightening," adding that the "weaknesses of the novel may be summed up as a tendency to be too explicit" (Hewett in Nelson, p. 4). James Stern, however, admired the allegorical elements in *Lord of the Flies*, writing in *The New York Times Book Review*, "With undertones of '1984' and 'High Wind in Jamaica,' this brilliant work is a frightening parody on man's return (in a few weeks) to that state of darkness from which it took him thousands of years to emerge . . . even the most skeptical reader will be carried away by the story's plausibility and power, by the skillfully worked-out progress, by the perfection of its characterization, dialogue and prose" (Stern in Nelson, p. 7). Dan Wickenden, in the *New York Herald Tribune*, was also enthusiastic, calling *Lord of the Flies* "an exciting and ultimately powerful narrative. The boys themselves are altogether convincing: the style is vivid and crystalline; the sense of mounting terror is brilliantly conveyed" (Wickenden in Nelson, p. 9). *Lord of the Flies* has its shortcomings, but all told it is a distinguished performance" (Wickenden in Nelson, p. 9).

—Albert Labriola and Pamela S. Loy

For More Information

Biles, Jack I. *Talk: Conversations with William Golding*. New York: Harcourt Brace Jovanovich, 1970.

Cesarani, David, and Tony Kushner, eds. *The Internment of Aliens in Twentieth Century Britain*. London: Frank Cass, 1993.

Dick, Bernard F. *William Golding*. Boston: Twayne, 1987.

Dunnigan, James F., and Albert A. Nofi. *Victory at Sea: World War II in the Pacific*. New York: William Morrow, 1995.

Epstein, E. L. "Biographical and Critical Notes." In *Lord of the Flies*. New York: Capricorn Books, 1959.

Golding, William. *Lord of the Flies*. New York: Berkeley, 1954.

Hickey, Michael. *The Korean War: The West Confronts Communism*. Woodstock, N.Y.: Overlook, 2000.

Kedward, H. R. *Fascism in Western Europe 1900–45*. New York: New York University Press, 1971.

Lukacs, John. *The Hitler of History*. New York: Alfred A. Knopf, 1997.

Maddox, Robert James. *Weapons for Victory: The Hiroshima Decision Fifty Years Later*. Columbia: University of Missouri Press, 1995.

Mosley, Leonard. *Backs to the Wall: London under Fire 1939–45*. London: Weidenfeld & Nicolson, 1971.

Moss, Joyce, and George Wilson. *Peoples of the World: Eastern Europe and the Post-Soviet Republics*. Detroit: Gale Research, 1993.

Nelson, William. *William Golding's "Lord of the Flies": A Source Book*. Indianapolis: Odyssey Press, 1963.

Sanders, Andrew. *The Short Oxford History of English Literature*. Oxford: Clarendon, 1996.

Midnight's Children

by

Salman Rushdie

THE LITERARY WORK

A magical realist novel, set in India and Pakistan from 1915 to 1977; published in 1981.

SYNOPSIS

The fantastic life of a "child of midnight" allegorically embodies India's dream of independence, as well as the devastating effects of a colonial legacy and of partition on the goal of national unity.

On June 19, 1947, just two months before India's independence and partition, (Ahmed) Salman Rushdie was born in Bombay, India. Like his father, Rushdie was well educated—first at Cathedral school in Bombay, then at his father's alma mater, King's College, Cambridge, in Great Britain. He earned a Master of History degree in 1968, focusing on Arabic and Islamic civilization, but aspired to be a writer like his hero, Urdu poet Faiz Ahmad Faiz. Upon graduation Rushdie moved to Karachi, Pakistan, where his family had relocated in 1964, intending to pursue a career in television writing. In 1969 he returned to London, frustrated by censorship in Pakistan, and for the next ten years made his living as an advertising copywriter, while devoting his off-hours to fiction. In 1975 his first novel, *Grimus,* was published to less-than-critical acclaim but his subsequent novel, *Midnight's Children,* won the Booker Prize, launching Rushdie's career and introducing a new type of novel in Britain. The novel's scathing attacks on political dynasties, corruption, and the legacy of British colonialism are tempered with abundant humor and self-deprecating jokes, yet it gave offense. Foreshadowing the political turmoil that would embroil his later career (the 1989 religious edict from Iran condemning him to death for his *The Satanic Verses*), India's Prime Minister Indira Gandhi sued Rushdie and his publisher for libel, forcing them to make a public apology. But that did not deter Rushdie from tackling controversial subjects. Following the publication of *Midnight's Children* he appeared frequently on talk shows and wrote nonfiction pieces attacking the Thatcher government in Britain and the nostalgic 1980s film and television revivals of the old British Raj, or ruling colonial government, in India. Considered by many to be "the great Indian novel," *Midnight's Children* had a profound impact on British literature by giving voice to those affected most by colonialism and partition.

Events in History at the Time of the Novel

Toward independence. After nearly two centuries of colonial rule, in 1918 the British Raj passed reforms that granted the people of India "complete responsibility as conditions permit" and created a new "dyarchy" in which power would be shared between the British and elected

Salman Rushdie

Indian representatives (Wolpert, p. 297). Coinciding with the reforms, however, was the passage of the Rowlatt Acts (March 1919), which imposed wartime emergency measures to combat "seditious conspiracy" (Wolpert, p. 298). In real terms, the Rowlatt Acts, which extended the 1915 Defense of India Act, denied basic civil rights and due process and censored the press. Disparaged as the "Black Acts," they encountered universal opposition from Indian members of the Imperial Legislative Council and even prompted several members to resign, including Muhammad Ali Jinnah, a prominent Muslim politician and the future "Father of Pakistan." He lambasted the government as an "incompetent bureaucracy" and declared that "the fundamental principles of justice have been uprooted and the constitutional rights of the people have been violated" (Jinnah in Wolpert, p. 298). Mohandas Karamchand Gandhi, a pacifist grassroots leader of the independence movement, called the Acts symptoms of a "deep-seated disease in the governing body" and urged citizens to peacefully defy them (Gandhi in Wolpert, p. 298). He proclaimed a *hartal*, or national strike, to be "accompanied by fasting and prayer, which was normally associated with mourning a loved one

(Chandra, p. 182). In the novel, Naseem, the protagonist's grandmother, wonders why there is a call for fasting and prayer when no one is dead, but her husband, Dr. Aziz, understands. He murmurs, "The British are wrong to turn back the clock. It was a mistake to pass the Rowlatt Act" (Rushdie, *Midnight's Children,* p. 34). Indeed, it proved to be a grave mistake, leading not only to death but to a tragedy of unimaginable proportions.

While Indians heeded Gandhi's call for a strike, paralyzing the railway system and business operations nationwide, Sikhs in particular, led by Drs. Kitchlu and Satyapal, organized meetings to discuss their response to Rowlatt. Fearing the potential action, British officials in Amritsar had Kitchlu and Satyapal arrested and deported on April 10. But instead of defusing the situation, the arrests outraged supporters and prompted them to march en masse to the British commissioner's camp. Raj troops opened fire on the crowd as they approached, killing several and turning the remainder into a terrorized mob that set fire to British banks and attacked English men and women in the streets. Order was restored when Brigadier-General R. E. H. Dyer arrived on the scene, but only temporarily. Three days later, on April 13, a crowd of 10,000 men, women, and children gathered in a park on a Sunday afternoon, not for political reasons but to celebrate a Hindu festival. Upon hearing that Sikhs had gathered at Jallianwala Bagh—in defiance of his order forbidding public assembly—Dyer's troops marched there, cornered the picnicking peasants, and, without warning, opened fire. "Dyer's troops fired for ten minutes, pouring 1,650 rounds of live ammunition into the unarmed mass of trapped humanity at point blank range. Some four hundred Indians were left dead, and twelve hundred wounded, when the brigadier and his force withdrew at sunset from the garden they had turned into a national graveyard" (Wolpert, p. 299). In the novel, Dr. Aziz is at the scene of the massacre. When he returns home covered in blood, Naseem cries out, "'But *where* have you *been,* my *God!*' 'Nowhere on earth,' he said, and began to shake in her arms" (*Midnight's Children*, p. 37).

News of the Jallianwala Bagh Massacre spread quickly and enraged not only Sikhs but Hindus and Muslims across India. The event turned even the staunchest loyalists of the British Raj into Indian nationalists, and calls for independence and the end of British rule echoed far and wide. The Raj, led by Viceroy Montagu, responded by relieving Dyer of his command (though he was given a hero's welcome in England, hailed as the "Saviour of the Punjab"). Montagu promised to implement immediate reforms, but Indian National Congress President Motilal Nehru (father/founder of the Nehru dynasty) called promises made by an "irresponsible executive and military" a "mockery," and leaders looked to their own means of achieving independence (Wolpert, p. 299).

Voices of division and unity. Though Indian leaders agreed on the urgent need for independence, they strongly disagreed on the form the new nation or government should take. Under Gandhi's influence, Congress had become an all-inclusive political entity dedicated to nationhood and Hindu-Muslim unity. But India was 70 percent Hindu, with the Hindu-dominated (though nominally secular) Congress as its primary mouthpiece; many Muslims therefore felt under-represented and distrusted Hindu leaders to heed their concerns. Moreover, using "divide and conquer" tactics, the British system of government had instituted separate electorates for Hindus and Muslims, thereby splitting leadership along religious lines and enhancing divisions. Congress President Jawaharlal Nehru proposed abolishing this system in a new Indian constitution, but Muslim League President Muhammad Ali Jinnah wanted to maintain it in order to guarantee Muslims one-third of the seats in the legislature. Nehru, like Gandhi, was opposed to division along religious lines, and Congress put forward a proposal to redistribute provincial boundaries on a linguistic basis. But Jinnah strongly denounced the proposal and warned that unless a new constitution assured Muslims greater security, there would be "revolution and civil war" (Jinnah in Wolpert, p. 312).

During the next 20 years, negotiations between Congress and the Muslim League over the issue of representation deteriorated as the positions of the two groups became more polarized. In 1930 Jinnah began to speak of partition, arguing that Hindus and Muslims belong to "two different religious philosophies, social customs, and literatures . . . indeed, they belong to two different civilizations," and in 1939 he and Fazlul Huq of Bengal drafted the Lahore Resolution that first put forward the idea of Pakistan as a separate nation (Jinnah in Wolpert, p. 331). Gandhi called the Resolution the "vivisection of India" and tried to persuade both sides to compromise. But he could not convince either Congress or the League to make any significant con-

cessions, and as World War II began, prospects of forging a consensus greatly diminished.

Independence and partition. By the end of World War II, the British had lost all desire to maintain rule in India. In February 1947, British

---

"EVENTS OF INDEPENDENCE"

1885 Indian National Congress founded to promote Indian self-rule.

1906 Muslim League founded.

1919 Rowlatt Acts; Jallianwala Bagh Massacre.

1920 *Satyagraha* campaign of "non-violent non-cooperation" and boycott of British goods and services, led by Mohandas Karamchand (M. K.) Gandhi.

1929 Constructive campaign of self-sufficiency, led by M. K. Gandhi, featuring "homespun" drive.

1930 Independence Day proclaimed by Jawaharlal Nehru (Jan. 26); Gandhi defies British salt tax.

1938 Sir Muhammad Iqbal murdered (April 21).

1939 Lahore Resolution—articulating demands that Pakistan become a separate nation comprised of the Muslim-majority provinces in eastern and northwestern India.

1942 Quit India movement, led by M. K. Gandhi, to oust the British Raj.

1946 Direct Action Day riots in Calcutta (Aug. 16); beginning of "civil war of secession"—5,000 dead, 100,000 homeless.

1947 Independence and partition (Aug. 15); 1-5 million die in communal violence; Congress leader Jawaharlal Nehru named first prime minister of independent India.

1948 M. K. Gandhi assassinated (Jan. 30); Muhammad Ali Jinnah dies (Sept. 1).

1951 Liaquat Ali Khan assassinated (Oct. 16).

1958 Pakistan military coup brings General Muhammad Ayub Khan to power.

1962 War with China over Himalayan border conflict; major military defeat for India.

1964 Jawaharlal Nehru dies of heart attack.

1965 India-Pakistan War over Kashmir—ends in stalemate in 22 days.

1971 Bangladesh War and independence (Dec. 16).

1975 State of Emergency declared by Indian Prime Minister Indira Gandhi.

1977 Emergency ends; Mrs. Gandhi defeated by Morarji Desai in national elections.

Prime Minster Clement Attlee announced that no later than June 1948, His Majesty's Government would transfer power to India and sent Lord Louis Mountbatten to serve as new Viceroy to oversee the operation. Mountbatten met with Jawaharlal Nehru and Liaquat Ali Khan (who represented the Muslim League and would become the first prime minister of Pakistan), and on April 20 Nehru agreed to the partition of the country.

On July 15, 1947—a year ahead of schedule—Mountbatten announced that independence and partition would take place in one month. Sheer pandemonium set in at his abrupt announcement. While government officials attempted to tally and divide India's assets and liabilities equally between two new nations in less than 30 days—82.5 percent for India, 17.5 percent for Pakistan—10 million Hindus and Muslims scrambled from their homes to find new ones, unsure of the exact borders they needed to cross or what they would encounter en route or at their final destinations. Tragically, what millions did encounter was a savage butchery perpetrated by all sides. From one to five million Indians—Muslim, Sikh, Jain, and Hindu—are estimated to have been killed in August 1947. Trainloads of slaughtered Muslims who arrived in Lahore, Pakistan, with the message "A present from India" written in blood across the car were answered with trainloads of murdered Hindus and Sikhs with the bloody message "A present from Pakistan" scrawled back (Mosley, p. 243). Muslims abducted, raped, and killed Hindu women; Hindus abducted, raped, and killed Muslim women; children caught in the wrong Hindu- or Muslim-controlled region were picked up by the feet, their heads dashed against the wall; neighbors turned guns on one another, buildings and farms were torched, land and life's work were lost, and families were torn apart forever. "There is no way of knowing how many parents were lost to their children in the sweep of this history, no way of knowing how many of them were lost by accident and how many by design" (Butalia, p. 41).

Whatever the final count, on all fronts the loss was catastrophic and the blame widespread. British haste and lack of adequate supervision during the transfer of power was grossly irresponsible, and the carnage and destruction perpetrated by Hindus and Muslims were indefensible. "Step by step, Delhi (Mountbatten) had been advised of the increasing gravity of the situation in the Punjab. The Viceroy had at least three chances to avert a massacre, and each

time—from weariness, from lack of foresight, or from aversion to another clash with Jinnah—he looked the other way. The result was disastrous" (Mosley, p. 216). Independence had finally come, but it was, in the words of Urdu poet Faiz Ahmad Faiz, "a scarred daybreak, a night-bitten dawn" (Ahmad Faiz in Tully, p. 13). In *Midnight's Children* Saleem and Shiva are born at the moment of India's independence and partition. The offspring of a violent and difficult birth, both the characters and the countries came about "in the age of darkness; so that although we found it easy to be brilliant, we were always confused about being good" (*Midnight's Children*, pp. 196-97).

Democratic underdevelopment. Redeeming his nation's "tryst with destiny," Jawaharlal Nehru became India's first prime minister; he sought "life and freedom" for the country after two centuries of foreign domination (Nehru in Wolpert, p. 349). However, he inherited a nation beset with problems that could not be easily overcome. As historian Bipin Chandra notes, "All the euphoria of freedom in 1947 could not hide the ugly reality of the colonial legacy that India inherited—the misery, the mud and filth . . . the changes that had come had led only to the development of underdevelopment" (Chandra in Tully, p. 149).

The development that the British had undertaken had indeed led to underdevelopment of the masses, as well as to the creation of an elite ruling class. Teeming with natural resources and a vast potential market for British goods, India had been a business enterprise for the British Empire, and the actions it took were designed to further those interests. The railway system was built to facilitate industry, the educational system to groom civil servants, and, while the majority of Indians remained illiterate, an elite group was singled out for privilege. The British created a vast bureaucratic network—the Indian Civil Service—and staffed it with their chosen elite, which included the Nehru family. These Anglicized, upper-caste and predominantly urban Indians became ICS administrators and politicians and alone were granted the vote (they comprised 14.2 percent of the population). Within the confines of this framework, class divisions widened, preparing only a select few for independence and leaving the majority uneducated, ostracized, agrarian, and wholly unfamiliar with the democratic process. This resulted in the "chosen elite" becoming a virtual monarchy at independence and created a political dynasty of the Congress Party and Nehru family in particular, who en-

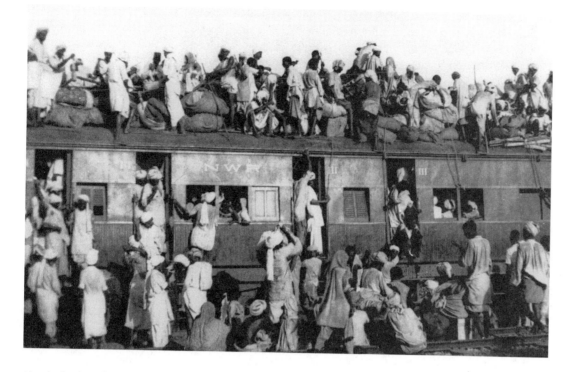

Hundreds of Muslim refugees crowd atop a train leaving New Delhi for Pakistan in September 1947, when India became independent of its British colonizers.

joyed an almost uninterrupted rule for the first 30 years.

1965 Indo-Pak War. In Pakistan the transition from independence to nationhood was not smooth, either. Jinnah died shortly after independence in 1948, Prime Minister Liaquat Ali Khan was assassinated in 1951, and a military coup in 1958 brought General Muhammad Ayub Khan to power. The territory of Kashmir had been disputed since partition, and at Nehru's death in 1964 tensions led to war. In the spring of 1965 the two nations began "sparring" in the Rann of Kutch, a desolate region both claimed, and the fighting escalated from there to Kashmir and the Punjab in August. Though Pakistan's Zulfikar Ali Bhutto officially denied that Pakistani soldiers were fighting in Kashmir, India's new Prime Minister Lal Bahadur Shastri declared that Pakistan's forces had invaded and vowed that "force and aggression against us will never be allowed to succeed" (Shastri in Wolpert, p. 375). Indian troops were sent to the Uri-Pooch "bulge" in Kashmir and also attacked Lahore in Pakistan. In the novel, Saleem insists the war was actually started by smugglers, working for the powerful Zulfikar family, whom Pakistani soldiers mistook for the Indian Army. "The story . . . is likely to be true as anything," Saleem says, "that is to say,

except what we were officially told" (*Midnight's Children*, p. 324). Whatever the cause, fighting easily escalated with the aid of propaganda on both sides. With memories of the bloody partition still fresh and easily exploitable, the governments of India and Pakistan each bolstered support through wild exaggerations. "In the first five days of the war Voice of Pakistan announced the destruction of more aircraft than India had ever possessed; in eight days, All-India Radio massacred the Pakistan Army down to, and considerably beyond, the last man" (*Midnight's Children*, pp. 328-29). On September 23, 1965, a UN-sponsored cease-fire took effect—just three weeks after the war had begun. Both sides were low on ammunition, more than 2,000 were dead, and neither had made any significant gains (India conquered 500 square miles of Pakistan, Pakistan 340 square miles into Indian-controlled Kashmir). Pre-war borders were restored exactly as they had been before the conflict, and an icy peace again developed.

1971 Indo-Pak War. Six years later, the legacy of partition laid its claim to the present again. Pakistan, now under another military ruler, General Yahya Khan, held its first nationwide popular election in December 1970. Sheikh Mujibur Rahman—an East Pakistani lobbying for Bengali autonomy—swept the elections, which put him in line to become prime minister. Yahya Khan was vehemently opposed to Bengali leadership in West Pakistan and immediately canceled the meeting of the National Assembly that would officially vote in Sheikh Mujib (Mujibur Rahman). In March 1971 talks to resolve the conflict broke down, and Mujib proclaimed East Pakistan to be "Bangladesh," a free country. As national flags

"NEHRU DYNASTY"

In Indian politics no family has been more influential than the so-called Nehru dynasty, which has ruled for more than 40 of the first 50 years of independence. Motilal inaugurated their life in government as the first president of the Indian National Congress. His son, Jawaharlal, followed his footsteps and became the first prime minister of India after independence in 1947. Two years after Jawaharlal's death in 1964, his daughter Indira Gandhi (no relation to M. K. Gandhi—she married a Parsi businessman, Firoze Gandhi, in 1952) became prime minister and served from 1966 to 1984, when she was assassinated (for three years, from 1977-80, she was out of office). Her sons, Sanjay and Rajiv, followed her into politics—Sanjay enthusiastically, Rajiv reluctantly. Sanjay, Mrs. Gandhi's close advisor who was being groomed to become prime minister, was killed in a plane crash in 1980, after *Midnight's Children* was written. Instead Rajiv became prime minister in 1984, then he too was assassinated in 1991. His widow, Sonia (an Italian), is currently head of the Congress party, serving in the Lok Sabha, or legislature, and has made several bids to become prime minister. Highly critical of this dynasty, Rushdie accuses Nehru and the Congress party of "clutching Time in their mummified fingers and refusing to let it move" (*Midnight's Children*, p. 317). He asserts that true democracy and progress will not take place in India until there is an end to this political legacy and a real changing of the guard.

were unfurled in Dacca (now Dhaka), Yahya Khan sent his crack troops to East Pakistan, where they attacked the capital, arrested Mujib, and brought him back to Karachi. Fierce fighting broke out as the cry of "Jai Bangla!—Victory to Bengal!" filled the streets. But Bengalis were seriously outgunned, and, fearing slaughter, millions of terrified citizens poured across the border to India. India appealed to the United Na-

tions to intervene and to United States President Richard Nixon to stop the flow of arms to West Pakistan. But Nixon refused (in fact, he was using Yahya Khan as a go-between to set up his summit with China) and, despite internal and international opposition, continued to supply weapons.

Bengali refugees flooded the Indian border—the largest mass exodus in history. By September 1971, 8-10 million were living in refugee camps, costing India $200 million a month to feed. Prime Minister Indira Gandhi, who had just overwhelmingly won her second term in office, realized that India had to intervene militarily. In December she sent Indian troops to attack Yahya Khan's forces in East Pakistan and maintain a "holding action" to contain his forces in the West. With both air superiority and mass popular support, the Indian Army advanced easily in the east and closed in quickly on Yahya Khan's forces in Dacca. On December 15 Pakistan surrendered and Mrs. Gandhi proclaimed, "Dacca is now the free capital of a free country!" (Wolpert, p. 390). Mujib was released, returned to Dacca, and became the first prime minister of Bangladesh in January.

Neocolonial nepotism. The 1971 war victory was a major triumph for Mrs. Gandhi and greatly broadened her power base, enabling her to push a sweeping reform package through the Indian parliament. Included in her program was a vow to eliminate corruption and nepotism—two of India's "oldest traditions" (Wolpert, p. 394). However, the Gandhi-Nehru family was as guilty as anyone in these practices. In fact, as she announced the crackdown on nepotism, she had just appointed her son Sanjay to be one of her top government advisors and given him a plum management job at India's new automobile factory (Maruti). As Saleem laments in the novel, "O endless sequence of nefarious sons-of-the-great!" (*Midnight's Children*, p. 323). In Pakistan, Saleem is quick to point out, the corruption, lies, and nepotism were equally prevalent—they just took different forms. In Pakistan, "a country where truth is what it is instructed to be," he says, "reality quite literally ceases to exist, so that everything becomes possible except what we are told is the case" (*Midnight's Children*, p. 315).

Though certainly perpetuated by post-colonial society, the British colonial legacy greatly contributed to corruption and the practice of nepotism in India and Pakistan. By creating elite ruling classes, the Raj vested power in privileged families who continue to run the nations' businesses and governments. With the creation of the ICS (which became the Indian Administrative Service) the British virtually institutionalized bribery and favoritism in a red-tape-engulfed bureaucratic system that rulers and administrators perfected through years of practice. It is a system, known in India as the "Neta-Babu Raj" (Politician Bureaucrat Government), that has thwarted progress and has become, in the eyes of many, the "bane" of India's national situation (Tully, p. 104; Fernandez in Tully, p. 48). As Rushdie notes, midnight's children, or the citizens born at independence, became both the "masters and victims of their own times"—victimized by the colonial systems they inherited and learned to master (*Midnight's Children*, p. 443).

Indira Raj and the Emergency. Though her popularity soared after India's military victory in 1971, Mrs. Gandhi found herself in political turmoil just four years later. In June 1975, with social unrest brewing due to massive inflation, allegations of corruption, and widespread poverty, Mrs. Gandhi was found guilty of election fraud in the 1971 elections—a charge that carried with it a mandatory penalty of banishment from public office for six years. Her political opponents—chiefly Jaya Prakash (known as J. P.) Narayan and Morarji Desai of the *Janata Morcha* (People's Front)—called for her immediate ouster and declared a national strike. Like "the spring of a cornered tigress determined to survive and keep her grip on what she had," Mrs. Gandhi responded by dissolving the government, arresting agitators, and declaring a state of emergency (Fishlock, p. 87). Much like the Rowlatt Acts, the Emergency suspended civil rights, dispensed with due process, and censored the press.

By August more than 10,000 of her political opponents were in jail, and Mrs. Gandhi put into effect her Twenty-Point Program of radical reforms. Included in the Program were two very unpopular reforms, led by her son Sanjay: slum eradication and forced sterilization. "Forced sterilization spread terror among the poor and illiterate. Village men fled at the sound of a jeep. In population control, as in slum clearance, officials felt licensed to act as brutally as they wished, as if the end justified even the cruellest of means" (Fishlock, p. 88). Sanjay—India's "man of tomorrow"—led the nation's youth movement (the Sanjay Youth Central Committee), forcing sterilization on the lower-class masses. At the same time, as part of the civic beautification program, bulldozers rolled through the big cities, leveling urban slums and leaving tens of thousands homeless. In the novel, Mrs. Gandhi and her programs prove to be Saleem's chief enemy. His dwelling is flattened by her government-sponsored bulldozers, his wife killed in the process, and he is sterilized, leaving him, he feels, without any future. "Test- and hysterectomized, the children of midnight were denied the possibility of reproducing themselves . . . but they drained us of more than that: hope, too, was excised" (*Midnight's Children*, p. 423). For India's poor, the inability to procreate was a devastating blow economically as well as psychologically. Children meant workers, and workers meant income. Therefore the inability to reproduce robbed them of their livelihood as well as of their progeny. Rushdie, vehemently opposed to Mrs. Gandhi's suspension of democracy, says his children of midnight are "a metaphor of hope" whose purpose was ultimately "destroyed by Mrs. Gandhi" (Rushdie in Weatherby, p. 47).

In 1977 the Emergency ended and Mrs. Gandhi was ousted in national elections by Morarji Desai. But as Saleem notes in the novel, like most his is an "amnesiac nation," and just months later "the Emergency was rapidly being consigned to the oblivion of the past" (*Midnight's Children*, p. 428). Indeed, before publication Mrs. Gandhi and the Congress party were back in power.

The Novel in Focus

Plot summary. Sitting in a Bombay pickle factory near the end of his life, Saleem begins telling his fantastic life story to his fiancée, Padma. A "child of midnight" born at the exact moment of India's independence and partition, Saleem is bestowed with not only an incredible life but with extraordinary gifts. He discovers he has the power of telepathy at age 10, and when his sinuses are drained he gains an uncanny sense of smell. His life becomes "embroiled in Fate"—specifically the fate of post-independence India as seen through the eyes of an English-educated Muslim boy from Bombay: "I have been a swallower of lives; and to know me, just the one of me, you'll have to swallow the whole lot" (*Midnight's Children*, p. 11). With this pronouncement, Saleem begins the story of his grandfather, Aadam Aziz, a doctor educated in Germany who returns to practice in Kashmir. A Muslim with an orthodox clientele, Dr. Aziz is repeatedly called to treat a young woman who seems to suffer from every ailment. Religious mores dictate that he can only examine the virgin Naseem through a hole in a perforated sheet, and he falls in love with her three square inches at a time. They marry and move to Amritsar, where Dr. Aziz finds himself in the midst of the Jallianwala Bagh massacre and cheats death due to the opportune timing of a sneeze.

Dr. Aziz becomes a supporter of Mian Abdullah's Islamic movement, which brings him into contact with Nadir Khan, Abdullah's secretary. When Abdullah is murdered, Nadir Khan is forced to go into hiding in Dr. Aziz's basement. While there, he falls in love with the doctor's daughter Mumtaz (an ebony-skinned beauty), and the two live underground in a Taj Mahal of their own making. But their happiness is short-lived; Nadir Khan is forced to divorce Mumtaz when he fails to consummate their marriage.

Mumtaz then marries Ahmed Sinai, who had been courting her sister Alia, and renames herself Amina. They move to Old Delhi, which is in the grip of the Ravana gang (*Ravana* is also the name of the villain of the Hindu epic *Ramayana*). An anti-Muslim band, the Ravana gang extort money and destroy those who don't pay. The gang ultimately burns down Sinai's business, but he is left with enough insurance money to begin a new life. At this time, Amina is pregnant and troubled by a prophecy told by a local fortuneteller about the son in her womb. The soothsayer, Ramram Seth, says, among other things: "There will be two heads—but you shall only see one. . . . Newspapers praise him, two mothers raise him! Sisters will weep, cobra will creep . . . spittoons will brain him—doctors will drain him . . . soldiers will try him—tyrants will fry him" (*Midnight's Children*, p. 87). In short, everything the soothsayer predicts comes true, but it's all riddles to Amina and serves only to disturb her sleep.

It is the summer of 1947, and at the behest of friends who tell Ahmed that the price of land is "dirt cheap" in Bombay, he takes the insurance money and moves his family west. They move into a large villa atop a hill purchased from an exiting Englishman, William Methwold. Two months later, at the stroke of midnight, August 15, 1947, Saleem is born to the Sinais. Actually Shiva is born to the Sinais, and Saleem is born to a poor woman named Vanita as Mr. Methwold's illegitimate child. But ayah (nanny) Mary Pereira switches the babies at birth, performing her own revolutionary act—giving the illegitimate child a life of privilege and the rich-born child a life of poverty. Just as the soothsayer predicted, *The Times of India* hails Saleem as the first baby of in-

dependence and posts his picture on the front page. He and 1,000 other children of midnight will grow with the nations. A letter from Nehru predicts that Saleem's fate will "in a sense mirror the country's," and Saleem proceeds to fulfill that prophecy (*Midnight's Children*, p. 122).

Book Two brings us to Saleem's childhood in Bombay. He is greatly influenced by the cosmopolitan city in which he grows up, particularly by the glitz and escapism of Bombay's film industry, or "Bollywood." He keeps in touch with his fellow midnight children by organizing conferences he facilitates with the help of his mind—he can bring everyone together through the power of telepathy he gains on his tenth birthday. There are 581 in his "club" (which represents the number of seats in the Lok Sabha or lower house of the Indian parliament; the other 419 did not survive their first decade of life), and he "plunged whenever possible into the separate, and altogether brighter reality of the five hundred and eighty-one" (*Midnight's Children*, pp. 194-95). While the distance grows between his father and mother as his father falls deeper and deeper into alcoholism, and they ignore him and his sisters annoy him, Saleem escapes into his other world. Repeatedly he "turns inwards to my secret Children" where he finds companionship and kinship (*Midnight's Children*, p. 247).

Saleem becomes a teenager and the family moves to Pakistan. Far from his children of midnight now, his telepathic ability dwindles, but when his sinuses are drained he gains incredible olfactory powers instead. His new power of smell is uncanny, and he begins to perfect a "science of nasal ethics" (*Midnight's Children*, p. 308). He can smell the good and the bad in people and events and creates his own moral hierarchy of odors. The problem is, he prefers the baser odors to those morally superior and starts to question his own moral fiber.

Just after the move to Pakistan, war with India breaks out (the Indo-Pak War of 1965). Aunt Alia, who moved to Karachi in the wake of Amina's marriage to her "rightful" husband, finally gets revenge against her sister. Both she and the war literally destroy the Sinai family—all but Saleem and his sister Jamila Singer escape falling bombs. Saleem is hit on the head with that prophesied spittoon, however, and the blow, combined with the sudden death of his parents and the trauma of the war, devastates him. Over the next six years, he becomes extremely withdrawn and introspective; the narration dubs him "the Buddha."

When war again breaks out in 1971, Saleem puts his keen olfactory powers to work and becomes a "man-dog," a tracker for the West Pakistani Army. He is the one who sniffs out Mujib in Dacca, but the deed causes him to question his actions and loyalties. Luckily, at this point a fellow Midnight Child, Parvati the witch, finds him and smuggles him back to Delhi with a band of circus magicians. Saleem comes to live in the magicians' ghetto with Parvati and marries her when he discovers she is pregnant with Shiva's child. By this point, Shiva has become a war hero and local playboy. He is working for Sanjay Gandhi's slum eradication campaign, whose bulldozers one day clear the magician's ghetto, killing Parvati. But the baby and Saleem live, and along with his snake-charmer friend, Picture Singh, they return to Bombay, where, Saleem discovers, Mary has made a fortune manufacturing pickles (highly apropos, considering the pickle she made of his life). He goes to work for the only mother he has left and meets his fiancée, Padma, there. Certain that his death is imminent, he begins telling his life's story to Padma in order that "one day, perhaps, the world may taste the pickles of history" (*Midnight's Children*, p. 444). Saleem marries Padma once the "pickles" are preserved, that is, once his history has been recorded and, while winding through the crowd after the ceremony, at last comes into contact with his destiny. Saleem foresees that he will be trampled by the crowd, but he has already preserved his life, as well as insured the future—through his son who is not his son and his history preserved in pages and pickles that are "waiting to be unleashed upon the amnesiac nation" (*Midnight's Children*, p. 443). Like the other children of midnight, he is trampled underfoot, but he will never be silenced. "A thousand and one children have died, because it is the privilege and the curse of midnight's children to be both masters and victims of their times, to forsake privacy and be sucked into the annihilating whirlpool of the multitudes, and to be unable to live or die in peace" (*Midnight's Children*, p. 446).

Methwold's legacy. Linking the microcosm to the macrocosm, Salman Rushdie uses the clever analogy of William Methwold fathering Saleem and abandoning his responsibility to illustrate the devastating long-term effects of British colonialism on India. Methwold represents the British Raj, Saleem the Indian born to chaos at midnight when the nation gains independence. Methwold, anxious to leave, sells out cheap to Saleem's family and exits hastily, leaving behind influences

and institutions intended and unintended, just as the British did in August 1947.

Intentionally Methwold leaves behind his mansions—his institutions—modeled after the best in Europe: Versailles, Buckingham, Escorial, Sans Souci. They are the palaces of Europe "sold on two conditions: that the houses be bought complete with every last thing in them, that the entire contents be retained by the new owners; and that the actual transfer should not take place until midnight on August 15, [1947]" (*Midnight's Children*, p. 95). Like the Raj, Methwold leaves his enormous Roman structures behind—an allegory of the vast bureaucratic and democratic frameworks that the British implemented and abruptly abandoned. They built their European monstrosities and filled them with their "things," which were of little or no use to the average Indians who inherited them. Amina has no use for portraits of "old Englishwomen" or Methwold's clothes in the cupboards (*Midnight's Children*, p. 96). In fact, there are so many British things cluttering the house, there is no place for any of her family's possessions or traditions. In Rushdie's analogy, Methwold's estate is the British government's colonial legacy—a vast entanglement of European institutions and systems that are preventing India from implementing its own democracy.

"I'm transferring power, too," Methwold tells Ahmed. "Got a sort of itch to do it at the same time the Raj does" (*Midnight's Children*, p. 96). But even he realizes that the British are pulling out too abruptly and leaving too much of a mess behind. "Bad show. Lost their stomachs for India. Overnight. . . . Seemed like they washed their hands—didn't want to take a scrap with them" (*Midnight's Children*, p. 96). As in Rushdie's allegory, after 200 years the British pulled up stakes and hurried back to England and like Methwold left more than just dirty laundry behind. They left a legacy; they left a people partly fathered by the British who now had to "live like those Britishers" and, as Amina says, clean up the stains that they left on the carpets (*Midnight's Children*, p. 96).

Like Mr. Methwold's conquest, the susceptible Vanita who bore his child, many Indians succumbed to British charms and seductive offers. When groomed for prime civil service positions, many eagerly accepted. In this way, as in the coupling of Vanita and Methwold, the Raj fathered a whole new class within India—the ICS bureaucracy and political dynasty that would linger long after the British pulled out. But, as with

Methwold's progeny, some offspring of this union were unintentional. The British seeds surely impregnated these "chosen elite," but, as in the case of Saleem, they also produced unplanned and illegitimate heirs. These "unintentional" children born at midnight represented the masses who were left to rebuild and to contend with the British institutions left behind. Like Saleem, these bastard children were impeded by the massive foreign structures that barred their entry, while others, like Indira Gandhi—part of the legitimate "chosen elite"—were born into those halls and held power so tightly that no others could wrest it away.

In this elaborate analogy, Rushdie also attributes the bloody communal violence at independence to Methwold's charms and powers of illusion. His hair—perfectly parted down the middle—is a gorgeous vision of India unified and equally divided. But, as Padma says, it is "too good to be true" and turns out to be a wig (*Midnight's Children*, p. 113). It is a hairpiece masking a barren landscape. It comes off as the lid comes off in India and communal rioting tears the nation apart. Methwold's hair is as slick as his talk and just as false. When the truth is revealed, he "distributes, with what looks like carelessness, the signed title—deeds to his palaces; and drives away" (*Midnight's Children*, p. 113). And Saleem, though he's never seen his father, finds him "impossible to forget," as does the rest of India, who are left with his colonial legacy (*Midnight's Children*, p. 113).

Using the allegory of Methwold, Rushdie mingles history and fantasy to show the lasting effects of colonialism on India. Like Saleem, the nation of India is the illegitimate offspring of the English. Saleem is both Ahmed and William's son-who-is-not-their-son and repeats the process with a son-who-is-not-his-son (but Shiva's son). In fact, all the children of Saleem's generation are born with this dual legacy and lineage. "All over the new India, the dream we all shared, children were being born who were only partially the offspring of their parents—the children of midnight were also the children of the time: fathered, you understand, by history" (*Midnight's Children*, p. 117). Through these relationships—these illegitimate children—Rushdie's novel shows that the neocolonial pattern will persist until there is real change in India. It seems to be arguing that until the European chains are broken and there is a substantive restructuring of the institutions and dynasties left behind, neocolonialism will continue to thwart Indian democracy and progress.

Sources and literary context. Though it is set at the independence of India, Pakistan, and Bangladesh and traces many related events, Rushdie himself hesitates to call *Midnight's Children* a "historical" novel. He describes it as a "political novel which transcends politics" (Rushdie in Weatherby p. 47). Clearly impacted by the Emergency of 1975 and the colonial legacy that contributed to it, Rushdie bases much of the novel and characters on actual people and events. But he is also quick to point out that the main characters are not based on himself or his family—in fact, the "most autobiographical things in the book are the places. Saleem's house is the house I grew up in . . . the school that he goes to is my school . . . those things are certainly based on my childhood" (Rushdie in May, p. 415). Rushdie cites the novel's literary influences, crediting, in addition to Gabriel García Márquez, Laurence Sterne, and Günter Grass, Nicolai Gogol, and Franz Kafka. He draws equally on Western and Eastern influences, consciously choosing the imagery of Saleem's family nose to invoke "The Nose" (Gogol), *Tristram Shandy* (Sterne), *Cyrano de Bergerac* (Edmond Rostand), and Ganesh (the elephant-headed god of good fortune, as well as the patron deity of literature in the Hindu pantheon). He also uses the Hindu gods Shiva and Parvati as characters and evokes Krishna often.

The structure of the novel draws from Indian epics like the *Mahabharata* and the *Ramayana* and is indebted to the traditions of oral cultures. Most obviously, the storyteller Saleem serves as a bard who relates his version of an epic tale, recording individual histories to convey a universal truth. Rushdie also blends the grandeur of epic with the melodrama of Bombay cinema. Not only does the novel's reproduction of memory imitate the long shots and close-ups of cinematic technique, but scenes in the novel conjure up the "Bombay talkies" of which Rushdie was enamored during his childhood. Children's classics and fairy tales, such as *The Arabian Nights,* clearly influence the content and structure of the novel as well. It is no coincidence that there are 1,001 children of midnight—the novel is at once a fantasy and a morality tale designed to entertain and enlighten its audience.

Reception. Upon publication, *Midnight's Children* was almost universally acclaimed. It won the 1981 Booker Prize for fiction, garnering praise as "comic, exuberant, ambitious, and stylistically brilliant" (May, p. 412). Anita Desai declared that Rushdie had painted a new portrait of India, and wrote, "*Midnight's Children* will surely be recognized as a great tour de force, a dazzling exhibition of the gifts of a new writer of courage, impressive strength, the power of both imagination and control and sheer stylistic brilliance" (Desai, p. 13). Writing for the *New York Times*, Clark Blaise said Rushdie's novel provided the ingredient Indian fiction had been missing: "a touch of Saul Bellow's Augie March brashness, Bombay rather than Chicago-born and going at things in its own special Bombay way" (Blaise, p. 18). Robert Towers in the *New York Review of Books* wrote that "no one should pick up *Midnight's Children* in the expectation of a rousing good story" and discredited its movement as "constantly impeded, dammed up, clogged." But despite that criticism, the review concluded by saying that Rushdie was one of the most important writers to come out of the English-speaking world in this generation (Towers, p. 30). The novel signified a bold new direction in British literature and was called the "great Indian Novel" (Weatherby, p. 41). It later won the Best of the Bookers award in 1993 as the best novel of the first 25 years of the prize's history.

—Diane Renée

For More Information

Blaise, Clark. Review of *Midnight's Children*, by Salman Rushdie. *New York Times Book Review*, 19 April 1981, 18.

Butalia, Urvashi. *The Other Side of Silence*. Durham, N.C.: Duke University Press, 2000.

Chandra, Bipan, Mridula Mukherjee, et al. *India's Struggle for Independence*. New Delhi: Penguin India, 1989.

Desai, Anita. Review of *Midnight's Children*, by Salman Rushdie. Book World, *Washington Post*, 15 March 1981, 13.

Fishlock, Trevor. *Gandhi's Children*. New York: Universe Books, 1983.

May, Hal, ed. *Contemporary Authors*. Vol. 111. Detroit: Gale Research, 1984.

Mosley, Leonard. *The Last Days of the British Raj*. New York: Harcourt Brace and World, 1961.

Reder, Michael R. ed. *Conversations with Salman Rushdie*. Jackson: University Press of Mississippi, 2000.

Rushdie, Salman. *Midnight's Children*. New York: Knopf, 1989.

Tharoor, Shashi. *India: From Midnight to the Millennium*. New York: Arcade, 1997.

Towers, Robert. Review of *Midnight's Children*, by Salman Rushdie. *New York Review of Books*, 24 September 1981, 30.

Tully, Mark. *India: 40 Years of Independence*. New York: George Braziller, 1988.

Weatherby, W. J. *Salman Rushdie: Sentenced to Death*. New York: Carroll & Graf, 1990.

Wolpert, Stanley. *A New History of India*. New York: Oxford University Press, 1997.

The Moonstone

by
Wilkie Collins

⌢

A prolific writer, Wilkie Collins (1824-89) authored some 25 novels, along with numerous articles, short stories, and plays. He was a close friend and collaborator of his elder contemporary, the novelist Charles Dickens (1812-70), who also served as editor of periodicals. Beginning in the 1850s, Dickens serialized Collins's novels in his periodicals *Household Words* (1850-59) and its successor *All the Year Round* (1859-88). The two friends also worked together on a number of short stories for the periodicals, and jointly wrote, produced, and acted in plays for Dickens's stage company as well. Best known among Collins's novels are, *The Woman in White* (1860) and *The Moonstone* (1868); both were serialized in *All the Year Round* and later adapted by Collins for production on the stage. Collins's tales are memorably dramatic, featuring strong villains and victimized heroines. In *The Moonstone* these plot elements are combined with crime and detection in a way that would distinguish the book, in the eyes of many modern critics, as the first true detective novel in English. Present-day critics have also seen deeper concerns at work in Collins's novels, which question many of the assumptions on which Victorian society rested. At the heart of his social critiques lies Collins's contempt for abuses of power, whether at home in Britain or abroad in the British Empire. It is with one such abuse that *The Moonstone* begins, when a British army officer plunders a famous diamond from the palace of a defeated local ruler in India.

THE LITERARY WORK

A novel set primarily in Yorkshire and London in 1848-50; first published in London in 1868.

SYNOPSIS

After a fabled Indian diamond disappears under mysterious circumstances from an English country house, attempts to recover it lead to intrigue and murder.

Events in History at the Time of the Novel

The British Raj. Britain's presence in India began in the seventeenth century, when the English East India Company established a handful of coastal trading posts (called "factories") at sites from Surat in the west (1619) to Calcutta in the east (1690). Only in the middle of the eighteenth century, however, with the breakup of India's Mughal Empire into warring states, did British influence begin to extend inland from the coast. In attempting to improve the East India Company's commercial and strategic position within India, the British faced stiff competition from the French, who wished to further their own commercial and colonial interests. The colonial rivalry continued until Britain's victory in the Napoleonic Wars in 1815, though the British had gained the upper hand in India by the 1760s. French influence in the final decades of the eighteenth century was limited to backing Indian

Wilkie Collins

rulers hostile to the East India Company, whose large armies now controlled the region of Bengal (today's Bangladesh) and were poised to expand British power further.

After the 1760s, France's best chance at upsetting British momentum in India came in 1798, when one of those anti-British rulers, Tipu Sultan of Mysore, took up negotiations with the French intending to arm himself against the raj, as British rule in India was known. At the same time, Napoleon Bonaparte occupied Egypt, posing a threat to the English since the brilliant French commander could use Egypt as a springboard from which to launch the overthrow of British rule in India. This so-called "scare of 1798" ended when the British Navy under Admiral Nelson shattered the French Mediterranean fleet in August of that year, and British forces under General David Baird captured Tipu Sultan's capital of Seringapatam in May 1799. The victorious British troops pillaged Tipu's opulent palace; in fact, Baird himself was reported to have participated in the widespread looting. This well-known historical event, the storming of Seringapatam, provided Collins with an exotic origin for his tale, which begins when a fictional British officer, Colonel John Herncastle, loots a sacred diamond known as the Moonstone from Tipu's palace.

While the events of 1799 open the story, the main action is set half a century later, in 1848-50, when the diamond is bequeathed to Herncastle's niece, Rachel Verinder. By that time, Britain had expanded its control throughout India, so that virtually the entire subcontinent was ruled either by the British directly or by states dependent on Britain. In 1849, the East India Company annexed the Punjab in the northwest, the last major region in India to remain independent. Yet less than a decade later, the British would be shocked by a stark demonstration of Indian resentment at foreign domination. In 1857, Indian troops, called *sepoys*, revolted against their British commanders. When the troops' discontent was picked up and amplified by Indian society at large, the revolt grew into more than simply a military problem for the British. The British have referred to the unrest as the Great Mutiny; today, Indians call it their First War for Independence. Fighting was bloody, and atrocities were committed by both sides, including the well-publicized murders of hundreds of British women and children. Only after a protracted military campaign were the British able to restore control in 1859, but the now enfeebled East India Company was dissolved and henceforth India was ruled directly by the British government.

The rebellion had been caused, of course, by Britain's assuming the role of superior power and, less obviously, by its insensitivity to Hindu customs. For example, orthodox Hindus were considered to be polluted if they crossed the sea, yet British commanders insisted on posting Indian troops overseas. In *The Moonstone* three determined Brahmins (Hindu priests) journey overseas to England to recover the diamond, which Collins describes as holding religious significance for them. By incurring this pollution, they thus willingly sacrifice their high status as Brahmins. Collins, writing a decade after the unrest of 1857-59, could have counted on many of his readers to recall its background, and understand the implications tied to the Brahmins' actions. He used this and other details to increase the novel's verisimilitude.

Victorian Britain and the outside world. Queen Victoria (ruled 1837-1901) gave her name to an era that saw dramatic advances for Britain both at home and abroad. While rapid changes brought prosperity at home, increasing power abroad, and the pride of an imperial nation to Britain, they also created social tensions, bleak social problems, and, for many, a reflexive fear of anything foreign. Like the British raj, considered the "jewel in the crown" of Britain's worldwide empire, British society itself by the middle of the nineteenth century possessed a veneer of assurance and arrogance that overlaid deeper insecurities.

Historians commonly divide the Victorian era into three periods roughly spanning the length of Queen Victoria's reign: early Victorian (about 1830 to 1850); middle Victorian (about 1850 to 1875); and late Victorian (about 1875 to 1900). Rapid industrialization, overcrowded cities, and economic dislocation made the early period one of social and political turbulence. This turmoil was expressed by two movements in particular: that of the Chartists, who agitated for political reform (such as abolishing the property qualification for Parliament); and the campaign to repeal the Corn Laws, which kept grain prices artificially high. The Chartists, whose petition to Parliament in 1839 was rejected despite having garnered over 1.2 million signatures, held huge demonstrations in London in 1842 and 1848. The demonstration in 1848 led many to fear a revolution in Britain similar to those occurring throughout Europe in that tumultuous year. For readers of The Moonstone, the character of the poor but fiery girl called Limping Lucy would have recalled this fear: "the day is not far off," she declares, "when the poor will rise against the rich" (Collins, The Moonstone, p. 248). But the Corn Laws, which (like the laws to which Chartists objected) favored wealthy, aristocratic landowners at the expense of the poor, were repealed in 1849. Their repeal, along with growing economic prosperity in the 1850s, eased much of the unrest that dominated the 1840s.

Perhaps the biggest boost to the economy in the 1850s was the completion of a national rail system. By 1850 about 5,000 miles of track had been laid, reaching most parts of the country and allowing for rapid travel and vastly expanded commerce. The effects of rail transportation revolutionized life for everyone. For example, London newspapers could now be delivered overnight to Scotland; fresh foods could bring variety to diets in areas that had not changed eating habits for centuries. At the Verinder country home in Yorkshire, the remote setting of much of the novel, railway timetables are posted in the front hall for the convenience of guests returning to London. Steamships, too, likewise sped up sea travel, and were coordinated with trains for the convenience of international travelers. When Franklin Blake, the hero of The Moonstone, goes abroad, he takes a "tidal train," a class of train flexibly scheduled to connect with a steamship leaving on the outgoing tide (The Moonstone, p. 250).

Further technological advances came rapidly in the two decades between the novel's setting and its composition. Most significantly, improvements in the telegraph (invented earlier in the century) meant that by 1854, when lines across Europe were finished, messages that had taken weeks or even months could now be sent in seconds. By 1866 a transatlantic cable had linked Europe with North America. The Victorian world was shrinking rapidly—but the results were not always comforting. For example, the 1850s also brought the Crimean War, which was the first war to be covered by foreign correspondents. These innovative reporters took advantage of the improvements in communication to send firsthand reports from the front lines. In this war, which lasted for two years (1854-56)

INDIAN MYTHOLOGY AND THE MOONSTONE

In Indian mythology Chandra, or Soma, is the name of the Moon god. The moon gem, or the Chandrakanta, serves a purpose. It absorbs the rays of the moon, then transforms and emits them as cool, unadulterated moisture.

and pitted Britain and France against Russia, military disasters and gruesome casualties could thus be described with an immediacy that many found shocking. Rapid communication similarly allowed the Great Mutiny of 1857 to be widely publicized in Britain, leading to a growing public awareness not only of Britain's imperial role, but also of the dangers inherent in it.

Crime and literature: "detective-fever." While crime rates in the Victorian era are thought to have been generally lower than in earlier times, they were higher in the 1840s than at any other time in the century. Urban growth (by 1850 half the nation's population would live in cities) and economic dislocation had created a new concern for public safety. In 1842, the London Metropolitan Police, which had been established in 1829, set up a detective department called Scotland Yard after its original location. Staffing it were two inspectors and six sergeants. By the 1850s, other cities had begun forming their own police forces and crime rates dropped steadily for the rest the century.

As police constables became a familiar sight on city streets, improved communications and the growth of mass media such as newspapers, magazines, and books helped both to create and to satisfy a growing public interest in crime and law enforcement. Just as with so many other Victorian literary trends, Collins's influential friend Charles Dickens led the way in 1850, writing two articles based on the exploits of a real-life police detective for his magazine *Household Words*. Dickens's subject was one of Scotland Yard's two original inspectors, Jonathan Whicher, whom he called Witchem in the articles. In 1860, amid great publicity, Whicher was called on to help solve the sensational Constance Kent murder case, in which the victim, a four-year-old boy named Francis Kent, had been found with his throat brutally slashed at his home in the small

---

SCOTLAND YARD

The famed British police detective force was originally located at Great Scotland Yard, the sight where Scottish royalty were housed when visiting London. Scotland Yard was reorganized and expanded in 1878, when it established its Criminal Investigation Division (C.I.D.). Shortly thereafter, it was relocated, but the name "Scotland Yard" stuck despite the detective force's moves to new quarters in 1890 and 1967.

---

village of Road in southwestern England. Whicher suspected the boy's sister, Constance, but was unable to locate a nightgown belonging to her that he believed must have been stained with Francis's blood. Without this key piece of evidence, Constance was acquitted, though in 1865 she confessed to the crime and to destroying the nightgown. Whicher's reputation suffered further when he arrested an innocent man in a separate case the following year, and public opinion forced Whicher to retire in disgrace.

In the 1850s and 1860s, such widely followed cases created what one character in *The Moonstone* calls "detective-fever" (*The Moonstone*, p. 182). Collins himself followed the Constance Kent case carefully, and critics have noted several details that he incorporated into *The Moonstone*: a stained and missing nightgown is one of the novel's central clues, for example, though it

is stained with paint, not blood; and the novel's professional detective, Sergeant Cuff, who like Whicher is wily and experienced, also proves to be fallible.

The Novel in Focus

Plot summary. The plot unfolds in a series of narratives, journal entries, and letters recorded by those characters in the tale who witnessed certain key events. A prologue purports to be taken from Herncastle family papers relating to the storming of Seringapatam in 1799, and to the subsequent theft of the Moonstone by Colonel John Herncastle. A large yellow diamond, the Moonstone was originally set in the forehead of a statue of the Hindu moon god before being stolen from its temple by a Mughal emperor and, much later, acquired by Tipu Sultan. Herncastle steals it from Tipu's palace, though he knows that a curse supposedly hangs over anyone who lays hands on the famous diamond. He has also heard that the three Brahmin priests of the temple from which the Moonstone was originally taken, priests who are the descendants of the three original guardians, have dedicated their lives to recovering it.

The first and longest narrative begins in 1848 and is told by Gabriel Betteredge, the head servant at the Verinder house near Frizingham, on the Yorkshire coast. Lady Verinder, whose husband is deceased, is the younger sister of John Herncastle. As Betteredge relates, the household is expecting the arrival that evening of Franklin Blake, a young nephew of Lady Verinder's, who has been studying abroad. That afternoon, the house is visited by three Indians dressed as traveling jugglers, whom Betteredge sends on their way. He also has to discipline one of the maids, Rosanna Spearman, a plain girl with a deformed shoulder who is unpopular with the other servants. She has left her work to go for a walk, claiming to need fresh air. Betteredge follows Rosanna to the Shivering Sand, a desolate patch of quicksand on the coast near the house that he knows is her favorite spot. While Betteredge and Rosanna sit talking at the Shivering Sand, they are surprised by the appearance of Franklin Blake, who has arrived at the house early and immediately sought out Betteredge. When Rosanna sees Blake, she blushes and awkwardly excuses herself.

Blake explains his early arrival. He has been followed in London for several days by "a certain dark-looking stranger" and thinks his

A reproduction of an 1883 wood engraving featuring visitors to Scotland Yard's Metropolitan Police Criminal Museum.

watcher might be connected with the three jugglers Betteredge saw earlier that afternoon (*The Moonstone*, p. 82). Indeed, he suspects that the Indians are after the Moonstone, which he then shocks Betteredge by producing from his pocket. Herncastle, ostracized both by English society and by his own family because of his actions at Seringapatam, has left the diamond to his niece, Rachel Verinder, Lady Verinder's young daughter. She is to take possession of it on her eighteenth birthday. Blake's father, as Herncastle's executor, has given Blake the task of delivering it to his cousin Rachel, whose birthday is approaching. Knowing the diamond's past, Blake wonders if the spiteful Herncastle has deliberately left "a legacy of trouble and danger" to Rachel in revenge for his rejection by Lady Verinder and the rest of the family (*The Moonstone*, p. 88).

In the days leading up to Rachel's birthday party, she and Blake spend time together painting a floral design on Rachel's bedroom door. They finish the task on the afternoon of the party. Blake has a rival for Rachel's attentions, however, in a third cousin, Godfrey Ablewhite, who has

also arrived several days before the party. The party itself is subdued, although Rachel is pleased with the diamond. The atmosphere worsens when Blake, who suffers from sleeplessness after quitting smoking, argues with Mr. Candy, a surgeon, over the effectiveness of modern medicine in dealing with such ailments. (A surgeon is addressed in Britain as Mister, while a physician is addressed as Doctor.) Another guest, Mr. Murthwaite, who has traveled extensively in India, identifies the three Indians (again seen nearby) as Brahmins, members of the highest priestly caste. Despite warnings, Rachel insists on wearing the valuable diamond and on keeping it that night in an unlocked drawer in her bedroom. The next morning, the Moonstone is gone.

When the local police superintendent proves unable to trace the missing diamond, Blake arranges for Lady Verinder to hire the celebrated Sergeant Richard Cuff of Scotland Yard. Cuff quickly rules out the Indians, whom the local superintendent had suspected, and directs his attention to a small smear on Rachel's newly painted door. Questioning the members of the household, he establishes that the smear had to have been made between the time Rachel went to bed and 3 A.M., when the paint would have been completely dry. Therefore, it was likely made during the theft. Find the garment with a smear of paint, Sergeant Cuff declares, and it will lead to the thief. But a search of the house fails to turn up either a stained garment or the missing diamond.

While both Blake and Betteredge (who catches what he calls "detective-fever") take an active interest in assisting the investigation, Rachel surprisingly appears uninterested, even obstructive. Furthermore, she seems inexplicably hostile to Blake for his efforts to uncover the thief. Cuff concludes that she has stolen the diamond herself to pay a secret debt of some sort. He sug-

KEY CHARACTERS IN *THE MOONSTONE*

Gabriel Betteredge	Head servant in the Verinder household
Lady Julia Verinder	Colonel Herncastle's younger sister
Rachel Verinder	Lady Verinder's young daughter
Franklin Blake	Rachel's cousin
Godfrey Ablewhite	Rachel's cousin
Rosanna Spearman	A servant in the Verinder household
Limping Lucy	A friend of Rosanna's
Miss Clack	A distant Verinder relative
Mr. Candy	The Verinders' doctor
Ezra Jennings	Mr. Candy's assistant
Sergeant Cuff	A police detective
Matthew Bruff	The Verinders' lawyer
Mr. Murthwaite	An expert on India
Septimus Luker	A London moneylender

gests she was assisted by Rosanna Spearman, who had been given her job despite a record as a thief, and who has acted suspiciously since the diamond's disappearance. Rosanna, who has fallen hopelessly in love with Blake, drowns herself in the Shivering Sand. To protect her daughter, Lady Verinder dismisses Sergeant Cuff from the case. Closing her house in Frizingham, she takes Rachel to London, and the broken-hearted Franklin Blake embarks on a long voyage abroad. Thus ends Gabriel Betteredge's narrative.

The story is then taken up by Drusilla Clack, another relative of the Verinders' who was also present at the birthday party. Humorously portrayed as a hypocritical and interfering "Evangelical," the pious Miss Clack lives in London, where she and Godfrey Ablewhite, whom she reveres, are active in a number of charitable causes. As Miss Clack relates, Ablewhite has been mysteriously attacked by an unknown assailant, who lures him into an empty apartment, ties him up, searches him, and then leaves. Also attacked in the same way is Mr. Septimus Luker, a London moneylender whom Rosanna Spearman had known, and from whom the attackers steal a receipt for "a valuable of great price" (*The Moonstone*, p. 264). When rumors spread in London society linking Ablewhite with Luker (to whom Ablewhite is thought to have pawned the diamond), Rachel is distressed. She declares that she positively knows her cousin Ablewhite to be innocent of the theft. Soon afterward, Lady Verinder dies from a heart condition, and Rachel agrees to marry Godfrey Ablewhite, whose father (Rachel's uncle) has become her guardian. The Verinder family lawyer, Mr. Bruff, then contributes a brief narrative. He tells how he has accidentally learned that Ablewhite is deeply in debt and is only marrying Rachel for her money. Bruff informs Rachel, and she breaks the engagement. Consulting with Murthwaite, the guest who traveled to India, Bruff also concludes that the Indians, who seem to have been responsible for the attacks on Ablewhite and Luker, are planning to intercept the diamond when Luker takes it out of the bank where he has deposited it.

At this point Franklin Blake, returned from his travels, picks up the story. He calls on Rachel after arriving in England, but, suspecting him of stealing the diamond, she refuses to see him or to answer his letters. Deciding that the only way to overcome her enmity is to recover the diamond, Blake goes to the Verinder house at Frizington, in hopes that he and Betteredge can take up the investigation where they left off. Betteredge takes him to Rosanna's friend, Limping Lucy, who gives him a letter that Rosanna had left with her. In the letter, Rosanna instructs Blake to go to the Shivering Sand, where she has secreted something that will explain her strange behavior before her suicide. Following her instructions, Blake and Betteredge go to the Sand and retrieve a watertight box in which Rosanna has secreted another letter and the missing stained nightgown. Blake is shocked to find that the nightgown is his own. The accompanying letter discloses Rosanna's love for him and tells him that she had found the nightgown when straightening his room the morning after the theft. Realizing its significance, she had then hidden it to protect him from being discovered as the thief.

Confused and disturbed, Blake then returns to London where, with the connivance of Mr. Bruff, he contrives a meeting with Rachel. She tells him that she saw him take the Moonstone with her own eyes, and that she too has kept the secret to protect him. Now desperate for an explanation, Blake interviews the enigmatic Ezra Jennings, the surgeon Mr. Candy's assistant, a terminally ill outcast who is shunned by the townspeople for his strange appearance. Jennings had saved Candy's life the night of the party, when Candy returned from the Verinders' with a high fever. The illness, which lasted days and almost killed the surgeon, impaired Candy's memory, and Jennings took over Candy's medical practice. While delirious with fever, Candy revealed that, smarting from the dinner argument with Blake, Candy had secretly slipped Blake a dose of opium as a joking rebuttal to Blake's attack on the effectiveness of modern medicine. The opium, thought Candy, would prove his point by relieving Blake of the insomnia about which Blake complained.

Jennings, who had recorded Candy's ravings and now reveals this intended joke to Blake, suggests that Blake, concerned for the Moonstone's safety, might have unknowingly taken the diamond himself under the drug's influence. Jennings also proposes that they reconstruct the conditions of that night as closely as possible to test his theory. The experiment is recorded in Jennings's journal. Blake again quits smoking; and after Jennings gives him opium, Blake gets up in the night and takes a stand-in gem from Rachel's unlocked drawer. He collapses before revealing what he did next, however, and remembers nothing of the incident the next morning. Rachel, who has agreed to be present for the experiment, loved him all along but had been heartbroken to believe him a thief.

Returning to London, Blake resumes the narrative, relating that in the meantime Mr. Bruff, the lawyer, has had Luker watched. The moneylender is seen to leave his house one morning accompanied by two guards. Blake and Bruff then hurry to Luker's bank, from which they see him exit and pass something to a tall bearded man who looks like a sailor, and whom Bruff's assistant follows to a dockside inn. Sergeant Cuff, whom Blake has recalled to the case, accompanies Blake and Bruff to the inn the next morning, where they discover the sailor's body in one of the rooms. When Cuff pulls off the fake beard, the body is revealed as Godfrey Ablewhite's.

Cuff, having interrogated Luker, contributes a brief narrative that reconstructs the sequence of events. As Luker has revealed, Blake in his opium-induced stupor had entrusted Ablewhite with the Moonstone after taking it from Rachel's room. Deeply in debt and leading a licentious double life, Ablewhite had kept the diamond to save himself from exposure and disgrace. He had pawned it to Luker, explaining how he had obtained it; despite his disguise, when he redeemed it from the moneylender, the Indians followed him to the inn, where they killed him and took back the Moonstone. Finally, in a letter from Murthwaite to Bruff, we learn that Murthwaite (traveling again in India) has witnessed the ceremony in which the Moonstone was restored to the forehead of the Hindu moon-god.

COLLINS AND OPIUM

Collins suffered from a painful condition called gout, for which he began taking opium before beginning *The Moonstone*. Opium was commonly prescribed for pain, as well as for a wide range of psychological ailments that the Victorians called "nervousness" or "hysteria." Like Ezra Jennings, Collins soon became accustomed to doses that would kill another person; he would continue taking the drug until his death in 1889. Just as Jennings's use of opium helped him deduce part of the mystery's solution, Collins's use contributed to his creation of the puzzle, by offering personal experience of the drug's effects.

Uneasy legacies. Critics have observed that the Indian elements in the story—the three Brahmins, and what Betteredge calls the "devilish Indian Diamond" itself—collectively constitute an alien threat that at first looms darkly over the cozy tranquility of the story's English setting (*The Moonstone*, p. 88). The Indians' menacing presence in the novel's early pages would have struck a responsive chord with a readership in which deep fears and racial hatred remained fresh after the bloody events of 1857. Popular attitudes after the uprising of 1857 were expressed bluntly by Collins's friend Charles Dickens, who wrote that if given the chance he would wipe the entire Indian race off the face of the earth.

But Collins's reaction to India and what it represented was more measured and sympathetic than his friend's. Indeed, it has been argued that the novel (particularly in its portrayal of the rapacious Herncastle) amounts to a biting and subversive indictment of British imperialism. British greed incites the Indians' behavior, and the foreign threat turns out to be less dire than the domestic one. The Moonstone, John Herncastle's uneasy legacy, is stolen by a second greedy and opportunistic Englishman, while the three ominously lurking Indians of the novel's early pages end up representing such honorable ideals as duty and religious devotion.

Just as critics have suggested that *The Moonstone* challenged Britain's imperial values, they have also seen the novel as questioning the values of British society at home. Most obviously, in the ludicrously self-righteous Miss Clack, Collins lampoons the hypocrisy of the do-gooder whose pious professions cloak less noble motives

THE DETECTIVE NOVEL

The Moonstone established many of the criteria for the classic English detective novel:

• A single mysterious crime in a remote country house
• Suspicion thrown on a number of characters in turn, after which an unlikely (or the least likely) suspect is shown to be guilty
• A bungled initial investigation, after which a famous detective is called in
• A mystery that follows the "rules of fair play," i.e. the reader encounters the same clues as the detective(s)

(Miss Clack, for example, affects disregard for Lady Verinder's will, but secretly has her hopes set on a bequest). The novel's villain, Godfrey Ablewhite, at first seems more genuinely to epitomize Victorian piety and respectability, though his hypocrisy too is progressively exposed to the reader. In contrast, Collins's deepest sympathy seems reserved for the novel's outcasts from respectable society, whose physical grotesqueness accompanies an essential sincerity: the deformed and unpopular Rosanna Spearman, tormented by her socially inappropriate love for Franklin Blake; and the sharp-minded but equally tormented Ezra Jennings, who ultimately performs the novel's most impressive feat of deduction. Both reveal key parts of the story but die before it ends. The truth is their uneasy legacy in *The Moonstone*, just as greed is the uneasy legacy of a "civilized" empire.

Sources and literary context. In addition to the Constance Kent murder case, another real life crime also inspired parts of *The Moonstone*. In July 1861, a man named William Murray was lured to an address in London, attacked from behind, and shot in the head. Despite his wound, Murray resisted and mortally injured his assailant, whose name was William Roberts. While Murray at first claimed that Roberts was a complete stranger to him, it later appeared the two had quarreled over Murray's wife. The case never attracted the wide attention of the Kent mystery, but it did receive ample coverage. Collins used its basic ingredients for the episode in which Ablewhite and Luker are lured to two London addresses and attacked by mysterious assailants about whom they claim to know nothing, but with whom they are in fact involved.

Collins took pains to be accurate in his details. His research sources included C. W. King's *Natural History, Ancient and Modern, of Precious Stones* (1865) for diamonds and diamond lore; Theodore Hook's *Life of Sir David Baird* (1832) for the storming of Seringapatam and the looting of Tipu Sultan's palace by English officers; and the eighth edition of the *Encyclopedia Britannica* for facts about diamonds and India. Collins also consulted John William Shaw Wyllie, who (like Murthwaite in the novel) was an experienced Indian traveler. Wyllie verified the authenticity of Collins's portrayal of Hinduism, particularly the plausibility of suggesting that the three Brahmins would willingly pollute themselves by journeying overseas to recover a sacred object.

Along with Gothic and popular "sensation" novels, *The Moonstone*'s literary predecessors include the colorful *Memoirs* (1828-29) of Eugène François Vidocq (1775-1857), a French policeman who founded the first detective department in France, then audaciously organized a robbery and investigated it himself. Vidocq's life inspired the first fictional detective, the French sleuth C. Auguste Dupin, who appears in several of Edgar Allen Poe's short stories, including *The Murders in the Rue Morgue* (1841), considered the earliest detective story. Vidocq is also thought to have been the inspiration for other short stories written in the 1860s by Émile Gaboriau and featuring a detective named Inspector Lecoq, who first appeared in 1866, two years before *The Moonstone* was published.

Reception. Victorian reviewers tended to dismiss *The Moonstone* as a mere puzzle story. For instance, the earliest review (by novelist Geraldine Jewsbury, writing in July 1868, just before the last installment of the serial) praised Collins's "carefully elaborate workmanship" but decried the "somewhat sordid detective element" (Jewsbury in *The Moonstone*, p. 543). Another reviewer that same month compared *The Moonstone* contemptuously to crossword puzzles and anagrams, allowing that if readers liked that sort of thing they might find the novel rewarding. Apparently readers did like that sort of thing, for the circulation of *All the Year Round* surged during *The Moonstone*'s serialization from January to August 1868, and the three-volume edition of the novel (published in July 1868) sold well both in Britain and in the United States. The novel has never been out of print, testimony to its continued popularity.

Later critics proved more generous, particularly those who have written detective stories themselves. For instance, detective novelists Dorothy L. Sayers and J. I. M. Stewart both helped to boost Collins's literary reputation in the first half of the twentieth century. No words of praise, however, are as often quoted as those of English poet T. S. Eliot, who, in his introduction to a 1928 edition of *The Moonstone*, called it "the first, the longest, and the best of modern English detective novels" (Eliot in *The Moonstone*, pp. 10-11).

—Colin Wells

For More Information

Collins, Wilkie. *The Moonstone*. Ed. Steve Farmer. Peterborough, Ontario: Broadview, 1999.

Hellar, Tamar. *Dead Secrets: Wilkie Collins and the Female Gothic*. New Haven: Yale University Press, 1992.

James, Lawrence. *Raj*. London: Little, Brown, 1997.

Lonoff, Sue. *Wilkie Collins and His Victorian Readers: A Study in the Rhetoric of Authorship*. New York: AMS, 1982.

Mitchell, Sally. *Daily Life in Victorian England*. Westport, Conn.: Greenwood, 1996.

Newsome, David. *The Victorian World Picture*. London: John Murray, 1997.

Peters, Catherine. *The King of Inventors: A Life of Wilkie Collins*. Princeton: Princeton University Press, 1993.

Reed, John R. "English Imperialism and the Unacknowledged Crime of Wilkie Collins' *The Moonstone*." *Clio* 2 (1973): 281-90.

Mrs. Dalloway

by
Virginia Woolf

Mrs. Dalloway was Virginia Woolf's fourth novel, although many scholars consider it the first of her great works. Like the novel that preceded it, *Jacob's Room* (1922), *Mrs. Dalloway* deals obliquely with the events and social issues surrounding the First World War, focusing on the thoughts and emotions of a variety of characters who all experience these times from differing perspectives. Woolf, born in 1882 in London, was a member of the same upper middle class as most of the characters in *Mrs. Dalloway*, although her family's interests leaned toward intellectual pursuits instead of political ones. Her father, Sir Leslie Stephen, was a respected nineteenth-century scholar. As part of the collection of writers, artists, and intellectuals called the Bloomsbury Group, Woolf was close to people involved in politics; among these political activists were the noted economist Maynard Keynes (who was on the staff of the British delegation to the postwar peace negotiations) and Woolf's husband, Leonard Woolf, who was literary editor of the left-wing journal *The Nation* when *Mrs. Dalloway* was written and published. Many readers attribute the novel's sympathetic depiction of Septimus Warren Smith's shell shock to Woolf's own recurring battle with mental illness.

Events in History at the Time of the Novel

Faltering postwar reconstruction. During World War I, the British government made many ide-

---

THE LITERARY WORK

A novel set in London on a single day in June 1923, and, through memory, some 30 years earlier; published in 1925.

SYNOPSIS

An upper-middle-class politician's wife prepares for and throws a party. On the same day, a shell-shocked veteran of the First World War commits suicide.

---

alistic promises to the populace about postwar social improvements—plans for health programs, expanded educational programs, universal unemployment insurance, and major home-building projects. These commitments were viewed as necessary to keep the population motivated to sustain the war effort, and also to forestall a socialist uprising like the Bolshevik Revolution that overthrew Tsarist Russia in 1917. But in the years following the end of the war in 1918, political and economic realities made fulfilling these promises extremely difficult for the British government.

In 1917, the government's Reconstruction Committee predicted that the most crucial issue the government would confront after the war would be minimizing the disruptions caused by demobilization of the men in the military and the shutting down of wartime industries, such as the manufacture of arms and ammunition. The com-

Virginia Woolf

mittee accurately predicted that unemployment would be the most serious problem the British government would face. Although there was a short postwar boom between 1918-19, by 1920 rising inflation, high taxes (necessary to pay off the nation's large war debt), and a weak market for the export of manufactured goods all combined to create an economic slump that drove unemployment up rapidly. By 1921, over 1.8 million workers eligible for government assistance were unemployed (Davis, p. 148).

High unemployment created particular problems for the country's leaders because it was politically untenable to refuse unemployment assistance to men who had fought for their country in the war. Whereas prior to the war the government's unemployment insurance programs had all been based on contributions made by the worker, postwar programs eliminated many of these requirements, creating "the dole" for the very first time: government assistance could now come in the form of a handout rather than a return on one's prior financial contributions. The government also tried other measures to ease the pressures of high unemployment, such as the 1922 Empire Settlement Act, which provided government funds to encourage emigration to the Dominions. The program, which met with little success, is echoed in Lady Bruton's emigration scheme in *Mrs. Dalloway*.

These internal difficulties contributed to political instability within the British government. During the war, British Prime Minister Lloyd George had forged a coalition between the traditionally Conservative party and the Liberals he represented. But by 1922, the idealist goals for reconstruction that had held this coalition together were obviously not coming to fruition, and the coalition fell apart. The Conservatives—Richard Dalloway's part in the novel—came into power, under the leadership of Bonar Law, who was forced by illness to retire less than a year into his tenure as prime minister. His successor, Stanley Baldwin, was beholden to keep one of Law's promises, however: to hold an election in 1923 to ascertain whether there was genuine public support for a Conservative program of tariff reform to establish protectionist policies as one way to combat inflation and unemployment. Both Conservatives and Liberals opposed the socialist agenda underpinning the working-class third party, Labour. Liberals, however, held to a belief in free trade, and, in an election perceived as a referendum against socialism, voters who might have supported the Conservatives instead voted against them. The Conservatives lost what had been a substantial majority in parliament and were forced to accede control to a Labour-Liberal alliance that resulted in Britain's first Labour government in early 1924. That government was short-lived, losing power in the next election in 1924, but it revealed the precariousness of Conservative power and indicated that the upperclass leaders of Britain's past were losing their authority. This Labour government came and went within the time between *Mrs. Dalloway*'s setting and its publication, but our knowledge of it colors our reading of the novel's descriptions of the governing class and its political characters, including the Prime Minister, who appears quite pitiable as a guest at Clarissa's party: "He looked so ordinary . . . poor chap, all rigged up in gold lace" (Woolf, *Mrs. Dalloway,* p. 172).

More choices for middle-class women. Women in the 1920s benefitted from tumultuous decades of agitation and change. In the nineteenth century, women had struggled for and achieved the right to own property on equal terms with men (through the Married Women's Property Acts of 1882 and 1883), and toward the end of the century they had begun to break free of the social conventions that prevented middle- and upperclass women from earning their own living in all but a very few respectable professions. By the 1890s the "New Woman" was becoming a fix-

THE EX-OFFICER PROBLEM

~

Many of the issues surrounding demobilization and employment for men who had served their country were particularly acute for the thousands of "temporary gentlemen" created by wartime field promotions. Historically, officers in the military were drawn from the educated upper and upper middle classes; being an officer and being a "gentleman" went hand in hand. During World War I, however, the great need for additional officers to lead the enormous mobilized forces resulted in field promotions for many soldiers of more humble backgrounds—men like *Mrs. Dalloway*'s Septimus Warren Smith, who "served with distinction" and was promoted (*Mrs. Dalloway*, p. 96). At first, they were labeled "temporary gentlemen" pejoratively, for their education, tastes, manners, and speech made it obvious that they were not from the same social class as the officers with whom they were now military equals. By the time the war ended, however, many of these men had earned a great deal of respect at the front, and both the government and these officers themselves struggled to reintegrate them into a civilian society where their military rank carried little weight. It was difficult, certainly, for men who had grown accustomed to leadership roles and officers' salaries to return to the lower-paying, lower-status jobs they had left before the war, but it was even more difficult to decide what sorts of retraining and unemployment benefits to offer them. Benefits for officers were based on assumptions about private income that looked back to the time when most officers were in fact "gentlemen" with means of their own in civilian life; so in certain cases the benefits were lower than those available to enlisted men. Similarly, the placement and retraining programs implemented for officers after the war generally presumed levels of education and past experience that many of the field-promoted officers did not possess, making it difficult for them to take advantage of these services. By the early 1920s, ex-officers suffering under the same economic pressures as the rest of Britain's population were often working at menial jobs—if they were working at all. These circumstances were especially distressing to this group of men, whose wartime successes had given them greater expectations and aspirations than they had before the war.

ture in the popular mind and culture of Britain. Often quite scandalous because of her independence, and sometimes because of her apparent sexual liberation, the New Woman was unmarried and self-supporting; moreover, she worked in shops or offices instead of the more genteel women's professions of the governess or schoolteacher. Her job relied on skills and knowledge unrelated to the supposedly inherent nurturing qualities of women, so by the very nature of her occupation, she defied the gender assumptions of the times.

In the years leading up to World War I, the women's movement in Britain made significant strides forward in the political arena, with the campaign for women's suffrage garnering much publicity. From the turn of the century onward,

two major groups organized and agitated to obtain the vote for women: the moderate National Union of Women's Suffrage Societies (NUWSS), which advocated working with the legal system to achieve change, and the militant Women's Social and Political Union (WSPU). In the years just before the war, the militants were the ones who made headlines. Frustrated after years of broken promises from political leaders who claimed to support women's suffrage but failed to vote for it in parliament, the militants—derisively labeled with the diminutive "suffragettes" by the media—turned to tactics that ranged from nonviolent demonstrations and heckling speakers at political rallies to violent and destructive activities such as window-smashing and arson. Their strategy demonstrated that they could use physical

A 1913 suffragist parade in London's Victoria Park. This political activism helped increase roles and options for women in early-nineteenth-century Britain.

force, a reality that surprised many, and that they were willing to suffer for their cause. They were careful that no people should be harmed through their activities—only property—but they suffered themselves when arrested and jailed as political prisoners. In prison, suffragists who went on hunger strike to protest their incarceration were sometimes force-fed through the nose, a humiliating and painful procedure that caused several of them to die as a result of broken blood vessels. All of these events brought the issue of women's suffrage to the forefront of the public stage, but they were displaced from the headlines by the outbreak of war in 1914. The women's movement prior to the war began a process of change that the war itself would accelerate. Afterwards the 1918 Qualification of Women Act would grant the vote to women over 30 who were wives of men on the register, or who were householders on the local government register, occupiers of property with an annual value of £5, or university graduates. The act acknowledged that the place of women in British society had decidedly changed.

Militant suffragism before the war and gaining the vote after it may have been the most visible aspect of the early-twentieth-century women's movement, but it was far from the only front upon which women experienced change. If working middle-class women were visible in the New Woman of the prewar years, they became commonplace during the war itself. While work was obviously nothing new for working-class women, who had been employed in factories from the beginnings of the industrial revolution, World War I brought many upper- and middle-class women out into the workforce for the first time. With so many men mobilized in the armed forces, women were encouraged to fill the job vacuum as their part of the war effort. They worked as nurses and ambulance drivers near the front, and in industry and agriculture at home. They ran supply depots and war charities, and drove trams and buses. Although most of these women were encouraged—and often forced—to give up their positions once the war ended and the demobilized soldiers returned home in search of jobs, the war years proved women were as capable of a full spectrum of work as men, and gave many young women a taste for economic independence.

By the 1920s, a young woman like Clarissa Dalloway's daughter, Elizabeth, could ponder a variety of career possibilities that had been unavailable to women who needed work in earlier decades and for the most part unthinkable to women such as her mother, who managed through luck of birth or marriage to be well provided for by men. By this time, marriage was one choice among many for young women, as were a variety of possible professions, including clerical work, medicine, or careers in banking and accounting. Women continued to face obstacles—in conventional thinking, in unequal pay, and in laws that prohibited them from working in some jobs considered too dangerous for females; however, it was now possible for a young woman of the upper or middle class to pursue a professional career without calling her moral character into question. This was certainly important to Woolf, who wrote in *A Room of One's Own* (1928) that economic independence was far more crucial to her than the vote.

Britain's diminishing status as an international power. The postwar settlements actually extended British influence in some regions, including Mesopotamia (Iraq), Palestine, and Persia (Iran). These areas were considered important to security in India, still the "jewel in the crown" of the British Empire. But the tide had turned on British imperialism, and in the years following the war a number of events and trends signaled the waning of Britain's power on the world stage.

Under a League of Nations mandate or Britain's own treaty (a 1919 Anglo-Persian agreement), the British were to govern certain regions of the Near and Middle East. These regions were highly volatile, and required an expensive military presence to sustain order and control. In Palestine, Arab and Jewish communities shared a simmering hostility, and the Arab majority resisted the creation of any political institutions that might be construed to imply their acceptance of the 1917 Balfour Declaration, in which British Foreign Secretary Arthur Balfour stated Britain's support for a Jewish homeland in the region. In Mesopotamia, a 1920 Arab rebellion against British control claimed 10,000 lives.

In Egypt, under a full British Protectorate, nationalists began to demand independence in response to wartime food shortages, inflation, and forced labor by Egyptian civilians for the British army. After these demands were refused in 1918 and the nationalist leader Sa'd Zaghlul was exiled in 1919, military force was required to suppress nationalism. Similar troubles brewed in India at this time, where Mahatma Gandhi led and inspired the nationalist movement. Indians were particularly angered by Britain's use of force in the Amritsar massacre of 1919, in which British troops fired on unarmed demonstrators, killing nearly 400 people.

Amidst all of this turmoil, it soon became clear that the British government, struggling with its war debt and problems at home, could not sustain the costs of maintaining the empire by force. Instead, British leaders sought to establish local authorities who would protect British interests, a shift that presaged the eventual breakup of the British Empire in the second half of the twentieth century.

In *Mrs. Dalloway* this dwindling power is suggested not so much through discussions of the situations in the Middle East or India (despite Peter Walsh's recent return from the subcontinent), but through Richard Dalloway's service on a parliamentary committee attempting to address the Armenian question. The Armenian people lived, historically, in an area between Turkey and Russia, and disputed by both. In the late nineteenth century, Britain had insisted (for its own security) that the Armenian lands and people be returned from Russian control to that of the Ottoman Empire, despite well-known attempts by Ottoman authorities to drive out Armenian peoples from the area. Britain promised that it would promote reform in Turkey to protect the Armenians, but it failed to do so. In 1915, Turkish massacres of the Armenian people killed thousands in what some historians consider the first genocide of the twentieth century. The post-World-War-I era saw Britain, a victor, negotiating with Turkey over the breakup of the Ottoman Empire. The postwar settlement included discussion of the need for protection of minorities and a possible homeland for the Armenians, a position the British public largely supported. But when the Treaty of Lausanne was signed in July of 1923—just a few weeks after *Mrs. Dalloway* is set—these provisions were abandoned. Despite rhetoric about human rights and its theoretical position of world leadership, the British government failed to take responsibility for the suffering of a people whose plight it had helped create. Like the nationalist unrest in India, Egypt and the Middle East, this incident reveals the weakening of the Empire.

The Novel in Focus

Plot summary. It could be said that *Mrs. Dalloway* is a novel without a plot. Although there is certainly a beginning, middle, and end to the day in June that the novel depicts, the boundaries of the day are frequently blurred by the narrative's excursions into the memories of various characters. Moreover, readers looking for a series of interesting events will find very few in this novel—although it does contain some deeply significant ones. Large portions of the narrative are devoted to people's thoughts, memories, and emotional reactions; what happens inside the minds of its characters is the real substance of *Mrs. Dalloway.*

The novel begins with Clarissa Dalloway's setting out to purchase flowers for a party she will host that evening. Stepping out into the streets of Westminster seems to her a "lark" and a "plunge," just as stepping out onto the terrace of her father's country house, Bourton, had seemed to her as a girl (*Mrs. Dalloway*, p. 3). On her walk she meets an old friend, Hugh Whitbread, which sets her to thinking of a past suitor, Peter Walsh, whom she loved dearly but rejected in favor of the less-demanding Richard Dalloway. While walking, she also thinks about how much she loves London; her gratitude that the war is over; her daughter Elizabeth and her hatred for Elizabeth's friend and teacher, Miss Kilman; and her theory of transcendence, in which people are connected to each other and the places they inhabit and in which they survive even after their individual deaths.

At the flower shop Clarissa is startled by the backfiring of a motorcar on the street, which strikes her at first as a pistol shot. Outside on the street, this same noise also jars Septimus Warren Smith, a shell-shocked veteran who has, to his wife's distress, threatened to kill himself. The motorcar itself creates quite a stir, as people in the street wonder and whisper to each other about which important personage may be inside, for the neighborhood is Westminster, the seat of the government. The crowd then becomes interested in some skywriting overhead, with which Septimus's wife attempts to distract him. Septimus, however, is lost in the world of his madness, seeing visions of unity, beauty, and, eventually, the return of his beloved dead officer, Evans.

Upon returning home Clarissa is disappointed to learn that her husband has been invited to lunch without her. She goes upstairs to her small, solitary bedroom—where her weak heart can get the rest it needs without being disturbed if her husband, a member of parliament, comes in late after meetings. There Clarissa ponders her muted feelings towards men and marriage, and remembers her passionate love for a girlfriend, Sally Seton, in her youth.

She next begins mending a tear in the dress she will wear to her party that evening, but is interrupted by an unexpected visit from Peter Walsh, who has returned quite suddenly from India, where he works in the Civil Service. Having fallen in love with the wife of an officer stationed there, Peter has come back to England to arrange a divorce for her. Their meeting is full of mixed emotions, which both of them try to conceal. Their affection for each other remains deep, although the pain caused by Clarissa's refusal to marry Peter still haunts them both. They are interrupted by the entrance of Clarissa's daughter Elizabeth, and Peter goes out to walk in Regent's Park, where he ponders his own memories of their youthful romance.

At the park, Peter passes Septimus and Rezia Warren Smith sitting on a bench, and the narrative returns to them. Septimus's "revelations" continue, and in a terrifying moment he mistakes Peter for Evans, the dead officer. While Peter goes on thinking about Clarissa and the other people they knew at Bourton in their youth, Rezia takes Septimus to an appointment with Sir William Bradshaw, a well-respected doctor specializing in cases like Septimus's. On the way, the narrative flashes back through Septimus's and Rezia's individual memories to tell us still more about his visions, about how the two of them met and married at the end of the war, and about Rezia's loneliness and fear.

Dr. Bradshaw has been recommended by Dr. Holmes, the general practitioner who had been treating Septimus. Bradshaw's philosophy centers on "proportion," and his diagnosis is grounded in the idea that Septimus has lost his sense of proportion and can, through willpower, gain it back; Bradshaw prescribes isolation in a mental institution to recover it (very much like the "rest cure" often prescribed for hysterical women in the late nineteenth century, whose symptoms were often akin to those of shell-shocked soldiers). This upsets both Septimus and Rezia. Septimus determines that Dr. Bradshaw and Dr. Holmes are the agents of "human nature," punishing him for the crimes he believes he has committed in not feeling things as people expect one to—neither grief for Evans nor love for his wife, whom he married in response to his panic that "he could not feel" (*Mrs. Dalloway*, p. 86).

The narrative then turns to the lunch at Lady Bruton's, to which Richard Dalloway has been invited without Clarissa. Hugh Whitbread is also a guest, and we learn that Lady Burton has invited them because she seeks their help in writing a letter to the *London Times* to promote an emigration scheme encouraging young people to move to Canada. Returning home, Richard thinks of how he loves Clarissa, and buys flowers with the determination to tell her so directly.

He finds that he cannot do it, however; the flowers alone must suffice. Both are thinking of Bourton, and Peter Walsh, whose presence in London has inspired a twinge of jealousy in Richard. Richard settles Clarissa on the sofa for the hour's rest she is supposed to have every afternoon because of her heart, and then departs for a committee meeting.

Resting, Clarissa thinks about her parties, and how others do not understand that she considers them her gift—her offering—to the people around her. Her daughter Elizabeth comes in with Miss Kilman; they are going out shopping and for tea. Clarissa thinks again of her hatred for Miss Kilman, whom she perceives as a rival for her daughter's affection.

At the store and over tea, Miss Kilman thinks about her troubles and the injustices she has suffered. Elizabeth pities her but also wishes to be free of her. Since Miss Kilman is very poor, Elizabeth pays for their tea, then leaves her to finish alone. Miss Kilman goes to a church to pray, while Elizabeth boards an omnibus to ride through London and think. Elizabeth imagines possible careers for herself, but realizes that her mother would oppose this, and that most people view her as a romantic or sexual object with a conventional marriage ahead of her. Nevertheless, Elizabeth delights in the freedom of other possibilities.

While Elizabeth rides her omnibus, Septimus and Rezia are sharing a surprisingly happy afternoon in their small flat, trimming a hat together. Septimus emerges briefly from his visions and anxiety, and both he and Rezia laugh contentedly over the hat and their private jokes. Rezia assures Septimus that she will not allow the doctors to separate them. Soon thereafter Dr. Holmes comes to fetch Septimus and barges into their apartment despite Rezia's objections. Determined that Holmes and Bradshaw will not get him, Septimus flings himself out of their window onto the spiked iron railing below.

Peter Walsh, returning to his hotel to dress for the evening, sees the ambulance carrying Septimus's body. As he dresses and eats dinner, Peter thinks still more about Clarissa, love, and his place in the world. Weighing his options, he chooses to go to her party that evening.

At the party, Clarissa worries that it will be a failure, but is reassured as she sees people become immersed in their conversations. Much to Clarissa's surprise, her girlfriend Sally Seton—now Lady Rosseter—appears, having been in London and having heard about the party from an acquaintance. Bustling about in her role of hostess, Clarissa cannot stop to speak to Peter and Sally, but the two settle down together and talk over old times.

SHELL SHOCK
〜

As the Great War stalemate of the trenches set in, many men in the armed forces developed symptoms of psychological stress. Lesser symptoms included nightmares, exhaustion and irritability; serious cases could display psychosomatic disorders such as paralysis or complete mental breakdown. These "psychiatric casualties" of the war were all labeled "shell shock" when enlisted men were afflicted; if the victim was an officer, the more genteel diagnosis of "neurasthenia" was often applied (Winter and Baggett, p. 212). The term "shell shock" originated from a theory that exploding shells were literally disturbing cerebro-spinal fluid and thus disrupting the biological workings of the brain, although it soon became evident that psychiatric, rather than medical, treatment was required. Today we would most likely diagnose these cases as Posttraumatic Stress Disorder.

Accounts written by soldiers suffering from shell shock describe symptoms very much like those Septimus Warren Smith suffers: trembling, anxiety, and sudden shifts of mood from cheerfulness to terror. Certainly by the early 1920s shell shock was a well-documented, if not yet well-understood, phenomenon. In *Mrs. Dalloway*, part of what makes Dr. Bradshaw so reprehensible is his failure to acknowledge that the condition merits understanding, his assumption that Septimus's illness is largely a failure of will on the part of the sufferer. The rest cure he prescribes is much like treatments prescribed for Woolf's own mental illness, treatments that she angrily resented and associated with private tyranny.

Clarissa is also pleased at the arrival of the Prime Minister, which adds importance to her gathering. She enjoys greeting the Bradshaws much less, for she too dislikes Dr. Bradshaw. Lady Bradshaw tells Clarissa about Septimus's suicide, startling her by introducing death into the party. Escaping to an empty room, Clarissa thinks about this young man whom she has never met, and what his death means to her. She experiences a profound sympathy for him—she understands the evil a man like Bradshaw can do by "forcing your soul"—but is also strangely invigorated by Septimus's gesture of rebellion (*Mrs. Dalloway*, p. 184). This empathetic moment brings Clarissa and Septimus together at the center of the web of acquaintances and crossed paths that structures the novel.

Mrs. Dalloway closes with a conversation between Peter and Sally about their youth and their relationships with Clarissa. Just as they are about to leave the dwindling party, Clarissa returns, which fills Peter with both terror and ecstasy. Thus the novel ends, as it began, with a character's subjective experience.

Marriage in *Mrs. Dalloway*. Woolf is known as a feminist writer, and some of her nonfiction books, such as *A Room of One's Own* and *Three Guineas* (1938) are classics in the feminist canon. But readers seeking a feminist heroine in *Mrs. Dalloway* are often perplexed because Clarissa is conventional in so many ways. Nevertheless, the novel does make a feminist statement through a critique of an institution in 1920s England—the conventional marriage, in which a wife is traditionally subordinated to her husband.

The most prominent example of this traditional model in *Mrs. Dalloway* is Lady Bradshaw, who has lost her individual personality to her domineering husband: "Fifteen years ago she had gone under. It was nothing you could put your finger on; there had been no scene, no snap; only the slow sinking, water-logged, of her will into his" (*Mrs. Dalloway*, p. 100). Clarissa, too, sometimes feels submerged in her husband's identity: "She had the oddest sense of being herself invisible" and finds "astonishing . . . this being Mrs. Dalloway; not even Clarissa any more" but simply "Mrs. Richard Dalloway" (*Mrs. Dalloway*, p. 11). Thinking about Clarissa, Richard, and the expectation that wives will adopt their husbands' points of view, Peter Walsh considers it "one of the tragedies of married life" that "with twice his wits, [Clarissa] had to see things through [Richard's] eyes" (*Mrs. Dalloway*, p. 77).

Therefore, it is not surprising that Elizabeth Dalloway resists people's romantic conceptions of her as a young woman soon to "come out" in society (through the season of parties and dances that introduced young women to the social world as candidates for marriage) and instead revels in the new professional opportunities available to middle- and upper-class women. Elizabeth minds people's objectification of her as a romantic object: "People were beginning to compare her to poplar trees, early dawn, hyacinths, fawns, running water, and garden lilies, and it made her life a burden to her"; instead "she would like to have a profession" (*Mrs. Dalloway*, pp. 134, 136). Miss Kilman has emphasized to Elizabeth that she has opportunities for economic independence that her mother or Miss Kilman never had: "every profession is open to women of your generation, said Miss Kilman," so Elizabeth thinks of what she might be (*Mrs. Dalloway*, p. 136):

> She liked people who were ill. . . . So she might be a doctor. She might be a farmer. Animals are often ill. She might own a thousand acres and have people under her. She would go and see them in their cottages . . . she liked the feeling of people working. . . . In short, she would like to have a profession. She would become a doctor, a farmer, possibly go into Parliament, if she found it necessary.
>
> (*Mrs. Dalloway*, p. 136)

It is by no means certain that Elizabeth will pursue one of these dreams. From a privileged family, she does not need to work for money and, as she admits to herself, she is also "rather lazy" (*Mrs. Dalloway*, p. 136). But Elizabeth thinks about these professional opportunities as alternatives to the marital career conventionally expected for women of her class. Marriage seemed like an inevitable catastrophe to her mother (*Mrs. Dalloway*, p. 34); in contrast, for Elizabeth a profession offers the possibility of supporting herself well and respectably. Within the space of a generation marriage has become an option, which women of her class are free to take up or reject as they wish.

Homoerotic relationships in *Mrs. Dalloway*. Although neither relationship is sexually consummated in the novel, Clarissa's love for Sally and Septimus's for Evans are both strikingly homoerotic. Despite "a scruple picked up Heaven knows where" Clarissa believes that sometimes "she did undoubtedly feel what men felt" for a woman (*Mrs. Dalloway*, pp. 31, 32). "It was a sudden revelation . . . an illumination; a match burning in a crocus; an inner meaning almost expressed" (*Mrs. Dalloway*, p. 32). Like the rest of the passage from which it comes, the visual imagery of female sexuality in the match in the crocus, suggests lesbian eroticism. Similarly suggestive is a brief description of the relationship between Septimus and Evans. In the trenches,

Septimus drew "the attention, indeed the affection of his officer, Evans by name. It was a case of two dogs playing on a hearth-rug. . . . They had to be together, share with each other, fight with each other, quarrel with each other" (*Mrs. Dalloway*, p. 86). While this last sentence could easily describe a marriage, the physicality of the image of the two dogs suggests a sexual relationship as well (indeed, in her diaries and letters Woolf often represented lovers as pairs of animals). Certainly Septimus's visions of Evans and the connection between Evans's death and Septimus's inability to feel suggest a relationship much more powerful than simple camaraderie.

These homoerotic pairings bolster the novel's critique of conventional marriage by offering passionate alternatives. Moreover, they reflect the range of relationships Woolf and her circle of friends accepted despite their taboo status in the culture as a whole. Although she resisted defining herself as a "Sapphist" (one contemporary term for a lesbian identity) just as she resisted other limiting categories, Woolf had multiple intimate relationships with women (Lee, p. 484). Her diaries and letters reveal that these affairs were sometimes quite passionate, though Woolf did not record details of possible sexual encounters. Moreover, several of her male friends were homosexual, including the well-known writers Lytton Strachey and E. M. Forster.

All male homosexual activity, public or private, was illegal in England under the 1885 Criminal Law Amendment Act (female homosexual activity was not addressed), and the widely publicized trial and conviction of Oscar Wilde for gross indecency in 1895 had reinforced the very real risks inherent in active homosexuality around the turn of the century. Nevertheless, research in the developing field of scientific "sexology," along with general trends toward a less rigid society, led to some changing attitudes towards homosexuality in the early twentieth century. Sexologists began to discuss sexuality in medical and psychological terms—rather than religious and moral ones—which facilitated a growing tendency to relate homosexuality to one's identity rather than simply one's choice of activity. By the 1920s, candid descriptions of homosexual love were beginning to appear in British literature, although these books were often banned. Radclyffe Hall's *The Well of Loneliness* (1928), about a young girl's attachment to an older woman, is a good example; Woolf publicly supported the novel when its publisher was taken to trial on obscenity charges. More subtle homoeroticism, as in Woolf's *Mrs. Dalloway*, allowed authors to suggest the possibilities of homosexual romance while avoiding censorship.

Sources and literary context. *Mrs. Dalloway* is drawn from Woolf's observations of the people and society around her. She wrote in her diary, "In this book I have almost too many ideas. I want to give life & death, sanity & insanity; I want to criticize the social system, & show it at work, at its most intense" (Woolf, *The Diary*, vol. 2, p. 248). Intentionally, then, the novel is grounded in the actual politics and society of England in 1923.

The novel is also embedded in the developing literary culture of modernism, which embraced experimental novels that rejected straightforward, realistic depictions of an objective world in favor of the subjective experience of individual consciousness. *Mrs. Dalloway* is often compared to James Joyce's **Ulysses** (1922; also in *WLAIT 4: British and Irish Literature and Its Times*) because the novel takes place in just a single day and concentrates on the thoughts and memories of its characters. *Mrs. Dalloway* is also associated with "stream-of-consciousness" writing, which in England was pioneered by the feminist novelist Dorothy Richardson beginning in 1915. In fact, *Mrs. Dalloway* is not pure stream of consciousness, for, like *Ulysses*, it jumps from mind to mind, incorporating the consciousnesses of dozens of characters, both major and minor; in so doing, it portrays the life of a whole community across a bustling urban landscape.

In addition to the Prime Minister, who is not named but probably modeled on Stanley Baldwin, Woolf based at least one character in *Mrs. Dalloway* on a real person. Rezia Warren Smith was drawn from Lydia Lopokova, Russian companion to the British economist Maynard Keynes. Woolf's diary records that she intentionally observed Lydia "as a type for Rezia" and at least once she slipped and called Lydia "Rezia" while she was at work on the novel (Woolf, *The Diary*, vol. 2, pp. 265, 310). Although Woolf made fun of Lydia's foreign eccentricities when Maynard first brought her into their social set, Rezia is a sympathetically drawn character, suggesting a concern on Woolf's part about the prevalence of anti-alien sentiment in British society in the postwar years.

Reception. Reviews of *Mrs. Dalloway* were generally either positive or ambivalent, and tended to emphasize the book's formal experiments (the single-day unity and the stream-of-consciousness technique). The comparatively negative reviews often responded to the character of Clarissa Dalloway, whom many reviewers found excessively prim, snobbish, and useless. Woolf herself had mixed feelings about Clarissa, writing in her diary that she thought the character might be "too stiff—too glittering & tinsely" (Woolf, *The Diary,* vol. 2, p. 272). The *Times Literary Supplement* called the novel's attempt at a new form a "thrilling and hazardous enterprise" and decided that, although the experiment had failings, "something real has been achieved; for, having the courage of her theme and setting free her vision, Mrs. Woolf steeps it in an emotion and irony and delicate imagination which enhance the consciousness and the zest of living" (*Times Literary Supplement,* p. 34). Writing for the *Literary Digest International Book Review,* H. L. Pangborn was less impressed, describing the novel's experiment in form as "literary tight-rope dancing" that Woolf performs well, but without real purpose (Pangborn, p. 617). Alice Beal Parsons also had reservations about some aspects of *Mrs. Dalloway,* but declared that Woolf's prose style was such that "readers will think of her not as a novelist, but as poet," concluding, finally, that "in a book so beautiful as this reservations, even if sustained, can do no more than brush a little of the bloom off the butterfly's wings" (Parsons, p. 5).

—Michelle N. Mimlitsch

For More Information

Bolt, Christine. *The Women's Movements in the United States and Britain from the 1790s to the 1920s.* Amherst: University of Massachusetts Press, 1993.

Bowlby, Rachel. *Virginia Woolf: Feminist Destinations.* Oxford: Basil Blackwell, 1988.

Davis, John. *A History of Britain, 1885-1939.* London: MacMillan, 1999.

Lee, Hermione. *Virginia Woolf.* New York: Knopf, 1997.

Pangborn, H. L. Review of *Mrs. Dalloway,* by Virginia Woolf. *Literary Digest International Book Review* (August 1925): 617.

Parsons, Alice Beal. "Re-enter People." Review of *Mrs. Dalloway,* by Virginia Woolf. *New York Herald Tribune,* 31 May 1925, 5.

Petter, Martin. "'Temporary Gentlemen' in the Aftermath of the Great War: Rank, Status and the Ex-Officer Problem." *The Historical Journal* 37 (1994): 127-152.

Review of *Mrs. Dalloway,* by Virginia Woolf. *Times Literary Supplement,* 21 May 1925, 34.

Tate, Trudi. "*Mrs Dalloway* and the Armenian Question." *Textual Practice* 8 (1994): 467-486.

Winter, Jay, and Blaine Baggett. *The Great War and the Shaping of the 20th Century.* New York: Penguin, 1996.

Woolf, Virginia. *The Diary of Virginia Woolf.* 5 vols. Ed. Anne Olivier Bell. San Diego: Harcourt Brace Jovanovich, 1977-1984.

———. *Mrs. Dalloway.* San Diego: Harcourt Brace Jovanovich, 1990.

"My Last Duchess" and Other Poems

by

Robert Browning

Born in Camberwell, London, in 1812, Robert Browning was the son of a bank clerk, a learned man who kept an extensive library. Browning attended a boarding school near Camberwell as a boy, and later attended the University of London for a time. However, he preferred to pursue his education at home. Aside from being tutored in subjects such as foreign languages, music, boxing, and riding, Browning read widely. His diverse interests provided him with a store of knowledge from which he drew when composing his poems. In 1833 Browning published his first poem, *Pauline*, anonymously: the work failed to sell and went virtually unnoticed by critics. Browning took trips to Russia in 1834 and Italy in 1837, from which he would draw for future poems. *Pauline* was followed by *Paracelsus* (1835); published at Browning's father's expense, it too was ignored, and *Sordello* (1840) was a critical failure that actually impeded Browning's poetic reputation. Browning briefly experimented with writing plays, but soon abandoned the stage, though his fascination with the dramatic monologue appears to date from that time. Between 1841 and 1846, Browning produced an eight-volume series of poetic pamphlets, *Bells and Pomegranates*. In the series was a collection of monologues that included "My Last Duchess"; also in the series was *Dramatic Romances and Lyrics* (1845), which contained the companion poems "Meeting at Night" and "Parting at Morning." Browning undertook a correspondence with the poet Elizabeth Barrett, whom he married a year later. The couple

---

THE LITERARY WORK

Four poems—one set in sixteenth-century Italy, three set in an unspecified time and place; published in 1842, in 1846, and one in 1864 (the middle two originally published together as one poem, "Night and Morning").

SYNOPSIS

In "My Last Duchess," an Italian duke relates the history of his previous marriage to an emissary; in "Meeting at Night" and "Parting at Morning," a man trysts with his lover by night and leaves her in the morning; in "Prospice," a male speaker envisions his death and the afterlife.

---

afterwards emigrated from England to Italy, where Browning sets "My Last Duchess."

Events in History at the Time of the Poems

Victorians and the past. The Victorian interest in the past found its most dramatic expression in the growing fascination with medievalism, which can be traced back to the late 1700s. Scholars, antiquarians, and artists of the Romantic period fell increasingly under the spell of the Middle Ages, taking its artifacts, architecture, legends, and values to heart. As early as the eighteenth century, medieval people came to be re-

Robert Browning

garded by some artists and intellectuals as more vital, uncorrupted, and closer to nature than their modern counterparts, a belief that persisted well into the nineteenth century and the onset of the Victorian Age. As rapidly advancing technology transformed England from a primarily agricultural nation into a major industrial power, many Victorians turned nostalgically to contemplation of the medieval world for a sense of harmony and stability that eluded them in the present. The literature of the times often reflected authors' sympathy with the medieval period, from the historical novels of Sir Walter Scott to the Arthurian poems of Lord Tennyson and William Morris. Ever an original, Robert Browning was *not* among the poets who became enamored of medieval subjects and legends. One literary scholar observes that, "In an age when the poets were mostly interested in escaping to the past . . . , Browning almost alone wrote of contemporary ideas and contemporary life, often in colloquial and contemporary phrase" (DeVane, p. 282). Another scholar argues that Browning did a brilliant job of evoking earlier periods than his own, but for him, the qualities of vigor, variety, sweeping change, and unfettered imagination "belong[ed] primarily to the Renaissance and later periods"; moreover, Browning's poems set in the past evinced an interest in "a world of history more than a world of myth or literary legend" (Taylor

in Peterson, pp. 58, 61). His duke in "My Last Duchess" seems representative of a particular Renaissance type, with values peculiar to that specific time period and society, rather than as a hero of timeless legend. He also bears a striking resemblance to a particular duke.

The real duke of Ferrara. Although Browning's arrogant, autocratic duke in "My Last Duchess" is an original creation in many respects, the poet drew at least in part on his knowledge of the powerful Este family, who ruled Ferrara, a duchy in northern Italy. Browning did not actually visit Ferrara when he traveled through Italy in June 1838, but he had read extensively on its history while composing his poem, *Sordello*. At the same time, Browning was engaged in reviewing R. H. Wilde's *Conjectures and Researches concerning the Love Madness and Imprisonment of Torquato Tasso*; Browning's research into the life of Tasso—an Italian poet—uncovered the figure of Alfonso II, fifth and last duke of Ferrara, who was Tasso's patron and the one who consigned him to a mental hospital after the poet experienced delusions and exhibited violent behavior.

Alfonso II (1533-1597) was the son of Ercole II and Renee of France. As the scion of a noble family and the heir to a dukedom, Alfonso received an extensive literary and social education, mastering such languages as Latin and French and devoting himself to courtly pursuits like hunting, fighting in tourneys, and attending plays and festivals. Owing to his French ancestry, Alfonso was sympathetic to France as a nation. He defied his father—who wanted his duchy Ferrara to remain neutral—by fighting beside his French cousin, Henry II, in a war against Charles V, emperor of the Holy Roman Empire. With the help of Cosimo I de Medici, Duke of Tuscany, the father, Ercole II managed to negotiate a peace with the emperor that included restoration of confiscated Ferrara lands. To strengthen the alliance between the Este and the de Medici families, Alfonso, then 25 years old, entered into an arranged marriage with Cosimo's 14-year-old daughter, Lucrezia de Medici, in 1558. Three days after the wedding, Alfonso returned to France, where he continued to fight in Henry II's wars.

After the death of Ercole II in 1559, Alfonso returned to Ferrara to assume his responsibilities as duke. In February 1560, Alfonso II sent for his wife—described as a serious, devout girl of not much education—to join him. Extensive details of their marriage are not known but Lucrezia, then 17, died on April 21, 1561. There were suspicions—which remained unproven—that she had been poisoned. Soon after Lucrezia's death, Alfonso began negotiating with Ferdinand, Count of Tyrol and son of Emperor Ferdinand I of Austria, for the hand of the emperor's daughter, Barbara. Ferdinand used an envoy—Nikolaus Madriz of Innsbruk—to negotiate the match to its successful conclusion. The marriage between Alfonso II and Barbara of Austria took place in 1565. Like her predecessor, Barbara died young—in 1572—and, like the duke's first marriage, his second was without issue. Alfonso then married Margherita Gonzaga in 1579 but she too bore him no children. Although Alfonso tried to have his illegitimate cousin Cesare named as his successor, his efforts were ultimately unsuccessful, in large part because of a papal bull (decree) in 1567 that prevented the investiture of illegitimate heirs with church lands. With the death of Alfonso II, the male line of the House of Este in Ferrara became extinct and the duchy reverted to the possession of the Church. The court of Ferrara—among the most brilliant in Italy for 200 years—fell into eclipse.

Browning did not name the duke and duchess in the first published version of his poem—it was not until 1849 that he added the subtitled "Ferrara" to "My Last Duchess." But the situation of the speaker negotiating for a new bride through a count's envoy encourages identification with the story of Alphonso II and Lucrezia de Medici. Literary scholar William Clyde DeVane observes, "In almost every respect Alfonso II meets the requirements of Browning's Duke. He was a typical Renaissance grandee: he came of the proud Este family, rulers in Italy for hundreds of years, not merchants and upstarts like the Medici; he was cold and egotistical, vengeful and extremely possessive; and a patron of the arts, painting, music, and literature" (DeVane, p. 108). While it is unclear how closely Browning's duchess resembles Lucrezia de Medici, the circumstances surrounding both women's deaths remain mysterious. Asked about his duchess's fate, Browning refused to commit himself to a definitive explanation. The poem's lines in which the duke "gave commands; / Then all smiles stopped together" prompted a question to Browning about what happened to her (Browning, *Poetry*, "My Last Duchess," line 46). In response, the poet first said that "the commands were that she should be put to death," then almost immediately added, "or he might have had her shut up in a convent" (Browning in DeVane, p. 109).

Public vs. private life. Despite their brevity, Browning's companion poems "Meeting at Night" and "Parting at Morning"—originally published together in 1845 as one poem "Night and Morning"—comment on the middle-class Victorian drive toward separate public and private lives.

ART AND PATRONAGE

Renaissance princes were often patrons of the arts and the Estes of Ferrara were no exception, their collection of adornments in an already splendid court benefitting from their generous support of talented painters and poets. Alfonso I, third duke of Ferrara and grandfather to Alfonso II, was a patron to several painters, including Dosso Dossi, Giovanni Bellini, Titian, and Raphael. In the last case, the relationship between patron and artist did not always run smoothly. At one point, Raphael promised to paint a picture for Alfonso I (*A Triumph of the Bacchus in India*), but Raphael already had so many commissions in Rome that he never even started it. Three years later, the angry duke wrote to the Ferrara ambassador in Rome:

> We wish you to find him and tell him . . . that it is now three years since he has given us only words; and that this is not the way to treat men of our rank; and that, if he does not fulfill his promise toward us, we shall make him know that he has not done well to deceive us. And then, as though from yourself, you can tell him that he had better take care not to provoke our hatred, instead of the love we bear him; for as, if he keeps his promise, he can hope for our support, so on the contrary, if he does not, he can expect one day to get what he will not like.
>
> (Alfonso I in Prescott, p. 236)

In Browning's poem, the duke of Ferrara is a patron to two artists: monastic painter Fra Pandolf, who paints the portrait of the last duchess, and the sculptor Claus of Innsbruck, who crafted a statue of Neptune taming a seahorse. Both artists are imaginary, although a painter named Giovanni Antonio Pandolfi was employed by the Este family to paint a portrait of Alfonso II's sister in 1570, and classical subjects in sculpture—such as Neptune taming a sea horse—were typical of the period.

They are indeed something of a parody of this desire. In general, the middle class created a mythology of individual spheres of existence consisting of the world of work, duty, and service—dominated by men—and the world of home and domestic concerns (and love), traditionally the province of women. In a famous 1865 lecture, the Victorian intellectual John Ruskin described, albeit from a very conservative point of view, gender roles prescribed for middle-class couples:

> The man's power is active, progressive, defensive. He is eminently the doer, the creator, the discoverer, the defender. His intellect is for speculation and invention; his energy for adventure, for war, and for conquest whenever war is just, whenever conquest is necessary. But the woman's power is for rule, not for battle—and her intellect is not for invention or creation, but for sweet ordering, arrangement, and decision. . . . The man, in his rough work in the open world, must encounter all peril and trial. . . . But he guards the woman from all this, within his house, as ruled by her, unless she herself has sought it, need enter no danger, no temptation, no cause of error or offence. This is the true nature of home—it is the place of Peace; the shelter, not only from all injury, but from all terror, doubt, and division.
>
> (Ruskin in Mitchell, p. 266)

According to this broadly painted conception, middle-class men were considered the breadwinners and warriors of public life, and women were often designated the guardians of private life. How far these myths extended into actual lives or even into a general belief system is unclear, but one feminine ideal of the mid-nineteenth century was the Angel in the House, a term derived from the title of a popular Victorian poem by Coventry Patmore. According to the poem (as often parodied as it was honored), this self-sacrificing domestic saint devoted herself entirely to the affairs of her household, tended to the needs of her husband and children, and provided through her own pure morals an example of Christian virtues in action. This Angel in the House never questioned her position nor attempted to prevent the men in her family from assuming their own places in the outside world. Some moralists of the day, such as Baldwin Brown, praised "women whose hearts are an unfailing fountain of courage and inspiration to the hard-pressed man . . . and who send forth husband or brother each morning with new strength for his conflict, armed, as the lady armed her knight of old, with a shield which he may not stain in any unseemly conflicts, and a sword which he dares only use against the enemies of truth, righteousness, and God" (Baldwin in Houghton, pp. 351-352). The Angel in the House also respected the boundary between public and private life: she kept the softer emotions, especially love, confined to the home so that the man in the family could perform his work in the world without distractions. Of course, this figure was in large part a projection of somewhat sappy wishful thinking, and many Victorians, Browning included, recognized the menacing patriarchal power lurking behind the adoration.

In Browning's companion poems, the heady bliss of a private romantic encounter—as two lovers tryst in a farmhouse, their "two hearts beating each to each!" (Browning, *Poetry*, "Meeting at Night," line 12)—gives way to a presumably inevitable separation as the sun rises and the male lover recalls "the need of a world of men for me" (Browning, *Poetry*, "Parting at Morning," line 4). Many years after these poems appeared in print, Browning was asked if the speaker was a woman lamenting the departure of her lover or else the loss of her purity. Browning replied, "Neither: it is *his* confession of how fleeting is the belief (implied in the first part) that such raptures are self-sufficient and enduring—as for the time they appear" (Browning in DeVane, p. 178). Browning thus casts these poems as existential laments, resisting the comfortable gender politics by which they often were (and are) read.

FROM "THE ANGEL IN THE HOUSE" BY COVENTRY PATMORE

Becoming one of the best-selling poems in Victorian England, "The Angel in the House" (1854-56) concerns a husband's intense love for his wife, describing their courtship and marriage. The poem reveals little about the nature of Victorian home life but fully expresses the feminine ideal of woman being queen of the domestic sphere, a separate world in which she "exercise[d] power in secret and subtle ways" (Hellerstein, et al, p. 134).

> Why, having won her, do I woo? . . .
>   Because, although in act and word
> As lowly as a wife can be,
> Her manners, when they call me lord,
>   Remind me 'tis by courtesy . . .
> Because, though free of the outer court
>   I am, this Temple keeps its shrine
> Sacred to Heaven; because, in short,
>   She's not and never can be mine.
>
> (Patmore in Hellerstein, pp. 139-40)

Religious doubt and certainty. At the start of the Victorian Age, many Dissenting Christians in England, that is, many of those who dissented from the mainstream Anglican Church, tended towards a literal reading of the Bible. They considered the Scriptures infallible and free of error; challenging this belief at the time was geological evidence and linguistic criticism, developed especially in Germany, which traced changes and inconsistencies in key texts. Meanwhile, scholars were conducting their own investigations, comparing biblical events with historical records and exploring, from an archaeological standpoint, the lifestyles in ancient cultures, like those of Egypt and Palestine.

Religious certainties were further undermined by sectarian conflicts, several of which originated in the earliest decades of the nineteenth century. One such conflict involved Utilitarianism—a philosophy founded by Jeremy Bentham (1772-1832)—which held that all institutions of society should be examined in the light of reason to discern whether they were "useful," that is, contributed to the greatest happiness of the greatest numbers. Benthamite Utilitarians tended to agree that established religion was not useful, but rather an outmoded superstition. This viewpoint, in turn, was challenged by religious conservatives, like John Henry Newman, who insisted that a powerful, dogmatic, and traditional religious institution was the best defense against mechanistic and secular Benthamism. Other scholars and intellectuals—including Thomas Carlyle—abandoned institutional Christianity but held that people needed some kind of religious faith to sustain them.

As a result of these ongoing religious debates, coupled with the emergence of scientific theories such as Charles Darwin's theory of human evolution, many Victorians suffered crises of faith. "Doubt arose . . . because of evangelical religion's emphasis on progress and reform. Was it really possible to accept the idea of hell, everlasting punishment, and a jealous deity who demanded obedience? The struggles to reconcile conflicting beliefs gave religion its active presence in many lives—and often, when faith failed, the struggle to live well by works of reform grew even stronger" (Mitchell, p. 247). Doubtless some Victorians came to believe that their reward, their claim to immortality, would rest on their accomplishments in the earthly world, rather than whatever they were granted in a possibly nonexistent heaven. The scholar Walter E. Houghton cogently sums up this position: "There may be a

God—and maybe not. And if there is, is there a life after death? in a heaven? or a hell? Let us forget the insoluble questions and plunge into some useful career" (Houghton, p. 258).

Despite this resolve, questions about the nature of God, the afterlife, and immortality continued to vex and trouble Victorian thinkers and writers, including Alfred Tennyson and Robert Browning. Both poets explored the nature of spiritual crises in their works—Tennyson, most notably, in his famous elegy, **In Memoriam** (also in WLAIT 4: *British and Irish Literature and Its Times*). Browning was to return time and again to the subject of faith in such poems as "Cleon," "Karshish," and "Saul." After facing his own religious doubts in his younger years, the mature Browning explored many positions, ranging from satiric nihilism (in his poem "Caliban Upon Setebos") to a kind of stoicism, close to belief. In "Prospice," composed soon after the death of Browning's wife, the speaker, imagining his own death, envisions an afterlife in which love somehow survives.

The Poems in Focus

The contents. "My Last Duchess" begins as the Duke of Ferrara points out to his listener the lifelike portrait of his late wife. Inviting the listener to "sit and look at her," Ferrara mentions the artist, Fra Pandolf, and remarks on how strangers who beheld the portrait seemed mesmerized by "the depth and passion of [the duchess's] earnest glance" and curious about how she came to wear such an expression ("My Last Duchess," lines 5, 8). Ferrara reveals that the flush on the duchess's cheek might have been evoked not only by her husband's presence but by Fra Pandolf's compliments.

Warming to his theme, Ferrara describes his late wife as having "a heart—how shall I say?—too soon made glad, / Too easily impressed; she liked whate'er / She looked on, and her looks went everywhere" ("My Last Duchess," lines 22-24). The duke goes on to list the many things that pleased the duchess, ranging from wearing her husband's favour, to sunsets, boughs of cherries, and white mules. He recalls how his wife seemed to thank men as though their gifts to her were all of the same value, including the duke's own gift of "a nine-hundred-years-old name" ("My Last Duchess," line 32). Ferrara wonders aloud how a man in his exalted position could criticize this habit of the duchess without somehow lowering or embarrassing himself in the process: "E'en then would be some stooping; and I choose / Never to stoop" ("My Last Duchess," lines 42-43).

After noticing how the duchess's smiles seem bestowed on everyone she encounters, Ferrara reveals that he "gave commands; / Then all smiles stopped together. There she stands / As if alive" ("My Last Duchess," lines 45-47). Immediately after that disclosure, the duke addresses his visitor—now identified as an envoy of a count, whose daughter Ferrara wishes to wed if she comes with the desired dowry. He invites the envoy to rise and go with him to meet the rest of the company downstairs. As Ferrara insists that he and the envoy go together, he points out to him a final masterpiece in his art collection: "Notice Neptune, though, / Taming a sea-horse, thought a rarity, / Which Claus of Innsbruck cast in bronze for me!" ("My Last Duchess," lines 54-56).

"Meeting At Night" begins as a man sails eagerly by moonlight towards a distant cove. Leaving his boat on the sands, he hurries across "a mile of warm, sea-scented beach" and three fields to reach a farm. He taps at the pane to be let in, a match is quickly struck, and his lover welcomes him with equal fervor. However, as the companion poem "Parting at Morning" reveals, when the sun rises, the male lover prepares for his inevitable departure and the resumption of his worldly duties: "And the sun looked over the mountain's rim: / And straight was a path of gold for him, / and the need of a world of men for me" ("Parting at Morning," lines 14-16).

"Prospice"—meaning "look forward"—opens with the question "Fear death?" and segues into the speaker's vision of what he might experience after death: "The power of the night, the press of the storm, / The post of the foe; / "Where he stands, the Arch Fear in a visible form, / Yet the strong man must go" (Browning, *Poetry*, "Prospice," lines 5-8). The speaker senses that "a battle's to fight ere the guerdon be gained"; he welcomes the impending conflict, "I was ever a fighter, so—one fight more, / The best and the last" ("Prospice," lines 13-15). Determined to face death bravely, like "the heroes of old," the speaker imagines the darkness and pain yielding ultimately to joy and a reunion with his lost love:

> And the elements' rage, the fiend-voices that
>   rave,
> Shall dwindle, shall blend,
> Shall change, shall become first a peace out of
>   pain,

> Then a light, then thy breast,
> O thou soul of my soul! I shall clasp thee
>   again,
> And with God be the rest!
>   ("Prospice," lines 23-28)

Victorian love. Overall, Victorians of the vocal but still small middle class tended to speak of love in highly idealized terms. As opposed to lust and sensuality, love—which presumably led to marriage and children—purified and strengthened the (male) lover against sin and temptation. Love represented "not only the supreme experience of life but its end and object—the very means by which the soul is saved" (Houghton, p. 373). Lovers' lives were defined by the moment in which each met and recognized the other as

> the one person in the wide world who was made for him or her, made to be loved forever, here and hereafter. After finding one's affinity, to draw back . . . out of timidity or apathy or any consideration of 'the world's honours,' is failure in life. Success is to seize the predestined moment and love on, even if love is unrequited . . . even if the beloved is dead—always to be faithful until, in heaven, the perfect union is achieved or renewed.
>   (Houghton, pp. 373-74)

The literature of love, as written in the 1840s and 1850s, often seems to reflect (or mock) what might be called the official line on love: "Love is not something carnal and evil to be ashamed of but something pure and beautiful; it is not a temptation to be struggled against but a great ethical force which can protect men from lust and even strengthen and purify the mortal will" (Houghton, p. 375).

Much of Browning's verse falls within the purview of love poetry and engages these notions in many ways, usually playfully or ironically. While the exact nature of the lovers' relationship in "Meeting at Night" is never specified, the headlong ecstasy of the man to reach his beloved is, at least on one level, presented sympathetically, even exultantly, and with imagery that slyly suggests a consummation even before the reunion: "And the startled little waves that leap / In fiery ringlets from their sleep, / As I gain the cove with pushing prow, / And quench its speed i' the slushy sand" ("Meeting at Night," line 3-6). Meanwhile, "Prospice" captures the Victorian ideal of the perfect love that transcends death itself when the speaker reunites with his beloved—"thou soul of my soul!" ("Prospice," line 27)—at the poem's conclusion.

Even a resoundingly unromantic poem like "My Last Duchess" can be explored in the context of Victorian love. The duke, however oddly sympathetic, is the exact antithesis of the ideal Victorian lover, a man who has in fact failed in his life because he cared too much for "the world's honors," specifically, his "gift of a nine-hundred years' old name" ("My Last Duchess," line 33). "Browning, observes one literary historian, could not have created the complex ironies of 'My Last Duchess' (1842)—in which the Duke complains about the inadequacy of his first wife while negotiating the dowry for his second—if he had not been able to set the Victorian reader's presumed expectations about marital relations against the duke's renaissance views" (Tucker, p. 89). Ferrara and his first wife seem emotionally and spiritually incompatible. Possessive and arrogant, the duke cannot tolerate, understand, or love a duchess who prizes sunsets, white mules, and cherry-boughs at the same worth as his own offerings, nor one who smiles upon all whom she beholds. Having rid himself of her, the duke chooses to concentrate instead upon his art collection, including the portrait of the duchess, which he can control as he never could the living woman. Even the bride he now courts is to become another piece in his collection, as he assures the envoy that "[the Count's] fair daughter's self, as I avowed / At starting, is my object" ("My Last Duchess," lines 52-53).

Sources and literary context. While researching the historical background of his poem *Sordello*, Browning discovered the Este family of Ferrara, particularly the figure of Alfonso II, the real-life model for the duke in "My Last Duchess." His sources most likely included *Biographie universelle* (1822)—a reference text Browning had consulted on several previous occasions—and Muratori's *Della Antichita Estensi*, both of which Browning had also used for *Sordello*. R. H. Wilde's *Conjectures and Researches concerning the Love Madness and Imprisonment of Torquato Tasso*, of which Browning was writing a review in spring of 1842, may have provided further details on Alfonso II, who was Torquato Tasso's patron.

The companion poems "Meeting at Night" and "Parting at Morning" do not appear to be rooted in any historical situation. "Prospice," by contrast, shows definite autobiographical influences: it was written shortly after the death of Elizabeth Barrett Browning in 1861 and was interpreted as an expression of Browning's own ideas about love and immortality transcending

death. Well aware of his wife's failing health, Browning nursed her patiently and devotedly through her final illness: she died in his arms. Writing to inform his father and sister of Elizabeth's death, Browning told them not to worry about him and asserted that his own life was to be devoted to the upbringing of his son, and that something of Elizabeth's spirit still sustained him, "I have some of her strength, really, added to mine"; in a postscript, Browning reflected on

---

THE ROMANCE OF THE CENTURY?

During the mid-1840s, Robert Browning became less famous for his poetry than for the role he played in what has been considered one of the most famous love stories in the Victorian Age. In January 1845, Browning wrote his first letter to the poetess Elizabeth Barrett, six years his senior and a semi-invalid living in her father's house. The letter was in response to a compliment she had paid his verse in one of her own poems ("Lady Geraldine's Courtship"). Praising Barrett's own work, Browning boldly declared, "I do, as I say, love these verses with all my heart—and I love you too" (Browning in Markus, p. 3). Startled by the young man's audacity, yet intrigued as well, Barrett continued to correspond with him by letter. They at last met face to face in May 1845, and, soon after, Browning initiated a clandestine courtship, clandestine because Elizabeth's father was a domestic tyrant who had forbidden any of his eleven children to marry. In 1846, the two poets were secretly married; a few days later, they eloped to Italy, for which Mr. Barrett never forgave his daughter. The Brownings nevertheless lived happily in Florence for the next 15 years, writing poetry, raising a son, Robert Weidemann Barrett Browning, and, in Elizabeth's case, becoming involved in local politics. After her death in 1861, Browning and his son returned to England; he never remarried.

---

his last sight of his wife, "How beautiful she looks now—how perfectly beautiful!" (Browning in Markus, pp. 333, 334). Even Browning, however, could not remain stoic forever; some weeks later, he broke down in front of Isa Blagden, a female friend, gasping in uncontrollable grief, "I want her, I want her" (Browning in Markus, p. 332). The prospect of being reunited with Elizabeth after death may indeed have been in his mind.

Alfonso II, the fifth duke of Ferrara, Italy, served as a
real-life model for the duke in "My Last Duchess."

"Meeting at Night," "Parting at Morning," and
"Prospice" fall within the category of lyric poetry,
brief pieces which convey the mood or state of
mind of a single speaker. "My Last Duchess,"
however, is a dramatic monologue, a form that
Browning helped make famous. The dramatic
monologue as executed by Browning and others
was characterized by a single character—clearly
not the poet himself—who delivers his speech in
a specific temporal and situational context while
interacting with one or more silent auditors.
Browning's taste for the theatrical often led him
to choose particularly dramatic situations for his
characters: thus, the avaricious bishop in "The
Bishop Orders his Tomb at St. Praxed's Church"
is on his deathbed, the rebellious monk in "Fra
Lippo Lippi" has just been apprehended in the
red-light district by the night watchman, and the
duke of "My Last Duchess" is on the brink of re-
marrying. Fittingly, "My Last Duchess" marked
what was to be a rewarding new direction in
Browning's poetry. Literary scholar William
Clyde DeVane observed, "The poem far surpasses
its source in subtlety and suggestiveness. In the
character of the Duke, Browning makes his first
brilliant study of the culture and morality of the
Italian Renaissance . . . 'My Last Duchess,' though
one of the earliest of Browning's dramatic monologues, has always been considered one of his
greatest" (DeVane, p. 109).

Reception. For much of Browning's youth, critical and popular success as a poet eluded him.
Many critics complained of his rough, unmusi-
cal style and eclectic choice of subject matter,
which some tended to find either obscure or disturbing. In 1846, an anonymous reviewer of his
eight-pamphlet series *Bells and Pomegranates*
made the following pronouncement in *The Eclectic Review*:

> Mr. Browning would be a poet of high order, if
> he could free himself from his affectations, and
> set before himself a great aim in poetry . . .
> besides muddiness of style, Mr. Browning has
> also much muddiness of matter to get rid of.
> There is a sensual trait about his writings which
> will bring him one day a bitterness that no
> amount of reputation will be found an antidote
> for. Let him purify his style and his spirit, and
> we shall hope to meet him again on a future
> day in a far higher and nobler position.
>
> (Litzinger and Smalley, p. 113)

The *Athenauem* reviewer of Browning's *Dramatic
Lyrics* (1842)—in which "My Last Duchess" first
appeared—expressed similar reservations about
his style, declaring "that what Mr. Browning
may, perhaps, consider as an evidence of his
strength is a sign of weakness—what he may regard as a portion of his wealth, is a witness of
its limitation. The inaptitude for giving intelli-
gible expression to his meanings . . . is a defect,
lessening the value, in any available sense of the
meanings themselves" (Litzinger and Smalley,
p. 84).

While these are harsh evaluations, the young
Browning had his defenders as well. John Forster,
writing for *The Examiner*, declared that "in the
simple but manly strain of some of these *Dramatic Lyrics*, we find proof of the firmer march
and steadier control. Mr. Browning will win his
laurel" (Forster in Litzinger and Smalley, p. 82).
Forster also singled out "My Last Duchess"—then
titled "Italy"—and other monologues in the 1842
volume as "full of the quick turns of feeling, the
local truth, and the picturesque force of expression, which the stage so much delights in"
(Forster in Litzinger and Smalley, p. 83). After
the publication of *Dramatic Romances and Lyrics*
(1845)—which included "Meeting at Night" and
"Parting at Morning"—an increasing number of
reviewers found favorable things to say about
Browning's poetry. One critic, writing for *The Examiner*, noted,

> His writing has always the stamp and freshness
> of originality. It is in no respective imitative or
> commonplace. Whatever the verse may be, the

man is in it: the music of it echoing to his mood. When he succeeds, there have been few so successful in the melodious transitions of his rhythm. In all its most poetical and most musical varieties, he is a master; and to us it expresses, in a rare and exquisite degree, the delicacy and truth of his genius.

> (Litzinger and Smalley, p. 104)

A reviewer for *The Oxford and Cambridge Review and University Magazine* concurred,

> Mr. Browning has many faults which, were we disposed to be severe, might be mentioned with proper censure; but his beauties are exceedingly more numerous, and on these we are better pleased to enlarge.
>
> (Litzinger and Smalley, p. 107)

After the publication of his epic, *The Ring and the Book* (1868-69), Browning acquired a large following, which lionized him for the very things he had been criticized for in his youth. Much of his earlier work was reevaluated in light of his new fame. "Meeting at Night" and "Parting at Morning" were praised by *Athenaeum* reviewer Walter Theodore Watts for their lyricism and for the way in which the "'still, sad music of humanity' floats over all the passion" (Watts in Litzinger and Smalley, p. 447). And "My Last Duchess" came to be regarded as one of Browning's best dramatic monologues. *The Saturday Review* described the poem as "a page long since placed near Mr. Tennyson's "Ulysses" by the admirers of exquisite poetical characterization" (Litzinger and Smalley, p. 264), while Richard Henry Stoddard, writing for *Appleton's Journal*, contended that "[Browning] excels Shakespeare, I think, in the art—if it be art—with which he makes his characters betray what they really are. They may deceive themselves, but they cannot deceive us. 'My Last Duchess' is a fine instance of this art" (Stoddard in Litzinger and Smalley, p. 372).

—Pamela S. Loy

For More Information

Browning, Robert. *Robert Browning's Poetry*. ed. James F. Loucks. New York: Norton, 1980.

DeVane, William Clyde. *A Browning Handbook*. New York: Appleton-Century-Crofts, 1955.

Erickson, Lee. *Robert Browning: His Poetry and His Audiences*. Ithaca: Cornell University Press, 1984.

Hair, Donald S. *Robert Browning's Language*. Toronto: University of Toronto Press, 1999.

Hellerstein, Erna Olafson, Leslie Parker Hume, and Karen M. Offen. *Victory Women: A Documentary Account of Women's Lives in Nineteenth-Century England, France, and the United States*. Stanford, Calif.: Stanford University Press, 1981.

Houghton, Walter E. *The Victorian Frame of Mind, 1830-1870*. New Haven: Yale University Press, 1957.

Litzinger, Boyd, and Donald Smalley, eds. *Browning: The Critical Heritage*. London: Routledge & Kegan Paul, 1970.

Markus, Julia. *Dared and Done: The Marriage of Elizabeth Barrett and Robert Browning*. New York: Alfred A. Knopf, 1995.

Mitchell, Sally. *Daily Life in Victorian England*. Westport: Greenwood Press, 1996.

Peterson, William S. ed. *Browning Institute Studies*. Vol. 8. New York: The Browning Institute, 1980.

Prescott, Orville. *Princes of the Renaissance*. New York: Random House, 1969.

Ryals, Clyde de L. *The Life of Robert Browning: A Critical Biography*. Cambridge, Mass.: Blackwell, 1993.

Tucker, Herbert F., Jr. *Browning's Beginnings: The Art of Disclosure*. Minneapolis: University of Minnesota Press, 1980.

Nights at
the Circus

by
Angela Carter

THE LITERARY WORK

A novel set in London, St. Petersburg, and Siberia in 1899; published in 1984.

SYNOPSIS

A winged *aerialiste* tells her life story to a reporter. Afterwards the reporter joins the circus himself, following the performer on a world tour.

Nights at the Circus is the eighth of nine novels written by Angela Carter (1940-92) before she died of cancer at the age of 51, in her literary prime. Raised in Yorkshire and London by middle-class parents, Carter began writing in the 1960s, publishing her first novel while still an undergraduate at Bristol University. After her initial successes, Carter moved to Japan from 1969 to 1972, a period she cites as extremely influential on her later work. In Japan she gained a new sense of what it meant to be a woman, and the experience radicalized her. Carter's fiction is complex, densely allusive, sexually explicit, frequently derisive, and always subversive. Although it makes much use of themes and images from myth and fairy tales, she defined myth as "consolatory nonsense," declaring herself to be in the demythologizing business (Carter in Peach, p. 9). The novelist Salman Rushdie (see **Midnight's Children,** also in *WLAIT 4: British and Irish Literature and Its Times*) once described Carter's books as drawing "their strength, their vitality, from all that is unrighteous, illegitimate, low" (Rushdie, p. 5). Following in this tradition, *Nights at the Circus* recounts the rise of a female foundling who is raised by prostitutes and becomes a celebrated circus performer; she serves as a vital symbol of the new vistas for women that would unfold in the twentieth century.

Events in History at the
Time the Novel Takes Place

Victoria, industry, and urban disparity. The novel is set in 1899, a turning point, in many

ways, for British and world history. In Britain, it was the end of the Victorian era, named for the reign of Queen Victoria (1837-1901), who, with her husband Prince Albert, set an example of duty and decorum, emphasizing adherence to a strict code of propriety. This image of prim morality was partially undercut at the end of the Victorian era by the behavior of Victoria's eldest son, Edward, the Prince of Wales, to whom the British throne would soon pass. Edward embarrassed the court and entertained the public with his scandalous and highly publicized lifestyle of gambling, drinking, and womanizing. In the novel, Prince Edward is a nightly spectator at London's Alhambra Theater where Fevvers, the novel's winged heroine, performs her trapeze act. There he sits "stroking his beard and meditating upon the erotic possibilities of her ability to hover and the problematic of his paunch vis-à-vis the missionary position" (Carter, *Nights at the Circus*, p. 18).

Angela Carter

During Victoria's reign, Britain had consolidated its position as the world's first industrialized nation. By the end of the nineteenth century, 80 percent of the population lived in town, making Britain the world's first urban nation as well. Britain's industrial strength allowed British imperialism, driven by trade, to extend British influence to parts of Asia, Africa, the Caribbean, and the South Pacific—which by this time had been subsumed by the British Empire. The heart of the British Empire was London, a city that, like other great cities of the day, contained within its ever-widening boundaries great disparities in fortune. The most prosperous Londoners had their homes in the glamorous West End of town with its majestic houses, decorous gardens, and wide well-lit streets. The East End, characterized by dark narrow alleys, omnipresent filth, and crowded dilapidated dwellings, was notoriously the poorest part of town, but poor parts surrounded the small enclave of rich London on all sides.

Towards the end of the nineteenth century, conditions began to materially improve for the working classes. Trade unions gained some power, which enabled them to offer their members sickness and unemployment benefits. Wages increased, and housing and diet began to improve. Workers even gained a little leisure time, and small amounts of spending money to enjoy it. The divide between the two Londons, rich and poor, was bridged to some extent by a more complex class system as the middle class expanded and diversified with the opening of new jobs in the service sector. Still, despite these changes, by century's end nearly 30 percent of London remained in abject poverty.

Victorian women. Just as the two Londons were separated by a gulf of difference, middle- and upper-class women of the Victorian era were regarded as altogether different from working-class women. Restriction to the sphere of home seemed necessary for respectable Englishwomen of the middle and upper classes. Working women, in contrast, could not afford this luxury. The working-class perspective, moreover, did not view the public world as a place of dangerous impropriety for women. With families of seven children sharing a single room, or even a part of a room in a boarding house, the city streets of poor London formed a necessary annex to home; in fact, they were known as "the drawing-room of the poor," a place where women as well as men conducted much of their lives (Barret-Ducrocq, p. 9). Such mixing of the sexes and lack of privacy made modesty—considered essential by middle- and upper-class women—an impossibility for the working-class woman. In respect to clothing too, there were glaring differences. As Victorian fashion dictated more and more articles of clothing for women, the poor woman, who could not afford so many superfluous items of dress, were seen as shockingly underdressed; the literature of the day went so far as to characterize poor women as naked for simply failing to wear gloves, hats, or the requisite number of petticoats. Such circumstances resulted in a middle-to-upper-class concept of the poor in general, and poor women in particular, as individuals who were necessarily immoral.

The phenomenon of working-class children born out of wedlock was seen as a symptom of this immorality. In actuality, working-class children born out of wedlock were the product of a different morality, a more traditional rural ethic whereby premarital sex was condoned as long as there was a definite engagement. This ethic was not shared by the middle and upper classes, who had come to regard such behavior as shocking. Reflecting their outrage, "bastardy clauses," negating an unmarried mother's right to compensation by the child's father, were added to the Poor Law when it was reformed in 1834. The reformers reasoned that the Poor Law, which gave unwed mothers the legal right to demand marriage or monetary compensation from unwed fathers, encouraged moral laxity, and also led to the entrapment of some "innocent" men. Unsurprisingly, many late-nineteenth-century unwed fathers took advantage of this change in the law and the changing mores of their time to desert their pregnant girlfriends.

What was a pregnant, unwed working woman to do? There was no social safety net at this time, and wages for working women, barely enough to keep a single person alive, could in no way pay for a nurse to care for a child while the mother worked. Some women tried the dangerous drugs offered illegally by certain chemists to induce abortion, but these often failed to produce the desired effect. The first foundling hospital was established in London in 1741, but the rules for admission were stringent, and many could not meet the strict requirements. *Nights at the Circus* presents one possibility, no doubt resorted to by many unfortunate women: the infant Fevvers is found abandoned in a basket on the front steps of a stately London house, which turns out to be a brothel.

Victorian prostitution. Prostitution was seen as the ultimate expression of the supposed immorality of working-class women. In fact, in nineteenth-century London, it was not unusual for working-class women to resort to prostitution, either occasionally or as a full-time profession. Poverty wages, long off-seasons for many kinds of work, and 12-hour workdays filled with difficult, tedious labor made prostitution an alluring option for some women.

Social workers and charitable organizations of the time compiled information on London prostitutes from which the following picture emerges: most were "unskilled daughters of the unskilled classes," exchanging futureless careers as maids or low-wage laborers for what seemed a relatively profitable, independent line of work (Abraham Flexner in Walkowitz, p. 15). The late teens was the usual age for a young woman, usually an orphan, to become a prostitute, and most left the trade in their mid-twenties. Although some London prostitutes catered to the upper and middle classes, the majority served a working-class clientele. A few made enough money to put some aside for the future, but the average prostitute barely scraped by, earning about as much as she would at other low-wage jobs open to women at the time, though she usually enjoyed more autonomy than she would in these other jobs.

Most prostitutes were streetwalkers—only a small minority lived in brothels, largely because of autonomy. In a brothel, explained one woman, "You ain't your own master, and I always like my freedom" (Walkowitz, p. 24). The novel describes a rare yet realistic situation in which prostitutes live together in an outwardly respectable establishment, whose "inmates had achieved a 'quiet' truce with the police" (Walkowitz, p. 24). The camaraderie and literary interests of the novel's prostitutes likewise reflect reality. Victorian prostitutes were known to pool resources to help one of their number; some prostitutes even formed small communistic societies where all earnings were shared and spent according to need. And on several occasions social workers were shocked by the intellectual level of a prostitute, who had "really superior books lying about" in her abode (Walkowitz, p. 28).

In the mid-nineteenth century, prostitution attracted public attention when the 1864 Contagious Diseases Act forced prostitutes to undergo regular internal examinations for venereal disease. The aim was to control infection among members of the armed forces, who had frequent recourse to prostitutes at this time. The 1864 measure, and especially the protests against it, brought to light an aspect of British society that hitherto had been largely ignored. Although some feminists protested forced examination as violence against women, most protesters objected to the seeming legitimization of vice that the Act entailed. In response to this legitimization, a movement to wipe out prostitution was born.

There was disagreement as to the root cause of prostitution. A few progressives saw prostitution as directly linked to the lack of economic opportunities open to women. Evangelical reformers tended to see prostitution as one symptom of the immorality of the poor, led astray by their "promiscuous" living conditions and the decline in churchgoing and traditional values. Still others saw the problem of prostitution as inherent to female sexuality; only severe social and legal restraints could keep women from their natural depravity. In the novel, Fevvers argues against this fairly common misogynist view: "though some of the customers would swear that whores do it for pleasure, that is only to ease their own consciences, so that they will feel less foolish when they fork out hard cash for pleasure that has no real existence unless given freely" (*Nights at the Circus*, p. 39). The Contagious Diseases Act was repealed in 1886. But moral crusaders continued to wage a social-purity campaign, which in the end led not to the demise of prostitution but only to more difficulties for its women, because of added attention from the crusaders and police.

Russia 1899. After leaving London, the novel moves to St. Petersburg, capital of Russia from 1703 to 1918. Although Russia formed trade and political alliances with countries to the west, life there remained quite different from life in nineteenth-century western Europe. Russia's leader, the tsar, was an autocratic dictator; the Orthodox Church strictly controlled many aspects of Russian culture; and the masses remained peas-

---

VICTORIAN FEMINISM

Although the term "feminism" was not coined until the end of the nineteenth century, several Victorian social movements can be described as feminist. For example, Josephine Butler led the fight to repeal the Contagious Diseases Act, Emily Davies fought for the right of women to be admitted to universities, and Millicent Garrett Fawcett organized the women's suffrage movement. All three of these feminist movements had broad support among men as well as women. At the time, feminism was informed by a strong sense of the differences believed to exist between men and women. Women were regarded as natural nurturers, the moral superiors of men. The belief was that a woman had greater ability to empathize with the weak; consequently she had greater responsibility to take their part against the strong.

---

ants, living in slavelike serfdom, a possession of either the state or the noble on whose land they dwelt. Some saw these factors as the source of Russia's might, others perceived them to be barriers to Russia's potential greatness. In western Europe, Russia was generally regarded as a backwards nation.

In 1899, the reigning emperor in Russia's capital was Nicholas II. His wife, the Empress Alexandra, was a German granddaughter of England's Queen Victoria, but despite this connection with constitutional England, Nicholas adhered to the principles of autocracy, openly ridiculing the idea of representative government. He had enemies. Bolshevik leader Vladimir Lenin published his first major work, *The Development of Capitalism in Russia,* in 1899. The political

movement that would lead to the unsuccessful Russian Revolution six years hence was growing at home and among Russian dissidents abroad, notably in Britain. In the novel, Fevvers's socialist foster-mother, Lizzie, sends news of the movement in St. Petersburg to Russian revolutionaries in London exile.

From the days of Peter the Great (1672-1725), Russia had been expanding her boundaries to form an empire of her own. Over time, Russia gained control of Poland, Finland, western Turkey, Georgia and the Caucasus. Western Europe feared and resisted Russia's expansion. Britain, in particular, cast a wary eye on Russian inland encroachment on India, the "jewel in the crown" of the British Empire. In the nineteenth century, Russia and Britain were each other's chief adversaries, not only because of this imperial dispute, but also because Russian autocracy and British liberalism represented opposing poles on the spectrum of European politics.

Siberia 1899. While western Europe viewed Russian expansion to the west and south with concern, Russia was also extending her control to the east, over Siberia in northern Asia. Siberia spreads from the Ural mountain range in the west all the way to the Pacific Ocean in the east. It comprises three distinct geographic zones: the north, a barren tundra covered in snow for much of the year; the taiga, a middle forest belt; and the south, a hot, dry desert. Like the landscape, the native peoples vary greatly, from pastoral nomads in the south, to reindeer-herders in the north, from hunters and gatherers in the taiga, to the peoples of the northern and eastern coasts, who live almost exclusively off sea mammals. All Siberians were essentially nomadic prior to Russian rule.

In the sixteenth century, several leaders of Siberian peoples were induced to sign treaties acknowledging the power of the Russian Tsar and pledging tribute. Russia, however, did not seriously turn its attention to Siberia until the nineteenth century. Construction of the Trans-Siberian Railroad, the only means of access to the region other than by human or animal foot, had not begun until 1891. By its completion in 1905, it would stretch from Chelyabinsk in the Ural Mountains through the taiga to Vladivostok on the Sea of Japan. At 5,500 miles, it was the world's longest railroad. In the novel, Fevvers's circus company takes the Trans-Siberian Express to get from Russia to Japan.

The Russian government came to view exile as a means of populating this eastern frontier, punishing all kinds of infractions from treason to fortune telling with expulsion to Siberia. Some exiles were sentenced to hard labor in Siberia's gold, silver, and coal mines—others were merely forced to settle the land and forbidden to return across the Urals. For many, this was punishment enough: the country was desolate, and the journey itself dangerous, with 10 to 15 percent of exiles dying en route. Nearly a million Russians were exiled to Siberia over the course of the nineteenth century; by the century's end, Russia was sending an unprecedented 19,000 exiles to Siberia each year.

The Siberian peoples suffered under pressure from Russian exiles and Russian rule in general. By the nineteenth century, native Siberians had been weakened by smallpox, influenza, and syphilis, first caught, it seems, from Russian settlers. Unscrupulous Russian officials demanded ever greater tributes of furs and other raw materials from the native peoples, who fell into a state of indebted pauperism. Meanwhile the environment that had for centuries provided their livelihood was slowly but surely being destroyed through the overhunting of Siberia's fur-bearing animals and the felling of its forests to provide farmland.

The circus. The first modern circus was presented in London in the 1770s by Philip Astley, an ex-soldier who delighted his audiences with equestrian shows and performing animals. After Astley began the circus tradition in Europe, some who had been his collaborators traveled to the United States and began to present circus entertainments there. By far, the most famous U.S. circus proprietor was American-born Phineas T. Barnum, who said there was a sucker born every minute and called himself "Prince of Humbugs." Barnum began his circus career exhibiting Joice Heth, an African-American woman whom he presented as the 161-year-old former nurse of the infant George Washington. When ticket sales started to flag, Barnum wrote an anonymous letter to the editor of a local paper claiming that Joice Heth was actually a contraption made of "India-rubber, whalebone, and concealed springs and that her speech was produced by a ventriloquist" (Croft-Cooke and Cotes, p. 59). This incident is obviously referenced in the novel when U.S. circus owner Colonel Kearney attempts to boost flagging ticket sales by writing a similar letter to the editor to the effect that "Fevvers is not a woman at all but a cunningly constructed automaton made up of whalebone, india-rubber and springs" (*Nights at the Circus*, p. 147). In both

instances, the raising of doubt actually spurs public curiosity, and the exhibition is a great success.

Barnum did not establish his first successful large-scale traveling circus until 1870, when he was 60 years old, many years after the Joice Heth exhibition. In 1880, another leading U.S. circus owned by James A. Bailey joined forces with Barnum's show to become "Barnum and Bailey, The Greatest Show on Earth." In 1888, Barnum and Bailey brought their show to England, where it was attended by Prince Edward and Prime Minister William Gladstone. Barnum later wrote a book entitled *The Humbugs of the World*. In Carter's novel, the character Walser considers using the title "Great Humbugs of the World" for the series of interviews that will include the life story of winged trapeze artist Fevvers.

Trapeze artists had been a fixture of circuses since the eighteenth century, but it was not until the innovations of Frenchman Jules Léotard (for whom the leotard is named) in 1859, that the flying trapeze was used. Before Léotard, trapezes had been fixed bars on which gymnasts performed, but with the flying trapeze, which swung through the air on ropes, a new kind of aerial act was born. Using the flying trapeze, Lena Jordan performed the world's first forward triple somersault in Sydney, Australia, in 1897. It is the most impressive of trapeze-artist feats—one that for many has ended in a broken neck. In order to achieve the triple somersault the artist must traverse the air at 62 miles per hour, but in the novel, Fevvers manages to perform the feat at a mere 25 miles per hour, thanks to her wings.

The Novel in Focus

Plot summary. The novel, which takes place in 1899, is divided into three sections: London, St. Petersburg, and Siberia. In London, 25-year-old U.S. reporter Jack Walser is taking a rest from his career as a roving war correspondent for the *New York Times* in order to recover from a dose of yellow fever incurred in the line of duty. He has decided to pass the time writing a few human interest stories, which takes him to the dressing room of famous English aerialiste Sophie Fevvers. He is interviewing her for a series of articles tentatively titled "Great Humbugs of the World," which applies to Fevvers, thinks Walser, because she claims to have wings that are natural appendages of her anatomy.

Fevvers is famous for her wings and for aerial acrobatics that she has performed to much ac-

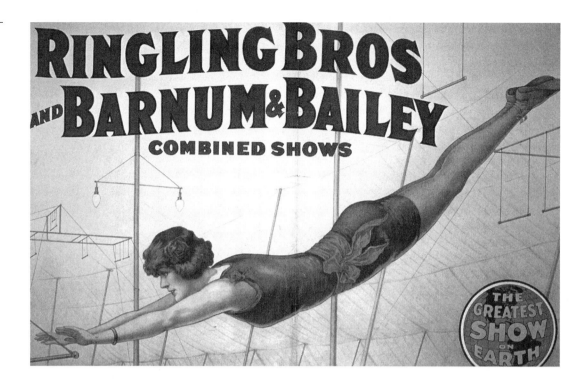

An advertisement for the Ringling Brothers and Barnum & Bailey Circus depicting the death-defying trapeze act. Barnum and Bailey brought their show to England in 1888, shortly before the setting of *Nights at the Circus,* whose heroine herself achieves fame as a trapeze artist.

claim in the great cities of Europe. Known as "the Cockney Venus," at six feet two inches tall, the blond Fevvers deliberately plays upon the controversy and uncertainty surrounding her wings, even taking as her publicity slogan the question "Is she fact or is she fiction?" (*Nights at the Circus*, p. 7). Indeed, as seen through Walser's eyes, Fevvers is a woman of many contradictions. She washes down eel pies with bottle after bottle of the finest champagne, pausing occasionally to belch and fart. She is mercenary yet boundlessly generous, crass yet charming. Throughout his interview with her, Walser is never sure how much of what Fevvers says he should believe.

In her cramped, smelly dressing room, Fevvers tells Walser her life story with occasional assistance from her "dresser" Lizzie, whom we later learn is Fevvers's foster mother. Abandoned as an infant on the steps of a London brothel, Fevvers was taken in and lovingly raised by a group of suffragist prostitutes led by an unusual madame called "Nelson," who wore an eye-patch and had a habit of dressing in military uniform. The prostitutes named the foundling "Fevvers," a cockney pronunciation of the word "feathers," because when they found her she had soft down growing on her shoulder blades, and it appeared that the child was "going to sprout Fevvers!" (*Nights at the Circus*, p. 12). In the brothel, Fevvers is never called upon to take up the trade, but she earns her keep as a young girl by portraying Cupid with a tiny golden bow and arrows, posing as a sort of living tableau in the drawing room alcove. Fevvers grows at a prodigious rate, her burgeoning bosom matched in development by two lumps on her back, from which wings burst forth when she is 14. Flight, however, does not come naturally; Fevvers must study the birds that nest on window ledges, as well as books on aerodynamics from the well-stocked brothel library, in order to learn this skill. She exchanges her role as Cupid for that of Winged Victory, posing with a sword that she adopts as her mascot and always wears on her person.

Not long after, the madame, Nelson, dies in a freak accident, and her nasty cleric brother comes to claim the brothel mansion. All the prostitutes are heartbroken, but must go their separate ways. Lizzie and Fevvers move in with Lizzie's sister until the family falls into dire financial straits and Fevvers decides there is nothing else to do but to sell herself to Madame Schreck in order to support her friends. Madame Schreck is a ghoulish woman who runs a "museum of woman monsters," as she describes it. In fact, it is another brothel of sorts, staffed by persons with physical abnormalities and frequented by men who are "troubled in their . . . souls" (*Nights at the Circus*, p. 57). Fevvers lives as a virtual prisoner in a barred cell in Madame Schreck's house, until one day Madame Schreck sells her to a man who goes by the name Christian Rosencreutz. Rosencreutz believes he can achieve eternal youth for himself through Fevvers's blood, but before he can sacrifice her on his May Day altar, Fevvers fends him off with her trusty sword and flies to freedom. Afterwards, Fevvers begins her career as an aerialiste, and the rest is history.

Over the course of the interview, Walser has become utterly fascinated with his subject. He decides to join Colonel Kearney's Grand Imperial Tour, the circus that has booked Fevvers for a tour across Russia to Japan and then on to the United States, in order to write a more comprehensive piece on the Cockney Venus. The Colonel, a Kentucky gentleman who wears the stars and stripes held together with a dollar-sign belt buckle, and whose motto is "bamboozlem," has misgivings, but his prophetic pig Sibyl advises him to hire Walser as a clown, and, unbeknownst to Fevvers, Walser travels with the circus to their first stop in St. Petersburg.

In St. Petersburg, the circus is a smashing success. Walser learns the art of clowning from Buffo the Great, a London-bred alcoholic clown whose comic antics belie a profound sorrow, and who characterizes clowns as "whores of mirth" (*Nights at the Circus*, p. 119). Fevvers eventually discovers Walser's presence, but is not displeased that he has followed her. An incipient romance manifests itself between the two.

After the final show in St. Petersburg, Fevvers, lured by the promise of a diamond necklace, accepts the invitation of a certain Grand Duke to visit his remote estate. It seems the Duke believes the hype about Fevvers being an automaton, and wishes to add her to his collection of elaborate toys. Although Fevvers loses her sword in the confrontation, she manages to escape the Duke and board the Trans-Siberia Express with the rest of the circus.

The train makes its long way through the frozen wastes of Siberia until an explosion on the tracks causes a fiery wreck. All are unharmed, except for Fevvers, who has a broken wing. It turns out that the explosion was caused by a band of outlaws, who are fleeing punishment for the vengeance they took on corrupt nobles and officials who had "forcibly dishonoured" the outlaws'

sisters, wives, and daughters (*Nights at the Circus*, p. 230). Fevvers has been touted in the gutter press as the fiancée of the Prince of Wales, and the outlaws believe she can intercede on their behalf with her royal mother-in-law, Queen Victoria, who is a distant relative of the Russian tsar. Hoping to convince Fevvers to take their part, the outlaws bring the whole circus troupe back to their hideout in the forest—except for Walser, who has been knocked senseless and lies hidden beneath the train wreckage. Walser is soon rescued by a group of women who have just escaped from a correctional facility in the Siberian wastes and who plan to form their own all-woman lesbian society somewhere in the vast wilderness. Walser is not allowed to accompany them but does meet a friendly shaman from among local Siberians, and, remembering nothing of his past, Walser is taken on as shaman's apprentice.

Meanwhile, after Fevvers dashes the outlaws' hopes by revealing her lack of royal connections, they die in a blizzard, too disconsolate to seek shelter. The clowns also lose their will to live, joining the outlaws in their frozen fate. But Fevvers, Lizzie, and the rest of the circus troupe survive. Making their way back to civilization, they come across Walser in the camp of the local Siberians, a group of reindeer-herders.

Fevvers, whose spirits have been at a low ebb since St. Petersburg, is revitalized by the looks of awe she receives from the native Siberians; suddenly she is back on stage, and all is well with the world. The sight and sound of Fevvers restores Walser's memory, and the novel ends when the two make love in the shaman's shack, with Walser imagining the sensation his story will cause and a future of wedded bliss with "Mrs. Sophie Walser."

Fevvers and the New Woman. In *Nights at the Circus*, Fevvers is an allegorical figure representing new womanhood on the eve of the twentieth century. Carter herself has spoken about the meaning of her writing: "I do put everything in a novel to be *read*, read the way allegory was intended to be read, the way you are supposed to read **Sir Gawain and the Green Knight** [in *WLAIT 3: British and Irish Literature and Its Times*]—on as many levels as you can comfortably cope with at the time" (Carter in Day, p. 8).

> "'Oh, my little one, I think you must be the pure child of the century that just now is waiting in the wings, the New Age in which no women will be bound down to the ground.'"
> (Ma Nelson to Fevvers in *Nights at the Circus*, p. 25)

The symbolism is made explicit at several points in the novel, and Carter has described it in an interview, explaining that the novel "is set at exactly the moment in European history when things began to change. It's set at that time quite deliberately, and [Fevvers] is the new woman" (Carter in Day, p. 172). The six-foot-tall winged working girl of humble origins and immodest ambitions is a powerful symbol of the possibilities for women inherent at the end of the nineteenth century—a time when the concept of the "new woman" gained currency. It was a concept that achieved notoriety in 1894, through Sarah Grand's article "The New Aspect of the Woman Question," in which she popularized the notion of the "new woman," one who defies traditional roles and restrictions.

The concept of the new woman pointed to real-life trends. The education of girls, which had improved and expanded with the passage of key education acts in 1870 and 1880, began to bear fruit in the 1890s, as the educated daughters of the middle and upper classes confronted the world with a set of expectations different from those of their mothers. At the same time, better employment opportunities were opening up for women as a result of expansion in the service sector of the economy, and the British government began allowing women to serve on various committees and the Board of Education. These factors doubtless played a part in the phenomenon of a number of young middle- and upper-class women who shocked turn-of-the-century society by rejecting chaperones, engaging in sport and other strenuous activities, adopting "rational dress" (divided skirts, bloomers), smoking, and refusing to promise to "obey" their husbands in marriage ceremonies. These were the new women, harbingers of a coming era viewed by some with hope, by many with alarm.

In the wake of Sarah Grand's article, other writers took up the theme of the new woman, mostly in a ridiculing, disapproving tone. The new woman was represented as mannish, shrieking, unnatural, and humorless; her demands for equality were treated as obviously absurd. One literary scholar suggests that Fevvers is an apt representative of the new woman at the turn of the century:

> In 1899 hardly anyone had seen a mentally and emotionally newly constituted woman, in the same way as no one had seen a woman with wings. The difficulty we might have in coming to terms with the notion of a woman who literally possesses wings enacts the difficulty that was felt in the late nineteenth century . . . in coming to terms with mentally and emotionally "new" or reconstructed women.
>
> (Day, p. 176)

Like the new woman of the 1890s, Fevvers makes people uncomfortable. Her role as Winged Victory at Ma Nelson's brothel is a hopeful omen for the future of women in the coming century, but the presence of the sword-brandishing living statue makes the brothel's male clientele nervous, causing business to fall off. Fevvers's motto: "Is she fact or is she fiction?" further speaks to the disbelief and puzzlement that greeted the advent of the new woman, just as her stint at the museum of female monsters reflects the popular consensus that judged the new woman to be monstrously unnatural.

But, as suggested above, it is the presence of Fevvers's wings that is most striking. The physical freedom they afford her can be understood to foreshadow the new personal and political freedoms women would enjoy in the coming century. Fevvers's wings also link her to an image of women popular in the nineteenth century, the "Angel in the House." In Coventry Patmore's 1856 poem of that name, he idealizes his wife as an angel of the domestic sphere, purified by her seclusion in the nurturing realm of home. In the latter half of the nineteenth century, woman as the "angel in the house" was seen to transcend the public sphere, and so could be denied a place in it. The dark side of this idealization is shown in the novel when Fevvers is abducted by "Christian Rosencreutz," who calls her by angelic names but wishes to sacrifice her so that he can gain eternal youth for himself by imbibing her essence. Fevvers reveals Rosencreutz's true identity only to Walser, not to the reader. She does, however, hint at his identity:

> I saw in the paper only yesterday how he gives the most impressive speech in the House on the subject of Votes for Women. Which he is against. On account of how women are of a different soul-substance from men, cut from a different bolt of spirit cloth, and altogether too pure and rarefied to be bothering their pretty little heads with things of *this* world, such as the Irish question and the Boer War.
>
> (*Nights at the Circus*, pp. 78-79).

The comment alludes to British Prime Minister from 1868 to 1894, William Gladstone, whose diaries reveal prostitution to be "the chief burden of [his] soul," making the former Prime Minister a likely candidate for the role of Rosencreutz (Walkowitz, p. 32). The otherwise liberal Gladstone consistently rejected any proposal to give women the parliamentary vote.

Whoever Rosencreutz may be, his attempt to sacrifice Fevvers for his own well-being suggests an ulterior motive for the idealization of women as angels. But just as the characterization of Fevvers resists idealization ("the *aerialiste*, who now shifted from one buttock to the other and—'better out than in, sir'—let a ripping fart ring round the room"), Fevvers rejects her role as sacrificial angel and escapes the trap Rosencreutz sets for her (*Nights at the Circus*, p. 11). This is another important aspect of her wingedness, the ability to escape the many snares set for her, mostly by sadistic men. Yet Fevvers's career is checkered, marked by brushes with catastrophe. Does this portend a troubled future for the new woman? Lizzie's reaction to Fevvers's optimism bodes ill:

> "And once the old world has turned on its axle so that the new dawn can dawn, then, ah, then! all the women will have wings, the same as I. . . . The dolls' house doors will open, the brothels will spill forth their prisoners, the cages, gilded or otherwise, all over the world, in every land, will let forth their inmates singing together the dawn chorus of the new, the transformed—
> "It's going to be more complicated than that," interpolated Lizzie. "This old witch sees storms ahead, my girl."
>
> (*Nights at the Circus*, pp. 285-86)

In short, as an allegorical figure, Fevvers represents the hope and freedom for women on the eve of the twentieth century, but also the struggle and uncertainty that faced them.

Sources and literary context. *Nights at the Circus* features fantastic elements, but grounds them in history, referencing many real people, places, and events from the late nineteenth century. As discussed above, Gladstone seems to be portrayed in the figure of Christian Rosencreutz, and Colonel Kearney seems to be an incarnation of P. T. Barnum. To the material of history, Angela Carter brings a rich assortment of literary and theoretical influences; the novel abounds in allusions to Greek myth, European fairy tales, Shakespeare, William Blake, T. S. Eliot, Baudelaire, Michel Foucault, and the Marquis de Sade, to name just a few. Fevvers describes the attitudes of the brothel's clientele, for example, saying "I put it down to the influence of *Baudelaire* . . . a poor fellow who loved whores not for the pleasure of it but, as he perceived it, the *horror* of it" (*Nights at the Circus*, p. 38). The reference

here is to the Frenchman Baudelaire's verses about his mulatto mistress Jeanne Duval, whom he depicted as "demon," "serpent," and "satan" (Baudelaire, pp. 69, 71, 83).

In regard to the form of *Nights at the Circus*, Carter "purposely used a certain eighteenth century fictional device, the picaresque, where people have adventures in order to find themselves in places where they can discuss philosophical concepts without distractions" (Carter in Day, p. 169).

ANGELA CARTER AND THE FAIRY-TALE TRADITION

Angela Carter is known for her politically pointed retellings of fairytales. *Nights at the Circus* alludes several times to the European fairy-tale tradition. Walser, for instance, is likened to "the boy in the fairy story who does not know how to shiver" (*Nights at the Circus*, p. 10). Fevvers's teeth are "big and carnivorous as those of Red Riding Hood's grandmother" (*Nights at the Circus*, p. 18). Before Fevvers (the princess) can rescue Walser (the prince) from his Siberian exile in an inversion of a common fairy-tale motif, Lizzie warns her that "The Prince who rescues the Princess from the dragon's lair is always forced to marry her, whether they've taken a liking to one another or not. That's the custom" (*Nights at the Circus*, p. 281). The one fairy tale referenced over and over again is "Sleeping Beauty." St. Petersburg is described as a "Sleeping Beauty of a city . . . longing yet fearing the rough and bloody kiss that will awaken her" (*Nights at the Circus*, p. 97). In the "museum of female monsters," one of Fevvers's fellow freaks is nicknamed the Sleeping Beauty because of her narcolepsy, a malady that dates to the onset of her puberty, just when the lengthy sleep began for the fairy-tale character.

Events in History at the Time the Novel Was Written

Britain 1984. The period between the novel's setting (1899) and publication (1984) comprises most of the twentieth century, a time of great incident and transformation, including the Russian revolutions of 1905 and 1917, and World Wars I and II (1914-1918; 1939-1945). "I am the pure product," explained Carter, "of an advanced, industrialized, post-imperialist country in decline" (Carter in Peach, p. 13). World War II left Britain with an enormous national debt, which led to austerity measures at home and the forfeiture of colonies overseas. Postwar economic troubles coupled with disastrous government "solutions" resulted in a drop in living standards during the 1970s, a time when other nations of western Europe were increasing their standards of living. Some saw the demands of labor unions, who were trying to negotiate a better deal for their constituents at this time, as contributing to the nation's decline. A rash of strikes by public service workers in the "winter of discontent" in 1978-79 resulted in mountains of uncollected trash and even unburied bodies, and many grew disenchanted with labor's cause. They acted by electing the conservative prime minister Margaret Thatcher in 1979, whose privatizing measures only intensified the economic woes of the majority of British people. By 1983, unemployment had reached a record high of over 15 percent, as factories and mills closed down. Thatcher claimed to support Victorian values, which she defined as self-sufficiency, personal responsibility, and minimal reliance on government intervention. *Nights at the Circus* provides a counterpoint to such nostalgic yearnings, presenting the Victorian era as a time when women looked to the future for better values than those that informed their own day. Were their hopes justified?

British women in the 1980s. With the prime ministry of Margaret Thatcher, it seemed that women had finally achieved power on an equal footing with men in British society. Yet, although some achieved wealth and power in 1980s Britain, the majority of women suffered under Thatcher's policies, which mostly benefitted the rich and hurt the poor. The government cut social services such as maternity leave, childcare, and subsidized school lunches, and wages dropped for working women, aggravating their difficulties.

Because a few women, like Margaret Thatcher, attained positions of power, some argued that sex discrimination was no longer an issue. However, women were still largely excluded from business. Lending institutions tended to deny loans to female entrepreneurs, and even by the late 1980s, women held only 15 percent of management-level jobs, and these were mostly in lower management. Finally, women in the Thatcher years suffered twice as much as underemployment as men. Society had hardly become equal.

In the 1980s, adultery, illegitimacy, and divorce were much less stigmatized than in the Victorian era, yet in some ways, the "Victorian values" that Margaret Thatcher extolled had never really disappeared. The same hypocrisy that had trapped women between a middle-class homebound ideal and an exploited working-class reality in the Victorian era existed in a new guise in the 1980s. Thatcher's Conservative Party stressed women's role in the home and devalued women's role in the workplace, yet many industries and sectors of the service economy relied on cheap female labor to keep Britain's financial wheels turning. The moral outcry against "permissiveness" that had characterized the end of the nineteenth century was repeated in the 1980s with the same pairing of strange bedfellows that saw Conservative forces join with feminist groups in protesting pornography, strip clubs, and prostitution. As before, this increase in public outrage made it harder for prostitutes to ply their trade, yet business did not drop off. Finally, despite much talk of family values, sex scandals surfaced under Thatcher's Conservative government, again echoing the hypocrisy of a Victorian era in which moral propriety was undercut by the promiscuous exploits of Prince Edward. Certainly there had been change, but in many ways the female plight had remained the same.

Reviews. Angela Carter's fiction is characterized by reviewers in the manner of a circus act: highly theatrical, larger than life, risky, and requiring a keen sense of balance. Reviews of *Nights at the Circus* focus on the perceived success or failure of Carter's daring high-wire act. One reviewer, after praising the first London-based section of the book, takes issue with the concluding two thirds, where he believes Carter loses her delicate balance between the realistic and the impossible, because impossibilities are presented straightforwardly, not, the way they are in the first section, as part of the questionable narrative of Fevvers. Other reviewers also saw Carter's task as one of balance, but were generally awed by the author's ability to keep the story brilliantly aloft. For them, the novel does indeed have an overwhelming, oftentimes overdone effect, but this only adds to its allure, making it "a luscious and gooey dessert of a book, doled out in sinful proportions" (Banks, p. 1). Another reviewer concurs, summing up *Nights at the Circus* as Carter's "finest achievement so far and a remarkable book by any standards" (Nye in Bristow and Broughton, p. 5).

—Kimberly Ball

For More Information

Banks, Carolyn. "Angela Carter's Flights of Fancy." *The Washington Post*, February 3, 1985, Book World, 1, 13.

Barret-Ducrocq, Françoise. *Love in the Time of Victoria: Sexuality, Class and Gender in Nineteenth Century London*. Trans. John Owe. London: Verso, 1991.

Baudelaire, Charles-Pierre. *Baudelaire: Selected Poems*. Ed. Joanna Richardson. Harmondsworth, England: Penguin, 1975.

Bristow, Joseph, and Trev Lynn Broughton, eds. *The Infernal Desires of Angela Carter: Fiction, Femininity, Feminism*. London: Longman, 1997.

Carter, Angela. *Nights at the Circus*. New York: Penguin, 1993.

Croft-Cooke, Rupert, and Peter Cotes. *Circus: A World History*. London: Paul Elek, 1976.

Day, Aidan. *Angela Carter: The Rational Glass*. Manchester: Manchester University Press, 1998.

Forsyth, James. *A History of the Peoples of Siberia: Russia's North Asian Colony 1581-1990*. Cambridge: Cambridge University Press, 1992.

Morgan, Kenneth O. *The People's Peace: British History 1945-1989*. Oxford: Oxford University Press, 1990.

Peach, Linden. *Angela Carter*. New York: St. Martin's, 1988.

Riasanovsky, Nicholas V. *A History of Russia*. Oxford: Oxford University Press, 1984.

Rushdie, Salman. "Angela Carter, 1940-92: A Very Good Wizard, a Very Dear Friend." *The New York Times Book Review*, 8 March 1992, 5.

Walkowitz, Judith R. *Prostitution and Victorian Society: Women, Class, and the State*. Cambridge: Cambridge University Press, 1989.

On the Origin of Species

by

Charles Darwin

The most influential scientific writer of the nineteenth century, Charles Robert Darwin (1809-82) sought a quiet life in rural Kent, where he was nonetheless plagued by gastrointestinal troubles, likely due to a tropical disease but undoubtedly exacerbated by worry. Charles was born to a wealthy Whig family, who had, after a couple of generations of vocal liberalism and Unitarian dissent, settled down into "Anglican respectability" (Desmond and Moore p. 19). Infinitely more interested in natural history than medicine (for which his family originally sent him to the University of Edinburgh) or divinity (for which he read at Cambridge University), Darwin put other pursuits on hold and accepted the post of naturalist and companion to Captain Fitzroy of the HMS *Beagle*. The voyage was decisive. Darwin spent five years on the *Beagle* (1831-36), exploring the world and gathering enough material to keep him busy for decades to come. Darwin's books enjoyed tremendous success. *The Descent of Man, and Selection in Relation to Sex* (1871), together with its predecessor *On the Origin of Species*, is considered the keystone of Darwin's work. Even his first book, which we now know as *The Voyage of the Beagle* (1839), was a dazzling success. But it took Darwin 20 years, after becoming convinced of the truth of its central ideas, to publish *On the Origin of Species*. He was fully sensitive to the potentially disturbing nature of his own work and to the social and familial upheavals it would ferment. Only the independent discovery of natural selection by another naturalist, Alfred Russel

THE LITERARY WORK

An essay on the question of how species develop; published in London in 1859.

SYNOPSIS

Positing a mechanism called "natural selection" for the evolution of new species from old, *On the Origin of Species* accounts for the presence of every species on earth through two simple principles: variation and selection.

Wallace, finally drove Darwin to publish "the book that shook the world" (Mayr, p. vii).

Events in History at the Time of the Essay

Economics and industry. Darwin observes in *On the Origin of Species* that "the struggle for existence" is "the doctrine of Malthus applied with manifold force to the whole animal and vegetable kingdom" (Darwin, *On the Origin of Species,* p. 63). He refers there to the sociological and economic principles put forth by Thomas Robert Malthus in his *Essay on Population* (1798), which Darwin read in 1838. Arguing that population, unchecked, always increases faster than its food supply, Malthus paints a grim picture of the miseries attendant on human overpopulation. These arguments take on particular poignancy in light

Charles Darwin

of certain economic shifts of the mid-nineteenth century. In 1831, the year that Darwin sets off on the *Beagle*, the national census revealed 24 million people in Britain. This astonishing figure meant that the population had doubled in only 30 years. Meanwhile, the food supply began to look insufficient. Since 1815, the Corn Laws had protected agricultural interests in England by keeping up the price of domestic corn (a term that referred to grains such as wheat, barley, and oats rather than the American on-the-cob variety) and preventing the import of cheaper corn from abroad. Manufacturers, who wished to open up what came to be called "free trade" and to secure lower food prices for workers and higher profits for themselves, began to agitate for the repeal of the Corn Laws. In the end, however, what finally brought about their repeal was very bad weather. The year 1845 witnessed nearly incessant rains. Bad crops at home and potato famine in Ireland, which drove over a million Irish out of the country in search of food, painted an all-too-vivid picture of Malthusian scarcity. In 1846, parliament passed a three-year plan to lift the Corn Laws—a decision that may have had more symbolic than economic impact. The price of corn remained relatively unchanged, but the repeal of the Corn Laws made it clear that popular agitation could effectively bring about governmental change and that England was no longer the predominantly agrarian state it had once been.

Industry had come to stay, and the mid-nineteenth century was the era for many to enjoy it—in particular, the many who belonged to the burgeoning middle class. England thrived on its industrial progress, dominating the world's coal, cotton goods, and steel markets. With economic success abroad came considerable changes at home, including the migration of hundreds of thousands of workers into cities such as London and Manchester. The rapid increase in urban populations and industry strained resources of food and raw materials. Apparently abundance and scarcity went hand in hand.

Religion, reform, and natural theology. By the early nineteenth century, the Church of England (the Anglican Church) had dominated the religious and, in many ways, the political life of the country for centuries. Indeed, anyone attending Oxford or Cambridge had to swear to the "Thirty-nine Articles of the Anglican Faith." Dissenters, that is, protestants who did not belong to the Anglican Church, were thus barred from university education and from virtually all positions of power within England. But the period during which Darwin researched and wrote witnessed considerable change in the position of the Church and in official religious tolerance. In 1837, the year after Darwin returned from his voyage on the *Beagle*, the Registration Act lifted the Anglican monopoly on performing marriages, burials, and baptisms. The Catholic Emancipation Act of 1829 had made it possible for Catholics to hold office, and by 1862 even Oxford and Cambridge—the last bastions of Anglican-only higher education—were admitting Dissenters.

Meanwhile, there was considerable variety of opinion within the Church. By no means did all Anglicans subscribe to the literal truth of the Bible. Nor was all religious thought easily separable from scientific thought. During the first half of the nineteenth century, natural theology, based on the conviction that man could and should come to know God through reason and the senses, was at the height of its popularity in England. While still at Cambridge, Darwin read William Paley's *Natural Theology* (1802), in which Paley laid out his famous version of the "argument from design." Just as the workings of a watch imply a watchmaker, he argued, the complexity of creation attests to the presence of a creator. And if Paley's work was starting to look a bit dated towards mid-century, a series of eight works published in the 1830s, known as the "Bridgewater Treatises," reinvigorated the argument from design. Indeed, Darwin draws one of the epigraphs for *On the Origin of Species* from William Whewell's treatise: "But with regard to the material world, we can at least go so far as this—we can perceive that events are brought about not by insulated interpositions of Divine power, exerted in each particular case, but by the establishment of general laws" (Whewell in *Origin*, p. ii).

Dinosaurs, embryos, and women. In 1842, Sir Richard Owen coined the term "Dinosaria" in order to distinguish Megalosaurus, Iguanadon, and Hylaeosaurus from other ancient reptiles. Arguing that these were higher-order reptiles than the ones that succeeded them, Owen proposed the category in part to argue against the progressive implications of early evolutionary theory. His notion of the "archetype" proposed a "primal" pattern on which all vertebrates were based, a static pattern that could not change or evolve. Opposed to Owen's static view of species were many early evolutionists like Herbert Spencer and T. H. Huxley. Among the evolutionists was Ernst Haeckel, who is responsible for the phrase "ontogeny recapitulates phylogeny." His is the most famous articulation of the theory known as "parallelism," which connects the stages of development of the individual (ontogeny) with the stages of development of the species (phylogeny) or, for non-evolutionists, connects the stages of development of the individual with the hierarchical rungs of a static scale of being. Parallelism implied that as a person developed to adulthood, he or she went through all the lower stages of life, spending some time (usually as an embryo) in a fish stage, a reptile stage, and so on.

From the flip side, parallelism (or "recapitulation" as the theory is sometimes called) implied that the more youthful an individual seemed, the less evolved that individual was. Thus, recapitulation was often used to argue for hierarchical relations among humans. Not only children, but also non-whites and women (because, like children, they were smaller than men and lacked facial hair), were often taken to be less evolved than white men. In this way, evolutionary theory was used to reinforce social structures already in place. The first half of the nineteenth century witnessed a considerable constriction in the role of women, who were in-

creasingly thought of as "angels in the home" for whom both public life and sex drives seemed inappropriate and incongruous. This view of women, as well as a confidence in women's good taste, is reflected in Darwin's theory of sexual selection (proposed in the *Origin*, but not explored at length until the *Descent*). Throughout the animal kingdom, vigorous and active males pursue relatively passive females, who nonetheless contribute to the strength and beauty of their species by choosing always the best and brightest among their suitors.

THE GREAT EXHIBITION AND THE CRYSTAL PALACE

In 1851, England seemed to be in a fine position indeed. It was wealthy and powerful, the center of a mighty empire. In fact, the world had not seen such an empire since the famous Roman one. Many took the opening of the Great Exhibition held in London's Hyde Park that year to be a sign of the might as well as the right of all things British. An international showcase of arts and manufactures, the Great Exhibition was the first world's fair in history. It opened on May 1 in the giant Crystal Palace, built of glass and iron and designed for the occasion by Joseph Paxton. The edifice itself inspired reverence and awe as well as a sense that industrial capitalism and progressive reform would lead to enduring national success. In essence, the dazzling spectacle secured an admiring nation's commitment to science. Six million people visited the Crystal Palace, witnessing its enormous engines, tropical plants, and artwork before it was disassembled in 1852 and taken to Sydenham in South London. Darwin enjoyed this new site rather more than he had enjoyed the original exhibition. Here the Palace was rebuilt with beautiful gardens and ornamental lakes, and here Richard Owen erected his life-size concrete dinosaurs, which still stand.

Wars abroad, unrest at home. Readers of *On the Origin of Species* will find it suffused with the language of war. Indeed, just one paragraph from the section on sexual selection yields a long list of war words: *shield, sword, spear, battle, weapons, courage* and *victory*. This may seem out of step for a country enjoying an extended domestic peace, but war could not be too far from the consciousness of the English at almost any time during the nineteenth century. Though the defeat of Napoleon in 1815 brought considerable relief, the war left Britain extremely sensitive to the possibility of revolution. The upper classes especially were anxious to avoid the kind of horrors that had taken place just over the channel in the French Revolution of 1789. A series of revolutions in Austria, Germany, Italy, and France in 1848 fueled the fear of class uprisings. Indeed, the Reform Bills of 1832, 1867, and 1884-85 can be understood as part of the attempt to rectify peacefully some of the class grievances settled so violently on the European continent. Designed to reapportion representation in Parliament in order to accommodate the growth of industrial cities in the north and designed also to extend the vote to a much larger number of people (male householders), these acts were revolutionary in that they allowed the middle classes to share power with the upper classes. Indeed, the acts can be said to mark the emergence of a new *species* of citizenry.

Though legislative reform kept life relatively peaceful at home, colonial interests led to trouble abroad. Fearful of Russian designs on India, Britain fought, along with France and Austria, in what was known as the Crimean War (1854-56); the goal was to keep Turkey out of Russian control. Though successful, the war was poorly run and evoked considerable public criticism. Moreover, the Indian Mutiny of 1857, though quickly suppressed, suggested that Indian nationalists would not always tolerate British rule and the westernization of Indian culture. Thus, the events of the 1850s would not only keep the fact of war before the eyes of the British, they would also begin to unsettle confidence in the dominance and permanence of the British empire. *On the Origin of Species* itself would reproduce the ambivalence of its culture, serving at once to foster and to assuage the anxieties attached to ideas of empire in Britain, even as that empire reached unprecedented heights.

The Essay in Focus

Contents summary. Though Darwin modestly terms its 500 pages and 14 chapters an "Abstract," the *Origin* is a rich piece of writing that reveals a mastery of a wide array of Victorian sciences, including botany, zoology, anatomy, paleontology, and geology. In London, Darwin was admitted to two clubs for pigeon fanciers, and a practical dimension infuses his writing. It displays a vast knowledge of the everyday experience of breeders and farmers, whose accounts furnish many of Darwin's examples throughout

the *Origin*. These permeate the first chapter, "Variation under Domestication," in which Darwin eases his readership into an understanding of his radical view of nature through an extremely familiar, analogous case. If we wish to understand the variation and modification of species in nature, Darwin reasons, our knowledge of "variation under domestication" must be "the best and safest clue" (*Origin*, p. 4). He cites (to name a few) the Italian greyhound, the Spanish pointer, and the Blenheim spaniel; the Ribston-pippin apple and the Codlin apple; and a dazzling array of pigeons—the English carrier, the runt, the pouter, the barb, the short-faced tumbler, the Jacobin, the trumpeter, the laugher, and the fantail. Darwin thus paints a picture of the rich variety among domestic productions. But though the breeders who are his sources maintain almost indignantly that each domestic breed stems from a unique wild species, Darwin argues that even very distinct breeds descend from common wild ancestors. Indeed, it is from the very plasticity of form that breeders observe, from their capacity to select consciously or unconsciously for desired traits and to breed out undesirable ones, and from their ability to substantially alter a breed this way, that Darwin becomes convinced—and convinces his reader—of his two central ideas: first, individuals of a breed or species exhibit a range of differences or variations; and second, these individual differences, when selectively accumulated over the course of many generations, form the basis of larger differences, such as those that distinguish the prize Hereford from the wild longhorn. Thus, "nature gives successive variations; man adds them up in certain directions useful to him" (*Origin*, p. 30). In other words, nature provides variety; man selects and breeds for those variations that he deems desirable.

Darwin then reasons by analogy. What man can do, nature can do better. Of course, for selection to occur, there must be something to select; there must be variation. Thus, Darwin devotes his second chapter to "Variation under Nature." It is here that his concern with the individual distinguishes him from the "systematists" who precede him. The same differences that other works on natural history gloss over in order to present a coherent picture of a "type" become Darwin's central obsession. "These differences blend into each other in an insensible series; and a series impresses the mind with an actual passage" (*Origin*, p. 51). In this way, Darwin suggests that we can infer from the *variety* currently visible in nature, a series of *changes* that have taken place over time.

It remains for the next chapter, "Struggle for Existence" to posit a mechanism that can explain how species arise in nature. Here, Darwin elaborates a complex "economy of nature" in which both individuals and species compete for resources that, at some time or another, will be insufficiently abundant. The term "Struggle for Existence" often evokes a rather bloody picture—two carnivores fighting over the same piece of meat, or what Alfred, Lord Tennyson described as "Nature red in tooth and claw" in his poem **In Memoriam** (Tennyson, 56.15; also in *WLAIT 4: British and Irish Literature and Its Times*). But Darwin's chapter concerns something much larger and more metaphorical, "including dependence of one being on another, and including (which is more important) not only the life of the individual, but success in leaving progeny" (*Origin*, p. 62). It is here that Darwin first coins the term "natural selection," the subject of Chapter 4 and the keystone of Darwin's theory. "Natural selection"—a term intended to evoke the analogy to "man's power of selection"—is the process through which variations, however slight, that give an individual an advantage in the struggle for existence will accumulate (*Origin*, p. 61). Advantaged individuals will have more success in leaving progeny, who, in turn, may enjoy similar advantages and reproduce successfully, and so on, until small variations add up to large ones, individual differences yield new varieties, and varieties yield new species. Thus nature, like man, selects for profitable variations.

In Chapter 5, "Laws of Variation," Darwin connects the rich variety in nature established in earlier chapters to his theory of natural selection. It is here that he begins to address "the ordinary view of each species having been independently created," a view which he finds completely inadequate in explaining either the visible variations within species or the similarities between species (*Origin*, p. 155).

The chapters that follow address many of the difficulties associated with this theory. Chapters 6-8 take up a series of troubling questions; Chapters 9-12 consider the challenges (to and from natural selection) of geology, paleontology and geography; and Chapter 13 returns to the difficulties of classification, with a view to explaining these difficulties by the theory of descent with modification. Why, Darwin asks and answers, if species develop out of other species, don't we see more intermediate gradations that connect disparate but related forms through a complete spectrum of forms in between? Why do species appear so well defined? How can we believe that natural selection produces small and insignificant as well as vital and complex structures within a species? How does natural selection explain the development of complex instinctual behaviors—such as those that result in the elaborate social structures of certain ants or the exquisite architecture of the hive-bee's cell?

The first of these questions points to a recurring emphasis in these chapters: the close relation between natural selection and extinction. We don't see more intermediate forms in nature, Darwin argues in Chapter 4, precisely because the success of the species that we do observe implies their success *over* those species or varieties with whom they have competed in the struggle for existence. Species, he argues, are more likely to compete with, and therefore lead to the extinction of, species like themselves. Thus, competition leads to diversification in nature. So competition explains why species appear distinct in nature; however, it fails to explain why we do not see more transitional forms among *extinct* species. Darwin returns to this question—which is the challenge posed by geology and paleontology to the theory of natural selection—in chapters 9 and 10. With extreme care, he enumerates the multiple causes that have conjoined to make the fossil record extremely imperfect and full of gaps through which species have come and gone without leaving a trace.

Finally, following two chapters on geographical distribution, Darwin revisits the major points of *On the Origin of Species*. In this final chapter, he comes to consider the reasons why so many naturalists and geologists have clung to the view that species are immutable, even though variation within species is everywhere evident and clear distinctions cannot be drawn between species and well-marked varieties. In addressing this question, he addresses nothing less than the question of how science, indeed thought, works. Anticipating "the load of prejudice by which this subject is overwhelmed," Darwin—perhaps inadvertently—evokes the interpretive nature of what we call facts, which nevertheless take shape only in light of the theories through which we view them (*Origin*, p. 482). He leaves it predominantly to the future to embrace his theory, and predicts an impact almost as great as the one *On the Origin of Species* has turned out to have. Winding up the treatise, Darwin ends with a sense of awe inspired by the view of nature he has articulated. He finds in this view a grandeur all its own, that from the simple beginnings of a few or only one species "endless forms most beautiful and most wonderful have been, and are being, evolved" (*Origin*, p. 490).

Evolution and empire. A great deal of the fascination with *On the Origin of Species* comes from the fact that while producing a brilliant and influential work of science, Darwin reveals how much he is a man of his times. However much his *theories* may be separated from their social applications, his *language* speaks to an audience deeply concerned about the endurance of the empire.

There can be no doubt that when Darwin published *On the Origin of Species* in 1859, the British empire was strong and growing stronger. The essay—like much of the science that preceded it—carried the potential to shatter this confidence. In particular, the fear of extinction wrought by Victorian paleontology and inseparable (as Darwin emphasizes) from natural selection, suggested that species—even apparently powerful species like the dinosaurs—could and very likely would eventually die out. Since Victorians often confounded the concepts of species, race, and nation, the fear of extinction readily spilled over into a fear of racial or national decline. For the reader looking for reassurance that Great Britain did indeed rule the waves and would continue to do so, the essay provides plenty of material. Certainly, any sufficiently devout nationalist will find a source of pride in the assertion that "the whole body of English racehorses have come to surpass in fleetness and size the parent Arab stock" (*Origin*, p. 35). Within the struggle for existence, the practice of forcibly occupying another nation can look quite natural, "for in all countries, the natives have been so far conquered by naturalised productions [species who are not indigenous], that they have allowed foreigners to take firm possession of the land" (*Origin*, p. 83 *sic*). Also, in spite of the frightening facts of the fossil record, natural selection implies for Darwin that "forms of life which are now dominant tend to become still more dominant" (*Origin*, p. 59). In a way that seems to reinforce the rightness and even the inevitability of the imperial project (or class divisions, or gender disparity, according to the inclinations of the reader), Darwin develops a mechanism that explains how "the forms of life throughout the universe become divided into groups subordinate to groups" (*Origin*, p. 59).

Nonetheless, not all colonial practices were viewed equally within England. In the early part of the nineteenth century, the question of colonialism was hardly separable from the question of slavery. England officially ended its slave trade in 1807 (though this proved rather hard to enforce) and in 1834, Parliament put into effect a bill that would abolish slavery throughout the British empire. The abolitionist sentiment that effected these changes remained strong in England for the three succeeding decades during which slavery remained legal in the United States. In light of the prevailing sentiment, it is surprising that, at least on the face of things, *On the Origin of Species* seems to treat slavery as quite natural—instinctual, if only in ants. On closer inspection, however, Darwin's discussion of the slavemaking instinct reads like a cautionary tale. These remarkable ants have so developed this instinct, so thoroughly established the division of labor, that "The males and fertile females do no work. The workers or sterile females, though most energetic and courageous in capturing slaves, do no other work" (*Origin*, p. 219). They no longer can. The slavemaking ants live in a state of abject dependence on their slaves. Indeed, "so utterly helpless are the masters" that when shut up without a slave, "they could not even feed themselves and many perished of hunger" (*Origin*, p. 219). Thus though *On the Origin of Species* implicitly offers reassurances about the endurance of empire, it also portends evil for those who would carry such power too far. Its complex (sometimes seemingly contradictory) implications, moreover, anticipate the wide array of uses to which Darwin's theories would eventually be put under the very broad rubric of "Social Darwinism."

Sources and literary context. By the middle of the nineteenth century, evolutionary ideas suffused Victorian popular and scientific thought. No well-read and educated Victorian (including Darwin) could have been unfamiliar with the best-loved, most-read, and most-quoted work of mid-Victorian literature: Alfred, Lord Tennyson's **In Memoriam**, a consolatory poem written in memory of his friend Arthur Henry Hallam that articulated many of the broader fears and hopes of its moment (also in *WLAIT4: British and Irish Literature and Its Times*). The poem raises, and in many ways resolves some of the anxieties wrought by the same sciences that influenced Darwin. Though Darwin was critical of Robert Chambers's *Vestiges of the Natural History of Creation* (published anonymously in 1844), Tennyson was fascinated. Chambers's book helped him reconcile his belief in God's love with his perception of nature's violence. In his poem he attempts to resolve the clash between evolutionary and Christian thought by developing a narrative of evolutionary progress that links the ape and tiger up through man to the divine itself. His poem indicates how thoroughly evolutionary ideas were already in the air while Darwin was writing (often in distressing ways, as in the perception of nature's violence mentioned above).

Moreover, Darwin was not the first scientist to develop a theory of evolution. His particular contribution was to posit a compelling mechanism—natural selection—to explain the process through which species could evolve. There were quite a few scientific theories of evolution in place before Darwin started writing. One of these was the work of Darwin's grandfather, Erasmus Darwin, a poet and physician, whose *Zoönomia* (1794) Darwin had read with enthusiasm as a teenager. Erasmus Darwin believed in the mutability of species, in the possibility of adaptation and variation in organisms, and in the importance of such changes for individual and species survival. Though influenced by these ideas, his grandson Charles did not embrace them or their implications wholesale. Yet Charles Darwin was no doubt disposed to be relatively sympathetic to some of the ideas of Lamarckian evolution when he encountered these first at Edinburgh. Jean-Baptiste de Lamarck, best known for his *Philosophie zoologique* (1809), posited a dynamic scale of nature in which organisms progressed up the scale of nature, becoming more and more complex because of the gradual accumulation of adaptations over many generations. Though Darwin would reject certain well-known Lamarckian ideas, such as spontaneous generation and the inheritance of characteristics acquired by an individual during its lifetime, *On the Origin of Species* would also adopt many important aspects of Lamarckian evolution, such as the possibility of transformation (or "transmutation") of species as well as the incredible long time scales required to make such changes. The controversy surrounding such works, moreover, may have influenced Darwin's decision whether and when to publish. Intrigued by such early evolutionary writings, he was nevertheless rather nervous lest his own ideas meet with similar rejection, and this nervousness accounts, in part, for his waiting so long to publish *On the Origin of Species*.

It was not, however, only the evolutionary sciences that influenced Darwin's thinking. In the 1830s, when Darwin was still very much a ju-

nior member of the scientific community, two schools of thought dominated and divided geological thinking. "Uniformitarians" contended that geological processes of the past were of the same kind and operated in the same degree as the processes now operating. "Catastrophists," on the other hand, depicted the earth's past as punctuated by violent and rapid upheavals, like volcanoes and floods, which would account for the changes in landscape and living forms indicated by the fossil record. Though Darwin's early training was steeped in catastrophism, he read Charles Lyell's *Principles of Geology* while on board the *Beagle*. Lyell's book was perhaps the foremost articulation of uniformitarian principles, and it not only shaped much of Darwin's geological thinking while on board the *Beagle*, but also laid the foundational premises necessary to develop the concepts he would eventually put forth in *On the Origin of Species*. In advocating the uniform nature of geological processes, Lyell emphasized a steady state view of the earth in which decay and formation are perpetually in process, a view that implied no particular progression or direction in terrestrial events, a view which would enable a scientist to explain the phenomena of the past by observing the events and causes of the present.

Reception and impact. The first edition of *On the Origin of Species* sold out the day it was published (November 24, 1859). A second edition, with very slight changes, was released just a month later (December 28). These changes, Darwin's first hurried response to some of the religious objections to the first edition, were clearly intended to make God more visible in his theory. In spite of such gestures to render *On the Origin of Species* compatible with religious thought, the most vehement resistance to Darwin's ideas came from religious thinkers—scientists among them. They objected on two counts. First, there were objections to the insufficient space left by natural selection for the intervention of God in the form of creation or miracles, and second, there were objections to the essay's failure to maintain a special place for humanity in the order of things. Though Darwin does attempt to address the first objection, he makes little mention of humankind (except as breeders) in the essay at all, saving that discussion for *The Descent of Man*. Actually, the disturbing closeness of humans to apes had already crept into British thought (indeed had been there for more than a century), and the essay's readers immediately picked up on its implications for the "monkey question." Perhaps the most famous clash over

Illustration of the HMS *Beagle* in the Straits of Magellan. Darwin spent five years on the *Beagle,* an experience that would stimulate his future writings.

this question was the 1860 debate between the Bishop Samuel Wilberforce and Thomas Henry Huxley—an extremely vocal proponent of Darwinism, whose enthusiasm earned him the nickname "Darwin's bulldog."

The response to *On the Origin of Species,* however, was by no means limited to a simple clash between science and religion. Even religious opinion was divided. While some found the essay deeply offensive, other religious readers saw in it evidence of the richness and complexity of God's methods. Scientific readers were similarly divided. Undoubtedly, the essay marked a complete shift in the status of evolution in the scientific community. Earlier evolutionary theories were always on the fringes of biological thought; Darwin brought evolution to the center. Certainly by 1875, probably by 1865, virtually every British biologist was an evolutionist. Nonetheless, there remained considerable dissension regarding the *mechanism* of evolution, as evolutionists debated whether natural selection could do all that Darwin claimed. Even those who accepted that natural selection could accumulate small changes in visible ways debated whether these could ever be significant enough to yield new species. Outside of biology, perhaps the most vocal scientific opponents of Darwinism

were the physicists, especially William Thomson, Lord Kelvin. The laws of thermodynamics, articulated and popularized at just about this time, put a limit on the age of the earth and sun that was far too short to accommodate the very long time scales required by evolutionary theory. Not until the discovery of radiation at the turn of the century did it look like the sun could endure long enough for evolution to make sense to physicists.

Darwin's ideas were also widely rejected and widely accepted by the general public. Needless to say, many Victorian readers objected to Darwinism for religious reasons. However, many found it quite satisfying to apply Darwinian principles to the social sphere. Such ideas, known collectively as "social Darwinism," could be used to argue for the rightness of extreme laissez-faire economics or for English imperialism, based on the notion that competition would insure that the best—people, class, nation—would rise above the rest. Extrapolating from Darwin, people modified his line of thought; to some, it implied *progress* (rather than just *change,* which was Darwin's more modest focus). Herbert Spencer (1820-1903), who began to develop an evolutionary model of society even before the publication of *On the*

Origin of Species, was responsible for articulating many of the doctrines of social Darwinism. Indeed, it was Spencer who coined the term "survival of the fittest"—a term often associated with Darwin, who was eventually sufficiently influenced by Spencer's work to include this term in the fifth edition (1869) of *On the Origin of Species*. In spite of the fact that most of Darwin's twentieth-century fans would like to clear him of all charges of social Darwinism, he was rather divided on the subject himself, sometimes rejecting the notion that his ideas could be applied to social situations (as when he was accused of having proven that might makes right), sometimes worrying that modern social and medical practice (such as vaccination) were actually preserving the unfit. But whether accepted or rejected, Darwin's ideas found their way into virtually every area of Victorian thought, from race, empire, economics, politics, and religion to sexuality, childrearing, birth control, music, medicine and architecture. Certainly his ideas greatly affected the literature of the age, influencing works as varied as George Eliot's **Middlemarch** (1871-72; in *WLAIT 3: British and Irish Literature and Its Times*), Robert Louis Stevenson's **The Strange Case of Dr. Jekyll and Mr. Hyde** (1886), H. G. Wells's **The Time Machine** (1895), and Virginia Woolf's *The Voyage Out* (1915) (Eliot's and Stevenson's works also in *WLAIT 4: British and Irish Literature and Its Times*).

—Barri Gold

For More Information

Beer, Gillian. "Introduction." *The Origin of Species*. 2d ed. New York: Oxford University Press, 1996.

———. *Darwin's Plots: Evolutionary Narrative in Darwin, George Eliot and Nineteenth-Century Fiction*. London: Ark, 1985.

Dale, Peter Allen. *In Pursuit of a Scientific Culture: Science, Art, and Society in the Victorian Age*. Madison: University of Wisconsin Press, 1989.

Darwin, Charles. *On the Origin of Species*. A facsimile of the first edition. Cambridge: Harvard University Press, 1998.

Desmond, Adrian, and James Moore. *Darwin: The Life of a Tormented Evolutionist*. New York: Norton, 1991.

Levine, George. *Darwin and the Novelists: Patterns of Science in Victorian Fiction*. Chicago: University of Chicago Press, 1988.

Lightman, Bernard, ed. *Victorian Science in Context*. Chicago: University of Chicago Press, 1997.

Mayr, Ernst. "Introduction." *On the Origin of Species*. Cambridge: Harvard University Press, 1998.

Ruse, Michael. *The Darwinian Revolution: Science Red in Tooth and Claw*. Chicago: University of Chicago Press, 1979.

Tennyson, Alfred. *In Memoriam*. Ed. Robert H. Ross. New York: Norton, 1973.

Peter Pan: Peter and Wendy

by

James Barrie

James Barrie was born into a Scottish weaver's family in 1860. When Barrie was six, his 13-year-old brother died, leaving Barrie with an enduring image of the perfect child who would never grow up, and a melancholy mother, who then pinned all her hopes on James Barrie. From an early age Barrie was a passionate reader with dreams of being a writer. Deferring to his mother, he postponed this career to attend Edinburgh University but, in 1885, settled in London to work as a freelance journalist, novelist, and playwright. Barrie's first taste of success came in 1891, with the publication of *The Little Minister*. Set in a fictionalized version of his birthplace, Kirriemuir, the novel established Barrie as a leading writer of the "Kailyard" school—fiction writers who sentimentally stereotyped the Scottish lowlanders. The following year, Barrie had great success with his play, *Walker, London*, in which he cast as lead actress Mary Ansell, the woman whom he would marry. In the next few years came several novels that dealt with Barrie's major subject—the desirability of boyhood: *Sentimental Tommy* (1896), *Tommy and Grizel* (1900), and *The Little White Bird* (1902). Eventually Barrie concentrated on writing for the stage. No work brought him more fame and fortune than *Peter Pan*, first performed for the 1904 Christmas pantomime season. *Peter and Wendy*, the 1911 novel, is based directly on the play; its significant addition is a narrator's voice—by turns playful, sentimental, nostalgic. The novel assimilates and responds to elements of classic boys' adventure

THE LITERARY WORK

A novel adapted from the play, set in an Edwardian London home and on the fantasy island Neverland; published in 1911.

SYNOPSIS

The three Darling children fly with eternally young Peter Pan to a dreamland of mermaids, lagoons, pirates and Indians. Here the Darlings join the orphaned "lost boys" and Peter Pan in a string of adventures that culminate with their battle against the pirates, led by the notorious Captain Hook.

stories—an island setting and attacks by pirates and Indians—melding them with a scathing portrayal of bourgeois English domesticity in the Edwardian period.

Events in History at the Time of the Novel

British imperialism. At the time Barrie wrote *Peter and Wendy*, the British Empire was at its height. Great Britain had become the richest country in the world, its empire the largest and the most successful. Britain's colonies covered more than a quarter of the earth's land and citizens. By 1900, the British Empire controlled the following territories:

J. M. Barrie

Aden, Antigua, Ascension, Australia, the Bahamas, Barbados, Basutoland, Bechuanaland, Bermuda, British Guiana, British Honduras, British North Borneo, British Solomon Islands, British Somaliland, Brunei, Burma, Canada, Cape of Good Hope, Cayman-Turks-Caicos Islands, Ceylon, Christmas Island, Cocos-Keeling Islands, Cook Islands, Cyprus, Dominica, the East African Protectorate, Egypt, Falkland Islands, Fiji, Gambia, Gibralter, Gilbert and Ellice Islands, Gold Coast, Grenada, Hong Kong, India, Jamaica, Labuan, Lagos, Leeward Isles, Malay States, Maldive Islands, Malta, Mauritius, Montserrat, Natal, New Zealand, Newfoundland, Nigeria, Norfolk Island, Northern Rhodesia, Nyasaland, Papua, Pitcairn, St. Kitts and Nevis, St. Helena, St. Lucia, St. Vincent, Sarawak, Seychelles, Sierra Leone, Singapore, Southern Rhodesia, Straits Settlement (Singapore, Penang, Malacca), Sudan, Swaziland, Tonga, Trinidad and Tobago, Tristan da Cunha, Uganda, Virgin Islands, Windward Isles, Zanzibar.

(Mitchell, p. 284)

Most of the world had been mapped and divided by turn of the twentieth century, and a time of relative peace ensued among the European powers. Great Britain focused its energy on the details of governing through such British agencies as the Foreign, India, War, and Colonial Offices. The empire had reached its apex, while James

Barrie's island paradise, Neverland, looks back to its sixteenth-century beginnings. As the narrator says, "Of all delectable islands the Neverland is the snuggest and most compact; not large and sprawly, you know, with tedious distances between one adventure and another, but nicely crammed" (Barrie, *Peter and Wendy,* p. 74).

The imperialist project reinforced ideas of British cultural and racial superiority, with the empire enlisting many messengers of such propaganda. Official government propaganda was less pervasive than that found in the military, the schools, churches, and popular entertainment. Juvenile literature, in particular, adventure tales and novels, played a key role. The most popular story for boys in the nineteenth century, R. M. Ballantyne's *The Coral Island* (1858), presents at a relatively early date the many elements of the imperialist tale: the boy hero as colonizer, the conquest of nature, the savagery of the indigenous, salvation at the hands of an English missionary, the glories of British civilization, and the evils of those outside it. Ballantyne's novel was Barrie's favorite as a boy. He wrote in his notebook: "Want to stop everybody in street & ask if they've read 'The Coral Island.' Feel sorry for if not" (Birkin, p. 12). Another classic island adventure, *Treasure Island*, by Barrie's idol Robert Louis Stevenson, appeared in 1883. Both novels are nineteenth-century rewritings of Daniel Defoe's *Robinson Crusoe* (1719) and precursors to the Peter Pan saga, which makes full use of the desert island, the stereotypic indigenous "savage," and ruthless pirates. In fact, *The Coral Island, Treasure Island,* and *Peter and Wendy* all invoke imperialist themes, though not as stridently as novels that dominated the end of the nineteenth century. Such authors as G. A. Henty, who wrote over a hundred novels for boys between 1868 and the century's end, articulated the mission of young Englishmen: to spread superior British values around the globe.

In the latter part of the nineteenth century, "penny dreadfuls," cheap boys magazines, such as *The Bad Boys' Paper*, glamorized crime and accompanied it with a crude imperialism. *Boys of England*, published between 1866 and 1899, featured the widely popular Jack Harkaway, who runs away from school to have a myriad of adventures against the backdrop of the empire. Barrie himself was a great fan of the penny dreadfuls; as he wrote of his young self, "He buys his sanguinary tales surreptitiously in penny numbers" (Barrie, *Peter Pan*, p. xiv). Improving, or improvement-oriented, magazines such as the popular *The Boy's Own Paper* arose in response to the penny dreadfuls. Established in 1879, *The Boy's Own Paper* included writings by G. A. Henty and R. M. Ballantyne. Along with other similar magazines, *The Boy's Own Paper* pushed a well-received imperialist ideology, based, as its title suggests, partly on an affirmation of the Victorian notion of separate spheres for men and women. Boys live adventurously and for themselves; girls stay at home and care for others. More dramatically, these magazines reinforced racial hierarchies. In stories of private school life, colonial wars, and emigration adventures, "the world," as John M. MacKenzie writes, "became a vast adventure playground in which Anglo-Saxon superiority could be repeatedly demonstrated *vis-à-vis* all other races, most of whom were depicted as treacherous and evil" (MacKenzie, p. 204).

Racism and the indigenous. A sense of racial superiority provided a rationale for imperialism. The eighteenth-century view that human nature was universal yielded to the view that racial differences were essential and unchanging. Racial others, "half-devil and half-child," in Rudyard Kipling's words, needed to be subdued and governed by the Anglo-Saxon race, who were fulfilling the "White Man's burden" (Kipling in Porter, p. 24).

In *Peter and Wendy*, Barrie populates his island with an amalgam of indigenous peoples.

> On the trail of the pirates, stealing noiselessly down the war-path . . . come the redskins, every one of them with his eyes peeled. They carry tomahawks and knives, and their naked bodies gleam with paint and oil. Strung around them are scalps, of boys as well as pirates, for these are the Piccaninny tribe, and not to be confused with the softer-hearted Delawares or the Hurons. . . . Bringing up the rear, the place of greatest danger, comes Tiger Lily, proudly erect, a princess in her own right. . . . [T]here is not a brave who would not have the wayward thing to wife, but she staves off the altar with a hatchet.
>
> (*Peter and Wendy*, pp. 115-16)

A caricature of native Americans, the "redskins" are also called "Piccaninnies," a word introduced by colonizing Europeans to apply to black and aboriginal children. These "redskins" speak a stereotyped Indian speech ("me his velly nice friend"), and are portrayed in the novel as one step up from the beasts (*Peter and Wendy*, p. 157). In the adventures of Neverland, the pirates chase the lost boys, the Indians steal after the pirates, and the beasts stalk the Indians. Living on a tropical island of the imagination, these American Indians stand in for all conquered indigenous peoples and hark back to a romanticized period of colonization that involved war rather than rule.

PIRATES
≈

The "Golden Age" of piracy occurred in the first quarter of the eighteenth century, when an unprecedented number of pirates attacked the growing merchant fleets crossing the Atlantic Ocean. Although piracy exists today, for the most part the practice has become the stuff of legend and story, whose main features were in place in literature by 1800. Literary pirates distinguished themselves by their "filthy habits" and rapaciousness; they displayed earrings, tattoos, and their own bare chests; they searched for buried gold with treasure maps (Rogozinski, pp. xi-xiv). Not only did pirates make frequent appearances in nineteenth-century stories for boys, from the penny dreadfuls to Robert Louis Stevenson's *Treasure Island*; they also found their way onto the stage in Victorian melodramas. In 1879, W. S. Gilbert and Arthur Sullivan parodied these stage pirates in *The Pirates of Penzance*.

J. M. Barrie placed his pirates amidst those from literature and history. Captain James Hook, the narrator states, "was Blackbeard's bo'sun [boatswain]. . . . He is the only man of whom Barbecue was afraid (*Peter and Wendy*, p. 108). Blackbeard was one of the many names of an English pirate also known as Edward Teach, who operated in the Atlantic Ocean and Caribbean Sea in the first part of the eighteenth century, and who had a reputation for appalling ferocity. Barbecue is another name for Long John Silver, the great pirate of *Treasure Island*. Barrie's pirate Skylights is "Morgan's Skylights" (*Peter and Wendy*, p. 114); that is, a crewmember of Sir Henry Morgan, the famous seventeenth-century Welsh buccaneer. Barrie incorporated other legendary aspects of piracy in his own pastiche. The name of Captain Hook's pirate ship, *The Jolly Roger*, is the term for the pirate flag itself. First used at the beginning of the eighteenth century, the Jolly Roger featured a white symbol of death (for example, a skeleton, skull, or sword) on a black background. Captain Hook orders the Darling boys and the lost boys "to walk the plank," a brutal punishment exacted only by literary pirates. With eyes blindfolded, victims were forced to walk along a narrow plank extended over the ship's edge, until they fell or were tipped into the water, or were shot.

Barrie's imagination may have been fueled not only by the adventure stories he loved but also by the continual spectacle of American Indians in London. Wood engravings, based on photographs, brought the Indian Wars to a British audience. Barrie moved to London in 1885, two years before Buffalo Bill's (William Frederick Cody's) "Wild West" show arrived in the city. From shows came details that contributed to stereotypes of Indian behaviors. An exhibit performed for Queen Victoria began on the Great Plains of America with the Indians sleeping in their tents, then emerging at dawn to dance a war dance. Then a messenger announced the approach of hostile Indians, whereupon the whites who were alerted made a rush for their weapons and horses, and a loud battle was simulated. Barrie invokes comparable "codes" of Indian behavior in *Peter and Wendy*: "By all the unwritten laws of savage warfare it is always the redskin who attacks, and with the wiliness of his race he does it just before the dawn" (*Peter and Wendy*, p. 173). "The Great White Father," one of Barrie's early titles for *Peter Pan*, emphasizes the racial difference between the novel's protagonist and its caricatured natives, as well as spotlighting the overlap between British imperialism and paternalism.

Middle-class childhood. Barrie wrote *Peter and Wendy* during the period often called "The Golden Age of Children's Literature." E. Nesbit's *The Railway Children* was published in 1906; Kenneth Grahame's *The Wind in the Willows* appeared in 1908; Frances Hodgson Burnett's *The Secret Garden* was released in 1911, the same year as *Peter and Wendy*. Stellar writers for children often worked closely with highly talented artists, such as Arthur Rackham, Edmund Dulac, and Charles Robinson. Using advances in color printing, they produced gift books like the Rackham illustrated *Peter Pan in Kensington Gardens*.

Was this also a golden age for children? It is fair to say that life for British children had improved dramatically over the previous century. Most children were healthy; fewer children were put to work; Balfour's Education Act of 1902 led to the formation of a truly national school system. In regard to social attitudes towards children, however, we must carefully distinguish between the idealized child of art and literature, and the actual child who lived in the confines of Edwardian domesticity.

The Edwardians, like the Victorians, were child-worshippers. They celebrated the innocence, energy, and creativity of childhood. The writers who expressed this cultural longing were not on the margins of their societies, but central to it. Jackie Wullschläger makes this case by pointing to the books embraced by each period, and the dominant roles of children in these books. A partial list would include Charles Dickens's *Oliver Twist* (1837-39), the young Jane in Charlotte Brontë's *Jane Eyre* (1847), Lewis Carroll's *Alice's Adventures in Wonderland* (1865), Frances Hodgson Burnett's *Little Lord Fauntleroy* (1886) and *Sarah Crewe* (1888); and Kipling's *Kim* (1901) (***Jane Eyre*** and ***Kim*** also in *WLAIT 4: British and Irish Literature and Its Times*). Barrie's *Peter Pan* (1904) falls in line next. However, Wullschläger claims that there is a significant difference between the Victorian and Edwardian eras: the Victorians adored little girls, while the Edwardians preferred little boys (Wullschläger, p. 109).

Wullschläger points to historical and artistic phenomena to explain the new emphasis on boyhood, which began about 1880:

> The new image . . . was encouraged by the role of Edward, the Prince of Wales, as the irresponsible, pleasure-seeking playboy of Europe, and by the Edwardian decade the image had crystalised. Virile, outward-bound, ever-young men are the cult figures of the 1890s and 1900s, and a sense that life beyond youth was not worth living contributed to the fervour for youthful martyrdom that came in 1914 [in World War I]. Leading up to it, the model of the dangerously attractive young man, immortal but in some way doomed, 'the lad who will never grow old', stands at the heart of thirty years of English culture.
>
> (Wullschläger, p. 109)

Actual middle-class Edwardian children lived not in an idyll, but within a tightly ruled family and school system. At home, their father was firmly in charge, even if he scarcely saw his children. At school, corporal punishment kept students in line. There were plenty of books at home, and summer holidays at the sea, but as Robert Cecil notes, "many of the same adults [who applauded *Peter Pan*] exercised a resolute, if discreet, tyranny in the home and repressed with a stern hand the waywardness that sounded so captivating in the mouths of Peter and Wendy" (Cecil, pp. 160-61).

Edwardian boys and girls grew up in a world still tightly controlled by their gender. Respectable married women did not work. Their lives revolved around the comfort of their husbands and the management of the children and home. Parents believed that choosing the right

Mary Martin as Peter in a 1984 benefit performance of *Peter Pan* at the Davies Symphony Hall in San Francisco.

school for their boys was very important. The private schools attended by boys were bastions of a smug conservatism that continued to emphasize the classics and athleticism. Parents were not so concerned with their daughters' education. Prior to World War I, it was still common for girls to receive much of their education under a governess, at home. Moreover, the goal of her education was not scholastic achievement but social advantage. Children's gender roles groomed them for their proper part in Britain's large empire. Boys needed to demonstrate independence and courage; girls, as J. S. Bratton indicates, "had to learn to be wife and mother to the pioneer and the soldier, and therefore the depository of the 'home values' and the guarantor of 'higher' feelings and motives for the men's conquests" (Bratton, p. 196).

Children's extracurricular activities served a similar function. In 1907, Robert Baden-Powell, a great fan of Barrie's *Peter Pan*, held an experimental Boy Scouts camp. In 1908, he published *Scouting for Boys*, and the following year conducted his first official camp. Though the Boy Scouts would appeal to all classes, the original intent had been to prevent the further "degeneracy" of working-class children, to make them healthier and more fit—should it be necessary—to defend Great Britain. The Girl Guides formed in 1909. Baden-Powell clearly wanted the two organizations to be separate. There was no mili-

---

THE NARRATOR OF *PETER AND WENDY*

No character in *Peter and Wendy* is more important than the shifting narrator. Sometimes the narrator addresses a child reader: "If you could keep awake (but of course you can't) you would see your own mother doing this" (*Peter and Wendy*, p. 73). Sometimes the narrator addresses an adult reader: "On these magic shores children at play are for ever beaching their coracles. We too have been there; we can still hear the sound of the surf, though we shall land no more" (*Peter and Wendy*, p. 74). Sometimes the narrator seems to be a child himself: "Off we skip like the most heartless things in the world, which is what children are, but so attractive; and we have an entirely selfish time; and then when we have need of special attention we nobly return for it, confident that we shall be embraced instead of smacked" (*Peter and Wendy*, p. 166). The narrator's varied modes of address reinforce the conflicts in the novel between children and adults, setting them in separate categories, and defining them as separate audiences. At the same time as the narrator indicates the distance between childhood and adulthood, he communicates the culture's nostalgic desire for childhood, either by playing the adult who longs to be a child, or by magically transforming into a child himself.

---

tarism in the Girl Guides. Its leader, Agnes Baden-Powell, Robert Baden-Powell's sister, had no intention of imitating the Boy Scouts. Instead, the Girl Guides set out to teach girls how to be fine housewives and mothers to guide the next generation. The Girl Guides, explained Agnes Baden-Powell, aimed only to make participants more capable in the "womanly" areas of life (Agnes Baden-Powell in Dyhouse, p. 111). By all measures, scouting was a success. By the time Barrie wrote *Peter and Wendy* in 1911, there were more than 100,000 participants.

The Novel in Focus

Plot summary. *Peter and Wendy* opens with the narrator's statement that "All children, except one, grow up" (*Peter and Wendy*, p. 69). That one is Peter Pan, and the novel charts his effect on the Darling family, whose staid London life provides the novel's frame. Mr. Darling, who knows about "stocks and shares," works in the financial district of London (*Peter and Wendy*, p. 70). Mrs. Darling, the ideal mother, nurtures Wendy, John, and Michael. The family has little money, but a great concern for respectability; thus, they employ a Newfoundland dog as a nurse. On the night the story begins, Mr. and Mrs. Darling are preparing for a dinner party. Mr. Darling is petulant; first, because he cannot fasten his tie; secondly, because his practical jokes misfire; ultimately, because he feels he does not get enough respect, from his family or from Nana, the dog who serves as "nurse." In a fit of pique, he ties Nana outside, leaving the nursery open to the arrival of Peter Pan.

Accompanied by the fairy Tinker Bell, Peter Pan flies in through the nursery window, seeking his lost shadow. It is not his first visit. He has always lived in the dreams of the Darling children. And it was a week before this night that he awakened Mrs. Darling; Nana sprang at him and tore off his shadow. On this evening, one week later, his sobs over his shadow awaken Wendy. He tells her that he ran away from his parents on the day he was born, so he would not have to grow up. Now he lives in Neverland with the lost boys, children who have fallen out of their carriages and remained unclaimed by their parents.

Peter is charmed by Wendy's knowledge of fairy tales. Wendy, enticed by Peter's description of Neverland, has visions of flying, mermaids, and the chance to play mother to the lost boys. She awakens John and Michael. Peter teaches them all how to fly, and away they go, "Second to the right, and straight on till morning," to Neverland (*Peter and Wendy*, p. 102).

The book now moves to Peter Pan's and the Darling children's adventures in Neverland, the scene of most of the novel. Wendy recreates Victorian domesticity in their underground home. She cooks, sews, keeps schedules, and quizzes the boys on their home life; that is, she reminds them daily of the civilization they have left behind. Meanwhile, they are engaged in adventures with the other occupants of the island and its waters: Indians and pirates.

Boyhood fantasies have become reality. The Indians, of the "Piccaninny tribe," carry tomahawks and adorn themselves with scalps. Though the "redskins" are fierce, the pirates pose a greater challenge because of the long enmity between their captain, James Hook, and Peter Pan. Hook, sinister yet of impeccably good breeding, lost his hand to Peter Pan and awaits his revenge. Hook is followed by a crocodile; having tasted Hook's right hand, the crocodile searches for the rest of him. Not only did the crocodile swallow Hook's hand, but a clock; thus, his arrival is always heralded by a familiar "tick tick."

The adventure at the Mermaid's Lagoon displays the personalities of all these players. Captured by Hook, the dangerous Tiger Lily, daughter of the Indian chief, has been left on a rock to drown. Peter Pan tricks the pirates into setting her free by imitating Captain Hook's voice. Even though he has achieved his objective, Peter Pan cannot refrain from playing games with Hook. The two engage in a guessing game in which Hook comes closer and closer to discovering his nemesis. Finally Peter Pan, much taken with his own courage, identifies himself by name. Hook attacks, and the pirates and the lost boys do battle. Of course, Hook does not fight fairly. He bites Peter Pan and claws him with his iron hand, but is prevented from doing further mischief by the arrival of the crocodile. Meanwhile, Peter and Wendy, stranded on a rock in the middle of the lagoon, seem fated to die. Wendy floats away on the tail of a kite, whereupon Peter prepares to die by "standing erect on the rock again, with that smile on his face and a drum beating within him. It was saying, 'To die will be an awfully big adventure'" (*Peter and Wendy*, p. 152). However, Peter Pan does not die. The Never Bird floats a nest his way, which Peter uses to reach home. Because he saved Tiger Lily, he becomes the "Great White Father" to the Indians; thus an alliance is forged between the lost boys and the Indians.

The adventures in Neverland might continue forever, but the Darling children fear that their parents will forget them. They decide to return home, and bring the lost boys with them. Just as the decision is made, the pirates attack the Indians, breaking the pattern of Indian warfare by striking first and thus defeating them. Tricking the children into believing the Indians have won, the pirates successfully ambush the Darlings and the lost boys, and bring them back to the pirate ship. Peter Pan, alone in the underground home, has fallen asleep, which leaves him defenseless in the presence of Captain Hook. Hook poisons Peter Pan's medicine. Soon after, Tinker Bell arrives and breathlessly informs Peter Pan that the pirates have captured his friends. Peter leaps up to rescue Wendy and decides to take his medicine first. Tinker Bell intercedes, drinks the poison, and prepares to die. Maybe, she says, she could recover if enough children believed in fairies. In a passage of the book that borrows closely from one of the play's most famous scenes, Peter flings out his arms.

> There were no children here, and it was nighttime; but he addressed all who might be dreaming of the Neverland. . . . "Do you believe?" he cried. . . . "If you believe," he shouted to them, "clap your hands; don't let Tink die."
>
> (*Peter and Wendy*, p. 185)

CHILDREN ABROAD

The lost boys, abandoned children sent to Neverland, have their Edwardian counterparts in the destitute children shipped abroad. In the latter part of the Victorian period, reformers such as Thomas Barnardo (1845-1905) zealously took up the idea of forcing children to emigrate. Between 1875 and 1925, 80,000 children went to rural Canada, where reformers believed they would profit from a better environment than the British cities. Barnardo's National Waif's Association sheltered and fed vagrant children. The "Guiding Principles" of his homes included not only that no destitute child would ever be refused admission, but also that the homes would constitute England's largest emigration agency for the young. Despite the good intentions of such people as Barnardo, emigration frequently led to great suffering for the young. Children sent to Canada were often treated cruelly, distrusted by the farming families that boarded them, and sometimes sent away from all that remained of their own families in Britain.

Tink is saved, and Peter Pan can now attend to freeing Wendy and killing Hook: "Hook or me this time," he swears (*Peter and Wendy*, p. 186).

The last scene in Neverland takes place on the pirate ship, the *Jolly Roger*. Captain Hook, melancholy and musing, finds himself tortured by considerations of "good form" (*Peter and Wendy*, p. 188). As a graduate of a famous public school (namely Eton), does he still show his good breeding? Meanwhile, Wendy has been tied to the mast, and the lost boys are set to walk the plank. Peter, imitating the ticking crocodile, boards the *Jolly Roger*, and hides in the cabin. Any pirate who ventures in is killed by the hidden Peter as if by a phantom. Finally it is time for one more battle between the lost boys and the pirates, and the final sword fight between Hook and Peter. James Hook, "not wholly unheroic," says the narrator, fights to the end in good form, before plunging into the sea and the crocodile's maw (*Peter and Wendy*, p. 204). After some time at playing pirates, the Darling children fly home to London with the lost boys.

Back in London, Mr. Darling has condemned himself for his role in the children's departure—his removing Nana allowed Peter Pan to whisk away his children unimpeded. He has taken to living in the kennel until his children return. Mrs. Darling waits, and keeps the house ready for Wendy, John, and Michael. In the window fly the children, to a place they barely remember and into bed they creep, as if they had never left. Mrs. Darling sees them as if in a dream, and a joyful family reunion occurs. Peter Pan, looking at them through the window, sees "the one joy from which he must be for ever barred" (*Peter and Wendy*, p. 214).

The novel, however, does not end at this point, where the play always did (except for once in 1908). The novel's final chapter, "When Wendy Grew Up," describes the fate of the Darlings and the lost boys. Adopted by the Darlings, the lost boys quickly forget about their lives in Neverland. Twice in the coming years, Wendy goes to Neverland for a week to help with spring cleaning; after that, she does not see Peter Pan until she is grown up with a daughter of her own. It becomes Jane's turn and then Jane's daughter's turn, to accompany Peter to Neverland, "and thus it will go on, so long as children are gay and innocent and heartless" (*Peter and Wendy*, p. 226).

Barrie and the golden age of childhood. In *Peter and Wendy*, the three Darling children are born into a family with tenuous middle-class status and strict gender divisions. Barrie satirizes middle-class concerns in his depiction of the Darling parents, especially the father, "one of those deep ones who knows about stocks and shares" (*Peter and Wendy*, p. 70). Mr. Darling works in the financial district of London, where, as a note in the play tells us, "he sits on a stool all day, as fixed as a postage stamp . . . so like all the others on stools that you recognise him not by his face but by his stool" (*Peter Pan*, p. 11). Mr. Darling's white-collar job is the result of a burgeoning number of clerical positions in Britain's economy. The novel clearly expresses middle-class concerns over money and respectability. When the first Darling child is born, "it was doubtful whether they [Mr. and Mrs. Darling] would be able to keep her, as she was another mouth to feed" (*Peter and Wendy*, p. 70). Maintaining one's status meant keeping up appearances, which entailed employing at least one servant, an attitude that Barrie mocks in the Darling family's choice of a dog as a nurse: "Mrs. Darling loved to have everything just so, and Mr. Darling had a passion for being exactly like his neighbours; so, of course, they had a nurse. As they were poor, owing to the amount of milk the children drank, this nurse was a prim Newfoundland dog, called Nana" (*Peter and Wendy*, p. 71). The Darlings have only one other servant, a young girl whom they sometimes refer to as "the servants."

If Mr. Darling is responsible for financial security, Mrs. Darling is in charge of psychological security. With a kiss permanently in the corner of her mouth, Mrs. Darling is the "angel in the house." In other words, she tells the fairy tales, keeps the peace, and follows "the nightly custom of every good mother," to survey her children's sleeping minds and "put things straight for next morning" (*Peter and Wendy*, p. 73). The narrator indicates his own partiality by saying about Mrs. Darling, "Some like Peter best and some like Wendy best, but I like her best" (*Peter and Wendy*, p. 210).

The children, therefore, have clear gender and class role models, which they emulate throughout the novel, from the very first scene in which Wendy and John play at parenting. Wendy is as maternal as a little girl can be. Her first step in Neverland is to recreate Victorian bourgeois domesticity in the house under the ground. It is from this house that the lost boys, the Darling boys, and Peter Pan go out to have adventures. Wendy is either absent from them—at home sewing and cooking—or a spectator, rather than an actor. By contrast, Peter Pan, the quintessential boy, who "hates lethargy," is all energy, activity, and instinct (*Peter and Wendy*, p. 112). The lost boys, adept at woodland skills, bear some resemblance to Baden-Powell's Boy Scouts. They are hardy and independent, scarcely needing a mother at all.

Peter and Wendy, thus, is a typical Edwardian production in its idolization of boyhood. The novel takes boyish games and desires—to play at pirates and Indians all day—and gives them literary status. As Barrie said, "The next best thing to being boys is to write about them" (Barrie in Wullschläger, p. 1). This idolization, though, is not always sentimental. Though *Peter and Wendy*'s narrator describes children as "gay and innocent and heartless," (*Peter and Wendy*, p. 226), Peter Pan's dreams make him cry in his sleep. The novel touches on childhood fears of abandonment and rejection. Though Wendy speaks of the greatness of mother love, Peter Pan tells a different story:

> Long ago . . . I thought like you that my mother would always keep the window open for me; so I stayed away for moons and moons and moons, and then flew back; but the window was barred, for mother had forgotten all about me, and there was another little baby sleeping in my bed.
>
> (*Peter and Wendy*, p. 167)

In Peter Pan's experience, children are replaceable. The situation of the lost boys may be even worse. As Peter Pan explains, "they are the children who fall out of their perambulators when the nurse is looking the other way. If they are not claimed in seven days they are sent far away to the Neverland to defray expenses" (*Peter and Wendy*, pp. 94-95). The lost boys are like mislaid packages. They have been abandoned to their own fate. Even the opening of the novel, which shows Mr. Darling calculating the expense of a new child, invokes such fairy tales as "Hansel and Gretel," in which parents "lose" their children in the woods because they can't afford to feed them. Though children may be as "savage" as the pirates and Indians they emulate, it is adults who are truly immoral in Barrie's world.

Sources and literary context. As noted, *Peter and Wendy* continues a line of island adventure stories stretching back to Daniel Defoe's *Robinson Crusoe*. In fact, *Robinson Crusoe* was the first book the boy Barrie and his mother read together.

Famous Island Adventure Stories

1719:	Daniel Defoe's *Robinson Crusoe*
1812-1813:	Johann David Wyss's *Swiss Family Robinson*
1841:	Frederick Marryat's *Masterman Ready*
1858:	R. M. Ballantyne's *The Coral Island*
1874:	Jules Verne's *The Mysterious Island*
1883:	Robert Louis Stevenson's *Treasure Island*
1911:	J. M. Barrie's *Peter and Wendy*
1954:	William Golding's *Lord of the Flies*.

Barrie states about this young self that "the reading he is munching feverishly is about desert islands; he calls them wrecked islands" (Barrie, *Peter Pan*, p. xiv). Even when he began to write plays, he remembers "quaking a little lest some low person counts how many islands are in them" (Barrie, *Peter Pan*, p. xv).

Barrie, however, pays far more credit to the inspiration provided by the Llewelyn Davies boys; collectively, they were the muse that inspired the many versions of *Peter Pan*. The swashbuckling boy hero of the play was largely the product of Barrie's own meeting in 1897 in Kensington Gardens with George, Jack, and Peter Llewelyn Davies—later on came two more boys, Michael and Nicholas. Barrie grew close to the Llewelyn Davies family; he recorded his early intimacy in a privately published fantasy, complete with photographs, of his summer adventures with the three older boys: *The Boy Castaways of Black Lake Island*. Barrie claims that this slight volume and the five Davies boys themselves were the main sources of the play. In its dedication, Barrie pays tribute to them and the fantasy games he played with them:

> What I want to do first is to give Peter to the Five without whom he never would have existed. . . . You had played it [Peter Pan] until you tired of it, and tossed it in the air and gored it and left it derelict in the mud and went on your way singing other songs; and then I stole back and sewed some of the gory fragments together with a pen-nib.
>
> (Barrie, *Peter Pan*, pp. v, viii)

Barrie played Captain Swarthy, the pirate who would become Captain Hook; Peter, Jack, and George were the wrecked survivors; Barrie's St. Bernard, Porthos, played any number of supporting roles.

When Barrie wrote *Peter Pan*, he incorporated the names of the Davies children. Peter's name was used for Peter Pan, Jack and Michael for John and Michael Darling, and George for Mr. Darling. Barrie believed Sylvia Llewelyn Davies, the mother of the Davies boys, to be a model of motherhood, and used her to create Mrs. Darling. Andrew Birkin argues that Mr. Darling is, in fact, a caricature of Arthur Llewelyn Davies (Birkin, p. 46). The name "Wendy" has a different origin. Barrie invented the name for the play, taking it from Margaret Henley, the young daughter of editor and poet W. E. Henley. Margaret lispingly called Barrie "My Wendy," meaning "My Friendy," and thus the name was born. Though Margaret Henley died when she was six, the name she invented and the cloak she wore were immortalized in Barrie's play.

Barrie's sentence—"There never was a simpler, happier family until the coming of Peter Pan"—can be read, as Birkin does, with a certain self-irony about Barrie's own disruptive role in the life of the Davies family (Birkin, p. 46; *Peter and Wendy*, p. 72). Barrie himself, then, is also a model for Peter Pan. A man of short stature, under the influence of his mother for a long time, unable, biographers speculate, to consummate his marriage, consumed with childhood games and talk, Barrie refused to let go of boyhood. As Max Beerbohm wrote in reviewing the play, Barrie "has never grown up. He is still a child, absolutely" (Beerbohm in Birkin, p. 118). Barrie came to a similar conclusion in 1922: "It is as if long after writing *Peter Pan* its true meaning came to me—desperate attempt to grow up but can't" (Barrie in Wullschläger, p. 131).

BARRIE'S GIFT TO SICK CHILDREN

~

In 1929, Barrie gave the royalties from *Peter Pan* to London's Great Ormond Street Hospital for Sick Children. When Barrie died, he reconfirmed the gift, and requested that the amount received by the hospital be kept secret. In 1987, the copyright expired. A year later the British Parliament acted to maintain the royalties to the hospital.

Before and after the novel *Peter and Wendy*, elements of the story appeared in various forms, the key source being the play *Peter Pan, or the Boy Who Wouldn't Grow Up*. Barrie had written the play *Peter Pan* for the Christmas pantomime season. Pantomime, which literally means "an imitator of all," was a popular form of drama in eighteenth- and nineteenth-century England. Incorporated into Barrie's play are basic pantomime principles: a boy hero played by a girl; a villain scorned by the audience; many roles for children; and audience involvement.

Elements of the Peter Pan story surfaced in works harking back to the beginning of the twentieth century.

Peter Pan's Major Appearances

1901: *The Boy Castaways of Black Lake Island*. A memoir by Barrie of his summer adventures with three older boys: George, Jack, and Peter, of the Llewelyn Davis family. Two copies were privately published; one was kept by Barrie, the other given to Arthur Llewelyn Davies, the boys' father.

1902: *The Little White Bird*. A novel that contains chapters on Peter Pan as a baby who flies to Kensington Gardens and remains always one week old.

1904: First performance of the play *Peter Pan, or the Boy Who Would Not Grow Up*.

1906: *Peter Pan in Kensington Gardens* (based on the Peter Pan chapters of *The Little White Bird*, and illustrated by Arthur Rackham).

1911: *Peter and Wendy*.

Reception. James Barrie was an immensely popular writer in his time, and no writings of his have been more popular or lasted longer than his incarnations of Peter Pan. The play was enthusiastically received, and has become the most popular children's play ever. In London, the *Daily Telegraph* wrote that the play is "of such originality, of such tenderness, and of such daring, that not even a shadow of doubt regarding its complete success was to be discerned in the final fall of the curtain. . . . It is so true, so natural, so touching, that it brought the audience to the writer's feet and held them captives there" (*Daily Telegraph* in Hanson, p. 45). The play opened subsequently in Washington, D.C., and traveled across North America, where an American critic wrote that "it is a bit of pure phantasy by the writer who, since the death of Robert Louis Stevenson, has most truly kept the ear and mind of a child" (*Outlook* in Dunbar, p. 146).

Peter and Wendy, published with illustrations by F. D. Bedford, was greeted with as much applause as the play. Critics praised Barrie's portrayal of "the motherheart and child-nature," his "delicious humour," and his ability to write a book that is "neither a boy's book, nor a girl's book, nor a fairy book, nor anything but just a *book* which is a delight for everybody" (Markgraf, pp. 230-232). A review in *Punch* made the following assessment:

[*Peter and Wendy* is] not merely the play of *Peter Pan* with "observed he" and "remarked she" stuck in all through to make it look like a book; it is packed with island lore that is new to us. . . . It is the whole play, and yet so much more than the play. . . .

(Punch in Markgraf, p. 232)

—Danielle Price

For More Information

Barrie, J. M. *Peter and Wendy*. In *Peter Pan in Kensington Gardens; Peter and Wendy*. Ed. Peter Hollindale. Oxford: Oxford University Press, 1991.

———. *Peter Pan; or, the Boy Who Would Not Grow Up. The Plays of J. M. Barrie*. New York: Scribner, 1928.

Birkin, Andrew. *J. M. Barrie and The Lost Boys: The Love Story that Gave Birth to Peter Pan*. New York: Clarkson N. Potter, 1979.

Bratton, J. S. "British Imperialism and the Reproduction of Femininity in Girls' Fiction, 1900-1930." In *Imperialism and Juvenile Literature*. Ed. Jeffrey Richards. Manchester: Manchester University Press, 1989.

Cecil, Robert. *Life in Edwardian England*. London: B. T. Batsford; G. P. Putnam's, 1969.

Dunbar, Janet. *J. M. Barrie: The Man Behind the Image*. Newton Abbot: Readers Union, 1971.

Dyhouse, Carol. *Girls Growing Up in Late Victorian and Edwardian England*. London: Routledge, 1981.

Hanson, Bruce K. *The Peter Pan Chronicles: The Nearly 100 Year History of "The Boy Who Wouldn't Grow Up."* New York: Carol, 1993.

MacKenzie, John M. *Propaganda and Empire: The Manipulation of British Public Opinion, 1880-1960*. Manchester: Manchester University Press, 1984.

Markgraf, Carl. *J. M. Barrie: An Annotated Secondary Bibliography*. Greensboro, N.C.: ELT Press, 1989.

Mitchell, Sally. *Daily Life in Victorian England*. Westport, Conn.: Greenwood, 1996.

Porter, Andrew, ed. "Introduction." *The Nineteenth Century*. Vol. 3 of *The Oxford History of the British Empire*. Oxford: Oxford University Press, 1999.

Rogozinski, Jan. *Pirates! Brigands, Buccaneers, and Privateers in Fact, Fiction, and Legend*. New York: Facts on File, 1995.

Wullschläger, Jackie. *Inventing Wonderland: The Lives and Fantasies of Lewis Carroll, Edward Lear, J. M. Barrie, Kenneth Grahame and A. A. Milne*. New York: Free Press, 1995.

The Playboy of the Western World

by

John Millington Synge

John Millington Synge was born in 1871, to an Irish Protestant family in Rathfarnham, near Dublin. As a young man, he left Ireland for the Continent and spent several years in Germany and France, studying various literatures and trying his hand at poetry and the essay. In Paris in 1896, his path crossed with that of another aspiring Irish writer, the poet William Butler Yeats. This meeting has become famous: as Yeats recounts in his "Autobiographical Writings," he encouraged Synge to abandon his rather moody and bohemian literary lifestyle in France and return to Ireland to rediscover the language and the folk culture that survived among the rural peasantry, and among the population of the Gaelic-speaking Aran Islands in particular (Yeats in Finneran, p. 293). Synge spent many summers in the west of Ireland getting to know the stories, songs, and social mores of the country people. As Synge writes in the introduction to *The Playboy of the Western World*, listening to the gossip of the servant girls through the chink in the floorboards of a house in county Wicklow brought him "more aid than any learning could have given" (Synge, "Preface," *The Playboy of the Western World*, p. 96). Synge believed that he was resurrecting and portraying an authentic and vital layer of Irish culture, and audiences seemed to agree with him, for his early plays, such as *Riders to the Sea* (1904) and *The Well of the Saints* (1905), were popular with the nationalist audiences at the newly opened Abbey Theatre. But

THE LITERARY WORK

A comedy in three acts, set in a remote corner of the West of Ireland in the early years of the twentieth century, first staged at the Abbey Theatre in Dublin in 1907.

SYNOPSIS

In an isolated village on the County Mayo coast, Pegeen Mike, a young, single but soon-to-be-married woman, has her life changed by the arrival of a mysterious young man on the run who claims to have committed a terrible crime.

The Playboy of the Western World (here "playboy" has the older, mainly Irish meaning of an amusing, interesting but not really trustworthy young man, or an attractive rogue) was greeted with hostile and violent reactions on the part of the theatergoing public when first staged in January 1907. Its image of Ireland did not fit with the desires of Dublin audiences both to be nationalist in the sense of a cultural distinction from England and to honor their respectable Catholic middle-class values. Only two years later, in 1909, Synge, who suffered from Hodgkin's disease, died at the age of 39. Gradually the originality of his work and the scale of his contribution to both Irish and world drama would be recognized, even by nationalist critics who had previously attacked him.

J. M. Synge

Events in History at the
Time the Play Takes Place

Killing Home Rule by kindness. John Synge's *Playboy of the Western World* is set, as the program notes indicate, on the "wild coast of Mayo" in the first few years of the twentieth century. The play refers to the South African War of 1899–1902 (also called the Boer War), which suggests that the play takes place in 1903 or 1904. By the time Synge was visiting that part of Ireland, the great Famine of the late 1840s was nothing more than a grim memory. The cycle of emigration and community decline had, however, not let up since that watershed in Irish history. Many historians of population and demographics have argued that the west of Ireland was actually overpopulated and that somehow the numbers of people living on the land had to be reduced if those remaining were to have any kind of a life. Whether this is an arguable view or not, the historical reality is that Ireland moved into the twentieth century with over 2 million people less than it had when it entered the nineteenth century, and the bulk of the population losses were in the western third of the country.

The British government had some ideas for the depopulated west that would also address general Irish concerns. During the glory days of the Irish Party under Charles Stewart Parnell (roughly 1879–92), Irish activists fought for land reform and the quasi-independence of Home Rule with rent strikes and boycotts in the Irish countryside and with passionate debates in the House of Commons in London. Worried about the political forces that had been unleashed, the British government came up with the notion of "killing Home Rule by kindness." Put more plainly, it was thought that if the long-overdue farm ownership reforms were carried out, and money was put into developing the infrastructure of the remoter parts of Ireland to raise the standard of living and nurture the economic vitality of these areas, the political demands for Home Rule would dissipate. (Home Rule was to consist of autonomy and self-government, but under the British Crown as head of state.) By and large, these reforms were instituted and the infrastructural development took place. By 1914, for example, when World War I broke out, the west of Ireland had one of the most comprehensive local rail networks anywhere in the British Isles.

This failed, however, to really stem the tide of emigration. Some commentators have suggested that the British government's policies were destined to fail, given the subsistence economy in which much of the west of Ireland lived. The paucity of good agricultural land in the west meant that key elements of the plan—loans to smallholders and other policies to encourage farm modernization and consolidation—could never have the desired effect in areas such as the village in Synge's play, where people lived on the output of farms as small as a half-acre with bad soil, seasonal fishing, and the like. In general, the potential for agricultural and economic development was much more limited in the west than in the midlands or in the rich dairy industry of the "Golden Vale" in southwest Ireland. There, land was well-suited to both grazing and crops, and many farms were, or could become, big enough to generate an income that could support at least a small family.

The other dimension of the failure of the state-driven "modernization" of the west was a cultural one. This was, and still is to some extent, the part of Ireland in which the most substantial numbers of people spoke Irish, or Gaelic, as their mother tongue. Outside this region, the Irish language had gone into massive and seemingly terminal decline throughout the nineteenth century—a decline encouraged by the expulsion of this language from the public school system at its inception in 1844. Gaelic had become either the second or the forgotten language for much of the population of Ireland. Census returns indicate that, in 1901, out of a total population of around 4.5 million, only about 640,000 spoke Gaelic as a first language (about 14.4 percent of the total); in 1911 this had declined to around 580,000, or 13.3 percent (Grote, p. 34). Although most people in the west wanted their children to speak English fluently for practical reasons, a part of them also wanted to hold fast to their Gaelic culture. This made the west somewhat more resistant to encroachments by the English language and the administrative interventions of the British administration in the seat of government at Dublin Castle.

Synge, for his part, did not just visit the west for literary inspiration. He had traveled there in 1905, accompanied by the painter Jack B. Yeats, brother of the poet William Butler Yeats (see **"Easter 1916"** and **"September 1913,"** also in *WLAIT 4: British and Irish Literature and Its Times*). Specifically, Synge had traveled around county Mayo (northwest of Galway, the one urban center of the region) on a journalistic assignment for an English newspaper, the *Manchester Guardian*. Synge published a series of 12 articles on the situation in western Ireland, with illustrations by Jack Yeats. The articles deal with a recognition that struck Synge many times during his travels—a vital and authentic folk culture can coexist with poverty, isolation, and deprivation. It is very likely that Synge's subtle interweaving of poetic fantasy and grim realism in *The Playboy of the Western World* was rooted in experiences such as this research trip.

Emigration and marriage. The poverty and desolation that Synge and many others observed in parts of Ireland at the beginning of the century were intensified by the continual exodus of young people, both men and women, to the urban centers of Dublin in Ireland, and Liverpool and Manchester in England, as well as to emigrant ships headed for the United States, a more popular destination for westerners. In fact, an unkind assessment of the infrastructural development of the west of Ireland might say that the improved transport network had simply made it easier for people to get to the harbor and the passenger ship. The supposed "remoteness" of even the very isolated areas of Clare, Galway, Mayo, and Sligo had never been a bar to emigration. In any case the hard part was not so much getting the fare together as enduring the psychological trauma of parting from family and friends, perhaps forever, certainly for a long time.

It is fairly obvious in *The Playboy of the Western World* that the village has a shortage of young men. Although the term *emigration* itself is never mentioned, Pegeen Mike's complaint to Shawn Keogh in Act 1 points in this direction as she reviews the pretty unimpressive qualities shown by her various neighbors:

> PEGEEN: . . . I wouldn't bother with this place where you'll meet none but Red Linahan, has a squint in his eye, and Patcheen is lame in his heel, or the mad Mulrannies were driven from California and they lost in their wits.
> (Synge, *Playboy of the Western World*, p. 100)

Indeed, Pegeen's betrothal to Shawn, her cousin, has more of a resigned acceptance of the best offer from a bad bunch than anything else. Shawn's wimpish personality and the fact that they are related would have reduced to zero the likelihood of Pegeen marrying him if she had any real alternative.

Historically this shortage of eligible males seemed to lead not only to the decline of a community as marriage rates fell, but also to a loss of self-respect and sense of direction on the part of many of those men (older, usually) who had not emigrated. Success became identical with getting out, moving away. A man who stayed was by definition a failure, or loser. This idea, many nationalists observed at the time, mirrored the more political reality of Ireland's being trapped in the status of a loser vis-à-vis Great Britain, the successful imperial power. The relationship of the different parts of the Irish population to Ireland's colonial situation was complex, particularly if one includes the Protestants of the northeast, who favored union with England. There was a clear relationship, however, between depopulation in poor regions of Ireland and one's sense of Irishness. In respect to the Catholic population of these regions, emigration became a kind of negative solution to the lack of prospects felt by both individuals and communities: people were convinced that there could be no future at home, and the continuous stream of departures tended to confirm that very belief.

The deeper issue, and one that would become a controversy generated by *The Playboy of the Western World*, was the effect of the Catholic Church and its almost unchallenged power over the social values of Irish Catholic society in rural areas, particularly in the west. At the turn of the century, when the play is set, the whole direction of Catholic education in Ireland was, first, to make marriage and children seem like the next-best option after entering Holy Orders, and second, to nurture a kind of prudish fear of the opposite sex in young people (Lyons, p. 74). This contradictory message, many would assert, often led to groundless sexual problems in adulthood and contributed to a tendency toward late marriages, which made rural Ireland an oddity in the European context in the first half of the twentieth century. Other countries had conservative cultures when it came to marriage and women's role in society, but only Ireland showed almost a pervasive postponement of marriage and family in surprisingly large numbers.

The picture was not so simple, however. The communities in the remote western region were, as manifested in Synge's play, in a strange border area between Irish Catholic orthodoxy and the surviving energies of a pagan culture. In these Gaelic-speaking areas, there was often a kind of earthy, good-humored recognition of the realities of sexuality and reproduction that was far from the prudish sensitivities of the urban middle classes in the Irish cities of Cork and Dublin. This sense of a different, more primitive but more honest and vital culture would become a major issue for Synge's audiences and, in some ways, for the whole Irish Literary Revival. The Revival was committed to creating new kinds of drama, poetry, and prose that would use distinctly Irish folk sources and materials to establish an independent sense of national culture and identity. It was not a monolithic body; there were many areas of disagreement. Still, it was a movement in which Synge's work would play one of the most significant roles.

The Play in Focus

Plot summary. Act 1 begins in a small village pub and store on the Mayo coast. Margaret Flaherty, known as Pegeen Mike (Little Peg, daughter of Michael James Flaherty), is laboriously composing a letter ordering the food and drink for her wedding party, which is to take place shortly when she marries her cousin, Shawn Keogh. She is going to be left alone in the store on a stormy night; her father, Michael James, plans to go to a wake some miles away and may be gone until dawn. Shawn, her fiancé, arrives to see her. He does not want to keep her company until her father returns, in nervous anticipation of the local parish priest's reprimand were he to stay overnight with Pegeen before their wedding (they are waiting for the special dispensation to marry that they require as first cousins). Shawn is a rather ineffectual young man, and it becomes

clear very quickly that Pegeen Mike does not have a lot of respect or admiration for him, or expect much from him as a future husband.

Shawn reveals that he has heard what could be the groans of a man out on the road, but, much to Pegeen's disgust, he was afraid to investigate what was going on: "Well, you're a daring fellow! And if they find his corpse stretched above in the dews of the dawn, what'll you say to them peelers or the Justice of the Peace?" (*Playboy,* p. 101). When her father comes in, flanked by his two drinking buddies Jimmy and Philly, she scolds him for leaving her alone in the pub on such a night. Michael James then tries to pressure Shawn into staying after all, but Shawn, still terrified of Father Reilly's possible reaction, runs out of the store, much to the amusement of the others, and to Pegeen's irritation and embarrassment. A few seconds later Shawn returns, having fled the injured man he had heard earlier.

The man enters the pub. He is young, and he looks tired and dirty as if he has been traveling a long way on foot. He seems very unsure of himself, as if he cannot be certain whether he should trust the people in the pub. He asks about the likelihood of police checking out the premises and is relieved when he hears that they have no reason to come by. Michael James, Pegeen Mike, and the others begin to question him about what he has done that makes him afraid of the law, but he is very vague at first, responding practically in riddles. The others are increasingly curious, and finally the young man, who later introduces himself as Christy Mahon, admits his dramatic deed: he has murdered his father. To the shock and amazement, as well as the growing admiration, of his listeners—Pegeen in particular—he explains that his father had always bullied and disrespected him, and that one day he just picked up a loy (a sharp, shovel-like tool for cutting turf) and struck his father over the head, splitting his skull and killing him.

Pegeen's obvious interest in the stranger begins to worry Shawn Keogh, who attempts to keep an eye on things when it looks like Christy is going to stay the night in the store. When her father and his friends leave for the wake, Pegeen hustles Shawn out also, saying that he had the chance to stay before, and didn't take it, so now he can forget it. Pegeen makes some supper for Christy, and they both become increasingly delighted in each other's company, Pegeen because she thinks she has found a real man at last, and Christy because he seems never to have had an intimate conversation with a woman before. He is relieved when he discovers—her response to his query is not very candid—that she is not married:

> CHRISTY: (drawing a little nearer to her) You've a power of rings, God bless you, and would there be any offence if I was asking are you single now?
> PEGEEN: What would I want wedding so young?
> (*Playboy*, p. 109)

The moment is disrupted by the arrival of the Widow Quin, who despite her name is not meant to be much more than 30 years old. Tainted by the mysterious death of her husband, which Pegeen implies was foul play, the Widow Quin sets out to play the mature older woman to Pegeen Mike's brazen youthfulness in a contest for Christy's affection. She announces to Pegeen's indignant astonishment that Shawn Keogh and Father Reilly have instructed her to remove Christy to her house. Christy manages to escape this plan, and stay in the pub, but the Widow Quin indicates that she has every intention of pursuing her interest in Christy whether Pegeen likes it or not.

Act 2 takes place the following morning. By now, the story of Christy's murder of his father has spread throughout the neighborhood, and the young women of the village are enthralled. Three girls, Sarah, Honor, and Susan, decide to call on Christy to see what a real hero looks like. Bringing him their gifts of eggs, butter, and a small chicken, they demand to hear his story. The Widow Quin arrives to say that she has entered Christy into the various competitions and races that are going to take place at the fair that afternoon. Increasingly comfortable with being regarded as a hero, Christy basks in the admiration of the young girls. Pegeen arrives back from an errand and bursts in upon the scene. Furious, she orders the other women out and tells Christy that if he wants to stay out of trouble, boasting to talkative girls is not a good idea. Pegeen begins to see the other side of Christy now, his sense of being hunted and lonely rather than the handsome daredevil with the dramatic story, and finds herself intrigued by this glimpse into a more complex personality.

Shawn and the Widow Quin return to try and bribe Christy to leave the village. Putting a complicated plot in motion to rescue Shawn's wedding plans by marrying Christy herself, the Widow Quin gives Christy a new set of clothes for the sporting competitions in which he will participate. While he is admiring himself in the new attire, Christy suffers a terrific shock. He sees his father, whom he believes he has killed, walking up the street. Terrified, he hides. The Widow Quin is therefore the only person to greet Old Mahon, Christy's father, who turns out to be anything but dead, although he has a large bandaged head wound that he shows anyone who is interested. He is determined to find his son and exact revenge for the attempted murder. Entering the pub, Old Mahon talks about Christy as a weak, timid boy, afraid for his life of girls and unable to handle a pint of beer. The Widow succeeds in putting Old Mahon off the track and sends him in the direction of the nearest harbor town. Realizing that she has a hold over Christy now, knowing as she does that his story is not quite true, the Widow Quin tries to get him for herself, but Christy remains true to his feelings for Pegeen Mike and begs Quin to help him. Impressed by this despite herself, she agrees, but she demands future compensation in the form of farm produce and a new right-of-way, to be paid after Christy and Pegeen are married and he becomes master of the house.

Act 3 opens with Old Mahon reappearing in the pub, apparently having been distracted by a bar or two on the way to the harbor, and never having reached his destination. Hoping that they do not make the connection to Christy, the Widow Quin tries to convince Jimmy and Philly that Mahon's diatribe about sons who try to murder their fathers is just the ravings of a madman. Suddenly, they hear shouts from the strand that seem to be for the winner who is just about to cross the line in the main race of the day. Seeing the winner raised up by the crowd, Old Mahon is astonished to see his son, Christy. The Widow Quin manages to convince Old Mahon that he is deranged and that the winner cannot possibly be Christy if his son is as useless and incapable as the father has been claiming. Once again, he leaves after this successful diversion by the Widow Quin. Christy and Pegeen enter then, both excited and happy after Christy's victory. Pegeen finally tells Shawn plainly that she has no intention of marrying him. As she says: "Wouldn't it be a bitter thing for a girl to go marrying the like of Shaneen, and he a middling kind of a scarecrow with no savagery or fine words in him at all?" (*Playboy*, p. 139). Her father agrees: "A daring fellow is the jewel of the world" (*Playboy*, p. 140).

Suddenly Old Mahon rushes back into the store, knocks Christy down, and begins to beat him. Realizing the truth, the villagers turn on Christy. Pegeen Mike is stunned by the revela-

Pegeen Mike prepares to attack Christy with burning coal at the climax of Act 3 in this stage production of *The Playboy of the Western World*.

tion that Christy's story might have been just that, a story. At this point, Christy picks up a loy and chases his father out of the pub, threatening to knock him down. There is the sound of an altercation offstage, suggesting that the son has made good his threat. Christy re-enters the pub, alone, whereupon the others turn on him, frightened by witnessing the violent deed he only spoke of before.

Although the Widow Quin tries to help Christy escape, Michael James and the others manage to get a rope around him, either to hang him or to tie him down until the police come. Crying with disappointment and anger, Pegeen eggs them on, at one point taking a burning coal from the fire and singeing Christy's leg with it.

When he suddenly manages to free himself, Christy finds himself face to face with his father. The relationship is changed; now Christy is in charge, and father and son recognize this. They leave together, both proud of the dramatic story they can tell to earn their supper in the future. Realizing that her dream has shattered, Pegeen Mike shoves aside Shawn Keogh—who understands nothing of what has happened and is just pleased that Christy has finally gone—then utters the famous last line: "Oh my grief, I've lost him surely. I've lost the only playboy of the western world" (*Playboy*, p. 146).

The deed and the story. Pegeen Mike's contemptuous remark to Shawn about a man who has neither fine words nor savagery in him at all encapsulates the problem with which the play wrestles. Shawn Keogh, and by implication much of the male population in general, has the qualities of neither a poet nor a storyteller nor of a folk hero with a fighting reputation. In some cultures, these two types of characteristics would be assigned to separate regions of existence. The poet's responsibility is song, but the man of action is generally known for silence. Silence is power, as it were. This is the traditional cultural configuration in Mexico, for example, as discussed by the writer Octavio Paz in *The Labyrinth of Solitude*. In Ireland, however, the cultural and psychological poles are reversed, and the ability to enchant with words is at least as powerful as, if not superior to, the charisma lent by an act of violence, particularly one that embodies a primal sin such as parricide, the killing of the father. Words, not silence, are where power lies.

The location of the words-as-power, in *The Playboy of the Western World*, is Christy. Pegeen Mike sees in him the transforming power of the heroic deed that also makes good poetry. It is as if a man has walked in where before there were only emasculated beings: Shawn is weak and intimidated by the local parish priest; Michael James and his clique travel to wakes and get hopelessly drunk; the other males in the area appear to be, in keeping with Pegeen's above-cited description of them to Shawn in Act 1, a collection of physically disabled half-wits. There is no "match," in either sense of the word, for a woman of Pegeen's intelligence and energy. The suggestion of a dangerous shortage of marriage partners in the small community is clearly articulated when the play makes Pegeen and Shawn cousins. Beyond this, *The Playboy of the Western World* uses the relationship between Christy and Pegeen— and among the characters in general—to suggest that one of the problems Irish society and the nationalist movement face is the discrepancy between romantic rhetoric and grim reality.

Parallels can be drawn to the Irish national movement. One such parallel involves the confusion of rhetoric with reality, rhetoric that creates an ideal Ireland or Irish culture that average human beings could never live up to; another parallel can be seen in England's embodying a male-like authority and identity whose dominance presents a problem that can only be solved by the violent removal of the patriarchal entity. There is a third possible parallel, too, between Pegeen Mike in the play and the female symbol of an Ireland waiting for its heroes to wake up and rescue her, the figure of "Cathleen ni Houlihan" in W. B. Yeats's early nationalist drama, for example. Pegeen Mike's desire for a hero and poet speaks to a search for something real, something more than just a story. Hopeful, Pegeen Mike thinks that Christy personifies this something, at least for a while; of course, both deed and story crumble away when the "dead" father returns to life.

The play seems to suggest that both the men and women are perhaps too open to being enchanted by words, too inclined to take the poetry of Irish national identity as equivalent to reality. In the play, reality dawns traumatically on Pegeen Mike, as revealed in a bitter comment to Christy: "I'll say a strange man is a marvel with his mighty talk; but what's a squabble in your back yard and the blow of a loy, have taught me that there's a great gap between a gallous story and a dirty deed" (*Playboy*, p. 144). Pegeen Mike realizes that behind Christy's story is a small-time incident of family violence and that perhaps more than just his story ends that way; there is no guarantee that other so-called heroic tales will always retain their aura of glory and wonder.

The final victory of rhetoric over reality is, of course, Christy's reconnection with his father under new rules, so to speak. They patch up their disagreement after Old Mahon survives the second attack by Christy—"Are you coming to be killed a third time or what ails you now?"—and leave together, clearly for a life of travel and profitable storytelling as an entertaining double-act: the son who killed his father and the father who returned from the dead (*Playboy*, p. 146). The one chance of a real life for Christy, marrying Pegeen, has been ruined, but she alone bitterly laments the lost future. Christy goes off with his father, resuming the male-male type of existence they seem to have led before Christy met Pegeen Mike (there is no mention in the play of his mother). He has challenged his father, and the relationship has indeed changed, but Christy feels empowered less because of that experience and more because he now has a story. Women, it seems, would somehow get in the way of the storytelling. Thus, in contrast to traditional comedy, which culminates in marriage and the promise of fertility, this Irish comedy ends with the woman alone and the men heading off down the road together.

Sources and literary context. There are two principal elements that make up the environment in which Synge wrote *The Playboy of the Western World* and his other plays. One is the search for new forms of dramatic language and theatrical performance that began in the late nineteenth and continued well into the twentieth century. The other important element is the Irish Literary Revival, the campaign waged by writers such as W. B. Yeats, George Moore, and Douglas Hyde, as well as actors and journalists, to provide the Irish people with a literature and drama that drew upon native traditions and ideas rather than merely copying the British models that were so nearby and so attractive. Both these elements play important but different roles in the literary context out of which Synge's work emerged.

There was a desire on the part of writers to create more challenging, less reassuring plays and a wish on the part of actors and producers to experiment with smaller, less technically standardized, and more intimate theatrical environments. Norway's Henrik Ibsen (1828–1906) became identified with the attempt to explore the grimmer side of contemporary human relations, embodied in the movement known as naturalism. Plays by Ibsen such as *Hedda Gabler* (1890) and *Master Builder* (1892) put issues of female sexual desire, infidelity, and middle-class hypocrisy on the European stage, creating controversy in Germany, England, and Denmark, as well as in his native Norway. As playwright George Bernard Shaw put it in his 1895 essay "The Problem Play": "Every social question, arising as it must from a conflict between human feeling and circumstances, affords material for drama" (Shaw in Dukore, p. 634). (For discussion of Shaw's own work, see **Pygmalion**, also in *WLAIT 4: British and Irish Literature and Its Times*). Synge, although engaged in a similar search for a new dramatic form, represented another direction. He rejected the dry sound of realistic, conversational dialogue—the "joyless and pallid words" he calls them in his "Preface"—in favor of a poetic lyricism that sounded specifically Irish, a kind of language in which the style and inflexions of Gaelic completely dominated the actual spoken English ("Preface," *Playboy*, p. 96). Such language manifests itself, for example, in a speech to Pegeen in Act 1:

> CHRISTY: . . . I've said it nowhere till this night, I'm telling you, for I've seen none the like of you the eleven days I am walking the world, looking over a low ditch or a high ditch on my north or south, into stony scattered fields, or scribes of bog, where you'd see young limber girls, and fine prancing women making laughter with the men.
>
> (*Playboy*, p. 109)

The other line of approach taken by dramatists in the late nineteenth and early twentieth century was to look to rural and/or peasant traditions to create an earthier, perhaps even more basic, kind of drama. Away from the urban centers, it was thought, people live starker, more elemental lives, and these provide more food for dramatic art than the domestic problems of the middle and upper classes. In Ireland, this turn to rural themes and images fit in neatly with the ideological interests of proponents of the national Literary Revival and its dramatic showcase, the Abbey Theatre. Not only did this trend draw on authentic native traditions, thought Yeats and other Irish Literary Revival leaders, but it also put Ireland on the map, as the search for a "native" art was something about which nationalist writers in many colonial situations across the world—and many African American authors—were passionately concerned. In Synge's case, his *Playboy of the Western World,* by its very subject matter and language, constituted a resistance to the cultural norms of the British literary mainstream and the notion that what was English was also, by virtue of this fact alone, culturally defining.

Events in History at the Time the Play Was Written

"Standing in their shifts." *The Playboy of the Western World* was certainly successful in attracting attention when it opened in Dublin at the Abbey Theatre in January 1907. One could say that it made history. Before Synge's play made its debut, rumors had been floating around the city that the new play was indecent, risqué, or shocking in some way. When it opened, audiences were primed to look for the evidence. They found it toward the end of the play, in Act 3, when Christy says to the Widow Quin that he has no interest in any women but Pegeen Mike: "It's Pegeen I'm seeking only, and what'd I care if you brought me a drift of chosen females standing in their shifts itself maybe, from this place to the Eastern World" (*Playboy,* p. 143). The actor playing Christy also ad-libbed a change to these lines on the opening night of the play, substituting "Mayo girls" for "chosen females." His change only aggravated the situation. The image of a line of exotic young women in their slips, or underdresses, was now an image of a bunch of innocent Irish country girls in the same scanty clothing. Shouts and catcalls were hurled at the stage by the first-night audience, and the situation grew worse on succeeding nights.

On the second night of the play, the cast was physically threatened, whereupon Lady Gregory, in her capacity as a director of the Abbey Theatre, called the police to restore order. This was followed by a week of performances under police protection, a considerable and uncomfortable irony, as the leaders of the national cultural revival were now presenting their art behind the police lines of the Royal Irish Constabulary, the uniformed manifestation of the British Crown's authority over Ireland. This particular irony revealed the fault lines in what many had seen as a unified nationalist movement, in which cultural issues and political demands were part and parcel of the same totality. The Abbey Theatre now needed police protection from the very audience to whom, in its mind, the institution was pitching its work.

A number of developments had come together in the last few years of the nineteenth and the first few years of the twentieth century to create a new model for Irish nationalism. The failure of Home Rule under Parnell and the split undergone by the Irish Parliamentary Party after his fall from leadership and death had led to the formation, in 1908, of a new political party called Sinn Féin, or "Ourselves Alone." Sinn Féin had a more radical program of independence, going beyond the demands for Home Rule to complete national autonomy, with only a modest titular role for the British Crown. This fell short of the independent republic and the complete removal of any link with the United Kingdom demanded by the most extreme nationalist voices, but it was significantly more than what Parnell had wanted. Flanking this new political party were three autonomous organizations that were seeking to give Irish nationalism a cultural identity of its own: the Gaelic Athletic Association (or GAA), the Gaelic League, and the Abbey Theatre Company.

The GAA, destined to become a major force in Irish life throughout the twentieth century, rediscovered, or invented, games such as hurling and camogie that would provide for the physical education and cultural independence of Irish youth in a way that also rejected the legitimacy of British sports in Ireland, such as soccer and cricket. The Gaelic League, under the committed leadership of Douglas Hyde, conducted a remarkable campaign of public education and advocacy to revitalize the Irish language, which, as mentioned earlier, seemed to have gone into terminal decline over the course of the nineteenth century. The Irish National Theatre Society, generally known as the Abbey Theatre after it had obtained permanent premises, was the last component in this equation. Started by the actor W. G. Fay and taken in hand by Yeats and Lady Augusta Gregory, its aim was to be the showcase for a new national drama that would, along with other kinds of literature, provide an authentic culture to underpin the desire for political independence. Although the three organizations were in many ways working toward the same goals, there were significant differences. The GAA, the

OPENING UP THE STORY

The early twentieth century in Ireland was marked by an intensified rhetoric of cultural independence and nationalist ardor, a rhetoric that the Irish National Theatre Company and the figures of the Literary Revival had played a major role in promoting. Yet the political situation seemed to offer no real opening for change. To Synge at the beginning of the 1900s the prospects for even limited autonomy seemed bleak (although another legislative attempt at Home Rule for Ireland would in fact pass the British House of Commons in 1912, only to be eclipsed by the outbreak of World War I in 1914).

Moreover, to his distress, Ireland appeared dependent upon Britain in every way—not just economically but culturally too, not just socially but also psychologically. It seemed as if Ireland was condemned to the kind of paralysis that frustrated James Joyce (see *Ulysses,* also in *WLAIT 4: British and Irish Literature and Its Times*), a kind of historical groove of rebellion and failure from which nobody could escape. In 1916, seven years after Synge's death, an armed nationalist rising would take place, surprising many who had believed that it was all just talk. Synge would almost certainly have rejected violence as a political tool, but he might have recognized a moment in history where Ireland was suddenly no longer trapped in someone else's story.

largest by far, was rural-based and distinctly Catholic in its orientation, the Gaelic League was more urban and middle-class, and the Abbey was dominated by the Anglo-Irish, Protestant, and rather elitist coterie around W. B. Yeats.

The situation on the opening night of *The Playboy of the Western World* can thus be described as follows: in a theater claiming to be dedicated to elevating Irish culture and presenting it to the world is a play of rural ignorance, pagan morality, and sexual suggestiveness, touted as a comedy and, worst of all, set in the remote west of Ireland, where the pure, unspoiled values of the Irish country people were supposedly to be found. Moreover, the play focused on violence and its appeal, a particularly infuriating aspect for the audience. As Declan Kiberd remarked: "The situation was, of course, rich in ironies, the most obvious being that the protesters shouted 'We Irish are not a violent people' and then sprang at the actors to prove their point—confirming Synge's conviction that *some* were" (Kiberd, p. 168).

EVOLUTION OF THE ABBEY

The Abbey Theatre is still in existence today as the national theater of Ireland. Its history, however, has often been as much a cultural burden as an artistic inspiration. Despite the original shock-effect of plays like Synge's *Playboy of the Western World*, the Abbey was eventually domesticated, after national independence, into a state-funded showcase of Irish theater that tended very much to offer the tragic or comic rural drama as its staple product, much to the delight of tourists and much to the dismay of serious playwrights in Ireland. By mid-twentieth century the sense of cutting-edge literary experiment and challenging the public taste had become an attribute of the past, and in the early 1950s the old Abbey Theatre building was destroyed in a fire, and the company had to move. In 1966, a new Abbey Theatre was finally opened to the public. The reborn Abbey proved more willing to produce the work of younger writers and began to move away from the Irish "peasant play" that Synge and others of his generation had come to represent (though Synge continued to be recognized as a preeminent dramatist). A kind of junior Abbey, called the Peacock Theatre, was established specifically to produce more experimental and offbeat drama and to nurture writers who were just beginning their careers.

The so-called "Playboy Riots" showed the nationalist spectrum as being rather wide and the parts not at all in synch with one another. A broad gulf divided the average Irish Catholic theatergoer from the experimental and disturbing vision of John Synge, just as the cultural gap between Irish Protestants and Irish Catholics was always present—even in the case of those Irish Protestants who committed themselves to the nationalist cause and indeed regarded themselves

as its intellectual and literary avant-garde. Clearly the Dublin middle classes were uncomfortable with Synge's ideas about violence and language and his innovations in dramatic content and style. The Abbey audience heard only the indecent suggestiveness of "shifts" and either could not or did not want to perceive the lyrical intensity of Christy's declarations of love, for example, as echoing the rhythm and style of the Irish language as Synge had experienced it in his travels in the west.

Reception. Quite apart from the famous events of the opening week, when there seemed to be more drama on the street outside the theater than on the stage, *The Playboy of the Western World* received the same confused-to-hostile response from magazine and newspaper reviewers that earlier Irish National Theatre offerings had provoked. As Cheryl Herr commented in her study of Irish popular theater around the turn of the century, the very successful Queen's Theatre, providing a profitable diet of comedies and romantic patriotic plays by writers such as Dion Boucicault, had trained Dublin audiences and press reviewers to expect a certain kind of play. What the Abbey was offering was offbeat and seemed elitist. A columnist named W. MacA., writing at the time in *The Irish Playgoer*, reflected a commonly held feeling when describing the Irish National Theatre productions as "the curious group of plays produced the last two years . . . claiming to be representative of the country" (Herr, pp. 17-19). Reviewing *The Playboy of the Western World* a few years later, the mainstream nationalist press was more plainspoken: the influential *Freeman's Journal* called it "an unmitigated, protracted libel upon Irish peasant men and, worse still, upon Irish peasant girlhood" (Lyons, p. 69).

Synge became a target for all that the bedrock nationalists disdained in the world of theater and culture: he seemed more interested in exploring strange dramatic stories than entertaining the public with uplifting patriotic plays or harmless comedies; he suggested a complex world of struggling moralities and violent desire; he asserted the right of the artist to portray the truth as he saw it; he was a Protestant. Although his work continues to be performed by the Abbey Theatre, it was only in the 1960s in Ireland that the distrust harbored by the cultural nationalists for his work dissipated and his contribution to Irish literature received more objective assessment. The question of Synge's relationship with, and sources of inspiration in,

Gaelic was first investigated thoroughly by Declan Kiberd in *Synge and the Irish Language* (1979). "Our view of him has never been more than one-dimensional," points out Kiberd. "He has always been presented as a great Anglo-Irish writer and he is certainly that, but he is also a vital artist in the Gaelic tradition. . . . Until we can learn to see his work as a fusion of both traditions, we shall never truly know him at all" (Kiberd, p. 16).

—Martin Griffin

For More Information

Corkery, Daniel. *Synge and Anglo-Irish Literature: A Study*. Cork: Cork University Press, 1947.

Dukore, Bernard F., ed. *Dramatic Theory and Criticism: Greeks to Grotowski*. New York: Holt, Rinehart & Winston, 1974.

Finneran, Richard J., ed. *The Yeats Reader: A Portable Compendium of Poetry, Drama, and Prose*. New York: Scribner, 1997.

Greene, David H., and Edward M. Stephens. *J. M. Synge: 1871–1909*. New York: Macmillan, 1959.

Grote, Georg. *Torn between Politics and Culture: The Gaelic League, 1893–1993*. New York: Waxmann, 1994.

Herr, Cheryl. *For the Land They Loved: Irish Political Melodramas, 1890–1935*. Syracuse, N.Y.: Syracuse University Press, 1991.

Kiberd, Declan. *Inventing Ireland: The Literature of the Modern Nation*. London: Random House, Vintage, 1996.

————. *Synge and the Irish Language*. London and Basingstoke: Macmillan, 1979.

Lyons, F. S. L. *Culture and Anarchy in Ireland, 1890–1939*. New York: Oxford University Press, 1979.

Synge, John Millington. *The Playboy of the Western World and Other Plays*. New York: Oxford University Press, 1995.

The Power and
the Glory

by
Graham Greene

Born in 1904, Graham Greene grew up in a world where duty, tradition, and moral virtue were primary emphases in a boy's upbringing. His father, Charles Greene, was headmaster of a well-regarded boarding school that Greene attended. Young Graham was expected not only to exhibit exemplary behavior, but to inform his father when his fellow pupils misbehaved—that is, engaged in sexual vice. Charles Greene believed masturbation to be a physically degenerate act that would lead boys to perdition. Offenders were summarily expelled. In this stifling atmosphere, the son rapidly learned to be quiet and unobtrusive—secretive, even. This behavior continued in his university career at Oxford, where Greene entertained German spies in his room. Indeed, many of his relatives (and Greene himself) engaged in more or less regular professional spycraft. Greene did a fair amount of professional spy work, in an official capacity during the Second World War and as a freelance agent-for-hire well into the 1970s. If it was unusual for a novelist to serve as a paid intelligence agent, it was not unusual for a novelist to write about spies, which Greene did throughout his life. Some of his novels were bald thrillers, others more serious stories, but virtually all of them featured deeply troubled protagonists in the throes of moral dilemma, personal treachery, and tortured religious identity. Greene converted to Roman Catholicism in 1926, and Catholic themes of good and evil, guilt and redemption, and the nature of faith appear in many of his novels, including *Brighton Rock* (1938), *The Power and the*

THE LITERARY WORK

A novel set in Mexico in the 1930s; first published in 1940.

SYNOPSIS

An unnamed priest struggles with fear and a sense of unworthiness in a region of Mexico where it is a capital offense to function as a priest. Pursued by a relentless police lieutenant, the priest ultimately meets with a dire fate.

Glory (1940), *The Heart of the Matter* (1948), *The End of the Affair* (1951), *A Burnt-Out Case* (1961), and *Monsignor Quixote* (1982). *The Power and the Glory* stands out as Greene's most single-mindedly Catholic novel, leaving other favorite topics (politics, espionage, and adultery) aside, as the protagonist struggles with the most basic elements of his faith.

Events in History at the Time of the Novel

Revolutionary Mexico. After a period of intermittent civil war (*c.* 1867–76) under the progressive but ineffectual president Benito Juárez, the infamous Porfirio Díaz seized power in 1876, maintaining an iron control over Mexico until 1910. The length and stability of Díaz's regime were unprecedented in Mexican political his-

Graham Greene

tory. First a fighter for reform, he later became a dictator who monopolized power for his own sake. Lower-class Mexicans grew poorer during Díaz's regime, many losing their lands because of legal maneuvering. Mexico grew ripe for rebellion, and in 1910 it descended into a state of unrest and revolution from which it would not emerge for 30 years.

It is perhaps a misnomer to speak of "the" Mexican Revolution; it was actually a series of insurrections, civil wars, guerrilla campaigns, and regional conflicts, punctuated by various periods of anarchy and relative peace. The principal characters were multiple, and they had wildly varying motives and goals. In 1924, after a series of rebellions, counter-rebellions, and assassinations, the presidency fell to Plutarco Calles, the architect of the Mexican socialist revolutionary state. Calles energetically furthered the process of wresting control of the country from the wealthy landowners, but he was no humanitarian—his methods were brutal and oppressive, and he and his supporters profited handsomely from the new order. He campaigned vigorously against the Catholic Church, doing his utmost to eliminate it entirely from Mexican society. This provoked a series of uprisings by forces loyal to the Church, and much blood was shed on both sides. Calles had to leave office in 1928 (the constitution allowed for one four-year term, with no

provision for reelection), and Alvaro Obrégon had his eye on the job. He was elected but was then assassinated before he could take office. Pascual Rubio was elected to replace Obrégon, but Calles remained in the background, taking the title of *Jefe Maximo* (Supreme Chief) and continuing to exercise power. Disgusted with Calles's interference, Rubio resigned in 1932, and Abelardo Rodríguez was appointed to finish Rubio's term. The year 1934 saw the inauguration of Lázaro Cárdenas, a capable army general; he succeeded in expelling Calles from the country in 1936. In a bold move that carried his predecessors' socialist programs into uncharted waters, Cárdenas in 1938 seized all foreign-owned oil companies operating in Mexico; these firms had long flouted Mexico's labor laws. The last major rebellion was suppressed in 1938, and in 1940 Cárdenas peacefully and voluntarily left office. Political stability had returned to Mexico.

The Power and the Glory is not a political novel, nor does it concern itself much with the issues that drove the Mexican Revolution (with the notable exception of the campaign against the Catholic Church). Nevertheless, the Revolution is the situational context of the story, and it provides the motivation for one of its main characters, the lieutenant; without revolutionary ideology, he could not exist. In him, revolutionary ideals are personified in a pure and uncorrupted form; the revolutionary leaders were often ambitious, treacherous, vain, and rapacious, but the lieutenant is none of these things. His firm belief in the program of national reform is supported by a fundamentally principled and honest disposition. He pursues the priest not because he will profit by his capture, but because he firmly believes that priests are a threat to the revolution. He succeeds in attaining his object, but other revolutionary programs are depicted as failures in the novel because they are under the control of unprincipled, self-seeking men. For example, liquor was outlawed by the government because alcohol abuse was viewed as a social evil. The law, however, was ineffectual because smuggling and the illegal sale of liquor are common practices; in the novel, the cousin of the governor is happy to sell brandy to the priest. In a more general sense, the overall revolutionary goals of establishing and maintaining equality, peace, and contentment among the people, of ensuring the availability of food and education for all, are not met. Instead there is rampant hunger, profiteering, cronyism, and bullying by the police. To whatever degree the Mexican Revolution might ultimately achieve anything, little progress had been made by the time the novel takes place.

The Church vs. the state. The long history of anticlericalism in Mexico began in 1857, with the ascendancy of Benito Juárez. In that year and under his direction, Mexico issued a new constitution that sought to break the awesome power of the Catholic Church—a power that had almost invariably maintained a staunch alliance with conservative political interests and the landed aristocracy. Some provisions of the constitution seem quite modest to twenty-first-century ears: It promised freedom of religion, the recognition of civil marriages, and the establishment of free public schools. Other provisions were more extreme: the constitution mandated that the extensive landholdings of the Church be nationalized, Church schools be closed, the income of the Church be subject to taxation, and the activity of the clergy be suppressed. The degree to which these provisions were enacted and the length of time they were observed varied from region to region. During the presidency of Porfirio Díaz (1876–1911), they were ignored almost completely. By 1911, the Church had reacquired vast real-estate holdings, enjoyed a virtual monopoly on quality education, and wielded considerable political influence. In short order, this would change radically.

The constitution issued by the administration of President Carranza in 1917 decreed that the Church be entirely subject to state control. This was in keeping with the revolutionary ideology that informed his presidency; socialist movements worldwide (Mexico was no exception) saw religious establishments as obstacles to their quest for political supremacy and as vast holders of land and wealth to be plundered and redistributed. Faced with such a threat, the Church in Mexico allied itself with conservative politics and the wealthy landowning classes and declared itself an implacable enemy of the revolution from the beginning. Mexico's 1917 constitution consequently enacted strong anticlerical legislation designed to break the Church's power and hold over the people. The Church was forbidden to operate schools of any kind and was deprived of its legal status as an institution: it could not own property, take legal action, collect revenues, or receive a legacy in a will; in short, in the eyes of the government, it ceased to exist. As a result of this official stance, parochial schools, convents, monasteries, seminaries, and churches were closed and despoiled of their property and furnishings. What was once the Church became simply a group of individuals, whose activities were severely regulated by a series of complex laws that were often overlapping and contradictory. Public religious activity was outlawed; active clergymen had to be of Mexican birth; and if they were of Mexican birth, they lost their citizenship. Though these measures were far more draconian than those promulgated by Juárez, the degree of their enforcement varied from state to state and from year to year. In some regions the Church was effectively wiped out; in others it simply had to keep a very low profile. The presidency of Calles (1924–28) saw a renewed wave of persecution; the laws of 1917 began to be more strictly enforced, and many priests lost their lives. Finally driven to armed insurrection, supporters of the Church, who called themselves

---

CALLES AND THE CHURCH

Calles has been described as inconsistently ruthless. As president, he upheld the rights of the Indian masses but was an oppressor of the Yaquis Indians. He formed strong political ties with organized labor, but he struck out at workers who went on strike at a friend's mine in Sonora, having them machine gunned. He was a rich man but hated the rich. He was a large landowner but condemned landowners as a class. In two things he was consistent. One was his abiding enmity for the Catholic Church. The other was the zeal with which he put down real or suspected opposition.

(Johnson, pp. 279-80)

Cristeros, began an organized challenge to the authority of the government. Shouting their battle cry of *"Viva Cristo Rey"* ("Long live Christ the King"), they seized partial control of a number of states, including Jalisco, Colima, Michoacán, Zacatecas, and Nayarit. At one point there were 50,000 Cristeros in the field, and the government army only escaped being overwhelmed with difficulty. Cristeros also engaged in guerrilla activity, such as blowing up trains full of government soldiers. In the end, appalling atrocities were committed by both sides; the uprising claimed 80,000 Mexican lives.

The rebellion subsided when the government relaxed enforcement of some of the more restrictive anticlerical measures, but Calles and his successors in the 1930s never failed to suppress

Mexican federal troops battle Catholic rebels at Durango, Mexico, circa 1927, an instance of the anticlerical violence that ensued between the state and Church during the Cristero Rebellion (1926-29).

and oppress Church activity and clergy when the opportunity arose. As before, the level of persecution varied by state. In some states, such as Tabasco (the model for the unnamed state in which *The Power and the Glory* is set), religious activity was driven almost completely underground, and priests were regularly hunted down and killed. Such extreme measures more or less ceased with the renewed stability that came with the peaceful transfer of power in 1940, but several decades passed before the Church was fully integrated back into Mexican society.

The Novel in Focus

Plot summary. Part 1 of the novel opens in a city in 1930s revolutionary Mexico. The Catholic Church has been suppressed, and the socialist government now wields moral authority. Liquor is banned outright, and even beer is a government monopoly, sold at a prohibitively high rate. Mr. Tench, a dentist and expatriate Englishman, is on his way down to the river to meet a boat. A lifeline to the outside world, the *General Obregon* means a new supply of ether (an anesthetic used by dentists in the days before Novocain) for Mr. Tench and a means of escape for a hunted priest waiting on the riverbank. This priest is un-

named and remains so throughout the novel. They meet, strike up a conversation, and decide to return to Tench's office to share the priest's bottle of brandy. The priest sympathetically listens to the dentist's account of his troubled life. He has a wife and son back in England with whom he has not communicated in years, is unable to earn enough money to return home, and exudes a deep sense of sadness and futility. The first chapter ends with the priest leaving the city on the back of a mule; in response to the plea of a child (who evidently knows his true identity), he abandons his intention to flee the state on the *General Obregon* and sets off to attend to the child's sick mother. He does so with ill will (thinking the child's mother is probably not sick at all) and prays to God for his own capture.

The reader is then introduced to the priest's nemesis—a lieutenant (also unnamed) who will pursue the priest throughout the novel. Unlike the priest, he is a man of firm resolve and iron discipline. For him, the Church is a cancer that eats away at the strength of Mexico and its people, and yet his beliefs have an almost religious quality to them:

> It infuriated him to think that there were still people in the state who believed in a loving and merciful God . . . what he had experienced was

vacancy—a complete certainty in the existence
of a dying, cooling world, of human beings who
had evolved from animals for no purpose at all.
He knew.

(Greene, *The Power and the Glory*, pp. 24-25)

The lieutenant learns of the priest's existence and
resolves to apprehend him. He also must look
out for James Calver, an escaped American murderer and bank robber, who has been seen in the
region.

Other significant figures appear early in the
novel as well. One is Luis, a boy whose pious
mother nightly reads aloud to him accounts of
Mexican priests, who ministered to their flocks
with bravery and devotion before being caught
and executed by the authorities. Meant to instill
a sense of devotion and religious identity (especially since the family can no longer attend
church), these stories unsettle the boy. He is
openly critical of their message and asks questions about the two priests with whom he has
been in recent contact. One is Padre José, a local
priest who, rather than flee the state or go underground, has decided to conform to the law by
ceasing to serve as a priest and by taking a wife.
According to Luis's mother, he is a disgrace to the
Church. The ex-priest is fat and timid, his wife is
a vulgar harridan, and the neighboring children
mock him mercilessly. The other is the hunted
priest himself, who stayed briefly with Luis's family. His predilection for drink became obvious to
them, and Luis's mother worried that his defects
would set a bad example for her children. She
tells her husband a story she has heard about the
priest—that once, the worse for liquor, he had
baptized an infant boy with the name of Brigitta.
Later in the novel, it is revealed that Brigitta is the
name of the priest's illegitimate daughter.

Finally the reader is introduced to Coral Fellows, the young daughter of an English banana
merchant. Captain Fellows is a hale and amiable
man, his wife Trix a somewhat quarrelsome semi-
invalid, and his daughter Coral a quiet but
thoughtful girl on the verge of adolescence. Mrs.
Fellows is educating Coral at home through a
mail-order series of courses from England, to
which Coral applies herself diligently. When the
reader first encounters her, she has just allowed
the priest (now on the run from the lieutenant)
to hide in her father's barn. Not Catholic or even
religious, she is oddly (even fiercely) solicitous
for his safety. Before he goes on his way, they
discuss his situation. He confesses to her his
sense of unworthiness and despair and his desire
to be caught. Quite logically, she suggests that

he give himself up. His answer is that he does
not possess the necessary resolve either to suffer
execution or abandon his sense of duty: "There's
the pain. To choose pain like that—it's not possible. And it's my duty not to be caught. You see,
my bishop is no longer here. . . . This is my
parish" (*The Power and the Glory*, p. 40).

Time passes. The priest, shabby and careworn, arrives at a poor village. The people have
not seen a priest in five years, and there is much
to do—baptisms, the hearing of confessions, the
saying of mass. Amid visible displays of anger
and resentment, the priest does his job. Back in
the main town, the ex-priest Padre José does not.
At the burial of a young child, he is asked by the
grieving family to say a brief prayer, and after a
struggle with his conscience he refuses—word

FROM GREENE'S RECORD OF HIS TRAVELS IN REVOLUTIONARY MEXICO

In *The Lawless Roads*, Greene interviews a resident of
Tabasco, a state with particularly harsh anticlerical laws: "He
said the church schools were far better than those that existed
now . . . there were even more of them, and the priests in
Tabasco were good men. . . . I asked about the priest in Chi-
apas who had fled. "Oh," he said, "he was just what we call
a whisky priest." He had taken one of his sons to be baptized,
but the priest was drunk and would insist on naming him
Brigitta. He was little loss, poor man . . . but who can judge
what terror and hardship and isolation may have excused him
in the eyes of God?" (*The Lawless Roads*, p. 150).

would get out; he would be caught and punished.
He returns home in a sink of despair while the
children's mocking voices ring in his ears. Young
Luis meets the lieutenant on the street and is
transfixed by the sight of his gun. The manifest
potency of the weapon enthralls the boy, and the
lieutenant is hit with an overwhelming sense of
mission:

> It was for these he was fighting. He would
> eliminate from their childhood everything
> which had made him miserable, all that was
> poor, superstitious, and corrupt. They deserved
> nothing less than the truth—a vacant universe
> and a cooling world, the right to be happy in
> any way they chose. He wanted to begin the
> world again with them, in a desert.
>
> (*The Power and the Glory*, p. 58)

Affectionately pinching the boy's ear, the lieutenant departs, "a little dapper figure of hate carrying his secret of love" (*The Power and the Glory*, p. 58).

Part 2 opens with the priest arriving at a village he knows quite well—it is the poor and squalid home of his onetime mistress Maria and their daughter, Brigitta. His presence causes a stir among the villagers. They welcome his pastoral ministration, but it also puts them in danger. Maria provides for his lodging. However, she treats him somewhat contemptuously, and Brigitta (who does not know her father) is a detestably unpleasant child. He says mass quickly, preaching a sermon on the joys of heaven: "Heaven is where there is no jefe, no unjust laws, no taxes, no soldiers and no hunger. Your children will not die in heaven" (*The Power and the Glory*, pp. 69-70). As he finishes, the lieutenant arrives. Possessing only an old photo of a younger, plumper version of the priest, the lieutenant does not recognize him, and the priest successfully passes himself off as a poor farmer. Assembling the villagers together, the lieutenant announces that he is searching for a priest and, in a way, preaches his own sermon:

> You're fools if you still believe what the priests tell you. All they want is your money. What has God ever done for you? Have you got enough to eat? Instead of food they talk to you about heaven. Oh, everything will be fine after you are dead, they say. I tell you—everything will be fine when *they* are dead, and you must help.
> (*The Power and the Glory*, p. 74)

When no one will admit to knowing the priest's whereabouts, the lieutenant declares that he will take a hostage. If he discovers that the priest has in fact been in the village, he will execute the hostage. The priest attempts to volunteer, but is refused, and the lieutenant departs with a villager in tow. Taking his leave first of Maria and then Brigitta (both encounters are hostile and recriminatory), the priest soon departs too.

On his way to Carmen (the village of his birth), the priest encounters a persistently disagreeable fellow, a mestizo (person of mixed Indian and European ethnicity). The mestizo immediately suspects that he is a priest and insists on following him. Talkative and very demanding, the mestizo pleads poverty and illness and makes continual reference to the idea of Christian charity. The priest *must* help him, *must* trust him, *must* not abandon him, because he is called to a standard of conduct that requires nonjudg-

mental love for one's fellow man. After parrying the mestizo's questions for a while, the priest eventually admits to being what he is, knowing that the man will eventually betray him. The mestizo is quite open about his moral dilemma. He is poor, he argues, and so how can he be blamed for turning in the priest for the substantial reward money? Nevertheless, he promises, he will not do so. The priest is not fooled. The mestizo's very appearance proclaims his wickedness; his gait is shambling, his manner furtive, and he has canine teeth that protrude like fangs. As they proceed towards Carmen, the mestizo sickens, and finally the priest must give up his place on the mule. Nearing the village, the priest changes his mind—he will not go there after all. His plans for betrayal thwarted, and now physically unable to pursue the priest, the mestizo is furious: "Of course, he had every reason to be angry: he had lost seven hundred pesos" (*The Power and the Glory*, p. 102).

Needing wine to perform the rites of mass, the priest attempts to obtain some in the main city of the province (home to Padre José, Luis, and Dr. Tench). A helpful beggar leads him to the house of a local gentleman—the cousin of the governor and a purveyor of illegal drink. The priest manages to make a deal for the purchase of a bottle of wine, but he is coerced not only into buying a bottle of brandy as well, but into opening the bottle of wine and sharing it with the Governor's cousin and the local chief of police—the lieutenant's boss, who is not nearly so diligent and incorruptible as his underling. The precious wine is slowly consumed, with the priest suffering wretchedly. He had only enough money for the one bottle. The priest consoles himself with the brandy. When the wine is gone, he leaves, walking the streets with the half-empty bottle of brandy in his pocket. When he is momentarily jostled by some young soldiers, his pocket gives a telltale clink, and he is forced to produce the illegal bottle. With the soldiers in hot pursuit, he flees but is apprehended, brought to the police station and charged with possession of illegal spirits. Unable to pay the fine of five pesos, he is sentenced to a night in jail, followed by a morning of work. The lieutenant is there but does not recognize him. Thrust into a pitch-black, crowded cell, the priest encounters the stench of unwashed prisoners and their excrement. A pair copulates noisily in the corner as he makes his way blindly to a vacant space on the floor.

The priest spends a long night in conversation with the other prisoners in the cell. In a moment of epiphany, he realizes that he is guilty of the sin of pride. The call of duty that had kept him a fugitive is suddenly revealed as a delusion, a self-serving conviction of his that he was better than the priests who had conformed to the law by renouncing their priestly duties and taking wives, better than the people he was supposed to be serving with humility. On impulse, he not only confesses to them that he is a priest, but that he is a bad priest—a drunk, a coward, and the father of an illegitimate child. Some of his fellow inmates respond with charity, some with indifference, and some with hatred and scorn, but he emerges in the morning feeling somewhat cleansed and ready to meet his fate. While performing his prescribed duties (emptying the latrine buckets from the cells of the prison), he encounters a guest (not an inmate) of the prison—the mestizo. Recognizing him immediately, the mestizo realizes the inadvisability of turning the priest in; the mestizo has been fed and housed for some time by the authorities while helping them in their search for the priest, but if he accuses the priest while the priest is in custody, he will not receive any reward money. Openly he announces his decision to the priest; he will keep silent and allow the priest to be released, then find him "out there" and take his reward. Upon the completion of his duties, the priest is led into the presence of the lieutenant, who treats his prisoner kindly and, before releasing him, gives him a five-peso coin, the same amount charged by the priest to say a mass. Astonished, the priest tells him that he is a good man.

On the run again, the priest returns to the banana station of the Fellows family and finds it deserted, except for a starving dog who weakly strives with him over a bone with some meat still on it. The house is in disorder, showing signs of a hasty departure. He does not know it, but Coral Fellows has fallen ill and died. A storm breaks, and he seeks shelter in a nearby hut. Inside he finds a three-year-old Indian boy, drenched in blood and dying. Outside an Indian woman warily darts to and fro. She is unwilling to abandon her child but is clearly afraid of the priest. The Indian woman speaks almost no Spanish, but he finally manages to convey to her that he is a priest. Despite his frantic efforts, the child dies, and the woman keeps saying a word—*Americano*. The priest wonders whether the child's death has something to do with the escaped American gangster. The woman straps her dead son to her back, and she and the priest walk into

the mountains. After a considerable distance, they arrive at an Indian graveyard, full of bizarre crosses and grave markers. No priest, the priest thinks to himself, had ever been here. The Indian woman deposits her child at the foot of a large cross and goes on her way. Afterward, the priest struggles on through the mountains until he arrives at signs of civilization and meets a man with a gun. Automatically, he tells him not to worry—he is a priest, but he is moving on and will not bring them any trouble. The man's reaction is unexpectedly joyful and welcoming. Unintentionally, the priest has crossed into a neighboring province, where priests are uncommon but not subject to the death penalty.

Part 3 opens several days later with the priest sitting comfortably on the veranda of Mr. and Miss Lehr (brother and sister), who run a successful farming compound. It was their man who found the priest in the forest, and they have invited him to stay as their guest. Setting immediately to work, the priest schedules masses, baptisms, and confessions. Each service carries a price, and he expects to make a substantial amount of money very quickly. His epiphany in the jail cell becoming a distant memory, he becomes somewhat haughty and demanding. He at the same time continues to drink, arranging with a local merchant for the purchase of a large quantity of brandy. He cannot, though, rid himself of an overwhelming sense of his own sin. The priest thinks to himself, "A virtuous man can almost cease to believe in Hell, but he carried Hell about with him" (*The Power and the Glory*, p. 176). After he earns enough money for the journey, he plans to travel to Las Casas, where the Church is alive and relatively unpersecuted. There he can confess his sins and receive absolution from a fellow priest.

While preparing for departure, the priest again encounters the mestizo. He has come, the mestizo explains, on an errand of mercy. The American fugitive has been shot by the police and is dying. A Catholic, he wishes to receive absolution from a priest before the end. His sins have been great. The priest learns that while fleeing the police, the American attempted to use the Indian boy as a shield, and the boy was hit. The mestizo produces a scrap of paper as evidence. Coincidentally, it is a school essay of Coral Fellows, a discussion of the indecision of Hamlet. On the reverse side, the American had written, "For Christ's sake, father. . . ." Though the mestizo protests his good intentions, the priest is naturally suspicious and questions him about the exact location of the American. It is just this side of the border, the mestizo promises—you will be safe. Now certain of the man's treachery, the priest comes to a sudden decision. His duty is with the persecuted church, and his destiny does not lie in Las Casas. Giving his newfound wealth to the local schoolmaster to buy food and books for the local children, he follows the mestizo back into the forest, knowing full well that death awaits him.

After a considerable journey, the priest discovers that the mestizo had not been lying entirely. The American lies wounded in a small hut and will not last much longer. He is indeed Catholic but is unwilling to confess. He keeps insisting that the priest get away while he can, and savagely calling the police "bastards." The American dies while attempting to convince the priest to take the American's knife and flee, and as the priest is intoning the words of conditional absolution, the lieutenant enters the hut and asks him whether he has finished. He is surprised to learn that the priest was expecting him.

Of course, the mestizo betrayed him, but the priest does not seem to mind. His duty is done, and his fate awaits him. The lieutenant is curious about the character of his long-pursued quarry, and they have an extensive discussion. As always, the lieutenant is firm, businesslike, and unshakable in his convictions. He bears the priest no personal animosity, telling him, "You're a danger. That's why we kill you. I have nothing against you, you understand, as a man" (*The Power and the Glory*, p. 193). The priest surprises him by essentially agreeing with the nature and implications of this distinction; in a moment reminiscent of his night in the jail cell, he confesses his many faults to the lieutenant, but he affirms the moral superiority of the Church he unworthily represents. He also commends the lieutenant for his sense of duty and self-discipline and, to a certain extent, his humanity:

> That's another difference between us. It's no good your working for your end unless you're a good man yourself. And there won't always be good men in your party. Then you'll have all the old starvation, beating, get-rich-anyhow. But it doesn't matter so much my being a coward—and all the rest. I can put God into a man's mouth just the same—and I can give him God's pardon. It wouldn't make any difference to that if every priest in the Church was like me.
>
> (*The Power and the Glory*, p. 195)

In spite of himself, the lieutenant is impressed and wonders why, of all the priests in the region,

this man was the one who stayed true, the one who did not conform to the law and marry, who did not flee to safer provinces. Upon their return to the city, the priest is put in a cell, and the lieutenant, trying to make his prisoner's final hours easier, asks if there is anything he can get the prisoner. The priest wishes to make a final confession, but the only priest available is Padre José, and he refuses to come. Moved by pity, the lieutenant tells him that his death will be painless, and he leaves him alone in the cell with a bottle of brandy. Throughout the night, the priest struggles with a sense of failure, a feeling that he has made no difference in the world at all.

The fourth and final part of the novel is short, touching on the lives of the people who have in fact been affected by the priest—for the better. Dr. Tench is in his office attending to the Chief of Police, who suffers from an agonizing toothache. Leaving the Chief in pain for a moment, Tench looks out his window to witness the execution of the priest. It upsets Tench. He remembers that the priest spoke with him about his wife and son, and he resolves to return to England as soon as possible to be reunited with them. Mr. Fellows attends his sickly wife, who is as quarrelsome as ever and is unwilling to recognize the grief they both feel over the death of Coral. Recalling the brief stay of the priest, Mr. Fellows ponders the change that it wrought in their daughter and her apparent sense that he stood for something important. Finally, young Luis (who had watched the lieutenant returning to the city with the captive priest) renounces his ambivalence about the Church. After spending another evening with his mother and the stories of martyr-priests, he asks her about the priest who was just shot. His mother (forgetting her earlier antipathy) replies that he was a true martyr and very likely a saint. Going to the window on his way to bed, he looks out to the street and sees the lieutenant walking by—and he spits on him. Later in the evening there is a knocking at the door; a new priest has arrived in the province, and Luis welcomes him into the house.

The problem of evil. Any religious system must at some point confront the problem of evil. Why do bad things happen to good people? Why do the wicked prosper? How can a world created by a perfectly just and infinitely benevolent God contain disease, earthquakes, and murderers? And what is the duty of a good man (or a bad man who wants to be good) in response to this situation? *The Power and the Glory* involves a situation where the above difficulties are combined into an almost worst-case scenario. The priest is haunted by the fact of his own sins (which are substantial) and by his sense of failure and worthlessness (which is even greater). His nemesis embodies everything that he is not. The lieutenant is purposeful, sober, incorruptible, and unflinchingly dedicated to his beliefs. The world in which these two men play out their drama is in many ways a hell on earth. The poor starve, the rich are parasites, and an authoritarian government casts an oppressive pall over the citizenry. Even the hope of heaven is denied to the people because the government tells them that it does not exist. In this setting, the novel presents the problem of evil in a distinctly modern form, and the question is raised—how can religious faith supply an adequate response?

The 1930s were a time of intellectual and social turmoil throughout the world. Socialist political movements, on both the right and the left, existed in all major countries of the world. Joseph Stalin's Soviet Union, Adolf Hitler's Germany, and Calles's Mexico all sought to remake the fabric of society in a manner never before seen in the world. The government was to be socialist yet authoritarian, egalitarian yet oppressive, and, perhaps most significantly, militantly secular. Religion was seen as a threat, both to the centralized power of the state and to the social well-being of the people. The reason for this is succinctly stated by the lieutenant in the novel: organized religion caused people to look for happiness in the afterlife, rather than in this world. The socialist agenda, whether communist or fascist, was predicated on the notion of the perfectibility of society, that man's true goal was to serve the cause of the state. His only function, his only value, was as a member of the social group, and his individual life and happiness were meaningless. Good and evil were therefore social concepts rather than norms for individual behavior, and there was no permanent or objective referent for judging behavior. The only meaningful standards were the immediate needs of the state.

Greene formulated a response to this ideology in *The Power and the Glory*, one that was fully orthodox in terms of Catholic doctrine, but which also borrowed certain elements from the seeming moral vacuum of socialist ideology. In his long conversation with the priest at the end of the novel, the lieutenant is surprised to discover that he and the priest agree on a number of issues and that he finds himself gaining considerable respect for the priest. The priest represents the same Church that the lieutenant passionately

hates—the wealthy and complacent Church that pervaded Mexico before the revolution. However, that Church no longer exists, and the priest is not defending it; indeed, he is not even defending himself. The lieutenant, as a true and dispassionate socialist, bears the priest no ill-will and will execute him not because he believes him to be a wicked man, but because he believes the interests of the state demand it. The priest, who has learned the virtues of humility and resignation, similarly does not hate the lieutenant (quite the opposite, in fact) and goes to his death simply hoping that he is worthy of martyrdom. For both men, personal good and evil are lacking in larger significance. The priest realized in the darkness of his crowded prison cell that he was guilty of inordinate pride, and it was in fact this pride that led him to stay in his parish rather than flee. In other words, the motive was evil, but the object was good. This could work in the opposite way, too; he loved his daughter so much that he offered up his own damnation to God in exchange for her safety, but how was it proper to love the fruit of his sin? This time, his motive (parental love) was good, but the object, his daughter, was evil—at seven years of age, she exhibited a precocious level of moral degeneracy. The inference to be made by the reader is clear: if the priest can love his daughter so, despite her sinful birth and repellent character, then God can love him. God's love is the great leveler, something that the priest tries to explain to the lieutenant as they converse beside the body of the dead gangster. God embraces the good and the bad, all of whom in some measure reflect his nature; even the mestizo, for all his faults, possesses qualities (his sense of justice, perhaps?) that stem from his creator. He is evil, and yet his demands for charity must be answered. The Church and the anticlerical state each have aims, motivations, means, and ends that are both good and evil, and the priest, with his newfound humility, is as unable to deny the defects of the Church as he is the wickedness of the world in general.

The sorrows of this world are real and cannot be escaped or explained. The universe is perennially hostile to human life and happiness. What can be done? For the priest, the answer is that all will be made right in heaven, but by the end of the novel he does not expect anyone to be comforted by this. There is a sadness at the core of his faith, one that remains with him to his death.

Sources and literary context. The literary context for *The Power and the Glory* is not to be found in the literature of the Mexican Revolution. Greene visited Mexico in 1938 to report on the persecution of the Catholic Church there (his nonfiction account of what he found, *The Lawless Roads,* was published in 1939). His visit certainly provided Greene with much of the authenticating detail and local "color" of the novel, but the story he tells is not, in the final analysis, as much about Mexico as about a human soul in torment. While the novel literally concerns a hunted priest in anticlerical Mexico of the 1930s, the moral dilemmas that lie at the heart of the book transcend any particular time or place. The

HOW CAN A SINFUL PRIEST SERVE GOD?

Like the Mexican Church in the 1920s and 1930s, the early Church had its share of martyrs and also its share of apostates—those who chose to save their lives by renouncing their faith. One of the heresies that confronted the Church centered around what to do with these failed Christians. A body of Christians (known as Donatists) held that apostates were not to be readmitted to the Church and that if they were priests, any sacraments administered by them were invalid. In 411 C.E. the Church categorically affirmed that this view was an error and that sacramental grace proceeded from God through the priest to the recipient irrespective of the moral status of the priest. It is this idea, perhaps above all others, that gives the priest in *The Power and the Glory* the will to persevere. Acutely conscious of his own grave sin, he nevertheless knows that he can still administer valid sacraments. The Church may be persecuted, and individual Christians may fail to live up to their obligations, but the Church itself will live on because its power and glory remain undiminished by such individual lapses.

priest could just have easily have been a fugitive Jesuit in Elizabethan England, when the Protestant queen routinely executed Catholic priests caught in her realm. The charge was even the same—treason. In fact, the literature that largely informs *The Power and the Glory* is that of persecuted Christianity (deriving from the first through the fourth centuries of the Christian era, when Christians suffered under Roman oppression) and persecuted Catholicism (deriving from sixteenth- and seventeenth-century Protestant England, when professing Catholics were punished as traitors to the crown). Many of these texts were known as "saints' lives"—biographical accounts of the lives and (in most cases) martyrdoms of steadfast Christians, who heroically suffered death rather than renounce their faith.

As an English Catholic, Greene was acutely conscious of the long and troubled relationship between his Church and his country. From c. 1533 (when Henry VIII separated the English Church from papal authority) until well into the nineteenth century, Catholics were not regarded as full citizens of England. When they were not actively persecuted, they still had to pay fines for not attending Anglican church services, they could not serve in the governmental or legal professions, they could not attend English universities, and so forth. In fact, it was only in 1926 that most of the remaining legal disabilities were removed, and some remain to this day. The Catholic Church in revolutionary Mexico and sixteenth-century England suffered in similar ways, and Greene's awareness of the marginal status of Catholicism in England figures into *The Power and the Glory*. Other important contexts for *The Power and the Glory* are the literatures of modernism and existentialism—narratives that tended to feature flawed, psychologically damaged protagonists confronting an empty and uncaring cosmos. While Greene cannot be conveniently grouped with either of these schools of thought, they both exercised considerable influence on his literary method. The existentialist dilemma—how to live when the only measure of one's life is personal experience, and how to face the world when only personal experience is useful or relevant—is one that confronts the hunted priest, but it does not overcome him. Literature in the modernist school, such as T. S. Eliot's *The Waste Land* (also in *WLAIT 4: British and Irish Literature of Its Times*), poses the problem of an empty world full of hollow men, but it gives no solution. The only sane response is disillusionment, even despair. In contrast, Greene's priest does accept the answers provided by his faith. Greene himself was fond of a quote by the Spanish writer Unamuno that aptly expresses the kind of faith that is meant:

> Those who believe that they believe in God, but without passion in their heart, without anguish of mind, without uncertainty, without doubt, without an element of despair even in their consolation, believe only in the God Idea, not in God Himself.
>
> (Unamuno in Sharrock, p. 23)

Reception and impact. The reception of the novel was a mirror of the state of "Catholic" literature (in English) at the time. If the position of the Catholic Church in England was somewhat marginal, so was that of its literature; there was a general suspicion that it was narrow and intellectually lightweight and an expectation among many Catholics that it should serve more or less uncritically to promote Catholic teachings. *The Power and the Glory* fulfilled neither role, but it was a bestseller, and reviewers for the most part praised it highly. *The Power and the Glory* sold 30,000 copies in 1940–41, an amazing figure given the fact that this was the time of severe wartime austerity measures and that German bombs were raining down on London on a regular basis. The book also won Greene the prestigious Hawthornden Prize for 1940.

On the other hand, the Vatican's reaction was strongly negative. In 1953 Cardinal Pizzardo, Secretary of the Holy Office, wrote to the Archbishop of Westminster (the Catholic primate in England) to complain:

> The author's aim was to bring out the victory of the power and the glory of the Lord in spite of man's wretchedness, but this aim is not attained, since it is the latter element which appears to carry the day, and in a way which does injury to certain friendly characters, and even to the priesthood itself.
>
> (Shelden, p. 271)

For the most part, though, Greene enjoyed a combination of commercial and critical success that most authors only dream about. In many ways, the continuing success of his works stems from the initial reception of *The Power and the Glory*; it first brought Greene to the world's notice, and in it readers found the unique treatment of Catholic themes that have always been such a major element in his appeal. Novelist and literary critic David Lodge sums up this appeal neatly, writing that Greene "made Catholicism, from a literary point of view, interesting, glamorous, and prestigious. There were no Anglican novelists, or Methodist novelists . . . but there was, it seemed, such a creature as a Catholic novelist" (Lodge in Shelden, p. 130).

—Matthew Brosamer

For More Information

Britton, John A. *Revolution and Ideology: Images of the Mexican Revolution in the United States.* Lexington, Ky: The University Press of Kentucky, 1995.

De Vitis, A. A. *Graham Greene.* Boston: Twayne, 1986.

Greene, Graham. *The Lawless Roads.* 3rd ed. London: Eyre & Spottiswode, 1950.

———. *The Power and the Glory.* 1940. Reprinted, New York: Penguin, 1971.

Johnson, William Weber. *Heroic Mexico: The Violent Emergence of a Modern Nation.* Garden City, N.Y.: Doubleday, 1968.

Kelley, Francis Clement. *Blood-Drenched Altars.* Milwaukee: Bruce, 1935.

Meyer, Michael C., and William L. Sherman. *The Course of Mexican History.* 2nd ed. New York: Oxford University Press, 1983.

O'Prey, Paul. *A Reader's Guide to Graham Greene.* London: Thames & Hudson, 1988.

Ruiz, Ramón Eduardo. *Triumphs and Tragedy: A History of the Mexican People.* New York and London: Norton, 1992.

Sharrock, Roger. *Saints, Sinners and Comedians: The Novels of Graham Greene.* Notre Dame, Ind.: University of Notre Dame Press, 1984.

Shelden, Michael. *Graham Greene: The Man Within.* London: Heinemann, 1994.

The Prime of Miss Jean Brodie

by

Muriel Spark

Born in 1918 in Edinburgh, Scotland, Muriel Spark (née Camberg) was the daughter of Bernard and Sarah Elizabeth Maud Camberg. Muriel's father was Jewish, her mother Protestant. Educated at the James Gillespie's School in Edinburgh, Muriel married S. O. Spark in 1937, and the couple moved to Rhodesia (present-day Zimbabwe). The marriage ended in divorce, but Spark retained her ex-husband's surname when she returned to Britain in 1944. In the mid-to-late 1940s, Spark became editor of the *Poetry Review*, then founded her own literary journal, *Forum*, which lasted only two issues. In 1950 she edited another journal, *European Affairs*, and around this time began writing short stories, many of which were based on her experiences in Africa. Spark took an increasing interest in Catholicism, particularly in the writings of Cardinal John Henry Newman, and joined the Roman Catholic Church in 1954. Soon after, she was approached by the Macmillan publishing house about writing a novel. Her first such work, *The Comforters* (1957), became an immediate success and was followed by *Robinson* (1958), *Memento Mori* (1959), *The Ballad of Peckham Rye* (1960), and *The Bachelors* (1960). Then came *The Prime of Miss Jean Brodie* (1961), which has been lauded for its complex themes, intricate narrative structure, eccentric, charismatic, yet dangerous title character, and vivid evocation of 1930s Edinburgh.

THE LITERARY WORK

A novel, set primarily in Edinburgh, Scotland, in the early 1930s with several flash-forwards up to the early 1960s; published in 1961.

SYNOPSIS

An unconventional teacher at a girls' school attempts to mold her students in her own image, but her unsavory motives are ultimately exposed by one of them.

Events in History at the Time of the Novel

Economic depression in interwar Scotland. The period between the two world wars was especially difficult for Britain economically. With the end of the First World War, manufacturers and financiers innocently expected a return to prewar prosperity—in the shape of an eager demand for British goods. But many European countries, hit hard by the war, simply could not afford to buy British goods, while countries outside Europe, cut off from those goods during the war, had either developed their own industries or sought rival sources of supply. From the 1920s onward, the three basic industries—coal, ship-building, and textiles—that sustained Great

Muriel Spark

Britain's economy were in decline, and they never entirely recovered from the slump. As a result, an increasing number of workers found themselves without employment over the next two decades. By mid-1921, unemployment had climbed to more than a million, and it continued rising to more than 2.75 million in 1933. Though the problem would ease with the coming of the next global conflict, unemployment would not disappear: "on the eve of the Second World War in 1938 [it] still stood at over 1.25 million" (Seaman, p. 35). Of this total, 170,000 or 10.6 percent of insured workers in Scotland were still unemployed (Rait and Pryde, p. 213).

The decade got off to a rocky start for Scotland, with a worldwide depression that affected it terribly.

> Scotland, too dependent on heavy industry and textiles, both now suffering from severe foreign competition, was harder hit than England and suffered even worse unemployment. At the height of the slump in 1931 as many as 65 per cent of the shipyard workers on the Clyde were unemployed. Agriculture, too, was depressed. The result was widespread suffering and demoralization on a scale which was . . . to lead in the long run to dangerous and continuing depopulation.
>
> (Maclean, p. 211)

In the novel, Miss Brodie's class witnesses Scotland's economic hardships when their teacher takes them on a walk through Edinburgh in the winter of 1931. For the first time in their sheltered lives, the young girls are exposed to Scottish slums and the unemployed, waiting to receive their government dole, or unemployment funds. Sandy Stranger is particularly affected by the sight of men entering the labor bureau: "She saw the slowly jerking file tremble with life, she saw it all of a piece like one dragon's body which had no right to be in the city and yet would not go away and was unslayable. . . . She wanted to cry as she always did when she saw a street singer or a beggar" (Spark, *The Prime of Miss Jean Brodie*, p. 60).

The rise of fascism in the 1930s. The political movement commonly known as fascism—which came to be applied to any right-wing, nationalist, totalitarian movement or regime—spread throughout Europe in the aftermath of the First World War, establishing itself in the governments of Italy (1922–43), Germany (1933–45), and Spain (1939–75). While fascist regimes differed somewhat from country to country, they all shared common features: 1) the absolute primacy of the state; 2) the submission of the individual will to the united will of the people, as represented by the state; 3) complete obedience to the leader who embodies the state; 4) the celebration of martial virtues, combat, and conquest; 5) the rejection of liberal democracy, bourgeois values, and rationalism (that is, rejection of the notion that human reason, rather than authority, experience, or spiritual revelation is the correct basis for action). Many fascist governments also expressed belief in a glorious destiny for the state and the people who composed it. Italy's Mussolini, for example, prophesied a rebirth of the Roman empire, while Germany's Adolf Hitler declared great benefits in store for the so-called "master (Aryan) race."

Historian H. R. Kedward notes that, in Italy, Mussolini's regime waged "a constant 'warfare' against internal enemies. . . . It became a hallmark of his system. Opposition parties were first prohibited then crushed. Critics were mostly silenced by imprisonment or forced into exile" (Kedward, p. 109). In Germany, Hitler's fascist program contained more detailed plans for national and racial power and security than that of Mussolini, but both regimes operated under the same totalitarian principles. Within six months of the 1933 passage of the Enabling Act, which allowed Hitler to rule by dictatorial powers, his party exercised almost complete control:

> Nazism had a stranglehold on all aspects of German life except the army. The trade unions lost all power of collective bargaining and were then abolished; the political parties were disbanded one by one and the Nazi Party remained the only political organization in the country. The various states of federal Germany were forced to surrender their independence and for the first time in history Germany became a centralized nation. . . .
>
> (Kedward, p. 117)

Civil War erupted in Spain in 1936. On one side were the Nationalists, comprised of the army, the Catholic Church, the large landowners, and the right-wing political parties—specifically, the *Falange Espanola*; on the other side were the Republicans, including many who subscribed to communist ideas and favored the revolutionary values of the working class. Both Mussolini and Hitler supported the Nationalists, supplying them with arms and reinforcements to use against the Republicans. In 1939 General Francisco Franco, who had emerged as leader of the Nationalists, established himself as a military dictator; his government would be recognized by Britain and France. A conservative army officer with a love for conventional Spain, Franco employed methods like those of fellow fascists Mussolini and Hitler, quashing rival political parties and factions.

In Spark's novel, Miss Jean Brodie regales her young charges with tales of her holidays abroad, including her perceptions of the spread of fascism through Europe. To Miss Brodie, "Mussolini is one of the greatest men in the world, far more so than [British Prime Minister] Ramsay MacDonald," for Mussolini had "performed feats of magnitude" and successfully abolished unemployment (*The Prime of Miss Jean Brodie*, pp. 66-67). Miss Brodie even ornaments the wall of her classroom with a picture of the Italian dictator's blackshirted Fascisti. Later she expresses a similar admiration for the Nazi regime, informing her students of her plans to visit Germany, "where Hitler was become Chancellor, a prophet-figure like Thomas Carlyle, and more reliable than Mussolini" (*The Prime of Miss Jean Brodie*, p. 143). Miss Brodie's belief in the efficacy of fascism leads her to encourage another student to run away to Spain to fight for Franco. The girl's subsequent death in Spain fuels Sandy's decision to denounce Miss Brodie to the headmistress as "a born Fascist" (*The Prime of Miss Jean Brodie*, p. 182).

Ironically, despite the formation of some fascist groups in the 1920s and 1930s—most notably the British Union of Fascists (BUF), founded in 1932 by Sir Oswald Mosely—fascism never took a firm hold in Britain. The nation's economic recovery around 1934, coupled with the lack of a charismatic leader like Hitler or Mussolini and such ugly incidents as the beating of anti-fascist hecklers at BUF rallies in Olympia and, abroad, Hitler's slaughter of over 80 "traitors to the Reich," helped undermine the movement in Britain, though it maintained a presence for the rest of the 1930s (Kedward, p. 121). The British Union of Fascists went so far as to promulgate a political platform: rewrite the British Constitution to include only one party—the BUF; organize the House of Commons by occupation, lawyers voting for lawyers, miners for miners, housewives for housewives, and so forth; replace the House of Lords with an Upper House of occupational experts. The BUF emblem, after 1935, was a flash of lightning in a circle, which from a distance resembled the Nazi swastika. By then they were waging a virulent campaign against the Jewish community of Great Britain and teaching that people were unequal from the start—some born to lead, others to follow. But the effect of all these efforts was minimal. "Even at its height, British Fascism had never made much impact. . . . British Fascism's pretensions were massive: its performance, dismal and squalid. It never posed a convincing alternative in the 1930s" (Thorpe, pp. 57-58).

In Scotland the BUF never attracted many followers, but the Scottish organized fascist clubs of their own in Edinburgh, Aberdeen, Dundee, and Glasgow. The Italian government took a census in 1933 that counted close to 50 percent of Scottish Italians as members of the Fascist Party. When Mussolini declared war on Britain (June 10, 1940), the Scottish Italian community would pay dearly for the affiliation. Riots broke out all over Britain, leading to destruction and the pillaging of British Italian businesses, and those in Scotland were especially virulent. With the onset of war, the British government imprisoned anyone thought to endanger the realm, which led to the jailing of 747 British Fascists and the outlawing of organizations such as the BUF (Thorpe, p. 57).

Public education in Scotland. Scottish education passed into secular hands in the nineteenth century after 300 years of control by the Church. In the first half of the century, many varieties of schools came into being, including the privately endowed school and the "Assembly" schools (provided by Scotland's General Assembly in the neediest locations). The Education Act of 1872 capped the transfer to secular hands, shifting responsibility for all Presbyterian schools in burgh and parish to elected school boards and making attendance compulsory from ages 5 to 13.

The early twentieth century saw various reforms, such as raising the school-leaving age to 14, and two new codes of rules, one for elementary (later called primary) and the other for secondary schools. In the years leading up to World War II, the elementary curriculum consisted mainly of reading, writing, and arithmetic—along with physical exercises, drawing, poetry, and, for female students, needlework. Seniors—those in their last year at elementary school—might take courses in history and geography as well. The daily educational routine tended to be formal and factual. Methods of instruction might vary with class size and room shape, but such variation was often impractical: "In many urban schools classes of well over fifty were common in the twenties and thirties, making experiment impossible" (Scotland, p. 52).

As the twentieth century progressed, the term "primary" began to replace "elementary," implying "that all children were entitled to at least two stages of education. What was not yet accepted . . . was that the second stage need be in 'secondary schools'" (Scotland, p. 57). Indeed, before World War II, secondary education was mainly a privilege of the middle and upper classes—or of bright children who could win scholarships, as Muriel Spark did. Typical subjects at a girls' secondary school included English grammar and literature, French, Latin, arithmetic, biology, needlework or cookery, music, and art. Though in the novel Miss Brodie loves to lecture on history and geography (if defined broadly enough to include her stories about the beloved soldier she lost in the First World War or her adventures in Egypt), the two did not become curriculum subjects until 1939. There were after-school activities, commonly hockey or netball (a slower-paced variation of basketball). Otherwise girls might engage in gymnastics, as Eunice does in the novel; act in a drama society, as Sandy's friend Jenny does; or write for a school magazine, as Spark herself did.

Scottish teachers in the 1930s tended to be women and were often "old-fashioned" for their day. All female teachers were single, since marriage would disqualify them from the job. (This threat helps explain why Miss Brodie is reluctant to get married.) Typically, instruction consisted of one of these teachers reading from a book while her students took notes. Rarely would she engage her students in a discussion; self-expression and critical thinking were not encouraged. On the other hand, bodily punishment was permissible. Students who talked out of turn or otherwise misbehaved risked physical rebuke, the threat of which made the classroom a tense environment.

"FOR COMMUNISM AND FOR LIBERTY"

For many Britons, the Spanish Civil War acquired a romantic, heroic image, with tremendous implications. Western intellectuals saw the struggle between the Republicans and the Nationalists not only as a battle between communism and fascism, but as a conflict that would determine the future of Europe, which seemed poised on the brink of another world war. Some Britons felt so strongly about the Republican cause that they voluntarily joined the International Brigade to fight on the Republican side in Spain.

> Organized by Communists from all over Europe, these Brigades were composed largely of two groups: workers drawn straight from factories and mines and intellectuals who were passionately anti-Fascist. They were the only help gained by the hard-pressed Republic from the democratic countries. Almost as soon as war broke out the governments of Britain and France suggested and carried through a Non-Intervention Pact according to which no military aid should go to either side.
>
> (Kedward, pp. 128-29)

Among the Britons who joined the Brigade was English poet John Cornford, who expressed in verse the idealism of those on the Republican side: "Our fight's not won till the workers of all the world / . . . Swear that our dead fought not in vain, / Raise the red flag triumphantly / For Communism and for liberty" (Cornford in Kedward, p. 128). Cornford was killed in Spain on his twenty-first birthday. Another British volunteer for the Republicans was novelist and essayist George Orwell (see **"The Lion and the Unicorn,"** also in *WLAIT 4: British and Irish Literature and Its Times*). Instead of the Brigade, Orwell joined the Workers' Party of Marxist Unification; he documented his wartime experience in *Homage to Catalonia*, which, contrary to the romantic image, focuses on aspects such as the daily drudgery endured by soldiers and internal dissension among people on the same side.

In the novel, Spark situates the fictional Marcia Blaine School for Girls in the history of the Scottish educational system when she describes the institution as "a day school which had been partially endowed by the middle of the nineteenth century by the wealthy widow of an Edinburgh book-binder" (*The Prime of Miss Jean Brodie*, p. 11). But the Marcia Blaine School is also distinctive in that it contains both primary and secondary—here called Junior and Senior—schools. The so-called Brodie set of girls first comes under Miss Brodie's influence as 10-year-olds in the Junior school, spends two years in her class, then proceeds to the Senior school as worldly 12-year-olds, indelibly changed by her methods. In disgust, a disapproving headmistress describes the Brodie set as "vastly informed on a lot of subjects irrelevant to the authorised curriculum . . . and useless to the school as a school. These girls were discovered to have heard of the Buchmanites and Mussolini, the Italian Renaissance painters, the advantages to the skin of cleansing cream and witch-hazel over honest soap and water, and the word 'menarche'" (*The Prime of Miss Jean Brodie*, p. 10).

The Novel in Focus

Plot summary. Most of the action in *The Prime of Miss Jean Brodie* takes place in the 1930s, with frequent flash-forwards that reveal the ultimate fates of the characters. The novel begins in 1936, as a group of 16-year-old girls from the Marcia Blaine School for Girls in Edinburgh await their teacher, Miss Jean Brodie, outside the school gates. Known by the rest of the school as the "Brodie set," the group is comprised of distinct individuals, each associated with particular traits or abilities. At school they are renowned for these marks of distinction: Monica Douglas, for mathematics and anger; Rose Stanley, for sexual allure and experience; Eunice Gardner, for gymnastic and swimming ability; Sandy Stranger, for small eyes and her vowel sounds; Jenny Gray, for grace and prettiness; and Mary Macgregor, for being a lumpish nonentity who gets blamed when things go wrong. A rich new student, Joyce Emily Hammond, aspires to become one of the "Brodie set" but is still regarded as an outsider by the others. Miss Brodie finally emerges from school and rounds up her group of followers, whom she invites to supper the next night and informs of the latest plot by the school to force her to resign. The Brodie girls express support for their teacher, who announces grandly, "I shall remain at this

education factory. . . . Give me a girl at an impressionable age and she is mine for life" (*The Prime of Miss Jean Brodie*, pp. 15-16).

The novel then flashes back to 1930, when the girls were 10 years old and first came under Miss Brodie's influence. Although she is a teacher for the Junior School at Marcia Blaine, she spends the time allotted for history and literature lessons discussing art, culture, politics (namely, her admiration for Italian dictator Benito Mussolini), her own life (including her engagement to Hugh, a young man killed in the First World War), and the necessity of recognizing the years of one's prime, which is "the moment one was born for" (*The Prime of Miss Jean Brodie*, p. 19). Miss Brodie asserts that these are the years of *her* prime, during which she will impart the benefit of her own experiences to her students. During the two years that this particular class spends with Miss Brodie—from ages 10 to 12—she selects "her favorites, or rather those whom she could trust" from among them (*The Prime of Miss Jean Brodie*, p. 39). Miss Brodie takes these favored girls—the beginning of the "Brodie set"—on special expeditions, escorting them to art galleries and museums and even inviting them to her home for tea. On one memorable occasion Miss Brodie leads her class on a walk through Old Town in Edinburgh, where they behold not only cathedrals and castles, but lower-class slums and the labor bureau, the latter swarming with the unemployed.

The impressionable girls succumb to Miss Brodie's forceful personality; her life becomes an object of endless fascination and speculation to them. Sandy and Jenny, who are best friends, even collaborate on a romantic story about Miss Brodie and her fiancé, miraculously returned from the dead. But these fictitious adventures pale beside Monica's claim, during the girls' second year at the Junior School, that she found Miss Brodie and Teddy Lloyd, the art master for the Senior school and a one-armed war veteran, kissing in the art room one afternoon. The girls are pleasurably scandalized—Mr. Lloyd is a married man—and watch Miss Brodie for signs of pregnancy that never materialize. Miss Brodie blooms in other ways, however; in the autumn of 1931, she begins an affair with Gordon Lowther, the unmarried singing master at Marcia Blaine School, whom she dominates as completely as she does her students. Sandy and Jenny fictionalize a steamy correspondence between the two teachers, which they later bury in a cave by the sea.

Edinburgh's lower-class Old Town.

The following year the girls advance to the Senior school. Its headmistress, Miss Mackay, who has long disapproved of Miss Brodie's experimental methods, attempts to break up the "Brodie set" by placing them in different school houses. Despite her efforts, the girls remain united by their loyalty to their former teacher, who continues to invite her old set to tea on Saturday afternoons. The girls are further connected by their art lessons with Mr. Lloyd, in whom Miss Brodie continues to be deeply interested, although she still sees Mr. Lowther and is in fact a weekend visitor to his house in Cramond. As the Brodie set matures, Rose Stanley attracts the attention of Mr. Lloyd, who asks to paint her portrait. The finished product, however, turns out to look like Miss Brodie, as Sandy, now 15, notices when she visits the Lloyd family home. During that same visit, Sandy notices additional sketches of Monica and Eunice, which also resemble Miss Brodie, and then is startled by a kiss from Mr. Lloyd. Sandy recoils, but the art teacher assures her that she is "just about the ugliest little thing [he's] ever seen in life" and has nothing to fear (*The Prime of Miss Jean Brodie*, p. 150). Mr. Lloyd goes on to paint more pictures of the girls, all of which end up looking like Miss Brodie, who is gratified by this revelation.

Meanwhile, after proposing several times to Miss Brodie, Mr. Lowther grows discouraged at her refusals. Oblivious to his discontent, Miss Brodie continues to fixate on Mr. Lloyd and selects one girl from her set—Sandy—in whom to confide about her private life. One afternoon, while they are playing golf together, Miss Brodie reveals to Sandy that she considers Sandy and Rose to be the most promising of the set: "Sandy dear, all my ambitions are for you and Rose. You have got insight, perhaps not quite spiritual, but you're a deep one, and Rose has got instinct, Rose has got instinct" (*The Prime of Miss Jean Brodie*, p. 157). To her amazement, Sandy learns that Miss Brodie is attempting to manipulate Rose and Mr. Lloyd into having an affair, and that Sandy herself is to keep her teacher informed of it. While Miss Brodie is concocting this plan, however, Mr. Lowther announces his forthcoming marriage to Miss Lockhart, the science teacher at school. Initially shocked by this development, Miss Brodie recovers and focuses her energy on her plans involving Mr. Lloyd, Rose, and Sandy.

In 1937 the Brodie girls reach the age of 17 and acquire more outside interests, yet they remain connected by their loyalty to Miss Brodie, whose methods come under increasing attack from the headmistress, Miss Mackay. The headmistress is forced to acknowledge that, except for the lumpish Mary Macgregor, the Brodie girls are among the brightest at the school. That same year, Joyce Emily Hammond, the outsider hoping to join the Brodie set, runs away to Spain to fight in the civil war and is killed when the train in which she is traveling is attacked. The school holds a memorial service for her.

The following year, Mary leaves to become a typist and Jenny enters a school of dramatic art. The remaining members of the Brodie set pursue training for their respective careers—Monica in mathematics, Eunice in foreign languages, and Sandy in psychology. Rose marries soon after leaving school, but first continues to gain sexual experience by having a number of flings with several local boys. Miss Brodie becomes convinced that Rose and Mr. Lloyd will be lovers soon, but in the summer of 1938, it is Sandy who has the affair with Lloyd, and Rose who informs Miss Brodie of it. The teacher is shocked by the news but reassured when she learns from Sandy that Mr. Lloyd's portraits still resemble her and that she remains the art teacher's muse. At this juncture, Miss Brodie lets slip that she had encouraged Joyce Emily to go to Spain and fight on the side of Franco: "However, she didn't have the chance to fight at all, poor girl" (*The Prime of Miss Jean Brodie*, p. 181).

That autumn Sandy visits Miss Mackay at the school and hears that Miss Brodie is forming another impressionable set. The headmistress expresses concern over how precocious and out of step with the rest of the students these girls have become. Sandy asks if Miss Brodie's politics have ever been questioned and informs Miss Mackay that Miss Brodie is "a born Fascist" who must be stopped (*The Prime of Miss Jean Brodie*, p. 182). Miss Brodie is forced to retire in 1939 on the grounds that she has been teaching fascism; Miss Mackay takes pleasure in telling Miss Brodie that one of her own set betrayed her.

In future years, none of the Brodie set fulfill the lofty ambitions their teacher had for them. As noted, Rose marries soon after leaving school; clumsy, incompetent Mary dies in a hotel fire at age 23; Eunice becomes a nurse who weds a doctor; Jenny becomes a middling actress; Monica's life is marred by her anger—her scientist husband demands a separation after she throws a live piece of coal at his sister; and Sandy writes a psychological treatise ("The Transfiguration of the Commonplace"), converts to Roman Catholicism (the faith of Mr. Lloyd, her former lover), and becomes a nun. The year before Sandy enters the convent, she has tea with Miss Brodie at

the Braid Hills Hotel. The formerly confident teacher is defeated and subdued; she admits to Sandy that Teddy Lloyd had been "the great love of [her] prime," that she had renounced him because he was married, and that she had an affair with Gordon Lowther (*The Prime of Miss Jean Brodie*, p. 83). Miss Brodie then acknowledges that she is now "past [her] prime" and obsesses over which one of her girls betrayed her all those years ago (*The Prime of Miss Jean Brodie*, p. 82). Later that year, at age 56, she dies.

After Sandy enters the convent, her old schoolmates visit her from time to time and discuss Miss Brodie. On one visit, Monica reveals

A SURPLUS OF WOMEN

The huge casualties suffered by Great Britain in the First World War—an estimated 750,000 lives—deprived the nation of an entire generation of young men (Seaman, p. 16). The young women, who in different circumstances might have married those young men, faced uncertain futures in the 1920s and 1930s. However, the turn of events was not wholly negative. Many chose to pursue career opportunities that had become newly available to them during the war years. Unmarried working-class women had filled positions as factory laborers and as bus conductors during the war, while middle-class spinsters were employed as typists and office personnel. Though the return of the men from the front led to the dismissal of many of these women, the existence of a female work force could not be wholly expunged. Middle-class women managed to land jobs as teachers and public servants. In the novel, Spark reveals that Miss Brodie belongs to that particular generation of women who had to find other outlets than marriage for their energies and talents: "There were legions of her kind during the nineteen-thirties, women from the age of thirty and upward, who crowded their war-bereaved spinsterhood with voyages of discovery into new ideas and energetic practices in art or social welfare, education or religion" (*The Prime of Miss Jean Brodie*, p. 62).

that before her death, Miss Brodie suspected Sandy of betraying her. Sandy replies, "It's only possible to betray where loyalty is due" and refuses to discuss the subject (*The Prime of Miss Jean Brodie*, p. 186). But one day, when another visitor asks her about the effect of her school days, Sandy tells him that the main influence on her "was a Miss Jean Brodie in her prime" (*The Prime of Miss Jean Brodie*, p. 187).

Faith and betrayal. In the novel, religious conflict, as well as political disagreements, sow the seeds for Miss Brodie's eventual betrayal by one of her students and her forced retirement from teaching. Sandy Stranger, the girl who commits the betrayal, comes to view her teacher not merely as a born Fascist but as a symbol of a faith whose tenets she must reject, specifically Calvinism—also known as Presbyterianism—the dominant religion in Scotland. Founded by French theologian John Calvin and introduced to Scotland by John Knox, Calvinism preached the doctrine of predestination. It decreed that people were chosen by God to be saved ("the divine elect") or to be damned.

As portrayed by Spark, says literary scholar Peter Kemp, Calvinism is "a creed which, also built around a concept of the chosen and the rejected, occupies a place in theology similar to that of Fascism in politics" (Kemp, p. 73). In the Edinburgh of Spark's novel, "the name of [John] Knox sounds out; doctrines of predestination and divine election hover" (Kemp, p. 73). Sandy, however, has long felt excluded from a true understanding of this significant aspect of her environment, and at age 15 she seeks to correct this gap in her education: "In fact, it was the religion of Calvin of which Sandy felt deprived, or rather a specified recognition of it. She desired this birthright; something definite to reject. . . . In some ways the most real and rooted people whom Sandy knew were Miss Gaunt and the Kerr sisters who made no evasions about their belief that God had planned for practically everybody before they were born a nasty surprise when they died" (*The Prime of Miss Jean Brodie*, pp. 158-59). Sandy later reads Calvin's writings, confirming for herself that the God of Calvin does indeed "implant in certain people an erroneous sense of joy and salvation, so that their surprise at the end might be the nastier" (*The Prime of Miss Jean Brodie*, p. 159). Those who believe they are among the elect may actually find out that they are the damned; only God knows for certain which souls he means to save.

Sandy's spiritual education coincides with her growing understanding of Miss Brodie's manipulations of the lives in her charge; eventually, the two blend in Sandy's mind. It is not that Miss Brodie is an unbeliever—indeed, she attends Sunday services in all denominations except Roman Catholicism, which she regards as a super-

stitious faith. It is that she experiences no qualms or remorse over any of her actions: "She was not in any doubt, she let everyone know she was in no doubt, that God was on her side whatever her course, and so she experienced no difficulty or sense of hypocrisy while at the same time she went to bed with the singing master" (*The Prime of Miss Jean Brodie*, p. 126). As the maturing Sandy acquaints herself more with Calvinism, she begins "to sense what went to the makings of Miss Brodie who had elected herself to grace in so particular a way" (*The Prime of Miss Jean Brodie*, p. 160). After Miss Brodie confides in Sandy about her plans to manipulate Rose into having an affair with Teddy Lloyd, Sandy realizes that "[Miss Brodie] thinks she is Providence, . . . she thinks she is the God of Calvin, she sees the beginning and the end" (*The Prime of Miss Jean Brodie*, p. 176). Miss Brodie and her teachings become part of the "birthright" Sandy feels she must reject to discover her own identity.

By the same token, Roman Catholicism comes to represent, for Sandy, the antithesis of everything for which Calvinism and Miss Brodie stand. In fact, Miss Brodie overtly rejects Roman Catholics, dismissing them as "the only people who did not want to think for themselves" (*The Prime of Miss Jean Brodie*, p. 125). The novel's omniscient narrator, however, observes that Miss Brodie's attitude was a strange one, for "by temperament [she was] suited only to the Roman Catholic Church; possibly it could have embraced, even while it disciplined, her soaring and diving spirit, it might even have normalised her" (*The Prime of Miss Jean Brodie*, p. 125).

Whether Sandy comes to hold these views herself is never fully revealed. Her own conversion occurs as a result of her affair with Teddy Lloyd; losing interest in Mr. Lloyd himself, she becomes increasingly fascinated by his Roman Catholicism: "Her mind was as full of his religion as a night sky is full of things visible and invisible. She left the man and took his religion and became a nun in the course of time" (*The Prime of Miss Jean Brodie*, p. 180). Sandy's conversion, however, does not guarantee her peace of mind, any more than her betrayal of Miss Brodie does. In the ranks of the Catholic Church, she soon discovers "quite a number of Fascists much less agreeable than Miss Brodie" (*The Prime of Miss Jean Brodie*, p. 183). Sandy is last glimpsed at the convent, clutching "at the bars of her grille more desperately than ever" while visitors question her about her psychological treatise—"The Transfiguration of the Commonplace"—and inquire about the early influences that shaped her life (*The Prime of Miss Jean Brodie*, p. 186).

In the centuries leading up to Catholic Emancipation in 1829, Roman Catholics were for the most part unwelcome in such an overwhelmingly Protestant nation as Scotland. An unofficial census of 1755 counted the Roman Catholic community at only about 33,000, an estimated 2.6 percent of Scotland's population (Pryde, p. 103). From the 1820s onward, however, Scotland's Roman Catholic population increased steadily as a result of large-scale immigration of Irish laborers and their families. Catholic churches and schools were set up to accommodate the expanding community. Although Irish immigration to Scotland eventually decreased, the number of Roman Catholics in Scotland continued to rise during the first half of the twentieth century, during the years in which Spark's novel takes place. In 1931, Roman Catholics in Scotland numbered around 607,000, approximately one-eighth of the population (Pryde, p. 309). By 1952, the official estimate of Roman Catholics in Scotland had climbed to 748,463, or 14.7 percent of the population (Rait and Pryde, p. 276).

Sources and literary context. Although *The Prime of Miss Jean Brodie* is not an autobiographical novel, Spark did draw upon some real-life people and places. The Marcia Blaine School for Girls was based on James Gillespie's School in Edinburgh, which Spark attended for 12 years from the age of five. There was no exact counterpart for Spark's Miss Brodie, but Spark did experience the thrill of an inspiring teacher, a Miss Christina Kay, whom Spark described in her autobiography, *Curriculum Vitae*, as "exhilarating and impressive" (Spark, p. 58). Like Miss Brodie, Kay was passionately interested in art, frequently entertained her classes with exciting accounts of her travels in various countries, and occasionally took a few of her most promising students, including Spark herself, to concerts and plays. But unlike Miss Brodie, Kay was a devout Christian who would never have had an affair with the art master or singing master. Spark herself writes,

> In a sense Miss Kay was nothing like Miss Brodie. In another sense she was far above and beyond her Brodie counterpart. If she could have met 'Miss Brodie' Miss Kay would have put the fictional character firmly in her place. And yet no pupil of Miss Kay's has failed to recognize her, with joy and great nostalgia, in the shape of Miss Jean Brodie in her prime.
>
> (Spark, *Curriculum Vitae*, p. 57)

Like many of Spark's novels, *The Prime of Miss Jean Brodie* is difficult to classify. On one level, the novel can be read as a bildungsroman, a "coming of age" story, in which a group of young protagonists succumb to or reject the influence of a charismatic authority figure. But the novel also targets such issues as sex, respectability, and religion. Overall, Spark's work is frequently compared to that of other "Catholic" novelists, such as Graham Greene and Evelyn Waugh (see ***The Power and the Glory*** and ***Brideshead Revisited***, also in *WLAIT 4: British and Irish Literature and Its Times*). However, literary scholar Dorothea Walker insists that, unlike Greene and Waugh, "[Spark's] Catholicism fails to embrace ordinary Catholics . . . It has been remarked that no one would be tempted to become a Catholic from reading her novels" (Walker, "Preface"). Moreover, her novels do not evince the same concern for realism about the sordid aspects of life so plainly featured in other post-World War II novels. Spark, asserts Walker, is unique. Adept at complex plots, witty dialogue, and innovative characters, she "shows in each novel an innate originality. She cannot be categorized" (Walker, "Preface").

Reviews. *The Prime of Miss Jean Brodie* was, on the whole, enthusiastically received by critics. Some reviewers admitted to not understanding Spark's overall purpose in the novel. Most critics, however, had high praise for the work. Frank Tuohy wrote in the *Spectator*, "*The Prime of Miss Jean Brodie* is Miss Spark's most realistic work so far, and I think her best" (Tuohy, p. 634). Writing for *Commonweal*, Samuel Hynes describes the novel as "intelligent, witty, and beautifully constructed, and it is new. . . . Mrs. Spark's powers of invention are apparently inexhaustible" (Hynes, p. 567). In the *New Republic*, R. W. Flint praised the novel's style and humor, calling it, "[a] short, tidy, but richly composed and affectionate comic novel in the Joycean manner" (Flint, p. 17). Unsurprisingly, Spark's handling of religious themes elicited comment. Granville Hicks observed in the *Saturday Review* that "[Spark's] religion makes itself felt in almost everything she has written. She is a gloomy Catholic . . . more concerned with the evil of man than with the goodness of God," but Hicks concluded that "the book is admirably written, beautifully constructed, extremely amusing and deeply serious" (Hicks, p. 18). Other critics expressed fascination with the nature of the relationship between Miss Brodie and her students, especially the treacherous Sandy. Writing for

Punch, Malcolm Bradbury summed up what he considered the main achievement: "It is in the deft placing of intellectual positions and in the depiction of the influence of minds upon one another that Miss Spark here excels" (Bradbury, p. 696).

—Pamela S. Loy

For More Information

Bradbury, Malcolm. Review of *The Prime of Miss Jean Brodie. Punch* 241, 8 November 1961, 696.

Flint, R. W. Review of *The Prime of Miss Jean Brodie. New Republic* 146, 29 January 1962, 17.

Hicks, Granville. Review of *The Prime of Miss Jean Brodie. Saturday Review* 45, 20 January 1962, 18.

Hynes, Samuel. Review of *The Prime of Miss Jean Brodie. Commonweal* 75, 23 February 1962, 567.

Kedward, H. R. *Fascism in Western Europe 1900–45.* New York: New York University Press, 1971.

Kemp, Peter. *Muriel Spark.* London: Elek Books Limited, 1974.

Maclean, Fitzroy. *A Concise History of Scotland.* New York: The Viking Press, 1970.

Pryde, George S. *Scotland from 1603 to the Present Day.* London: Thomas Nelson & Sons, 1962.

Rait, Sir Robert, and George S. Pryde. *Scotland.* New York: Frederick A. Praeger, 1955.

Scotland, James. *The History of Scottish Education.* Vol. 2. London: University of London Press, 1969.

Seaman, L. C. B. *Life in Britain between the Wars.* London: B. T. Batsford, 1970.

Spark, Muriel. *Curriculum Vitae.* Boston: Houghton Mifflin, 1993.

———. *The Prime of Miss Jean Brodie.* 1961. Reprinted, New York: Harper Perennial, 1994.

Thorpe, Andrew. *Britain in the 1930s: The Deceptive Decade.* Oxford: Blackwell, 1992.

Tuohy, Frank. Review of *The Prime of Miss Jean Brodie. Spectator* 207, 3 November 1961, 634.

Walker, Dorothea. *Muriel Spark.* Boston: Twayne, 1988.

Pygmalion

by

George Bernard Shaw

George Bernard Shaw was born in 1856 in Dublin, Ireland. He was the only son of an Anglo-Irish family that belonged to the upper-middle-class Protestant section of Irish society but, despite its status, had little money. Shaw's father, a civil servant, experienced little professional success. An alcoholic, he neglected Shaw as well as Shaw's two sisters, as did his wife, so the three were raised mainly by servants. At age 15, after attending several different Irish schools, Shaw took a job as an office boy for Uniacke Townshend and Company, a firm of estate agents; he later became a clerk for this same firm. In 1876 Shaw joined his mother and sisters in London, where they had moved 5 years before, leaving Shaw's father behind. For several years, Shaw attempted to establish himself as a novelist without much success. He made his mark in other ways, however. Becoming passionately interested in social reform, in 1884 Shaw helped found the Fabian Society, an organization dedicated to the establishment, by gradual stages, of a socialist government in England. During the late 1880s, he began to make a name for himself in the literary world as a music critic, writing for such journals as the *London* and the *World*. In 1895, Shaw became dramatic critic for the *Saturday Review*, a London periodical; his provocative reviews galvanized contemporary audiences and introduced a slew of controversial ideas about plays and acting. Meanwhile, Shaw embarked on a playwrighting career, in which he was to achieve lasting success; his first play, *Widowers' Houses*, which dealt with the problem of

THE LITERARY WORK

A play set in London, England during the 1910s; first performed in 1913; published in 1914.

SYNOPSIS

A professor of phonetics makes a wager to pass off a London flower girl as a high-society lady by refining her speech, manner, and appearance.

slum landlordism, was produced in 1892. Most of Shaw's plays explored social issues—prostitution in *Mrs. Warren's Profession* (1893), war in *Arms and the Man* (1894), and evangelism in *Major Barbara* (1907). *Pygmalion* (1912), arguably Shaw's best-known play to modern audiences, is considered not only an effective comedy, but a brilliant study of the connection between accent and social class in England.

Events in History at the Time of the Play

Upstarts, social climbers, and class-consciousness. Early in the play, Henry Higgins declares, "This is an age of upstarts. Men begin in Kentish Town with £80 a year and end in Park Lane with a hundred thousand" (Shaw, *Pyg-*

George Bernard Shaw

malion, p. 15). His words accurately describe the changes overtaking British society in the late nineteenth and early twentieth centuries. Although, in theory, society continued to be as rigidly hierarchical as ever, in reality, wealth and power were no longer exclusively held by the landed aristocrats. Fortunes had been made in the 1800s by the spread of the railway, the conversion of sailing to steamships, the construction of factories, and the discovery of distant markets for products. Many of these rich industrialists became favorites of the Prince of Wales, later King Edward VII, who found his mother's social circle—royal relatives from Europe and a few members of the old nobility—dull and staid. In contrast, the newly wealthy could entertain Edward VII in the lavish style that he favored, thus cementing their popularity with him.

It is not to be supposed that the English aristocracy was pleased by the influx of nouveaux riche into what had formerly been regarded as elite social circles. Many aristocratic families became increasingly obsessed with demonstrating their superiority—in birth, breeding, and social graces—over these extravagant newcomers. According to historian Ronald Pearsall, "Arrogance and irritability marked many of the old gentry in both town or country. It was as if they were aware they were a dying breed. . . . In the women there was a note of petulance when confronted with

the changed conditions" (Pearsall, p. 74). He goes on to quote some aristocrats, namely, the Countess of Cardigan and Lancastre. "The lavish expenditure and the feverish pursuit of pleasure that constitute Society do not appeal to me any more than the restaurant life, which did not exist in my day. . . . Nowadays money shouts, and birth and breeding whisper!" (Countess of Cardigan and Lancastre in Pearsall, p. 74). Given this class-conscious attitude, it is not surprising that formal occasions such as dinner parties and country-house visits often became social battlefields. Wealthy social climbers sought to prove themselves worthy of inclusion in the upper ranks of society. On the other hand, those born to upper-class status continued to emphasize the importance of qualities that could not be bought and proved quick to snub or patronize newcomers who did not measure up to their aristocratic standards. Even the domestic staff of a great estate could enter into the game of social one-upmanship: "At one great country house, a footman kept a meticulous record of all the bad English and 'ignorance' he heard while waiting at table, and related the choicer items, with names and dates, to the servants of later visitors" (Pearsall, p. 73).

In *Pygmalion*, Higgins attacks the artificiality and snobbery that he sees reflected in the British class system by teaching Eliza Doolittle, the lower-class flower girl, to look, act and, even more importantly, *speak* like a duchess. Higgins explains to his astonished mother, "But you have no idea how frightfully interesting it is to take a human being and change her into a quite different human being by creating a new speech for her. It's filling up the deepest gulf that separates class from class and soul from soul" (*Pygmalion*, pp. 63-64). Later, after being criticized by Eliza herself for his rudeness and bad manners, Higgins lends a retort that reveals his true feelings about class distinctions: "The great secret, Eliza, is not having bad manners and good manners or any other particular sort of manners, but having the same manner for all human souls. . . . The question is not whether I treat you rudely, but whether you ever heard me treat anyone else better" (*Pygmalion*, p. 98).

The London poor. The luxury and comfort enjoyed by the wealthy and privileged during the Edwardian Age formed a stark contrast to the wretched, squalid lives of the poor in the same period. The years before World War I were marked by vigorous consumer spending and conspicuous display, and a growing economic gap: "The poor were getting poorer and the rich were getting richer. . . . The poor, it was considered, were poor because they deserved to be, and were largely made up of idlers and scroungers who could get jobs if they were less work-shy" (Pearsall, p. 103). For the most part, the poor remained downtrodden and apathetic during the early 1900s, resenting their situation but helpless to remedy it.

Poverty tended to be a more pressing concern in urban areas than in rural areas. In London alone, the number of paupers increased by 15,800 during the period from 1880 to 1907. In the East End of London and in some of its boroughs were a number of perpetually unemployed citizens. "The poor married too young, had large families, were riddled with venereal disease, and drank" (Pearsall, p. 109). Local government offices did little to improve the morale or living conditions of the poor and indigent. Boards of Guardians, comprised of elected officials, were responsible for the organization and running of urban workhouses. Often these boards employed poorly trained or incompetent men to serve as relieving officers, many of whom dispersed money carelessly, without sufficient regard for the needs of the applicants. Seldom did the relieving officers inquire into the resources of the applicants, or bother to verify the facts behind each plea for aid. The Guardians were frequently corrupt as well; many were estate agents, slumowners, and public-house and saloon owners who had a vested interest in keeping the amount of financial relief quite low and readily gave away the money to friends, relatives, and customers. Meanwhile, the poor shied away from the overcrowded, unsanitary, and otherwise hateful workhouse, many of them choosing starvation or suicide over going into the workhouse.

The cost of living increased in the early twentieth century, but there was no corresponding rise in working-class wages so that even those in a somewhat better financial position often had to struggle to make ends meet. In 1903, the minimum living wage for a family of five was considered to be 21 shillings, 8 pence a week, but in 1914 nearly a quarter of male wage earners garnered less than 25 shillings a week. Working women in sweatshops and factories often fared worse than their male counterparts. In the East End tailoring district, makers of artificial flowers, which were often used to trim gowns and hats, earned 8 to 12 shillings a week, corset makers 8 to 16 shillings a week, and umbrella makers 10 to 18 shillings a week (Priestley, p. 74).

Workdays lasted up to 12 or 14 hours, and working conditions were usually appalling—crowded, dirty, poorly lit, and inadequately ventilated.

Many of the same complaints could also be made about the workers' *living* conditions. The poorest Londoner lived in filthy, vermin-ridden slums, possessed no furniture beyond a straw pallet and some orange crates to sit on, and had no access to lavatories. Workers with more money could usually find cleaner quarters, but living conditions remained unsatisfactory for them as well. Author J. B. Priestley, who grew up during the Edwardian period, describes a third of the population as overworked, underpaid, and packed into slum quarters that should have been pulled down years earlier. In fact, "conditions were so bad that it was believed that they were producing degenerate physical types, anemic mothers of rickety children, young men who were incapable of defending the Motherland and Empire" (Priestley, pp. 72-73).

Pygmalion's flower girl, Eliza, reveals her own slum background during her first meeting with Higgins. Alarmed by Higgins's observation that she came from Lisson Grove, a slum area in West London, Eliza wails, "Oh, what harm is there in my leaving Lisson Grove? It wasnt fit for a pig to live in; and I had to pay four [shillings]-and-six [pence] a week" (*Pygmalion*, p. 12). At this point in the play, Eliza's present accommodations represent a small improvement but are not in the least palatial. In the stage directions, Shaw describes Eliza's living quarters as *"the irreducible minimum of poverty's needs: a wretched bed heaped with all sorts of coverings that have any warmth in them, a draped packing case with a basin and jug on it and a little looking glass over it, a chair and table, the refuse of some suburban kitchen, and an American alarum clock on the shelf above the unused fireplace: the whole lighted with a gas lamp with a penny in the slot meter. Rent: four shillings a week"* (*Pygmalion*, p. 19). Given her living conditions, it is not surprising that Eliza ultimately leaps at the chance of something better.

Social rituals and the season. Much of the action in *Pygmalion* takes place against the background of the "London Season," a giddy round of social events lasting from May through July that consumed the attention of the wealthy and well-established. Traditionally, a private gallery exhibition at the Royal Academy of Arts in May began the Season; other important social events included horse races at Ascot, the Henley regatta, cricket matches between the schools of Eton and

Harrow and Oxford and Cambridge, and, of course, countless private balls and parties.

The Season also had a serious side: Parliament was in session, and the social events provided a convenient venue for men who occupied high places in government to conduct political business and form useful alliances among colleagues. Moreover, the Season, even in the early years of

AFTERNOON CALLS AND AT-HOMES

Throughout the year, women of leisure exchanged calls—short visits lasting from 15 to 30 minutes, during which tea and light refreshments were usually offered. The purpose was not only to chat and socialize but to further an acquaintance that might prove useful or advantageous in the future. During the Victorian period (1837-1901), visitors hoping to call upon the mistress of a certain house often left small cards bearing their names with her servants. Social contact was established if, on reading the cards, the lady invited the visitors inside, sent them a card of her own in return, or paid them a visit at their homes instead. The usual hours for paying calls were between 3 P.M. and 6 P.M.—however, these visits were referred to as "morning calls" because callers wore "morning dress" (daytime clothes rather than evening dress). If the lady of the house was busy, indisposed, or disinclined to visit with anyone, she often instructed her servants to inform prospective callers that she was not "at home" or, rather, not receiving visitors that day. The excuse was generally not intended as a snub or a slight. Often a woman had a designated At-Home day, with predetermined hours—again, usually between 3 and 6 P.M.—during which friends and acquaintances could call upon her, in full expectation of finding her available. In *Pygmalion*, Higgins commandeers his mother's At-Home day for Eliza's first test as a "lady." As a new acquaintance, Eliza stays for the minimum amount of time at Mrs. Higgins's house, though not before making several outlandish remarks that Higgins just manages to explain away as "the new small talk" (*Pygmalion*, p. 59).

the twentieth century, still revolved around the no-less-serious business of marrying off middle- and upper-class young girls to eligible young men. Debutantes were presented to English royalty at drawing rooms in St. James's Palace, then made the rounds at countless parties, balls, dances, and other festive occasions.

Evening parties tended to fall into two categories: those with dancing and those without dancing. Among the latter were the grand receptions—nicknamed "drums" in the nineteenth century—at which guests were invited to meet others of equal or superior social consequence. Historical novelist Rona Randall writes, "The highest level of reception included those given by the wives of cabinet ministers or ambassadors; at the opposite scale were those boring little drums for a few elegant ladies in someone's drawing room very late in the afternoon" (Randall, p. 27). The most formal of the evening receptions tended to begin around 10 or 11 P.M. and feature superbly dressed guests, even if they planned on only staying a short while before leaving to attend some rival party. Apparently "the whole reason for being there was to see and be seen, to be able to say that you had met such-and-such a person at such-and-such a house, the more imposing the better" (Randall, p. 27).

In the play, Higgins and Pickering use the events of the Season as venues to test Eliza's progress at speaking and behaving like a lady. Although the former flower girl makes several verbal gaffes at Mrs. Higgins's tea party, held during the older woman's At-Home day, she later manages to pass muster among the cream of high society at a garden party, a dinner, and an Embassy reception, all held on the same day! Exhausting as such a schedule may sound, it was not unusual to attend a string of social events lasting from morning until night during the height of the London Season.

The birth of modern phonetics. Shaw enjoyed making the claim that *Pygmalion* was primarily a didactic work that explored the importance of phonetics, the study of speech sounds, that is, of their physiological production and acoustic qualities. Phoneticians study the configuration of the vocal tract used to produce speech sounds (articulatory phonetics), the acoustic properties of speech sounds (acoustic phonetics), their effect on the ear (auditory phonetics) and the manner in which sounds combine to make syllables, words, and sentences (linguistic phonetics).

In Britain, modern phonetics began towards the mid-nineteenth century with the work of Sir Isaac Pitman (1813-97), an English inventor. In *Stenographic Shorthand* (1837), Pitman set forth a shorthand system based on phonetic rather than orthographic principles (later called "phonography"). His system was adapted to more than a dozen languages and soon became one of the most widely used methods in the world, replacing all the older forms of shorthand. During the 1840s, Pitman collaborated with another phonetician, Alexander John Ellis, to produce a series of phonetic alphabets. The final result of their collaboration—Phonotypic alphabet no. 10—was published in 1847. Their labors "during the ten years that preceded the 1847 alphabet can be said to have established phonetics as a modern science in Great Britain" (Kelly in Asher and Henderson, p. 262). The two brought a great deal of innovation to the field. While Pitman poured energy into effecting reforms, Ellis showed an unparalleled knack for observation, description, and experimentation, setting new standards in the study of phonetics.

Alexander Melville Bell (1819-1905)—a Scottish-American educator and the father of telephone inventor Alexander Graham Bell—was another important pioneer of modern phonetics. Bell's *Visible Speech* (1867) introduced a physiological or visible alphabet composed of symbols that were intended to represent every sound of the human voice. Called Steno-Phonography, Bell's system won the admiration of Henry Sweet (1845-1912), an English phonetician and philologist. Sweet, an authority on Anglo-Saxon and the history of the English language, had studied the widely used Pitman system but considered it "one of the poorest systems in existence, on account of its geometric-shaped symbols, its use of the thick/thin distinction and its inherent character of brevity" and irritably dubbed it the "Pitfall" system instead (MacMahon in Asher and Henderson, pp. 265-66).

From 1869 to the 1880s, Sweet relied on Bell's system for his own studies, but eventually acknowledged that there were some inadequacies there as well: "One defect was . . . the method of indicating a consonant's place of articulation by the angle of the slope of the symbol" (MacMahon in Asher and Henderson, p. 266). In 1892, Sweet published an improved version of Bell's system, which relied more on cursive writing and less on geometric shapes. In Current, as Sweet's version was called, the symbols were based on whole letters of the alphabet, on parts of letters, or on innovative ways to combine parts of letters. Current avoided the "angularity, jerkiness, sprawliness, and hand-cramping movements" of the geometric based shorthands, "especially Pitman's" (MacMahon in Asher and Henderson, pp. 268-69). While Current failed to supplant the Pitman system, Sweet's efforts were encouraged and commended by friends and colleagues. Shaw, who corresponded with Sweet and met

him on a few occasions, became an admirer of his work and of Sweet himself. In his Preface to *Pygmalion*, Shaw paid tribute to Sweet, who died the year the play was written:

> His great ability as a phonetician (he was, I think, the best of them all at his job) would have entitled him to high official recognition, and perhaps enabled him to popularize his subject, but for his Satanic contempt for all academic dignitaries and persons in general who thought more of Greek than of phonetics. . . . He was, I believe, not in the least an illnatured man: very much the opposite, I should say; but he would not suffer fools gladly; and to him all scholars who were not rabid phoneticians were fools.
>
> (Shaw in *Pygmalion*, pp. 1-2)

Sweet, in fact, became the model for Henry Higgins in *Pygmalion*. While Shaw denied that Hig-

---

THE COCKNEY DIALECT

During the late nineteenth-century, the speech of the London working class became generally known as "Cockney" (from "coken-ay," meaning a cock's egg, or a worthless thing). The term, dating back to the late 1400s, originally applied to the language of all Londoners who were not part of the court. However, by the 1900s, the Education Acts, which insisted on the use of "proper English" in schools, had helped transform speech and London working-class talk "was fast becoming the Cockney of caricature and stereotype. . . . The appearance of Eliza Doolittle in *Pygmalion* with her 'kerbstone English' of *flars* and *garn* (go on) and *Ay-ee, Ba-yee, Cy-ee* (A, B, C) consummated the marriage of [the poor] East End and Cockney" (McCrum, p. 275). In the published version of the play, Shaw attempted to recreate Eliza's exact manner of speech as a flower-girl in her first scene:

Cockney: "Ow, eez y -ooa son, is e? Wal, fewd dan y' d -ooty bawmz a mather should, eed now bettern to spawl a pore gel's flahrzn then ran awy athaht pyin. Will y -oo py me f'them?"

(*Pygmalion*, p. 9).

Translation: "Oh, he is your son, is he? Well, if you had done your duty by him as a mother should, he would know better than to spoil a poor girl's flowers and then run away without paying. Will you pay me for them?"

(*Pygmalion*, p. 120)

gins was an exact portrait, he conceded that "there are touches of Sweet in the play," adding, "With Higgins's physique and temperament Sweet might have set the Thames on fire" (Shaw in Pygmalion, p. 4).

The Play in Focus

Plot summary. The play begins one rainy summer night, in the Covent Garden area of London. A crowd of people have taken shelter from the

---

COVENT GARDEN

As well as providing a location for a theatre and an Opera House, Covent Garden—a corruption of the phrase "convent garden" because it used to be the garden of the abbot of Westminster—served as the principal fruit, flower, and vegetable market of London for over 300 years. The market was first established in 1670 and rebuilt in 1830. During the nineteenth century, Covent Garden market did a booming trade—fruit sellers, costermongers, porters, florists and flower girls arrived in the square during the early hours of the morning to start their day's work. In the mid-1800s, Henry Mayhew described the "bustle and confusion" of the market on a typical morning: "[I]n the paved square the people pass and cross each other in all directions, hampers clash together, and excepting the carters from the country, every one is on the move. . . . Cabbages are piled up into stacks as it were. Carts are heaped high with turnips, and bunches of carrots like huge red fingers, are seen in all directions. Flower girls with large bunches of violets under their arms, run past, leaving a trail of perfume behind them" (Mayhew, pp. 103-104). From 1884 to 1904, the market underwent a period of great expansion, prompting numerous public complaints about crowds, traffic, and vegetable refuse.

---

downpour in a church portico, among them an upper-class mother, daughter, and son. As the son searches for a taxi, he collides with a young flower girl who startles his family by calling him by his name, "Freddy." Fearing a possible indiscretion, Freddy's mother quickly buys flowers from the girl who, encouraged by her increased business, approaches a gentleman in a similar vein. The flower girl becomes alarmed, however, when a bystander informs her that another man is writing down everything she says. The crowd's

attention quickly shifts to the note taker, Henry Higgins, who claims that he can identify everyone's place of origin from his or her speech, then proceeds to demonstrate that ability. Higgins proudly explains to his impressed audience that he is a phonetician, one who studies the science of speech. Higgins also claims that he could pass off the flower girl as a duchess at a garden party in three months' time, simply by changing the way she speaks.

At this point, one of the bystanders to whom Higgins has been talking reveals himself to be Colonel Pickering, another phonetician. Favorably impressed by each other's work, Higgins and Pickering agree to meet to discuss their shared profession in more detail. Pickering invites Higgins to sup with him, and the two men depart as Higgins flings some money into the flower girl's basket. The astonished girl treats herself to a taxi ride home.

The next day, at his home on Wimpole Street, Higgins proudly shows off his laboratory and the results of his studies to Pickering. Their conversation is interrupted by the arrival of Eliza Doolittle, the flower girl they met at Covent Garden the previous night. Eliza tells an astonished Higgins that she wants to hire him to teach her to "talk more genteel" so she can work in a flower shop instead of selling flowers on the street. At first Higgins rejects Eliza's proposal, but Pickering challenges him to prove his skill by teaching the flower girl to pass for a duchess and offers to pay for Eliza's lessons. Higgins gleefully accepts the challenge and instructs his housekeeper, Mrs. Pearce, to take the thoroughly confused Eliza in hand and make her presentable.

While Eliza is being bathed, Mrs. Pearce warns Higgins that he must set a good example for the girl by curbing some of his own bad habits, including swearing and slovenliness. An irritable Higgins agrees, then privately complains to Pickering that Mrs. Pearce is "firmly persuaded that I'm an arbitrary, overbearing bossing kind of fellow" (*Pygmalion*, p. 38). Meanwhile, Alfred Doolittle, Eliza's father and a London dustman (so called because his trade involves collecting the dust—ashes and other refuse—from people's dustbins), calls on Higgins, demanding his daughter's return. Higgins correctly interprets Doolittle's indignant display as a plot to extort money and calls his bluff, telling him to take Eliza away. Doolittle quickly changes tactics, expresses approval of Eliza's wish to improve her speech, and attempts to engage Higgins and Pickering's sympathies on his behalf, as Eliza's father and

Mrs. Patrick Campbell as Eliza, Edmund Gurney as Alfred Doolittle, and Sir Herbert Tree as Henry Higgins in the first English stage production of *Pygmalion* at His Majesty's Theatre in London in 1914.

one of the "undeserving poor." The term refers to idlers and scroungers, and Doolittle makes no pretense to being deserving. Amused, Higgins at last gives Doolittle a five-pound note; the dustman departs, though not before seeing a clean, immaculately dressed Eliza. All three men are astonished by her improved appearance.

For the next few months, Higgins relentlessly drills Eliza on her speech, often driving her to tears of frustration. He schedules her first test in society by inviting her to his mother's At-Home. Mrs. Higgins is dismayed by this last-minute addition to her guest list but, on learning of her son's project, reluctantly consents to include Eliza. The Higginses' conversation is cut short by the arrivals of Pickering and the Eynsford Hills,

the same mother, daughter, and son trio whom Eliza encountered that night at Covent Garden. Higgins recognizes them, but fortunately the Eynsford Hills—genteel but financially straitened—do not recognize him or Eliza in her fashionable new clothes. Freddy Eynsford Hill is especially struck by Eliza's beauty. At first, Eliza's deportment and conversation are quite proper, if a bit stilted, but as the visit continues, her speech becomes more colorful and less appropriate. Higgins manages to pass off her utterances as the "new small talk" and ushers her discreetly out of the house, although Eliza shocks Mrs. Higgins's other guests by using the word "bloody" as she departs (*Pygmalion*, p. 59). After the Eynsford Hills leave, Mrs. Higgins remonstrates with

Higgins and Pickering for not giving sufficient thought to what they will do with Eliza if or when they succeed in transforming her. Both men airily dismiss her concerns and resume their project of "inventing new Elizas" (*Pygmalion*, p. 64).

Six months after Eliza began her speech lessons, Higgins and Pickering take her to an ambassador's evening reception. This time Eliza's appearance, deportment, and speech are faultless; the other guests react to her as though she were a princess. Even Nepommuck, a foreign interpreter who was Higgins's first pupil, is convinced that she is Hungarian royalty. Pickering informs a nervous Eliza that she has won Higgins's bet "ten times over" and the trio quickly exits (*Pygmalion*, p. 71).

Back at Higgins's house, the two men congratulate each other on their victory and loudly express relief that their experiment is over, oblivious to Eliza's presence and growing distress. After Pickering leaves the room, Eliza explodes at Higgins, berating him for his thoughtlessness and asking him what is to become of her now. Taken aback by her passionate outburst, Higgins nonetheless refuses to take Eliza's concerns seriously, enraging her further. Their quarrel ends with Higgins accusing Eliza of ingratitude and storming from the room.

Upstairs, Eliza changes into walking clothes, gathers up a few personal belongings, and leaves the house. Outside, she encounters the lovestruck Freddy Eynsford Hill who has been haunting the neighborhood in the hopes of seeing her again. In need of comfort, Eliza encourages his devotion and asks him to accompany her on a taxi ride through London while she sorts out her predicament.

The following morning, Higgins and Pickering, distraught over Eliza's mysterious departure, show up at Mrs. Higgins's house. Mrs. Higgins scolds both men for sending the police out to look for Eliza "as if she were a thief, or a lost umbrella," but does not let them know that the girl has taken refuge with her (*Pygmalion*, p. 84). Then, Alfred Doolittle, who has been searching for Higgins, appears; to everyone's surprise, the dustman is splendidly dressed, as though for a fashionable wedding. Doolittle glumly confesses that, owing to a legacy from a wealthy American, he is no longer a member of "the undeserving poor" but now a gentleman besieged by requests for money and obliged to uphold "middle-class morality" (*Pygmalion*, p. 86). Doolittle blames Higgins for letting the American know of his existence. (Higgins, in fact, has mentioned Doolit-

tle's name and unusual outlook on morality to the American benefactor.) The subject of Eliza comes up and Mrs. Higgins reveals that Eliza has been staying with her since that morning, then criticizes the astonished Higgins and Pickering for their unthinking, unappreciative treatment of their former protégé. After making the two men promise to mind their manners, Mrs. Higgins has Eliza join them in the drawing room.

Now poised and self-possessed, Eliza thanks Pickering for the kindness and courtesy he consistently showed her during her lessons, crediting him with teaching her self-respect. She also makes several barbed comments about Higgins's lack of manners, which infuriates the professor. Despite Pickering's entreaties, Eliza declines to return to Wimpole Street with him and Higgins. At this point, Doolittle startles his daughter by stepping forward, revealing his newfound wealth to her, and announcing that he is to marry her "stepmother" that afternoon. Although Eliza despises the bride as a "low common woman," she reluctantly agrees to attend the wedding (*Pygmalion*, p. 95).

While everyone else readies themselves to go to the church, Eliza and Higgins are finally left alone. Once again they clash, widening the gulf between them. Eliza demands to be treated with respect and consideration, while Higgins, with equal obstinacy, refuses to change his nature for anyone. He can offer her nothing more than a platonic relationship, yet he becomes indignant when he learns that Freddy is her suitor and outraged when Eliza threatens to go to work for the interpreter Nepommuck and teach phonetics. Irritated but intrigued by this independent new Eliza, Higgins invites her to return to Wimpole Street with him and Pickering and be "three old bachelors together instead of only two men and a silly girl" (*Pygmalion*, p. 104). As Mrs. Higgins re-enters, Eliza coolly refuses, tells him they will not be seeing each other again, and makes a majestic exit. As the play ends, the incorrigible Higgins continues to call out domestic instructions to her and laughs uproariously at the thought of Eliza marrying Freddy.

An independent woman. Shaw's play recalls the Greek myth of Pygmalion—in which a sculptor carves a statue of the ideal woman and falls in love with his creation, then brings it to life by his prayers to the love goddess Aphrodite. The play does not so much update the Greek myth as invert it. Shaw's biographer Michael Holroyd points out, "Higgins [creates] a petrified social statue of Eliza. Under his tutelage she becomes a doll of 'remarkable distinction and beauty . . . speaking with pedantic correctness of pronunciation and great beauty of tone'. . . . This dummy figure replaces the 'draggle tailed guttersnipe . . . more brute than being' whose life Higgins acknowledges to have been real, warm, and violent" (Holroyd, p. 327). Calling her son and Pickering "a pretty pair of babies playing with your live doll," the acerbic Mrs. Higgins questions whether their experiment will do Eliza more harm than good (*Pygmalion*, p. 63). They have not considered what is to be done with her afterward, once they have given her manners that disqualify her from earning her living as a flower girl without furnishing her with an income.

Mrs. Higgins's words prove prophetic. Having passed in high society as a duchess and won Higgins's wager, a despairing Eliza asks her former teacher, "What am I fit for? What have you left me fit for? Where am I to go? What am I to do? Whats to become of me?" (*Pygmalion*, p. 76). The unthinking Higgins is forced to admit that he has never given much consideration to the subject. His vague suggestion that Eliza might marry "some chap or other" that his mother picks out meets with the scornful response, "We were above that in Tottenham Court Road. . . . I sold flowers. I didnt sell myself. Now youve made a lady of me I'm not fit to sell anything else" (*Pygmalion*, p. 77).

Significantly, the final stage of Eliza's metamorphosis—from guttersnipe to doll-like duchess to living woman—takes place only after she breaks with Higgins. While Galatea, the statue in the original legend came to life to wed Pygmalion, her modern counterpart ultimately rejects her creator and the life of "three old bachelors together" that he offers her, in favor of a possible career as a teacher and marriage to the feckless Freddy Eynsford Hill, who loves her. (*Pygmalion*, p. 104). Threatening to set herself up as a rival in Higgins's own field of phonetics, Eliza revels in his discomfiture:

> You cant take away the knowledge you gave me. You said I had a finer ear than you. And I can be civil and kind to people, which is more than you can. . . . Oh, when I think of myself crawling under your feet and being trampled on and called names, when all the time I had only to lift up my finger to be as good as you, I could just kick myself.
>
> (*Pygmalion*, pp. 103-104).

Despite being taken aback by Eliza's defiance, the unpredictable Higgins declares, "By George, Eliza, I said I'd make a woman of you; and I have.

I like you like this. . . . Five minutes ago you were like a millstone round my neck. Now you're a tower of strength: a consort battleship" (*Pygmalion*, p. 104).

Eliza's startling declaration of independence coincides with historical changes in the lives of women in the early twentieth century. Even in the late Victorian Age, a growing number of middle- and upper-class women became less content to accept marriage and motherhood as their sole lot in life. Indeed, the surplus of women in Great Britain meant that many would end up as spinsters. Nor were such women content to be only governesses and schoolteachers; with the founding of women's colleges at Oxford and Cambridge during the 1870s, higher education for women became increasingly possible. Some of these New Women, the term for the increasing number of middle- and upper-class women of the 1880s and '90s who sought lives beyond the domestic sphere, followed the example of Florence Nightingale, the famous nurse of the Crimean War, studying medicine and even qualifying as doctors. Others tried to enter the law courts. Meanwhile, women of the working- and lower-classes began to aspire to higher-status positions than laborers in factories or sweatshops. Some became secretaries in banks and commercial houses.

Also, the campaign for women's suffrage ignited during the Edwardian Age. In 1903 Mrs. Emmeline Pankhurst formed a new, more militant women's suffrage movement. Pankhurst's followers were far more insistent and aggressive than previous campaigners had been—holding vigorous public demonstrations, visiting the House of Commons and shouting the slogan "Votes for Women," while dropping leaflets onto the heads of startled members of Parliament, and, on a few occasions, even damaging public property in an attempt to make themselves heard. For their efforts, the suffragists were harassed, arrested, jailed, and subjected to brutal force-feeding if they staged hunger strikes in jail. The British public refused to take the suffragists seriously until one of them, Emily Wilding Davidson, threw herself in front of the king's horse on Derby Day, 1913. When her injuries proved fatal, the suffragist movement acquired its first martyr to the cause; the opposition was sufficiently "startled and roused" by Davidson's actions to wonder what harm could truly result from granting women the vote (Minney, p. 171). In 1918, women over the age of 30 at last gained the vote as well as the right to sit in Parliament;

ten years later, the vote was extended to all women aged 21 and older.

Sources and literary context. Shaw took the title of his play from the Greek legend of Pygmalion described above, in which a statue of a beautiful woman becomes the object of its creator's desire. Like his mythical counterpart, Shaw's Henry Higgins "creates" a woman out of unpromising material—in this case, the "squashed cabbage leaves of Covent Garden"

PYGMALION IN PRODUCTION

It was perhaps a minor miracle that the English production of *Pygmalion* managed to be staged at all. Shaw, Sir Herbert Beerbohm Tree, who played Higgins, and Mrs. Patrick Campbell, who played Eliza, were each accustomed to having his or her own way. Plays seldom had an official producer during the early twentieth century. Rather, theatrical companies and the productions as well were usually run by the chief actor in the troupe, who was often called the Actor-Manager. Shaw, however, had very specific ideas of how he wanted *Pygmalion* to be performed, so he himself served as the producer, overseeing rehearsals and demanding that the actors perform their roles according to his directions. Quarrels frequently erupted between the playwright and his two stars. Years later, Mrs. Patrick Campbell recalled the experience in a letter to Shaw: "At long last came the rehearsals—Oh my God! . . . I was 25 years too old for the part . . . you bullied me unmercifully. I was having infinite trouble with the accent, I wanted to get rhythm into it, and no comic adenoid effects—nothing to worry the audience—I have one letter of yours, written just before the first night, that would have made a weaker woman commit suicide" (Campbell in Shaw, p. xix). The male star, Tree, presented other difficulties, the most obvious being his desire to play Higgins as a romantic hero and imply that, despite Shaw's insistence to the contrary, Higgins and Eliza were united in the end. After *Pygmalion* opened in England and Shaw stopped attending performances, Tree essentially threw out the playwright's directions in favor of his own interpretation, which included a scene at the end in which Higgins threw flowers and blew kisses to a departing Eliza. Shaw, on hearing about this, was enraged. Tree defended his changes: "My ending makes money, you ought to be grateful," whereupon Shaw fired back, "Your ending makes nonsense, you ought to be shot" (Huggett, p. 162).

(*Pygmalion*, p. 92). In the myth, however, Pygmalion the sculptor marries the woman into which the statue turns, whereas the relationship between Higgins and Eliza remains undetermined at the end of the play. Shaw maintained to the end of his life that the two did not marry, although filmmakers and modern audiences have often disagreed with him.

While there was no one-to-one correspondence between real-life originals and the characters in *Pygmalion*, Shaw, as mentioned, based Henry Higgins in part on the revolutionary phonetician Henry Sweet, who died while the play was being written. The part of Eliza was created for Mrs. Patrick Campbell, a leading actress of Shaw's day with whom, for a time, he was in love.

As a play, *Pygmalion* combines elements of comedy, satire, farce, and biting social commentary. Shaw himself insisted that *Pygmalion* was a didactic work, intended to demonstrate how phonetics could break apart an antiquated and artificial class system. He, however, conceded that there were elements of "romance" in *Pygmalion*, though not in the sense that the hero and heroine were to be romantically involved:

> I call it a romance because it is the story of a poor girl who meets a gentleman at a church door and is transformed by him into a beautiful lady. That is what I call a romance. It is also what everybody else calls a romance, so for once we are all agreed. She does not marry anybody. I draw the line at that. She can marry whom she pleases when the curtain comes down, but I have something better for her to do when it is up.
>
> (Shaw in Huggett, p. 111)

Reception. To the considerable indignation of the British theatrical establishment, which criticized Shaw for disloyalty, *Pygmalion* actually premiered abroad, making its debut in Vienna on October 16, 1913. The play was a resounding success from the start, whetting English appetites for the London premiere, which took place 6 months later, on April 11, 1914. Despite a horrendous and stormy rehearsal process, the English production, like Vienna's, proved to be a triumph.

There were some complaints about the venue: the reviewer for the *Westminster Gazette* argued that His Majesty's Theatre was large for such an intimate play, but conceded that the play is full of good qualities. The reviewer singled out Alfred Doolittle—an audience favorite—for special praise, calling the character "one of the most entertaining in the whole Shaw theatre" (Evans, pp. 224-25). In the *Nation,* H. W. Massingham, agreed, and also showered praise on Tree and Mrs. Patrick Campbell: "Sir Herbert is a large, filling personality, he does well for the blustering Professor. . . . Mrs. Campbell's beauty is not the beauty of a London flower-girl; but she simulated it with great skill and humor" (Massingham in Evans, p. 229). Other critics praised Shaw's verbal brilliance. Alex M. Thompson, writing for the *Clarion,* observed in *Pygmalion* an "abundance of bold and startling wit, most of which probably no other author would have thought of, and much of which assuredly no other author would have dared to offer to any audience" (Thompson in Evans, p. 226). Finally, in the *New Statesman,* the prominent drama critic Desmond MacCarthy, called *Pygmalion* "an exhilarating, amusing, and often a deep comedy," adding

> Like all good comedies, it is full of criticism of life; in this case criticism of social barriers and distinctions, of the disinterested yet ferocious egotism of artists, of genteel standards, of the disadvantages of respectability, of the contrast between man's sense of values and women's, and of the complexity and misunderstanding which a difference of sex introduces into human relations, however passionately one of the two may resolve to sink the He and She.
>
> (MacCarthy, p. 108)

—Pamela S. Loy

For More Information

Asher, R. E., and Eugénie J. A. Henderson, eds. *Towards a History of Phonetics.* Edinburgh: Edinburgh University Press, 1981.

Crow, Duncan. *The Edwardian Woman.* New York: St. Martin's, 1978.

Evans, T. F., ed. *Shaw: The Critical Heritage.* London: Routledge & Kegan Paul, 1976.

Holroyd, Michael. *Bernard Shaw.* Vol. 2. New York: Random House, 1990.

Huggett, Richard. *The Truth about Pygmalion.* New York: Random House, 1969.

MacCarthy, Desmond. *Shaw's Plays in Review.* New York: Thames and Hudson, 1977.

Mayhew, Henry. *Mayhew's London.* London: The Pilot Press, 1949.

McCrum, Robert, William Cran, and Robert MacNeil. *The Story of English.* New York: Viking Penguin, 1986.

Minney, R. J. *The Edwardian Age.* Boston: Little, Brown, 1964.

Pearsall, Ronald. *Edwardian Life and Leisure.* Newton Abbot: David & Charles, 1973.

Priestley, J. B. *The Edwardians.* New York: Harper & Row, 1970.

Randall, Rona. *The Model Wife, Nineteenth-Century Style.* London: The Herbert Press, 1989.

Shaw, George Bernard. *Pygmalion.* Burnt Mill: Longman, 1983.

The Remains of
the Day

by

Kazuo Ishiguro

Born in Nagasaki, Japan, in 1954, Kazuo Ishiguro moved to England with his family in 1960. While the family lived in an upper-middle-class London suburb and Ishiguro attended English schools, he spoke Japanese at home, where his parents maintained his familiarity with Japanese culture. Ishiguro received a bachelor's degree in philosophy and literature from the University of Kent in 1978, and a master's degree in creative writing from the University of East Anglia in 1980. He published several short stories in an anthology of work by new writers while working on his master's degree, and shortly thereafter he sold his first novel, *A Pale View of Hills* (1982). The following year, *A Pale View of Hills* won the Winifred Holtby Award from the Royal Society of Literature. Ishiguro's second novel, *An Artist of the Floating World* (1986) won the Whitbread Book of the Year Award in 1986. Both novels examine cultural tensions between Japan and the West: *A Pale View of Hills* follows the story of Etsuko, a Japanese woman who marries an Englishman and immigrates to Britain, while *An Artist of the Floating World* is set in a small Japanese town in the aftermath of Japan's defeat in World War II. Ishiguro's third novel, *The Remains of the Day* (1989), abandons Japanese themes to focus more closely on English life. An international bestseller, it won the coveted Booker Prize in 1989, consolidating Ishiguro's critical reputation as one of Britain's most promising young authors.

THE LITERARY WORK

A novel set in England over six days in July 1956; published in London in 1989.

SYNOPSIS

During an automobile journey in the summer of 1956, Stevens, an aging English butler, meditates on his past and confronts the reality of his former employer's pro-Nazi sympathies in the years leading up to World War II.

Events in History at the Time
the Novel Takes Place

Britain and Germany between two world wars. In World War I (1914-18), Britain and France, along with their allies, triumphed over the so-called Central Powers, led by Germany and her neighbor, the Austro-Hungarian Empire. Some 10 million soldiers died during a war that deeply shocked both combatants and noncombatants alike because of its brutality and scope. Virtually an entire generation of young European men was wiped out by the carnage. Europe, it was thought, had fought, "the war to end all wars." Yet the scale and horror of World War I were dwarfed by World War II (1939-45), in which approximately 50 million people died around the world. More civilians than soldiers

Kazuo Ishiguro

were killed, including some six million Jews targeted for genocide by the German Nazi government, and over 100,000 Japanese incinerated by the two American atomic bombs dropped at Hiroshima and Nagasaki (many more were maimed or poisoned by the blasts). *The Remains of the Day* is set in 1956, about a decade after the end of World War II, but much of the story relates to the fragile peace of the 1920s and 1930s, the period between the World Wars.

Historians have largely attributed the outbreak of the second war to the punitive peace terms imposed on Germany at the end of the first. The terms of the peace had been agreed upon during the Paris Peace Conference, which took place in 1919, after the German surrender that ended World War I. Germany and the other defeated Central Powers were not represented at the conference, which was attended only by the victors, including Britain, France, Italy, and the United States (which had entered the war in 1917). Under the resulting Treaty of Versailles (1919), Germany was forced to give up territory, to disarm, to admit guilt for the war, and to pay heavy reparations (cash payments meant to defray the costs of the war) to the victors. These conditions meant that the German government

in the 1920s—a fragile democracy known as the Weimar Republic—labored under a double burden of national humiliation and crippling financial obligations.

In the novel's early chapters, Stevens, the narrator and the aging butler at the magnificent English country estate of Darlington Hall, remembers supervising the accommodations for a high-level diplomatic meeting there in 1923. His employer, then the English aristocrat and politician Lord Darlington, was working on Germany's behalf to help soften the treaty's harsh terms. The fictional French representative, Dupont, rejects any softening of the Allied terms, an element of the novel that reflects historical reality, for of all the allies, France's attitude toward Germany was the most hostile. In the Paris negotiations and in the diplomatic maneuvering that followed, Britain and the United States often played the role of mediator between these bitter enemies. As for the verisimilitude of the event, the fictional meeting in the novel is not based on any single real-life conference. But such meetings did in fact occur in the early 1920s when the allies discussed the question of how strictly the treaty should be enforced.

In 1923, the same year as the novel's diplomatic conference at Darlington Hall, a small right-wing political group, the National Socialist German Workers, or Nazi Party, attempted to overthrow the Weimar government in an abortive coup known as the Beer Hall Putsch. Founded two years earlier, the Nazi party was led by Adolf Hitler, an embittered former corporal in the German army who, like many Germans, deeply resented the peace terms that Germany had been forced to accept. After the failed coup, Hitler was sentenced briefly to prison, where he wrote a book, *Mein Kampf,* or "My Battle," blaming Communists and Jews, among others, for what he characterized as the betrayal of Germany at the end of the war. Rabidly nationalistic and anti-Semitic, the book proposed that Germans comprised a superior race threatened by the admixture of alien, inferior blood from groups such as Jews and Slavs.

While Hitler and the Nazi Party won few followers in the 1920s, when the Weimar government managed to stabilize the German economy, severe economic hardship during the Great Depression of the 1930s created a more receptive audience for Hitler's ideas. From 1929 to 1933, he built the Nazi Party into the largest party in the Reichstag, or German Parliament. In 1933 Hitler became Chancellor of Germany, and over the next three years he dismantled the Weimar democratic system and replaced it with a heavily policed Nazi dictatorship under his own direct personal control. Through state investment in industry and public works, Hitler reduced unemployment and restored German prosperity. At the same time he dramatically expanded the German army, using the threat of this revived military force to abrogate the Versailles Treaty, which he and other Germans still saw as a humiliation. By 1936 Hitler was preparing a campaign of conquest to provide Germany with the *Lebensraum* or "living space" that he publicly declared was needed for continued economic growth.

Hitler's rise did not occur in political isolation. Many of the ideas around which his Nazi state cohered had also found expression in countries other than Germany. In Italy, Benito Mussolini had seized dictatorial power in the 1920s on similar right-wing ideological principles, which he called *fascismo* (from the Latin *fasces*, bundles of rods symbolizing Roman authority). As democratic capitalism appeared to be collapsing in the unprecedented turmoil of the Great Depression, fascism seemed to some Europeans to be the only viable alternative to communist socialism, which had only recently become a potent ideological force when the Soviet communist government took power after the Russian revolution of 1917.

In Britain, fascism played on elitist, authoritarian sympathies and on preexisting anti-Semitism, holding a definite if limited appeal to a British minority that consisted largely (but not exclusively) of the upper class. During the 1930s, British anti-Semitism was most openly expressed by the British Union of Fascists, which was founded in 1932 by Sir Oswald Mosley, a baronet, and supported by other British aristocrats such as the newspaper tycoon Viscount Rothermere, and Mosley's wealthy father-in-law (after 1936), Baron Redesdale. In the middle of *The Remains of the Day*, Stevens, remembering events of the 1930s and alluding to later unfavorable press reports about Lord Darlington, attempts to discount "any talk linking his lordship" to the British Union of Fascists by saying that "Sir Oswald Mosley, the gentleman who led the 'blackshirts,' was a visitor at Darlington Hall on, I would say, three occasions at the most" (Ishiguro, *The Remains of the Day*, p. 137). The passage comes in the context of Stevens's affirmations that Lord Darlington was not an anti-Semite—"except, perhaps, in respect to one very minor episode in the thirties which has been

blown up out of all proportion" (*The Remains of the Day*, p. 137). That episode turns out to be Darlington's order that Stevens dismiss two maids employed in the household because they were Jewish.

Appeasement. Demoralized by the Great Depression, the major democratic powers—Britain, France, and the United States—each fell back on its own passive strategy for coping with an increasingly belligerent Nazi Germany in the late 1930s. While the United States declared neutrality, and France relied on a series of fortifications (called the Maginot Line) along its German border, British leaders followed a policy known as appeasement—that is, giving in while hoping for no further demands. From 1936 to 1939, under the premierships first of Stanley Baldwin

---

OSWALD MOSLEY AND BRITISH FASCISM

Despite Oswald Mosley's charismatic leadership, fascism in Britain never won the wide following—particularly among the working classes—that it did in countries such as Germany and Italy. Membership in Mosely's British Union of Fascists peaked in 1934, when the group filled the 13,000-seat Olympia Stadium in London with supporters for a party rally. Violence erupted between several thousand anti-fascist demonstrators and the B.U.F.'s blackshirted "stewards" (whose paramilitary-style uniforms were modeled on similar uniforms worn by German and Italian fascists). In the public outcry that followed, much of Mosley's upper-class following abandoned the B.U.F., as Stevenson implies that Darlington did in the novel.

(1935-37) and then of Neville Chamberlain (1937-40), Britain and the other democracies stood by as Hitler's newly rearmed Germany took over more and more territory. Although these moves directly contravened the Versailles Treaty, the democracies did nothing more than protest, relying on German assurances that each takeover was the last:

- **1936:** Germany reoccupies the Rhineland, an important industrial area ceded from Germany to France under the Versailles Treaty.
- **1938:** Hitler engineers German *Anschluss* (unification) with neighboring Austria, then annexes the Sudetenland, part of Czechoslovakia. German occupation of Czech lands is ratified by Britain and other powers at Munich Conference.

• **1939**: Germany occupies further Czech territory; appeasement ends, as Britain and France guarantee to defend Poland against Germany. Nazi-Soviet Non-Aggression Pact is signed; Germany and Soviet Union invade Poland and divide it between themselves. Under the treaty agreement to protect Poland, Britain and France declare war on Germany.

In pursuing appeasement, Chamberlain and other British leaders naively assumed that the Nazi diplomats were negotiating in good faith. The most effective Nazi diplomat was Joachim von Ribbentrop, ambassador to Britain from 1936 to 1938. Before assuming that post, Ribbentrop negotiated the Anglo-German Naval Agreement of 1935, which sanctioned German naval rearmament. During Ribbentrop's ambassadorship, which in large part coincided with appeasement, he assuaged British fears about Germany's territorial aggression in the Rhineland, Austria, and Czechoslovakia. After leaving the ambassadorship, he concluded German alliances with Japan and Italy, as well as temporarily neutralizing the Soviets with perhaps his boldest stroke, the Nazi-Soviet Non-Aggression Pact, which kept the Soviets out of the war until 1941, the year that Hitler ordered the invasion of the Soviet Union.

Once war broke out, Ribbentrop's importance to Hitler's plans diminished, but during his tenure as ambassador to Britain, Ribbentrop played a crucial role in lulling the British with false promises. Ishiguro's novel injects Ribbentrop and other actual historical figures—such as the British Foreign Secretaries Anthony Eden (1935-38; 1940-45) and Lord Halifax (1938-40)—into Stevens's memories of the story's fictional events. For example, Stevens recalls Ribbentrop's numerous visits to Darlington Hall as ambassador, rebuking those who later behaved "as though Lord Darlington was alone in believing Herr Ribbentrop an honourable gentleman and developing a working relationship with him" (*The Remains of the Day*, p. 136). Stevens recalls that Lord Halifax met there with Ribbentrop a number of times, doing so reluctantly and only after Darlington's insistence.

With the outbreak of war, Chamberlain and appeasement were thoroughly discredited, and a special wartime coalition government was formed under the leadership of Winston Churchill, the only British politician who had doggedly called for opposing the Nazis from the beginning. Indeed, Churchill had long publicly characterized Hitler as evil; in the end, his spirited and optimistic defiance of early German military gains would help lead Britain to ultimate victory in World War II.

Postwar Britain. Victory, however, came at a high cost. Britain's role as a world power—a status that had seemed secure at the beginning of the twentieth century—was now drastically eroded. Britain possessed neither the resources nor the will to retain her colonies, which fell away one by one as the peoples of the once mighty British Empire claimed their rights to political self-determination (examples include India in 1947 and Burma, now Myanmar, in 1948). Instead, the postwar world was dominated by the two states whose armed might and industrial capacity had defeated Germany and her allies, and that now stood alone as the world's two superpowers: the United States and the Soviet Union. In the novel, America's relative wealth after the war is reflected in the character of Mr. Farraday, the amiable American millionaire who has recently become Stevens's employer, having purchased Darlington Hall after Lord Darlington's death in 1953.

Economically exhausted, the British turned to socialism for many answers, as the Labour Party under Prime Minister Clement Atlee took over from Churchill's wartime coalition government after a landslide victory in 1945. Medicine, utilities, coal and steel production, telecommunications, and public transportation were among the many aspects of British life now owned and operated by the government. Labour governments held power throughout much of the postwar period, and the Labour-sponsored nationalization of important British industries remained in place into the 1980s. Near the end of the novel, Stevens discusses politics with a group of townspeople, including a doctor who approves of both the new National Health Service (Britain's socialized medicine program offering all British subjects free hospital, medical, and dental care) and the ongoing process of granting independence to the various parts of the empire.

The Novel in Focus

Plot summary. The novel takes place during a six-day automobile journey that Stevens, the butler at Darlington Hall, undergoes in July 1956, to ascertain whether a former fellow-employee, Miss Kenton, would be interested in returning to work at Darlington Hall again. Miss Kenton, who was housekeeper at Darlington Hall from 1922 to 1936, left to get married (though she is now

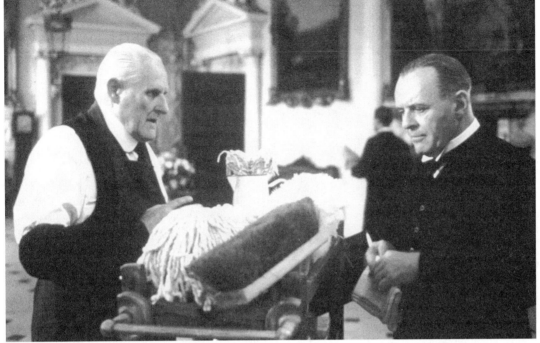

Peter Vaughan (left) as Stevens, Sr., and Anthony Hopkins as Stevens in the 1993 film version of *The
Remains of the Day.*

officially Mrs. Benn, Stevens most often refers to her as Miss Kenton). After Lord Darlington's death three years earlier, the estate was run by a "skeleton team" of six, until Darlington's family sold Darlington Hall to its new and often absent American owner, Mr. Farraday, who asked Stevens to further reduce the staff to four (*The Remains of the Day*, p. 6). Stevens has had difficulty accommodating the reduction, and when, in a recent letter of Miss Kenton's, he finds signs of a collapsing marriage, "an unmistakeable nostalgia for Darlington Hall, and—I am quite sure of this—distinct hints of her desire to return here," he tells himself that her proven efficiency would be a valuable asset to the estate's staff (*The Remains of the Day*, p. 9). Mr. Farraday, whose bantering conversational style makes Stevens uncomfortable, has suggested that Stevens take a short driving holiday, offering to pay for gas and to supply his own car, a comfortable Ford. Stevens decides that—for strictly professional reasons, he assures the reader—he will use the opportunity to approach Miss Kenton.

Stevens's slow four-day westward journey across southern England takes him from Darlington Hall in Berkshire (west of London) to the Cornwall village of Little Compton (in England's southwest corner), where he meets Miss Kenton.

At each stop Stevens recounts the day's travels, offers a few details about his accommodations, and engages in ruminations about the past. His story takes a narrative hiatus for two days following his meeting with Miss Kenton. The story resumes with Stevens's stopping on his return journey in the Dorset seaside resort of Weymouth, and here the novel ends. It thus takes place during a U-shaped, approximately 150-mile trip of six days.

The reader soon learns that Stevens is an unreliable narrator. His presentation of the story's events often reveals more about them than Stevens himself perceives—or more than he allows himself to perceive. On the first night of the trip, for example, Stevens stops at a guest house in the city of Salisbury, where, when he gives his address as "Darlington Hall," he sees the landlady "look at me with some trepidation, assuming no doubt that I was some gentleman used to such places as the Ritz or the Dorchester" (*The Remains of the Day*, p. 26). Rather than thinking him accustomed to great luxury hotels, however, the landlady has more likely associated Darlington Hall with the well publicized pro-Nazi sympathies of its former owner, Lord Darlington.

Such realizations come to the reader from scattered and unwitting hints that Stevens drops rather than from forthright revelations on his part. The overzealous denials of Darlington's fascist affinities and anti-Semitism (mentioned above) use dramatic irony to supply such hints, which make a case opposite to the one Stevens intends. Similar clues let the reader know that deeper motives underlie Stevens's desire to see Miss Kenton than the business reasons that he professes. These two parallel lines of revelation—one political, one personal, but both domestic—comprise the novel's twin focus, as the butler moves painfully towards openness with himself

BUTLERS AND BRITAIN'S GREAT HOUSES

While Stevens and Darlington Hall are fictional, the depiction in *The Remains of the Day* of the impeccable English butler and the magnificent household that he oversees reflects historical reality. In medieval times, the butler was in charge of the ale and wine that would be served to the house's aristocratic master (the word comes from the French *bouteillier*, "bottle-bearer"). Later, the position evolved into one of responsibility for managing the entire household. "Not the least qualification of the butler was that he should be a bachelor," writes E. S. Turner in a history of household service, using terms that recall Stevens's credo in the novel: "A butler who married was guilty of selfishness as well as vulgarity. His duty was to be dignified, and the sight of a butler with a nagging wife and children was . . . offensive and subversive to discipline" (Turner, p. 159). While Stevens perfectly chooses to observe this code of behavior, in real life he could have opted to marry and leave Lord Darlington's service. Many butlers married housekeepers with whom they worked, leaving domestic service and often setting up successful hotels. An example is London's stylish Claridge's hotel, established by just such a couple, a Mr. and Mrs. Claridge.

and with the reader about his former employer's true nature and about a personal relationship that he let slip away.

Ultimately, both revelations are prompted by the question that Stevens asks himself as he begins his trip: "what is a great butler?" (*The Remains of the Day*, p. 31). At first, Stevens (who remembers discussing the matter with other butlers during his service to Lord Darlington) believes that a butler's greatness rests on "dignity," which Stevens argues "has crucially to do with a

butler's ability not to abandon the professional being he inhabits" (*The Remains of the Day*, p. 42). Stevens tells several anecdotes to illustrate this point, including two about the early career of his father, also a butler. Later in his career, the elder and by then infirm Stevens came to Darlington Hall, appearing around the same time as Miss Kenton (1922), and entered a sort of semi-retirement, serving under the son. It is in this context that the reader is told about the diplomatic meeting at Darlington Hall in 1923 to discuss postwar German penalties. Stevens proudly recalls his ability to focus on his pressing duties during the conference; he steadfastly remained at his post even though his father lay dying upstairs at the time. Stevens excuses his behavior to the shocked Miss Kenton by saying that his father would have wanted it that way.

By the second day of his journey, however, Stevens has revised his conception of what makes a great butler. While refusing to retract his earlier ideas about "'dignity' and its crucial link with 'greatness,'" Stevens now suggests that in order to attain true greatness, a butler must concern himself "with the *moral* status of an employer" and must indeed serve an employer who was "furthering the progress of humanity" (*The Remains of the Day*, pp. 113, 114). Stevens clearly intends this assertion to back his own implicit (though strenuously denied) title to greatness as a butler, for he has already made precisely such a moral claim for Lord Darlington, in connection with Darlington's attempts to alleviate the harsh terms of the Versailles Treaty.

Stevens wonders why this moral dimension never occurred to him before during the many previous discussions of "greatness" he has had with other butlers. Perhaps, he concludes, it is because of the interruption in his journey that day when the Ford overheated owing to an empty radiator. Approaching a nearby house, Stevens found a man to identify and repair the trouble. The peaceful interlude, Stevens says, offered him an unusual opportunity for reflection. Yet to the reader it is clear that other factors may have prompted his train of thought. For example, when the man who is helping him learns where Stevens works and inquires if Stevens actually worked for Lord Darlington, Stevens denies it and disingenuously implies that he had recently been hired by the new owner, Mr. Farraday. Stevens recalls an earlier incident in which he had also denied working for Lord Darlington, then dismisses both "white lies" as merely "the simplest means of avoiding unpleasantness" stemming from "the nonsense" people repeat about his former employer (*The Remains of the Day*, p. 126).

On the third morning Stevens recalls the visits to Darlington Hall of Ribbentrop, Halifax, and others during the era of appeasement. Later that day he again has a mishap with the car, running out of gas near Tavistock in Devon. As he waits at a house nearby, where a kindly couple offers him a night's room until he can get more gas the next day, he muses on the charges of anti-Semitism aired against Lord Darlington. His denials to the reader of Darlington's anti-Semitism then lead him to recount his dismissal of the two Jewish maids on Darlington's orders, Miss Kenton's outrage at their dismissal, and her subsequent promise to quit. She does not do so, however, blaming herself for cowardice (she fears that she will fail to find another job if she quits). Relations between the two, once warm if formal, turn chilly, even though Stevens later tells her that privately he shared her sense of unfairness at the maids' dismissal. Soon afterward, in 1936, Miss Kenton leaves to get married.

As he spends that evening in the village where he ran out of gas, Stevens meets a group of local townspeople with whom he discusses politics. Though he impresses them by naming Eden, Halifax, and other famous statesmen he has met, once again he declines to identify himself as Lord Darlington's butler. He can no longer maintain his claims about Darlington's moral worth to the reader, acknowledging privately that "the passage of time has shown that Lord Darlington's efforts were misguided, even foolish," but denying that he himself has any reason to feel ashamed (*The Remains of the Day*, p. 201).

The next day, having arrived early at the village where he is to meet Miss Kenton, Stevens recalls the time she gave notice in 1936. Darlington was meeting that day with "the British Prime Minister, the Foreign Secretary and the German Ambassador" (*The Remains of the Day*, p. 221). A young reporter, a friend of the Darlington family, arrived too, remonstrating with Stevens that Darlington was trying to persuade the Prime Minister to visit Hitler and was even suggesting that the King himself might also do so. The reporter says frankly that Darlington is a pawn of Hitler's, and suggests that Stevens's passivity calls his own loyalty into question—both to his employer and to his country. Miss Kenton tries to gain Stevens's attention, but the "events of great importance" unfolding in the house prevent him from responding; he remembers his im-

pression, though, that she was crying at the time (*The Remains of the Day*, p. 226).

Stevens's narrative breaks off at this point, resuming two days later, during the evening of day six, as Stevens sits on a pier in the seaside town of Weymouth. He recounts his bittersweet meeting two days earlier with Miss Kenton, who says she has decided to stay with her husband but still thinks sometimes "about a life I may have had with you, Mr. Stevens" (*The Remains of the Day*, p. 239). Stevens, for his part, acknowledges to the reader "a certain degree of sorrow" in hearing her words: "Indeed—why should I not admit it—

BRITISH ANTI-SEMITISM

A recent historian has called anti-Semitism "the glue which held the ideas of British fascism together" in the period between 1934 and the outbreak of war in 1939 (Renton, p. 14). Yet British antipathy towards Jews differed from that commonly found on the European continent, which may help explain fascism's limited appeal in Britain. Historians have suggested that British anti-Semitism was generally passive in nature, rejecting active persecution while endorsing tacit discrimination. This peculiarly British attitude was captured by the writer Harold Nicolson in 1945, in a diary entry written just as the Allies were liberating Jews from Nazi concentration camps: "although I loathe anti-semitism I do dislike Jews" (Nicolson in Kushner, p. 156). Nicolson, an aristocrat, apparently made this statement without any intention of irony. The fictional Lord Darlington, who (according to Stevens) later declares that he was wrong to have dismissed two maids because of their Jewishness, may reflect similar sentiments.

at that moment, my heart was breaking" (*The Remains of the Day*, p. 239). They both agree that it is too late to turn back the clock, and part company with warm wishes for each other's future.

Now as he sits on the pier overlooking the sea and a crowd of sightseers, Stevens converses with a man who turns out to have worked as a butler himself. Stevens talks openly of his service to Lord Darlington, finally breaking down in tears: "All those years I served him, I trusted I was doing something worthwhile. I can't even say I made my own mistakes. Really—one has to ask oneself—what dignity is there in that?" (*The Remains of the Day*, p. 243). Stevens refers here to having suppressed his own judgment in favor of his master's, whose choices (mistakes) he blindly followed. The other man, who has retired, gently advises Stevens to take advantage of the time he has left, telling him that for many people the evening is the best part of the day. The man leaves, and while Stevens watches evening fall, he decides to follow the man's advice and "make the best of what remains of my day" (*The Remains of the Day*, p. 224). As the narrative closes, Stevens looks to the future and, given the chatty style of his new employer, resolves to practice bantering, the better to please Mr. Farraday.

Dignity, democracy, and self-delusion. When Stevens talks with the group of villagers near the end of the novel, they raise the question of what it is that makes a gentleman. Stevens, echoing his own earlier answer to the question of what makes a great butler, suggests dignity. In response, one villager—with the quintessentially common name of Harry Smith—declares, "Dignity isn't just something gentlemen have. Dignity's something every man and woman in this country can strive for and get" (*The Remains of the Day*, p. 185-86). Moreover, Smith explicitly connects dignity with democracy, not just as a social ideal but also as a political system: in England, he asserts, "no matter if you're rich or poor, you're born free and you're born so that you can express your opinion freely, and vote in your member of parliament or vote him out. That's what dignity's really about" (*The Remains of the Day*, p. 186). He further asserts that the English fought against Hitler as a free people, to preserve those rights and that freedom. If Hitler had won, he says, "we'd just be slaves now" and "there's no dignity to be had in being a slave" (*The Remains of the Day*, p. 186).

Stevens's discussion with the townspeople marks a crucial stage in his odyssey of self-discovery, for it is what brings Stevens, the following day, finally to acknowledge the moral dubiousness of Lord Darlington's misguided efforts. It also seems to prompt him to remember the young journalist's rebuke (which resembles Smith's remarks) of Stevens for refusing to question Darlington's activities. Stevens's conception of dignity, in which the perfect butler never abandons his subservience, is exactly opposed to Smith's proposition that "there's no dignity to be had in being a slave"—a thrust that breaches Stevens's wall of self-delusion. In blindly trusting the anti-democratic Lord Darlington to know best, in persistently refusing to voice his own opinions and feelings even to himself or to the

reader—much less to his employer or to a woman who seems to love him—Stevens ultimately realizes that he has in fact lost his dignity rather than enhanced it.

At the time, however, true to his earlier conception of dignity, Stevens declines to voice his disagreement with the townspeople. Privately, he approves of the more authoritarian views held in the 1930s by Lord Darlington, who once told him: "Look at Germany and Italy, Stevens. See what strong leadership can do if it's allowed to act. None of that universal suffrage stuff there" (*The Remains of the Day*, pp. 198-99). Stevens's own views changed, though. In moving to a new conception of dignity as being based on political self-expression, he also moves closer to the democratic views that prevailed in the mainstream of British society, and for which Britons such as Harry Smith fought against the Nazis.

Literary context. While the era of the world wars generated a great volume of English literature, few novels have examined British pro-German sympathies between the wars. As a recent historian writing on that subject points out, "the reason it has been neglected lies almost entirely in the picture we British like to present of our role in the war," a picture that is centered around the idea "of heroic resistance against the odds" (Weale, p. 2). Churchill, not Chamberlain, captures this remembered self-image, and defiance, not appeasement, characterizes the way many British would like to remember the 1930s.

Appropriately, therefore, Ishiguro's novel focuses the reader's attention on the ambiguity and unreliability of its narrative voice, that of Stevens, whose memory of events is often transparently self-serving. The literary technique of the unreliable narrator is essentially ironic—that is, it tells the reader something other than what the speaker ostensibly intends to say. It is a technique developed in earlier works such as the psychologically realistic novels of Joseph Conrad (1857-1924). The novel commonly viewed as best exemplifying the technique is Ford Madox Ford's *The Good Soldier* (1915), which like *The Remains of the Day* examines conflicts between rigid ideas of class, duty, and morality, and the shifting and often contradictory impulses of human emotions and sexuality. While in other works (for example, *A Pale View of Hills*) Ishiguro extends the narrator's unreliability to the reporting of actual events, *The Remains of the Day* follows such earlier novels in limiting the speaker's unreliability to his interpretations of the events.

Events in History at the Time the Novel Was Written

The Thatcher years. Britain in the 1980s underwent a period of reappraisal, in which the government, led by Conservative Prime Minister Margaret Thatcher, rolled back much of the system of state ownership put in place after World War II. Called privatization, this process involved the selling off of state-owned industries (such as telecommunications and other systems) into private ownership. By decade's end, much of the rest of the world, too, had begun shaking off the patterns into which it had settled after World War II. The Cold War, or competition between the United States and Soviet Union for world leadership, ended and the Soviet-dominated communist nations of Eastern Europe began moving towards democracy. In 1989, the year the novel was published, the Berlin Wall—symbol of the postwar settlement that divided Germany into separate democratic and communist regions—was dismantled, and Germany began the process of reunification. At the same time, in Britain as in the rest of Europe, there was a resurgence of fascist ideas among some young people that worried observers; of particular concerns were the racial and ethnic hostilities displayed by the loose neo-Nazi grouping known as skinheads. By the late 1980s in Britain, for example, hate crimes were rising sharply, as urban skinheads targeted black and Asian immigrants from former British colonies such as the West Indies, Pakistan, and India. The skinheads were represented by a political organization called the British Movement; other right-wing groups included the white supremacist British National Party (see **The Buddha of Suburbia**, also in *WLAIT 4: British and Irish Literature and Its Times*).

Reception. Nearly all critics praised *The Remains of the Day,* many of them singling out the stylistic subtlety and consistency with which Ishiguro captures Stevens's butlerish tone and severe emotional repression. Critics also lauded the author's ability to provoke an emotional response from the reader by the very dryness of the narrator's voice, and noted the way in which the novel interweaves historical events with Stevens's domestic and personal life. Writing in the *Times Literary Supplement,* for example, Galen Strawson called the work "as strong as it is delicate, a very finely nuanced and at times humourous study of repression" in which the author often conveys "a massive charge of pathos in a single unremarkable phrase" (Strawson, p. 535). Not everyone concurred. In a review for *The New Statesman,* Geoff Dyer wondered "if the whole idea of irony as a narrative strategy hasn't outlived its usefulness," although he conceded the novel's persuasiveness in implicating "a broader segment of the ruling class in the rise of fascism while emphasizing the complicity of a huge army of subordinates that led ultimately to the Holocaust" (Dyer, p. 34). But Dyer's response is atypical; more common assessments come from Lawrence Graves. In the *New York Times Book Review,* Graves praised Ishiguro's "dazzling" stylistic virtuosity; it is "remarkable," he adds, "that as we read along in this strikingly original novel, we continue to think not only about the old butler, but about his country, its politics and its culture" (Graves, p. 3).

—Colin Wells

For More Information

Dyer, Geoff. Review of *The Remains of the Day*, by Kazuo Ishiguro. *New Statesman* 2 (May 26, 1989): 34.

Graves, Lawrence. Review of *The Remains of the Day,* by Kazuo Ishiguro. *New York Times Book Review,* 8 October 1989, 3.

Ishiguro, Kazuo. *The Remains of the Day.* London: Faber & Faber, 1989.

Keegan, John. *The Second World War.* London: Penguin, 1989.

Kushner, Tony, and Kenneth Lunn, eds. *The Politics of Marginality: Race, the Radical Right and Minorities in Twentieth Century Britain.* London: Frank Cass, 1990.

Renton, Dave. *Fascism, Anti-Fascism and Britain in the 1940s.* New York: St. Martin's, 2000.

Strawson, Galen. Review of *The Remains of the Day,* by Kazuo Ishiguro. *Times Literary Supplement,* 19 May 1989, 535.

Turner, E. S. *What the Butler Saw.* London: Michael Joseph, 1962.

Weale, Adrian. *Renegades: Hitler's Englishmen.* London: Weidenfeld & Nicolson, 1994.

The Sea, The Sea

by

Iris Murdoch

Iris Murdoch (1919-99) was born in Dublin to Anglo-Irish parents, but the Murdoch family moved to London while Iris was still an infant, causing the author to regard herself thereafter as "a kind of exile, a displaced person" (Murdoch in Conradi, p. 10). After studying classics and philosophy at Oxford and Cambridge, Murdoch worked as a civil servant during World War II and its aftermath, assisting literally displaced persons in Belgium and Austria before returning to England to teach philosophy at Oxford University. While working in continental Europe, Murdoch encountered the philosophical movement known as existentialism, the main principle of which is "existence precedes essence," positing the absolute freedom of the individual to create meaning in a world of otherwise absurd meaninglessness. Murdoch took exception to existentialism's picture of the human being "as a brave naked will" independent of the surrounding world and instead called for a vision of the individual "against a background of values, of realities, which transcend him"; accordingly her novels present each character as "related to a rich and complicated world from which, as a moral being, he has much to learn" (Murdoch in Byatt, p. 8). Iris Murdoch published numerous philosophical articles and books in her lifetime, and also addressed such concerns in her poems, plays, and novels. *The Sea, The Sea*, for which she won the Booker Prize in 1978, reflects Murdoch's concern that art express the inherent messiness of reality—what she refers to in her philosophical works as "contingency"; it deals also with

THE LITERARY WORK

A novel set on the northern English coast and in London circa the 1970s; published in 1978.

SYNOPSIS

A famous theatrical director retires to a remote house on the English coast where he writes his memoirs and is confronted by his personal demons.

what has been identified as Murdoch's "central preoccupation"—the problem of ethical goodness, which in *The Sea, The Sea* is explored in relation to the tenets of Buddhism and the quest to escape egoism (Ramanathan, p. 2).

Events in History at the Time of the Novel

Changing mores. The novel is set in the 1970s, a time of tremendous social change in England. Observers sometimes characterize this decade as permissive, a conclusion that can be drawn from the range of personal situations in Murdoch's novel. Several characters are divorced, some are homosexual, and most engage in adulterous affairs with little or no sense of shame or social stigma. Non-traditional relationships are attempted, and women pursue careers and personal happiness outside the scope of marriage, motherhood, and family. Such things were to

Iris Murdoch

some extent acceptable when the novel was published in 1978 because of legal and social changes initiated in the 1960s.

A new sexual freedom for women was heralded by two developments in late 1960s Britain affecting women's reproductive control: the advent of the contraceptive pill and the passing of the Abortion Act. The pill was more reliable than other forms of contraception previously available, and unlike other forms was under the complete control of the woman, giving women for the first time the same kind of sexual freedom as men. It was not until the 1970s, however, that British doctors began to prescribe the pill to unmarried women. The 1967 Abortion Act legalized abortion, giving women even more control over their reproductive life. At the same time, the stigma against unmarried mothers began to lessen, so, although the illegitimacy rate rose in the 1960s and remained high through the 1970s, the number of babies put up for adoption declined.

Another development that transformed English society in the 1970s was the passing of the 1967 Sexual Offenses Act, which partially legalized male homosexual behavior. In a strange twist of the sexual double standard, lesbian sexual behavior had never been outlawed in the first place. In the wake of the new decriminalization of male homosexuality, the Gay Liberation Front

(GLF) formed in 1970 to promote openness in homosexuality, counteracting a long history of shame in which criminalized homosexuality had necessarily been hidden. As the decade progressed, a much greater openness was achieved, though prejudice persisted. The GLF related their own oppression to that of women, yet the membership of the GLF remained overwhelmingly male, and lesbians found it an unaccommodating environment for their own issues.

One factor that contributed to openness toward homosexuality, and sexuality in general, was the great change in censorship laws of the fifties and sixties. In 1959, the Obscene Publications Act reduced the censorship restrictions on published materials, and by the 1960s, cases of criminal obscenity in published works brought to trial before juries were being decided almost entirely in the publishers' favor. British juries simply refused to ban books. In 1968, the Theatres Act had a similar effect in the theatre world by taking away the Lord Chamberlain's powers of censorship over stage plays. Prior to the Theatres Act, before any play could be performed it had to gain the approval of the Lord Chamberlain, and he routinely banned plays that made any reference to homosexuality or showed an irreverent attitude towards religion, royalty, or "the family." The Theatres Act, the Obscene Publications Act, and the more tolerant attitudes of the public meanwhile resulted in less self-censorship by publishers, theatre directors, radio producers, and television networks, who no longer had to worry much about legal prosecution. In this way, the whole notion of what was indecent or offensive changed in Britain.

As the new openness in sexuality gained acceptance, a more relaxed and pragmatic attitude toward relationships also took hold. The Divorce Act, which passed in 1967 and took effect January 1, 1971, marked a significant change in attitudes toward marriage. Before the Divorce Act, divorce was only allowed if one marriage partner could be proven to have committed a "matrimonial offense," such as desertion, cruelty, or adultery, against the other. If the charge of matrimonial offense was challenged by the accused partner, the matter was decided by a judge through a process very much like a criminal trial with cross-examinations of witnesses. Two people who simply wished to end their marriage amicably could not circumvent this often ugly process; one had to be publicly labeled the guilty party and one the innocent in order for a divorce to be granted. Moreover, if one partner desired a divorce while the other did not, there was no way to force the issue as long as the spouse who wished to stay married could not be shown to have committed a matrimonial offense. The Divorce Act helped make divorce more accessible and more socially acceptable by allowing for "no-fault" divorce and divorce on the grounds of individual or mutual unhappiness.

Women's movement. One of the major forces of change in the 1970s was the Women's Liberation Movement, which held its first British national conference in 1970. Although the Movement soon faded as a national organization, unofficially it expanded as individuals and groups pursued feminist objectives and achieved several significant milestones:

1970 Equal Pay Act
Called for equal pay for men and women engaged in equivalent kinds of work

1975 Sex Discrimination Act
Allowed women and men to bring their employers before a special tribunal on counts of sexual discrimination

1976 Domestic Violence Act
Allowed women to seek the arrest of the husbands or boyfriends who beat them

Of course, the impact of these acts depended greatly on the extent of their enforcement. One of the women in *The Sea, The Sea* speaks of her husband's abuse to herself and her child, mentioning that a private group, the "prevention of cruelty people," had come to their home some years ago (Murdoch, *The Sea, The Sea*, p. 225). Before the Domestic Violence Act, the British legal system left the rescue of abused wives and girlfriends largely in the hands of private organizations. And even after the Domestic Violence Act, many police officers hesitated to enter into what was still frequently regarded as a private matter. Likewise, the Equal Pay Act did little to balance the wages for women's work and men's work because women's and men's jobs were so deeply segregated at this time. Three quarters of working women in 1971 held traditional women's jobs—for example, secretary, maid, nurse, hairdresser, waitress, primary school teacher—and these continued to pay less than men's jobs regardless of the Equal Pay Act.

Likewise the Sexual Discrimination Act did little; placing the onus of proof on the employee, it resulted in only a handful of actions against employers. The act failed as well in its mandate to eliminate differences in educational opportunity based on gender. As in the past, schools en-

Feminists march in London in 1971 for equal pay and expanded opportunities for women. The 1970s women's liberation movement helped foster a more permissive society than ever before in England.

couraged girls to take "light" courses such as home economics, boys to take career-oriented subjects like science and math. Even educational employment was segregated, with women filling the less prestigious, lower-paying jobs in primary and secondary education while men filled management and university-level positions. Iris Murdoch, in her university post, was an exception to this rule.

Yet despite the failure of these legal measures, they both reflected and helped foster a fundamental change in mores. Britain in the 1970s had become a very different, more "permissive" society than ever before.

The London theatrical world. After the novel's Charles Arrowby finishes his secondary education, he decides to attend acting school in London. His parents are not pleased. For a long time, acting was a profession held in disrepute in Britain. The public often assumed that pursuit of the acting profession entailed a life of sexual promiscuity, and that the portrayal of characters with low moral standards must redound to the dishonor of the actor.

In the latter half of the nineteenth century, people gradually began to think of acting as a reputable profession. The payment of playwrights came to be based on royalties rather than flat fees and hence potentially more lucrative; thus, the profession started attracting members of the middle and upper classes, who wrote plays set in the social milieu with which they were most familiar. The 1860s saw more realistic dramas beginning to be performed on the London stage, characters in the plays of Oscar Wilde and others became more reputable, and so did the actors portraying them (see **The Importance of Being Earnest**, also in *WLAIT 4: British and Irish Literature and Its Times*). Also amateur acting gained popularity at the country homes of the upper classes, and at the universities of Oxford and Cambridge.

In the early 1900s, the first acting schools opened in London, just as members of the middle and upper classes began to view an acting career as a viable occupation for them. From the turn of the century until the end of World War II, actors originated overwhelmingly from the middle and upper classes, and their status certainly did not suffer from the association with the profession. On the contrary, they pursued glamorous, high-status lifestyles, mixing with royalty and aristocracy in London's fashionable clubs and restaurants. It is during this period that Charles Arrowby moves to London to pursue his acting career, and it is probably with this image of the high-status actor in mind that the husband of Charles's first love, who, unlike Charles, has not risen above the class into which he was born, rejects a social invitation from Charles, explaining that "We aren't your sort" (*The Sea, The Sea*, p. 151).

In the 1930s, theaters began to receive competition from films and, in the 1950s, from television. The new mediums took away much of the theatrical audience for light entertainment, and theaters responded by concentrating more and more on serious artistic works. Plays began to portray working-class heroes and heroines, and correspondingly, actors began to be drawn from the working classes. The era of the glamorous high-status stage-actor was over.

In the novel, several of Charles Arrowby's ex-lovers are actresses. From the seventeenth through the nineteenth century actresses were typically regarded on the same social level as prostitutes. Gradually the status of female actresses improved, but the twentieth century saw continuing inequities. There were generally more than twice as many roles available to men as to women in British theater, and men occupied most of the high-status behind-the-scenes positions as directors, playwrights, and the like. This began to change in the 1970s, as small, fringe touring companies, including women's theatre groups set out to raise political consciousness by bringing works by female playwrights to the public.

Britain, Buddhism, and Tibet. In *The Sea, The Sea,* the character James Arrowby is "sent on a secret mission into Tibet to investigate Soviet activity there" following World War II (*The Sea, The Sea*, p. 64). His involvement in Tibet leads him to adopt the practices of Tibetan Buddhism, the tenets of which held interest for the novel's author Iris Murdoch.

Tibet, the once independent country that became a part of the People's Republic of China in the 1950s, is situated between India and Nepal to the southwest, and China to the north and east. Buddhism began in approximately 528 B.C.E. with a young Indian nobleman known as Siddharta Gautama. Siddharta taught a spiritual practice that he called "The Middle Way," a path between the two extremes of self-mortification and self-indulgence. Siddharta, called the Buddha, taught that ordinary human existence entails a great deal of misunderstanding one must overcome in order to achieve nirvana, a state of bliss and freedom from misery. The Buddha's teachings, Buddhism, soon became an established dogma, with his students arguing over fine points and eventually forming different schools of Buddhism. The earliest forms of Buddhism are collectively known as Hinayana Buddhism, and focus on renunciation of the world and pursuit of personal enlightenment in monasteries. Around the time of Christ, a new form of Buddhism, Mahayana Buddhism, was developed. Mahayana Buddhism stresses the importance of living in the world, maintaining social connections and furthering the spiritual evolution of all sentient beings, rather than merely concentrating on one's own enlightenment. Hinayana Buddhism spread from India to Ceylon and Burma, while Mahayana Buddhism spread to Japan, China, and Tibet. Tibet quickly became a major center of Buddhist scholarship, and Buddhism came to permeate every aspect of Tibetan society. Approximately one third of the male population in Tibet were Buddhist monks, and Tibet was ruled by a Buddhist spiritual leader, the Dalai Lama.

In 1720, the Chinese Empire helped Tibet oust Mongol invaders, and in return Tibet became a part of the Chinese Empire, retaining a separate, but subject, government. At the end of the nineteenth century, under the now not-so-strong Chinese thumb, Tibet became the focus of a rivalry between the three great imperial powers Britain, Russia, and China. In the wake of the weakening Chinese empire, Britain tried to beat Russia to Tibet and sent a diplomatic and military delegation there in 1903 demanding a conference with the Tibetans and Chinese. Both refused British demands, and the Tibetan army attacked the British troops. As violence mounted, the Dalai Lama fled the capital, and the British representative rounded up a few minor government figures and convinced them to sign a treaty with Britain on Tibet's behalf, making Tibet a British protectorate. A few years later, realizing that Russia hadn't the slightest foothold in Tibet, Britain acceded to Chinese demands to acknowledge that Tibet was a part of the Chinese Empire. This state of affairs changed yet again in 1914 when, in a moment of Chinese weakness, Britain convinced Tibetan leadership to sign a new treaty granting the British Empire a chunk of Tibetan territory and switching suzerainty from China to Britain. Tibet became a British protectorate, but its status was far from clear. From World War I to beyond World War II, Britain wavered between regarding Tibet as a British protectorate and as a part of China. The British showed little interest in maintaining their hold on Tibet after World War II, when they began dismantling their empire. In 1947 India achieved independence from Britain, and Britain ceded her rights in Tibet to India.

The 1949 communist victory in China inspired Tibet to step up efforts it had already begun to be recognized as an independent nation. Despite U.S. pleas for British intervention, Britain, who did not share the United States's absolute horror of communism, maintained its distance. India did not wish to risk entering a conflict with China and likewise maintained a hands-off policy. In 1950, Tibet turned to the United Nations for help, but none of the powers proved ready to risk conflict by supporting tiny Tibet. Chinese troops proceeded to establish a garrison in Tibet's capital, Lhasa, claiming the country as a part of the People's Republic of China. Interested in converting Tibet to a modern Marxist state, the Chinese tried to root out the Buddhism that formed the basis of Tibetan culture. In 1959, after almost a decade of Chinese occupation, Tibetans staged an armed revolt to drive out the Chinese, but it failed. Fear-

ing reprisal, the Dalai Lama and several of his advisors fled across the Indian border, with thousands of ordinary Tibetans following the leader into exile. Some of these exiles brought Tibetan Buddhism to the West.

Meanwhile, in Tibet in 1965 China's Red Guards embarked on the Great Proletarian Cultural Revolution. Inspired by the writings of Chinese leader Mao Zedong, they banned traditional Tibetan ways and attempted to destroy all Buddhist temples and artifacts. The next decade saw a softening in Chinese policy toward Tibet to the point that China even began negotiations with the Dalai Lama. In 1976, after Mao Zedong died, China admitted that it had been brutal in its treatment of Tibet but remained in control of the country, a dominance that would endure throughout the twentieth century.

The Novel in Focus

Plot summary. Charles Arrowby, famous actor, playwright, and director, decides to retire from the London theater world. "I just knew," explains Arrowby, "that if I stayed in it any longer I would begin to wilt spiritually" (*The Sea, The Sea*, p. 4). Arrowby is "over sixty years of age," comfortable but not rich, and single (*The Sea, The Sea*, p. 3). He has bought a house ("Shruff End") on a remote part of the English coast, where he wishes to "abjure magic and become a hermit," searching for that "something" which he has not yet lost, and to this end writing his memoirs (*The Sea, The Sea*, p. 2). Shruff End is an odd, dilapidated dwelling built near the turn of the century and lacking electricity or gas. Perched on a rocky cliff, it commands an impressive view of the sea, the changing face of which is described in detail at intervals of the novel. The house lies a short distance from Narrowdean, the quaint erstwhile fishing village where Arrowby buys supplies.

The novel is in Arrowby's voice. It is his "memoir," which also serves as a diary of daily events at Shruff End. The autobiographical sections interspersed throughout the novel reveal the following: Charles Arrowby grew up in the Forest of Arden near Stratford-Upon-Avon, the birthplace of Shakespeare in the English midlands. His father, Adam Arrowby, was a clerk, and the family lived modestly, outshone in every respect by the family of Adam's brother Abel Arrowby, a successful businessman who married an American "heiress." Abel Arrowby's son James, Charles's cousin, thus enjoyed a more privileged upbringing with ponies, better education, and travel, for which Charles envied him terribly. Throughout his life, Charles has felt condescended to and threatened by James, who "shone" and left Charles feeling like "a provincial barbarian" (*The Sea, The Sea*, p. 62-63). Only when James decided, after serving in World War II, to make a career for himself in the armed forces, a move judged by all to have been "a wrong turning," did Charles begin to feel that he would beat James in their lifelong rivalry (*The Sea, The Sea*, p. 64). At the time of the novel, both Charles's and James's parents are dead, but the cousins maintain infrequent communication, mostly on the initiative of James, who has become a Buddhist while serving in the armed forces in Tibet, but is now back in London where he works in the Ministry of Defence and appears to be "a disappointed man" (*The Sea, The Sea*, p. 57). Although Charles regards his relationship with James primarily as a competition, James seems to feel a deep love for Charles.

The other major figure in Charles Arrowby's childhood was a girl named Mary Hartley Smith (known to Charles as "Hartley"), whom he considers his first and only love. The two were friends since early childhood and fell for each other at the age of 12. "Ours was a solemn holy happiness," Charles recalls, "that was love of a purity which can never come again and which I am sure rarely exists in the world at all" (*The Sea, The Sea*, pp. 79-80). Charles and Hartley agreed that they would marry at age 18. In the meantime, Charles decided not to go to university as his parents expected, but to attend a London acting school instead. From London, Charles wrote Hartley daily and visited her each weekend, but when the time came, Hartley changed her mind about marrying Charles. She gave no clear reason for the break-up, saying only, "I can't go on with it, I just can't" (*The Sea, The Sea*, p. 82). Afterwards, Hartley disappeared, and though Charles searched England for her, he could not find her. He finally learned from a mutual acquaintance that she had married someone else.

In the wake of Hartley, Charles decided he could never truly love again, and focused on his career. He first achieved success as an actor on the London stage then derived more satisfaction from writing and directing his own plays. Charles became quite famous at this. Only later, however, when he became a Shakespearean director did he find his true calling, and it is this aspect of his career for which he is chiefly celebrated at the time of the novel. Despite his self-professed

inability to love, Charles had a series of mistresses, all actresses, but in each case Charles remained emotionally detached and ultimately broke off the relationship. First, when Charles was twenty, there was Clement Makin, a glamorous actress twice Charles's age. Theirs was a relationship that evolved into different configurations until Charles finally became Clement's caretaker as she died of cancer some time before the novel begins. While Clement was still alive, Charles began a romance with another actress, Rosina Vamburgh, the wife of Charles's actor friend Peregrine Arbelow. After convincing Rosina to divorce her husband, Charles tired of the constant fights of which tempestuous Rosina was so fond, and broke off the relationship, for which Rosina never forgave him. Next there was Lizzie Scherer, another actress, who fell in love with Charles as he directed her in a series of Shakespearean plays. Although Charles broke off that relationship as well, Lizzie remains devoted to Charles, despite a sort of platonic marriage she maintains with a gay actor friend, Gilbert Opian. At the time Charles comes to Shruff End, he is romantically unattached and ready to pursue hermithood—or so he believes.

Soon after his arrival at Shruff End, and immediately after Charles begins to write his memoirs, he has an experience "so extraordinary and so horrible" that he is shaken to his depths (*The Sea, The Sea*, p. 1). While gazing out over the sea, Charles sees a giant sea-monster coiling up out of the water. Charles attempts to explain the perception as an LSD flashback from the days he took the drug, but he is unnerved by it for the rest of the novel. Then, disconcerting things begin to happen inside the house. An antique vase and mirror are smashed, seemingly of their own accord, and Charles begins to see faces looking at him through windows. Eventually Charles discovers that he is being "haunted" by his second mistress Rosina Vamburgh, who, in her hatred for Charles and out of jealousy of Lizzie, with whom she believes Charles to be still having an affair, has been entering Shruff End while Charles is not there, breaking things. Charles assures her that there is nothing between himself and Lizzie, and Rosina leaves, after which life returns to normal.

Normality does not last long, however, for one day in the village of Narrowdean Charles sees a "funny old woman" who bears a striking resemblance to his first love, Hartley (*The Sea, The Sea*, p. 145). Then he realizes that it *is* Hartley, and he has found his one true love again at last. He approaches her, and she recognizes him, but Hartley, now a stout, ill-kempt, elderly-looking woman, only seems embarrassed and confused at the meeting with her famous first love, as if she would rather have never seen Charles again. Enraptured, Charles tells Hartley, "You are my love," and learns, to his disappointment, that she is still married (*The Sea, The Sea*, p. 116). Although Hartley vaguely agrees to contact him in the future, Charles becomes impatient, and begins to visit her and her husband, Benjamin, uninvited, at their cottage in the village. Through a combination of Hartley's testimony and his own observation, Charles soon discovers that Benjamin is an insanely jealous, abusive husband, and the principle object of Benjamin's jealousy over the years has been Charles himself. The couple has an adopted son, Titus, and Benjamin believes that Titus is actually the son of Charles and Hartley, refusing to see the absurdity of this suspicion or his unfounded belief that Charles and Hartley have kept up an affair throughout the years of their marriage. Both Titus and Hartley suffered abuse because of Benjamin's twisted beliefs, and Titus ultimately ran away from home; his parents haven't seen him for years. Charles's appearance in the village only confirms Benjamin's suspicions.

Charles still loves Hartley intensely and wants to save her from the "hateful tyrant" Benjamin, but Hartley shows no inclination to be saved. Then one morning, Titus appears at Shruff End, asking Charles if he is his father. Charles tells Titus the truth, that he is not his son but that he wishes him to be his son, and Hartley to be his wife. Titus, an attractive, intelligent young man who wants to become an actor, decides to stay with Charles and help him win back Hartley, and Charles secretly invites Hartley to Shruff End to see her son. While Hartley and Titus talk in private, Charles sends a letter to Benjamin, telling him that Hartley is with him and Titus and that she wishes to stay. When Hartley learns what Charles has done, she becomes hysterical, and, fearing that she will hurl herself into the sea, Charles locks her in a room, hoping she will come to her senses and realize that she should leave Benjamin.

Soon thereafter Charles receives a flood of visitors, including cousin James and Peregrine Arbelow, from whom he attempts to conceal Hartley's presence. Despite Charles's efforts, however, the guests soon learn of Hartley's captivity and eventually convince Charles to allow her to return to her husband as she wishes. After driving Hartley home, Charles goes for a walk on the rocks and is suddenly shoved by unseen hands into "Minn's cauldron," a churning pool of water surrounded by sheer rock walls from which there is seemingly no escape. Charles is, however, somehow rescued, and the next thing he knows he is being resuscitated on the rocks by his cousin James. Charles assumes it was Benjamin who pushed him in as reprisal for abducting Hartley, but finds out eventually that it was Peregrine, who, despite professing friendship for all these years, actually hates Charles for stealing Rosina from him.

Shortly afterwards, Titus drowns in the ocean, and Charles feels responsible for not warning him about the dangers of swimming off the rocks of Shruff End. Charles is devastated by the death, but when he visits Hartley and Benjamin a short time afterwards at their invitation, the couple seem somehow relieved by the death of their adopted son. In fact, the couple appear to be quite happy and loving, and announce their plans to move to Australia.

James comes to visit Charles once more at Shruff End, and for the first time the cousins discuss James's experiences in Tibet and his Buddhism. James reveals that he has the ability to perform certain "tricks," like consciously controlling his body temperature. After James's visit, Charles remembers details about his brush with death in the sea. He recalls that in the sea with him was the sea monster he had seen when he first moved to Shruff End, and he recalls that it was James who rescued him. James had apparently used one of his "tricks," for Charles remembers him scaling down the sheer rock face of Minn's Cauldron on hands and knees "like a lizard," and pulling him to safety (*The Sea, The Sea*, p. 468). After remembering this, Charles tries to get in touch with James, but learns that his cousin has just died, apparently consciously willing himself to death. James has left his fortune to Charles, who moves out of Shruff End and into James's London flat, filled with Buddha statues.

In the end, Charles comes to various realizations that have been developing over the course of his stay at Shruff End. Charles regrets that his rivalry with James prevented him from ever truly knowing his cousin. He realizes that he has used his love for Hartley as an excuse to avoid the potential pain of emotional attachment, and that the most important relationship in his life was with Clement Makin. He finally comes to see other people as fully realized human beings in their own right rather than as mere characters in his own life drama. Charles has lost the possibility of Rosina's love, as she and Peregrine have reconciled and remarried. He has lost Lizzie, who is finally truly happy in her life with Gilbert. And he has lost Hartley again, only this time there is no mystery about her motives, and he must accept that she simply does not want him. At the close of the novel Charles contemplates mortality as he experiences mysterious chest pains, and he gradually settles back into life in London, a somewhat wiser man.

Monsters of the deep. "Out of a perfectly calm empty sea, at a distance of perhaps a quarter of a mile (or less), I saw an immense creature break the surface and arch itself upward. At first it looked like a black snake, then a long thickening body with a ridgy spiny back followed the elongated neck. There was something which might have been a flipper or perhaps a fin. I could not see the whole of the creature, but the remainder of its body, or perhaps a long tail, disturbed the foaming water round the base of what had now risen from the sea to a height of (as it seemed) twenty or thirty feet" (*The Sea, The Sea,* p. 19).

Since ancient times, people around the world have reported seeing unusually large and monstrous creatures rising from bodies of water. The twentieth century brought what is perhaps the best-known sea monster to public attention, Scotland's Loch Ness Monster. No scientific "proof" has ever been found for the existence of sea monsters, and sightings of such creatures are usually explained as tricks of the eye, basking sharks, or (in the case of sailors) the result of excessive drinking. Sea monsters, then, are frightening creatures of doubtful reality, akin to the apparitions encountered in the post-death experiences Buddhists call the *bardos.*

Buddhism, along with other non-Western spiritual practices, became popular in Britain in the 1960s and 1970s as young people in particular began to question the traditions of their parents and seek an approach to spirituality more based on personal experience than institutional doctrine. Buddhism is not a religion. The subject of whether or not there is a god does not come up in Buddhist teachings, except when such speculations are discouraged as a waste of time in pursuit of what is ultimately unknowable. The most basic tenet of Buddhism is that there are buddhas. The word *buddha* comes from the Sanskrit root *budh,* meaning "to wake up" or "to know," hence, buddhas are individuals who have

become aware of something about which most people are "asleep." The most basic principle that a buddha realizes is *anatman,* the principle that there is no such thing as a soul, or self, as it is usually understood. Instead, there are processes, events. Put differently, *anatman* is the knowledge that "what we call 'I,' or 'being,' is only a combination of physical and mental aggregates, which are working together interdependently in a flux of momentary change within the law of cause and effect, and that there is nothing permanent, everlasting, unchanging and eternal in the whole of existence" (Rahula, p. 66). The practice of Buddhism involves careful examination of one's own consciousness, and a complete reexamination of what one has taken for granted about one's relationship to the external world and to other people. Such an examination, it is hoped, will ultimately free one from the *samsaric,* or ego-centered, state of mind that attaches one to the world. When Charles contemplates his reasons for seeking "recollection in tranquility" at Shruff End, he suggests that it might be "To repent a life of egoism? Not exactly, yet something of the sort" (*The Sea, The Sea,* p. 1).

Strictly speaking, since there is no self, according to Buddhism, there is no afterlife *per se,* and yet Buddhists believe that some part of individual consciousness does survive and undergo frightening experiences, known as *bardos,* after death. The bardos must be handled correctly for the consciousness to escape the cycle of suffering through rebirth; the *Tibetan Book of the Dead* is a sort of bardo instruction manual. According to this Buddhist text, in the first bardo one perceives a great light that is the purest essence of one's psyche. One should recognize this light as the source of one's own consciousness and merge with it, but most people are unable to do this, and thus pass to the next bardo, wherein one encounters apparitions that are actually manifestations of one's own consciousness. At first, the apparitions are peaceful deity figures, but as time goes on, they become more and more frightful. The thing to do is "own" the apparitions, for it is only by recognizing them as aspects of oneself that one may become free of the karmic wheel of reincarnation. In the novel, James explains the apparitions of the bardos to Charles as the "attendant demons" that "very few people are without" (*The Sea, The Sea,* p. 385). Indeed, the novel seems to be very much about the gods and monsters that populate the psyche, and the necessity for individuals to get rid of them in order to see the truth.

In the novel, Charles's sea serpent is a monster with green eyes who represents the primary green-eyed monster in Charles's life, the monster of jealousy. Jealousy is the primary motivation behind most of the plot. Charles's jealousy for his cousin James is the defining emotion of his childhood. It creates the tension in their relationship that prevents Charles from ever truly knowing his cousin, and Charles cites this jealousy of James as the motivation that drove Charles himself to become a success in the London theatre world. It is the jealousy of Hartley's Ben that makes him a monstrous husband. Jealousy of Charles's relationship with Lizzie drives Rosina to "haunt" Charles, and jealousy of Charles's relationship with Rosina drives her husband to push Charles into Minn's Cauldron. Appropriately, the French proverb, "Jealousy is born with love, but does not always die with it," is invoked repeatedly in the novel.

The sea serpent is explicitly connected with jealousy in the novel. When Charles looks at Rosina as she explains her intense jealousy of Lizzie, he sees momentarily "a snake-like head and teeth and pink opening mouth of my sea monster" in the place where Rosina's face ought to be (*The Sea, The Sea*, p. 105). As a Buddhist, Charles's brother James represents freedom from the destruction wrought by emotions such as jealousy (represented by the sea monster). Later, on a trip to London's Tate Gallery, Charles is reminded of his serpent when he sees Titian's painting of Perseus and Andromeda, depicting the Greek legend wherein Perseus slays the sea monster before it can devour Andromeda. The painting reflects what Charles believes he is doing in rescuing Hartley from Ben, made monstrous through jealousy; it also reflects what comes to pass later in the novel when James saves Charles from the monster in Minn's Cauldron after Charles is pushed in by a very jealous Peregrine. James represents salvation from the monster of jealousy that torments Charles until the novel's end, when Charles finally comes to realize, "I let loose my own demons, not least the sea serpent of jealousy" (*The Sea, The Sea*, p. 492). By the novel's end, then, he better understands himself, achieving an objective that many in his generation pursue.

Sources and literary context. When Iris Murdoch began writing novels in the early 1950s, a reaction was afoot in Britain against the literary modernism of writers such as Virginia Woolf (see *Mrs. Dalloway*, also in *WLAIT 4: British and Irish Literature and Its Times*). Modernism, argued its critics, attended to form and device at the expense of "truth." Writers of this period, such as Kingsley Amis, John Wain, and C. P. Snow, attempted to return to the social realism of the eighteenth- and nineteenth-century English novel, an attempt in which they were ultimately deemed to be not very successful. Murdoch was initially classed with these writers as one of the "Angry Young Men," or a related group known as the Movement, although her writing betrayed little interest in the social protest for which the Angry Young Men were known. Iris Murdoch herself claimed to be a realist in the tradition of George Eliot and Jane Austen (see *Middlemarch* and *Sense and Sensibility*, both in *WLAIT 3: British and Irish Literature and Its Times*). But Murdoch's elaborate (and, as some see them, contrived) plots have caused critics to question the validity of this claim. A more just comparison may perhaps be made between Murdoch's densely complex fiction and that of nineteenth-

> **"THE GRAVEYARD BY THE SEA"**
>
> The title of Iris Murdoch's novel, *The Sea, The Sea*, is taken from a poem entitled "The Graveyard by the Sea" by French poet Paul Valéry: "The Sea, The Sea perpetually renewed! / Ah what a recompense, after a thought, / A prolonged gazing on the calm of gods!"
>
> (Valéry, p. 213)

century Russian novelists—especially Feodor Mikhailovich Dostoyevsky, whom Murdoch so admired.

The Sea, The Sea contains much reference to Shakespeare; it is apparently most connected with *The Tempest*, Iris Murdoch's favorite of Shakespeare's plays. *The Tempest* is the story of elderly scholar and wizard, Prospero, a deposed duke who retires to an island with his daughter Miranda. The two live here happily for a time, but a shipwreck intrudes a host of other characters into their solitude, including a young man with whom Miranda falls in love. Prospero attempts to thwart the romance, knowing that it will mean separation from his daughter if allowed to progress, but eventually the lovers are successful, and Prospero is convinced to return to civilization with his daughter and new son-in-law. The character Charles Arrowby is likened by critics to Prospero, whom he resembles in his determination to "abjure magic and become a hermit" at Shruff End, only to return to London's civilization some time later, after a tempest of events has shaken his sense of himself (*The Sea, The Sea*, p. 2). According to Murdoch, *The Tempest* "is to do with reconciliation and virtue and the triumph of virtue," which also describes the essence of *The Sea, The Sea* (Murdoch in Conradi, p. 232).

Reviews. Although Iris Murdoch's novels often received critical accolades and always sold quite well, reviewers, as noted, frequently took issue with what they perceived as the improbability or contrived nature of her novels' complex plots. Such reviewers, however, typically considered Murdoch's defects admissible in exchange for "such richness of imagination and such grandeur of intellect" as could be found in *The Sea, The Sea* (King, p. 17). The novelist Joyce Carol Oates, who was Murdoch's contemporary, took *The Sea, The Sea* to task for too many "sketchy characters," and too many ideas that were "brilliant," but "inadequately embodied in narrative" (Oates, p. 30). In the words of another reviewer, "Iris Murdoch's novels are made easy to criticize because she attempts so much and because the things she is good at are so various as to leave awkward spaces in between" (Irwin, p. 345). Still other readers appreciate the magnitude of Murdoch's novels as approximating the complexity (and often, awkwardness) of reality itself. *The Sea, The Sea* was proclaimed by several reviewers at the time of its publication to be Murdoch's best novel so far, and in retrospect to have been her best novel altogether.

—Kimberly Ball

For More Information

Anderson, Walt. *Open Secrets: A Western Guide to Tibetan Buddhism*. Harmondsworth: Penguin, 1980.

Bright, Charles. *Sea Serpents*. Bowling Green: Bowling Green State University Popular Press, 1991.

Byatt, A. S. *Iris Murdoch*. Harlow: Longman, 1976.

Conradi, Peter J. *Iris Murdoch: The Saint and the Artist*. London: Macmillan, 1986.

Grunfeld, A. Tom. *The Making of Modern Tibet*. London: Zed, 1987.

Irwin, Michael. Review of *The Sea, The Sea*, by Iris Murdoch, *Times Literary Supplement*, 25 August 1978, 345.

King, Francis. "Love's Spell and Black Magic." *The Spectator*, 26 August 1978, 15-17.

Murdoch, Iris. *The Sea, The Sea*. New York: Viking, 1980.

Oates, Joyce Carol. Review of *The Sea, The Sea*, by Iris Murdoch, *New Republic*, 18 November 1978, 27-31.

Ramanathan, Suguna. *Iris Murdoch: Figures of Good*. New York: St. Martin's Press, 1990.

Shellard, Dominic. *British Theatre Since the War*. New Haven: Yale University Press, 1999.

Valéry, Paul. *Charms*. Trans. David Paul. Princeton: Princeton University Press, 1971.

"September 1913" and "Easter, 1916"

by

William Butler Yeats

Often considered the foremost poet of the twentieth century, William Butler Yeats was born in 1865 in Sandymount, Ireland, a district on the outskirts of Dublin. Yeats's childhood was spent between London and Dublin—the cities in which his father sought to earn a living as an artist—and the Irish countryside of Sligo, where he spent vacations with his extended family, soaking in the folklore and legends that would permeate much of his early poetry. While enrolled in Dublin's Metropolitan School of Art, Yeats met the budding mystic, George Russell, and the Irish nationalist, John O'Leary, who became his much-admired mentor. Through O'Leary's introduction in 1889, Yeats met and fell in love with Maud Gonne, a fiery Irish nationalist and feminist, who became the muse that would inspire and haunt much of his poetry. He offered her countless proposals of marriage throughout his life, but she continually turned him down, claiming that they would always have a "spiritual marriage" rather than a bodily one. Embracing this emphasis on spiritual concerns, Yeats developed an interest in occult practices, became involved in Madame Blavatsky's circle of psychics, and was initiated into London's Hermetic Order of the Golden Dawn, a Rosicrucian, mystical cult. Torn between the contemplative life of mysticism and the active life of politics, he continually oscillated between extremes. With the help of his patron, Lady Augusta Gregory, Yeats played a prominent role in advocating the cultural nationalism of the Irish Literary Revival, which sought to elevate the

> ## THE LITERARY WORK
>
> Two poems set in Dublin, Ireland, in 1913 and 1916 respectively; "September 1913" first published as "Romance in Ireland" in 1913, later published in *Responsibilities* in 1914; "Easter, 1916" privately published for Yeats's friends in 1916, publicly published in *Michael Robartes and the Dancer* in 1921.
>
> ## SYNOPSIS
>
> In "September 1913," the poet mocks the acquisitive mentality of the Catholic middle classes, portraying them as incapable of rising to revolutionary heroism, in contrast to the nationalist martyrs of the past. In "Easter, 1916," he retracts the 1913 satire.

distinct folklore, legends, and traditions of a golden Gaelic past. His play *The Countess Cathleen* (1892) helped launch the Irish National Theatre in 1899—later called the Abbey Theatre—while his early poems, in collections such as *The Rose* (1893) and *The Wind Among the Reeds* (1899), sought to awaken an interest in Celtic legendary material. By 1913, Yeats had turned his poetic attention towards the arena of political action. Various disputes related to the revival, along with the 1913 labor strike, increased his sense of alienation and removed him from Irish politics for a time. Not until the Easter Rising of 1916 would Yeats fully re-enter Irish politics, ac-

William Butler Yeats

knowledging that the same generation he had thought incapable of heroic sacrifice had indeed risen to the revolutionary challenge.

Events in History at the Time of the Poems

Political nationalism. Throughout his life, Yeats claimed to be a "nationalist of the school of John O'Leary," whom he had met in 1885 after O'Leary returned from imprisonment and exile for his activities in the Irish Republican Brotherhood (IRB). Founded in 1858 by James Stephens, the IRB was an oath-bound secret society that sought to lay the groundwork for the overthrow of English rule in Ireland, and its participants in both America and Ireland came to be known as "Fenians." While many nationalists advocated the use of violence to attain their revolutionary ends, O'Leary instead condemned terrorism, discouraged agrarian agitation, and withheld endorsement of parliamentary action at Westminster, England, where the British and Irish lawmakers met. As the leader of the Dublin Fenians in the 1880s, O'Leary sought to keep the organization intact and prevent terrorist acts until the time when a general rising became a viable possibility. Because he was a landlord dependent on rents, he remained suspicious of Charles Stewart

Parnell's vision of Home Rule, or self-government, for Ireland, especially following the Land War of 1879-82, which helped transfer power from the Protestant ascendancy to former tenant farmers.

Yet Parnell's popularity soared in the 1870s and 1880s, as he proved to be a powerful and astute political leader, capable of combining pressure at Westminster with the threat of agrarian agitation in the Irish countryside. Disrupting parliamentary procedure with "obstruction" tactics by speaking for hours at a time, Parnell and other members of the Irish Parliamentary Party forced the English-dominated Parliament at Westminster to pay attention to Irish grievances and to take the idea of Home Rule seriously. During the agrarian crisis of 1877-79, when the potato crops were flooded, landlords continued to demand rent and to evict tenants. In an effort to halt these evictions and lower rents, Parnell and Michael Davitt founded the Land League in 1879, well aware of the benefits of linking Home Rule politics with agitation for land reform. In the same year, agrarian protest erupted, resulting in the Land War of 1879-82. The violence in the Irish countryside forced the British government to take coercive action and arrest members of the Land League, including Parnell. Upon Parnell's release, William Gladstone, the leader of the British Liberal party, urged Parnell to use his influence to curb rural unrest and to give the 1881 Land Act a chance to operate, which would provide fair rent and fixed tenure for tenants. By 1882 the worst effects of the depression had passed, and Parnell turned his attention to advancing the cause of Home Rule.

In April 1886, Gladstone introduced the first Home Rule Bill, which would have devolved power to a new Irish legislature, but the bill was defeated by a vote of 343-313. Parnell would soon face his own personal defeat, after his love affair with Katherine O'Shea became known to the public and was denounced from the Catholic pulpits. After being voted out of the Irish Parliamentary Party, Parnell returned to Ireland, where he toured the countryside trying to rouse support for Home Rule, but his health began to fail, and he died in 1891, a few months after marrying Katherine. Held in Dublin, his funeral drew 200,000 mourners. The seemingly indefatigable Gladstone introduced a second Home Rule Bill in February 1893, which emphasized British control over a new Irish parliament, but the House of Lords defeated this bill by a vote of 419-41.

During the rest of the 1890s, Home Rule was off the political agenda at Westminster, and the Irish Parliamentary Party found itself engaged in bitter factional fighting. Ireland's Chief Secretary Gerald Balfour spoke of "killing Home Rule with kindness," and a 1903 Land Act encouraged landlords to sell their estates to their tenants, with the Treasury providing £12 million in direct cash payments to these landlords. The new policy sought to carry out farm ownership reforms and to finance the development of remote parts of Ireland in the interest of raising the standard of living and thereby dissipating the demand for Home Rule. The strategy resulted in a massive land transfer. Nearly 9 million acres passed from landlords to tenants in approximately 300,000 sales between the years of 1903 to 1920; by the time World War I began, nearly 70 percent of former Irish tenants owned their own holdings (Rees, p. 48).

Cultural nationalism. After the fall of Parnell, many Irish citizens became disillusioned with political nationalism and turned instead to the new cultural nationalism espoused by the Gaelic Athletic Association (GAA), the Gaelic League, and the Irish Literary Revival. Founded in 1884, the GAA promoted Irish sports such as hurling, football, and handball, encouraging local patriotism and fueling nationalism in rural areas. While the GAA made headway in the countryside, the Gaelic League fostered interest among the middle-class urban intelligentsia and also enjoyed clerical support. Founded by Douglas Hyde in 1893, the Gaelic League advocated "de-Anglicization" and the revival of the Irish language as the best protection against English influence, which Hyde saw as having eroded Irish cultural distinctiveness. Hyde led successful campaigns to establish St. Patrick's Day as a national holiday and to force the post office to accept letters and parcels in the Irish Gaelic language. The League also established new Gaelic journals, published Irish literature and textbooks, sponsored literacy camps, and introduced the Irish language into the national school curriculum.

Along with Hyde, Yeats and Lady Gregory initiated the Irish Literary Revival when they established the Abbey Theatre to develop a national drama, and when they collected and published Irish folktales, reviving centuries-old heroic legends and lore in an effort to prove Ireland the cultural equal of any European nation. Writers of the Irish Literary Revival promoted a backward-looking idealization of a golden Gaelic past as a necessary fiction for the development of a literary and cultural renaissance, something James Joyce would later rebel against as he escaped to the continent and urged a turn towards a broader, cosmopolitan outlook (see *Ulysses*, also in *WLAIT 4: British and Irish Literature and Its Times*). Irish revivalist writers, such as Yeats, J. M. Synge, and Standish O'Grady, sought to define themselves in opposition to English culture by creating a new literature based on the oral rather than on the written tradition, a literature that opposed the patriarchal, standardizing forces of English literature. Yet Yeats experienced difficulty in popularizing his ideas beyond his elite circle of friends, and he recognized the contradiction inherent in seeking to create a distinct Irish literature that continued to be written in English.

Although Hyde said he wanted to use the Irish "language as a neutral playing field upon which all Irishmen might meet," regardless of religion, the number of Protestant members in the Gaelic League decreased after 1900, and the Gaelic revival soon drew attention to divisions between Protestants and Catholics (Rees, p. 77). The journalist D. P. Moran clearly articulated these divisions in his newspaper *The Leader*, where he called for an "Irish Ireland," identifying true nationalism with Catholicism, taking issue with Yeats and his Anglo-Irish Protestant friends, denouncing Synge's *The Playboy of the Western World* (1907; also in *WLAIT 4: British and Irish Literature and Its Times*) as an immoral and pagan play. As for Yeats, few questioned his nationalism after seeing his play *Cathleen ni Houlihan* (1902), in which an old woman who symbolizes Ireland calls men into battle against England, promising them eternal glory and the liberation of their country if they sacrifice their lives. Many years after the Easter Rising of 1916 and near the end of his life, Yeats wondered, "Did that play of mine send out/ Certain men the English shot?" (Yeats, "The Man and the Echo," *Collected Poems*, p. 345).

Labor unrest and gallery disputes. At the turn of the twentieth century, nearly one-third of all Dubliners lived in tenement dwellings—some unfit for habitation—and over two-thirds of these tenement dwellers lived in a single room (Kiberd, p. 219). The death rate, 44 in every thousand, exceeded that of any major European city, and was even worse than in the slums of Calcutta, India (Kiberd, p. 219). When called before the commission that inquired into the causes of Dublin's 1913 strike and lockout, labor leader Jim Larkin pointed out that the horrible accommodations in

A burned-out car in front of bombed buildings during the 1916 Easter Rising.

Mountjoy Prison were far superior to a residence in the Dublin slums (Kiberd, p. 220).

Five years earlier, in 1908, the labor leaders James Connolly and Jim Larkin had organized the Irish Transport and General Workers' Union (ITGWU). The union steadily increased its membership until 1913, when William Martin Murphy, Dublin's most prominent businessman, vowed to break the union's power. Murphy was a former anti-Parnellite, the owner of the *Irish Independent* newspaper, and the chair of the Dublin United Tramway Company. Growing alarmed and combative when Larkin sought to enroll United Tramway workers in the ITGWU, Murphy fired those workers who opted to become union members. On August 26, 1913, 200 tramdrivers went on strike, but on September 3, Murphy retaliated by convincing the leading businessmen of the city to lock out of their offices all members of the ITGWU. Nearly 24,000 men were jobless by the third week of September, and over the next few months, starvation, rioting, and mass demonstrations ensued. When several social workers concocted a plan in October to ship the starving children of Dublin dockworkers to sympathetic families in England, the Catholic hierarchy—at Murphy's behest—condemned and interfered with the plan, claiming that the children would be drawn away from the Catholic

faith by being placed in Protestant homes. By January of 1914, the strikers had been defeated, but not before Connolly had formed the Irish Citizen Army for the protection of the workers, a militia that would prove instrumental during the Easter Rising of 1916. Connolly's socialist demands soon took a back seat as a third Home Rule Bill made its way through Westminster and as the crisis of World War I loomed on the horizon.

In October 1913, Yeats witnessed crowds attempting to blockade the ports and railway stations to keep workers from sending their children to England. Appalled by the actions of the mob, he sent a letter to Connolly's newspaper, *The Irish Worker*, objecting to the police's failure to protect the rights of citizens and charging the newspapers "with appealing to mob law day after day, with publishing the names of workingmen and their wives for purposes of intimidation" (Yeats, *Uncollected Prose*, p. 406). Yeats also denounced the use of clerical pressure to support Murphy's economic blockade. Scholars have often puzzled over his reaction, viewing it as an anomaly in the poet's generally right-wing politics, but Yeats consistently took issue with the acquisitive mentality of the Catholic middle classes and not with the lower, working classes, for whom he could occasionally express sympathy. He decried the rise of a new urbanite middle class that exalted the crassness of the marketplace while it denigrated the traditional aristocratic values of wasteful expenditure and sovereignty of the few. Conor Cruise O'Brien argues that Yeats saw Murphy as a particularly loathsome member of this new middle class, which had risen to power with the Land League and which often used clerical pressure to attain its ends (O'Brien, p. 27). Elizabeth Cullingford claims that Yeats took Larkin's side in the strike of 1913 because he had been affected by "O'Leary's praise of artisans, Morris's championship of the workers, Maud Gonne's devotion to the poor" (Cullingford in Brown, p. 201).

Yeats and Larkin also shared a common enemy in Murphy, who played a prominent role in opposing Sir Hugh Lane's proposed art gallery, a project important to Yeats and Lady Gregory. Larkin supported Lane's gallery—likely to annoy Murphy—and while Murphy's newspapers declared that the proposal was too expensive and would take money away from the poor, Yeats and Larkin were quick to point out that Murphy had no altruistic tendencies, as evidenced by his war with the trade unionists. Hugh Lane, Lady Gregory's nephew and a distinguished art collector, had offered a collection of French Impressionist paintings to Dublin, provided that the city would earmark funds for a gallery spanning the River Liffey, designed by the English architect, Sir Edwin Lutyens. Disliking the idea of employing an English architect, the city planners squabbled over his proposal, calling it a "monument at the city's expense," and ultimately envisioning it as a condescending act of the Protestant Ascendancy towards Dublin citizens (Brown, p. 201). Lane withdrew his proposal by the autumn of 1913, instead offering the collection of paintings to the National Gallery in London. In an unwitnessed codicil to his will, Lane returned the paintings to Dublin, but he drowned in the sinking of the *Lusitania* in 1915, leaving Lady Gregory and Yeats with the task of fighting to return the collection to Dublin. An agreement was ultimately reached whereby Dublin and London would share the collection, which now spends half of each year at the National Gallery in London and half of each year at the Hugh Lane Municipal Gallery of Modern Art in Dublin.

Yeats wrote in his notes to *Responsibilities* that three public controversies had stirred his imagination during the thirty years in which he had been reading Irish newspapers: the Parnell controversy, the dispute over *The Playboy of the Western World,* and the Lane debacle (Jeffares, p. 105). These three conflicts typified everything Yeats had come to despise about materialistic Ireland and its middle-class pieties, and he rails against this alliance of religion and acquisitiveness in "September 1913," originally entitled "Romance

---

MIDDLE-CLASS HYPOCRISIES?

In *Vale,* his 1914 account of the Irish Literary Revival, George Moore parodies Yeats's actions and rhetoric during the Lane controversy, especially mocking his identification with the aristocracy:

> We . . . could hardly believe our ears when . . . he began to thunder like Ben Tillett against the middle classes, stamping his feet, working himself into a great temper, and all because the middle classes did not dip their hands in their pockets and give Lane the money he wanted for his exhibition. When he spoke the words, the middle classes, one would have thought that he was speaking against a personal foe, and we looked round asking each other with our eyes where on earth our Willie Yeats had picked up the strange belief that none but titled and carriage-folk could appreciate pictures. And we asked ourselves why our Willie Yeats should feel himself called upon to denounce his own class; millers and shipowners on one side, and on the other a portrait-painter of distinction. . . .
>
> We have sacrificed our lives for Art; but you, what have you done? What sacrifices have you made? He asked, and everybody began to search his memory for the sacrifices Yeats had made, asking himself in what prison Yeats had languished, what rags he had worn, what broken victuals he had eaten. As far as anybody could remember, he had always lived very comfortably, sitting down invariably to regular meals, and the old green cloak that was in keeping with his profession of romantic poet he had exchanged for the magnificent fur coat which distracted our attention from what he was saying, so opulently did it cover the back of the chair out of which he had risen. But, quite forgetful of the coat behind him, he continued to denounce the middle classes, throwing his arms into the air, shouting at us.

(Moore in Jeffares p. 100)

---

in Ireland / (On reading much of the correspondence against the Art Gallery)." While the poem was overtly written to deride the middle classes for refusing to give financial support to Hugh Lane's proposed art gallery, Yeats may also be calling into question the behavior of the middle class towards the working class during the labor strike and lockout of 1913. Disillusioned by the Lane controversy, the labor strike, and the acquisitive mentality of the Catholic middle classes, Yeats turned away from Irish politics and moved to England for a few years, living and working in literary collaboration with the poet Ezra Pound in Sussex.

Easter Rising. When the third Home Rule Bill came before Parliament in May 1912, the Ulster Unionists—Protestants who favored maintaining a legislative union with England—increased their opposition to the proposal, organizing local militias and importing guns from Germany without interference from the British. The Irish Volunteers, a militia in the south of Ireland, declared themselves as a countervailing force to the Ulster Unionists, but when they also attempted to smuggle weapons into Ireland at the end of 1913, British troops fired upon an unarmed Dublin crowd, killing three and injuring 38. The Home Rule Bill passed in May 1914, despite these disturbances, with a proviso that allowed counties to opt out of the plan if they so chose. The bill became law in September 1914, but its implementation was suspended for the duration of World War I.

During the first year of the war, many of the Irish who enlisted to fight were drawn from the working class of Dublin, where living conditions remained severely below the British standard. Rural Ireland, however, experienced economic gains because the war heightened the demand for Irish produce, and sons often stayed home to work the land rather than fight in the war. Taking advantage of the situation, the IRB and Sinn Féin—a political party founded by Arthur Griffith in 1905—began to recruit these sons to the nationalist cause and to plan covertly for an insurrection while England's attention was distracted. Many of these sons had grown up under the influence of the Gaelic League and the Gaelic Revival, which had attracted a whole generation to cultural nationalism. Patrick Pearse, a leader of the Easter 1916 Rising, lauded this generation of cultural revivalists, urging them to win nationhood through bloodshed. He described the sacrifice "as a cleansing and sanctifying thing," saying that "the nation which regards it as the final horror has lost its manhood. There are many things more horrible than bloodshed; and slavery is one of them" (Pearse in Rees, p. 196-97).

The threat of potential conscription to fight in World War I fueled anti-British sentiment. Meanwhile, the Irish Volunteers drilled with fake guns, scheduling "exercises" for Easter Sunday 1916 that were actually a cover for revolutionary activity, which the Military Council of the IRB had been planning for a year. The Military Council included Patrick Pearse, James Plunkett, Eamonn Ceannt, Thomas Clarke, Sean MacDermott, Thomas MacDonagh, and lastly, James Connolly, who had decided that the goals of socialism and nationalism could not be dissevered. The rebels expected a shipment of German arms, but when the *Aud* sailed into Tralee Bay with this cargo on April 19, 1916, the ship failed to establish contact with the shore. Intercepted by the British Navy, it was escorted to Queenstown Harbor, Ireland, where the skipper sank the ship with its cargo of 20,000 rifles. Roger Casement, who had visited Germany in an attempt to rouse support for the Irish insurrection, planned to return to Ireland to warn the Military Council against pursuing any revolutionary activities, but when he was smuggled into County Kerry by a German submarine on April 20, he was immediately arrested. Casement's capture, along with the sinking of the *Aud* and a notice in the newspapers canceling the Easter Sunday maneuvers, convinced British authorities that they had no need to fear an insurrection, but the Military Council planned to rise on Monday instead. In the absence of any real hope for success, Pearse returned to his doctrine of blood sacrifice, claiming that Ireland could only be redeemed through bloodshed and the creation of martyrs who would give their lives for their land. In choosing Easter for the rising, Pearse intentionally invoked Christian symbolism of sacrificial death and rebirth.

Nearly 1,600 insurgents, including the Irish Volunteers, the Irish Citizen Army, and numerous women, participated in the Easter Rising, which began April 24, 1916, as the troops occupied Dublin's key buildings, including the Post Office, Four Courts, St. Stephen's Green, Jacob's Biscuit Factory, and Boland Flour Mills, the last under the command of a young Eamon de Valera. As the President of the Provisional Government, Pearse stood on the front steps of the Post Office and read the "Proclamation from the Provisional Government" to a crowd of surprised onlookers, a document that urged Irishmen and Irishwomen to "sacrifice themselves for the common good" and that referred obliquely to the Germans, "our gallant allies in Europe," ensuring that the British would view this rebellion as an act of serious treason (Rees, p. 207). The insurgents held their positions for a few days as the Dublin poor went on a looting spree and as the British began shelling the rebels' positions with artillery barrages. Most of Sackville Street was destroyed, the Post Office caught fire, and Connolly was seriously wounded. Sixty-four rebels, more than 100 British troops, and over 200 civilians were killed, while another 2,614 were wounded (Rees, p. 207). To prevent further loss of life, Pearse and Connolly surrendered, and the rising, which lasted only one week, was over. The rebels were arrested, including 60 women who had served as cooks, nurses, and couriers, and who had held up food vans at gunpoint. Approximately 30 more women in the Irish Citizen Army had played a more active role, including Countess Constance Markievicz, an old friend of Yeats and Gonne, who was Michael Mallin's second-in-command in St. Stephen's Green. Indeed, according to Russell Rees, the "memory of the flamboyant 48-year-old countess in her military uniform with revolver in hand remains one of the most powerful images of the rising" (Rees, p. 208).

At first, most Dubliners thought the rebellion had been an act of folly and expressed outrage over the loss of lives and property, but their attitudes changed dramatically as the British authorities imposed martial law and ordered large-scale arrests of 3,500 people, two times the number who had participated in the rising. The British shipped most of these prisoners off to detention camps in North Wales, which, ironically, became the training ground for new nationalists and new members of the IRB. Commanding the British, Major-General Sir John Maxwell sought to make examples of the revolutionaries at a time of international crisis and war, but he drastically mishandled a delicate situation, infuriating Dubliners with the secret trials and executions of the 15 ringleaders. Ninety rebels were sentenced to death, including Maud Gonne's husband, John MacBride, while 75 received sentences of penal servitude, including Countess Markievicz, on account of her sex, and Eamon de Valera, who claimed United States citizenship. Various tales of the martyrs' heroism, humanity, and devotion to the Catholic faith aroused public sympathy. The seriously wounded Connolly had to be strapped to a chair before facing the firing squad. Plunkett was married to Grace Gifford on the night before his execution, but the couple was not allowed to spend any time alone together. Before marching out to join the Rising, Thomas MacDonagh taught his last class, on Jane Austen, the topic revealing that he did not reject English influence, but rather the British imperial system,

which denied freedom to its subjects. Almost everyone executed received the last rites.

Another incident that inflamed public opinion was the murder of Francis Sheehy-Skeffington, a popular journalist and eccentric, renowned throughout Dublin for his pacifist, feminist, and socialist soapbox speeches. Along with two other journalists, Sheehy-Skeffington had witnessed Captain J. C. Bowen-Colthurst murder an unarmed Dublin youth during the rising. Bowen-Colthurst took the three journalists into custody,

---

PROCLAMATION OF THE IRISH REPUBLIC READ BY PATRICK PEARSE ON THE STEPS OF THE POST OFFICE AT THE BEGINNING OF THE EASTER RISING

Poblacht na h-Éireann The Provisional Government of the Irish Republic to the People of Ireland

Irishmen and Irishwomen: In the name of God and of the dead generations from which she receives her old tradition of nationhood, Ireland, through us, summons her children to her flag and strikes for her freedom.

Having organized and trained her manhood through her secret revolutionary organization, the Irish Republican Brotherhood, and through her open military organizations, the Irish Volunteers, and the Irish Citizen Army . . . she now seizes that moment, and supported by her exiled children in America and by gallant allies in Europe, but relying in the first on her own strength, she strikes in full confidence of victory.

We declare the right of the people of Ireland to the ownership of Ireland, and to the unfettered control of Irish destinies, to be sovereign and indefeasible. The long usurpation of that right by a foreign people and government has not extinguished the right, nor can it ever be extinguished except by the destruction of the Irish people. . . . Standing on that fundamental right and again asserting it in arms in the face of the world, we hereby proclaim the Irish republic as a sovereign independent state, and we pledge our lives and the lives of our comrades-in-arms to the cause of its freedom, of its welfare, and of its exaltation among the nations. . . .

Signed on behalf of the provisional government,

THOMAS J. CLARKE, SEAN MACDIARMADA, THOMAS MACDONAGH, P. H. PEARSE, EAMONN CEANNT, JAMES CONNOLLY, JOSEPH PLUNKETT.

The Times, 1 May 1916
(Reiss and Hepburn, vol. 2, pp. 149-50)

murdered them without a trial, and buried their bodies in quicklime inside Portobello Barracks. Bowen-Colthurst was later found guilty, but insane, and his act of brutality profoundly increased anti-British sentiment. In the end, as Terence Brown notes, "it was the British response—swift, surgical, and uncomprehending of the ghosts they were reawakening—which helped to make of a botched rebellion the sacrificial act of national renewal some of the doomed participants had hoped it might be" (Brown, p. 226).

Yeats heard about the Rising from England, where he had moved in self-imposed exile after his alienating experiences with the middle classes in 1913. Shocked and saddened by the recent turn of events, Yeats wrote to Lady Gregory of the emotions inspired in him by the Dublin tragedy:

> I am trying to write a poem on the men executed—'terrible beauty has been born again'. . . . I am very despondent about the future. At the moment I feel that all the work of years has been overturned, all the bringing together of the classes, all the freeing of Irish literature and criticism from politics.
>
> (Yeats in Wade, p.612).

The Poems in Focus

Contents summary. "September 1913." Yeats opens the ballad with a stanza that mocks the avariciousness of the middle classes, who "fumble in a greasy till / And add the halfpence to the pence / And prayer to shivering prayer"; preoccupied with hoarding their money and saving their souls, they believe that "men were born to pray and save" (Yeats, *Collected Poems,* "September 1913," lines 2-4). In the refrain that closes each stanza, Yeats contrasts this new materialism with the heady idealism of the past, declaring that "Romantic Ireland's dead and gone, / It's with O'Leary in the grave" ("September 1913," lines 7-8). For Yeats, the 1908 death of nationalist John O'Leary was a watershed moment, when the noble and generous values of one generation gave way to the self-serving values of the next.

In the second stanza, Yeats contrasts the present greed of the middle classes with the self-sacrificial mentality of heroes of the past, whose names "stilled" his "childish play," and who "have gone about the world like wind," an image of energetic and wasteful expenditure that contrasts sharply with the pinched, sterile asceticism of the

middle classes ("September 1913," lines 10-11). Yeats notes that the nationalist heroes had little time to pray since the hangman's rope was waiting to cut short their lives.

The third stanza asks if the sacrificial martyrs of the past died in vain, only to support an Ireland enslaved to greed, an Ireland unable to appreciate aesthetic beauty or offer aid to the poor: "Was it for this the wild geese spread / The grey wing upon every tide; / For this that all that blood was shed. . . ?" ("September 1913," lines 17-19). The "wild geese" were Irishmen who served in the armies of France, Spain, and Austria, due to the Penal Laws, or anti-Catholic measures, passed after 1691. Nearly 120,000 "wild geese" left Ireland between 1690 and 1730. In France, England's longtime rival, they formed the Irish Brigade, which fought on the side of the French until the 1789 Revolution (Jeffares, p. 110). Yeats next invokes the names that "stilled his childish play," including Edward Fitzgerald (1763-98), a romantic nationalist who served in America and later joined the United Irishmen, the group that brought a French force to Ireland in 1798. Wolfe Tone (1763-98) founded the United Irishmen and petitioned the French for military support; Robert Emmet (1778-1803) led a thwarted revolt in 1803 and was hung for high treason.

In the final stanza, Yeats wonders what would happen if the years could be turned back and the exiles recalled, but he realizes that the middle classes would neither understand the nationalists' love of their land nor the call of Cathleen ni Houlihan, who urges men to sacrifice their lives for their country: "You'd cry, 'Some woman's yellow hair / Has maddened every mother's son'" ("September 1913," line 29). He underscores the generosity of the martyrs, who "weighed so lightly what they gave," whereas the middle classes weigh and save each "pence" and "prayer" ("September 1913," lines 3-4). At the end, Yeats relinquishes his rhetorical questions and throws up his hands in despair, acknowledging that the heroic ghosts should not be reawakened: "let them be, they're dead and gone, / They're with O'Leary in the grave" ("September 1913," lines 31-32).

"Easter, 1916." After the Easter Rising, Yeats observed that his poem "September 1913" sounded old-fashioned and that no matter how one might question the wisdom of the Dublin Rising, it was undeniably heroic. The generation that Yeats thought incapable of self-sacrifice had indeed risen to the revolutionary challenge in the Easter Rebellion. His "Easter 1916" is a palinode, a poetic retraction, in which Yeats rescinds the criticism of "September 1913" and performs his bardic duty of memorializing and naming the fallen heroes.

In the first stanza, Yeats recalls encounters with casual acquaintances on the streets of Dublin, whom he would pass "with a nod of the head / Or polite meaningless words," never suspecting that these ordinary people would later be transformed into the martyrs of the Easter Rising (Yeats, "Easter, 1916," *Collected Poems,* lines 5-6). Even as he lingered briefly for meaningless conversations with these acquaintances, his attention would already be distracted by the thought of a joke or tale to tell other friends "around the fire at the club," since he remained "certain that they and I / But lived where motley is worn" ("Easter, 1916," lines 12-14). Referring to the jester's multi-colored costume, Yeats reveals his earlier belief that Ireland would always play the fool at the courts of the British, but now he realizes how wrong he was. His refrain invokes the oxymoron of "terrible beauty": "All changed, changed utterly: A terrible beauty is born" ("Easter, 1916," lines 15-16).

In the second stanza, Yeats deliberately postpones naming the heroes and instead refers obliquely to them, first describing Constance Markievicz, his old friend from Sligo, whose "sweet" aristocratic voice had turned "shrill" from nights spent in heated political argument. Yeats then describes the poet and idealist Patrick Pearse, the man who "had kept a school / And rode our wingèd horse," a reference to Pegasus, the horse of the Muses ("Easter, 1916," lines 24-25). Pearse had opened the bilingual St. Enda's school in 1908, promoting the study of Irish language, history, and legends, and attracting pupils from the most prominent families in the Gaelic revival. His "helper and friend" was Thomas MacDonagh, an assistant lecturer in English at University College, Dublin, who "might have won fame in the end" with his "sensitive nature" and his "daring" and "sweet" thought ("Easter, 1916," lines 26, 28-30). In describing Maud Gonne's ex-husband John MacBride, Yeats writes, "This other man I had dreamed / A drunken, vainglorious lout. / He had done most bitter wrong / to some who are near my heart" ("Easter, 1916," lines 31-34). Yet even this lout has been transformed into a martyr, and Yeats will not neglect to "number him in the song" ("Easter, 1916," lines 35-37).

The third stanza marks a shift in tone and content, as Yeats reveals his uncertainty and ambivalence towards the martyr's unflinching ob-

session with a cause, contrasting images from nature that exist in perpetual motion with the stony rigidity of the martyrs' hearts. As he describes horses splashing in the stream and "birds that range / From cloud to tumbling cloud," Yeats depicts nature as a restorative force because it changes "minute by minute" and does not offer the transcendent stasis that the sacrificed martyrs embody ("Easter, 1916," lines 46-48). Indeed, the poem opposes the continual motion of nature to the rigid "hearts with one purpose alone" that have become "enchanted to a stone / To trouble the living stream" ("Easter, 1916," lines 41, 43-44).

"Too long a sacrifice / Can make a stone of the heart," Yeats claims in the final stanza, lamenting the fixation on a single cause that has hardened the hearts of the martyrs ("Easter, 1916," lines 57-58). Yeats wonders when their sacrifices will suffice, but he leaves that question up to Heaven; instead, the poet's part is "to murmur name upon name, / As a mother names her child / When sleep at last has come / On limbs that had run wild" ("Easter, 1916," lines 60-64). Yet Yeats still postpones the moment of naming, remaining ambivalent towards the martyrs' sacrifice, wondering if "England may keep faith / For all that is done and said" ("Easter, 1916," line 68-69). And "what if excess of love bewildered them till they died?" Yeats asks, drawing the phrase "excess of love" from Pearse's writings and drawing upon the dual definitions of "bewilder," one denoting confusion, the other denoting the loss of a path—appropriate for those who have wandered away from the natural flux of life ("Easter, 1916," lines 72-73).

When Yeats finally performs his bardic duty and names the martyrs, he blatantly uses an active, present verb tense—a rare occurrence in this poem—and ensures that he receives the credit for memorializing the passive heroes, for transforming them into household names, baptized and reborn into the immortality of art: "*I write it out in verse*— / MacDonagh and MacBride / And Connolly and Pearse / Now and in time to be, / Wherever green is worn, / Are changed, changed utterly: / A terrible beauty is born" ("Easter, 1916," lines 74-80, italics added).

Aristocrats and feminists. In many of his poems, Yeats laments the loss of the Irish aristocracy, showing himself to be nostalgic for the "custom and ceremony" of a leisurely, gracious life, where one can avoid the crass utilitarianism of the marketplace and find time to delight in aesthetic pursuits. As he bemoans the disappearance of the aristocracy, Yeats also deplores the fate of Maud Gonne and Countess Markievicz, two beautiful women who turned away from their aristocratic heritage to join the ugly world of politics, a world where Yeats believed women did not belong.

In "Easter, 1916," he contrasts the shrillness of Countess Markievicz's political voice with the sweetness of her voice during her aristocratic youth, when she was engaged in leisurely, pastoral pursuits in County Sligo. When Constance Markievicz, née Gore-Booth (1868-1927) was presented at the court of Queen Victoria in 1887 and pronounced "the new Irish beauty," her fate as an ornamental socialite appeared incontrovertible. Though she married the Polish Count Markievicz in 1900, she would refuse to remain a passive member of the nobility, instead becoming involved in feminist, socialist, and nationalist politics, joining Maud Gonne's feminist group Inghinidhe na hÉereann (The Daughters of Ireland), supporting the labor strike of 1913, and participating as Michael Mallin's second-in-command during the Easter Rising. She told the court martial at her trial, "I did what was right and I stand by it" (Gar Media). When the British refused to execute her on account of her being a woman, Markievicz was dismayed and reportedly said, "I do wish your lot had the decency to shoot me" (Gar Media).

Sources and literary context. With their emphasis on mysticism and otherworldly lore, Yeats's early poems stand in stark contrast to "September 1913" and "Easter, 1916." The latter titles eschew the dreamy mists of legend for the arena of political action, as do other poems of Yeats's middle age. In *Responsibilities,* the volume in which "September 1913" appeared, Yeats included a series of poems that launch a satirical assault on the philistinism of the middle classes, including "Paudeen," "To a wealthy man who promised a second subscription to the Dublin Municipal Gallery," and "To a friend whose work has come to nothing." In "Paudeen," for example, Yeats mocks the middle classes, contrasting their avariciousness with the sacrificial generosity of Parnell.

Michael Robartes and the Dancer, the volume in which "Easter, 1916" appeared, features other poems about the Easter Rising, including "The Rose Tree," which explores the sacrificial imagery of the Rising, "On a Political Prisoner," which describes Countess Markievicz in prison, and "Sixteen Dead Men." When Yeats names and immortalizes the fallen martyrs in "Easter, 1916,"

he draws upon a long tradition of Irish poetic tributes, including ballads such as John Kells Ingram's "The Memory of the Dead," Dion Boucicault's "The Wearing of the Green," Caroll Malone's "The Croppy Boy," and Eileen O'Connell's "Lament for Art O'Leary."

In drama, Sean O'Casey takes a jaundiced look at the Easter Rising in his play *The Plough and the Stars* (1926), which satirizes the "boyscoutish vanity" of the rebel leaders with their swords and kilts and Celtic jewelry (Kiberd, p. 225). Unlike Yeats, who raises the fallen heroes into the immortality of art, O'Casey questions the motives of the rebels and their rhetoric of blood sacrifice.

Yeats's own drama had an influential effect on his poetry. When he wonders, "Did that play of mine send out / Certain men the English shot?" he refers to his play, *Cathleen ni Houlihan* (1902), which drew upon the image of the motherland as symbolized by the Poor Old Woman or "Shan van Vocht" (sean bhean bhocht) of ancient Celtic legend, who is transformed into a beautiful queen. As presented in Yeats's play *Cathleen ni Houlihan,* the Poor Old Woman calls Irishmen to sacrifice their lives for their country and to regain the "four beautiful green fields" of Ireland (*Cathleen ni Houlihan,* p. 10-11). Yeats's play, in which Maud Gonne starred in the leading role, did indeed arouse the fanatical devotion that caused Yeats to question his own culpability in the Easter Rising. For P. S. O'Hegarty, a republican rebel, the drama became a "sort of sacrament," and to Countess Markievicz, it became a "kind of gospel" (Kiberd, p. 200).

Publication and reception. Perhaps wary of further inflaming public opinion, Yeats did not formally publish "Easter, 1916" until 1921 and instead privately circulated 25 copies among friends in 1916. According to Terence Brown, Yeats's social successes in England made him think he could "influence affairs of state in private conversation," and he withheld a very partisan poem in order to keep such channels open and to allow diplomatic negotiations about the Lane bequest to continue, a project he and Lady Gregory were pursuing in 1916-17 (Brown, p. 235).

When Yeats circulated copies of "Easter, 1916" among his friends, Maud Gonne told him in no uncertain terms that she disliked the poem and resented the idea that "England may keep faith." In a letter to Yeats, she wrote, "No I don't like your poem, it isn't worthy of you & above all it isn't worthy of the subject" (Gonne in Brown, p. 234). That "Easter, 1916" has since been more highly lauded than "September 1913" indicates that posterity disagreed.

"September 1913" received indirect praise as part of the volume *Responsibilities* (1914). The American poet Ezra Pound gave it a favorable review, stating that the collection as a whole represented a shift in Yeats's style away from his early Celtic romantic "glamour" and towards a "greater hardness of outline" (Pound, p. 188). On the other hand, it maintained a successful effect of Yeats's earlier verse:

> Perhaps the highest function of art [is] that it should fill the mind with a noble profusion of sounds and images, that it should furnish the life of the mind with such accompaniment and surrounding. At any rate Mr. Yeats's work has done this in the past and still continues to do so.
> (Pound, p. 189)

—Kathryn Stelmach

For More Information

Brown, Terence. *The Life of W. B. Yeats.* Dublin: Gill & Macmillan, 1999.

Caufield, Max. *The Easter Rebellion.* Dublin: Gill & Macmillan, 1995.

GAR Media. "Constance Markievicz: The Countess of Irish Freedom." *The Wild Geese Today-Erin's Far Flung Exiles.* 1997. http://www.thewildgeese.com/pages/ireland.html (30 Dec. 2000).

Jeffares, A. Norman. *A New Commentary on the Poems of W. B. Yeats.* Stanford: Stanford University Press, 1984.

Kiberd, Declan. *Inventing Ireland.* Cambridge: Harvard University Press, 1995.

O'Brien, Conor Cruise. "Passion and Cunning: An Essay on the Politics of W. B. Yeats." In *Passion and Cunning and Other Essays.* London: George Weidenfeld and Nicolson, 1988.

Pound, Ezra. "Ezra Pound on Yeats's Change of Manner." In *W. B. Yeats: The Critical Heritage.* Ed. A. Norman Jeffares. London: Routledge & Kegan Paul, 1977.

Rees, R., and A. C. Hepburn, eds. *Ireland: 1905-1925: Text and Historiography.* 2 vols. Newtonards: Colourpoint Books, 1998.

Yeats, W. B. *Uncollected Prose.* Ed. John P. Frayne and Colton Johnson. Vol. 2. London: Macmillan, 1975.

———. *The Collected Poems of W. B. Yeats.* Ed. Richard J. Finneran. New York: Simon and Schuster, 1996.

———. *Cathleen ni Houlihan.* London: A. H. Bullen, 1909.

Wade, Allan, ed. *The Letters of W. B. Yeats.* London: Rupert Hart-Davis, 1954.

Sonnets from the Portuguese

by

Elizabeth Barrett Browning

Born in 1806 in County Durham, England, Elizabeth Moulton-Barrett was the eldest of 11 surviving children. Although, like most young girls of the time, she had no formal schooling, she shared a tutor with the brother closest to her in age, studying Latin and Greek. Elizabeth Barrett furthered her education by extensive readings in history, philosophy, and literature. She also began to compose poetry at an early age; *The Battle of Marathon* was privately printed by her father in 1820. In 1825 her poem "The Rose and the Zephyr" was published in the *Literary Gazette*, and the following year, a collection of poetry, *An Essay on Mind with Other Poems,* appeared in print. Over the next two decades, Elizabeth Barrett continued to write poems and essays, publishing several volumes, including *Prometheus Bound and Miscellaneous Poems* (1833), *The Seraphim and Other Poems* (1838), and *Poems* (1844). Plagued by chronic ill-health since adolescence, she became increasingly reclusive as an adult, a tendency that her domineering father, who had forbidden any of his children to marry, did not discourage. A chance correspondence with Robert Browning in 1845, however, led to an eventual meeting between the two poets, which, in turn, resulted in a secret romance, culminating in marriage and departure for Italy in 1846, where the couple lived until the death of Barrett, now named Barrett Browning, in 1861. Her *Sonnets from the Portuguese* (1850) depicts the stages of the poets' developing romance, while introducing innovation into a lyric form brought to its

THE LITERARY WORK

A sequence of sonnets, set in nineteenth-century England; published in 1850.

SYNOPSIS

A female poet depicts the progression of her romance with a male poet, from the first tentative stages of courtship to the fulfillment of commitment.

height nearly 500 years earlier, the Petrarchan or Italian sonnet.

Events in History at the Time of the Poems

The Barrett-Browning courtship. One of the most famous romances of the Victorian period began quietly enough with a compliment from one poet to another. In her poem "Lady Geraldine's Courtship," Elizabeth Barrett, who by this time had won some renown for her own verse, paid tribute to the work of a rising younger poet, Robert Browning. She had recently become acquainted with his pamphlet series, *Bells and Pomegranates.* Alluding to certain verses read by the poet-narrator to Lady Geraldine, Barrett mentioned that very series: "Or from Browning some 'Pomegranate,' which, if cut deep down the middle, / Shows a heart within blood-tinctured, of a veined humanity" (Barrett Browning in Porter

Elizabeth Barrett Browning

and Clarke, vol. 2, p. 292). Browning's response to this compliment, when he learned of it, was characteristically ardent. In a letter dated January 10, 1845, Browning declared, "I love your verses with all my heart, dear Miss Barrett" and later reiterated, "I do, as I say, love these books with all my heart—and I love you too" (Browning in Karlin, p. 1). Barrett herself responded warmly the following day, "I thank you, dear Mr. Browning, from the bottom of my heart. . . . Such a letter from such a hand! Sympathy is dear—very dear to me: but the sympathy of a poet & of such a poet, is the quintessence of sympathy to me! Will you take back my gratitude for it?" (Barrett Browning in Karlin, p. 2). Shortly thereafter, the two poets embarked on a regular correspondence, declaring themselves delighted with each other's letters. Barrett asserted that "everybody likes writing to somebody—& it [would] be strange and contradictory if I were not always delighted both to hear from *you* and to write to *you*" (Barrett Browning in Karlin, p. 10).

In many respects, Barrett and Browning could not have been more different. The only son of middle-class parents, the 32-year-old Browning enjoyed travel and moved easily and freely through literary society in London, though his works had not yet found great favor with the critics or the public. By contrast, Barrett was six years

Browning's senior and an invalid. Ill-health had troubled her since adolescence; moreover, she had been devastated by several deaths in the family, including that of her favorite brother, Edward (nicknamed "Bro"), who had drowned in a sailing accident in 1840. Inheritances from her grandmother and uncle made Elizabeth the only one of the Barrett children to be independently wealthy. Because of their father's opposition to the idea of his children's marrying, all remained at the family home on Wimpole Street in London. Her physical frailty kept Barrett confined to her bedroom: family members—and occasionally friends—visited her there, bringing her whatever she asked. Relieved of domestic responsibilities because of her poor health, she became a voracious reader and prolific writer—of letters, poems, and essays. By the time she and Browning exchanged their first letters, Barrett was England's most famous woman poet, a celebrity whose work had found favor on both sides of the Atlantic, in America as well as England.

After several months of correspondence, Barrett at last consented to a personal meeting; on May 20, 1845, Browning paid his first visit to 50 Wimpole Street and was received by Barrett in her own room. A few days later he apparently wrote the one letter of their correspondence which does not survive—Barrett returned it to him at his request and he destroyed it. Most Browning scholars agree that the letter most likely contained a declaration of love. Barrett reproached Browning in her reply: "[Y]ou do not know what pain you give me in speaking so wildly. . . . You have said some intemperate things . . . fancies—which you will not say over again, nor unsay, but *forget at once, & for ever, having said at all,*—and which (so) will die out between *you & me alone*, like a misprint between you and the printer" (Barrett Browning in Karlin, p. 57). Moreover, if Browning ever alluded to the subject again "*I must not . . . I WILL not see you again—& you will justify me later in your heart*" (Barrett Browning in Karlin, p. 58). After Browning apologized for his intemperance, the letters and visits—Browning was to record 91 visits to Wimpole Street in the course of their courtship—resumed. (Virginia Woolf's *Flush* is the story of these visits from the perspective of Barrett Browning's dog.)

By August, the friendship between the two poets had reached a point at which Browning felt emboldened to speak again, "Let me say now—*this only once*—that I loved you from my soul, and gave you my life, so much of it as you would take" (Browning in Karlin, p. 109). Barrett, oppressed by ill-health, a sense of her own unworthiness, and the tyrannical strictures of her widowed father, replied more cautiously, "The subject will not bear consideration—it breaks in our hands. But that God is stronger than we, cannot be a bitter thought to you but a holy thought. . . . While He lets me, as much as I can be anyone's, be only yours" (Barrett Browning in Karlin, p. 119).

In the autumn of 1845, Dr. Chambers, Barrett's physician, prescribed that she go abroad for her health to avoid spending another winter in London. Pisa, Italy, was suggested as a destination; two of Barrett's siblings would accompany her (unknown to anyone but Elizabeth was the plan for Browning to show up wherever she spent the winter). Barrett's father, however, disapproved so thoroughly of the Pisa scheme that it was ultimately abandoned, a development that led Barrett to question whether he really cared for her welfare or not. Browning responded to her distress by declaring, "I would marry you now and thus—I would come when you let me and go when you bade me, . . . when your head ached I should be *here*" (Browning in Karlin, p. 131). Touched, Barrett at last capitulated, "Henceforward I am yours for everything but to do you harm . . . if [God] should free me within a moderate time from the trailing chain of this weakness, I will then be to you whatever at that hour you shall choose . . . whether friend or more than friend" (Barrett Browning in Karlin, pp. 132-33).

During the winter months, Barrett began to take some exercise outdoors, and her health improved noticeably. By spring, she and Browning were planning their future together—amazingly, they had managed to conceal their entire romance from her father—and on September 12, 1846, the couple were married secretly at St. Marylebone Church in London, with only her maid and his cousin as witnesses.

Barrett Browning returned to Wimpole Street afterwards but did not inform her siblings of her marriage. A week later, the Brownings—accompanied by Barrett Browning's maid and her King Charles spaniel, Flush—set off for Italy where they were to live for the whole of their married lives. Mr. Barrett never forgave his daughter for her elopement. Two other children, Henrietta and Alfred, who married in his lifetime, were also disinherited.

During the lovers' courtship, Barrett Browning was at work on *Sonnets from the Portuguese*.

The poems' exact dates of composition remain unknown, but thoughts expressed in her letters to Browning found their way into the sonnets. Barrett Browning's realization that she had resigned herself to an early death before meeting Browning—"I had done *living*, I thought, when you came & sought me out!"—resonates through several sonnets in the sequence, most notably in the first sonnet, in which "a mystic Shape" yanks the weeping speaker "backward by the hair" and proves to be "Not Death, but Love" (Barrett

A MYSTERY ILLNESS

The cause of Elizabeth Barrett Browning's ill-health has never been conclusively determined. As a child, she had been quite healthy, a tomboy who enjoyed the outdoors. But in autumn 1821, Elizabeth and her sisters, Henrietta and Arabella, all fell ill with what appeared to be the same ailment. Symptoms included headaches, pains in the side, and muscle spasms. While Henrietta and Arabella recovered quickly, Elizabeth did not; she was still experiencing malaise when she contracted measles the following summer. Not too surprisingly, she became preoccupied with thoughts of her ill-health. One physician, Dr. Coker, thought she suffered from a "nervous disorder" and prescribed opium—a common remedy of the time—to which, unfortunately, Elizabeth became habituated for the rest of her life. At another point, it was thought that Elizabeth might have a disease of the spine—as a result, she was sent to a spa in Gloucester, where she spent long periods of time in a spine crib, a kind of hammock, so that the condition might manifest itself and thus be treated. The treatment appeared to have little effect and Elizabeth returned home nearly a year later. Her health continued to be uncertain in adulthood—she suffered severe bronchial attacks that became more frequent as she kept increasingly to her bedroom, shunning fresh air and exercise. By the time Robert Browning became her correspondent, Elizabeth had resigned herself to ill-health and, in all likelihood, an early death, as some of the verse in *Sonnets from the Portuguese* reveals. Referring to herself as "a poor, tired wandering singer" leaning against a "cypress tree" (a traditional symbol of death), the speaker argues that she and her lover are incompatible in life because "The chrism is on thine head—on mine the dew,—/And Death must dig the level where these agree" (Barrett Browning, *Sonnets from the Portuguese*, 3:11, 12, 13, 14).

Browning in Karlin, p. 125; *Sonnets*, 1:10-11, 14). Incidents from the poets' courtship were also immortalized in verse, including their exchanging locks of hair in Sonnets 18 and 19, her rapturous rereading of his letters to her in Sonnet 28, and her asking him to call her by her pet-name ("Ba") in Sonnet 33. However, no reference to Barrett Browning's composition of the sonnets appeared in her letters to Browning of the time. It was not until 1849, nearly three years after their marriage, that she at last found the courage to show him these highly personal poems.

Unmarried women. During the nineteenth century, marriage was, for the most part, regarded as a woman's natural destiny, a highly probable

---

LOVING BANTER

From a letter in which Barrett asks Browning to use her pet-name:

"I am glad that you do not despise my own right name too much, because I was never called Elizabeth by anyone who loved me at all, & I accept the omen—So little it seems my name that if a voice said suddenly 'Elizabeth,' I should as soon turn round as my sisters would . . . no sooner. Only my own right name has been complained of for want of euphony . . . Ba."

(Barrett Browning in Karlin, p. 189)

From Browning's response:

"You never before heard me love and bless and send my heart after . . . 'Ba'—did you? Ba . . . and that is you! I TRIED—(more than wanted—) to call you that, on Wednesday!"

(Browning in Karlin, p. 190)

---

if not inevitable milestone in her life. While such factors as social class and level of affluence still influenced courtship and marriage practices, women in general had more personal freedom in choosing whom to wed than their mothers and grandmothers had. Historians Estelle B. Freedman and Erna Olafson Hellerstein contend,

> The weakening of external controls on courtship was in fact a mixed blessing for women. To the extent that it lessened the surveillance over their romantic and sexual behavior, it brought greater personal autonomy; but at the same time it left them unprotected as they ventured into a larger world. . . . Women's

sexual and economic vulnerability, their desire for respectability and security, and their longing (in many cases) for children combined with the growing ordeal of romantic love to place great pressure on them to marry. Spinsterhood was, in fact, rare in the nineteenth century—by the end of the century, more than 90 percent of all American women married, as did 85-88 percent of the women in England and France.

> (Freedman and Hellerstein in Hellerstein et al, p. 121)

Spinsters did exist, however, from all walks of life. Historian Sally Mitchell notes that, in Victorian England, "[t]here were more women in their twenties and thirties than men to marry them (largely because of male emigration and colonial service), but not all single women were unhappy old maids. In the working classes, women in well-paid trades were more apt to remain single than those whose earnings were too low to provide adequate support. Among the middle and upper classes, too, it was quite possible for women to earn decent incomes and live contented, independent lives" (Mitchell, p. 269).

Financial independence made a huge difference in an unmarried woman's quality of life, as did race, class, and nationality. White middle-class women with independent means could create comfortable existences for themselves and, if necessary, become teachers, writers, lecturers, or social reformers. For much of the period, however, it was considered socially unacceptable for middle-class women to do paid work; in general, a middle-aged, middle-class spinster with no money of her own was expected to stay with her parents until their deaths. After that, she could keep house for an unmarried brother or move in with a married sibling who had a large family and serve as an unpaid companion or nurse to her nieces and nephews.

The situation of Barrett and her siblings was at once typical and atypical of the preceding scenario. Mr. Barrett opposed marriage for all his children, apparently desiring to keep every one of them under his control. As noted, Barrett herself had an independent income from legacies bequeathed to her by her grandmother and uncle; so she did not need to write for her living. She furthermore chose to remain in the family home because of her poor health, her love for her siblings, and her love for her father. Even in her youth, before illness took such a firm hold on her, Barrett apparently had no inclination to marry. In a diary she kept as a child, Barrett declared, "My mind is naturally independent and spurns that subserviency of opinion which is generally considered necessary to feminine softness!" (Barrett Browning in Forster, p. 29). As an adolescent, Barrett read Mary Wollstonecraft's *Vindication of the Rights of Woman* (in *WLAIT 3: British and Irish Literature and Its Times*) and came to sympathize with many of its views. She also observed in her parents' marriage an example of women's subservience to men, which she evidently deplored. Years later, she described to Browning her late mother—who had died suddenly when Barrett was 22:

> A sweet gentle nature, which the thunder a little turned from its sweetness—as when it turns milk—One of those women who never can resist,—but in submitting & bowing on themselves, make a mark, a plait, within, . . . a sign of suffering. Too womanly she was—it was her only fault—Good, good, & dear—& refined too!
>
> (Barrett Browning in Karlin, p. 293)

Intriguingly, Barrett alludes several times to her lost mother in *Sonnets from the Portuguese*—specifically, in Sonnets 18 and 33—but never once refers in these poems to the father who dominated much of her adult life.

Women and writing. While many middle-class Victorian women who did not marry eventually became housekeepers, companions, and nurses in the households of married relatives, a significant number turned to yet another means to support themselves and became writers. Some even found lasting fame as authors, including George Eliot (see *Middlemarch,* in *WLAIT 3: British and Irish Literature and Its Times*), the journalist Harriet Martineau, and Elizabeth Barrett Browning herself. Historians Leslie Parker Hume and Karen M. Offen contend: "During the first half of the nineteenth century the best English writing was nourished in rural parsonages or country cottages, as the careers of the Brontë sisters and Jane Austen attest; . . . there were many women who turned to writing to supplement their incomes; this was one of the few types of work in which a needy middle-class woman could engage without losing social status" (Hume and Offen in Hellerstein et al, p. 280).

Nonetheless, women who wrote professionally faced their share of difficulties. Although most of them worked in the home (considered women's proper sphere), "their vocation brought them into direct conflict with the cultural bias that defined writing as intellectual and therefore unwomanly" (Hume and Offen in Hellerstein et

al, p. 280). Female would-be authors were not supposed to aspire to the same lofty literary goals as their male counterparts. Some women writers of the nineteenth century chose male pseudonyms, either to help them find publishers or to ensure that their work was given a fair hearing by critics and the public: Marian Evans became George Eliot, while Charlotte, Emily, and Anne Brontë took the names, respectively, of Currer, Ellis, and Acton Bell. Other writers, including Elizabeth Gaskell and Dinah Maria Mulock, emphasized the elements of domesticity or morality in their work to offset charges of being "unwomanly."

Unlike many of her contemporaries, Elizabeth Barrett did not have to write for her living for financial reasons. Not only did she have the bequests from her uncle and grandmother, but also she belonged to an upper-middle-class family of considerable means, even though financial reverses in the 1830s had led to Mr. Barrett's selling their country property—Hope End in Herefordshire—and eventually moving the family to London. Nor did Barrett need to resort to a male pseudonym—by the 1840s, she had become a literary celebrity in her own right. Nonetheless, Barrett herself often regretted the dearth of women poets whom she could emulate and by whom she could be inspired, once writing wistfully, "I look everywhere for grandmothers and see none" (Barrett Browning in Bristow, p. 1). Literary analyst Dorothy Mermin explains,

> Women had written good poetry in English, had even been published and read, before [Barrett] . . . but in the nineteenth century their works were almost invisible. The popular "poetesses" who adorned the literary scene when she began to write—Joanna Baillie, Felicia Hemans, Letitia Landon, and others of smaller merit and renown, inspired her as both positive and negative examples, but theirs was not the noble lineage with which she wished to claim affiliation. . . . Lacking female precursors (or grandmothers), she became such a precursor herself.
>
> (Mermin, pp. 1-2)

Throughout *Sonnets from the Portuguese,* Barrett Browning exhibits a distinct awareness of her own role as a poet. While the speaker often presents herself as inferior to her lover in health, vigor, and talents, she never forgets that she too is a professional and it is as a poetic peer that she most often addresses him. Moreover, when earthly differences are stripped away and their "two souls stand up erect and strong, / Face to face, silent, drawing nigh and nigher," the lovers are revealed as true spiritual equals (*Sonnets*, 22:1-2).

The Poems in Focus

Plot summary. Like many sonnet sequences, *Sonnets from the Portuguese* contains a narrative of sorts, as the various stages of a love relationship unfold. The sequence begins as the speaker recalls how the Greek poet Theocritus sang nostalgically of "the sweet years, the dear and wished-for years" (*Sonnets*, 1:2). These musings lead her, in turn, to remember "the melancholy years, / Those of my own life, who by turns had flung / A shadow across me" (*Sonnets*, 1:7-9). Memories of past sorrows and all that she has missed cause the speaker to weep, but suddenly "a mystic Shape did move / Behind me, and drew me backward by the hair; / And a voice said in mastery, while I strove,— / "Guess now who holds thee?'" (*Sonnets*, 1:10-13). The speaker replies, "Death," but is speedily contradicted: "The silver answer rang, —'Not Death but Love'" (*Sonnets*, 1:14).

Surprised by love, the speaker initially expresses disbelief that her lover, a fellow poet, desires her. To her mind, they are so dissimilar in every way that she imagines that their "ministering two angels look surprise / On one another as they strike athwart / Their wings in passing" (*Sonnets*, 3:3-5). Her lover is a "guest for queens to social pageantries," eminently suited to the role of "chief musician" (*Sonnets*, 3:6, 9). She, by contrast, is a "poor, tired, wandering singer, singing through / The dark, and leaning up a cypress tree" (*Sonnets*, 3:11-12). Several times, the speaker exhorts her suitor to "go from [her]," even as she realizes it is already too late because she feels that he has become a part of her: "What I do / And what I dream include thee, as the wine / Must taste of its own grapes" (*Sonnets*, 6:1, 10-12).

The speaker ponders her changed circumstances: having resigned herself to an early death, she instead finds herself "caught up into love, and taught the whole / Of life in a new rhythm" (*Sonnets*, 7:6-7). She also wonders what she can give her lover in return in exchange for "the gold / And purple of thine heart" which he has offered to her, fearing that "frequent tears have run / The colors from my life, and left so dead / And pale a stuff, it were not fitly done / To give the same as pillow to thy head" (*Sonnets*, 8:2-3, 10-13). Despite her misgivings, however, the speaker ul-

timately concludes that "love, mere love, is beautiful indeed / And worthy of acceptation" (*Sonnets*, 10:1-2). Moreover, when the speaker at last admits to the lover, "*I love thee*—in thy sight, / I stand transfigured, glorified aright, / With conscience of the new rays that proceed / Out of my face towards thine" (*Sonnets*, 10:6-9). Her love transforms her into a being worthy of love.

Having openly acknowledged her love for her suitor, the speaker takes her first steps towards accepting their relationship. She urges her lover not to love her for such changeable things as "her smile—her look—her way / Of speaking gently" but to "love me for love's sake, that evermore / Thou mayst love on, through love's eternity" (*Sonnets*, 14:3-4, 13-14). As their romance progresses, the lovers exchange tokens—in this case, locks of hair—and rejoice in their growing bond, which compensates for whatever differences exist between them. Midway through the sequence, the speaker reaches a point where she can fully commit herself to life because of her love: "As brighter ladies do not count it strange, / For love, to give up acres and degree, / I yield the grave for thy sake, and exchange / My near sweet view of Heaven, for earth with thee!" (*Sonnets*, 23:11-14).

The latter half of *Sonnets from the Portuguese* reflect mainly positive developments in the lovers' ongoing relationship. As their feelings for each other deepen and mature, the speaker reflects upon the changes love has wrought in her world. Even the life of the mind, which formerly contented her, seems inadequate compared to the love that has transformed her whole existence. She describes how, years ago, she "lived with visions for my company, / Instead of men and women" but when those bright visions faded, "Thou didst come—to be, / Beloved, what they seemed" (*Sonnets*, 26:1-2, 8-9). Her beloved provides her with "satisfaction of all wants: / Because God's gifts put man's best dreams to shame" (*Sonnets*, 26:13-14). The speaker feels her being increasingly twined in that of her lover; she enjoins him to call her by the "pet-name" she had in childhood and so "catch the early love up in the late" and thus become all in all to her (*Sonnets*, 33:12).

Despite the totality of her commitment to her lover, the speaker is occasionally troubled by fears that their love might not be strong enough to withstand the similarly strong pull of her home and family: "Shall I never miss / Home-talk and blessing and the common kiss / That comes to each in turn, nor count it strange, / When I look up to drop on a new range / Of walls and floors, another home than this?" (*Sonnets*, 35:2-6). Nonetheless, she remains determined to make the attempt, if he remains constant: "Open thine heart wide, / And fold within the wet wings of thy dove" (*Sonnets*, 35:13-14).

The speaker's love for her suitor and her confidence in their future together continue to grow, culminating in the moment when she asks herself and him the question, "How do I love thee?" (*Sonnets*, 43:1). The thoughts, ideals, and experiences of her life mingle in her reply: "I love thee freely, as men strive for Right; / I love thee purely, as they turn from Praise. / I love thee with the passion put to use / In my old griefs, and with my childhood's faith. / I love thee with a love I seemed to lose / With my lost saints" (*Sonnets*, 43:7-12). Turning from contemplation of one world to the next, she goes on to assert that "if God choose, / I shall but love thee better after death" (*Sonnets*, 43:13-14).

In the final sonnet of the sequence, the speaker recalls the "many flowers" her beloved has brought to her during their courtship and now, in turn, she makes him an offering of her own: "So, in the like name of that love of ours, / Take back these thoughts which here unfolded too, / And which on warm and cold days I withdrew / From my heart's ground" (*Sonnets*, 44:1, 5-8). Although the garden of her heart still contains "bitter weeds and rue" and requires his careful tending, she nonetheless entrusts what *has* bloomed in that place to his care: "[T]ake them, as I used to do / Thy flowers, and keep them where they shall not pine / Instruct thine eyes to keep their colors true, / And tell thy soul their roots are left in mine" (*Sonnets*, 44:9, 11-14).

Women, love, and modernity. For much of the nineteenth and twentieth centuries, the prevailing image of Elizabeth Barrett Browning has been that of the ailing, fragile maiden lying on her couch, rescued by a dashing poet from the domestic tyranny of her overbearing father. While those elements certainly formed a part of the famous romance between Elizabeth Barrett and Robert Browning, Barrett's own role in the proceedings was by no means passive, nor was *Sonnets from the Portuguese* a conventionally sentimental tribute from the poet to her new husband. Death, morbidity, loneliness, and self-doubt resonate through the poems as much as love, joy, and awakening passion. And for a woman to express these emotions as nakedly as Barrett does through her female speaker was in itself an innovation, during a period when purity, modesty, and reticence were expected of the "womanly"

Robert Browning.

(middle-class) woman. Her female speaker was, moreover innovative in terms of Barrett Browning's own poetry to date, as scholar Margaret Reynolds argues:

> The *Sonnets from the Portuguese* mark a radical change in the character of Elizabeth Barrett Browning's poetry, or rather in the character of Barrett Browning's poet. In the earlier work, her first-person poetic persona is either male, as in *Lady Geraldine's Courtship*, or is sexless, as in *A Vision of Poets*, so that she does not contravene the law of silence for women. In the *Sonnets*, however, a *woman* speaks and she speaks as a *poet*, the equal of a man poet, fit to barter and compete with him.
>
> (Reynolds, p. 60)

The genre of poetry in which Barrett Browning chose to express these radical changes is also significant, as noted by literary scholar Angela Leighton:

> To write a sonnet sequence is to trespass on a male domain. Dante, Petrarch, Sidney and Shakespeare are the eminent 'grandfathers' of this predominantly male line, and Barrett Browning is one of the first granddaughters. She thus enters into a tradition in which the roles are sexually delineated: there is the man who speaks, and there is the woman who is admired, described, cajoled and pleaded with from a distance. . . . Barrett Browning must not only

reverse the roles, but she must also be sensitive to the fact that Robert was a lover and a poet in his own right, and disinclined to be cast in the role of the superior muse.

(Leighton, pp. 98-99)

Barrett Browning's version of the sonnet sequence thus does not cast the woman solely as the lover who entreats a distant male beloved to

---

THE SONNET FORM

Popular since the fourteenth century, the sonnet consists of a single stanza of 14 lines in iambic pentameter—five metric feet in which an unstressed syllable is followed by a stressed syllable—connected by an intricate rhyme scheme. The two most popular forms are the Italian (or Petrarchan) and English (or Shakespearean) sonnet. The Italian sonnet form contains an octave rhyming *abbaabba*, followed by a sestet rhyming *cdecde* or *cdcdcd*. Frequently, the octave puts forth a problem or situation, which is then resolved in the sestet. By contrast, the English sonnet consists of three quatrains (*abab cdcd efef*), followed by a couplet (*gg*), which gives an epigrammatic turn to the subject explored in the preceding quatrains. While both forms of sonnet have been utilized by generations of poets, it has been argued that the Italian sonnet is the more challenging of the two forms for English speakers to master. Elizabeth Barrett Browning employs the Italian sonnet form throughout *Sonnets from the Portuguese*. In sensibility, however, she was far more like her English literary predecessors, especially William Shakespeare and John Milton (see Milton's **Paradise Lost** in *WLAIT 3: British and Irish Literature and Its Times*). While most sonneteers—including Petrarch, Sidney, and Spenser—wrote *about* their idealized beloveds, Shakespeare, Donne, and Barrett Browning often spoke directly *to* their lovers, engaging them in discussion and debate.

---

return her affections. Instead, the woman speaker is both subject and object in the poems. She is the speaker and sonneteer but, at the same time, she is also the one who inspires love in her poet suitor, love that she is, if not unwilling, then, reluctant to accept: "O my fears, / That this can scarce be right! We are not peers, / So to be lovers; and I own, and grieve, / That givers of such gifts as mine are, must / Be counted with the ungenerous!" (*Sonnets*, 9:6-10).

Yet for all her apparent self-abnegation, the speaker knows herself to be capable of passion and power, despite the sorrows that have blighted her life. Comparing her "heavy heart" to Electra's sepulchral urn that supposedly held the ashes of her dead brother, she reveals both those sorrows and the potential for passion to her lover: "Behold and see / What a great heap of grief lay hid in me, / And how the red wild sparkles dimly burn / Through the ashen greyness" (*Sonnets*, 5:1, 6-10). The "red wild sparkles" of passion could be stamped out by her suitor's foot if he scorns them, but if blown to new life, she warns, those few embers could ignite a powerful and dangerous blaze and "those laurels on thine head, / O my Beloved, will not shield thee so, / That none of all the fires shall scorch and shred / The hair beneath" (*Sonnets*, 5:11-14).

The turning point of the sequence, Sonnet 10, also represents a marked departure from poetic tradition. Despite her qualms, the speaker acknowledges the beauty of love and accepts it in this pivotal sonnet: Her love, she says, "is fire" (*Sonnets*, 10:5). The speaker's revelation in this sonnet alone distinguishes *Sonnets from the Portuguese* from its poetic predecessors, in which declarations of mutual love are eternally deferred. Moreover, as the lovers' relationship matures and approaches romantic fulfillment, Barrett's sonnet sequence becomes, increasingly, the product not only of her sex but of her particular time.

> Like almost all Victorian amatory sequences, and unlike most Renaissance ones, [*Sonnets from the Portuguese*] assumes that marriage—the social affirmation of love, the affective bond holding society together—is love's proper end. . . . By surrendering to love, the speaker is repudiating (as many Victorian poets felt it necessary to do) art bred in isolation. . . . And as in most Victorian sequence poems, lyric utterance is set in a context of humdrum, unromantic, unheroic, everyday life.
>
> (Mermin, p. 130)

This celebration of the ordinary harks back not to Petrarch or to Shakespeare but to far more recent poets, to William Wordsworth and Samuel Taylor Coleridge at the turn of the nineteenth century (see **Lyrical Ballads** in *WLAIT 3: British and Irish Literature and Its Times*).

Given her familiarity with classical and English literature, Barrett Browning was likely aware of the ways in which her sonnet sequence differed from those of her literary "grandfathers." Indeed, if a letter composed early in her correspondence with Browning is any indication, she may have deliberately reinvented the genre to create a new poetry more suited to her day:

> I am inclined to think that we want new *forms* . . . as well as thoughts—The old gods are dethroned. Why should we go back to the antique moulds . . . classical moulds, as they are so improperly called. . . . Let us all aspire to *Life*—& let the dead bury their dead. If we have but courage to face these conventions, to touch this love ground we shall take strength from it instead of losing it. . . . For there is poetry *everywhere* . . . the 'treasure' (see the old fable) lies all over the field.
>
> (Barrett Browning in Karlin, p. 36)

Sources and literary context. The autobiographical nature of *Sonnets from the Portuguese* was no secret to the Brownings themselves. In 1849, while the couple were living in Pisa, Elizabeth informed her husband, depressed over the recent death of his mother, that she had once written some poems about him, and she showed them to him. She described Browning's reaction to the poems as "touched and pleased" and before long, he was encouraging her to have them published (Barrett Browning in Forster, p. 237). Because Elizabeth felt the poems were too personal to be published under her own name, the Brownings decided to disguise the sonnet sequence as a translation. They chose the title *Sonnets from the Portuguese* for two reasons: Browning's nickname for Elizabeth—because of her olive complexion—was "my little Portuguese," and he was intrigued by her earlier poem, "Catarina to Camoëns," which dealt with a Portuguese poet and his beloved.

Sonnets from the Portuguese helped to revive the sonnet sequence, a literary genre that had flourished during the fourteenth, fifteenth, and sixteenth centuries. The Italian poet, Petrarch, is usually credited with originating the genre through a series of sonnets that explored his undying and unrequited love for the beautiful but married Laura. Many Elizabethan poets emulated Petrarch by writing linked sonnets that depicted the various aspects of a relationship between lovers; the most famous of these Elizabethan sonnet sequences include Sir Philip Sidney's *Astrophel and Stella* (1580), Edmund Spenser's *Amoretti* (1595), and William Shakespeare's untitled sonnets, which appear to be addressed, alternately, to a handsome young man and a beguiling dark woman. After several centuries in eclipse, the sonnet form and sequence became popular again during the nineteenth century. William Wordsworth's *The River Duddon*,

Dante Gabriel Rossetti's *The House of Life*, Elizabeth Barrett Browning's *Sonnets from the Portuguese*, and Christina Rossetti's *Monna Innominata* are all examples of this revived poetic genre. *Sonnets from the Portuguese*, however, was the first sonnet sequence, written by a woman, to give the woman's perspective on the relationship between lovers. Moreover, *Sonnets from the Portuguese* was one of the few sonnet sequences that ended happily, with the lovers achieving fulfillment rather than disappointment.

Reviews. *Sonnets from the Portuguese* was published in Barrett Browning's *Poems* in 1850. At the time, the volume attracted little critical notice, perhaps because it contained much reprinted material. Most of the reviews that it did inspire were positive, with the lone exception of the one from the *Spectator,* which complained, "Mrs Browning has given no single instance of her ability to compose finished works. Diffuseness, obscurity, and exaggeration, mar even the happiest efforts of her genius" (*Spectator* in Taplin, pp. 238-239). Other reviewers were more enthusiastic. H. F. Chorley, writing for the *Athenaeum*, declared, "Mrs. Browning is probably, of her sex, the first imaginative writer England has produced in any age:—she is, beyond comparison, the first poetess of her own" (Chorley in Taplin, p. 237). Elizabeth scoffed at the "of her sex"—faint praise indeed. The *English Review* similarly asserted that Barrett Browning held "high rank among the bards of England" and noted "her especial beauties—in the combination of romantic wildness with deep, true tenderness and most singular power" (*English Review* in Taplin, p. 237).

More specifically, the reviewer for the *Examiner* wrote that *Sonnets from the Portuguese* comprised a "remarkable series," though, as the Brownings had intended, he seemed unaware of the autobiographical significance. The critic for *Fraser's Magazine* was similarly misled by the title but nonetheless appreciated the unique quality of the sonnets, remarking, "From the Portuguese they may be: but their life and earnestness must prove Mrs. Browning either to be the most perfect of all known translators, or to have quickened with her own spirit the framework of another's thoughts, and then modestly declined the honour which was really her own" (*Fraser's Magazine* in Taplin, p. 238). Full-fledged acknowledgement of the poems' prowess came from a knowing audience, though, to whom they were originally directed. Robert Browning proclaimed them "the finest sonnets written in any language since Shakespeare's" (Browning in Radley, p. 90).

The sequence become better known and more widely praised after Barrett Browning's death in 1861. The following year, a critic for the *Christian Examiner* wrote of *Sonnets from the Portuguese*, "Such purity, sweet humility, lofty self-abnegation, and impassioned tenderness have never before found utterance in verse. Shakespeare's sonnets, beautiful as they are, cannot be compared with them, and Petrarch's seem commonplace beside them" (*Christian Examiner* in Taplin, pp. 408-409). By the end of the nineteenth century, *Sonnets from the Portuguese* had secured a place in the affection of late-Victorian readers and critics. In his *Victorian Poets* (1895), Edmund Clarence Stedman ranked *Sonnets from the Portuguese* among

the finest subjective poetry in our literature . . . it is no sacrilege to say that their music is showered from a higher and purer atmosphere than that of the Swan of Avon. . . . Mrs. Browning's Love *Sonnets* are the outpourings of a woman's tenderest emotions, at an epoch when her art was most mature and her whole nature exalted by a passion that to such a being comes but once and for all. Here, indeed, the singer rose to her height. Here she is absorbed in rapturous utterance, radiant and triumphant with her own joy.

(Stedman, p. 137)

—Pamela S. Loy

For More Information

Bristow, Joseph, ed. *Victorian Women Poets: Emily Brontë, Elizabeth Barrett Browning, Christina Rossetti*. London: Macmillan, 1995.

Barrett Browning, Elizabeth. *Sonnets from the Portuguese and Other Love Poems*. New York: Doubleday, 1990.

Donaldson, Sandra, ed. *Critical Essays on Elizabeth Barrett Browning*. New York: G. K. Hall, 1999.

Forster, Margaret. *Elizabeth Barrett Browning*. New York: Doubleday, 1988.

Hellerstein, Erna Olafson, Leslie Parker Hume, and Karen M. Offen, eds. *Victorian Women*. Stanford: Stanford University Press, 1981.

Karlin, Daniel, ed. *Robert Browning and Elizabeth Barrett: The Courtship Correspondence 1845-1846*. Oxford: Clarendon Press, 1989.

Leighton, Angela. *Elizabeth Barrett Browning*. Bloomington: Indiana University Press, 1986.

Mermin, Dorothy. *Elizabeth Barrett Browning: The Origins of a New Poetry*. Chicago: University of Chicago Press, 1989.

Mitchell, Sally. *Daily Life in Victorian England*. Westport: Greenwood, 1996.

Porter, Charlotte, and Helen A. Clarke, eds. *The Complete Works of Elizabeth Barrett Browning*. Vol. 2. New York: AMS, 1973.

Radley, Virginia L. *Elizabeth Barrett Browning*. Boston: Twayne, 1972.

Reynolds, Margaret. "Love's Measurements in Elizabeth Barrett Browning's *Sonnets from the Portuguese*." In *Studies in Browning and His Circle* 21 (21 November 1977): 53-67.

Stedman, Edmund Clarence. *Victorian Poets*. Boston: Houghton, Mifflin, 1895.

Taplin, Gardner B. *The Life of Elizabeth Barrett Browning*. New Haven: Yale University Press, 1957.

Sour Sweet

by

Timothy Mo

Timothy Mo was born in Hong Kong in 1950 to a Chinese father and an English mother who divorced soon after his birth. When Mo was ten, he moved to England to live with his mother, where he later received a B.A. degree in history from Oxford University and studied creative writing at the University of East Anglia. While Mo, who speaks and writes little Chinese, considers his novels to address matters of universal significance, those larger issues are framed by issues that reflect his dual Chinese and European background. His first novel, *The Monkey King* (1978), is set in Hong Kong in the 1950s and features a half-Chinese, half-Portuguese main character who slowly comes to value the mixed heritage that he at first despises. Most of Mo's later books—*An Insular Possession* (1986), *The Redundancy of Courage* (1991), and *Brownout on Breadfruit Boulevard* (1995)—are also set in Asia. Of his novels to date only the second, *Sour Sweet*, is set in Britain. Like the others, it has an Asian focus, taking place entirely within London's Chinese immigrant community.

Events in History at the Time of the Novel

Hong Kong. Britain's Chinese immigrant community has been profoundly shaped by the British Empire's colonial presence in Eastern Asia, and that presence is exemplified above all by the former British trading colony of Hong Kong. Hong Kong has been and remains central

THE LITERARY WORK

A novel set in London in the early 1960s; published in 1982.

SYNOPSIS

Having emigrated from Hong Kong, the Chen family struggles to adapt to life in London, where Mr. Chen unwittingly becomes a target of the Chinese international crime syndicate known as the Triad Society.

to the experience and identity of Chinese immigrants in Britain.

Britain and Hong Kong have an intertwined history that goes back to the city's foundation by British merchants in the 1820s, before which the infertile and mountainous Hong Kong Island was occupied by a few small fishing settlements. Around the middle of the nineteenth century, Britain fought two wars with China in order to impose the Hong Kong-based and British-controlled importation of opium into China. The settlements of these wars confirmed British possession of Hong Kong by treaty: in the First Opium War (1839-42) China ceded Hong Kong Island to the British; in the Second Opium War (1856-60) China ceded the area called Kowloon on the mainland opposite the island. Thus, the British secured both the eastern and western approaches to the island's magnificent natural anchorage, Victoria Harbour. On July 1, 1898, Britain signed

Timothy Mo

a 99-year lease with China for a large inland area north of Kowloon known as the New Territories, along with over 200 nearby islands. By that time, both commercial development and population had expanded rapidly, so that over 300,000 people, mostly Chinese, lived in urban Hong Kong. By contrast, in the larger and less developed New Territories, small villages continued to exist and would endure through the time the novel takes place. In *Sour Sweet* Mr. Chen, the head of the immigrant family whose story the novel tells, comes from a village in the New Territories.

Hong Kong was one of many so-called "treaty ports" around which the European colonial powers had carved out spheres of influence in China by the end of the nineteenth century. While Hong Kong and nearby Macao (ceded to Portugal) were the only actual territorial concessions, each European power had a number of Chinese commercial centers in which it controlled trade. All major Chinese ports and many inland cities were "opened" in this way to British, French, Portuguese, or other European traders, as the tottering and unpopular Manchu Qing Dynasty (1644-1911) used European support to maintain its grip on power. These centers all attracted Chinese traders, merchants, and settlers.

From its early years, Hong Kong has exerted an especially strong attraction for Chinese seeking economic prosperity or political refuge. Im-

migration into Hong Kong was unrestricted, and the flow of Chinese immigrants increased in times of trouble. Thousands of Chinese refugees, for example, arrived after the Japanese invasion of China in 1937. Hong Kong itself fell to the Japanese in 1941, and the flow of refugees reversed during World War II, with the population falling from 1.6 million to about 650,000 as many fled back to mainland China. With the resumption of British rule after the end of the war in 1945, hundreds of thousands of Chinese began returning to Hong Kong, largely Cantonese-speakers from the neighboring provinces of Guangxi and Guangdong. The city's growing population was further swollen in 1949 by refugees from China's civil war between the Nationalists and the Communists. Communist victory that same year created the People's Republic of China, with the defeated Nationalists occupying the offshore island of Taiwan, which like Hong Kong would remain a literal island of capitalism close to the Communist mainland. In the novel, Mr. Chen's wife, Lily, is the daughter of a martial arts expert from Guangxi who was killed fighting for the Nationalists when she was 11. Lily and her sister Mui, four years older, joined the flood of immigrant refugees into Hong Kong, where she worked in a shoe factory until marrying Mr. Chen.

In 1982, the year the novel was published, Britain and China opened negotiations to hand Hong Kong back to China, as the July 1997 expiration of the New Territories treaty approached. China's position had long been that both the lease and the original treaties had been imposed by force and were therefore invalid, and the British agreed to return the entire colony to Chinese control. More and more residents emigrated in the late 1970s because of uncertainty about Hong Kong's future, but emigration would not increase sharply until the late 1980s.

Chinese immigrants in Britain. Small Chinese immigrant communities have been recorded in Britain as early as the late eighteenth century, but only in the period after World War II did the numbers of Chinese-born British residents surpass a few thousand. Postwar immigration from China increased sharply in the late 1940s, as a result of various factors. The 1948 British Nationality Act officially gave citizens of the United Kingdom and Colonies and of the Independent Commonwealth Countries (former British colonies, such as Canada and India) the right to enter the United Kingdom and find employment there without restriction. Other factors also combined to spur immigration. There was an increased demand for labor in Britain as its economy recovered from the war. At the same time, cheap rice imports into Hong Kong from Thailand began to undercut local rice growers from the New Territories villages, creating an incentive for emigration. *Sour Sweet* speaks of cheap Thai rice imports putting financial pressure on Mr. Chen's father, a carpenter in a village where few can afford to build; during the course of the novel Mr. Chen joins his son's family in Britain.

The following figures from the British census show the increasingly important role that Hong Kong played in Chinese immigration:

Chinese Population in Postwar Britain by Place of Birth

Year	China	Hong Kong	Singapore	Malaysia	Total
1951	8,636	3,459	3,255	4,046	19,396
1961	9,192	10,222	9,820	9,516	38,750
1971	13,495	29,520	27,335	25,680	96,030
1981	17,569	58,917	32,447	45,430	154,363

(adapted from Parker, p. 63)

While the numbers of Hong Kong-born Chinese rose faster than any other segment of the Chinese British population, Hong Kong's influence was even greater than these numbers may suggest at first glance. First, like the novel's Lily Chen, many or even most of the China-born immigrants settled in or passed through Hong Kong before arriving in Britain. Many of the others had kinship ties with Hong Kong. Second, immigrants from Singapore and Malaysia (both British colonies whose populations were largely ethnic Chinese) tended to be wealthier and better educated than those born in Hong Kong or China. Many were students or professional trainees, such as doctors and nurses, who intended to return home on completing a course of study or training; Hong Kong-born and China-born immigrants tended to stay longer or to settle permanently in Britain. Finally, in contrast with the closed nature of the mainland Communist system, Hong Kong's vital popular culture, in the form of print and other media, remained accessible to the immigrant community and offered all Chinese in Britain a way to keep in touch with their Chinese roots. Cantonese, Hong Kong's dominant Chinese language, thus also became the main language of Chinese immigrants in Britain.

Restaurants, takeaways, and racism. After the war, new tastes and more disposable income among the British created an economic niche in the food service business that Chinese immi-

grants were quick to fill. There were various reasons for this alacrity, including discrimination. As shown in later decades, Asians who applied for jobs often suffered "racial disadvantage," which narrowed the options (Ramdin, p. 326).

Chinese immigrants often opted to begin their own enterprises. Starting in the 1950s, a rapidly growing number of Chinese restaurants appeared in Britain's cities. Restaurant work suited the needs of many immigrants, since it was labor-intensive employment that did not require special skills or much knowledge of the English language. At the beginning of the novel, Mr. Chen works in London's Chinatown (located in the city's Soho district). Such restaurants were at first staffed almost entirely by men. Between 1945 and 1970, the number of Chinese food service establishments in Britain rose tenfold, from about 100 to about 1000.

By the early 1960s, women were joining this immigrant labor force. As immigrant men increasingly arranged for their families to join them in Britain (or, like the novel's Mr. Chen, returned to Hong Kong to find a wife to bring back to Britain), those who had formerly worked as waiters in Chinese restaurants began establishing their own smaller, family-run businesses. The Chen family starts such a business, moving away from London's Chinatown and opening a takeaway shop, a small restaurant without tables where customers can purchase quickly prepared food to eat away from the premises. In the late 1960s the small family-owned takeaway would start to play a central role in the Chinese immigrant community, largely though not completely displacing the larger partner-owned restaurants that had predominated earlier. By the 1970s Chinese takeaway shops had become a familiar sight in many British cities and towns. Subsequently many Chinese opened takeaway fish-and-chips shops that specialized in this traditional English favorite (as Chen's sister-in-law Mui does at the end of the novel). Other ethnic-based fast foods likewise became popular in Britain: the Chens, for example, compete with a Pakistani takeaway nearby.

Meanwhile, the immigration picture changed, which affected the number of Chinese British in food service occupations. In 1962 the British Commonwealth Immigrants' Act abolished the automatic right of British citizenship for Commonwealth citizens. Now unskilled Commonwealth applicants could win approval for immigration only if they could obtain a voucher from an employer showing that they already had a job waiting in Britain. But the 1962 Act also distinguished between British colonies in the Commonwealth and independent Commonwealth nations, allowing the dependents of immigrants from British colonies (such as Hong Kong) continued access. In the novel Mr. Chen's father is allowed entry as a dependent, although, as Lily's sister Mui observes, "English people don't want many foreign persons here. . . . Authorities are much stricter than when I came," that is before the 1962 Act (Mo, *Sour Sweet*, p. 208).

Over time, the changes brought about by the 1962 Act had the effect of funneling Chinese immigrants even more sharply into food service, by

---

RACISM AND TAKEAWAYS

Immigration was a major political issue in Britain in the 1960s, as popular reaction set in to unprecedented levels of immigration after 1948. Some have associated racist motivations with attempts to limit immigration, since many of the immigrants were dark-skinned (such as those from the former colonies in India, Pakistan, and the West Indies). *Sour Sweet* does not depict overt racism against its protagonists, but racism is constantly in the novel's background. For example, Chen and Lily both feel camaraderie with Pakistani and black West Indian bus conductors, and Lily warns her son not to get on the bus if the conductor is white. Chinese immigrants did in fact commonly encounter racist behavior in mid-twentieth-century Britain, behavior that ranged from hostile looks and comments to physical violence. Young Chinese women working in takeaways were particularly vulnerable to such behavior, often being exposed late at night to hostile, drunken groups of young male customers coming in for food after the eleven o'-clock pub closing hour.

---

giving employers greater control over prospective immigrants. These changes also encouraged the opening of family-run takeaways, giving increased importance to family and village connections as a way of landing a job before immigration, or of finding a place as a dependent who could help with the business (as the elder Mr. Chen does in the novel). By 1985, a few years after the novel was published, a British government survey indicated that 90 percent of Chinese in Britain worked in the food service industry (Parker, p. 72).

The Triads. Parallel to the story of the Chen family, *Sour Sweet* also depicts a dramatic feud involving a very different kind of familial organization, the Chinese crime syndicate known to its members as the Hung family, but to the English-speaking world as the Triad Society. This secret brotherhood originated in the seventeenth century, when loyalists of the overthrown Ming Dynasty banded together to overthrow the usurping Manchu Qing Dynasty and restore Ming rule. In Triad legend the society's founders were warrior monks of the Shao Lin Monastery, whose martial arts skills incurred the wrath of the Manchu emperor, provoking him ultimately to destroy the monastery. After the last Qing emperor abdicated in 1911, the society—as one of the many factions that had helped bring about the dynasty's downfall—enjoyed enhanced power and prestige. With its original purpose of overthrowing the Qing Dynasty accomplished, however, the society now increasingly moved into criminal activity, its once strong central authority giving way to largely independent branches.

Always strongest in southern China, these criminal Triad Societies were already well established in Hong Kong when the Communists took power in mainland China in 1949. (Hong Kong police officer and author W. P. Morgan, in his 1960 book *Triad Societies of Hong Kong*, employs the plural to distinguish the new, criminal organizations from the old society.) As supporters of the Nationalists, they were targeted on the mainland by the Communists, so that after 1949 Hong Kong became a major stronghold. At the same time, struggles for power over the limited but lucrative Hong Kong turf erupted between rival branches. Morgan describes a series of confrontations between the newer so-called 14K branches and the older Wo and other societies in the 1940s and 1950s. As Morgan points out, the Triads' powerful grip extended wherever Chinese settled: in the novel Mo dramatizes a bloody (and fictional) power struggle between the 14K and the Wo societies in London's Soho Chinatown.

The Novel in Focus

Plot summary. Most of the narrative follows the Chen family: Mr. Chen, Lily, their 2½-year-old son Man Kee, and Mui, Lily's elder sister, who immigrated after Man Kee's birth to help look after the boy. However, the action periodically shifts to related events unfolding as the Wo society prepares to fend off challenges to its Chinatown turf by the 14K branch. At the onset of the novel, the Chens have been living in London's Chinatown for more than three years, and Mr. Chen works at a Chinese restaurant called Excellence. The couple has been married for four years, Mr. Chen having returned to Hong Kong to find a wife. He and Lily met at a dance in the New Territories village where he grew up, a gathering arranged so that visiting emigrants could meet single women. They married soon after. Each month Chen sends a remittance to his parents, a money order upon which the elderly couple relies heavily, like many other couples in the village.

Lily and Mui have no surviving relatives. Since their parents had no male children, their father, a martial arts expert and renowned fighter, trained Lily in Chinese martial arts techniques before he was killed fighting the Communists. Thus, Mui, though four years older than Lily, is more compliant and submissive (more ladylike in traditional Chinese terms). The athletic and strong-willed Lily actually worries that since arriving in Britain after Man Kee's birth, Mui has rarely left the apartment and watches TV constantly.

At Lily's urging, Chen quits his restaurant job and the family moves out of Chinatown into a small flat in a south London neighborhood. On the bottom floor of the flat, they open a small takeaway, finding ready customers among the truck drivers who frequent the garage nearby. Lily, however, does not know that the real reason Chen has agreed to this step is that he has secretly accepted money from the Wo society, in a deal brokered by a fellow waiter who is a runner, or heroin dealer, for the society. The money, which the society ostensibly offers as a gift, is for medical attention needed by Chen's father in Hong Kong. Knowing that he is now under an obligation that can bring him only deeper and more dangerous involvement with the society, Chen's agreement to move and start a business is really a desperate attempt to hide.

The business prospers, however, and a potential dispute with the garage owner, Mr. Constantinides—who complains that some of the truck drivers who patronize the Chens' takeaway are blocking his entrance—is averted when he and Chen strike a mutually advantageous arrangement whereby the drivers will park in the garage, from where Constantinides will phone in their orders. Mui, whose TV watching has resulted in her English improving more than Chen's or Lily's, collects good tips delivering the drivers' orders. In a reversal of her earlier timidity, she now becomes the family's informal rep-

resentative to the British world. Chen cooks and Lily handles the counter, impassively and silently as possible helping the English customers, who sit on homemade benches in the small front room as they wait for the food.

Gradually the immigrants' world broadens: they purchase a battered old van, visit the seashore for a picnic, and survive baffling encounters with British bureaucracy in the forms of a lady who wishes to put them on the local voting rolls and, more alarmingly, the tax man. Lily's reaction to both is guarded and skeptical—she suspects the kind of "licensed brigandry" that similar officials in China might engage in—but Mui acts as interpreter and buffer (*Sour Sweet*,

REMITTANCES

In the 1960s whole villages in the rural New Territories began relying on remittances from young men working abroad, as villages had in many parts of China since the previous century. Remittances not only provided material support for the worker's family, but lent the whole family social distinction as well. As Chen reflects in the novel, if he stopped sending money home his family would be subject to humiliating gossip. Some of the young male workers were sojourners, temporary immigrants who planned to work for a few years before returning home. Others planned to stay. In Hong Kong, Britain was the preferred destination for both sojourners and permanent immigrants.

p. 163). The family gains more exposure to British ways when Man Kee starts school, which to Lily's chagrin he enjoys.

Lily is even more dismayed when it transpires that Mui—normally plump but now seeming to get "fatter by the day"—is in fact six months pregnant (*Sour Sweet*, p. 184). Refusing to tell Lily who the father is, and wanting to keep her pregnancy secret, Mui acquiesces to Lily's plan that she move into the Chinatown house of their friend Mrs. Law, the wealthy older widow of a Hong Kong shipping magnate. Lily tells Chen vaguely that Mui will be back "soon" and enlists Man Kee, now old enough to take the bus to school by himself (in fact he instructs Lily on bus procedure), to help at the counter (*Sour Sweet*, p. 201). However, after Mui has the baby, a girl, she does not wish to bring her daughter back to the Chens' small flat as Lily had planned. Instead, Mrs. Law has offered to support the newborn, and has extended her a permanent room in the house. Mui agrees; she will move back in with Lily and Chen and visit her daughter as often as possible.

Just as they begin this new arrangement, news arrives that Chen's mother has died, leaving Chen's elderly and infirm father with no place to go:

> He had spent his son's remittance money on feasting and gambling, quite legitimately of course as was his right, instead of building the kind of two-storey concrete and corrugated iron pill-box that other sons and other remittances had constructed on the settlement's outskirts.
>
> (*Sour Sweet*, p. 207)

TAKEAWAY CHINESE

"The food they sold, certainly wholesome, nutritious, colourful, even tasty in its way, had been researched by Chen. It bore no resemblance at all to Chinese cuisine. They served from a stereotyped menu, similar to those outside countless other establishments" (*Sour Sweet*, p. 105). Like the fictional Chens, Chinese for decades have carefully tailored the food they serve the British public to fit the public's taste, while continuing to enjoy more authentic dishes themselves. "We didn't actually touch the stuff," said one young Chinese woman who worked in her father's takeaway in the 1990s: "Dad stuffed the other food full of M.S.G. (Monosodium Glutamate) for the customers, we had the authentic food for ourselves" (Parker, p. 99). Customer favorites featured in *Sour Sweet* include "lurid orange sweet and sour pork with pineapple chunks;" authentic dishes consumed by the Chens include "white, bloody chicken and yellow duck's feet" (*Sour Sweet*, p. 61).

None of Chen's brothers have room to take their father in their tiny houses, so they have decided that he must join Chen's family in Britain. Lily is happy to have this chance to honor her father-in-law, and Mui arranges permission for the old man to immigrate.

The normally stolid Chen, however, is panic-stricken: all these highly visible arrangements will undoubtedly reveal his whereabouts to the Wo society. His fears have more basis than he knows, for (as the reader has learned) the run-ner who arranged his earlier gift from the society has falsely blamed him for the loss of money that the runner himself embezzled. One of the Wo members, White Paper Fan, plots to topple Red Cudgel, a leader of a unit of the society (the Soho lodge), by using Red Cudgel's plan to assassinate Chen as a lever. Though White Paper Fan knows that Chen is innocent, he aims to take advantage of Red Cudgel's mistaken assassination of an innocent man to discredit Red Cudgel. The plan works, and the reader learns that Chen was taken and killed with "neither fear nor pain" (*Sour Sweet*, p. 263).

As far as Lily knows, however, Chen simply walks off one day and disappears. To conceal their mistake (assassinating an innocent man would cause the society to lose face if the Chinese community at large found out) the Wo society sends Lily a monthly stipend. This allows Lily to imagine that Chen has merely taken a temporary job abroad and will one day return to his family. Even as she holds out hope for his return, however, she begins to adjust to life without him, and even to relish her own newfound freedom. Although she loved Chen—loves him still, she tells herself—she feels "as if a stone had been taken off her and she had sprung to what her height should have been" (*Sour Sweet*, p. 278). Using the Chinese mode of referring to family members, she thinks to herself that "she might have lost Husband for a while, but she still had Son. Who could take him away from her?" (*Sour Sweet*, p. 278).

Family, duty, and acculturation. While strikingly different in tone and content, the intertwined narratives in *Sour Sweet*—that of the Chen family and that of the Triads—both dramatize Chinese concepts of family and duty. Indeed, for both groups family and duty seem closely related, even synonymous. For the Triad gangsters, however, both have become abstract: the notion of family has become an empty metaphor, and self-interest has displaced the ancient ideas of duty that once dominated the secret society. For the Chens, by contrast, and especially for Lily, the link between duty and family remains real and immediate.

At various points each of the three adults in the Chen household is described as dutiful, each in a subtly different way that suits his or her character, but always in the context of family. Lily's sense of duty is rigid and deeply internalized, though it has more traditional and less traditional elements. In the novel's opening pages, for instance, we are told that Lily always prepares a snack of soup for Chen after his shift as a waiter is over. Though he doesn't get home till 1:00 A.M., she feels that she would be "failing in her wifely duties" otherwise (*Sour Sweet*, p. 2). Lily is also the one who personally sends the remittance on the same date each month, always enclosing a brief personal note to Chen's parents, and her very Chinese sense of filial loyalty is outraged by the way the British ignore their old people. Yet Lily shocks Mui by boldly taking it upon herself to learn how to drive the van, which Mui had assumed Chen, as the man of the family, would do (in a highly comic scene, he proves completely incapable of learning).

Chen's sense of duty is described in ways that make it seem more conventional, almost a matter of politeness, and less the result of any deep inner conviction. For instance, he drinks the soup "dutifully," even though it is salty and leaves him suffering from thirst all night (*Sour Sweet*, p. 2). And while he sent the remittances regularly when he was single, Lily's sterner sense of duty acts as an insurance policy in case Chen's should slip: "He was a dutiful son. She would have made sure he was anyway" (*Sour Sweet*, p. 60). Whereas Lily analyzes situations constantly, the stolid Chen responds to the demands of duty without much analysis, and it gets him killed.

In contrast to Lily, who has shouldered her duties by conviction and choice, and Chen, who rotely goes through the motions, Mui has had her sense of duty forcibly imposed on her. Their strict father brought her up to be a traditional Chinese woman: "uncomplaining, compliant, dutiful, considerate, unselfish . . . utterly submissive to the slightest wishes of her superiors, which included women older than herself and the entire male sex, including any brothers she might acquire in the future" (*Sour Sweet*, pp. 10-11). This artificially imposed sense of duty collapses like a thin veneer when Mui immigrates. She shakes off her traditional Chinese sense of duty, becomes pregnant out of wedlock (shocking Lily), and begins making choices for herself. By the end of the novel, she is planning to marry, and partly by virtue of her acculturation has replaced her sister as the dominant one in the family.

While Lily makes certain accommodations, her more strongly internalized sense of duty remains essentially intact, withstanding the assaults of Western culture to the end. One of her strongest duties, she feels, is to raise her son as Chinese. Near the end of the novel, she is determined that Man Kee will attend Chinese school in Chinatown on weekends, and her

greatest fear is that he will "grow into a foreign devil boy" (*Sour Sweet*, p. 236). Despite Lily's final and optimistic reflection that no one can take her son from her, however, the novel has made it clear that Britain is already claiming Man Kee; as with other second-generation immigrants, he would soon find himself acculturated in ways that his parents could never share.

Sources and literary context. For *Sour Sweet*'s passages describing Hong Kong and its people,

THE WO SOCIETY *VS.* 14K

Like the Chen family, the Triad societies that came from Hong Kong to London with the Chinese immigrants were forced to adapt to new ways of doing business. In *Sour Sweet* the societies are undergoing two conflicts between old and new: one pits the more traditional Wo society against the upstart 14K society; the other opposes the old-fashioned criminal techniques —street fighting, violence, brute strength—against the newer, streamlined methods that rely as much on bookkeeping as on leg-breaking. In the novel, Red Cudgel, leader of the Wo society, epitomizes the old, blunt warriors of the past, while his lieutenant, White Paper Fan, represents the new business-oriented style. The novel refers to the Triad members by their positions in the organization. "Red Cudgel," for example, is the position of enforcer, and each unit or lodge of the Triad would have a Red Cudgel as its chief strongarm man. Leadership did not rest with any specific position; instead the leader was chosen from a pool of high-ranking members. White Paper Fan was responsible for bookkeeping and administration, and in the novel it is the holder of this position who displaces the Wo lodge's Red Cudgel as leader. While not based closely on actual events, the fictional conflict in the novel does generally reflect a turf war between the real-life Wo and 14K societies that occurred in both Hong Kong and London in late 1950s and early 1960s.

Mo could draw from his own extensive personal experience as someone born there. Similarly, as an immigrant from Hong Kong to Britain, he had his own experience to guide him in the emotions and perceptions that accompany acculturation. His presentation of this material has been compared to that of great nineteenth-century novelists such as Dickens and Flaubert, but the choice of material itself is highly original, for Mo is the first novelist working in English to write seriously of the Chinese immigrant experience in Britain (and also one of the first to write about Hong Kong). Mo's most important literary source for the Triads was Morgan's *Triad Societies of Hong Kong*, which he cites in a brief bibliographical note at the end of *Sour Sweet*. In addition, Mo also used *The Triad Society* (1900), by William Stanton, who like Morgan was an English Hong Kong police officer, and Dutch scholar Gustave Schlegel's 1866 translation of collected Triad Society documents, *Thian Thi Hui, the Hung League*.

Reception. *Sour Sweet* has met with the warmest reception, both from critics and from the reading public, of Mo's works to date. Short-listed for the Booker Prize in 1982, it won the Hawthornden Prize from the Society of Authors the following year. Writing in the *New Statesman*, Michael Poole called *Sour Sweet* "a brilliantly observed study in the first-generation immigrant experience" (Poole, p. 27). On the other hand, John Sutherland and Peter Lewis found Mo's handling of the Triads to be less satisfactory than the rest of the book, faulting his characterizations of the Triad members as comparatively shallow and unoriginal depictions of stereotyped gangsters. At the same time, both reviewers found much to praise in Mo's portrayal of the Chen family. The two critics disagreed, however, on the author's tone. Writing in the *London Review of Books*, Sutherland highlighted Mo's comedic touch and original perspective, praising the "fresh and consistently comic . . . way in which familiar British situations are reflected off an alien ethnic surface" (Sutherland, p. 18). Using similar language, Peter Lewis praised the same reflection but seemed to find it mildly disturbing:

he wrote in the *Times Literary Supplement* of a "new *frisson*" that the novel created with its "apparent discrepancy between location and action, between modern England and a largely self-contained and alien society functioning within it" (Lewis, p. 502). Despite the novel's many comic moments, Lewis continued in a similar vein, "the final effect is far from comic" (Lewis, p. 502).

—Colin Wells

For More Information

Ho, Elaine Yee Lin. *Timothy Mo*. Manchester: Manchester University Press, 2000.

Lewis, Peter. "Hong Kong London." Review of *Sour Sweet*, by Timothy Mo. *Times Literary Supplement*, 7 May 1982, 502.

Mo, Timothy. *Sour Sweet*. London: Abacus, 1982.

Morgan, W. P. *Triad Societies in Hong Kong*. Hong Kong: Government Press, 1960.

Pan, Lyn. *The Encyclopedia of the Chinese Overseas*. Richmond, England: Curzon, 1998.

Parker, David. *Through Different Eyes: The Cultural Identities of Young Chinese People in Britain*. Aldershot, England: Averbury, 1995.

Poole, Michael. Review of *Sour Sweet*, by Timothy Mo. *New Statesman* 103 (April 23, 1982): 27.

Ramdin, Ron. *Reimaging Britain: 500 Years of Black and Asian History*. London: Pluto, 1999.

Solomos, John. *Race and Racism in Britain*. London: MacMillan, 1993.

Sutherland, John. "Nationalities." Review of *Sour Sweet*, by Timothy Mo. *London Review of Books*, 6 May 1982, 18.

Wah, Yung Yung, Burjor Avari, and Simon Buckley. *British Soil, Chinese Roots*. Liverpool: Countyvise, 1996.

Ward, J. S. M., and W. G. Stirling. *The Hung Society*. 3 vols. London: Baskerville Press, 1925.

"Station Island"

by

Seamus Heaney

Seamus Heaney was born in 1939 to a farming family in Mossbawn, County Derry, about 30 miles northwest of Belfast, Ireland. He has written that this rural childhood attuned his ear to the conflicting claims in the sounds of words, as local Irish voices contrasted with "the official idioms" of radio reports from England and that it opened his eyes to the etymology of local place-names and their legendary origins (Heaney, "The Nobel Lecture," *Opened Ground*, p. 418). Heaney left Mossbawn in 1951 for college at St. Columb's in Londonderry and Queen's University in Belfast, where he would later teach as a member of the English Department. During his time there he published his first two books of poems, *The Death of a Naturalist* (1966) and *Door into the Dark* (1969). In 1972, Heaney left this "perfectly agreeable job" in Belfast for a small farm in Glanmore, County Wicklow, south of Dublin in Republican Ireland. There, Heaney proposed to concentrate exclusively on writing, "to put the practice of poetry more deliberately at the centre of my life" (Heaney, *Preoccupations*, p. 11). Four years later, after completing many of the poems in *Wintering Out* (1972), *North* (1975), and *Field Work* (1979), he returned to teaching, first at Caryfort College in Dublin, then at Harvard University, where he still works. *Station Island* (1985), written in the first years after Heaney's return from Glanmore, takes its name from the central sequence in which the poet faces shades from his personal and literary past. Along with his translations of *Beowulf* (2000), Sophocles's *Philoctetes* (as *The Cure at Troy*, 1991) and

> ## THE LITERARY WORK
>
> A poem in 12 sections, set at Lough Derg in County Donegal, Ireland; first published in 1984.
>
> ## SYNOPSIS
>
> Heaney travels to an ancient pilgrimage site and, as he undertakes its rituals, confers with the spirits of the dead.

the medieval Irish poem *Buile Suibhne* (as *Sweeney Astray*, 1983), "Station Island" is among Heaney's most ambitious work. In it, he emerges as a poet of deep concern for history and for his own time.

Events in History at the Time of the Poem

"The Troubles." Conflict over British governance of Ireland dates back to the medieval period, and the twentieth century saw this conflict rise to armed rebellion. After the 1916 rising, in which Irish rebels (the Sinn Féin) seized and held sections of Dublin, the Anglo-Irish Treaty (1921) provided independence for the 26 southern counties, predominantly Catholic, where resistance had been strongest; the new Irish Free State (later Éire, or the Republic of Ireland) had its capitol in Dublin. The United Kingdom retained control over the six predominantly Protestant counties of Northern Ireland (or Ulster), gov-

Seamus Heaney

A political conference in Republican Ireland at the end of the year saw the Sinn Féin split over the best means for reclaiming Ulster. The more radical or aggressive side of this schism formed the Provisional IRA (or "Provos"), a group committed to the destruction of British rule in Ulster by any means. The Irish Republican Army, or IRA, had always been the military wing of the Sinn Féin; the Provos, however, would direct and foment guerrilla and terrorist attacks on targets in Northern Ireland itself. The year 1971 saw a string of such attacks (shootings and bombings) that brought about the formation of small Protestant paramilitary groups to balance the Provos. Ulster police and British troops were granted powers of internment without trial against anyone suspected of terrorist (specifically Provisional IRA) activity.

On January 30, 1972 ("Bloody Sunday"), police fired into the crowd at an agitated Catholic protest rally, killing thirteen. Later that year Northern Ireland's Prime Minister was dismissed by Britain's Edward Heath, and Ulster came under direct British control. The guerrilla violence escalated, and Belfast became the site of almost-daily protests (which often included assaults on troops or police called out to monitor the crowds), gunfire, and bombings. Between 1970 and 1995, more than three thousand people were killed in the sectarian violence in Northern Ireland, and blame seems impossible to assign: like the spirits released from Pandora's box, or like fire spilled from a censer, the violence of the Troubles was easily released, and impossible to contain.

This was the Belfast in which Heaney lived during the late 1960s (and until 1972), a city under siege from within, where random violence could erupt without warning—although when asked about the violence he found himself answering, "things aren't too bad in our part of the town: a throwaway consolation meaning that we don't expect to be caught in crossfire if we step into the street" (Heaney, *Preoccupations*, p. 30). Heaney, by temperament, is chiefly interested in the local effects of this political strife: the nearby sound of gunfire or rumbling of a bomb, the sectarian murder (or accidental shooting) of an acquaintance, the tense silence in a period of relative peace. "We survive explosions and funerals," Heaney wrote, as if the two threats, of death and grief, are almost equivalent, "and live on among the families of the victims" (Heaney, *Preoccupations*, p. 30).

St. Patrick's Purgatory, Lough Derg. Lough Derg is a fair-sized body of water in the south-

erned by a local parliament that met in Belfast. This compromise, like any other, left many unsatisfied on both sides of the new border. Irish Unionists (Fenians) in the South pressed for Home Rule for the whole island, and Northern Catholics found themselves marginalized and disempowered in an increasingly sectarian Northern state. Political relations between the Republic of Ireland and Great Britain went through cycles of strain and relative amicability over much of the twentieth century, the stakes of their contention being rule of the six counties of the North.

Tensions rose between Ulster's Protestant majority and the Catholic minority during the 1960s, a decade of Catholic civil-rights protests modeled on the protests in the interest of African Americans in the southern United States. In August 1969, after a difficult general election and the resignation of Terence O'Neill as Northern Ireland's Prime Minister, rioting erupted in the streets of Derry and Belfast: small mobs of one sect or party attacked buildings or organizations belonging to another, and retributions escalated. Police found themselves uncomfortably in the middle of this chaos, besieged with rocks and homemade gasoline grenades from both sides. By the end of the month, British troops were on the streets to help manage the crowds, a temporary solution that naturally brought tensions higher.

ern part of Donegal, Republican Ireland's northernmost county. Because the twentieth-century lines of partition between Ulster and the Republic are demographic and not geographic, County Donegal has a much longer border with Northern Ireland than with County Sligo, the only fellow Republican Irish county that it borders. It is therefore difficult to reach Lough Derg from Dublin without crossing the patrolled border twice (Byron, pp. 15-19); for similar reasons, Lough Derg may have taken on especially strong significance for Northern Catholics during the last eighty years. (The Lough Derg of Heaney's poem should not be confused with the larger lake of the same name that borders Counties Galway, Clare, and Tipperary, farther south in the interior of the Irish Republic.)

The island within Lough Derg called Station Island or (more properly) St. Patrick's Purgatory has been the site of religious pilgrimage for Catholics seeking penance or religious vision for many centuries, possibly since the advent of Christianity in Ireland. St. Patrick, Ireland's patron saint, is said to have spent a week on an island in Lough Derg during his missionary work in the late fifth century, and to have been granted there "a vision of Purgatory and the torments of Hell," though neither Patrick's writings nor historical evidence place the patron saint at Lough Derg for any length of time (Cunningham, p. 11). Station Island may have received visitors even in St. Patrick's era, and we know it to have been a site of monastic settlement in the ninth century and again in 1135 (Curtayne, p. 27).

It seems likely that the legend of Patrick's vision is a combination of local lore with later tales of missionaries and pilgrims. For example, the lake takes its name (*derg* is Irish for "red") from its ruddy color, legendarily drawn from the blood of a monstrous worm or serpent slain there by Conan, the son of the Irish giant-hero Finn McCool. Unable to injure the creature's hide, Conan arranged to be swallowed along with the monster's daily ration of cattle, then hacked it apart from the inside. Other versions of the legend have the serpent slain by St. Patrick, or, in a curious mixture, St. Patrick helping Conan by pinning the mortally wounded serpent to the lake-bottom as it bled to death. The actual ruddiness of Lough Derg's waters is due to iron oxides from nearby rocks, but tension between the Christian and pagan origin myths of Lough Derg may be as important as the facts of chemistry.

The tradition of Patrick's vision of Purgatory and Hell may also be related to the twelfth-century narrative of the Knight Owen, a wandering Crusader who came to Station Island to fast and to do penance. (The later narrative may have crept back into the legends about St. Patrick, or the earlier story may have colored the tale of the Knight Owen. From this historical distance, it is nearly impossible to tell, since both men are known chiefly by the fantastic narratives told about them.) Part of this penance exercise

---

"ONE OF THE MOST HARROWING MOMENTS . . ."

One of the most harrowing moments in the whole history of the harrowing of the heart in Northern Ireland came when a minibus full of workers being driven home one January evening in 1976 was held up by armed and masked men and the occupants of the van ordered at gunpoint to line up at the side of the road. Then one of the masked executioners said to them, "Any Catholics among you, step out here." As it happened, this particular group, with one exception, were all Protestants, so the presumption must have been that the masked men were Protestant paramilitaries about to carry out a tit-for-tat sectarian killing of the Catholic as the odd man out, the one who would have been presumed to be in sympathy with the IRA and all its actions. It was a terrible moment for him, caught between dread and witness, but he did make a motion to step forward. Then, the story goes, in that split second of decision, and in the relative cover of the winter evening darkness, he felt the hand of the Protestant worker next to him take his hand and squeeze it in a signal that said no, don't move, we'll not betray you, nobody need know what faith or party you belong to. All in vain, however, for the man stepped out of the line; but instead of finding a gun at his temple, he was pushed away as the gunmen opened fire on those remaining in line, for these were not Protestant terrorists, but members, presumably, of the Provisional IRA.

(Heaney, "The Nobel Lecture," *Opened Ground*, pp. 421-22)

---

was a 24-hour vigil kept while sealed in a cave, and when the Knight Owen's vigil began, he had a vision of the afterlife, in which he "struggled with demons and was consoled by angels; he walked through Hell; he was admitted to the portals of Paradise" (Curtayne, p. 30). This possibly apocryphal, or fictitious, story, recorded by Friar Henry of Saltrey, was accepted as fact and incorporated into the chronicles of numerous medieval historians, with many resulting variations on the story's details and the name of its central knight. The fame of Station Island naturally grew in the centuries that followed, and numerous penitents and pilgrims from around Europe traveled there for absolution and holy visions. Predictably, as the site's reputation grew, so did the number of visions of the afterlife, and the expectation for direct communication with the dead (Curtayne, pp. 30-50). In 1397 Raymond de Perelhos, a Spanish count in the court of Pope Benedict XII, traveled to the cavern on Station Island to receive information from the recently deceased King John of Aragon—and reported success in his spiritual conference, though the King would not tell why he had been consigned to Purgatory (Curtayne, pp. 44-45). Station Island had become permanently associated, in local history and European lore, with visions of the afterlife and the dead. This visionary furor seems to have lasted until 1497, when a scandal involving fraud and simony (the practice of charging fees for church offices) brought about a papal order that the small cavern be sealed. It is not clear whether this order was followed, or whether the sealed cavern was not Station Island but a "false" visionary cave on nearby Saints' Island, where the local monastery was situated, but the sixteenth century saw a great diminishment in fantastic tales of the underworld from Station Island (Curtayne, pp. 50-55).

The island remains, however, an important holy site, though the modern pilgrim does not visit the cavern in which the Knight Owen had his vision. Modern visitors to Station Island keep a three-day fast (except for water and small portions of bread) and, while on the island, a twenty-four-hour vigil, barefoot walking, repeated circling of stone "beds" (said to be the remnants of medieval monastic cells), and repetition of vocal prayer. These are the exercises Heaney undertakes during his own pilgrimage and his literary visions of the dead.

The Poem in Focus

Plot summary. "Station Island" has Heaney traveling to St. Patrick's Purgatory, or Station Island, in County Donegal to perform a ritual of penance. While he undertakes this pilgrimage, Heaney is visited by a number of spirits or shades of the dead, both from his personal acquaintance and from his store of literary forefathers: a boyhood schoolmaster, a cousin killed by Protestant

terrorists, the poet Patrick Kavanagh, the novelist James Joyce. (The narrator clearly seems to be the poet himself, and we are to suspect that the trip to Station Island, if not the visions, was Heaney's own.) While there is a strong tradition linking Station Island to visions of the afterlife, the poet, Heaney seems to be running against the grain of the island's rituals: often in the moments when he sees the apparitions, he has drawn apart from the crowds of pilgrims, or faces against the direction of their procession. This seems to register both the poet's need for spiritual contact or consolation and his doubts about the ritual motions through which he's pacing. Though the ghosts seem at first determined to undermine the poet's faith in both Catholicism and his writing, the poem ends with a qualified confirmation of both, sending the man-poet back from Station Island with a renewed sense of purpose.

The first of the poem's 12 sections occurs before Heaney arrives on the island itself. Crossing a field of grain and summoned by church-bells, he is confronted by the spirit of an old neighbor, the tinker Simon Sweeney, "an old Sabbath-breaker / who has been dead for years" (Heaney, "Station Island," *Station Island*, 1.19-20). Sweeney resists this simple identification, claiming to be a sort of bogeyman from Heaney's childhood, haunting him now as then. Holding a bow-saw "like a lyre" ("Station Island," 1.12) and curiously concerned with the hazel bushes, Simon Sweeney seems to evoke the legendary mad Irish poet-king who shares his name. As Heaney draws away from Sweeney and into the crowd called to Mass, Sweeney warns, "Stay clear of all processions!"—advice that ironically follows the poet through the pilgrimage to come ("Station Island," 1.65).

The second section finds Heaney stumbling on another shade, this one farther from his personal acquaintance: a footnote reveals this "someone walking fast in an overcoat" to be the nineteenth-century Irish author William Carleton, whose narrative "The Lough Derg Pilgrim" (1828) describes his own pilgrimage to Station Island, on which he is adored and robbed, coming and leaving, by two old women, who at first mistake him for a young priest ("Station Island," 2.4). Carleton's narrative, written after his conversion to Protestantism from Catholicism, inveighs against the "mechanical spirit" of the pilgrimage exercises, and his appearance here seems to be a second warning to the poet against the rituals of Station Island (O'Brien, pp. 57-58). Carleton's ghost appears angry that Heaney is on his way to Lough

Derg ("O holy Jesus Christ, does nothing change?" he asks ["Station Island," 2.19]); and he challenges Heaney as a writer to match the political strife of his times ("If times were hard, I could be hard too," ["Station Island," 2.34]). Heaney insists instead on the virtues of local peace and harmony, calling up images of a tamer sectarian struggle—"a band of Ribbonmen play[ing] hymns to Mary" near his childhood home, "not that harp of unforgiving iron / the Fenians strung"; or simple images of farming and rustic nature ("Station Island," 2.43-49). Carleton gets the last word, however, as he interrupts, insisting, "We are earthworms of the earth, and all that / has gone through us is what will be our trace," a metaphor that calls for a greater poetic appetite at the same time as it belittles the entire endeavor of writing ("Station Island," 2.67-68).

Sections 3 and 4 have Heaney recalling a young invalid girl (his father's sister, according to Corcoran, p. 112). He also sees the shade of Terry Keenan, a missionary priest and early acquaintance of Heaney's who later died in the tropics. Like several of his other encounters, these tread a careful line between reminiscence and vision. The girl's treasured toy or souvenir appears to Heaney in Section 3, for example, within the frame of his memory. The souvenir carries the narrative of her sickness in its physical presence as a reliquary might hold a saint's bones: "A seaside trinket floated then and idled / in vision, like phosphorescent weed . . . / pearls condensed from a child invalid's breath / into a shimmering ark" ("Station Island," 3.9-14). The apparition of Section 4 might be only a "malarial priest, home from the missions," one of the pilgrims surrounding Heaney as he walks the island's stations (O'Brien, p. 55); however, he is not, for he vanishes suddenly at line 56 as the section is ending. Heaney seems to have known the priest at Mossbawn, for the poet ventures, "I'm older now than you when you went away" ("Station Island," 4.33): that is, the priest was once his senior, but now, in the purgatorial suspension of death, Heaney is the elder. Keenan has stayed one age while Heaney has grown older.

Like the ghost of Carleton, the missionary priest questions the value of Heaney's pilgrimage, accusing him of the same easy comforts and pieties their neighbors felt in the priest's homely presence back at Mossbawn. The priest says Heaney has made it "clear" of religious practice only to "walk into [it] / over again" ("Station Island," 4.50-51). "What are you doing," he asks,

"going through these motions?"—and *going through motions* is an apt description of the barefoot circular pacing and repetitions of vocal prayer undertaken on Station Island ("Station Island," 4.52). The priest answers his own question, suggesting that Heaney might be "taking the

SWEENEY AND ST. RONAN

Roughly contemporary with St. Patrick are the legends of Sweeney (or Suibhne), a seventh-century Ulster king who rebelled against and then was accepted by Christianity as it arrived in Ireland. Hearing the bell of St. Ronan announcing the founding of a church within his kingdom, the pagan king rushes out to do battle, as his story *Buile Suibhne* (*Sweeney Astray*) begins. He strikes St. Ronan's bell with his spear, and flings the cleric's richly illuminated psalter into a lake. An otter miraculously delivers the book from the lake-bottom, undamaged by its time underwater, and St. Ronan calls down a curse with the bell that had so angered Sweeney: the one-time king is transformed into a mad bird-man, who spends the rest of his days flying through Ireland and Scotland, mourning his plight and composing poetry. Through his hardships—more "purgatorial" than any endured on Station Island—Sweeney comes to accept "with saint-like grace the Christian shaping of his story, whilst living in the wild and pagan world of his exile" (Byron, pp. 46-47). Near the end of his life, Sweeney is pitied by St. Moling, who cannot restore his body or his senses, but who provides the former king with food and offers benedictions over his death.

Heaney not only translated *Buile Suibhne*; he also speaks, as it were, in the voice of the transformed Sweeney in the third section of the book that contains "Station Island." And so when the tinker Simon Sweeney is called "an old Sabbath-breaker," particularly with the sound of church-bells ringing around him and with his eyes fixed on the hazel bushes nearby, Heaney invokes not only unshaped fears from his childhood but the mad bird-king of his recent literary work ("Station Island," 1.19).

last look" at a religion he is giving up, and Heaney's silence at this point implies some measure of doubt ("Station Island," 4.55).

In Section 5, Heaney sees the ghosts of two schoolmasters (who taught him Latin and literature at Anahorish) and the shade of Patrick

Kavanagh, a fellow Ulster poet Heaney has else-where credited with a strong influence on his work, and whose 1942 poem "Lough Derg" is one of the literary precedents or undertexts of "Station Island." Like the other literary figures that visit Heaney, Kavanagh complains about the poet's old-fashionedness: "Forty-two years on / and you've got no farther!" ("Station Island,"

ROMANTIC TERRORIST

In his essay on "Station Island," Neil Corcoran identifies the ghost that appears to Heaney in Section 9 as Francis Hughes, a young member of the Provisional IRA who died while on a hunger strike in May 1981. A guerrilla with other Catholic factions for several years before joining the Provisional IRA in 1974, Hughes quickly developed a reputation in County Derry for effective terrorist work and for a brash, freewheeling style that had him telephoning his police opponents and walking through patrolled roadblocks. Hughes captured a certain Romantic imagination by being both a deadly gunman and a man of principles: "I don't want to be shooting them," he said, "But what other way do I have to protest, can you tell me? . . . I hate what I'm doing. I really hate it. But I'm going to keep doing it" (Hughes in Bell, pp. 538-39).

On the night before St. Patrick's Day, 1978, Hughes was seriously wounded by return fire in an unplanned attack on a police outpost in a field near Maghera, in County Derry, not far from Heaney's childhood home. He was captured and in a trial ten months later received a life sentence for two of the attacks of which he was suspected. In January 1981, from prison, he joined a hunger strike designed to call world attention to the troubles in Ireland. Branded as "the Bellaghy Butcher" and suspected now of over 26 deaths, he did little to draw public support for the protest, though others did. Ever a man of his convictions, Hughes died on May 12, 1981, the fifty-ninth day of his fast. He was neither the first nor the last to die in this protest, but his local fame in southeast County Derry lends him special relevance for Heaney.

5.59-60). Again, Heaney has only silence as an answer to this challenge.

Section 6 returns to a vision of Heaney's child-hood, this one more thoroughly transporting in that scenery and events return, not only the spirits of the dead. Heaney, walking against the flow of his fellow pilgrims again, stands in the shade

of an oak and remembers a girl, apparently a first love, peeped at through keyholes and atoned for in the confessional, and the innocent ardor of their nicknames and whispered secrets. The section, touching especially for its presence among scenes of doubt and penitence, is made ironic only by the "parting shot" Kavanagh's ghost has given in the preceding section: "In my own day, / the odd one came here on the hunt for women" ("Station Island," 5.62-63). The seventh and eighth sections give voice to two recently deceased shades, a shopkeeper acquaintance (William Strathearn) and a cousin (Colum McCartney, for whom an elegy, "The Strand at Lough Beg," appears in Heaney's *Field Work*)—both murdered in the sectarian violence that haunted Heaney's adulthood in Belfast. These two sections are among Heaney's most direct treatments of that violence, and Section 8 in particular shows his sense of guilt, or inadequacy for his difficult times: like the earlier ghost of Carleton, McCartney's shade accuses Heaney of evasiveness, saying that his atonement at Station Island may be—or *should* be—"for the way you whitewashed ugliness and drew / the lovely blinds of the *Purgatorio* [the second poem in Dante's *Divine Comedy*, which supplies the epigraph to "The Strand at Lough Beg"] / and saccharined my death with morning dew" ("Station Island," 8.73-75). The shopkeeper's ghost is less accusatory, though Heaney asks him for absolution ("Forgive my timid circumspect involvement," he asks, whereupon the shopkeeper simply brushes him off: "Forgive / my eye" ["Station Island," 7.79-80]). In both cases, Heaney seems to want or need a forgiveness the ghosts are unable to give, and this refusal of consolation seems an important part of the penance Heaney has undertaken.

The ninth section, the dark midnight end of Heaney's 24-hour vigil, has him visited by what seems will be the last of his ghosts, an unnamed gunman (whom Neil Corcoran identifies as Francis Hughes, an IRA hunger-striker [Corcoran, p. 114]). Within the poem, Hughes is marked as Catholic only by the "mass cards / at his shrouded feet" in his funeral service ("Station Island," 9.16-17). Heaney participates, briefly, in the gunman's experience, seeing what he had seen from his hayloft perch, then turns to a standard elegiac maneuver (modified by modern circumstances). He addresses the dead gunman who has just spoken to him in the dark: "Unquiet soul, they should have buried you / In the bog where you threw your first grenade, / Where only helicopters and curlews / Make their maimed music" ("Station Island," 9.22-25). Then, as if to reject this consolation in poetry, a new vision appears, a living but non-human thing that Heaney describes as a "Strange polyp" or sea anemone, "like a huge corrupt / Magnolia bloom, surreal as a shed breast" ("Station Island," 9.31-32). Faced with this apparition of the inhuman and unintelligible, and with its implications of violence done to human flesh, Heaney recants against his "unweaned" life of half-conscious complacency, and wakes the next morning full of self-reproach ("Station Island," 9.35). He recognizes, however, that the reproach itself offers him no new path, no converted life: he compared himself to "someone / Drunk in the bathroom during a party, / . . . repelled by his own reflection, / . . . As if a stone . . . could grind itself down to a different core" ("Station Island," 9.61-68).

The next two sections offer an unexpected consolation, in precisely the places where Heaney had previously found only discomfort: memory and poetry. In Section 10, Heaney sees at the pilgrims' breakfast a mug or dipping cup that recalls, abruptly and exactly, a glazed earthenware cup that had been a family treasure, visible (but forgotten, perhaps, until now) throughout his childhood like a private Holy Grail. He compares this return of the unchanged, unbroken cup across the decades to the return of St. Ronan's book of psalms, fished from the lake-bottom undamaged by an otter. Section 11 has Heaney working a sort of poetic equivalent to saying the rosary: writing a translation (presented in the poem and requested by a monk) of a poem by St. John of the Cross, the refrain of which ("although it is the night") recalls the disturbing visions of Section 9, and in its way tames them—bringing them to the poet's service, repeating the words until they are less frightening.

His penance done, and his pilgrimage complete, Heaney returns from the island to the lake shore in Section 12, and finds himself, unexpectedly, taking the hand of another ghost, whom he does not at first recognize. Before the ghost begins to speak, however, Heaney takes him for James Joyce, the novelist who is surely among the most prodigious figures in Ireland's literary pantheon. Perhaps it is strange that a poet would receive his final visitation from Joyce and not from William Butler Yeats, Ireland's major early-twentieth-century poet and a notorious spiritualist (see **"September 1913"** and **"Easter, 1916"**, also in *WLAIT 4: British and Irish Literature and Its Times*). However, Heaney's connec-

tion to Joyce is immediate and powerful: the poet charges a passage in Joyce's *Portrait of the Artist as a Young Man* (1916) with having opened his eyes to the etymological power of his local dialect. The "Feast of the Holy Tundish," as Heaney calls it, celebrates a conflict between Joyce's protagonist Stephen Dedalus and a Jesuit dean over the words *funnel* and *tundish*, the latter being Stephen's familiar Dublin dialect—and, as Joyce reveals, "good old blunt English too" (Corcoran, p. 118). The etymological discovery—that *tundish* and, by extension, local dialect words in general are as legitimate, as close to the source, as the pedagogue's standard vocabulary—is also, for Heaney, "a revelation / set among my stars" because, by coincidence, the date of Stephen's diary entry (April 13) is also Heaney's birthday ("Station Island," 12.36-37).

The instructions Heaney gives himself in the guise of Joyce's ghost chiefly concern striking an independent, individual voice—"it's time to swim / out on your own," the shade tells him ("Station Island," 12.48-49). Although in a way this is something Heaney has been doing all along, swimming against the current of the pilgrims milling about him, the surety of Joyce's phrasing (which combines encouragement with rebuke) makes it clear that Heaney's pilgrimage has been of value, though not for orthodox reasons. Heaney does not comment on Joyce's advice and admonitions, but only shows the phantom walking straight off into the rain; however, Joyce's chief command is that Heaney keep on writing, that he place his faith there, and the rest of Heaney's work is evidence that he has followed this command.

A poet's social obligation. As an Ulster Catholic and a man of public stature, Heaney has been berated by some on both sides of the Northern Irish conflict for not taking a stronger political stand in his poetry—for writing chiefly about the personal and the local; the quiet rural landscapes of Mossbawn or Glanmore, instead of the pitched demonstrations that echoed around him in the Belfast of the 1970s. In his Nobel Prize address, Heaney describes this atmosphere as "a situation of ongoing political violence and public expectation, . . . not [for] poetry as such but [for] political positions variously approvable by mutually disapproving groups" (Heaney, "The Nobel Lecture," *Opened Ground*, p. 418). To write for either side, Heaney says, would have been unjust and would have made enemies of many committed friends. Remaining silent, however, was a compromise against social responsibility. In "Ex-

A masked IRA gunman stands near a roadblock in Londonderry, Northern Ireland in 1970.

posure," one of the poems initially published in *North* (1975), Heaney writes that he would like to find motivation in

> my friends'
> Beautiful prismatic counseling
> And the anvil brains of some who hate me
>
> As I sit weighing and weighing
> My responsible *tristia*.
> (Heaney, "Exposure," *Opened Ground*, p. 135)

He imagines a poetry that not only describes but transforms the world, that creates a new clarity "like the impatient thump which unexpectedly restores the picture to the television set" (Heaney, "The Nobel Lecture," *Opened Ground*, p. 420).

After all, poets as various as Percy Shelley and William Butler Yeats—or, for that matter, Patrick Kavanagh—had turned their verse to political purposes.

A certain measure of guilt for his compromise of non-involvement seems to haunt Heaney in "Station Island," and, in large measure, it is for having avoided political themes that he seems to seek atonement. Faced with the visibly wounded ghost of a friend shot by Protestant thugs, Heaney surprises himself by asking, "Forgive the way I have lived indifferent— / forgive my timid, circumspect involvement" ("Station Island," 7.77-78). Looking on this man's injuries, Heaney feels the obligation to have spoken for him, a social responsibility for a murdered friend. However, this is not the *only* obligation of the poet, as Heaney apparently sees it. He writes that even in a country injured by sectarian violence, there is a tension "between two often contradictory commands: to be faithful to the collective historical experience and to be true to the recognitions of the emerging self" (Heaney, "Envies," p. 19). Heaney's poems about the violence of his times, like the middle sections of "Station Island," or parts of "Singing School" in *North*, are personal accounts, anecdotes, and encounters. This is the compromise for which he asks forgiveness, a forgiveness that the ghosts of William Strathearn and Colum McCartney in "Station Island" seem unwilling to grant.

However, in the poem's final section, Heaney takes the hand of James Joyce, and finds, in the advice given by the elder writer's shade, some measure of absolution for his own writerly guilt. Joyce first says that the pilgrimage to Station Island has been misdirected, the atonement not sufficient:

> Your obligation
> is not discharged by any common rite.
> What you must do must be done on your
>   own
>
> so get back in harness. The main thing is to
>   write
> for the joy of it.
>
>   ("Station Island," 12.17-23)

It is as clear here as at any point in "Station Island" that the reason for Heaney's pilgrimage is a thread of doubt not in religion, which has never played a dominant role in Heaney's writing, but in the *writing* itself. "Station Island" is in its way an attempt to atone for having taken craft more seriously than social and political strife. Heaney's move from Belfast to rural, Republican Glanmore in 1972 might have been seen as a kind of flight; Joyce's advice refigures that return to the country as a necessary step for Heaney's *poetic* obligation—an obligation described in agricultural terms: like an ox or a draft-horse, Heaney must do his work "in harness" ("Station Island," 12.22).

Joyce's advice finishes with an invocation not of the violence that killed many of Heaney's specters, but with the imagery of love seen in Section 6, familiar too from the many beautiful love lyrics in the rest of Heaney's work. Joining love to field-work—both endeavors being, after all, personal as well as social—Joyce tells Heaney to

> Cultivate a work-lust
> that imagines its haven like your hands at
>   night
> dreaming the sun in the sunspot of a breast.
> You are fasted now, light-headed, dangerous.
> Take off from here. And don't be so earnest,
>
> let others wear the sackcloth and ashes.
> Let go, let fly, forget.
> You've listened long enough. Now strike your
>   note.
>
>   ("Station Island," 12.23-30)

The "sackcloth and ashes" of religious penitence suggests here the earnestness of the poet of strict social responsibility. Joyce directs Heaney away from this sort of commitment, saying, "You lose more of yourself than you redeem / doing the decent thing" ("Station Island," 12.46-47). The counsel from Joyce that ends the poem returns Heaney to his previous practice—writing personal lyrics and accounts like "Station Island" itself—but leaves him seeing this choice not as a compromise, but as brave independence, walking straight away from the social tumult: not ignoring the rumble of bomb-blasts or the clamor of political rhetoric, but (in such silence as they allow) striking one's own note.

Sources and literary context. Heaney's use of William Carleton as representative of the nineteenth-century writer's "The Lough Derg Pilgrim," or Patrick Kavanagh as representative of the modern poet's "Lough Derg," are discussed briefly above, but the clearest literary forebear for "Station Island" is Dante's *Divine Comedy*, in which Dante encounters numerous shades of the recent dead, some of which upbraid him much as Heaney's do. Heaney discusses this relation himself in a talk titled "Envies and Identifications: Dante and the Modern Poet." Although sections of "Station Island" approximate Dante's verse form, what seems to have interested Heaney is not the epic's form or structure, but its "local intensity, the vehemence and fondness attaching to individual shades" (Heaney, "Envies," p. 18). Heaney sees in this individual or *local* attention an answer to, or compromise between, the competing claims of history on the one hand and the poet's individuality on the other (Heaney, "Envies," p. 19).

Of course, narratives of conversation with the dead occur at least as early as Homer's *Odyssey*, and certain aspects of "Station Island" seem to resemble Odysseus's travels more than Dante's. For instance, Heaney, like Odysseus, summons his shades through ritual, not by traveling to their realm. Similarly, Heaney seems to receive the apparitions for specific reasons: warnings, admonitions, or advice. Here he seems to partake in the medieval lore and tradition surrounding St. Patrick's Purgatory and the visions of the Knight Owen as closely as he follows Dante.

Reception. Seamus Heaney was already a major figure in poetry when *Station Island* appeared in 1984. *The Times Literary Supplement, The New York Review of Books, The Yale Review,* and *The New Yorker* all hailed the new collection of poems with articles of several pages, generally focusing their praise on the book's 12-part eponymous central sequence, "Station Island." In the *Yale Review,* Robert B. Shaw called it "a book of great imaginative vitality," and one that cast Heaney's work to date into a clear shape by "defining more keenly than ever before the unanswerable questions" that "[spur] this Irish poet into song" (Shaw, p. 581). Many also saw *Station Island* as a chance for Heaney to remake or reinvent his poetic persona, a turn from the short, personal lyrics of his earlier volumes to a social, even religious poetry, more involved with his times while still in vital contact with tradition: the *Times Literary Supplement* wrote, "As every new book by a major writer should, it gives us a rather different poet from the one we thought we knew" (Morrison, p. 1191). The critics' early sense of the importance of "Station Island" has been confirmed, as it—along with the bog-people poems of *North* (1975) and, most likely, the new translation of **Beowulf** (2000; in *WLAIT 3: British and Irish Literature and Its Times*)—has become the most noted and most recognized of the works of this important late-twentieth-century poet. Heaney received the Nobel Prize for Literature in 1995.

—Isaac Cates

For More Information

Bell, J. Bowyer. *The Irish Troubles: a Generation of Violence, 1967-1992.* New York: St. Martin's, 1993.

Byron, Catherine. *Out of Step: Pursuing Seamus Heaney to Purgatory.* Bristol: Loxwood Stoneleigh, 1992.

Corcoran, Neil. "Writing a Bare Wire: *Station Island.*" *New Casebooks: Seamus Heaney.* Ed. Michael Allen. New York: St. Martin's, 1997.

Cunningham, John B. *Lough Derg: Legendary Pilgrimage.* Monaghan: R. & S., 1984.

Curtayne, Alice. *Lough Derg: St. Patrick's Purgatory.* London: Burns Oates & Washbourne, 1944.

Heaney, Seamus. "Envies and Identifications: Dante and the Modern Poet." *Irish University Review* 15, no. 1 (spring 1985): 5-19.

———. *Preoccupations: Selected Prose 1968-1978.* New York: Farrar, Straus and Giroux, 1980.

———. *Opened Ground: Selected Poems 1966-1996.* New York: Farrar, Straus and Giroux, 1998.

———. "Station Island." In *Station Island.* New York: Farrar, Straus, and Giroux, 1985.

Morrison, Blake. "Encounters with Familiar Ghosts." *Times Literary Supplement,* 19 October 1984, 1191-1192.

O'Brien, Darcy. "Piety and Modernism: Seamus Heaney's 'Station Island.'" *James Joyce Quarterly* 26, no. 1 (fall 1988): 51-65.

Shaw, Robert B. "Heaney's Purgatory." *The Yale Review* 74 (summer 1985): 581-587.

Tapscott, Stephen. "Poetry and Trouble: Seamus Heaney's Irish Purgatorio." *Southwest Review* 71 (autumn 1986): 519-535.

Vendler, Helen. *Seamus Heaney.* Cambridge, Mass.: Harvard University Press, 1998.

The Time Machine

by

H. G. Wells

Herbert George Wells (1866-1946) was born in the southern English town of Bromley, where his parents operated a small shop. The family had little money, but as a boy Wells won a scholarship to the Normal School of Science in South Kensington, London. This prestigious school attracted some of the foremost thinkers of the day, including the famous and controversial biologist T. H. Huxley, who became Wells's teacher and mentor there. With *The Time Machine* (1895), his first novel, Wells embarked on a prolific and varied writing career, dominating the British literary scene into the 1930s. His massive output (some 120 books, along with numerous articles and stories) falls into four major categories. First came the popular "scientific romances," including *The Time Machine*, *The Island of Doctor Moreau* (1896), *The Invisible Man* (1897), and *The War of the Worlds* (1898). Wells then wrote several comic novels, such as *Love and Mr. Lewisham* (1900) and *Kipps* (1905), and a series of novels focusing on social issues: *Ann Veronica* (1909), for instance, deals with women's emancipation, and *Tono-Bungay* (1909) with class, capitalism and scientific progress. At the same time, his books of history (*The Outline of History*; 1920) and futuristic speculation (*Anticipations*, 1901; *A Modern Utopia*, 1905; *The Shape of Things to Come*, 1933) kept Wells's often radical social opinions more directly before the public eye. His deep interest in human society is present as well in the early romances: not just in *The Time Machine* (often considered his finest work) but also in other gripping tales of his that helped establish the modern genre of science fiction.

THE LITERARY WORK

A novella set near London in the 1890s and in the distant future; first published in serial form in 1894 and in book form in 1895.

SYNOPSIS

A "time machine" takes its inventor into the future: first to the year 802,701, when he finds that humans have evolved into two separate but equally debased species, and then to witness the extinction of the sun and the end of life on earth.

Events in History at the Time of the Novella

Science, society, and the idea of progress. The late Victorian era (c. 1875-1900) was a time in which science and scientific ideas acquired an unprecedented importance in British society at large. As the first popular British author with a formal education in science, H. G. Wells had received the training that enabled him to reflect the public's new regard for science. He obtained his degree in biology from London University in 1890, but it was his earlier studies under Thomas Henry Huxley that made the deepest impression on him. Like his famous teacher, Wells would

H. G. Wells

become a leading popularizer of scientific ideas. Huxley, a brilliant debater and public speaker, was a biologist, and the most influential single idea in all of late-nineteenth-century Western culture had come straight from biology: Charles Darwin's controversial theory of evolution. Darwin himself disliked controversy, and so after he had published his theory in his book **On the Origin of Species** (1859; also in *WLAIT 4: British and Irish Literature and Its Times*) it had fallen to others to defend his ideas. Huxley, nicknamed "Darwin's Bulldog" for his aggressive public defense of evolutionary theory, was the man who did so most effectively.

Much of the impact of Darwin's ideas came from their apparent relevance to areas that lay outside of biology itself. The late Victorians applied evolutionary theory—summed up in the phrase "survival of the fittest"—to their own society in two major ways. First, thinkers such as Herbert Spencer used it to justify the exercise of power at home (by the rich) and abroad (by British imperialists). Because nature herself favored "the fittest," went the logic, the powerful deserved their privileged position in society and in the world at large. This contention, called "Social Darwinism," took what was originally a biological explanation and turned it into a moral and political justification.

Second, the late Victorians found it easy to equate Darwinian evolution, in which organisms change over the generations in adaptation to their local environments, with the attractive idea of progress, which holds out a reassuring expectation of perpetual improvement. Their era brought to a close a century of industrial growth, confident imperial expansion (Britain ruled a worldwide empire by the 1890s), and advances in science and technology. Progress seemed to characterize every area of British endeavor, so it was natural to apply it to evolution as well.

Social Darwinism and the notion of evolutionary progress exerted deep influence on popular attitudes at the end of the nineteenth century, yet both of these concepts reflect misunderstandings of Darwin's original ideas. Wells, trained by Darwinian theory's chief exponent, would address both of these misunderstandings in his writings. In *The Time Machine*, which depicts future humans as having evolved into less sophisticated, less intelligent creatures, he offers a fanciful corrective to the second one in particular: the popular misconception that evolution means progress.

Scientific and technological progress. A series of remarkable achievements in other areas of science and technology helped inspire the late Victorians' firm belief in progress. They too form the novella's intellectual background, most notably in the fields of geology (Wells's other major area of study at the Normal School) and physics.

A major influence on Darwin's ideas was the work of Charles Lyell (1797-1875), often referred to as "the father of geology," who suggested that the earth was shaped by forces that worked slowly and steadily over long stretches of time. Before Lyell's work, the world was thought to be at most several thousand years old; Lyell showed instead that geological history goes back millions and millions of years. Lyell divided the deep past into the ages (for example, the Jurassic Age), comprising millions of years each, familiar to geology students today. Paleontology (the study of prehistoric life) was also born from Lyell's realization of the immensity of the past, and soon fossils of dinosaurs and other ancient animals were being studied enthusiastically. Wells refers to Lyell's geologic ages and to dinosaurs at the end of the novella, when the Time Traveller is imagined as journeying to the "abysses of the Cretaceous Sea; or among the grotesque saurians, the huge reptilian brutes of the Jurassic times" and as "wandering on some plesiosaurus-haunted Oolitic reef, or beside the lonely saline lakes of the Triassic Age" (Wells, *The Time Machine*, p. 91).

In physics, the British scientists Michael Faraday (1791-1867) and James Clerk Maxwell (1831-79) achieved, respectively, the practical and theoretical understanding of electricity and electromagnetism that would allow the electronic wonders of the twentieth century. A number of scientists across Europe, including Sadi Carnot, James Joule, and William Thomson (Lord Kelvin), contributed to the discovery of the first and second laws of thermodynamics: energy can be transferred but not created or destroyed (conservation of energy); and heat cannot pass from a cooler body to a hotter one. This second law led German physicist Rudolph Clausius to formulate the principle of entropy, which dictates that in the transfer of energy some will always be dissipated in the form of heat, so that closed systems will always lose energy. Since the universe (scientists assumed) is a closed system, it too should eventually wind down into cold and darkness. It is this so-called "heat death" that the Time Traveller witnesses near the end of the novella, as the sun cools and all life on earth perishes.

In step with such scientific breakthroughs, technology progressed rapidly during the late nineteenth century. Several contemporary technological developments figure in the novella:

- **The bicycle:** In the 1880s the development of the chain drive, equal size wheels, and the pneumatic tire made the bicycle (invented in the 1870s) more comfortable and efficient. A bicycling craze in the mid-1890s resulted in an estimated 1.5 million bicyclists in Britain by 1896. The bicycle was seen as a symbol of the future, and Wells's description of the Time Machine would bring bicycles to the reader's mind—especially its "saddle," the British term for a bicycle seat (*Time Machine*, p. 9).
- **The Kodak camera:** On his second voyage the Time Traveller takes a Kodak camera, the small portable camera invented in 1888 by American George Eastman, founder of the Eastman Kodak Company. This simple and popular camera made photography available to amateurs for the first time.
- **The motion picture:** Wells's descriptions of time travel may be based on the effects produced by running a movie faster, slower, and backwards. In 1894 Wells might have seen a London demonstration of the Edison Kinetoscope, a precursor to the motion picture. The Theatrograph, the first motion picture publicly shown in London, was demonstrated in 1896 (the year after the novella was published), and Wells claimed to have helped invent it.
- **Electrical power:** Wells alludes pointedly to the gas lights, candles, and kerosene lamps of the Time Traveller's house, located in the London borough of Richmond. The Electric Lighting Act of 1888 had given local authorities the right to veto the new electrical power (as the borough of Richmond did), so London in general was modernizing only haphazardly. In contrast, by the mid-1890s cities like Chicago and Berlin had built centralized light and power systems extending into their suburbs.

DARWIN'S BULLDOG AND HUMAN EVOLUTION

Charles Darwin's monumental book *On the Origin of Species* (1859) established that evolution occurs and offered a theory, called natural selection, to explain how it works. Natural selection suggests that different species evolve from common ancestors, through small changes over long periods of time. Such random changes or mutations occur regularly when individual organisms reproduce. Every once in a while a mutation will help an individual survive by offering an advantage in its environment; such changes (called adaptations) have a better chance of being passed on to the next generation than those that do not favor survival. Over many generations, these adaptations spread through the population, shaping the species.

Wells's teacher T. H. Huxley was known as "Darwin's Bulldog" because he devoted much of his life to explaining and advocating natural selection. Huxley's 1863 book *Evidence as to Man's Place in Nature* is usually considered to be the first attempt to apply the theory to human evolution. Some three decades later, Huxley's former student H. G. Wells would use Darwinian ideas to speculate on a possible future for human evolution in *The Time Machine*.

New visions of society: socialism and class struggle. By the 1880s the Industrial Revolution was more than a century old in Britain, and nearly as old in the other leading industrialized European countries. As early as the 1830s, Victorian social critics such as Thomas Carlyle (1795-1881) had pointed out the injustices of nineteenth-century industrial capitalism, in which the means of economic production were held by private individuals without state regulation. In response to the plight of poor and exploited workers, the French philosopher Henri de Saint-Simon (1760-1825), the German economist and philosopher Karl Marx (1818-83), and other thinkers had formulated the political ideology called socialism, in which the means of production would be owned by the state. Beginning with their seminal work *The Communist Manifesto* (1848), Marx and his colleague Friedrich Engels (1820-95) elaborated a version of socialism called communism, in which property would be owned by all and shared according to need. Marx, Engels, and later their followers defined history in terms of the struggle between classes, that is between labor (the workers) and capital (the wealthy).

EVOLUTIONARY "PROGRESS"

"Progress" in evolution is always relative to specific environments; absolute progress—the sense in which the Victorians used the word—is an illusion, since environments change and therefore call for new adaptations. Evolutionary change does not—as many have assumed—necessarily imply increasing strength and intelligence. A creature can be superbly adapted to its environment and lack both; while many beings find strength useful, intelligence has evolved in only a handful of species. In fact, then, the phrase "survival of the fittest" refers neither to strength nor to intelligence. It simply means that those individuals who best "fit" their environment will be more likely to survive and thus to pass their adaptations on to future generations.

In his satirical novel *Sartor Resartus* (1833), Carlyle had offered a caricature of the class struggle, pitting the useful drudges (the workers) against the useless dandies (the wealthy). Just over a decade later, in his novel *Sybil* (1845), the British author and future prime minister Benjamin Disraeli wrote metaphorically of the divide between rich and poor:

> [The rich and poor are] two nations; between whom there is no intercourse and no sympathy; who are as ignorant of each other's habits, thoughts and feelings, as if they were dwellers in different zones, or inhabitants of different planets: who are formed by different breeding, are fed by a different food, are ordered by

different manners, and are not governed by the same laws.

(Disraeli in Stover, p. 8)

The Time Machine, a social fable as much as a scientific adventure story, fancifully applies evolutionary theory to Disraeli's well known "two nations" view of British society. The novella pictures a future in which these two classes have actually evolved into separate species: the Eloi, who live an aimless life of ease and comfort above ground; and the Morlocks, brutish and apelike predators who live underground.

By the 1870s workers in Britain and elsewhere had begun organizing themselves into labor unions. The unions' aim was to present a cohesive force to oppose the perceived injustices of their wealthy employers. Supported by Marxist socialists in Britain, for example, dock workers in 1889 led the Great London Dock Strike, which won for unskilled labor the right to unionize. Then in the so-called Coal War of 1893 the coal miners' union shut down every coal mine in Britain, where virtually all homes used coal for heat, and industry relied primarily on coal for power. This successful strike won British labor the right to form its own political organization, which became the Labour Party (today one of Britain's two major political parties).

As with the Great Dock Strike, the Marxist socialists had strongly supported labor in the Coal War, while the anti-Marxists—including Wells—viewed such strikes as dangerous threats to society. The Coal War generated a surge of Marxist writing in support of the miners. Wells answered it with *The Time Machine*, in which he imagines the sinister, subterranean Morlocks as the descendants of the coal miners, whose own nickname for themselves was "mollocks."

The Novella in Focus

Plot summary. Less than 100 pages in most editions, the tale is short. Yet its narrative structure is complex, involving an "Inner Narrator" (that is, the unnamed Time Traveller) whose account is "framed" by that of an "Outer Narrator." This Outer Narrator is one of the audience of friends who has heard the Time Traveller's tale of his adventures; he himself is recounting it to the reader three years later, long after the Time Traveller's final disappearance into an unspecified time. Only two members of this audience of friends are named: Filby, "an argumentative person with red hair" whom critics have taken as a caricature of George Bernard Shaw, and Hillyer, whom critics have presumed to be the Outer Narrator, though the text does not make this clear (*The Time Machine*, p. 3). Most of the rest are referred to by their professions: the Medical Man, the Psychologist, the Journalist, the Editor, the Provincial Mayor. In addition, the inner narrator calls one the Silent Man (taken to be a caricature of William Morris) and one the Very Young Man.

The novella opens with the Outer Narrator relating the events of one Thursday evening, the regular time that the group of friends meets at the Time Traveller's house. The Time Traveller, a scientist and an inventor, is discussing the concept of time travel. "I shall have to controvert one or two ideas that are almost universally accepted. The geometry, for instance, they taught you at school is founded on a misconception," he asserts (*The Time Machine*, p. 3). He goes on to claim that, in addition to the three spatial dimensions of conventional geometry, a fourth dimension, time, can also be thought of as existing in space. Since it exists in space, like space it can be traversed. In fact, he argues, we move through it every day, jumping back briefly in our memories or forward in our imaginations. What he has done, he says, is to construct a machine that can do the same thing, only in a more lasting way, moving freely around "as the driver determines" not only through space but also through time (*The Time Machine*, p. 7).

He shows them a working toy-size model of his machine, which he says took him two years to make, then takes the group to his laboratory, where he shows them the time machine itself. The following Thursday, they meet again at the Time Traveller's house, where he has left a note saying he may be late. When he does appear, limping, dirty, and pale, with a half-healed cut on his chin, he is obviously exhausted. He tells the following story.

That morning he had used the time machine for the first time. Pushing the lever, he saw the room go dark. He then saw his housekeeper come in and "shoot across the room like a rocket" (*The Time Machine*, p. 18). He pushed the lever over further:

> The night came like the turning out of a lamp, and in another moment came tomorrow. . . . As I put on pace, night followed day like the flapping of a black wing. The dim suggestion of the laboratory seemed presently to fall away from me, and I saw the sun hopping swiftly across the sky. . . .
>
> (*The Time Machine*, pp. 18-19)

Repeatedly jarred and disoriented, he finally brings the machine to an abrupt stop, tumbling out to a "sound like a clap of thunder" (*The Time Machine*, p. 21).

Having landed in the future, The Time Traveller finds himself in a garden dominated by a large white sphinxlike statue set on a bronze pedestal. The machine's dial registers the year: 802,701. After a few minutes he is approached by eight or ten small creatures, beautiful and graceful "but indescribably frail," all with the same curly hair, large eyes, and little pink hands (*The Time Machine*, p. 23). Chattering among each other with soft cooing voices, they seem completely uncurious about the Time Traveller's sudden appearance. These are the Eloi, among

---

SAINT-SIMON AND MARX: TWO SOCIALISMS

⁓

British socialists were divided into two camps: the Marxist socialists, led by the poet, artist, and intellectual William Morris and others; and the anti-Marxists, led by playwright George Bernard Shaw and others. Wells, who was an anti-Marxist socialist, drew (like Shaw and the others) on the ideas of Henri de Saint-Simon. A major distinction between the two socialisms was that the Marxists advocated the overthrow of capital by labor, while the anti-Marxists followed Saint-Simon and Thomas Carlyle in calling for harmonious cooperation between the classes. *The Time Machine* imagines a future outcome of the class struggle, and the novella features humorous caricatures of the two socialist leaders: Morris, whose views Wells attacks, and Shaw.

---

whom the Time Traveller will spend eight days. They live and dine communally, eating only fruit, for there seem to be no farm animals in the future: "horses, cattle, sheep, dogs, had followed the Ichthyosaurus into extinction" (*The Time Machine*, p. 27). Indeed, he sees no insects or wild animals either. There are no small houses—only large halls where the childlike creatures eat and sleep together—and a number of large abandoned ruins. The creatures seem to be practicing communism.

The Time Traveller speculates further that, having conquered nature completely, and having supplied all of its own needs through scientific and technological advances, humankind had peaked. After a period of achievement and strength, he concludes, humans had begun a long slow evolutionary decline. Their deterioration was promoted by the evolutionary force of their new surroundings, an artificial man-made environment that favored complacency and weakness:

> Under the new conditions of perfect comfort and security, that restless energy, that with us is strength, would become weakness. Even in our own time, certain tendencies and desires, once necessary to survival, are a constant source of failure. Physical courage and the love of battle, for instance, are no great help—and may even be hindrances—to a civilised man. And in a state of physical balance and security, power, intellectual as well as physical, would be out of place.
>
> (*The Time Machine*, p. 33)

THE TIME MACHINE AND EINSTEIN'S THEORY OF RELATIVITY

∾

"Scientific people," the Time Traveller tells his audience in the novella's opening pages, "know very well that Time is only a kind of Space" (*The Time Machine*, p. 5). Two decades after *The Time Machine*'s publication, Albert Einstein published the General Theory of Relativity, in which he treats time and space as a single entity, space-time. Einstein's work was based partly on the revolutionary geometry of Georg Friedrich Riemann (1826-66), which successfully challenged the universality of conventional three-dimensional Euclidean geometry by showing the mathematical possibility of geometry in four or more dimensions. Some critics have seen the Time Traveller's scientific ideas as an anticipation of Relativity theory—as Wells himself later boasted. Others call the Time Traveller's science simply the "patter . . . of a stage magician," contending that even after Einstein's work Wells never achieved a clear understanding of Relativity theory (Stover, p. 35).

That night, when he returns to the statue called the White Sphinx, his time machine is gone. After shouting ineffectually at some of the sleeping Eloi, he goes to sleep in a mood of despair. The next morning he finds signs that the time machine was dragged into the White Sphinx's pedestal, which seems hollow. Again he rages at one of the Eloi. Exploring later that day, he notices what seem like wells and ventilation towers in the ground, and hears a deep mechanical thudding coming from one of the wells.

The following day, he makes a friend: a young female he calls Weena, whom he rescues from drowning, and who responds by attaching herself to him like a young child. Like the other Eloi, Weena seems to dread the night. That night, he glimpses what appear to be white, apelike animals in the dark.

On the morning of the fourth day, he gets a closer look at one of these apelike creatures, which vanishes down a ventilation shaft. He realizes that humans have split into two species, and that "this bleached, obscene, nocturnal Thing" he has just seen is one of them (*The Time Machine*, p. 47). Evolution has stepped into "the present merely temporary and social difference between the Capitalist and the Labourer" and widened it into a biological one (*The Time Machine*, p. 49). The Eloi, he decides, live in comfort above ground, ruling over the brutish, subterranean Morlocks (as he calls the two species). On the sixth day he descends a well and investigates the underground world of the Morlocks, who flee when he strikes a match. In a large cavern he finds the remains of a meal, including meat, and some machinery. Running low on matches, he climbs back up the well, pursued by several Morlocks, who are emboldened as the matches run out. He now suspects that far from ruling over the Morlocks, the Eloi are their victims. The Morlocks prey on the Eloi at night—perhaps even keep them like cattle for eventual slaughter. This, he fears, explains the meat he saw in the cavern.

That afternoon, accompanied by Weena, he heads for a large building he has seen several miles in the distance, which he calls the Palace of Green Porcelain. Reaching the deserted and ruined palace, they discover it to be the remains of a museum. Inside the Time Traveller finds dinosaur and other fossils, before moving on to uncover the crumbling remains of decayed books. From some huge machinery whose purpose remains unclear he takes a hefty lever to use for protection against the threatening Morlocks. He also finds a box of matches and some camphor (a flammable substance) that have survived in one of the airtight display cases. While fleeing through some woods on the return journey that night, the Time Traveller tries to use fire against the Morlocks but loses his matches. Then, as he beats away Morlocks with the heavy lever, dry underbrush ignites, creating a forest fire. In the confusion, Weena disappears. The next day the Time Traveller reaches the White Sphinx, where the doors of the bronze pedestal have been

This small portable camera, invented by George Eastman in 1888 and thus the first Kodak camera, is the one the Time Traveler takes on his second journey.

opened, revealing the time machine within. The Morlocks have opened the doors in order to ambush him, but as they close in he takes the time machine forward into the future.

Moving headlong through time, he sees the sun grow larger and redder as it cools and eventually stands still in the sky. He slows down and stops at a time when the place (which is always the same—time changes, not the location) has become a desolate beach under a dim red sun that leaves stars glowing in the dark sky. He sees "something like a huge white butterfly" and "a monstrous crab-like creature" (*The Time Machine*, p. 83). When another crab-like creature approaches him, he propels the machine forward through time again and sees many of them. Continuing on, he makes stop after stop. Finally, "more than thirty million years hence," in the frigid snow of the nearly lifeless planet, all that is left of life is a round, soccer-ball size creature with tentacles (*The Time Machine*, p. 83). The Time Traveller sends his machine back to his own present, slowing down and finally stopping as the dial turns to the correct date and time.

He ends his story, whose truthfulness is questioned by a few skeptics in the audience. As they disperse, the Time Traveller admits that he himself wonders whether perhaps he dreamed it all.

But when the Outer Narrator returns to the Time Traveller's house the next day, he finds the Time Traveller preparing for another journey, this time with his camera (which he had forgotten before). He asks the Outer Narrator to wait for him for a half-hour or so—but that was three years ago. The Time Traveller never returned.

Progress and degeneration at the *fin-de-siècle*. A corollary to the idea that evolutionary competition leads towards greater strength and intelligence is the assumption that if such competition is removed, strength and intelligence must inevitably decline. While he avoids the error of assuming evolutionary progress, Wells bases his depiction of future humanity in the novella on its equally fallacious corollary:

> What, unless biological science is a mass of errors, is the cause of human intelligence and vigour? Hardship and freedom: conditions under which the active, strong, and subtle survive and the weaker go to the wall. . . . Humanity had been strong, energetic, and intelligent, and had used all its abundant vitality to alter the conditions under which it lived. And now came the reaction of the altered conditions. . . . We are kept keen on the grindstone of necessity, and, it seemed to me, that here was that hateful grindstone broken at last!
> (*The Time Machine*, pp. 32-34)

Of course, simply breaking the grindstone will not dull the blade. While Wells recognizes that "conditions" shape evolution, he fudges the conditions that, by the time of the Morlocks and the Eloi, could remove such an improbable but successful adaptation as the human intellect. It remains unclear whether he does this for literary reasons or because he shared a commonly held misunderstanding of evolutionary change. Progress, it turns out, is not a scientifically founded phenomenon; there is only change to fit environments.

The ends of centuries have historically encouraged apocalyptic and time-related anxieties among Christian European peoples. As the nineteenth century drew to a close, its version of such anxieties was naturally shaped by the imposing presence of Darwinian theory. Darwin had brought new subjects into common discourse, not only evolution but also concepts such as extinction. The overwhelmingly vast majority of species, it became clear, had disappeared from the earth. So, although the late Victorians were fixated on progress, they were also faced with the possibility of extinction. To explain extinction, they appealed to progress's equally unfounded opposite, which they called degeneration. One, it seems, could not exist without the other: evolutionary degeneration is the shadow concept of evolutionary progress.

By century's end, degeneration was tied to other increasingly common pseudo-scientific ideas, especially that of racial purity. As the next century unfolded, the relationship between degeneration and racial purity would grow into a particularly virulent offshoot of Darwinism. Wells, who reflects *fin-de-siècle*, or end-of-the-century, fears of degeneration in *The Time Machine*, would live a further half-century to see the horrors of World War II, which drew diabolical inspiration from these same unfounded fears.

Sources and literary context. When Hungarian-born writer Max Nordau used it as the title of his widely read book *Degeneration* (1893), the term was already a commonplace opposite for progress. The book argues that humans as a species are hopelessly degenerating; more exactly, it describes "a Dusk of the Nations in which all suns and all stars are gradually waning and mankind with all its institutions and creations is perishing in the midst of a dying world" (Nordau in Jarrett, p. 159). This metaphorical description becomes a literal circumstance in Wells's novella. Also influential were the "dandies" and "drudges" of Thomas Carlyle's *Sar-*

tor Resartus and the "two nations" of Benjamin Disraeli's *Sybil,* elements that helped inspire the Eloi and Morlocks in *The Time Machine.*

Wells's thought was shaped as well by the tradition of utopian and antiutopian fiction, exemplified by writers from ancient times (Plato in fourth century B.C.E. Greece) through the Renaissance (Sir Thomas More, 1478-1535) and the Enlightenment (Jonathan Swift, 1677-1745). This literary current broadened in the late nineteenth century, taking on an edge of futuristic speculation combined with a social agenda: examples include Samuel Butler's *Erewhon* (1872), American Edward Bellamy's *Looking Backward* (1887), and William Morris's *News from Nowhere* (1891). In *The Time Machine* Wells implicitly attacks Morris's views, which are represented by the Time Traveller's first and ultimately naïve assumption that the Eloi live in communistic bliss.

The 1890s saw the rapid decline of the long Victorian novel in favor of shorter works. The reasons for this transition are complex, but they include the end of a virtual lock on the market for new novels by libraries. Earlier in the Victorian period, libraries had been able to keep the price of new novels artificially high—partly by demanding that they come in three volumes—which discouraged their purchase by consumers. As the price of new fiction fell, authors became freer to experiment with new forms. Wells's *The Time Machine,* along with the other short, science-based novels that followed it, established the genre that would become known as "scientific romance," which was a precursor of modern science fiction. The scientific romances harked back to the works of writers such as America's Edgar Allen Poe (1809-49) and especially France's Jules Verne (1828-1905), whose science-based adventures include *Journey to the Center of the Earth* (1864) and *Around the World in 80 Days* (1873). Along with Verne, Wells is considered one of the founders of science fiction.

Publication and reception. *The Time Machine*'s unusually complex and lengthy publication history can be outlined as follows:

- **1888:** Wells publishes a short story called "The Chronic Argonauts" in the student magazine at the Normal School of Science. Aside from time travel and one or two snatches of dialogue, this early story has nothing in common with *The Time Machine* as published later.
- **1889-92:** Wells revises the story "The Chronic Argonauts" in two separate versions, both of which have been lost.

- **1894**: *National Observer* editor W. E. Henley solicits material from Wells, who produces the first version of *The Time Machine*. Shorter than later versions, the serialized story leaves the Eloi unnamed, though it does name the Morlocks; the two species have no contact. The Time Traveller is called "the Philosophical Inventor."
- **1895**: Encouraging Wells to expand the story, Henley moves to the *New Review*, where a longer version is serialized in five parts (January-May 1895). In May, two separate versions are also published in book form: a U.S. edition by Henry Holt & Co. (May 7); and a British edition by William Heinemann (May 29). The Heinemann edition, based on the *New Review* version, becomes the most familiar version.
- **1924**: The Heinemann text is reprinted with minor revisions in Volume I of *The Atlantic Edition of the Works of H. G. Wells*. Many modern versions reproduce this version; others retain the Heinemann text.

Reviews of the commercially successful 1895 Heineman edition ranged from positive to enthusiastic, with one reviewer calling the novella "a strikingly original performance" that "grips the imagination as it is only gripped by genuinely imaginative work" (Geduld, p. 9). Another saw it as a "brilliant little romance" that was "worthy of [Jonathan] Swift, and possibly not devoid of satirical reference to 'the present discontents,'" by which the reviewer presumably meant the labor movement (Zangwill in Geduld, p. 10). Writing in 1895, the influential journalist W. T. Stead called Wells "a man of genius," an opinion that would soon become standard (Stead in McConnell, p. 315). Catapulted to overnight fame by the 1895 edition of the novella, Wells would be accorded a lofty status for the rest of his long career.

—Colin Wells

For More Information

Batchelor, John. *H. G. Wells*. Cambridge: Cambridge University Press, 1985.

Bergonzi, Bernard. *H. G. Wells: A Collection of Critical Essays*. Englewood Cliffs, N.J.: Prentice-Hall, 1976.

Geduld, Harry M. *The Definitive Time Machine: A Critical Edition of H. G. Wells's Scientific Romance With Introduction and Notes by Harry M. Geduld*. Bloomington: Indiana University Press, 1987.

Jarrett, Derek. *The Sleep of Reason: Fantasy and Reality from the Victorian Age to the First World War*. London: Weidenfeld and Nicolson, 1988.

Harrison, J. F. C. *Late Victorian Britain 1875-1901*. London: Routledge, 1991.

McConnell, Frank D., ed. *H. G. Wells: The Time Machine/The War of the Worlds*. New York: Oxford University Press, 1977.

Smith, David C. *H. G. Wells: Desperately Mortal*. New Haven: Yale University Press, 1986.

Stableford, Brian. *Scientific Romance in Britain 1890-1950*. New York: St. Martin's, 1985.

Stover, Leon, ed. Introduction to *The Time Machine: An Invention*, by H. G. Wells. Jefferson, N.C.: McFarland, 1996.

Wells, H. G. *The Time Machine/The Island of Doctor Moreau*. Oxford: Oxford University Press, 1996.

Troubles

by
J. G. Farrell

*T*roubles is the first part of the "Empire Trilogy," a series of novels by J. G. Farrell published in the 1970s depicting moments of crisis and decline in the history of the British Empire. Prior to *Troubles,* Farrell was a relatively unknown novelist who had achieved only moderate success. He was born on January 25, 1935, in Liverpool to an English father and Irish mother, and spent his childhood years in both England and Ireland. His Anglo-Irish heritage would prove to be an important influence in his writing. An athletic and confident youth who excelled at sports, in October 1956, Farrell went up to Brasenose College, Oxford University, to study law. But within weeks of his arrival he was seriously ill, struck down with the crippling disease of polio. He spent many weeks paralyzed in an iron lung, and although he would recover, the polio left his body irreparably damaged; he permanently lost some mobility, especially in his upper half. Not surprisingly perhaps, his early novels combined a sense of existential bleakness with a subtly redemptive, if often bizarre, sense of humor. His style (and fortunes) changed considerably, however, when he turned to historical matters in his Empire Trilogy novels. The first in the series, *Troubles* (1970), concerns the end of British rule in Ireland. The second, *The Siege of Krishnapur* (1973), focuses on the so-called Indian "mutiny" of 1857. Third and longest, *The Singapore Grip* (1978) examines the fall of Singapore to Japanese forces in 1942. In the year after its publication, Farrell moved to Ireland and bought a cot-

THE LITERARY WORK

A novel set in Ireland between 1919 and 1921; published in 1970.

SYNOPSIS

A First World War veteran travels from London to the south of Ireland to stay with his fiancée in the crumbling Majestic Hotel during the last days of British rule.

tage on the coast. On Saturday, August 11, 1979, while fishing on some rocks, the 44-year-old Farrell was washed out to sea in a freak storm and drowned. At the time of his death, he left an unfinished seventh novel, *The Hill Station,* published in 1981. It is, however, for his masterpiece, *Troubles,* that he is best remembered. In it, Farrell managed to bring together the melancholy, absurdist vision of his earlier writing with a well-researched, unsympathetic view of British colonial history in a way that greatly influenced later novelists keen to treat the violence and injustices of British colonialism.

Events in History at the Time the Novel Takes Place

Nationalism, "Home Rule" and the Irish Free State. *Troubles* begins with the arrival of its central character, Major Brendan Archer, at the Majestic Hotel in Kilnalough, Ireland, in the sum-

J. G. Farrell

mer of 1919. It ends with his departure in the late summer of 1921. The years bracketed by these dates contained some of the most traumatic and bloody events in twentieth-century Irish history, as British rule came to an end for the 26th of its 32 counties with the declaration of the Irish Free State in December 1921. Although "the Troubles" is more often used to refer to the political situation in the north of Ireland after 1968, it has also been used in relation to the years 1919-1921—hence the title of Farrell's novel.

During the nineteenth century, there had been various attempts to challenge the Act of Union (1800) between England and Ireland that had abolished the Irish Parliament and made the country subservient to government from Westminster, England. Toward the end of the century, Charles Stuart Parnell had galvanized the predominantly poor Catholic population of Ireland into a nationalist movement and, during the 1880s, negotiated with England's Prime Minister, William Gladstone, for a form of Irish "Home Rule" that would return limited domestic powers to the country. Home Rule was an alarming prospect for the affluent Irish Protestant population, which constituted a minority throughout the island as a whole but a significant majority in the six counties of the north of Ireland collectively known as "Ulster." As successive British governments attempted to introduce Home Rule in the

early years of the twentieth century, they met with increasing hostility from the Ulster Protestants, who were committed to the maintenance of the Union with England. The Home Rule proponents likewise clashed with frustrated Catholic Irish nationalists who felt that the measure did not go far enough; instead they demanded the establishment of an Irish Republic completely free from British influence. On Easter Monday, 1916, a nationalist insurrection occurred on the streets of Dublin. British soldiers were attacked by nationalist troops, and a statement declaring the creation of a provisional Irish Republic was read from the steps of the General Post Office on Sackville Street. Within days the insurrection had been defeated. In the following weeks its leaders were executed, creating a public outcry; the memory of Easter 1916 and the fate of its leaders would act as a powerful emotive force in the years leading up to independence.

By 1919 armed nationalist forces—originally referred to as the "Volunteers" but gradually known as the Irish Republican Army (IRA)—had begun taking action under the leadership of Michael Collins. His group and others began a series of guerrilla attacks on police and military targets (and on Irish Catholics deemed "traitors" to the nation), with the aim of bringing Ireland to its knees. The violence began in January with the murder of two constables of the Royal Irish Constabulary (RIC) by the "Volunteers" Dan Breen and Sean Treacy (the event is recorded near the beginning of *Troubles*). As these attacks increased, brutal reprisals by the RIC became common occurrences, often involving the burning of houses and attacks on Irish men and women. In response to the escalating violence from 1919 into 1920, the British government sent two forms of reinforcements to Ireland to support the RIC. Rather than restoring British law and order, each form seemed to make the situation worse. The first, the Black and Tans, arrived in March 1920 and soon attracted a reputation for bloody retaliation and violence against the insurgent Catholic Irish. The second, the Auxiliaries, arrived in July of that year and also established a reputation for aggression (a detachment of Auxiliaries stays at the Majestic Hotel in *Troubles*). For example, in September 1920 the Auxiliaries burned and sacked the city center of Cork after the IRA destroyed RIC barracks in the area. In July 1921, the British Prime Minister, Lloyd George, increasingly alarmed at the escalating bloodshed and chaos in Ireland, invited Irish nationalist leaders to London. On

Bomb-damaged buildings on Dublin's Sackville Street, remnants from the Civil War of 1922-23.

December 6, 1921, the Anglo-Irish Treaty was signed, giving 26 of the Irish counties autonomy over their own affairs as the Irish Free State, but retaining the six Protestant-majority counties in the north as part of the Union. However, this effective partition of the country, as well as the controversial aspects of the treaty (ministers of the new Irish Free State still had to take an oath of allegiance to the British crown), created a set of problems that led to the Irish Civil War of 1922-23 and would remain very much a part of Irish politics through the twentieth century.

Nationalist resistance throughout the Empire. By 1919 the British Empire was at its zenith. In addition to Ireland, its colonial possessions included much of South Asia, numerous lands in Africa; the Middle Eastern territories; and a variety of Caribbean islands; as well as the Dominions of Australia, New Zealand, South Africa and Canada. The defeat of Germany in the First World War meant that German colonies—including Cameroon, Togo and Tanganyika—also became British Mandates. By 1919 the British Empire had become one of the largest empires the world had ever seen.

Ostensibly Britain seemed to occupy a position of imperial force. However, this impression masked incidents of continual opposition and resistance to British rule throughout the colonies,

often by nationalist forces in colonized lands. At the turn of the century, these challenges found strong expression in the Empire's "settler" colonies: those countries in the American and Australasian continents featuring large populations descended from European settlers. The settler colonies agitated for forms of self-government achieved when they became "Dominions" of the British Empire, self-governing states that pledged an allegiance to the British Crown. Canada was the first to receive Dominion status in 1867; Australia followed in 1900, New Zealand in 1907, South Africa in 1909. Additionally, during the early decades of the twentieth century, a variety of pressure groups were formed throughout the colonies in order to give focus to anticolonial and nationalist energies, especially in Africa and Asia. For example, the South African National Native Congress (later the African National Congress) originated in 1914, while in 1921 Mohandas Gandhi began the Non-Cooperation movement in India. This momentum against the rule of empire would grow steadily, culminating for many colonies in the achievement of independence after the Second World War (1939-1945).

During the early decades of the century, resistance movements often met with brutality at the hands of the British. To choose just one example, on April 13, 1919, at the Jallianwallagh (a public park) in Amritsar, India, a crowd of peaceful demonstrators were gunned down by Indian Army troops led by Brigadier-General R. E. H. Dyer. In *Troubles* the Major reads about the Amritsar Massacre in the newspaper at the Majestic Hotel, and on several other occasions news reaches Ireland of anticolonial unrest in South Africa, India, and elsewhere. Indeed, one of *Troubles*'s most important characteristics is its careful linking of the anti-British violence in Ireland with those anticolonial struggles overseas that to some degree influenced and encouraged Irish nationalism—which, in turn, were subsequently affected by events in Ireland. Although produced by a unique history and specific to Ireland, Irish nationalist resistance was in fact linked to these wider, transnational forms of resistance against empire that surfaced in countries throughout the world.

Protestantism and the Anglo-Irish Ascendancy. For centuries Ireland has been riven by tensions between two communities, Catholics and Protestants. While Irish Catholics have been in the majority throughout the island, they have constituted the peasant and working classes, historically remote from power and authority. Contrarily, from the late seventeenth century until the War of Independence (1919-21) Protestants comprised a rich and powerful landowning elite more centrally involved in Irish politics and the economy. The reasons behind this divide, and the consequent tensions between the two communities, lie in a long and complex Irish history.

Elizabeth I's conquest of Ireland in the latter part of the sixteenth century established English government in a Gaelic, predominantly Catholic country that, significantly, had remained unaffected by the Protestant Reformation in Renaissance Europe. Elizabeth met with resistance from Gaelic chiefs and lords, the most famous being the Earl of Tyrone's stand against Elizabethan rule in Ulster in 1598. But by 1601 Tyrone had been defeated. He received a royal pardon for his treason, but in 1607 fled the country. His lands in Ulster were forfeited to the British Crown, and in 1610 there began the "Plantation of Ulster." English and Scottish Protestants settled in the north in an attempt to stabilize the volatile relations between Ireland and the rest of the British isles. These settlers, and those born to them, were fiercely proud of their Protestant identity and traditions and deeply suspicious of the Catholic Irish, who became their tenants or laborers. Tensions between the two faiths were inevitable. In

1641 there occurred a bloody uprising of Catholic Irish in an attempt to recover the lands lost to the settlers, in which Protestants were slaughtered. Eight years later the anti-Catholic Oliver Cromwell, fresh from his victories in the English civil war, arrived in Ireland to fight both those troops stationed there loyal to England's King Charles II and the Irish Catholics. Catholics were given little mercy in the violence that ensued; any lands remaining in Catholic hands were seized and redistributed. Robert Kee estimates that the percentage of land owned by Catholics was 59 percent in 1641, 22 percent in 1649, 14 percent in 1659 and 7 percent in 1714 (Kee, p. 48). Both Cromwell's ruthlessness in reasserting the authority of Protestantism in Ireland, and the Catholic Uprising of 1641, remain emotive memories for Ireland's divided communities to this day.

Protestant power in Ireland was clinched in the late seventeenth century. Concerned by the crowning of the Catholic James II in England, who seemed willing to restore lands to Irish Catholics, Irish Protestants again began to fear for their safety. When news arrived in 1688 in Londonderry, Ulster, that Catholics were murdering Protestants as a response to the news from England that James II was being succeeded by a new king, the Protestant William of Orange, Londonderry's citizens refused to admit a Catholic garrison of the King's troops. Soon both James II and William of Orange were fighting each other in Ireland. William completely defeated the King's Catholic forces in 1691. As Robert Kee puts it, "This was the foundation of that triumph of Protestant over Catholic, Orange over Green, still perpetuated in memory by Protestants in Northern Ireland" (Kee, p. 50).

The eighteenth century saw the establishment of a Protestant landowning class, often called the "Anglo-Irish Ascendancy." This is an odd name, perhaps, as many of the Protestant landowning families had been settled in Ireland for generations and knew very little of England. However, the term "Anglo-Irish" emphasizes the fact that the Ascendancy remained firmly Protestant and treasured its close religious and political affiliations with Britain. The thought of Irish independence was anathema to the Ascendancy, which feared an Ireland ruled by Catholics beyond the jurisdiction of the British state. Although suffering a decline in the nineteenth century, the Ascendancy held considerable influence at the time of the War of Independence, especially in Ulster, although its power was indeed waning as Catholic Irish nationalism gained momentum. It is into the early twentieth-century world of the Anglo-Irish Ascendancy in decline that Farrell takes us in *Troubles*.

The Novel in Focus

Plot summary. *Troubles* consists of two parts of equal length (like the country it depicts, it has been divided into two). In the first, "A Member of the Quality," Major Brendan Archer arrives at the illustrious Majestic Hotel in Kilnalough, a fictional Irish village on the east coast of Ireland, to meet up with his fiancée, Angela Spencer, to whom he became rashly engaged in Brighton while on leave in 1916. Angela is the eldest daughter of Edward Spencer, who purchased the Majestic Hotel on his return from India some years earlier. Although Edward is not of the Irish landowning Protestant Ascendancy, the so-called "Quality," his wealth and power aligns him with them while pointing to the continued collusion between the Protestant Irish and the English. Like the Irish Protestants, he too fears and distrusts the Catholic Irish.

The Majestic has fallen into disrepair and retains only a shadow of its former glory as an exclusive and fashionable establishment for members of the "Quality." The Major has read all about the Majestic and the Spencers in Angela's letters, yet on his arrival he is disconcerted to find that both the hotel and the family are not at all what he imagined. Inhabited mainly by old ladies and administered by a skeleton staff of local Irish characters, including the mysterious Irish servant Murphy, the Majestic is a vast, rambling building, full of hidden passageways and staircases. Litters of cats can be found gamboling in the deserted rooms. The hotel features crumbling masonry, and the Palm Court is filled with comically overgrown foliage.

The Major meets Angela's family—her father Edward, her brother Ripon, and her twin sisters Faith and Charity (her mother died some years previously). Gradually he is drawn into the bizarre day-to-day rhythm of life at the hotel. Angela herself proves elusive. She rarely appears at meals, and mysteriously disappears from the Major's view altogether. Soon he meets other key figures in Kilnalough, including Sarah Devlin, an outspoken Irish Catholic girl occasionally confined to a wheelchair due to an unspecified illness. Within a few weeks the Major has decided that his engagement to the mysterious Angela is a bad idea and decides to leave the Majestic. He travels to Dublin to see the Peace Day parade on July 19, 1919, and, while there, he witnesses the gunning down of an Irish Volunteer who had just assassinated a retired British Army Officer working at Dublin Castle. Disconcerted and baffled by the escalating violence around him, the Major decides to quit Ireland immediately. But a telegram arrives to tell him that Angela has died from leukemia, and the Major makes his way back to the Majestic in a melancholy frame of mind.

After the funeral, at the end of the summer, the Major returns to London but stays in touch with Sarah Devlin, who visits him some weeks later. Throughout the next few months he develops a burgeoning love for Sarah, which draws him back to Kilnalough in May 1920. The Majestic seems in a greater state of disrepair than ever. A sinister warning has been erected at the entrance to the hotel by the IRA telling of the dire consequences for those abetting "traitors" to Ireland; the Major soon learns that a group of Auxiliaries are staying in the hotel. One morning the Major notices that the starving Kilnalough villagers have begun to steal corn from Edward Spencer's fields. This is because Edward is in dispute with the villagers about their access to the land—from which, no doubt, they derive their only source of income—and has forbidden them to reap their usual harvest. During the night, he is woken up to witness the corn fields blazing, an action that Edward suspects is the doing of the IRA, keen to turn the Kilnalough villagers' opinion against him by spreading the word that the fire was Edward's doing. Very gradually, the Major detects the violence and hostility he witnessed in Dublin making its presence felt in the daily lives of those in Kilnalough.

In Part Two of the novel, the violence at large in Ireland exerts greater impact on Kilnalough, causing Edward Spencer to become more defensive and hostile towards the Irish. Living absurdly amidst the old ladies at the Majestic and spending his days wandering the hotel or playing cards, the Major attempts to pursue his relationship with Sarah, but her capricious behavior frequently frustrates his intentions and he becomes suspicious of her growing intimacy with Edward. Meanwhile, the Majestic gradually grows more decrepit. In one particularly ironic episode, the capital "M" of the hotel's name, which hangs on its exterior wall, detaches itself and falls to the ground, leaving the moniker "ajestic" in its place (the hotel has literally become "a jest"). Fueled by their rivalry for Sarah, the Major and Edward begin to argue; the Major objects to the colonial, racist attitude typical of the Ascendancy that Edward takes towards the Catholic Irish, (who are, incidentally, spotted daily foraging desperately amongst the hotel's bins for scraps of food to eat). By Christmas 1920 the atmosphere at large in the country has become increasingly tense, and there is a palpable sense of the community at the Majestic living in a state of siege (revolvers are laid on the dinner table, along with knives and forks). Madly perhaps, Edward decides to throw a party. A ball at the Majestic, he thinks, may restore some splendor and grandeur to the establishment and to the Anglo-Irish Ascendancy it represents.

FROM *THE TIMES*, SATURDAY, SEPTEMBER 2, 1920
"DISTRICT INSPECTOR MURDERED"

"A police officer was killed yesterday evening in a lonely part of Co. Sligo and two policemen who were with him were wounded. An official report of the outrage, which was received in Dublin to-day, states that a motor police patrol was ambushed at half-past 5 between Bunnanadden and Tubbercurry. District-inspector Brady was shot dead and Constable O'Hara was seriously wounded. Constable Browne was also wounded in the head. . . .

Following the shooting of District-inspector Brady, the town of Tubbercurry was visited by armed men in lorries during the night and many houses were wrecked. The firing of rifles and the bursting of bombs terrified the inhabitants, several of whom fled to the fields. Afterwards the party drove into the country, and this morning the Ballyara and Achonry creameries were found to have been burned."

(*Times*, p. 10)

The ball is attended by many of the "Quality," but it serves only to underline their declining fortunes in the Ireland of 1921. Disrupted by the hooligan behavior of the Auxiliaries and the mysterious disappearance of Edward Spencer at its height, it is also an evening of failed hopes for the Major. Sarah refuses his offer of marriage, and the Major soon discovers evidence of a sordid liaison between Sarah and Edward. She disappears with a brutal British soldier, Captain Bolton, during the night. After the failure of the ball, the Major realizes that the Majestic's days are numbered, a fact exacerbated by the shooting of an Irishman by Edward, who had suspected the Irishman to

be a member of the IRA. Fearful of reprisals the Major convinces Edward to leave the Majestic and put the hotel up for sale. Next, he persuades the old ladies that they too must leave for their own safety and sees them safely onto a train leaving Kilnalough. In the novel's closing pages he is left alone at the Majestic to greet the arrival of an RIC officer concerning Edward's killing of the IRA suspect.

During the visit, the RIC officer and the Major are attacked, buried up to their necks in sand on the Kilnalough shore and left to drown. In a scene typical of Farrell's ability to combine pathos with the bizarre, the Major is rescued by the old ladies, whose scheduled train has been canceled, forcing them to return to the hotel. Meanwhile, Edward's Irish servant, Murphy, gleefully burns the Majestic to the ground. The novel ends with news of the Major's recovery from his ordeal and departure for London in autumn 1921; still troubled by thoughts of Sarah, he has rescued the statue of Venus from the entrance hall of the ruined Majestic to take home with him.

The problem of writing history. After witnessing the killing of the Volunteer in Dublin, the Major reads about the incident in the newspaper the following day. He reflects upon the difference he notices between his experience of the incident and the subsequent reporting of it as a significant historical event, which converts a senseless act of violence into something portrayed as "normal and inevitable" (Farrell, *Troubles*, p. 102). This leads him to consider the amount of everyday life that historical representations leave out: "A raid on the barracks, the murder of a policeman in a lonely country road, an airship crossing the Atlantic, a speech by a man on a platform, or any other random acts, mostly violent, that one reads about every day: this was the history of the time. The rest was the mere 'being alive' that every age has to do" (*Troubles*, p. 102).

In its self-consciousness concerning the problem of narrating history, *Troubles* is typical of a more general "crisis in historicity" that pervaded the late 1960s in literature, philosophy, and history itself. Intellectuals such as Roland Barthes and Michel Foucault in France were arguing that history should not be thought of as a reliable witness of the past; rather, history was merely one more discourse among others, and there was essentially no significant difference between historical writing and imaginative writing. To this way of thinking, historical documents were compromised by the views and prejudices of those who both produced and read them. The documents left out of the picture more things than were recorded, and thus any historical narrative could be only a partial, limited view of a vanished era. In time this line of thinking would earn the name "postmodernism"; postmodernist thought declared the relativity of all points of view and cast doubt on the ability of language to reflect accurately the past and the present. These ideas exerted great impact on British and American literary culture in the late 1960s, as a growing number of writers began to produce novels where the practice of representing the past became profoundly problematic. The most famous example is perhaps John Fowles's novel **The French Lieutenant's Woman** (1969; also in *WLAIT 4: British and Irish Literature and Its Times*), a tale of mid-Victorian England in which the narrator frequently interrupts the story to share with readers the difficulties that he is having in trying to give an accurate picture of life at the time, and doubts his, and his readers', ability to discover any truth about the past. Although less overtly worried about its representation of history, *Troubles* is similarly preoccupied with how best to bear witness to the past.

Farrell believed that historical experience was not to be found in the official records and grand narratives of the historian, but in the day-to-day, seemingly incidental and insignificant details of life. In contrast to the conventional historian's craft, Farrell's focus is on the microcosmic, the particular, the curious. In his view, history is not "composed of treaties being signed or pincer movements. It's smoke in your eyes or having a blister on your foot" (Farrell in Binns, p. 21). Significantly, *Troubles* is punctuated by extracts from newspaper reports (it is not resolved if these are real extracts from 1919-21 or invented by Farrell). The reports record the gradually worsening situation in Ireland, and bring news of other conflicts throughout Europe and the British Empire. Yet the bulk of the novel's action is set at a slight angle to these historical events, which, for much of the novel, seem to have only an incidental impact on life at the Majestic. Significantly the novel's setting is *not* Dublin, the capital of the nation, but rather a seemingly minor coastal village in Ireland. This is *not* a story of great leaders or heroes in the vanguard of history. Instead, its focus is on the "being alive" that every age does. The characters are minor, marginal participants at an important moment in history over which they have no overall control. The

Major, a veteran of the First World War, has already experienced life undergoing history, has already followed orders from those directing the course of the war, and has already witnessed the suffering and bloodshed of the trenches (these experiences are responsible for the frequently melancholy moods that characterize him in the novel). It is a typical Farrell witticism that the name most frequently used for him, the Major, is ironic. In fact, the Major relinquished his military commission after completing his service in the British army; he is a Major in name only and not in any more meaningful sense.

In a similar fashion, the events depicted in *Troubles* both are and are not major. Although hostilities throughout the country are always on the edge of the reader's vision, most of the action concerns seemingly trivial incidents. Yet it is clear that there is a definite historical relationship between seemingly unconnected "major" and "minor" events. The most innocuous and bizarre occurrences are just as much a result of the war of independence as are grander events. For example, Edward's son, Ripon, falls in love with Máire Noonan, the daughter of a prominent Irish Catholic. Their relationship is a controversial one within each family as it crosses the borders of religion and nationality. In the interests of decency, Mr. Noonan decides to meet Edward at the Majestic. On his arrival, Edward, who is digging in the garden, mistakes Noonan for a rather insolent elderly telegraph boy and sends him up to the house, while Noonan takes Edward to be the gardener. Soon both men are wandering through the Majestic looking for each other, each thinking of the political and religious troubles that are, indirectly, responsible for their absurd wanderings through the labyrinthine Majestic on this particular day. In the seemingly unsensational incident of two elderly fathers wandering aimlessly through the hotel, merely "being alive," the novel suggests many of the "major" events directing their lives: the prejudices of Catholics and Protestants that add to their mutual misrecognition of each other; the historical situation that makes Edward wish to close ranks and not admit an Irish Catholic into his family; the failure of those on opposite sides of the divide in Ireland to meet on common ground. Indeed, the mundane incident of two men branching off in different directions in the Majestic, fated never to meet amicably, acts as a vivid and novel representation of the troubled situation in Ireland as a whole. *Troubles* invites readers to speculate that the true significance of history is best discovered in such microcosmic and bizarre consequences. In so doing, it makes its own contribution to debates at the time concerning the crisis of historicity.

Sources and literary context. Farrell's influences were various, and he drew from several different sources throughout his career. His favorite writers included Joseph Conrad, Richard Hughes and Malcolm Lowry. He was particularly taken by Lowry's novel *Under the Volcano* (1947); Chris Ackerley has written at length on the influence of Lowry in Farrell's writing (see Ackerley in Crane, pp. 19-35). Farrell's first three novels

---

THE DISINTEGRATING EMPIRE: TRAGEDY OR FARCE?

~

As John Spurling has noted, "From a seat in the gods the British in their short-lived Empire—in Ireland, in India or Malaya at those particular moments of disintegration—look tragic; but when you get down amongst them, the thing is a farce" (Spurling, p. 165). In depicting the end of British rule in Ireland, Farrell's fiction is by no means nostalgic or elegiac for the vanishing empire. Indeed, the variety of tone in the novel is one of its greatest triumphs. Through the character of the Major, the war veteran, we are never allowed to forget that bloody conflict exacts a morbid price. But existing alongside such melancholy is a highly comic atmosphere that delights in indulging black and bizarre humor, often created through Farrell's penchant for the unexpected metaphor. For example, at Angela's funeral the Major glances down into her grave and sees a "neat oblong trench along the sides of which the white knuckles of roots showed like nuts in a slice of fruit cake" (*Troubles,* p. 105). A mixture of black humor and the bizarre contributes to the depiction of Edward and the Anglo-Irish "Quality" as farcical buffoons left increasingly moribund by historical events—remnants of an older, terminal world who are rapidly being turned into oddities and anachronisms in the historical present of 1919-1921. In the latter part of the novel, Edward takes to conducting a series of bizarre scientific experiments, one of which involves him firing a shotgun at his servant Murphy in order to measure the reduction of saliva in the human mouth when frightened. But his experiments only point up the increasing meaninglessness of Edward's life, and the extent to which the history he is undergoing is rapidly leaving him as well as the rest of the "Quality" washed up and abandoned in its wake.

---

were influenced by Albert Camus, Jean-Paul Sartre and French existentialism, and the Empire Trilogy bears the traces of their absurdist view of human life as temporary and meaningless. In addition, Farrell admitted owing much to Russian novelist Leo Tolstoy and French writer Stendhal, who served as good examples of writers attempting to depict the experience of "undergoing history" (Binns, p. 210).

In writing *Troubles*, Farrell made a conscious decision to employ Ireland, the country where he spent part of his childhood each year, and he drew upon a variety of literary and historical resources. One important literary influence was the genre of the Big House novel. As Ronald Tamplin explains, "From Maria Edgeworth's *Castle Rackrent* (1800) on, a considerable number of Irish writers produced novels set in, often dominated by, a Big House, the type of grand house in which Anglo-Irish landowning families lived, drawing rent from the tenant farmers around and occupying something of a feudal relation to the locality, though not always accepting a feudal responsibility" (Tamplin in Crane, p. 49; see *Castle Rackrent* in *WLAIT 3: British and Irish Literature and Its Times*). Examples from twentieth-century literature would include Elizabeth Bowen's *The Last September* (1929), Henry Green's *Loving* (1945) and John Banville's *Birchwood* (1973). The Majestic's infernal fate is very much part of the conventions of Big House fiction, and it in fact bears witness to the fortunes of many Big Houses during the transitional months of Irish independence. As Richard Gill notes, the burning of the Big House "was more dramatically linked with revolutionary social change: the home passed away with the Anglo-Irish establishment. During the Troubles, the house was usually burned to the ground and as a charred ruin became a monument to a vanished order" (Gill, p. 168).

The fiery fate of the Majestic, then, invokes a conventional novelistic representation of the end of British rule in Ireland. One vital difference between Farrell's Big House and the Big Houses of convention, though, is the status of the Majestic as a hotel. This status underlines the temporary nature of Britain's accommodation in Ireland. It also signals the fact that, while *Troubles* uses aspects of the Big House novel, it is not a typical or conventional Big House novel. Indeed, *Troubles* is characterized by a postmodernist self-consciousness on the part of Farrell who makes it plain to his readers that he is cheerfully playing with the conventions of the genre and not following them faithfully. We are never allowed to forget that the novel is not a faithful representation of Ireland in 1919-21 but a fictional recreation from a later age; the reader is always aware that the world of *Troubles* is first-and-foremost a fictional illusion. On this point the "factual" newspaper extracts which intrude into and punctuate the text are absolutely vital: they make sure that the reader never forgets that the narrative he or she is reading stands at a remove from more conventional or reliable forms of historical documentation. This self-consciously literary approach offsets the more documentary aspects of the novel, and accounts for its haunting atmosphere. Farrell's Ireland is caught somewhere between the worlds of history and illusion, fact and fiction.

Two further influences are important to the creation of the Majestic. First, Farrell exploits the conventions of gothic fiction. The Majestic is a dark, at times sinister and mysterious location with hidden horrors. His first night at the hotel, the Major's attempts to sleep are disturbed by a peculiar smell that pervades his room. On investigation he is terrified to find a rotting sheep's head infested with maggots, and he vomits copiously at the discovery. The servant, Murphy, is an ancient figure who moves mysteriously through the hotel; indeed, he seems the only character who knows each twist and turn of the vast building, and he startles the guests with his sudden appearances. At the end of the novel he is glimpsed standing amongst the inferno of the hotel with "his clothes a cloak of fire, his hair ablaze: Satan himself! Then he vanished and was never seen again in Kilnalough" (*Troubles*, pp. 443-44). Farrell's biographer, Lavinia Greacen, has recently revealed another major influence on the creation of the Majestic Hotel—the burnt ruin known as Ocean View Hotel on Block Island, New York, which Farrell visited in May 1967 (Greacen, pp. 224-25). Inspired by the ruin, Farrell spent the next weeks researching the history of life at the formerly prestigious hotel.

Events in History at the Time the Novel Was Written

The troubles of 1969. Farrell conceived of writing a book about Ireland in 1967 while living in New York. He had moved there the previous year to take up a Harkness Fellowship, which he finished in London in 1969. By an act of remarkable historical coincidence of which Farrell was keenly aware, during the very period in which

he was writing about the troubles of 1919-21, the modern "troubles" in Northern Ireland emerged. As Lavinia Greacen notes, "Jim often took the tube home from North London or Bloomsbury surrounded by commuters reading the *Evening Standard* accounts of disturbances that mirrored events he had just been unearthing" (Greacen, pp. 254-55). As he quipped to Caroline Moorehead in an interview, "I couldn't help feeling that in some way I had evoked what was happening" (Moorehead, p. 12). Indeed, there is little doubt that Farrell's sense of the troubles of 1919-21 was heightened by the conflict in Northern Ireland, which exploded at the time he was writing his novel.

EDWARD SPENCER AND EDMUND SPENSER

The proprietor of the Majestic Hotel, Edward Spencer, is modeled on the sixteenth-century English poet Edmund Spenser, who spent a great deal of his adult life in Ireland, first as secretary to the Governor General of Ireland and later as the Sheriff of Cork. Edmund Spenser owned a three-thousand-acre estate, Kilcolm Castle, on which he intended to settle a community of English immigrants. His advocacy of colonialism in Ireland was eloquently expressed in his treatise *A View to the Present State of Ireland*. Like the Majestic, Kilcolm Castle was burned in October 1598 during a rebellion and Spenser was driven back to England. So, in modeling the fictional Edward Spencer on the real-life Edmund Spenser, Farrell deliberately called attention to the long history of the British colonial presence in Ireland, and resistances to it, offering another important historical context in which to read the troubles of 1919-21.

As explained, the Anglo-Irish treaty of December 6, 1921, had effectively created two countries: the Irish Free State and Northern Ireland. The latter consisted of the six counties of Antrim, Armagh, Down, Fermanagh, Londonderry (or Derry) and Tyrone. Collectively known to some as Ulster, the area's population was predominantly Protestant although a significant number were Catholics. Fiercely opposed to the idea of an all-Ireland republic ruled from Dublin, Protestant Northern Ireland had a form of devolved government with its own prime minister and chamber at Stormont. But Catholic nationalist sentiment in Northern Ireland had never gone away, and it began to mount in the 1960s. Increasingly angered at the discriminatory policies and activities in Northern Ireland, under which Protestants received preferential treatment in government posts, employment, and housing, in 1964 the Catholic communities formed the Northern Ireland Civil Rights Association to protest the undemocratic conditions they were suffering. They organized a number of marches during subsequent months. One march, in January 1969, was violently attacked by a Protestant mob; significantly, the Royal Ulster Constabulary (RUC) arrested 80 Catholic marchers but not a single Protestant attacker. To many Catholics it seemed that the RUC often quickly sided with Protestants when any conflict arose between the two communities. In August 1969 riots flared in Belfast and British troops were deployed to restore law and order. On July 12, for example, there was an annual Apprentice Boys march of Ulster Protestants through Derry to commemorate the siege of Londonderry against the forces of King James II. The march triggered a three-day riot between police and Derry's Catholic community that would become known as the Siege of the Bogside. The modern Irish "troubles" had truly begun.

The end of the year saw the re-emergence of the IRA as the organizer and instigator of violent protest against the perceived persecution of Irish Catholics in Northern Ireland. In calling for a united Irish Republic, and in portraying itself as defender of the north, who had little if any faith in the ability of RUC to uphold law and order with impartiality, the IRA won popular support in some parts of Northern Ireland's Catholic community. Recalling the guerrilla tactics of Michael Collins during the War of Independence of 1919-21, the IRA carried out a series of attacks in both Northern Ireland and mainland Britain. In fact, during the period in which he wrote *Troubles,* J. G. Farrell was stopped by police outside Victoria Station in London as the IRA bombing campaign intensified. The IRA proved themselves to be a ruthless and formidable terrorist organization for many years to come, making RUC officers and police stations focal points of attack, much as the RIC officers were in 1919-21. In August 1971, a year after the publication of *Troubles,* Brian Faulkner, Prime Minister of Northern Ireland, would introduce "internment" in the province in an attempt to regain control of the increasingly chaotic and violent situation. Internment allowed the RUC to arrest and hold without trial anyone suspected of being involved in IRA activities. But the situation failed to improve. On January 30, 1972, 13 unarmed Catholic civilians were shot dead by British troops in Derry. Remembered as Bloody Sunday, the incident would prove a turning point in Northern Ireland's history. As violence escalated in its wake, the Stormont administration was dissolved on March 20, 1972, by the British prime minister, Edward Heath, and the administration of Northern Ireland became the full responsibility of parliament in Westminster, England.

Reviews. The Empire Trilogy changed Farrell's life considerably, winning him critical acclaim and securing his reputation as one of Britain's most promising and inventive postwar writers. *Troubles* kicked off the acclaim, receiving a mostly positive reception. The anonymous reviewer in the *Times Literary Supplement* enjoyed the hallucinogenic qualities of the novel: "Everything in the book, or almost everything, is observed, as it were, at a remove, through curtains of fine lawn hung blowily and shabbily at leaky windows; and these impose a blurred, half ghostly outline on scenes and situations" (*Times Literary Supplement,* p. 85). But the poet James Fenton, writing in the *New Statesman,* was less impressed. He described the novel as "an unhappy mixture of the historical, political and fantastical" and commented that "the essential arbitrariness of the whole conception in imaginative terms undermines its well-researched political and documentary observations" (Fenton, p. 14). However, the judgement of novelist William Trevor would prove more accurate, as evidenced by the subsequent success of the novel. In his estimation, as expressed in the *Guardian, Troubles* was "a *tour de force* of considerable quality" (Trevor in Greacen, p. 266). The literary world agreed with him. On May 6, 1971, Farrell was awarded the Geoffrey Faber Memorial Prize and received a check for £250. As Lavinia Greacen puts it, "Overnight, and without any other further call on his own resources, he was a literary star" (Greacen, p. 267).

—John McLeod

For More Information

Binns, Ronald. *J. G. Farrell.* London: Methuen, 1986.

Crane, Ralph, ed. *J. G. Farrell: The Critical Grip.* Dublin: Four Courts Press, 1999.

Dean, Malcolm. "An Insight Job." *Guardian,* 1 September 1973, 11.

"District Inspector Murdered." *The Times* (London), 2 September 1920, 10.

Donnelly, Brian. "The Big House in the Recent Irish Novel." *Studies: Irish Quarterly Review* 14 (1975): 133-42.

"End of a Dream." Review of *Troubles,* by J. G. Farrell, *Times Literary Supplement,* 22 January 1971, 85.

Farrell, J. G. *Troubles.* London: Flamingo, 1970.

Fenton, James. "Victims." *New Statesman,* 9 October 1970, 464.

Gill, Richard. *Happy Rural Seat: The English Country House and the Literary Imagination.* New Haven: Yale University Press, 1972.

Greacen, Lavinia. *J. G. Farrell: The Making of a Writer.* London: Bloomsbury, 1999.

Kee, Robert. *Ireland: A History.* Rev. ed. London: Abacus, 1995.

Moorehead, Caroline. "Writing in the Dark, and Not a Detail Missed." *Times,* 9 September 1978, 12.

Spurling, John. "As Does the Bishop." In *A. G. Farrell, The Hill Station: An Unfinished Novel and an Indian Diary.* Ed. John Spurling. London: Flamingo, 1981.

Ulysses

by

James Joyce

～

James Augustine Aloysius Joyce was born February 2, 1882, in Rathgar, a suburb of Dublin. He was the eldest of 16 children born to Mary Jane Joyce and John Stanislaus Joyce. John Joyce worked first in business, then as a civil servant, establishing a tenuous middle-class economic position. This position steadily eroded during James's youth, as his father often drank, neglected his affairs, and borrowed money. According to contemporaries, John Joyce was a jolly, bibulous, pugnacious good fellow, notorious in Dublin for his extravagance, biting wit, and monocle. His son James inherited some of his traits—an interest in Irish politics, a love of music, a lively sense of humor, a distrust of the clergy, and spendthrift habits. From age 6 to 9, James Joyce attended Clongowes Wood College, considered the best Jesuit school in Ireland; from 11 to 15, Belvedere College; and from 16 to 20, University College, Dublin. When Joyce was just 9, he wrote his first poem, a tribute to his father's hero, Charles Stewart Parnell, leader of the late-nineteenth-century Irish Home Rule movement. By 1902 several of Joyce's college essays had been published, including "Ibsen's New Drama" in *The Fortnightly Review,* a prominent English journal. His first book of poems, *Chamber Music,* was published in 1904. That same year, he met Nora Barnacle, a young woman from Galway working in Dublin as a chambermaid— the couple's first walk together is memorialized by the date on which *Ulysses* is set. Later in 1904, the couple left Ireland, settling first in Trieste, Italy, then in Zurich, Switzerland (during World

---

> **THE LITERARY WORK**
>
> A novel set in Dublin, Ireland, on June 16, 1904; published serially in *The Little Review* from March 1918 to December 1920, in book form in 1922.
>
> **SYNOPSIS**
>
> *Ulysses* follows the wanderings of Leopold Bloom, a middle-aged advertising salesman, and Stephen Dedalus, a young artist, as they cross and recross Dublin on a single summer day.

War I), and finally in Paris, France. They had two children, Giorgio and Lucia, and Joyce continued his writings. Early versions of three of the short stories that would comprise *Dubliners* appeared in 1904 in *The Irish Homestead,* edited by the Irish poet George Russell (A.E.). Though *Dubliners* was largely completed by 1905, Joyce did not find a publisher willing to print it until 1914. His autobiographical novel *A Portrait of the Artist As a Young Man* (1916) was received coolly by the Irish reading public, but nonetheless contributed to his success by attracting the attention of respected literary figures, including the American poet and editor Ezra Pound, who, together with the Irish poet W. B. Yeats, helped Joyce secure patronage. *Ulysses* appeared in 1922 but was banned in the United States until 1933 and in the United Kingdom until 1936. Joyce's final

James Joyce

work, *Finnegan's Wake,* appeared in 1939. He died in Zurich, Switzerland, on January 13, 1941, after an operation for a duodenal ulcer. *Ulysses* presents Joyce's distinctive variety of an Irish novel through its cosmopolitan inclusiveness, meanwhile lending a mythic dimension to the routines of middle-class life in 1904 Ireland.

Events in History at the Time of the Novel

Beleaguered Ireland. Since *Ulysses* makes reference to much of Irish history, a basic knowledge of that history's major events and actors is instrumental in understanding the novel's complexities. From its prehistory, Ireland has been subject to a series of invasions, incursions, and settlements by outsiders. Its legendary background includes mythic occupiers such as crude and earthy Firbolg, heroic Tuatha Da Danann, and the Milesians, free spirits and artists regarded as the ancestors of the Irish royal clans. The third century (C.E.) marked the high point of the kingship of Tara, the "golden age" of heroic sovereigns who ruled "justly, peacefully, prosperously, and truthfully" (Connolly, p. 534). In the early fifth century, the British-born St. Patrick embarked on his mission to convert the Irish to Christianity.

Ireland was invaded in the ninth century by Norsemen and in the twelfth by the recent Norman conquerors of England. England would subsequently dominate Ireland largely through the Anglo-Irish nobility (descendants of Norman invaders, in contrast to native Irish). In 1155 the only Englishman to become Pope, Adrian VI, was reputed to have issued a Papal Bull (apparently fictitious) granting England's king Henry II sovereignty over Ireland; Henry assumed full charge of an invasion of Ireland by his nobility in 1171-72. Not until the sixteenth century, however, did the English—under King Henry VII of the Tudor dynasty—begin the political and economic domination that would eventually reduce Ireland to the status of an impoverished English colony.

The early sixteenth century saw England's King Henry VIII break with the Roman Catholic Church and inaugurate the Protestant Reformation in England. Henry himself became supreme head of the Church of England and sought to reform the church power structure in Ireland as well, but some Irish chiefs resisted his usurpation of their ancient prerogatives. Judging that the Irish would continue to revolt if unmonitored, Henry set out to completely replace the Catholic, Irish-speaking chieftain class with a Protestant administration that would be controlled from London. He established the Church of England in 1534—and its Irish branch, the Church of Ireland in 1536. A few years later, in 1541, Henry declared himself king of Ireland. Henceforth the Irish courts, churches, and landed estates would be governed directly by the English or their Anglo-Irish Protestant representatives. To enforce this new arrangement, the English Parliament passed a set of discriminatory codes that barred Catholics from all legal and government professions in Ireland, and that subjected the meetings and legislative drafts of the Irish Parliament to the control of the English king and council. The Irish did not suffer these indignities quietly. Their resistance led to a declaration of independence during the English Civil War (1642-51) that produced disastrous consequences. In 1649 England's Oliver Cromwell mounted an invasion that thoroughly devastated Ireland; he and his relentless Puritan army massacred several thousand and confiscated all Irish lands. The rights of Catholics were further curtailed. By the middle of the eighteenth century, the Protestant Ascendancy in Ireland was complete, leaving followers of the Church of England—only about one-tenth of the population—in control of land and political office. Through discriminatory penal laws, not only Catholics but also Presbyterians and Nonconformists would be deprived of civil rights in Ireland for more than a hundred years.

Irish resistance. Not surprisingly, England's oppression led to the beginning of the modern Irish independence movement. Patriotic opposition in the Irish Parliament, spearheaded by Henry Flood and Henry Grattan, resulted in the moderate reforms of 1782, which included limited Irish self-government. During this period some minor disabilities suffered by Catholics in Ireland were abolished, but this slight relaxation of English control only intensified the Irish desire for self-rule. At the end of the eighteenth century, when the English were distracted by the French Revolution, the Irish saw an opportunity to advance their cause. In 1791, hoping to unite Protestants and Catholics in the movement for an independent constitutional republic, Theobald Wolfe Tone (1763-98) and others formed the Society of United Irishmen. Tone's movement sought sweeping parliamentary reform, universal suffrage, and full Catholic emancipation. By 1795 the United Irishmen had adopted a revolutionary stance, and actively sought assistance from France against England. After unsuccessful attempts by the French to invade and wrest control of Ireland, Tone led the United Irishmen in a series of abortive uprisings. The uprisings, staged in 1798, were brutally suppressed by the English. Afterwards, to centralize more legislative power in English hands, British Prime Minister William Pitt engineered the union of the British and Irish Parliaments. The Act of Union, which took effect January 1, 1801, dissolved the 500-year-old Irish Parliament and merged the kingdoms of Great Britain and Ireland into the United Kingdom. To patriots such as Flood and Grattan, the Act of Union signaled the end of the Irish nation. A failed rebellion led by Robert Emmet in 1803 was the last protest of the United Irishmen. Early in the nineteenth century, Irish Catholic politician Daniel O'Connell ("The Liberator"), using both legal and illegal means, led a lengthy and arduous nationalistic movement that resulted in the British Parliament's voting for Catholic emancipation in 1829. O'Connell organized immense meetings at which as many as 250,000 Irishmen gathered in support of his agenda. Their emancipation consisted of the repeal of the final anti-Catholic measures. O'Connell tried but failed to repeal the Act of Union.

British political domination had enormous social effects. Probably the most significant histor-ical event for nineteenth-century Ireland was The Great Famine (1845-49). Prompted by a potato blight that destroyed the staple of a large portion of the Irish population, the famine led to widespread starvation and death. British rule, both in previously confining Ireland to an agrarian economy and in failing to act to alleviate immediate conditions, aggravated the suffering enormously. In three years, the population of Ireland fell by 1.5 million (due to death and emigration). Some who remained rebelled once more, again without success. The British military promptly suppressed the Young Ireland uprising (1848) mounted during the Great Famine, as well as the subsequent Fenian revolt (1867). Fenianism (named after Fianna, the legendary band of Irish warriors led by Finn McCool) was a revolutionary movement that arose in the last third of the nineteenth century. At the heart of the movement was a secret society of Irish nationalists who espoused a radical republican ideology that rejected any connection with the British crown. Around the same time, other political movements, fearing renewed famine, saw land-reform as the crucial element in efforts to undermine England's political control. The Home Rule League, founded in 1870 by Isaac Butt, and the Irish Land League, Michael Davitt's 1879 organization, thought the chief means to Irish political autonomy rested in fair rents, secure tenant tenure, and the free sale of tenant's interest, with the ultimate purpose of transforming the tenant farmers into owners of their holdings.

Meanwhile, newly elected Anglo-Irish Party leader Charles Stewart Parnell was seeking to work a Home Rule bill through the British Parliament. By the early 1880s Parnell had galvanized the predominantly poor Catholic population of Ireland into a nationalist movement, and he took the British Parliament hostage by using the single voting block of the Irish Party as a means of obstruction and filibuster, thus forcing the Irish Question to the center stage of English politics. Parnell negotiated with British Prime Minister William Gladstone for a form of Irish Home Rule that would grant Ireland limited domestic powers. But in 1882, two prominent British officials, Lord Frederick Cavendish, chief secretary for Ireland, and his undersecretary, Mr. Burke, were murdered in Phoenix Park, Dublin, by an Irish revolutionary group, the "Invincibles." The resulting political violence undermined Parnell's campaign, and a Home Rule bill introduced in parliament in 1886 was defeated. When Parnell became embroiled in a divorce case in 1889, and revelations of his decade-long liaison with Kitty O'Shea became public, he fell from power, dying in 1891. The devastation to the cause of Irish nationalism by Parnell's ruin was overwhelming: the country's political party was hopelessly divided into Parnellite and anti-Parnellite factions, with Ireland's Catholic Church siding against Parnell and the Parnellite factions accusing the Church of caving in to the interests of the British. Parnell's supporters in the Church, meanwhile, accused him of putting his own interests before the interests of his party. The bitter factionalism that Parnell's fall caused among Irish nationalists, sometimes even within families, receives memorable treatment in Joyce's novel *A Portrait of the Artist As a Young Man,* as the Dedalus family's Christmas dinner turns into a rancorous argument over Parnell's "betrayal." Parnell, the fallen hero, also haunts *Ulysses,* as memories of the Irish patriot recur repeatedly both to Bloom and Dedalus. In the end, constitutional home-rule for Ireland never materialized under Gladstone, and Irish nationalist ambitions were frustrated for the next 20 years.

Nationalism and the Irish Literary Revival. As the Irish Party in parliament fell into disarray with the disgrace of Parnell, the energy behind the movement for national independence began to express itself culturally rather than politically. In 1893, Gaelic scholar Douglas Hyde founded the Gaelic League, a nationalist organization of Roman Catholics and Protestants dedicated to preserving and extending Irish language (Gaelic) and culture. That same year Hyde delivered an address to the Irish Literary Society on "The Necessity for De-Anglicizing Ireland." He intended not simply to rid Ireland of English lawmakers; Hyde wished to rid it as well of all traces of English cultural imperialism, a force that by the end of the nineteenth century had gone far toward obliterating Gaelic and many Irish customs and folkways. To this end, he and other like-minded nationalist scholars established institutions such as the School for Irish Learning, which opened in 1903 and offered classes in Irish history, folklore, dance, and, of course, the Gaelic language. Cultural-defense organizations also developed at this time, such as D. P. Moran's Irish Ireland campaign, which sought to exclude all Protestant influence from Irish nationalism, and the Gaelic Athletic Association, which promoted the revival of Irish sports such as hurling—something of a cross between lacrosse and field hockey. These groups urged nationalists and non-nationalists alike to stop imitating the English and assert respect for Irish culture.

The most enduring assertion of Irish cultural nationalism was the Irish literary renaissance, a movement of poets, prose writers, and playwrights, who, between about 1890 and 1914, sought inspiration in Irish mythology, folklore, and popular culture. The domination of the movement by Irish writers from middle- and upper-class Protestant backgrounds, such as W. B. Yeats, John Millington Synge, and Lady Augusta Gregory, and its preoccupation with using Gaelic material as the basis of a revitalized Irish literature in English, has encouraged the alternative label "Anglo-Irish revival." Hyde's book *A Literary History of Ireland* (1899) was among the most influential works of the revival, introducing many Irish people to an indigenous Irish literary tradition that they were not even aware they possessed.

Joyce maintained an ambivalent relation to the Irish literary renaissance and Irish nationalism in general. On the one hand, as an avowed socialist, he supported the cause of Irish independence and welcomed the revival of Irish letters. On the other hand, he always asserted a catholic and cosmopolitan sensibility in his works, an inclusive European attitude.

The rise of the social sciences. Joyce drew upon the voluminous research of nineteenth-century social science in constructing a mythic and heroic background for the otherwise rather unspectacular actions of Bloom and Dedalus in *Ulysses.* In particular, the emerging fields of modern anthropology, comparative mythology, sociology of religion, and psychology offered Joyce a fertile harvest of ideas for his "mythical method," as T. S. Eliot called it (Eliot in Gray, p. 228).

Popular interest in anthropology had been stimulated in the late nineteenth century by studies of contemporary preliterate cultures, such as that of American Indian peoples and Australian aborigines, and by the disinterment of dead civilizations, such as that of Minoan Crete (begun in 1898 by Sir Arthur Evans) and Troy (by Heinrich Schliemann from 1876-85). In addition, works such as J. G. Frazer's *The Golden Bough* (1890, reissued in 12 volumes, 1907-15) put religion itself in a new light. *The Golden Bough* surveyed spiritual beliefs and practices worldwide, with special emphasis on myths of regeneration (like those that inform the reveries of Leopold Bloom in *Ulysses*). Such writings suggested that, however much religions might claim to differ, their sacred narratives, dogmas, and practices

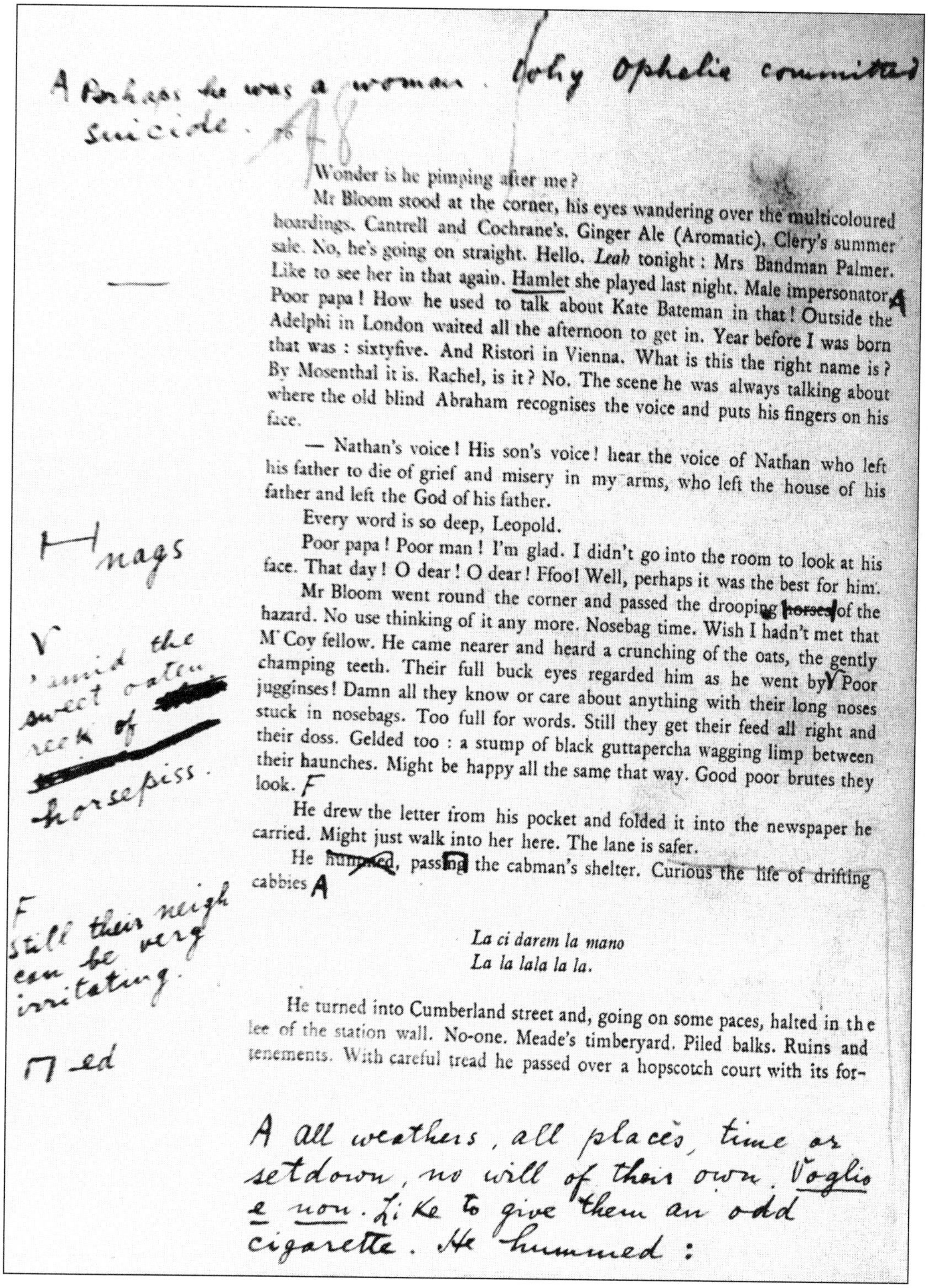

A Perhaps he was a woman. Why Ophelia committed suicide. A

Wonder is he pimping after me?

Mr Bloom stood at the corner, his eyes wandering over the multicoloured hoardings. Cantrell and Cochrane's. Ginger Ale (Aromatic). Clery's summer sale. No, he's going on straight. Hello. *Leah* tonight: Mrs Bandman Palmer. Like to see her in that again. Hamlet she played last night. Male impersonator. Poor papa! How he used to talk about Kate Bateman in that! Outside the Adelphi in London waited all the afternoon to get in. Year before I was born that was: sixtyfive. And Ristori in Vienna. What is this the right name is? By Mosenthal it is. Rachel, is it? No. The scene he was always talking about where the old blind Abraham recognises the voice and puts his fingers on his face.

— Nathan's voice! His son's voice! I hear the voice of Nathan who left his father to die of grief and misery in my arms, who left the house of his father and left the God of his father.

Every word is so deep, Leopold.

Poor papa! Poor man! I'm glad I didn't go into the room to look at his face. That day! O dear! O dear! Ffoo! Well, perhaps it was the best for him.

Mr Bloom went round the corner and passed the drooping horses of the hazard. No use thinking of it any more. Nosebag time. Wish I hadn't met that M'Coy fellow. He came nearer and heard a crunching of the oats, the gently champing teeth. Their full buck eyes regarded him as he went by. Poor jugginses! Damn all they know or care about anything with their long noses stuck in nosebags. Too full for words. Still they get their feed all right and their doss. Gelded too: a stump of black guttapercha wagging limp between their haunches. Might be happy all the same that way. Good poor brutes they look. F

He drew the letter from his pocket and folded it into the newspaper he carried. Might just walk into her here. The lane is safer.

He hummed, passing the cabman's shelter. Curious the life of drifting cabbies A

La ci darem la mano
La la lala la la.

He turned into Cumberland street and, going on some paces, halted in the lee of the station wall. No-one. Meade's timberyard. Piled balks. Ruins and tenements. With careful tread he passed over a hopscotch court with its for-

Handwritten annotations:
H nags
'amid the sweet oaten reek of horsepiss.
F still their neigh can be very irritating.
□ ed

A all weathers, all places, time or setdown, no will of their own. Voglio e non. Like to give them an odd cigarette. He hummed:

Pages from the fourth set of corrected proofs for the 1922 edition of *Ulysses,* showing how Joyce painstakingly reworked his fiction.

conformed to a few simple motifs and patterns found all over the world, and that highly developed theologies were rooted in ideas associated with primitive magic.

As important as the British advances in anthropology was the work of French sociologist Emile Durkheim, whose book *The Elementary Forms of Religious Life* (1915) was published while

Joyce was writing *Ulysses*. Durkheim's pioneering works of the 1890s had helped broaden and transform the sociological study of law, economics, linguistics, ethnology, and art history not only in France but throughout Europe. His religious theories, which caused considerable controversy, may have appealed to Joyce for the emphasis they give to the communal function of religion.

Parallel to the advances in anthropology were those of psychology. Modern psychology, especially as it was developing at the turn of the twentieth century around the Viennese school of Sigmund Freud, was throwing new light upon the influence of unconscious mental processes in human thought and behavior. Freud's studies offered intriguing explanations of dreams, slips of the tongue and pen, processes of verbal association, jokes, forgetting, and many other ingredients of psychology, all of which play a part in Joyce's novel. Joyce is known to have read and discussed Freud's work as early as 1911, and to have been intrigued particularly by slips of the tongue (Davison, p. 129). Of special importance for *Ulysses* were studies by a student of Freud, Otto Rank, whose work on hero myths, the incest motif in literature, and the trauma of birth all contribute to ideas at work in the novel. Joyce would later have personal contact with another student of Freud, the Swiss psychologist Carl Jung; in 1934, Jung treated Joyce's daughter, Lucia, for the mental illness that darkened the happiness of Joyce's later years, when he had finally achieved a measure of fame and financial security.

Joyce's trademark stream-of-consciousness narrative style, which he claimed to have borrowed from the minor French novelist Valéry Larbaud, might owe something to associationist theories of psychology, particularly to those of the German physiological psychologist Wilhelm Wundt. However these factors may have influenced him, Joyce himself drew a connection between *Ulysses* and contemporary psychology in his description of what the novel achieved: "I have recorded, simultaneously, what a man says, sees, thinks" and how all this activity affects "what you Freudians call the subconscious" (Joyce in Ellmann, p. 524).

The Novel in Focus

Plot overview. The characters and events in *Ulysses* parallel in an ingenious and frequently subtle manner the *Odyssey* of Homer, the ancient Greek epic and touchstone of the Western literary canon. Almost every detail of Homer's epic, which features Odysseus, a hero who journeys home from the Trojan War to recover his house and kingdom, can be found echoed or transformed in Joyce's novel, often to comic effect. Joyce's *Ulysses* is divided into three large sections that roughly correspond to the traditional divisions of the *Odyssey*. Homer's epic begins with the "Telemachia," which recounts the effort of Odysseus's son Telemachus to find his father and defend the honor of his mother, Penelope. The middle books of the *Odyssey* describe the many adventures of Odysseus and his men, and the concluding books, called the "Nostos," or homecoming, describe Odysseus's ultimate return and reestablishment of his rule in Ithaca, his island homeland. The 18 chapters of Joyce's modern epic *Ulysses*—the title comes from the Latin name for Odysseus—mirror Homer's three-part scheme: Chapters 1 through 3 comprise a Telemachia, with Stephan Dedalus, the youthful poet and protagonist of Joyce's earlier novel *A Portrait of the Artist As a Young Man*, corresponding to Telemachus. Chapters 4 through 15 of *Ulysses* mostly detail the adventures of Leopold Bloom, an Irish-Jewish Odysseus and a partial projection of Joyce's own middle-aged self. Chapters 16 through 18 form the Nostos of the novel, as Leopold Bloom, his wife Molly, and Stephen Dedalus all converge at the Bloom's home at 7 Eccles Street in Dublin. Not only is Homer's large three-part division reproduced in *Ulysses*, but each chapter of Joyce's novel corresponds to an episode in Homer's *Odyssey*, according to a schema for the novel that Joyce circulated among friends. The correspondences, however, are often disguised.

Plot summary. What follows is a chapter-by-chapter summary of the basic plot line of the novel, prefaced by their Homeric equivalents in brackets. Readers should be aware, however, that *Ulysses* is intentionally designed to thwart simple summaries.

1. [Telemachus]: The first episode takes place about 8 A.M. in the Martello Tower at Sandycove, a coastal suburb of Dublin, where Joyce lived for a short time in the spring of 1904. The squat tower was one of 15 battlements built in 1804, when a French invasion of Britain was threatened. The chapter introduces Stephen Dedalus, a self-styled poet and schoolteacher, who has recently returned from Paris on the news of his mother's

THREE CHAPTERS FROM JOYCE'S ORIGINAL SCHEMA FOR *ULYSSES*

∿

As the chart below shows, Joyce assigned a complex system of correspondences to his labyrinthine novel. Not only does each chapter correspond to a scene from Homer's *Odyssey,* but most chapters also have an associated bodily organ (e.g., the ear for the musical Sirens chapter), art (in the broad sense, as in the art of medicine), symbol, and technique. While some of these correspondences hardly seem apparent, and some are clearly far more significant than others, the chart exhibits the painstaking attention to minute detail characteristic of Joyce's writing.

Title	Hour	Scene	Bodily organ	Art	Symbol	Technique
10. Wandering Rocks	3 P.M.	streets	blood	mechanics	citizens	labyrinth
11. Sirens	4 P.M.	concert room	ear	music	barmaids	Fuga per canonem
12. Cyclops	5 P.M.	tavern	muscle	politics	Fenian	gigantism

(Adapted from Gilbert, pp. 227, 240, 258)

terminal illness. He has been living in the tower with his erstwhile friend, Buck Mulligan, a medical student. Stephen still wears a black mourning suit for his mother, though it has been months since her funeral; his refusal to pray at his mother's deathbed in spite of her pleading will torment him throughout the day. Stephen and Mulligan are joined at breakfast by Haines, an Oxford acquaintance and guest of Mulligan, who has recently also been living in the tower. Haines is a wealthy English tourist in Ireland doing research for a book on Irish folk sayings. He condescendingly speaks to the old Irishwoman who delivers the men their morning milk, addressing her in Gaelic, a language she does not know. At the end of the chapter, shortly before swimming in the nearby ocean, Mulligan gets Stephen to give him the key to the tower.

2. [Nestor]: Events of the chapter are based on Joyce's experiences as a teacher at Clifton School in Dalkey in 1904. Stephen queries his students about the ancient battle of Asculum (279 B.C.)—which occasioned the phrase "Pyrrhic victory"—and hears a declamation of Milton's elegy "Lycidas." Later he is paid his monthly wages by Mr. Deasy, the aged and opinionated headmaster. Deasy lectures the polite Stephen on financial responsibility, meanwhile expressing Anglo-Irish loyalty and anti-Semitism. Before he departs,

Stephen agrees to help get Deasy's letter about foot-and-mouth disease published.

3. [Proteus]: Having left the school, Stephen wanders along the seacoast at Sandymount Strand while waiting to meet Mulligan for lunch (Stephen later joins the men from the newspaper office instead). His mind wanders over his considerable store of abstruse learning, as well as events in his life thus far. Philosophical and theological matters mingle with Irish history, his childhood artistic ambitions, his unproductive time in Paris, his estranged relations with his family, his lack of a woman's love, and his complex bond with Mulligan, who both fears him and lords it over him, much like the "usurpers" of Odysseus's household in the Greek epic. On the beach, he sees two midwives, the corpse of a drowned dog, and a gypsy couple with their dog; the gypsy woman inspires him to scribble a line of verse (on a torn-off end of Deasy's letter), which he subsequently abandons on the beach. At the end of the chapter, he urinates and leaves his dried snot on a rock.

4. [Calypso]: Leopold Bloom is introduced in this chapter, the events of which take place at about 8 A.M. at 7 Eccles Street, the home of Leopold and Molly Bloom. (The fourth, fifth and sixth chapters roughly recapitulate the times of the first, second and third chapters.) The uxorious Bloom prepares breakfast

for his wife, affectionately feeds the cat, goes to the butcher shop for a kidney (forgetting to take his latch key), has a bowel movement, and performs a host of other trivial domestic labors. Meanwhile, his mind wanders from half-informed scientific speculations to visions of an exotic Orient, the body of the maidservant in front of him at the butcher's, and the past and present situation of the Jews and their homeland. Molly remains in bed during the entire chapter, clearly accustomed to Bloom's service; she queries her husband about a term—"metempsychosis"—in a book he has obtained for her from a library and with characteristic frankness complains that "there's nothing smutty" in the novel (Joyce, *Ulysses*, 4.355). The Blooms receive mail from their daughter Milly, who works away from home and has just celebrated her fifteenth birthday; Molly also gets a letter from Blazes Boylan, an advertising man (like Bloom) and an impresario, whose arrangements for Molly's impending concert tour involve his coming to the Blooms' house later that day. At the end of the chapter, Bloom expresses sympathy for his dead acquaintance, Paddy Dignam, whose funeral he is about to attend.

5. [Lotus Eaters]: Awaiting Dignam's funeral, Bloom strolls about central Dublin; he takes the opportunity to check, at a post office distant from his home, for mail from a woman, Martha Clifford, with whom he has initiated a correspondence under the pseudonym Henry Flower. After being distracted by an encounter with an acquaintance, Bloom reads Martha's letter, to which she has pinned a flower, which appeals to Bloom's somewhat masochistic sexuality. After watching the end of a mass at a Catholic church, Bloom orders a refill of Molly's lotion and a bar of lemon soap at a nearby druggist. Shortly before entering a public bath, where he contemplates masturbating while rereading Martha's letter, he encounters another acquaintance, Bantam Lyons. In order to get rid of Lyons, who wants to know the odds on the English Ascot horse race later that day, Bloom hands him his newspaper. At the end of the chapter, Bloom lies floating in the bath, his penis "a languid floating flower" (*Ulysses*, 5.571-72).

6. [Hades]: Bloom attends the funeral of Paddy Dignam in the company of several Dubliners, including Simon Dedalus, Stephen's father. The chapter resembles a descent into the realm of the dead, including images that recall Odysseus's encounter with the underworld in Book 11 of the Greek epic. En route to the funeral, the carriage passes Stephen (on his way to Sandymount), whom Bloom notices; Blazes Boylan, whom Bloom refuses to recognize; and a Jew, the occasion of mild anti-Semitic remarks from Bloom's companions. The conversation during the ride reveals Bloom's outsider status. He attempts to ingratiate himself to these men but his thoughts—and occasionally his speech—reflect his divergence from typical Irish sentiments. Bloom thinks of Dignam's red nose as evidence of alcoholism, the real reason of his death, while he openly asserts that the declared reason, heart attack, is the best way to go: quick, with little suffering. The sentiment contradicts Catholic doctrine, which requires time to receive sacramental forgiveness for sins before death. Though the episode reminds Bloom of the two deaths closest to him—his father's (a suicide) and his son Rudy's (after 11 days)—Bloom is able to joke, sing, and approach death from the perspective of a commonsensible agnostic. The graveyard contains the remains of the Irish nationalists O'Connell and Parnell as well as Stephen's mother. At the end of the chapter, Bloom watches a large rat crawl into a grave site and imagines—without any faintness of heart—its meal of decaying flesh. His mind then returns from the realm of the dead; re-engaging life, he thinks of Molly.

7. [Aeolus]: In this chapter, the book adopts a single timeline, in which Bloom and Stephen cross paths until they ultimately meet (chapter 14). The chapter begins at the office of the *Freeman's Journal,* where Bloom works as an advertising salesman. Anxious to renew an ad for Alexander Keyes (a tea, wine, and spirit merchant), Bloom applies to the newspaper's foreman, who agrees to the arrangement if Keyes renews for three months. This sets Bloom—the only Irishman in the chapter engaged in productive activity—off to the newspaper office of the *Evening Telegraph,* where he asks the editor, Myles Crawford, if he can phone Keyes. Bloom then goes out to meet Keyes. At the end of the chapter, Bloom returns to the *Telegraph*'s offices, where an irritable Crawford is leading a group of Irishmen out to drink. Included are an unsuccessful lawyer, a questionable "professor,"

the drunken Crawford, and the leech Lenehan (who, like many minor characters in *Ulysses*, first appears in Joyce's *Dubliners*). The group also includes Stephen Dedalus, who enters the *Telegraph*'s office just after Bloom leaves to meet Keyes. Stephen, who has delivered Deasy's letter, listens willingly to the talk, mostly of past glories and lost causes. He offers his own Dublin story, "The Parable of the Plums," which is at odds with the empty and windy rhetoric of other characters. The chapter is stylistically notable for its newspaper-like headline; actually parodies of headlines, they introduce sections of the action, to which they sometimes seem only remotely relevant.

8. [Lestrygonians]: Bloom eats. In the course of further wanderings about Dublin—with the later meeting between Boylan and his wife feeding on his mind—he is handed a flyer, feeds some seagulls, pities the ragged Dilly Dedalus (Stephen's little sister), meets an old flame (Josie Breen), initially stops for lunch at a hotel but is put off by the swinish manners of the diners, helps a blind boy cross the street, and finally has a glass of wine and a cheese sandwich at Davy Byrne's. Bloom's hunger tends to darken his thoughts; he thinks nostalgically about his past, his mind flitting to apparently happier days with Molly, and to his lost son, Rudy. He also muses on the unhappy condition of many Irishwomen, something he attributes to Catholic doctrine, and the tendency of the Irish to forsake their leaders, such as Parnell. At the end of the chapter, Bloom manages to avoid a direct confrontation with Boylan by quickly ducking into the Dublin National Museum.

9. [Scylla and Charybdis]: Stephen presents his interpretation of Shakespeare, in the office of the National Library of Dublin, which was intended for Haines, the English tourist-researcher. Since Haines fails to appear, Stephen must perform for some local Dublin intellectuals: the author A.E. (pseudonym of the poet George Russell)—who leaves soon after Stephen begins—the librarians Thomas Lyster, Richard Best, and John Eglinton (pseudonym of essayist William Magee). Later Mulligan joins the group. Meanwhile, Bloom lurks in the background, seeking a copy of a previous ad for Keyes. Though the chapter alludes to a wide variety of Shakespearean interpretations, Stephen's is highly

personal: Shakespeare's life is everywhere in his art. In particular, Shakespeare identified with dispossessed and cuckolded Hamlet the father (rather than Hamlet the son). Stephen presents his evidence in seemingly haphazard fashion, according to the whims of his skeptical listeners. At the end of the seemingly inconclusive performance, Bloom leaves the library, passing between Stephen and Mulligan, that is, between the whirlpool of idealism and the rock of materialism. Stephen apparently takes little notice.

10. [Wandering Rocks]: As one of two omnibus chapters in *Ulysses* (the other being 15), this segment is a miniature of the whole. Nearly all the characters in *Ulysses* appear in the chapter's 19 subsections, each moving simultaneously and relatively to the others throughout a time-space nexus of the city, carefully plotted by Joyce. The three chief characters of the novel—Molly, Bloom, and Stephen—are reduced to the level of all other Dubliners. In this chapter, we learn the opinions of others in the novel about the main characters: Lenehan credits Bloom with having a touch of the artist in him; Mulligan views Stephen's artistic aspirations with disdainful skepticism. Here we also learn the date of the book, June 16, 1904, and have the single glimpse into Boylan's mind: "A young pullet," he thinks, looking at a serving girl's cleavage (*Ulysses*, 10.327). A montage of Dublin moments and characters, the chapter begins with the walk of Father Conmee and ends with a procession of the (English) viceroy of Dublin, which is a secular counterpart to Father Conmee's introductory walk.

11. [Sirens]: Set in the Ormond Hotel, where first Boylan stops on his way to visit Molly, and then Bloom writes back to Martha while eating another meal, this chapter is an elaborate verbal imitation of a musical composition. The chapter uses stylistic techniques such as tonal contrasts, rhythmic variations, contrapuntal phrases, percussives, and Wagnerian leitmotifs. Some 58 different musical themes are laid out in the opening, which is often described as an introductory enunciation of the musical motifs, and marks the most substantial departure from conventional narrative form thus far in the novel. Boylan and Molly's sexual encounter—at the Bloom's home—is indirectly suggested by activities in the Ormond's bar, including

Bloom's vicarious enjoyment of the song sung by Simon Dedalus and other "sirens." Leaving the hotel, Bloom adds his contribution to the musical chapter—his farting covered by the passing streetcar's noise.

12. [Cyclops]: The meaner aspects of Dublin life are exposed in this segment, which is narrated by a Dublin barfly. In Barney Kiernan's pub we encounter a number of male Dubliners, including "the citizen," an ultranationalist member of the Gaelic League. The lot of them are somewhat the worse for drinking. Bloom is there to meet with Martin Cunningham about financial support for Paddy Dignam's family. The chapter contrasts Bloom to the citizen, his polar opposite. Bloom is humane and nonviolent, preaching the Judeo-Christian doctrine of love, while the citizen is a xenophobic Fenian committed to savage attacks upon the English and against all but the most chauvinistic Irish patriots. Personal attacks on Bloom reach a climax when the patrons of the pub, misinformed by Bantam Lyons into thinking that the "Jew," Bloom, has won money betting on "Throwaway" (the winner of the Ascot Race), resent his not treating them to drinks. The episode ends with the citizen's shouting anti-Semitic abuse, hurling a biscuit tin at Bloom (recalling the Cyclops who hurls boulders at Odysseus in the *Odyssey*), and setting his mangy dog after him. Bloom, hustled into a passing car by Cunningham, is stylistically transformed into "Oben Bloom Elijah amid clouds of angels," a reference to the Hebrew prophet Elijah, carried skyward, says the Bible, in a chariot of fire (*Ulysses*, 12.1916-17).

13. [Nausica]: After visiting Dignam's widow, the generous Bloom strolls along Sandymount Strand, stopping, as evening falls, to sit on the same rocks where Stephen had rested earlier that morning. Bloom is biding his time, deliberately postponing his return home. Also on the beach is Gerty MacDowell, a young lower-middle-class woman. The first half of the chapter, presented from Gerty's perspective in a sentimentalized ladies-magazine style, details her troubled home life and romanticizing attitudes. As she recognizes that Bloom's gaze—from a distance—is focused upon her, her not unperceptive fantasy about him becomes increasingly sexual. At the end of her narrative, she deliberately exposes her undergarments to the surreptitiously masturbating Bloom and walks away limping (she is lame). The second half of the chapter shifts to Bloom's postorgasmic reflections, largely about women. Though he is grateful for Gerty's participation in his sexual release (and recognizes that she also enjoyed herself), his mind returns again and again to Molly. He muses about the events of the day, acknowledging the *fait acccompli* of his wife's adultery and the cyclical nature of one's existence. After finding the scrap of paper left by Stephen, whose writing he cannot decipher, Bloom futilely attempts to write a message in the sand for Gerty, which he then erases. At the end of the chapter, he falls asleep on the rocks.

14. [Oxen of the Sun]: Bloom next proceeds to the Holles Street Maternity Hospital to check on an acquaintance, Mina Purefoy, in her third day of labor. He joins a group of medical students and acquaintances—including Stephen, Lenehan and Stephen's college friend from *A Portrait of the Artist As a Young Man,* Lynch, who engage in coarse and irreverent conversation in the hospital's cafeteria. Topics include procreation, pregnancy, contraception, venereal disease, and birth, as well as Irish history and politics. Bloom largely remains silent, but observes Stephen with paternal solicitude, inwardly concerned about the young man's increasing drunkenness. He reflects upon his own sexual life, his relationship to Molly and Milly, and his dead son Rudy. During the episode, Mulligan arrives, Haines makes a brief appearance, and Mrs. Purefoy gives birth to a son. Eventually the group decamps to a pub; Stephen and Lynch then head to Nighttown, Dublin's brothel district. In accord with the theme of birth and development, the chapter is narrated in a historical range of English literary styles (especially those used by Anglo-Irish writers), from Latinate beginnings to modern Dublin slang and journalese.

15. [Circe]: Bloom follows Stephen to Nighttown, and in a phantasmagoria of literary modernism—in which soap bars talk, dead and imaginary characters walk the streets, and Bloom changes sex and bears a child—he encounters the now thoroughly drunken Stephen at Bella Cohen's brothel. The chapter is presented in drama form, but is akin to a psychodrama, animated by apparitions and hallucinations. Almost every previous element of *Ulysses*, including the most seem-

ingly trivial, is here recapitulated, often in a surreal manner, and it is difficult to separate reality from illusion. Bloom has guilt-ridden sexual fantasies, which include his ambivalent response to Molly's adultery, as well as images of his personal empowerment and humiliation. These fantasies externalize Bloom's conscious and unconscious feelings. At the climax of the chapter, Stephen, in terror at an alcohol-induced vision of his dead mother, smashes a lampshade and rushes from the brothel. Bloom placates Bella Cohen, pays for the lamp, and follows Stephen—by now abandoned by Lynch—to the street. There he finds Stephen confronted by two drunken English soldiers. Despite Bloom's efforts to defuse the situation, Stephen ultimately provokes one soldier into knocking him down. Though the police arrive, Bloom manages to prevent the unconscious Stephen from being arrested. As the chapter ends, Bloom, attempting to revive Stephen, has a vision of an 11-year-old Rudy.

16. [Eumaeus]: Bloom and Stephen travel a short distance to a cabman's shelter, where Bloom buys Stephen some coffee and a bun. The two exhausted Irishmen—it is now past midnight—share desultory remarks, often amusing in the deadpan style of the chapter. Bloom does most of the talking—Stephen is still recovering from the soldier's attack and the effect of drinking all day. Topics include Stephen's careless behavior, Irish politics (specifically Parnell and the Phoenix Park murders), and writing as a profession. Bloom is polite, discreet and solicitous; Stephen is curt and brusque. Both men are mystified by a sailor, W. B. Murphy, who has been entertaining those in the shelter with his stories, and who claims, without evidence, to know Simon Dedalus. After showing Molly's portrait to an apparently uncomprehending Stephen, Bloom, who is now plotting to have Stephen tutor his wife in Italian, suggests that Stephen follow him home. Taking his arm, Bloom escorts him out. On the way to Eccles Street, they discuss their shared love of music.

17. [Ithaca]: Bloom and Stephen continue their walk to 7 Eccles Street. Upon their arrival, Bloom finds that he has forgotten to take the latch key. He resourcefully climbs down into the area railing, lets himself in through the kitchen, and admits Stephen through the front door. Bloom then serves Stephen cocoa in the kitchen, and the two men continue their conversation. Though Stephen politely refuses Bloom's offer to spend the night, both men tentatively agree that Stephen should give Molly Italian lessons, and she give him vocal lessons. They also plan to undertake further conversations. Bloom returns the money that he has held for Stephen since the Nighttown excursion, and both men exit through the back garden. They contemplate the early morning sky and urinate together. Stephen leaves as the nearby church bells ring the 2 A.M. hour. Reentering the house, Bloom, bumping his head against the sideboard, recognizes that the front-room furniture has been rearranged. He straightens up and proceeds to bed, where he encounters further evidence (food crumbs, the imprint of a human form) of Boylan's earlier presence. Reflecting philosophically on his wife's adultery, he kisses her rear end, which arouses him sexually. She awakes and questions him about his day. He gives her an abbreviated account and then falls asleep, his head at her feet, as is his wont. The chapter's rigidly objective, question-and-answer catechismal style offers a great deal of apparently true information about the three main characters. Included is the fact that the Blooms have not had complete "carnal intercourse" for more than ten years, following the death of Rudy, as well as a host of other seemingly unimportant issues (including the route of the water Bloom draws to make the cocoa, from reservoir to faucet) (*Ulysses*, 17.2280-84).

18. [Penelope]: The final chapter of *Ulysses* is the 20,000-word, eight-paragraph, wholly unpunctuated stream-of-consciousness monologue of Molly Bloom, the earthy frankness of which shocked many of Joyce's readers. Almost all of the action of the episode is mental, involving Molly's reflections upon and memories of the day, Dublin, its inhabitants, and her former life. She does, however, urinate, menstruate, and perhaps masturbate. Also she is conscious of the time—she hears the church bells strike 4 A.M.—and the presence of her sleeping husband. Her thoughts range from her rather lonely youth in Gibraltar, where she grew up without a mother or close friends her own age, to her children, Milly and the dead Rudy. Although she mentions several possible lovers and fantasizes about Stephen, her recent sexual intercourse

with Blazes Boylan is perhaps her first affair since she has been married. Always her thoughts return to Bloom. Her monologue—and the book—ends with her sensual recollection of the day he proposed marriage: "and I thought well as well him as another and then I asked him with my eyes to ask again yes and then he asked me would I yes to say yes my mountain flower and first I put my arms around him yes and drew him down to me so he could feel my breasts all perfume yes and his heart was going like mad and yes I said yes I will Yes" (*Ulysses*, 18.1604-09).

JEWS IN EARLY-TWENTIETH-CENTURY IRELAND

Ulysses's Leopold Bloom exhibits an assimilationist response to Dublin life, which was fairly common among Irish Jews at this time. Though Jewish law calls for circumcision, he has not been circumcised. On the other hand, he has received the Catholic sacrament of baptism three times. Bloom's ethnic identity is a complex one. In fact, the history of the Jews generally in Ireland is a complex story of exile and assimilation. By the end of the eighteenth century, the Dublin Jewish population was decimated due to pressures to emigrate, convert, or otherwise assimilate, reducing the small population of 40 families to two. As naturalization laws began to ease in the mid-nineteenth century, Jews were allowed a relative amount of religious and cultural freedom: Jewish marriages were given legal status; proscription from holding public office was eliminated; and dress codes were relaxed and finally eliminated. Due to new laws, Jewish refugees and émigrés, fleeing from pogroms and political oppression in Eastern Europe and Russia, began arriving in the late nineteenth century. By 1901, Jews in Dublin numbered 3,000, but they were still denied access to many public and private institutions, such as Trinity College, and anti-Semitism remained prevalent. When an anti-Semitic outburst took place in Limerick, Ireland, in 1904, the nationalist Arthur Griffith defended the anti-Semitic remarks of the priest Father Creagh. In a front-page column of the *United Irishman*, the Catholic priest had warned against the "usurious toils" of the Jews, naming them as an "economic evil" in Ireland (Creagh in Manganiello, p. 131-33). Such realities account for the frequent presence of anti-Semites in *Ulysses*.

Joyce's reservations about Irish nationalism. The Cyclops chapter of *Ulysses* offers perhaps Joyce's most pointed critique of Irish nationalism, especially of the movement's racist and chauvinistic tendencies. In "Cyclops," a group of pub denizens—including one character called "the citizen"—perfectly embody the racist strain in extreme Irish nationalism. The slogan of these ultranationalists was "Ireland for the Irish," meaning for the Irish Catholics, to the exclusion of Jews, Protestants, Italian immigrants, and so forth. The citizen and others in the pub insult Bloom, behind his back as well as to his face, asking, "Is he a jew or a gentile or a holy Roman or a swaddler or what the hell is he?" (*Ulysses*, 12.1631-32). "Saint Patrick would want to land again at Ballykinlar and convert us, says the citizen, after allowing things like that to contaminate our shores" (*Ulysses*, 12.1671-72). As Bloom departs, the citizen shouts after him, "Three cheers for Israel!" (*Ulysses*, 12.1791). Bloom's reply—"Mendelssohn was a jew and Karl Marx and Mercadante and Spinoza. And the Saviour was a jew and his father was a jew. Your God"—inflames the citizen further: "By Jesus, says the citizen, I'll brain that bloody jewman for using the holy name. By Jesus, I'll crucify him so I will. Give us that biscuitbox there" (*Ulysses*, 12.1804-05. 12.1811-12). Hurling the tin at Bloom but missing, the citizen sets his dog after Bloom. This portrait exhibits the blind rage and invincible ignorance of ferocious Irish nationalism. Joyce responded to the political and cultural conflicts of his country largely through his art, asserting Irish independence by means of claims that ran counter to the dominant nationalist ideology. Instead of an Ireland made up of "pure" Gaels from a single race, *Ulysses* presents an Ireland made up of Greeks, Jews, Spaniards, and Italians, all of whom are still specifically and locally Irish. Instead of a literary tradition focused on Irish literature to the exclusion of the English and European traditions, *Ulysses* incorporates the entire corpus of the Western canon while simultaneously questioning its dominant hierarchies. Joyce felt the nationalist revival was "educating the people of Ireland on the old pap of racial hatred" (Joyce in Manganiello, p. 127). While certainly not all Irish nationalists were racist, Joyce found the ideology of the extremists no less stifling or conservative than the repressive church-rule of Catholicism or than British imperialism, all of which he felt were paralyzing the country and from which he moved to the Continent to escape. Although Joyce considered himself a nationalist—if one did not insist on the Irish language—he thought the way to save Ireland was to make the country international, heterodox, egalitarian, and cosmopolitan, rather than isolationist, exclusionary, reactionary, and feudalistic, as nationalists like the citizen in *Ulysses* sought to do. Joyce created a rich fusion in his art between European, Irish, and English literary traditions, and he filled the Dublin of *Ulysses* with the lower-middle-class character types among whom he was raised. The novel evokes a city of secondhand clothes, recruiting posters, and pubs, along with the constant colonial presence of police, soldiers, and English officials. The novel also shows the numerous foreign-born inhabitants of Dublin, whom Joyce portrays as Irishmen and Irishwomen as genuine as any others. *Ulysses* is literature hardly typical of the Irish Literary Revival, but it shows that Joyce remained heavily invested in the fate of Ireland.

Sources. It is no overstatement to say that Joyce marshals the entire Western intellectual heritage as material for *Ulysses.* The seemingly limitless range of his learning makes an account of the novel's sources a daunting prospect. Nevertheless, an immense volume of literary-critical scholarship has accumulated around *Ulysses* during the twentieth century, helping illuminate many of Joyce's sources, some of great obscurity, others of extreme ephemerality. Still others remain unknown. The present sketch can only suggest the rich allusiveness of Joyce's epic. Along with the Greco-Roman literary and mythological tradition, which provides the novel its title and general framework, Joyce drew heavily on Judeo-Christian literature, particularly the Bible—there are 65 quotations from the Gospel of Matthew—and on the Roman Catholic liturgical and sacramental tradition. Nearly 150 Catholic saints are mentioned in the text, together with numerous references to Church ritual. Irish mythology also figures prominently in the novel, particularly *The Book of Invasions*, a popular medieval fable about the early settlement of Ireland. Norse, Germanic, and Hindu mythology play significant roles in *Ulysses* as well. The most conspicuous of Joyce's philosophical and theological sources can be grouped chronologically. Among the ancient sources are Homer, the philosophers Plato and Aristotle, and the theologian St. Augustine. Medieval influences of greatest note are the poet Dante and theologian St. Thomas Aquinas. Joyce's modern sources include the philosophers Giambattista Vico, Giordano Bruno, Arthur Schopenhauer, and Friedrich Nietzsche. On the

subject of literary influences on Joyce much ink has been spilled and many library shelves filled. It would take far less room to list the English-language authors who are not among Joyce's sources than those who are. Of central importance is Shakespeare and perhaps the decisive near-contemporary influences are, in Britain, Walter Pater and John Henry Newman, and, on the Continent, Henrik Ibsen, Anton Chekhov, and Gabriele D'Annunzio. As the Oxen of the Sun chapter suggests, Joyce owed a debt, which he paid in full, to every age of English literature. Music as well provided an array of sources. Joyce had a good tenor singing voice, according to his contemporaries, and his great love of music, both sacred and secular, is evident in the novel's nearly 200 songs. His ear was furthermore attuned to the musicality of language—hence the 50 nursery and street rhymes that are found in *Ulysses*—and he spoke Italian as smoothly as English, flawless French, fluent German, knew some 12 other tongues including Lapp, and numerous dialects. Finally, not least among Joyce's sources are the many people he knew in Dublin who served as models for characters in the novel. For example, Stephen's father, Simon Dedalus, is based on Joyce's own father; Molly on Joyce's wife, Nora; and the citizen on Michael Cusack, founder of the Gaelic Athletic Association and a rabid Irish nationalist.

Events in History at the Time the Novel Was Written

Nationalism revisited. While Joyce was writing *Ulysses,* continental Europe and Ireland were each in a state of military and social upheaval. World War I was decimating the Great Powers, while Ireland's slow progress toward Home Rule exploded in the Easter Uprising of 1916 and the guerrilla warfare campaign that followed. Joyce had complex reactions to both events. Like Leopold Bloom, Joyce supported Sinn Fein leader Arthur Griffith's nationalist policy of passive resistance, a strategy of parliamentary obstruction that seemed to Joyce appropriately forceful but nonviolent. When he learned of the 1916 Easter Uprising, in which a small number of Irish nationalists—1200 at the largest count—seized the national post office, raided Dublin Castle, dynamited the British armory, and held out for almost a week—his first reaction was a patriotic *Erin go bragh!* (Ireland forever!). But as the death toll mounted and the British began shelling Dublin, the pacifistic Joyce felt that the rebels were needlessly wasting lives. Although he sympathized with the cause of Irish independence, he felt that violence would not solve anything for Ireland. It seemed to Joyce that his figure of the rabid nationalist, the citizen from the Cyclops chapter, had finally been unleashed on Ireland, hurling bombs rather than biscuit tins.

Reception. From the first, responses to *Ulysses* typically tended toward extremes of either praise or condemnation. The book was at first judged legally obscene and banned in Ireland, England, and the United States. Of the second printing of 2,000 copies, 500 were burned in New York by the U.S. Post Office, and the English customs authorities confiscated and destroyed 499 copies of the third edition of 500 copies. But wherever *Ulysses* was banned, it was smuggled in; bowdlerized, pirated, and forged editions soon appeared in the United States. Early reactions ranged from the Irish poet A.E.'s "greatest fiction of the twentieth century" to the English poet Alfred Noyes's "It is simply the foulest book that has ever found its way into print" (A.E. and Noyes in Kunitz, p. 737). The *Dublin Review* declared, "A great Jesuit-trained talent has gone over malignantly and mockingly to the powers of evil" (*Dublin Review* in Kunitz, p. 737). Edmund Gosse wrote that *Ulysses* was a "cynical appeal to sheer indecency" (Gosse in Ellmann, p. 528). More complimentary, Virginia Woolf singled out Joyce as the most original and important of the younger writers on the scene, despite what she considered the narrowness of his focus and—it is the complaint voiced most often by the first readers of *Ulysses*—the "emphases laid, perhaps didactically, upon indecency" (Woolf, pp. 154-56). On the other hand, the American novelist Ernest Hemingway, in a letter to fellow novelist Sherwood Anderson, exclaimed that "Joyce has written a most goddamn wonderful book," and the European literary avant-garde generally agreed (Hemingway in Ellmann, p. 529). Though banned in Ireland, the novel earned approval from a few Irish writers living in England. Yeats recognized something specifically Irish in the work, an "Irish cruelty and an Irish strength," and George Bernard Shaw saw the "hideously real" Dublin that he had left 20 years before (Yeats and Shaw in Ellmann, pp. 507, 531).

Recent critics have looked closely at Joyce's investment in specifically Irish political and social issues, a dimension previously minimized. By the end of the twentieth century, the judgment of A.E. seems to have proven accurate, for Joyce is generally regarded as the century's defining novelist. Joyce once said of *Ulysses,* "I've put in so many enigmas and puzzles that it will keep the professors busy for centuries arguing over what I mean, and that's the only way of insuring one's immortality" (Joyce in Ellmann, p. 535). However mocking Joyce's attitude may have been, at the dawn of the twenty-first century, all signs indicate that his wish for immortality will be fulfilled.

—James Caufield

For More Information

Blamires, Harry. *The New Bloomsday Book: A Guide through Ulysses.* London: Routledge, 1996.

Cheng, Vincent. *Joyce, Race, and Empire.* Cambridge: Cambridge University Press, 1995.

Connolly, S. J. *The Oxford Companion to Irish History.* New York: Oxford University Press, 1998.

Davison, Neil R. *James Joyce,* Ulysses, *and the Construction of Jewish Identity.* Cambridge: Cambridge University Press, 1996.

Ellmann, Richard. *James Joyce.* 2nd ed. New York: Oxford University Press, 1982.

Gilbert, Stuart. *James Joyce's* Ulysses: *A Study.* New York: Vintage, 1955.

Gray, Wallace. *Homer to Joyce: Interpretations of the Classic Works of Western Literature.* New York: Macmillan, 1985.

Joyce, James. *Ulysses.* Ed. Hans Walter Gabler. London: Bodley Head, 1986.

Kunitz, Stanley, and Howard Haycraft. *Twentieth Century Authors.* New York: H. H. Wilson, 1942.

Manganiello, Dominic. *Joyce's Politics.* London: Routledge, 1980.

Tymoczko, Maria. *The Irish Ulysses.* Berkeley: University of California Press, 1994.

Woolf, Virginia. "Modern Fiction." In *The Common Reader.* New York: Harcourt, Brace and World, 1953.

Under Milk Wood

by

Dylan Thomas

Dylan Thomas (1914-53), Wales's most renowned modern poet, was born in the seaport town of Swansea on the southern Welsh coast. From his father, a school teacher with literary interests and atheistic beliefs, the young Dylan Thomas early acquired a love of poetry and literature; from his mother, a warm and highly religious woman from a large rural family, he inherited a spiritual if undogmatic sensibility, along with a love of nature and the countryside. As critics have discovered by examining his early notebooks, the vast majority of his poems were conceived (if not necessarily put into final form) before Thomas was 21. In addition to several collections of poetry, he also wrote a number of prose works, often autobiographical in nature: a book of short stories (*Portrait of the Artist As a Young Dog*, 1940); an unfinished novel (posthumously published as *Adventures in the Skin Trade*, 1955); essays (posthumously collected as *Quite Early One Morning*, 1954); and the brief sketch *A Child's Christmas in Wales* (1955). This last piece, like the play *Under Milk Wood*, richly evokes Welsh daily life; both the sketch and the play were originally written to be performed on the radio, but they have proven to be Thomas's most widely read works. *A Child's Christmas in Wales* offers a child's-eye view of a Welsh holiday household. Depicted in *Under Milk Wood* are the adult passions and foibles of a small Welsh village's inhabitants.

THE LITERARY WORK

A play for voices set around the middle of the twentieth century in a small coastal village in Wales; first performed in 1953; produced for radio and published in 1954.

SYNOPSIS

In a series of brief vignettes, a wide cast of characters, both dead and living, recalls the past and experiences moments from the course of a single day in the fictional Welsh fishing village of Llareggub.

Events in History at the Time of the Play

Wales and the Welsh. To understand Welsh culture in the twentieth century, it is necessary first to grasp the unusual historical forces that shaped it. The Welsh are descended from the Celtic peoples who inhabited much of Western Europe in prehistoric times. In the first century B.C.E. Celts in southern Britain came under Roman rule, and by the fourth and fifth centuries C.E. they had adopted Christianity along with the rest of the Roman Empire. After the decline of Roman power in the late fifth century, Germanic peoples from Northern Europe, led by the Angles and Saxons, invaded and settled southern

Dylan Thomas

500 C.E. who took a stand in Wales against the incoming Anglo-Saxons. Another high-profile aspect of Welsh culture is the popular institution the *eisteddfod*. Featuring competitions in poetry, music, and folk dancing, many of these Welsh folk festivals are held annually throughout the land, attracting international tourists as well as British travelers from outside Wales. The largest and most famous of them all is the National Eisteddfod of Wales, held yearly at a site that alternates between North and South Wales. The *eisteddfodau* (plural) are run by officers who trace their status back to the ancient pre-Christian Druid religion of the Celts, which was overthrown by the coming of the Romans and Christianity. King Arthur, the *eisteddfodau*, and the Druids are all mentioned in a poem recited by the poet-preacher Eli Jenkins in *Under Milk Wood* (see below).

After the Norman conquest of England in the eleventh century, England's Norman rulers conducted a determined campaign to conquer Wales, which they succeeded in doing, despite Welsh resistance, by the end of the thirteenth century. In the fifteenth century the Welsh nobleman Henry Tudor took the English throne as King Henry VII, followed by his son, Henry VIII, and his granddaughter, Elizabeth I. Under Henry VIII (reigned 1509-47), the Acts of Union of 1536 and 1543 unified Wales and England under a single political and administrative system. By the mid-twentieth century, around 30 percent of the Welsh people spoke the native language, though English was encroaching ever more swiftly on their daily lives.

Dylan Thomas's parents could both speak Welsh but used English in their home. Thomas, therefore, like most of his Welsh contemporaries, grew up speaking and writing only English. Yet Thomas's English is deeply influenced by Welsh rhythms and cadences, which give even his prose writings a distinctive poetic feel. For example, *Under Milk Wood*'s famous opening lines poetically evoke nighttime in the tiny darkened village: "starless and bible-black, the cobblestreets silent and the hunched courters'-and-rabbits' wood limping invisible down to the sloeblack, slow, black, crowblack, fishingboat-bobbing sea" (Thomas, *Under Milk Wood*, p. 1). (The phrase "courters'-and-rabbits' wood" refers to Milk Wood, which stands near the town and attracts courting couples; sloe berries are deep black in color.)

Britain, where they became the English (whose appellation comes from the name of the Angles). Unsuccessfully resisting these numerous and aggressive incomers, the Celts over time were pushed west and north in Britain. By about 800 C.E. Celts in Britain were limited to these remote areas, where their descendants live today: the Cornish of southwest England, and the Welsh (the Irish are also of Celtic descent).

Isolated from other Celts, the Welsh developed their own distinctive Celtic language and culture over the coming centuries, but their identity would always be influenced by the presence of their powerful English neighbors. The English names for the land and people, for example, both come from the Anglo-Saxon *wealas*, or "strangers." It was in the early Middle Ages, when the borders of modern Wales had been established, that the Welsh first referred to themselves as *Cymry*, "compatriots," the term still used in Welsh today.

Despite the progressive anglicization of Wales, Celtic elements remained strong in the Welsh consciousness, and many entered the mainstream of British culture. For example, one version of history holds that the legendary King Arthur, if he existed, was a British king of around

Welsh livelihoods, worship, and leisure. Just as Welsh linguistic rhythms seep into Dylan

Thomas's poetic idiom, so does Wales's rich cultural history permeate what Thomas, in a letter to a friend, called the imaginary "never-never Wales" of *Under Milk Wood* (Thomas in Ackerman, *A Dylan Thomas Companion*, p. 243). Welsh livelihoods have historically centered around mining, farming, or (as in *Under Milk Wood*) the sea. In the first half of the twentieth century, Welsh ships carried industrial products such as coal and slate from Welsh mines and quarries to overseas markets, returning with loads of timber for shoring up the mines or with phosphates used in smelting ore. Smaller ships called smacks or schooners traded along the Welsh coast, and fishing or oyster boats sailed from most coastal towns and villages. Dylan Thomas grew up in the southern seaport city of Swansea, and later in life he lived in the much smaller coastal village of Laugharne, the real-life inspiration for the village in *Under Milk Wood*. In both Swansea and Laugharne, maritime livelihoods, such as shipping and fishing, provided the economic center of town life. Thomas underscores the sea's importance to the village in the play by frequently employing nautical images (boats, sailors, and pirates), by describing village locations in terms of their position relative to the sea, and by including whimsical characterizations of village personalities (such as blind old Captain Cat, a retired sea captain who reminisces about his long-dead lover, and Sinbad Sailors, who sits and drinks beer in the local pub, the Sailors Arms).

In religious life Wales has been dominated since the eighteenth century by the Protestant denomination of Methodism. Methodism started as a branch of the Anglican Church in the 1730s, when an Anglican minister named John Wesley began focusing his attention on the poor and downtrodden, who felt ignored by the larger Anglican establishment. Wesley first preached to coal miners in England, and thereafter the rapidly growing movement—which officially split from the Anglican Church in 1795, four years after Wesley's death—appealed most strongly in Britain's industrialized areas, including Wales. After the split from Anglicanism, Methodism was considered a Nonconformist sect (one that did not "conform" to Anglicanism, the official state religion), which only increased its attractiveness to the Welsh. Methodism, as well as other Nonconformist sects, appealed to the desire of the Welsh people to differentiate themselves from the English-dominated British establishment.

On another level, the lively, rollicking hymns featured in Methodist and other Nonconformist chapels also attracted the Welsh, for singing has always been a central part of their culture. The play itself features a number of poems and songs recited or sung by various characters; Thomas's music for the songs is included after the text in most printed editions. After one of the songs, the town's preacher, Reverend Eli Jenkins, exclaims (with unintentional irony), "Praise the Lord! We are a musical nation!" (*Under Milk Wood*, p. 60). (The praise invokes the Lord to applaud a song [full of double entendre] about sex and the singer's love life.) To a Welsh audience, Jenkins would have represented a well-known social type, the fiery, bardic, Nonconformist preacher. The rhythmical oratory and emotional enthusiasm of such preachers brings to mind the ancient mystical element that had produced the Druid

---

BARDIC TRADITIONS AND ARTHURIAN LEGEND

For centuries poetry has stood at the center of Welsh culture, harking back to the ancient poets called bards, oral storytellers whose poems celebrated the deeds of legendary warriors, heroes, and kings. The bardic tradition dates back to the Celtic culture of pre-Roman Britain, when the bards' prestige derived from their ability to dramatize the exploits of great warriors in battle. The most famous group of bardic tales survives in the medieval work known as the **Mabinogion** (in *WLAIT 3: British and Irish Literature and Its Times*), a collection of much older stories featuring a variety of native Welsh heroes, including King Arthur.

---

religion of the pre-Roman Celts: the Welsh author Jan Morris writes that "the stylized rhetoric of the preachers was not unlike the chanting of the old priests" (Morris, p. 112). A poet with a "bard's white hair" who sermonizes about King Arthur, dreams of the *eisteddfodau*, and wears "a druid's seedy nightie" as he sleeps, Jenkins points to an element of harmony between Nonconformism and more ancient Welsh traditions (*Under Milk Wood*, pp. 27, 23).

Attitudes towards love and sex. Its Nonconformist past, Welsh historian Kenneth Morgan writes, has made Wales "traditionally a puritannical . . . land, its ethos created by chapels of sepulchral austerity and by the flamboyant pulpit oratory which preached hell and eternal damnation" (Morgan, p. 352). However, in the period after World War II, Morgan continues, old attitudes began to change as the Nonconformist chapels lost their traditional hold on Welsh behavioral standards. Morgan cites the play in order to contrast its humorous portrayal of a small town preacher with the reality of a more permissive postwar society:

> But the chapels depended above all on the sanctions that controlled everyday social behavior, like the spiritual power exercised by Roman Catholic priests in rural Ireland or Italy. In a much less puritannical age, these were simply disappearing, or else becoming the butts for irreverent humour in radio and television comedy programmes. The Reverend Eli Jenkins in *Under Milk Wood* still preserved his dignity, pride, and sense of cultural tradition. Many of his real-life equivalents felt that they were losing theirs.
>
> (Morgan, p. 353)

As Morgan observes, however, small rural villages such as that depicted in the play had already fostered their own idiosyncratic but practical brand of sexual openness. If a rural woman bore a child out of wedlock, for example (as the play's Polly Garter has repeatedly done), she would generally incur little or no social censure. Furthermore, the child itself would often be adopted by its grandmother and would thus become "relegitimized in the eyes of the community" (Morgan, p. 351). As far back as the nineteenth century, such "permissiveness was always there in rural communities, flavoured, then as later, by the exquisite, aphrodisiac taste of forbidden fruit" (Morgan, p. 351). Conventional morality in a small village could thus function to enhance the very pleasures it ostensibly opposed, and in the play Thomas focuses on precisely this paradoxical and potentially humorous aspect of village life.

The Play in Focus

Contents summary. *Under Milk Wood* has no plot, no character development, and little action by its more than 60 characters, all citizens of the tiny Welsh fishing village of Llareggub. Instead, chronology provides the play's only structure, as the listener or reader follows a single day in the village through the voices of both its dead and its living inhabitants. These voices are framed by two others, the First Voice and the Second Voice, who serve as omniscient narrators, describing the town and introducing the various characters who make their brief vocal appearances in the se-

quence. The only interaction comes on those occasions when two of the characters conduct a brief dialogue. Often, however, a single voice is heard, sometimes picking up or breaking off in the middle of a sentence. There are no act or scene divisions; the continuous interweaving of voices takes the reader or listener from pre-dawn darkness on one spring day to the same still hour of the following day.

As the vignettes follow each other in sequence, the play most commonly moves from one to the next by using the First or Second Voice to introduce the next character or characters. When the play begins, it is still night, and the characters are asleep: the reader eavesdrops, as it were, on their dreams. In these early episodes, the First Voice typically introduces the character, while the Second Voice interrupts and takes over for the description of the dream. Depending on the length of the dream vignette, other voices featured in the dream may then be heard, as in the opening vignette, for example. The major characters are introduced through the dream vignettes, which make up the first third of the play. The series of dream vignettes ends, as day breaks, with the "Voice of a Guide-Book" that offers a tourist's description of the village, calling it a "backwater of life" whose inhabitants nonetheless have "a salty individuality of their own" and manage to retain "some of that picturesque sense of the past so frequently lacking in towns and villages which have kept more abreast of the times" (*Under Milk Wood*, pp. 25-26).

- The play opens with the First Voice's description of the small town at night as all the people are sleeping. In his description the First Voice mentions several of the characters whose voices will be heard, among them "Captain Cat, the retired blind sea captain, asleep in his bunk in the seashelled, ship-in-bottled, shipshape best cabin of Schooner House" (*Under Milk Wood*, p. 3). The Second Voice breaks in to describe Captain Cat's dreams, which include the voices of five of his drowned comrades and that of his long-dead love, Rosie Probert, who exclaims, "Come on up, boys, I'm dead" (*Under Milk Wood*, p. 4). The voices of Captain Cat's former shipmates, identified in the text as First Drowned, Second Drowned, and so forth, wistfully interrogate Captain Cat about the world of the living: "And who brings coconuts and shawls and parrots to *my* Gwen now?" asks Fifth Drowned;

"What's the smell of parsley?" First Drowned inquires plaintively (*Under Milk Wood*, pp. 5-6).

Later Captain Cat and Rosie Probert, "the one love of his sea-life," conduct a dialogue in verse that celebrates their love in nautical imagery with sexual overtones (*Under Milk Wood*, p. 76). "Lie down, lie easy. / Let me shipwreck in your thighs" the old man says: moments later a child's voice remarks that Captain Cat is crying in the window of Schooner House (*Under Milk Wood*, p. 77).

- Miss Price, the seamstress, dreams of Mr. Edwards, the draper (someone who sells cloth). These two have conducted a love affair exclusively by mail, passionately writing each other every day from opposite ends of town. Though they see each other frequently in passing, they have never spoken, nor do they feel a need to. "I love you more than all the flannelette and calico, candlewick, dimity, crash and merino, tussore, cretonne, crépon, muslin, poplin, ticking and twill in the whole Cloth Hall of the world," he declares in her dream; "I will knit you a wallet of forget-me-not blue, for the money to be comfy," she responds (*Under Milk Wood*, p. 7).

- Black Jack the cobbler, a prudish but prurient man, "sleeps with his nightshirt tied to his ankles with elastic" but dreams of chasing "bare bold girls" who are carrying on with young men (*Under Milk Wood*, p. 8). Later we learn that his main pleasure in life is to persecute lovers, whom he views as sinful. He sees Milk Wood, a grove that stands above the town and is a favorite spot for romantic couples, as a dark and terrible place.

- Evans the Death, the undertaker, dreams of his mother and his childhood. Next door, in a "little pink-eyed cottage," stout philandering Mr. Waldo with his "fat pink hands palm up over the edge of the quilt" dreams of his own mother, who recited "This little piggy" to him when he was a boy (*Under Milk Wood*, p. 9). His mother's voice is followed by others: those of his boyhood neighbors commenting on his misbehavior as they gossip about his father's love affairs, similar to his own adult ones; that of his accusing wife; and those of his various romantic partners.

- Mrs. Ogmore-Pritchard ("widow, twice, of Mr. Ogmore, linoleum, retired, and Mr.

Pritchard, failed bookmaker") dreams of assigning cleaning and hygiene tasks to her two dead husbands (*Under Milk Wood*, p. 15). She runs a boardinghouse but allows no guests because they would detract from her house's cleanliness. "Before you let the sun in, mind it wipes its shoes," she tells Mr. Pritchard in her dream (*Under Milk Wood*, p. 18). Later, as she goes to sleep again that evening, her only boarders—the ghosts of her two dead husbands—wait somewhat reluctantly to visit her once more. "After you," each tells the other (*Under Milk Wood*, p. 85).

- Gossamer Beynon, the butcher's daughter, dreams of searching her father's slaughterhouse and finding "with no surprise, a small rough ready man with a bushy tail" who will be her true love (*Under Milk Wood*, p. 18). A demure schoolteacher, she appears prim and proper, but she daydreams about brutish lovers who are "all cucumber and hooves" (*Under Milk Wood*, p. 67). She is also the object of male sexual fantasies in the village.

At breakfast, Butcher Beynon, Gossamer's father, will horrify his wife by telling her that the liver they are eating is from a cat. "Yesterday," he tells the hysterical woman, "we had mole," preceded by shrews on Tuesday and otter on Monday (*Under Milk Wood*, p. 39). "Now," he says, "I'm going out after the corgies [dogs] with my little cleaver" (*Under Milk Wood*, p. 40).

- Cherry Owen, the drunkard, dreams of drinking. His wife (we learn later) loves him because in a single man she gets two husbands, one who is sober by day and one who is drunk at night. That evening Sinbad Sailors offers to buy him a drink at the local pub, the Sailors Arms. When Sinbad asks, "What'll you have?" Cherry replies, "Too much" (*Under Milk Wood*, pp. 88-89).

- Willy Nilly, the postman, dreams of knocking on doors; his wife dreams of how he spanks her before bed each night. Later in the day she will steam open the mail and read a love letter from Mr. Edwards to Miss Price.

- Sinbad Sailors sleeps over the Sailors Arms and "hugs his damp pillow, whose secret name is Gossamer Beynon" (*Under Milk Wood*, p. 21). Later he will be one of many males who undress Gossamer with their eyes as she walks down the street.

- Seventeen-year-old Mae Rose Cottage dreams that she "peals [sic] off her pink-and-white skin in a furnace in a tower in a cave in a waterfall in a wood and waits there raw as an onion for Mister Right" (*Under Milk Wood*, p. 21). At dusk, desperate for romance, she listens to the nannygoats she is herding, and plans to "sin till I blow up" (*Under Milk Wood*, p. 86).

- Bessie Bighead, a homely girl who works on a farm and will be "alone until she dies," dreams of picking flowers to put on the grave of a boy "who kissed her once by the pig-sty when she wasn't looking and never kissed her again although she was looking all the time" (*Under Milk Wood*, p. 21). She was conceived in Milk Wood.

- Reverend Eli Jenkins dreams of the *Eisteddfodau*. Soon the Second Voice will describe him rising and going to his front doorway. There, as he looks out at the town, we hear him recite his own poetry celebrating the town's beauty, complete with references to the *Mabinogion*, other Welsh folkloric commonplaces, and the names of actual rivers and other actual geographic features near Laugharne.

- Mr. Pugh, the schoolmaster, dreams of murder; as we learn later, he and his wife enjoy a balanced and satisfying relationship in which she is fulfilled by nagging him constantly and he is fulfilled by forever plotting her death.

- Eighty-five-year-old Mary Ann Sailors, Sinbad's grandmother, dreams of Eden, which bears an exact resemblance to Llareggub. She believes that the village is "the Chosen Land" and that the River Dewi, which flows nearby, is the River Jordan. (*Under Milk Wood*, p. 54).

- Dai Bread, the baker, dreams of "harems" (*Under Milk Wood*, p. 25). He has two wives, we learn later: one fat, maternal, and jolly, the other slender and gypsy-like. The resulting threesome gets along quite happily.

- Polly Garter dreams of "babies" (*Under Milk Wood*, p. 25). We will learn that she has many illegitimate children because she loves infants but can't limit herself to having them with only one man. Later she sings about some of the men she has loved.

- Nogood Boyo, the local delinquent, dreams of "nothing" (*Under Milk Wood*, p. 25). "I want to be *good* boyo," he says later, "but nobody'll let me" (*Under Milk Wood*, p. 80).

During the remainder of the play, we look in upon the characters in seemingly random order, as they go about their daily lives. Shifts of scene are often abrupt, though usually signaled by the First Voice or the Second Voice. The sketch of the major characters that follows adopts the same order in which they are introduced in the dream vignettes. However, much of what the reader or listener finds out about them is imparted later, as the characters make brief reappearances during the course of the day.

As the day draws to a close and night falls again on the village, with cries of "Off to Gomorrah" Black Jack goes out to chastise lovers in Milk Wood, where philandering Mr. Waldo and promiscuous Polly Garter indeed enjoy a tryst (*Under Milk Wood*, p. 87). Milk Wood means many different things to the various townspeople, the First Voice tells us in conclusion. It is a Satanic place, for example, in the eyes of Black Jack, but a place of innocence to Eli Jenkins, as the play's final words make clear:

> The Wood, whose every tree-foot's cloven in the black glad sight of the hunters of lovers, that is a God-built garden to Mary Ann Sailors, who knows there is Heaven on earth and the chosen people of His kind fire in Llareggub's land, that is the fairday farmhands' wantoning ignorant chapel of bridesbeds, and, to the Reverend Eli Jenkins, a greenleaved sermon on the innocence of men, the suddenly wind-shaken wood springs awake for the second dark time this one Spring day.
>
> (*Under Milk Wood*, p. 95)

Freedom, repression, and humor. In a 1951 letter, Dylan Thomas included a detailed discussion of the work-in-progress that became *Under Milk Wood*. Mentioning the various characters and their eccentricities, when he comes to the reproving Black Jack he writes: "and, oh, the savour his cries of Gomorrah add to the pleasures of the small town" (Thomas, *Collected Letters*, p. 814). In other words, Thomas humorously suggests, not only the lover-chasing cobbler but also the lovers he chases—and indeed, the rest of the townspeople, who are depicted as watching the chases—obtain enjoyment from the pursuit. In contrast to Black Jack's persecution of those he condemns as sinners, Thomas continues that "the First Voice, and the poet preacher, never judge nor condemn but explain" the townspeople's often strange behavior (Thomas, *Collected Letters*, p. 814).

This contrast points to something of a paradox in Welsh culture. Despite the emotional sermons and rowdy hymns, like other Nonconformists (such as the Puritans), Methodists have held to strict standards when it comes to social and sexual propriety. However, the stern morality preached in the many small-town chapels—not all of them Methodist, for Quakers and some other Nonconformist sects attracted many Welsh converts—have often conflicted with the fun-loving Welsh temperament. Writing of this strict moral code, Jan Morris observes that "to many Welshmen down to our own times, it has seemed repulsively pietist and kill-joy," but "to many more Welsh people . . . chapel morality was Welsh morality, self-restrained [and] teetotal" (Morris, p. 114). In the play Black Jack represents this "chapel morality": as Dylan Thomas's biographer the scholar John Ackerman notes, "the severe moral code of Welsh Nonconformity is evident in the cobbler's obsessions with sexual sinfulness" (Ackerman, *A Dylan Thomas Companion*, p. 244). Other characters also reflect the same code to varying degrees (for example, nagging Mrs. Pugh suggests that Polly Garter should be arrested for having babies). By contrast, we can easily imagine the drunk Cherry Owen, for example, among those who would find it "repulsively pietist and kill-joy."

The play focuses on and pokes fun at this conflict, drawing humorously on the constant tension between, on the one hand, human appetites and passions and, on the other hand, the repressive and puritanical norms that govern social behavior in the small town. The work clearly comes down on the side of freedom from such repression. Yet the play dramatizes the conflict with such humor and affection for all the characters that, like the First Voice and the poet preacher, it offers amusement in place of condemnation.

Sources and literary context. Thomas first visited Laugharne, the village on which Llareggub is modeled, in the 1930s, making a home there with his family in the 1940s. The Welsh-looking name of the village in the play—actually the English expletive "Bugger all" spelled backwards—comes from a story that Thomas wrote in 1935. In 1939 he decided that "What Laugharne really needs is a play about well-known Laugharne characters," and he appropriated the name for the project that became *Under Milk Wood* (Thomas in Sinclair, p. 192). Thomas spent hours at a time in the pub at Brown's Hotel in Laugharne, and according to Thomas's wife Caitlin, the proprietress Ivy Williams introduced Thomas to many of the people upon whom he

based the characters in *Under Milk Wood*. Some of Captain Cat's sailing adventures, for example, may have been based on tales that Thomas heard from a retired sea captain named Johnnie Thomas, who had sailed a schooner and became blind as an old man. Mr. Edwards the draper, described as wearing "a butterfly-collar and straw-hat" in the play, took his outfit from Laugharne's actual draper, who dressed similarly. The play's butcher, Mr. Beynon, resembles Laugharne's butcher, Mr. Eynon, who later recounted how Thomas said with a smile that he was writing a play and that he would put Mr. Eynon in it. Other local personalities who recognized themselves in the play, however, took offense at the work, feeling that they had been unfairly ridiculed.

In developing the play, Thomas was heavily influenced by American poet Edgar Lee Masters's *Spoon River Anthology* (1914), in which the dead and living citizens of a small town speak of their lives and dreams in poetry. Thomas worked on a radio piece about Masters for the British Broadcasting Corporation (BBC) in the early 1950s. Like *Under Milk Wood*, *Spoon River Anthology* (which includes a "First Voice" and "Second Voice" who serve as narrators) shocked many readers with its sexual frankness and its mockery of small town Puritanism. Thomas was also influenced by another American masterpiece, Thornton Wilder's Pulitzer Prize-winning stage play *Our Town* (1938), in which a character called the "Stage Manager" presents episodes from life in a small town. Finally, critics have also found literary precedent for the play's chronological structure and carefully rendered quotidian details in the famous "Nighttown" section of Joyce's **Ulysses** (1922; also in *WLAIT 4: British and Irish Literature and Its Times*).

Reception. After its first group reading at the Poetry Center in New York City on May 14, 1953, *Under Milk Wood* received 15 curtain calls from an extraordinarily enthusiastic audience. Later that year the Poetry Center opened its season program with the play, just weeks before Thomas's death in New York in November. The play first reached British audiences in January 1954, when it was produced for the BBC in London; it was published in London later that year. Reviews of both the early performances and the initial publication were generally, though not exclusively, favorable. An unsigned review in the *Times* of London described the play as "the most gaily gruesome of bawdy rhetorical fantasies," calling Thomas's outlook (both in the play and in his other works) "adolescent" (*Times Literary Supplement*, p. 148). Also some Welsh listeners "bridled" when they heard the play on the BBC, "taking special offence at the bawdy passages" (Ferris, p. 289).

Yet the play became a bestseller in Britain, where 25,000 copies were sold within the half year after Thomas's death. "The printed words give the reader, at every turn, the Welsh voice," wrote critic John Arlott in the *Spectator*, characterizing the play's portrayal of Wales as "mischievously and . . . wittily true" (Arlott, p. 441). Subsequent readers—and audiences of the frequently performed play—have borne out another early assessment, this one by American scholar Jacob Korg in his 1954 review of the publication in the United States: "*Under Milk Wood* is delightful and not difficult to understand, and it will probably become Thomas's most popular work" (Korg, p. 360).

—Colin Wells

For More Information

Ackerman, John. *A Dylan Thomas Companion: Life, Poetry and Prose*. London: Macmillan, 1991.

———. *Welsh Dylan: Dylan Thomas's Life, Writing and his Wales*. Bridgend, Wales: Poetry Wales Press, 1998.

Arlott, John. Review of *Under Milk Wood*, by Dylan Thomas. *The Spectator*, 9 April 1954, 441.

Ferris, Paul. *Dylan Thomas*. New York: Dial, 1977.

Korg, Jacob. *Dylan Thomas*. New York: Twayne, 1992.

———. Review of *Under Milk Wood*, by Dylan Thomas. *The Nation* 178 (24 April 1954): 360.

Morgan, Kenneth O. *Rebirth of a Nation: Wales 1880-1980*. Oxford: Oxford University Press, 1981.

Morris, Jan. *The Matter of Wales: Epic Views of a Small Country*. Oxford: Oxford University Press, 1984.

Review of *Under Milk Wood*, by Dylan Thomas. *Times Literary Supplement*, 5 March, 1954, 148.

Sinclair, Andrew. *Dylan Thomas: No Man More Magical*. New York: Holt, Rinehart and Winston: 1975.

Thomas, Dylan. *Collected Letters*. Ed. Paul Ferris. London: J. M. Dent, 1985.

———. *Under Milk Wood*. New York: New Directions, 1954.

Waiting for Godot

by
Samuel Beckett

Samuel Barclay Beckett was born in Foxrock, Dublin, in 1906. Though his early interests were athletic—he played on the cricket and rugby teams at the Portora Royal School in Northern Enniskillen—he studied and excelled in French and Italian at Trinity College in Dublin. In 1928 Beckett began a two-year-exchange fellowship at *l'Ecole Normale Supérieure* in Paris, where he befriended the Irish writer James Joyce and became a member of his intellectual and social circle. A decade later, in 1937, after teaching in Dublin and traveling through Europe, he decided to take up permanent residence in Paris. With the outbreak of World War II in September 1939, Beckett became a member of the French Resistance Movement, whose objective was subversive and sabotage activity against the Nazis to assist the advance of the Allied armed forces. Afterwards he was awarded the *croix de guerre* and other citations for his work in the French underground. For approximately two years in the postwar era, Beckett concentrated on writing fiction, most notably novels such as *Mercier & Camier, Murphy, Molloy, and Malone Dies.* He acquired the habit of writing first in French, then translating his works into English, believing that in this way he avoided verbal superfluity. Without any experience in theatrical production, Beckett ventured into composing drama as a respite from his flurry of fiction writing. From 1952 to 1956, *En Attendant Godot* and its English translation, *Waiting for Godot,* catapulted Beckett to international prominence. In 1969 Beckett received the Nobel Prize for literature, and before his death in 1989, he

---

THE LITERARY WORK

A play set on a country road in an unspecified era; written in 1948-49; published in French (as *En Attendant Godot*) in 1952, in English in 1954.

SYNOPSIS

Two men pass the time by a tree near a roadway as they await the arrival of Godot, who does not appear. Through a boy messenger, Godot sends word that he will appear the next day. This recurs in the second act, leaving the two men in a state somewhere between hope and despair.

---

composed close to 30 works of fiction and more than 30 plays, poems, translations, and critical commentaries. *Waiting for Godot* portrays the major issues that preoccupied Beckett in his lifetime: the instability of one's own existence, the failure to communicate with others, and both the loneliness and camaraderie of the human condition. The play grows out of, and casts these concerns in, Beckett's experience of Europe in the years surrounding World War II.

Events in History at the Time the Play Takes Place

The French underground. France capitulated to World War II's Nazi aggressors in June 1940. Just days before the conquest, Samuel Beckett fled

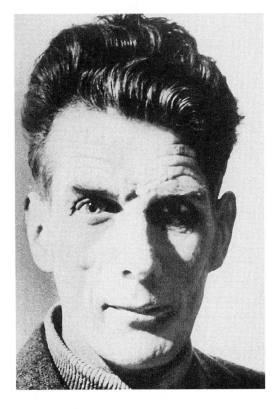

Samuel Beckett

south for a few months, then returned to Paris. After the arrest of Paul Léon, a Jewish friend, who was ultimately tortured to death, Beckett joined the Resistance. More exactly, he joined a circuit of the British secret service, or Special Operations Executive (SOE). The mission of the SOE was to coordinate and promote clandestine sabotage against the Nazis, which it did through various sections—one supplied clothing, another forged documents, a third conducted passengers along escape routes out of France, and the so-called F section, the main body of British agents organizing subversion in France, destroyed telephone switchboards, transformers that powered factories, and railroad yards that transported German supplies. Almost 100 independent circuits of the F section operated on French soil, each as a network of subversive agents, of whom Beckett himself was one. Together they armed thousands of resisters at perilous risk to life and limb; some 100 of the 400 or so F agents sent to France never returned, among them Beckett's colleague, Alfred Péron. Arrested after one of the circuit's members was tortured into confession, Péron was sent to Mauthausen concentration camp, where he endured hard labor and malnourishment as long as possible, so poignantly reciting poetry in the

midst of the nightmare that a capo, a Nazi commandant, came to him in search of a poem for his wife on their anniversary. As a member of the circuit, Beckett collected information on German troop movements, which he would decode and type to prepare for its being smuggled out to London. Once the secrecy of the circuit was compromised, he fled south to the small inconspicuous rural community of Rouissillon, where Beckett engaged in more subversion, aiding and abetting the *maquis,* the guerrilla units formed by young men, who, instead of reporting for service as forced laborers for the Nazis, took to the hills to combat them. (*Maquis* is a Corsican word, designating the thick local brushwood.)

In Rouissillon, as elsewhere, there was a paramount need for secrecy in the Resistance, so dire a need that no one used real names, and two agents on the same mission manipulated circumstances so as not to see each other. That way, if they were caught and subjected to torture, they would have nothing to confess. When an agent guided an escapee to a prearranged drop-off spot, a park bench, for example, the agent would disappear and the escapee would wait maybe 15 minutes before being collected by a second agent, who never laid eyes on the first. Similarly, messengers carried information between agents in coded language the messenger did not understand, again so that nothing could be divulged to the enemy.

Days were filled with waiting and nights with clandestine activity and writing for Beckett. (He is said to have begun his plan for *Waiting for Godot* during his two and a half years in Rouissillon [1942-45]). Afterwards, film footage made public the horror of the concentrations camps of Bergen-Belsen, Dachau, and Auschwitz, while Georges Loustaunau-Cacau wrote books about life in Mauthausen, where Beckett's friend Péron perished, after carrying coal and reciting poetry in the midst of hellish camp life. "These are the kinds of human issues that inform the varied relationships between the characters in [Beckett's] play," which features not only two tramps committed to each other but also another pair of men, a master wielding a whip over a menial, who dances, sings, recites, and carries, recalling, among others, the abused, poetry-reciting, coal-carrying Péron (Knowlson, p. 345).

In the midst of World War II's human degradation and cruelty were the sacrifice and nobility of the Resistance.

> By D day, 30,000 Resistance and maquis had been executed; another 30,000 had been killed

in battles with the enemy. Of the 115,000 deported to the Buchenwald, Ravensbruck, Dachau, and Mauthausen camps, and countless others deported for forced labor only 35,000 returned.

(Gordon, p. 167)

Meanwhile, in France, many more abided the German oppressor, taking "the easier road of *attentisme . . .* of 'rolling with the punch' or waiting for outside salvation," even as the two tramps await salvation in *Waiting for Godot* (Wright, p. 402).

From tragedy to comedy—the music hall. Characters in *Waiting for Godot* wear bowlers, play musical hats, fall down, and try to help each other up, only to all fall down in slapstick fashion, reminiscent of variety theater in Beckett's day. In fact, before becoming an expatriate in Paris in 1928, Beckett regularly attended variety in Dublin. Its antecedent was the music hall, which gave way to "variety" after World War I, though the two terms have often been used interchangeably. An amalgamation of acts, music hall harked back to 1852, the opening of Canterbury Hall, a type that would soon become widespread. By the end of the century, music hall featured animal acts, dancers, serious singers of stirring patriotic tunes and ballads, and the most popular act of all, the comics. There were solo comics who appeared as character types—an egg salesman, for example, the humor stemming not from jokes but from the character sketch. Strong social satire in the early days of music hall gave way to performers who seemed to "preach ironic acceptance of a hard life" during the decline of this form of entertainment (1913-23) and the rise of variety (Wilmut, p. 14). Variety would endure for roughly 40 years (1919-60), enduring difficult times for much of the 1930s, during the economic depression, but rallying at the end of the decade. In revue-like style, variety featured a series of unconnected routines whose performers composed a momentary ensemble, only to afterwards part company and move on to other locations, where they would appear with totally new sets of performers. Variety saw the rise of the double act: two comedians teamed up, one delivering the funny lines, the other acting as his stooge, the dialogue between the straight man and funny man becoming known as "cross talk." The two "often indulged in 'turns,' borrowing each other's hats, boots and even trousers, or doing slapstick with ladders and chairs" (Cronin, p. 57). They engaged in a rhythmic type of patter with each other: the straight man would question what the comic said by repeating it and then the comic would repeat it again. There is dialogue in Beckett's play that echoes this sort of patter, just as the relationship between the two main characters echoes the distinctive comedy of the double act.

> **From *Waiting for Godot***
>
> Estragon [speaking about Lucky, a carrier]: Why doesn't he put down his bags?
>
> . . .
>
> Vladimir: Damn it haven't you already told us?
> Pozzo: I've already told you?
> Estragon: He's already told us?
>
> (Beckett, *Waiting for Godot*, p. 43)

ECHOES OF THE RESISTANCE

In writing the play, Beckett at first gave one of the tramps a Jewish name, Lévy, evoking the persecution of World War II, but then made their two names Vladimir and Estragon. The tramps have other appellations—Didi and Gogo, respectively, which could be cryptic ways of mutual recognition by members of the French underground. Each name has four letters, or two syllables, the latter repeating the former, an apt way of generating a sign and the countersign. In addition, the setting of the play—a country road with a solitary tree—typifies a landmark for a clandestine location; at such a site members of a circuit could conduct their rendezvous safely and apart from outside surveillance. Also the meeting of Vladimir and Estragon may reenact a rendezvous of two members of a circuit at a location from which they anticipate departure under the direction of a guide—Godot, perhaps also a code name. When Godot does not arrive, Vladimir and Estragon separate for the night, then return to the same setting on the following eve to wait. This activity mimics procedures that would compartmentalize members of a circuit, reducing their knowledge of one another's whereabouts, and minimizing the damage to the circuit as a whole from the capture of a single member.

Most renowned in the interwar period was the double act of Bud Flannagan and Chesney Allen. Their act entailed a complicated sort of word play that called into question communication, something Beckett's characters struggle with less comically; in the dialogue above, there is a sharp undertone of seriousness associated with the seemingly vain attempt to exchange information. On the variety stage, the attempt is equally vain, but the dialogue remains slapstick, going no deeper than the surface:

From Flannagan and Allen's Double Act

FLANNAGAN: I went down to the docks.
ALLEN: Oh, you saw the ships?
FLANNAGAN: Yes, I saw all the ships coming into whisky.
ALLEN: Coming into port.
FLANNAGAN: Coming into port—oh, a marvellous sight. . . . See all the labradors at work.
ALLEN: The what?
FLANNAGAN: The labradors.
ALLEN: The labradors—the salvadors!
FLANNAGAN: The stevedores, you fool—oi!

(Adapted from Wilmut, p. 61)

TRAGICOMIC SONG, TRAGICOMIC DANCE

Integrated into *Waiting for Godot* is both song and dance. Opening Act 2, the song "A dog came in" tragically recounts how a dog, having stolen a crust of bread, is beaten to death by a ladle-wielding cook. Tending to their own, other dogs assemble to dig a grave for the victim: Then all the dogs came running / And dug the dog a tomb— / And dug the dog a tomb (*Godot*, p. 64). Likewise, dance assumes tragic overtones in the play, when one character entertains the others with his less-than-fancy footwork:

POZZO: He used to dance the farandole, the fling, the brawl, the jig, the fandango, and even the hornpipe. He capered. For joy. Now that's the best he can do. Do you know what he calls it?
ESTRAGON: The Scapegoat's Agony.
VLADIMIR: The hard stool.
POZZO: The Net. He thinks he's entangled in a net.

(*Godot*, p. 42)

From their initial performance in 1931 until they retired in 1945, Flannagan and Allen remained the most popular double act in the business. What distinguished them from other comedians was the bond of affection they conveyed on stage.

Usually the straight man in such acts showed complete irritation with the antics of the funny man, but no matter how irritating Flannagan's antics were, Allen still emoted a tenderness for the man. Similarly, Vladimir and Estragon show deep-seated affection for each other in Beckett's play. "I'll never walk again," complains Estragon,

rather comically after trying to comfort the weeping passerby Lucky, who promptly kicks his would-be benefactor; "I'll carry you," volunteers Vladimir "(*tenderly*)," then pauses and adds a comical "if necessary" (*Waiting for Godot*, p. 32).

Beckett and philosophy. An avid reader of philosophy, Beckett declared that he himself was no philosopher, yet his literature resounds with ideas peculiar to his time. Various related philosophies flourished during the World War II era, particularly in France, where they manifested themselves in such works as Albert Camus's novel *L'Étranger* (1942; *The Stranger*) and his essay *Le Mythe de Sisyphe* (1942; *The Myth of Sisyphus*). Camus saw humanity as confronting a universe that is unintelligible. In his view, the universe provides no answers to profound questions about where one comes from or where one is going, a situation he considered absurd.

Drama too gave expression to philosophies of the era, with Jean-Paul Sartre's *Huis clos* (1945; *In Camera*, also titled *No Exit*) featuring existential philosophy. Coined by French journalists in the World War II era, *existentialism* became a popular term for a family of philosophies of despair, though much in existential writing did not fit this definition. The philosophies aimed to interpret human existence. A human being has no God-given or nature-given essence, taught the existentialists; instead each being makes himself or herself to be what he or she is through his or her choices and actions. Building on prior philosophers (such as Søren Kierkegaard and Martin Heidegger), the existentialists became preoccupied with ideas like 1) nothing truly exists, 2) even if something does exist, it cannot truly be known, and 3) even if it can be known, it cannot be truly communicated to others. Taken together, these ideas comprise the skeptical extreme known as "nihilism." Existentialism became preoccupied too with death and suicide. One must face death, taught Heidegger, to enter into "authentic" being. Sartre addressed the subject of a person's social responsibility. Human consciousness, he taught (in *Existentialism and Humanism,* 1946), gives rise to the freedom of the individual, and freedom, to social responsibility. The individual, said the existentialists, is not a detached observer in this world but a participant—again, humans define themselves by the choices they make, the way they act. Actually the existentialists were philosophers of creation. One can better take their full measure by distinguishing between their diagnosis of humanity's current condition and the possibilities for an ethical life that their diagnosis opened up. As shown, Sartre's view does not ultimately lead to despair but to engagement, pointing to the responsibility of the individual to make life worth living.

Beckett did not identify himself with any of these thinkers per se; in fact, he "distanced himself from existentialism" (Kern, p. 170). Yet Beckett's literature addresses many of these same subjects, as well as those posed by other philosophers, such as Arthur Schopenhauer (1788-1860), whom Beckett avidly read and whose teachings support his view that suffering is the norm for humanity. Beckett did not, however, prefer one philosopher to the exclusion of others or develop a system of philosophy separate from his drama and fiction. He nevertheless has been regarded as a philosophical writer, and his works mined for ideas of modern life, perhaps because of his overall intent. Beckett aimed, he said, "to imitate the universal mess. . . . To find a form that accommodates the mess, that is the task of the artist now" (Beckett in Cormier and Pallister, p. 118). In the process, he evokes "existential" and other ideas about existence—the condition of irremediable solitude, the experience of cosmic absurdity, the failure to communicate.

Of course, historical events as well as philosophy impinged on Beckett's outlook. His, it should be remembered, was a lifetime that before the brutalities of World War II had witnessed the bloody carnage of the First World War and of the Irish Civil War, whose "cumulatory effect . . . was a general cynicism and disbelief in either virtue or decency, in goodness or uprightness or honesty" (Gordon, p. 20). However, Beckett's personal theater, or field of battle, was neither the Irish Civil War nor the First World War but rather the civilian underground in World War II France, and it did *not* present him with unrelieved human depravity. There were the activists in the Resistance—everyday teachers, farmers, and parents—who risked life and limb to combat the Nazis. Also, to the south of Beckett's rural refuge, Roussillon, was another village, Le Chambon, a Protestant town whose ordinary citizens took bold yet unobtrusive action, sneaking into the protective folds of their homes hundreds of Jewish children and raising them as their own. Such valiance paled beside the butchery of millions in the Nazi gas chambers, or the torture of Resistance agents captured by the Nazis, or the passive attitudes toward Nazi evils adopted by many other citizens. Still, it existed, validating the idea of "suffering redeemed

through camaraderie" that "would resound throughout [Beckett's] work and life," and that would surface in the not unrelieved despair of *Waiting for Godot* (Gordon, p. 17).

The Play in Focus

Plot summary. A drama in two acts, *Waiting for Godot* spans two days. The first act begins in the evening and ends with the onset of nightfall, and the second act occurs during the same time the next day. Onstage the action takes place only at the darkening stages of twilight. The setting consists of a country road and a tree; nearby are a mound and a ditch, a type of area one might find in rural France. In the first act, the tree has no leaves, but in the interval between the first and second acts, it sprouts four to five leaves. Near the tree, the two major characters of the play, Vladimir and Estragon, wait for the coming of Godot, whom they have never met and about whom they know nothing, except his name. As they wait, they become very time-conscious and experience nervous agitation, which they strive to alleviate by conversation. Seemingly inconsequential chatter, at moments their conversation verges on profound deliberation. But they never wish to face the implications of what they say.

At the beginning of Act I Vladimir wakens Estragon, who complains "Why will you never let me sleep?" to which Vladimir replies "I felt lonely" (*Godot,* p. 10). Estragon rather comically struggles to pull off his boots, which are too small. They contemplate hanging themselves, but decide they cannot, for Vladimir is too heavy for the hanging to work, and, without Estragon, he would be left alone. "Well?" asks Vladimir, "What do we do?" to which Estragon replies "Nothing," because doing nothing is safer (*Godot,* p. 13).

Interrupting them as they wait for Godot are Pozzo, owner of the land on which they wait, and Lucky, whom Pozzo leads on a rope like a dog and who carries his bag, basket, and stool. "He carries," complains Pozzo, "like a pig. It's not his job" (*Godot,* p. 30). Clearly Lucky has come down in the world; he can sing, dance, and think, less effectively than he once did but better than any of the others there. Lucky dances, feebly, and he thinks for them, also feebly.

Pozzo treats Lucky abusively, and speaks of plans to sell him, whereupon Lucky weeps and Estragon attempts to comfort him, but gets kicked violently by Lucky for his pains. The conversation wanders. All four men wear bowler hats and Vladimir observes sarcastically what a

Peter Woodthorpe, Paul Daneman, and Peter Bull in a 1955 production of *Waiting for Godot* at London's Arts Theatre.

charming evening they are having; worse, he says than "the music-hall" (*Godot,* p. 35). Estragon introduces himself to Pozzo as Adam, the world's first man; later he compares himself to Christ and still later, in a comical interchange, equates Pozzo with Abel. At the time, Pozzo is lying in a helpless heap on the ground.

> VLADIMIR: I tell you his name is Pozzo.
> ESTRAGON: We'll soon see. (He reflects.) Abel! Abel!
> POZZO: Help!
> ESTRAGON: Got it in one!
>
> (*Godot,* p. 95)

The names conjure the image of universal human being that other action in the play promotes. Pozzo and Lucky take their leave, and a Boy enters, a messenger who reports that Godot is not coming; he will be there tomorrow. Asked if he is unhappy, the Boy, who minds goats, says he does not know. "You're as bad as myself," ventures Vladimir, continuing to equate one instance of humanity with another (*Godot,* p. 56). The Boy, it turns out, has a brother, who minds the sheep and suffers beatings, as does Estragon, who is beaten during the day. As night falls and Act I ends, Estragon and Vladimir contemplate hanging themselves again, discuss Estragon's attempted suicide in former days when they har-

vested grapes by the Rhone, and recall how long they have been together—50 years maybe. "I sometimes wonder if we wouldn't have been better off alone," muses Estragon, "each one for himself" (*Godot,* p. 58).

Act 2 opens as Vladimir and Estragon reunite on the same ground, again at twilight. Vladimir wants to embrace Estragon, but Estragon protests, for he has been beaten, but he wants Vladimir to stay with him. "I wouldn't have let them beat you," volunteers Vladimir protectively, saying he would have stopped Estragon from doing whatever angered them; but, protests Estragon, "I wasn't doing anything" (*Godot,* p. 65).

The two converse again, so they won't have to hear "all the dead voices" or think about "all these corpses," "these skeletons," references perhaps to World War II, as well as to a more general dance of death (*Godot,* p. 71). They notice that the tree has sprouted leaves and marvel that this happened in a single night. Was it only yesterday that they were there? "Yes," says Estragon, "now I remember, yesterday evening we spent blathering about nothing in particular. That's been going on now for half a century" (*Godot,* p. 73). Comically again, Estragon staggers around trying on a pair of boots he finds by the roadside. Lucky left his hat there yesterday, so they engage in a game of musical bowlers—exchanging one hat for another and then another. They play too at being Pozzo and Lucky. Estragon leaves momentarily, returns, and falls into Vladimir's arms.

> ESTRAGON: There you are again at last! . . .
> VLADIMIR: Where were you? I thought you were gone for ever.
>
> (*Godot,* p. 82)

They rejoice at the sound of someone approaching, thinking Godot has finally arrived, but it is only Pozzo, now blind, and Lucky, now dumb. Lucky and Pozzo fall down, and Estragon and Vladimir consider whether to help them up gladly or subordinate their good offices to certain conditions for some tangible reward. Vladimir grows decisive, energetic:

> Let us not waste our time in idle discourse! (Pause. Vehemently.) Let us do something, while we have the chance. It is not every day that we are needed. Not indeed that we personally are needed. Others would meet the case equally well, if not better. To all mankind they were addressed those cries for help still ringing in our ears! But at this place, at this moment of time, all mankind is us, whether we like it or not. Let us make the most of it, before it is too late! Let us represent worthily for once the foul brood to which a cruel fate consigned us!
>
> (*Godot,* p. 90)

Comically and tragically, Vladimir tries to pull Pozzo up and stumbles down himself, then Estragon pulls Vladimir and stumbles and falls as well. Estragon observes that Pozzo, who again cries "help," is all humanity. Vladimir and Estragon get up and help Pozzo up, who does not recall meeting them yesterday. Pozzo explains that Lucky cannot sing or recite or even groan for them: "one day he went dumb, one day I went blind, one day we'll go deaf, one day we were born, one day we shall die, the same day, the same second, is that not enough for you?" (*Godot,* p. 103). Pozzo and Lucky leave.

Vladimir and Estragon continue to wait for Godot. Exasperated, Estragon cannot sleep because again Vladimir wakes him to stave off loneliness. Vladimir refuses to hear about Estragon's dream, and the two wonder if Pozzo could have been Godot. Struggling with his boots again, Estragon cries "help me!" whereupon Vladimir has a fit of remorse;

> Was I sleeping, while the others suffered? Am I sleeping now? To-morrow, when I wake, or think I do, what shall I say of to-day? That with

Estragon my friend, at this place until the fall of night, I waited for Godot? . . . But in all that what truth will there be?
>
> (*Godot,* p. 104)

Vladimir muses about how habit deadens the cries for help that are everywhere in the air.

The Boy messenger arrives again to say Mr. Godot will not keep the appointment today but will come tomorrow. "Tell him that you saw me," says Vladimir, somewhat frantically, as if questioning his own existence (justifiably, in light of Pozzo's not having remembered him). ". . . You're sure you saw me, you won't come and tell me to-morrow that you never saw me!" (*Godot,* p. 106). The Boy leaves, and Vladimir and Estragon contemplate suicide again. Will they hang themselves tomorrow, or will Godot come, in which case they would be saved, or would they be? As the curtain falls, the two characters are immobile, and the audience is left wondering.

A brave new world—or not? "Let us not then speak ill of our generation," philosophizes Pozzo in the play. "It is not any unhappier than its predecessors. (Pause.) Let us not speak well of it either. Let us not speak of it at all," he adds, unwilling to dwell on the subject (*Godot,* p. 32).

Written in the 1940s, the play speaks to a World War II and postwar generation that spanned extremes, ranging from grim wartime horrors to high postwar hopes for a greatly improved society. These hopes surfaced in both Britain and Beckett's adopted home, France. In England, earlier than most, George Orwell expressed an idealistic vision in his 1941 essay **"The Lion and the Unicorn"** (also in *WLAIT 4: British and Irish Literature and Its Times*), which anticipated an entirely new social order, one that did away with the class system and inaugurated a practical type of socialism in Britain. The war, it was thought, had fortified the commitment to general human decency and justice for all. People had sacrificed together to combat Nazism, and to protect British independence in a way that excited hopes for a more equitable postwar Europe. Beckett himself referred to such hopes in a 1946 BBC radio broadcast. After the war, he labored with the Irish Red Cross to build a hospital in a ravaged French community. In just one night, explained Beckett, Saint-Lô had been bombed to pieces.

> [People] continue two years after the liberation, to clear away the debris, literally by hand. . . . [S]ome of those who were in Saint-Lô [to build the hospital] will come home realising that they

got at least as good as they gave, that they got indeed what they could hardly give, a vision and sense of a time-honoured conception of humanity in ruins, and perhaps even an inkling of the terms in which our condition is to be thought again.

(Beckett, "Capital of the Ruins," pp. 75-76)

Would there be a fundamentally new order in postwar Britain? Political developments were encouraging at first. By a wide margin, the people elected into power the Labour Party under Clement Attlee on a platform of sweeping reforms: the Labour Party would provide decent housing for all, effect full employment, and initiate the welfare state. Labour's government, which endured from 1945 to 1951 (Beckett was in France during these years, writing *Waiting for Godot*), did indeed establish the modern-day British welfare state. The government passed the National Health Service Act (1946), which provided free health care to all, constructed council housing for the homeless, and achieved full employment of the workforce. There was a failure, however, to change underlying structures in a revolutionary way that would lead to a more equitable society. "The Labour Party was in the end unable to use the institutions of the state to bring about the social transformation many of its supporters had hoped for. . . . 'The welfare measures . . . did not of themselves produce a more egalitarian or open society'" (Williamson, pp. 84, 85). Discussion of social revolution filled the air, yet postwar society remained class-riven and class-conscious. By the early 1950s, British leaders stopped envisioning a government that would take collective responsibility for the welfare of everyone by providing services and benefits to all.

People blamed the Cold War for the failure. A competition for world leadership between the Soviet Union and the United States and their respective allies, the Cold War "destroyed any socialist vision, dragooned people into flocks of Atlanticist sheep or pro-Soviet goats, and blocked off any 'third way'" (Thompson in Williamson, p. 61). The global competition dashed hopes for a socialist Europe, instead holding the continent hostage to the specter of one superpower's threatening another with nuclear death. Britain linked itself to the United States after World War II, securing U.S. loans. If, thought its leaders, we do not ally with America, then Europe will remain under the threat of Soviet domination. So the Cold War took precedence over any fundamental reorganization of society in Britain. Postwar France went through a similar experience: "It is

true enough that much of the wartime idealism soon curdled; that resistance dreams of a wholly new era . . . were quickly shattered; that the Fourth Republic as a political system turned out to be not very much different from the Third" (Wright, p. 401). Neither Britain nor France experienced pivotal institutional change; nor was there much fundamental change in human interaction.

Racist and abusive behavior blights some of the human relations in *Waiting for Godot*. As noted, Pozzo abuses Lucky in a way reminiscent of the Nazi capo's abuse of Jews in World War II's extermination camps. There was little bald anti-Semitism in Britain after the war, but controversy over Palestine led to attacks on Jewish shops and to individual remarks such as one editor's in the press that "'The Jews, indeed, are a plague on Britain'" (Caunt in Williamson, p. 52). British law prosecuted the editor, but the instance illustrated that racism persisted. And with post World War II immigration from the far reaches of the dwindling empire—India, Pakistan, the Caribbean, and Hong Kong—racism flared. A 1948 survey showed that schoolbooks in Britain promoted misguided stereotypes of these immigrants, a "sophisticated" example of the failure to communicate that plagues characters in *Waiting for Godot*.

At the same time, there were improvements in postwar British society. Welfare legislation eased poverty, concluded a 1950 study of York, and also expanded everyone's rights (Williamson, p. 77). The 1944 Education Act, to cite a specific example, guaranteed free secondary education to all. With good cause, then, one might echo Pozzo's lines in the play: let us not speak ill of postwar humanity; let us not speak well of it. As in the wartime era, humanity afterwards had some successes, and it had some profound failures.

Sources and literary context. Beckett's sources for *Waiting for Godot* are multiple and various, ranging from his own real-life experience in World War II and as a fan of the music hall (described above) to paintings and readings. According to Beckett himself, the visual setting of the play stemmed from a painting he saw by Caspar David Friedrich. At the end of each act in the play, Vladimir and Estragon stand by the tree as the moon rises, forming silhouettes against the evening sky. The image resembles two paintings by Friedrich—*Two Men Contemplating the Moon* (1819) and *Man and Woman Observing the Moon* (1824). Exactly which one inspired Beckett re-

INFECTIOUS CINEMA

Along with the music hall, Beckett drew on his experience as a purveyor of early cinema. In the 1920s, film was the newest medium of entertainment. Influenced by music-hall entertainment, early cinema was often humorous. Beckett, a young man in his late teens and early twenties at the time, regularly frequented the cinema in Dublin. There he saw the films of Charlie Chaplin, Laurel and Hardy, and Harold Lloyd, all of whom began their careers as vaudevillians. When the Marx Brothers began to make films, he saw them too. Among the hallmarks of these films were physical humor—slapstick, pratfalls, cross-talk, and the like. Also, ill-fitting clothes, hats, and shoes or boots were integrated into the humor. Charlie Chaplin, for instance, wore a tight jacket but baggy trousers. Beyond the physical and verbal humor, the deadpan demeanor of the performers was crucial to the success of early cinema. Chaplin, Buster Keaton, and Laurel and Hardy—the so-called stoic comedians—perfected the deadpan demeanor in cinema. In effect, the stoic comedians maintained straight faces despite the laughter that they evoked from their audiences. (Later cinema would feature Keaton in Beckett's one venture into moviemaking— the 1964 production *Film*.)

Like the stoic comedians of early cinema, the protagonists in *Waiting for Godot* have a complementary relationship. The first to appear in the play is Estragon, typically played by a short, fat man. Vladimir is taller and leaner, if not gaunt. In stage productions, both men wear hats like the bowlers of early cinema as well as variety theater. Humor derives from Vladimir's reaction to his hat, just as it does from Estragon's annoyance with his boots. As Vladimir removes his hat, knocks on the crown, and seems intent on dislodging a foreign object, Estragon removes one of his boots, turns it upside down, and shakes it. Their actions mix humor into the tragedy, another resemblance between *Waiting for Godot* and early cinema. Melodrama informed some of the comedians' theatrics with tragedy until a reversal in fortune resulted in their happiness. The audience's response would shift from one extreme to the other—from fear and anxiety, on the one hand, to joy, on the other. But ultimately the tragic threat gave way to a comic resolution, and here the resemblance ends, as this is not the case at the end of *Waiting for Godot*.

mains unclear. In the first, two men in cloaks, viewed from behind, gaze at a full moon pictured against the dark branches of a great leafless tree.

Literary influences include philosophers such as René Descartes, Martin Heidegger and Albert Camus, as well as Arthur Schopenhauer, mentioned above. When asked what dramatist influenced his own playwrighting the most, Beckett named John Millington Synge, whose mingling of tragedy and comedy Beckett particularly admired. The French playwright Racine also influenced Beckett greatly. Racine aimed for the classic unity of action, place, and time, a dramaturgic device ultimately derived from the doctrine of Aristotle. Certainly *Waiting for Godot* observes a unity of place and action. As for time, "Racine

and French classical criticism had extended the allowable period to twenty-four hours," the extent of Beckett's play (Cronin, p. 60). A familiar complaint about Racine's plays was that nothing much happened, except that pairs of characters went on chattering to each other, an influence on Beckett that needs no elaboration. Also, in the manner of French classical drama, which taught that the setting should not be specific, Beckett's is nondescript—"A country road. A tree. Evening" (*Godot*, p. 1). Other possible sources include Christian writings, specifically the *Confessions* of St. Augustine, which may have inspired the "fifty-fifty chance of salvation that runs through [Beckett's] play" (Knowlson, p. 343).

Beckett's storyline—waiting for a person to arrive or an event to occur that might change a situation—resounds in drama he knew. John Millington Synge's **The Playboy of the Western World,** (1907; also in *WLAIT 4: British and Irish Literature and Its Times*), whose heroine seizes on a young man to deliver her from a tedious future is one example; W. B. Yeats's *At the Hawk's Well* (1916), whose characters must wait for the dry bed of a well to fill before they can drink its waters of youth and immortality, is another.

That other drama of the day addressed philosophical concerns has already been noted in the case of Jean-Paul Sartre's *No Exit* (1944), which focuses on three characters who have recently died and are trapped in the eternal damnation of the hold they have on each other. Other contemporary drama includes Eugène Ionesco's *The Bald Soprano* (1950), which features meaningless dialogue between two couples that degenerates into babbling. Ionesco's play was part of the theater of the absurd, a new genre that reduced setting and action to the minimum, strove to generalize characters, sometimes to the point of not naming them, and incorporated elements from the circus, like the marionette or the clown, as well as from the music hall. In contrast to others, Beckett did not see himself as part of the new genre; in fact "public association with Ionesco . . . and the 'theatre of the absurd' would always annoy him" (Cronin, p. 525).

Reception. *Waiting for Godot* opened in France at the Théâtre de Babylone 5 January, 1953. The curtain fell, reported Sylvain Zegel in *Libération,* before a confused audience that nevertheless realized they had just seen an important play. Preeminent French playwright Jean Anouilh cemented its success with his review in *Arts-Spectacle.* "Godot," he said is "a masterpiece that will cause despair for men in general and for playwrights in particular" (Anouilh in Cronin, p. 421). Dazzled by the reviews, crowds stormed into the playhouse for every performance but often left after the first act, confused by it and, many of them, bored. Yet the praise from critics continued; a month after the play's opening Alain Robbe-Grillet observed that though "made out of nothingness," *Waiting for Godot* flowed forward seamlessly "without an empty space" (Robbe-Grillet in Cronin, p. 423).

Outside France, *Waiting for Godot* was a resounding success. The audience in Ireland appears to have been more steadfast about staying for the duration. In *The Irish Times* (February 18, 1956), Vivian Mercier contended that Beckett has "achieved a theoretical impossibility—a play in which nothing happens, that yet keeps audiences glued to their seats" (Mercier in Andonian, p. 95). In England's *The Spectator* (August 12, 1955), Anthony Hartley described *Waiting for Godot* as "a play of great power and skill (the dialogue is masterly)" (Hartley in Andonian, p. 92). Brooks Atkinson, who reviewed the American production on Broadway for the *New York Times,* sensed "an illusion of faith flickering around the edges of the drama. It is as though Mr. Beckett sees very little reason for clutching at faith, but is unable to relinquish it entirely" (Atkinson, p. 21). The play prompted not only such comments but also a flurry of interpretation. All the interpretation distressed Beckett, who thought it reflected a fundamental misunderstanding of the intent of *Waiting for Godot.* "'The end,' Beckett said, 'is to give artistic expression to something hitherto almost ignored—the irrational state of unknowingness where we exist . . . which is beyond reason'" (Beckett in Cronin, p. 457).

—Albert Labriola and Joyce Moss

For More Information

Andonian, Cathleen Culotta. *The Critical Response to Samuel Beckett.* Westport, Conn.: Greenwood, 1998.

Atkinson, Brooks. Review of *Waiting for Godot. New York Times,* 20 April 1956, 21.

Beckett, Samuel. "The Capital of the Ruins." In *As No Other Dare Fail.* London: John Calder, 1986.

———. *Waiting for Godot: A Tragicomedy in Two Acts.* Trans. Samuel Beckett. New York: Grove, 1954.

Cormier, Ramona, and Janis L. Pallister. *Waiting for Death: The Philosophical Significance of Beckett's En Attendant Godot.* University, Ala.: University of Alabama Press, 1979.

Cronin, Anthony. *Samuel Beckett: The Last Modernist.* New York: HarperCollins, 1997.

Foot, M. R. D. *SOE in France: An Account of the Work of the British Special Operations Executive in France 1940-1944.* London: Her Majesty's Stationery Office, 1966.

Gordon, Lois. *The World of Samuel Beckett.* New Haven, Conn.: Yale University Press, 1996.

Kern, Edith. *Existential Thought and Fictional Technique.* New Haven: Yale University Press, 1970.

Knowlson, James. *Damned to Fame: The Life of Samuel Beckett.* New York: Simon & Schuster, 1996.

Williamson, Bill. *The Temper of the Times: British Society since World War II.* Oxford: Basil Blackwell, 1990.

Wilmut, Roger. *Kindly Leave the Stage! The Story of Variety 1919-1960.* London: Methuen, 1985.

Wright, Gordon. *France in Modern Times.* Stanford: Norton, 1987.

The Waste Land

by

T. S. Eliot

B orn in St. Louis, Missouri, on September 26, 1888, Thomas Stearns Eliot spent his youth in St. Louis and New England. Eliot earned his A.B. and an M.A. degrees in philosophy at Harvard University in 1906. He spent the next few years abroad (London, Paris, and Marburg, Germany) before settling in London in 1914. Since his early days at Harvard, Eliot had been writing poetry, but it was not until he met Ezra Pound in September 1914, that his work received any special attention. Pound was so impressed with Eliot's poem "The Love Song of J. Alfred Prufrock," that he sent it to Harriet Monroe, renowned editor of *Poetry*, proclaiming it "the best poem I have yet had or seen from an American" (Pound in Ackroyd, p. 44). "Prufrock" was published in June 1915, and that same month, Eliot married Englishwoman Vivien (also spelled Vivienne) Haigh-Wood. In 1917, Eliot began work as a clerk for Lloyd's Bank in the Colonial and Foreign Department. Meanwhile, he continued to write poetry and, that same year, took a position as assistant editor at *The Egoist*, a prominent literary magazine. In 1922 in the English journal *Criterion*, Eliot published *The Waste Land*, a work that would revolutionize modern poetry with its radical use of free verse, multiple perspectives, and literary allusion. Eliot adopted British citizenship in 1927 and became a devoted member of the Anglican Church. His subsequent literary and critical works would reflect a growing political and religious conservatism. Eliot won the Nobel Prize for literature in 1948, married his second wife, Valerie

---

THE LITERARY WORK

A long poem consisting of five sections set in post-World War I London, though parts were written as early as 1914; first published in 1922.

SYNOPSIS

A complicated montage of voices conveys a sense of the decadence, confusion, and despair prevalent in post-World War I Western culture.

Fletcher, in 1957, and died in 1965. *The Waste Land* remains one of the most dramatic expressions of the atmosphere pervading Britain after the First World War.

Events in History at the Time of the Poem

World War I. T. S. Eliot left Marburg, Germany, in early August 1914 just as World War I began. Since Harvard had awarded him a travel grant, he went to England and taught there at Oxford University. As a citizen of the United States, which would not enter the war until April 1917, the poet had a unique perspective on the toll it was taking on England and her people. Food had already become scarce when he arrived in London, and it was impossible to overlook the news-

T. S. Eliot

paper headlines announcing the tremendous numbers of British causalities.

Historians still debate the initial causes of the war, but there is little room for argument about its effects. The British government, led by Lloyd George, had done its best to inspire patriotism and high spirits among the country's young men. Thousands volunteered for service, dedicating themselves to fight for the honor and glory of England. A century had passed since England had fought in a major war. Everyone imagined that this contest would "be an affair of great marches and great battles, quickly decided" (Fussell, p. 21). The enthusiasm and the expectation of a quick outcome were soon dashed, however, by the technological nightmares of the war itself: chemical weapons, machine guns, trench warfare. These "innovations" resulted in the slaughter of hundreds of thousands of young men as well as the destruction of farms, churches, cities, and, it seemed, much of Western civilization. During the Battle of Somme, for example, in July 1916, of the 110,000 men who attacked the German front, 60,000 were killed or injured (Fussell, p. 13). A year later, the third Battle of Ypres (July 1917), turned into a siege of several months that resulted in 370,000 British casualties. Soldiers were dead, wounded, sick, or frozen, and thousands of them literally drowned in the mud of the battlefield (Fussell, p. 16).

Though he did his best to enlist when the United States entered the war in 1917, Eliot himself never saw combat. Poor health prevented his passing the requisite physical exam. He tried to obtain a position in Naval Intelligence, but by the time the paperwork was completed, the war had run its course. Despite his lack of firsthand experience, the war had a tremendous impact on the poet. It would have been impossible to be in London during wartime and not notice the multitudes of refugees or the absence of young English men on the city streets. In addition to hearing the horror stories of those returning from the front, Eliot lost a very close personal friend, the talented young French poet Jean Verdenal, who drowned at Gallipoli in 1915.

Aftermath of the Great War. *The Waste Land* does not deal with life in London *during* the war, but with the aftermath of the war. Trying to figure out how to resume one's life after four years of horror preoccupied Londoners once the peace had been signed. A sense of waste and desolation filled the air. Many of the men who managed to survive the war suffered from severe neuroses associated with shell shock or post-traumatic stress disorder. To many veterans, the urban landscape itself appeared transformed: no longer did it seem a place of promise and excitement, but rather it took on a gloomy, ominous, even unreal aspect, as though it had lost its health.

Most significant is the shift in attitudes regarding technology. In the decades leading up to the war, people celebrated the idea of progress and the newfound conveniences of technology. But after the war a more sober appreciation of the destructive potential of technology emerged. The machine gun was a vivid example of the deadly power that technology had loosed on the world. Even a more benign device such as the typewriter lost any innocence it might once have possessed. Instead of making people's lives easier, it seemed to have dehumanized them and transformed individual "life" into mechanical routine.

Vivien Eliot, *née* Haigh-Wood. On June 26, 1915, T. S. Eliot married Vivien (also spelled Vivienne) Haigh-Wood, an Englishwoman whom he had known for only a few months. Most critics agree that this unfamiliarity was the source of much unhappiness over the course of the couple's life together. Vivien was unlike any of the women Eliot had ever known. She struck him as "adventurous and vivacious," traits to which the young intellectual was understandably attracted

(Ackroyd, p. 63). For her part, Vivien saw the young Eliot as "a good-looking foreigner who could rescue her from the world of Edwardian respectability" (Ackroyd, p. 63). Her family belonged to the upper middle class, and she very likely felt stifled by a world of strict class divisions and social hierarchy.

Unknown to her fiancé, Vivien had suffered "nervous disorders"—migraines, mood swings, and insomnia—for quite some time; in fact, she had a history of illness dating back to childhood. He would learn this soon enough, for shortly after the wedding, Vivien suffered a nervous collapse. Actually, Eliot himself often succumbed to fits of nerves, and caring for his wife aggravated this tendency. No doubt the combination of their respective nervous conditions made the relationship unusually trying for both parties.

It is important to note that the Eliots' relationship went beyond a patient-nurse dynamic. Vivien not only had unrealized literary aspirations of her own, she also read and commented on her husband's work. A revealing example of Vivien's commentary appears in the manuscript of *The Waste Land*. The middle interlude of the second section of the poem, "A Game of Chess," which begins with, "My nerves are bad tonight . . ." is generally understood as an autobiographical description of the Eliots' marriage and one of Vivien's breakdowns; in the margin, Vivien has written, "WONDERFUL!" (Eliot, *The Waste Land*, lines 111-116).

Ezra Pound. An American poet and critic born in Hailey, Idaho, in 1885, Ezra Pound was one of the most influential men of letters in the early twentieth century. Pound moved to Europe in 1908 because he felt frustrated with the provincialism of American culture. He settled in London and for a time worked closely with Irish poet W. B. Yeats (see **"September 1913,"** also in *WLAIT 4: British and Irish Literature and Its Time*). Later Eliot became involved in the British avant-garde, taking special interest in Imagism and Vorticism, literary movements that attempted to convey concrete images instead of abstract impressions.

In some ways, Pound is responsible for T. S. Eliot's success. When the two men met in 1914, Pound was the more established of the pair. In fact, Pound professed to "have more or less discovered [Eliot]" (Pound to John Quinn in *The Waste Land*, p. 1). Indeed Pound, who had been acquainted with London's literary and artistic circles since 1908, did take the young Eliot under his wing. Not only did Pound introduce the London newcomer to other writers, but he also went to great lengths to get Eliot's work published. Besides sending Eliot's poetry to Harriet Monroe at the important journal *Poetry*, Pound encouraged Eliot to submit his work to the journals *Blast*, *The Egoist*, and *The Dial*.

The two often critiqued each other's poetry, suggesting revisions, and in the end, Pound played an instrumental role in Eliot's revision of *The Waste Land*. As evinced in the published manuscripts, he made several drastic editorial changes in the poem. Pound seemed to have a better sense of the overall structure of the poem, and so made editorial suggestions aimed at tightening the work. In retrospect, some critics believe that Pound gave the work a streamlined, polished shape and highlighted themes that Eliot had difficulty expressing, while others believe he misunderstood Eliot's message completely. Eliot himself considered Pound's advice invaluable and in recognition of such efforts, he dedicated *The Waste Land* to Pound, "*il miglior fabbro,*" a quote taken from Alighieri Dante's poem *Purgatorio*, which means "the better craftsman" (Southam, p. 136).

Lloyd's Bank. Eliot had hoped to make his living as a man of letters lecturing and writing reviews. Unfortunately, as of 1917, this plan had not yet worked out, and he was forced to resign his teaching position and gain regular employment to make ends meet. Eliot took a job in the Lloyd's bank Colonial and Foreign Accounts department as a temporary employee, then worked his way into a permanent position. For Eliot, the position was ideal. He found the work interesting, it gave him an opportunity to write in the evenings, and it proved less draining than his teaching position had been. Soon, however, the bank position would become stressful too. By 1920, Eliot had been promoted to the information department of the head office, where he worked on the prewar debts between Lloyd's and Germany. Although he apparently welcomed the assignment, he began to resent the time it took away from his literary ambitions. Ezra Pound tried to raise enough money for Eliot to subsidize his income so that he could quit his job at the bank. Living expenses, however, combined with Vivien's poor health, kept Eliot there through the initial publication of *The Waste Land* until the mid-twenties.

The Poem in Focus

Contents overview. Divided into five sections, *The Waste Land* has no single narrative thread. It has perhaps been most aptly described as "a web of subcutaneous nerve cells whose synapses fire periodically as we proceed through the poem" (Sigg, p. 195). There is no linear plot development or even a consistent timeframe: the poem jumps around in both time and space across centuries and continents. There is, though, a common focus. The poem features a variety of voices that all speak to life in the urban world of postwar London.

In addition to the five verse sections of the poem, *The Waste Land*, also has its own footnotes. The notes were not published with the poem in its initial serial form but appended to it by Eliot for the book publication. Some controversy has been stimulated by the notes. Readers have either viewed them as a key to solving the mystery of the poem, or they have scorned the notes as, in Eliot's own words, "bogus scholarship" meant to lead scholars on a "wild goose chase" (Eliot in Litz, p. 10). On one hand, the notes may provide a sense of Eliot's own intellectual trajectory during the poem's composition; on the other hand, they do not offer any overall interpretation of its meaning. A unified, self-sufficient work, the poem stands entirely on its own terms.

Contents summary. "In the Cage." *The Waste Land*'s epigraph comes from Petronius's *Satyricon*. In the *Satyricon*, Trimalchio, a rich, drunken millionaire, tries to surpass the outlandish tales told by his guests at a lavish banquet. The tale he tells is of the Cumaen Sibyl, a woman with prophetic powers who asked the Greek god Apollo for as many years as there were grains in her fistful of sand. Unfortunately, she forgot to ask for eternal youth to accompany immortality. Apollo granted her request, and as she aged, her body deteriorated until she was nothing but a bottle of dust. For his epigraph, Eliot chose the following quote: "Yes, and I myself with my own eyes even saw the Sibyl hanging in a cage; and when the boys cried at her: 'Sibyl, Sibyl, what do you want?' 'I would that I were dead,' she said in answer" (translation from Southam, p. 133). Setting the tone of the poem that follows, the question (cited in the original Latin and Greek) conveys a sense of eternal despair and futility. The quote's context, Trimalchio's drunken feast, may also suggest the widespread decadence and apathy of Eliot's own age.

"The Burial of the Dead." The title of this section is the title of the official burial service of the Anglican church. Its famous first lines contain a multitude of references from Geoffrey Chaucer's *Canterbury Tales* (in *WLAIT 3: British and Irish Literature and Its Times*) to Walt Whitman's "When Lilac's Last in the Dooryard Bloomed." Readers might feel an immediate sense of disorientation because April and spring, the time in which the section is set, are generally thought to be periods of regeneration and festivity, rather than of funeral services. Introduced in this section are a variety of images that all carry a sense of bleakness and sterility, in which a strange melancholy and nostalgic lyricism are mingled. The section includes references to a number of infertile gardens and "stony places," and uses several different voices and scenarios to depict modern life as a type of hell on earth: "Unreal City, / Under the brown fog of a winter dawn" where "death had undone so many" (*Waste Land*, lines 60-61, 63).

Aside from the initial medley of images attached to the seasons, the poem's opening serves to invoke or awaken a multitude of speakers. Many of these speakers are anonymous and it is often difficult to tell where one voice ends and another begins. After the opening, we meet Marie, whose persona is based on a Lithuanian countess; she reminisces about sledding in the mountains as a young girl, feeling frightened yet free. The next episode features an unidentified voice whose dark prophesies, mixing biblical with modern idioms, seem to be a direct address to the reader: "Son of man, / You cannot say, or guess, for you know only / a heap of broken images" (*Waste Land*, lines 20-22). We then hear from the Hyacinth Girl, who has a rendezvous in the Hyacinth Garden that results not in intimacy but incomprehension; looking into the "heart of light" afterwards, one sees only the sea—alien (its description is given in German), empty, and silent (*Waste Land*, line 41). Rather than the source of life, it is presented as cold and barren—a reflection of the city. After this, Madam Sosostris, another prophet, gives an enigmatic tarot reading. Finally, readers are forced to experience the numbness of the London commuters, traveling to and from work in a wintry haze that starts to resemble the circles of hell found in Dante's *Inferno*.

All of these episodes suggest that the world of the poem is in decline. Each of the voices is searching for a way to escape its present environment, whether through memory, travel, sex, the occult, or the comfort of routine. The problem is that nothing seems to work. Readers not only witness this failure, but they also become implicated in its truth.

"A Game of Chess." The title of this section comes from a play by Thomas Middleton (1580-

HE DO THE POLICE IN DIFFERENT VOICES: Part II.

A Game of Chess.

IN THE CAGE.

The Chair she sat in, like a burnished throne
Glowed on the marble, where the swinging glass
Held up by standards wrought with golden vines
From which one tender Cupidon peeped out
(Another hid his eyes behind his wing)
Doubled the flames of seven-branched candelabra
Reflecting light upon the table as
The glitter of her jewels rose to meet it,
From satin cases poured in rich profusion;
In vials of ivory and coloured glass
Unstoppered, lurked her strange synthetic perfumes
Unguent, powdered, or liquid- troubled, confused
And drowned the sense in odours; stirred by the air
That freshened from the window, these ascended,
Fattening the candle flames, which were prolonged,
And flung their smoke into the laquenaria,
Stirring the pattern on the coffered ceiling.
Upon the hearth huge sea-wood fed with copper
Burned green and orange, framed by the coloured stone,
In which sad light a carved dolphin swam;
Above the antique mantel was displayed
In pigment, but so lively, you had thought
A window gave upon the sylvan scene,
The change of Philomel, by the barbarous king
So rudely forced, yet there the nightingale
Filled all the desert with inviolable voice,
And still she cried (and still the world pursues)
Jug Jug, into the dirty ear of death, lust,
And other tales, from the old stumps and bloody ends of time
Were told upon the walls, where staring forms
Leaned out, and hushed the room and closed it in.
There were footsteps on the stair,
Under the firelight, under the brush, her hair
Spread out in little fiery points of will
Glowed into words, then would be savagely still.

"My nerves are bad tonight. Yes, bad. Stay with me.
"Speak to me. Why do you never speak. Speak.
"What are you thinking of? What thinking? What?
"I never know what you are thinking. Think".

I think we met first in rats' alley,
Where the dead men lost their bones.

"What is that noise?"

                    The wind under the door.

"What is that noise now? What is the wind doing?"

A page from the original manuscript of *The Waste Land,* with Eliot's handwritten notations.

1627). In the scene to which the poem refers, a game of chess serves as a metaphor for seduction, in which the movement of chess pieces corresponds to the maneuvers of the man and woman. The larger structure of the poem's "A Game of Chess" can be broken into three main parts: lines 77-110, 111-138 and 139-172. All three segments involve "romantic" scenarios, but they differ according to the socioeconomic status of the characters.

The first subsection is characterized by elevated description and heightened rhetoric. It opens with an allusion to Shakespeare's Cleopatra on her "burnished throne" (*Waste Land*, line 77; see ***Antony and Cleopatra*** in *WLAIT 3: British and Irish Literature and Its Times*). The woman described here lives like a queen in luxury, surrounded by tapestries, paintings, and perfumes. Amidst the elegance and opulence of the scene, the poem not only uses inflated language but it is also overtly sexual and artificial. The scene seems ripe for romance and seduction, until we realize that at least one of the pictures hanging on the wall is a rape scene from the classical myth of Philomel, who was turned into a nightingale after revealing the sordid details of being raped by her brother-in-law. This image of Philomel and the other "withered stumps of time" decorating the room seem to usher us out and down the stairs, as its female inhabitant sits brushing her hair. Though rich and sumptuous, the scene is sterile; there is no promise of passion here (*Waste Land,* line 104).

The second subsection of the poem leaves this world of luxury and affluence and shifts to a middle-class husband and wife. Readers witness a very strange exchange as both parties seem to be suffering from anxiety and nervous strain. The woman displays many of the same tendencies as Eliot's own wife, while the man might be experiencing shell shock. He is haunted by memories of the war and life in the trenches, and he might even be experiencing hallucinations and flashbacks. As in the first scene of the section, there is no romance or seduction here, despite the desperate attempts at conversation. Instead there is a failure to talk to, or at least understand each other. Both parties seem unstable and unable to see past their own anxieties to connect with the other.

Finally, in the third subsection, we are privy to a gossipy conversation taking place in a lower-class pub. Punctuated by the barman's calls of "HURRY UP PLEASE IT'S TIME," the account concerns Lil, friend of the subsection's anonymous speaker. Lil's husband gave her money to have her teeth pulled, and Lil has just spent it for another purpose—an abortion. (The delivery of her last child almost killed her.) Presently Lil is not feeling well, having taken the pills the druggist gave her to bring off the abortion. Not only is the speaker completely unsympathetic with Lil; she actually sides with the husband, telling Lil she should be ashamed to look so "antique" at 31: "Think of poor Albert / he's been in the army four years, he wants a good time / and if you don't give it him, there's others will" (*Waste Land*, lines 164, 148-149). The verse paints a degrading picture of lower-class married life. Such marriage, according to the poem, is all about sex and reproduction. There is no possibility of understanding or love; it is merely another sort of wilderness.

No matter which class one belongs to, "A Game of Chess" is just that, a game. Romance and friendship have mostly been reduced to unfeeling manipulation and strategic maneuvers, while lovers have become mere players, if not pawns. Ultimately, this section of the poem challenges modern assumptions about emotional intimacy and suggests that, if such intimacy is not already extinct, there may no longer be a place for it in contemporary urban society.

"The Fire Sermon." The title of this section of the poem originates in Buddhism. The Fire Sermon "was preached by Buddha to warn mankind against the fires of lust, anger, envy and the other passions that consume men" (Southam, p. 164). Accordingly, the poem presents several such scenarios. Echoes of Andrew Marvell's "To His Coy Mistress" run through this episode, foregrounding the idea of seduction and casting a dark shadow of urgency over the entire section. First, we visit the banks of the Thames River, apparently the recent scene of some festive summer evenings, but the magic of those evenings has dissipated and all that remains are garbage and disease. The focus zooms in on a rat crawling along the riverbank, recalling perhaps life, or rather death, in the wartime trenches, where rats fed on corpses strewn across the battlefield. (The middle-class husband, in the previous section, describes his home as a "rats' alley"—*Waste Land,* line 115). The riverbank sparks the memory of a shipwreck, as well as an Australian ballad from World War I about a brothel-keeper named Mrs. Porter, who was infamous for spreading venereal disease. From the low humor of the lines "O the moon shone bright on Mrs. Porter / And on her daughter / They wash their feet in soda water," the poem shifts to a rather mordant nightingale's, echoing the rape of Philomel from "A Game of Chess" (*Waste Land*, lines 119-201). Then we find ourselves back on the streets of London, only now it is later in the day and the commuters we met in "Burial of the Dead" are on their way home from work. The juxtaposition of such images of disease and defeat with images of domestic and commercial life, the tones—ranging from the lyrical to the bathetic—suggests something of the complexity of modern urban existence, conceived as simultaneously cheerful and sordid.

This section introduces Tiresias, whom Eliot conceived as "the most important personage in the poem, uniting all the rest" (*Waste Land*, p. 148). In "The Fire Sermon," Tiresias witnesses one of the poem's central events, an encounter between "the young man carbuncular" (carbuncles are large puss-filled acne) and the typist (*Waste Land*, line 231). In this brief portrayal, at once sober and acid, what begins as dinner evolves into a sexual encounter that seems mechanized and unemotional. The typist is bored, while the vain young man, apparently interested only in the sex, welcomes her indifference. Tiresias indicates that the scene is all too common, at least among the working class, and the poem incorporates an Elizabethan sonnet, which serves to further satirize the sentimentality of conventional love in a modern, urban setting. Any further thoughts on the event are cut off by the gramophone, which silences the typist's thoughts and takes the reader out of her flat and down to the Strand, where music can be heard from apartments, restaurants, and churches along the way.

The rest of the episode consists of additional voices from various times in history, each telling a tale of "love." First, the poem takes us onboard Queen Elizabeth's sixteenth-century barge, where the Queen flirts with the Earl of Leicester not because of any romantic interest, but as a part of a political power play. From the river barge, the poem travels to twentieth-century Moorgate, London's financial district, and then to Margate Sands, the resort where Eliot spent time in 1921 recovering from nerves and assembling the first three sections of *The Waste Land*. The section nears its close in ancient Carthage, recalling Vergil's *Aeneid* and the suicide of Queen Dido, who threw herself on a funeral pyre when her lover Aeneas left her to found Rome. Concluding the section are fragments of the *Confessions of Saint Augustine,* a self-examining treatise that discloses his uneasy youth and spiritual journey before finding refuge in the Roman Catholic Church.

"Death by Water." By far the shortest section of the poem, "Death by Water" originated as a much longer piece, but Pound excised the bulk of it. The title refers back to Madam Sosostris and her tarot reading: "Fear death by water" (*Waste Land*, line 55). In this short section, a Phoenician sailor's body drifts underwater as an anonymous speaker laments the tragedy of his early death.

Phlebas the Phoenician may represent Eliot's young friend Jean Verdenal, who drowned in the war, in which case this part of the poem could be elegizing Verdenal's premature death. Various implications can be discerned in the lines. They perhaps suggest the inevitability of death, or the process of material economic exchange, or the importance of self-knowledge. Certainly the ocean imagery connects to the other images of fluidity in the poem. The section might also refer to the Christian ceremony of baptism, which purifies souls for admission to the church. The ceremony's use of water, depending on the spe-

---

TIRESIAS

In his footnotes, Eliot claims that Tiresias serves, not as the poem's main character or central figure, but as its unifying persona. "What Tiresias *sees*, in fact, is the substance of the poem. . . . Just as the one-eyed merchant, seller of currants, melts into the Phoenician sailor, and the latter is not wholly distinct from Ferdinand Prince of Naples, so all the women [in the poem] are one woman, and the two sexes meet in Tiresias" (*Waste Land*, p. 148). Tiresias, according to Greek mythology, had lived as both a man and a woman. Because of these experiences, he was called to settle an argument between Zeus and Hera, the king and queen of the gods. They asked him whether a man or a woman experienced greater pleasure during physical intimacy. Tiresias supported Zeus's claim that the woman enjoyed it more, and as a result, Hera struck him blind. In Eliot's version of the myth, Tiresias is not only blind, but also shares male and female physical attributes: he is an "old man with wrinkled female breasts" (*Waste Land*, line 219).

---

cific practices of individual denominations, ranged from sprinkling a few drops on one's forehead to complete corporeal immersion.

"What the Thunder Said." Of "What the Thunder Said," Eliot observed that it was "not only the best part of the poem, but the only part that justifies the whole, at all" (Eliot in Southam, p. 185). Apparently Ezra Pound agreed with Eliot's assessment, because he made virtually no changes or suggestions to this final section of the poem. There are at least three layers of meaning interwoven into the section, all concerned with the question of salvation.

The title provides a key to the three layers: Christianity, the Grail Legend, and Eastern philosophy. In relation to Christianity, "What the Thunder Said" might contain a reference to Revelations and John's prophecy of the apocalypse, which was given to him as a scroll to eat. This scroll contained the mysteries of God. Themes of Christian damnation and salvation run through "What the Thunder Said." There are possible allusions to the plagues and droughts that God set upon the Egyptians and promised to deliver in Revelations. There are several references to Christ's last hours, from his last night spent in prayer in the garden of Gethsemane, to his betrayal by Simon with the cock's crow at dawn. There is "frosty silence in the gardens," and we hear the rooster cry "Co co rico co co rico" (*Waste Land,* lines 323, 392). The poem might also fore-

---

DADAISM

Some scholars have postulated that the "DA" of "What the Thunder Said" might also contain a contemporary reference to an anti-aesthetic art movement called Dadaism, which thrived from 1916-1922. The Dadaists, many of whom were close friends with Ezra Pound, celebrated the absurd and irrational. By its use of the term, *The Waste Land* may be suggesting that we as readers need to look beyond logical solutions to what resists systematic arrangement. Perhaps redemption can only come out of the complete breakdown and transformation of the waste land as we know it.

---

cast Christ's subsequent arrest by the Roman soldiers and the crucifixion: "the agony in stony places / The shouting and the crying" and "He who was living is now dead" (*Waste Land,* lines 324-25, 328). In lines 359-365, we walk with the disciples along the road to Emmaus (a village some distance from Jerusalem) on the day of Christ's resurrection. They are accompanied by a person whom they do not recognize, and in the poem an unidentified voice asks "Who is the third who is always beside you? / When I count, there are only you and I together / But when I look ahead up the white road / There is always another one walking beside you / Gliding wrapped in a brown mantle" (*Waste Land,* lines 359-363). The Gospel of Luke later reveals this unknown figure to be Christ after his resurrection. In addition to the Christian interpretation,

the third figure anecdote, says the poem's notes, recalls a memoir of an Antarctic expedition by the famous explorer Ernest Shackleton, in which the exhausted explorers hallucinate and imagine an additional traveler with them.

A second layer of meaning emerges from the section's references to Jesse Weston's study of Sir Galahad's quest for the Holy Grail. In this section of Eliot's poem, Sir Galahad approaches the Chapel Perilous, where the knight must face a final test of his courage before attaining the grail. We know that Galahad must bear witness to grotesque things, like "bats with baby faces, in the violet light"—an image belonging as much to the ambiance of European expressionism in the years before the Great War as to the world of medieval Gothic; we do not, however, know if Galahad passes his test and actually acquires the Grail (*Waste Land*, line 379). Late in the poem a rooster appears, recalling the disciple Peter's final betrayal of Christ; it may also be signaling the departure of the ghosts and terrible spirits from the Chapel, something that would signify Galahad's success. But the poem is ambiguous to the end and refuses to offer conclusive evidence of a new day.

The last layer of "What the Thunder Said" is rooted in "The Three Great Disciplines" of the *Upanishads*, treatises in the Sanskrit language on Hindu theology. Three groups of creatures approach their creator, Prajapti: gods, men, and demons. Each of them asks him for advice. To all, he answers, "DA." The gods interpret this as "control," as in "control yourselves." The men interpret it as "give," as in "give alms." Finally, the demons interpret it as "sympathize." After each interpretation, the poem offers a cryptic response about what each of these might mean. For example, after the command is interpreted as "Give," the poem asks "What have we given?" and posits: "The awful daring of a moment's surrender / Which an age of prudence can never retract" (*Waste Land*, lines 401, 402-403). The important point about the incorporation of the Sanskrit word is that it suggests that perhaps Christianity is not the solution to the problems of the Waste Land, nor is placing all faith in Sir Galahad's Holy Grail quest.

As the poem ends, its text accelerates and spins out of control. The phrases of the verse get shorter, and the languages change even more frequently until the world it has created explodes. We are left with "*shantih shantih shantih,*" a phrase that translates approximately to "the peace which passeth understanding." Perhaps the *Waste Land* we have experienced has been annihilated. If the poem has succeeded, it might be because, by its last line, we have escaped from this waste land and reached a completely new and unfamiliar place that we cannot yet understand because we do not recognize it.

Psychoanalysis. "My nerves are bad tonight," says a speaker in the second section of *The Waste Land*, bringing to the forefront the individual's psychological condition (*Waste Land*, line 111). In 1922, the *New York Evening World* proclaimed psychoanalysis "our most popular science" (North, p. 65). This trend was not limited to the United States. By the early 1920s, psychoanalysis, especially as represented by Sigmund Freud, had become extremely popular in Great Britain also. Suddenly pamphlets addressing anxiety, nervousness and how to cope with one's repressed instincts appeared, and consumers could purchase "products which promised to 'control Stage-Fright and other forms of nervousness' in addition to preventing colds and headaches" (North, p. 66).

In England, the acute problem of shell shock had amplified the urgency of psychological questions. A psychological condition that affected many survivors of the First World War, shell shock is more commonly known today as Post-Traumatic Stress Disorder. Sufferers typically experienced an event that aroused intense horror and/or could have resulted in their death. Soldiers who witnessed the deaths of fellow combatants, as well as nurses and doctors who tried to help the wounded and dying, often suffered from the trauma of these experiences. Symptoms might include intense flashbacks to the event, recurring dreams, or severe reactions to cues that resemble or remind the sufferers of their original trauma.

Initially, psychoanalysts thought that shell shock was linked to hysteria (a common female malady thought to result from over-stimulation). The prescribed treatment often involved some version of the Rest Cure, which required isolation, bed rest and no stimulation from the external world. In other words, patients should not think or talk about their experiences, nor should they attempt to read or otherwise distract themselves. Instead, they should simply relax.

This treatment was not only prescribed to those soldiers who suffered from shell shock. It was a much more general cure for a multitude of psychological ailments. T. S. Eliot and his wife, for example, suffered from nervous disorders, and both sought refuge in sanitariums at various stages of their union. It should be noted, how-

ever, that sanitariums do not have the same connotations of disease and mental illness that they may carry today. Indeed, Margate Sands, where Eliot spent three weeks in October of 1921 recovering from excessive stress, was a fashionable seaside resort. In any case, psychological disorders and anxieties were not regarded as criminal or deviant. The public accepted them as illnesses that were both explainable and scientifically treatable.

In England, the Bloomsbury set, a group of prominent artists and thinkers including Lytton Strachey, Clive Bell, Roger Fry, and Virginia Woolf, began to introduce Freud and psychoanalytic ideas to the general public. Lytton Strachey's brother, James Strachey, published English translations of Freud, and the project was subsequently adopted by Woolf's Hogarth Press. Not only did the writers of Bloomsbury publish these editions of Freud, but they also wrote pamphlets about the possible applications of psychoanalytic methods to understanding art.

When Freudian concepts such as repression and the unconscious became part of mainstream culture, the general public tended increasingly to focus on them. Psychoanalysis began to affect, if not produce, the behavior it sought to explain; it became obligatory to develop complexes (North, p. 67). People began to accept both the idea that they harbored a deep, impenetrable emotional region with themselves, and the idea that their behavior might not always stem from rational causes. They started to look for psychological explanations of patterns of behavior, and to acknowledge that the unconscious might influence individuals in peculiarly oblique ways.

The proliferation of these ideas had a significant impact on many fields of endeavor, such as politics, advertising, and literature. For example, the notion that advertising might do more than simply notify consumers of the availability of a product had not occurred to anyone before (North, p. 77). Now the popular enthusiasm for psychology encouraged advertisers to consider ways of manipulating the customer's desires.

The complicated relationship of "modern" literature to psychology was likewise becoming widely recognized. Works like *The Waste Land*, James Joyce's **Ulysses,** and Virginia Woolf's **Mrs. Dalloway** (also in *WLAIT 4: British and Irish Literature and Its Times*) were all regarded as psychological studies. This affiliation of literary works to psychology helps explain the extreme critical reactions that such works inspired. Readers might find the perceived exploration of an individual's psychology offensive (especially in the case of a character like Joyce's Leopold Bloom, who thinks about "base" matters such as masturbation and digestion) or they might find such an exploration fascinating. Probably the association helped *The Waste Land* get published, since it could be regarded as "a most distressingly moving account of Eliot's own agonized state of mind during the years which preceded his nervous breakdown" (Bush in North, p. 81). Marketing the poem as an extreme case study, given the popularity of all things psychological, might make it more appealing to readers.

Sources. Eliot's poetry assumes knowledge of a wide range of literary and cultural sources. *The Waste Land* draws upon classical mythology; English, French, and Italian poetry; Shake-

---

HE DO THE POLICE IN DIFFERENT VOICES

~

Originally, Eliot planned to call the poem, "He Do the Police in Different Voices," a quotation from *Our Mutual Friend*, by Charles Dickens. In this novel, "Sloopy is a foundling adopted by old Betty Higden, a poor widow. 'I do love a newspaper,' she says. 'You mightn't think it, but Sloopy is a beautiful reader of a newspaper. He do the Police in different voices'" (*The Waste Land*, p. 125). The title would have pointed up the dramatic nature of the poem and the different voices readers encounter along their journey through its landscape.

---

spearean drama; German opera; contemporary London landmarks; popular ballads; scientific and other learned treatises; biblical literature; and even Eastern philosophy. When the poem first appeared, its frequent deployment of allusions and quotations aroused widespread controversy. Many critics faulted the work for what they perceived as a lack of originality and even went so far as to accuse Eliot of plagiarism. However, other readers have suggested that Eliot's use of these sources represents an attempt to revitalize the great works of the past and reconstruct literary traditions.

Two main sources have often been used as "keys" to unlocking *The Waste Land*: Jesse Weston's *From Ritual to Romance* (1920) and Sir James Frazer's *The Golden Bough* (12 vols. 1890-1915). In the notes to the poem, Eliot implies that the secret to understanding *The Waste Land* lies in *Ritual to Romance*. In this work, Weston

investigates the occult myth of the Fisher King, an impotent king whose land is cursed to endure infertility until a stranger arrives to take up specific challenges. Eliot and Weston connect this myth to Christ and the Holy Grail (Southam, p. 128). In the Christian myth, the Grail is the cup used by Christ and his disciples at the Last Supper and later to catch the blood from his side at the crucifixion. The Grail gets lost, and a knight (in Arthurian legend, Sir Galahad) must find it in order to bring healing and restoration to the dying kingdom. The knight's quest takes him to the Chapel Perilous, where, like the stranger in the Fisher King myth, he must answer certain questions about the Grail to lift mankind's curse.

Eliot studied James Frazer's *The Golden Bough* while at Harvard and claimed to draw upon Frazer's elaborate study of primitive myth and ritual, especially the vegetation ceremonies that were meant to appease the "powers of nature and ensure the continuing cycle of the seasons, with the life of the new year to be born out of the old" (Southam, p. 129). Other important sources for *The Waste Land* include (but are not limited to) Dante's *Inferno* and *Purgatorio*, *The Confessions of St. Augustine*, the Bible, *The Tempest*, the Upanishads, and Baudelaire's *Fleurs du Mal*.

Eliot's practice of allusion has encouraged readers to search for a key to the poem somewhere outside its borders. Instead of grappling with the poem itself, they expect to find what it *means* in sources like *The Golden Bough*. But even a careful consideration of *The Waste Land*'s notes and sources does not provide a recipe for interpretation. The sources may help explain some of Eliot's own thought processes, or bring references into sharper relief, or promote an understanding of the poem's many echoes and voices. Ultimately, however, the disorientation experienced when reading *The Waste Land* cannot be remedied by an outside source, for this shock effect comprises the heart of the poem.

Literary context. The form of *The Waste Land* is unlike that of any work Eliot's contemporaries had ever encountered. It attempts, many critics agree, to mirror the so-called modern condition. According to this view, experience is broken, fragmented, alien and alienating. The world is out of joint and hopelessly equivocal. Thus, the poem consists of a montage of voices, echoes, and quotations. Inherent in this polyphonic form, in Eliot's ventriloquism, may be the suggestion that everything one can experience is necessarily secondhand. There is no truly original thought or expression—only the great storehouse of cultural forms waiting to be revived like discarded fashions. The decay of the life of language is reflected in the routinized and disembodied existence of human beings in the modern metropolis. In the face of such a drying up of the immediate sources of life, the poet can only wonder: "What shall [we] do now? What shall [we] do?" (*Waste Land*, line 130).

On the other hand, the poem can be viewed as attempting to inject new life into a culturally dead world. Though fragmentary, the quotations and echoes may be the only available lifeline out of the waste land of the modern world. Perhaps by harking back to the best thoughts and ideas of the past, the poem will somehow be able to rejuvenate a sense of literary tradition or culture. In any case, the consensus is that, in his rendering of the shattering incongruities of modern civilization, Eliot's poetic design and linguistic modulation are both groundbreaking and powerfully expressive. Unlike many other poets of the early twentieth century, Eliot did not write directly in conventional poetic forms. He incorporated them, usually ironically, when it suited his purpose, but he believed that poetry must change itself drastically in order to represent life in the modern world. In his view, conventional forms were not adequate to the modern condition because they implied a vision of order that was artificial and contrived.

Reception. Few poems have provoked such strong reactions from their readers as *The Waste Land*. Critics' original responses fell into two sharply opposed camps. While readers either loved the work or hated it, everyone recognized the impact that it would have on poetry and literature. The poem was undeniably innovative. Written in free verse, it made heavy use of literary allusions, refused linear or logical interpretations, and relied more on emotional impact than on any rational argument.

The opinions of the poem's detractors may best be represented by Louis Untermeyer, who shared his disdain in the *Freeman,* dismissing the verse as "a pompous parade of erudition, a lengthy extension of earlier disillusion, a kaleidoscopic movement in which the bright pieces fail to atone for the absence of an integrated design" (Untermeyer in Grant, p. 151). He also complained that "Mr. Eliot does not disdain to sink to doggerel that would be refused admission to the cheapest of daily columns" (Untermeyer in Grant, p. 152). Untermeyer faults the poet for writing about "low" subject matter, topics that are inappropriate for the newspaper, let

alone literature. The poem, said this and other reviews, had nothing real to say to the world. Instead it was merely a showcase of Eliot's own personal erudition. The references to Dante and Shakespeare were plain arrogance and episodes like the one featuring the "young man carbuncular" were included for their shock value alone.

In the *Double Dealer,* another more sympathetic reviewer charged that, though the poem

---

BRITISH OR AMERICAN?

~

T. S. Eliot was born and raised in St. Louis, Missouri. He spent his formative years in the United States, and he attended Harvard University. Only afterwards did he spend a significant amount of time abroad and move to England. It was not until 1927 that Eliot joined the Anglican church and adopted British citizenship—five years after *The Waste Land* was published. Why then, is it considered one of the landmark texts of twentieth-century British literature? Yes, *The Waste Land* features London landmarks and recalls many of the hallmarks of Britain's literary traditions, but it does not identify with these places or conventions. In fact, the sense of profound alienation the poem conveys depends on a lack of identification. Still many critics favor a retroactive inclusion of his works in the British canon. It can be argued that Eliot's religious conversion and adopted citizenship justify his inclusion. But a better explanation might be found in the sheer impact of *The Waste Land* on the mass of British literature to follow. No matter how Eliot saw himself, British or American, one cannot deny the monumental influence *The Waste Land* has had on subsequent generations of British writers. Certain poets, such as W. H. Auden, would follow Eliot's lead and write verse whose form reflected the condition of the modern world as they understood it. Others, like Philip Larkin, would rail against such "gibberish," which he thought was esteemed only for its outrageousness, and revert to traditional poetic forms that could more faithfully represent the human condition (Larkin, p. 23).

---

might make perfect sense to Mr. Eliot, to the average reader who "cannot read through Mr. Eliot's spectacles, it must remain a hodge-podge of grandeur and jargon" (J.M. in Grant, p. 170). While *The Waste Land* may well be a masterpiece, asserts this review, most readers will likely not find the poem satisfactory. Yes, it does contain "passages of extreme beauty," but only the poet can appreciate all of its intellectual and emotional associations because their significance is of such an individual nature (J.M. in Grant, p. 171).

Finally, there were critics who thought the poem a work of genius. Their reviews attempt to justify the disorientation that most readers experienced. Conrad Aiken, for example, claimed that the poem "has an emotional value far clearer and richer than its arbitrary and rather unworkable logical value" (Aiken in Grant, p. 160). Aiken praised the overall emotional impact, concluding his review with the proclamation that "the poem succeeds . . . by virtue of its incoherence . . . [and] its ambiguities" (Aiken in Grant, p. 161). What would otherwise be flaws become virtues because they are honest representations of modern experience.

—Erin Templeton

For More Information

Ackroyd, Peter. *T. S. Eliot: A Life*. New York: Simon & Schuster, 1984.

Eliot, T. S. *The Waste Land: A Facsimile and Transcript of the Original Drafts Including the Annotations of Ezra Pound*. Ed. Valerie Eliot. New York: Harcourt Brace Jovanovich, 1971.

————. *On Poetry and Poets*. London: Faber, 1957.

Fussell, Paul. *The Great War and Modern Memory*. New York: Oxford University Press, 1975.

Gordon, Lyndall. *Eliot's Early Years*. New York: Oxford University Press, 1977.

Grant, Michael, ed. *T. S. Eliot: The Critical Heritage*. 2 vols. Boston: Routledge and Kegan Paul, 1982.

Larkin, Philip. *All What Jazz*. London: Faber, 1970.

Litz, A. Walton. *Eliot and His Time*. Princeton, N.J.: Princeton University Press, 1973.

North, Michael. *Reading 1922: A Return to the Scene of the Modern*. New York: Oxford University Press, 1999.

Sigg, Eric. *The American T. S. Eliot: A Study of the Early Writings*. Cambridge: Cambridge University Press, 1989.

Southam, B. C. *A Guide to The Selected Poems of T. S. Eliot*. New York: Harcourt, Brace and Company, 1994.

What the Butler Saw

by

Joe Orton

The eldest of four children, Joe Orton was born to working-class parents in Leicester, England, on January 1, 1933, as John Kingsley Orton. After Joe failed his 11 plus exam, his mother, Elsie, sent him to the local Clark's College, a secretarial school, after which Joe worked for two years as a clerk. He hated clerking but developed an interest in acting, participating in a local amateur dramatic society. In 1951 Orton won a scholarship to the Royal Academy of Dramatic Art (RADA) in London, where he met his lifelong partner, Kenneth Halliwell. Together with Halliwell, Orton embarked upon a largely unsuccessful literary collaboration during the 1950s. In 1962 their collaboration came to an end when Orton and Halliwell were sentenced to six months imprisonment for defacing library books in north London's Islington Library. Prison represented a turning point for Orton. "Being in the nick," he told the *Leicester Mercury* in 1964, "brought detachment to my writing. I wasn't involved any more" (Orton in Lahr, p. 152). Orton learned also to despise "society," developing a style that came to be described as "Ortonesque"—"a peculiar mix of farce and viciousness, especially as it expresses itself in the greed, lust and aggression that lie just beneath the surface of British middle-class proprieties" (Charney, p. 124). Throughout his short period of critical and popular acclaim, Orton continued to live with Kenneth Halliwell, although the relationship was not monogamous, as Orton's sexually explicit diaries make clear. Halliwell suffered in-

---

THE LITERARY WORK

A farcical drama set in a private psychiatric clinic sometime in the 1960s; written in 1967 and first performed posthumously in 1969.

SYNOPSIS

As Dr. Prentice, a psychiatrist, attempts to seduce a young woman, he is interrupted by the arrival of his wife, and she is confronted by a hotel page boy with whom she had a liaison the night before. Chaos ensues through cross-dressing and concealment in a comedy of anarchic misrule.

---

creasingly from depression, in the end finding life, and life with Orton, unbearable: on August 10, 1967, Halliwell brutally murdered Joe Orton before taking his own life with 22 sleeping pills. From 1963 to 1967, Orton had completed a radio play followed by six theater plays (*The Ruffian on the Stair,* 1963; *Entertaining Mr. Sloane,* 1963-64; *The Good and Faithful Servant,* 1964; *Loot,* 1964-66; *The Erpingham Camp,* 1965; *Funeral Games,* 1966; and *What the Butler Saw,* 1967). Orton's most critically acclaimed farce, *What the Butler Saw* satirizes his struggle with Halliwell and the "sexual and psychological exploitation that dominated not only their own lives, but also the public imagination" (Lahr, p. 312).

Joe Orton

Events in History at the
Time of the Play

The Wolfenden Report on Homosexuality, 1957. The setting of the play has no specific date other than that it takes place sometime in the 1960s (Act One refers to the no-nonsense men and women of the sixties who are members of the local council). Indeed, many of the play's concerns can be understood as an expression of and dialog with the social and cultural climates of Britain in the relatively repressive 1950s and liberal 1960s.

Homosexuality was still a criminal offense while Orton was writing the play during the 1960s, although "Orton's involvement in theater spans the crucial period when the scope for homosexuals, both in British society and in the theater, was sharply contested" (Sinfield, p. 259). Up until the late nineteenth century, sodomy (legally any homosexual act was subsumed under this specific activity) was punishable by death. In practice, though, as social historian Jeffrey Weeks points out, "the death penalty was not applied after the 1830s and was finally removed in 1861 (to be replaced by sentences of between ten years and life imprisonment)" (Weeks, p. 100). The pioneering work of Sigmund Freud (1856-1939), contributed to moving homosexuality from its criminal status to the area of medicine.

Indeed, from the mid-1950s, social attitudes towards homosexuality and the representation of homosexuality in the theater began to change, as is evident from the findings and recommendations of the Wolfenden Report and the lifting of the Lord Chamberlain's ban on plays dealing with homosexual themes.

> The sickness theory of homosexuality was to have profound social resonance from the 1930s onwards, but even earlier many homosexuals themselves had a deeply rooted belief that they were sick. Oscar Wilde complained in prison that he had been led astray by 'erotomania' and extravagant sexual appetite which indicated temporary mental collapse. . . . With such a deeply rooted self-conception often went a willingness to accept a hegemony of (often dubious) medical knowledge and that in turn encouraged would-be cures, from hypnotism through to chemical experimentation and in the 1960s to aversion therapy. . . . The existence of a medical model was profoundly to shape the individualisation of homosexuality, and contribute to the construction of the notion of a distinct homosexual person.
>
> (Weeks, p. 105)

Orton is clearly skeptical and satirical about the methods and conclusions of the psychiatric profession, which he depicts in Dr. Rance's often erroneous analyses in *What the Butler Saw*.

The Wolfenden Report of 1957 was a bold step in the removal of private homosexual behavior from the sphere of public legislative interventions. In 1954 British Parliament appointed a Home Office departmental committee of 15 men and women to look into the laws on homosexual practices and the courts' treatment of people charged with homosexual offences. The Committee was chaired by Lord Wolfenden, and his Report on the Committee of Homosexual Offences and Prostitution (known as the Wolfenden Report) was published on September 3, 1957.

The Report recommended the decriminalization of homosexuality, a recommendation that would not be enshrined in law until July 27, 1967—a fortnight before Orton was killed. On that date, the Sexual Offences Act received Royal Assent, and homosexuality was partially decriminalized. Sex between men was legal if there were only two of them, they were over 21, and they were "in private" (i.e., no one else was in the house). Moreover, they could not be in the armed forces or the Merchant Navy, and the law applied only to England and Wales. Life imprisonment for sodomy was now reduced to two, five, or ten years, depending upon who was involved.

Orton was writing, then, in a climate of progressive social and sexual change, but it was one in which his own sexuality, and the sexuality he described in his plays, was still outlawed. In 1958 the Lord Chamberlain (a crown or royal official who was responsible for censoring the content of plays) removed the ban on drama with homosexual themes (in 1968 the office of Lord Chamberlain itself would be removed). This is, of course, not to say that dramatists hadn't found ways of incorporating homosexual issues in their earlier work. As Alan Sinfield argues: "In the heyday of Noel Coward (1930s-50s) audiences divided according to whether they could pick up hints of homosexuality. From the mid-1960s the split was hardly over decoding competence, but around a contest as to what could be said in public" (Sinfield, p. 264). In his play *Entertaining Mr. Sloane,* Orton wanted to explore different combinations of sexual relationships, and the bisexual Mr. Sloane, the play's central character, ends up being shared by brother and sister Ed and Kath: they will each have him for six months of the year. Orton was keen, too, to use the myth of Oedipus, and while the Freudian dynamics of the mother-son relationship are strongly hinted at in *Entertaining Mr. Sloane,* Orton doesn't quite break the taboo, as he does in *What the Butler Saw*: Mr. Sloane, it turns out, isn't really the son Kath had once given up for adoption. In *Sloane,* however, Orton was already subverting notions and constructions of conventional family life. These constructions of the family as bulwark of the state were ones that the government had been keen to protect: in a sense, Orton grew up with them. As Jeffrey Weeks observes: "The continuing official concern with the future of the family was demonstrated in a series of major commissions and reports, including those of Beveridge in 1942, the Curtis Committee on children in care in 1946, the Population Commission in 1949, the Morton Commission on Divorce in 1955, the Wolfenden Committee on homosexuality and prostitution in 1957, the Ingleby Committee on Children and Young Persons in 1960" (Weeks, p. 236).

In *What the Butler Saw* Orton stages moral outrage when a character expresses a desire for anything other than sex within heterosexual monogamous marriage. By staging outrage, he is also feigning outrage, since heterosexual marriage is clearly only one of many sexual identities available. His play features transvestitism, incest, homosexuality, bisexuality, and nymphomania, presided over not just by corrupt and imbecilic authority/parental figures, but also the revered politician and statesman, Sir Winston Churchill. By invoking Churchill, Orton was ridiculing a figure revered and respected in British Society, and he was also making an explicit (and irreverent) connection between politicians and sexual behavior. This was a timely connection: at the time of the play's performance, the Profumo Affair was still a fairly recent event, an affair that brought down the Conservative Government led by Churchill a decade earlier (1950-55).

The 1960s and the Profumo Affair. The front cover of Methuen's 1993 edition of Joe Orton's *Complete Plays* shows him mimicking what has

FROM LORD WOLFDEN'S REPORT ON HOMOSEXUALITY

Further, we feel bound to say this. We have outlined the arguments against a change in the law [for decriminalizing homosexuality], and we recognise their weight. We believe, however, that they have been met by the counter-arguments we have already advanced. There remains one additional counter-argument which we believe to be decisive, namely, the importance which society and the law ought to give to individual freedom of choice and action in matters of private morality. Unless a deliberate attempt is to be made by society, acting through the agency of the law, to equate the sphere of crime with that of sin, there must remain a realm of private morality and immorality which is, in brief and crude terms, not the law's business.

(Wolfenden, p. 24)

become an iconographic image of the 1960s: he imitates Christine Keeler's infamous pose, sitting astride a chair, ostensibly naked. The photograph marks Orton as being indelibly of the 1960s. By association, the photograph also invites us to regard him as scandalous, and the source of the scandal, the story behind the photograph, is both sexual and political.

What has come to be known as the "Profumo Affair" was a scandal that took place in 1963 while Orton was writing *Entertaining Mr. Sloane,* his first successful stage play. In the sordid real-life scandal, Christine Keeler was a high-class call girl who had an affair with John Profumo, then the British Defense Minister. The two were introduced by Stephen Ward, a homosexual who went on to commit suicide during the trial. Ward had also set Keeler up to have an affair with a Russian military attaché, and anxiety was particularly high since this was also the era of the Cold War, or the competition between communism and democracy for world supremacy. Anxiety prevailed about the vulnerability of state secrets. Profumo lied at first about his relationship with Keeler, but when the truth came out, he was forced to resign, and the scandal eventually brought down the Conservative Government.

John Lahr has argued that from a more recent vantage, the Profumo Affair seems "trivial." Yet it also was a vehicle through which to ask questions about authority figures. It was, says Lahr, "one of the decade's watersheds" (Lahr, p. 186). And it ushered in a new attitude. Evidence of this new attitude can be seen in *What the Butler Saw*'s satiric treatment of the revered wartime and post-war British Conservative Prime Minister, Sir Winston Churchill, who held office between 1940-45 and 1950-55. The play has much fun with sexual innuendo in relation to a statue of Sir Winston destroyed in a gas explosion that kills Geraldine Barclay's stepmother, known in the play as Mrs. Barclay. A missing part of the former Prime Minister (who died in 1965, two years before Orton wrote the play) is believed to have been embedded in Mrs. Barclay. The reappearance of this "missing part" becomes crucial to the play's denouement, though what the part is remains subject to innuendo; the audience must decide what is revealed in the box that Geraldine has at the end of the play. Whether it is a phallus or cigar, Orton is clearly drawing on a traditional symbol used in farce. In his essay "The dawn of farce: Aristophanes," Gregory Doborov points out that "the phallus was most likely the stock-in-trade of Old Comedy. Phallic jokes abound in [Aristophanes'] extant plays" (Doborov in Redmond, p. 21). The fate of the statue of Winston Churchill can be seen, then, as an anarchic gesture during a period of political and sexual instability and revision: Winston Churchill was (and to some extent still remains) the potent symbol of the British nation during a period of World War, but, for Orton, the representative of political authority is quite literally (and anarchically) castrated in his last play, with the removal and flaunting of his cigar/phallus.

Having fun with Freud. *What the Butler Saw* draws on more than changes in attitudes towards sexuality, politics and authority figures. The play satirizes the psychiatric profession, and in particular Dr. Rance, the government-appointed representative, whose "psychoanalytic prattle twists experience into meanings all its own" (Lahr, p. 314).

In an interview with the *Evening News*, shortly before his death, Orton commented specifically about psychiatrists and their apparent desire to make everything explicable. Orton himself remained open to the notion that perhaps things weren't meant to be taken too seriously, and it is the enormous wish to explain everything that his play mocks through the character of Dr. Rance, who invokes the psychoanalytic theories of Sigmund Freud (1856-1939).

Freud is widely regarded as the founding father of psychoanalysis. Collaborating with Joseph Breuer in the mid-1880s, Freud developed his theory that hysteria was symptomatic of a trauma that the patient was repressing. Although Freud would part company with Breuer, the theory endured, turning into the practice that we now recognize as psychoanalysis. Freud's greatest discovery was that of the existence of the unconscious: the site of primitive, often sexual, desires that are at odds with what is socially acceptable and civilized behavior. "Investigations along this path," says James Strachey (Freud's first German-English translator) "were what led Freud to his discoveries of the long-disguised secrets of the sexual life of children and of the Oedipus complex" (Strachey in Freud, pp. 21-22). Part of Freud's work was to uncover unconscious mental processes and "to understand why there is such strong resistance to their becoming conscious" (Freud, p. 21). *What the Butler Saw* clearly parodies this resistance when Dr. Rance cross-examines Geraldine: "She may say 'Yes' when she means 'No'. It's elementary feminine psychology" (Orton, *What the Butler Saw*, p. 26).

Freud postulated that both the infant boy and girl experience an Oedipal conflict prior to acquiring language and being socialized, although each gender experiences that conflict differently. The little girl, Freud believed, assumes that there is no difference between herself and the little boy and that her own sexual organs will grow to match those of the little boy, an assumption made possible by her unconscious acceptance that she has been castrated. "Her Oedipus complex culminates," Freud argued, in desire:

> [A] desire, which is long retained, to receive a baby from her father as a gift—to bear him a child. One has an impression that the Oedipus complex is then gradually given up because this wish is never fulfilled. The two wishes—

to possess a penis and a child—remain strongly cathected in the unconscious and help to prepare the female creature for her later sexual role.

(Freud, p. 321)

In Orton's play, Dr. Rance's analysis of Geraldine is seen to be entirely inappropriate and as self-deluding as he believes Geraldine to be: "It's also obvious to the meanest amateur, [Dr.] Prentice, that you resemble the patient's [Geraldine's] father. That is why she undressed herself. When I arrived on the scene she was about to re-enact the initial experience with her parent" (*What the Butler Saw*, p. 27). Orton's play parodies the assertiveness of Freudian thinking, which still informed attitudes towards sexuality and homosexuality in the 1950s and 1960s.

The Play in Focus

Plot summary. Act One begins in "A room in a private clinic" in the morning, though as we soon learn, the purpose of the clinic "isn't to cure, but to liberate and exploit madness" (*What the Butler Saw*, p. 32). Dr. Prentice, a specialist in "complete breakdown" is interviewing Geraldine Barclay, a young woman applying for the position as his new secretary. In the course of the questioning, she reveals that she has not seen her mother for some time, never knew her father, and had been brought up by a Mrs. Barclay, who has been recently killed in a gas explosion. The only other victim of the disaster was a statue of Sir Winston Churchill, parts of which were found embedded in her stepmother. Also in the course of the questioning, Dr. Prentice reveals that he himself once stayed overnight in the Station Hotel, where Geraldine's mother, who had worked there as a chambermaid, was "the victim of an unpleasant attack" (*What the Butler Saw,* p. 8). He then asks Geraldine to undress, as though this were part of the normal procedure for an interview. But just as she has undressed and is lying naked behind the consulting-room screen, Mrs. Prentice appears unexpectedly, demanding to know to whom Dr. Prentice is talking.

Mrs. Prentice has returned unexpectedly from a meeting with a women's group to which she belongs; prior to the meeting, she had spent the night in the aforementioned Station Hotel, where she had encountered Nicholas Beckett, a hotel page boy, and with whom she had entered into some sort of sexual liaison. He then arrives and threatens Mrs. Prentice with blackmail over some pornographic photographs he had taken of her,

and he also demands the post of secretary to Dr. Prentice. Mrs. Prentice disappears into the psychiatric ward, and Dr. Prentice (for no apparent reason) presses money into Nick's hand before turning to Geraldine, who is still naked and hiding behind the curtain. The doctor asks Geraldine to leave. But each time he tries to return her clothing, he is caught in the act, which leads Mrs. Prentice to assume that he has taken up cross-dressing.

The other character who accelerates the pace of the farce is Dr. Rance, a psychiatrist and government representative. Upon discovery of the naked Geraldine, he believes Dr. Prentice's assessment that she is a patient suffering from the delusion that she had applied for the post of Dr. Prentice's secretary. Geraldine's predicament worsens; as the farce develops, Dr. Rance certifies her insane and commits her to his psychiatric institution. The plot then turns upon the search for the "missing" Geraldine, Mrs. Prentice's attempts to secure the secretarial post for Nick, and Dr. Prentice's increasingly manic attempts to conceal Geraldine's clothes. Just when it appears that things cannot get any more complicated for Dr. Prentice, a policeman, Sergeant Match, appears at the door.

Nick fears that he will be turned over to the police. As he confesses to Dr. Prentice, Mrs. Prentice was unwilling for their sexual encounter to go very far, so he turned his attentions to a group of schoolgirls at the hotel, and it's for this that he fears arrest. But Dr. Prentice realizes that he himself is also in a terrible predicament since Geraldine is still in the psychiatric clinic, but is also being pursued as a missing person. Fortuitously Nick has just returned Mrs. Prentice's dress and wig from the dry cleaners, which prompts Dr. Prentice to suggest that Nick impersonate Geraldine by wearing Mrs. Prentice's clothes. Nick's impersonation will help conceal the fact that the real Geraldine is still concealed in the clinic. As Nick undresses down to his underwear, Mrs. Prentice returns, leading her to assume (we presume) that her husband has homosexual desires towards Nick: "This folly will get you struck off the Register" (*What the Butler Saw*, p. 41).

As Dr. Rance prepares to enter the room, Geraldine, now cross-dressed in Nick's hotel uniform, hides behind the curtains while Nick enters from the dispensary also cross-dressed in Mrs. Prentice's clothing. Mrs. Prentice enters at precisely this moment, and the cross-dressed Nick takes her by surprise; she thinks she rec-

Richard Wilson and Debra Gillet in a 1995 stage production of *What the Butler Saw* at London's National Theatre.

ognizes Geraldine, whom Nick is now impersonating. Sergeant Match then enters and accuses Nick/Geraldine of possessing the missing part of Winston Churchill.

Act Two, which begins only a minute later in terms of the action of the drama, focuses on the relationship between biological sex, gender identity, and sexual identity. Geraldine accuses Dr. Prentice of scandalous conduct. Duped by her clothing, Sergeant Match thinks she is a boy, not a girl, and so assumes that Geraldine/Nick is accusing Dr. Prentice of making homosexual advances towards a minor. After a series of verbal wranglings between Dr. Prentice, Dr. Rance and Sergeant Match, Rance decides that he should conduct an examination of Geraldine. As Geraldine tries to extricate herself from this fate, she lets slip that she would not enjoy sex because she might become pregnant, leading Dr. Rance to suppose that the "boy" thinks he is a girl, which prompts Geraldine to exclaim in despair, "I'm not a boy! I'm a girl!" (*What the Butler Saw*, p. 57). Her assertion of the facts can only lead to Dr. Rance's psychoanalytic distortion of them, leaving him to conclude that the "boy" needs to think of himself as a girl in order to minimize "his" guilt about "his" homosexuality.

Dr. Rance, still convinced that Geraldine is a boy, takes "him" off to a padded cell, since "Rampant hermaphroditism must be discouraged" (*What the Butler Saw*, p. 63). As the sheer absurdity of the play mounts, Nick suggests that he impersonate the Sergeant so that he can arrest himself. Once arrested, he reasons, "we can write me off" (*What the Butler Saw,* p. 63). Nick then reappears pretending to be his own brother, now dressed as a policeman, and claiming to have arrested Nick—which would account for his apparent disappearance. The Sergeant takes the tranquilizers offered by Dr. Prentice as Nick disappears to the summer house to finish getting dressed. There follows a series of farcical moments with characters leaving and entering the stage—Dr. Prentice leaves as Mrs. Prentice enters and Nick re-enters wearing only his underpants and Sergeant Match's helmet. Mrs. Prentice declares that the clinic is like a madhouse—whereupon Dr. Rance enters and, once again, misreads a statement of factual truth for fantasy: when she says she keeps seeing naked men, Dr. Rance wants to know "When did these delusions start?" (*What the Butler Saw*, p. 66).

In the meantime, Dr. Prentice and Nick reconvene, whereupon they find the drugged

Sergeant and dress him in Mrs. Prentice's dress. Mrs. Prentice sees Dr. Prentice carrying the drugged and cross-dressed body of the real Sergeant into the shrubbery, and thinks he is dragging a woman into the bushes, which leads Dr. Rance to assume that Dr. Prentice has murdered his secretary. In Dr. Rance's mind, the episode confirms his hypothesis that this is a story of "incest, buggery, outrageous women and strange love cults catering for depraved appetites" (*What the Butler Saw*, p. 71).

Events begin to climax when Nick asks Dr. Prentice to put on the straitjacket; Sergeant Match appears wearing a leopard-spotted dress and declaring himself ready for examination; and Geraldine, wearing Nick's uniform, staggers in from the garden. Dr. Prentice tries to reassert order by asking everyone to return their rightful clothes to each other. But more chaos ensues—clothes are only half swapped and returned. Eventually, with all the characters assembled, Dr. Prentice confesses that he had been about to seduce Geraldine, Geraldine corroborates this, and Dr. Rance asserts his belief that Geraldine has been the victim of an incestuous attack, which will turn out to be technically true, since Dr. Prentice will soon be revealed as Geraldine's biological father.

Geraldine, to her sorrow, has lost part of an elephant charm. Rance produces the brooch from his pocket, whereupon Nick declares that he has one too—and when they are pieced together, they make a pair. Mrs. Prentice then announces that when she was a young woman she was raped in a linen cupboard—and the man who raped her left the brooch as a partial payment for what he had done. As a result of the rape (oddly, what Mrs. Prentice calls her own misdemeanor) she bore twins, but, engaged as she was to a promising young psychiatrist, she left the twins as foundlings at either end of the town in which she lived. In fact, she is Nick and Geraldine's mother. Dr. Prentice then comes forward—he gave the brooch to the chambermaid and so is revealed as the father of the twins. The moment of their conception, it turns out, was precious to both Dr. and Mrs. Prentice and seemed to be an act of mutual consent.

Sergeant Match then descends as a *deus ex machina*, asking for the missing part of Winston Churchill. Geraldine confesses that she has a box that the undertaker handed to her after her stepmother's funeral. Dr. Rance is filled with admiration at the sight of the missing part. With the resolution of the play, a lot of them leave "weary,

bleeding, drugged and drunk" as they climb the rope ladder "into the blazing light" (*What the Butler Saw*, p. 92).

Seventeenth-century parallels. The play carries an epigraph from *The Revenger's Tragedy*, which has prompted at least one critic to read *What the Butler Saw* in the tradition of Jacobean tragedy, a popular literary genre during the reign of James I (1603-25).

> *What the Butler Saw* is a virtual compendium of the most outrageous excesses of Jacobean drama transposed into a modern context—an assimilation of such standard motifs as the changeling, inadvertent incest, madness, and tragicomic violence into a twentieth-century setting.
>
> (Hutchings in Redmond, p. 228)

"Lunatics are melodramatic," says Dr. Rance in the play, an allusion to the twentieth-century context (*What the Butler Saw,* p. 71). The twentieth-century setting of a seventeenth-century genre is readable in terms of the questions that were evolving during the 1960s about authority figures (the psychologist, the politician), as well as in what this more recent drama was now allowed to express. As we see in the play, every time Dr. Prentice tries to make good his misdemeanors, his situation becomes more chaotic; meanwhile, each time Dr. Rance, representative of Her Majesty's Government, tries to interpret the situation, he misreads and gets wrong what has in fact happened. Dr. Rance, as the representative of both Government and Crown, is unable to see the disorder and madness around him. Moreover, argues Hutchings, in the light of Orton's satire upon those in positions of authority—politicians, policemen, psychiatrists—Rance is responsible for perpetuating forms of madness, seeing only what he wants to see, and pathologizing what appears to be non-pathological. Finally, Rance's name "contains an obvious pun on 'rants'—that most frequent of all symptoms of theatrical madness in the Renaissance" (Hutchings in Redmond, p. 228).

Literary context. On March 14, 1967, Orton noted in his diary that he had just seen a poster advertising a film called "LIBIDO MEANS LUST":

> It said "What happens when a sadistic sex-maniac falls in love!" On the way home I noticed a crit [critical review] of THE DIARY OF A MADMAN which is being presented, for four weeks, at the Duchess with Nicol Williamson. I thought how fashionable madness is at the moment. The film of the *Marat/Sade* is just out.

Of course it's the perennial fascination of most people with watching lunatics. Four hundred years ago they'd've gone to Bedlam for the afternoon. Now a director and actors recreate a madhouse in a theater. Let's look at mad people. At queer people. They only have to look in their mirrors. Kenneth H. said "In *What the Butler Saw* you're writing of madness." "Yes," I said, "but there isn't a lunatic in sight—just doctors and nurses."

(Orton, *The Orton Diaries*,
Diary 14, March 1967, p. 115)

But if Orton was inspired by a spate of fashionable madness, he was also aware of contemporary productions of classical farces: Victorien Sardou's *Let's Get a Divorce*; Georges Feydeau's *A Flea in Her Ear*, and Tom Stoppard's *Rosencrantz and Guildenstern Are Dead*.

The difference between comedy and farce, for John Dryden, was that "Comedy presents us with the imperfections of human nature. Farce entertains us with what is monstrous and chimerical" (Marcoux in Redmond, p. 132). According to this definition, to see Orton's achievement as comedy is to ignore the savagery of his writing and his humor. *What the Butler Saw* invokes many of the familiar features of traditional farce (for example, disguises, mistaken identities, and foundlings). "With the possible exception of Tom Stoppard," declared literary scholar William Hutchings, "no contemporary English playwright has written with more conscious awareness of the literary tradition within which he works" (Hutchings in Redmond, p. 227). The characteristics of ancient Greek farce are present, too, that is, the farce of Aristophanes: "rebellion, the destruction of authority, the mechanical, tit-for-tat, deception, the violent, the festive, the 'inflexible mind-set', and the absurd" (Doborov in Redmond, p. 26). These features can be seen partly in the unremittingly violent and bleak end to the play when the characters exit "drunk, dumb, bruised and bloody" (*What the Butler Saw*, p. 92). The violence accords with descriptions of farce that require the innocent to suffer along with the guilty, the co-presence of physical and psychological violence, and a loss of control veering towards disaster. In such farce, argues J. Paul Marcoux, "Plot seems little more than a chain of events, while motives are either non-existent or obviously forced" (Marcoux in Redmond, p. 132). While *What the Butler Saw* conforms to much of what he describes as farce, it is also a tightly plotted play that does have a rationale in its satiric purpose.

Reception—"Brighton Old Ladies Shocked." *What the Butler Saw* was performed posthumously at the Queen's Theatre in London, March 5, 1969, with an esteemed cast: Stanley Baxter played Dr. Prentice, Coral Browne played Mrs. Prentice, and Dr. Rance was performed by the veteran actor Sir Ralph Richardson. The play's initial reception was troubled. Prior to its West End debut at the Queen's Theatre, the play had been tried out in the more provincial setting of Brighton. At this performance, Stanley Baxter recalled old ladies violently destroying their programs. Sir Ralph seemed ill at ease with Orton's language and was faulted by the critic Hilary Spurling for a performance in which he seemed not to actually know what he was saying. On opening night at the Queen's Theatre, Stanley Baxter perceived the mood to be one of "militant hate" (Lahr, p. 333). Someone shouted for Sir Ralph to return his knighthood.

Critics were divided. Charles Marowitz in his book *Confessions of a Counterfeit Critic* thought that the audience's initial response to the play accounted for one of the "grossest miscarriages of theatrical justice ever annaled" and that *What the Butler Saw* "is Orton's masterpiece" (Marowitz, p. 155). Harold Hobson, on the other hand, felt that the play was "a wholly unacceptable exploitation of sexual perversion," and he went on to see in this degradation the seeds of Orton's violent end (Hobson in Lahr, p. 334). Among those who disagreed was Frank Marcus, writer of *The Killing of Sister George*, a play dealing explicitly with lesbian relationships. Marcus predicted, correctly, as it turned out, that *What the Butler Saw* would be "a comedy classic of English literature" (Marcus in Lahr, p. 334). It was in 1975, when Lindsay Anderson staged a revival of Orton's plays at London's Royal Court Theatre, that the reputation of the play was secured.

—Tracy Hargreaves

For More Information

Charney, Maurice. *Joe Orton*. London: Macmillan, 1984.

Denning, Alfred. *The Profumo Affair*. London: Pimlico, 1992.

Freud, Sigmund. "The Dissolution of the Oedipus Complex." In *On Sexuality*. Pelican Freud Library. London: Penguin, 1987.

Lahr, John. *Prick Up Your Ears: The Biography of Joe Orton*. London: Penguin, 1978.

Marowitz, Charles. *Confessions of a Counterfeit Critic: A London Theatre Notebook*. London: Eyre Methuen, 1973.

Orton, Joe. *Complete Plays.* London: Methuen, 1993.

———. *The Orton Diaries.* Ed. John Lahr. London: Methuen, 1986.

———. *What the Butler Saw.* London: Methuen, 1969.

Redmond, James, ed. *Themes in Drama: Farce.* Cambridge: Cambridge University Press, 1988.

Sinfield, Alan. "Who Was Afraid of Joe Orton?" *Textual Practice* 4 (1990):259-277.

Weeks, Jeffrey. *Sex, Politics & Society: The Regulation of Sexuality since 1800.* 2nd ed. London: Longman, 1989.

Wolfenden, Sir John. *Report of the Committee on Homosexual Offences and Prostitution.* London: HMSO, 1957.

Women in Love

by

D. H. Lawrence

D. H. Lawrence, son of a coal miner and a former schoolteacher, was born in the English Midlands in 1885. Lawrence attended Nottingham High School as a scholarship student and later Nottingham University College, where in 1912 he met and eloped with Frieda von Richthofen, the aristocratic German wife of one of his teachers. In 1913 he published his great autobiographical novel *Sons and Lovers*, and began work on a long novel with a female protagonist, to be called *The Sisters*. Eventually this project split in two. The first half, now called *The Rainbow*, was published in 1915, and immediately suppressed for obscenity. The second half, *Women in Love*, was rewritten between 1915 and 1917, during World War I—a period of intense bitterness in Lawrence's life. Because of the fate of *The Rainbow*, and because of the threat of libel suits, *Women in Love* was first published privately in the United States in 1920, and only later published in England. After the war Lawrence and Frieda wandered the world, searching for a congenial culture and a climate that would be favorable to Lawrence's tuberculosis. Lawrence died in Vence, France, in 1930. His *Women in Love*, though focused on personal relationships, reflects a broader disillusionment in postwar British society.

Events in History at the Time of the Novel

World War I—the Great War. Lawrence wrote in the Foreword to the first American edition of

---

THE LITERARY WORK

A novel set in England and Austria just before or after World War I (1914-18); published in 1920.

SYNOPSIS

The sisters, Ursula and Gudrun Brangwen, are attracted, respectively, to Rupert Birkin, a school-inspector and misanthropic philosopher, and Gerald Crich, the son of a wealthy coal-mine owner. Ursula and Birkin end up happily, if unconventionally, married, but Gudrun's affair with Gerald falls into a destructive spiral, ending in Gerald's death.

Women in Love: "it is a novel which took its final shape in the midst of the period of war, though it does not concern the war itself. I should wish the time to remain unfixed, so that the bitterness of the war may be taken for granted in the characters" (Lawrence in Farmer, p. 485). At one point, Lawrence thought of calling the novel *Dies Irae*, the "Day of Wrath." Mark Kinkead-Weekes perceptively calls it "a 'war novel' no less for being set in a world apparently at peace," because the impulse to violence is so near the surface in all of the characters (Kinkead-Weekes, p. 334).

The Great War of 1914-18, which we now call World War I, caused "bitterness" in many, many people besides D. H. Lawrence. It ended a long period in which Europeans had allowed

D. H. Lawrence

themselves to believe that civilization had reached an unprecedented pinnacle, and that moral progress would inevitably accompany material progress. The novelist Henry James wrote, "The plunge of civilization into this abyss of blood and darkness . . . is a thing that so gives away the whole long age during which we have supposed the world to be, with whatever abatement, gradually bettering" (James in Fussell, p. 8). But beyond any abstract significance, there were the brute facts of the war itself, its unprecedented and futile waste of human life. The industrialization of warfare had made "battles" and battlefields obsolete, and produced two evenly matched forces, equipped with punishing artillery, machine guns, and poison gas, but unable to defeat each other. For four years, the trenches faced each other for 400 miles, from the North Sea to the Swiss border. Most of the time, Fussell reminds us, the soldiers spent "sitting or lying or squatting in place below the level of the ground"; but even in these "quietest times, some 7,000 British men and officers were killed and wounded daily" (Fussell, p. 41). In a major assault, as at the Somme River in France on July 1, 1916, 60,000 (half of the attacking force) could be killed or wounded in one day (Fussell, p. 13). Moreover, until near the end of the war, all of the major assaults, on both sides, failed, either because of poor planning or because the dec-

imated armies could not hold on to their conquests. People joked, half-seriously, that the war would still be going on in 1950 (Fussell, p. 73).

Lawrence had opposed the war from the start. He even planned to collaborate with Bertrand Russell, despite their very different philosophies, on an antiwar magazine. But as Paul Delany points out in *D. H. Lawrence's Nightmare*, he did not take the professed causes of the war very seriously, or even hold for long to the socialist view that a corrupt ruling class was to blame. "What really mattered," to Lawrence, explains Delany, "were the deep currents of emotion in the masses of all European countries that made them eager to join in. Fundamentally, this had to be a collective desire for death" (Delany, p. 29).

As the war dragged on, conditions at home worsened. Universal conscription was introduced, and the Defense of the Realm Act permitted the government to take action against dissidents with only the barest semblance of due process. That Lawrence had a German wife—a cousin, moreover, of the notorious German aviator, the Red Baron—did not help. The Lawrences were interrogated by the police a number of times, and finally evicted from their home in Cornwall, for fear that they were signaling to German submarines. Lawrence was repeatedly called up for humiliating draft physicals, though he was always let off on the grounds of incipient consumption (which, of course, he did not want to admit he had). Looking back on this period later, Lawrence saw it as the end of all that was valuable in English civilization. "It was at home the world was lost. . . . At home stayed all the jackals, middle-aged, male and female jackals. And they bit us all" (Lawrence in Fussell, pp. 89-90). Lawrence shows a fury here that, the historian Paul Fussell reminds us, was not unique; it was shared by many disillusioned soldiers returning from the war front, who regarded the smugly patriotic stay-at-homes as their exploiters and oppressors. None of this is explicit subject matter in *Women in Love*. The war is clearly not going on during the novel; whether it takes place before the war, or in some putative after, we cannot tell. Only once, at the very end—when Ursula contemplates Gerald's corpse, and Birkin's hopeless sorrow—is the war evoked: "Ursula could not but think of the Kaiser's: "Ich habe es nicht gewollt" [I didn't want this]" (Lawrence, *Women in Love*, p. 581). Here the frame is broken, and Lawrence's intent becomes clear: the real and the fictional tragedies are interchangeable, both victories of the collective desire for death.

Coal-mining towns. Great Britain ranked highest in the world in coal output in the early 1900s, and coal was the country's major male employer. In 1911, 24.5 percent of the British male workforce consisted of miners. Gerald Crich's father in *Women in Love* owns a coal mine. Such a father would in reality occupy a central position in local society. Lawrence's own father worked for the mine owner Thomas Barber of Barber Walker Company in Eastwood in Nottinghamshire. A charitable business magnate, Barber apparently took a somewhat paternalistic interest in the miners' lives. He contributed to religious denominations in the community, encouraged his company managers to involve the miners in sports, ran an Ambulance Training Corps for the local youth, and otherwise promoted a sense of belonging to the company. He was an ostensibly benevolent mine owner, and there were a few more like him.

Below the mine owner were managers and engineers, and beneath them were "butties." Until the middle of the nineteenth century, a company would sink a shaft into earth, then contract with a butty to provide the working capital to operate the mine; the butty would hire, supervise, and pay the work force, often in goods rather than cash. Among the richest in town, the butty commanded an interest in local shops where the miners would spend their pay. The power of the butty diminished as the century wore on, and mining methods changed. A so-called "little butty system" gained prominence. Longwall mining involved 30-50 meter stretches of the face of a mine, which were worked in teams of about ten men. In charge of the men was a little butty, a supervisor who no longer paid for the running of a mine pit as in the past nor had any say in how it was worked. All that the little butty controlled was a small gang of men whom he recruited and paid from the contract price for working his stretch. There was a concomitant drop in the butty's status. Now he was not part of the genuine middle-class, but he anyway retained a higher status and income than ordinary miners, who showed continuing resentment for the butties. Lawrence's father was a little butty for the Barber Walker Company.

Other changes transpired in Nottinghamshire and other mining regions from the nineteenth century into the early twentieth century. New industries and developments in transportation transformed the village into the town and a town like Nottingham into a modern metropolis. In the coalfield districts, the majority of the inhabitants became occupants of medium-sized towns. The transformation was riveting: "From an agricultural community to a village of skilled workmen and from such a community to a mining and factory town and finally to a fully urbanised and partly suburbanised area. . . . These changes have forced upon the workers a paroxysm of social readjustment" (Gilbert, p. 169).

Helping the miners cope with the readjustment to changing work patterns was the union, or Nottinghamshire Miners' Association (NMA). The union hired a small group of paid officials, not more than six in the 1910s, and its early leaders were proponents of conciliation rather than conflict. Most of the unions' leading personalities were butties, and they identified with conservative or right-wing politics. In fact, a vice-president of the NMA in 1919, William Holland, was also leader of the right-wing political group known as the British Workers' League (BWL).

The right wing thrived in the Barber Walker Company mine pits, where Lawrence's father worked. At the Moor Green pit, a butty named Joe Birkin enjoyed extremely close relations with owner Thomas Barber. "Major Barber," recalled Birkin wistfully during a 1926 labor dispute, "was a coalowner, but he was a gentleman in every sense . . . if only all the coalowners . . . had the same feeling for justice" (Gilbert, p. 183).

The *Women in Love* character Thomas Crich is clearly modeled on Thomas Barber, and the reforms that his son Gerald introduces were actually going on in Lawrence's time:

> New machinery was brought from America. . . . [A]ll the control was taken out of the hands of the miners, the butty system was abolished. Everything was run on the most accurate and delicate scientific method, educated and expert men were in control everywhere, the miners were reduced to mere mechanical instruments. They had to work hard, much harder than before, the work was terrible and heartbreaking in its mindlessness.
> (*Women in Love*, p. 304)

Lawrence, in his editorial voice, calls this kind of automation "the first great phase of chaos, the substitution of the mechanical principle for the organic" (*Women in Love*, p. 305).

Changing sexual roles. The status of women was changing enormously in Lawrence's lifetime. According to literary historians Sandra M. Gilbert and Susan Gubar, the years 1900 to 1920 saw in America, a "1000 per cent" increase in the number of women enrolled in public colleges, and the increase in England was "almost equally impressive" (Gilbert and Gubar, vol. 1, p. 33). In addition to the advances in education, the era of the First World War (1914-18) called for massive numbers of women to enter the work force, filling previously male-occupied places in industry. As a result, men often felt as assaulted on the home front as they were on the military front itself" (Gilbert and Gubar, vol. 1, p. 34). All this advancement was capped by what people of the time perceived as ultimate triumph for females: women's winning the right to vote in England and in America. Women were becoming prominent in many disciplines—the arts, psychology, anthropology. Research in anthropology, some of it conducted by women, encountered evidence that, in prehistory, a Great Mother goddess had preceded the patriarchal gods. Thanks to Sigmund Freud and Havelock Ellis, among others, there was "a radical alteration in the very conception of female sexuality" (Gilbert and Gubar, vol. 1, pp. 34-35). Much on the public mind, in place of the old image of women as angel in the house, contentedly nurturing her husband and raising their children, was a stereotype of the New Woman—professionally ambitious and willing to consider sexual relations outside of marriage. As *Women in Love* begins, Ursula and Gudrun are having a cynical conversation about marriage that would have fit the stereotype perfectly. The sense of "male dispossession" and anxiety in the face of these changes is, Gilbert and Gubar argue, one of the great and neglected themes of modernism—the literary movement that had gained currency during their time.

Lawrence himself makes an interested, mixed case in this regard. As a child, he identified with his mother much more than with his father. Also, in the first flush of his marriage with Frieda, while he was writing his initial novel about Ursula Brangwen, *The Rainbow*, Lawrence felt "that men should go to women to get their 'souls fertilized by the female' . . . in order to access a vision, one that 'contains awe and dread and submission' on the part of the man, 'not pride or sensuous egotism and assertion'" (Nixon, p. 15). But by 1915, the marriage with Frieda was going less smoothly, and, Gilbert and Gubar argue, Lawrence was participating in a general male feeling that women who benefitted economically by the war—or even more, those who tried to shame men into fighting—were essentially vampires. Gilbert and Gubar quote a poem of Lawrence's from 1915: "Why am I

bridegroom of War, war's paramour? . . . / And why do the women follow us, satisfied, / Feed on our wounds like bread, receive our blood / Like glittering seed upon them for fulfillment?" (Lawrence in Gilbert and Gubar, vol. 2, p. 262). By 1922, when he published *Fantasia of the Unconscious*, Lawrence was convinced that the culture had become feminized, and that the man who saw his "highest moment" as "the emotional moment when he gives himself up to the woman" (as Lawrence himself had earlier) was risking not only his manhood but even his life (Lawrence, *Fantasia*, p. 98).

> [I]n certain periods, such as the present, the majority of men concur in regarding woman as the source of life, the first term in creation: woman, the mother, the prime being. . . . Man has now entered onto his negative mode. . . . This being so, the whole tendency of his nature changes. Instead of being assertive and rather insentient, he becomes wavering and sensitive. He begins to have as many feelings—nay, more than a woman. . . . He worships pity and tenderness and weakness, even in himself. In short, he takes on very largely the original role of woman. Woman meanwhile becomes the fearless, inwardly relentless, determined positive party. She grips the responsibility. The hand that rocks the cradle rules the world. Nay, she makes man discover that cradles should not be rocked, in order that her hands may be left free. She is now a queen of the earth, and inwardly a fearsome tyrant. She keeps pity and tenderness emblazoned on her banners. But God help the man whom she pities. Ultimately she tears him to bits.
>
> (Lawrence, *Fantasia*, pp. 98-99)

These are the ideas that Lawrence first tries out in Birkin's mouth in the *Women in Love* chapter "Man to Man." It is no wonder, then, that Birkin is reluctant to say that he "loves" Ursula in the conventional, romantic way. Meanwhile, Gerald, who accepts the outward "pity" and the hidden power-struggles of conventional love, is indeed torn to bits.

Homosexuality. Only 20 years had passed since the trial and imprisonment of the playwright Oscar Wilde for sodomy (see **The Importance of Being Earnest**, also in *WLAIT 4: British and Irish Literature and Its Times*). Yet the same scientists who broached a new view of female sexuality also opened male homosexuality to public discussion. It was not the taboo subject it had been in Wilde's time; sometimes such relationships were even publicly avowed, especially in the Bloomsbury circle surrounding Lytton Strachey, Virginia

After the two eloped in 1912, Lawrence married Frieda von Richthofen Weekley on July 13, 1914. Shown here are Lawrence (left), Katherine Mansfield, Frieda, and John Middleton Murry on the Lawrences' wedding day.

Woolf, and John Maynard Keynes. Lawrence is known to have been deeply shocked by his encounter with this milieu on a visit to Cambridge in 1915. Yet he himself clearly considered a world of men by themselves an alternative to the dangers he saw in heterosexuality. He had strong homoerotic feelings toward John Middleton Murry, to whom he proposed blood-brotherhood, as Birkin does to Gerald in the novel. He may even have had a physical relationship with a young farmer in Cornwall (Delany, pp. 309-15). He wrote a Prologue to *Women in Love* in which Birkin is quite conscious of his physical desire for men, and then omitted it from the final draft. Cornelia Nixon has suggested, in *Lawrence's Leadership Politics and the Turn Against Women*, that Lawrence's ambivalence explains many of the more controversial aspects of *Women in Love*: the emphasis on ideal male bonding; the distrust of conventional heterosexual lovemaking, and the hints about anal intercourse; the animus against openly "decadent" characters like Loerke.

The Novel in Focus

Plot summary. Ursula and Gudrun Brangwen are living with their parents and teaching school in the mining town of Beldover. After gaining some reputation as a sculptor in London, Gudrun has returned home for uncertain reasons. They have a conversation about marriage. Gudrun is more drawn to the idea of a "highly attractive individual of sufficient means," but both agree that they cannot imagine the daily proximity of "any man one knows" (*Women in Love*, pp. 54-55). Dissatisfied with the conversation and with each other, they go out to observe the wedding of the local mine owner's daughter, Laura Crich. Watching from the adjoining churchyard, Gudrun feels immediately attracted to Laura's brother Gerald, "a young, good-humored, smiling wolf" (*Women in Love*, p. 61). Ursula is more intrigued by the wedding guest Rupert Birkin, a school-inspector, though he for the moment is clearly attached to Hermione Roddice, a local noblewoman and patron of the arts. Back at the wedding reception, Birkin shares with Gerald's mother his conviction that "not many people are anything at all" and that "it would be better if they were just wiped out" (*Women in Love*, p. 73). He is aware of a strong mutual attraction between him and Gerald, yet they can't seem to help arguing—first about patriotism and war, then about the need for social rules and conventions. On both issues, Birkin takes an anarchist position; Gerald argues that without rules "We should have everybody cutting everybody else's throat in five minutes"; Birkin suggests that "That means you would like to be cutting everybody's throat," or perhaps even that Gerald "desires to be murdered" (*Women in Love*, p. 82). Birkin remembers that Gerald did, in fact, accidentally kill his brother, as a boy, and wonders whether anything truly happens by accident.

Over the succeeding weeks, the characters continue to run across each other. Birkin and Gerald meet on a train to London and discuss a newspaper article that calls for a strong leader to save Western civilization. Birkin confesses that he feels only a deep monogamous relationship with a woman would set him spiritually on track. Gerald proceeds to follow Birkin into the bohemian world of the Pompadour café. There he meets and has a brief affair with a model nicknamed "The Pussum," who seems to be involved in a strange power struggle with her former lover, Halliday.

The noblewoman Hermione invites the Brangwen sisters, along with Gerald and Birkin, to a weekend party at her country house, Breadalby. But before much can develop, Hermione, who senses Birkin's imminent rejection of her, and his disgust with her wilful, to him almost insane, self-control, attempts to murder him by slamming a lapis lazuli paperweight down on his head. Birkin deflects the blow with a book, then wanders out, stunned, into the countryside. He lies down naked in a thicket, and has a brief vision of how he could live happily in a world without human beings. When he gets home, he is ill for a week or two.

Ursula and Gudrun encounter Gerald while waiting for a train to pass. Gerald has ridden his mare right up to the crossing; when she is frightened by the train and tries to bolt, he forces her to stand, using his spurs. Ursula screams at him to stop; Gudrun seems to experience a kind of ecstasy, though afterwards, "like a witch," she cries out, "'I should think you're proud'" (*Women in Love*, p. 171).

In the meantime, Birkin, having recovered, is furnishing a mill-house he has rented in the country. Ursula comes upon him during an afternoon walk. He confesses to her his feeling of his own failure to live and his fantasy of a depopulated earth. Ursula feels at once drawn to his "quick" and "alive" energy but put off by his need to preach and save the world; she brashly sticks to her belief in love, and in "just be[ing]

oneself, like a walking flower" (*Women in Love*, pp. 186). Hermione interrupts them; she has come, with Gerald in tow, to help with the furnishing. Ursula is piqued by her continued prominence in Birkin's life, and withdraws. But soon after, Birkin invites Ursula to tea at his rooms in town. He proposes a kind of "strange conjunction," a "star equilibrium," with her, but still avoids using, and mocks, the terms of romantic love (*Women in Love*, p. 210). She accuses him of really wanting male supremacy—a "satellite," not a double star (*Women in Love*, p. 213). But when she tells him her past history, the tension breaks; they end up embracing.

The four protagonists meet again at the annual "Water-Party" that the Crich family gives for the whole community. Gerald has his hand bandaged; he has caught it in a machine. The Brangwen sisters are immediately put off by the crowd; Gerald lends them a rowboat to escape to the far end of the lake. There, Gudrun does a "eurhythmic" dance while Ursula sings. A cluster of cattle come up to watch, and Gudrun starts to dance, provocatively, in their direction. Just then, Gerald and Birkin arrive, and Gerald drives the cattle away. Infuriated by his interference, Gudrun slaps him across the face. "You have struck the first blow," he says. "And I shall strike the last," she replies (*Women in Love*, p. 237).

But after nightfall, out rowing, Gudrun begins to feel that she is in love with Gerald. At that very moment, a cry rings out. One of the younger Crich daughters has fallen into the water. A young doctor dives in to try to rescue her. Gerald himself dives in many times to rescue his sister but is hampered because he has an injured hand, and there is utter darkness under the surface. Finally everyone gives up hope, and Birkin is commissioned to open the sluice to drain the lake. Ursula comes with him, and they make love, but a voice in his mind protests, "Not this, not this" (*Women in Love*, p. 255). The next day, the bodies are recovered; it is clear that Diana Crich has embraced and drowned the doctor, her would-be rescuer. All that day, Ursula waits for Birkin to come to her. But when he does arrive, it is too late, and he is clearly becoming ill again. She is repelled, and passes into a "pure and gemlike" hatred of him (*Women in Love*, p. 268). During his illness, Birkin, in turn, reaches a pinnacle of misogyny. Woman, he concludes, "had such a lust for possession, a greed of self-importance in love. . . . Everything must be referred back to her, to Woman, the Great Mother of everything"; "the hot narrow intimacy between man and wife was abhorrent" to him; "he wanted something clearer, more open, cooler, as it were" (*Women in Love*, pp. 269-70). When Gerald comes to visit him, Birkin proposes that they swear blood-brotherhood to each other, but Gerald temporizes, saying he does not understand the idea.

In the meantime, Gerald's father is dying of cancer. He worries particularly about his youngest daughter, Winifred; at Hermione's suggestion, Gudrun comes to Shortlands, the Crich's estate, to be Winifred's art teacher and unofficial companion. The first time she encounters Gerald, he rescues her when she is trying to subdue a rabbit for Winifred to sketch. Both are badly clawed, and feel a "mutual hellish recognition," looking at each other's wounds (*Women in Love*, p. 317).

After Birkin recovers from his illness, he goes away to the South of France. Not knowing he has returned, Ursula stumbles on him at the millpond one night. He is throwing stones at the moon's reflection on the water, and cursing the Great Mother goddess. When Ursula comes out of hiding and asks him to stop, their mutual affection returns. The next day, he decides to ask her to marry him. Unfortunately, he encounters her father first, and tells him his intentions. When Ursula returns, the cantankerous Will Brangwen asks her "what do you say"; she flies into a rage and accuses them both of "want[ing] to bully me" (*Women in Love*, pp. 338-39).

Birkin leaves and goes straight to Shortlands, where he finds Gerald in a state of profound ennui; the purposelessness of his life, apart from work, is beginning to dawn on him. Agreeing that they both need a drastic break of some kind, Birkin offers to teach Gerald Jiu-jitsu. They wrestle until they pass out against each other's naked bodies. Afterwards both feel relieved but slightly embarrassed; Birkin says, "We are mentally, spiritually intimate, therefore we should be more or less physically intimate too—it is more whole" (*Women in Love*, p. 351).

Birkin and Ursula go for a drive. When she finds out that he has to get home for a dinner with Hermione, they have a violent quarrel. He gives up his dinner plans, and they drive on aimlessly, suddenly completely at peace with each other. They stop for tea at an inn; Ursula kneels and caresses the backs of Birkin's thighs. Birkin proposes that they both resign from their jobs so that they can start a completely new life. They end up spending the night in the open in Sher-

wood Forest, in an "unspeakable communication in touch" (*Women in Love*, p. 403).

As Thomas Crich nears his end, Gerald finds that Gudrun is the only person he can turn to for sympathy. Three nights after his father's death, he cannot stand being alone. He walks to Beldover, sneaks into the Brangwen house, and finds Gudrun's room. She lets him stay and make love to her. Afterwards he falls asleep, "perfect as if he were bathed in the womb again," but she is awake and despairing, "left with all the anguish of consciousness" (*Women in Love*, pp. 430-32).

Birkin and Ursula decide to get married. Gerald considers marrying Gudrun too, but cannot quite make up his mind. The four spend Christmas together at a ski resort in the Tyrol, despite Gudrun's fear that, since Gerald and Birkin have planned this together, they are "arranging an outing with some little type they'd picked up" (*Women in Love*, p. 468).

On their way to Austria, Gerald and Gudrun stop in London, and go to the Pompadour café. They encounter the model, Pussum, confirming Gudrun's worst suspicions about Gerald's relations with "little types." But when they overhear Pussum's former lover Halliday making fun of a letter from Birkin in Birkin's high-sounding prophetic mode, Gudrun snatches the letter away, and runs from the restaurant. On the boat crossing the Channel to mainland Europe, Ursula and Birkin both feel they have indeed embarked on a new life, "like one closed seed of life falling through dark, fathomless space" (*Women in Love*, p. 479). At Innsbruck, Austria, they rejoin Gerald and Gudrun. The four ascend into a beautiful but inhuman landscape, where "the last peaks of snow" are "like the heart petals of an open rose" (*Women in Love*, p. 491). The German guests at the inn welcome them heartily; after a boisterous party, Birkin and Ursula are inspired to sexual experiment, to "mocking brutishness" (*Women in Love*, p. 505). But Gudrun is beginning to feel afraid of Gerald's intrusion on her self-conscious inner world.

One of their fellow guests is a little German sculptor named Loerke. He is a believer in art for art's sake, but also something of a Futurist, who holds that "art should interpret industry, as it once interpreted religion" (*Women in Love*, p. 518). Though he apparently has a male lover, Leitner, he immediately focuses on Gudrun. The women spend hours talking with him, though Gerald hates him, and Birkin dismisses him as "the wizard rat that swims ahead" in "the river of corruption" (*Women in Love*, p. 523).

Ursula decides that she cannot stand the atmosphere (climatic or emotional), and she and Birkin leave for Italy. Left alone, Gerald and Gudrun's relationship deteriorates rapidly. She accuses him of wanting her rather than loving her; though he cannot contradict her, he feels that "a strange rent had been torn in him . . . he had been torn apart and given to Gudrun," and that he cannot give up this "cruelest joy" (*Women in Love*, p. 543). As she seems more and more clearly to have an understanding with the sculptor Loerke, Gerald begins to fantasize about killing her. She decides to leave. On the day before her departure, Gerald comes upon her and Loerke having a picnic in the snow. He knocks Loerke down and begins to strangle Gudrun. But when Loerke breaks his concentration with a sarcastic remark, Gerald lets go and wanders away. He climbs higher and higher into the mountains, with no destination. Finally, feeling that "somebody was going to murder him" and "he could feel the blow descending," he collapses and falls asleep in the snow (*Women in Love*, pp. 574-75).

When his frozen body is discovered, Gudrun summons Birkin and Ursula back from Italy. Birkin is in despair, feeling that if Gerald had accepted his offer of love, it would have saved him. He reassures Ursula that "You are enough for me, as far as woman is concerned," and that "We shan't have any need to despair, in death," but the novel ends with them disagreeing about his wish for "two kinds of love" (*Women in Love*, pp. 582-83).

Birkin—character or mouthpiece? *Women in Love* still has the power to provoke deeply polarized reactions in its readers, for its ideology as much as for its art. Those who hate the novel tend to consider Birkin the authorial voice, even in his most neurotic, misanthropic, misogynist pronouncements. They see Ursula as capitulating to him and forfeiting the potential for an independent life that she developed in *The Rainbow* (Adelman, pp. 508-510).

Those who love the novel tend to feel—often after repeated readings—that it is a work in which even negative characters like Hermione and Loerke are sometimes right and that the polarities are too profound ever to be resolved in one direction. As Birkin himself says, in a self-dissatisfied moment, "There wouldn't have to be any truth, if there weren't any lies" (*Women in Love*, p. 322). From this point of view, Birkin profoundly needs the correction he gets from Ursula, and both are changed by the end of the book. If Ursula adopts some of Birkin's opinions,

Birkin learns from her how to live in the moment, to set aside his need to be right when the urgencies of human interaction demand it.

One episode that particularly reveals the unresolved tensions between the different views Lawrence's characters espouse is that of the horse and the train. When Gerald forces his mare to stand still at the crossing, it seems a precise analogue to what he has done in his industrial reforms. The natural, organic impulse—whether in the horse, or in the miners—is completely sacrificed to the imposed order of the machine. This is how Ursula understands it. Moreover, Gudrun's conflicted, but partly ecstatic, reaction underlines an important concept in the novel: that sadomasochistic sexuality and the power relations of industrial society are connected. In Lawrence's view, both are manifestations of a collective desire for death.

When Birkin, however, first hears the story about the horse and train, he sides with Gerald. The whole scene appeals to his anti-sentimental, hierarchical side, and to his desire for male supremacy. "Nothing is so detestable as the maudlin attributing of human consciousness to animals," he says, and later adds, gratuitously, "And woman is the same as horses. . . . With one will she wants to subject herself utterly. With the other she wants to bolt, and pitch her rider to perdition" (*Women in Love*, pp. 201-2). When Birkin says this, we are in for some surprises. First, Hermione agrees with him and draws an analogy to her own reliance on rigid self-control in dealing with her inner chaos. Then, Ursula and Hermione join forces, for the only time in the novel, expressing mutual distrust for Birkin's "criticism and analysis of life," his inability to "see things in their entirety, with their beauty left to them" (*Women in Love*, p. 203). It is a criticism that the plot seems, at least partly, to bear out; it is only when Birkin lets go, acts on impulse and risks himself in the face of setbacks rather than insisting on dominance that his relationship with Ursula begins to succeed.

A further plot-irony makes clear the relevance of all this to Gerald's eventual fate. When we next see him, he has his hand bandaged from an industrial accident. Hermione's analogy has proved accurate, though not quite in the way she meant it: the excessive need for control will ultimately turn against the other within the self, as well as external others, animal or human. That is, this need will lead one to wreak havoc on oneself. The industrial accident reveals Gerald's unconscious self-destructiveness; and surely it reflects

Lawrence's own diagnosis of the illness of the entire culture, in the light of the War. In the culture, as in Gerald, the loss of a sense of cosmic connection, through excessive reliance on reason and power, leads to a failure of the will to live, which leads, in turn, to the need to murder or be murdered. The "substitution of the mechanical principle for the organic" is, to quote Lawrence's dictum again, "the first great phase of chaos" (*Women in Love*, p. 305).

Sources and literary context. Just how far *Women in Love* was taken as a *roman à clef*, a portrait of literary London with identifiable characters, may be judged from the lawsuits it almost spawned. To this day, the character Pussum is called "Minette," in some editions because an ex-friend, Philip Heseltine, had a mistress who was nicknamed "The Puma." The alteration, plus fifty pounds, kept Heseltine from filing a lawsuit against Lawrence (Kinkead-Weekes, p. 698).

The case of Lady Ottoline Morrell was more serious, and actually delayed publication by three years. Lady Ottoline was famous, a patron of the arts and liberal causes. She had an affair with the philosopher Bertrand Russell, and the guests at her country house, Garsington, included Virginia Woolf, T. S. Eliot, and E. M. Forster, as well as the Lawrences. She and Lawrence's wife Frieda had quarreled by the time Lawrence rewrote *Women in Love*; and she felt her manner and dress, as well as her public role, were cruelly caricatured in the figure of Hermione. Lawrence responded that obviously Hermione wasn't Ottoline, since he and Ottoline had never had an affair. (In the novel Birkin, presumed to have been modeled on Lawrence, does have an affair with Hermione.) But to the real-life Ottoline, the very suggestion that they might have had one only made matters worse.

That Birkin is essentially Lawrence, no one has ever questioned. Ursula plays the role in his life that Frieda played in Lawrence's; and when Ursula is angry, she doubtless shows some of Frieda's "God Almightiness" (Kinkead-Weekes, p. 72). But her background is that of Lawrence's ex-fiancée, Louie Burrows. All in all, it seems fairest to call her an imagined character. The disastrous attempt of writers John Middleton Murry and Katherine Mansfield to live with the Lawrences in Cornwall doubtless stands behind the foursome plot. But Gerald, like Ursula, is an invented character; all he has in common with Murry is that both refused the offer of blood-brotherhood. Gudrun, on the other hand, may be quite a close portrait of Katherine Mansfield,

the great short-story writer. Both have a gift for satire that miniaturizes, in their art and conversation. Mansfield wrote some witty remarks about Lawrence himself: "the 'dear man' in him whom we all loved is hidden away . . . like a little gold ring in that immense German Christmas pudding which is Frieda" (Mansfield in Delany, p. 229). Like the character Gudrun, Mansfield could be fiercely loyal; in fact, she snatched a book of Lawrence's poems out of the hands of two aesthetes who were making fun of it, at the Cafe Royal. Also like Gudrun, she was sexually unconventional. She left Murry for a brief affair with the painter Mark Gertler, the inspiration for the sculptor Loerke in *Women in Love*.

With Gertler, as perhaps with Lady Ottoline, Lawrence ended up making savage fictional use of someone he had initially liked personally. Lawrence's first response to Gertler's painting "The Merry-Go-Round" was to call it "the best modern picture I have seen"; like the frieze for the factory in Cologne created by Loerke in the novel, the painting shows how "the machine works [man], instead of he the machine" (*Women in Love*, p. 519). But, as Lawrence clearly understood, the intent of "the combination of blaze, and violent mechanical rotation . . . and ghastly, utterly mindless human intensity of sensational extremity" was satire, not, as in Loerke's case, affirmation of industry (Lawrence in Delany, p. 259). That the men in the painting were soldiers made it specifically a satire on industrialized warfare. That Gertler, a German-Jewish artist, was not allowed to exhibit it, filled Lawrence the war-protestor with fellow-feeling. Why, then, does Loerke come across as such a negative character? Perhaps Lawrence was still angry at Gertler on Murry's behalf; or perhaps his "Day of Wrath" simply needed a wide panoply of damned souls.

Reception. Lawrence, no doubt anticipating that the pre-publication scandals surrounding the book would affect its reception, wanted no review copies sent out in England—a request that his publisher only partly respected. Lawrence was largely right in his fears. In the *Times Literary Supplement*, the poet Edmund Blunden, now a protege of Lady Ottoline's, found that Lawrence's "conception of love" was one of "jubilant brutality," and that Hermione alone stood out as a figure of "immense dignity" (Blunden in Farmer, p. liii). John Middleton Murry, who had even more of a vested interest, wrote that Lawrence had "murdered his gifts," that the characters were indistinguishable, and that "they writhe continually, like the damned, in a frenzy of sexual awareness" (Murry in Kinkead-Weekes, pp. 671-72). Other reviews dismissed the novel humorously; one even called for its suppression. "Apart from the purely hostile reviews," Farmer and his co-editors tell us, "the early notice . . . was characterised by a sense that Lawrence was more a poet than a novelist, more interested in philosophy and sex than in writing convincing fiction. The extraordinariness of the book was seen as an effort (and as a failure) to enliven psychological drama" (Farmer, p. lv). The most positive reviewer, Rebecca West, thought Lawrence successful in conveying "the spiritual truth with which he is concerned at the moment," though at the cost of a "distortion of life's physical appearances"; she did, however, allow that the novel was "a work of genius" (West in Farmer, p. lv).

The American reviews were, on the whole, more positive than the British. John Macy, writing in the *New York Evening Post Literary Review*, saw Lawrence as a "tragic poet." If the emotions of his characters were "more frequent and more violent than the ordinary human soul can enjoy or endure," still Lawrence knew "what goes on inside the human head"; and even his outward portraiture had "a fidelity not surpassed by [British novelist] Mr. [Arnold] Bennett" (Macy in Kinkead-Weekes, p. 657). This was about as good as it got, in 1921. It would be a few years before some critics, beginning with F. R. Leavis, agreed with Lawrence's own assessment: "I con-sider this the best of my books" (Lawrence in Farmer, p. xxxix).

—Alan Williamson

For More Information

Adelman, Gary. "The Man Who Rode Away: What D. H. Lawrence Means to Today's Readers." *Tri-Quarterly* 107/108 Winter-Summer 2000: 508.

Delany, Paul. *D. H. Lawrence's Nightmare: The Writer and His Circle in the Years of the Great War.* New York: Basic, 1978.

Farmer, David, Lindeth Vasey, and John Worthen, eds. *Women in Love, by D. H. Lawrence.* The Cambridge Edition. Cambridge: Cambridge University Press, 1987.

Fussell, Paul. *The Great War and Modem Memor.* Oxford: Oxford University Press, 1975.

Gilbert, David. *Class, Community, and Collective Action: Social Change in Two British Coalfields, 1850-1926.* Oxford: Clarendon Press, 1992.

Gilbert, Sandra M., and Susan Gubar. *No Man's Land.* 2 vols. New Haven: Yale University Press, 1988-89.

Kinkead-Weekes, Mark. *D. H. Lawrence: Triumph to Exile, 1912-1922.* Cambridge: Cambridge University Press, 1996.

Lawrence, D. H. *Fantasia of the Unconscious and Psychoanalysis and the Unconscious.* London: Penguin, 1977.

——. *Women in Love.* Ed. Charles L. Ross. London: Penguin, 1986.

Nixon, Cornelia. *Lawrence's Leadership Politics and the Turn Against Women.* Berkeley: University of California Press, 1986.

Index